KU-507-235

GREAT BRITAIN
ROAD ATLAS

Contents

Map pages and distance chart	inside front cover
Route planning	**II–XVII**
Route planner	II–VII
Channel hopping and the Isle of Wight	VIII–IX
Ferries to Ireland and the Isle of Man	X
Scotland and North Sea ferries	XI
Caravan and camping sites in Britain	XII–XV
Traffic signs	XVI–XVII
Motorways	**XVIII–XXV**
Restricted junctions	XVIII–XXI
M25 London Orbital motorway	XXII
M6 Toll motorway	XXIII
Smart motorways	XXIV–XXV
Map pages	**XXVI**
Road map symbols	**1**
Road maps	**2–173**
Britain 1:200,000 scale Some islands are shown at slightly smaller scales	2–169
Ireland 1:1,000,000 scale	170–173
District maps	**174–185**
Birmingham	174–175
Glasgow	176–177
London	178–181
Manchester	182–183
Tyne & Wear	184–185
Street map symbols	**186**
Towns, ports and airports	**187–237**
Town plans	188–234
Major airports	235–237
Port plans	VIII–XI
Channel Tunnel terminals	27
Central London	**238–253**
Central London street map	238–247
Central London index	248–253
Index to place names	**254–302**
County, administrative area map	254
Place name index	255–302
Map pages and distance chart	inside back cover

34th edition June 2019

© AA Media Limited 2019

Original edition printed 1986.

Cartography: All cartography in this atlas edited, designed and produced by the Mapping Services Department of AA Publishing (A05690).

This atlas contains Ordnance Survey data © Crown copyright and database right 2019 and Royal Mail data © Royal Mail copyright and database right 2019.

Contains public sector information licensed under the Open Government Licence v3.0

Ireland mapping and distance chart contains data available from openstreetmap.org © under the Open Database License found at opendatacommons.org

Publisher's Notes: Published by AA Publishing (a trading name of AA Media Limited, whose registered office is Fanum House, Basing View, Basingstoke, Hampshire RG21 4EA, UK. Registered number 06112600).

ISBN: 978 0 7495 8133 6 (leather)
ISBN: 978 0 7495 8132 9 (standard)

A CIP catalogue record for this book is available from The British Library.

Disclaimer: The contents of this atlas are believed to be correct at the time of the latest revision, it will not contain any subsequent amended, new or temporary information including diversions and traffic control or enforcement systems. The publishers cannot be held responsible or liable for any loss or damage occasioned to any person acting or refraining from action as a result of any use or reliance on material in this atlas, nor for any errors, omissions or changes in such material. This does not affect your statutory rights.

The publishers would welcome information to correct any errors or omissions and to keep this atlas up to date. Please write to the Atlas Editor, AA Publishing, The Automobile Association, Fanum House, Basing View, Basingstoke, Hampshire RG21 4EA, UK. E-mail: *roadatlasfeedback@theaa.com*

Acknowledgements: AA Publishing would like to thank the following for information used in the creation of this atlas: Cadw, English Heritage, Forestry Commission, Historic Scotland, National Trust and National Trust for Scotland, RSPB, The Wildlife Trust, Scottish Natural Heritage, Natural England, The Countryside Council for Wales. Award winning beaches from 'Blue Flag' and 'Keep Scotland Beautiful' (summer 2018 data): for latest information visit *www.blueflag.org* and *www.keepscotlandbeautiful.org*. Road signs are © Crown Copyright 2019. Reproduced under the terms of the Open Government Licence. Transport for London (Central London Map), Nexus (Newcastle district map).

Ireland mapping: Republic of Ireland census 2016 © Central Statistics Office and Northern Ireland census 2016 © NISRA (population data); Irish Public Sector Data (CC BY 4.0) (Gaeltacht); Logainm.ie (placenames); Roads Service and Transport Infrastructure Ireland

Printer: 1010 Printing International Ltd

Scale 1:200,000
or 3.16 miles to 1 inch

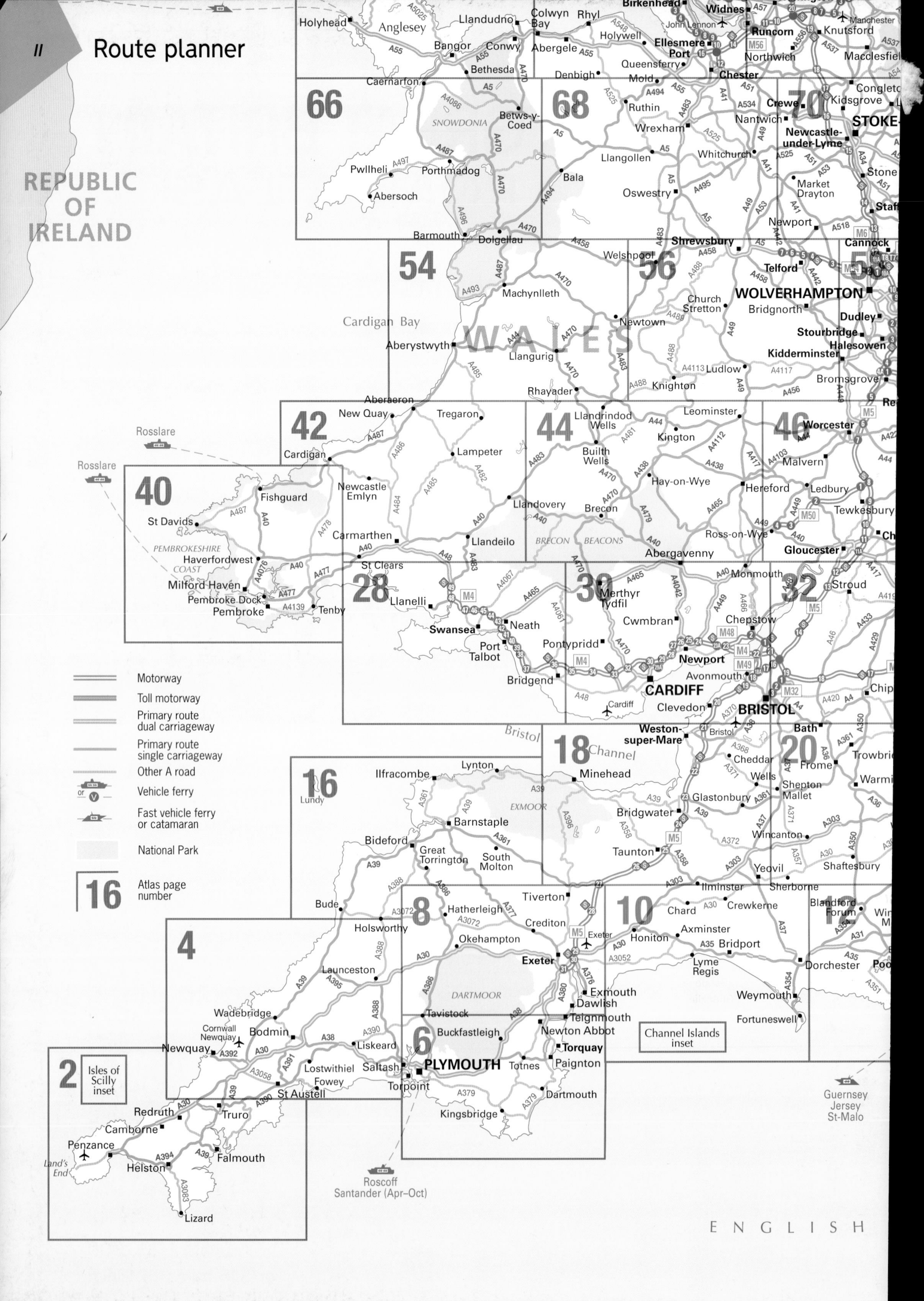

REPUBLIC
OF
IRELAND

WALES

Cardigan Bay

BRECON BEACONS

Bristol Channel

DARTMOOR

EXMOOR

PEMBROKESHIRE COAST

SNOWDONIA

ENGLISH

Map panel numbers

66 68 70 STOKE
54 56
42 44 46
40 28 30 32
16 18 20
8 10 12
4 6
2 Isles of Scilly inset

Channel Islands inset

Legend

Motorway
Toll motorway
Primary route dual carriageway
Primary route single carriageway
Other A road
Vehicle ferry
Fast vehicle ferry or catamaran
National Park
16 Atlas page number

Place names

Holyhead
Anglesey
Bangor
Caernarfon
Bethesda
Conwy
Llandudno
Colwyn Bay
Rhyl
Abergele
Holywell
Queensferry
Mold
Denbigh
Ruthin
Chester
Ellesmere Port
Northwich
Runcorn
Widnes
Knutsford
Manchester
John Lennon
Macclesfield
Pwllheli
Porthmadog
Abersoch
Betws-y-Coed
Bala
Llangollen
Wrexham
Oswestry
Whitchurch
Nantwich
Crewe
Kidsgrove
Newcastle-under-Lyme
Market Drayton
Stone
Stafford
Barmouth
Dolgellau
Welshpool
Shrewsbury
Newport
Cannock
Machynlleth
Newtown
Church Stretton
Bridgnorth
Telford
WOLVERHAMPTON
Dudley
Stourbridge
Halesowen
Kidderminster
Aberystwyth
Llangurig
Rhayader
Knighton
Ludlow
Bromsgrove
Aberaeron
New Quay
Tregaron
Lampeter
Llandrindod Wells
Kington
Leominster
Worcester
Cardigan
Newcastle Emlyn
Builth Wells
Hay-on-Wye
Hereford
Ledbury
Malvern
Tewkesbury
Fishguard
St Davids
Haverfordwest
Milford Haven
Pembroke Dock
Pembroke
Tenby
Carmarthen
Llandeilo
Llandovery
Brecon
Abergavenny
Monmouth
Ross-on-Wye
Gloucester
Stroud
Rosslare
Llanelli
Swansea
Neath
Port Talbot
Bridgend
Merthyr Tydfil
Cwmbran
Pontypridd
Newport
CARDIFF
Chepstow
BRISTOL
Avonmouth
Clevedon
Bath
Weston-super-Mare
Cheddar
Wells
Shepton Mallet
Frome
Trowbridge
Warminster
Ilfracombe
Lynton
Minehead
Lundy
Barnstaple
Bideford
Great Torrington
South Molton
Bridgwater
Glastonbury
Taunton
Wincanton
Bude
Holsworthy
Hatherleigh
Tiverton
Crediton
Exeter
Honiton
Axminster
Bridport
Crewkerne
Chard
Ilminster
Yeovil
Sherborne
Shaftesbury
Blandford Forum
Dorchester
Poole
Launceston
Okehampton
Tavistock
Buckfastleigh
Newton Abbot
Torquay
Paignton
Exmouth
Dawlish
Teignmouth
Lyme Regis
Weymouth
Fortuneswell
Wadebridge
Bodmin
Newquay
Liskeard
Saltash
PLYMOUTH
Torpoint
Totnes
Dartmouth
Kingsbridge
Lostwithiel
Fowey
St Austell
Truro
Redruth
Camborne
Penzance
Helston
Falmouth
Lizard
Land's End
Roscoff
Santander (Apr–Oct)
Guernsey
Jersey
St-Malo

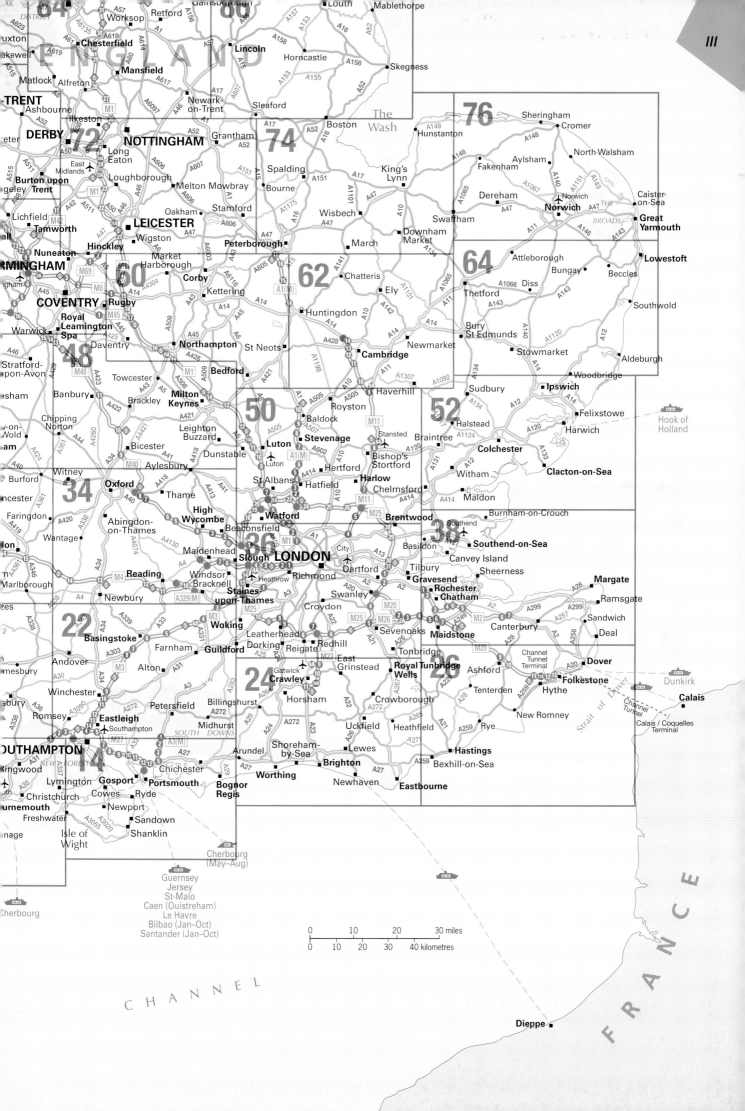

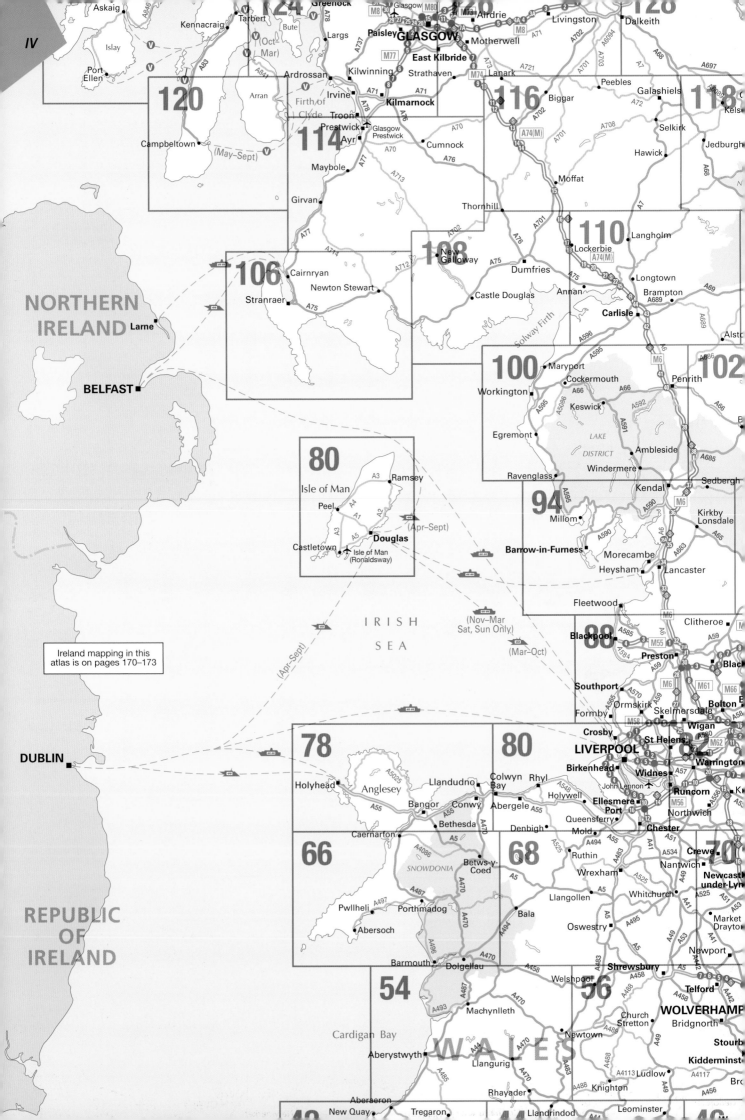

Ireland mapping in this atlas is on pages 170–173

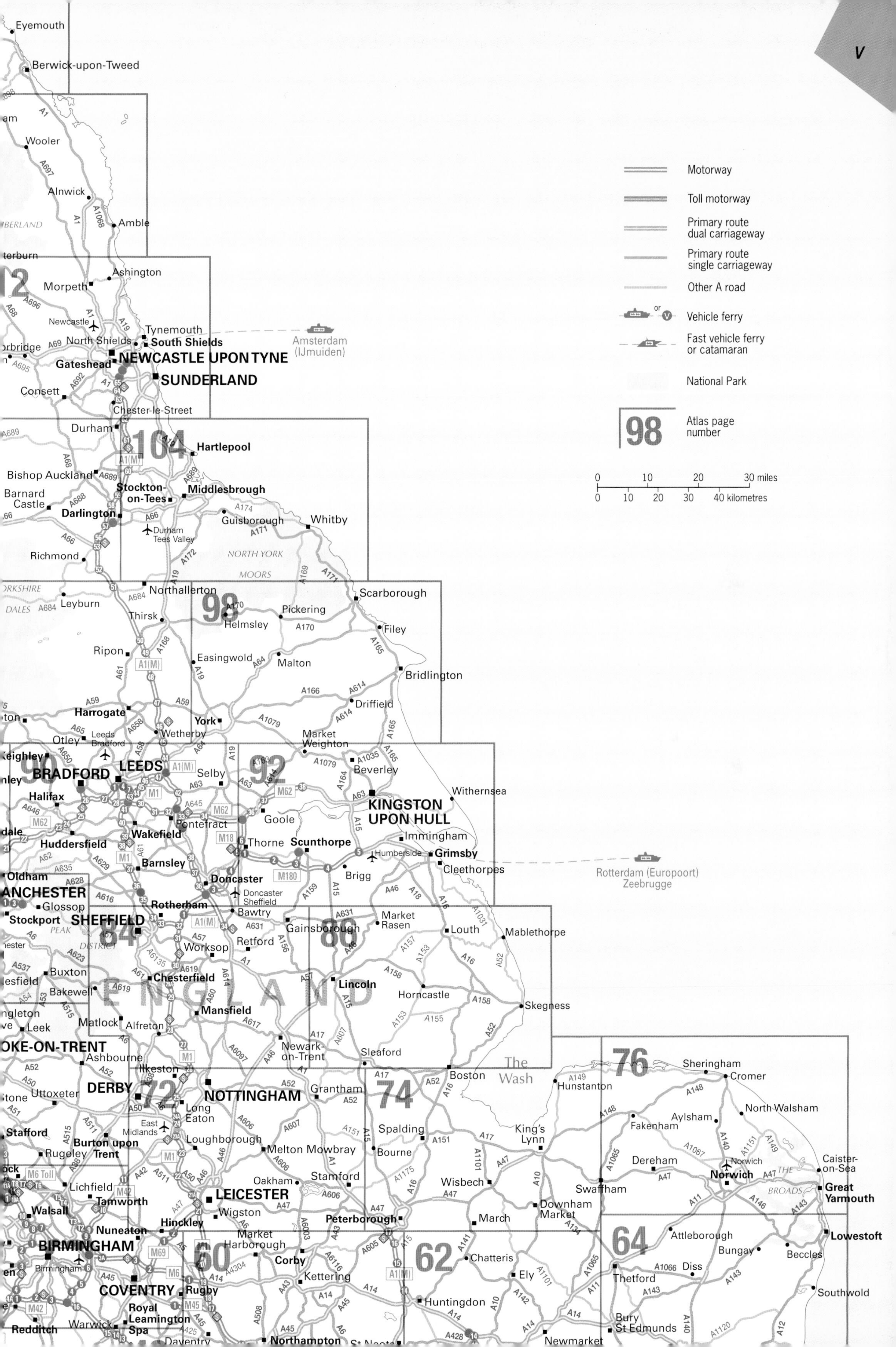

Legend

Motorway

Toll motorway

Primary route dual carriageway

Primary route single carriageway

Other A road

or V · Vehicle ferry

Fast vehicle ferry or catamaran

National Park

98 Atlas page number

```
0        10        20        30 miles
0    10   20   30   40 kilometres
```

Eyemouth
Berwick-upon-Tweed
Wooler
Alnwick
Amble
Morpeth
Ashington
Newcastle
North Shields
Tynemouth
South Shields
NEWCASTLE UPON TYNE
Gateshead
SUNDERLAND
Consett
Chester-le-Street
Durham
Hartlepool
Bishop Auckland
Stockton-on-Tees
Middlesbrough
Barnard Castle
Darlington
Richmond
Guisborough
Whitby
Durham Tees Valley
NORTH YORK MOORS
Northallerton
Leyburn
Thirsk
Scarborough
Pickering
Helmsley
Filey
Easingwold
Malton
Ripon
Bridlington
Driffield
Harrogate
Market Weighton
York
Wetherby
Otley
Leeds Bradford
BRADFORD
LEEDS
Selby
Beverley
Keighley
Halifax
Huddersfield
Pontefract
Goole
KINGSTON UPON HULL
Withernsea
Wakefield
Thorne
Scunthorpe
Immingham
Barnsley
Humberside
Grimsby
Doncaster
Cleethorpes
Oldham
Glossop
MANCHESTER
Doncaster Sheffield
Brigg
Stockport
Rotherham
SHEFFIELD
Bawtry
Market Rasen
PEAK DISTRICT
Worksop
Gainsborough
Louth
Mablethorpe
Buxton
Chesterfield
Retford
Bakewell
Lincoln
Matlock
Alfreton
Mansfield
Horncastle
Skegness
Leek
STOKE-ON-TRENT
Ashbourne
Newark-on-Trent
Ilkeston
Sleaford
The Wash
Uttoxeter
DERBY
NOTTINGHAM
Grantham
Boston
Stafford
Long Eaton
East Midlands
Spalding
King's Lynn
Burton upon Trent
Loughborough
Bourne
Rugeley
Melton Mowbray
Oakham
Stamford
Wisbech
Lichfield
LEICESTER
Wigston
Tamworth
Peterborough
March
Downham Market
Walsall
Hinckley
Market Harborough
Nuneaton
BIRMINGHAM
Corby
Kettering
Ely
Huntingdon
COVENTRY
Rugby
Attleborough
Bungay
Royal Leamington Spa
Warwick
Thetford
Redditch
Daventry
Northampton
Newmarket
Bury St Edmunds
Sheringham
Cromer
North Walsham
Aylsham
Fakenham
Hunstanton
Dereham
Norwich
Caister-on-Sea
Swaffham
Great Yarmouth
THE BROADS
Lowestoft
Diss
Beccles
Southwold

Amsterdam (IJmuiden)
Rotterdam (Europoort) Zeebrugge

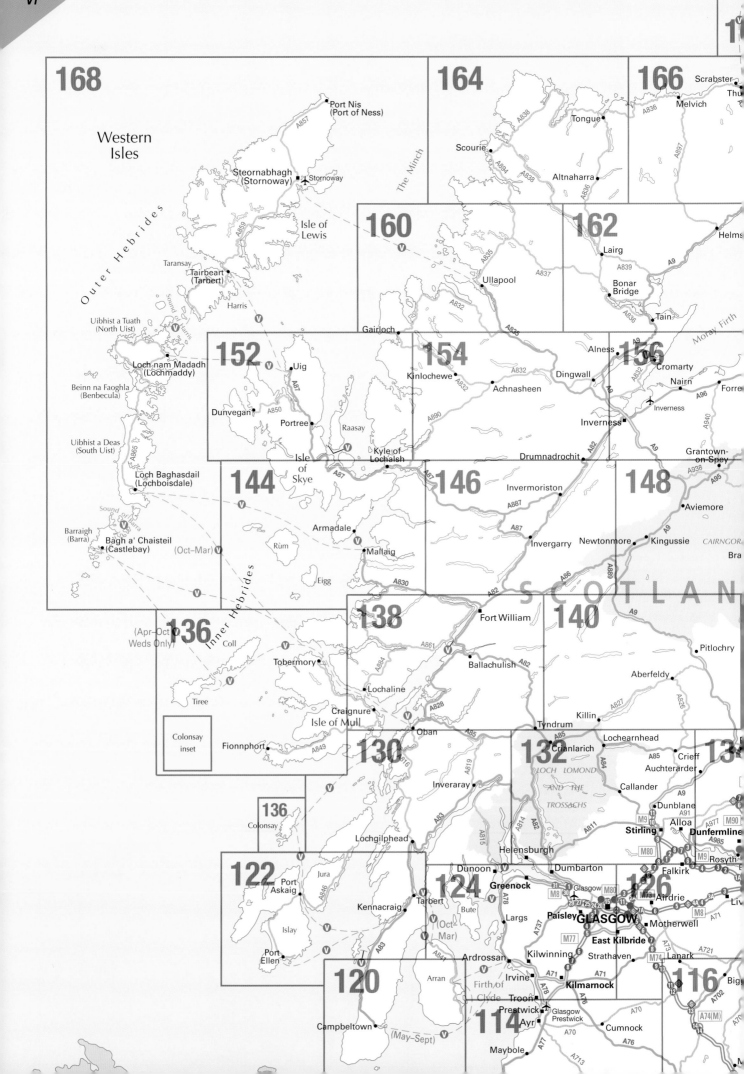

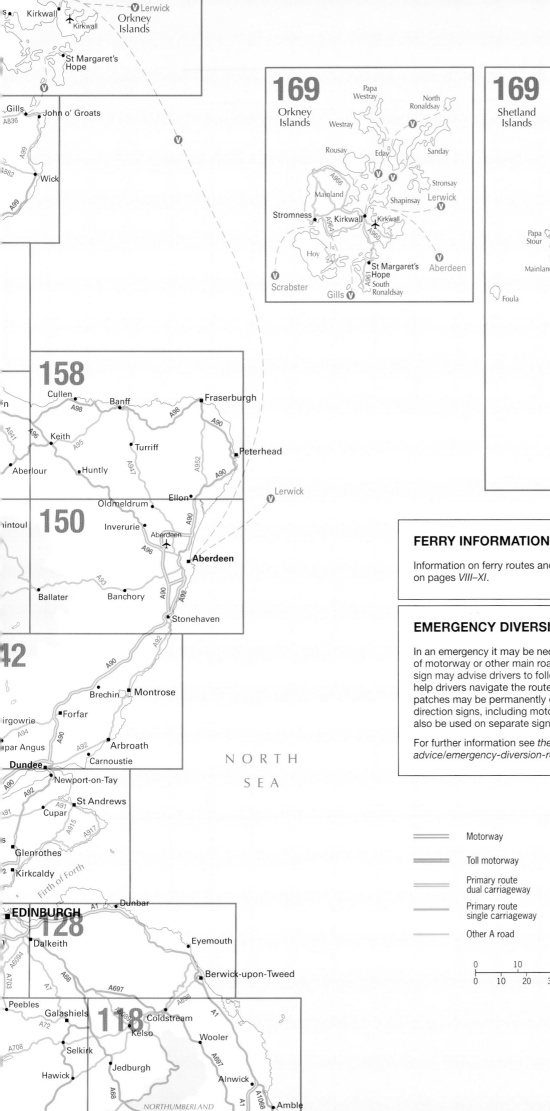

FERRY INFORMATION

Information on ferry routes and operators can be found on pages *VIII–XI*.

EMERGENCY DIVERSION ROUTES

In an emergency it may be necessary to close a section of motorway or other main road to traffic, so a temporary sign may advise drivers to follow a diversion route. To help drivers navigate the route, black symbols on yellow patches may be permanently displayed on existing direction signs, including motorway signs. Symbols may also be used on separate signs with yellow backgrounds.

For further information see *theaa.com/breakdown-cover/ advice/emergency-diversion-routes*

Channel hopping and the Isle of Wight

For business or pleasure, hopping on a ferry across to France, the Channel Islands or Isle of Wight has never been easier.

The vehicle ferry services listed in the table give you all the options, together with detailed port plans to help you navigate to and from the ferry terminals. Simply choose your preferred route, not forgetting the fast sailings (see 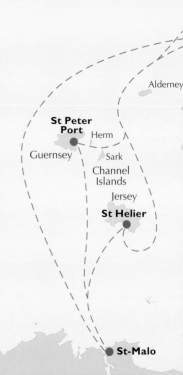). Bon voyage!

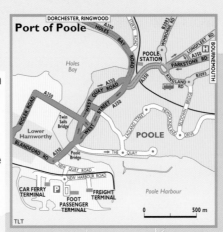

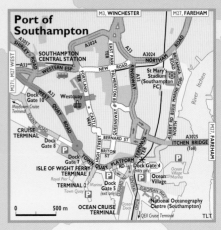

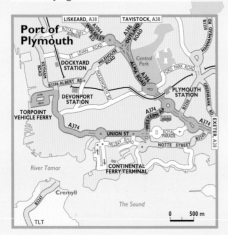

Plymouth

Roscoff

ENGLISH

Alderney

St Peter Port
Herm
Guernsey
Sark
Channel Islands
Jersey
St Helier

St-Malo

ENGLISH CHANNEL AND ISLE OF WIGHT FERRY CROSSINGS

From	To	Journey time	Operator website
Dover	Calais	1 hr 30 mins	dfdsseaways.co.uk
Dover	Calais	1 hr 30 mins	poferries.com
Dover	Dunkirk	2 hrs	dfdsseaways.co.uk
Folkestone	Calais (Coquelles)	35 mins	eurotunnel.com
Lymington	Yarmouth (IOW)	40 mins	wightlink.co.uk
Newhaven	Dieppe	4 hrs	dfdsseaways.co.uk
Plymouth	Roscoff	6–8 hrs	brittany-ferries.co.uk
Poole	Cherbourg	4 hrs 15 mins	brittany-ferries.co.uk
Poole	Guernsey	3 hrs 🚢	condorferries.co.uk
Poole	Jersey	4 hrs 30 mins 🚢	condorferries.co.uk
Poole	St-Malo	7–12 hrs (via Channel Is.) 🚢	condorferries.co.uk
Portsmouth	Caen (Ouistreham)	6–7 hrs	brittany-ferries.co.uk
Portsmouth	Cherbourg	3 hrs (May–Aug) 🚢	brittany-ferries.co.uk
Portsmouth	Fishbourne (IOW)	45 mins	wightlink.co.uk
Portsmouth	Guernsey	7 hrs	condorferries.co.uk
Portsmouth	Jersey	8–11 hrs	condorferries.co.uk
Portsmouth	Le Havre	5 hrs 30 mins	brittany-ferries.co.uk
Portsmouth	St-Malo	9–11 hrs	brittany-ferries.co.uk
Southampton	East Cowes (IOW)	1 hr	redfunnel.co.uk

The information listed is provided as a guide only, as services are liable to change at short notice. Services shown are for vehicle ferries only, operated by conventional ferry unless indicated as a fast ferry service (🚢). Please check sailings before planning your journey.

Travelling further afield? For ferry services to Northern Spain see brittany-ferries.co.uk.

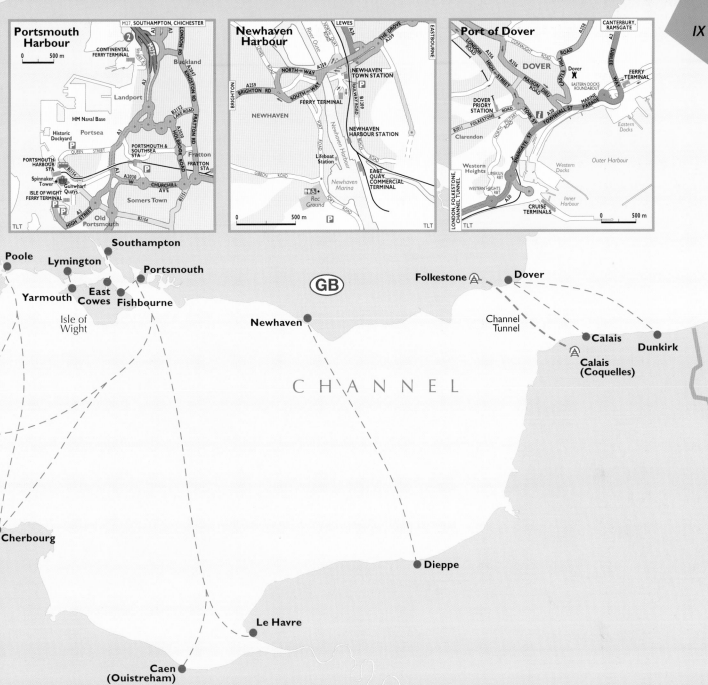

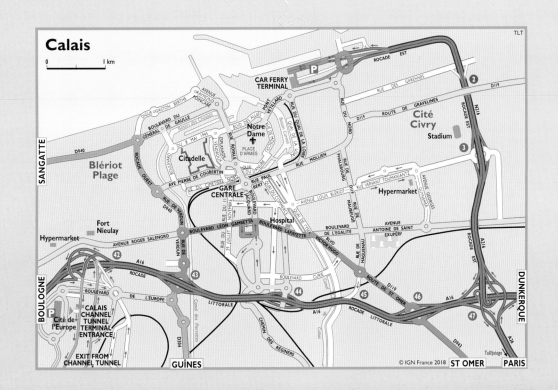

Ferries to Ireland and the Isle of Man

With so many sea crossings to Ireland and the Isle of Man the information provided in the table to the right will help you make the right choice.

IRISH SEA FERRY CROSSINGS

From	To	Journey time	Operator website
Cairnryan	Belfast	2 hrs 15 mins 🚢	stenaline.co.uk
Cairnryan	Larne	2 hrs	poferries.com
Douglas	Belfast	2 hrs 45 mins (April–Sept) 🚢	steam-packet.com
Douglas	Dublin	2 hrs 55 mins (April–Sept) 🚢	steam-packet.com
Fishguard	Rosslare	3 hrs 15 mins	stenaline.co.uk
Heysham	Douglas	3 hrs 45 mins	steam-packet.com
Holyhead	Dublin	2 hrs 🚢	irishferries.com
Holyhead	Dublin	3 hrs 15 mins	irishferries.com
Holyhead	Dublin	3 hrs 15 mins	stenaline.co.uk
Liverpool	Douglas	2 hrs 45 mins (Mar–Oct) 🚢	steam-packet.com
Liverpool	Dublin	8 hrs–8 hrs 30 mins	poferries.com
Liverpool (Birkenhead)	Belfast	8 hrs	stenaline.co.uk
Liverpool (Birkenhead)	Douglas	4 hrs 15 mins (Nov–Mar Sat, Sun only)	steam-packet.com
Pembroke Dock	Rosslare	4 hrs	irishferries.com

The information listed is provided as a guide only, as services are liable to change at short notice. Services shown are for vehicle ferries only, operated by conventional ferry unless indicated as a fast ferry service (🚢). Please check sailings before planning your journey.

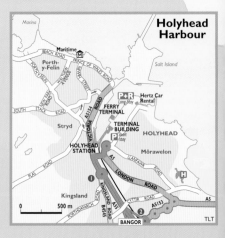
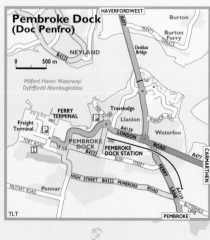
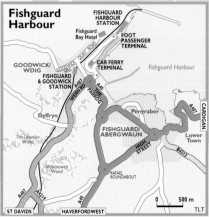
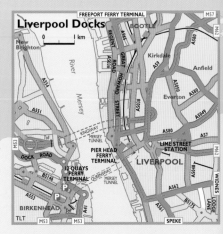

SCOTLAND FERRIES

From	To	Journey time	Operator website
Scottish Islands/west coast of Scotland			
Gourock	Dunoon	20 mins	*western-ferries.co.uk*
Glenelg	Skye	20 mins (Easter–Oct)	*skyeferry.co.uk*
Numerous and varied sailings from the west coast of Scotland to Scottish islands are provided by Caledonian MacBrayne. Please visit *calmac.co.uk* for all ferry information, including those of other operators.			
Orkney Islands			
Aberdeen	Kirkwall	6 hrs	*northlinkferries.co.uk*
Gills	St Margaret's Hope	1 hr	*pentlandferries.co.uk*
Scrabster	Stromness	1 hr 30 mins	*northlinkferries.co.uk*
Lerwick	Kirkwall	5 hrs 30 mins	*northlinkferries.co.uk*
Inter-island services are operated by Orkney Ferries. Please see *orkneyferries.co.uk* for details.			
Shetland Islands			
Aberdeen	Lerwick	12 hrs 30 mins	*northlinkferries.co.uk*
Kirkwall	Lerwick	7 hrs 45 mins	*northlinkferries.co.uk*
Inter-island services are operated by Shetland Island Council Ferries. Please see *shetland.gov.uk/ferries* for details.			

Please note that some smaller island services are day dependent and reservations are required for some routes. Book and confirm sailing schedules by contacting the operator.

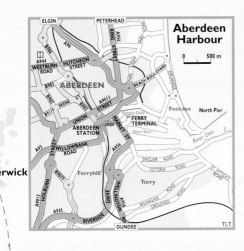

Aberdeen Harbour

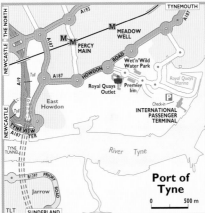

Port of Tyne

Port of Hull

For a port plan of Harwich see atlas page 53

NORTH SEA FERRY CROSSINGS

From	To	Journey time	Operator website
Harwich	Hook of Holland	7–8 hrs	*stenaline.co.uk*
Kingston upon Hull	Rotterdam (Europoort)	12 hrs	*poferries.com*
Kingston upon Hull	Zeebrugge	12 hrs	*poferries.com*
Newcastle upon Tyne	Amsterdam (IJmuiden)	15 hrs 30 mins	*dfdsseaways.co.uk*

The information listed on this page is provided as a guide only, as services are liable to change at short notice. Services shown are for vehicle ferries only, operated by conventional ferry. Please check sailings before planning your journey.

NORTH SEA

Caravan and camping sites in Britain

These pages list the top 300 AA-inspected Caravan and Camping (C & C) sites in the Pennant rating scheme. **Five Pennant Premier sites are shown in green,** **Four Pennant sites are shown in blue.**

Listings include addresses, telephone numbers and websites together with page and grid references to locate the sites in the atlas. The total number of touring pitches is also included for each site, together with the type of pitch available. The following abbreviations are used: **C = Caravan CV = Campervan T = Tent**

To find out more about the AA's Pennant rating scheme and other rated caravan and camping sites not included on these pages please visit *theAA.com*

ENGLAND

Alders Caravan Park
Home Farm, Alne, York
YO61 1RY
Tel: 01347 838722
alderscaravanpark.co.uk   **97 R7**
Total Pitches: 87 (C, CV & T)

Andrewshayes Holiday Park
Dalwood, Axminster
EX13 7DY
Tel: 01404 831225
andrewshayes.co.uk   **10 E5**
Total Pitches: 150 (C, CV & T)

Apple Tree Park C & C Site
A38, Claypits, Stonehouse
GL10 3AL
Tel: 01452 742362   **32 E3**
appletreepark.co.uk
Total Pitches: 65 (C, CV & T)

Atlantic Bays Holiday Park
St Merryn, Padstow
PL28 8PY
Tel: 01841 520855   **4 D7**
atlanticbaysholidaypark.co.uk
Total Pitches: 70 (C, CV & T)

Ayr Holiday Park
St Ives, Cornwall
TR26 1EJ
Tel: 01736 795855   **2 E5**
ayrholidaypark.co.uk
Total Pitches: 40 (C, CV & T)

Back of Beyond Touring Park
234 Ringwood Road,
St Leonards, Dorset
BH24 2SB
Tel: 01202 876968   **13 K4**
backofbeyondtouringpark.co.uk
Total Pitches: 80 (C, CV & T)

Bagwell Farm Touring Park
Knights in the Bottom,
Chickerell, Weymouth
DT3 4EA
Tel: 01305 782575   **11 N8**
bagwellfarm.co.uk
Total Pitches: 320 (C, CV & T)

Bardsea Leisure Park
Priory Road, Ulverston
LA12 9QE
Tel: 01229 584712   **94 F5**
bardsealeisure.co.uk
Total Pitches: 83 (C & CV)

Barn Farm Campsite
Barn Farm, Birchover, Matlock
DE4 2BL
Tel: 01629 650245   **84 B8**
barnfarmcamping.com
Total Pitches: 62 (C, CV & T)

Bath Chew Valley Caravan Park
Ham Lane,
Bishop Sutton
BS39 5TZ
Tel: 01275 332127   **19 Q3**
bathchewvalley.co.uk
Total Pitches: 45 (C, CV & T)

Bay View Holiday Park
Bolton le Sands, Carnforth
LA5 9TN
Tel: 01524 732854   **95 K7**
holgates.co.uk
Total Pitches: 100 (C, CV & T)

Beacon Cottage Farm Touring Park
Beacon Drive, St Agnes
TR5 0NU
Tel: 01872 552347   **3 J3**
beaconcottagefarmholidays.co.uk
Total Pitches: 70 (C, CV & T)

Beaconsfield Farm Caravan Park
Battlefield,
Shrewsbury
SY4 4AA
Tel: 01939 210370   **69 P11**
beaconsfieldholidaypark.co.uk
Total Pitches: 60 (C & CV)

Beech Croft Farm
Beech Croft,
Blackwell in the Peak,
Buxton
SK17 9TQ
Tel: 01298 85330   **83 P10**
beechcroftfarm.co.uk
Total Pitches: 30 (C, CV & T)

Bellingham C & C Club Site
Brown Rigg, Bellingham
NE48 2JY
Tel: 01434 220175   **112 B4**
campingandcaravanning club.co.uk/bellingham
Total Pitches: 64 (C, CV & T)

Beverley Park C & C Park
Goodrington Road, Paignton
TQ4 7JE
Tel: 01803 661961   **7 M7**
beverley-holidays.co.uk
Total Pitches: 172 (C, CV & T)

Blue Rose Caravan Country Park
Star Carr Lane, Brandesburton
YO25 8RU
Tel: 01964 543366   **99 N11**
bluerosepark.com
Total Pitches: 58 (C & CV)

Briarfields Motel & Touring Park
Gloucester Road, Cheltenham
GL51 0SX
Tel: 01242 235324   **46 H10**
briarfields.net
Total Pitches: 72 (C, CV & T)

Broadhembury C & C Park
Steeds Lane, Kingsnorth,
Ashford
TN26 1NQ
Tel: 01233 620859   **26 H4**
broadhembury.co.uk
Total Pitches: 110 (C, CV & T)

Budemeadows Touring Park
Widemouth Bay, Bude
EX23 0NA
Tel: 01288 361646   **16 C11**
budemeadows.com
Total Pitches: 145 (C, CV & T)

Burnham-on-Sea Holiday Village
Marine Drive,
Burnham-on-Sea
TA8 1LA
Tel: 01278 783391   **19 K5**
haven.com/burnhamonsea
Total Pitches: 781 (C, CV & T)

Burrowhayes Farm C & C Site & Riding Stables
West Luccombe, Porlock,
Minehead
TA24 8HT
Tel: 01643 862463   **18 A5**
burrowhayes.co.uk
Total Pitches: 120 (C, CV & T)

Burton Constable Holiday Park & Arboretum
Old Lodges, Sproatley, Hull
HU11 4LJ
Tel: 01964 562508   **93 L3**
burtonconstable.co.uk
Total Pitches: 105 (C, CV & T)

Caister-on-Sea Holiday Park
Ormesby Road, Caister-on-Sea,
Great Yarmouth
NR30 5NH
Tel: 01493 728931   **77 Q9**
haven.com/caister
Total Pitches: 949 (C &CV)

Caistor Lakes Leisure Park
99a Brigg Road,
Caistor
LN7 6RX
Tel: 01472 859626   **93 K10**
caistorlakes.co.uk
Total Pitches: 36 (C &CV)

Cakes & Ale
Abbey Lane, Theberton, Leiston
IP16 4TE
Tel: 01728 831655   **65 N9**
cakesandale.co.uk
Total Pitches: 55 (C, CV & T)

Calloose C & C Park
Leedstown, Hayle
TR27 5ET
Tel: 01736 850431   **2 F7**
calloose.co.uk
Total Pitches: 109 (C, CV & T)

Camping Caradon Touring Park
Trelawne, Looe
PL13 2NA
Tel: 01503 272388   **5 L11**
campingcaradon.co.uk
Total Pitches: 75 (C, CV & T)

Capesthorne Hall
Congleton Road, Siddington,
Macclesfield
SK11 9JY
Tel: 01625 861221   **82 H10**
capesthorne.com
Total Pitches: 50 (C & CV)

Carlyon Bay C & C Park
Bethesda, Cypress Avenue,
Carlyon Bay
PL25 3RE
Tel: 01726 812735   **3 R3**
carlyonbay.net
Total Pitches: 180 (C, CV & T)

Carnon Downs C & C Park
Carnon Downs, Truro
TR3 6JJ
Tel: 01872 862283   **3 L5**
carnon-downs-caravanpark.co.uk
Total Pitches: 150 (C, CV & T)

Cartref C & C
Cartref, Ford Heath,
Shrewsbury
SY5 9GD
Tel: 01743 821688   **56 G2**
cartrefcaravansite.co.uk
Total Pitches: 44 (C & CV & T)

Carvynick Country Club
Summercourt, Newquay
TR8 5AF
Tel: 01872 510716   **4 D10**
carvynick.co.uk
Total Pitches: 47 (C & CV)

Castlerigg Hall C & C Park
Castlerigg Hall, Keswick
CA12 4TE
Tel: 017687 74499   **101 J6**
castlerigg.co.uk
Total Pitches: 68 (C, CV & T)

Charris C & C Park
Candy's Lane, Corfe Mullen,
Wimborne
BH21 3EF
Tel: 01202 885970   **12 G5**
charris.co.uk
Total Pitches: 45 (C, CV & T)

Cheddar Mendip Heights C & C Club Site
Townsend, Priddy, Wells
BA5 3BP
Tel: 01749 870241   **19 P4**
campingandcaravanningclub. co.uk/cheddar
Total Pitches: 90 (C, CV & T)

Chy Carne Holiday Park
Kuggar, Ruan Minor,
Helston
TR12 7LX
Tel: 01326 290200   **3 J10**
chycarne.co.uk
Total Pitches: 30 (C, CV & T)

Clippesby Hall
Hall Lane, Clippesby,
Great Yarmouth
NR29 3BL
Tel: 01493 367800   **77 N9**
clippesbyhall.com
Total Pitches: 120 (C, CV & T)

Cofton Holidays
Starcross, Dawlish
EX6 8RP
Tel: 01626 890111   **9 N8**
coftonholidays.co.uk
Total Pitches: 450 (C, CV & T)

Concierge Camping
Ratham Estate, Ratham Lane,
West Ashling, Chichester
PO18 8DL
Tel: 01243 573118   **15 M5**
conciergecamping.co.uk
Total Pitches: 15 (C, CV & T)

Coombe Touring Park
Race Plain, Netherhampton,
Salisbury
SP2 8PN
Tel: 01722 328451   **21 L9**
coombecaravanpark.co.uk
Total Pitches: 50 (C, CV & T)

Corfe Castle C & C Club Site
Bucknowle, Wareham
BH20 5PQ
Tel: 01929 480280   **12 F8**
campingandcaravanning club.co.uk/corfecastle
Total Pitches: 80 (C, CV & T)

Cornish Farm Touring Park
Shoreditch, Taunton
TA3 7BS
Tel: 01823 327746   **18 H10**
cornishfarm.com
Total Pitches: 50 (C, CV & T)

Cosawes Park
Perranarworthal, Truro
TR3 7QS
Tel: 01872 863724   **3 K6**
cosawes.co.uk
Total Pitches: 59 (C, CV & T)

Cote Ghyll C & C Park
Osmotherley,
Northallerton
DL6 3AH
Tel: 01609 883425   **104 E11**
coteghyll.com
Total Pitches: 77 (C, CV & T)

Country View Holiday Park
Sand Road, Sand Bay,
Weston-super-Mare
BS22 9UJ
Tel: 01934 627595   **19 K2**
cvhp.co.uk
Total Pitches: 190 (C, CV & T)

Crealy Adventure Park and Resort
Sidmouth Road, Clyst St Mary,
Exeter
EX5 1DR
Tel: 01395 234888   **9 P6**
crealy.co.uk
Total Pitches: 120 (C, CV & T)

Crows Nest Caravan Park
Gristhorpe, Filey
YO14 9PS
Tel: 01723 582206   **99 M4**
crowsnestcaravanpark.co.uk
Total Pitches: 49 (C, CV & T)

Deepdale Backpackers & Camping
Deepdale Farm, Burnham
Deepdale
PE31 8DD
Tel: 01485 210256   **75 R2**
deepdalebackpackers.co.uk
Total Pitches: 80 (CV & T)

Dolbeare Park C & C
St Ive Road, Landrake,
Saltash
PL12 5AF
Tel: 01752 851332   **5 P9**
dolbeare.co.uk
Total Pitches: 60 (C, CV & T)

Dornafield
Dornafield Farm, Two Mile Oak,
Newton Abbot
TQ12 6DD
Tel: 01803 812732   **7 L5**
dornafield.com
Total Pitches: 135 (C, CV & T)

East Fleet Farm Touring Park
Chickerell, Weymouth
DT3 4DW
Tel: 01305 785768   **11 N9**
eastfleet.co.uk
Total Pitches: 400 (C, CV & T)

Eden Valley Holiday Park
Lanlivery, Nr Lostwithiel
PL30 5BU
Tel: 01208 872277   **4 H10**
edenvalleyholidaypark.co.uk
Total Pitches: 56 (C, CV & T)

Exe Valley Caravan Site
Mill House, Bridgetown,
Dulverton
TA22 9JR
Tel: 01643 851432   **18 B8**
exevalleycamping.co.uk
Total Pitches: 48 (C, CV & T)

Eye Kettleby Lakes
Eye Kettleby,
Melton Mowbray
LE14 2TN
Tel: 01664 565900   **73 J7**
eyekettlebylakes.com
Total Pitches: 130 (C, CV & T)

Fields End Water Caravan Park & Fishery
Benwick Road, Doddington,
March
PE15 0TY
Tel: 01354 740199   **62 E2**
fieldsendcaravans.co.uk
Total Pitches: 52 (C, CV & T)

Flower of May Holiday Park
Lebberston Cliff, Filey,
Scarborough
YO11 3NU
Tel: 01723 584311   **99 M4**
flowerofmay.com
Total Pitches: 503 (C, CV & T)

Freshwater Beach Holiday Park
Burton Bradstock,
Bridport
DT6 4PT
Tel: 01308 897317   **11 K6**
freshwaterbeach.co.uk
Total Pitches: 750 (C, CV & T)

Glenfield Caravan Park
Blackmoor Lane, Bardsey,
Leeds
LS17 9DZ
Tel: 01937 574657   **91 J2**
glenfieldcaravanpark.co.uk
Total Pitches: 31 (C, CV & T)

Globe Vale Holiday Park
Radnor, Redruth
TR16 4BH
Tel: 01209 891183   **3 J5**
globevale.co.uk
Total Pitches: 138 (C, CV & T)

Glororum Caravan Park
Glororum Farm,
Bamburgh
NE69 7AW
Tel: 01670 860256   **119 N4**
northumbrianleisure.co.uk
Total Pitches: 213 (C & CV)

Golden Cap Holiday Park
Seatown, Chideock, Bridport
DT6 6JX
Tel: 01308 422139   **11 J6**
wdlh.co.uk
Total Pitches: 108 (C, CV & T)

Golden Coast Holiday Park
Station Road, Woolacombe
EX34 7HW
Tel: 01271 872302   **16 H3**
woolacombe.com
Total Pitches: 431 (C, CV & T)

Golden Sands Holiday Park
Quebec Road, Mablethorpe
LN12 1QJ
Tel: 01507 477871   **87 N3**
haven.com/goldensands
Total Pitches: 1672 (C, CV & T)

Golden Square C & C Park
Oswaldkirk,
Helmsley
YO62 5YQ
Tel: 01439 788269   **98 C5**
goldensquarecaravanpark.com
Total Pitches: 129 (C, CV & T)

Goosewood Holiday Park
Sutton-on-the-Forest,
York
YO61 1ET
Tel: 01347 810829   **98 B8**
flowerofmay.com
Total Pitches: 100 (C & CV)

Green Acres Caravan Park
High Knells, Houghton,
Carlisle
CA6 4JW
Tel: 01228 675418   **110 H8**
caravanpark-cumbria.com
Total Pitches: 35 (C, CV & T)

Greenhill Farm C & C Park
Greenhill Farm, New Road,
Landford, Salisbury
SP5 2AZ
Tel: 01794 324117   **21 Q11**
greenhillfarm.co.uk
Total Pitches: 160 (C, CV & T)

Greenhill Leisure Park
Greenhill Farm, Station Road,
Bletchingdon, Oxford
OX5 3BQ
Tel: 01869 351600   **48 E11**
greenhill-leisure-park.co.uk
Total Pitches: 92 (C, CV & T)

Grooby's Pit
Bridgefoot Farm, Steeping Road,
Thorpe St Peter
PE24 4QT
Tel: 07427 137463   **87 N8**
fishskegness.co.uk
Total Pitches: 18 (C & CV)

Grouse Hill Caravan Park
Flask Bungalow Farm,
Fylingdales, Robin Hood's Bay
YO22 4QH
Tel: 01947 880543 **105 P10**
grousehill.co.uk
Total Pitches: 175 (C, CV & T)

Gunvenna Holiday Park
St Minver,
Wadebridge
PL27 6QN
Tel: 01208 862405 **4 F6**
gunvenna.com
Total Pitches: 75 (C, CV & T)

**Haggerston Castle
Holiday Park**
Beal, Berwick-upon-Tweed
TD15 2PA
Tel: 01289 381333 **119 K2**
haven.com/haggerstoncastle
Total Pitches: 1340 (C & CV)

Harbury Fields
Harbury Fields Farm, Harbury,
Nr Leamington Spa
CV33 9JN
Tel: 01926 612457 **48 C2**
harburyfields.co.uk
Total Pitches: 59 (C & CV)

**Harford Bridge
Holiday Park**
Peter Tavy, Tavistock
PL19 9LS
Tel: 01822 810349 **8 D9**
harfordbridge.co.uk
Total Pitches: 198 (C, CV & T)

**Haw Wood Farm
Caravan Park**
Hinton, Saxmundham
IP17 3QT
Tel: 01502 359550 **65 N7**
hawwoodfarm.co.uk
Total Pitches: 60 (C, CV & T)

Heathfield Farm Camping
Heathfield Road, Freshwater,
Isle of Wight
PO40 9SH
Tel: 01983 407822 **13 P7**
heathfieldcamping.co.uk
Total Pitches: 75 (C, CV & T)

**Heathland Beach
Caravan Park**
London Road,
Kessingland
NR33 7PJ
Tel: 01502 740337 **65 Q4**
heathlandbeach.co.uk
Total Pitches: 63 (C, CV & T)

Hele Valley Holiday Park
Hele Bay, Ilfracombe
EX34 9RD
Tel: 01271 862460 **17 J2**
helevalley.co.uk
Total Pitches: 50 (C, CV & T)

Hendra Holiday Park
Newquay
TR8 4NY
Tel: 01637 875778 **4 C9**
hendra-holidays.com
Total Pitches: 548 (C, CV & T)

Hidden Valley Park
West Down, Braunton,
Ilfracombe
EX34 8NU
Tel: 01271 813837 **17 J3**
hiddenvalleypark.com
Total Pitches: 100 (C, CV & T)

Highfield Farm Touring Park
Long Road, Comberton,
Cambridge
CB23 7DG
Tel: 01223 262308 **62 E9**
highfieldfarmtouringpark.co.uk
Total Pitches: 120 (C, CV & T)

Highlands End Holiday Park
Eype, Bridport,
Dorset
DT6 6AR
Tel: 01308 422139 **11 K6**
wdlh.co.uk
Total Pitches: 195 (C, CV & T)

Hill Cottage Farm C & C Park
Sandleheath Road, Alderholt,
Fordingbridge
SP6 3EG
Tel: 01425 650513 **13 K2**
hillcottagefarm
campingandcaravanpark.co.uk
Total Pitches: 95 (C, CV & T)

Hill of Oaks & Blakeholme
Windermere
LA12 8NR
Tel: 015395 31578 **94 H3**
hillofoaks.co.uk
Total Pitches: 43 (C & CV)

Hillside Caravan Park
Canvas Farm, Moor Road,
Knayton, Thirsk
YO7 4BR
Tel: 01845 537349 **97 P3**
hillsidecaravanpark.co.uk
Total Pitches: 50 (C & CV)

Holiday Resort Unity
Coast Road, Brean Sands,
Brean
TA8 2RB
Tel: 01278 751235 **19 J4**
hru.co.uk
Total Pitches: 1114 (C, CV & T)

Hollins Farm C & C
Far Arnside, Carnforth
LA5 0SL
Tel: 01524 701767 **95 J5**
holgates.co.uk
Total Pitches: 12 (C, CV & T)

Hylton Caravan Park
Eden Street, Silloth
CA7 4AY
Tel: 016973 31707 **109 P10**
stanwix.com
Total Pitches: 90 (C, CV & T)

Island Lodge C & C Site
Stumpy Post Cross,
Kingsbridge
TQ7 4BL
Tel: 01548 852956 **7 J9**
islandlodgesite.co.uk
Total Pitches: 30 (C, CV & T)

**Isle of Avalon
Touring Caravan Park**
Godney Road, Glastonbury
BA6 9AF
Tel: 01458 833618 **19 N7**
avaloncaravanpark.co.uk
Total Pitches: 120 (C, CV & T)

Jasmine Caravan Park
Cross Lane, Snainton,
Scarborough
YO13 9BE
Tel: 01723 859240 **99 J4**
jasminepark.co.uk
Total Pitches: 68 (C, CV & T)

**Kenneggy Cove
Holiday Park**
Higher Kenneggy, Rosudgeon,
Penzance
TR20 9AU
Tel: 01736 763453 **2 F8**
kenneggycove.co.uk
Total Pitches: 40 (C, CV & T)

**Kennford International
Caravan Park**
Kennford, Exeter
EX6 7YN
Tel: 01392 833046 **9 M7**
kennfordinternational.co.uk
Total Pitches: 87 (C, CV & T)

King's Lynn C & C Park
New Road, North Runcton,
King's Lynn
PE33 0RA
Tel: 01553 840004 **75 M7**
kl-cc.co.uk
Total Pitches: 150 (C, CV & T)

Kloofs Caravan Park
Sandhurst Lane, Bexhill
TN39 4RG
Tel: 01424 842839 **26 B10**
kloofs.com
Total Pitches: 125 (C, CV & T)

**Kneps Farm
Holiday Park**
River Road, Stanah,
Thornton-Cleveleys, Blackpool
FY5 5LR
Tel: 01253 823632 **88 D2**
knepsfarm.co.uk
Total Pitches: 40 (C & CV)

**Knight Stainforth Hall
Caravan & Campsite**
Stainforth, Settle
BD24 0DP
Tel: 01729 822200 **96 B7**
knightstainforth.co.uk
Total Pitches: 100 (C, CV & T)

**Ladycross Plantation
Caravan Park**
Egton, Whitby
YO21 1UA
Tel: 01947 895502 **105 M9**
ladycrossplantation.co.uk
Total Pitches: 130 (C, CV & T)

**Lady's Mile
Holiday Park**
Dawlish, Devon
EX7 0LX
Tel: 01626 863411 **9 N9**
ladysmile.co.uk
Total Pitches: 570 (C, CV & T)

Lakeland Leisure Park
Moor Lane, Flookburgh
LA11 7LT
Tel: 01539 558556 **94 H6**
haven.com/lakeland
Total Pitches: 977 (C, CV & T)

**Lamb Cottage
Caravan Park**
Dalefords Lane, Whitegate,
Northwich
CW8 2BN
Tel: 01606 882302 **82 D11**
lambcottage.co.uk
Total Pitches: 45 (C & CV)

**Langstone Manor
C & C Park**
Moortown, Tavistock
PL19 9JZ
Tel: 01822 613371 **6 E4**
langstonemanor.co.uk
Total Pitches: 40 (C, CV & T)

Lanyon Holiday Park
Loscombe Lane,
Four Lanes, Redruth
TR16 6LP
Tel: 01209 313474 **2 H6**
lanyonholidaypark.co.uk
Total Pitches: 25 (C, CV & T)

Lebberston Touring Park
Filey Road, Lebberston,
Scarborough
YO11 3PE
Tel: 01723 585723 **99 M4**
lebberstontouring.co.uk
Total Pitches: 125 (C & CV)

Lickpenny Caravan Site
Lickpenny Lane, Tansley,
Matlock
DE4 5GF
Tel: 01629 583040 **84 D9**
lickpennycaravanpark.co.uk
Total Pitches: 80 (C & CV)

Lime Tree Park
Dukes Drive, Buxton
SK17 9RP
Tel: 01298 22988 **83 N10**
limetreeparkbuxton.com
Total Pitches: 106 (C, CV & T)

**Lincoln Farm Park
Oxfordshire**
High Street, Standlake
OX29 7RH
Tel: 01865 300239 **34 C4**
lincolnfarmpark.co.uk
Total Pitches: 90 (C, CV & T)

**Little Lakeland
Caravan Park**
Wortwell, Harleston
IP20 0EL
Tel: 01986 788646 **65 K5**
littlelakeland
caravanparkandcamping.co.uk
Total Pitches: 58 (C, CV & T)

Littlesea Holiday Park
Lynch Lane, Weymouth
DT4 9DT
Tel: 01305 774414 **11 P9**
haven.com/littlesea
Total Pitches: 861 (C, CV & T)

Long Acres Touring Park
Station Road, Old Leake,
Boston
PE22 9RF
Tel: 01205 871555 **87 L10**
long-acres.co.uk
Total Pitches: 40 (C, CV & T)

Longnor Wood Holiday Park
Newtown, Longnor,
Nr Buxton
SK17 0NG
Tel: 01298 83648 **71 K2**
longnorwood.co.uk
Total Pitches: 47 (C, CV & T)

**Lower Polladras
Touring Park**
Carleen, Breage, Helston
TR13 9NX
Tel: 01736 762220 **2 G7**
lower-polladras.co.uk
Total Pitches: 39 (C, CV & T)

Lowther Holiday Park
Eamont Bridge, Penrith
CA10 2JB
Tel: 01768 863631 **101 P5**
lowther-holidaypark.co.uk
Total Pitches: 180 (C, CV & T)

**Manor Wood Country
Caravan Park**
Manor Wood, Coddington,
Chester
CH3 9EN
Tel: 01829 782990 **69 M4**
cheshire-caravan-sites.co.uk
Total Pitches: 45 (C, CV & T)

Marton Mere Holiday Village
Mythop Road, Blackpool
FY4 4XN
Tel: 01253 767544 **88 C4**
haven.com/martonmere
Total Pitches: 782 (C & CV)

Mayfield Park
Cheltenham Road, Cirencester
GL7 7BH
Tel: 01285 831301 **33 K3**
mayfieldpark.co.uk
Total Pitches: 105 (C, CV & T)

Meadowbank Holidays
Stour Way, Christchurch
BH23 2PQ
Tel: 01202 483597 **13 K6**
meadowbank-holidays.co.uk
Total Pitches: 41 (C & CV)

**Middlewood Farm
Holiday Park**
Middlewood Lane, Fylingthorpe,
Robin Hood's Bay, Whitby
YO22 4UF
Tel: 01947 880414 **105 P10**
middlewoodfarm.com
Total Pitches: 100 (C, CV & T)

Minnows Touring Park
Holbrook Lane, Sampford
Peverell
EX16 7EN
Tel: 01884 821770 **18 D11**
minnowstouringpark.co.uk
Total Pitches: 59 (C, CV & T)

Monkey Tree Holiday Park
Hendra Croft, Scotland Road,
Newquay
TR8 5QR
Tel: 01872 572032 **3 L3**
monkeytreeholidaypark.co.uk
Total Pitches: 700 (C, CV & T)

Moon & Sixpence
Newbourn Road, Waldringfield,
Woodbridge
IP12 4PP
Tel: 01473 736650 **53 N2**
moonandsixpence.co.uk
Total Pitches: 50 (C & CV)

Moor Lodge Park
Blackmoor Lane, Bardsey, Leeds
LS17 9DZ
Tel: 01937 572424 **91 K2**
moorlodgecaravanpark.co.uk
Total Pitches: 12 (C & CV)

Moss Wood Caravan Park
Crimbles Lane, Cockerham
LA2 0ES
Tel: 01524 791041 **95 K11**
mosswood.co.uk
Total Pitches: 25 (C, CV & T)

Naburn Lock Caravan Park
Naburn
YO19 4RU
Tel: 01904 728697 **98 C11**
naburnlock.co.uk
Total Pitches: 100 (C, CV & T)

New Lodge Farm C & C Site
New Lodge Farm, Bulwick,
Corby
NN17 3DU
Tel: 01780 450493 **73 P11**
newlodgefarm.com
Total Pitches: 72 (C, CV & T)

Newberry Valley Park
Woodlands, Combe Martin
EX34 0AT
Tel: 01271 882334 **17 K2**
newberryvalleypark.co.uk
Total Pitches: 110 (C, CV & T)

Newlands Holidays
Charmouth, Bridport
DT6 6RB
Tel: 01297 560259 **10 H6**
newlandsholidays.co.uk
Total Pitches: 240 (C, CV & T)

Newperran Holiday Park
Rejerrah, Newquay
TR8 5QJ
Tel: 01872 572407 **3 K3**
newperran.co.uk
Total Pitches: 357 (C, CV & T)

Ninham Country Holidays
Ninham, Shanklin, Isle of Wight
PO37 7PL
Tel: 01983 864243 **14 G10**
ninham-holidays.co.uk
Total Pitches: 135 (C, CV & T)

North Morte Farm C & C Park
North Morte Road, Mortehoe,
Woolacombe
EX34 7EG
Tel: 01271 870381 **16 H2**
northmortefarm.co.uk
Total Pitches: 180 (C, CV & T)

**Northam Farm Caravan
& Touring Park**
Brean, Burnham-on-Sea
TA8 2SE
Tel: 01278 751244 **19 K3**
northamfarm.co.uk
Total Pitches: 350 (C, CV & T)

**Oakdown Country
Holiday Park**
Gatedown Lane, Weston,
Sidmouth
EX10 0PT
Tel: 01297 680387 **10 D6**
oakdown.co.uk
Total Pitches: 150 (C, CV & T)

Old Hall Caravan Park
Capernwray, Carnforth
LA6 1AD
Tel: 01524 733276 **95 L6**
oldhallcaravanpark.co.uk
Total Pitches: 38 (C & CV)

Ord House Country Park
East Ord,
Berwick-upon-Tweed
TD15 2NS
Tel: 01289 305288 **129 P9**
ordhouse.co.uk
Total Pitches: 79 (C, CV & T)

Oxon Hall Touring Park
Welshpool Road,
Shrewsbury
SY3 5FB
Tel: 01743 340868 **56 H2**
morris-leisure.co.uk
Total Pitches: 105 (C, CV & T)

Padstow Touring Park
Padstow
PL28 8LE
Tel: 01841 532061 **4 E7**
padstowtouringpark.co.uk
Total Pitches: 150 (C, CV & T)

Park Cliffe C & C Estate
Birks Road, Tower Wood,
Windermere
LA23 3PG
Tel: 015395 31344 **94 H2**
parkcliffe.co.uk
Total Pitches: 60 (C, CV & T)

Parkers Farm Holiday Park
Higher Mead Farm,
Ashburton, Devon
TQ13 7LJ
Tel: 01364 654869 **7 K4**
parkersfarmholidays.co.uk
Total Pitches: 100 (C, CV & T)

Park Foot C & C Park
Howtown Road,
Pooley Bridge
CA10 2NA
Tel: 017684 86309 **101 N6**
parkfootullswater.co.uk
Total Pitches: 454 (C, CV & T)

Parkland C & C Site
Sorley Green Cross,
Kingsbridge
TQ7 4AF
Tel: 01548 852723 **7 J9**
parklandsite.co.uk
Total Pitches: 50 (C, CV & T)

**Pebble Bank
Caravan Park**
Camp Road, Wyke Regis,
Weymouth
DT4 9HF
Tel: 01305 774844 **11 P9**
pebblebank.co.uk
Total Pitches: 120 (C, CV & T)

**Perran Sands
Holiday Park**
Perranporth, Truro
TR6 0AQ
Tel: 01872 573551 **4 B10**
haven.com/perransands
Total Pitches: 1012 (C, CV & T)

Petwood Caravan Park
Off Stixwould Road,
Woodhall Spa
LN10 6QH
Tel: 01526 354799 **86 G8**
petwoodcaravanpark.com
Total Pitches: 98 (C, CV & T)

Polmanter Touring Park
Halsetown, St Ives
TR26 3LX
Tel: 01736 795640 **2 E6**
polmanter.co.uk
Total Pitches: 270 (C, CV & T)

Porthtowan Tourist Park
Mile Hill, Porthtowan,
Truro
TR4 8TY
Tel: 01209 890256 **2 H4**
porthtowantouristpark.co.uk
Total Pitches: 80 (C, CV & T)

Primrose Valley Holiday Park
Filey
YO14 9RF
Tel: 01723 513771 **99 N5**
haven.com/primrosevalley
Total Pitches: 1549 (C & CV)

Quantock Orchard Caravan Park
Flaxpool, Crowcombe, Taunton
TA4 4AW
Tel: 01984 618618 **18 F7**
quantock-orchard.co.uk
Total Pitches: 60 (C, CV & T)

Ranch Caravan Park
Station Road, Honeybourne, Evesham
WR11 7PR
Tel: 01386 830744 **47 M6**
ranch.co.uk
Total Pitches: 120 (C & CV)

Ripley Caravan Park
Knaresborough Road, Ripley, Harrogate
HG3 3AU
Tel: 01423 770050 **97 L8**
ripleycaravanpark.com
Total Pitches: 60 (C, CV & T)

River Dart Country Park
Holne Park, Ashburton
TQ13 7NP
Tel: 01364 652511 **7 J5**
riverdart.co.uk
Total Pitches: 170 (C, CV & T)

River Valley Holiday Park
London Apprentice, St Austell
PL26 7AP
Tel: 01726 73533 **3 Q3**
rivervalleyholidaypark.co.uk
Total Pitches: 45 (C, CV & T)

Riverside C & C Park
Marsh Lane, North Molton Road, South Molton
EX36 3HQ
Tel: 01769 579269 **17 N6**
exmoorriverside.co.uk
Total Pitches: 58 (C, CV & T)

Riverside Caravan Park
High Bentham, Lancaster
LA2 7FJ
Tel: 015242 61272 **95 P7**
riversidecaravanpark.co.uk
Total Pitches: 61 (C & CV)

Riverside Holiday Park
Southport New Road, Southport
PR9 8DF
Tel: 01704 228886 **88 E7**
riversideleisurecentre.co.uk
Total Pitches: 615 (C & CV)

Riverside Meadows Country Caravan Park
Ure Bank Top, Ripon
HG4 1JD
Tel: 01765 602964 **97 M6**
flowerofmay.com
Total Pitches: 80 (C, CV & T)

Robin Hood C & C Park
Green Dyke Lane, Slingsby
YO62 4AP
Tel: 01653 628391 **98 E6**
robinhoodcaravanpark.co.uk
Total Pitches: 32 (C, CV & T)

Rose Farm Touring & Camping Park
Stepshort, Belton, Nr Great Yarmouth
NR31 9JS
Tel: 01493 738292 **77 P11**
rosefarmtouringpark.co.uk
Total Pitches: 145 (C, CV & T)

Rosedale Abbey C & C Park
Rosedale Abbey, Pickering
YO18 8SA
Tel: 01751 417272 **105 K11**
rosedaleabbeycaravanpark.co.uk
Total Pitches: 100 (C, CV & T)

Ross Park
Park Hill Farm, Ipplepen, Newton Abbot
TQ12 5TT
Tel: 01803 812983 **7 L5**
rossparkcaravanpark.co.uk
Total Pitches: 110 (C, CV & T)

Rudding Holiday Park
Follifoot, Harrogate
HG3 1JH
Tel: 01423 870439 **97 M10**
ruddingholidaypark.co.uk
Total Pitches: 86 (C, CV & T)

Run Cottage Touring Park
Alderton Road, Hollesley, Woodbridge
IP12 3RQ
Tel: 01394 411309 **53 Q3**
runcottage.co.uk
Total Pitches: 45 (C, CV & T)

Rutland C & C
Park Lane, Greetham, Oakham
LE15 7FN
Tel: 01572 813520 **73 N8**
rutlandcaravanandcamping.co.uk
Total Pitches: 130 (C, CV & T)

St Helens Caravan Park
Wykeham, Scarborough
YO13 9QD
Tel: 01723 862771 **99 K4**
sthelenscaravanpark.co.uk
Total Pitches: 250 (C, CV & T)

St Ives Bay Holiday Park
73 Loggans Road, Upton Towans, Hayle
TR27 5BH
Tel: 01736 752274 **2 F6**
stivesbay.co.uk
Total Pitches: 507 (C, CV & T)

Salcombe Regis C & C Park
Salcombe Regis, Sidmouth
EX10 0JH
Tel: 01395 514303 **10 D7**
salcombe-regis.co.uk
Total Pitches: 110 (C, CV & T)

Sand le Mere Holiday Village
Southfield Lane, Tunstall
HU12 0JF
Tel: 01964 670403 **93 P4**
sand-le-mere.co.uk
Total Pitches: 89 (C & CV)

Sandy Balls Holiday Village
Sandy Balls Estate Ltd, Godshill, Fordingbridge
SP6 2JZ
Tel: 01442 508850 **13 L2**
awayresorts.co.uk
Total Pitches: 225 (C, CV & T)

Searles Leisure Resort
South Beach Road, Hunstanton
PE36 5BB
Tel: 01485 534211 **75 N3**
searles.co.uk
Total Pitches: 413 (C, CV & T)

Seaview Holiday Park
Preston, Weymouth
DT3 6DZ
Tel: 01305 832271 **11 Q8**
haven.com/seaview
Total Pitches: 347 (C, CV & T)

Seaview International Holiday Park
Boswinger, Mevagissey
PL26 6LL
Tel: 01726 843425 **3 P5**
seaviewinternational.com
Total Pitches: 201 (C, CV & T)

Severn Gorge Park
Bridgnorth Road, Tweedale, Telford
TF7 4JB
Tel: 01952 684789 **57 N3**
severngorgepark.co.uk
Total Pitches: 12 (C & CV)

Shamba Holidays
East Moors Lane, St Leonards, Ringwood
BH24 2SB
Tel: 01202 873302 **13 K4**
shambaholidays.co.uk
Total Pitches: 150 (C, CV & T)

Shrubbery Touring Park
Rousdon, Lyme Regis
DT7 3XW
Tel: 01297 442227 **10 F6**
shrubberypark.co.uk
Total Pitches: 120 (C, CV & T)

Silverdale Caravan Park
Middlebarrow Plain, Cove Road, Silverdale, Nr Carnforth
LA5 0SH
Tel: 01524 701508 **95 K5**
holgates.co.uk
Total Pitches: 80 (C, CV & T)

Skelwith Fold Caravan Park
Ambleside, Cumbria
LA22 0HX
Tel: 015394 32277 **101 L10**
skelwith.com
Total Pitches: 150 (C & CV)

Skirlington Leisure Park
Driffield, Skipsea
YO25 8SY
Tel: 01262 468213 **99 P10**
skirlington.com
Total Pitches: 930 (C & CV)

Sleningford Watermill Caravan Camping Park
North Stainley, Ripon
HG4 3HQ
Tel: 01765 635201 **97 L5**
sleningfordwatermill.co.uk
Total Pitches: 135 (C, CV & T)

Somers Wood Caravan Park
Somers Road, Meriden
CV7 7PL
Tel: 01676 522978 **59 K8**
somerswood.co.uk
Total Pitches: 48 (C & CV)

South Lytchett Manor C & C Park
Dorchester Road, Lytchett Minster, Poole
BH16 6JB
Tel: 01202 622577 **12 G6**
southlytchettmanor.co.uk
Total Pitches: 150 (C, CV & T)

South Meadows Caravan Park
South Road, Belford
NE70 7DP
Tel: 01668 213326 **119 M4**
southmeadows.co.uk
Total Pitches: 83 (C, CV & T)

Stanmore Hall Touring Park
Stourbridge Road, Bridgnorth
WV15 6DT
Tel: 01746 761761 **57 N6**
morris-leisure.co.uk
Total Pitches: 129 (C, CV & T)

Stanwix Park Holiday Centre
Greenrow, Silloth
CA7 4HH
Tel: 016973 32666 **109 P10**
stanwix.com
Total Pitches: 337 (C, CV & T)

Stowford Farm Meadows
Berry Down, Combe Martin
EX34 0PW
Tel: 01271 882476 **17 K3**
stowford.co.uk
Total Pitches: 700 (C, CV & T)

Stroud Hill Park
Fen Road, Pidley, St Ives
PE28 3DE
Tel: 01487 741333 **62 D5**
stroudhillpark.co.uk
Total Pitches: 60 (C, CV & T)

Summer Valley Touring Park
Shortlanesend, Truro
TR4 9DW
Tel: 01872 277878 **3 L4**
summervalley.co.uk
Total Pitches: 60 (C, CV & T)

Sumners Ponds Fishery & Campsite
Chapel Road, Barns Green, Horsham
RH13 0PR
Tel: 01403 732539 **24 D5**
sumnersponds.co.uk
Total Pitches: 86 (C, CV & T)

Swiss Farm Touring & Camping
Marlow Road, Henley-on-Thames
RG9 2HY
Tel: 01491 573419 **35 L8**
swissfarmhenley.co.uk
Total Pitches: 140 (C, CV & T)

Tanner Farm Touring C & C Park
Tanner Farm, Goudhurst Road, Marden
TN12 9ND
Tel: 01622 832399 **26 B3**
tannerfarmpark.co.uk
Total Pitches: 120 (C, CV & T)

Tattershall Lakes Country Park
Sleaford Road, Tattershall
LN4 4LR
Tel: 01526 348800 **86 H9**
tattershall-lakes.com
Total Pitches: 186 (C, CV & T)

Tehidy Holiday Park
Harris Mill, Illogan, Portreath
TR16 4JQ
Tel: 01209 216489 **2 H5**
tehidy.co.uk
Total Pitches: 18 (C, CV & T)

Tencreek Holiday Park
Polperro Road, Looe
PL13 2JR
Tel: 01503 262447 **5 L11**
dolphinholidays.co.uk
Total Pitches: 355 (C, CV & T)

Teversal C & C Club Site
Silverhill Lane, Teversal
NG17 3JJ
Tel: 01623 551838 **84 G8**
campingandcaravanningclub.co.uk/teversal
Total Pitches: 126 (C, CV & T)

The Laurels Holiday Park
Padstow Road, Whitecross, Wadebridge
PL27 7JQ
Tel: 01208 813341 **4 F7**
thelaurelsholidaypark.co.uk
Total Pitches: 30 (C, CV & T)

The Old Brick Kilns
Little Barney Lane, Barney, Fakenham
NR21 0NL
Tel: 01328 878305 **76 E5**
old-brick-kilns.co.uk
Total Pitches: 65 (C, CV & T)

The Old Oaks Touring Park
Wick Farm, Wick, Glastonbury
BA6 8JS
Tel: 01458 831437 **19 P7**
theoldoaks.co.uk
Total Pitches: 98 (C, CV & T)

The Orchards Holiday Caravan Park
Main Road, Newbridge, Yarmouth, Isle of Wight
PO41 0TS
Tel: 01983 531331 **14 D9**
orchards-holiday-park.co.uk
Total Pitches: 160 (C, CV & T)

The Quiet Site
Ullswater, Watermillock
CA11 0LS
Tel: 07768 727016 **101 M6**
thequietsite.co.uk
Total Pitches: 100 (C, CV & T)

Thornwick Bay Holiday Village
North Marine Road, Flamborough
YO15 1AU
Tel: 01262 850569 **99 Q6**
haven.com/parks/yorkshire/thornwick-bay
Total Pitches: 225 (C, CV & T)

Thorpe Park Holiday Centre
Cleethorpes
DN35 0PW
Tel: 01472 813395 **93 P9**
haven.com/thorpepark
Total Pitches: 1491 (C, CV & T)

Treago Farm Caravan Site
Crantock, Newquay
TR8 5QS
Tel: 01637 830277 **4 B9**
treagofarm.co.uk
Total Pitches: 90 (C, CV & T)

Tregoad Park
St Martin, Looe
PL13 1PB
Tel: 01503 262718 **5 M10**
tregoadpark.co.uk
Total Pitches: 200 (C, CV & T)

Treloy Touring Park
Newquay
TR8 4JN
Tel: 01637 872063 **4 D9**
treloy.co.uk
Total Pitches: 223 (C, CV & T)

Trencreek Holiday Park
Hillcrest, Higher Trencreek, Newquay
TR8 4NS
Tel: 01637 874210 **4 C9**
trencreekholidaypark.co.uk
Total Pitches: 194 (C, CV & T)

Trethem Mill Touring Park
St Just-in-Roseland, Nr St Mawes, Truro
TR2 5JF
Tel: 01872 580504 **3 M6**
trethem.com
Total Pitches: 84 (C, CV & T)

Trevalgan Touring Park
Trevalgan, St Ives
TR26 3BJ
Tel: 01736 791892 **2 D6**
trevalgantouringpark.co.uk
Total Pitches: 135 (C, CV & T)

Trevedra Farm C & C Site
Sennen, Penzance
TR19 7BE
Tel: 01736 871818 **2 B8**
trevedrafarm.co.uk
Total Pitches: 100 (C, CV & T)

Trevella Park
Crantock, Newquay
TR8 5EW
Tel: 01637 830308 **4 C10**
trevella.co.uk
Total Pitches: 165 (C, CV & T)

Trevornick
Holywell Bay, Newquay
TR8 5PW
Tel: 01637 830531 **4 B10**
trevornick.co.uk
Total Pitches: 688 (C, CV & T)

Truro C & C Park
Truro
TR4 8QN
Tel: 01872 560274 **3 K4**
trurocaravanandcampingpark.co.uk
Total Pitches: 51 (C, CV & T)

Tudor C & C
Shepherds Patch, Slimbridge, Gloucester
GL2 7BP
Tel: 01453 890483 **32 D4**
tudorcaravanpark.com
Total Pitches: 75 (C, CV & T)

Twitchen House Holiday Park
Mortehoe Station Road, Mortehoe, Woolacombe
EX34 7ES
Tel: 01271 872302 **16 H3**
woolacombe.com
Total Pitches: 569 (C, CV & T)

Two Mills Touring Park
Yarmouth Road, North Walsham
NR28 9NA
Tel: 01692 405829 **77 K6**
twomills.co.uk
Total Pitches: 81 (C, CV & T)

Ulwell Cottage Caravan Park
Ulwell Cottage, Ulwell, Swanage
BH19 3DG
Tel: 01929 422823 **12 H8**
ulwellcottagepark.co.uk
Total Pitches: 77 (C, CV & T)

Vale of Pickering Caravan Park
Carr House Farm, Allerston, Pickering
YO18 7PQ
Tel: 01723 859280 **98 H4**
valeofpickering.co.uk
Total Pitches: 120 (C, CV & T)

Wagtail Country Park
Cliff Lane, Marston, Grantham
NG32 2HU
Tel: 01400 251123 **73 M2**
wagtailcountrypark.co.uk
Total Pitches: 76 (C & CV)

Waldegraves Holiday Park
Mersea Island, Colchester
CO5 8SE
Tel: 01206 382898 **52 H9**
waldegraves.co.uk
Total Pitches: 30 (C, CV & T)

Warcombe Farm C & C Park
Station Road, Mortehoe, Woolacombe
EX34 7EJ
Tel: 01271 870690 **16 H2**
warcombefarm.co.uk
Total Pitches: 250 (C, CV & T)

Wareham Forest Tourist Park
North Trigon, Wareham
BH20 7NZ
Tel: 01929 551393 **12 E6**
warehamforest.co.uk
Total Pitches: 200 (C, CV & T)

Waren C & C Park
Waren Mill, Bamburgh
NE70 7EE
Tel: 01668 214366 **119 N4**
meadowhead.co.uk
Total Pitches: 150 (C, CV & T)

Warren Farm Holiday Centre
Brean Sands, Brean, Burnham-on-Sea
TA8 2RP
Tel: 01278 751227 **19 J3**
warrenfarm.co.uk
Total Pitches: 975 (C, CV & T)

Watergate Bay Touring Park
Watergate Bay, Tregurrian
TR8 4AD
Tel: 01637 860387 **4 D8**
watergatebaytouringpark.co.uk
Total Pitches: 171 (C, CV & T)

Waterrow Touring Park
Wiveliscombe, Taunton
TA4 2AZ
Tel: 01984 623464 **18 E9**
waterrowpark.co.uk
Total Pitches: 44 (C, CV & T)

Wayfarers C & C Park
Relubbus Lane, St Hilary,
Penzance
TR20 9EF
Tel: 01736 763326 **2 F7**
wayfarerspark.co.uk
Total Pitches: 32 (C, CV & T)

Wells Touring Park
Haybridge, Wells
BA5 1AJ
Tel: 01749 676869 **19 P5**
wellstouringpark.co.uk
Total Pitches: 72 (C, CV & T)

Wheathill Touring Park
Wheathill, Bridgnorth
WV16 6QT
Tel: 01584 823456 **57 L8**
wheathillpark.co.uk
Total Pitches: 25 (C & CV)

Whitecliff Bay Holiday Park
Hillway Road, Bembridge,
Whitecliff Bay
PO35 5PL
Tel: 01983 872671 **14 H9**
wight-holidays.com
Total Pitches: 653 (C, CV & T)

Whitefield Forest Touring Park
Brading Road, Ryde,
Isle of Wight
PO33 1QL
Tel: 01983 617069 **14 H9**
whitefieldforest.co.uk
Total Pitches: 90 (C, CV & T)

Whitemead Caravan Park
East Burton Road, Wool
BH20 6HG
Tel: 01929 462241 **12 D7**
whitemeadcaravanpark.co.uk
Total Pitches: 105 (C, CV & T)

Widdicombe Farm
Touring Park
Marldon, Paignton
TQ3 1ST
Tel: 01803 558325 **7 M6**
widdicombefarm.co.uk
Total Pitches: 180 (C, CV & T)

Wild Rose Park
Ormside,
Appleby-in-Westmorland
CA16 6EJ
Tel: 017683 51077 **102 C7**
harrisonholidayhomes.co.uk
Total Pitches: 226 (C & CV)

Wilksworth Farm
Caravan Park
Cranborne Road,
Wimborne Minster
BH21 4HW
Tel: 01202 885467 **12 H4**
shoreline.co.uk/camping-
touring-holidays/our-parks/
wilksworth-caravan-park
Total Pitches: 85 (C, CV & T)

Willowbank Holiday Home
& Touring Park
Coastal Road, Ainsdale,
Southport
PR8 3ST
Tel: 01704 571566 **88 C8**
willowbankcp.co.uk
Total Pitches: 87 (C & CV)

Wolds View Touring Park
115 Brigg Road, Caistor
LN7 6RX
Tel: 01472 851099 **93 K10**
woldsviewtouringpark.co.uk
Total Pitches: 60 (C, CV & T)

Wood Farm C & C Park
Axminster Road,
Charmouth
DT6 6BT
Tel: 01297 560697 **10 H6**
woodfarm.co.uk
Total Pitches: 175 (C, CV & T)

Wooda Farm
Holiday Park
Poughill, Bude
EX23 9HJ
Tel: 01288 352069 **16 C10**
wooda.co.uk
Total Pitches: 200 (C, CV & T)

Woodclose Caravan Park
High Casterton, Kirkby
Lonsdale
LA6 2SE
Tel: 015242 71597 **95 N5**
woodclosepark.com
Total Pitches: 22 (C, CV & T)

Woodhall Country Park
Stixwold Road, Woodhall Spa
LN10 6UJ
Tel: 01526 353710 **86 G8**
woodhallcountrypark.co.uk
Total Pitches: 115 (C, CV & T)

Woodland Springs Adult
Touring Park
Venton, Drewsteignton
EX6 6PG
Tel: 01647 231695 **8 G6**
woodlandsprings.co.uk
Total Pitches: 81 (C, CV & T)

Woodlands Grove C & C Park
Blackawton, Dartmouth
TQ9 7DQ
Tel: 01803 712598 **7 L8**
woodlandsgrove.co.uk
Total Pitches: 350 (C, CV & T)

Woodovis Park
Gulworthy, Tavistock
PL19 8NY
Tel: 01822 832968 **6 C4**
woodovis.com
Total Pitches: 50 (C, CV & T)

Yeatheridge Farm Caravan Park
East Worlington, Crediton
EX17 4TN
Tel: 01884 860330 **9 J2**
yeatheridge.co.uk
Total Pitches: 122 (C, CV & T)

SCOTLAND

Auchenlarie Holiday Park
Gatehouse of Fleet
DG7 2EX
Tel: 01556 506200 **107 P7**
swalwellholidaygroup.co.uk
Total Pitches: 451 (C, CV & T)

Beecraigs C & C Site
Beecraigs Country Park,
The Visitor Centre, Linlithgow
EH49 6PL
Tel: 01506 844516 **127 J3**
beecraigs.com
Total Pitches: 36 (C, CV & T)

Blair Castle Caravan Park
Blair Atholl, Pitlochry
PH18 5SR
Tel: 01796 481263 **141 L4**
blaircastlecaravanpark.co.uk
Total Pitches: 226 (C, CV & T)

Brighouse Bay Holiday Park
Brighouse Bay, Borgue,
Kirkcudbright
DG6 4TS
Tel: 01557 870267 **108 D11**
gillespie-leisure.co.uk
Total Pitches: 190 (C, CV & T)

Cairnsmill Holiday Park
Largo Road, St Andrews
KY16 8NN
Tel: 01334 473604 **135 M5**
cairnsmill.co.uk
Total Pitches: 62 (C, CV & T)

Craig Tara Holiday Park
Ayr
KA7 4LB
Tel: 0800 975 7579 **114 F4**
haven.com/craigtara
Total Pitches: 1144 (C & CV)

Craigtoun Meadows
Holiday Park
Mount Melville, St Andrews
KY16 8PQ
Tel: 01334 475959 **135 M4**
craigtounmeadows.co.uk
Total Pitches: 56 (C, CV & T)

Faskally Caravan Park
Pitlochry
PH16 5LA
Tel: 01796 472007 **141 M6**
faskally.co.uk
Total Pitches: 430 (C, CV & T)

Glen Nevis C & C Park
Glen Nevis, Fort William
PH33 6SX
Tel: 01397 702191 **139 L3**
glen-nevis.co.uk
Total Pitches: 380 (C, CV & T)

Hoddom Castle Caravan Park
Hoddom, Lockerbie
DG11 1AS
Tel: 01576 300251 **110 C6**
hoddomcastle.co.uk
Total Pitches: 200 (C, CV & T)

Huntly Castle Caravan Park
The Meadow, Huntly
AB54 4UJ
Tel: 01466 794999 **158 D9**
huntlycastle.co.uk
Total Pitches: 90 (C, CV & T)

Invercoe C & C Park
Ballachulish, Glencoe
PH49 4HP
Tel: 01855 811210 **139 K6**
invercoe.co.uk
Total Pitches: 66 (C, CV & T)

Linwater Caravan Park
West Clifton,
East Calder
EH53 0HT
Tel: 0131 333 3326 **127 L4**
linwater.co.uk
Total Pitches: 64 (C, CV & T)

Loch Ken Holiday Park
Parton, Castle Douglas
DG7 3NE
Tel: 01644 470282 **108 E6**
lochkenholidaypark.co.uk
Total Pitches: 40 (C, CV & T)

Lomond Woods Holiday Park
Old Luss Road, Balloch,
Loch Lomond
G83 8QP
Tel: 01389 755000 **132 D11**
woodleisure.co.uk
Total Pitches: 115 (C & CV)

Milton of Fonab Caravan Park
Bridge Road,
Pitlochry
PH16 5NA
Tel: 01796 472882 **141 M6**
fonab.co.uk
Total Pitches: 154 (C, CV & T)

River Tilt Caravan Park
Blair Atholl, Pitlochry
PH18 5TE
Tel: 01796 481467 **141 L4**
rivertiltpark.co.uk
Total Pitches: 30 (C, CV & T)

Sands of Luce Holiday Park
Sands of Luce, Sandhead,
Stranraer
DG9 9JN
Tel: 01776 830456 **106 F7**
sandsofluceholidaypark.co.uk
Total Pitches: 80 (C, CV & T)

Seaward Caravan Park
Dhoon Bay,
Kirkudbright
DG6 4TJ
Tel: 01557 870267 **108 E11**
gillespie-leisure.co.uk
Total Pitches: 25 (C, CV & T)

Seton Sands Holiday Village
Longniddry
EH32 0QF
Tel: 01875 813333 **128 C4**
haven.com/setonsands
Total Pitches: 640 (C & CV)

Silver Sands Holiday Park
Covesea, West Beach,
Lossiemouth
IV31 6SP
Tel: 01343 813262 **157 N3**
silver-sands.co.uk
Total Pitches: 140 (C, CV & T)

Skye C & C Club Site
Loch Greshornish, Borve,
Arnisort, Edinbane, Isle of Skye
IV51 9PS
Tel: 01470 582230 **152 E7**
campingandcaravanning
club.co.uk/skye
Total Pitches: 105 (C, CV & T)

Thurston Manor
Leisure Park
Innerwick, Dunbar
EH42 1SA
Tel: 01368 840643 **129 J5**
thurstonmanor.co.uk
Total Pitches: 120 (C & CV)

Trossachs Holiday Park
Aberfoyle
FK8 3SA
Tel: 01877 382614 **132 G8**
trossachsholidays.co.uk
Total Pitches: 66 (C, CV & T)

Witches Craig C & C Park
Blairlogie, Stirling
FK9 5PX
Tel: 01786 474947 **133 N8**
witchescraig.co.uk
Total Pitches: 60 (C, CV & T)

WALES

Bron Derw Touring Caravan
Park
Llanrwst
LL26 0YT
Tel: 01492 640494 **67 P2**
bronderw-wales.co.uk
Total Pitches: 48 (C & CV)

Bron-Y-Wendon Caravan Park
Wern Road, Llanddulas,
Colwyn Bay
LL22 8HG
Tel: 01492 512903 **80 C9**
bronywendon.co.uk
Total Pitches: 130 (C & CV)

Bryn Gloch C & C Park
Betws Garmon,
Caernarfon
LL54 7YY
Tel: 01286 650216 **67 J3**
campwales.co.uk
Total Pitches: 177 (C, CV & T)

Caerfai Bay Caravan
& Tent Park
Caerfai Bay, St Davids,
Haverfordwest
SA62 6QT
Tel: 01437 720274 **40 E6**
caerfaibay.co.uk
Total Pitches: 106 (C, CV & T)

Cenarth Falls Holiday Park
Cenarth, Newcastle Emlyn
SA38 9JS
Tel: 01239 710345 **41 Q2**
cenarth-holipark.co.uk
Total Pitches: 30 (C, CV & T)

Daisy Bank Caravan Park
Snead, Montgomery
SY15 6EB
Tel: 01588 620471 **56 E6**
daisy-bank.co.uk
Total Pitches: 80 (C, CV & T)

Dinlle Caravan Park
Dinas Dinlle, Caernarfon
LL54 5TW
Tel: 01286 830324 **66 G3**
thornleyleisure.co.uk
Total Pitches: 175 (C, CV & T)

Eisteddfa
Eisteddfa Lodge, Pentrefelin,
Criccieth
LL52 0PT
Tel: 01766 522696 **67 J7**
eisteddfapark.co.uk
Total Pitches: 100 (C, CV & T)

Fforest Fields C & C Park
Hundred House, Builth Wells
LD1 5RT
Tel: 01982 570406 **44 G4**
fforestfields.co.uk
Total Pitches: 120 (C, CV & T)

Fishguard Bay Resort
Garn Gelli, Fishguard
SA65 9ET
Tel: 01348 811415 **41 J3**
fishguardbay.com
Total Pitches: 102 (C, CV & T)

Greenacres Holiday Park
Black Rock Sands, Morfa
Bychan, Porthmadog
LL49 9YF
Tel: 01766 512781 **67 J7**
haven.com/greenacres
Total Pitches: 945 (C & CV)

Hafan y Môr Holiday Park
Pwllheli
LL53 6HJ
Tel: 01758 612112 **66 G7**
haven.com/hafanymor
Total Pitches: 875 (C, CV & T)

Hendre Mynach Touring
C & C Park
Llanaber Road, Barmouth
LL42 1YR
Tel: 01341 280262 **67 L11**
hendremynach.co.uk
Total Pitches: 240 (C, CV & T)

Home Farm Caravan Park
Marian-Glas, Isle of Anglesey
LL73 8PH
Tel: 01248 410614 **78 H8**
homefarm-anglesey.co.uk
Total Pitches: 102 (C, CV & T)

Islawrffordd Caravan Park
Tal-y-bont, Barmouth
LL43 2AQ
Tel: 01341 247269 **67 K10**
islawrffordd.co.uk
Total Pitches: 105 (C, CV & T)

Kiln Park Holiday Centre
Marsh Road, Tenby
SA70 8RB
Tel: 01834 844121 **41 M10**
haven.com/kilnpark
Total Pitches: 849 (C, CV & T)

Pencelli Castle C & C Park
Pencelli, Brecon
LD3 7LX
Tel: 01874 665451 **44 F10**
pencelli-castle.com
Total Pitches: 80 (C, CV & T)

Penisar Mynydd Caravan Park
Caerwys Road, Rhuallt,
St Asaph
LL17 0TY
Tel: 01745 582227 **80 F9**
penisarmynydd.co.uk
Total Pitches: 71 (C, CV & T)

Plas Farm Caravan
& Lodge Park
Betws-yn-Rhos, Abergele
LL22 8AU
Tel: 01492 680254 **80 B10**
plasfarmcaravanpark.co.uk
Total Pitches: 54 (C & CV)

Plassey Holiday Park
The Plassey, Eyton,
Wrexham
LL13 0SP
Tel: 01978 780277 **69 L5**
plassey.com
Total Pitches: 90 (C, CV & T)

Pont Kemys C & C Park
Chainbridge, Abergavenny
NP7 9DS
Tel: 01873 880688 **31 K3**
pontkemys.com
Total Pitches: 65 (C, CV & T)

Presthaven Sands
Holiday Park
Gronant, Prestatyn
LL19 9TT
Tel: 01745 856471 **80 F8**
haven.com/presthavensands
Total Pitches: 1102 (C & CV)

Red Kite Touring Park
Van Road, Llanidloes
SY18 6NG
Tel: 01686 412122 **55 L7**
redkitetouringpark.co.uk
Total Pitches: 66 (C & CV)

River View Touring Park
The Dingle, Llanedi,
Pontarddulais
SA4 0FH
Tel: 01635 844876 **28 G3**
riverviewtouringpark.com
Total Pitches: 60 (C, CV & T)

Riverside Camping
Seiont Nurseries, Pont Rug,
Caernarfon
LL55 2BB
Tel: 01286 678781 **67 J2**
riversidecamping.co.uk
Total Pitches: 73 (C, CV & T)

The Trotting Mare
Caravan Park
Overton, Wrexham
LL13 0LE
Tel: 01978 711963 **69 L7**
thetrottingmare.co.uk
Total Pitches: 65 (C, CV & T)

Trawsdir Touring
C & C Park
Llanaber, Barmouth
LL42 1RR
Tel: 01341 280999 **67 K11**
barmouthholidays.co.uk
Total Pitches: 70 (C, CV & T)

Trefalun Park
Devonshire Drive, St Florence,
Tenby
SA70 8RD
Tel: 01646 651514 **41 L10**
trefalunpark.co.uk
Total Pitches: 90 (C, CV & T)

Tyddyn Isaf Caravan Park
Lligwy Bay, Dulas,
Isle of Anglesey
LL70 9PQ
Tel: 01248 410203 **78 H7**
tyddynisaf.co.uk
Total Pitches: 80 (C, CV & T)

White Tower Caravan Park
Llandwrog, Caernarfon
LL54 5UH
Tel: 01286 830649 **66 H3**
whitetowerpark.co.uk
Total Pitches: 52 (C & CV)

CHANNEL ISLANDS

Daisy Cottage Campsite
Route de Vinchelez, St Ouen,
Jersey
JE3 2DB
Tel: 01534 481700 **11 a1**
daisycottagecampsite.com
Total Pitches: 29 (C, CV & T)

Fauxquets Valley Campsite
Castel, Guernsey
GY5 7QL
Tel: 01481 255460 **10 b2**
fauxquets.co.uk
Total Pitches: 120 (CV & T)

Rozel Camping Park
Summerville Farm, St Martin,
Jersey
JE3 6AX
Tel: 01534 855200 **11 c1**
rozelcamping.com
Total Pitches: 100 (C, CV & T)

Signs giving orders

**Signs with red circles are mostly prohibitive.
Plates below signs qualify their message**

Entry to
20mph zone

End of
20mph zone

Maximum
speed

National speed
limit applies

School crossing
patrol

Stop and
give way

Give way to
traffic on
major road

Manually operated temporary
STOP and GO signs

No entry for
vehicular traffic

No vehicles
except bicycles
being pushed

No cycling

No motor
vehicles

No buses
(over 8
passenger
seats)

No
overtaking

No
towed
caravans

No vehicles
carrying
explosives

No vehicle or
combination of
vehicles over
length shown

No vehicles
over
height shown

No vehicles
over
width shown

Give priority to
vehicles from
opposite
direction

No right turn

No left turn

No
U-turns

No goods vehicles
over maximum
gross weight
shown (in tonnes)
except for loading
and unloading

No vehicles
over maximum
gross weight
shown
(in tonnes)

Parking
restricted to
permit holders

No waiting

No stopping during
period indicated
except for buses

No stopping
(Clearway)

No stopping during
times shown
except for as long
as necessary to set
down or pick up
passengers

**Signs with blue circles but no red border mostly give
positive instruction.**

Ahead only

Turn left ahead
(right if symbol
reversed)

Turn left
(right if symbol
reversed)

Keep left
(right if symbol
reversed)

Vehicles may
pass either
side to reach
same
destination

Mini-roundabout
(roundabout
circulation – give
way to vehicles
from the
immediate right)

Route to be
used by pedal
cycles only

Segregated
pedal cycle
and pedestrian
route

Minimum speed

End of minimum
speed

Buses and
cycles only

Only
Trams only

Pedestrian
crossing
point over
tramway

One-way traffic
(note: compare
circular 'Ahead
only' sign)

With-flow bus and
cycle lane

Contraflow bus lane

With-flow pedal cycle lane

Warning signs

Mostly triangular

Distance to
'STOP' line
ahead

Dual
carriageway
ends

Road narrows on
right (left if
symbol reversed)

Road
narrows on
both sides

Distance to
'Give Way'
line ahead

Crossroads

Junction on
bend ahead

T-junction with
priority over
vehicles from
the right

Staggered
junction

Traffic merging
from left ahead

The priority through route is indicated by the broader line.

Double bend first
to left (symbol
may be reversed)

Bend to right
(or left if symbol
reversed)

Roundabout

Uneven road

Plate below
some signs

Two-way
traffic crosses
one-way road

Two-way traffic
straight ahead

Opening or
swing bridge
ahead

Low-flying aircraft
or sudden
aircraft noise

Falling or
fallen rocks

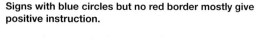
Traffic signals
not in use

Traffic signals

Slippery road

Steep hill
downwards

Steep hill
upwards

Gradients may be shown as a ratio i.e. 20% = 1:5

Tunnel ahead

Trams crossing ahead

Level crossing with barrier or gate ahead

Level crossing without barrier or gate ahead

Level crossing without barrier

Downward pointing arrows mean 'Get in lane'
The left-hand lane leads to a different destination from the other lanes.

The panel with the inclined arrow indicates the destinations which can be reached

Patrol

School crossing patrol ahead (some signs have amber lights which flash when crossings are in use)

Frail (or blind or disabled if shown) pedestrians likely to cross road ahead

No footway for 400 yds

Pedestrians in road ahead

Zebra crossing

Safe height 16'-6"

Overhead electric cable; plate indicates maximum height of vehicles which can pass safely

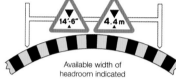
Available width of headroom indicated

Signs on primary routes - green backgrounds

On approaches to junctions

At the junction

Route confirmatory sign after junction

On approaches to junctions

On approach to a junction in Wales (bilingual)

Sharp deviation of route to left (or right if chevrons reversed)

STOP when lights show

Light signals ahead at level crossing, airfield or bridge

Red STOP
Green Clear
IF NO LIGHT - PHONE CROSSING OPERATOR

Miniature warning lights at level crossings

Blue panels indicate that the motorway starts at the junction ahead.
Motorways shown in brackets can also be reached along the route indicated.
White panels indicate local or non-primary routes leading from the junction ahead.
Brown panels show the route to tourist attractions.
The name of the junction may be shown at the top of the sign.
The aircraft symbol indicates the route to an airport.
A symbol may be included to warn of a hazard or restriction along that route.

Cattle

Wild animals

Wild horses or ponies

Accompanied horses or ponies

Cycle route ahead

Signs on non-primary and local routes - black borders

On approaches to junctions

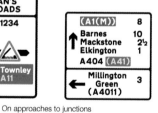

At the junction

Direction to toilets with access for the disabled

Ice

Risk of ice

Queues likely

Traffic queues likely ahead

Humps for ½ mile

Distance over which road humps extend

Hidden dip

Other danger; plate indicates nature of danger

Soft verges for 2 miles

Soft verges

Green panels indicate that the primary route starts at the junction ahead.
Route numbers on a blue background show the direction to a motorway.
Route numbers on a green background show the direction to a primary route.

Side winds

Hump bridge

Ford

Worded warning sign

Quayside or river bank

Risk of grounding

Emergency diversion routes

In an emergency it may be necessary to close a section of motorway or other main road to traffic, so a temporary sign may advise drivers to follow a diversion route. To help drivers navigate the route, black symbols on yellow patches may be permanently displayed on existing direction signs, including motorway signs. Symbols may also be used on separate signs with yellow backgrounds.

For further information visit:
theaa.com/breakdown-cover/advice/emergency-diversion-routes

Direction signs

Mostly rectangular

Signs on motorways - blue backgrounds

At a junction leading directly into a motorway (junction number may be shown on a black background)

On approaches to junctions (junction number on black background)

Route confirmatory sign after junction

Note: The signs shown in this road atlas are those most commonly in use and are not all drawn to the same scale. In Scotland and Wales bilingual versions of some signs are used, showing both English and Gaelic or Welsh spellings. Some older designs of signs may still be seen on the roads. A comprehensive explanation of the signing system illustrating the vast majority of road signs can be found in the AA's handbook *Know Your Road Signs*. Where there is a reference to a rule number, this refers to *The Highway Code*.

Restricted junctions

Motorway and primary route junctions which have access or exit restrictions are shown on the map pages thus:

M1 London - Leeds

Northbound
Access only from A1 (northbound)

Southbound
Exit only to A1 (southbound)

Northbound
Access only from A41 (northbound)

Southbound
Exit only to A41 (southbound)

Northbound
Access only from M25 (no link from A405)

Southbound
Exit only to M25 (no link from A405)

Northbound
Access only from A414

Southbound
Exit only to A414

Northbound
Exit only to M45

Southbound
Access only from M45

Northbound
Exit only to M6 (northbound)

Southbound
Exit only to A14 (southbound)

Northbound
Exit only, no access

Southbound
Access only, no exit

Northbound
No exit, access only

Southbound
Access only from A50 (eastbound)

Northbound
Exit only, no access

Southbound
Access only, no exit

Northbound
Exit only to M621

Southbound
Access only from M621

Northbound
Exit only to A1(M) (northbound)

Southbound
Access only from A1(M) (southbound)

M2 Rochester - Faversham

Westbound
No exit to A2 (eastbound)

Eastbound
No access from A2 (westbound)

M3 Sunbury - Southampton

Northeastbound
Access only from A303, no exit

Southwestbound
Exit only to A303, no access

Northbound
Exit only, no access

Southbound
Access only, no exit

Northeastbound
Access from M27 only, no exit

Southwestbound
No access to M27 (westbound)

M4 London - South Wales

For junctions 1 & 2 see London district map on pages 178–181

Westbound
Exit only to M48

Eastbound
Access only from M48

Westbound
Access only from M48

Eastbound
Exit only to M48

Westbound
Exit only, no access

Eastbound
Access only, no exit

Westbound
Exit only, no access

Eastbound
Access only, no exit

Westbound
Exit only to A48(M)

Eastbound
Access only from A48(M)

Westbound
Exit only, no access

Eastbound
No restriction

Westbound
Access only, no exit

Eastbound
No access or exit

Westbound
Exit only to A483

Eastbound
Access only from A483

M5 Birmingham - Exeter

Northeastbound
Access only, no exit

Southwestbound
Exit only, no access

Northeastbound
Access only from A417 (westbound)

Southwestbound
Exit only to A417 (eastbound)

Northeastbound
Exit only to M49

Southwestbound
Access only from M49

Northeastbound
No access, exit only

Southwestbound
No exit, access only

M6 Toll Motorway

See M6 Toll motorway map on page *XXIII*

M6 Rugby - Carlisle

Northbound
Exit only to M6 Toll

Southbound
Access only from M6 Toll

Northbound
Exit only to M42 (southbound) and A446

Southbound
Exit only to A446

Northbound
Access only from M42 (southbound)

Southbound
Exit only to M42

Northbound
Exit only, no access

Southbound
Access only, no exit

Northbound
Exit only to M54

Southbound
Access only from M54

Northbound
Access only from M6 Toll

Southbound
Exit only to M6 Toll

Northbound
No restriction

Southbound
Access only from M56 (eastbound)

Northbound
Exit only to M56 (westbound)

Southbound
Access only from M56 (eastbound)

Northbound
Access only, no exit

Southbound
Exit only, no access

Northbound
Exit only, no access

Southbound
Access only, no exit

Northbound
Access only from M61

Southbound
Exit only to M61

Northbound
Exit only, no access

Southbound
Access only, no exit

Northbound
Exit only, no access

Southbound
Access only, no exit

M8 Edinburgh - Bishopton

For junctions 7A to 29A see Glasgow district map on pages 176–177

Westbound
Exit only, no access

Eastbound
Access only, no exit

Westbound
Access only, no exit

Eastbound
Exit only, no access

Westbound
Access only, no exit

Eastbound
Exit only, no access

M9 Edinburgh - Dunblane

Northwestbound
Access only, no exit

Southeastbound
Exit only, no access

Northwestbound
Exit only, no access

Southeastbound
Access only, no exit

Northwestbound
Access only, no exit

Southeastbound
Exit only to A905

Northwestbound
Exit only to M876
(southwestbound)

Southeastbound
Access only from M876
(northeastbound)

M11 London - Cambridge

Northbound
Access only from A406
(eastbound)

Southbound
Exit only to A406

Northbound
Exit only, no access

Southbound
Access only, no exit

Northbound
Exit only, no access

Southbound
No direct access,
use jct 8

Northbound
Exit only to A11

Southbound
Access only from A11

Northbound
Exit only, no access

Southbound
Access only, no exit

Northbound
Exit only, no access

Southbound
Access only, no exit

M20 Swanley - Folkestone

Northwestbound
Staggered junction; follow
signs - access only

Southeastbound
Staggered junction; follow
signs - exit only

Northwestbound
Exit only to M26
(westbound)

Southeastbound
Access only from M26
(eastbound)

Northwestbound
Access only from A20

Southeastbound
For access follow signs -
exit only to A20

Northwestbound
Exit only, no access

Southeastbound
Access only, no exit

Northwestbound
Access only, no exit

Southeastbound
Exit only, no access

M23 Hooley - Crawley

Northbound
Exit only to A23
(northbound)

Southbound
Access only from A23
(southbound)

Northbound
Access only, no exit

Southbound
Exit only, no access

M25 London Orbital Motorway

See M25 London Orbital motorway map on page *XXII*

M26 Sevenoaks - Wrotham

Westbound
Exit only to clockwise
M25 (westbound)

Eastbound
Access only from
anticlockwise M25
(eastbound)

Westbound
Access only from M20
(northwestbound)

Eastbound
Exit only to M20
(southeastbound)

M27 Cadnam - Portsmouth

Westbound
Staggered junction; follow
signs - access only from
M3 (southbound). Exit
only to M3 (northbound)

Eastbound
Staggered junction; follow
signs - access only from
M3 (southbound). Exit
only to M3 (northbound)

Westbound
Exit only, no access

Eastbound
Access only, no exit

Westbound
Staggered junction; follow
signs - exit only to M275
(southbound)

Eastbound
Staggered junction; follow
signs - access only from
M275 (northbound)

M40 London - Birmingham

Northwestbound
Exit only, no access

Southeastbound
Access only, no exit

Northwestbound
No restriction

Southeastbound
For exit follow signs

Northwestbound
Access only, no exit

Southeastbound
Exit only, no access

Northwestbound
Exit only to M40/A40

Southeastbound
Access only from
M40/A40

Northwestbound
Exit only, no access

Southeastbound
Access only, no exit

Northwestbound
Access only, no exit

Southeastbound
Exit only, no access

Northwestbound
Access only, no exit

Southeastbound
Exit only, no access

M42 Bromsgrove - Measham

See Birmingham district map on pages 174–175

M45 Coventry - M1

Westbound
Access only from A45
(northbound)

Eastbound
Exit only, no access

Westbound
Access only from M1
(northbound)

Eastbound
Exit only to M1
(southbound)

M48 Chepstow

Westbound
Access only from M4
(westbound)

Eastbound
Exit only to M4
(eastbound)

Westbound
No exit to M4 (eastbound)

Eastbound
No access from M4
(westbound)

M53 Mersey Tunnel - Chester

Northbound
Access only from M56
(westbound). Exit only to
M56 (eastbound)

Southbound
Access only from M56
(westbound). Exit only to
M56 (eastbound)

M54 Telford - Birmingham

Westbound
Access only from M6
(northbound)

Eastbound
Exit only to M6
(southbound)

M56 Chester - Manchester

For junctions 1,2,3,4 & 7 see Manchester district map on pages 182–183

Westbound
Access only, no exit

Eastbound
No access or exit

Westbound
No exit to M6
(southbound)

Eastbound
No access from M6
(northbound)

Westbound
Exit only to M53

Eastbound
Access only from M53

Westbound
No access or exit

Eastbound
No restriction

M57 Liverpool Outer Ring Road

Northwestbound
Access only, no exit

Southeastbound
Exit only, no access

Northwestbound
Access only from A580
(westbound)

Southeastbound
Exit only, no access

M58 Liverpool - Wigan

Westbound
Exit only, no access

Eastbound
Access only, no exit

M60 Manchester Orbital

See Manchester district map on pages 182–183

M61 Manchester - Preston

Northwestbound
No access or exit

Southeastbound
Exit only, no access

Northwestbound
Exit only to M6
(northbound)

Southeastbound
Access only from M6
(southbound)

M62 Liverpool - Kingston upon Hull

Westbound
Access only, no exit

Eastbound
Exit only, no access

Westbound
No access to A1(M)
(southbound)

Eastbound
No restriction

M65 Preston - Colne

Northeastbound
Exit only, no access

Southwestbound
Access only, no exit

Northeastbound
Access only, no exit

Southwestbound
Exit only, no access

M66 Bury

Northbound
Exit only to A56
(northbound)

Southbound
Access only from A56
(southbound)

Northbound
Exit only, no access

Southbound
Access only, no exit

M67 Hyde Bypass

Westbound
Access only, no exit

Eastbound
Exit only, no access

Westbound
Exit only, no access

Eastbound
Access only, no exit

Westbound
Exit only, no access

Eastbound
No restriction

M69 Coventry - Leicester

Northbound
Access only, no exit

Southbound
Exit only, no access

M73 East of Glasgow

Northbound
No exit to A74 and A721

Southbound
No exit to A74 and A721

Northbound
No access from or exit to
A89. No access from M8
(eastbound)

Southbound
No access from or exit to
A89. No exit to M8
(westbound)

M74 and A74(M) Glasgow - Gretna

Northbound
Exit only, no access

Southbound
Access only, no exit

Northbound
Access only, no exit

Southbound
Exit only, no access

Northbound
No access from A74 and
A721

Southbound
Access only, no exit to
A74 and A721

Northbound
Access only, no exit

Southbound
Exit only, no access

Northbound
No access or exit

Southbound
Exit only, no access

Northbound
No restriction

Southbound
Access only, no exit

Northbound
Access only, no exit

Southbound
Exit only, no access

Northbound
Exit only, no access

Southbound
Access only, no exit

Northbound
Exit only, no access

Southbound
Access only, no exit

M77 Glasgow - Kilmarnock

Northbound
No exit to M8
(westbound)

Southbound
No access from M8
(eastbound)

Northbound
Access only, no exit

Southbound
Exit only, no access

Northbound
Access only, no exit

Southbound
Exit only, no access

Northbound
Access only, no exit

Southbound
No restriction

Northbound
Exit only, no access

Southbound
Exit only, no access

M80 Glasgow - Stirling

For junctions 1 & 4 see Glasgow district map
on pages 176–177

Northbound
Exit only, no access

Southbound
Access only, no exit

Northbound
Access only, no exit

Southbound
Exit only, no access

Northbound
Exit only to M876
(northeastbound)

Southbound
Access only from M876
(southwestbound)

M90 Edinburgh - Perth

Northbound
No exit, access only

Southbound
Exit only to A90
(eastbound)

Northbound
Exit only to A92
(eastbound)

Southbound
Access only from A92
(westbound)

Northbound
Access only, no exit

Southbound
Exit only, no access

Northbound
Exit only, no access

Southbound
Access only, no exit

Northbound
No access from A912
No exit to A912
(southbound)

Southbound
No access from A912
(northbound).
No exit to A912

M180 Doncaster - Grimsby

Westbound
Access only, no exit

Eastbound
Exit only, no access

M606 Bradford Spur

Northbound
Exit only, no access

Southbound
No restriction

M621 Leeds - M1

Clockwise
Access only, no exit

Anticlockwise
Exit only, no access

Clockwise
No exit or access

Anticlockwise
No restriction

Clockwise
Access only, no exit

Anticlockwise
Exit only, no access

Clockwise
Exit only, no access

Anticlockwise
Access only, no exit

Clockwise
Exit only to M1
(southbound)

Anticlockwise
Access only from M1
(northbound)

M876 Bonnybridge - Kincardine Bridge

Northeastbound
Access only from M80
(northbound)

Southwestbound
Exit only to M80
(southbound)

Northeastbound
Exit only to M9
(eastbound)

Southwestbound
Access only from M9
(westbound)

A1(M) South Mimms - Baldock

Northbound
Exit only, no access

Southbound
Access only, no exit

Northbound
No restriction

Southbound
Exit only, no access

Northbound
Access only, no exit

Southbound
No access or exit

A1(M) Pontefract - Bedale

Northbound
No access to M62
(eastbound)

Southbound
No restriction

Northbound
Access only from M1
(northbound)

Southbound
Exit only to M1
(southbound)

A1(M) Scotch Corner - Newcastle upon Tyne

Northbound
Exit only to A66(M)
(eastbound)

Southbound
Access only from A66(M)
(westbound)

Northbound
No access. Exit only to
A194(M) & A1
(northbound)

Southbound
No exit. Access only from
A194(M) & A1
(southbound)

A3(M) Horndean - Havant

Northbound
Access only from A3

Southbound
Exit only to A3

Northbound
Exit only, no access

Southbound
Access only, no exit

A38(M) Birmingham Victoria Road (Park Circus)

Northbound
No exit

Southbound
No access

A48(M) Cardiff Spur

Westbound
Access only from M4
(westbound)

Eastbound
Exit only to M4
(eastbound)

Westbound
Exit only to A48
(westbound)

Eastbound
Access only from A48
(eastbound)

A57(M) Manchester Brook Street (A34)

Westbound
No exit

Eastbound
No access

A58(M) Leeds Park Lane and Westgate

Northbound
No restriction

Southbound
No access

A64(M) Leeds Clay Pit Lane (A58)

Westbound
No exit (to Clay Pit Lane)

Eastbound
No access (from Clay Pit
Lane)

A66(M) Darlington Spur

Westbound
Exit only to A1(M)
(southbound)

Eastbound
Access only from A1(M)
(northbound)

A74(M) Gretna - Abington

Northbound
Exit only, no access

Southbound
No exit

A194(M) Newcastle upon Tyne

Northbound
Access only from A1(M)
(northbound)

Southbound
Exit only to A1(M)
(southbound)

A12 M25 - Ipswich

Northeastbound
Access only, no exit

Southwestbound
No restriction

Northeastbound
Exit only, no access

Southwestbound
Access only, no exit

Northeastbound
Exit only, no access

Southwestbound
Access only, no exit

Northeastbound
Access only, no exit

Southwestbound
Exit only, no access

Northeastbound
No restriction

Southwestbound
Access only, no exit

Northeastbound
Exit only, no access

Southwestbound
Access only, no exit

Northeastbound
Access only, no exit

Southwestbound
Exit only, no access

Northeastbound
Exit only, no access

Southwestbound
Access only, no exit

Northeastbound
Exit only (for Stratford
St Mary and Dedham)

Southwestbound
Access only

A14 M1 - Felixstowe

Westbound
Exit only to M6 & M1
(northbound)

Eastbound
Access only from M6 &
M1 (southbound)

Westbound
Exit only, no access

Eastbound
Access only, no exit

Westbound
Exit only to M11
(for London)

Eastbound
Access only, no exit

Westbound
Exit only to A14
(northbound)

Eastbound
Access only, no exit

Westbound
Access only, no exit

Eastbound
Exit only, no access

Westbound
Exit only to A11
Access only from A1303

Eastbound
Access only from A11

Westbound
Access only from A11

Eastbound
Exit only to A11

Westbound
Exit only, no access

Eastbound
Access only, no exit

Westbound
Access only, no exit

Eastbound
Exit only, no access

A55 Holyhead - Chester

Westbound
Exit only, no access

Eastbound
Access only, no exit

Westbound
Access only, no exit

Eastbound
Exit only, no access

Westbound
Exit only, no access

Eastbound
No access or exit.

Westbound
No restriction

Eastbound
No access or exit

Westbound
Exit only, no access

Eastbound
No access or exit

Westbound
Exit only, no access

Eastbound
Access only, no exit

Westbound
Exit only to A5104

Eastbound
Access only from A5104

Refer also to atlas pages 36–37 and 50–51

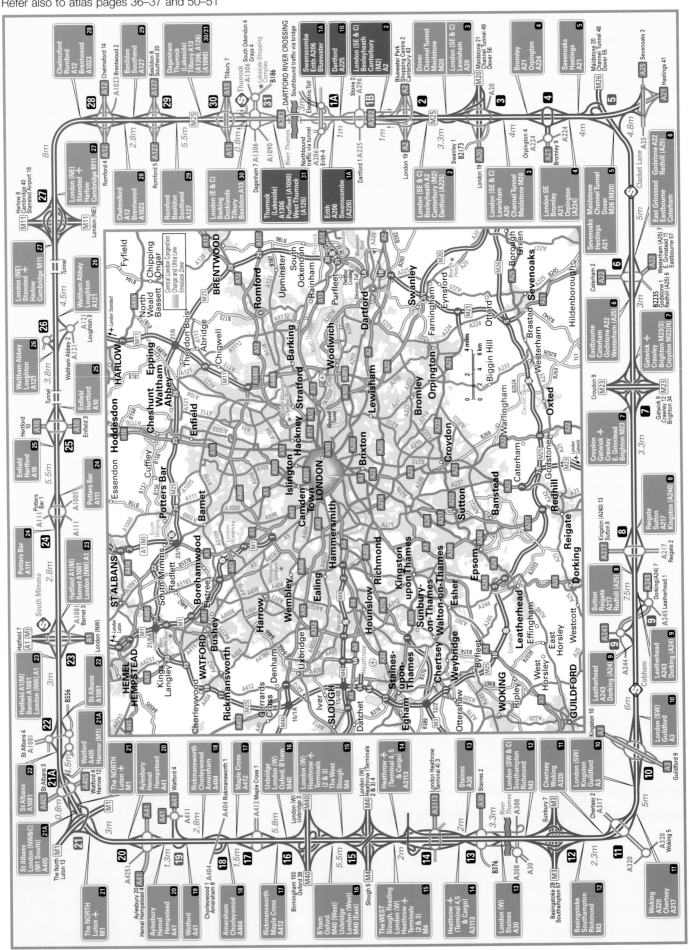

Refer also to atlas pages 58–59

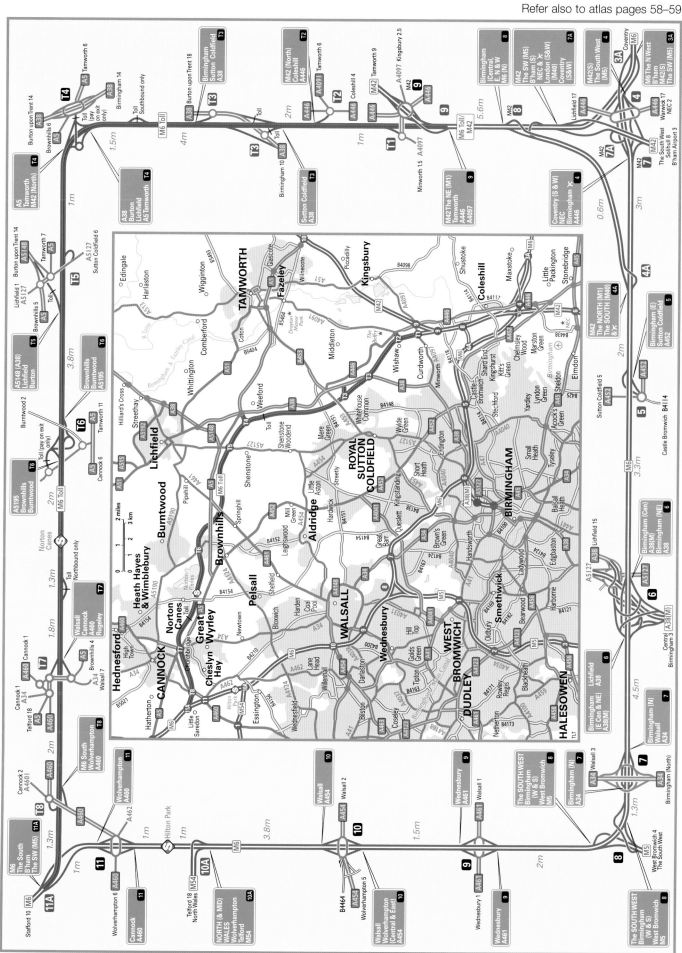

Smart motorways

Since Britain's first motorway (the Preston Bypass) opened in 1958, motorways have changed significantly. A vast increase in car journeys over the last 61 years has meant that motorways quickly filled to capacity. To combat this, the recent development of **smart motorways** uses technology to monitor and actively manage traffic flow and congestion.

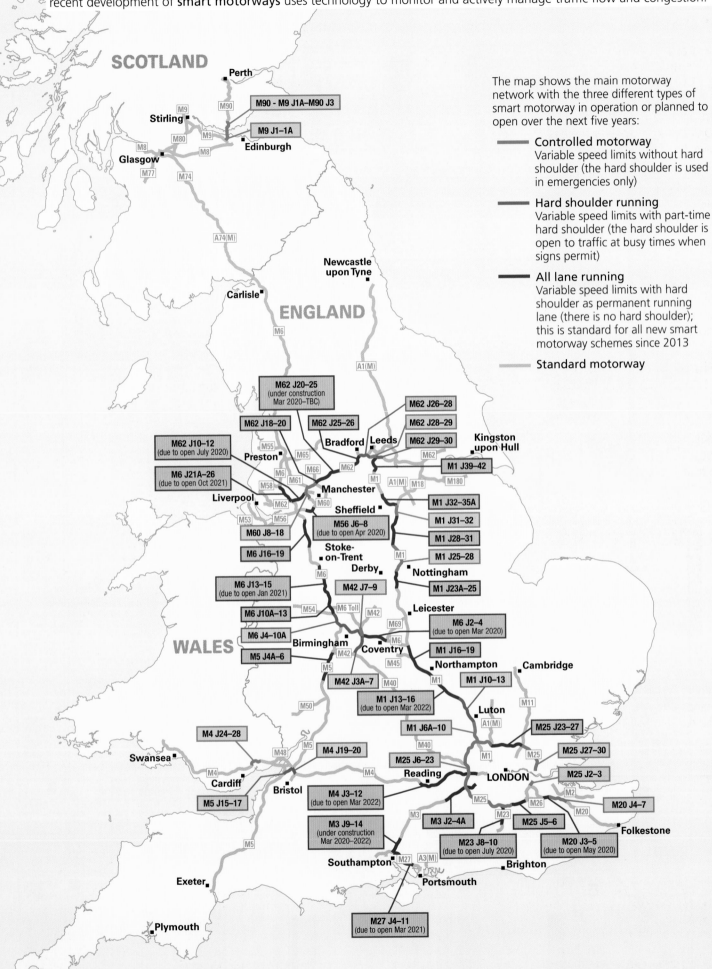

The map shows the main motorway network with the three different types of smart motorway in operation or planned to open over the next five years:

— **Controlled motorway**
Variable speed limits without hard shoulder (the hard shoulder is used in emergencies only)

— **Hard shoulder running**
Variable speed limits with part-time hard shoulder (the hard shoulder is open to traffic at busy times when signs permit)

— **All lane running**
Variable speed limits with hard shoulder as permanent running lane (there is no hard shoulder); this is standard for all new smart motorway schemes since 2013

— **Standard motorway**

SCOTLAND

Perth
M90 - M9 J1A–M90 J3
M90
M9
M9 J1–1A
Stirling
Edinburgh
M80
M9
M8
Glasgow
M8
M77
M74

A74(M)

Newcastle upon Tyne

Carlisle
ENGLAND
M6

A1(M)

M62 J20–25 (under construction Mar 2020–TBC)
M62 J26–28
M62 J25–26
M62 J28–29
M62 J18–20
M62 J29–30
Bradford Leeds
M55
Kingston upon Hull
M62 J10–12 (due to open July 2020)
M65
M62
M1 J39–42
Preston
M6
M66
M62
M6 J21A–26 (due to open Oct 2021)
M61
A1(M) M18
M180
M58
Liverpool
M62
Manchester
M1 J32–35A
M53
M56
M60
Sheffield
M1 J31–32
M60 J8–18
M56 J6–8 (due to open Apr 2020)
M1 J28–31
M6 J16–19
Stoke-on-Trent
M1 J25–28
Derby
Nottingham
M6 J13–15 (due to open Jan 2021)
M6
M42 J7–9
M1 J23A–25
M6 J10A–13
M54
M6 Toll
M42
Leicester
M6 J4–10A
M69
M6 J2–4 (due to open Mar 2020)
M5 J4A–6
WALES
Birmingham
M42
Coventry
M6
M1 J16–19
M5
M42 J3A–7
M45
Northampton
Cambridge
M40
M1
M50
M1 J13–16 (due to open Mar 2022)
M1 J10–13
M11
M4 J24–28
Luton
M1 J6A–10
A1(M)
M48
M5
M4 J19–20
M25 J23–27
Swansea
M4
M40
M25
M25 J6–23
Reading **LONDON**
M25 J27–30
Cardiff
Bristol
M4 J3–12 (due to open Mar 2022)
M25 J2–3
M5 J15–17
M3
M25
M20 J4–7
M3 J9–14 (under construction Mar 2020–2022)
M3 J2–4A
M23
M26
M20
M25 J5–6
M23 J8–10 (due to open July 2020)
M20 J3–5 (due to open May 2020)
Folkestone
Southampton
M27
A3(M)
Brighton
Exeter
Portsmouth
Plymouth
M5
M27 J4–11 (due to open Mar 2021)

Smart motorways (*Intelligent Transport Systems* in Scotland) are the responsibility of Highways England, Transport Scotland and Transport for Wales

How they work

Smart motorways utilise various active traffic management methods, monitored through a regional traffic control centre:

- Traffic flow is monitored using CCTV
- Speed limits are changed to smooth traffic flow and reduce stop-start driving
- Capacity of the motorway can be increased by either temporarily or permanently opening the hard shoulder to traffic

- Warning signs and messages alert drivers to hazards and traffic jams ahead
- Lanes can be closed in the case of an accident or emergency by displaying a red X sign
- Emergency refuge areas are located regularly along the motorway where there is no hard shoulder available

In an emergency

On a smart motorway there is often no hard shoulder so in an emergency you will need to make your way to the nearest **emergency refuge area** or motorway service area.

Emergency refuge areas are lay-bys marked with blue signs featuring an orange SOS telephone symbol. The telephone connects to the regional control centre and pinpoints your location. The control centre will advise you on what to do, send help and assist you in returning to the motorway.

If you are unable to reach an emergency refuge area or hard shoulder (if there is one) move as close to the nearside (left hand) boundary or verge as you can.

If it is not possible to get out of your vehicle safely, or there is no other place of relative safety to wait, stay in your vehicle with your seat-belt on and dial 999 if you have a mobile phone. If you don't have a phone, sit tight and wait to be rescued. Once the regional traffic control centre is aware of your situation, via the police or CCTV, they will use the smart motorway technology to set overhead signs and close the lane to keep traffic away from you. They will also send a traffic officer or the police to help you.

Refuge areas for emergency use only

Sign indicating presence of emergency refuge areas ahead

Emergency refuge area SOS

This sign is located at each emergency refuge area

Signs

Motorway signals and messages advise of abnormal traffic conditions ahead and may indicate speed limits. They may apply to individual lanes when mounted overhead or, when located on the central reservation or at the side of the motorway, to the whole carriageway.

Where traffic is allowed to use the hard shoulder as a traffic lane, each lane will have overhead signals and signs. A red cross (with no signals) displayed above the hard shoulder indicates when it is closed. When the hard shoulder is in use as a traffic lane the red cross will change to a speed limit. Should it be necessary to close any lane, a red cross with red lamps flashing in vertical pairs will be shown above that lane. Prior to this, the signal will show an arrow directing traffic into the adjacent lane.

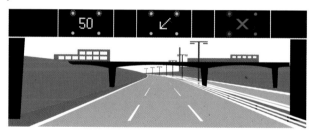

These signals are mounted above the carriageway with a signal for each traffic lane; each signal has two pairs of lamps that flash. You should obey the signal for your lane

Move to adjacent lane (arrow may point downwards to the right)

Leave motorway at next exit

Red lamps flashing from side to side in pairs, together with a red cross, mean 'do not proceed in the traffic lane directly below'. More than one lane may be closed to traffic

Where variable speed limit signs are mounted over individual lanes and the speed limit is shown in a red ring, the limit is mandatory. You will be at risk of a driving offence if you do not keep to the speed limit. Speed limits that do not include the red ring are the maximum speeds advised for the prevailing conditions.

Speed limits of 60, 50 and 40mph are used on all types of smart motorways. When no speed limit is shown the national speed limit of 70mph is in place (this is reduced to 60mph for particular vehicles such as heavy or articulated goods vehicles and vehicles towing caravans or trailers).

Quick tips

- Never drive in a lane closed by a red X
- Keep to the speed limit shown on the gantries
- A solid white line indicates the hard shoulder – do not drive in it unless directed or in the case of an emergency
- A broken white line indicates a normal running lane

- Exit the smart motorway where possible if your vehicle is in difficulty. In an emergency, move onto the hard shoulder where there is one, or the nearest emergency refuge area
- Put on your hazard lights if you break down

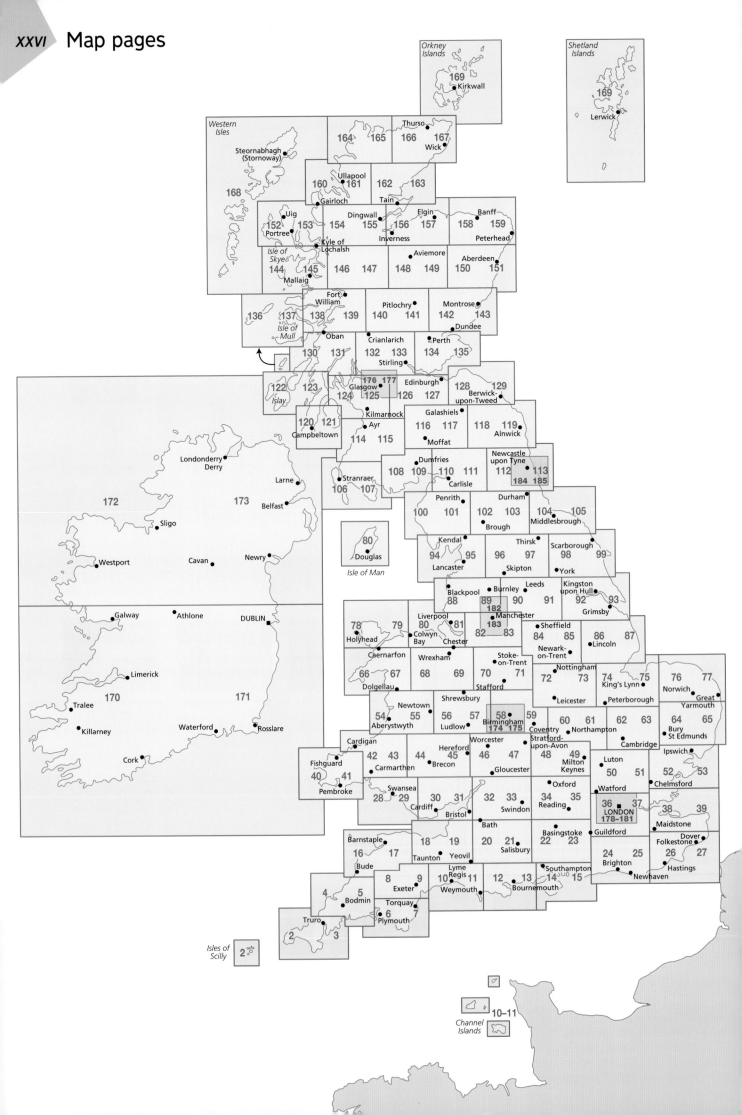

Motoring information

M4	Motorway with number	S	Primary route service area	⊧=======⊧	Road tunnel	Ⓕ	International freight terminal
Toll T4	Toll motorway with toll station	BATH	Primary route destination	Toll →	Road toll, steep gradient (arrows point downhill)	Ⓗ	24-hour Accident & Emergency hospital
6	Motorway junction with and without number	A1123	Other A road single/dual carriageway	▼ 5 ▼	Distance in miles between symbols	Ⓒ	Crematorium
5	Restricted motorway junctions	B2070	B road single/dual carriageway	⛴ or Ⓥ	Vehicle ferry	P+R	Park and Ride (at least 6 days per week)
Fleet S R	Motorway service area, rest area		Minor road more than 4 metres wide, less than 4 metres wide		Fast vehicle ferry or catamaran		City, town, village or other built-up area
	Motorway and junction under construction		Roundabout	----------	Railway line, in tunnel	628 ▲ 637 Lecht Summit	Height in metres, mountain pass
A3	Primary route single/dual carriageway		Interchange/junction	—o—✕—	Railway/tram station, level crossing		Snow gates (on main routes)
1	Primary route junction with and without number		Narrow primary/other A/B road with passing places (Scotland)	+++++++	Tourist railway		National boundary
3	Restricted primary route junctions		Road under construction	Ⓐ ✈ Ⓗ	Airport (major/minor), heliport		County, administrative boundary

Touring information To avoid disappointment, check opening times before visiting

	Scenic route	✳	Garden		Waterfall		Motor-racing circuit
Ⓩ	Tourist Information Centre	♣	Arboretum		Hill-fort		Air show venue
Ⓩ	Tourist Information Centre (seasonal)		Country park		Roman antiquity		Ski slope (natural, artificial)
Ⓥ	Visitor or heritage centre		Agricultural showground		Prehistoric monument		National Trust site
⚲	Picnic site		Theme park	✕ 1066	Battle site with year		National Trust for Scotland site
🚐	Caravan site (AA inspected)		Farm or animal centre		Steam railway centre	‡	English Heritage site
▲	Camping site (AA inspected)		Zoological or wildlife collection	⌒	Cave or cavern		Historic Scotland site
▲🚐	Caravan & camping site (AA inspected)		Bird collection	✖	Windmill, monument	✚	Cadw (Welsh heritage) site
⌂	Abbey, cathedral or priory		Aquarium		Beach (award winning)	★	Other place of interest
⌂	Ruined abbey, cathedral or priory	RSPB	RSPB site		Lighthouse	☐	Boxed symbols indicate attractions within urban areas
✖	Castle		National Nature Reserve (England, Scotland, Wales)	⚑	Golf course	◉	World Heritage Site (UNESCO)
🏛	Historic house or building		Local nature reserve		Football stadium		National Park and National Scenic Area (Scotland)
Ⓜ	Museum or art gallery		Wildlife Trust reserve		County cricket ground		Forest Park
	Industrial interest	....	Forest drive		Rugby Union national stadium		Sandy beach
	Aqueduct or viaduct	– – – –	National trail		International athletics stadium		Heritage coast
	Vineyard, brewery or distillery	☀	Viewpoint		Horse racing, show jumping		Major shopping centre

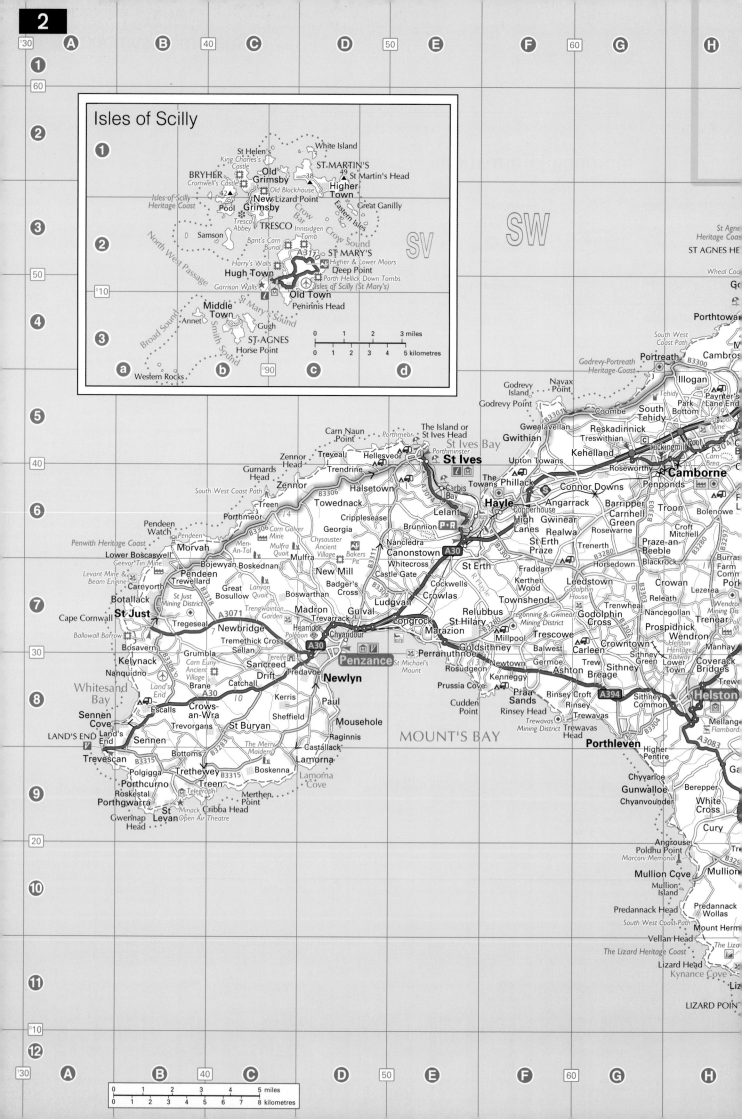

4

Newquay

0   200 m

Fistral
Beach
Atlantic Hotel
Memorial
KING EDWARD CRESCENT
HEADLAND ROAD
Newquay Golf Club
Fly Cove
Tithy Cove
Newquay Bay
BELMONT PLACE
HARBOUR VIEW
TOBY WAY
STONEY ROAD
Lifeboat Station
Towan Beach
Great Western Beach
The Island
Superstore
Tolcarne Beach
Great Western Hotel
Lifeguard Stn
(high season only)
Travelodge
NEWQUAY STATION
West End Bowling Green
The Train Track
Blue Reef
The Royal British Legion
Register Office
Christian Ctr
Hotel Victoria
Police Sta
Jobcentre Plus
Newquay School
Salvation Army
St John Ambulance
St Michael's
Pirate's Quest
Trenance Learning Academy
Ambulance Sta
Surgery
Superstore
Newquay H
ST COLUMB MINOR
Fire Station
Newquay AFC
Recreation Ground
Trenance Gardens
Tregunnel Park Caravan Park
River Gannel
GANNEL ROAD
GANNEL ROAD
MELLANVRANE ROUNDABOUT
A392
REDRUTH, BODMIN

SW

Pentire Point - Widemouth
Heritage Coast
Boscastle
Trevalga
TINTAGEL HEAD
Castle
Tintagel
Treth
Treth
Bossiney
Old Post Office
Penhallic Point
Tregatta
Treknow
Trewarme
Trebarwith
Penpethy
Treligga
Rockhead
Delabole
Pengell
South West Coast Path
Valley Tru
Westdowns
Lanteglos
Port Isaac
Bay
Helsto
Rumps
Point
Port Quin
Bay
Kellan
Head
Varley
Head
Port Gaverne
Trewalder
Stepper Point
New Polzeath
Port
Quin
Port Isaac
Trewetha
St Teath
Knightsm
Pentire Point
Padstow Bay
Polzeath
Plain Street
Trelights
Treve
Trebetherick
Long Cross
Pendoggett
Treharrock
Mic
Hayle Bay
Trevose Head
Heritage Coast
Gunver Head
Hawker's
Cove
Trevanger
Pityme
St Minver
Tregellist
St Endellion
Trelill
A39
Trenewth
Mother Ivey's Bay
Crugmeer
Harlyn Bay
Prideaux Place
Rock
Splatt
Stoptide
Tredrizzick
Trewethern
St Kew
St Kew Highway
Chapel Amble
Trequite
St Tudy
TREVOSE HEAD
Dinas Head
Trevose
Trevone
Treator
Padstow
Dinas
Hendra
Lank
Constantine Bay
Harlyn
Windmill
Tregonce
Tregunna
Bodieve
St Mabyn
Wenfordbridge
Blis
Constantine Bay
Treyarnon
Towan
St Merryn
Trevorrick
Edmonton
Trevanson
Trehemborne Shop
St Issey
Tredethy
Porthcothan
Little Petherick
Trenance
Whitecross
Wadebridge
Egloshayle
Croanford
Pencarrow House
Hellanbridg
Park Head
Treburrick
Penrose
Rumford
Tredinnick
Royal Cornwall
St Breock
Sladesbridge
Burlawn
Washaway
Hellan
Engollan
Downhill
St Ervan
Trelow
Hay
Polbrock
Camel Valley
Bedruthan Steps
Carnewas
St Eval
St Jidgey
St Breock Downs Monolith
Brocton
Lane End
Dunmere
Trenance
Camel Creek
Adventure Park
Nine Maidens
A39
Ruthernbridge
Boscarne
Berryl's Point
Mawgan Porth
B3274
Tregawne
Nanstallon
St Lawrence
Bodmin
Griffin's Point
Trevarrian
St Mawgan
Cornish Birds of Prey Centre
Rosenannon
Withielgoose
Tremore
Tregurrian
Carloggas
Talskiddy
St Wenn
Withiel
Retire
Lamorick
Lanivet
Trebyan
Lanhy
Watergate Bay
Cornwall Newquay
Gluvian
Reterth
Tregonetha
Demelza
Towan Head
Newquay Bay
St Columb Minor
St Columb Major
Castle-an-Dinas
Belowda
Victoria
Higher Town
Cornwall
A391
Bokiddick
Sw
Newquay
Fistral Bay
Porth
Trevithick
Trebudannon
Screech Owl Sanctuary
Lockengate
Helman Tor
Kelsey Head
West Pentire
Pentire
Colan
Bosoughan
Black Cross
Ruthvoes
A30
Tregoss
Roche
Criggan
Carbis
Bugle
Bodwen
Penhale
West Pentire
Treninnick
Mountjoy
Trevarren
Goss Moor
Tredinnick
Holywell Bay
Crantock
Lane
Quintrell Downs
A392
Enniscaven
Carne
Carnsmerry
Rosevean
Lanlivery
Penhale Point
Trenowah
Trevemper
Rosecliston
St Columb Road
Indian Queens
Fraddon
Blue Anchor
Whitemoor
Luxulyan
Holywell
Tresean
Treval
Kestle Mill
Retyn
Penhale
St Dennis
Stenalees
Carthew
Penwithick
Trethurgy
Luxulyan Valley
Ligger Point
Cubert
Trevoll
Trerice
Gummow's Shop
Cornish Dairyland
Farm World
Troan
St Enoder
A30
Treviscoe
Nanpean
Wheal Martyn
A391
Tywardreath Highway
Penp
Ligger or Perran Bay
Mount
St Newlyn East
Rejerrah
Trevilson
A3076
Summercourt
Burthy
Melbur
Foxhole
Wheal
St Blazey
Tywar
Rose
Lappa Valley
Steam Railway
Chapel Town
Treviscoe
Carpalla
Ruddlemoor
Carclaze
Tregrehan Mills
Eden Project
Pa
Perranzabuloe
Mitchell
Brighton
Scarcewater
3
Trethosa
High Street
Carland Cross
Menna
A3058
St Stephen
Ruddlemoor
Carclaze
Boscoppa
St Blazey Gate
Biscovey
A3082
Perranporth
Fiddlers Green
Goonhavern
Trendeal
Gwindra
St Austell
Trewoon
Holmbush
Cligga Point
Bolingey
Cocks
Coombe
New Mills
Trelion
Hay
St Mewan
Charlestown
Charlestown Bay
Polkerr
Trevellas Downs
Carnkiet
B3285
Perranwell
Zelah
Ladock
Coombe
Sticker
Carlyon Bay
Menab
St Agnes
Penhallow
St Allen
Trispen
London Apprentice
Polgooth
Tregorrick
Porthpean
St Austell Bay
Mithian
Barkla Shop
Callestick
Marazanvose
St Erme
Treverbyn
Grampound Road
Levalsa Meor
Hewas Water
Rescorla
Goonbell
Coldharbour
Silverwell
Allet Common
Treworgan
Probus
A390
Towan
Trenarren
Black Head
EAD
Mount Hawke
B3284
Agnes
Min. District
Averton Cross
Three
Ilian
Tresawle
River Fa
Tucoyse
Grampound Creek
St Ewe
Kestle
Tregiskey
Mevagissey Bay
Wheal
Menagissey
Blackwater
A390
Threemilestone
Probus
Tresawle
Penare

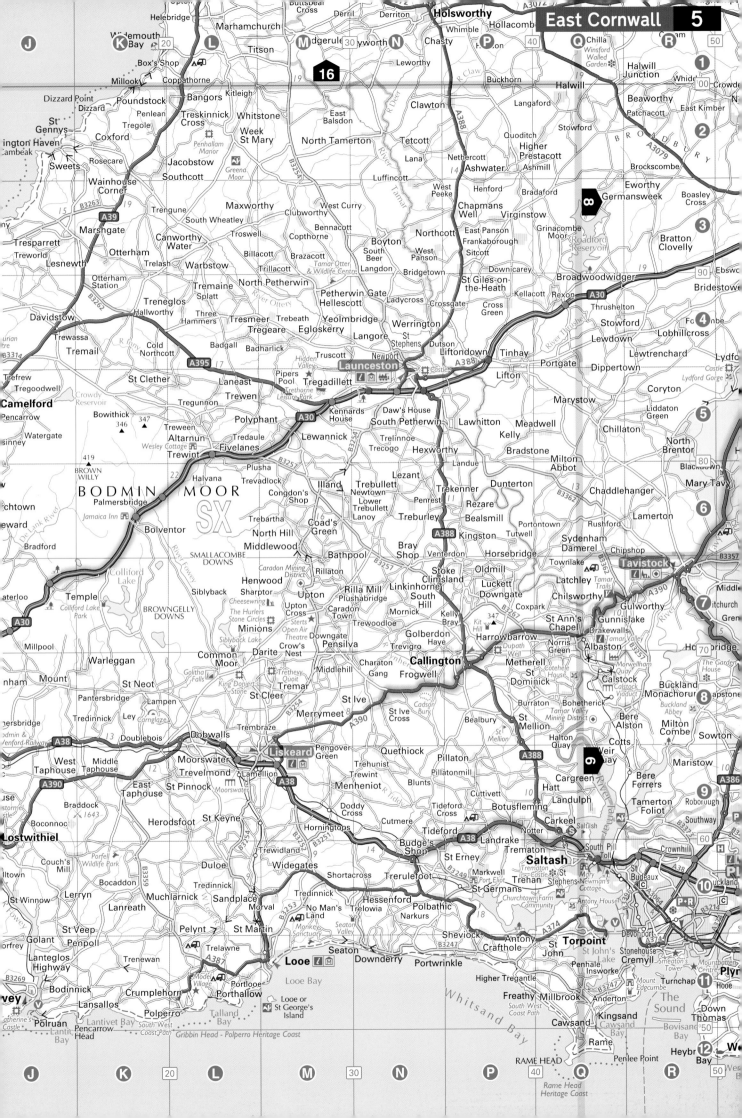

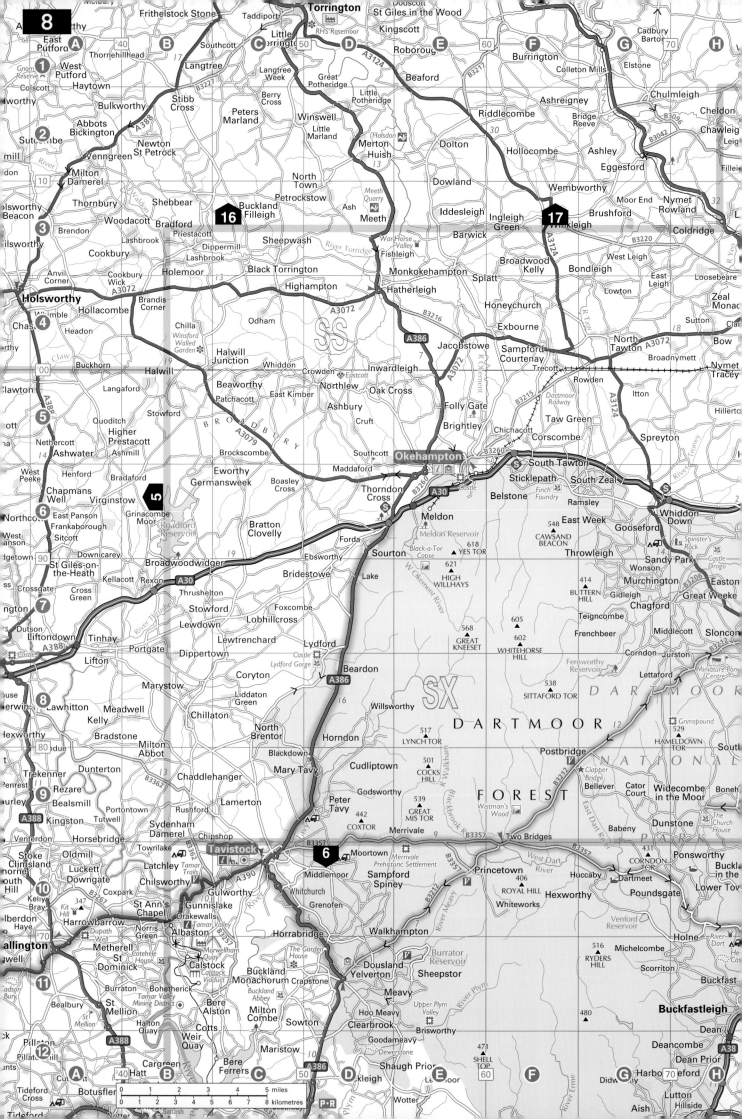

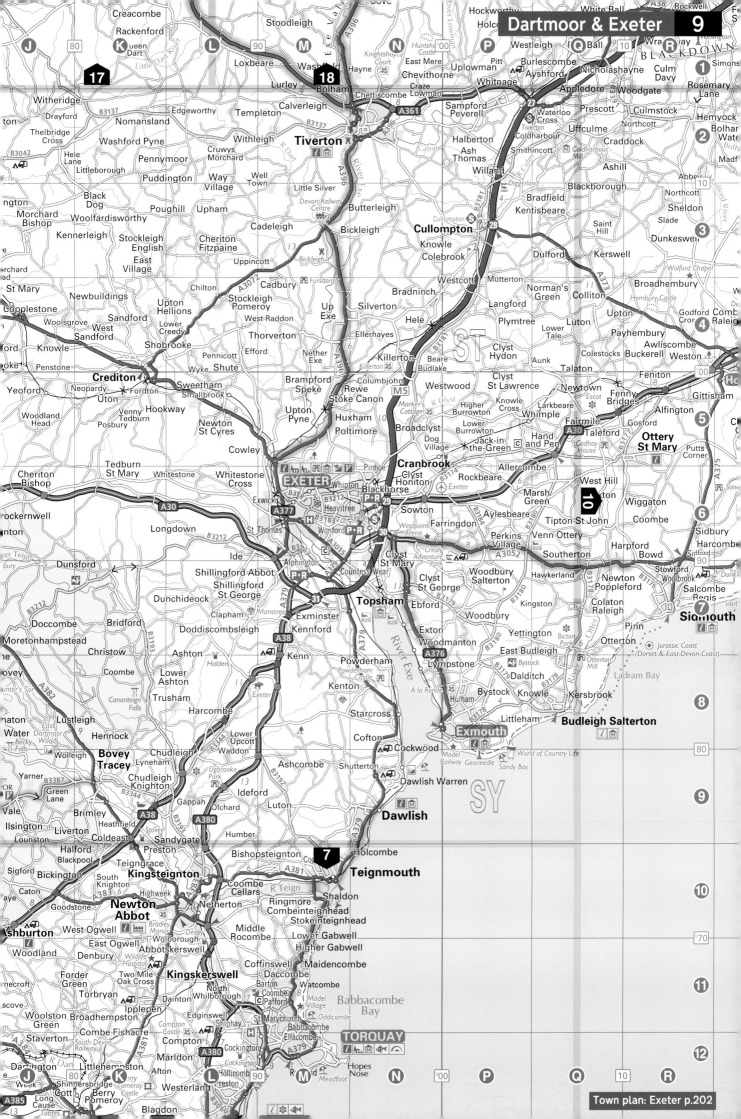

Jersey

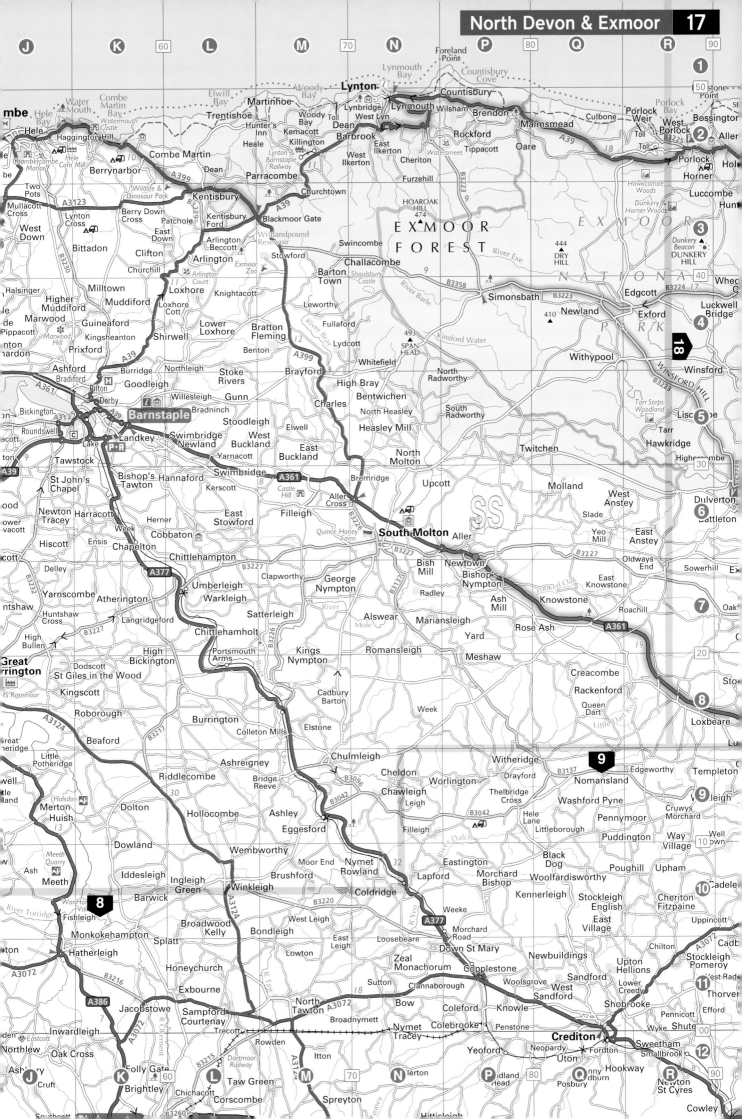

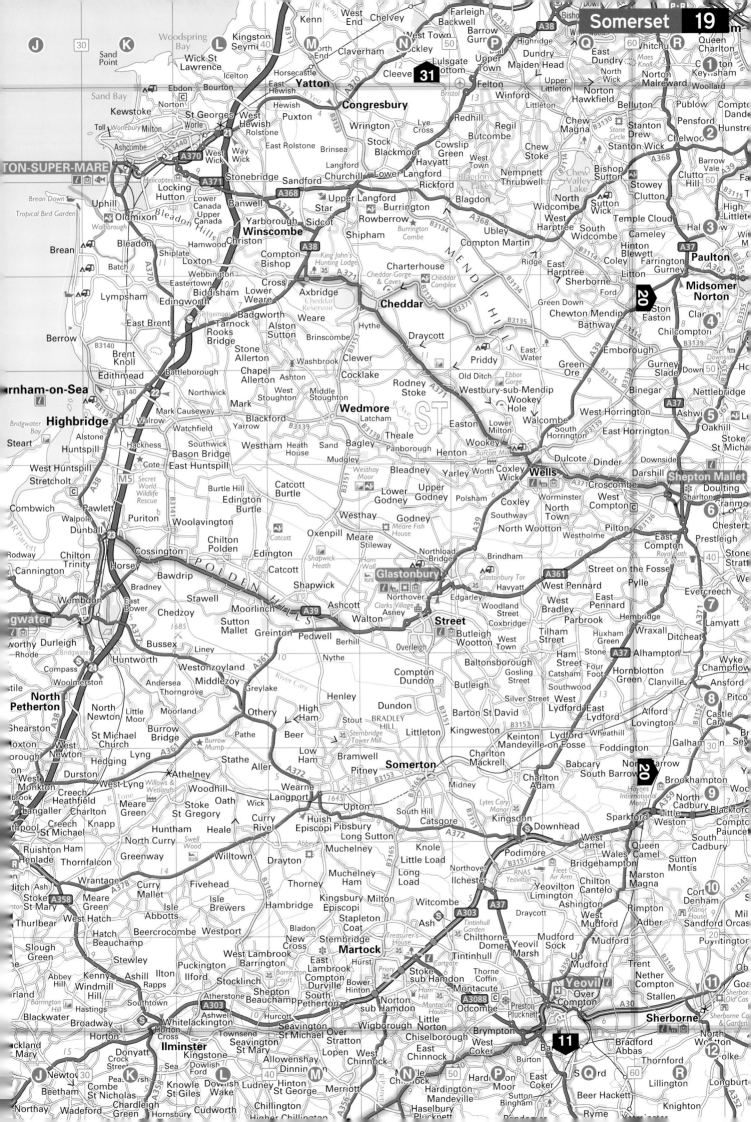

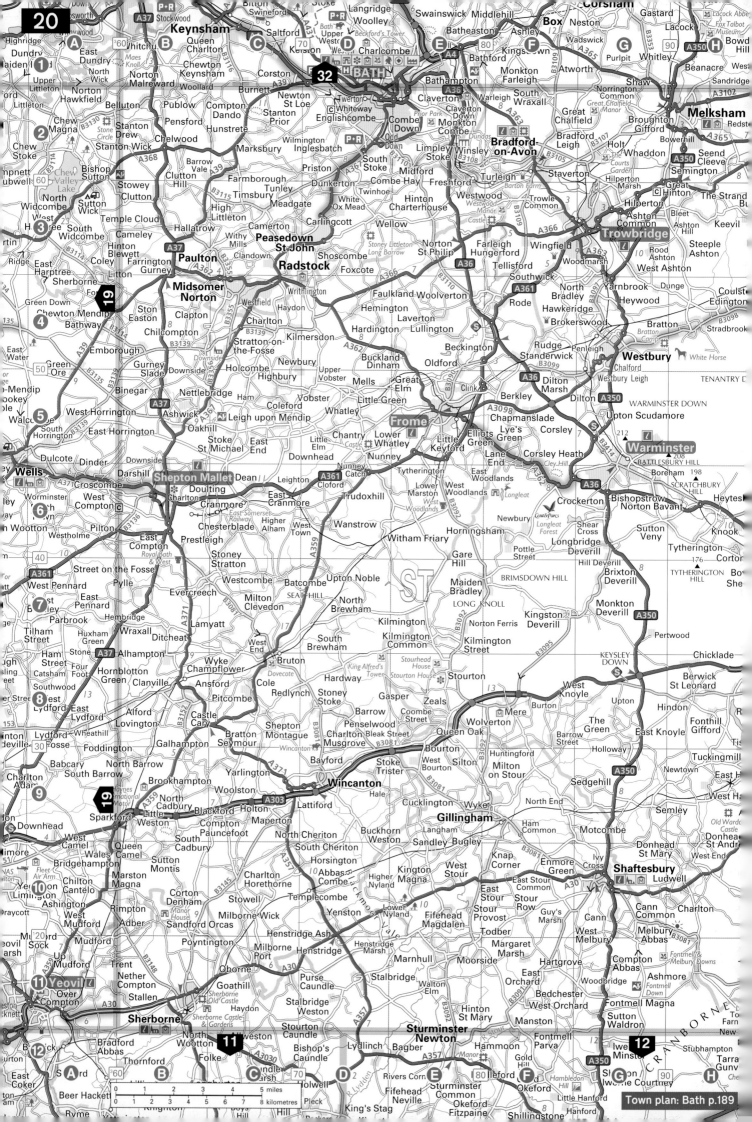

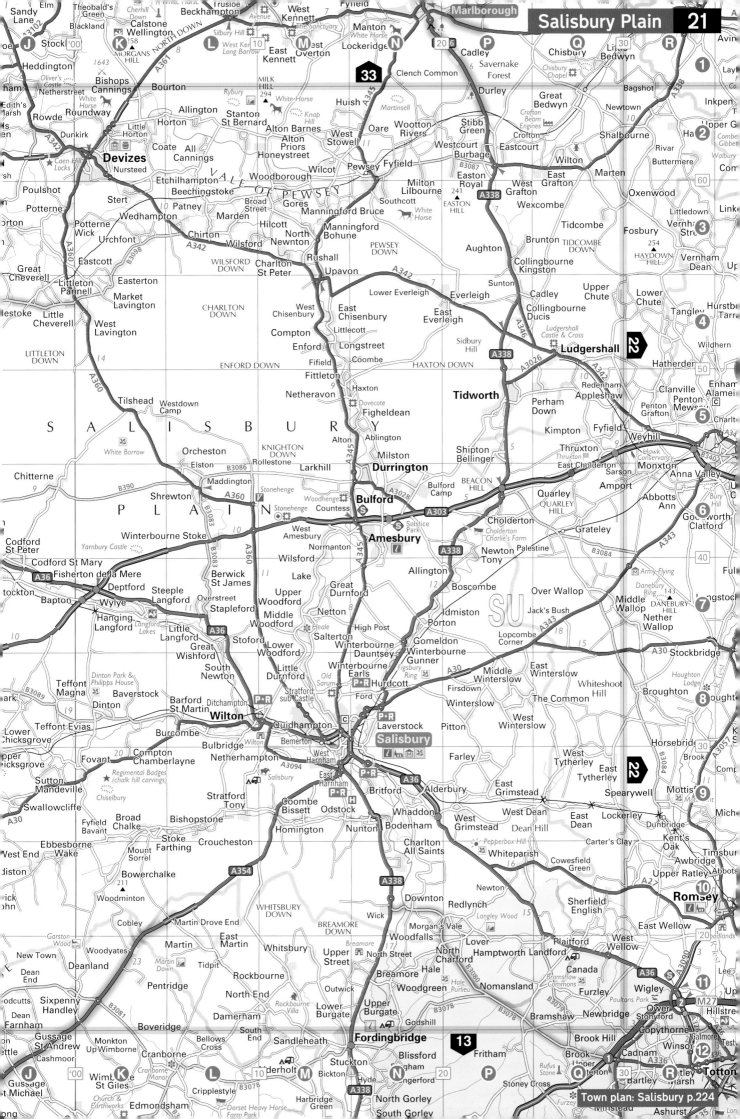

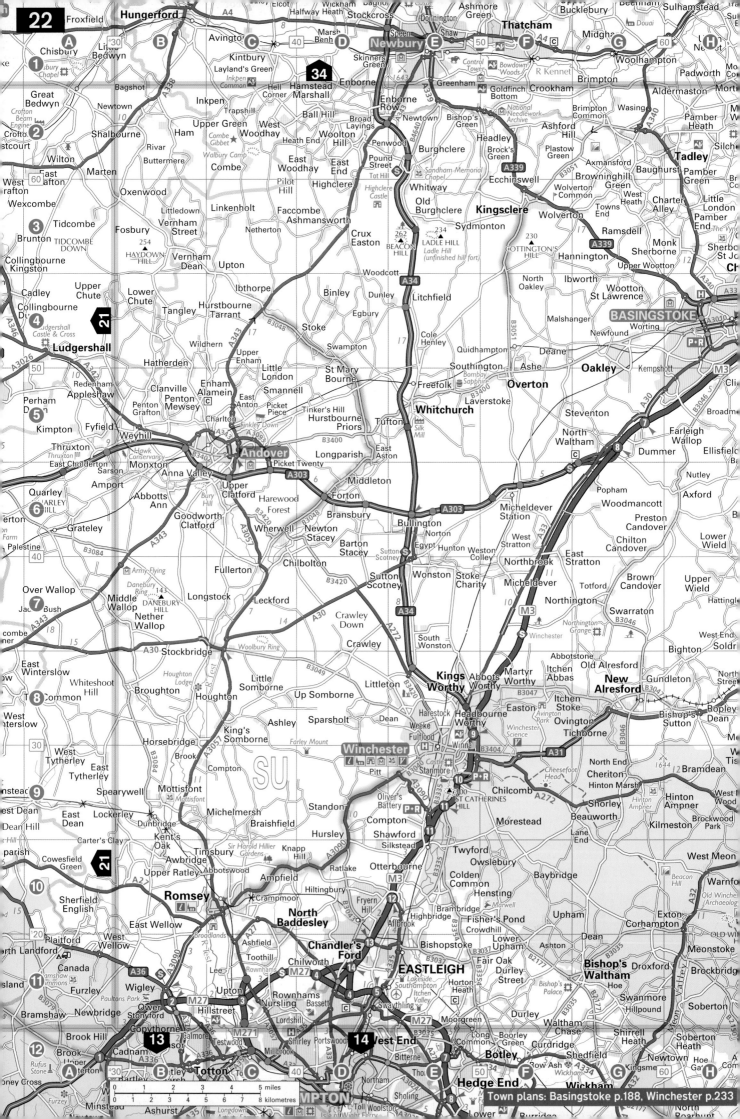

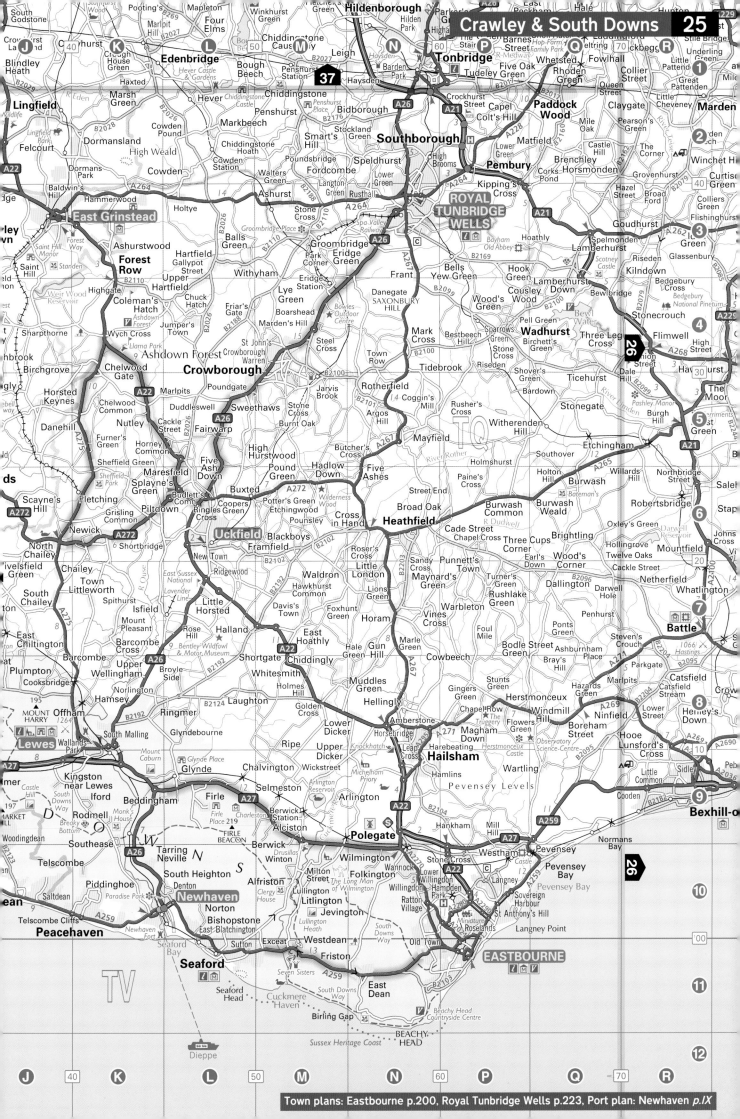

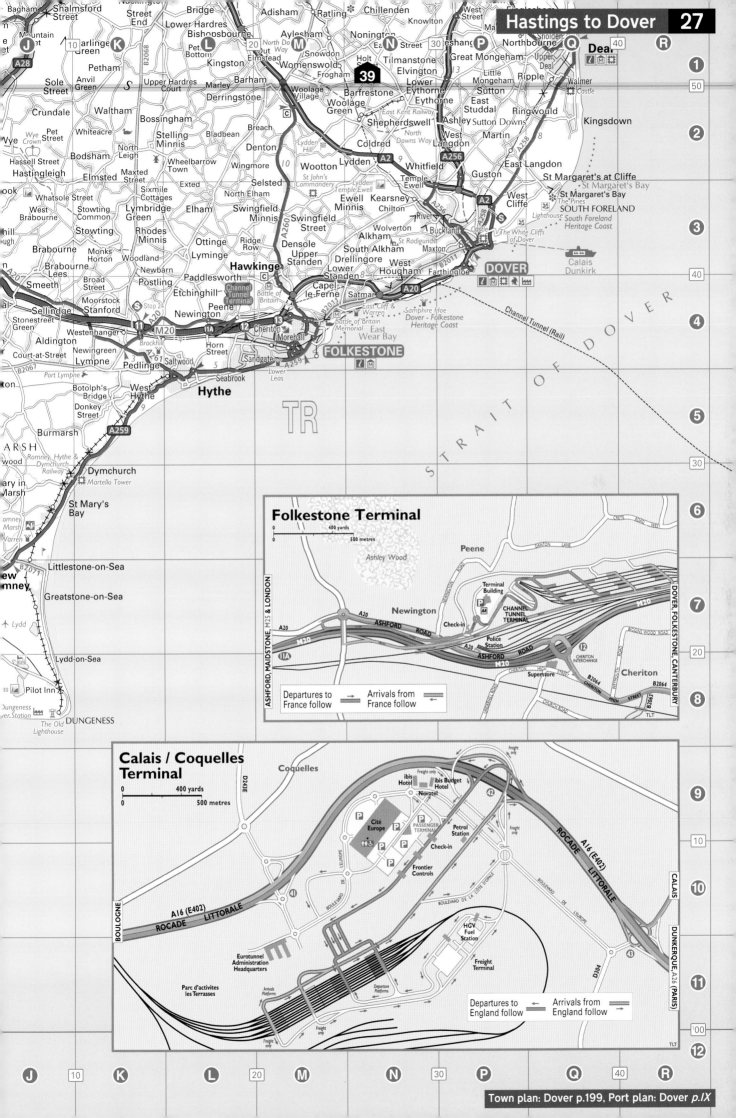

Folkestone Terminal

Departures to France follow →
Arrivals from France follow

Calais / Coquelles Terminal

Departures to England follow ←
Arrivals from England follow →

Town plan: Dover p.199, Port plan: Dover *p.IX*

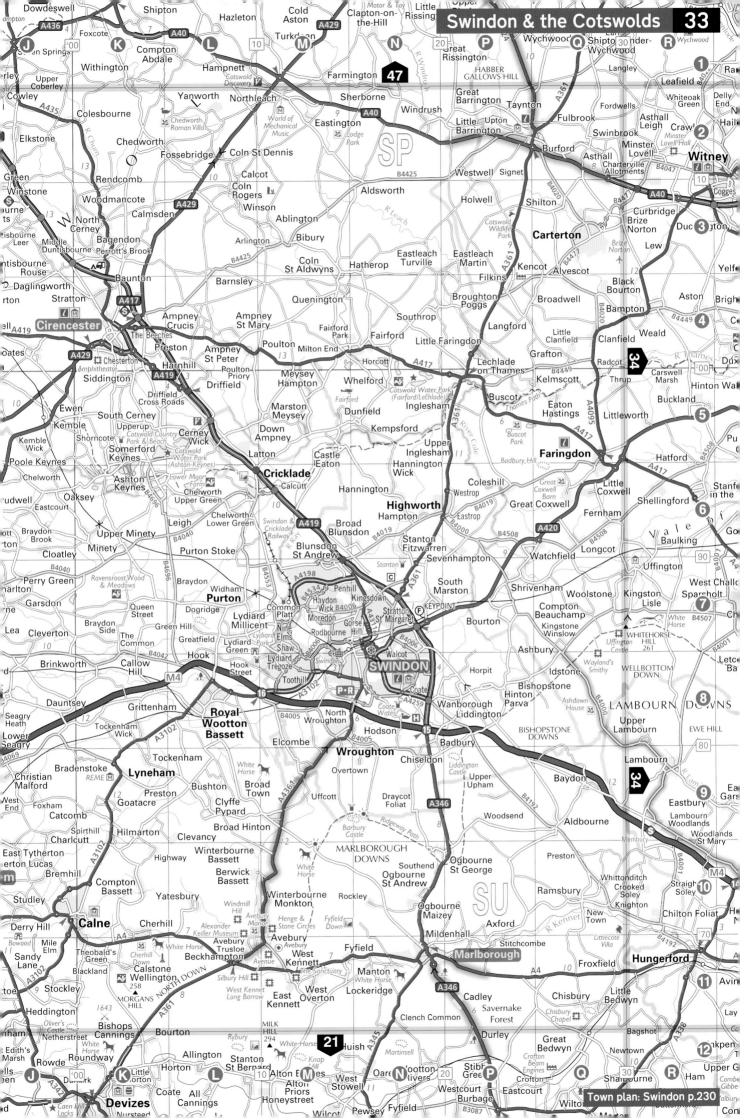

SM

SR

Rosslare

STRUMBLE HEAD

Pen Brush
Garn Fawr

Trefasser

Goodwick
(Wdig)

Pwll Deri

Manorowen

Pembrokeshire Coast Path

St Nicholas

Panteg

Ynys Daullyn

Granston

Carreg Sampson

Abercastle

Llangloffan

Jordans

SM

Porthgain

Trefin

Mathry

Castle Morris

Abereiddy

Llanrhian

Llangloffan Fen

Berea

Croes-goch

Square and Compass

Tretio

Treglemais

Treffynnon

Letterst

ST DAVID'S HEAD

Treleddyd-fawr

Carnhedryn

Cerbyd

River Solva

Llandeloy

Whitesands Bay

Rhodiad-y-brenin

Caer Farchell

Tancredston

Pont-yr-hafod

Bishop's Palace

Whitchurch

Middle Mill

Treffgarne Owen

Hayscastle

RAMSEY ISLAND

St Davids
(Tyddewi)

Hayscastle Cross

Nine Wells

Solva

178
DUDWELL MT

RSPB

Ramsey Sound

St David's Peninsula Heritage Coast

Penycwn

Lewe

Newgale

Roch

Wolfsdale

PEMBROKESHIRE COAST NATIONAL PARK

Roch Gate

Simpson Cross

St Brides Bay

Rickets Head

Nolton Haven

Nolton

Keeston

Cam

Ta

St Brides Bay Heritage Coast

Pelcomb Cross

Pelcom

Lambston

Pelcomb Bridge

Druidston

Sutton

Haroldston West

Portfield Gate

Broad Haven

Broadway

Dreen Hill

Little Haven

Walton West

Pembrokeshire Coast Path

Talbenny

Solbury

Tiers Cross

St Brides

Walwyn's Castle

SKOMER ISLAND

Wooltack Point

Marloes

Hasguard

Thornton

Broad Sound

Sandy Haven

Herbrandston

Steynton

Marloes & Dale Heritage Coast

St Ishmael's

Hubberston

Honeyboro

Waterston

SKOKHOLM ISLAND

Dale

Westdale Bay

Dale Point

Great Castle Head

Hakin

Llanstad

Milford Haven

Milford Haven
(Aberdaugleddau)

Pem
D

St Ann's Head

Angle

Angle Bay

Pwllcrochan

(Doc

Rosslare

Rhoscrowther

Freshwater West

Castlemartin Brook

Castlemartin

SR

Warren

Linney Head

Merr

PEMBROKESHIRE C
NATIONAL PA

Pembrokeshire Coast Path

0 1 2 3 4 5 miles
0 1 2 3 4 5 6 7 8 kilometres

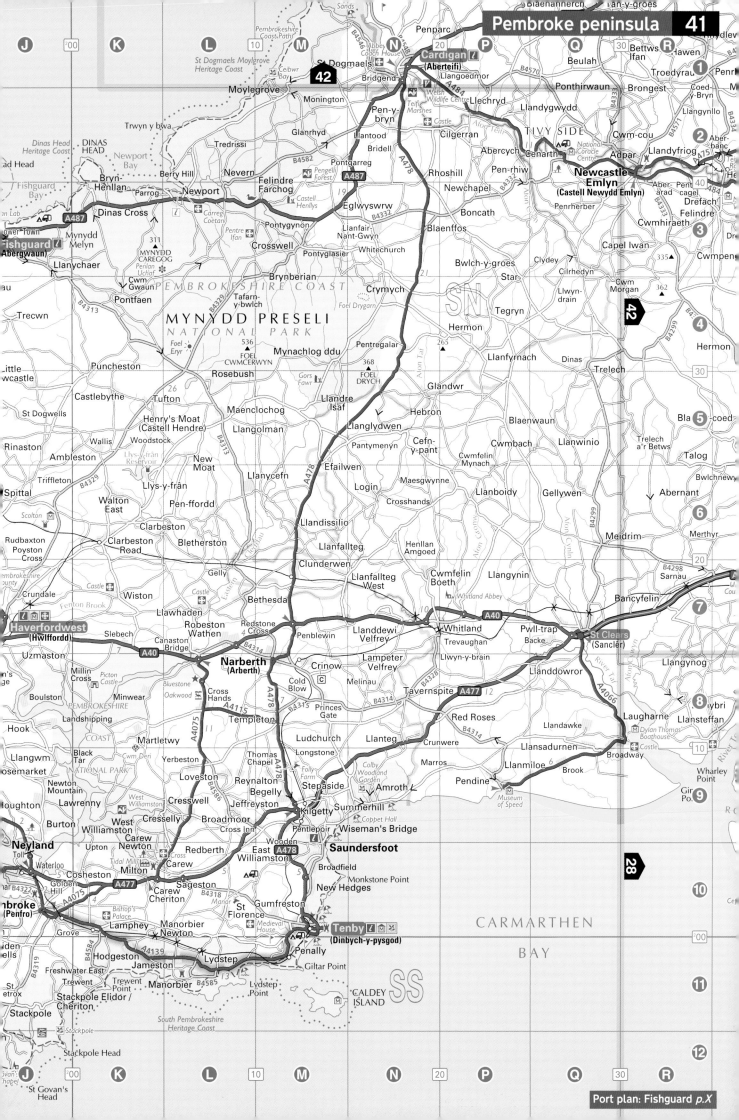

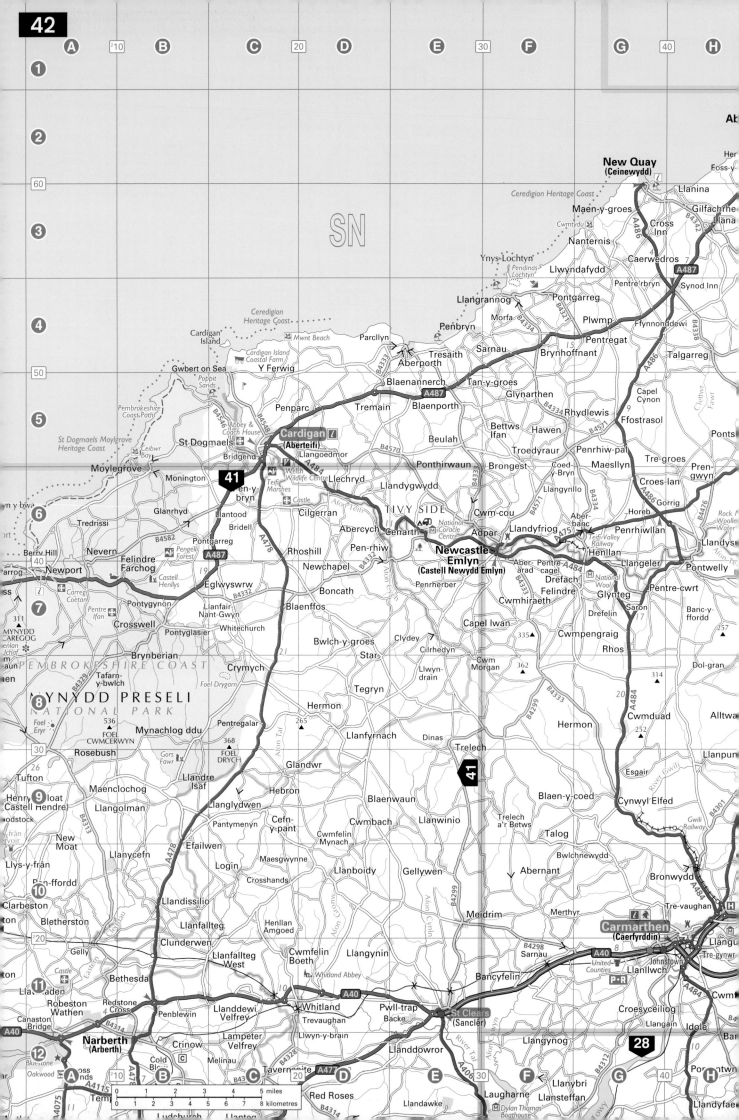

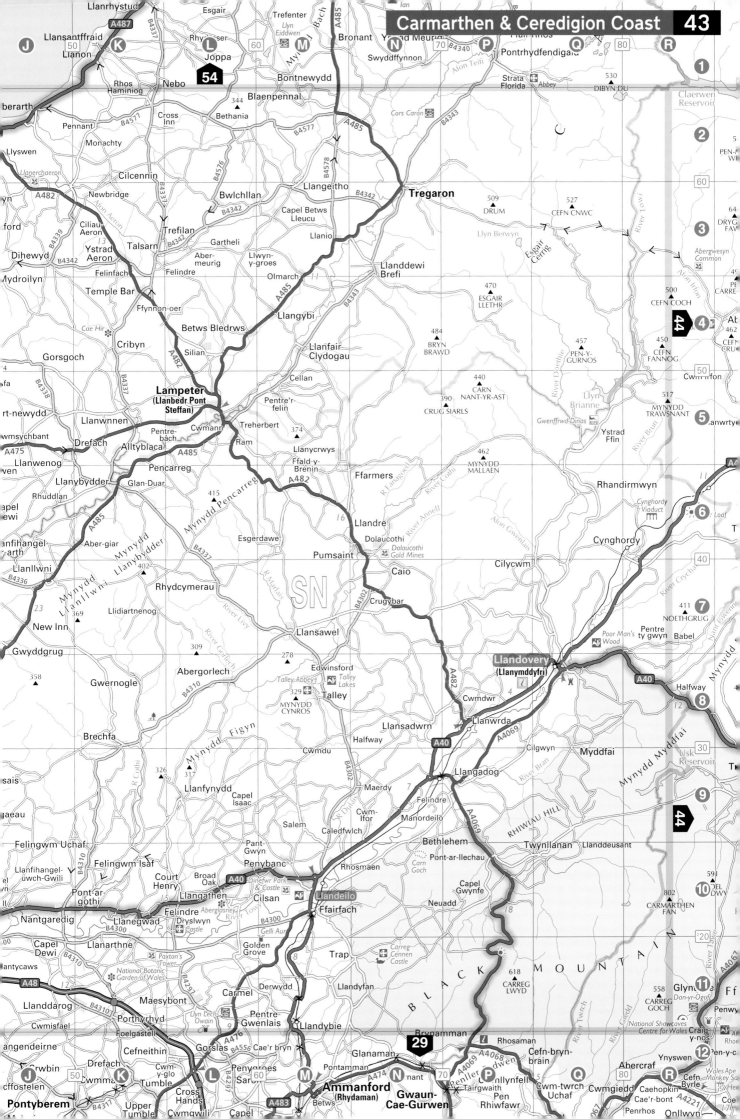

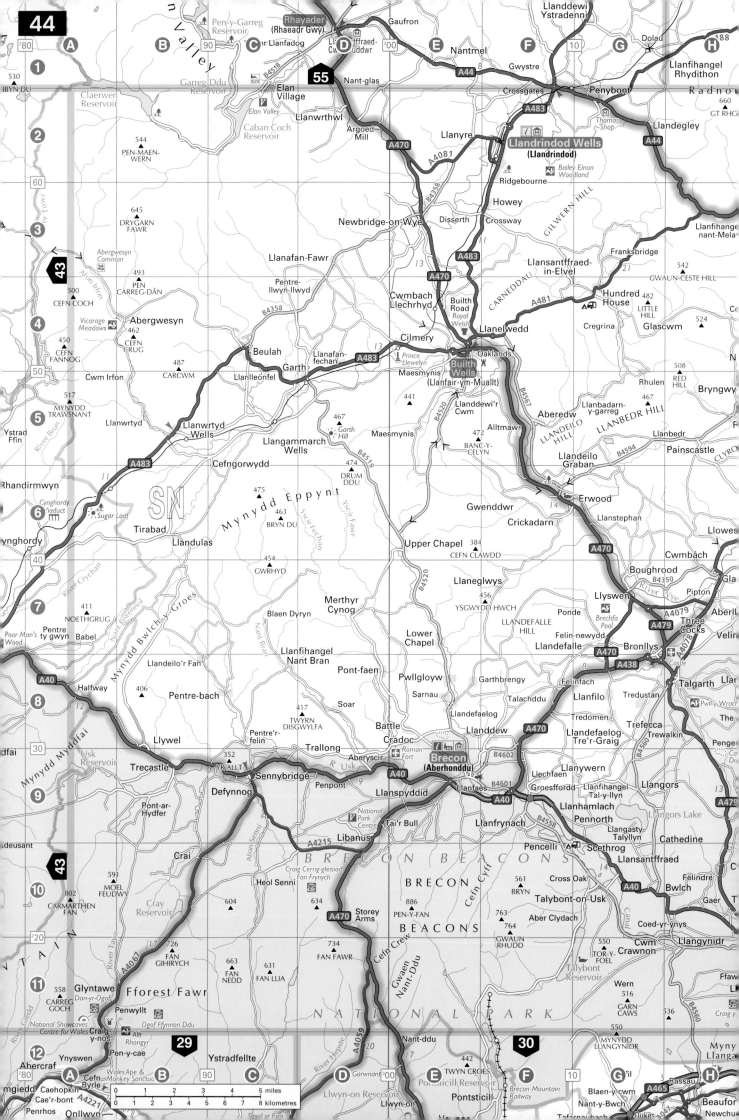

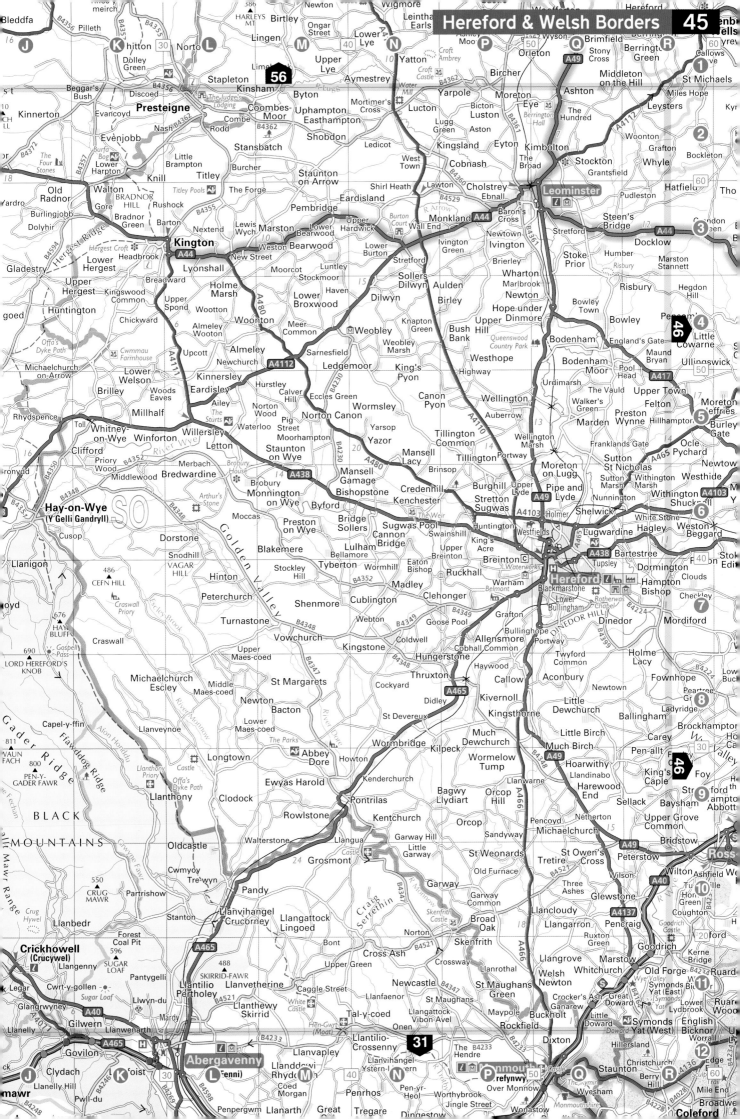

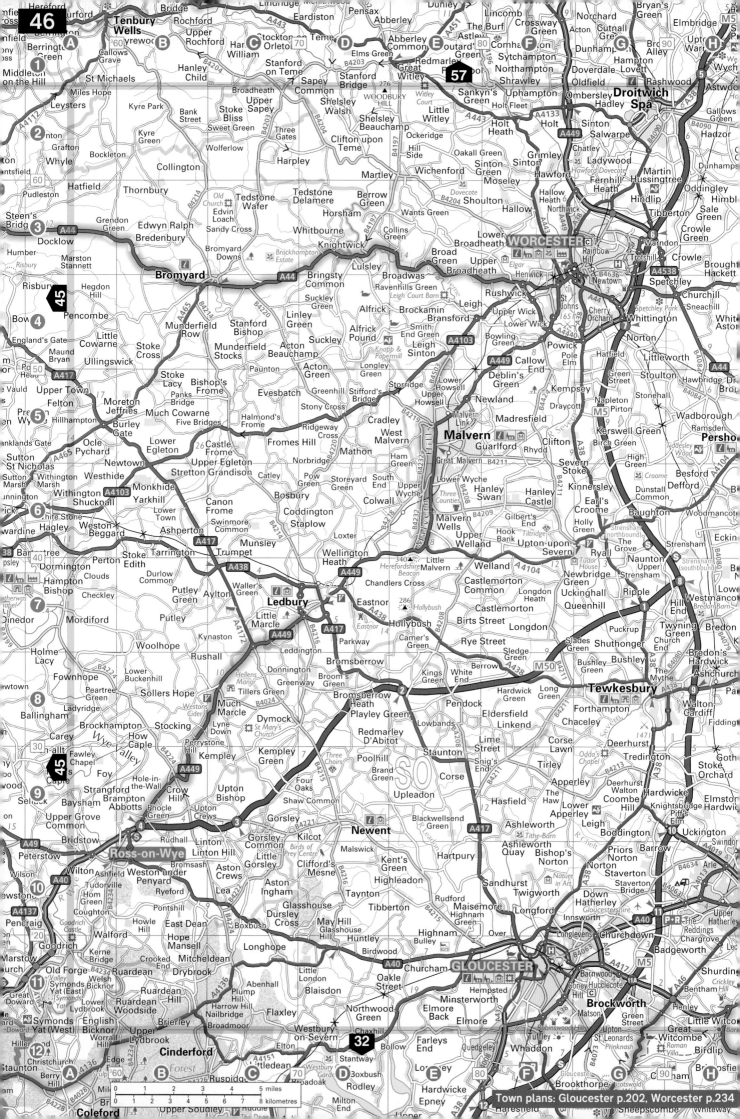

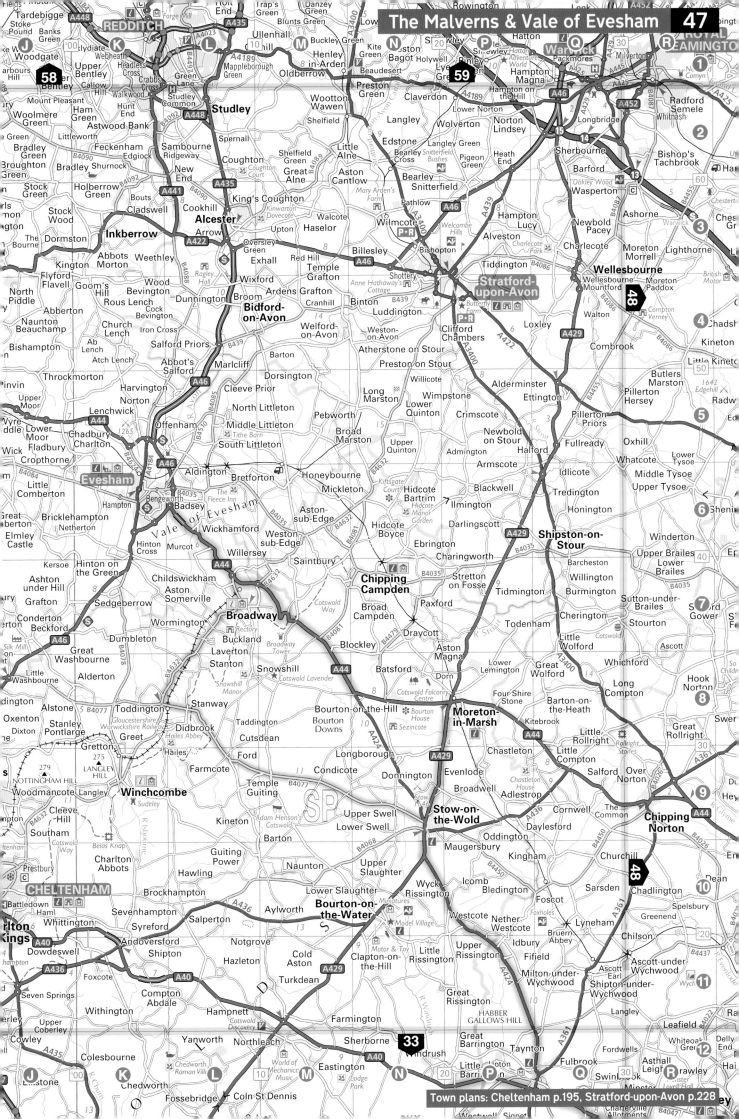

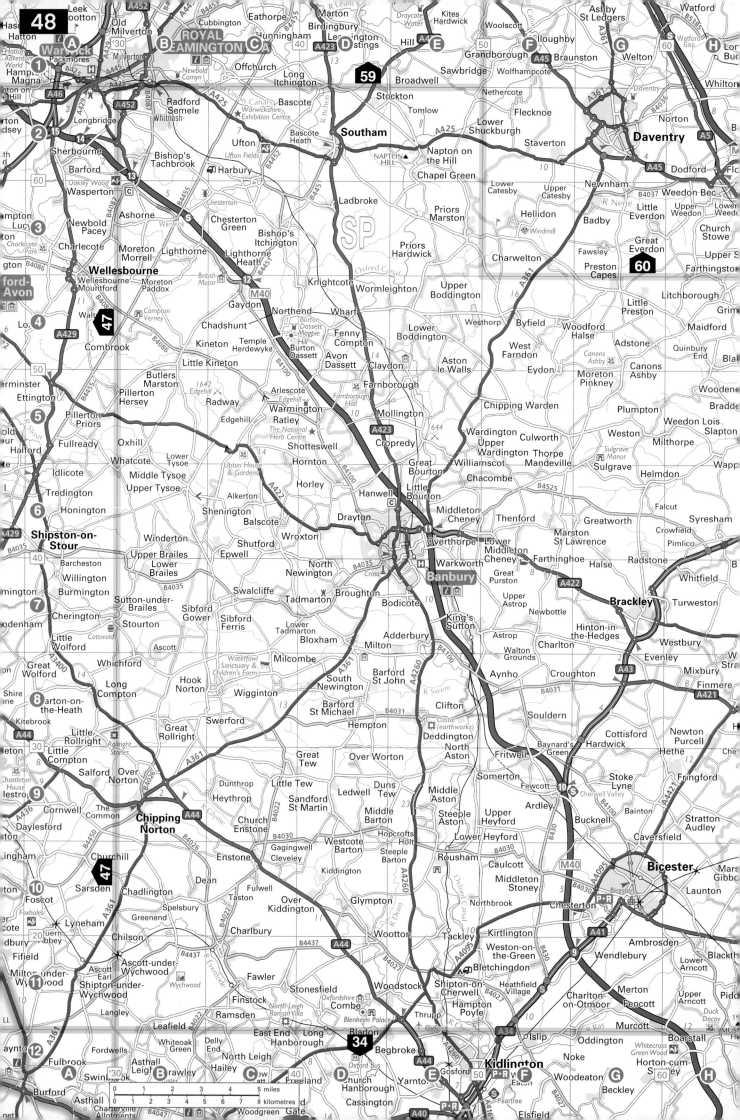

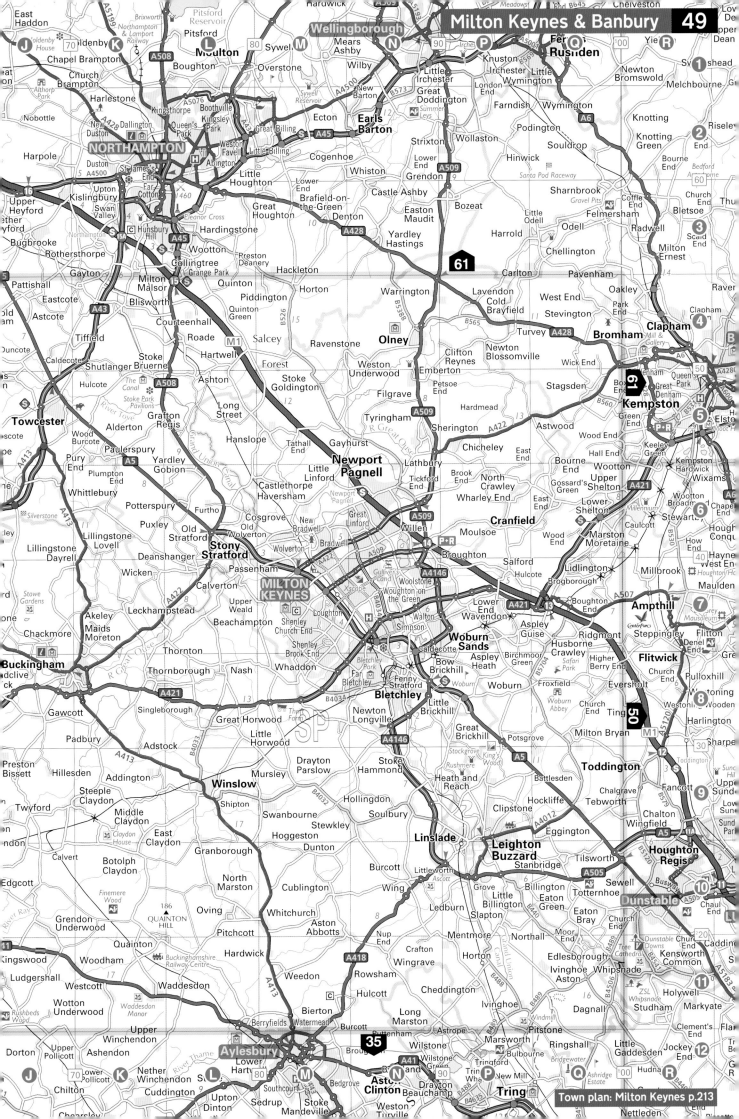

Harwich International Port

PASSENGER & CRUISE TERMINAL
HARWICH INTERNATIONAL STATION
CAR FERRY TERMINAL
FREIGHT TERMINAL
WEST DOCK
REFINERY ROAD
STATION ROAD
Parkeston
Harwich Industrial Estate
Superstore
PARKESTON ROUNDABOUT
ST NICHOLAS ROUNDABOUT
Superstore
Premier Inn
MAIN ROAD
PARKESTON ROAD
Dovercourt
Upper Dovercourt
A120
IPSWICH, COLCHESTER
HARWICH
A136
0   400 m

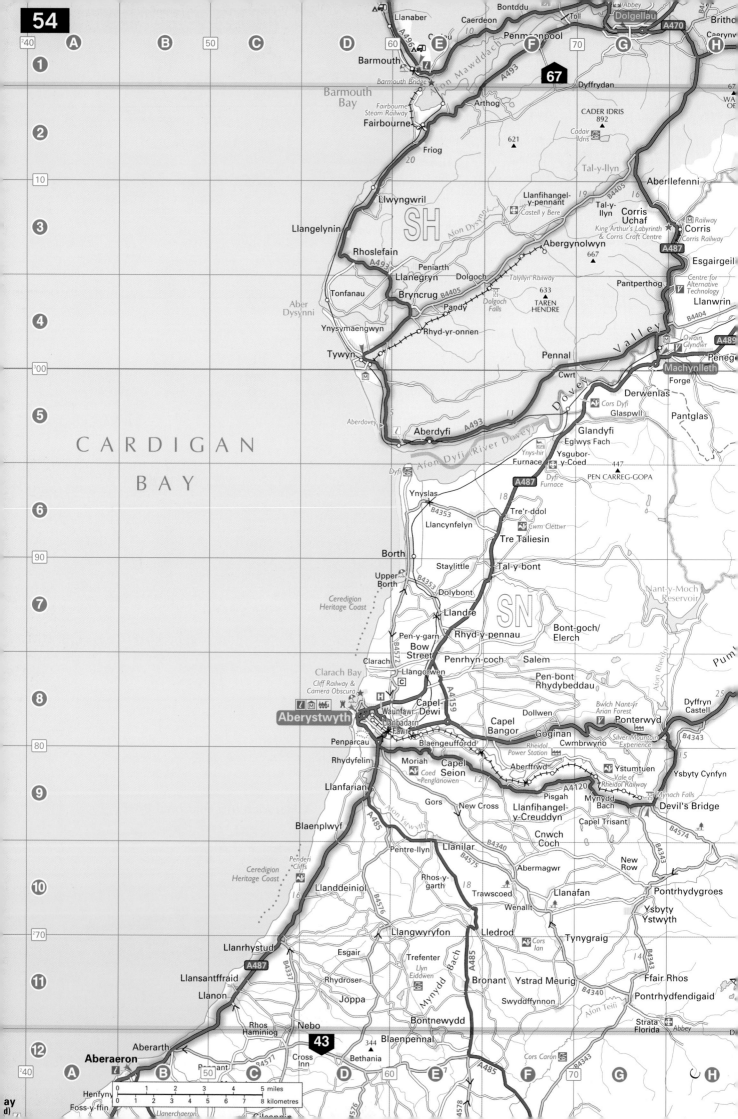

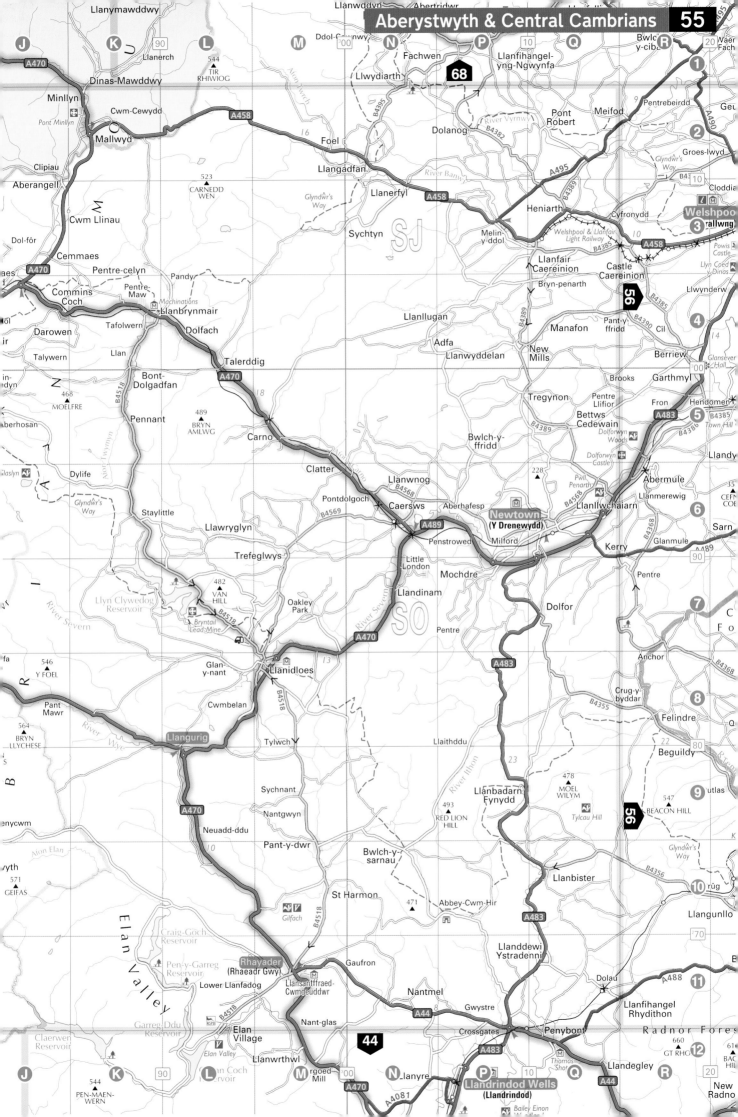

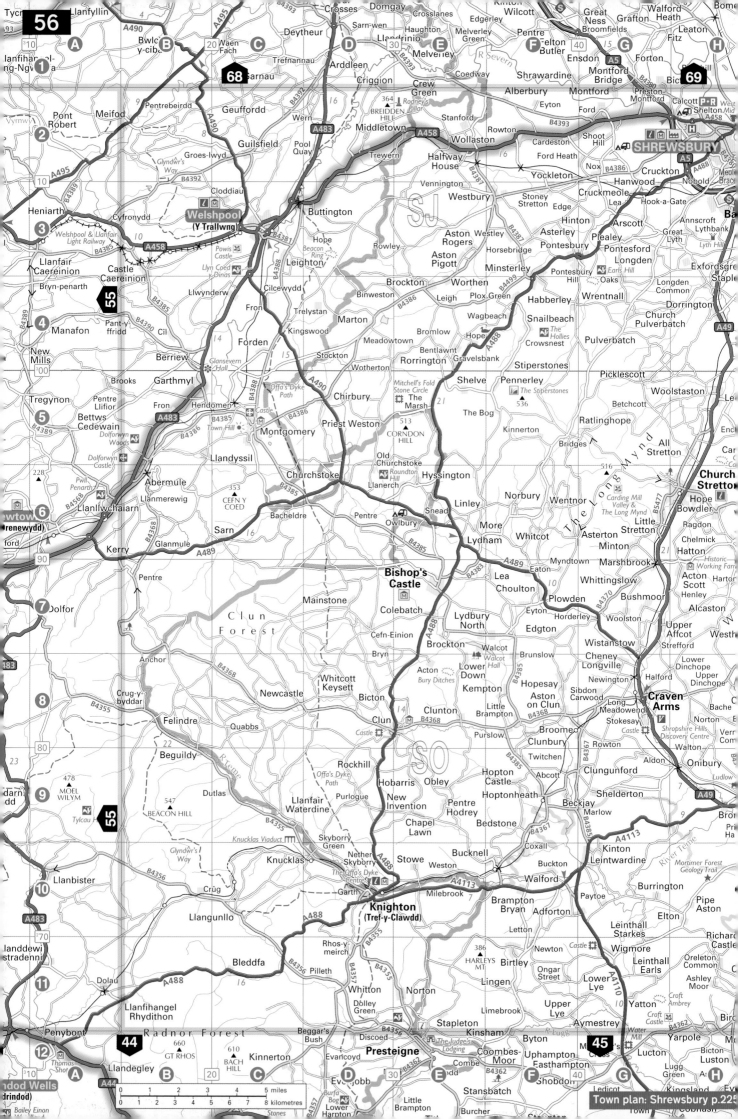

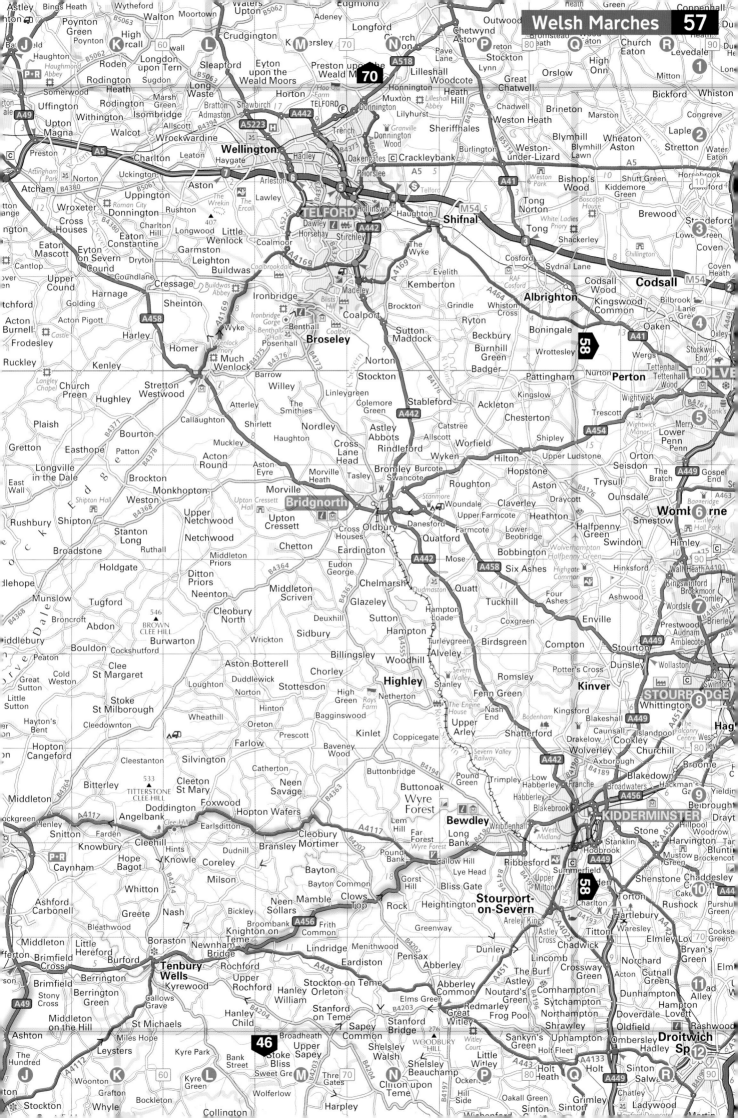

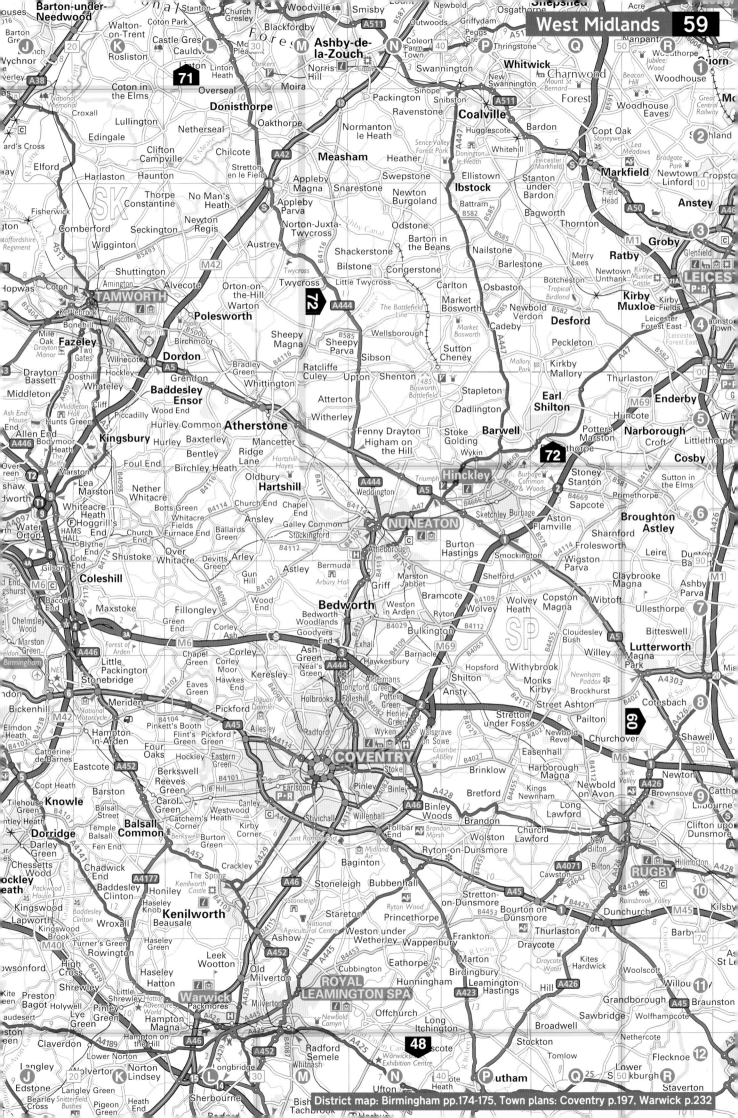

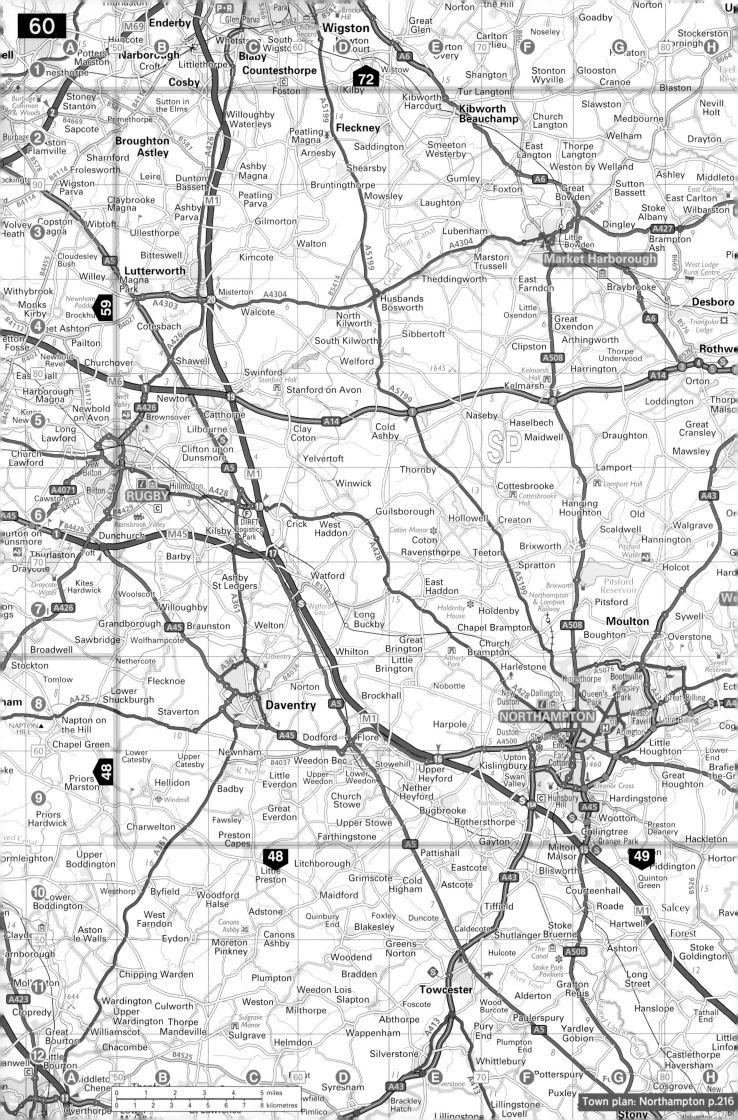

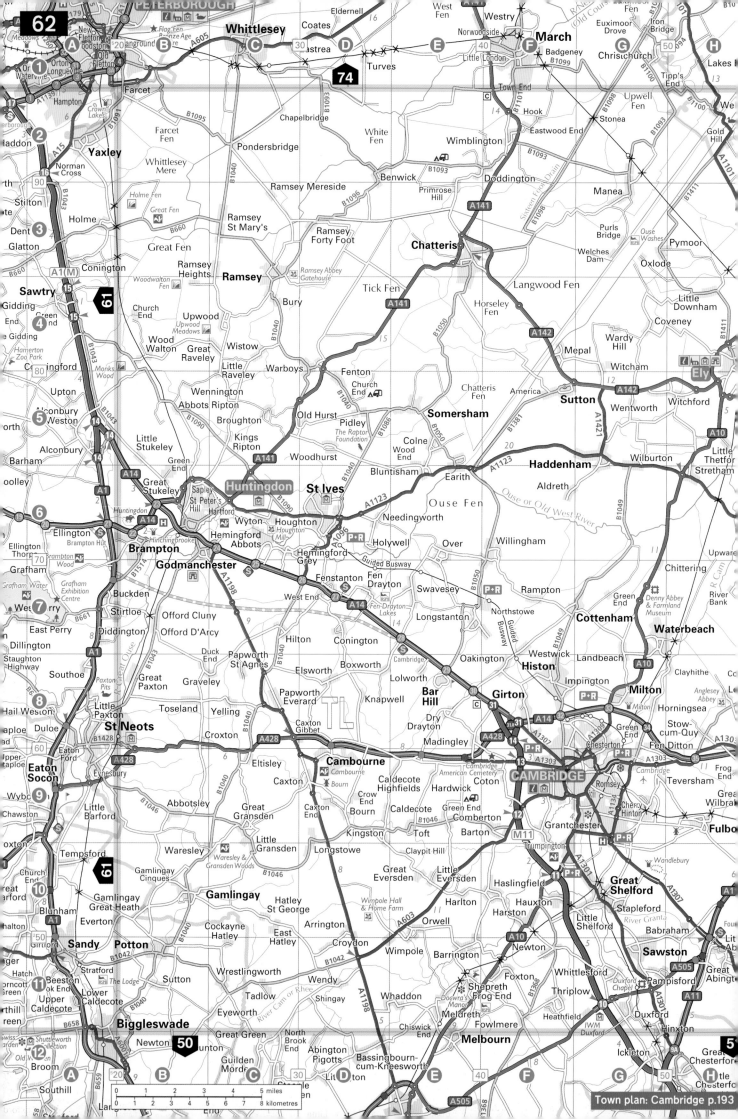

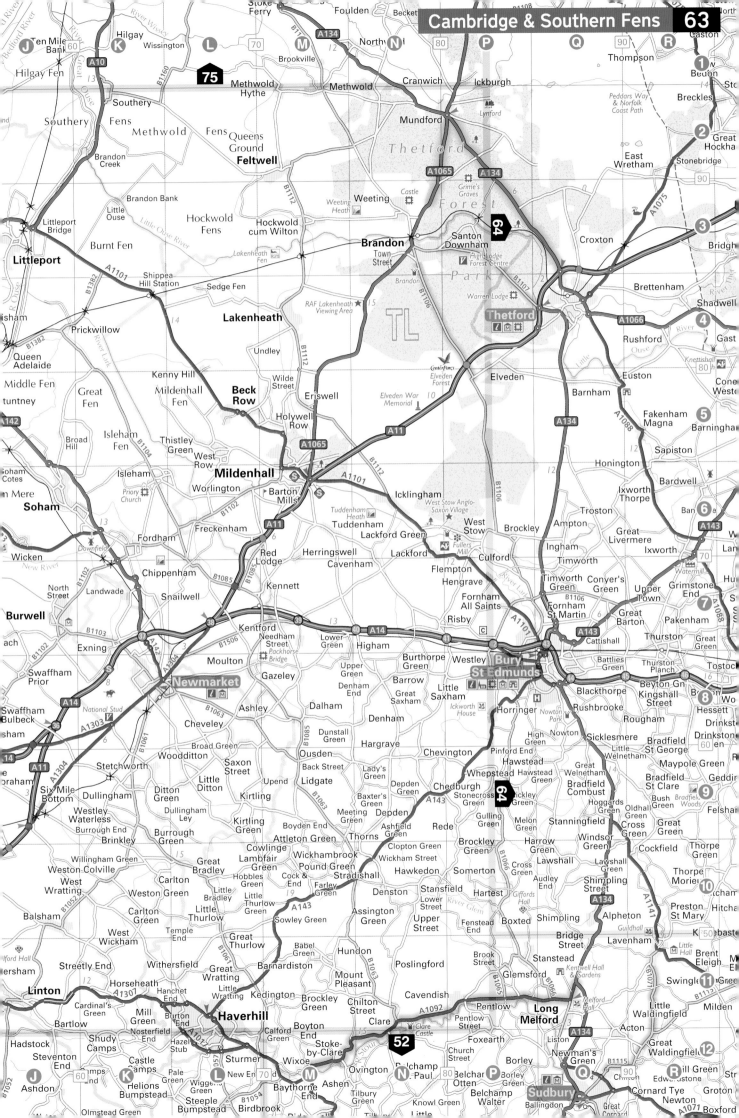

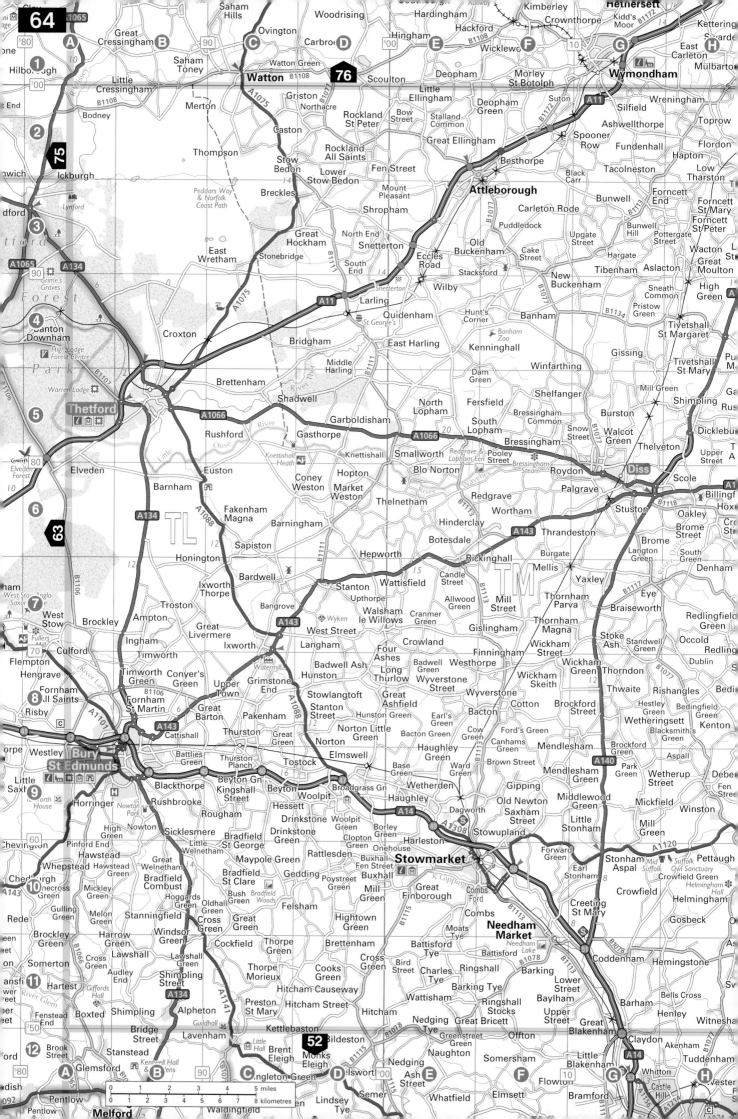

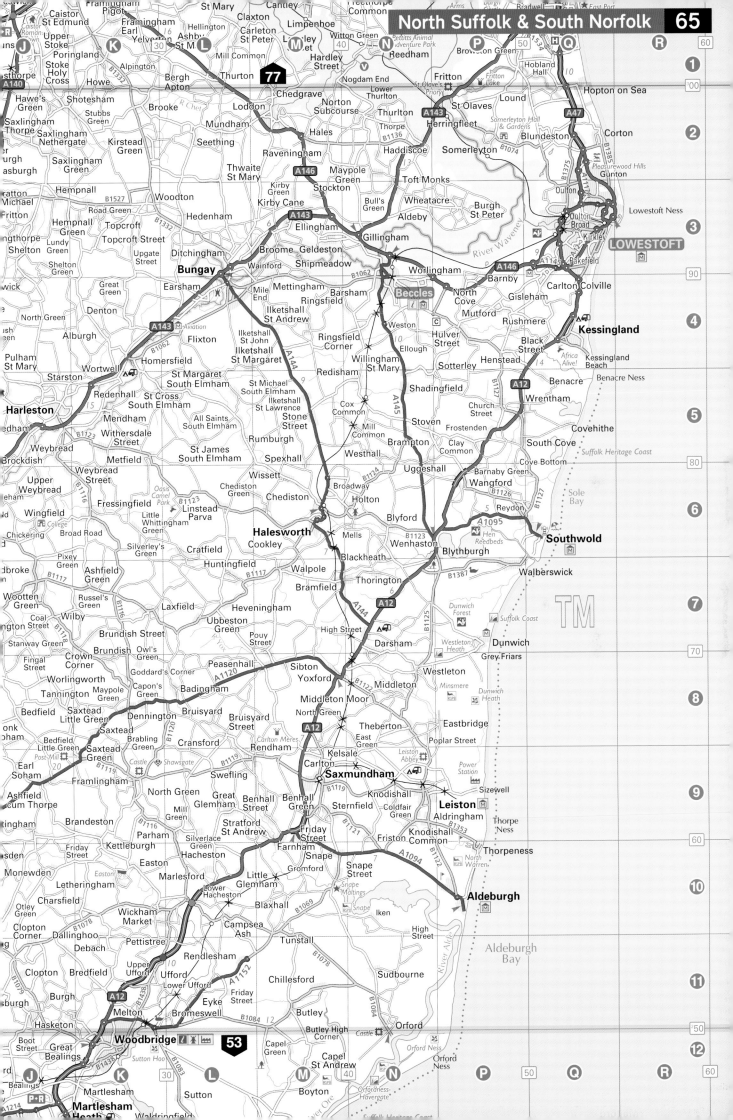

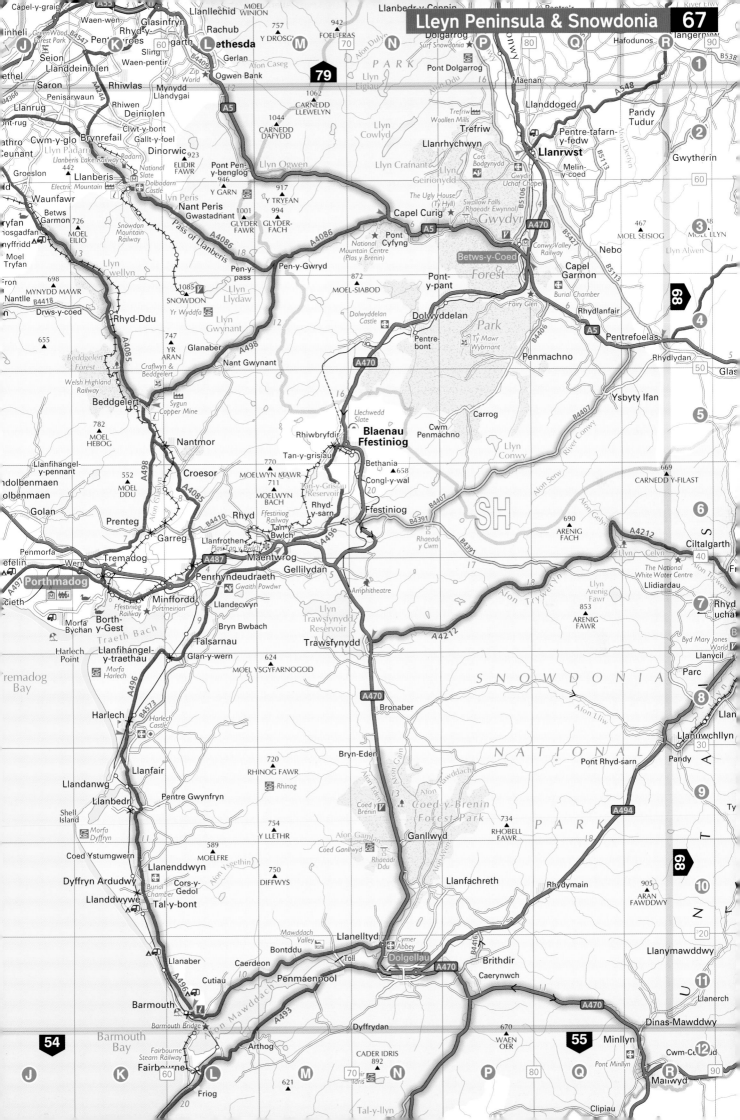

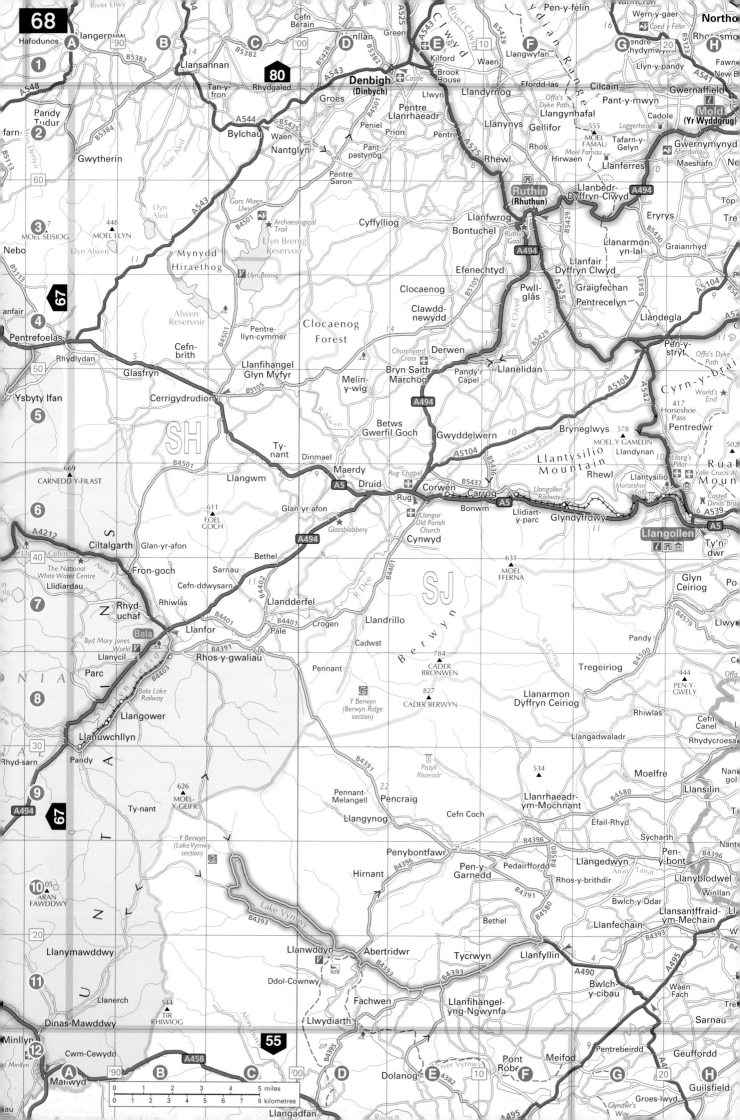

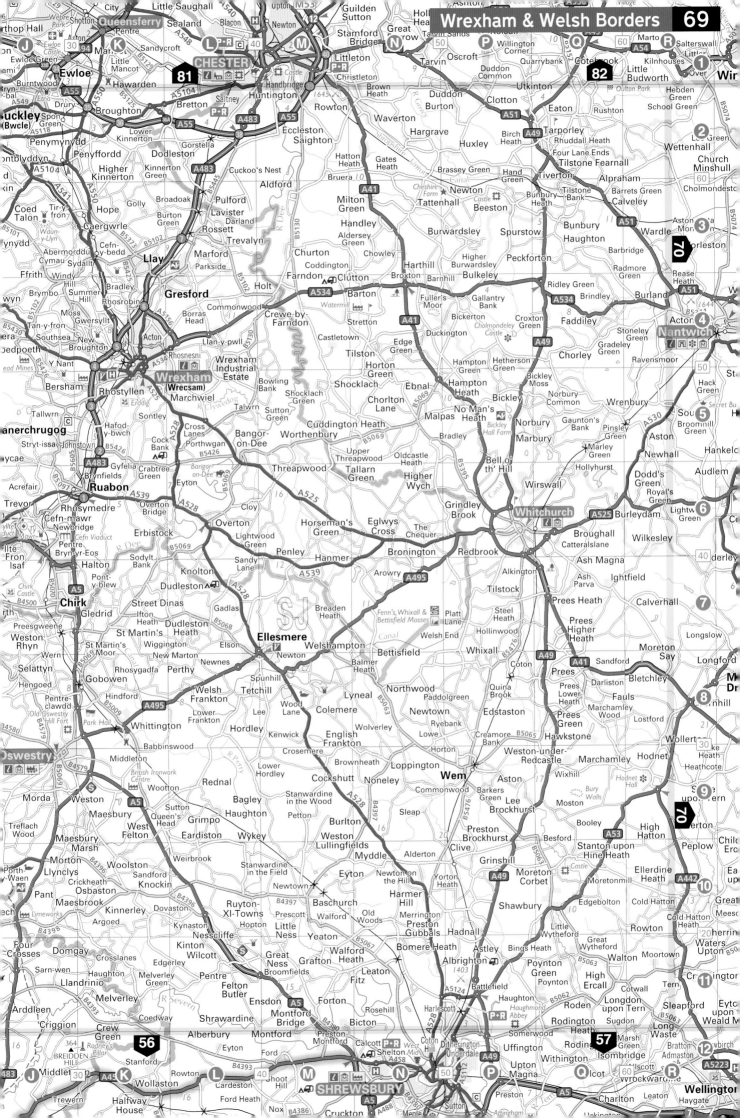

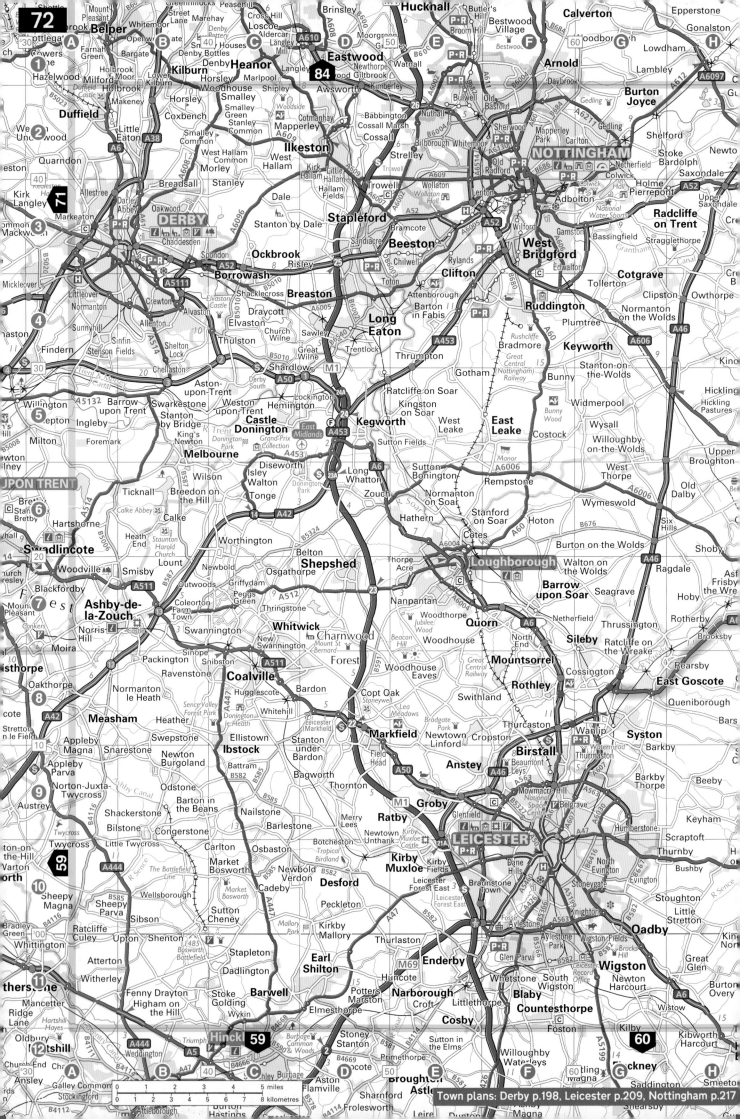

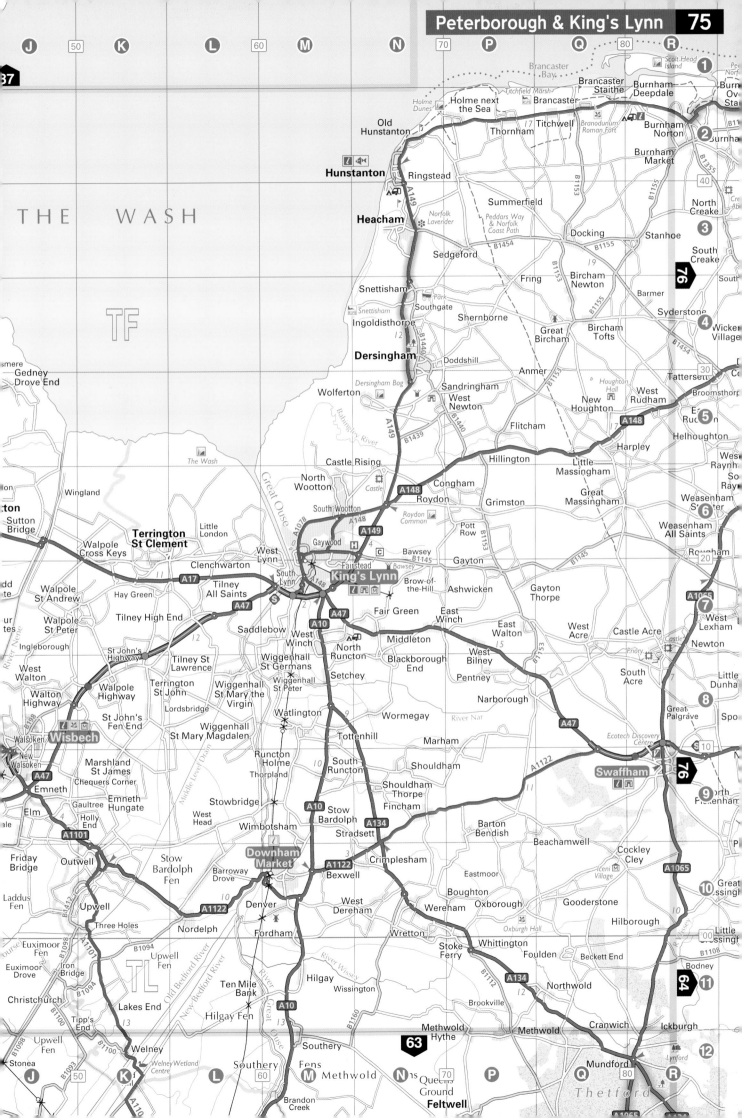

THE WASH

TF

Gedney
Drove End

Sutton
Bridge

Walpole
Cross Keys

Terrington
St Clement

Little
London

Wingland

Clenchwarton

West
Lynn

Tilney
All Saints

South
Lynn

King's Lynn

Hay Green

Walpole
St Andrew

Walpole
St Peter

Ingleborough

Tilney High End

St John's
Highway

Saddlebow

West
Winch

North Runcton

Fair Green

West Walton

Walton
Highway

Walpole
Highway

St John's
Fen End

Tilney St
Lawrence

Terrington
St John

Lordsbridge

Wiggenhall
St Mary the
Virgin

Wiggenhall
St Peter

Wiggenhall
St Germans

Watlington

Setchey

Blackborough
End

Middleton

West
Bilney

East
Winch

East
Walton

West
Acre

Narborough

Wisbech

Marshland
St James

Chequers Corner

Emneth

Emneth
Hungate

Gaultree

Holly
End

Walsoken

New
Walsoken

Elm

Friday
Bridge

Outwell

Stow
Bardolph
Fen

Barroway
Drove

Wiggenhall
St Mary Magdalen

Runcton
Holme
Thorpland

Stowbridge

West
Head

Wimbotsham

Downham
Market

South
Runcton

Tottenhill

Wormegay

Marham

Shouldham

Shouldham
Thorpe

Fincham

Barton
Bendish

Beachamwell

Laddus
Fen

Upwell

Three Holes

Nordelph

Denver

Fordham

Bexwell

Stradsett

Stow
Bardolph

Crimplesham

West
Dereham

Wereham

Boughton

Oxborough

Gooderstone

Hilborough

Cockley
Cley

Ceni
Village

Oxburgh Hall

Eastmoor

Euximoor
Fen

Iron
Bridge

Upwell
Fen

TL

Lakes End

Tipp's
End

Christchurch

Stonea

Welney

Welney Wetland
Centre

Ten Mile
Bank

Hilgay Fen

Hilgay

Wissington

Brookville

Methwold
Hythe

Methwold

Stoke
Ferry

Whittington

Foulden

Northwold

Cranwich

Beckett End

Bodney

Ickburgh

Mundford

Lynford

Thetford

Southery

Southery
Fens

Methwold

Feltwell

Queen's
Ground

Brandon
Creek

Old Hunstanton

Hunstanton

Heacham

Ringstead

Snettisham

Southgate

Ingoldisthorpe

Dersingham

Wolferton

Sandringham

West
Newton

Doddshill

Flitcham

Castle Rising

North
Wootton

South Wootton

Gaywood

West Lynn

Fairstead

Brow-of-
the-Hill

Ashwicken

Gayton
Thorpe

Gayton

Bawsey

Pott
Row

Grimston

Congham

Roydon

Roydon
Common

Hillington

Little
Massingham

Great
Massingham

Harpley

Helhoughton

West
Rudham

New
Houghton

Houghton
Hall

Anmer

Great
Bircham

Bircham
Newton

Bircham
Tofts

Fring

Shernborne

Summerfield

Sedgeford

Docking

Stanhoe

Syderstone

Tattersett

Broomsthorpe

Barmer

Holme next
the Sea

Holme
Dunes

Thornham

Titchwell

Brancaster

Brancaster
Staithe

Burnham
Deepdale

Burnham
Norton

Burnham
Market

Branodunum
Roman Fort

Brancaster
Bay

Titchfield Marsh

Norfolk
Lavender

Peddars Way
& Norfolk
Coast Path

North
Creake

South
Creake

Wicken
Village

Weasenham
St

Weasenham
All Saints

Rougham

Castle Acre

South
Acre

Great
Palgrave

West
Lexham

Newton

Little
Dunham

Great
Dunham

Swaffham

Ecotech Discovery
Centre

River Nar

Pentney

West
Walton

Scolt Head
Island

Great Ouse

Babingley River

Dersingham Bog

Snettisham

Wingland

River Nene

B1098

B1101

B1100

B1094

B1093

B1160

B1112

B1108

A17

A47

A148

A149

A47

A10

A134

A1122

A1101

A1065

A1078

A1140

A1439

B1145

B1153

B1155

B1454

B1439

The Wash

Middle Level Drain

Old Bedford River

New Bedford River

River Great Ouse

River Wissey

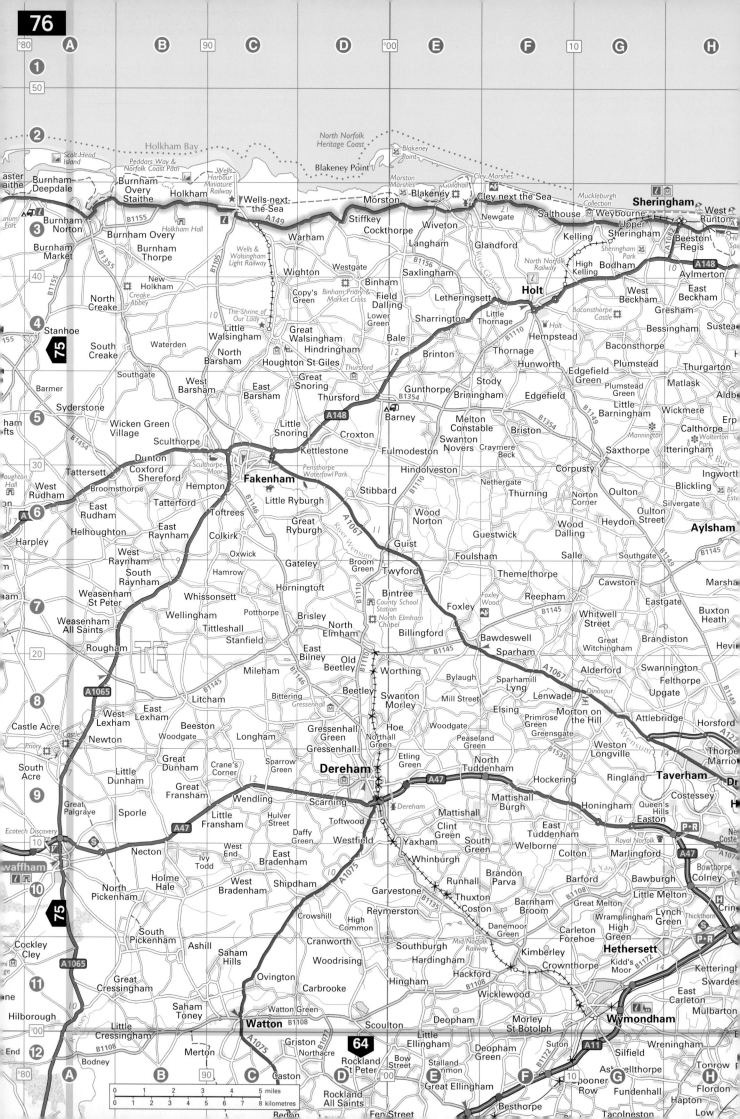

J K 30 L M 40 N P 50 Q R 60

1 50
2
3
40
4
5
30
6
7
20
8
9
10
10
11
00
12

Cromer
Overstrand
Sidestrand
Northrepps
A149
B1436
Crossdale Street
Trimingham
Southrepps
Gimingham
Mundesley
Stow Mill
Lower Street
Knapton
Paston
B1159
B140
Thorpe Market
Trunch
Bacton
Walcott
A149
Bradfield
Old Hall Street
Edingthorpe
Antingham
B1436
B1145
Suffield
Swafield
Pollard Street
Happisburgh
North Walsham
Edingthorpe Green
Witton
Ridlington
Banningham
B1145
Spa Common
Ridlington Street
Whimpwell Green
Felmingham
Tungate
Meeting House Hill
Crostwight
Happisburgh Common
Eccles on Sea
Hempstead
Skeyton Corner
Honing
Lessingham
Ingham Corner
Sea Palling
Tuttington
Westwick
A149
Briggate
East Ruston
Ingham
Waxham
burgh next Aylsham
Skeyton
Bengates
Worstead
Stalham
Calthorpe Street
Bure Valley Railway
Swanton Abbott
B1150
Frankfort
Dilham
Low Street
Stalham Green
Hickling
Horsey Corner
Oxnead Lamas
Scottow
Smallburgh
Sutton Fen
Sutton
Hickling Green
Horsey
Buxton
Badersfield
Fairstead
Barton Turf
Wood Street
Hickling Heath
Hill Common
Hickling Broad
Horsey Windpump
Stratton Strawless
Little Hautbois
Sco Ruston
Tunstead
Pennygate
Neatishead
Barton Broad
Catfield
Catfield Common
Martham Broad
East Somerton
St James
Crowgate Street
Irstead
Wroxham Barns
Sharp Green
Potter Heigham
West Somerton
Winterton-on-Sea
Horstead
Coltishall
B1354
Threehammer Common
Ludham
Martham
Belaugh
Hoveton
RAF Air Defence Radar
Johnson Street
Bastwick
Cess
Hemsby Hole
Frettenham
BeWILDerwood
A1062
Repps
Ormesby Broad
Newport
Wroxham
Upper Street
Horning
Thurne
Rollesby
Ormesby St Michael
Scratby
Newton St Faith
A1151
Woodbastwick
Broads Wildlife Centre
Thurne
B1152
Fleggburgh Burgh St Margaret
California
Horsham St Faith
Crostwick
Ranworth Broad
Pilson Green
Clippesby
Billockby
Ormesby St Margaret
Caister-on-Sea
Spixworth
A1270
Rackheath
Salhouse
Ranworth
Fairhaven
Cargate Green
Thrigby
Filby
New Rackheath
Little Plumstead
Panxworth
South Walsham
Upton
Stokesby
Thrigby Hall
Mautby
West End
Caister
West Caister
Sprowston
Thorpe End
B1140
Town Green
Burlingham Green
Acle
Runham
NORWICH
Great Plumstead
Blofield Heath
Hemblington
North Burlingham
Stracey Arms Windpump
A47
Thorpe St Andrew
Witton
A47
Damgate
Runham
Brundall
Blofield
Lingwood
Beighton
Tunstall
THE BROADS
Great Yarmouth
A1242
Postwick
Strumpshaw
South Burlingham
Moulton St Mary
Halvergate
Southtown
Norfolk Ski Centre
Buckenham
B1140
Freethorpe
Berney Marshes
Burgh Castle
Gorleston on Sea
Trowse Newton
Kirby Bedon
Surlingham
Hassingham
Southwood
Freethorpe Common
Wickhampton
Burgh Castle
Bradwell
Armingham
Bramerton
Rockland St Mary
Cantley
Wickhampton
Berney Arms Windmill
Belton
Caistor St Edmund
Framingham Pigot
Claxton
Carleton St Peter
Langley Street
Browston Green
Caistor Roman Town
Upper Stoke
Framingham Earl Yelverton
Ashby St Mary
Limpenhoe
Witton Green
Pettitts Animal Adventure Park
Reedham
Hobland Hall
Poringland
Stoke Holy Cross
Howe
B1332
Alpington
Mill Common
Hardley Street
Fritton
Fritton Lake
Hopton on Sea
A140
Hawe's Green
Shotesham
Bergh Apton
Thurton
Nogdam End
Lower Thurlton
St Olave's Priory
Lound
A47
Saxlingham
Stubbs Green
Brooke
R Chet
Loddon
Chedgrave
Norton Subcourse
65
Thurlton
St Olaves
Somerleyton Hall & Gardens
Corton
Saxlingham Nethergate
Kirstead Green
Seething
Mundham
Hales
A143
Herringfleet
Brundston
A47
Saxlingham Th
Raveningham
Haddiscoe
Maypole
A146
Thwaite
Pleasurewood Hills

J K 30 L M 40 N P 50 Q R 60

Holyhead Harbour

Marina
Maritime
BEACH ROAD
Porth-y-Felin
PRINCE OF WALES ROAD
PARK STREET
NEWRY STREET
WALTHEW AVENUE
PORTLAND STREET
VICTORIA ROAD
A5154
SOUTH STACK ROAD
PLAS ROAD
Stryd
Kingsland
KINGSLAND ROAD
A51
PORTHDAFARCH
B545
Salt Island
P+R Long Stay
Hertz Car Rental
FERRY TERMINAL
TERMINAL BUILDING
Short stay
HOLYHEAD
HOLYHEAD STATION
Môrawelon
A5
LLANFAWR ROAD
CYTTIR ROAD
A5153
A5
BANGOR
0   500 m
TLT

Holyhead Bay

The Skerries
Hen Borth
CARMEL HEAD
Llanfairynghornwy
Church Bay
Llanrhyddlad
Llanfaethlu
Dublin
Dublin
Porth Tywynmawr
North Stack
Gogarth Bay
Breakwater
South Stack
Ellin's Tower
Holyhead Mountain Heritage Coast
Penrhyn Mawr
Llaingoch
Holyhead Mountain Hut Circles
Holyhead (Caergybi)
Penrhos Feilw
Kingsland
Penrhos
Trefignath
A5
B4545
Trearddur Bay
HOLY ISLAND
Four Mile Bridge
Llanfair-yn-Neubwll
Rhoscolyn
Rhoscolyn Head
Cymyran Bay
Plas Cymyran
SH
Llanfwrog
Llanddeusant
Stryd-y-Facsen
Llanfachraeth
Llanynghenedl
Llanfihangel yn Nhowyn
Valley
A5025
Bodedern
Valley
Llechylched
Capel Gwyn
Rhosneigr
Ty Newydd
A4080
Ty Croes
Bryn Du
Llanfaelog
Pencarnisiog
Aberffraw Circuit
Bethel
Aberffraw
Aberffraw Bay
Barclodiad y Gawres
Porth Trecastell
Aberffraw Bay Heritage Coast
Malltraeth Bay
Llanddwyn Island
Llanddwyn Bay

North Anglesey Heritage Coast
Wylfa Head
Cemaes Bay
Cemaes
Tregele
Llanbadrig
Porth Wen
Bull Bay
Bull Bay
Amlwch
Llaneilian
Pengorffw
Poin
Burwen
Pentrefelin
Nebo
Rhosbeirio
Bodewryd
Penysarn
A5025
Llanfechell
Llanfflewyn
Rhosgoch
Carreglefn
Rhosybol
Gadfa
City Dulas
Llanbabo
Llyn Alaw
Capel Parc
Brynrefail
Rh
Din Llig
Elim
Gwredog
Llandyfrydog
Llantrisant
Pen-llyn
Llanfigael
Llanerchymedd
Hebron
Bachau
Maenaddwyn
Presaddfed
Llyn Llywenan
B5112
Llechcynfarwy
Capel Coch
Brynteg
Cors Erddreiniog
A N G L E S E Y
B5109
Trefor
Bodffordd
Llangwyllog
B5111
Tregaian
Llan
Rhosmeirc
Caergeiliog
Bryngwran
A55
Llynfaes
Gwalchmai
Cefni Reservoir
Oriel Ynys Môn
B5110
A5
Heneglwys
Anglesey
Rhostrehwfa
Llangefni
A5114
Ceint
Dothan
Cerrigceinwen
Capel Gwyn
A4080
Din-Dryfol
Henblas
B4422
Capel Mawr
Trefdraeth
Bodorgan
Llangadwaladr
Hermon
Bodorgan
Llangaffo
A4080
A5
A55
Llangristiolus
Pentre Berw
Gaerwen
Malltraeth
Llanddaniel F
Bodowyr Burial Chamber
Brynsiencyn
Castell Bryn Gwyn
Caer Lêb
Dwyran
B4419
Newborough
Pen-lôn
Anglesey Sea Zoo
Foel Farm Park
Caernarfon
Caernarfon Castle
Newborough W
Abermenai Point
Welsh Highland Railway

0 1 2 3 4 5 miles
0 1 2 3 4 5 6 7 8 kilometres

Llandudno

0   200 m

Great Orme Tramway
Tabor Hill
Old Road
Great Orme
Victoria Station
Ty-Coch Road
Plas Coch Road
Hill Terrace
Llandudno Pier
The Grand Hotel
War Memorial
North Shore Beach
Llandudno Bay

The Old Bank Gallery
Church Walks
Rectory Lane
Abbey Road
Llewelyn Avenue
New Street
Travelodge
GLODDAETH STREET
SOUTH PARADE
Mostyn Street
George Street
A546
St John's
The Promenade
Clifton Road
St Andrew's Avenue
Madoc Street
Town Hall
Caroline Road
Victoria
Holy Trinity
Our Lady Star of the Sea
Conwy Archive Service
Brookes Street
Trinity Square
Mostyn Gallery
THE PARADE
Medical Centre
Adelphi Street
Coach
Swimming Pool
MOSTYN BROADWAY
Venue Cymru
St Paul's
Mostyn Avenue
B5115
DEGANWY
A546
Maelgwyn Road
Lloyd Street
St David's Road
St Seiriol's Road
Claremont Road
Vaughan Street
CONWAY ROAD
CYLCH-TUDUR
Clarence Crescent
Clarence Drive
Cae Clyd
Maes Clyd
LLANDUDNO STATION
Police Station
Jubilee Street
Magistrates' Court
Parc Llandudno Retail Park
Mostyn Champneys Retail Park
Ysgol Craig Y Don
Ysgol Tudno
AVENUE
TRINITY
Norman Road
Builder Street West
Council Street West
Howard Road
Fire & Ambulance Station
Ffordd Penrhyn
Ffordd Tudno
Charlotte Street
Tudor Road
B5115
Kingsway
Ysgol Ffordd Dyffryn
Dinas Road
King's Avenue
Dennis Road
Mowbray Road
King's Drive
Coach
Ffordd Dulyn
Ffordd Dwyfor
Ffordd Dewi
Cwm Place
Wern Wylan
Ysgol Morfa Rhianedd
Ysgol John Bright
CONWAY ROAD
A470
TLT
Llandudno FC
Builder Street
A55, BETWS-Y-COED

SH

Seawatch Centre
Moelfre
anallgo
Marian-glas
Benllech
Red Wharf Bay
Goch
Red Wharf Bay
Pentraeth
Llanddona
Llangoed
Hafoty Medieval House
Llanfaes Gaol
B5109
Beaumaris Castle
Beaumaris
Courthouse
Llansadwrn
Llandegfan
Menai Bridge (Porthaethwy)
Bangor
Penrhos garnedd
Penrhyn Castle
Spinnies Abergowen
Glan-yr-afon
Caim
Puffin Island
Toll
Penmon
Penmon Priory
Black Point
Conwy Bay
Great Orme Heritage Coast
GREAT ORME'S HEAD
Great Orme Tramway
Toll
Llandudno
Deganwy
Llanrhos
Penrhynside
Penrhyn Bay
Little Ormes Head
Rhôs-on-Sea
Llandrillo-yn-Rhos
Colwyn B (Bae Colwyn)
Pydew
Esgyryn
Mochdre
Old Colwyn
A55
Llysfaen
Llanelian-yn-Rhos
Bryn-y-Maen
Dolwen
Betw
Dwygyfylchi
Conwy
Conwy Castle
Capelulo
Penmaenan
Penmaenmawr
Llanfairfechan
Gorddinog
Nant-y-pandy
Abergwyngregyn
Henryd
Llandudno Junction
Llansanffraid Glan Conwy
Bodnant
A470
B5106
B5381
Dawn
SNOWDONIA
TAL-Y-FAN 610
Rowen
Ty'n-y-Groes
Caerhun
Tal-y-Cafn
Graig Eglwysbach
Trofarth
NATIONAL
MOEL WNION 580
Aber Falls
Coedydd Aber
Afon Anafon
Castell
Llanbedr-y-Cennin
Tal-y-Bont
Dolgarrog
Surf Snowdonia
Pentre'r Felin
Vale of Conwy
Hafodunos
Llanc
Tregarth
Rhyd-y-groes
Glasinfryn
Llandygai
Tal-y-bont
Rhiwlas
Rachub
Gerlan
Llanllechid
Y DROSGL 757
942 FOEL-FRAS
Afon Dulyn
Afon Ddu
Pont Dolgarrog
Maenan
River Elwy
Bethesda
Ogwen Bank
Zip World
1062 CARNEDD LLEWELYN
1044 CARNEDD DAFYDD
Llyn Eigiau
Trefriw Woollen Mills
Llanddoged
Pandy Tudur
Menai Bridge
Britannia Bridge
Plas
Capel-y-graig
Waen-wen
Pentir
Mynydd Llandygai
ELIDIR FAWR 923
MOEL WINION
Llyn Ogwen
Llyn Cowlyd
Llanrhychwyn
Tre
Cors Bodgynyd
Penmach-tafarn-y-fedw
Llanrwst
Gwytherin
GreenWood Forest Park
Seion
Llanddeiniolen
Saron
Penisarwaun
Rhiwen
Deiniolen
Llanrug
Cwm-y-glo
Brynrefail
Clwt-y-bont
Gallt-y-foel
Dinorwic
Llanberis Lake Railway
Llyn Padarn
Pont Pen
National
A5
A55
A487
A470
A548
A544
A545

67
80

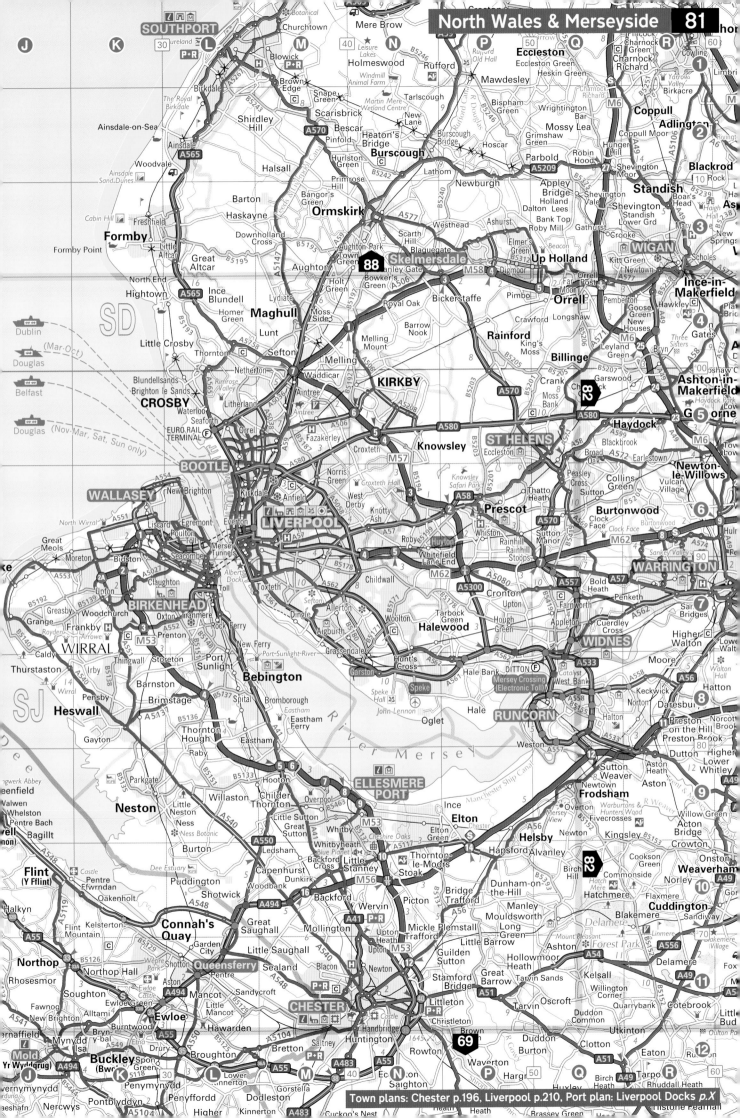

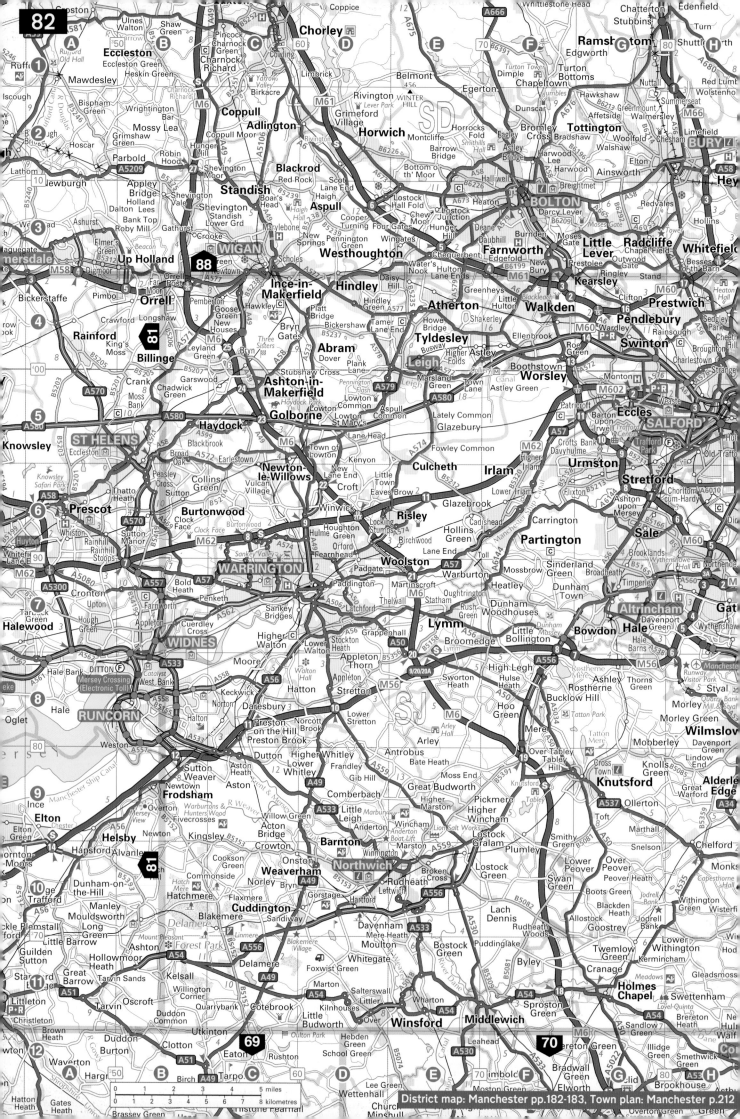

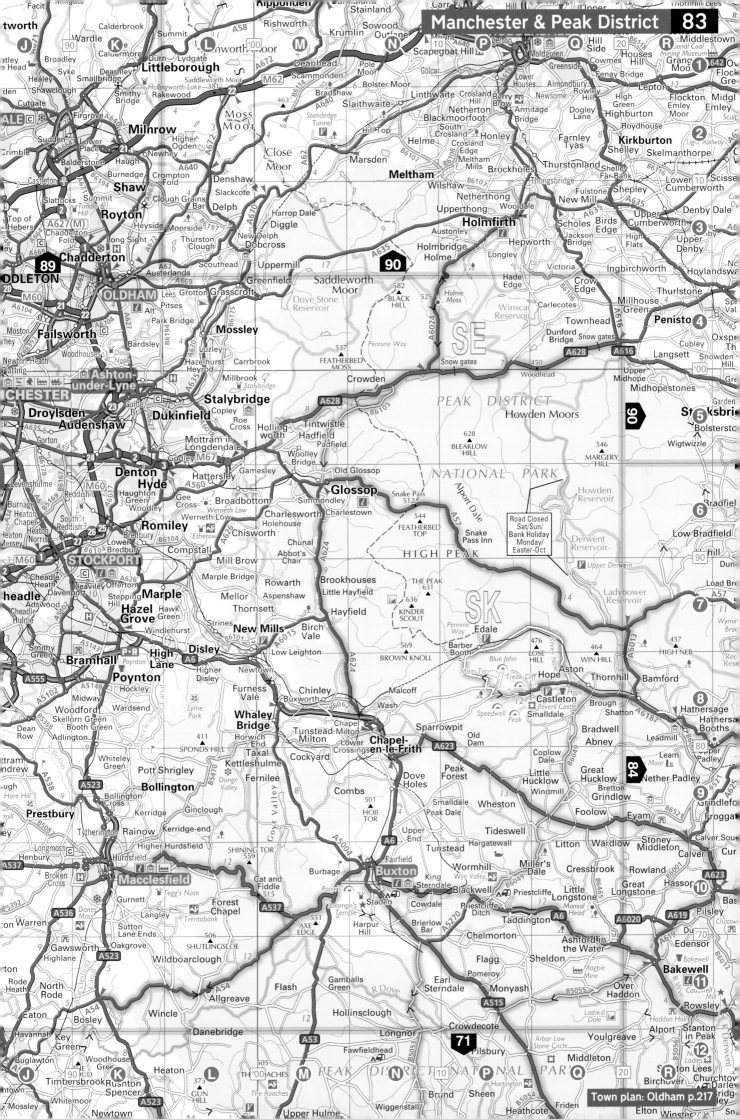

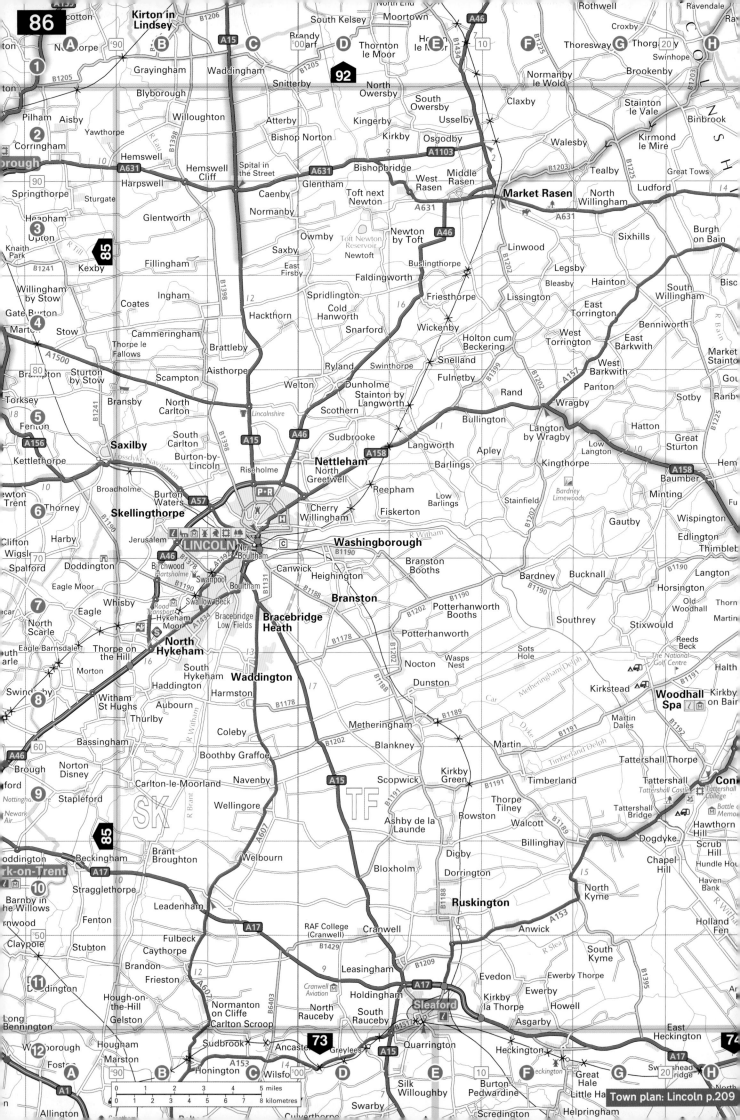

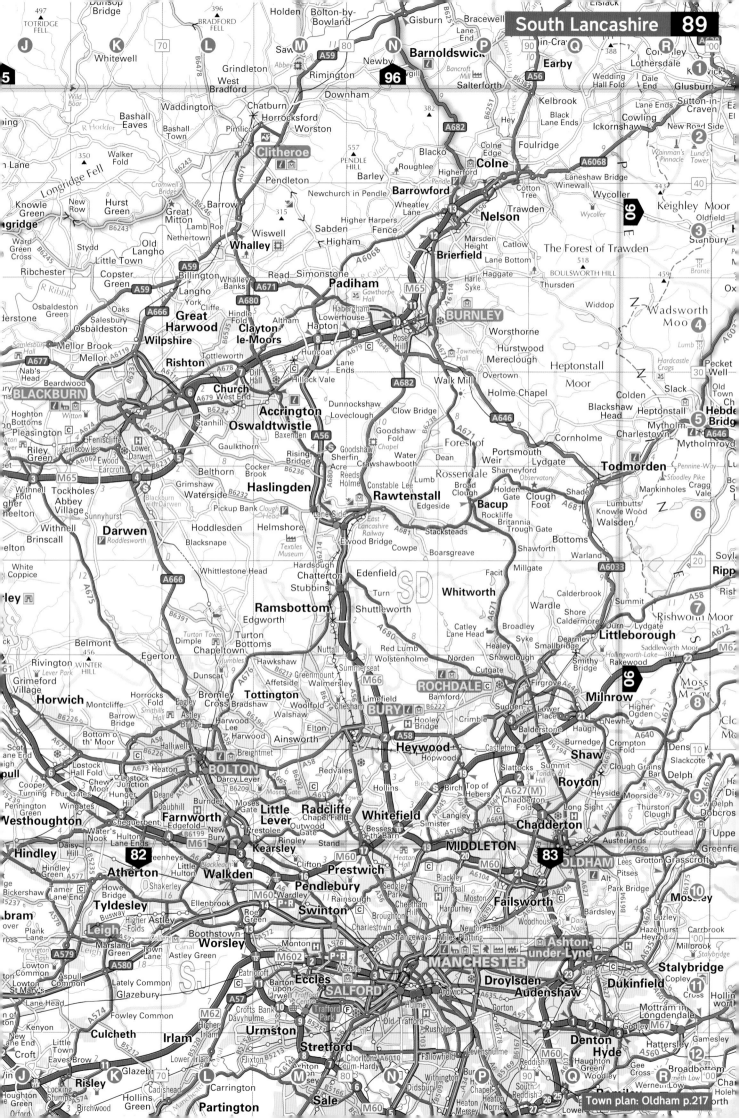

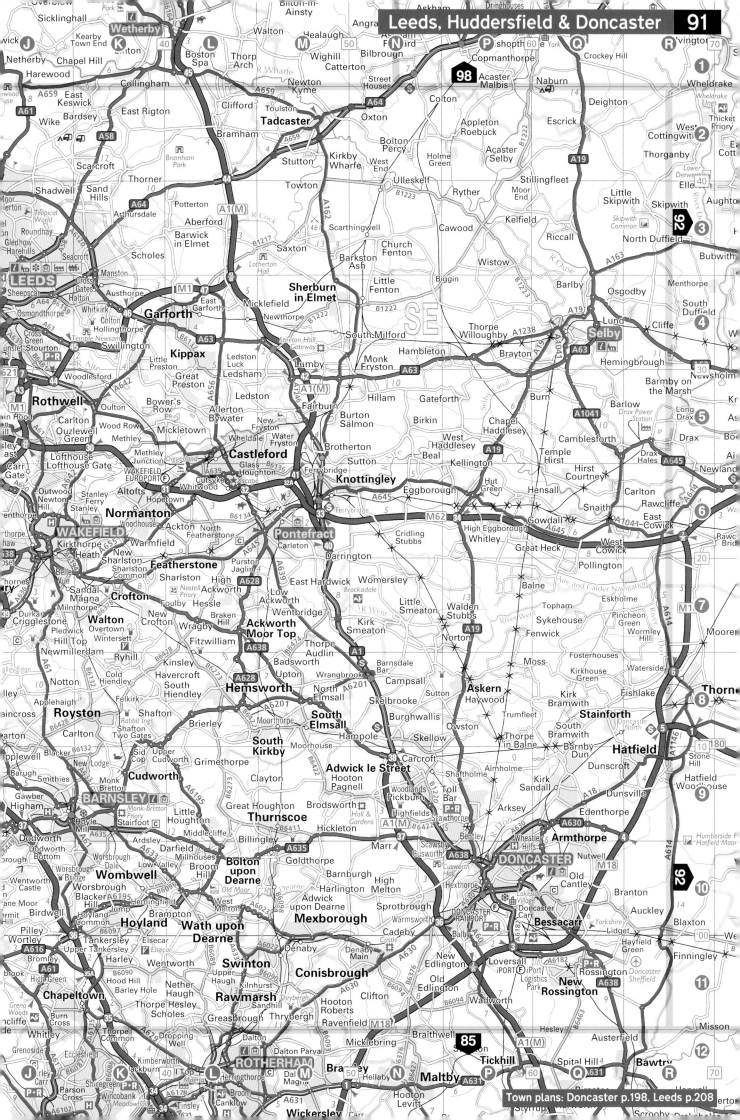

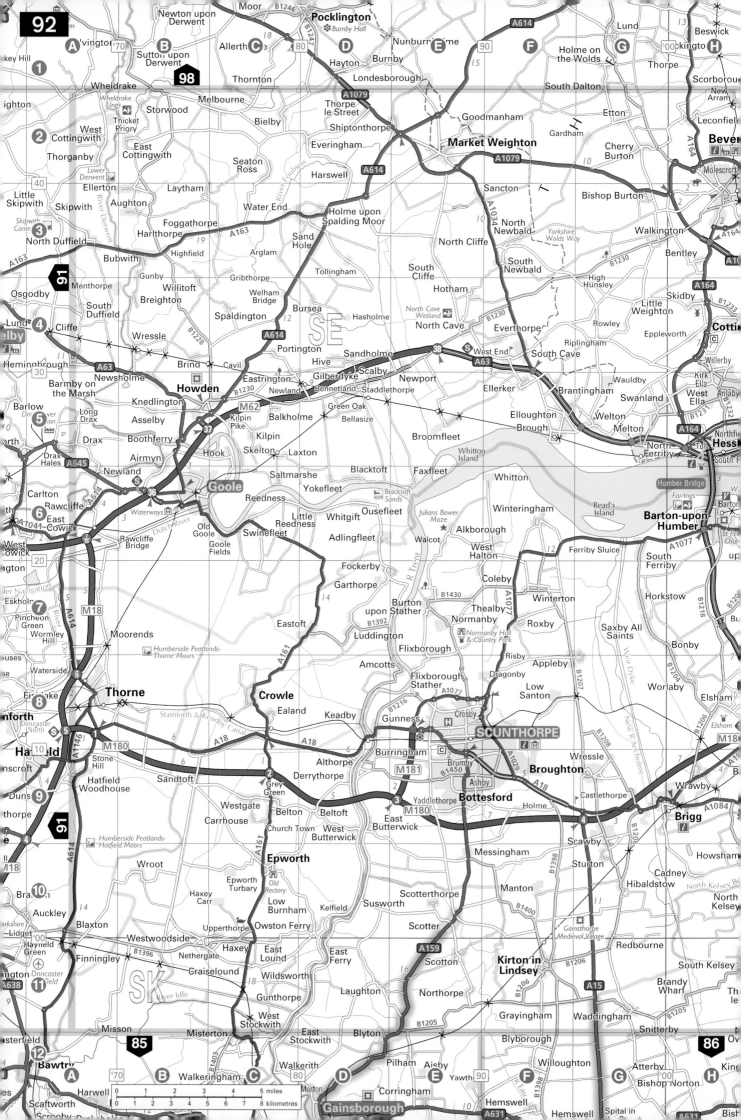

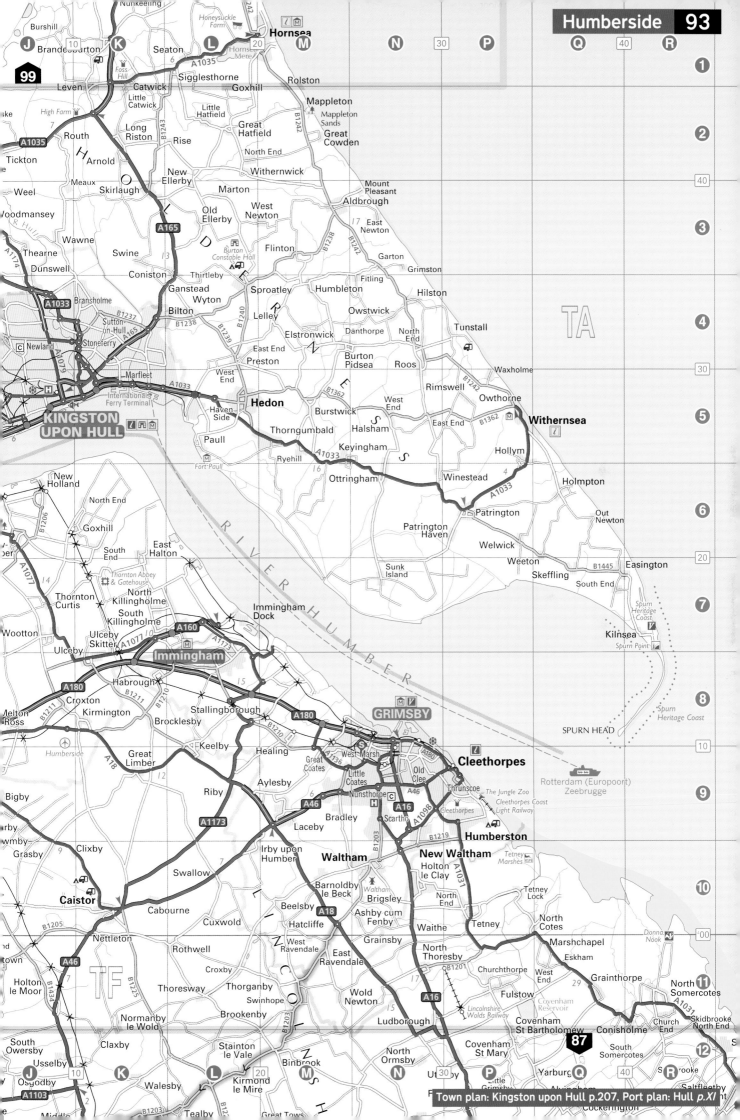

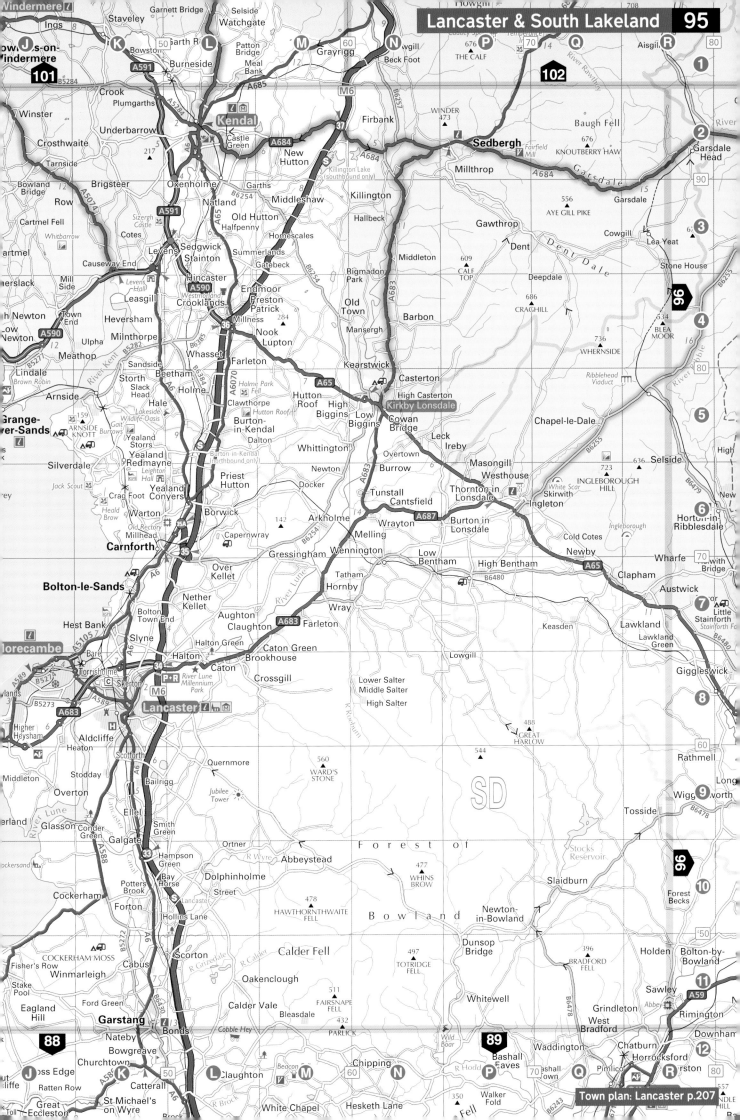

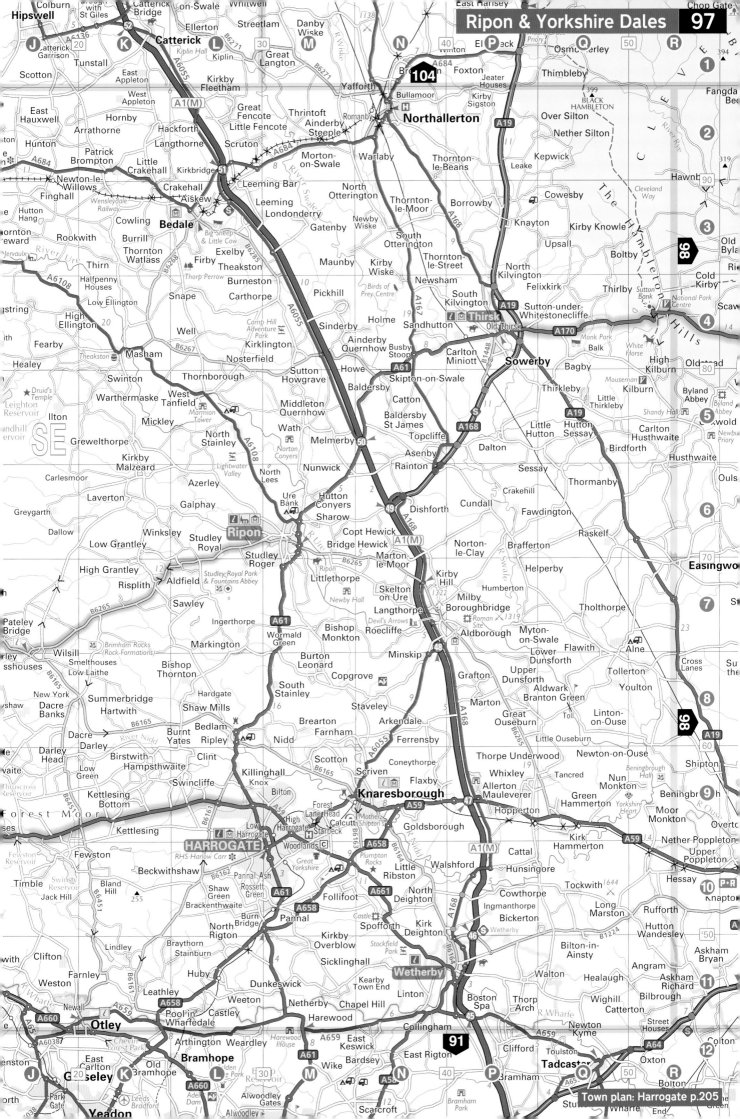

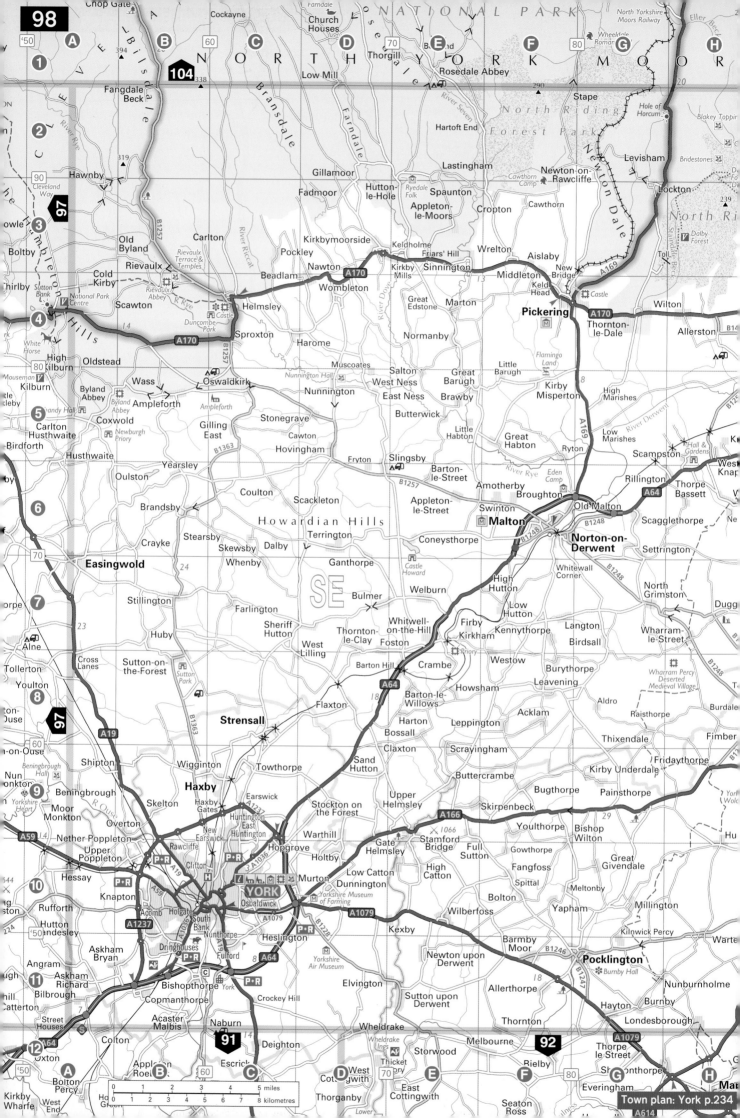

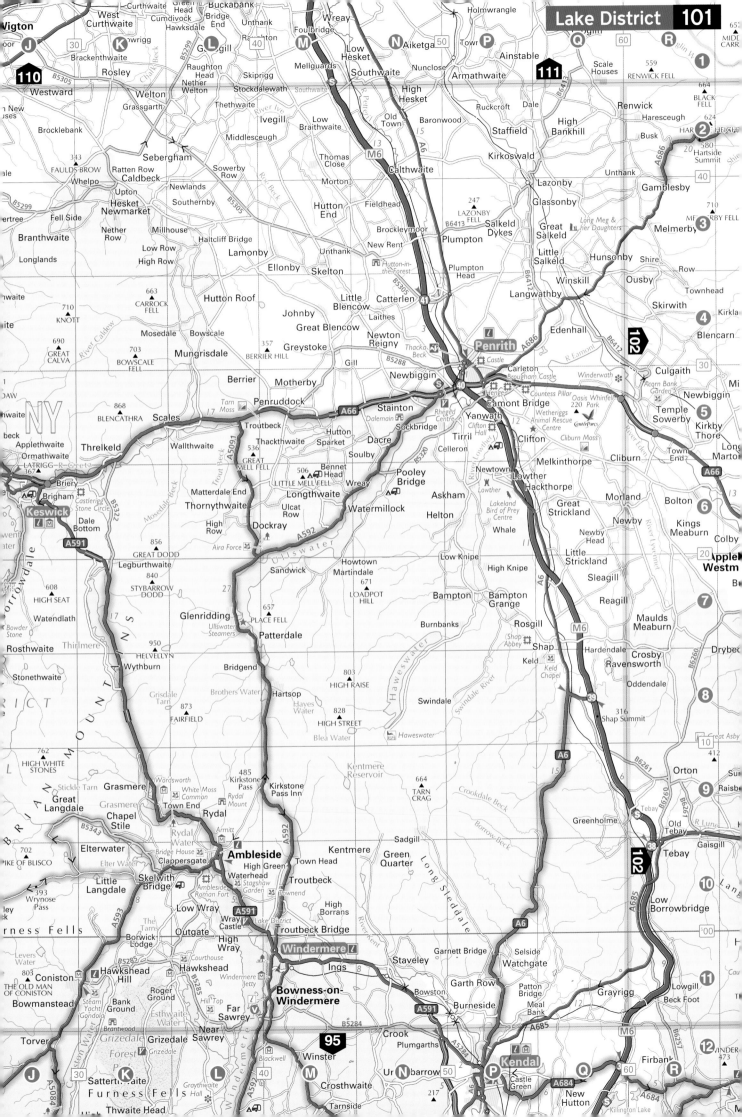

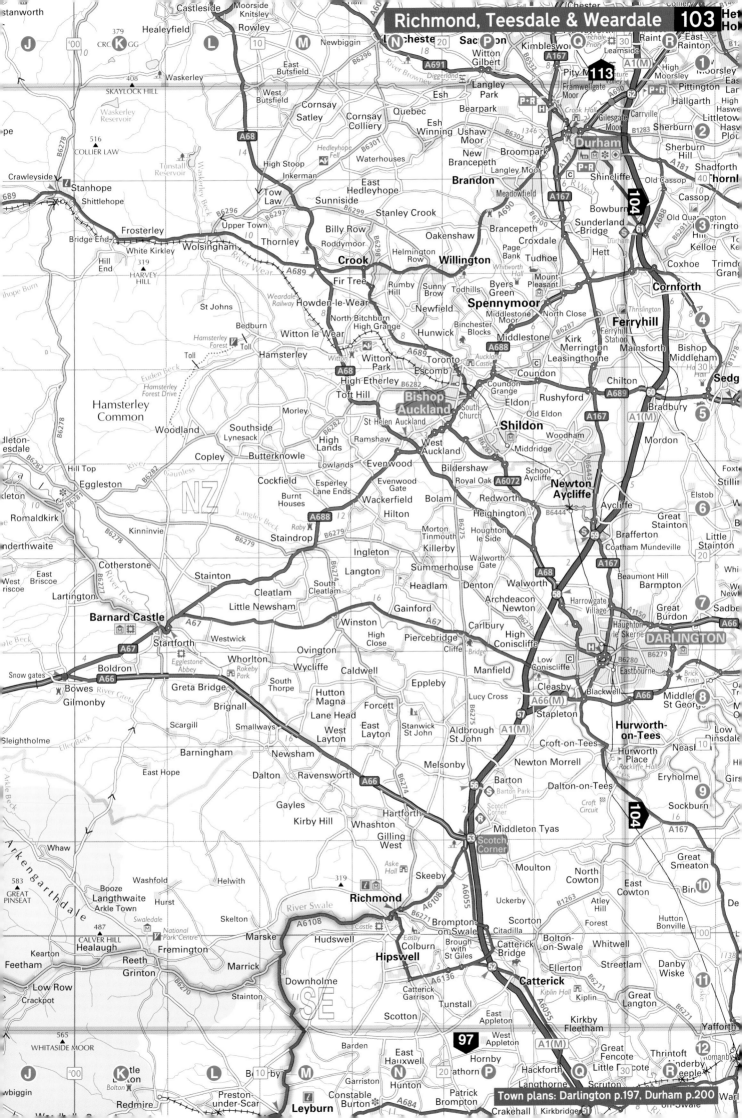

J 70 K L 80 M N 90 P Q R'00

NZ

Saltburn-by-the-Sea
Saltburn Smugglers
Brotton
Skelton
New Skelton
North Skelton
Lingdale
Kilton Thorpe
Kilton
Liverton
Stanghow
Woodhill
A171
Moorsholm
Gerrick
B1366
Scaling
Scaling Dam
22

New Brotton
Carlin How
Skinningrove
Hummersea Scar
Upton
Boulby
Ironstone Mining
Dalehouse
Easington
Staithes
Captain Cook & Staithes
Port Mulgrave
Hinderwell
Newton Mulgrave
Roxby
Handale
Borrowby
B1266
Mickleby
West Barnby
East Barnby
Ugthorpe

Runswick Bay
North Yorkshire and Cleveland Heritage Coast
Runswick
Kettleness
Goldsborough
Ellerby
A174
Lythe
Sandsend
Sandsend Wyke
Overdale Wyke

Whitby
Abbey
Saltwick Bay

Raithwaite
Dunsley
Newholm
Hutton Mulgrave
Ruswarp
Stainsacre
High Hawsker
B1410
Aislaby
Briggswath
Sneaton
Ugglebarnby
Low Hawsker
B1447
Ness Point or North Cheek
A171
Sleights
Iburndale
Sneatonthorpe
Raw
Robin Hood's Bay
Danby
The Moors National Park Centre
301
Stonegate
Castleton
Ainthorpe
Lealholm Side
Lealholm
River Esk
The Green
Egton
Glaisdale
Egton Bridge
Key Green
Grosmont
Esk Dale
A169
Blue Bank
Littlebeck
B1416
Fylingthorpe
Robin Hood's Bay
Old Peak or South Cheek
Danby Bottom
Street
Beck Hole
Goathland
Ravenscar
NORTH YORK MOORS
326
PIKE HILL
369
North Yorkshire Moors Railway
292
Staintondale
Shire Horse Centre
Hayburn Wyke
NATIONAL PARK
Rosedale
Thorgill
Low Bell End
Wheeldale Roman Road
Eller Beck
Harwood Dale
Cloughton Newlands
Cloughton Wyke
Rosedale Abbey
River Seven
290
Stape
HO R Y O R K M O O R S
Mill
Stape
North Riding
Hole of Horcum
99
Cloughton
Cromer Point
rtoft End
Levisham
Blakey Topping
Bridestones
Toll
Bickley
Broxa
Silpho
Suffield
Cleveland Way
Lastingham
Crosscliff
Langdale
Hackness

A '90 B C '200 D E 10 F G 20 H

1 80 114

2 Belfast
Currarie
Port

Larne

3 Corsewall Point
Milleur
Point
Lady
Bay

Barnhills
Portencalzie

Glen App

BENERAIRD 437

CARLOCK HILL 321

ALTIMEG HILL 387

Heronsford
Water of Tig

BENBRAKE 305
HILL

Southern
Upland
Way

Glenwhilly
Laggangairn
Standing Stones

4 70
B738
Kirkcolm
A718

Ervie
Loch
Connell
Low
Barbeth
B798

Knocknain
Leswalt
B7043

Low
Salchrie

Cairnryan
17

Penwhirn
Reservoir

Braid Fell

A77

ARTFIELD 271
FELL

New
Luce

5 Balgracie
Auchnotteroch

Loch Ryan

Castle of
St John

Stranraer
H

Innermessan
A751

A77

Aird

Black Loch
Castle
Kennedy
White
Loch

Chlenry

CRAIG 164
FELL

6 60
NW
Broadsea Bay
Portslogan

Black Head
Dunskey

Portpatrick
A77

B738

Lochans
181
CAIRN
PAT
8

Castle Kennedy
A75 10

Glenwhan
Dunragit

Glenluce Abbey
Glenluce

Kildrochet House
Piltanton Burn
B7077

B7084
Whitecrook

Luce Sands
Ringdoo
Point

A747

Milton
Stairhaven

7 50
B7042

Stoneykirk
A716
14

North
Milmain
18

19
B7084

Auchenmalg
Mull of Sinniness
Auchenmalg
Bay

8 Cairngarroch
Money Head

Kirkmadrine
Stones

Sandhead

High Ardwell
Ardwell Bay

Ardwell

9 40
Drumbreddon

Logan

Port Logan Bay
Port Logan

Chapel Rossan

Balgowan

L U C E   B

10 Garrochtrie
Clanyard Bay

Laggantalluch Head
Barncorkrie

B7065
A716

Kilstay

Kirkmaiden
High
Drummore

Drummore
Cailiness Point

Maryport

11 Damnaglaur
B7041

Cardryne

Cardrain
West
Cairngaan

12 30
MULL OF GALLOWAY

A '90 B '200 C D E 10 F G 20 H

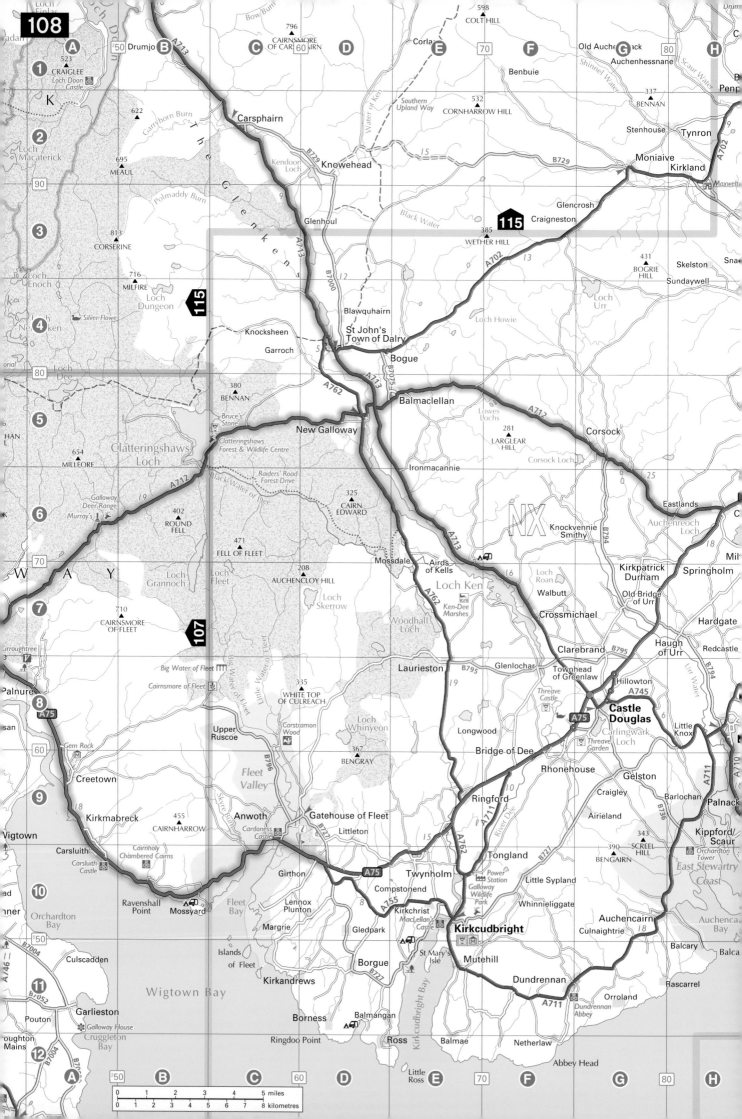

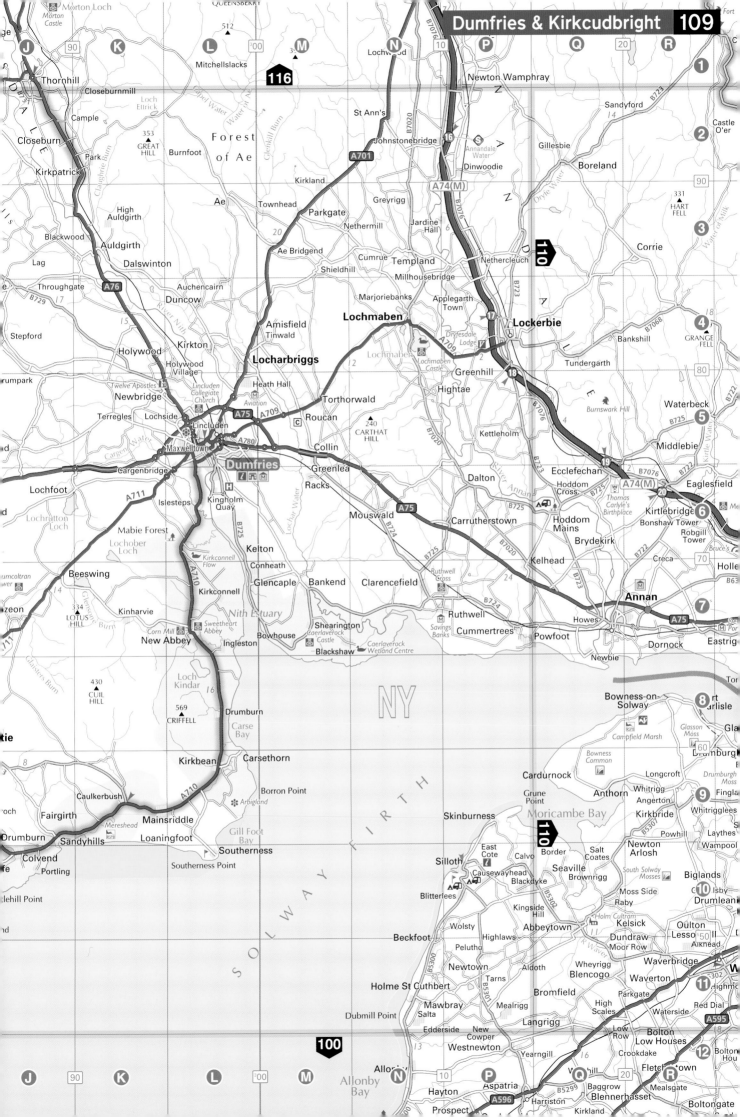

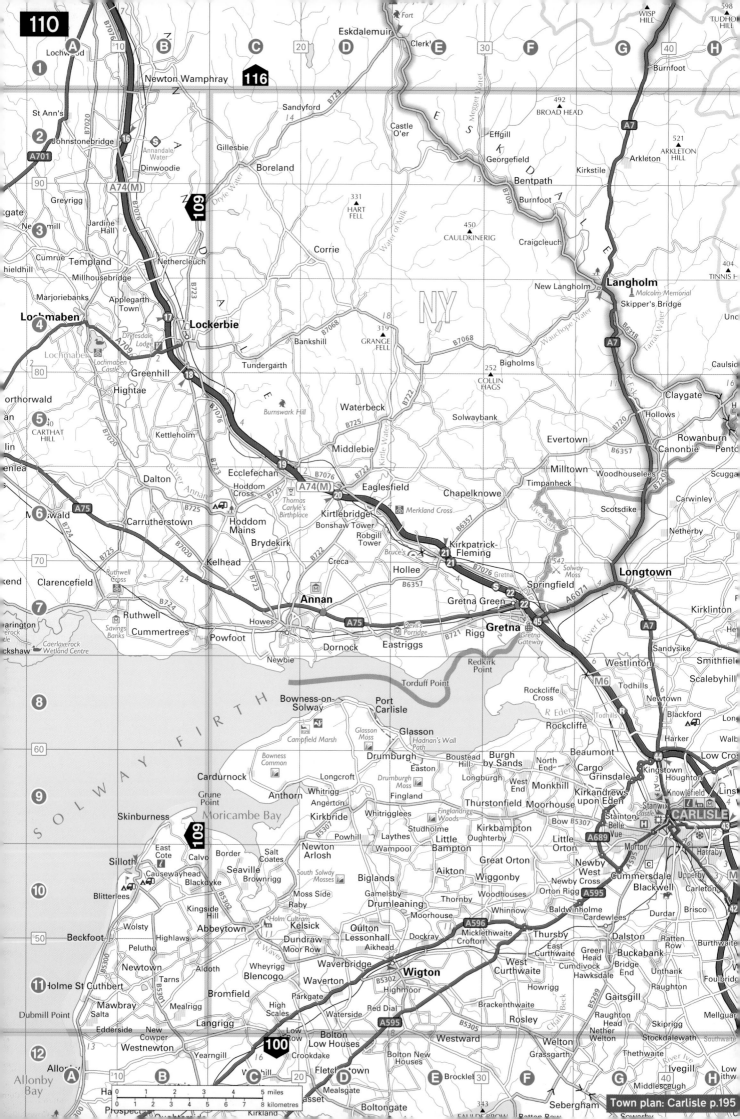

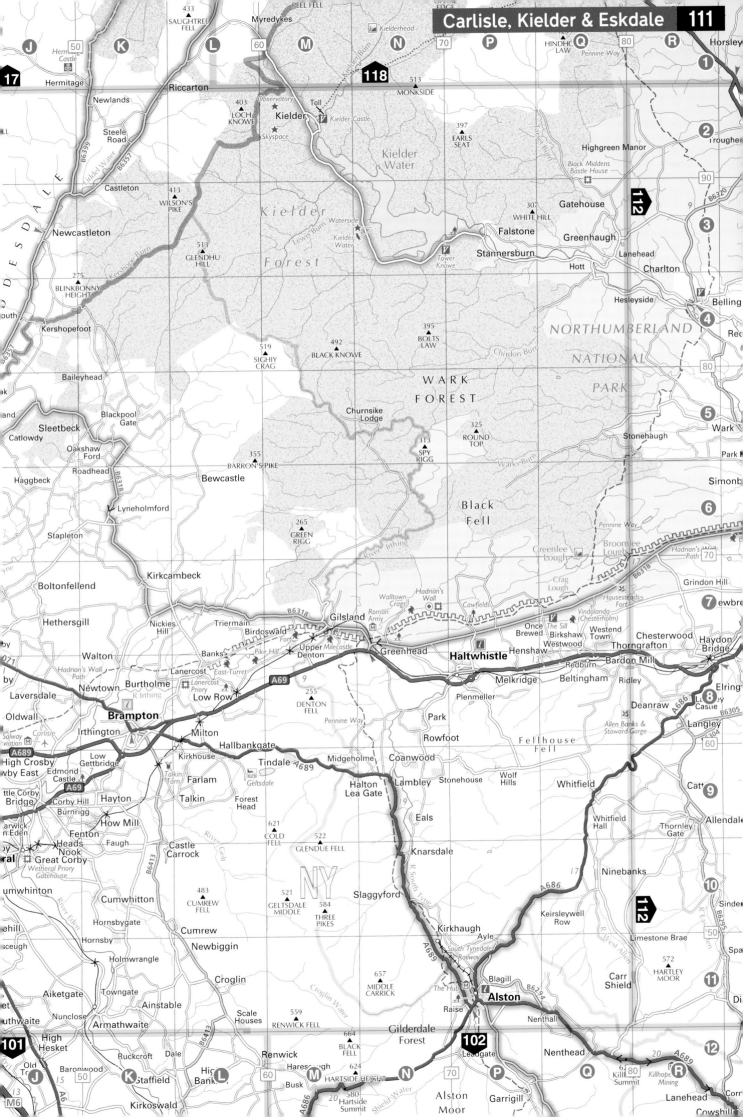

PEEL FELL
433 SAUGHTREE FELL
Myredykes
Kielderhead
EDGE
Horsley

J 50
K
L 60
M
N 70
P
Q HINDHC LAW
R Pennine Way

1

17 Hermitage
Hermits Castle
Riccarton
118
513 MONKSIDE
Troughe
90
B6320

Newlands
403 Observatory
Kielder
Toll
Kielder Castle
397 EARLS SEAT
Highgreen Manor
2

Steele Road
LOCH KNOWE
Skyspace
Black Middens Bastle House
3

B6399 B6357
Castleton
413 WILSON'S PIKE
Kielder Water
307 WHITE HILL
Gatehouse
Greenhaugh
Falstone
Laneheaed
112

Newcastleton
Waterside
Lewis Burn
Kielder Water
Stannersburn
Hott
Charlton
Hesleyside
Belling
4

513 GLENDHU HILL
Forest
Tower Knowe
80

275 BLINKBONNY HEIGHT
Kershope Burn
NORTHUMBERLAND
Red
Kershopefoot
492 BLACK KNOWE
395 BOLTS LAW
Chirdon Burn
NATIONAL
5

Baileyhead
519 SIGHTY CRAG
WARK
PARK
Stonehaugh
Wark
Park

Blackpool Gate
FOREST
Churnsike Lodge
325 ROUND TOP
Simonb
Sleetbeck
Oakshaw Ford
Catlowdy
355 BARRON'S PIKE
313 SPY RIGG
Warks Burn
6

Haggbeck
Roadhead
Bewcastle
Black Fell
Pennine Way
Greenlee Lough
Broomlee Lough
Hadrian's Path 70

Stapleton
Lyneholmford
265 GREEN RIGG
River Irthing
Crag Lough
B6318
Grindon Hill
7

Boltonfellend
Kirkcambeck
Walltown Crags
Hadrian's Wall
Cawfields
Housesteads Fort
Vindolanda (Chesterholm)
ewbre

Hethersgill
B6318
Gilsland
Roman Army
The Sill
Westend Town
Chesterwood
Thorngrafton
Haydon Bridge

Nickies Hill
Triermain
Birdoswald Fort
Milecastle
Once Brewed
Birkshaw
Westwood
Walton
Banks
Pike Hill
Upper Denton
Greenhead
Haltwhistle
Henshaw
Bardon Mill
Elring
8

Hadrian's Wall Path
Lanercost
East-Turret
Redburn
Beltingham
Ridley
Langley
B6305
B6304

Laversdale
Newtown
Burtholme
Lanercost Priory
Low Row
A69 9
Melkridge
Plenmeller
Park
Deanraw
Allen Banks & Staward Gorge
60

Oldwall
Brampton
Irthington
Milton
255 DENTON FELL
Pennine Way
Rowfoot
Fellhouse Fell
Whitfield

High Crosby
wby East
A689
Low Gettbridge
Kirkhouse
Hallbankgate
Midgeholme
Coanwood
Fell
Whitfield Hall
Catt

Edmond Castle
A69
Corby Hill
Hayton
Farlam
Tindale
A689
Lambley
Stonehouse
Wolf Hills
Thornley Gate
Allendal

ttle Corby Bridge
Burnrigg
How Mill
Talkin
Forest Head
Halton Lea Gate
Eals
9

arwick n Eden
Fenton
Heads Nook
Faugh
Castle Carrock
621 COLD FELL
522 GLENDUE FELL
Knarsdale
Ninebanks
10

Great Corby
Wetheral Priory Gatehouse
NY
584 THREE PIKES
Slaggyford
A686
17
112

mwhinton
Cumwhitton
483 CUMREW FELL
521 GELTSDALE MIDDLE
Kirkhaugh
Ayle
Keirsleywell Row
Limestone Brae
11

Hornsbygate
Hornsby
Cumrew
Newbiggin
South Tynedale Railway
Blagill
B6294
Carr Shield
572 HARTLEY MOOR

Holmwrangle
Croglin
657 MIDDLE CARRICK
The Hub
Alston
Raise
Nenthall

Aiketgate
Towngate
Ainstable
Scale Houses
559 RENWICK FELL
Croglin Water
Di

101
J 50
K Staffield
L 60
M HARTSIDE HEIGHT
N 70
P Leadgate
Q
R
12

High Hesket
Baronwood
Ruckcroft
Dale
B6413
Renwick
664 BLACK FELL
624 Harescugh
HARTSIDE HEIGHT
580 Hartside Summit
Gilderdale Forest
102
Nenthead
A689

M6
A6
Kirkoswald
Busk
Alston Moor
Garrigill
Kill Summit
Killhope Mining
Lanehead
Cowshi

Port of Tyne

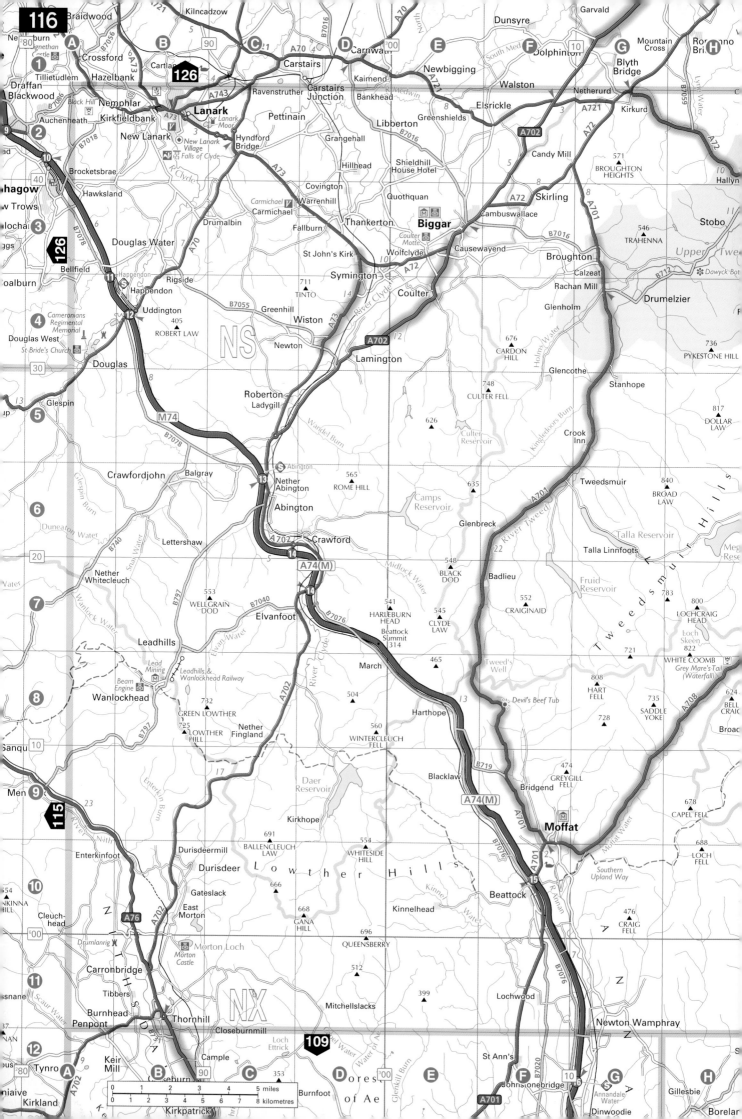

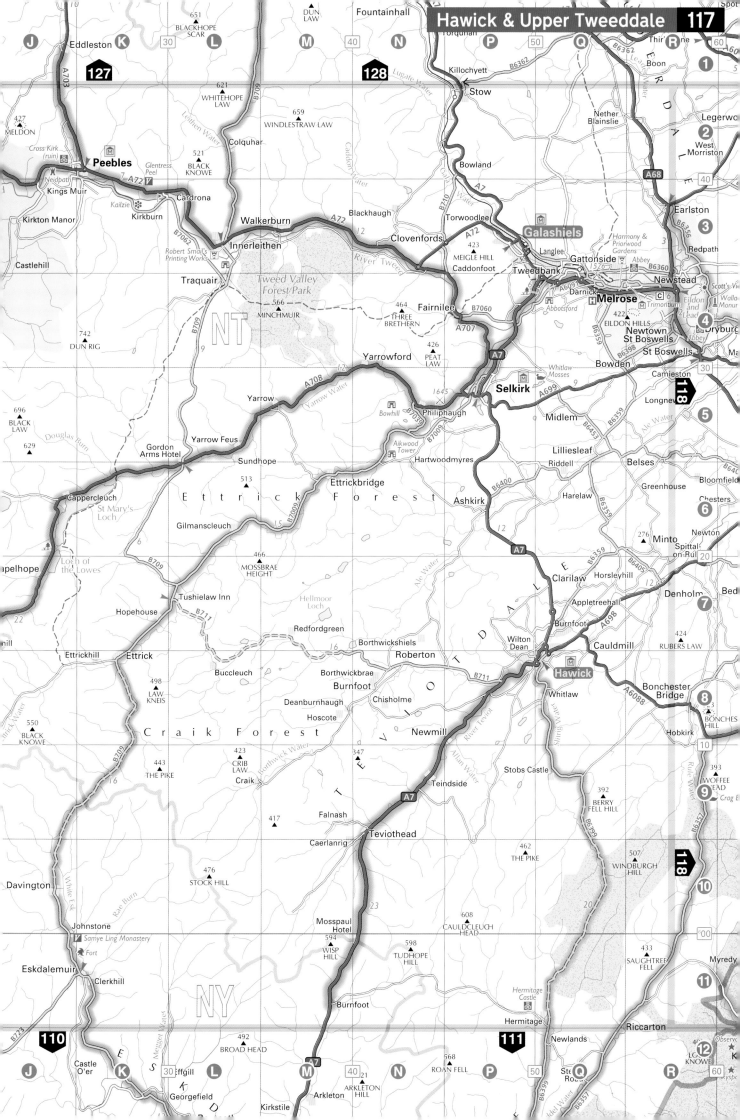

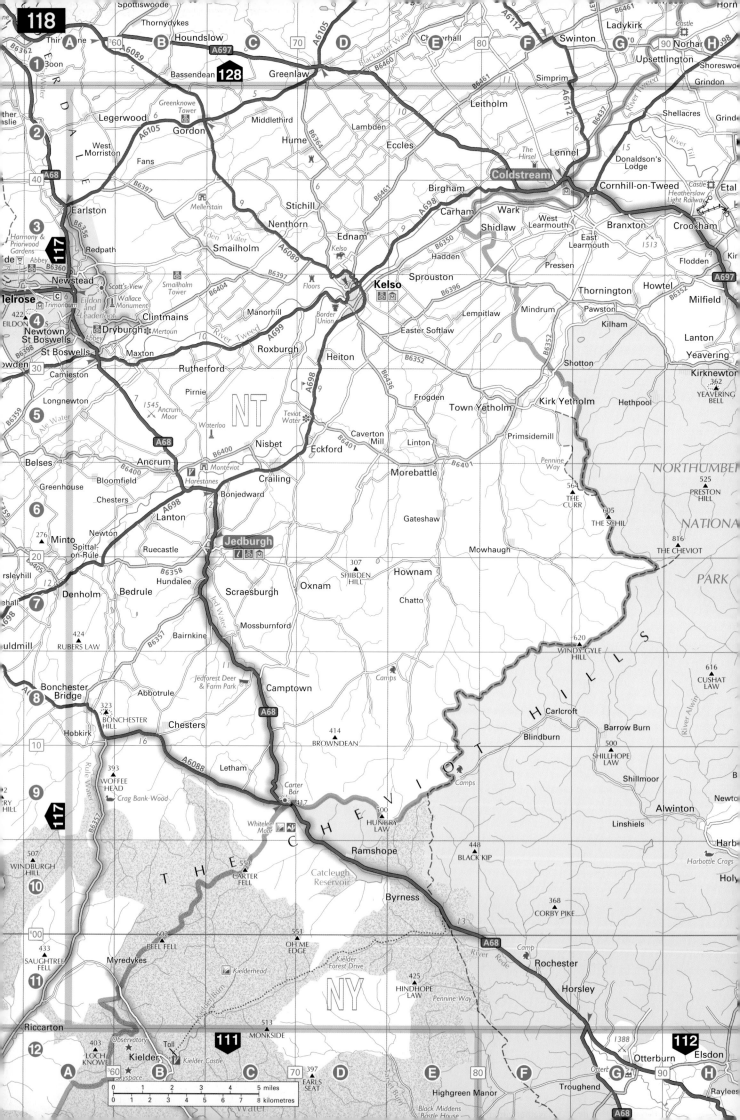

Sound of Bute

St B'ane's Church

J   K   L   Garrochty   M   Faslie Roads   N   P   Q   R   Be

Kilbirnie

Garroch Head   10   Little Cumbrae Island   Hunterston Power Station   20   Glengarnock   B784   B780   COMM   LAW   Barr   1

200   Drakemyre   Highfield   50   Bur   Thorn   1

A841   8   Chalmadale   Portencross   B7048   Farland Head   B781   B780   Munnoch   B780   Dalry   B707   Highfield   Auchen   de   2

124   Sannox   West Kilbride   A78   B714   Dalgarven   B778   Dalgarven Mill   A737   N   C   U   N

834   TEAL ABHAIL   Corrie   Seamill   B780   Kilwinning   Fergushill   B785   slie   3

874   GOATFELL   Brodick Castle, Garden & Country Park   Merkland Point   Ardrossan   Horse Isle   A78   A738   Stevenston   A78   Eglinton   Cunn   Per   3

Glen Rosa   Brodick Bay   124   Saltcoats   Ardeer   B780   B779   A78   Girdle Toll   40   Spring   N

512   CHRUACH   Brodick   Strathwhillan   FIRTH   Irvine   Maritime   Dreghorn   4

REAC   A841   Corriegills   OF   Fullarton   B708   Dryb   4

Lamlash   H   Clauchlands Point   CLYDE   Irvine Bay   Gailes   Castle   5

Margnaheglish   Lamlash Bay   Barassie   B746   A759   Loans   5

Cordon   Holy Island   V   Troon   B749   A78   30   5

4   Royal Troon   A79   6

Auchencairn   Kingscross   Knockenkelly   Lady Isle   Pr   ton   6

Carn Ban   Whiting Bay   Whiting Bay   (May-Sept, Sat only)   (May-Sept)   Prestwick   7

Glenashdale   Largymore   New Prestwick   B743   Whitlett   A7

Kilmory Water   Largybeg   V   NS   Ayr Bay   7

Kilmory   Dippin   Dippin Head   Wallace   Ayr   7

orrylin Cairn   Bennan   Kildonan   Doonfoot   A79   Belmont   8

Bennan Head   Pladda   Heads of Ayr   Burns Cottage   8

Fisherton   Heads of Ayr   A719   Alloway   Robert Bu   Birthplace   8

Dunure   Culroy   9

114   Drumshang   Croy Brae (Electric Brae)   Minishant   9

Knoweside   A77   B   9

Culzean Bay   Grimmet   10

Culzean Castle & Country Park   Pennyglen   B7023   Whitefaulds   Maybole   10

Maidenhead Bay   22   A719   Crossraguel Abbey   B7023   Kirkm   10

Maidens   Kirkoswald   Threave   10

Turnberry   12   Souter Johnnie's Cottage   Crosshill   10

Turnberry Bay   Roan of Craigoch

Wallacetown

Dipple   Kilgrammie   B741   Dailly   11

A77   Water of Girvan   00   11

Ailsa Craig   340   NX   Old Daily   B7035   12

Penkill   429   EFFIN FE   12

J   K   L   10   M   Girv   N   20   P   B734   Q   30   R   Lac

Dounepark   Dalquharran   River Stinch

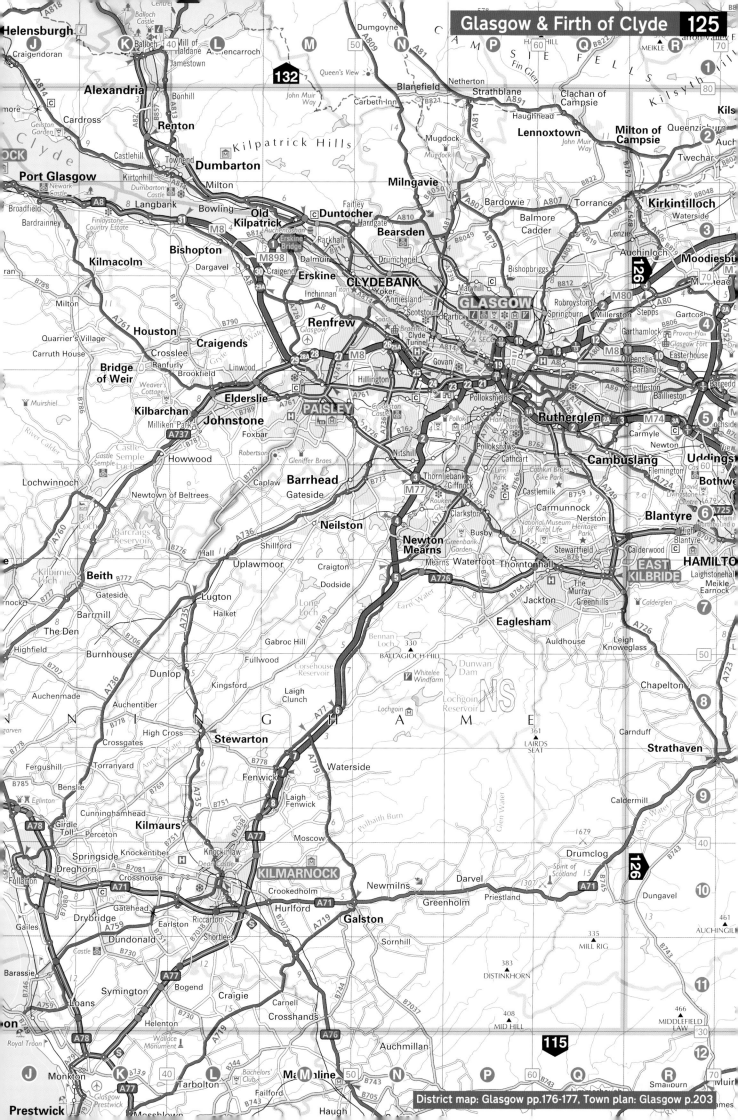

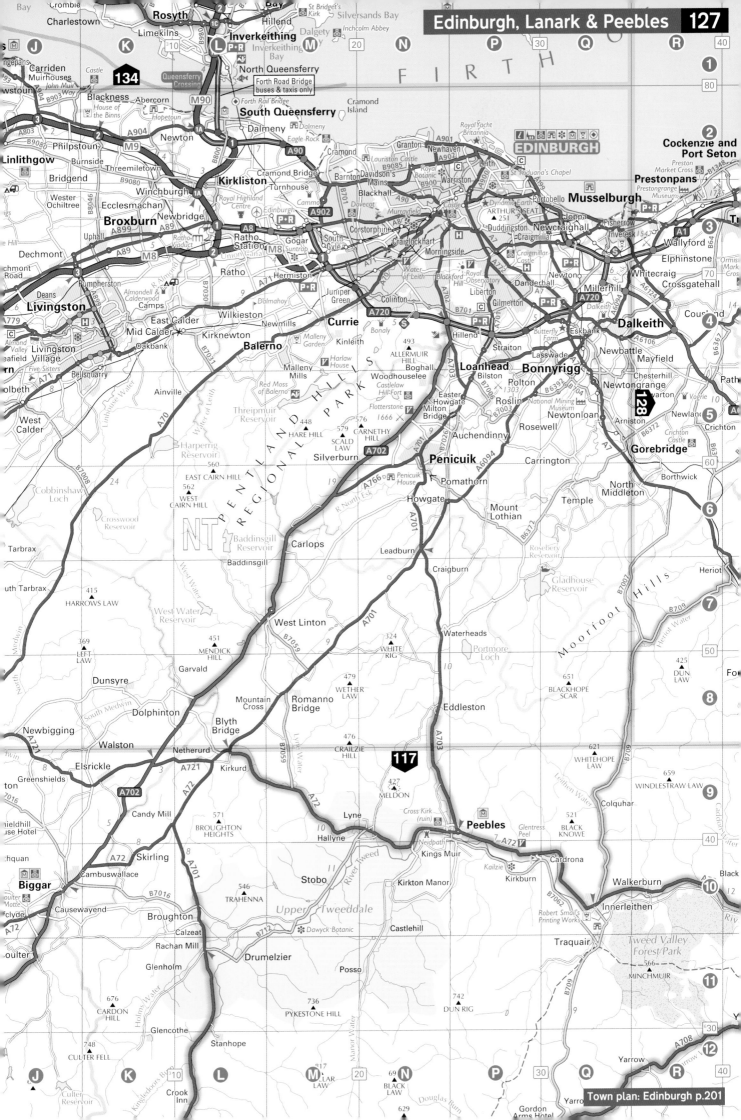

J K 80 L M 90 N P '00 Q R 10

1
90
2
3
80
4
5
70
6
7
60
8
9
50
10
11
40
12
10

Barns Ness
East Barns
Chapel Point
Skateraw
Torness Power Station
Thorntonloch
Crowhill
Reed Point
Cove Pease Bay
Dunglass Collegiate Church
319
COCKLAW HILL
Oldhamstocks
Cockburnspath
A1107
Pease Dean
Siccar Point
Fast Castle Head
ST ABB'S HEAD
196
BROWN RIG
Coldingham Loch
St Abbs
Ecclaw
391
HEART LAW
Southern Upland Way
Grantshouse
Coldingham
Coldingham Bay
Butterdean
Lye Water
21
Houndwood
Heugh Head
Cairncross
A1107 22
Eyemouth
Quixwood
262
HORSELEY HILL
Reston
Ayton
A1
Burnmouth
Abbey St Bathans
Edin's Hall Broch
14
B6438
Auchencrow
emford
325
COCKBURN LAW
Marygold
ster
B6355
Lintlaw
A6112
Lamberton
Primrosehill
Preston
Chirnside
B6437
B6355
Foulden
Marshall Meadows Bay
B6365
Cumledge
Edrom Church
Chirnsidebridge
15
Foulden Tithe Barn
1333
North Northumberland Heritage Coast
Edrom
Edington
Whiteadder Water
A6105
S
Manderston
Broadhaugh
Allanton
Hutton
Berwick-upon-Tweed
Duns
A6105
Paxton
Castle
Barracks & Main Guard
Gavinton
Blackadder
B6460
Hilton
Paxton
Town Ramparts
Tweedmouth
Polwarth
Nisbet Hill
Sinclair's Hill
Whitsome
13
Loanend
Spittal
Fogo
7
A6105
A6112
6
Horndean
Horncliffe
East Ord
Huds Head
Charterhall
Swinton
Ladykirk
Castle
Norham
A698
Murton
Thornton
Unthank
A1
Scremerston
Cheswick
Lambden
B6460
B6461
Leitholm
A6112
11
Upsettlington
Shoreswood
West Allerdean
Ancroft
118
Eccles
10
Simprim
Grindon
Felkington
119
Goswick
Haggerston
Beal
Lennel
The Hirsel
15
Shellacres
Grindonrigg
Bowsden
Berrington
B6525
15
Fenham
Coldstream
Cornhill-on-Tweed
Donaldson's Lodge
Duddo
B6353
West Kyloe
Lowick
Fenwick
Birgham
Castle
Etal
Heatherslaw Light Railway
Heatherslaw Corn Mill
Lady Waterford Hall
Buckton
Carham
Wark
West Learmouth
E M xton Crookr N
Ford
P
Q
R
10
Ednam
J
Kelso
K
80
idhlaw L
East Learmouth
90
1513
Flodden
14
Kimmerston
Hadden
B6350
St Cuthbert's
Holburn
Detchant
Middleton

NU

Causeway flooded at high tide

River Tweed
River Till
Blackadder Water

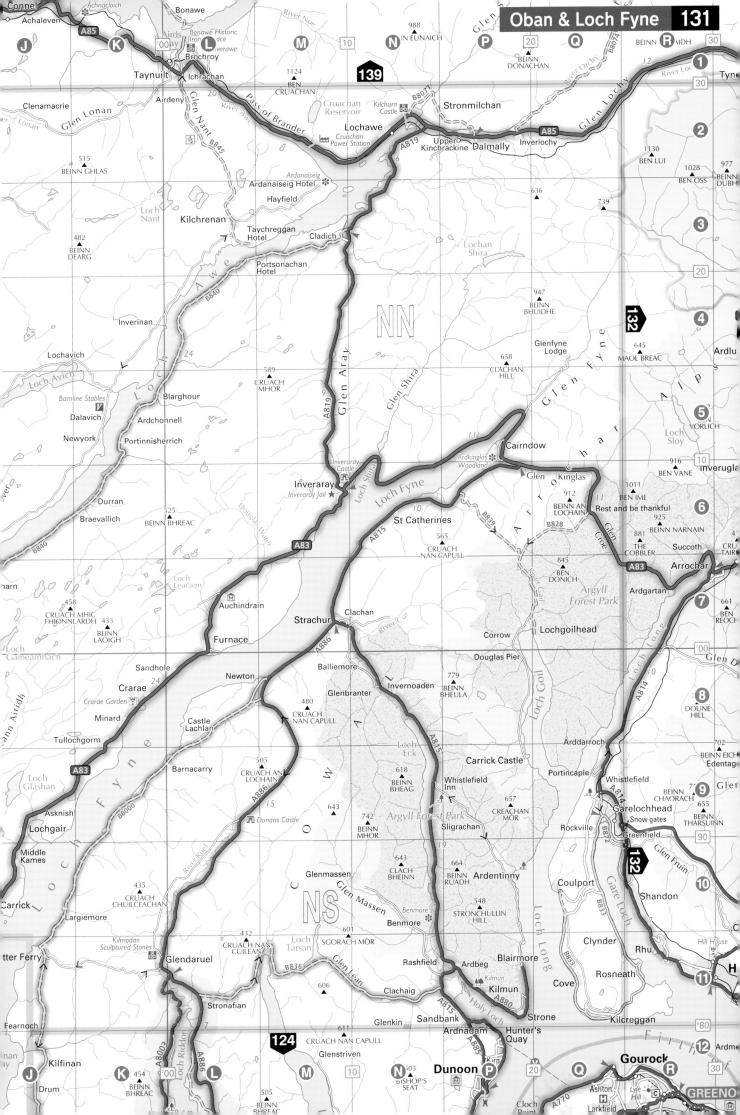

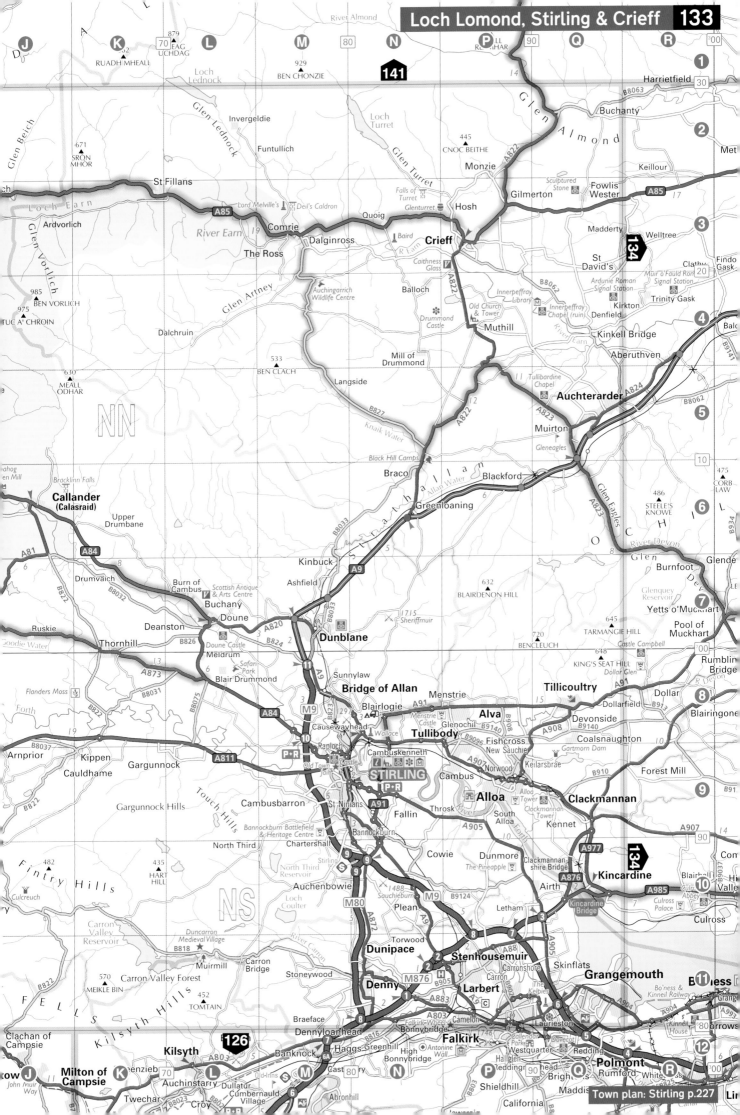

Town plan: Perth p.219

NL

NM

NR

Colonsay

COLONSAY

ORONSAY

COLL

TIREE

TRESHNISH
ISLES

IONA

Coll labels:
Eilean Mòr
Rubha Mòr
Rubha Sgor-in
Sorisda
Bousd
Cliad Bay
B8072
Arnabost
Grishipoll
Clabhach
Loch Clad
B8071
Hogh Bay
Ballyhaugh
Arinagour
B8070
Totronald
Feall Bay
Coll
Acha
Arileod
Uig
Loch Breachacha
Eilean Ornsay
Calgary Point
Crossapol Bay
Rubha Fàsachd
Gunna

Barra ferry label:
Bàgh a' Chaisteil
(Castlebay)
(Apr-Oct. Weds only)

Tiree labels:
Rubha Port Bhiosd
Clachan Mòr
Balephetrish Bay
Caoles
Rubha Dubh
B8069
Ruaig
Loch Bhasapoll
Hough Bay
Ballevullin
Cornoigmore
Kenovay
B8068
Gott Bay
Kilkenneth
B8068
Tiree
Moss
Heylipoll
Scarinish
B8065
Middleton
Crossapol
Barrapoll
B8065
Hynish Bay
Loch a' Phuill
B8067
Balemartine
Mannal
Rinn Thorbhais
Hynish
Balephuil Bay

Flo
Lunga
Bac Mòr or Dutchman's
Bac Beag

Soa Island
Erraid

Iona Abbey & Nunnery
Baile Mòr
MacLean's Cross
Sound of I

Colonsay inset labels:
Eilean Dubh
Kiloran Bay
Rubh' a' Geodha
143
CARNAN EOIN
Oban
Kiloran
Kilchattan
B8067
Scalasaig
B8086
Machrins
Colonsay
B8085
Garvard
Oronsay
Rubha Bàn
Dubh Eilean
Eilean Ghaoideamal
Port Askaig

0   1   2   3 miles
0   1   2   3   4   5 kilometres

0   1   2   3   4   5 miles
0   1   2   3   4   5   6   7   8 kilometres

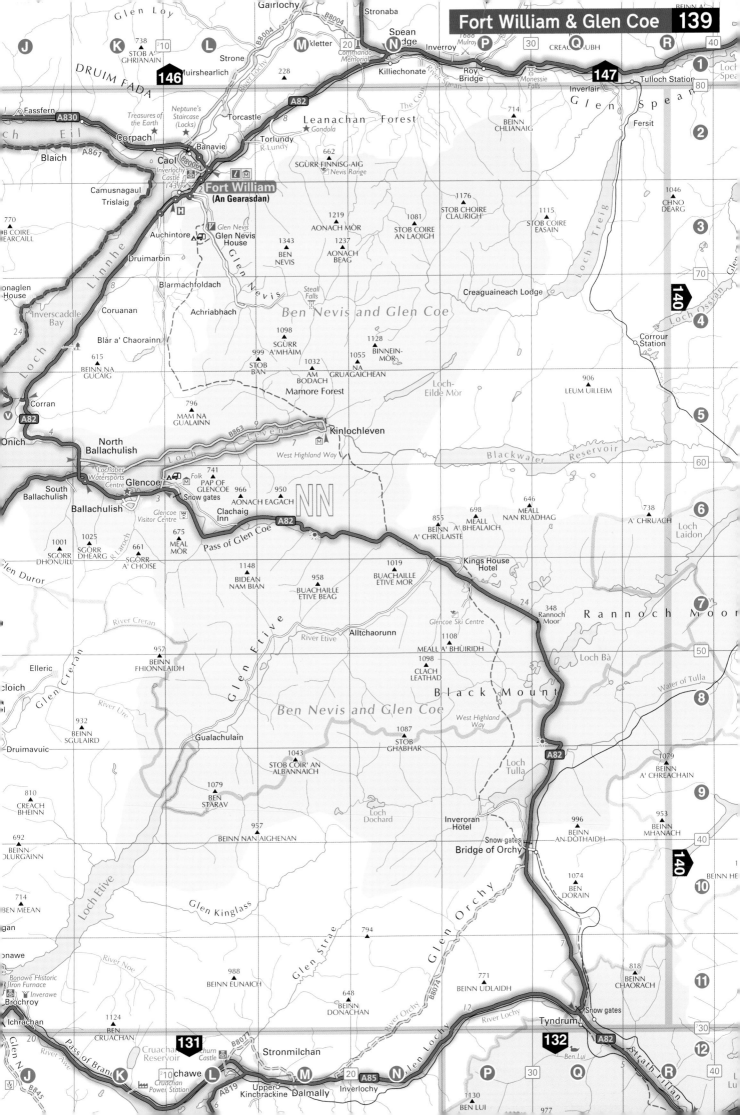

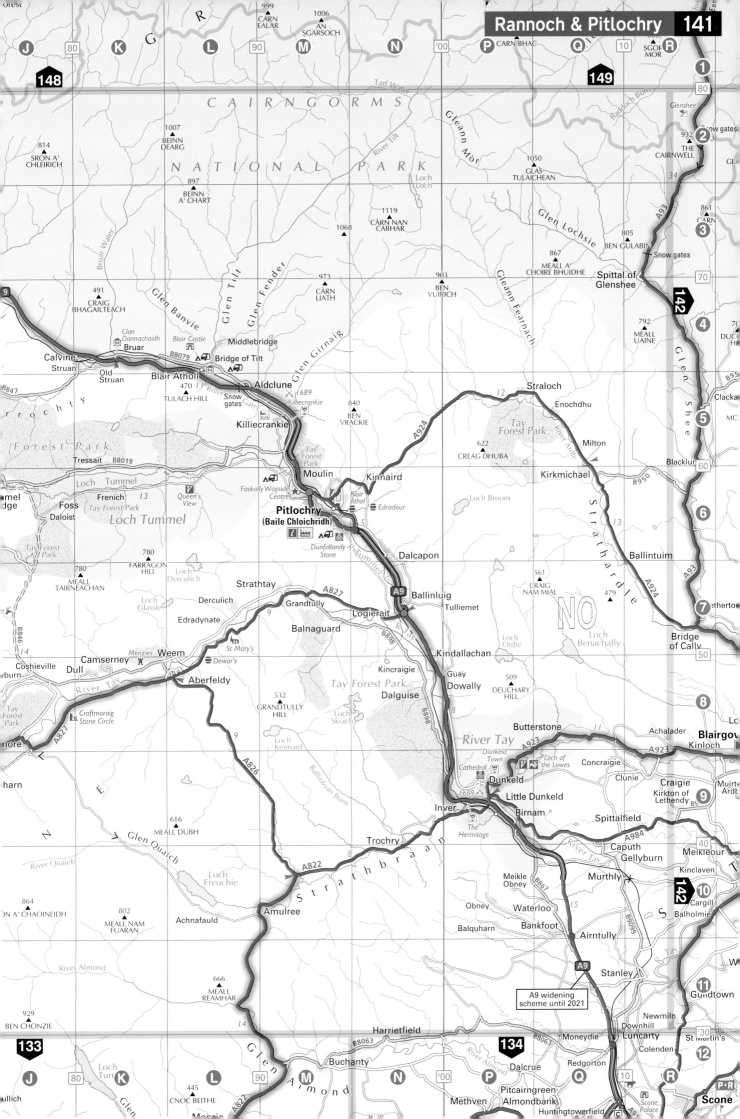

148

149

1

CAIRNGORMS

NATIONAL PARK

142

MOUNT
BATTOCK
J 475 **K** 60 **L** B974 **M** 465 70 **N** 80 Temple **P** **Q** **R** 90
HILL OF GOYLE Nev Mill Fiddes 80
FINGRAY HILL New Mill Drumlithie
475 454 Glenbervie Drumlithie `151` Fowlsneugh `1`
HILL OF Cairn O'Mount Mondynes 80 Crawton
FINGRAY
Glenesk Folk 414 Auchenblae Catterline
Snow gates FINELLA B967 `2`
Water of North Esk HILL Fordoun Grassic Gibbon Kinneff Todhead Point
544 Pittarrow Redmyre Arbuthnott Centre
STURDY Mains of B966 Inverbervie `3`
HILL Balnakettle 25 Bervie
605 Sauchieburn Mains of A92 Bay
BULG Fettercairn Haulkerton Laurencekirk Gourdon 70
677 Bogmuir B9120 Redford
HILL OF Edzell Laurencekirk Benholm
WIRREN Edzell Woods Dykelands 13 `4`
Bridgend Balfield Luthermuir Johnshaven
Dunlappie B9120 Craigo Marykirk Bush
Brown B9120 Craigo Lochside Milton Ness
Caterthun Inchbare Logie Logie Morphie St Cyrus `5`
Kirkton White Newtonmill Pert St Cyrus
Menmuir Caterthun Keithock Logie 60
Mains of Tigerton Trinity Hillside `6`
Balhall Little Maison Brechin Dun House of A92 Montrose
Lochty Brechin Dieu Chapel Dun Montrose Air Station
Careston (ruin) Caledonian Montrose NO
South Esk Railway Basin Scurdie Ness `6`
Netherton Haughs of Barnhead Ferryden
Sculptured Kinnaird Maryton Craig Usan `7`
Stones A933 Farnell Westerton
Aberlemno Mains of of Rossie Braehead Boddin Point `50`
Melgunds B9113 132 Lunan
emp's B9113 Bolshan WUDDY Lunan Lunan Bay `8`
Castle LAW Inverkeilor
llie Glasterlaw Kinnell Lunan Water `50`
urnside A932 Guthrie Boysack Friockheim 13 Chapelton Red Head `8`
Pitmuies C B965 Leysmill Cauldcots
ichen Letham Friockheim Letham
uld Colliston Grange Marywell `9`
aichie Redford St Vigeans Auchmithie
Greystone B961 Condor Carlingheugh
whillock Carmyllie B9127 6 St Vigeans Bay `40`
B9127 Elliot Water The Deil's
Bonnington Arbirlot Arbroath Head `10`
Kirkton Crombie B961 A92 `40`
of Monikie East Haven
Craigton B9128 Muirdrum 17 `10`
rlungie House Upper 7 Panbride
Victoria West Haven `11`
Barry Barry Mill Carnoustie
nifieth Carnoustie A930 `11`
BUDDON `135`
NESS `12`

J 60 **K** **L** 70 **M** **N** 80 **P** **Q** **R** 90
entsmuir Point 30

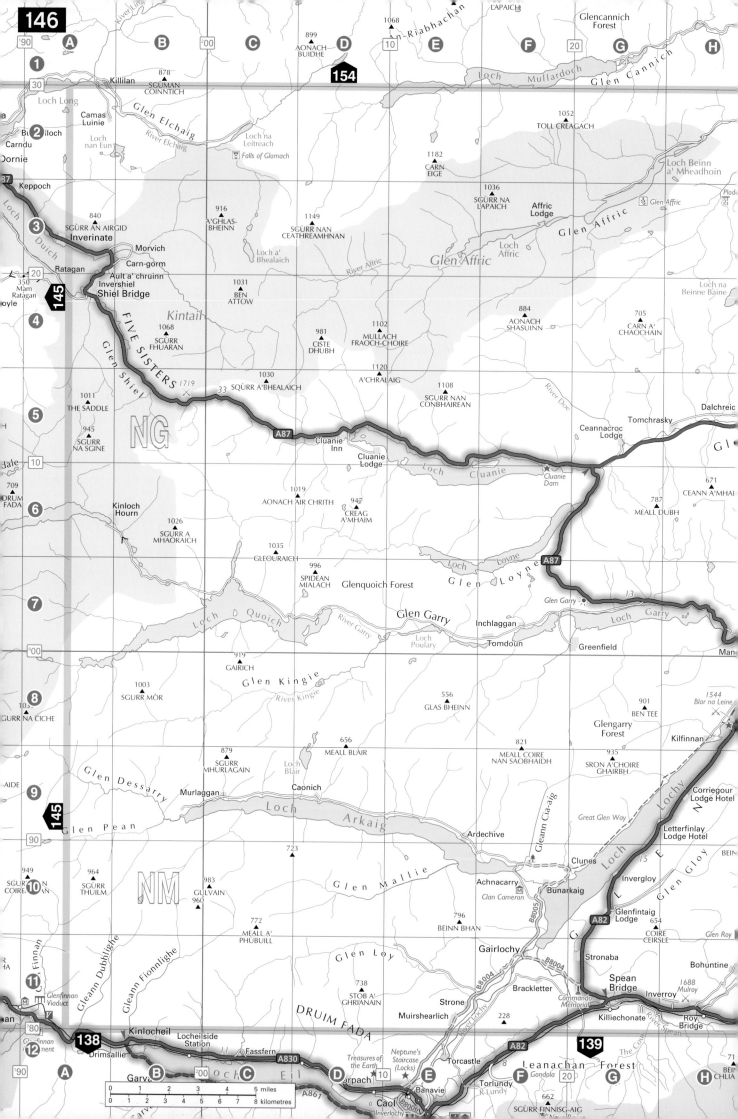

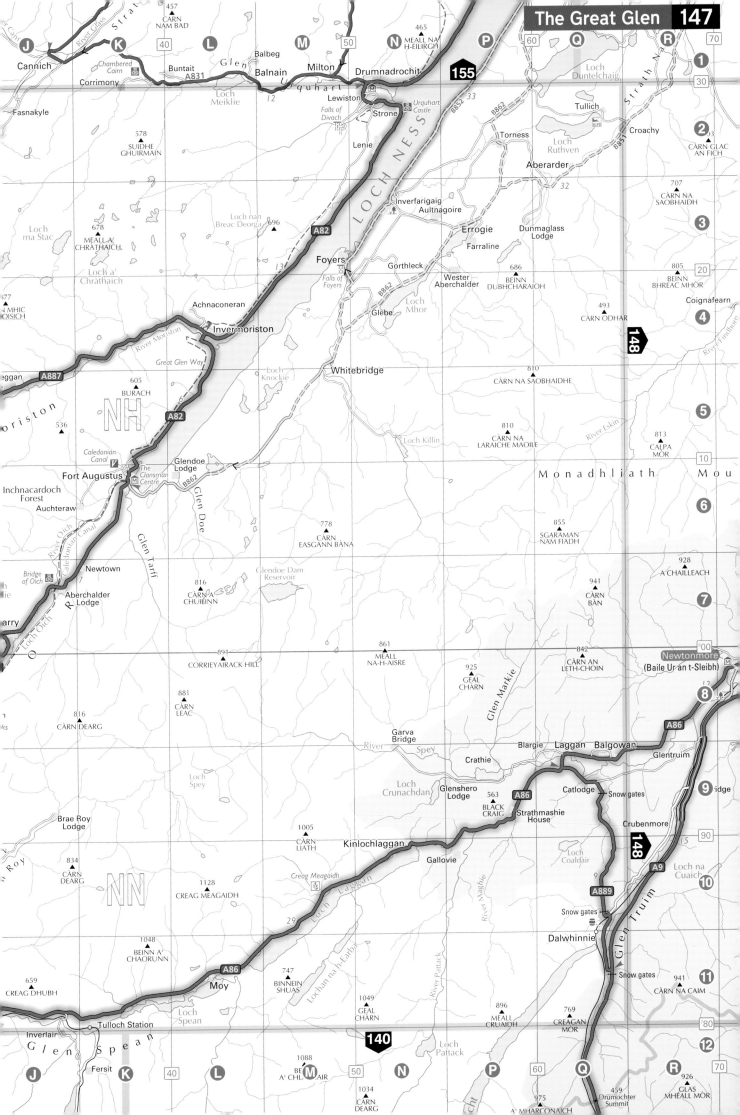

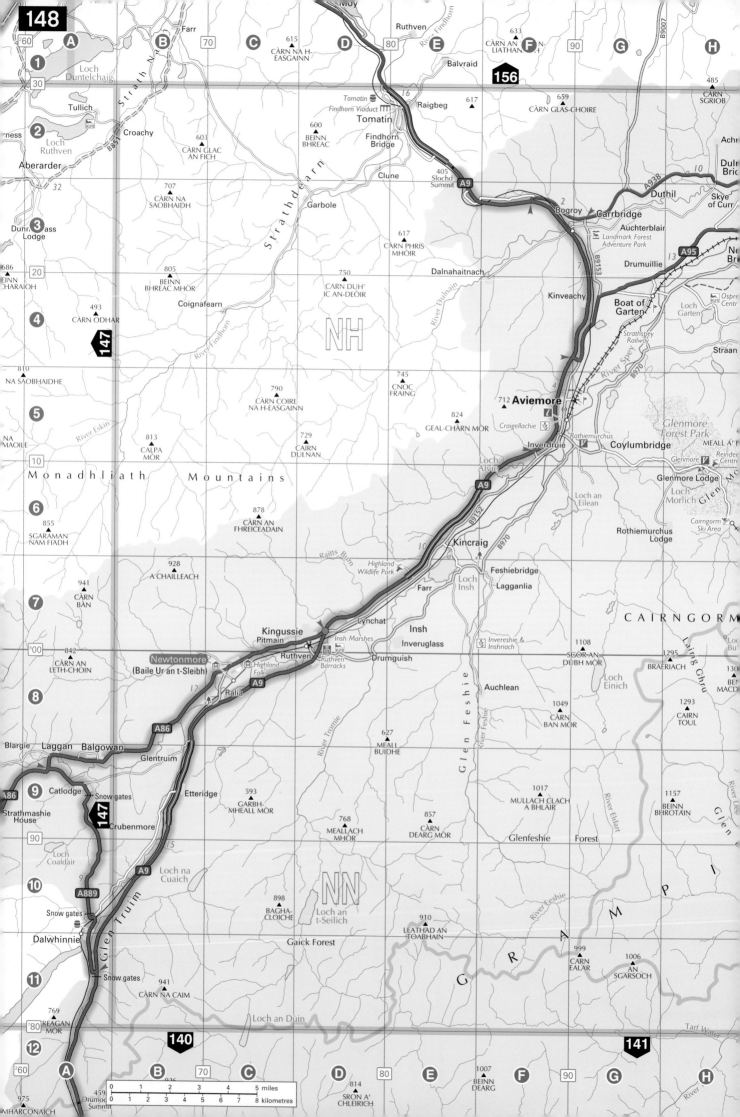

Lettoch
Delliefure
J **K** **L**
Mains of Dalvey
A910 14

Cromdale
Speybridge
own-Spey
Hills of Cromdale
River Spey
1690

157 Drumin
Shenval
Glenlivet
Auchbreck
1595
Glenlivet
M **N** B9009 19 **P** 30 **Q** **R**
B9009
North East 250 20
B9009
River Fiddich
Bridg **1**
30 30 **2**
ach
766
CORRYHABBIE
HILL
571
ROUND
HILL
Aldivalloch Aldunie

River Avon
Strath Avon 13
Speyside Way

Tomnavoulin
Auchnarrow
B9008
Clashnoir
Chapeltown
787

459
CÀRN NA
LOINNE
A939 14
Snow gates
Bridge of Brown
Snow gates
Bridge of Avon
Tomintoul
Glenlivet
Estate
Delnabo

NJ
803
CÀRN MÒR
637
THE
SOCACH
718

1595
THE B **3**
629
HILL OF THREE STONES
20
632
CREAG
AN EUNAN **4**
Badenyon
656
MOSS
HILL

Belnacraig
Kirkton of
Glenbuchat
Glenbuchat
Castle
Bellabeg Forbestown
Strathdon
Roughpark
Garchory
A944
Milltown
Colnabaichin

Lettoch
Dorback Lodge
River Nethy
606
CÀRN
TUADHAM
821
GEAL CHÀRN
803
CÀRN BHEADHAIR
730
MAIM
SUIM
710
CRAIG VEANN
792
CÀRN
EALASAID
Lecht Ski Area
Lecht
Summit
North East 250
Snow gates
Cock Bridge
Corgarff
Castle
Corgarff
Heughhead
10
5
6

CAIRNGORMS
Funicular
713
THE
BRUACH
741
BIG
GARVOUN
Loch Buiig
Glen Avon
829
BROWN
COW HILL
744
CÀRN A'
BHACAIN
A939
12
749
MONA GOWAN
872
MORVEN
Co

NATIONAL
Loch Avon
chachan
1083
BEINN A
CHAORRUINN
1196
NORTH
TOP
1171
BEN
AVON
River Cairn
M
O
U
N
T
A
I
N
S
7

UNTAINS
PARK
Glen Derry
930
BEINN
BHREAC
1177
SOUTH
TOP
1084
CÀRN
EÀS
900
CULARDOCH
North East 250
B9976
743
GEALLAIG HILL
Coilacriech
A93
Bridge
of Gairn
B972
Candacraig
800
Car
o'
Tullich
North East 250
8

Glen Lui
Linn of Dee
Quoich Water
618
MEALL
GORM
17
Crathie
Littlemill
B976
River Dee
Ballater
Inver
Easter
Balmoral
Balmoral
Castle
Royal
Lochnagar
Balnacroft
Birkhall
596
THE COYLES
OF MUICK
699
CAIRN LEUCHAN
9
90

Allanaquoich
Braemar
Keiloch
A93
Snow gates
Morrone
Birkwood
Inver
600
CREAG NAN GALL
Glen Gelder
**BALMORAL
FOREST**
River Muick
Glen Muick
150
10
938
MOU
KEEN

Inverey
859
MORRONE
HILL
NO
816
CÀRN
LIATH
1154
LOCHNAGAR
720
FASHEILACH
Glen Mar
11

919
CARN BHAC
886
SGOR
MÒR
Clunie Water
North East 250
Loch
Callater
996
BROAD
CAIRN
Loch
Muick
Spittal of
Glenmuick
832
EASTER BALLOCH
80
12

J **K** L A10 **L** **M** **N** Glen Doll **P** 30 **Q** **R** 40
1050
GLAS
932
670
THE
CAIRNWELL
Snow gates
1067
GLAS MAOL
1018
CÀRN AN
TUIRC
1045
CAIRN
TAGGART
957
TOM BU'
142
831
LAIR OF
ALDARARIE
Lee
Glenshee

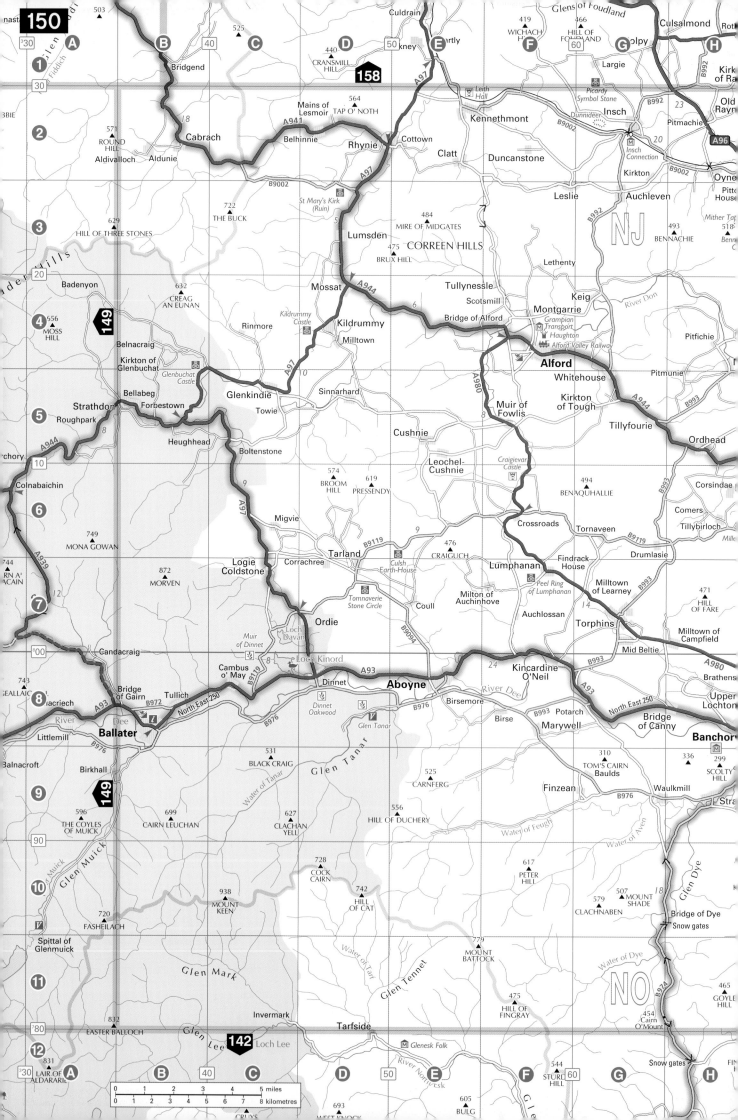

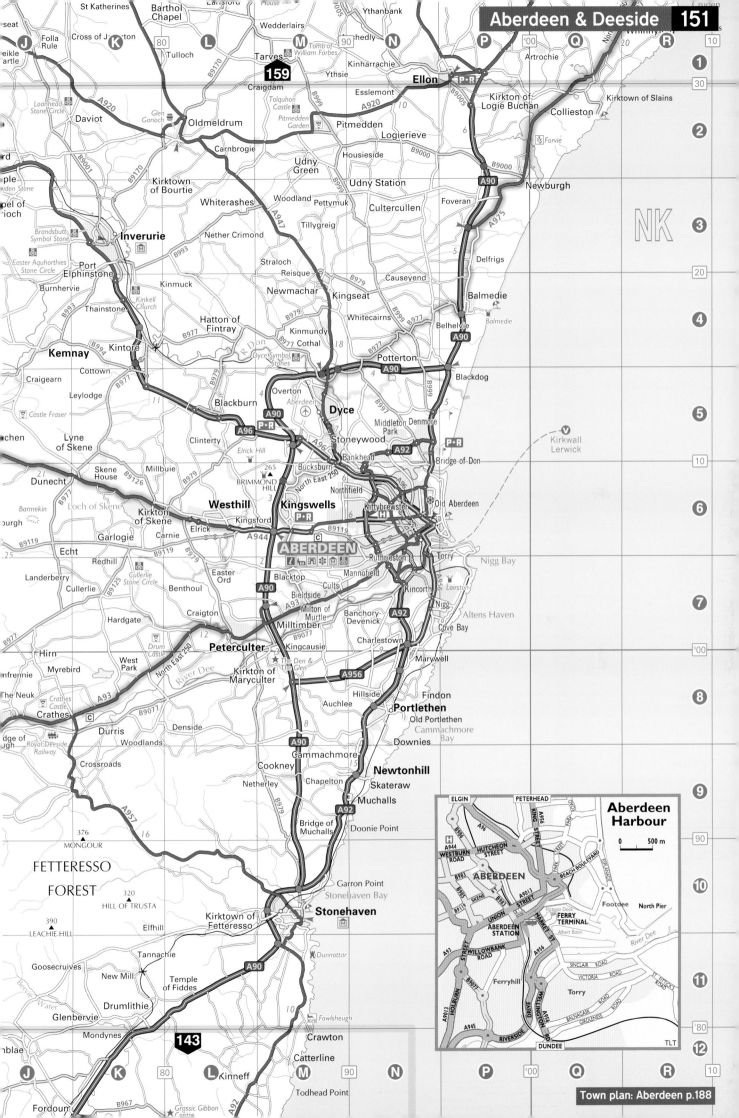

NK

159

143

Aberdeen Harbour

0   500 m

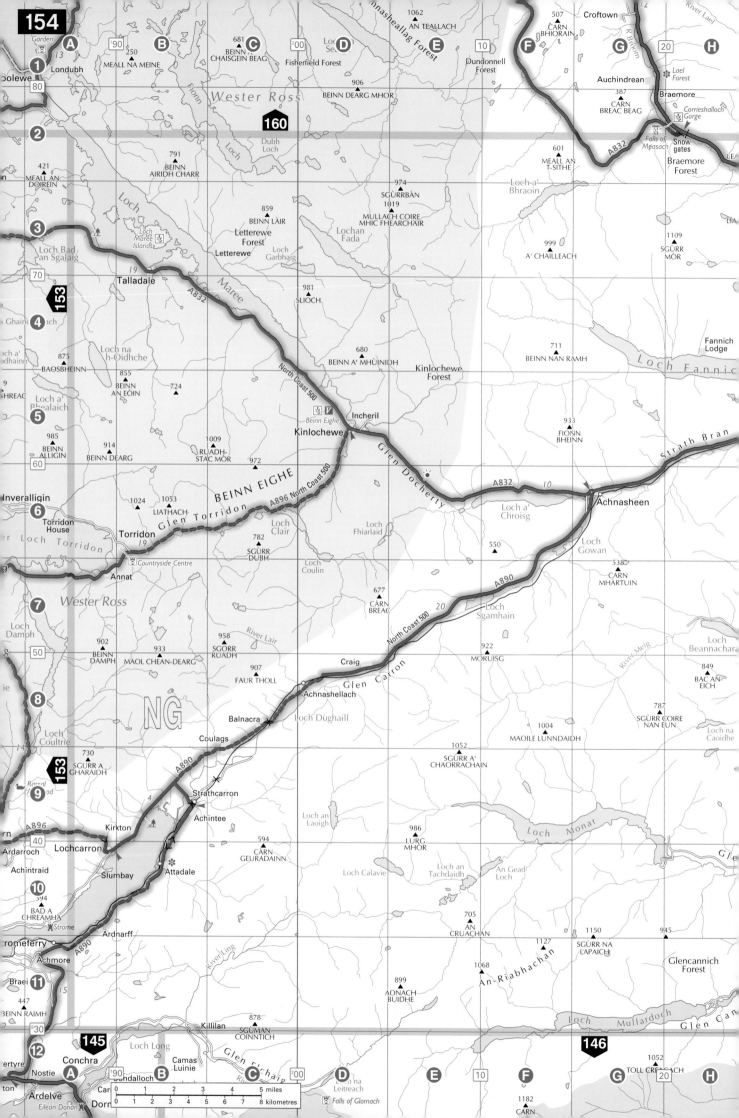

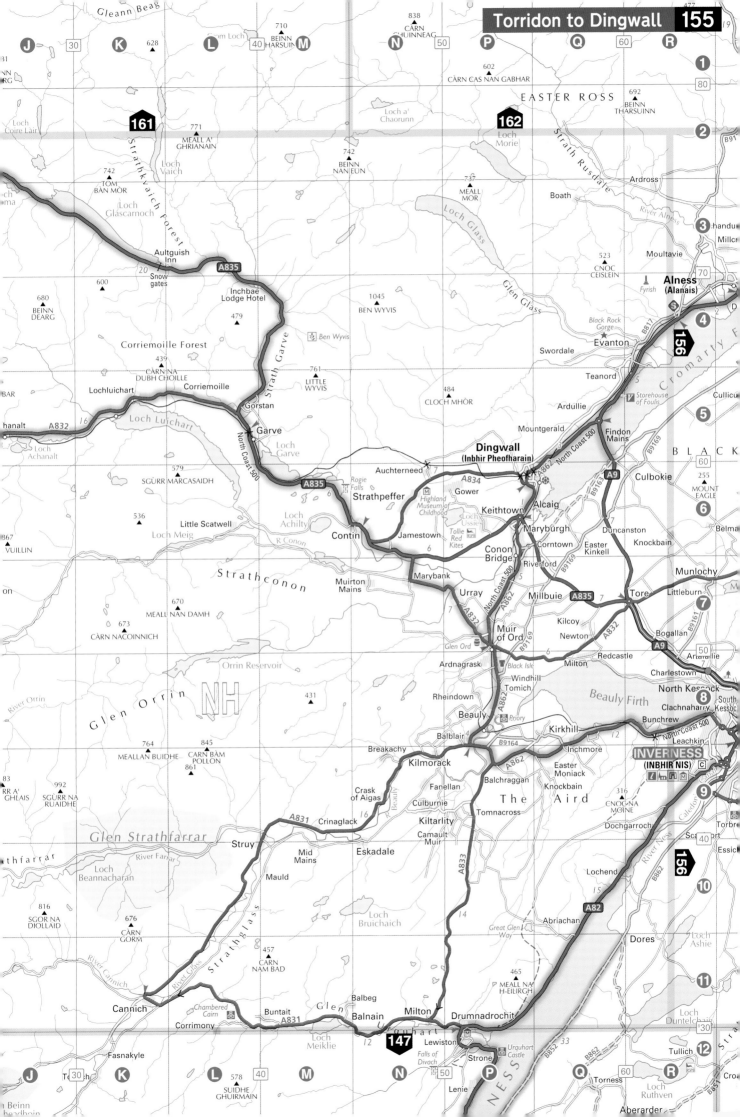

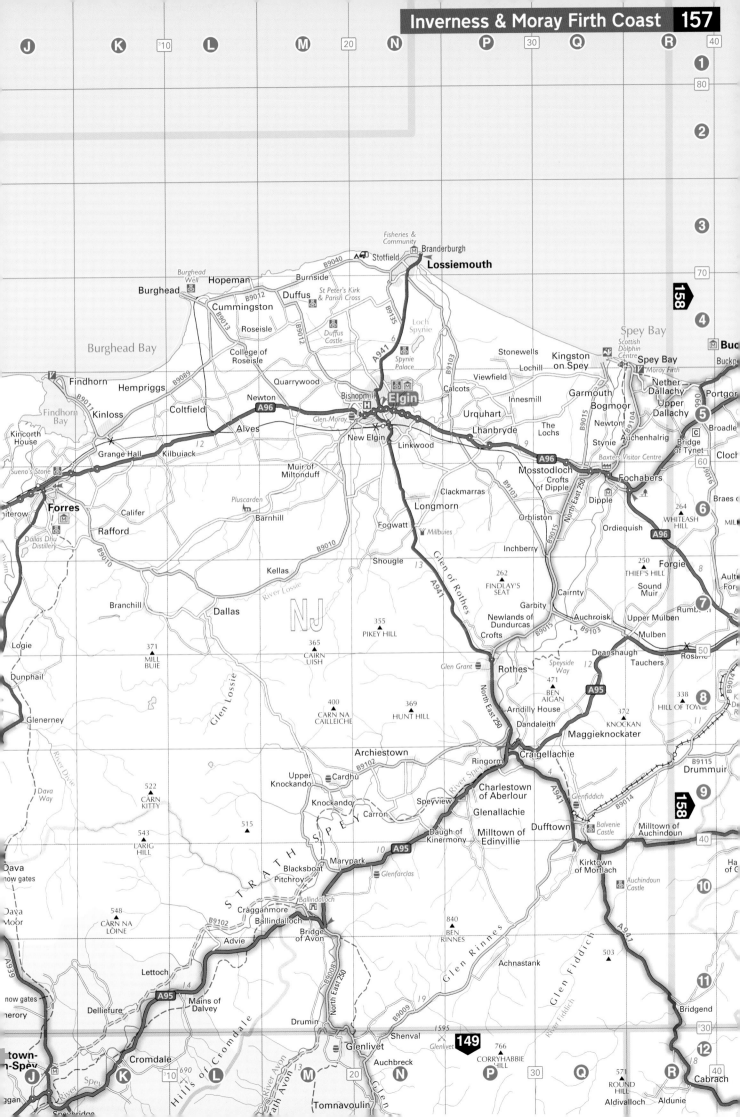

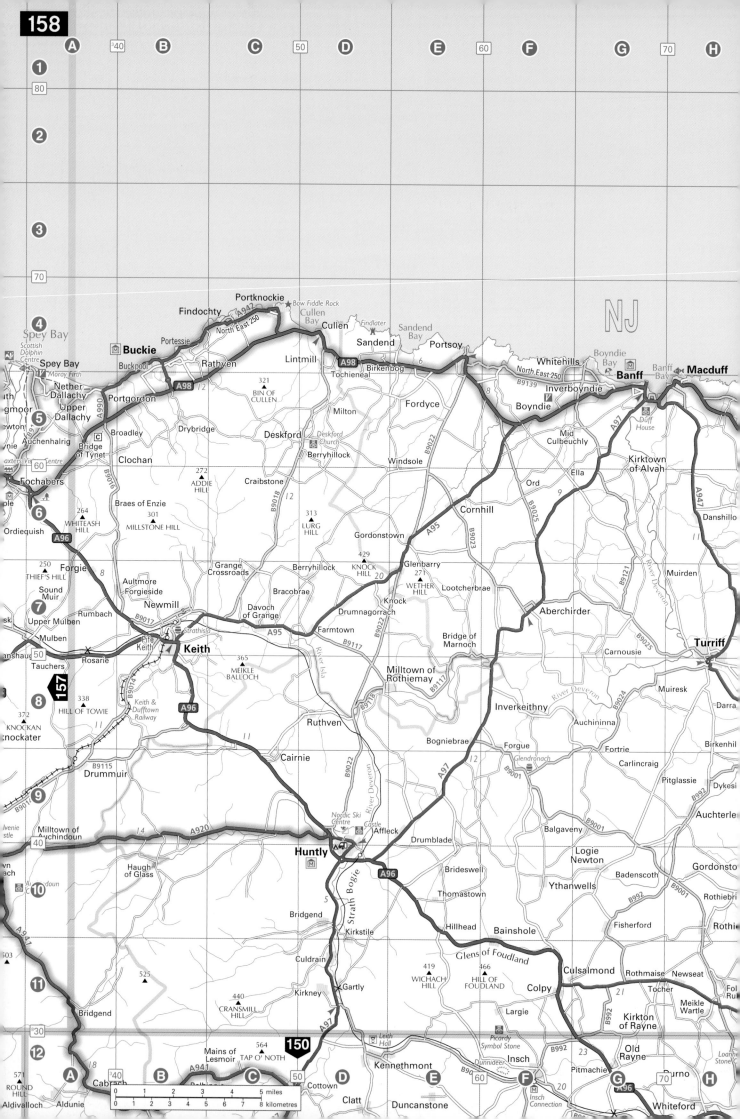

A B C D E F G H

1
2
3
4
5
6
7
8
9
10
11
12

NJ

Spey Bay
Scottish Dolphin Centre
Spey Bay
Moray Firth
Nether Dallachy
Upper Dallachy
Auchenhalrig
Baxters Vis Centre
Fochabers
Ordiequish

Buckie
Portessie
Buckpool
Rathven
Portgordon
Broadley
Clochan
Bridge of Tynet

Findochty
Portknockie
★ Bow Fiddle Rock
Cullen Bay
Cullen
Sandend
Sandend Bay
Portsoy
Findlater
North East 250

Lintmill
Tochieneal
Birkenbog
A98
6

321
BIN OF CULLEN
Milton
Drybridge
Deskford
Deskford Church
Berryhillock
Windsole
Fordyce

Whitehills
Boyndie Bay
Banff Bay
Banff ✈ **Macduff**
North East 250
B9139
Inverboyndie
Boyndie
Duff House
Mid Culbeuchly
Ella
Ord
Kirktown of Alvah
Danshillo
A947
Muirden
8

272
ADDIE HILL
B9018
12
Craibstone
313
LURG HILL
Gordonstown
Cornhill
B9022
B9025
9
11

A98
12
A990
A96

264
WHITEASH HILL
301
MILLSTONE HILL
Braes of Enzie
Grange Crossroads
Berryhillock
Bracobrae
429
KNOCK HILL
20
Glenbarry
271
WETHER HILL
Lootcherbrae
A95
B9023
Aberchirder
B9121
River Deveron

Forgie
THIEF'S HILL
250
8
Aultmore
Forgieside
Newmill
Davoch of Grange
Knock
Drumnagorrach
B9022
Bridge of Marnoch
B9025
Carnousie
Turriff

Sound Muir
Rumbach
B9017
Strathisla
A95
Farmtown
B9117
Milltown of Rothiemay
B9117
Inverkeithny
River Deveron
Muiresk
Darra

Upper Mulben
Mulben
Fife Keith
Keith
365
MEIKLE BALLOCH
River Isla
B9024
Auchininna
Auchterle

50
Tauchers
Rosarie
B9014
Keith & Dufftown Railway
Ruthven
Bogniebrae
Forgue
A97
12
Glendronach
B9001
Fortrie
Carlincraig
Pitglassie
B992
Dykesi
Darra

157
338
HILL OF TOWIE
A96
Cairnie
B9022
Birkenhil

372
KNOCKAN
Knockater
11
B9115
Drummuir
B9018
Nordic Ski Centre
Castle
Affleck
Drumblade
A97
Balgaveny
Forgue
B9001
Auchterle

B9017
Milltown of Auchindoun
venie Castle
A920
14
40
Haugh of Glass
Alddoun
A941
Bridgend
5
Strath Bogie
Kirkstile
Huntly
A96
Brideswell
Thomastown
Hillhead
Bainshole
Logie Newton
Badenscoth
Ythanwells
Gordonsto
B992
B9001
Rothiebri
Fisherford
Rothi

ROUND HILL
571
Aldivalloch
Aldunie
Cabrach
B40
A941
503
525
Bridgend
Culdrain
Bridgend
440
CRANSMILL HILL
Kirkney
Kirstile
Gartly
Largie
Glens of Foundland
419
WICHACH HILL
466
HILL OF FOUNDLAND
Colpy
Culsalmond
Rothmaise
Newseat
21
Tocher
Meikle Wartle
Fo Ru
B992

Mains of Lesmoir
564
TAP O' NOTH
150
Cottown
Clatt
Kennethmont
Duncanstone
Leith Hall
Picardy Symbol Stone
Dunnideer
Insch
Insch Connection
Pitmachie
Kirkton of Rayne
Old Rayne
Loanh Stone
Durno
A96
Whiteford

A941
A97
B90
B992
23
20

Scale:
0 1 2 3 4 5 miles
0 1 2 3 4 5 6 7 8 kilometres

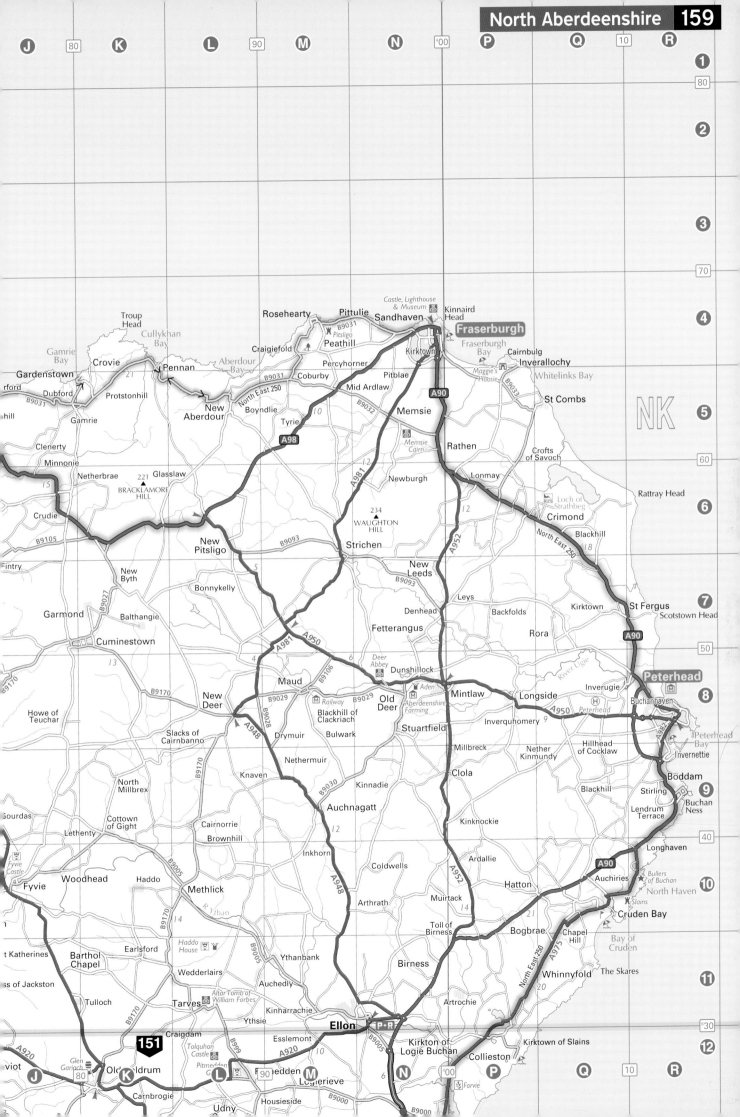

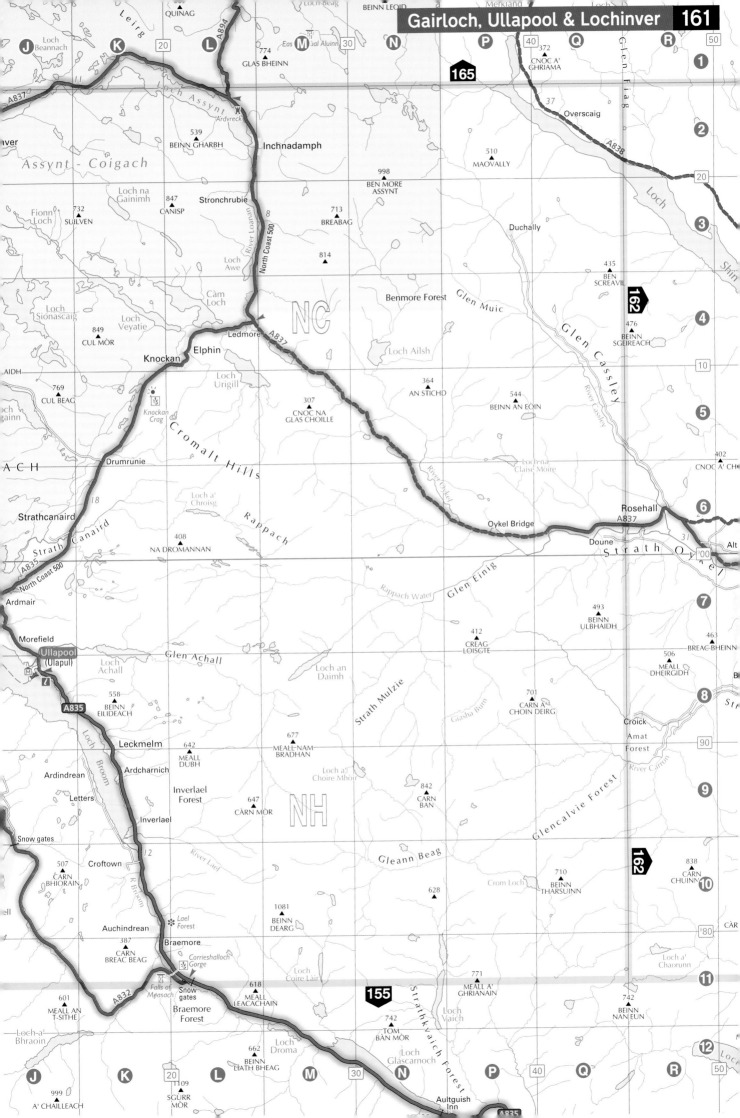

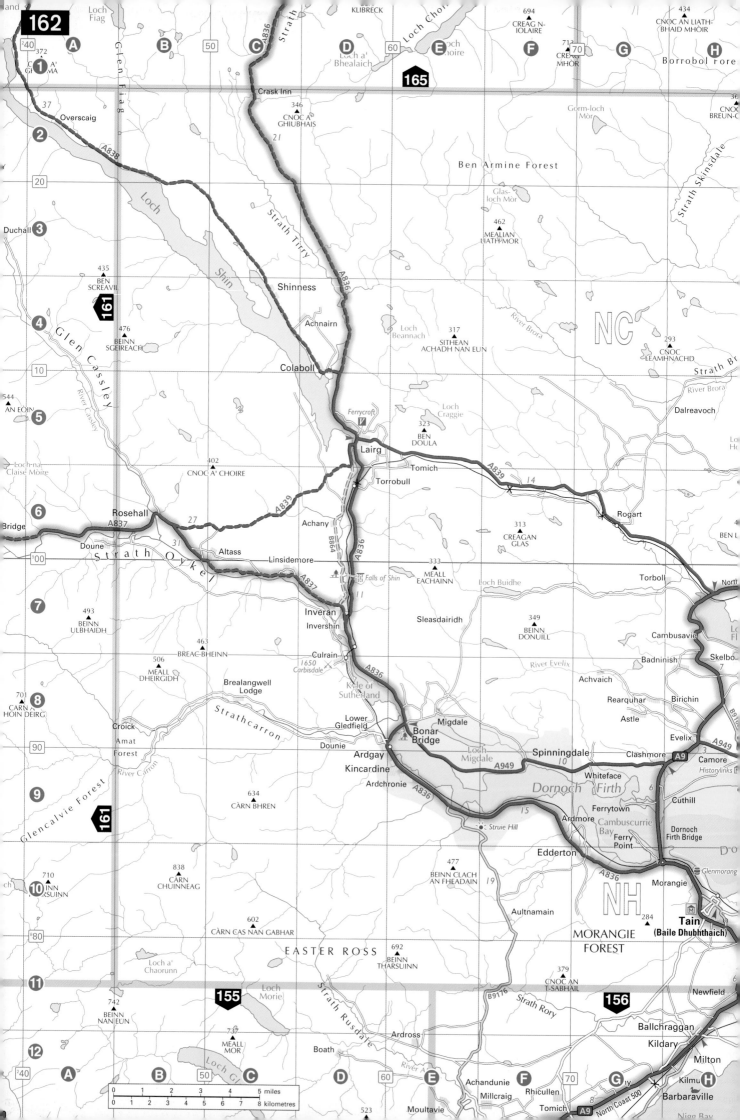

NA FEARNA

705 MORVEN

202 CNOC DAIL-CHAIRN

J **Strath Free** K 90 **Suisgill** L 518 **CNOC AN EIREANNAICH** M '00 N 626 **SCARABEN** P 10 Q **Knockally** **Snow gates** R 20

1

66 Loch Ascaig

167

Langwell Forest

Borgue

388 **CREAG NAM FIADH**

Learable Hill Cairns, Stone Row & Stone Circles

17

Newport

Langwell House

North Coast 500

Berriedale

2

20

554 **CREAG SCALABSDALE**

Kildonan Lodge

A9

Badbea Historic Village

20

337 CNOC NA H-INNSE MOIRE

Kildonan 416 **BEINN DUBHAIN** **A897** River Helmsdale Torrish

401 **CNOC NA MAOILE**

404 **CREAG THORARAIDH**

Ord of Caithness

3

421 **CNOC NAN CRÙBAG MÒR**

624 **BEINN DHORAIN**

Navidale Timespan M

Snow gates

20

Strath of Kildonan

591 **BEINN NA MÈILICH**

West Helmsdale

East Helmsdale

Helmsdale

Glen Loth

Gartymore

Portgower

ND

4

Balnacoil

539 **COL-BHEINN**

Lothmore

Lothbeg

10

5

Loch Brora

21

Dalchalm

Clynelish

378 **CAGAR FEOSAIG**

Brora

6

Doll

A9

Backies

Carn Liath

383 BHRAGGIE Rhives

Dunrobin Castle

'00

Golspie

7

Littleferry

street

urpenny

Embo

8

mbo Street

Royal Dornoch

90

ornoch

Tarbat Ness

9

Dornoch Point

Innis Mhor

Wilkhaven

Portmahomack

NJ

10

Inver B9165 Rockfield

Lower Arboll

Toulvaddie

Lochslin

80

Loch Eye

Rhynie

Hill of Fearn

Balmuchy

11

Fearn B9166 Tullich

Hilton of Cadboll Chapel (ruin)

Arabella

Hilton

Shandwick

Balintore

Ankerville

Shandwick Bay

12

igg

J K 90 L '00 M N P 10 Q R 20

B9040 A9

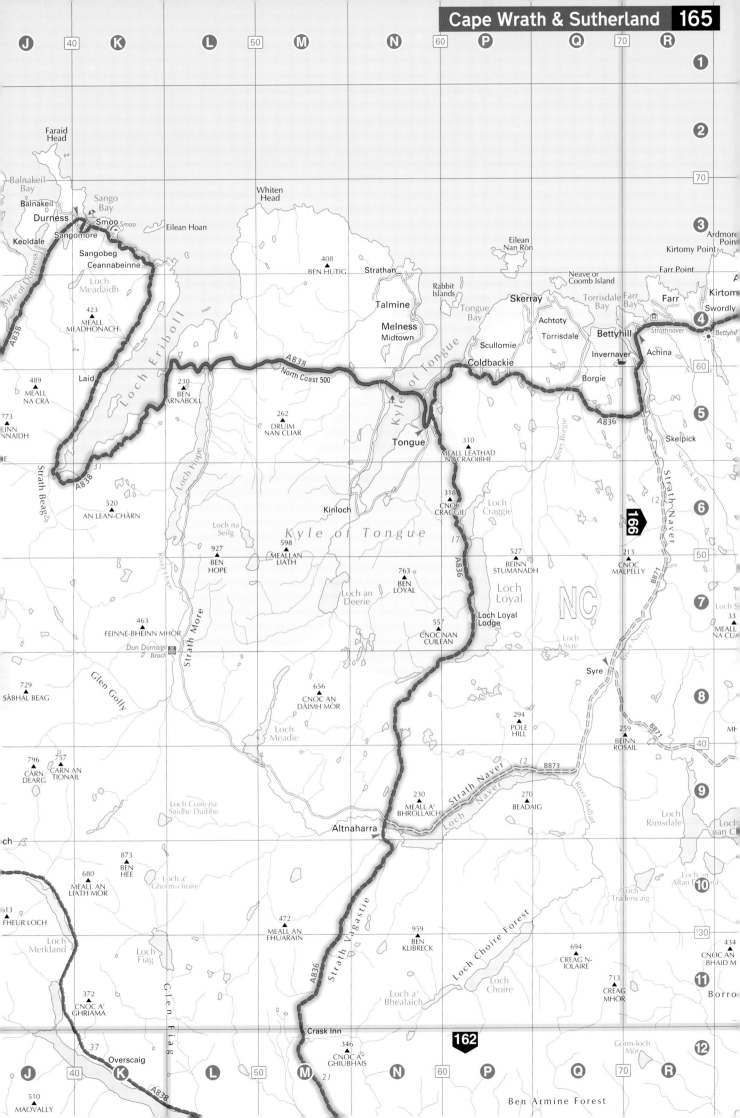

J 40 K 50 L M N 60 P Q 70 R

Faraid
Head

Balnakeil
Bay

Balnakeil
Durness
Keoldale
Sangomore
Sango
Bay
Smoo Smoo
Sangobeg
Ceannabeinne

Kyle of Durness
A838

Loch Meadaidh

423
▲
MEALL
MEADHONACH

489
▲
MEALL
NA CRÀ

773
▲
EINN
NNAIDH

Loch Eriboll

Strath Beag

A838 37

A838

Whiten
Head

Eilean Hoan

Laid

230
▲
BEN
ARNABOLL

262
▲
DRUIM
NAN CLIAR

520
▲
AN LEAN-CHÀRN

408
▲
BEN HUTIG

Strathan

Talmine

Melness
Midtown

A838

North Coast 500

Rabbit
Islands

Tongue
Bay

Skerray

Achtoty
Torrisdale

Scullomie

Coldbackie

Kyle of Tongue

Tongue

Loch Hope

Loch na
Seilg

598
▲
MEALLAN
LIATH

Kyle of Tongue

Eilean
Nan Ròn

Torrisdale
Bay

Farr
Bay

Farr

Bettyhill

Invernaver

Strathnaver

Kirtomy Point

Farr Point

Swordly

Kirtom

Bettyhil

Achina

M 60

Borgie

13

A836

River Borgie

Ardmore
Poin

L

Skelpick

Strath Naver

Skelpick Burn

310
▲
MEALL LEATHAD
NA CRAOIBHE

318
▲
CNOC
CRAGGIE

17

A836

Loch
Craggie

527
▲
BEINN
STUMANADH

213
▲
CNOC
MALPELLY

12

B871

166

50

927
▲
BEN
HOPE

Strath More

463
▲
FEINNE-BHEINN MHÒR

Dun Dornaigil
Broch

Glen Golly

729
▲
SÀBHAL BEAG

796
▲
CÀRN
DEARG

757
▲
CARN AN
TIONAIL

Loch an
Deerie

763
▲
BEN
LOYAL

557
▲
CNOC NAN
CUILEAN

Loch Loyal
Lodge

656
▲
CNOC AN
DÀIMH MÒR

Loch
Meadie

Loch Coire na
Saidhe Duibhe

613
▲
FHEUR LOCH

Loch
Merkland

680
▲
MEALL AN
LIATH MOR

873
▲
BEN
HEE

Loch a'
Ghorm-choire

Loch
Fiag

372
▲
CNOC A'
GHRIAMA

ch

Glen Fiag

472
▲
MEALL AN
FHUARAIN

Strath Vagastie

A836

Altnaharra

230
▲
MEALL A'
BHROLLAICH

Strath Naver

Loch Naver

959
▲
BEN
KLIBRECK

Loch
Loyal

NC

Loch
Syre

Syre

294
▲
POLE
HILL

270
▲
BEADAIG

12 B873

River Mallart

Loch Choire Forest

Loch a'
Bhealaich

Loch
Choire

694
▲
CREAG N-
IOLAIRE

713
▲
CREAG
MHOR

259
▲
BEINN
ROSAIL

B871

40

Loch
Rimsdale

Loch
Truderscaig

Loch an
Altan F na

30

434
▲
CNOC AN
BHAID M

Borro

Overscaig

A838

510
▲
MAOVALLY

J 40 K 37 L 50 M 60 N 60 P Q 70 R

346
▲
CNOC A'
GHIUBHAIS

Crask Inn

M 21

162

Gorm-loch
Mòr

Ben Armine Forest

33
▲
MEALL
NA CU

Loch S

50

7

MH

Loch
nan C

MEALL
NA CU

1
2
70
3
4
M 60
5
6
50
7
8
40
9
10
11
12

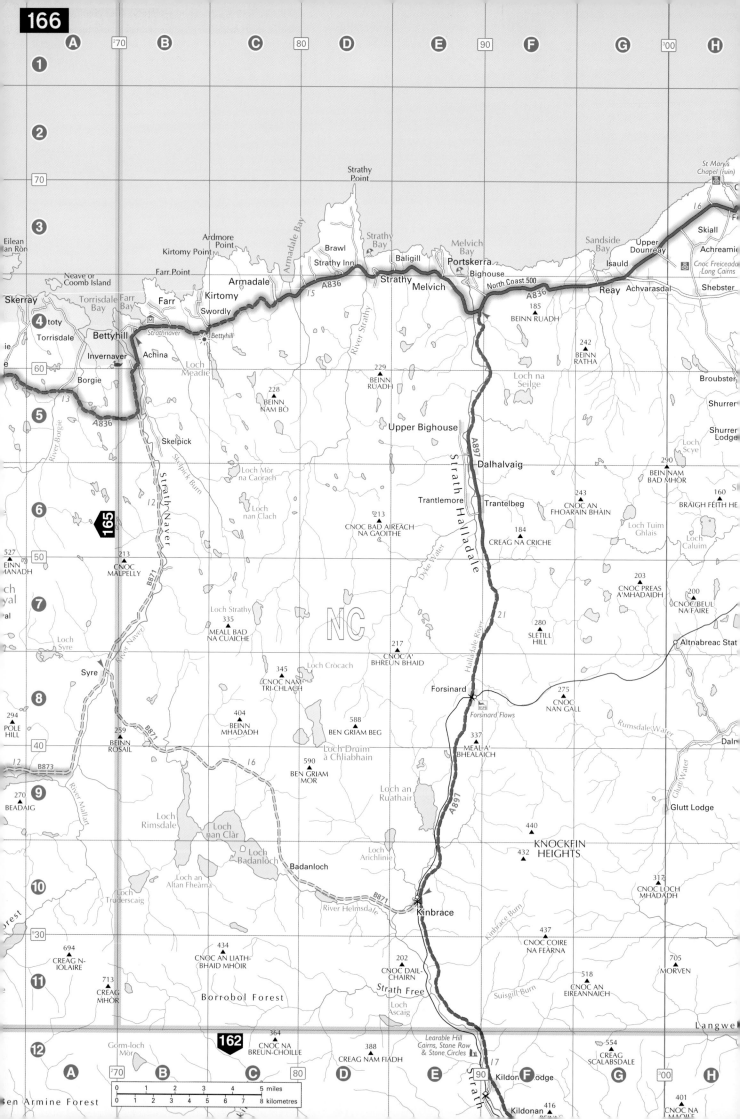

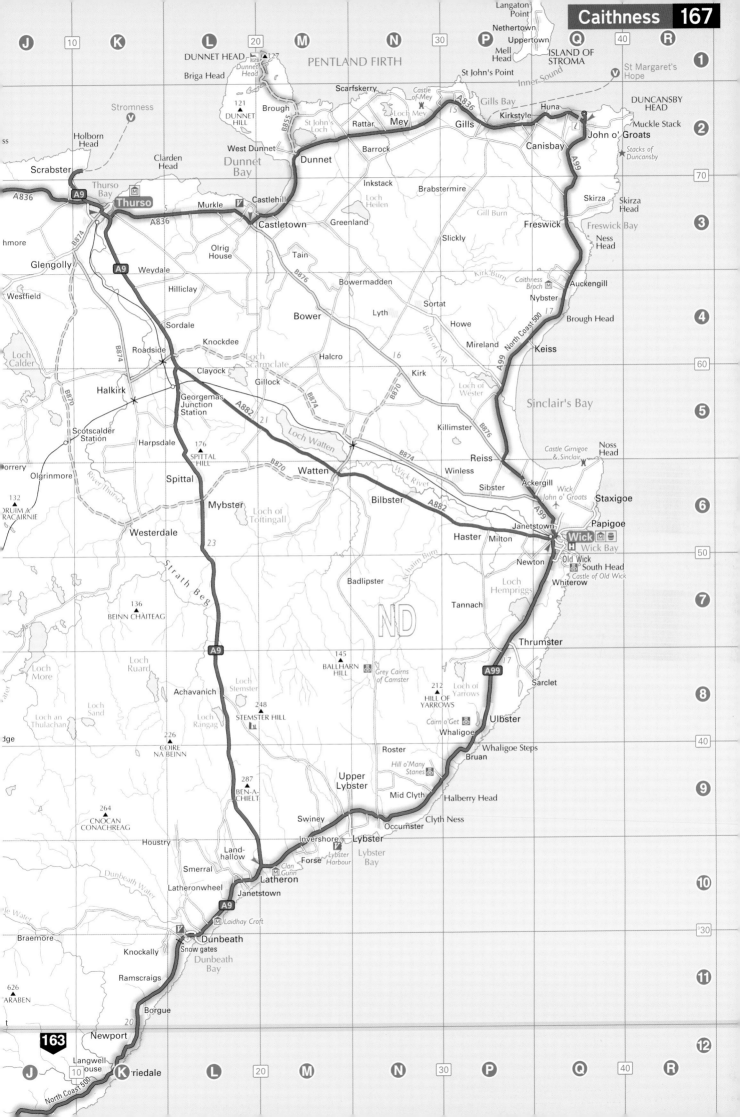

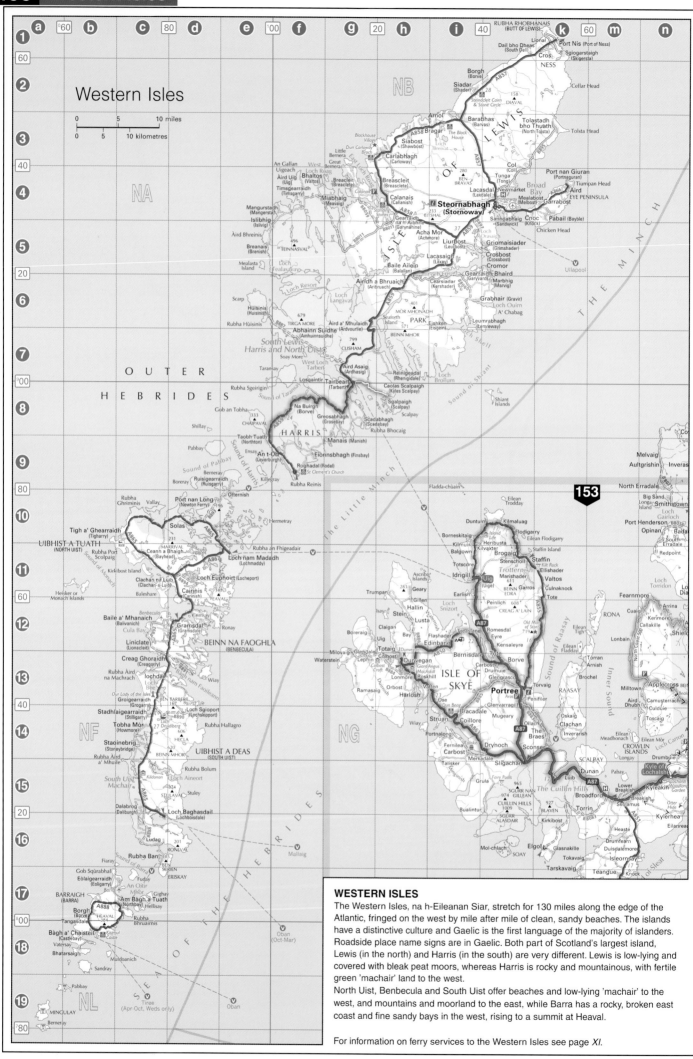

WESTERN ISLES

The Western Isles, na h-Eileanan Siar, stretch for 130 miles along the edge of the Atlantic, fringed on the west by mile after mile of clean, sandy beaches. The islands have a distinctive culture and Gaelic is the first language of the majority of islanders. Roadside place name signs are in Gaelic. Both part of Scotland's largest island, Lewis (in the north) and Harris (in the south) are very different. Lewis is low-lying and covered with bleak peat moors, whereas Harris is rocky and mountainous, with fertile green 'machair' land to the west.

North Uist, Benbecula and South Uist offer beaches and low-lying 'machair' to the west, and mountains and moorland to the east, while Barra has a rocky, broken east coast and fine sandy bays in the west, rising to a summit at Heaval.

For information on ferry services to the Western Isles see page XI.

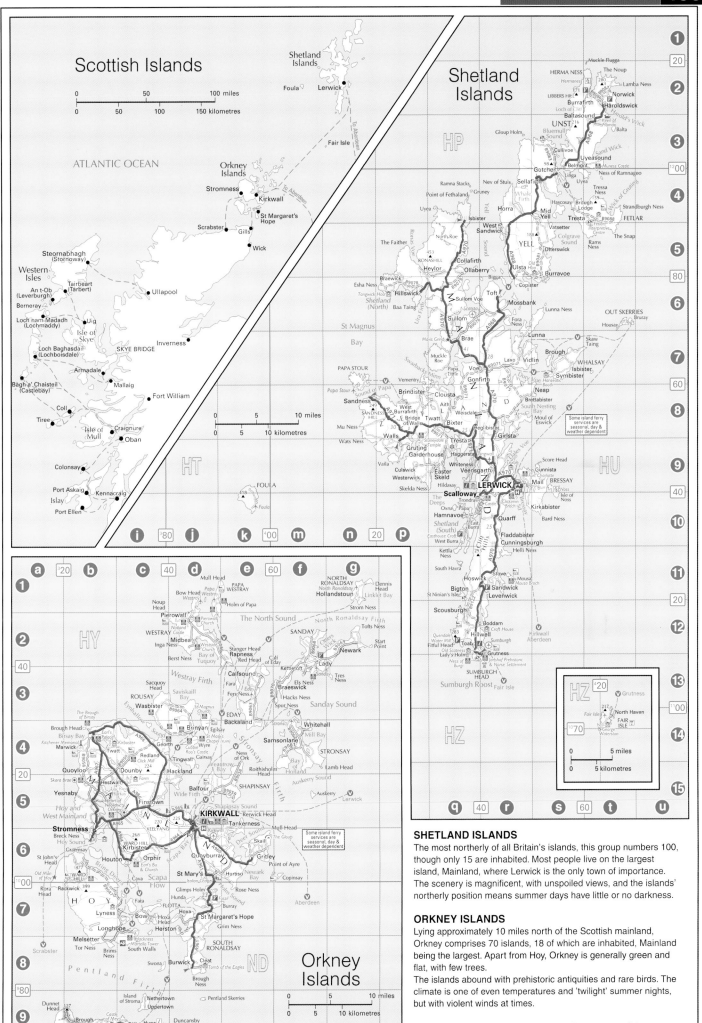

SHETLAND ISLANDS

The most northerly of all Britain's islands, this group numbers 100, though only 15 are inhabited. Most people live on the largest island, Mainland, where Lerwick is the only town of importance. The scenery is magnificent, with unspoiled views, and the islands' northerly position means summer days have little or no darkness.

ORKNEY ISLANDS

Lying approximately 10 miles north of the Scottish mainland, Orkney comprises 70 islands, 18 of which are inhabited, Mainland being the largest. Apart from Hoy, Orkney is generally green and flat, with few trees.

The islands abound with prehistoric antiquities and rare birds. The climate is one of even temperatures and 'twilight' summer nights, but with violent winds at times.

For information on ferry services to the Shetland and Orkney Islands see page XI.

Ireland index

Abbeydorney....C12
Abbeyfeale....D12
Abbeyleix....G11
Adamstown....H12
Adare....D12
Adrigole....C14
Aghalee....J5
Ahascragh....E9
Ahoghill....J4
Allenwood....H9
Allihies....B15
An Bun Beag....E4
An Charraig....E5
An Cheathrú Rua....C9
An Clochán Liath....E4
An Coireán....B14
An Daingean....B13
An Fál Carrach....F3
An Fhairche....C9
Annahilt....J6
Annalong....J7
Annascaul....B13
Annestown....G13
An Rinn....G13
An Spidéal....D9
Antrim....J5
Ardagh....D12
Ardara....E5
Ardee....H8
Ardfert....C12
Ardfinnan....F12
Ardglass....K6
Ardgroom....B14
Ardmore....F14
Ardnacrusha....E11
Arklow....J11
Armagh....H6
Armoy....J3
Arvagh....G7
Ashbourne....J9
Ashford....J10
Askeaton....D12
Athboy....H8
Athea....D12
Athenry....E9
Athleague....E8
Athlone....F9
Athy....H10
Augher....G6
Aughnacloy....H6
Aughrim....E9
Aughrim....J11
Avoca....J11

Bagenalstown....H11
Baile an Fheirtéaraigh....B13
Baile Chláir....D9
Baile Mhic Íre....D14
Baile na Finne....F4
Bailieborough....H7
Balbriggan....J8
Balla....D8
Ballacolla....G11
Ballaghaderreen....E7
Ballina....E11
Ballina....D7
Ballinafad....E7
Ballinagar....G9
Ballinagh....G7
Ballinamallard....G6
Ballinamore....F7
Ballinascarty....D14
Ballinasloe....E9
Ballincollig....E14
Ballindaggan....H12
Ballindine....D8
Ballineen....D14
Ballingarry....D12
Ballingarry....G12
Ballingeary....D14
Ballinlough....E8
Ballinrobe....D8
Ballinspittle....E14
Ballintra....F5
Ballivor....H9
Ballon....H11
Ballybay....H7
Ballybofey....F5
Ballybunion....C12
Ballycanew....J11
Ballycarry....K5

Ballycastle....J3
Ballycastle....C6
Ballyclare....J5
Ballyclerahan....F12
Ballyconneely....B9
Ballyconnell....G7
Ballycotton....F14
Ballycumber....F9
Ballydehob....C15
Ballyduff....C12
Ballyduff....E7
Ballyferriter....B13
Ballygally....J4
Ballygar....E9
Ballygawley....H6
Ballygawley....E6
Ballygowan....K5
Ballyhaise....G7
Ballyhalbert....K5
Ballyhaunis....E8
Ballyhean....D8
Ballyheige....C12
Ballyjamesduff....G8
Ballylanders....E12
Ballylickey....C14
Ballyliffin....G3
Ballylongford....H10
Ballylynan....H10
Ballymacarbry....F13
Ballymahon....F8
Ballymakeery....D14
Ballymena....J4
Ballymoe....E8
Ballymoney....H4
Ballymore....F9
Ballymore Eustace....H10
Ballymote....E7
Ballynacarrigy....G8
Ballynahinch....J6
Ballynure....J5
Ballyporeen....F13
Ballyragget....G11
Ballyroan....G10
Ballysadare....E6
Ballyshannon....F5
Ballyvaughan....D10
Ballywalter....K5
Balrothery....J8
Baltimore....C15
Baltinglass....H10
Banagher....F10
Banbridge....J6
Bandon....E14
Bangor....K5
Bangor Erris....C7
Bansha....F12
Banteer....D13
Bantry....C14
Barna....D9
Béal an Mhuirthead....B6
Béal Átha an Ghaorthaidh....D14
Bearna....D9
Belcoo....F6
Belfast....J5
Belgooly....E14
Bellaghy....H4
Belleek....F6
Belmullet....B6
Belturbet....G7
Benburb....H6
Bennettsbridge....G12
Beragh....G5
Bessbrook....J6
Bettystown....J8
Birr....F10
Blacklion....F6
Blackwater....J12
Blarney....E14
Blessington....H10
Boherbue....D13
Borris....H12
Borris-in-Ossory....F10
Borrisokane....F10
Borrisoleigh....F11
Boyle....E7
Bray....J10
Bridgetown....H13

Brittas....J9
Broadford....E11
Broadford....D12
Broughshane....J4
Bruff....E12
Bunbeg....E4
Bunclody....H11
Buncrana....G3
Bundoran....E6
Bunmahon....G13
Bunnyconnellan....D7
Bushmills....H3
Buttevant....E13
Bweeng....E13

Cadamstown....F10
Caherconlish....E12
Caherdaniel....B14
Cahersiveen....B14
Cahir....F12
Caledon....H6
Callan....G12
Caltra....E9
Camp....B13
Carndonagh....G3
Cappamore....E12
Cappawhite....E12
Cappoquin....F13
Carlanstown....H8
Carlingford....J7
Carlow....H11
Carna....C9
Carnew....J11
Carnlough....J4
Carragh....H9
Carraig Airt....F3
Carraroe....C9
Carrick....E5
Carrickfergus....K5
Carrickmacross....H7
Carrickmore....G5
Carrick-on-Shannon....F7
Carrick-on-Suir....G12
Carrigaline....E14
Carrigallen....F7
Carriganimmy....D13
Carrigart....F3
Carrigtwohill....E14
Carryduff....J5
Cashel....F12
Castlebar....D8
Castlebellingham....J7
Castleblakeney....E9
Castleblayney....H7
Castlebridge....J12
Castlecomer....G11
Castleconnell....E11
Castlederg....G5
Castledermot....H11
Castlegregory....B13
Castleisland....C13
Castlemaine....C13
Castlemartyr....F14
Castleplunket....E8
Castlepollard....G8
Castlerea....E8
Castlerock....H3
Castletownbere....B15
Castletownroche....E13
Castletownshend....D15
Castlewellan....J6
Cathair Dónall....B14
Causeway....C12
Cavan....G7
Celbridge....H9
Charlestown....D7
Charleville....E12
Cill Charthaigh....C9
Cill Chiaráin....C9
Clady....H4
Clane....H9
Clara....G9
Claregalway....D9
Claremorris....D8
Clashmore....F13
Claudy....G4
Cleggan....B8
Clifden....B9
Cliffoney....E6
Cloghan....F10
Clogheen....F13
Clogher....G6

Clogherhead....J8
Clogh Mills....J4
Clonakilty....D15
Clonaslee....G10
Clonbur....C9
Clondalkin....J9
Clonea....G13
Clones....G7
Clonmany....G3
Clonmel....F12
Clonmellon....H8
Clonroche....H12
Clough....K6
Cloughjordan....F10
Cloyne....F14
Coachford....D14
Coagh....H5
Coalisland....H5
Cobh....E14
Coleraine....H3
Collinstown....G8
Collon....H8
Collooney....E7
Comber....K5
Cong....D9
Convoy....F4
Cookstown....H5
Coole....G8
Cooraclare....C11
Cootehill....G7
Cork....E14
Cornamona....C9
Corr na Móna....C9
Corrofin....D10
Courtmacsherry....E15
Courtown....J11
Craigavon....H5
Craughwell....E10
Creeslough....F4
Croithlí....E4
Crolly....E4
Crookhaven....C15
Crookstown....D14
Croom....E12
Crossakeel....H8
Crosshaven....E14
Crossmaglen....H7
Crossmolina....D7
Crumlin....J5
Crusheen....D10
Culdaff....G3
Cullybackey....J4
Culmore....G4
Curracloe....J12
Curry....E7
Cushendall....J4
Cushendun....J3

Daingean....G9
Daingean Uí Chúis....B13
Delvin....H9
Derrinturn....H9
Derry....G4
Derrygonnelly....F6
Derrylin....G6
Dervock....H3
Dingle....B13
Doagh....J5
Donabate....J9
Donaghadee....K5
Donaghmore....H5
Donaghmore....H8
Donegal....F5
Donemana....G4
Doolin....C10
Doon....E12
Doonbeg....C11
Downings....F3
Downpatrick....K6
Dowra....F6
Draperstown....H4
Drimoleague....D14
Drogheda....J8
Droichead Nua....H10
Dromahair....E6
Dromara....J6
Dromcollogher....D12
Dromiskin....J7
Drommahane....E13
Dromod....F8
Dromore....J6

Dromore....G5
Dromore West....D6
Drumaness....K6
Drumfries....G3
Drumkeeran....F7
Drumlish....F8
Drumquin....G5
Drumshanbo....F7
Drumsna....F7
Duagh....C12
Dublin....J9
Duleek....J8
Dunboyne....J9
Dún Chaoin....A13
Dundalk....J7
Dundonald....K5
Dundrum....J6
Dunfanaghy....F3
Dungannon....H5
Dungarvan....G13
Dungiven....H4
Dunglow....E4
Dungourney....F14
Dunkineely....E5
Dún Laoghaire....J9
Dunlavin....H10
Dunleer....J8
Dunloy....J4
Dunmanway....D14
Dunmore....E8
Dunmore East....H13
Dunquin....A13
Dunshaughlin....H9
Durrow....G11
Durrus....C15
Dysart....E9

Easky....D6
Edenderry....H9
Edgeworthstown....G8
Eglinton....H4
Elphin....F8
Emyvale....H4
Enfield....H9
Ennis....D11
Enniscorthy....H12
Enniscrone....D6
Enniskean....D14
Enniskillen....G6
Ennistymon....D10
Eyrecourt....F10

Fahan....G4
Falcarragh....F3
Fanore....D10
Farranfore....C13
Feakle....E11
Fenagh....F7
Fenit....B13
Ferbane....F10
Fermoy....E13
Ferns....J12
Fethard....F12
Fethard....H13
Fintona....G6
Fintown....F4
Fivemiletown....G5
Foxford....D7
Foynes....D12
Freemount....D13
Frenchpark....E8
Freshford....G11

Galbally....E12
Galway....D9
Garrison....F6
Garvagh....H4
Gilford....J6
Glandore....D15
Glanworth....E13
Glaslough....H6
Glassan....F9
Gleann Cholm Cille....E5
Glenamaddy....E8
Glenarm....J5
Glenavy....J5
Glenbeigh....C13
Glencolumbkille....E5
Glenealy....J10
Glengarriff....C14
Glenties....E5

Glin....D12
Golden....F12
Goleen....C15
Goresbridge....H11
Gorey....J11
Gort....D10
Gorteen....E7
Gortin....H4
Gowran....H11
Graiguenamanagh....H12
Granard....G8
Grange....E6
Greencastle....H3
Greencastle....J6
Greenore....J7
Greyabbey....K5
Greystones....J10
Gulladuff....H4

Hacketstown....H11
Headford....D9
Hillsborough....J6
Hilltown....J6
Holycross....F12
Holywood....J5
Hospital....E12
Howth....J9

Inagh....D10
Inch....B13
Inchigeelagh....D14
Inishcrone....D6
Innishannon....E14
Irvinestown....F6

Johnstown....G11

Kanturk....D13
Keadue....F7
Keady....H6
Kealkill....C14
Keel....B7
Kells....J4
Kells....H8
Kenmare....C14
Kesh....F5
Kilbeggan....G9
Kilcar....E5
Kilcock....H9
Kilcolgan....D10
Kilconnell....E9
Kilcoole....J10
Kilcormac....F10
Kilcullen....H10
Kildare....H10
Kildorrery....E13
Kilfenora....D10
Kilfinane....E12
Kilgarvan....C14
Kilkee....C11
Kilkeel....J7
Kilkenny....G11
Kilkieran....C9
Kill....H9
Kill....G13
Killadysert....D11
Killala....D6
Killaloe....E11
Killarney....C13
Killashandra....G7
Killeagh....F14
Killenaule....F12
Killimer....C11
Killiney....J9
Killinick....J13
Killorglin....C13
Killough....K6
Killucan....G9
Killurin....G10
Killybegs....E5
Killyleagh....K6
Kilmacanogue....J10
Kilmacrenan....F4
Kilmacthomas....G13
Kilmaganny....G12
Kilmaine....D8
Kilmallock....E12
Kilmanagh....G11
Kilmeedy....D12
Kilmichael....D14
Kilmihil....C11
Kilmore Quay....H13

Kilmuckridge....J12
Kilpedder....J10
Kilrea....H4
Kilrush....C11
Kilsheelan....G12
Kiltegan....H11
Kiltimagh....D8
Kilworth....E13
Kingscourt....H7
Kinlough....E6
Kinnegad....G9
Kinnitty....F10
Kinsale....E14
Kinvarra....D10
Kircubbin....K5
Knock....D8
Knockcroghery....F8

Lahinch....C10
Lanesborough....F8
Laragh....J10
Larne....K4
Lauragh....C14
Laurencetown....F10
Leap....D15
Leenaun....C8
Leighlinbridge....H11
Leitrim....B9
Leitrim....F7
Leixlip....H9
Letterfrack....B8

Letterkenny....F4
Lifford....G4
Limavady....H4
Limerick....E11
Lisbellaw....G6
Liscarroll....D13
Lisdoonvarna....D10
Lisburn....J5
Lismore....F13
Lisnaskea....G6
Listowel....C12
Loghill....D12
Londonderry....G4
Longford....G8
Longwood....H9
Loughbrickland....J6
Loughglinn....E8
Loughrea....E9
Louisburgh....C8
Lucan....J9
Lurgan....J6
Lusk....J9

Macroom....D14
Maghera....H4
Magherafelt....H4
Maguiresbridge....G6
Maigh Cuilinn....D9
Malahide....J9
Málainn Mhóir....E5
Malin....G3

0   10   20 miles
0   10   20   30 kilometres

Malin More E5
Mallow E13
Manorhamilton F6
Markethill H6
Martinstown J4
Maynooth H9
Mayobridge J6
Midleton F14
Milford F4
Millstreet D13
Milltown C13
Milltown Malbay C11
Mitchelstown E13
Moate F9
Mohill F7
Monaghan H6
Monasterevin G10
Moneymore H5
Monivea E9
Mooncoin G13
Mountbellew E9
Mountcharles F5
Mountmellick G10
Mountrath G10
Mountshannon E10
Moville G3
Moy H6
Moycullen D9
Moynalty H8
Mucklagh G9
Muff G4

Muine Bheag H11
Mullagh H8
Mullaghmore E6
Mullinavat G12
Mullingar G9
Mulranny C7
Murrisk C8
Murroe E11

Naas H10
Na Dúnaibh F3
Naul J8
Navan H8
Nenagh E11
Newbawn H12
Newbliss G7
Newbridge H10
Newcastle J6
Newcastle West D12
Newmarket D13
Newmarket-on-
  Fergus D11
Newport C7
Newport E11
New Ross H12
Newry J6
Newtownabbey J5
Newtownards K5

Newtownbutler G7
Newtown-
  cunningham G4
Newtownforbes F8
Newtownhamilton ... H6
Newtownmount-
  kennedy J10
Newtownstewart G5
Nobber H8

Ogonnelloe E11
Oilgate H12
Oldcastle G8
Omagh G5
Omeath J7
Oola E12
Oranmore D9
Oughterard D9

Pallasgreen E12
Partry D8
Passage East H13
Passage West E14
Patrickswell E12
Pettigo G5
Piltown G12
Plumbridge G5
Pomeroy H5
Portadown H6
Portaferry K6
Portarlington G10

Portavogie K6
Portballintrae H3
Portglenone H4
Port Laoise G10
Portlaw G13
Portmagee B14
Portmarnock J10
Portnablagh F3
Portnoo E4
Portroe E11
Portrush H3
Portstewart H3
Portumna E11
Poyntzpass J6
Prosperous H9

Quin D11

Raharney G9
Ramelton F4
Randalstown J5
Raphoe G4
Rasharkin H4
Rathangan H10
Rathcoole J9
Rathcormac E13
Rathdowney G11
Rathdrum J10
Rathfriland J6
Rathkeale D12
Ráth Luirc E12

Rathmore D13
Rathmullan G4
Rathnew J10
Rathvilly H11
Ratoath J9
Recess C9
Rhode G9
Ringaskiddy E14
Ringville G13
Riverchapel J11
Riverstick E14
Rochfortbridge G9
Rockcorry H7
Roosky F8
Rosbercon H12
Roscommon F8
Roscrea F10
Rosscarbery D15
Rosses Point E6
Rosslare J13
Rosslare Harbour J13
Rosslea G6
Rossnowlagh F5
Rostrevor J7
Roundstone B9
Roundwood J10
Rush J9

Saintfield K6
St Johnston G4
Sallins H9

Salthill D9
Scarriff E11
Scartaglin C13
Schull C15
Seskinore G5
Shanagarry F14
Shannon D11
Shannonbridge F9
Shercock H7
Shillelagh H11
Shinrone F10
Shrule D9
Silvermines E11
Sion Mills G5
Sixmilebridge D11
Skerries J8
Skibbereen D15
Slane H8
Sligo E6
Smithborough G6
Sneem B14
Spanish Point C11
Spiddal D9
Sraith Salach C9
Stewartstown H5
Stoneyford G12
Strabane G4
Stradbally G10
Stradone G8
Strandhill E6
Strangford K6

Stranorlar F5
Strokestown F8
Summerhill H9
Swan G11
Swanlinbar F6
Swinford D7
Swords J9

Taghmon H12
Tagoat J13
Tallaght J9
Tallow F13
Tandragee J6
Tarbert C12
Templemore F11
Termonfeckin J8
Thomastown G12
Thurles F11
Timahoe G10
Timoleague D15
Tinahely J11
Tipperary F12
Tobercurry E7
Tobermore H4
Toomevara F11
Toomore C15
Toormore C15
Tower E14
Tralee C13
Tramore G13
Trim H8

Tubbercurry E7
Tulla D11
Tullamore G9
Tullow H11
Tulsk E8
Turlough D7

Urlingford G11

Virginia G8

Warrenpoint J7
Waterford G13
Watergrasshill E13
Waterville B14
Wellingtonbridge .. H13
Westport C8
Wexford J12
Whitegate E14
Whitehead K5
Wicklow J10
Woodenbridge J11
Woodford E10

Youghal F14

For Central London see pages 238-247

Town plan : Central London p.238-247

Street map symbols

Town, port and airport plans

2	Motorway and junction	→	One-way, gated/ closed road	⊷●	Railway station	**P P**	Car park, with electric charging point
4	Primary road single/ dual carriageway and numbered junction		Restricted access road	○	Light rapid transit system station	**P+R**	Park and Ride (at least 6 days per week)
37	A road single/ dual carriageway and numbered junction		Pedestrian area	✛	Level crossing		Bus/coach station
	B road single/ dual carriageway	-----	Footpath	●━●━●	Tramway	**H**	Hospital
	Local road single/ dual carriageway	- - - -	Road under construction	✈ Ⓗ	Airport, heliport	**H**	24-hour Accident & Emergency hospital
	Other road single/ dual carriageway, minor road	⌐-----⌐	Road tunnel	Ⓡ	Railair terminal		Beach (award winning)
	Building of interest	🗼	Lighthouse		Theatre or performing arts centre		City wall
	Ruined building	♜	Castle		Cinema		Escarpment
i	Tourist Information Centre	☀	Castle mound	†	Abbey, chapel, church		Cliff lift
V	Visitor or heritage centre	•	Monument, statue	✡	Synagogue		River/canal, lake
◉	World Heritage Site (UNESCO)	✉	Post Office	☾	Mosque		Lock, weir
M	Museum	📖	Public library	⚑	Golf course		Viewpoint
	English Heritage site		Shopping centre		Racecourse		Park/sports ground
	Historic Scotland site		Shopmobility		Nature reserve		Cemetery
	Cadw (Welsh heritage) site		Football stadium		Aquarium		Woodland
	National Trust site		Rugby stadium		Agricultural showground		Built-up area
	National Trust Scotland site		County cricket ground		Toilet, with facilities for the less able		Beach

Central London street map (see pages 238–247)

⊖	London Underground station	⊖	London Overground station
⊖	Docklands Light Railway (DLR) station		Central London Congestion Charge and Ultra Low Emission boundary

Royal Parks

Green Park	Park open 5am–midnight. Constitution Hill and The Mall closed to traffic Sundays and public holidays 8am–dusk.
Grosvenor Square Garden	Park open 7:30am–dusk.
Hyde Park	Park open 5am–midnight. Park roads closed to traffic midnight–5am.
Kensington Gardens	Park open 6am–dusk.
Regent's Park	Park open 5am–dusk. Park roads closed to traffic midnight–7am, except for residents.
St James's Park	Park open 5am–midnight. The Mall closed to traffic Sundays and public holidays 8am–dusk.
Victoria Tower Gardens	Park open dawn–dusk.

Traffic regulations in the City of London include security checkpoints and restrict the number of entry and exit points.

Note: Oxford Street is closed to through-traffic (except buses & taxis) 7am–7pm Monday–Saturday.

Central London Congestion Charge Zone (CCZ)

The charge for driving or parking a vehicle on public roads in this Central London area, during operating hours, is £11.50 per vehicle per day in advance or on the day of travel. Alternatively you can pay £10.50 by registering with CC Auto Pay, an automated payment system. Drivers can also pay the next charging day after travelling in the zone but this will cost £14. Payment permits entry, travel within and exit from the CCZ by the vehicle as often as required on that day.

The CCZ operates between 7am and 6pm, Mon–Fri only. There is no charge at weekends, on public holidays or between 25th Dec and 1st Jan inclusive.

For up to date information on the CCZ, exemptions, discounts or ways to pay, visit *www.tfl.gov.uk/modes/driving/congestion-charge*

Ultra Low Emission Zone (ULEZ)

All vehicles in Central London need to meet minimum exhaust emission standards or pay a daily Emission Surcharge. It applies to the same area covered by the Congestion Charge and operates 24 hours a day, every day of the year. The surcharge is £12.50 for motorcycles, cars and vans and is in addition to the Congestion Charge.

For further information visit *www.tfl.gov.uk/ULEZ*

In addition the Low Emission Zone (LEZ) operates across Greater London, 24 hours every day of the year and is aimed at the most heavy-polluting vehicles. It does not apply to cars or motorcycles. For details visit *www.tfl.gov.uk/LEZ*

Town Plans

Aberdeen	188	
Basingstoke	188	
Bath	189	
Birmingham	190	
Blackpool	189	
Bournemouth	191	
Bradford	191	
Brighton	192	
Bristol	192	
Cambridge	193	
Canterbury	194	
Cardiff	194	
Carlisle	195	
Cheltenham	195	
Chester	196	
Colchester	196	
Coventry	197	
Darlington	197	
Derby	198	
Doncaster	198	
Dover	199	
Dundee	199	
Durham	200	
Eastbourne	200	
Edinburgh	201	
Exeter	202	
Glasgow	203	
Gloucester	202	
Great Yarmouth	204	

Guildford	204
Harrogate	205
Huddersfield	205
Inverness	206
Ipswich	206
Kingston upon Hull	207
Lancaster	207
Leeds	208
Leicester	209
Lincoln	209
Liverpool	210
Llandudno	79
LONDON	238-247
Luton	211
Maidstone	211
Manchester	212
Margate	39
Middlesbrough	214
Milton Keynes	213
Newcastle upon Tyne	215
Newport	214
Newquay	4
Northampton	216
Norwich	216
Nottingham	217
Oldham	217
Oxford	218
Perth	219
Peterborough	219

Plymouth	220
Poole	222
Portsmouth	221
Preston	222
Ramsgate	39
Reading	223
Royal Tunbridge Wells	223
Salisbury	224
Sheffield	224
Shrewsbury	225
Southampton	226
Southend-on-Sea	225
Stirling	227
Stockton-on-Tees	227
Stoke-on-Trent (Hanley)	228
Stratford-upon-Avon	228
Sunderland	229
Swansea	230
Swindon	230
Taunton	231
Torquay	231
Warwick	232
Watford	232
Winchester	233
Wolverhampton	233
Worcester	234
York	234

Central London

PADDINGTON 238 | 239 | FINSBURY | 240 | 241 | CITY | STEPNEY
SOHO | 246 | 247
KENSINGTON 242 | 243 | 244 | 245 | SOUTHWARK | BERMONDSEY
WESTMINSTER
CHELSEA | KENNINGTON

Ferry Ports

Aberdeen Harbour	XI
Calais	IX
Dover, Port of	IX
Fishguard Harbour	X
Harwich International Port	53
Heysham Harbour	X
Holyhead Harbour	X
Hull, Port of	XI
Liverpool Docks	X
Newhaven Harbour	IX
Pembroke Dock	X
Plymouth, Port of	VIII
Poole, Port of	VIII
Port of Tyne	XI
Portsmouth Harbour	IX
Southampton, Port of	VIII

Channel Tunnel

Folkestone Terminal	27
Calais / Coquelles Terminal	27

Airports

Aberdeen	237
Birmingham	236
East Midlands	236
Edinburgh	237
Glasgow	237
Leeds Bradford	237
London City	236
London Gatwick	235
London Heathrow	235
London Luton	235
London Stansted	235
Manchester	236

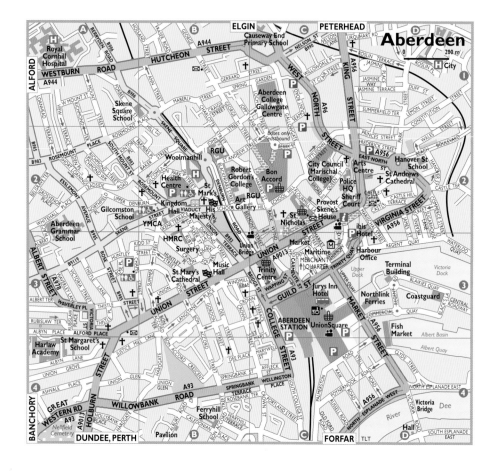

Aberdeen

Aberdeen is found on atlas page **151 N6**

Affleck Street	C4	Maberly Street	B1
Albert Street	A3	Marischal Street	D2
Albury Road	B4	Market Street	C3
Alford Place	A3	Nelson Street	C1
Ann Street	B1	Palmerston Road	C4
Beach Boulevard	D2	Park Street	D1
Belgrave Terrace	A2	Portland Street	C4
Berryden Road	A1	Poynernook Road	C4
Blackfriars Street	B2	Regent Quay	D3
Blaikies Quay	D3	Richmond Street	A2
Bon Accord Crescent	B4	Rose Place	A3
Bon Accord Street	B3	Rose Street	A3
Bridge Street	C3	Rosemount Place	A2
Caledonian Place	B4	Rosemount Viaduct	A2
Carmelite Street	C3	St Andrew Street	B1
Chapel Street	A3	St Clair Street	C1
Charlotte Street	B1	School Hill	C2
College Street	C3	Skene Square	B1
Constitution Street	D1	Skene Street	A3
Crimon Place	B3	Skene Terrace	B2
Crown Street	B3	South College Street	C4
Dee Street	B3	South Esplanade East	D4
Denburn Road	B2	South Mount Street	A2
Diamond Street	B3	Spa Street	B2
East North Street	D2	Springbank Street	B4
Esslemont Avenue	A2	Springbank Terrace	B4
Gallowgate	C1	Summer Street	B3
George Street	B1	Summerfield Terrace	D1
Gilcomston Park	B2	Thistle Lane	A3
Golden Square	B3	Thistle Place	A3
Gordon Street	B3	Thistle Street	A3
Great Western Road	A4	Trinity Quay	C3
Guild Street	C3	Union Bridge	B3
Hadden Street	C3	Union Grove	A3
Hanover Street	D2	Union Street	B3
Hardgate	B4	Union Terrace	B2
Harriet Street	C2	Upper Denburn	A2
Holburn Street	A4	Victoria Road	D4
Huntley Street	A3	Victoria Street	A3
Hutcheon Street	B1	View Terrace	A1
Jasmine Terrace	D1	Virginia Street	D2
John Street	B2	Wapping Street	C3
Justice Mill Lane	A4	Waverley Place	A3
King Street	C1	Wellington Place	C4
Langstane Place	B3	West North Street	C1
Leadside Road	A2	Westburn Road	A1
Loanhead Terrace	A1	Whitehall Place	A2
Loch Street	C1	Willowbank Road	A4

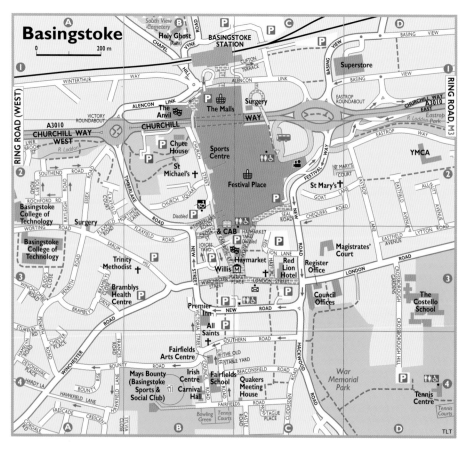

Basingstoke

Basingstoke is found on atlas page **22 H4**

Alencon Link	C1	London Street	C3
Allnutt Avenue	D2	Lower Brook Street	A2
Basing View	C1	Lytton Road	D3
Beaconsfield Road	C4	Market Place	B3
Bounty Rise	A4	May Place	C3
Bounty Road	A4	Montague Place	C4
Bramblys Close	A3	Mortimer Lane	A2
Bramblys Drive	A3	New Road	B3
Budd's Close	A3	New Road	B2
Castle Road	C4	New Street	B3
Chapel Street	B1	Penrith Road	A3
Chequers Road	C2	Rayleigh Road	A2
Chester Place	A4	Red Lion Lane	C3
Churchill Way	B2	Rochford Road	A2
Churchill Way East	D1	St Mary's Court	C2
Churchill Way West	A2	Sarum Hill	A3
Church Square	B2	Seal Road	C2
Church Street	B2	Solby's Road	A2
Church Street	B3	Southend Road	A2
Cliddesden Road	C4	Southern Road	B4
Clifton Terrace	C1	Stukeley Road	A3
Cordale Road	A4	Sylvia Close	B4
Council Road	B4	Timberlake Road	B2
Crossborough Gardens	D3	Victoria Street	B3
Crossborough Hill	D3	Victory Roundabout	A2
Cross Street	B3	Vyne Road	B1
Devonshire Place	A4	Winchcombe Road	A3
Eastfield Avenue	D2	Winchester Road	A2
Eastrop Lane	D2	Winchester Street	B3
Eastrop Roundabout	C1	Winterthur Way	A1
Eastrop Way	D2	Worting Road	A2
Essex Road	A2	Wote Street	C3
Fairfields Road	B4		
Festival Way	C2		
Flaxfield Court	A2		
Flaxfield Road	A3		
Flaxfield Road	B3		
Frances Road	A4		
Frescade Crescent	A4		
Goat Lane	C2		
Hackwood Road	C4		
Hamelyn Road	A4		
Hardy Lane	A4		
Hawkfield Lane	A4		
Haymarket Yard	C3		
Joices Yard	B3		
Jubilee Road	B4		
London Road	D3		

Bath

Bath is found on atlas page **20 D2**

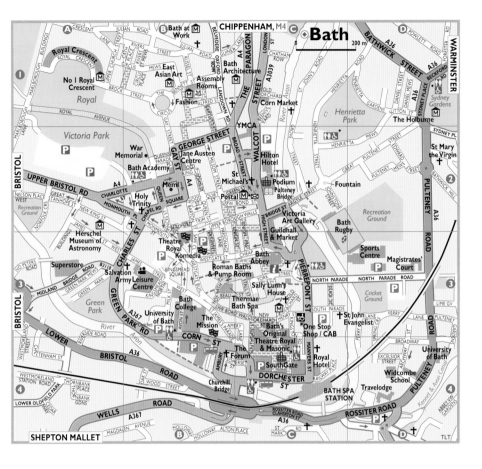

Archway Street	D4	Lower Borough Walls	B3
Argyle Street	C2	Lower Bristol Road	A3
Avon Street	B3	Lower Oldfield Park	A4
Bartlett Street	B1	Manvers Street	C3
Barton Street	B2	Midland Bridge Road	A3
Bathwick Street	D1	Milk Street	B3
Beauford Square	B2	Milsom Street	B2
Beau Street	B3	Monmouth Place	A2
Beckford Road	D1	Monmouth Street	B2
Bennett Street	B1	New Bond Street	B2
Bridge Street	C2	New King Street	A2
Broad Street	C2	New Orchard Street	C3
Broadway	D4	Norfolk Buildings	A3
Brock Street	A1	North Parade	C3
Chapel Road	B2	North Parade Road	D3
Charles Street	A3	Old King Street	B2
Charlotte Street	A2	Oxford Row	B1
Cheap Street	C3	Pierrepont Street	C3
Cheltenham Street	A4	Princes Street	B2
Circus Mews	B1	Pulteney Road	D2
Claverton Street	C4	Queen Square	B2
Corn Street	B4	Queen Street	B2
Daniel Street	D1	Railway Place	C4
Dorchester Street	C4	Rivers Street	B1
Edward Street	D2	Rossiter Road	C4
Ferry Lane	D3	Royal Avenue	A1
Gay Street	B1	Royal Crescent	A1
George Street	B2	St James's Parade	B3
Great Pulteney Street	C2	St John's Road	C1
Great Stanhope Street	A2	Saw Close	B3
Green Park Road	A3	Southgate Street	C4
Green Street	B2	South Parade	C3
Grove Street	C2	Stall Street	C3
Guinea Lane	B1	Sutton Street	D1
Henrietta Gardens	D1	Sydney Place	D1
Henrietta Mews	C2	The Circus	B1
Henrietta Road	C1	The Paragon	C1
Henrietta Street	C2	Thornbank Place	A4
Henry Street	C3	Union Street	B2
High Street	C2	Upper Borough Walls	B2
Hot Bath Street	B3	Upper Bristol Road	A2
James Street West	B3	Upper Church Street	A1
John Street	B2	Walcot Street	C2
Julian Road	B1	Wells Road	A4
Kingsmead North	B3	Westgate Buildings	B3
Kingston Road	B3	Westgate Street	B2
Lansdown Road	B1	Westmoreland Station Road	A4
London Street	C1	York Street	C3

Blackpool

Blackpool is found on atlas page **88 C3**

Abingdon Street	B1	Havelock Street	C4
Adelaide Street	B3	High Street	C1
Albert Road	B3	Hornby Road	B3
Albert Road	C3	Hornby Road	D3
Alfred Street	C2	Hull Road	B3
Ashton Road	D4	Kay Street	C4
Bank Hey Street	B2	Kent Road	C4
Banks Street	B1	King Street	C2
Belmont Avenue	C4	Leamington Road	D2
Bennett Avenue	D3	Leicester Road	D2
Bethesda Road	C4	Leopold Grove	C2
Birley Street	B2	Lincoln Road	D2
Blenheim Avenue	D4	Livingstone Road	C3
Bonny Street	B4	Lord Street	B1
Buchanan Street	C1	Louise Street	C4
Butler Street	C1	Milbourne Street	C1
Caunce Street	D1	Montreal Avenue	D3
Cedar Square	C2	New Bonny Street	B3
Central Drive	C4	New Larkhill Street	C1
Chapel Street	B4	Palatine Road	C4
Charles Street	C1	Palatine Road	D3
Charnley Road	C3	Park Road	D2
Cheapside	B2	Park Road	D4
Church Street	B2	Peter Street	D2
Church Street	C2	Pier Street	B4
Church Street	D2	Princess Parade	B1
Clifton Street	B2	Promenade	B1
Clinton Avenue	D4	Queen Street	B1
Cookson Street	C1	Raikes Parade	D2
Coop Street	C4	Reads Avenue	C3
Coronation Street	C3	Reads Avenue	D3
Corporation Street	B2	Regent Road	C2
Dale Street	B4	Ribble Road	C4
Deansgate	B2	Ripon Road	D3
Dickson Road	B1	Seasiders Way	B4
Edward Street	C2	Selbourne Road	D1
Elizabeth Street	D1	South King Street	C2
Fairhurst Street	D1	Springfield Road	B1
Fisher Street	C1	Stanley Road	C3
Fleet Street	C3	Talbot Road	B2
Foxhall Road	B4	Talbot Road	C1
Freckleton Street	D4	Topping Street	C2
General Street	B1	Vance Road	B3
George Street	C1	Victoria Street	B2
Gorton Street	D1	Victory Road	D1
Granville Road	D2	West Street	B2
Grosvenor Street	C1	Woolman Road	D4
Harrison Street	D4	York Street	B4

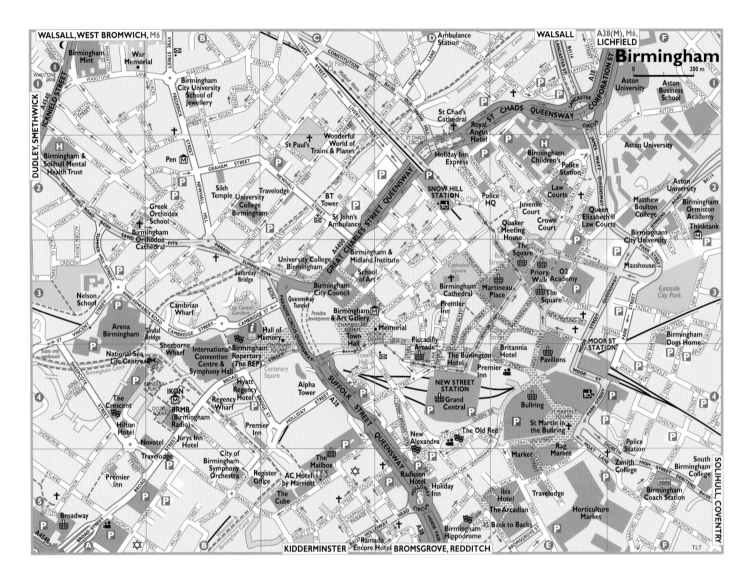

Birmingham

Birmingham is found on atlas page **58 G7**

Acorn Grove	A2	Caroline Street	B1
Albert Street	E3	Carrs Lane	E3
Albert Street	F3	Carver Street	A1
Albion Street	B2	Chamberlain Square	C3
Allison Street	F4	Chapmans Passage	C5
Anderton Street	A2	Charlotte Street	B3
Arthur Place	A2	Cheapside	F5
Aston Street	F1	Cherry Street	D3
Atlas Way	B4	Church Street	D2
Banbury Street	F3	Civic Close	B3
Barford Street	F5	Clement Street	A3
Bartholomew Street	F3	Cleveland Street	D1
Barwick Street	D3	Coleshill Street	F2
Bath Street	E1	Colmore Circus Queensway	E2
Beak Street	D4	Colmore Row	D3
Benacre Drive	F4	Commercial Street	C5
Bennetts Hill	D3	Constitution Hill	C1
Berkley Street	B4	Corporation Street	E1
Bishopgate Street	A5	Corporation Street	E3
Blucher Street	C5	Coventry Street	F4
Bond Street	C2	Cox Street	C1
Bordesley Street	F4	Dale End	E3
Bow Street	D5	Daley Close	A3
Bradford Street	F5	Dalton Street	E2
Bridge Street	B4	Dean Street	E5
Brindley Drive	B3	Digbeth	E4
Brindley Place	B4	Dudley Street	D4
Broad Street	A5	Eden Place	C3
Bromsgrove Street	E5	Edgbaston Street	E4
Brook Street	C2	Edmund Street	D3
Brunel Street	C4	Edward Street	B3
Bull Street	E3	Ellis Street	D5
Cambridge Street	B3	Essington Street	A5
Camden Drive	B2	Ethel Street	D4
Camden Street	A2	Etna Street	F2
Cannon Street	D3		

Exeter Street	D5	King Edward's Drive	A4
Fazeley Street	F3	King Edwards Road	A3
Fleet Street	C3	Ladywell Walk	D5
Fox Street	F3	Lancaster Circus	E1
Frederick Street	B1	Lancaster Street	E1
Freeman Street	E3	Lawson Street	E1
Gas Street	B4	Legge Lane	B2
George Street	B2	Lighthouse Avenue	A3
Gloucester Street	E5	Lionel Street	C3
Goodman Street	A2	Livery Street	C1
Gough Street	C5	Louisa Street	B3
Graham Street	B2	Loveday Street	E1
Granville Street	B5	Lower Loveday Street	D1
Great Charles Street		Lower Temple Street	D4
Queensway	C3	Ludgate Hill	C2
Grosvenor Street	F2	Margaret Street	C3
Grosvenor Street West	A5	Marshall Street	C5
Hall Street	B1	Martineau Way	E3
Hampton Street	D1	Mary Ann Street	C1
Helena Street	B3	Mary Street	C1
Henrietta Street	C1	Meriden Street	F4
High Street	E4	Mill Lane	F5
High Street Deritend	F5	Moat Lane	E4
Hill Street	C4	Moor Street	E4
Hinckley Street	D4	Moor Street Queensway	E4
Hingeston Street	A1	Moreton Street	A1
Holland Street	B2	Navigation Street	C4
Holliday Street	B5	Needless Alley	D3
Holloway Circus	D5	Nelson Street	A3
Holloway Head	C5	New Bartholomew Street	F4
Holt Street	F1	New Canal Street	F4
Horse Fair	D5	Newhall Hill	B2
Hospital Street	D1	Newhall Street	C2
Hurst Street	D5	New Meeting Street	E3
Icknield Street	A1	New Street	D3
Inge Street	D5	Newton Street	E2
James Street	B2	Northwood Street	C1
James Watt Queensway	E2	Old Snow Hill	D1
Jennens Road	F2	Old Square	E3
John Bright Street	D4	Oozells Square	B4
Kenyon Street	B1	Oxford Street	F5

King Edward's Drive	A4	Parade	B3
King Edwards Road	A3	Paradise Circus Queensway	C3
Ladywell Walk	D5	Paradise Street	C4
Lancaster Circus	E1	Park Street	E4
Lancaster Street	E1	Pemberton Street	A1
Lawson Street	E1	Pershore Street	E5
Legge Lane	B2	Pope Street	A1
Lighthouse Avenue	A3	Powell Street	A2
Lionel Street	C3	Price Street	E1
Livery Street	C1	Princip Street	E1
Louisa Street	B3	Printing House Street	E2
Loveday Street	E1	Queens Drive	D4
Lower Loveday Street	D1	Queensway Tunnel	C3
Lower Temple Street	D4	Rea Street	F5
Ludgate Hill	C2	Regent Parade	B1
Margaret Street	C3	Regent Place	B1
Marshall Street	C5	Regent Street	B1
Martineau Way	E3	Ridley Street	C5
Mary Ann Street	C1	Ruston Street	A5
Mary Street	C1	Ryland Street	A5
Meriden Street	F4	St Chads Queensway	E1
Mill Lane	F5	St Jude's Pass	D5
Moat Lane	E4	St Marks Crescent	A3
Moor Street	E4	St Martin's Square	E4
Moor Street Queensway	E4	St Paul's Square	C1
Moreton Street	A1	St Philip's Place	D3
Navigation Street	C4	St Vincent Street	A3
Needless Alley	D3	Sand Pitts	A2
Nelson Street	A3	Saturday Bridge	B3
New Bartholomew Street	F4	Scotland Street	B3
New Canal Street	F4	Severn Street	C5
Newhall Hill	B2	Shadwell Street	D1
Newhall Street	C2	Shaw's Passage	F4
New Meeting Street	E3	Sheepcote Street	A4
New Street	D3	Sherborne Street	A4
Newton Street	E2	Sloane Street	B2
Northwood Street	C1	Smallbrook Queensway	D5
Old Snow Hill	D1	Snow Hill Queensway	D2
Old Square	E3	Spencer Street	B1
Oozells Square	B4	Staniforth Street	E1
Oxford Street	F5	Station Street	D5

Steelhouse Lane	E2
Stephenson Street	D4
Suffolk Street Queensway	C4
Summer Hill Road	A2
Summer Hill Street	A2
Summer Hill Terrace	A2
Summer Lane	D1
Summer Row	B3
Swallow Street	C4
Temple Row	D3
Temple Row West	D3
Temple Street	D3
Tenby Street	A1
Tenby Street North	A1
Tennant Street	A5
The Priory Queensway	E3
Thorp Street	D5
Tindal Bridge	B3
Trent Street	F4
Union Street	E3
Upper Dean Street	E5
Upper Gough Street	C5
Vesey Street	E1
Victoria Square	C3
Vittoria Street	B1
Vyse Street	B1
Warstone Lane	A1
Washington Street	C5
Waterloo Street	C3
Water Street	C2
Weaman Street	D2
Whittall Street	E2
William Street	B5
Woodcock Street	F1

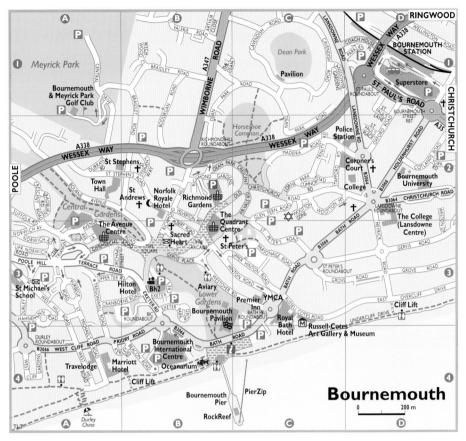

Bournemouth

Bournemouth is found on atlas page **13 J6**

Albert Road	B3	Old Christchurch Road	C2
Avenue Lane	A3	Orchard Street	A3
Avenue Road	A3	Oxford Road	D2
Bath Hill Roundabout	C3	Park Road	D1
Bath Road	B4	Parsonage Road	C3
Beacon Road	B4	Poole Hill	A3
BIC Roundabout	B3	Priory Road	A4
Bodorgan Road	B2	Purbeck Road	A3
Bourne Avenue	A2	Richmond Gardens	B2
Bournemouth Street		Richmond Hill	B3
Roundabout	D1	Richmond Hill Roundabout	B2
Bradburne Road	A2	Russell Cotes Road	C3
Braidley Road	B1	St Michael's Road	A3
Cavendish Road	C1	St Paul's Lane	D1
Central Drive	A1	St Paul's Place	D2
Christchurch Road	D2	St Paul's Road	D1
Coach House Place	D1	St Pauls Roundabout	D1
Commercial Road	A3	St Peter's Road	C3
Cotlands Road	D2	St Peter's Roundabout	C3
Cranborne Road	A3	St Stephen's Road	A2
Crescent Road	A2	St Stephen's Way	B2
Cumnor Road	C2	St Valerie Road	B1
Dean Park Crescent	B2	Stafford Road	C2
Dean Park Road	B2	Suffolk Road	A2
Durley Road	A3	Terrace Road	A3
Durley Roundabout	A4	The Arcade	B3
Durrant Road	A2	The Deans	B1
East Overcliff Drive	D3	The Square	B3
Exeter Crescent	B3	The Triangle	A3
Exeter Park Road	B3	Tregonwell Road	A3
Exeter Road	B3	Trinity Road	C2
Fir Vale Road	C2	Undercliff Drive	D3
Gervis Place	B3	Upper Hinton Road	C3
Gervis Road	D3	Upper Norwich Road	A3
Glen Fern Road	C2	Upper Terrace Road	A3
Grove Road	C3	Wellington Road	D1
Hahnemann Road	A3	Wessex Way	A2
Hinton Road	B3	West Cliff Gardens	A4
Holdenhurst Road	D2	West Cliff Road	A4
Kerley Road	A4	West Hill Road	A3
Lansdowne Gardens	C1	Weston Drive	D2
Lansdowne Road	C1	Westover Road	B3
Lansdowne Roundabout	D2	Wimborne Road	B1
Lorne Park Road	C2	Wootton Gardens	C2
Madeira Road	C2	Wootton Mount	C2
Meyrick Road	D3	Wychwood Close	B1
Norwich Avenue	A3	Yelverton Road	B2
Norwich Road	A3	York Road	D2

Bradford

Bradford is found on atlas page **90 F4**

Aldermanbury	B3	Lower Kirkgate	C2
Bank Street	B2	Lumb Lane	A1
Barkerend Road	D2	Manchester Road	B4
Barry Street	B2	Manningham Lane	A1
Bolling Road	C4	Manor Row	B1
Bolton Road	C2	Market Street	B3
Bridge Street	C3	Midland Road	B1
Broadway	C3	Morley Street	A4
Burnett Street	D2	Neal Street	B4
Canal Road	C1	Nelson Street	B4
Carlton Street	A3	North Brook Street	C1
Centenary Square	B3	Northgate	B2
Chandos Street	C4	North Parade	B1
Chapel Street	D3	North Street	C2
Cheapside	B2	North Wing	D1
Chester Street	A4	Otley Road	D1
Church Bank	C2	Paradise Street	A2
Claremont	A4	Peckover Street	D2
Croft Street	C4	Piccadilly	B2
Darfield Street	A1	Pine Street	C2
Darley Street	B2	Princes Way	B3
Drewton Road	A2	Randall Well Street	A3
Dryden Street	D4	Rawson Road	A2
Duke Street	B2	Rawson Square	B2
East Parade	D3	Rebecca Street	A2
Edmund Street	A4	St Blaise Way	C1
Edward Street	C4	St Thomas's Road	A2
Eldon Place	A1	Sawrey Place	A4
Filey Street	D3	Senior Way	B4
George Street	C3	Shipley Airedale Road	C1
Godwin Street	B2	Stott Hill	C2
Grattan Road	A2	Sunbridge Road	A2
Great Horton Road	A4	Tetley Street	A3
Grove Terrace	A2	Thornton Road	A3
Hallfield Road	A1	Trafalgar Street	B1
Hall Ings	B4	Tyrrel Street	B3
Hammerton Street	D3	Upper Park Gate	D2
Hamm Strasse	B1	Upper Piccadilly	B2
Holdsworth Street	C1	Valley Road	C1
Houghton Place	A1	Vicar Lane	C3
Howard Street	A4	Wakefield Road	D4
Hustlergate	B3	Wapping Road	D1
Infirmary Street	A1	Water Lane	A2
John Street	B2	Wellington Street	C2
Lansdowne Place	A4	Westgate	A2
Leeds Road	D3	Wharf Street	C1
Little Horton	A4	Wigan Street	A2
Little Horton Lane	B4	Wilton Street	A4

Brighton

Brighton

Brighton is found on atlas page **24 H10**

Ardingly Street	D3	Madeira Place	D4
Ashton Rise	D1	Manchester Street	C4
Bartholomew Square	B3	Margaret Street	D4
Black Lion Street	B3	Marine Parade	D4
Blaker Street	D3	Market Street	B3
Bond Street	B2	Marlborough Place	C2
Boyces Street	A3	Meeting House Lane	B3
Brighton Place	B3	Middle Street	B3
Broad Street	D4	Morley Street	D1
Buckingham Road	A1	New Dorset Street	B1
Camelford Street	D4	New Road	B2
Cannon Place	A3	New Steine	D4
Carlton Hill	D2	Nile Street	B3
Centurion Road	A1	North Gardens	B1
Chapel Street	D3	North Place	C2
Charles Street	C4	North Road	B1
Cheltenham Place	C1	North Street	B2
Church Street	A1	Old Steine	C3
Church Street	B2	Portland Street	B2
Circus Street	C2	Powis Grove	A1
Clifton Hill	A1	Prince Albert Street	B3
Clifton Terrace	A1	Prince's Street	C3
Devonshire Place	D3	Queen's Gardens	B1
Dukes Lane	B3	Queen Square	A2
Duke Street	B2	Queen's Road	B2
East Street	C3	Regency Road	A2
Edward Street	D3	Regent Hill	A2
Elmore Street	D1	Regent Street	C2
Foundry Street	B1	Robert Street	C1
Frederick Street	B1	St James's Street	D3
Gardner Street	B2	St Nicholas Road	A1
George Street	D3	Ship Street	B3
Gloucester Place	C1	Spring Gardens	B1
Gloucester Road	B1	Steine Street	C4
Gloucester Street	C1	Sussex Street	D2
Grand Junction Road	B4	Sydney Street	C1
Grand Parade	C2	Tichborne Street	B2
High Street	D3	Tidy Street	C1
Ivory Place	D1	Upper Gardner Street	B1
John Street	D2	Upper Gloucester Road	A1
Jubilee Street	C2	Upper North Street	A2
Kensington Gardens	C1	Vine Street	C1
Kensington Street	C1	Wentworth Street	D4
Kew Street	B1	Western Road	A2
King's Road	A3	West Street	A3
Kingswood Street	C2	White Street	D3
Leopold Road	A1	William Street	D2
Little East Street	B4	Windsor Street	B2

Bristol

Bristol is found on atlas page **31 Q10**

Anchor Road	A3	Passage Street	C2
Avon Street	D3	Pembroke Street	C1
Baldwin Street	B2	Penn Street	C1
Bath Bridge	D4	Pero's Bridge	B3
Bond Street	C1	Perry Road	A2
Bond Street	D2	Philadelphia Street	C2
Broadmead	C1	Portwall Lane	C4
Broad Plain	D2	Prewett Street	C4
Broad Quay	B3	Prince Street	B3
Broad Street	B2	Queen Charlotte Street	B3
Broad Weir	C2	Queen Square	B3
Canons Way	A3	Redcliffe Hill	C4
Canynge Street	C3	Redcliffe Parade West	B4
Castle Street	C2	Redcliffe Way	C4
College Green	A3	Redcliff Mead Lane	C4
Colston Avenue	B2	Redcliff Street	C3
Colston Street	B2	Royal Fort Road	A1
Commercial Road	B4	Rupert Street	B2
Corn Street	B2	St Augustine's Parade	A3
Countership	C3	St George's Road	A3
Cumberland Road	A4	St Matthias Park	D1
Deanery Road	A3	St Michael's Hill	A1
Denmark Street	A3	St Stephen's Street	B2
Explore Lane	A3	St Thomas Street	C3
Fairfax Street	C2	Small Street	B2
Ferry Street	C3	Somerset Street	C4
Friary	D3	Southwell Street	A1
Frogmore Street	A2	Tankards Close	A1
Great George Street	A3	Telephone Avenue	B3
Great George Street	D1	Temple Back	C3
Guinea Street	B4	Temple Back East	D3
Haymarket	C1	Temple Gate	D4
Hill Street	A2	Temple Street	C3
Horfield Road	B1	Temple Way	D3
Jacob Street	D2	The Grove	B4
King Street	B3	The Horsefair	C1
Lewins Mead	B2	The Pithay	C2
Lodge Street	A2	Tower Hill	D2
Lower Castle Street	D2	Trenchard Street	A2
Lower Church Lane	A2	Tyndall Avenue	A1
Lower Maudlin Street	B1	Union Street	C1
Marlborough Hill	B1	Upper Maudlin Street	B1
Marlborough Street	B1	Victoria Street	C2
Marsh Street	B3	Wapping Road	B4
Museum Street	A4	Welsh Back	B3
Newgate	C2	Whitson Street	B1
Old Market Street	D2	Wine Street	C2
Park Street	A2	Woodland Road	A1

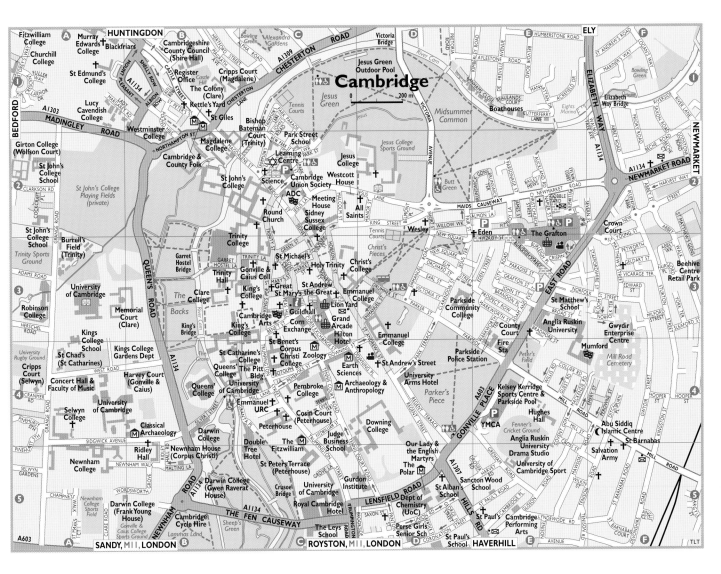

Cambridge

Cambridge is found on atlas page **62 G9**

Abbey Road	F1
Abbey Street	F2
Abbey Walk	F3
Acrefield Drive	E1
Adam and Eve Street	E3
Albion Row	B1
Alpha Road	C1
Auckland Road	E2
Aylestone Road	E1
Bailey Mews	E2
Banhams Close	D1
Beaulands Court	E1
Beche Road	F2
Belmont Place	D2
Belvoir Road	E1
Bene't Street	C3
Bloom Street	F3
Bradmore Street	E3
Brandon Place	E3
Bridge Street	C2
Broad Street	E3
Brookside	D5
Brunswick Gardens	E2
Brunswick Terrace	E2
Burleigh Place	E3
Burleigh Street	E3
Cambridge Place	E5
Castle Row	B1
Castle Street	B1
Champneys Walk	A5
Chesterton Lane	B1
Chesterton Road	C1
Christchurch Street	E2
City Road	E3
Clarendon Street	D3
Cobble Yard	E2

Collier Road	E4
Corn Exchange Street	C3
Coronation Street	D5
Covent Garden	E4
Crispin Place	E2
Cross Street	E4
Crusoe Bridge	B5
Cutler Ferry Close	E1
Cutterferry Lane	E1
De Freville Avenue	E1
Devonshire Road	F5
Ditchburn Place	F4
Downing Place	C4
Downing Street	C4
Drosier Road	D5
Drummer Street	D3
Earl Street	D3
East Road	E3
Eden Street	E3
Eden Street Back	E3
Edward Street	F3
Elizabeth Way	F1
Elm Street	D3
Emery Street	F4
Emmanuel Road	D3
Emmanuel Street	D3
Evening Court	E2
Fairsford Place	F3
Fair Street	E2
Fitzroy Lane	E2
Fitzroy Street	E3
Fitzwilliam Street	C4
Garret Hostel Bridge	B3
Garret Hostel Lane	B3
Geldart Street	F3
George IV Street	D5

Glisson Road	E5
Godstone Road	F2
Gonville Place	D4
Grange Road	A3
Grange Road	A4
Granta Place	B4
Green Street	C3
Gresham Road	E5
Gwydir Street	F4
Harvest Way	F2
Harvey Road	E5
Hertford Street	B1
Hills Road	D5
Hobson Street	C3
Humberstone Road	E1
James Street	E2
Jesus Lane	C2
Jesus Terrace	D3
John Street	E3
Kimberley Road	E1
King's Bridge	B3
King's Parade	C3
Kingston Street	F4
King Street	D2
Lady Margaret Road	A1
Lensfield Road	D5
Logan's Way	F1
Lwr Park Street	C2
Lyndewode Road	E5
Mackenzie Road	E4
Madingley Road	A1
Magdalene Street	B2
Magrath Avenue	B1
Maids Causeway	D2
Malcolm Street	C2
Malting Lane	B5
Manhattan Drive	E1
Manor Street	D2
Mariner's Way	F1
Market Street	C3
Mawson Road	E5

Milford Street	F3
Mill Lane	C4
Mill Road	E4
Mill Street	E4
Mortimer Road	E4
Mount Pleasant	B1
Napier Street	E2
Newmarket Road	E2
Newnham Road	B5
Newnham Walk	A5
New Park Street	C2
New Square	D3
New Street	F2
Norfolk Street	E3
Norfolk Terrace	F3
Northampton Street	B2
Occupation Road	F2
Orchard Street	D3
Panton Street	D5
Paradise Street	E3
Parker Street	D3
Park Parade	C1
Parkside	D3
Park Street	C2
Park Terrace	D4
Parsonage Street	E2
Peas Hill	C3
Pembroke Street	C4
Perowne Street	F4
Petworth Street	F3
Pound Hill	B1
Priory Road	F1
Prospect Row	E3
Queen's Lane	B4
Regent Street	D4
Regent Terrace	D4
River Lane	F1
Riverside	F1
St Andrew's Road	F1
St Andrew's Street	D3
St Barnabas Road	F5

St Mary's Street	C3
St Matthew's Gardens	F2
St Matthew's Street	F3
St Paul's Road	E5
St Peter's Street	B1
Salmon Lane	E2
Saxon Road	F1
Saxon Street	D5
Severn Place	F2
Shelly Row	B1
Short Street	D2
Sidgwick Avenue	A4
Sidney Street	C2
Silver Street	B4
Staffordshire Street	F3
Sturton Street	F3
Sussex Street	C3
Tenison Avenue	E5
Tenison Road	E5
Tennis Court Road	C4
Tennis Court Terrace	C4
The Fen Causeway	B5
Thompson's Lane	C2
Trinity Lane	C3
Trinity Street	C3
Trumpington Road	C5
Trumpington Street	C4
Union Road	D5
Vicarage Terrace	E3
Victoria Avenue	D1
Victoria Bridge	D1
Victoria Street	C3
Warkworth Street	E3
Warkworth Terrace	E4
Wellington Street	E2
West Road	A4
Wilkin Street	E4
Willis Road	E4
Willow Walk	D2
Wordsworth Grove	A5
Young Street	F3

University Colleges

Christ's College	C3
Clare College	A3
Clare College	B1
Clare College	B3
Corpus Christi College	C4
Darwin College	B4
Downing College	D4
Emmanuel College	C3
Emmanuel College	D3
Fitzwilliam College	A1
Girton College (Wolfson Court)	A2
Gonville & Caius College	C3
Gonville & Caius College	B4
Jesus College	C2
King's College	B3
Lucy Cavendish College	A1
Magdalene College	B2
Murray Edwards College	A1
Newnham College	A5
Pembroke College	C4
Peterhouse	C4
Queens' College	B4
Robinson College	A3
St Catharine's College	C4
St Edmund's College	A1
St John's College	B2
Selwyn College	A4
Sidney Sussex College	C2
Trinity College	B3
Westminster College	B1

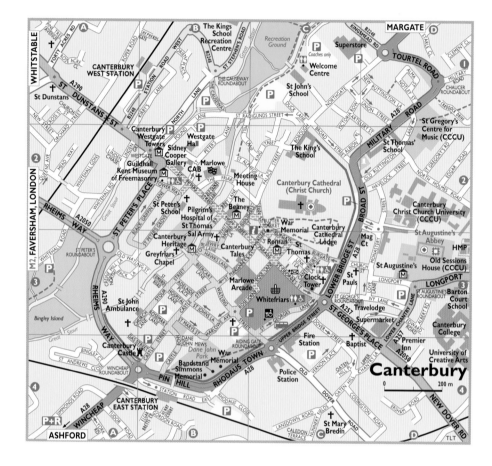

Canterbury

Canterbury is found on atlas page **39 K10**

Adelaide Place	B3	Nunnery Fields	C4
Albion Place	C2	Oaten Hill	C4
Alma Street	D1	Old Dover Road	C4
Artillery Street	C1	Old Ruttington Lane	D2
Beercart Lane	B3	Orchard Street	A2
Best Lane	B2	Palace Street	C2
Black Griffin Lane	A3	Parade	C3
Borough	C2	Pin Hill	B4
Broad Street	D2	Pound Lane	B2
Burgate	C3	Queens Avenue	A2
Butter Market	C2	Rheims Way	A3
Canterbury Lane	C3	Rhodaus Town	B4
Castle Row	B4	Rose Lane	B3
Castle Street	B3	Rosemary Lane	B3
Cossington Road	C4	St Alphege Lane	B2
Dover Street	C3	St Dunstans Street	A1
Duck Lane	C1	St Edmunds Road	B3
Edgar Road	D2	St George's Lane	C3
Edward Road	D3	St George's Place	C3
Ersham Road	D4	St George's Street	C3
Gas Street	A4	St Gregory's Road	D2
Gordon Road	B4	St Johns Lane	B3
Guildhall Street	B2	St Margaret's Street	B3
Havelock Street	D2	St Marys Street	B3
Hawks Lane	B3	St Peter's Grove	B3
High Street	B2	St Peter's Lane	B2
Hospital Lane	B3	St Peter's Place	A3
Ivy Lane	C3	St Peters Street	B2
Jewry Lane	B3	St Radigunds Street	B1
King Street	C2	Station Road East	B4
Kirby's Lane	B1	Station Road West	A1
Lansdown Road	C4	Stour Street	B3
Linden Grove	A2	Sturry Road	D1
Longport	D3	Sun Street	C2
Love Lane	D3	The Causeway	B1
Lower Bridge Street	C3	The Friars	B2
Lower Chantry Lane	D4	Tourtel Road	D1
Marlowe Avenue	B3	Tower Way	B2
Mead Way	A2	Tudor Road	A4
Mercery Lane	C3	Union Street	D1
Military Road	D2	Upper Bridge Street	C4
Mill Lane	B1	Vernon Place	C4
Monastery Street	D3	Victoria Row	C1
New Dover Road	D4	Watling Street	B3
New Ruttington Lane	D1	Whitehall Gardens	A2
North Lane	B1	Whitehall Road	A2
Northgate	C1	Wincheap	A4
Notley Street	D1	York Road	A4

Cardiff

Cardiff is found on atlas page **30 G9**

Adam Street	C3	Museum Avenue	B1
Adams Court	D2	Museum Place	B1
Adamscroft Place	D3	Newport Road	D1
Atlantic Wharf	D4	Newport Road Lane	D2
Boulevard de Nantes	B1	North Luton Place	D2
Bridge Street	C3	North Road	A1
Brigantine Place	D4	Oxford Lane	D1
Bute Street	C4	Oxford Street	D1
Bute Terrace	C3	Park Grove	B1
Callaghan Square	B4	Park Lane	B1
Caroline Street	B3	Park Place	B1
Castle Lane	D1	Park Street	A3
Castle Street	A2	Pellett Street	C3
Central Link	D3	Pendyris Street	A4
Charles Street	B2	Quay Street	A3
Churchill Way	C2	Queen Street	B2
City Hall Road	A1	Richmond Crescent	C1
City Road	D1	Richmond Road	C1
Crockherbtown Lane	B2	St Andrew's Crescent	B1
Custom House Street	B4	St Andrew's Lane	C1
David Street	C3	St Andrew's Place	B1
Davis Street	D3	St John Street	B2
Duke Street	A2	St Mary Street	B3
Dumfries Place	C2	St Peter's Street	C1
East Bay Close	D3	Salisbury Road	C1
East Grove	D1	Sandon Street	C3
Fford Churchill	C2	Saunders Road	B4
Fitzalan Place	D2	Schooner Way	D4
Fitzalan Road	D2	Stuttgarter Strasse	B1
Fitzhamon Embankment	A4	The Friary	B2
Glossop Road	D1	The Hayes	B3
Greyfriars Road	B2	The Parade	D1
Guildford Street	C3	The Walk	C1
Guildhall Place	A3	Trinity Street	B3
Havelock Street	B3	Tudor Street	A4
Hayes Bridge Road	B3	Tyndall Street	D4
Heol Siarl	B2	Vere Street	D1
Herbert Street	C4	Wesley Lane	C2
High Street	B3	West Canal Wharf	B4
High Street Arcade	B2	West Grove	C1
Hills Street	B3	Westgate Street	A3
King Edward VII Avenue	A1	Wharton Street	B3
Knox Road	D2	Windsor Lane	C2
Lloyd George Avenue	C4	Windsor Place	C1
Mary Ann Street	C3	Windsor Road	D3
Mill Lane	B4	Womanby Street	A3
Moira Place	D2	Wood Street	A4
Moira Terrace	D2	Working Street	B3

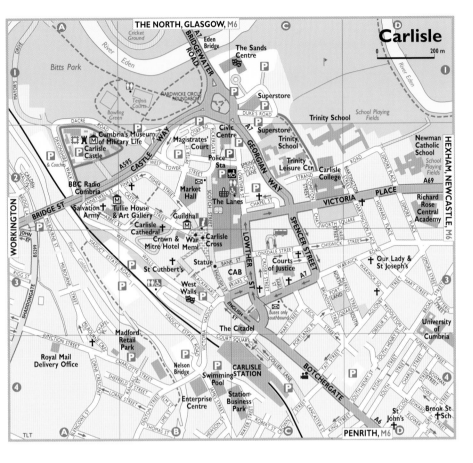

Carlisle

Carlisle is found on atlas page **110 G9**

Abbey Street	A2	Howard Place	D2
Aglionby Street	D3	Howe Street	D4
Annetwell Street	A2	James Street	B4
Bank Street	B3	John Street	A3
Blackfriars Street	B3	Junction Street	A4
Blencowe Street	A4	King Street	C4
Botchergate	C4	Lancaster Street	C4
Bridge Lane	A2	Lime Street	B4
Bridge Street	A2	Lismore Place	D2
Bridgewater Road	B1	Lismore Street	D3
Broad Street	D3	Lonsdale Street	C3
Brunswick Street	C3	Lorne Crescent	A4
Caldew Maltings	A2	Lorne Street	A4
Castle Street	B2	Lowther Street	C3
Castle Way	B2	Mary Street	C3
Cecil Street	C3	Mayor's Drive	A1
Chapel Place	A3	Milbourne Crescent	A3
Chapel Street	C2	Milbourne Street	A3
Charles Street	D4	Myddleton Street	D3
Charlotte Street	B4	North Alfred Street	D3
Chatsworth Square	C2	Orfeur Street	D3
Chiswick Street	C3	Peter Street	B2
Close Street	D4	Petteril Street	D3
Collier Lane	C4	Portland Place	C4
Compton Street	C2	Portland Square	C3
Corp Road	B2	Randall Street	B4
Court Square	B4	Rickergate	B2
Crosby Street	C3	Rigg Street	A3
Crown Street	C4	Robert Street	C4
Currie Street	C3	Rydal Street	D4
Dacre Road	A1	Scotch Street	B2
Denton Street	B4	Shaddongate	A3
Devonshire Walk	A2	Sheffield Street	A4
Duke's Road	C1	South Alfred Street	D3
Edward Street	D4	South Henry Street	D4
Elm Street	B4	Spencer Street	C2
English Street	B3	Spring Gardens Lane	C2
Finkle Street	B2	Strand Road	C2
Fisher Street	B2	Tait Street	C4
Flower Street	D4	Thomas Street	B4
Friars Court	C3	Viaduct Estate Road	A3
Fusehill Street	D4	Victoria Place	D3
Georgian Way	C2	Victoria Viaduct	B4
Grey Street	D4	Warwick Road	D3
Hartington Place	D2	Warwick Square	D3
Hartington Street	D2	Water Street	C4
Hart Street	D3	West Tower Street	B2
Hewson Street	B4	West Walls	B3

Cheltenham

Cheltenham is found on atlas page **46 H10**

Albion Street	C2	Montpellier Parade	B4
All Saints' Road	D2	Montpellier Spa Road	B4
Ambrose Street	B1	Montpellier Street	A4
Argyll Road	D4	Montpellier Terrace	A4
Back Montpellier Terrace	A4	Montpellier Walk	A4
Bath Road	B4	New Street	A1
Bath Street	C3	North Street	B2
Bayshill Road	A3	Old Bath Road	D4
Bayshill Villas Lane	A3	Oriel Road	B3
Bennington Street	B1	Parabola Lane	A3
Berkeley Street	C3	Parabola Road	A3
Burton Street	A1	Park Street	A1
Carlton Street	D3	Pittville Circus	D1
Church Street	B2	Pittville Circus Road	D1
Clarence Parade	B2	Pittville Street	B2
Clarence Road	C1	Portland Street	C1
Clarence Street	B2	Prestbury Road	C1
College Road	C4	Priory Street	D3
Crescent Terrace	B2	Promenade	B3
Devonshire Street	A1	Queens Parade	A3
Duke Street	D3	Regent Street	B2
Dunalley Street	B1	Rodney Road	B3
Evesham Road	C1	Royal Well Lane	A2
Fairview Road	C2	Royal Well Road	B2
Fairview Street	D2	St Anne's Road	D2
Fauconberg Road	A3	St Anne's Terrace	D2
Glenfall Street	D1	St George's Place	B2
Grosvenor Street	C3	St George's Road	A2
Grove Street	A1	St George's Street	B1
Henrietta Street	B1	St James' Square	A2
Hewlett Road	D3	St James Street	C3
High Street	A1	St Johns Avenue	C2
High Street	C2	St Margaret's Road	B1
Imperial Lane	B3	St Paul's Street South	B1
Imperial Square	B3	Sandford Street	C3
Jersey Street	D1	Selkirk Street	D1
Jessop Avenue	A2	Sherborne Street	C2
Keynsham Road	D4	Station Street	A1
King Street	A1	Suffolk Parade	B4
Knapp Road	A1	Swindon Road	B1
Lansdown Road	A4	Sydenham Villas Road	D3
Leighton Road	D2	Trafalgar Street	B4
London Road	D3	Union Street	D2
Malden Road	D1	Wellington Street	C3
Market Street	A1	Winchcombe Street	C2
Milsom Street	A1	Winstonian Road	D2
Monson Avenue	B1	Witcombe Place	C3
Montpellier Grove	B4	York Street	D1

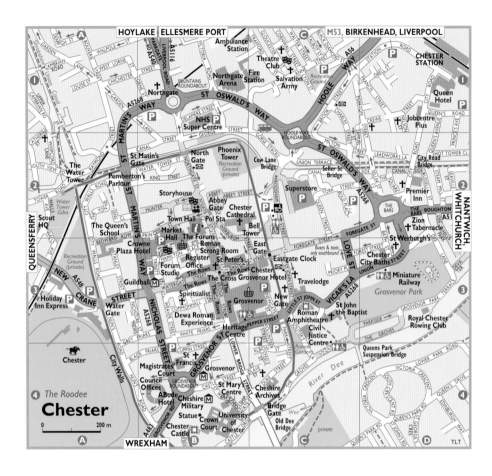

Chester

Chester is found on atlas page **81 N11**

Albion Street	C4	Nicholas Street	B3
Bath Street	D2	Northgate Street	B2
Black Diamond Street	C1	Nun's Road	A3
Boughton	D2	Parkgate Road	B1
Bouverie Street	A1	Park Street	C3
Bridge Street	B3	Pepper Street	C3
Brook Street	C1	Princess Street	B2
Canal Side	C2	Priory Place	C3
Castle Street	B4	Queen's Park Road	C4
Charles Street	C1	Queen's Road	D1
Chichester Street	A1	Queen Street	C2
City Road	D2	Raymond Street	A2
City Walls Road	A2	Russell Street	D2
Commonhall Street	B3	St Anne Street	C1
Cornwall Street	C1	St John's Road	D4
Crewe Street	D1	St John Street	C3
Cuppin Street	B4	St Martin's Way	A2
Dee Hills Park	D2	St Mary's Hill	B4
Dee Lane	D2	St Olave Street	C4
Delamere Street	B1	St Oswald's Way	B1
Duke Street	C4	St Werburgh Street	B2
Eastgate Street	B3	Samuel Street	C2
Egerton Street	C1	Seller Street	D2
Foregate Street	C2	Shipgate Street	B4
Forest Street	C3	Souter's Lane	C3
Francis Street	D1	South View Road	A2
Frodsham Street	C2	Stanley Street	A3
Garden Lane	A1	Station Road	D1
George Street	B2	Steam Mill Street	D2
Gloucester Street	C1	Steele Street	C4
Gorse Stacks	C2	Talbot Street	A2
Grosvenor Park Terrace	D3	Tower Road	A2
Grosvenor Road	B4	Trafford Street	C1
Grosvenor Street	B4	Trinity Street	B3
Hamilton Place	B3	Union Street	D3
Hoole Way	C1	Union Terrace	C2
Hunter Street	B2	Upper Cambrian Road	A1
King Street	B2	Vicar's Lane	C3
Leadworks Lane	D2	Victoria Crescent	D4
Little St John Street	C3	Victoria Road	B1
Liverpool Road	B1	Volunteer Street	C3
Lorne Street	A1	Walpole Street	A1
Love Street	C3	Walter Street	C1
Lower Bridge Street	B4	Watergate Street	B3
Lower Park Road	D4	Water Tower Street	B2
Milton Street	C2	Weaver Street	B3
New Crane Street	A3	White Friars	B3
Newgate Street	C3	York Street	C2

Colchester

Colchester is found on atlas page **52 G6**

Abbey Gates	C3	Middleborough	B1
Alexandra Road	A3	Middleborough Roundabout	A1
Alexandra Terrace	A4	Military Road	D4
Balkerne Hill	A3	Mill Street	D4
Beaconsfield Avenue	A4	Napier Road	C4
Burlington Road	A3	Nicholsons Green	D3
Butt Road	A4	North Bridge	B1
Castle Road	D1	Northgate Street	B1
Cedar Street	B3	North Hill	B1
Chapel Street North	B3	North Station Road	B1
Chapel Street South	B3	Nunn's Road	B1
Church Street	B3	Osborne Street	C3
Church Walk	B3	Papillon Road	A3
Circular Road East	C4	Pope's Lane	A2
Circular Road North	B4	Portland Road	C4
Creffield Road	A4	Priory Street	D3
Cromwell Road	C4	Queen Street	C3
Crouch Street	A3	Rawstorn Road	A2
Crouch Street	B3	Roman Road	D1
Crowhurst Road	A2	St Alban's Road	A2
Culver Street East	C2	St Augustine Mews	D2
Culver Street West	B2	St Botolph's Circus	C3
East Hill	D2	St Botolph's Street	C3
East Stockwell Street	C2	St Helen's Lane	C2
Essex Street	B3	St John's Avenue	B3
Fairfax Road	C4	St John's Street	B3
Flagstaff Road	C4	St Julian Grove	D3
Garland Road	A4	St Mary's Fields	A2
George Street	C2	St Peter's Street	B1
Golden Noble Hill	D4	Salisbury Avenue	A4
Gray Road	A3	Sheepen Place	A1
Headgate	B3	Sheepen Road	A1
Head Street	B2	Short Wyre Street	C3
Henry Laver Court	A2	Sir Isaac's Walk	B3
High Street	B2	South Street	B4
Hospital Road	A4	Southway	B3
Hospital Lane	A3	Stanwell Street	B3
Land Lane	D2	Trinity Street	B3
Lewis Gardens	D2	Walsingham Road	B3
Lexden Road	A3	Wellesley Road	A4
Lincoln Way	D1	Wellington Street	B3
Long Wyre Street	C2	West Stockwell Street	B1
Lucas Road	C4	West Street	B4
Magdalen Street	D3	Westway	A2
Maidenburgh Street	C1	Whitewell Road	C3
Maldon Road	A4	Wickham Road	A4
Manor Road	A3	William's Walk	C2
Mersea Road	C4	Winnock Road	D4

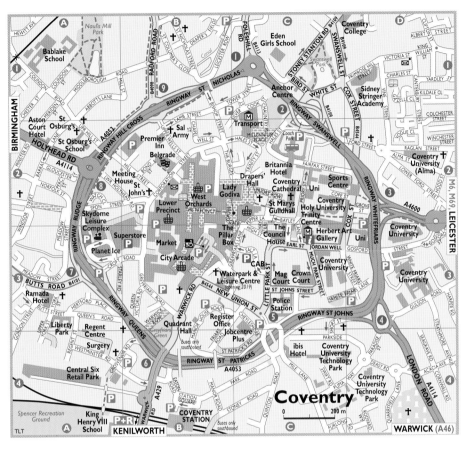

Coventry

Coventry is found on atlas page **59 M9**

Abbotts Lane	A1	Much Park Street	C3
Acacia Avenue	D4	New Union Street	B3
Alma Street	D2	Norfolk Street	A2
Barras Lane	A2	Park Road	B4
Bayley Lane	C2	Parkside	C4
Bird Street	C1	Primrose Hill Street	D1
Bishop Street	B1	Priory Row	C2
Broadgate	B2	Priory Street	C2
Butts Road	A3	Puma Way	C4
Butts Street	A3	Quarryfield Lane	D4
Canterbury Street	D1	Queen's Road	A3
Chester Street	A2	Queen Victoria Road	B3
Cheylesmore	C3	Quinton Road	C4
Cornwall Road	D4	Radford Road	B1
Corporation Street	B2	Raglan Street	D2
Coundon Road	A1	Regent Street	A4
Cox Street	D1	Ringway Hill Cross	A2
Cox Street	D2	Ringway Queens	A3
Croft Road	A3	Ringway Rudge	A3
Earl Street	C3	Ringway St Johns	C3
Eaton Road	B4	Ringway St Nicholas	B1
Fairfax Street	C2	Ringway St Patricks	B4
Foleshill Road	C1	Ringway Swanswell	C1
Gloucester Street	A2	Ringway Whitefriars	D2
Gosford Street	D3	St Johns Street	C3
Greyfriars Lane	B3	St Nicholas Street	B1
Greyfriars Road	B3	Salt Lane	B3
Grosvenor Road	A4	Seagrave Road	D4
Gulson Road	D3	Spon Street	A2
Hales Street	C2	Starley Road	A3
Hertford Place	A3	Stoney Road	B4
High Street	C3	Stoney Stanton Road	C1
Hill Street	B2	Strathmore Avenue	D3
Holyhead Road	A2	Swanswell Street	C1
Jordan Well	C3	The Burges	B2
Lamb Street	B2	Tower Street	B1
Leicester Row	B1	Trinity Street	C2
Little Park Street	C3	Upper Hill Street	B2
London Road	D4	Upper Wells Street	A4
Lower Ford Street	D2	Victoria Street	D1
Lower Holyhead Road	A2	Vine Street	D1
Manor House Road	B4	Warwick Road	B3
Manor Road	B4	Warwick Road	B4
Meadow Street	A3	Westminster Road	A4
Meriden Street	A1	White Friars Street	D3
Middleborough Road	A1	White Street	C1
Mile Lane	C4	Windsor Street	A3
Mill Street	A1	Yardley Street	D1

Darlington

Darlington is found on atlas page **103 Q8**

Abbey Road	A3	Maude Street	A2
Albert Street	D4	Melland Street	D3
Appleby Close	D4	Neasham Road	D4
Barningham Street	B1	Northgate	C2
Bartlett Street	B1	North Lodge Terrace	B2
Beaumont Street	B3	Northumberland Street	B4
Bedford Street	C4	Oakdene Avenue	A4
Beechwood Avenue	A4	Outram Street	A2
Blackwellgate	B3	Parkgate	D3
Bondgate	B2	Park Lane	D4
Borough Road	D3	Park Place	C4
Brunswick Street	C3	Pendower Street	B1
Brunton Street	D4	Pensbury Street	D4
Chestnut Street	C1	Polam Lane	B4
Cleveland Terrace	A4	Portland Place	A3
Clifton Road	C4	Powlett Street	B3
Commercial Street	B2	Priestgate	C3
Coniscliffe Road	A4	Raby Terrace	B3
Corporation Road	B1	Russell Street	C2
Crown Street	C2	St Augustine's Way	B2
Dodds Street	B1	St Cuthbert's Way	C2
Duke Street	A3	St Cuthbert's Way	C4
Easson Road	B1	St James Place	D4
East Mount Road	D1	Salisbury Terrace	A1
East Raby Street	B3	Salt Yard	B3
East Street	C3	Scarth Street	A4
Elms Road	A2	Skinnergate	B3
Elwin Lane	B4	Southend Avenue	A4
Feethams	C4	Stanhope Road North	A2
Fife Road	A3	Stanhope Road South	A3
Four Riggs	B2	Stonebridge	C3
Freeman's Place	C2	Sun Street	B2
Gladstone Street	B2	Swan Street	C4
Grange Road	B4	Swinburne Road	A3
Greenbank Road	A1	Trinity Road	A2
Greenbank Road	B2	Tubwell Row	B3
Hargreave Terrace	C4	Uplands Road	A3
Haughton Road	D2	Valley Street North	C2
High Northgate	C1	Vane Terrace	A2
High Row	B3	Victoria Embankment	C4
Hollyhurst Road	A1	Victoria Road	B4
Houndgate	B3	Victoria Road	C4
John Street	C1	West Crescent	A2
John Williams Boulevard	D3	West Powlett Street	A3
Kendrew Street	B2	West Row	B3
Kingston Street	B1	West Street	B4
Langholm Crescent	A4	Woodland Road	A2
Larchfield Street	A3	Yarm Road	D3

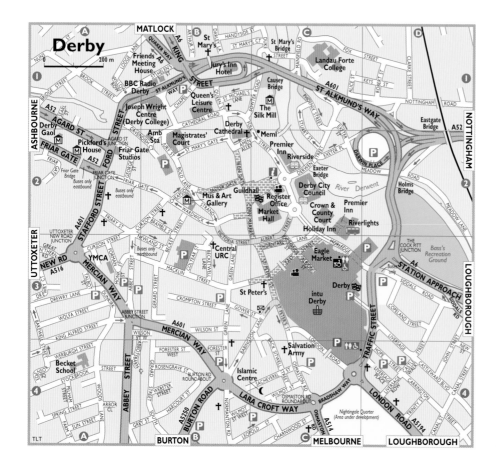

Derby

Derby is found on atlas page **72 B3**

Abbey Street	A4	King Alfred Street	A3
Agard Street	A1	King Street	B1
Albert Street	C3	Lara Croft Way	B4
Babington Lane	B4	Leopold Street	B4
Back Sitwell Street	C4	Liversage Row	D4
Becket Street	B3	Liversage Street	D3
Bold Lane	B2	Lodge Lane	A1
Bradshaw Way	C4	London Road	C3
Bramble Street	B2	Macklin Street	B3
Bridge Street	A1	Mansfield Road	C1
Brook Street	A1	Meadow Lane	D2
Burton Road	B4	Meadow Road	D2
Canal Street	D4	Mercian Way	B3
Carrington Street	D4	Morledge	C3
Cathedral Road	B1	Newland Street	A3
Cavendish Court	A2	New Road	A3
Chapel Street	B1	New Street	D4
Clarke Street	D1	Nottingham Road	D1
Copeland Street	D3	Osmaston Road	C4
Corn Market	B2	Phoenix Street	C1
Crompton Street	B3	Queen Street	B1
Curzon Street	A2	Robert Street	D1
Curzon Street	A3	Rosengrave Street	B4
Darwin Place	C2	Sacheverel Street	C4
Derwent Street	C2	Sadler Gate	B2
Drewry Lane	A3	St Alkmund's Way	C1
Duke Street	C1	St Helen's Street	B1
Dunkirk	A3	St Mary's Gate	B2
East Street	C3	St Peter's Street	C3
Exchange Street	C3	Siddals Road	D3
Exeter Place	C2	Sowter Road	C1
Exeter Street	C2	Spring Street	A4
Ford Street	A2	Stafford Street	A3
Forester Street West	B4	Station Approach	D3
Forman Street	A3	Stockbrook Street	A4
Fox Street	C1	Strand	B2
Friary Street	A2	Stuart Street	C1
Full Street	B1	Sun Street	A4
Gerard Street	B3	The Cock Pitt	D3
Gower Street	B3	Thorntree Lane	C3
Green Lane	B3	Traffic Street	D4
Grey Street	A4	Trinity Street	D4
Handyside Street	B1	Victoria Street	B2
Harcourt Street	B4	Wardwick	B2
Iron Gate	B2	Werburgh Street	A4
John Street	D4	Wilmot Street	C4
Jury Street	B2	Wolfa Street	A3
Keys Street	D1	Woods Lane	A4

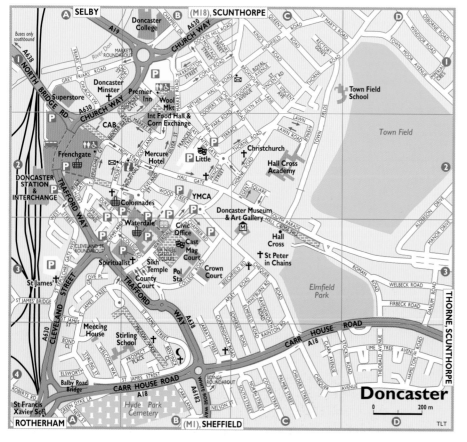

Doncaster

Doncaster is found on atlas page **91 P10**

Alderson Drive	D3	Nelson Street	B4
Apley Road	B3	Nether Hall Road	B1
Balby Road Bridge	A4	North Bridge Road	A1
Beechfield Road	B3	North Street	C4
Broxholme Lane	C1	Osborne Road	D1
Carr House Road	C4	Palmer Street	C4
Carr Lane	B4	Park Road	B2
Chamber Road	B3	Park Terrace	B2
Chequer Avenue	C4	Prince's Street	B2
Chequer Road	C3	Priory Place	A2
Childers Street	C4	Prospect Place	B4
Christ Church Road	B1	Queen's Road	C1
Church View	A1	Rainton Road	C4
Church Way	B1	Ravensworth Road	C3
Clark Avenue	C4	Rectory Gardens	C1
Cleveland Street	A4	Regent Square	C2
College Road	B3	Roman Road	D3
Cooper Street	C4	Royal Avenue	C1
Coopers Terrace	B2	St Georges Gate	B2
Copley Road	B1	St James Street	B4
Cunningham Road	B3	St Mary's Road	C1
Danum Road	D3	St Sepulchre Gate	A2
Dockin Hill Road	B1	St Sepulchre Gate West	A3
Duke Street	A2	St Vincent Avenue	C1
East Laith Gate	B2	St Vincent Road	C1
Elmfield Road	C3	Scot Lane	B2
Firbeck Road	D3	Silver Street	B2
Frances Street	B2	Somerset Road	B3
Glyn Avenue	C1	South Parade	C2
Green Dyke Lane	A4	South Street	C4
Grey Friars' Road	A1	Spring Gardens	A2
Hall Cross Hill	C2	Stirling Street	A4
Hall Gate	B2	Stockil Road	C4
Hamilton Road	D4	Theobald Avenue	D4
Harrington Street	B1	Thorne Road	C1
High Street	A2	Town Fields	D1
Highfield Road	C1	Town Moor Avenue	D1
Jarratt Street	B4	Trafford Way	A2
King's Road	C1	Vaughan Avenue	C1
Lawn Avenue	C2	Waterdale	B3
Lawn Road	C2	Welbeck Road	D3
Lime Tree Avenue	D4	Welcome Way	A4
Manor Drive	D3	West Laith Gate	A2
Market Place	A2	West Street	A3
Market Road	B1	Whitburn Road	C3
Milbanke Street	B1	White Rose Way	B4
Milton Walk	B4	Windsor Road	D1
Montague Street	B1	Wood Street	B2

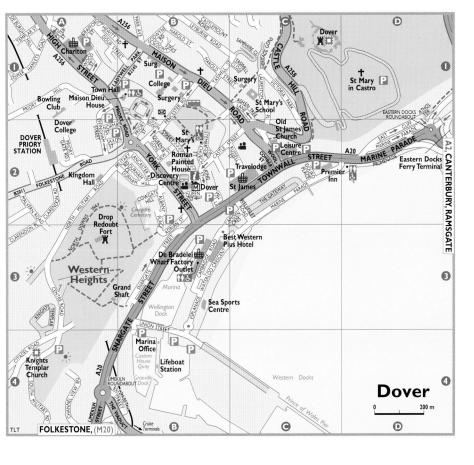

Dover

Dover is found on atlas page **27 P3**

Adrian Street	B3		Marine Parade	D2
Albany Place	B2		Military Road	B2
Ashen Tree Lane	C1		Mill Lane	B2
Athol Terrace	D1		New Street	B2
Biggin Street	B2		Norman Street	A2
Cambridge Road	B3		North Downs Way	A3
Camden Crescent	C2		North Military Road	A3
Castle Hill Road	C1		Park Avenue	B1
Castlemount Road	B1		Park Street	B1
Castle Street	B2		Pencester Road	B2
Centre Road	A3		Peter Street	A1
Channel View Road	A4		Priory Gate Road	A2
Church Street	B2		Priory Hill	A1
Citadel Road	A4		Priory Road	A1
Clarendon Place	A3		Priory Street	B2
Clarendon Road	A2		Promenade	D2
Cowgate Hill	B2		Queen's Gardens	B2
Crafford Street	A1		Queen Street	B2
De Burgh Hill	A1		Russell Street	B2
Douro Place	C2		Samphire Close	C1
Dour Street	A1		Saxon Street	A2
Durham Close	B2		Snargate Street	A4
Durham Hill	B2		South Military Road	A4
East Cliff	D2		Stembrook	B2
Eastern Docks			Taswell Close	C1
Roundabout	D2		Taswell Street	B1
Effingham Street	A2		Templar Street	A1
Elizabeth Street	A4		The Viaduct	A4
Esplanade	B3		Tower Hamlets Road	A1
Folkestone Road	A2		Townwall Street	C2
Godwyne Close	B1		Union Street	B3
Godwyne Road	B1		Victoria Park	C1
Harold Street	B1		Waterloo Crescent	B3
Harold Street	B1		Wellesley Road	C2
Heritage Gardens	C1		Wood Street	A1
Hewitt Road	A1		Woolcomber Street	C2
High Street	A1		York Street	B2
King Street	B2			
Knights Templar	A3			
Ladywell	A1			
Lancaster Road	B2			
Laureston Place	C1			
Leyburne Road	B1			
Limekiln Roundabout	A4			
Limekiln Street	A4			
Maison Dieu Road	B1			
Malvern Road	A2			
Marine Parade	C2			

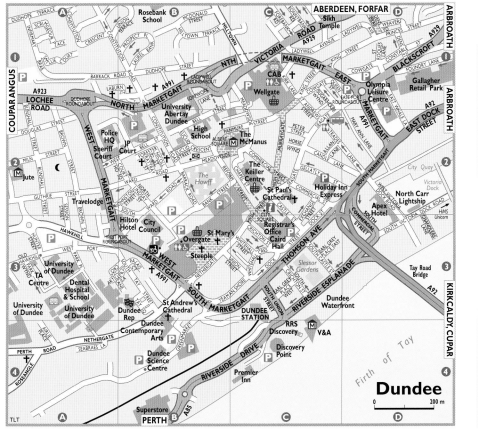

Dundee

Dundee is found on atlas page **142 G11**

Albert Square	B2		Laurel Bank	B1
Bank Street	B2		Lochee Road	A1
Barrack Road	A1		McDonald Street	D2
Barrack Road	B2		Meadowside	B2
Bell Street	B2		Miln Street	A2
Blackscroft	D1		Murraygate	C2
Blinshall Street	A1		Nethergate	A4
Blinshall Street	A2		North Lindsay Street	B2
Bonnybank Road	C1		North Marketgait	B1
Brown Street	A2		North Victoria Road	C1
Candle Lane	C2		Old Hawkhill	A3
Castle Street	C2		Panmure Street	B2
Chapel Street	C2		Perth Road	A4
City Square	C3		Princes Street	D1
Commercial Street	C2		Prospect Place	B1
Constable Street	D1		Queen Street	C1
Constitution Crescent	A1		Reform Street	B2
Constitution Road	A1		Riverside Drive	B4
Constitution Road	B2		Riverside Esplanade	C3
Court House Square	A2		Roseangle	A4
Cowgate	C1		St Andrews Street	C1
Cowgate	D1		Scrimgeour Place	A1
Crichton Street	C3		Seabraes Lane	A4
Dock Street	C3		Seagate	C2
Douglas Street	A2		Session Street	A2
Dudhope Street	B1		South Castle Street	C3
East Dock Street	D2		South Commercial Street	D3
East Marketgait	C1		South Crichton Street	C3
East Whale Lane	D1		South Marketgait	B3
Euclid Crescent	B2		South Tay Street	B3
Euclid Street	B2		South Union Street	C3
Exchange Street	C3		South Victoria Dock Road	D3
Forebank Road	C1		South Ward Road	B2
Foundry Lane	D1		Sugarhouse Wynd	D1
Gellatly Street	C2		Tay Road Bridge	D3
Greenmarket	B4		Tay Square	B3
Guthrie Street	A2		Thomson Avenue	C3
Hawkhill	A3		Trades Lane	C2
High Street	C3		Union Street	B3
Hilltown	B1		Union Terrace	A2
Hilltown Terrace	B1		Ward Road	B2
Hunter Street	A3		Weavers Yard	D1
Infirmary Brae	A1		West Marketgait	A2
Johnston Street	B2		West Port	A3
King Street	C1		West Victoria Dock Road	D2
Kirk Lane	C1		Whitehall Crescent	C3
Laburn Street	A1		Whitehall Street	C3
Ladywell Avenue	C1		Yeaman Shore	B3

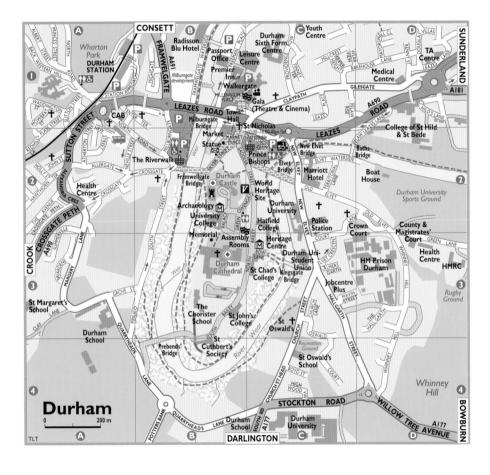

Durham

Durham is found on atlas page **103 Q2**

Albert Street A1
Alexandria Crescent..........A2
Allergate A2
Atherton Street A2
Back Western Hill............A1
Bakehouse Lane C1
Baths Bridge..................C2
Bow Lane C3
Boyd Street C4
Briardene A3
Church Lane C3
Church Street C4
Church Street Head C4
Clay Lane A3
Claypath......................C1
Court Lane C3
Crossgate....................A2
Crossgate Peth..............A3
Douglas Villas................D1
Elvet Bridge..................C2
Elvet Crescent................C3
Elvet Waterside..............C2
Finney Terrace................C1
Flass Street A2
Framwelgate..................B1
Framwelgate Bridge..........B2
Framwelgate Waterside B1
Freeman Place................B1
Gilesgate......................C1
Green Lane D3
Grove Street..................A3
Hallgarth Street C3
Hawthorn Terrace............A2
Highgate......................B1
High Road View..............C4
High Street C2
Hillcrest C1
Holly Street A2
John Street A2
Keiper Heights C1
Kingsgate Bridge............C3
Leazes Place C1
Leazes Road B1
Margery Lane A3
Market Square B2
Mavin Street C3
Mayorswell Close............D1
Milburngate Bridge B1

Millburngate..................B2
Millennium Place B1
Mowbray Street A1
Neville Street A2
New Elvet....................C2
New Elvet Bridge C2
New Street....................A2
North Bailey C3
North Road A1
Old Elvet C2
Oswald Court C3
Owengate....................B2
Palace Green..................B2
Palmers Garth C3
Pelaw Leazes Lane C2
Pelaw Rise....................C1
Pimlico........................A3
Potters Bank..................B4
Prebends' Bridge............B4
Princes' Street A1
Providence Row C1
Quarryheads Lane A3
Redhills Lane A2
Renny Street D1
Saddler Street................B2
St Hild's Lane................D1
Silver Street..................B2
South Bailey B3
South Road C4
South Street B3
Station Approach............A1
Stockton Road C4
Summerville..................A3
Sutton Street A2
Tenter Terrace A1
Territorial Lane..............C2
The Avenue..................A2
The Hall Garth D3
Waddington Street A1
Wear View....................C1
Whinney Hill D3
Willow Tree Avenue D4

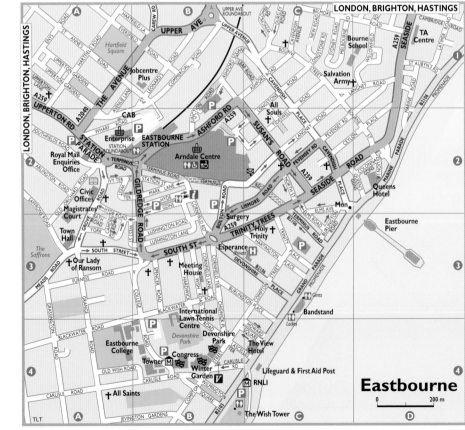

Eastbourne

Eastbourne is found on atlas page **25 P11**

Arlington Road..................A2
Ashford Road B2
Ashford Road C1
Ashford Square................B1
Avenue Lane A1
Belmore Road C1
Blackwater Road A4
Bolton Road B3
Bourne Street..................C1
Burlington Place................B3
Burlington Road................C3
Camden Road................A3
Carew Road..................B1
Carlisle Road..................A4
Carlisle Road..................B4
Cavendish Avenue C1
Cavendish Place................C1
Ceylon Place C2
Chiswick Place B3
College Road..................B3
Colonnade Gardens............D2
Commercial Road B1
Compton Street B4
Compton Street C3
Cornfield Lane..................B3
Cornfield Road................B2
Cornfield Terrace..............B3
Devonshire Place..............B3
Dursley Road..................C1
Elms Road C3
Enys Road A1
Eversfield Road A1
Furness Road A3
Gildredge Road B2
Grand Parade..................B3
Grange Road A3
Grassington Road A3
Grove Road A3
Hardwick Road B3
Hartfield Lane A1
Hartfield Road................A1
Hartington Place................C3
Howard Square C4
Hyde Gardens B2
Hyde Road....................A2
Ivy Terrace A2
Jevington Gardens............A4
Junction Road..................B2

Langney Road D1
Langney Road C2
Lascelles Terrace..............B4
Latimer Road D1
Leaf Road......................B1
Lismore Road B2
Longstone Road C1
Lushington Road B3
Marine Parade................D2
Marine Road D1
Mark Lane B2
Meads Road A3
Melbourne Road C1
Old Orchard Road A4
Old Wish Road A4
Pevensey Road................C2
Promenade C3
Queen's Gardens..............D2
Saffrons Road A2
St Anne's Road A1
St Aubyn's Road D1
St Leonard's Road B1
Seaside........................D1
Seaside Road C2
Southfields Road A2
South Street A3
South Street B3
Spencer Road A3
Station Parade................A2
Station Street B2
Susan's Road C2
Sutton Road..................B2
Sydney Road C1
Terminus Road A2
Terminus Road C3
The Avenue..................A1
Tideswell Road................C2
Trinity Place B3
Trinity Trees..................B3
Upper Avenue B1
Upperton Gardens............A1
Upperton Road................A1
West Street A3
West Terrace A3
Willowfield Road..............D1
Wilmington Square..........B4
Wish Road B3
York Road....................A3

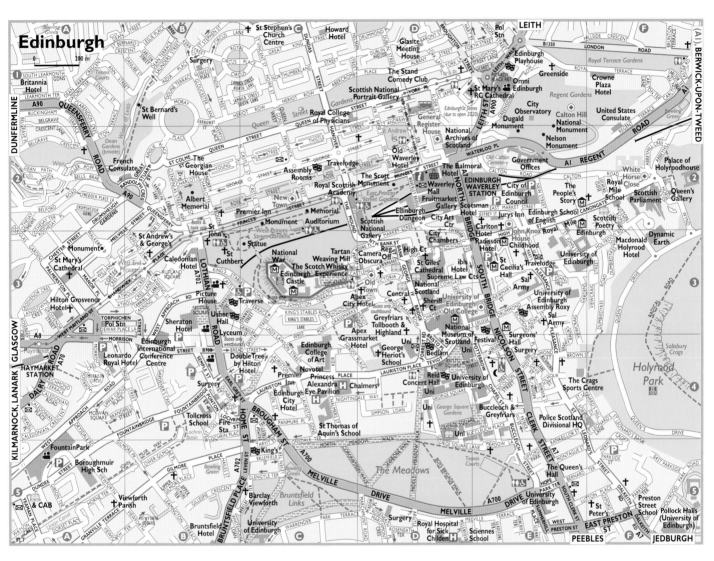

Edinburgh

Edinburgh is found on atlas page **127 P3**

Abbeyhill	F2	
Abercromby Place	C1	
Adam Street	E3	
Albany Street	D1	
Ann Street	A1	
Argyle Place	D5	
Atholl Crescent Lane	A3	
Bank Street	D3	
Barclay Terrace	C5	
Belford Road	A2	
Belgrave Crescent	A2	
Bernard Terrace	E5	
Boys Brigade Walk	D5	
Brandfield Street	A4	
Bread Street	B4	
Bristo Place	D4	
Brougham Street	C4	
Broughton Street	D1	
Broughton Street Lane	E1	
Brunton Terrace	F1	
Bruntsfield Place	B5	
Buccleuch Place	D4	
Buccleuch Street	E4	
Caledonian Place	A4	
Caledonian Road	A4	
Caledonian Street	A4	
Calton Road	E2	
Candlemaker Row	D3	
Canning Street	B3	
Canongate	E2	
Carlton Terrace	F1	
Castle Hill	C3	
Castle Street	C2	
Castle Terrace	B3	
Chalmers Street	C4	
Chambers Street	D3	
Chapel Street	E4	
Charlotte Square	B2	
Chester Street Gardens	A2	
Circus Lane	B1	
Circus Place	B1	
Clarendon Crescent	A1	
Clerk Street	E4	
Cockburn Street	D2	
Coronation Walk	C5	
Cowan's Close	E4	
Cowgate	D3	
Dalkeith Road	F5	
Dalry Road	A4	
Danube Street	B1	
Davie Street	E4	
Dean Park Crescent	A1	
Dean Street	A1	
Dewar Place Lane	A3	
Douglas Gardens	A3	
Doune Terrace	B1	
Drummond Street	E3	
Dublin Street	D1	
Dumbiedykes Road	F3	
Dunbar Street	B4	
Dundas Street	C1	
Dundee Street	A5	
Earl Grey Street	B4	
Easter Road	F1	
East Market Street	E2	
East Parkside	F5	
East Preston Street	F5	
Elder Street	D1	
Forrest Road	D4	
Forth Street	D1	
Fountainbridge	A4	
Frederick Street	C2	
Gardener's Crescent	B4	
George IV Bridge	D3	
George Square	D4	
George Square Lane	D5	
George Street	B2	
George Street	C2	
Gifford Park	E5	
Gillespie Crescent	B5	
Gilmore Park	A5	
Gilmore Place	B5	
Gilmour Street	E4	
Glenfinlas Street	B2	
Gloucester Lane	B1	
Granville Terrace	A5	
Great King Street	C1	
Great Stuart Street	B2	
Greenmarket	C3	
Greenside Row	E1	
Grindlay Street	B3	
Grosvenor Street	A3	
Grove Street	A4	
Haddon's Court	E4	
Hanover Street	C2	
Haymarket Terrace	A4	
Heriot Row	C1	
Hermits Croft	F5	
High Street	D3	
High Street	E3	
Hillside Crescent	E1	
Hill Street	C2	
Holyrood Park Road	F5	
Holyrood Road	E3	
Home Street	C4	
Hope Street	B2	
Horse Wynd	F2	
Howden Street	E4	
Howe Street	C1	
India Place	B1	
India Street	B1	
Jamaica Street South Lane	B1	
Jawbone Walk	D5	
Jeffrey Street	E2	
Johnston Terrace	C3	
Keir Street	C4	
Kerr Street	B1	
King's Stables Road	B3	
Lady Lawson Street	C3	
Lansdowne Crescent	A3	
Lauriston Gardens	C4	
Lauriston Place	C4	
Lauriston Street	C4	
Lawnmarket	D3	
Leamington Terrace	B5	
Leith Street	E1	
Leith Walk	E1	
Lennox Street	A1	
Leven Place	C5	
Lochrin Place	B4	
Lochrin Street	B4	
London Road	E1	
Lothian Road	B3	
Lower Gilmore Place	B5	
Lutton Place	E5	
Lynedoch Place Lane	A2	
Manor Place	A3	
Marchmont Crescent	D5	
Marchmont Road	D5	
Market Street	D2	
Meadow Lane	E5	
Melville Drive	C5	
Melville Street	A3	
Melville Terrace	D5	
Middle Meadow Walk	D5	
Millerfield Place	D5	
Miller Row	A2	
Moncrieff Terrace	E5	
Montague Street	E5	
Moray Place	B1	
Morrison Link	A4	
Morrison Street	A4	
Mound Place	D3	
Nelson Street	C1	
New Street	E2	
Nicolson Square	E4	
Nicolson Street	E4	
Nightingale Way	C4	
North Bridge	D2	
North Castle Street	C2	
North Meadow Walk	C5	
North St Andrew Street	D1	
North St David Street	D1	
Northumberland Street	C1	
Oxford Street	F5	
Palmerston Place	A3	
Panmure Place	C4	
Pleasance	E3	
Ponton Street	B4	
Potterrow	E4	
Princes Street	C2	
Queensferry Road	A1	
Queensferry Street	B2	
Queen Street	B2	
Radical Road	F3	
Ramsay Lane	C3	
Randolph Crescent	B2	
Randolph Lane	B2	
Rankeillor Street	E5	
Regent Road	E2	
Richmond Place	E3	
Rose Street	B2	
Roseneath Place	D5	
Rothesay Place	A3	
Royal Circus	B1	
Royal Terrace	E1	
St Andrew Square	D1	
St Bernard's Crescent	A1	
St Colme Street	B2	
St James Place	D1	
St Leonard's Bank	F4	
St Leonard's Hill	F4	
St Leonard's Lane	F4	
St Leonard's Street	E4	
St Patrick Street	E4	
St Stephen Street	B1	
St Vincent Street	C1	
Saunders Street	B1	
Sciennes	E5	
Semple Street	B4	
Shandwick Place	A3	
Simpson Loan	D4	
South Bridge	E3	
South Charlotte Street	B2	
South Clerk Street	E5	
South Learmonth Gardens	A1	
South St Andrew Street	D2	
South St David Street	D2	
Spittal Street	C4	
Stafford Street	B3	
Tarvit Street	C5	
The Mound	C2	
Thistle Street	C2	
Torphichen Street	A3	
Union Street	E1	
Upper Gilmore Place	B5	
Victoria Street	D3	
Viewcraig Gardens	E4	
Viewcraig Street	F3	
Viewforth	A5	
Walker Street	A3	
Warrender Park Terrace	C5	
Waterloo Place	D2	
Waverley Bridge	D2	
West Approach Road	A5	
West Maitland Street	A3	
West Nicolson Street	E4	
West Port	C4	
West Richmond Street	E4	
West Toll Cross	B4	
William Street	A3	
Yeaman Place	A5	
York Lane	D1	
York Place	D1	
Young Street	B2	

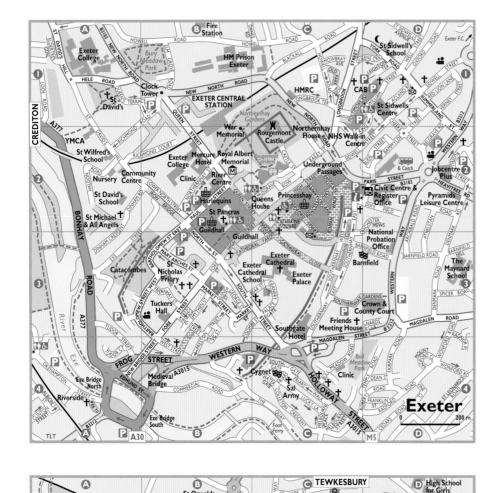

Exeter

Exeter is found on atlas page **9 M6**

Acland Road	D1	King Street	B3
Archibald Road	D3	King William Street	D1
Athelstan Road	D3	Longbrook Street	C1
Bailey Street	C2	Lower North Street	B2
Bampfylde Lane	C2	Magdalen Road	D3
Bampfylde Street	D2	Magdalen Street	C4
Barnfield Road	D3	Market Street	B3
Bartholomew Street East	B3	Martins Lane	C2
Bartholomew Street West	B3	Mary Arches Street	B3
Bear Street	C3	Musgrave Row	C2
Bedford Street	C2	New Bridge Street	A4
Belgrave Road	D2	New North Road	A1
Blackall Road	C1	Northernhay Street	B2
Bonhay Road	A2	North Street	B3
Bude Street	D2	Old Park Road	C1
Bull Meadow Road	C4	Oxford Road	D1
Castle Street	C2	Palace Gate	C3
Cathedral Close	C3	Paris Street	D2
Cathedral Yard	B3	Paul Street	B2
Cedars Road	D4	Preston Street	B4
Cheeke Street	D1	Princesshay	C2
Chichester Mews	C3	Queens Crescent	C1
Commercial Road	B4	Queen's Terrace	A1
Coombe Street	B3	Queen Street	B1
Deanery Place	C3	Radford Road	D4
Dean Street	D4	Richmond Court	B2
Denmark Road	D3	Richmond Road	A2
Dinham Crescent	A3	Roberts Road	C4
Dinham Road	A2	Roman Walk	C2
Dix's Field	D2	St David's Hill	A1
Eastgate	C2	Sidwell Street	C2
Edmund Street	A4	Sidwell Street	D1
Elm Grove Road	B1	Smythen Street	B3
Exe Street	A3	Southernhay East	C3
Fairpark Road	D4	Southernhay Gardens	C3
Fore Street	B3	Southernhay West	C3
Franklin Street	D4	South Street	B3
Friernhay Street	B3	Spicer Road	D3
Frog Street	A4	Summerland Street	D1
George Street	B3	Temple Road	D4
Guinea Street	B3	Tudor Court	A3
Haldon Road	A2	Tudor Street	A3
Heavitree Road	D2	Verney Street	D1
Hele Road	A1	Well Street	D1
High Street	C2	Western Way	B4
Holloway Street	C4	West Street	B4
Howell Road	B1	Wonford Road	D4
Iron Bridge	B2	York Road	D1

Gloucester

Gloucester is found on atlas page **46 F11**

Albert Street	D4	Millbrook Street	D4
Albion Street	B4	Montpellier	B4
All Saints' Road	D4	Napier Street	D4
Alvin Street	C2	Nettleton Road	C3
Archdeacon Street	B2	New Inn Lane	C3
Arthur Street	C4	Norfolk Street	B4
Barbican Road	B3	Northgate Street	C3
Barrack Square	B3	Old Tram Road	B4
Barton Street	D4	Over Causeway	A1
Bedford Street	C3	Oxford Road	D1
Belgrave Road	C4	Oxford Street	D2
Berkeley Street	B3	Park Road	C4
Black Dog Way	C2	Park Street	C2
Blenheim Road	D4	Parliament Street	B3
Brunswick Road	B4	Pembroke Street	C4
Brunswick Square	B4	Pitt Street	B2
Bruton Way	D3	Priory Road	B1
Bull Lane	B3	Quay Street	B2
Castle Meads Way	A2	Royal Oak Road	A2
Clarence Street	C3	Russell Street	C3
Clare Street	B2	St Aldate Street	C2
College Court	B2	St Catherine Street	C1
Commercial Road	B3	St John's Lane	B3
Cromwell Street	C4	St Mark Street	C1
Cross Keys Lane	B3	St Mary's Square	B2
Deans Walk	C1	St Mary's Street	B2
Eastgate Street	C3	St Michael's Square	C4
Gouda Way	B1	St Oswald's Road	B1
Great Western Road	D2	Sebert Street	C1
Greyfriars	B3	Severn Road	A3
Hampden Way	C3	Sherborne Street	D2
Hare Lane	C2	Sinope Street	D4
Heathville Road	D2	Southgate Street	B4
Henry Road	D1	Spa Road	B4
Henry Street	D2	Station Road	C3
High Orchard Street	A4	Swan Road	C1
Honyatt Road	D1	Sweetbriar Street	C1
Kings Barton Street	C4	The Cross	B3
Kingsholm Road	C1	The Oxebode	B3
King's Square	C3	The Quay	A2
Ladybellegate Street	B3	Union Street	C1
Llanthony Road	A4	Upper Quay Street	B2
London Road	D2	Vauxhall Road	D4
Longsmith Street	B3	Wellington Street	C4
Market Parade	C3	Westgate Street	A2
Merchants' Road	A4	Widden Street	D4
Mercia Road	B1	Worcester Parade	C2
Metz Way	D3	Worcester Street	C2

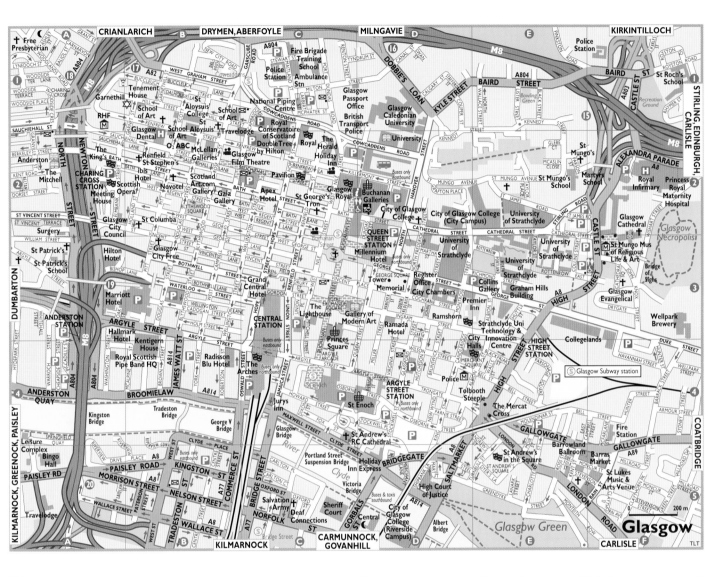

Glasgow

Glasgow is found on atlas page **125 P4**

Albert Bridge	D5	Candleriggs	D4
Albion Street	D4	Carlton Place	C5
Albion Street	E3	Carnarvon Street	A1
Alexandra Parade	F2	Castle Street	F1
Anderston Quay	A4	Castle Street	F2
Argyle Arcade	C4	Cathedral Square	F3
Argyle Street	A3	Cathedral Street	E3
Armour Street	F4	Centre Street	B5
Ashley Street	A1	Chalmer Street	F5
Bain Street	F5	Charing Cross	A1
Baird Street	E1	Charles Street	F1
Baliol Street	A1	Charlotte Street	E5
Barrack Street	F4	Cheapside Street	A4
Bath Lane	B2	Claythorn Avenue	F5
Bath Street	A2	Claythorn Park	F5
Bell Street	E4	Clyde Place	B4
Berkeley Street	A2	Clyde Street	C4
Blackfriars Street	E4	Cochrane Street	D3
Black Street	E1	Collins Street	D3
Blythswood Square	B2	Commerce Street	B5
Blythswood Street	B3	Couper Street	D1
Bothwell Lane	B3	Cowcaddens Road	C1
Bothwell Street	B3	Dalhousie Lane	B1
Bridgegate	D5	Dixon Street	C4
Bridge of Sighs	F3	Dobbie's Loan	D1
Bridge Street	C5	Dorset Street	A2
Broomielaw	B4	Douglas Street	B3
Brown Street	B4	Drury Street	C3
Brunswick Street	D4	Drygate	F3
Buccleuch Lane	B1	Duke Street	F4
Buccleuch Street	B1	Dundas Street	D3
Buchanan Street	C4	Dunlop Street	D4
Cadogan Street	B3	Dyer's Lane	E5
Calgary Street	D1	East Campbell Street	E4
Cambridge Street	C1	Elmbank Street	A2
Canal Street	D1	Fox Street	C4

Gallowgate	E4	Lanark Street	E5
Garnethill Street	B1	Larbert Street	C1
Garnet Street	B2	Lister Street	E1
Garscube Road	C1	London Road	E4
Garth Street	D3	Maitland Street	C1
George Square	D3	Martha Street	D3
George Street	E3	Mart Street	D5
George V Bridge	B4	Maxwell Street	C4
Glasgow Bridge	C5	McAlpine Street	B4
Glassford Street	D4	McAslin Close	E2
Glebe Court	E2	McFarlane Street	F4
Gorbals Street	C5	McPhater Street	C1
Gordon Street	C3	Merchant Lane	D5
Grafton Place	D2	Miller Street	D4
Granville Street	A2	Millroad Drive	F5
Greendyke Street	E5	Millroad Street	F5
Green Street	F5	Milton Street	C1
Hanover Street	D3	Mitchell Street	C4
High Street	E4	Moir Street	E5
Hill Street	B1	Molendinar Street	E4
Holland Street	B2	Moncur Street	E5
Holm Street	B3	Monteith Row	E5
Hope Street	C3	Montrose Street	D3
Howard Street	C4	Morrison Street	A5
Hunter Street	F4	Nelson Street	B5
Hutcheson Street	D4	New City Road	B1
Hydepark Street	A4	Newton Street	A2
Ingram Street	D3	New Wynd	D4
Jamaica Street	C4	Norfolk Street	C5
James Watt Street	B4	North Frederick Street	D3
John Knox Street	F3	North Hanover Street	D3
John Street	D3	North Portland Street	E3
Kennedy Street	D2	North Street	A2
Kennedy Street	E1	North Wallace Street	E1
Kent Road	A2	Osborne Street	C4
Kent Street	E5	Oswald Street	C4
Killermont Street	C2	Oxford Street	C5
Kingston Bridge	A5	Paisley Road	A5
Kingston Street	B5	Parnie Street	D4
King Street	D4	Parsonage Square	E4
Kyle Street	D1	Parson Street	E2

Paterson Street	B5	Steel Street	D5
Pinkston Road	E1	Stevenson Street	F5
Pitt Street	B2	Stewart Street	C1
Port Dundas Road	C1	Stirling Road	E2
Portland Street		Stockwell Place	D4
Suspension Bridge	C5	Stockwell Street	D4
Queen Street	C4	Suffolk Street	E5
Renfield Lane	C3	Sydney Street	F4
Renfield Street	C3	Taylor Place	E2
Renfrew Lane	C2	Taylor Street	E2
Renfrew Street	B1	Tradeston Bridge	B4
Renton Street	C1	Tradeston Street	B5
Rhymer Street	F1	Trongate	D4
Richmond Street	E3	Turnbull Street	D5
Riverview Drive	A4	Tyndrum Street	C1
Robertson Street	B4	Union Street	C3
Rose Street	B2	Virginia Street	D4
Ross Street	E5	Wallace Street	A5
Rottenrow	E3	Walls Street	E4
Rottenrow East	E3	Warroch Street	A4
Royal Exchange Square	C3	Washington Street	A4
Royston Road	F1	Waterloo Street	B3
Royston Square	F1	Wellington Lane	B3
St Andrew's Square	D5	Wellington Street	B3
St Andrew's Street	E4	Wellpark Street	F4
St James Road	E2	West Campbell Street	B3
St Mungo Avenue	D2	West George Lane	B2
St Vincent Lane	B3	West George Street	B2
St Vincent Place	C3	West Graham Street	B1
St Vincent Street	A2	West Nile Street	C3
St Vincent Terrace	A2	West Regent Lane	C2
Saltmarket	D5	West Regent Street	B2
Sauchiehall Lane	A2	West Street	B5
Sauchiehall Street	A1	William Street	A3
Sauchiehall Street	B2	Wilson Street	D4
Scott Street	B1	Wishart Street	F3
Shipbank Lane	D5	Woodlands Road	A1
Shuttle Street	E3	Woodside Crescent	A1
South Frederick Street	D3	Woodside Terrace	A1
Springfield Quay	A4	Woodside Terrace Lane	A1
Stafford Street	D1	York Street	B4

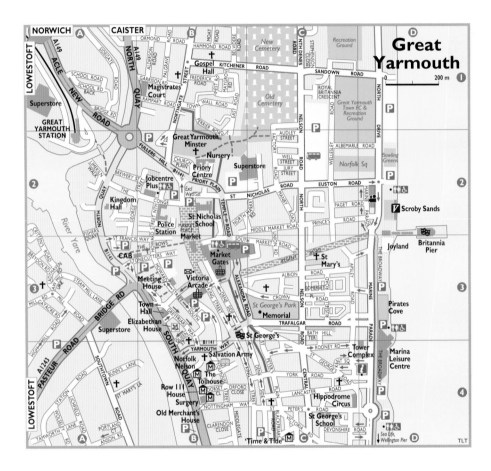

Great Yarmouth

Great Yarmouth is found on atlas page **77 Q10**

Acle New Road	A1	North Drive	D1
Albemarle Road	C2	North Market Road	C2
Albion Road	C3	North Quay	A2
Alderson Road	B1	Northgate Street	B1
Alexandra Road	B3	Nottingham Way	B4
Apsley Road	C3	Ormond Road	B1
Belvidere Road	B1	Paget Road	C2
Blackfriars Road	C4	Palgrave Road	B1
Brewery Street	A2	Pasteur Road	A4
Breydon Road	A3	Prince's Road	C2
Bridge Road	A1	Priory Plain	B2
Bridge Road	A3	Queen Street	B4
Bunn's Lane	A4	Rampart Road	B1
Church Plain	B2	Regent Road	C3
Critten's Road	A3	Rodney Road	C4
Crown Road	C3	Russell Road	C3
Dene Side	B3	St Francis Way	A3
Devonshire Road	C4	St George's Road	C4
East Road	B1	St Nicholas Road	B2
Euston Road	C2	St Peter's Plain	C4
Factory Road	C2	St Peter's Road	C4
Ferrier Road	B1	Sandown Road	C1
Fishers Quay	A2	Saw Mill Lane	A3
Frederick Road	B1	School Road	A1
Fullers Hill	B2	School Road Back	A1
Garrison Road	B1	Sidegate Road	A1
Gatacre Road	A3	South Market Road	C3
George Street	A2	South Quay	B3
Greyfriars Way	B3	Southtown Road	A4
Hammond Road	B1	Station Road	A4
High Mill Road	A3	Steam Mill Lane	A3
Howard Street North	B2	Stephenson Close	C1
Howard Street South	B3	Stonecutters Way	B3
King Street	B3	Tamworth Lane	A4
Kitchener Road	B1	Temple Road	B2
Ladyhaven Road	A3	The Broadway	D3
Lancaster Road	C4	The Conge	A2
Lichfield Road	A4	The Rows	B3
Limekiln Walk	A2	Tolhouse Street	B4
Manby Road	C2	Town Wall Road	B1
Marine Parade	D3	Trafalgar Road	C4
Maygrove Road	B1	Union Road	B1
Middle Market Road	C2	Victoria Road	C4
Middlegate	B4	Wellesley Road	C2
Moat Road	B1	West Road	B1
Nelson Road Central	C3	Wolseley Road	A4
Nelson Road North	C1	Yarmouth Way	B4
North Denes Road	C1	York Road	C4

Guildford

Guildford is found on atlas page **23 Q5**

Abbot Road	C4	Millmead	B3
Angel Gate	B3	Millmead Terrace	B4
Artillery Road	B1	Mount Pleasant	A4
Artillery Terrace	C1	Nightingale Road	D1
Bedford Road	A2	North Street	B3
Bridge Street	A3	Onslow Road	C1
Bright Hill	C3	Onslow Street	B2
Brodie Road	D3	Oxford Road	C3
Bury Fields	B4	Pannells Court	C2
Bury Street	B4	Park Street	B3
Castle Hill	C4	Pewley Bank	D3
Castle Street	C3	Pewley Fort Inner Court	D4
Chapel Street	B3	Pewley Hill	C3
Chertsey Street	C2	Pewley Way	D3
Cheselden Road	D2	Phoenix Court	B3
Church Road	B1	Porridge Pot Alley	B4
College Road	B2	Portsmouth Road	A4
Commercial Road	B2	Poyle Road	D4
Dene Road	D2	Quarry Street	B3
Denmark Road	D2	Sandfield Terrace	C2
Drummond Road	B1	Semaphore Road	D3
Eagle Road	C1	South Hill	C3
Epsom Road	D2	Springfield Road	C1
Falcon Road	C1	Station Approach	D1
Farnham Road	A3	Station View	A2
Fort Road	C4	Stoke Fields	C1
Foxenden Road	D1	Stoke Grove	C1
Friary Bridge	A3	Stoke Road	C1
Friary Street	B3	Swan Lane	B3
George Road	B1	Sydenham Road	C3
Guildford Park Road	A2	Testard Road	A3
Harvey Road	D3	The Bars	C2
Haydon Place	C2	The Mount	A4
High Pewley	D4	The Shambles	B3
High Street	C3	Tunsgate	C3
Jeffries Passage	C2	Upperton Road	A3
Jenner Road	D2	Victoria Road	D1
Laundry Road	B2	Walnut Tree Close	A1
Leapale Lane	B2	Ward Street	C2
Leapale Road	B2	Warwicks Bench	C4
Leas Road	B1	Wherwell Road	A3
London Road	D2	William Road	B1
Mareschal Road	A4	Wodeland Avenue	A3
Market Street	C3	Woodbridge Road	B1
Martyr Road	C2	York Road	B1
Mary Road	A1		
Millbrook	B3		
Mill Lane	B3		

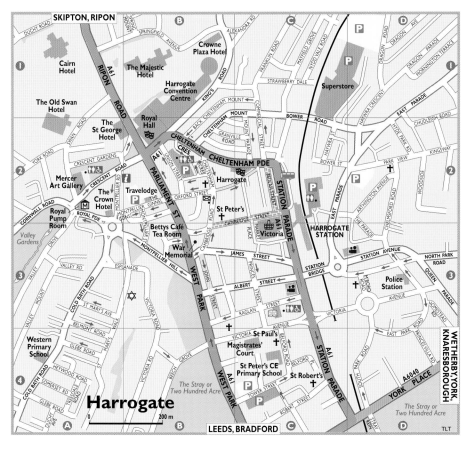

Harrogate

Harrogate is found on atlas page **97 M9**

Albert Street	C3	Montpellier Road	A2
Alexandra Road	B1	Montpellier Street	B2
Arthington Avenue	D2	Mornington Terrace	D1
Back Cheltenham Mount	B2	Mount Parade	C2
Beech Grove	B4	North Park Road	D3
Belford Place	C4	Nydd Vale Road	C1
Belford Road	C4	Oxford Street	B2
Belmont Road	A3	Park View	D2
Beulah Street	C2	Parliament Street	B2
Bower Road	C1	Princes Street	C3
Bower Street	C2	Princes Villa Road	D4
Cambridge Road	B3	Queen Parade	D3
Cambridge Street	C2	Raglan Street	C3
Chelmsford Road	D3	Ripon Road	A1
Cheltenham Crescent	B2	Robert Street	C4
Cheltenham Mount	B2	Royal Parade	A2
Cheltenham Parade	B2	St Mary's Avenue	A3
Chudleigh Road	D2	St Mary's Walk	A4
Cold Bath Road	A3	Somerset Road	A4
Commercial Street	C1	South Park Road	D4
Cornwall Road	A2	Springfield Avenue	B1
Crescent Gardens	A2	Spring Mount	B1
Crescent Road	A2	Station Avenue	D3
Dragon Avenue	D1	Station Bridge	C3
Dragon Parade	D1	Station Parade	C2
Dragon Road	D1	Strawberry Dale	C1
Duchy Avenue	A4	Stray Rein	D4
Duchy Road	A1	Swan Road	A2
East Parade	C2	The Ginnel	B2
East Park Road	D4	The Parade	D2
Esplanade	A3	Tower Street	C4
Franklin Road	C1	Treesdale Road	A4
Glebe Road	A4	Union Street	B2
Granville Road	B2	Valley Drive	A3
Haywra Street	C2	Valley Mount	A3
Heywood Road	A4	Valley Road	A3
Homestead Road	D3	Victoria Avenue	B4
Hyde Park Road	D2	Victoria Road	B3
Hywra Crescent	D2	West Park	B3
James Street	B3	West Park Street	B4
John Street	B3	Woodside	D2
King's Road	B1	York Place	D4
Kingsway	D2	York Road	A2
Market Place	C3		
Marlborough Road	D3		
Mayfield Grove	C1		
Montpellier Gardens	B2		
Montpellier Hill	B3		

Huddersfield

Huddersfield is found on atlas page **90 E7**

Albion Street	B4	New North Road	A2
Alfred Street	C4	New Street	B4
Back Union Street	C1	Northgate	C1
Bankfield Road	A4	Northumberland Street	C2
Bath Street	B1	Old Leeds Road	D2
Belmont Street	A1	Old South Street	B3
Brook Street	C2	Outcote Bank	B4
Byram Street	C2	Oxford Street	C1
Cambridge Road	B1	Page Street	C4
Carforth Street	D4	Park Avenue	A2
Castlegate	B1	Park Drive South	A2
Chancery Lane	B3	Peel Street	C4
Chapel Hill	B4	Portland Street	A2
Chapel Street	B4	Princess Street	B4
Church Street	C2	Prospect Street	A4
Clare Hill	B1	Quay Street	D2
Claremont Street	B1	Queen Street	C3
Cloth Hall Street	B3	Queen Street South	C4
Cross Church Street	C3	Queensgate	C4
Dundas Street	B3	Railway Street	B2
Elizabeth Queen Gardens	A2	Ramsden Street	B3
Elmwood Avenue	A1	Rook Street	B1
Firth Street	D4	St Andrew's Road	D2
Fitzwilliam Street	A2	St George's Square	B2
Fitzwilliam Street	B2	St John's Road	B1
Gasworks Street	D1	St Peter's Street	C2
Great Northern Street	C1	Southgate	C2
Greenhead Road	A3	Spring Grove Street	A4
Half Moon Street	B3	Spring Street	A3
High Street	B3	Springwood Avenue	A3
Highfields Road	A1	Stadium Way	D1
John William Street	B2	Station Street	B2
King Street	C3	Trinity Street	A2
King's Mill Lane	D4	Turnbridge Road	D2
Kirkgate	C3	Union Street	C1
Leeds Road	C2	Upper George Street	A3
Lincoln Street	D3	Upperhead Row	B3
Lord Street	C2	Viaduct Street	B2
Lower Fitzwilliam Street	C1	Victoria Lane	C3
Lynton Avenue	A3	Wakefield Road	D3
Manchester Road	A4	Water Street	A3
Market Place	C3	Watergate	D2
Market Street	B3	Waverley Road	A2
Merton Street	A3	Wentworth Street	A2
Milford Street	B4	Westgate	B3
Mountjoy Road	A1	William Street	C1
New North Parade	B2	Wood Street	C2
New North Road	A1	Zetland Street	C3

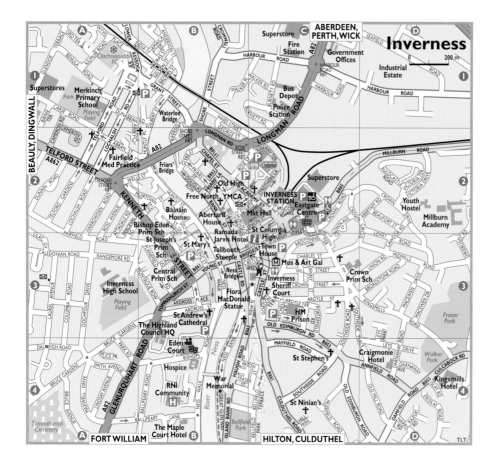

Inverness

Inverness is found on atlas page **156 B8**

Abertaff Road	D2	Glenurquhart Road	A4
Academy Street	B2	Gordon Terrace	C3
Anderson Street	B1	Grant Street	B1
Annfield Road	D4	Great Glen Way	B4
Ardconnel Terrace	C3	Harbour Road	C1
Ardross Street	B3	Harris Road	D4
Argyle Street	C3	Harrowden Road	A2
Argyle Terrace	C3	Haugh Road	B4
Ballifeary Lane	A4	High Street	C3
Ballifeary Road	B4	Hill Park	C4
Bank Street	B2	Hill Street	C3
Bellfield Terrace	C4	Huntly Street	B2
Benula Road	A1	Innes Street	B1
Birnie Terrace	A1	Kenneth Street	A2
Bishops Road	B4	King Street	B3
Bridge Street	B3	Kingsmills Road	D3
Broadstone Road	D3	Laurel Avenue	A4
Bruce Gardens	A4	Lindsay Avenue	A4
Bruce Park	A4	Lochalsh Road	A2
Burnett Road	C1	Longman Road	C2
Caledonian Road	A3	Lovat Road	D3
Cameron Road	A2	Lower Kessock Street	A1
Cameron Square	A2	Maxwell Drive	A4
Carse Road	A1	Mayfield Road	C4
Castle Road	B3	Midmills Road	D3
Castle Street	C3	Millburn Road	D2
Chapel Street	B2	Mitchell's Lane	C3
Charles Street	C3	Muirfield Road	C4
Columba Road	A3	Ness Bank	B4
Crown Circus	C2	Old Edinburgh Road	C3
Crown Drive	D2	Park Road	A4
Crown Road	C2	Planefield Road	B3
Crown Street	C3	Porterfield Road	C3
Culcabock Road	D4	Raasay Road	D4
Culduthel Road	C4	Rangemore Road	A3
Dalneigh Road	A4	Ross Avenue	A2
Damfield Road	D4	Seafield Road	D1
Darnaway Road	D4	Shore Street	B1
Denny Street	C3	Smith Avenue	A4
Dochfour Drive	A3	Southside Place	C3
Dunabban Road	A1	Southside Road	C4
Dunain Road	A2	Telford Gardens	A2
Duncraig Street	B3	Telford Road	A2
Eriskay Road	D4	Telford Street	A2
Fairfield Road	A3	Tomnahurich Street	B3
Falcon Square	C2	Union Road	D3
Friars' Lane	B2	Walker Road	C1
Glendoe Terrace	A1	Young Street	B3

Ipswich

Ipswich is found on atlas page **53 L3**

Alderman Road	A3	Key Street	C3
Anglesea Road	B1	King Street	B2
Argyle Street	D2	London Road	A2
Austin Street	C4	Lower Brook Street	C3
Barrack Lane	A1	Lower Orwell Street	C3
Belstead Road	B4	Museum Street	B2
Berners Street	B1	Neale Street	C1
Black Horse Lane	B2	Neptune Quay	D3
Blanche Street	D2	New Cardinal Street	B3
Bolton Lane	C1	Newson Street	A1
Bond Street	D3	Northgate Street	C2
Bramford Road	A1	Norwich Road	A1
Bridge Street	C4	Old Foundry Road	C2
Burlington Road	A2	Orchard Street	D2
Burrell Road	B4	Orford Street	A1
Cardigan Street	A1	Orwell Place	C3
Carr Street	C2	Orwell Quay	D4
Cecil Road	B1	Portman Road	A3
Cemetery Road	D1	Princes Street	A3
Chancery Road	A4	Quadling Street	B3
Charles Street	B1	Queen Street	B3
Christchurch Street	D1	Ranelagh Road	A4
Civic Drive	B2	Russell Road	A3
Clarkson Street	A1	St George's Street	B1
Cobbold Street	C2	St Helen's Street	D2
College Street	C3	St Margaret's Street	C2
Commercial Road	A4	St Matthews Street	B2
Constantine Road	A3	St Nicholas Street	B3
Crown Street	B2	St Peter's Street	B3
Cumberland Street	A1	Silent Street	B3
Dalton Road	A2	Sir Alf Ramsey Way	A3
Dock Street	C4	Soane Street	C2
Duke Street	D4	South Street	A1
Eagle Street	C3	Star Lane	C4
Elm Street	B2	Stoke Quay	C4
Falcon Street	B3	Suffolk Road	D1
Fonnereau Road	B1	Tacket Street	C3
Foundation Street	C3	Tavern Street	B3
Franciscan Way	B3	Tower Ramparts	B2
Geneva Road	A1	Tuddenham Avenue	D1
Grafton Way	B3	Turret Lane	C3
Great Gipping Street	A2	Upper Orwell Street	C3
Great Whip Street	C4	Vernon Street	C4
Grey Friars Road	B3	West End Road	A3
Grimwade Street	D3	Westgate Street	B2
Handford Road	A2	Willoughby Road	B4
Hervey Street	D1	Wolsey Street	B3
High Street	B1	Woodbridge Road	D2

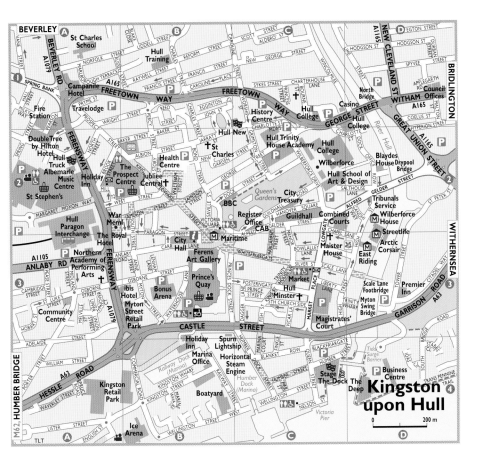

Kingston upon Hull

Kingston upon Hull is found on atlas page **93 J5**

Adelaide Street	A4	Market Place	C3
Albion Street	B2	Mill Street	A2
Alfred Gelder Street	C2	Myton Street	B3
Anlaby Road	A3	New Cleveland Street	D1
Baker Street	B2	New Garden Street	B2
Beverley Road	A1	New George Street	C1
Blackfriargate	C4	Norfolk Street	A1
Blanket Row	C4	Osborne Street	B3
Bond Street	B2	Osborne Street	A3
Brook Street	A2	Paragon Street	B2
Caroline Street	B1	Percy Street	B1
Carr Lane	B3	Porter Street	A3
Castle Street	B3	Portland Place	A2
Chapel Lane	C2	Portland Street	A2
Charles Street	B1	Posterngate	C3
Charterhouse Lane	C1	Princes Dock Street	B3
Citadel Way	D3	Prospect Street	A1
Commercial Road	B4	Queen Street	C4
Dagger Lane	C3	Railway Street	B4
Dock Office Row	D2	Raywell Street	B1
Dock Street	B2	Reform Street	B1
Durban Street	D1	Russell Street	A1
Egginton Street	B1	St Luke's Street	A1
Ferensway	A2	St Peter Street	D2
Freetown Way	A1	Saville Street	B2
Gandhi Way	D2	Scale Lane	C3
Garrison Road	D3	Scott Street	C1
George Street	B2	Silver Street	C3
George Street	D1	South Bridge Road	D4
Great Union Street	D1	South Church Side	C3
Grimston Street	C2	South Street	B2
Guildhall Road	C2	Spring Bank	A1
Hanover Square	C2	Spyvee Street	D1
Hessle Road	A4	Sykes Street	C1
High Street	C3	Tower Street	D3
Hodgson Street	D1	Upper Union Street	A3
Humber Dock Street	C4	Victoria Square	B2
Humber Street	C4	Waterhouse Lane	B3
Hyperion Street	D1	Wellington Street	C4
Jameson Street	B2	Wellington Street West	B4
Jarratt Street	B2	West Street	A2
King Edward Street	B2	Whitefriargate	C3
Kingston Street	B4	Wilberforce Drive	C2
Liddell Street	B1	William Street	A4
Lime Street	C1	Wincolmlee	C1
Lister Street	A4	Witham	D1
Lowgate	C3	Worship Street	C1
Margaret Moxon Way	A2	Wright Street	A1

Lancaster

Lancaster is found on atlas page **95 K8**

Aberdeen Road	D4	Lincoln Road	A3
Aldcliffe Road	B4	Lindow Street	B4
Alfred Street	C2	Lodge Street	C2
Ambleside Road	D1	Long Marsh Lane	A2
Balmoral Road	D4	Lune Street	B1
Bath Street	D3	Market Street	B3
Blades Street	A3	Meeting House Lane	A3
Bond Street	D3	Middle Street	B3
Borrowdale Road	D2	Moor Gate	D3
Brewery Lane	C3	Moor Lane	C3
Bridge Lane	B2	Morecambe Road	B1
Brock Street	C3	Nelson Street	C3
Bulk Road	D2	North Road	C2
Bulk Street	C3	Owen Road	C1
Cable Street	B2	Park Road	D3
Castle Hill	B3	Parliament Street	C2
Castle Park	A3	Patterdale Road	D2
Caton Road	C2	Penny Street	B4
Cheapside	C3	Portland Street	B4
China Street	B3	Primrose Street	D4
Church Street	B2	Prospect Street	D4
Common Garden Street	B3	Quarry Road	C4
Dale Street	D4	Queen Street	B4
Dallas Road	B3	Regent Street	B4
Dalton Road	D2	Ridge Lane	D1
Dalton Square	C3	Ridge Street	D1
Damside Street	B2	Robert Street	C3
Derby Road	C1	Rosemary Lane	C2
De Vitre Street	C2	St George's Quay	A1
Dumbarton Road	D4	St Leonard's Gate	C2
East Road	D3	St Peter's Road	C4
Edward Street	C3	Sibsey Street	A3
Fairfield Road	A3	South Road	C4
Fenton Street	B3	Station Road	A3
Gage Street	C3	Stirling Road	D4
Garnet Street	D2	Sulyard Street	C3
George Street	C3	Sun Street	B3
Grasmere Road	D3	Thurnham Street	C4
Great John Street	C3	Troutbeck Road	D2
Gregson Road	D4	Ulleswater Road	D3
Greyhound Bridge Road	B1	West Road	A3
High Street	B4	Westbourne Road	A3
Kelsey Street	A3	Wheatfield Street	A3
Kentmere Road	D2	Williamson Road	D3
King Street	B3	Wingate-Saul Road	A3
Kingsway	C1	Wolseley Street	D2
Kirkes Road	D4	Woodville Street	D3
Langdale Road	D1	Wyresdale Road	D3

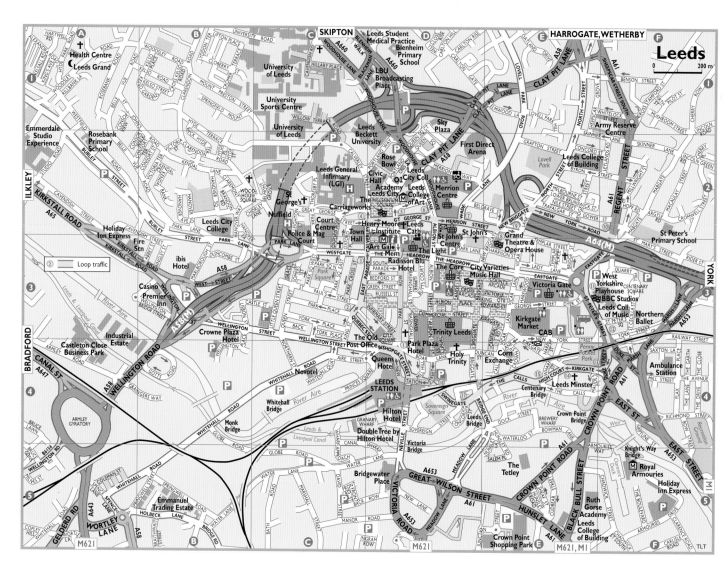

Leeds

Leeds is found on atlas page **90 H4**

Abbey Street B3	Calverley Street C2	Duke Street F4	King's Avenue A1	Northern Street C4	Springfield Mount B1
Aire Street C4	Canal Street A4	Duncan Street D4	King Street C3	North Street E2	Springwell Road B5
Albion Place D3	Canal Wharf C4	Duncombe Street.............B3	Kirkgate...........................E3	Oxford Place C3	Springwell Street B5
Albion Street D2	Carlton Hill D1	Dyer Street E3	Kirkstall Road A2	Oxford Row C3	Studio Road A2
Alexandra Road................A1	Carlton Rise D1	Eastgate...........................E3	Lady Lane E3	Park Cross Street C3	Swinegate D4
Argyle Road F2	Castle Street B3	East Parade C3	Lands Lane D3	Park Lane B2	Templar Street E3
Armley Gyratory................A4	Cavendish Road C1	East Street F4	Leighton Street C2	Park Place C3	The Avenue F4
Armley Road A4	Cavendish Street A2	Elmwood Lane E1	Leylands Road F2	Park Row D3	The Boulevard F5
Armouries Drive F5	Centenary Square F3	Flax Place F4	Lifton Place B1	Park Square East C3	The Calls E4
Armouries Way E4	Central Road E3	Front Street C5	Lincoln Green Road F1	Park Square North C3	The Headrow D3
Back Hyde Terrace B2	Chadwick Street F5	Geldard Road A5	Lisbon Street B3	Park Square West C3	Thoresby Place C2
Back Row C5	Cherry Row F1	George Street E3	Little Queen Street C3	Park Street C3	Trafalgar Street E2
Bath Road C5	Chorley Lane B2	Globe Road B4	Lovell Park Hill E1	Pilot Street F1	Upper Basinghall Street D3
Bedford Street D3	City Square D3	Gotts Road B4	Lovell Park Road E1	Portland Crescent D2	Vicar Lane E3
Belgrave Street D2	Claremont........................B2	Gower Street E2	Lower Basinghall Street D3	Portland Way D2	Victoria Road D5
Belle Vue Road A1	Clarence Road F5	Grace Street C3	Lower Brunswick Street E2	Princes Square C4	Victoria Street B2
Belmont Grove C2	Clarendon Road B1	Grafton Street E2	Lyddon Terrace B1	Quarry Hill F3	Victoria Terrace B2
Benson Street F1	Clay Pit Lane D2	Graingers Way A4	Mabgate............................F2	Quebec Street C3	Wade Lane D2
Bingley Street B3	Cloberry Street B1	Great George Street C2	Macaulay Street F2	Queen Square D2	Water Lane B5
Bishopgate Street D4	Commercial Street D3	Great Wilson Street D5	Manor Road C5	Queen Square Court D2	Waterloo Street E4
Black Bull Street E5	Concordia Street D4	Greek Street D3	Mark Lane D3	Queen Street C3	Wellington Bridge Street ...B3
Blackman Lane C1	Concord Street E2	Hanover Avenue B2	Marlborough Street C3	Railway Street F3	Wellington Road A4
Blenheim Walk C1	Consort Street B2	Hanover Lane B2	Marshall Street C5	Regent Street F2	Wellington Road A5
Boar Lane D4	Consort View A1	Hanover Square B2	Marsh Lane F3	Richmond Street F4	Wellington Street B3
Bowman Lane E4	County Arcade..................E3	Harewood Street E3	Maude Street E4	Rider Street F3	Westfield Road A1
Bow Street F4	Cromer Terrace B1	Harper Street E4	Meadow Lane D5	Rillbank Lane A1	Westgate...........................C3
Brandon Road B2	Cromwell Street F2	Harrison Street E3	Melbourne Street E2	Rosebank Road A1	West Street B3
Bridge End D4	Cross Arcade....................D3	Hartwell Road A1	Merrion Street D2	St Cecilla Street F3	Wharf Approach C4
Bridge Road B5	Cross Kelso Road B1	High Court E4	Merrion Way D2	St John's Road A1	Wharf Street E4
Bridge Street E2	Cross Stamford Street F1	Holbeck Lane B5	Millennium Square D2	St Mary's Street F3	Whitehall Quay C4
Bridge Street E3	Crown Point Road E5	Hope Road F2	Mill Street F3	St Paul's Street C3	Whitehall Road B3
Briggate D4	Crown Street E4	Hunslet Road E4	Millwright Street F2	St Peter's Square E3	Whitehall Road A5
Burley Street A2	Cudbear Street E5	Hunslet Road E5	Mount Preston Street B1	St Peter's Street E3	Whitelock Street F1
Butts Court D3	David Street C5	Hyde Park Road A1	Mushroom Street F1	Salem Place E5	Willow Terrace Road C1
Byron Street E2	Dock Street E4	Hyde Street B2	Neptune Street F4	Saxton Lane F3	Woodhouse Lane C1
Call Lane E4	Duke Street F4	Hyde Terrace B1	Neville Street D4	Sheepscar Grove E1	Woodhouse Square B2
		Infirmary Street D3	New Briggate E3	Sheepscar Street South F1	Woodsley Road A1
		Junction Street D5	New Lane D5	Skinner Lane E1	Wortley Lane A5
		Kelso Road B1	New Station Street D4	South Parade D3	Wortley Lane A5
		Kendal Lane B2	New York Road E2	Sovereign Street D4	York Place C3
		King Edward Street E3	New York Street E3	Spence Lane A5	York Street F3

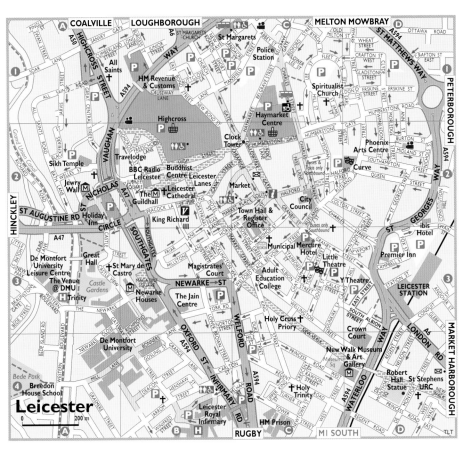

Leicester

Leicester

Leicester is found on atlas page **72 F10**

Albion Street	C3	Infirmary Road	B4
All Saints Road	A1	Jarrom Street	B4
Bath Lane	A2	Jarvis Street	A1
Bedford Street	C1	King Street	C3
Belgrave Gate	C1	Lee Street	C1
Belvoir Street	C3	London Road	D3
Bishop Street	C3	Lower Brown Street	B3
Bonners Lane	B4	Magazine Square	B3
Bowling Green Street	C3	Mansfield Street	B1
Burgess Street	B1	Market Place South	B2
Burton Street	D2	Market Street	C3
Calais Hill	C3	Mill Lane	A4
Campbell Street	D3	Morledge Street	D1
Cank Street	B2	Newarke Street	B3
Castle Street	A3	New Walk	C3
Charles Street	C1	Oxford Street	B3
Chatham Street	C3	Peacock Lane	B2
Cheapside	C2	Pocklington Walk	B3
Church Gate	B1	Princess Road East	D4
Clyde Street	D1	Princess Road West	C4
Colton Street	C2	Queen Street	D2
Conduit Street	D3	Regent Road	C4
Crafton Street West	D1	Regent Street	D4
Deacon Street	B4	Richard III Road	A2
De Montfort Street	D4	Rutland Street	C2
Dover Street	C3	St Augustine Road	A2
Duke Street	C3	St George Street	D2
Duns Lane	A3	St Georges Way	D2
East Bond Street Lane	B1	St James Street	C1
Erskine Street	D1	St Matthews Way	D1
Fleet Street	C1	St Nicholas Circle	A2
Friar Lane	B3	Sanvey Gate	A1
Gallowtree Gate	C2	Soar Lane	A1
Gateway Street	A3	South Albion Street	D3
Granby Street	C2	Southampton Street	D2
Grasmere Street	A4	Southgates	B3
Gravel Street	B1	Station Street	D3
Great Central Street	A1	The Newarke	A3
Greyfriars	B2	Tower Street	C4
Halford Street	C2	Vaughan Way	A2
Haymarket	C2	Waterloo Way	D4
Highcross Street	A1	Welford Road	C4
Highcross Street	B2	Welles Street	A2
High Street	B2	Wellington Street	C3
Hill Street	C1	Western Boulevard	A4
Horsefair Street	B3	West Street	C4
Humberstone Gate	C2	Wharf Street South	D1
Humberstone Road	D1	Yeoman Street	C2

Lincoln

Lincoln is found on atlas page **86 C6**

Alexandra Terrace	B2	Montague Street	D3
Arboretum Avenue	D2	Motherby Lane	B2
Baggholme Road	D3	Nelson Street	A2
Bailgate	C1	Newland	B3
Bank Street	C3	Newland Street West	A2
Beaumont Fee	B3	Northgate	C1
Belle Vue Terrace	A1	Orchard Street	B3
Brayford Way	A4	Oxford Street	C4
Brayford Wharf East	B4	Park Street	B3
Brayford Wharf North	A3	Pelham Street	C4
Broadgate	C3	Pottergate	D2
Burton Road	B1	Queen's Crescent	A1
Carholme Road	A2	Richmond Road	A1
Carline Road	A1	Rope Walk	A4
Cathedral Street	C2	Rosemary Lane	D3
Chapel Lane	B1	Rudgard Lane	A2
Charles Street West	A2	St Hugh Street	D3
Cheviot Street	D2	St Mark Street	B4
City Square	C3	St Martin's Street	C2
Clasketgate	C3	St Mary's Street	B4
Cornhill	B4	St Rumbold's Street	C3
Croft Street	D3	Saltergate	C3
Danesgate	C2	Silver Street	C3
Depot Street	A3	Sincil Street	C4
Drury Lane	B2	Spring Hill	B2
East Bight	C1	Steep Hill	C2
Eastgate	C1	Swan Street	C3
Free School Lane	C3	Tentercroft Street	B4
Friars Lane	C3	The Avenue	A2
Grantham Street	C2	The Sidings	A4
Greetwellgate	D1	Thorngate	C3
Gresham Street	A2	Triton Road	A4
Guildhall Street	B3	Union Road	B1
Hampton Street	A1	Unity Square	C3
High Street	B3	Victoria Street	B2
Hungate	C2	Victoria Terrace	B2
John Street	D3	Vine Street	D2
Langworthgate	D1	Waterside North	C3
Lindum Road	C2	Waterside South	C3
Lindum Terrace	D2	Westgate	B1
Lucy Tower Street	B3	West Parade	A2
May Crescent	A1	Whitehall Grove	A2
Melville Street	C4	Wigford Way	B3
Michaelgate	C2	Winnow Sty Lane	D1
Minster Yard	C2	Winn Street	D3
Mint Lane	B3	Wragby Road	D2
Mint Street	B3	Yarborough Terrace	A1
Monks Road	D3	York Avenue	A1

Lincoln

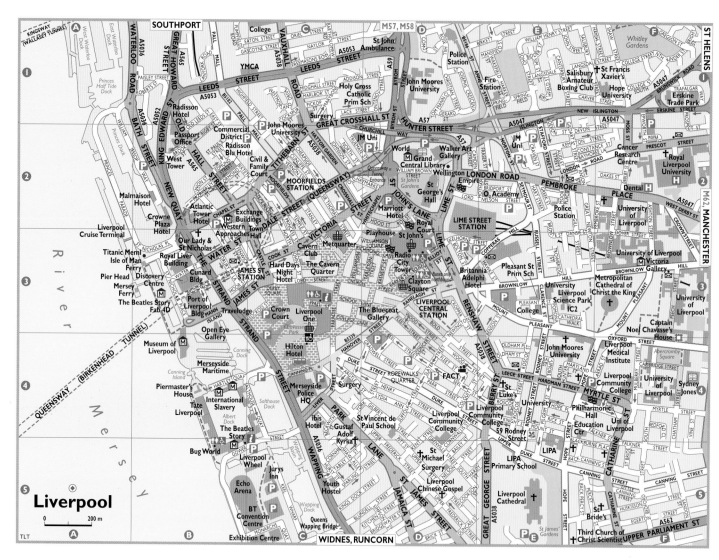

Liverpool

Liverpool is found on atlas page **81 L6**

Addison Street C1
Anson Street E2
Argyle Street C4
Arrad Street F4
Ashton Street F2
Audley Street E2
Back Canning Street E5
Baltimore Street E4
Bath Street B2
Beckwith Street C4
Bedford Street South F5
Benson Street E3
Berry Street E4
Bidder Street E1
Birkett Street D1
Bixteth Street B2
Blackburne Place E5
Blundell Street C5
Bold Street D3
Bosnett Street D3
Bridgewater Street D5
Bridport Street E2
Brook Street B2
Brownlow Hill E3
Brownlow Street F3
Brunswick Road F1
Brunswick Street B3
Byrom Street D1
Cambridge Street F4
Camden Street D2
Canning Place C4
Canning Street E5
Canterbury Street E1
Carver Street E1
Castle Street C3
Catharine Street F5

Cathedral Walk E3
Chapel Street B2
Chatham Street F4
Cheapside C2
Christian Street D1
Church Street C3
Churchill Way D2
Clarence Street E3
Cockspur Street C1
College Lane C3
College Street North F1
College Street South F1
Colquitt Street D4
Constance Street E2
Cook Street C3
Copperas Hill E3
Cornhill C5
Cornwallis Street D5
Craven Street E2
Cropper Street D3
Crosshall Street C2
Crown Street F2
Dale Street (Queensway) C2
Dansie Street E3
Daulby Street F2
Derby Square C3
Devon Street E2
Dover Street F3
Drury Lane B3
Duke Street D4
East Street B1
Eaton Street B1
Edmund Street B2
Egerton Street F5
Elliot Street D3
Epworth Street F1

Erskine Street F1
Falkner Street E4
Fazakerley Street B2
Fenwick Street B3
Fleet Street D3
Fontenoy Street D1
Fraser Street E2
Gascoyne Street B1
Gilbert Street D4
Gildart Street E2
Gill Street E2
Gower Street B5
Gradwell Street D4
Great Crosshall Street C1
Great George Street E5
Great Howard Street B1
Great Newton Street E2
Greek Street E2
Gregson Street F1
Grenville Street South D5
Hackins Hey C2
Hanover Street C4
Hardman Street E4
Harker Street E1
Hartley Quay B4
Hart Street E2
Hatton Garden C2
Hawke Street E3
Henry Street D4
Highfield Street B1
Hood Street D2
Hope Place E4
Hope Street E5
Hotham Street E2
Hunter Street D1
Huskisson Street F5
Islington E2
Jamaica Street D5
James Street B3
Johnson Street C2
Keel Wharf C5

Kempston Street E2
Kent Street D5
Kinder Street F1
King Edward Street B2
Kingsway (Wallasey Tunnel) ... A1
Kitchen Street D5
Knight Street E4
Lace Street C1
Langsdale Street E1
Leece Street E4
Leeds Street B1
Lime Street D2
Liver Street C4
London Road D2
London Road E2
Lord Nelson Street D2
Lord Street C3
Lydia Ann Street D4
Mann Island B3
Mansfield Street E1
Marybone C2
Maryland Street E4
Midghall Street C2
Moorfields C2
Moor Street B3
Moss Street F1
Mount Pleasant E3
Mount Street E4
Mulberry Street F4
Myrtle Street E5
Naylor Street C1
Nelson Street D5
Newington D4
New Islington E1
New Quay B2
North John Street C3
Norton Street E2
Old Hall Street B1
Oldham Street E4
Old Haymarket C2
Old Leeds Street B1

Ormond Street B2
Oxford Street F4
Paisley Street B1
Pall Mall B1
Paradise Street C3
Parker Street D3
Park Lane C4
Parr Street D4
Peech Street F3
Pembroke Place E2
Pembroke Street F2
Percey Street E5
Pilgrim Street E4
Pleasant Street E3
Pomona Street E3
Prescot Street F2
Princes Parade A2
Prospect Street F1
Queensway
(Birkenhead Tunnel) A4
Ranelagh Street D3
Redcross Street C3
Renshaw Street D3
Richmond Lane C3
Rigby Street B2
Rodney Street E4
Roscoe Street E4
Rose Hill D1
Russell Street E3
St Anne Street D1
St James Street D5
St John's Lane D2
St Josephs Crescent D1
St Nicholas Place B3
St Paul's Street B2
Salisbury Street E1
Salthouse Quay C4
Sandon Street F5
School Lane C3
Seel Street D4
Seymour Street E2

Shaw Street F1
Sir Thomas Street C2
Skelhorne Street D3
Slater Street D4
Soho Street E1
Sparling Street C5
Springfield E1
Stafford Street E2
Stanley Street C2
Strand Street B3
Suffolk Street D4
Tabley Street C5
Tarleton Street D3
Temple Street C2
The Strand B3
Tithe Barn Street C2
Trafalgar Way F1
Trowbridge Street E3
Trueman Street C2
Upper Duke Street E5
Upper Frederick Street D4
Upper Parliament Street F5
Upper Pitt Street D5
Vauxhall Road C1
Vernon Street C3
Victoria Street C3
Wakefield Street E1
Wall Street B1
Wapping ....
Waterloo Road A1
Water Street B3
West Derby Street F2
Westmorland Drive C1
Whitechapel D2
William Brown Street D2
William Henry Street E1
William Jessop Way A2
Williamson Square D3
Williamson Street D3
Wood Street D3
York Street C4

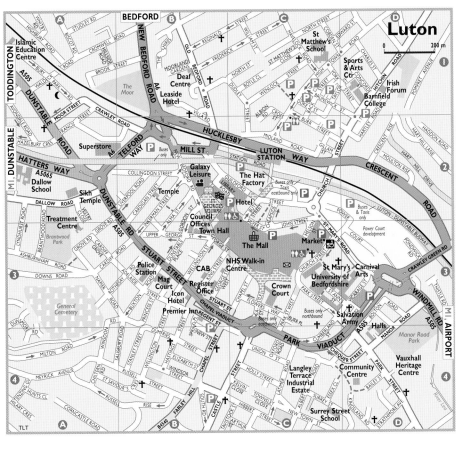

Luton

Luton is found on atlas page **50 C6**

Adelaide Street	B3	Hibbert Street	C4
Albert Road	C4	Highbury Road	A1
Alma Street	B2	High Town Road	C1
Arthur Street	C4	Hitchin Road	D1
Ashburnham Road	A3	Holly Street	C4
Biscot Road	A1	Hucklesby Way	B2
Brantwood Road	A3	Inkerman Street	B3
Brunswick Street	C1	John Street	C3
Burr Street	C2	King Street	B3
Bury Park Road	A1	Latimer Road	C4
Bute Street	C2	Liverpool Road	B2
Buxton Road	B3	Manor Road	D4
Cardiff Road	A3	Meyrick Avenue	A4
Cardigan Street	B2	Midland Road	C2
Castle Street	B4	Mill Street	C2
Chapel Street	B4	Milton Road	A4
Chapel Viaduct	B3	Moor Street	A1
Charles Street	D1	Napier Road	A3
Chequer Street	C4	New Bedford Road	B1
Church Street	C2	New Town Street	C4
Church Street	C3	Old Bedford Road	B1
Cobden Street	C1	Park Street	C3
Collingdon Street	B2	Park Street West	C3
Concorde Street	D1	Park Viaduct	C4
Crawley Green Road	D3	Princess Street	B3
Crawley Road	A1	Regent Street	B3
Crescent Road	D2	Reginald Street	B1
Cromwell Road	A1	Rothesay Road	A3
Cumberland Street	C4	Russell Rise	A4
Dallow Road	A2	Russell Street	B4
Dudley Street	C1	St Mary's Road	C3
Dumfries Street	B4	St Saviour's Crescent	A4
Dunstable Road	A1	Salisbury Road	A4
Farley Hill	B4	Stanley Street	B4
Flowers Way	C3	Station Road	C2
Frederick Street	B1	Strathmore Avenue	D4
George Street	B3	Stuart Street	B3
George Street West	B3	Surrey Street	C4
Gordon Street	B3	Tavistock Street	B4
Grove Road	A3	Telford Way	B2
Guildford Street	B2	Upper George Street	B3
Hart Hill Drive	D2	Vicarage Street	D3
Hart Hill Lane	D2	Waldeck Road	A1
Hartley Road	D2	Wellington Street	B4
Hastings Street	B4	Wenlock Street	C1
Hatters Way	A2	Windmill Road	D3
Havelock Road	C1	Windsor Street	B4
Hazelbury Crescent	A2	Winsdon Road	A4

Maidstone

Maidstone is found on atlas page **38 C10**

Albany Street	D1	Market Buildings	B2
Albion Place	D2	Marsham Street	C2
Allen Street	D1	Meadow Walk	D4
Ashford Road	D3	Medway Street	B3
Bank Street	B3	Melville Road	C4
Barker Road	B4	Mill Street	B3
Bedford Place	A3	Mote Avenue	D3
Bishops Way	B3	Mote Road	D3
Brewer Street	C2	Old School Place	D2
Broadway	A3	Orchard Street	C3
Broadway	B3	Padsole Lane	C3
Brunswick Street	C4	Palace Avenue	B3
Buckland Hill	A2	Princes Street	D1
Buckland Road	A2	Priory Road	C4
Camden Street	C1	Pudding Lane	B2
Chancery Lane	D3	Queen Anne Road	D2
Charles Street	A4	Reginald Road	A4
Church Street	C2	Rocky Hill	A3
College Avenue	B4	Romney Place	C3
College Road	C4	Rose Yard	B2
County Road	C1	Rowland Close	A4
Crompton Gardens	D4	St Anne Court	A2
Cromwell Road	D2	St Faith's Street	B2
Douglas Road	A4	St Luke's Avenue	D1
Earl Street	B2	St Luke's Road	D1
Elm Grove	D4	St Peters Street	A2
Fairmeadow	B1	Sandling Road	B1
Florence Road	A4	Sittingbourne Road	D1
Foley Street	D1	Square Hill Road	D3
Foster Street	C4	Staceys Street	B1
Gabriel's Hill	C3	Station Approach	A4
George Street	C4	Station Road	B1
Greenside	D4	Terrace Road	A3
Hart Street	A4	Tonbridge Road	A4
Hastings Road	D4	Tufton Street	C2
Hayle Road	C4	Union Street	C2
Heathorn Street	D1	Upper Stone Street	C4
Hedley Street	C1	Victoria Street	A3
High Street	B3	Vinters Road	D2
Holland Road	D1	Wat Tyler Way	C3
James Street	C1	Week Street	B1
Jeffrey Street	C1	Well Road	C1
King Street	C2	Westree Road	A4
Kingsley Road	D4	Wheeler Street	C1
Knightrider Street	C4	Woollett Street	C1
Lesley Place	A1	Wyatt Street	C2
London Road	A3		
Lower Stone Street	C3		

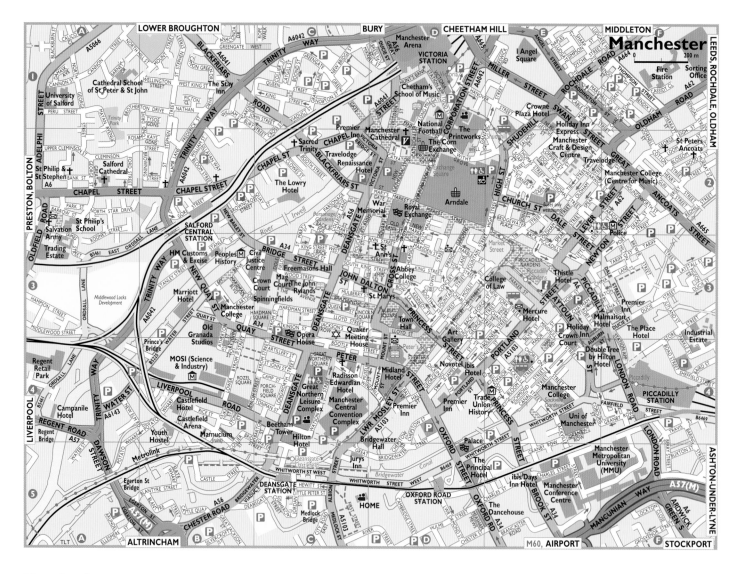

Manchester

Manchester is found on atlas page **82 H5**

Abingdon Street	E4
Addington Street	E1
Adelphi Street	A2
Albion Street	C5
Angel Street	E1
Ardwick Green South	F5
Artillery Street	C4
Atherton Street	B4
Atkinson Street	C3
Auburn Street	E4
Aytoun Street	E3
Back Piccadilly	E3
Bank Street	A2
Baring Street	F4
Barton Street	C4
Berry Street	F4
Blackfriars Road	B1
Blackfriars Street	C2
Blantyre Street	B5
Bloom Street	B2
Bloom Street	E4
Blossom Street	F2
Boad Street	F4
Boond Street	C1
Booth Street	D3
Bootle Street	C4
Brancaster Road	E5
Brazennose Street	C3
Brewer Street	F3
Bridge Street	C3
Bridgewater Place	E2
Bridgewater Street	B4
Bridgewater Viaduct	B5
Brook Street	E5
Brotherton Drive	A1
Browncross Street	B2

Browning Street	B2
Brown Street	D3
Bury Street	B1
Byrom Street	B4
Cable Street	E1
Cambridge Street	D5
Camp Street	C4
Canal Street	E4
Cannon Street	A1
Canon Green Drive	B1
Castle Street	B5
Cathedral Street	D2
Chadderton Street	F1
Chapel Street	A2
Charles Street	E5
Charlotte Street	D3
Chatham Street	E3
Cheapside	D3
Chester Road	B5
China Lane	E3
Chorlton Street	E4
Church Street	E2
City Road East	C5
Cleminson Street	A2
College Land	C2
Collier Street	C1
Commercial Street	C5
Copperas Street	E2
Cornell Street	F2
Corporation Street	D2
Cotton Street	F2
Crosskeys Street	F1
Cross Street	C2
Cross Street	D3
Dale Street	E2
Dantzic Street	D2

Dawson Street	A5
Deansgate	C4
Dickinson Street	D4
Duke Street	B4
Dulcie Street	F3
East Ordsall Lane	A3
Egerton Street	A5
Exchange Square	D2
Fairfield Street	F4
Faulkner Street	D4
Fennel Street	D1
Ford Street	A2
Fountain Street	D3
Frederick Street	B2
Garden Lane	B1
Gartside Street	B3
George Leigh Street	F2
George Street	D4
Gore Street	B2
Granby Row	E5
Gravel Lane	C1
Great Ancoats Street	F2
Great Bridgewater Street	C5
Great Ducie Street	D1
Great George Street	A2
Great Jackson Street	B5
Great John Street	B4
Greengate	C1
Greengate West	B1
Gun Street	F2
Hanover Street	D1
Hardman Street	C3
Hewitt Street	C5
High Street	E2
Hood Street	F2
Hope Street	E3
Houndsworth Street	F2
Hulme Street	D5
James Street	A3
Jersey Street	F2
John Dalton Street	C3

John Street	D1
John Street	E2
Joiner Street	E2
Jutland Street	F3
Kennedy Street	D3
King Street	C1
King Street	C3
King Street West	C3
Lamb Lane	B2
Laystall Street	F3
Left Bank	B3
Lena Street	F3
Lever Street	E2
Little Lever Street	E2
Little Peter Street	C5
Liverpool Road	B4
Lloyd Street	C3
London Road	F4
Long Millgate	D1
Longworth Street	B4
Lower Byrom Street	B4
Lower Mosley Street	C4
Lower Ormond Street	D5
Ludgate Street	E1
Major Street	E4
Mancunian Way	E5
Marble Street	D3
Market Street	D2
Marsden Street	D3
Marshall Street	E1
Mason Street	E1
Mayan Avenue	A1
Medlock Street	C5
Middlewood Street	A3
Miller Street	E1
Minshull Street	E4
Mirabel Street	C1
Mosley Street	D3
Mount Street	B1
Mount Street	D4
Museum Street	C4

Nathan Drive	B1
New Bailey Street	B2
New Bridge Street	C1
New Cathedral Street	D2
New Elm Road	A4
New George Street	E2
New Quay Street	B3
Newton Street	E3
New York Street	E3
Nicholas Street	D3
North George Street	A1
North Hill Street	A1
North Star Drive	A2
Norton Street	C1
Oldfield Road	A3
Oldham Road	F1
Oldham Street	E2
Ordsall Lane	A4
Oxford Road	D5
Oxford Street	D4
Pall Mall	D3
Parker Street	E3
Peru Street	A1
Peter Street	C4
Piccadilly	E3
Piccadilly Gardens	E3
Portland Street	D4
Port Street	F3
Potato Wharf	A5
Princess Street	D3
Quay Street	B3
Queen Street	C1
Queen Street	C3
Redhill Street	F2
Regent Road	A4
Reyner Street	D4
Rice Street	B4
Richmond Street	E4
Rochdale Road	E1
Rodney Street	A3
Rosamond Drive	A2

Sackville Street	E4
St Anns Square	C2
St Ann Street	C3
St James Square	C3
St James Street	D4
St Mary's Parsonage	C3
St Stephen Street	B2
Store Street	F3
Sharp Street	E1
Shudehill	E2
Silk Street	A1
Simpson Street	E1
South King Street	C3
Spear Street	E3
Spring Gardens	D3
Station Approach	F3
Swan Street	E1
Tariff Street	F3
Thomas Street	E2
Thompson Street	F1
Tib Lane	D3
Tib Street	E2
Todd Street	D1
Tonman Street	C4
Travis Street	F4
Trinity Way	A4
Turner Street	E2
Victoria Bridge Street	C2
Victoria Station Approach	D1
Victoria Street	D2
Warwick Street	E2
Watson Street	C4
Well Street	D2
West King Street	B1
West Mosley Street	D3
Whitworth Street	D5
Whitworth Street West	C5
Windmill Street	C4
Withy Grove	D2
Wood Street	C3
York Street	D3

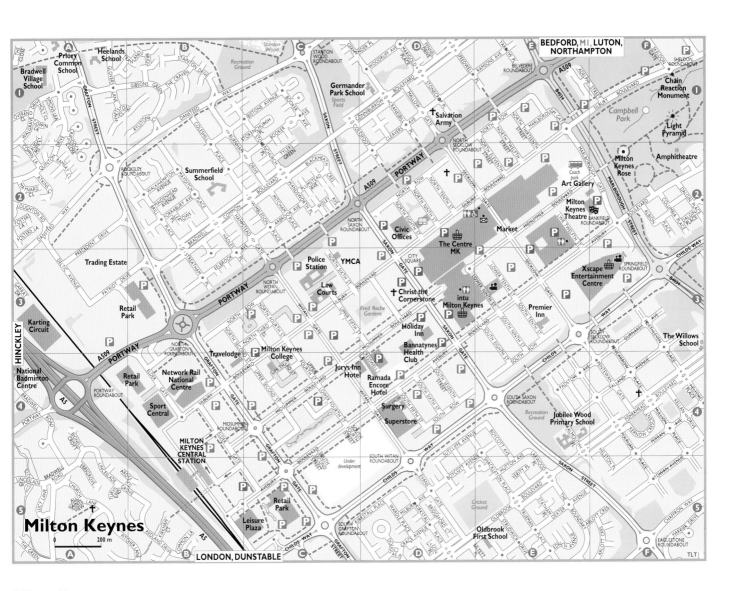

Milton Keynes

Milton Keynes is found on atlas page **49 N7**

Adelphi Street	E1	Craneshill Place	D1
Albion Place	F2	Cresswell Lane	D3
All Saints View	A5	Dalgin Place	F2
Arbrook Avenue	C2	Dansteed Way	A2
Ardys Court	A5	Dansteed Way	B1
Arlott Crescent	F5	Deltic Avenue	A3
Atkins Close	A2	Dexter Avenue	E5
Audley Mews	A2	Douglas Place	D5
Avebury Boulevard	C5	Eaglestone Roundabout	F5
Bankfield Roundabout	E2	Ebbsgrove	A5
Belvedere Roundabout	E1	Edrich Avenue	E5
Bignell Croft	A4	Eelbrook Avenue	B3
Blackheath Crescent	C2	Elder Gate	B4
Booker Avenue	C1	Evans Gate	D5
Boycott Avenue	D5	Falmouth Place	E4
Boycott Avenue	E4	Fennel Drive	D1
Bradwell Common Boulevard	B2	Fishermead Boulevard	F4
Bradwell Road	A4	Forrabury Avenue	B2
Bradwell Road	A5	Fosters Lane	A2
Bridgeford Court	D5	Garrat Drive	A3
Brill Place	B2	Germander Place	C1
Burnham Drive	B1	Gibsons Green	B1
Chaffron Way	F5	Glovers Lane	A1
Childs Way	C5	Grace Avenue	D5
Childs Way	F3	Grafton Gate	B4
Church Lane	A5	Grafton Street	A1
City Square	D3	Grafton Street	C5
Cleavers Avenue	D1	Gurnards Avenue	F3
Coleshill Place	B1	Hadley Place	B2
Coltsfoot Place	C1	Hampstead Gate	B2
Columbia Place	F2	Harrier Drive	F5
Common Lane	B5	Helford Place	F4
Conniburrow Boulevard	C1	Helston Place	E5
Coppin Lane	A2	Holy Close	A1
Craddocks Close	A1	Hutton Avenue	E5
		Ibistone Avenue	C1
Kellan Drive	F4	North Secklow Roundabout	D1
Kernow Crescent	F4	North Second Street	B3
Kirkham Court	B5	North Sixth Street	C3
Kirkstall Place	C5	North Tenth Street	D2
Larwood Place	E5	North Third Street	C3
Leasowe Place	B2	North Thirteenth Street	E3
Linceslade Grove	A5	North Twelfth Street	E1
Loughton Road	A2	North Witan Roundabout	C3
Lower Fourth Street	C4	Oldbrook Boulevard	E5
Lower Ninth Street	E3	Overend Close	A1
Lower Tenth Street	E3	Padstow Avenue	E4
Lower Twelfth Street	E2	Patriot Drive	A3
Lucy Lane	A5	Pencarrow Place	F3
Maidenhead Avenue	B2	Pentewan Gate	F4
Mallow Gate	D1	Perran Avenue	F4
Marigold Place	D1	Pitcher Lane	A5
Marlborough Gate	E1	Plumstead Avenue	C2
Marlborough Gate	E2	Polruan Place	F4
Marlborough Street	F2	Porthleven Place	F3
Mayditch Place	B2	Portway	B3
Maynard Close	A2	Portway Roundabout	A4
Midsummer Boulevard	C4	Precedent Drive	A3
Midsummer Boulevard	E2	Quinton Drive	A2
Midsummer Roundabout	B4	Ramsay Close	A2
Milburn Avenue	D5	Ramsons Avenue	E1
Mitcham Place	C2	Redland Drive	B5
Mullion Place	F4	Rooksley Roundabout	A2
North Eighth Street	D2	Rylstone Close	B1
North Eleventh Street	E1	Saxon Gate	D2
North Fourth Street	C3	Saxon Street	C1
North Grafton Roundabout	B3	Secklow Gate	D2
North Ninth Street	D2	Shackleton Place	E5
North Row	B3	Sheldon Roundabout	F1
North Row	D2	Silbury Boulevard	B4
North Saxon Roundabout	C2	Silbury Roundabout	B4
Simons Lea	A1	Tyson Place	D5
Skeldon Gate	F1	Ulyett Place	D5
South Eighth Street	E3	Upper Fifth Street	C3
South Fifth Street	D4	Upper Fourth Street	C4
South Fourth Street	C4	Upper Second Street	C4
South Grafton Roundabout	C5	Upper Third Street	C4
South Ninth Street	D4	Verity Place	E5
South Row	D4	Walgrave Drive	A1
South Saxon Roundabout	E4	Walkhampton Avenue	B2
South Secklow Roundabout	D3	Wandsworth Place	C2
South Second Street	C5	Wardle Place	D5
South Seventh Street	D4	Whetstone Close	A1
South Sixth Street	D4	Wimbledon Place	C2
South Tenth Street	E3	Wisely Avenue	C2
South Witan Roundabout	D5	Witan Gate	C3
Speedwell Place	B1	Woodruff Avenue	D1
Springfield Roundabout	F3	Yarrow Place	E1
Stainton Drive	B1		
Stanton Wood Roundabout	C1		
Statham Place	E5		
Stokenchurch Place	C1		
Stonecrop Place	D1		
Streatham Place	B3		
Strudwick Drive	E5		
Sutcliffe Avenue	D4		
Talland Avenue	F4		
The Boundary	E5		
The Close	A1		
The Craven	B1		
The Green	A5		
Towan Avenue	F5		
Tranlands Brigg	B1		
Trueman Place	E5		
Turvil End	A5		
Tylers Green	C2		

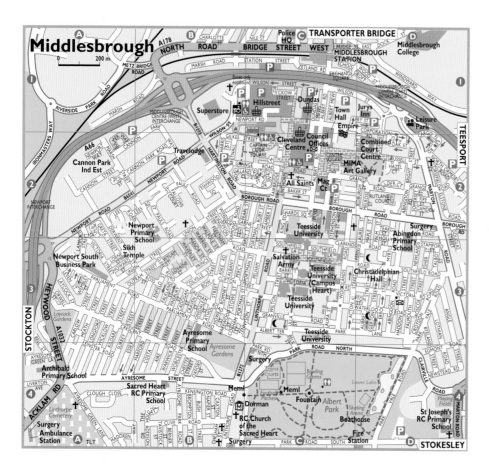

Middlesbrough

Middlesbrough is found on atlas page **104 E7**

Acklam Road	A4	Heywood Street	A3
Acton Street	C3	Ironmasters Way	A2
Aire Street	B4	Kensington Road	B4
Albert Road	C2	Kildare Street	A4
Amber Street	C2	Laurel Street	D3
Athol Street	B3	Lees Road	A2
Aubrey Street	D3	Linthorpe Road	B4
Ayresome Park Road	B4	Longford Street	B4
Ayresome Street	A4	Lorne Street	A3
Borough Road	C2	Lothian Road	D3
Bretnall Street	B2	Marsh Street	A2
Bridge Street East	C1	Marton Road	D2
Bridge Street West	C1	Melrose Street	D2
Bush Street	B4	Metz Bridge Road	A1
Cadogen Street	B3	Myrtle Street	D3
Camden Street	D2	Newlands Road	D3
Cannon Park Road	A2	Newport Road	B3
Cannon Park Way	A2	Palm Street	D3
Cannon Street	A2	Park Lane	C3
Carlow Street	A3	Park Road North	C4
Centre Square	C2	Park Vale Road	C4
Clairville Road	D4	Parliament Road	A3
Clarendon Road	C3	Pearl Street	C2
Clifton Street	B3	Pelham Street	C3
Corporation Road	D1	Portman Street	B3
Costa Street	B4	Princes Road	B3
Craven Street	B3	Riverside Park Road	A1
Crescent Road	A3	Ruby Street	C2
Croydon Road	D3	Russell Street	D2
Derwent Street	A2	St Pauls Road	B2
Diamond Road	B3	Southfield Road	C3
Egmont Road	D4	Station Street	C1
Emily Street	C2	Stowe Street	B3
Errol Street	D3	Tavistock Street	B4
Essex Street	A4	Tennyson Street	B3
Fairbridge Street	C2	Union Street	A3
Falmouth Street	D3	Victoria Road	C3
Finsbury Street	B3	Victoria Street	A3
Fleetham Street	B2	Warren Street	B2
Garnet Street	B2	Waterloo Road	D3
Glebe Road	B3	Waverley Street	A3
Grange Road	B2	Wembley Street	A3
Grange Road	D2	Wilson Street	B2
Granville Road	C3	Wilton Street	B2
Gresham Road	B3	Windsor Street	B2
Harewood Street	B3	Woodlands Road	A2
Harford Street	B4	Worcester Street	B4
Hartington Road	B2	Zetland Road	C1

Newport

Newport is found on atlas page **31 K7**

Albert Terrace	B3	Jones Street	B3
Allt-Yr-Yn Avenue	A2	Keynsham Avenue	C4
Bailey Street	B3	King Street	C4
Bedford Road	D2	Kingsway	C2
Blewitt Street	B3	Kingsway	C2
Bond Street	C1	Llanthewy Road	A3
Bridge Street	B2	Locke Street	B1
Bryngwyn Road	A3	Lower Dock Street	C4
Brynhyfryd Avenue	A4	Lucas Street	B1
Brynhyfryd Road	A4	Market Street	B2
Caerau Crescent	A4	Mellon Street	C4
Caerau Road	A3	Mill Street	B2
Cambrian Road	B2	North Street	B3
Caroline Street	D3	Oakfield Road	A3
Cedar Road	D2	Park Square	C4
Charles Street	C3	Queen's Hill	B1
Chepstow Road	D1	Queen's Hill Crescent	A1
Clarence Place	C1	Queen Street	C4
Clifton Place	B4	Queensway	B2
Clifton Road	B4	Risca Road	A4
Clyffard Crescent	A3	Rodney Road	C2
Clytha Park Road	A2	Rudry Street	D1
Clytha Square	C4	Ruperra Lane	C4
Colts Foot Close	A1	Ruperra Street	D4
Commercial Street	C3	St Edward Street	B3
Corelli Street	D1	St Julian Street	B4
Corn Street	C2	St Mark's Crescent	A2
Corporation Road	D2	St Mary Street	B3
Devon Place	B2	St Vincent Road	C2
Dewsland Park Road	B4	St Woolos Road	B3
Dumfries Place	D4	School Lane	C3
East Street	B3	Serpentine Road	A2
East Usk Road	C1	Skinner Street	C2
Factory Road	B1	Sorrel Drive	A1
Fields Road	A2	Spencer Road	A3
Friars Field	B4	Stow Hill	B3
Friars Road	B4	Stow Hill	B4
Friar Street	C3	Stow Park Avenue	A4
George Street	D4	Talbot Lane	C3
Godfrey Road	A2	Tregare Street	D1
Gold Tops	A2	Tunnel Terrace	A3
Grafton Road	C2	Upper Dock Street	C2
Granville Lane	D4	Upper Dock Street	C3
Granville Street	D4	Usk Way	D3
High Street	B2	Victoria Crescent	B3
Hill Street	C3	West Street	B3
John Frost Square	C3	Wyndham Stret	C1
John Street	D4	York Place	A4

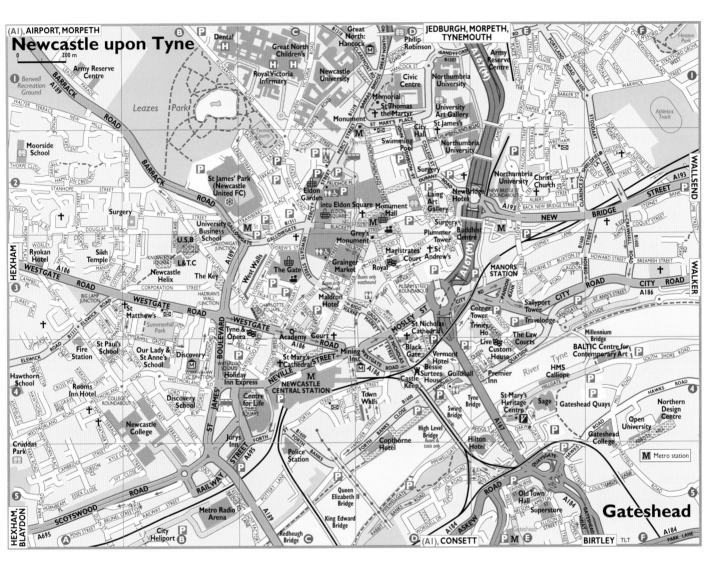

Newcastle upon Tyne

Newcastle upon Tyne is found on atlas page **113 K8**

Abbots Hill	F4	Clayton Street West	C4
Albert Street	E2	Cloth Market	D3
Argyle Street	E2	Colby Court	A4
Askew Road	D5	College Roundabout	A4
Avison Street	A2	College Street	D2
Back New Bridge Street	E2	Cookson Close	A3
Barker Street	E1	Copland Terrace	E2
Barrack Road	A1	Coppice Way	E1
Barras Bridge	D1	Coquet Street	F2
Bath Lane	B3	Corporation Street	B3
Belgrave Parade	A4	Cottenham Street	A3
Big Lamp Junction	A3	Coulthards Lane	F5
Blackett Street	C2	Crawhall Road	F2
Blagdon Street	E3	Cross Parade	A4
Blandford Square	B4	Cross Street	C3
Blandford Street	B4	Darnell Place	A2
Bottle Bank	E4	Dean Street	D3
Boyd Street	F2	Derby Street	B2
Breamish Street	F3	Diana Street	B3
Bridge Street	E4	Dinsdale Place	F1
Broad Chare	E3	Dinsdale Road	F1
Brunel Street	A5	Dobson Close	A5
Buckingham Street	B3	Douglas Terrace	A2
Buxton Street	E3	Duke Street	B4
Byron Street	E1	Dunn Street	A5
Cambridge Street	A5	Durant Road	D2
Camden Street	E2	East Street	E5
Campbell Place	A3	Edward Place	A3
Carliol Square	D3	Eldon Square	C2
Charlotte Square	C3	Ellison Street	E5
Chelmsford Grove	F1	Elswick East Terrace	B4
Chester Street	E1	Elswick Road	A3
City Road	E3	Elswick Row	A3
Claremont Road	D1	Essex Close	A5
Clarence Street	E2	Falconar's Court	C3
Clayton Street	C3	Falconer Street	E2

Fenkle Street	C3	King Edward Bridge	C5
Field Close	F2	King Street	E4
Fletcher Road	D5	Kirkdale Green	A4
Forth Banks	C4	Kyle Close	A5
Forth Banks Close	D5	Lambton Street	E5
Forth Street	C4	Leazes Crescent	C2
Friars Street	C3	Leazes Lane	C2
Gallowgate	B2	Leazes Park Road	C2
Gallowgate Junction	B3	Leazes Terrace	C2
Gateshead Highway	E5	Liddle Road	A2
George Street	B4	Lime Street	F2
Gibson Street	F3	Lombard Street	E4
Gladstone Terrace	E1	Longley Street	A2
Gloucester Terrace	A4	Lord Street	B4
Grainger Street	C3	Low Friar Street	C3
Grantham Road	E1	Maiden Street	B5
Great North Road	D1	Mansfield Street	A3
Grey Street	D3	Maple Street	B5
Groat Market	C3	Maple Terrace	A4
Hamilton Crescent	A2	Market Street	D3
Hanover Street	C5	Mather Road	A4
Harrison Place	E1	Melbourne Street	E3
Hawks Road	E5	Mill Road	F4
Hawthorn Place	A4	Milton Close	E1
Hawthorn Terrace	A4	Milton Place	E1
Helmsley Road	E1	Monday Crescent	A1
Henry Square	E1	Mosley Street	D3
High Bridge	D3	Napier Street	E1
High Level Road	D5	Nelson Street	C3
High Street	E5	Nelson Street	E5
Hillgate	E4	Neville Street	C4
Hood Street	D3	New Bridge Street	E2
Hopper Street	B3	Newgate Street	C3
Hornbeam Place	A5	Newington Road	F1
Houston Street	A4	New Mills	A1
Howard Street	F3	Northumberland Road	D2
Hudson Street	E5	Northumberland Street	D2
Ivy Close	A5	Nun Street	C3
Jesmond Road West	D1	Oakwellgate	E4
John Dobson Street	D2	Orchard Street	C4
Jubilee Road	E3	Ord Street	B5

King Edward Bridge	C5	Oxford Street	D2
King Street	E4	Pandon	E3
Kirkdale Green	A4	Pandon Bank	E3
Kyle Close	A5	Park Lane	F5
Lambton Street	E5	Park Road	A5
Leazes Crescent	C2	Peel Lane	B4
Leazes Lane	C2	Penn Street	A5
Leazes Park Road	C2	Percy Street	C2
Leazes Terrace	C2	Pilgrim Street	D2
Liddle Road	A2	Pink Lane	C4
Lime Street	F2	Pipewellgate	D5
Lombard Street	E4	Pitt Street	B2
Longley Street	A2	Portland Road	E1
Lord Street	B4	Portland Road	F1
Low Friar Street	C3	Pottery Lane	C5
Maiden Street	B5	Prospect Place	A2
Mansfield Street	A3	Prudhoe Place	C2
Maple Street	B5	Quarryfield Road	F5
Maple Terrace	A4	Quayside	E5
Market Street	D3	Quayside	F3
Mather Road	A4	Queen Street	E4
Melbourne Street	E3	Queen Victoria Road	C1
Mill Road	F4	Rabbit Banks Road	D5
Milton Close	E1	Railway Street	B5
Milton Place	E1	Red Barnes	E3
Monday Crescent	A1	Redheugh Bridge Road	B5
Mosley Street	D3	Richardson Road	B1
Napier Street	E1	Rock Terrace	E2
Nelson Street	C3	Rosedale Terrace	E1
Nelson Street	E5	Rye Hill	A4
Neville Street	C4	St Andrew's Street	C3
New Bridge Street	E2	St Ann's Street	F3
Newgate Street	C3	St James' Boulevard	B4
Newington Road	F1	St Mary's Place	D1
New Mills	A1	St Nicholas Street	D4
Northumberland Road	D2	St Thomas' Court	C2
Northumberland Street	D2	St Thomas' Street	C1
Nun Street	C3	Sandgate	E3
Oakwellgate	E4	Sandhill	D4
Orchard Street	C4	Sandyford Road	D1
Ord Street	B5		

Scotswood Road	A5	
Shieldfield Lane	F2	
Shield Street	E2	
Shot Factory Lane	C5	
Simpson Terrace	E2	
Somerset Place	A4	
South Shore Road	F4	
South Street	C4	
Stanhope Street	A2	
Stepney Bank	F2	
Stepney Lane	E3	
Stepney Road	F2	
Stoddart Street	F1	
Stowell Street	C3	
Stratford Grove West	F1	
Strawberry Place	C2	
Summerhill Grove	B3	
Summerhill Street	A3	
Summerhill Terrace	B4	
Swinburne Street	E5	
Tarset Road	F3	
Terrace Place	C2	
Tindal Street	A3	
Tower Street	E3	
Tyne Bridge	E4	
Union Street	F2	
Vallum Way	A3	
Victoria Street	B4	
Walter Terrace	A1	
Warwick Street	F1	
Waterloo Square	B4	
Waterloo Street	C4	
Wellington Street	B2	
Westgate Road	A3	
Westmorland Road	A4	
West Street	E5	
West Walls	C3	
Worley Close	A3	
Worsdell Drive	D5	
Wretham Place	E2	
York Street	A3	

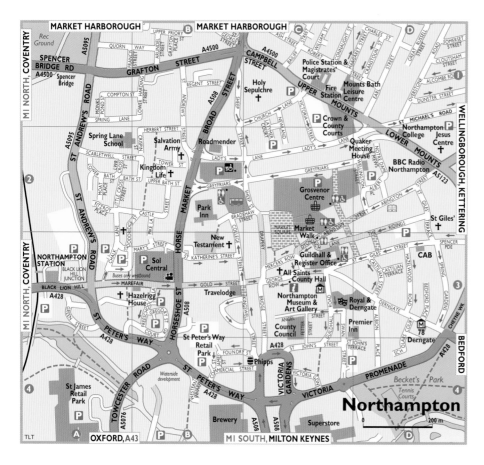

Northampton

Northampton

Northampton is found on atlas page **60 G8**

Abington Street	C2	Little Cross Street	A2
Albert Place	D2	Lower Bath Street	A2
Albion Place	D3	Lower Cross Street	A2
Angel Street	C3	Lower Harding Street	B1
Arundel Street	B1	Lower Mounts	D2
Ash Street	C1	Marefair	A3
Bailiff Street	C1	Margaret Street	C1
Black Lion Hill	A3	Market Square	C2
Bradshaw Street	B2	Mercers Row	C3
Bridge Street	C3	Moat Place	A2
Broad Street	B1	Monkspond Street	A1
Campbell Street	C1	Newland	B2
Castilian Street	D3	Notredame Mews	D2
Castle Street	B2	Overstone Road	D1
Chalk Lane	A3	Pike Lane	B3
Cheyne Walk	D3	Quorn Way	A1
Church Lane	C1	Regent Street	B1
College Street	B2	Robert Street	C1
Commercial Street	B4	St Andrew's Road	A2
Connaught Street	C1	St Andrew's Street	B1
Court Road	B3	St Giles' Street	D3
Cranstoun Street	D1	St Giles' Terrace	D2
Crispin Street	B2	St John's Street	C4
Derngate	D3	St Katherine's Street	B3
Doddridge Street	A3	St Mary's Street	A3
Drapery	C3	St Michael's Road	D1
Dunster Street	D1	St Peter's Way	B4
Dychurch Lane	C3	Scarletwell Street	A2
Earl Street	D1	Scholars Court	D4
Fetter Street	C3	Sheep Street	B1
Fitzroy Place	A2	Sheep Street	B1
Foundry Street	B4	Spencer Bridge Road	A1
Francis Street	A1	Spencer Parade	D3
Freeschool Lane	B3	Spring Gardens	D3
George Row	C3	Spring Lane	A2
Gold Street	B3	Swan Street	C3
Grafton Street	A1	Tanner Street	A4
Great Russell Street	D1	The Ridings	D2
Green Street	A3	Towcester Road	A4
Gregory Street	B3	Tower Street	A4
Greyfriars	B2	Upper Bath Street	B2
Guildhall Road	C3	Upper Mounts	C1
Hazelwood Road	D3	Upper Priory Street	B1
Herbert Street	B2	Victoria Gardens	C4
Horse Market	B3	Victoria Promenade	C4
Horseshoe Street	B3	Victoria Street	C1
Kingswell Street	C3	Wellington Street	D2
Lady's Lane	B2	Western Wharf	B4

Norwich

Norwich

Norwich is found on atlas page **77 J10**

All Saints Green	B4	Pottergate	A2
Bank Plain	C2	Prince of Wales Road	C2
Barn Road	A1	Princes Street	C2
Bedding Lane	C1	Quay Side	C1
Bedford Street	B2	Queens Road	B4
Ber Street	C4	Queen Street	C2
Bethel Street	A3	Rampant Horse Street	B3
Bishopgate	D1	Recorder Road	D2
Brigg Street	B3	Red Lion Street	B3
Calvert Street	B1	Riverside Road	D3
Castle Meadow	C3	Riverside Walk	D1
Cathedral Street	D2	Rose Lane	C3
Cattle Market Street	C3	Rouen Road	C3
Chantry Road	B3	Rupert Street	A4
Chapelfield East	A3	St Andrews Street	B2
Chapelfield North	A3	St Benedicts Street	A2
Chapelfield Road	A3	St Faiths Lane	D2
Cleveland Road	A3	St Georges Street	B1
Colegate	B1	St Giles Street	A2
Convent Road	A3	St Julians Alley	C4
Coslany Street	B2	St Marys Plain	B1
Cow Hill	A2	St Peters Street	B3
Davey Place	B3	St Stephens Road	A4
Dove Street	B2	St Stephens Square	A4
Duke Street	B1	St Stephens Street	A4
Elm Hill	C2	St Swithins Road	A2
Exchange Street	B2	St Verdast Street	D2
Farmers Avenue	C3	Surrey Street	B4
Ferry Lane	D2	Ten Bell Lane	A2
Fishergate	C1	Theatre Street	A3
Friars Quay	B1	Thorn Lane	C4
Gaol Hill	B3	Tombland	C2
Gentlemans Walk	B3	Unicorn Yard	A1
Goldenball Street	C3	Union Street	A4
Grapes Hill	A2	Unthank Road	A3
Haymarket	B3	Upper Goat Lane	A2
Heigham Street	A1	Upper King Street	C2
King Street	C2	Upper St Giles Street	A2
London Street	B2	Vauxhall Street	A3
Lower Goat Lane	B2	Walpole Street	A3
Magdalen Street	C1	Wensum Street	C1
Market Avenue	C3	Wessex Street	A4
Mountergate	D3	Westlegate	B4
Music House Lane	D4	Westwick Street	A1
Muspole Street	B1	Wherry Road	D4
New Mills Yard	A1	Whitefriars	C1
Oak Street	A1	White Lion Street	B3
Palace Street	C1	Willow Lane	A2

Nottingham

Nottingham is found on atlas page **72 F3**

Albert Street	B3	King Street	B2
Angel Row	B2	Lenton Road	A3
Barker Gate	D2	Lincoln Street	C2
Bath Street	D1	Lister Gate	B3
Bellar Gate	D3	London Road	D4
Belward Street	D2	Long Row	B2
Broad Street	C2	Lower Parliament Street	C2
Broadway	C3	Low Pavement	B3
Bromley Place	A2	Maid Marian Way	A2
Brook Street	D1	Market Street	B2
Burton Street	B1	Middle Hill	C3
Canal Street	C4	Milton Street	B1
Carlton Street	C2	Mount Street	A3
Carrington Street	C4	Norfolk Place	B2
Castle Boulevard	A4	North Circus Street	A2
Castle Gate	B3	Park Row	A3
Castle Road	B3	Pelham Street	C2
Chaucer Street	A1	Peveril Drive	A4
City Link	D3	Pilcher Gate	C3
Clarendon Street	A1	Popham Street	C3
Cliff Road	C3	Poultry	B2
Collin Street	B4	Queen Street	B2
Cranbrook Street	D2	Regent Street	A2
Cumber Street	C2	St Ann's Well Road	D1
Curzon Place	C1	St James's Street	A3
Derby Road	A2	St Marks Gate	C3
Exchange Walk	B2	St Marks Street	C1
Fisher Gate	D3	St Mary's Gate	C3
Fletcher Gate	C3	St Peter's Gate	B3
Forman Street	B1	Shakespeare Street	A1
Friar Lane	A3	Smithy Row	B2
Gedling Street	D2	South Parade	B2
George Street	C2	South Sherwood Street	B1
Glasshouse Street	C1	Spaniel Row	B3
Goldsmith Street	A1	Station Street	C4
Goose Gate	C2	Stoney Street	C2
Halifax Place	C3	Talbot Street	A1
Heathcote Street	C2	Thurland Street	C2
High Cross Street	C2	Trent Street	C4
High Pavement	C3	Upper Parliament Street	A2
Hockley	D2	Victoria Street	C2
Hollow Stone	D3	Warser Gate	C3
Hope Drive	A4	Weekday Cross	C3
Hounds Gate	B3	Wellington Circus	A2
Howard Street	C1	Wheeler Gate	B2
Huntingdon Street	C1	Wilford Street	B4
Kent Street	C1	Wollaton Street	A1
King Edward Street	C1	Woolpack Lane	C2

Oldham

Oldham is found on atlas page **83 K4**

Ascroft Street	B3	Napier Street East	A4
Bar Gap Road	B1	New Radcliffe Street	A2
Barlow Street	D4	Oldham Way	A3
Barn Street	B3	Park Road	B4
Beever Street	D2	Park Street	A4
Bell Street	D2	Peter Street	B3
Belmont Street	B1	Prince Street	D3
Booth Street	A3	Queen Street	C3
Bow Street	C3	Radcliffe Street	B1
Brook Street	D2	Ramsden Street	A1
Brunswick Street	B3	Regent Street	D2
Cardinal Street	C2	Rhodes Bank	C3
Chadderton Way	A1	Rhodes Street	C2
Chaucer Street	B3	Rifle Street	B1
Clegg Street	C3	Rochdale Road	A1
Coldhurst Road	B1	Rock Street	B2
Crossbank Street	B4	Roscoe Street	C3
Curzon Street	B2	Ruskin Street	A1
Dunbar Street	A1	St Hilda's Drive	A1
Eden Street	B2	St Marys Street	B1
Egerton Street	C2	St Mary's Way	B2
Emmott Way	C4	Shaw Road	D1
Firth Street	C3	Shaw Street	C1
Fountain Street	B2	Shore Street	D1
Franklin Street	B1	Siddall Street	C1
Gower Street	D2	Silver Street	B3
Grange Street	A2	Southgate Street	C3
Greaves Street	B2	South Hill Street	D4
Greengate Street	D4	Spencer Street	D2
Hardy Street	D4	Sunfield Road	B1
Harmony Street	C4	Thames Street	D1
Henshaw Street	B2	Trafalgar Street	A1
Higginshaw Road	C1	Trinity Street	B1
Highfield Street	A2	Tulbury Street	A1
High Street	B3	Union Street	B3
Hobson Street	B3	Union Street West	A4
Horsedge Street	C1	Union Street West	B3
John Street	A3	University Way	B4
King Street	B3	Wallshaw Street	D2
Lemnos Street	D2	Wall Street	B4
Malby Street	C1	Ward Street	A1
Malton Street	A4	Waterloo Street	C3
Manchester Street	A3	Wellington Street	B4
Market Place	B3	West End Street	A2
Marlborough Street	C4	West Street	B3
Middleton Road	A3	Willow Street	D2
Mortimer Street	D1	Woodstock Street	C4
Mumps	D2	Yorkshire Street	C3

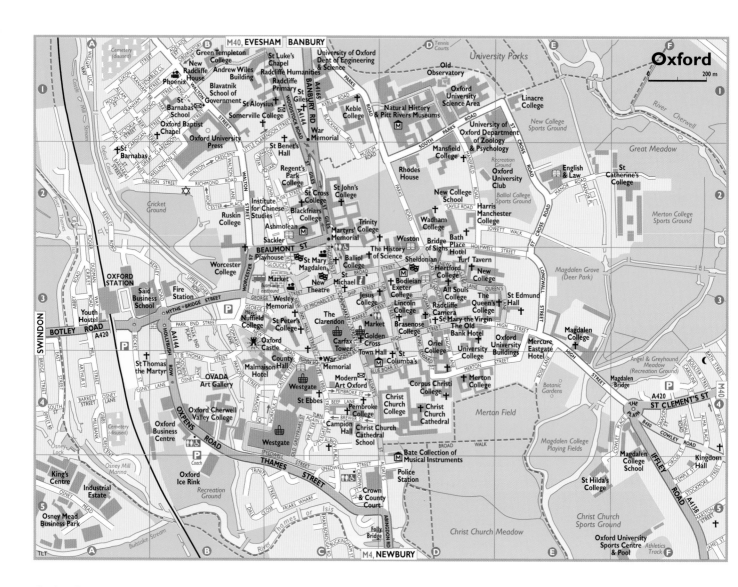

Oxford

Oxford is found on atlas page **34 F3**

Abbey Road	A3	Cromwell Street	C5
Abingdon Road	D5	Dale Close	B5
Adelaide Street	B1	Dawson Street	F4
Albert Street	A1	East Street	A4
Albion Place	C4	Folly Bridge	C5
Allam Street	A1	Friars Wharf	C5
Alma Place	F4	George Street	B3
Arthur Street	A4	George Street Mews	B3
Banbury Road	C1	Gibbs Crescent	A4
Barrett Street	A4	Gloucester Street	C3
Bath Street	F4	Great Clarendon Street	A2
Beaumont Street	C3	Hart Street	B1
Becket Street	A3	High Street	D3
Beef Lane	C4	High Street	E4
Blackhall Road	C1	Hollybush Row	B3
Blue Boar Street	C4	Holywell Street	D2
Bonn Square	C4	Hythe Bridge Street	B3
Botley Road	A3	Iffley Road	F4
Boulter Street	F4	James Street	F5
Brewer Street	C4	Jericho Street	A1
Bridge Street	A4	Jowett Walk	D2
Broad Street	C3	Juxon Street	A1
Broad Walk	D4	Keble Road	C1
Buckingham Street	C5	King Edward Street	D3
Canal Street	A1	King Street	B1
Cardigan Street	A2	Little Clarendon Street	B2
Caroline Street	F4	Littlegate Street	C4
Castle Street	C4	Longwall Street	E3
Catte Street	D3	Magdalen Bridge	E4
Circus Street	F5	Magdalen Street	C3
Cornmarket Street	C3	Magpie Lane	D3
Cowley Place	F4	Manor Place	E2
Cowley Road	F4	Manor Road	E2
Cranham Street	A1	Mansfield Road	D2
Cranham Terrace	A1	Market Street	C3
Cripley Road	A3	Marlborough Road	C5

Marston Street	F5	St Barnabas Street	A2
Merton Street	D4	St Clement's Street	F4
Millbank	A4	St Cross Road	E1
Mill Street	A4	St Cross Road	E2
Mount Street	A1	St Ebbes Street	C4
Museum Road	C2	St Giles	C2
Nelson Street	A2	St John Street	C2
New College Lane	D3	St Michael's Street	C3
New Inn Hall Street	C3	St Thomas' Street	B4
New Road	B3	Savile Road	D2
Norfolk Street	C4	Ship Street	C3
Observatory Street	B1	South Parks Road	D2
Old Greyfriars Street	C4	South Street	A4
Osney Lane	A4	Speedwell Street	C5
Osney Lane	B4	Stockmore Street	F5
Osney Mead	A5	Temple Street	F5
Oxpens Road	B4	Thames Street	C5
Paradise Square	B4	The Plain	F4
Paradise Street	B4	Tidmarsh Lane	B3
Park End Street	B3	Trinity Street	B5
Parks Road	C1	Turl Street	D3
Parks Road	D2	Turn Again Lane	C4
Pembroke Street	C4	Tyndale Road	F4
Pike Terrace	C4	Upper Fisher Row	B3
Pusey Lane	C2	Venables Close	A1
Pusey Street	C2	Victoria Street	A1
Queen's Lane	D3	Walton Crescent	B2
Queen Street	C4	Walton Lane	B2
Radcliffe Square	D3	Walton Street	B1
Rewley Road	A2	Wellington Square	B2
Rewley Road	B3	Wellington Street	B2
Richmond Road	B2	William Lucy Way	A1
Roger Dudman Way	A3	Woodbine Place	B4
Rose Lane	E4	Woodstock Road	C1
St Aldate's	C4	Worcester Place	B2
St Aldate's	D5	Worcester Street	B3

University Colleges

All Souls College	D3
Balliol College	C3
Brasenose College	D3
Christ Church College	D4
Corpus Christi College	D4
Exeter College	D3
Harris Manchester College	D2
Hertford College	D3
Jesus College	C3
Keble College	C1
Linacre College	E1
Lincoln College	D3
Magdalen College	E3
Mansfield College	D2
Merton College	D4
New College	D3
Nuffield College	B3
Oriel College	D3
Pembroke College	C4
Ruskin College	B2
St Catherine's College	F2
St Cross College	C2
St Hilda's College	E5
St John's College	C2
St Peter's College	C3
Somerville College	B1
The Queen's College	D3
Trinity College	C2
University College	D3
Wadham College	D2
Worcester College	B3

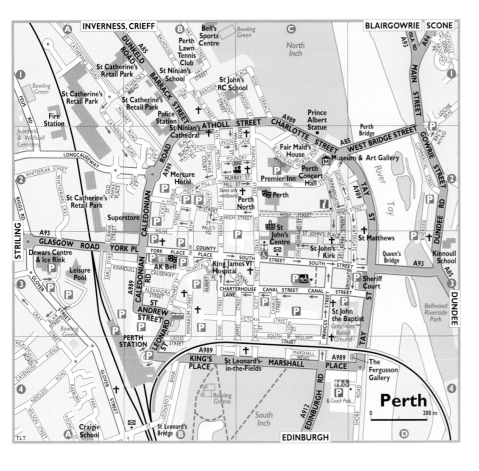

Perth

Perth is found on atlas page **134 E3**

Albert Place	B3	Melville Street	B1
Alexandra Street	B3	Mill Street	B2
Atholl Street	B1	Mill Street	C2
Back Wynd	D2	Milne Street	B2
Balhousie Street	B1	Monart Road	A1
Barossa Place	B1	Murray Street	B2
Barrack Street	B1	Needless Road	A4
Blackfriars Wynd	C2	New Row	B3
Black Watch Garden	B2	North Methven Street	B2
Caledonian Road	B2	North Port	C2
Caledonian Road	B3	North William Street	B2
Canal Street	C3	Old Market Place	A2
Cavendish Avenue	A4	Paul Street	B2
Charles Street	C3	Perth Bridge	D2
Charlotte Street	C2	Pickletullum Road	A4
Charterhouse Lane	B3	Pomarium Street	B3
Commercial Street	D2	Princes Street	C3
County Place	B3	Queen's Bridge	D3
Cross Street	B4	Raeburn Park	A4
Dundee Road	D3	Riggs Road	A2
Dunkeld Road	B1	Riverside	D3
Earls Dykes	A3	Rose Terrace	C1
Edinburgh Road	C4	St Andrew Street	B3
Elibank Street	A3	St Catherine's Road	A1
Feus Road	A1	St John's Place	C3
Foundry Lane	B2	St John Street	C3
George Street	C2	St Leonard's Bank	B4
Glasgow Road	A3	St Paul's Square	B2
Glover Street	A3	Scott Street	C3
Glover Street	A4	Shore Road	D4
Gowrie Street	D2	Skinnergate	C2
Gray Street	A3	South Methven Street	B2
Hay Street	B1	South Street	C3
High Street	B2	South William Street	C4
High Street	C2	Speygate	D3
Hospital Street	B3	Stormont Street	B1
Isla Road	D1	Tay Street	D2
James Street	C3	Tay Street	D4
King Edward Street	C3	Union Lane	B2
King's Place	B4	Victoria Street	C3
King Street	B3	Watergate	D2
Kinnoull Causeway	A3	West Bridge Street	D2
Kinnoull Street	C2	West Mill Wynd	B2
Leonard Street	B3	Whitefriars Crescent	A2
Lochie Brae	D1	Whitefriar Street	A2
Longcauseway	A2	Wilson Street	A4
Main Street	D1	York Place	A3
Marshall Place	C4	York Place	B3

Peterborough

Peterborough is found on atlas page **74 C11**

Albert Place	B3	New Road	C1
Bishop's Road	C3	Northminster	C1
Boongate	D1	North Street	B1
Bourges Boulevard	A1	Oundle Road	B4
Bridge Street	B3	Park Road	B1
Bright Street	A1	Pipe Lane	D2
Broadway	B2	Priestgate	A2
Brook Street	C1	Rivergate	B3
Cathedral Square	B2	River Lane	A2
Cattle Market Street	C1	Russell Street	A1
Chapel Street	C1	St John's Street	C2
Church Street	B2	St Peters Road	B3
Church Walk	C1	South Street	D2
City Road	C2	Star Road	D2
Cowgate	B2	Station Road	A2
Craig Street	B1	Thorpe Lea Road	A3
Crawthorne Road	C1	Thorpe Road	A2
Cromwell Road	A1	Trinity Street	B3
Cross Street	B2	Viersen Platz	B3
Cubitt Way	B4	Vineyard Road	C3
Deacon Street	A1	Wake Road	D2
Dickens Street	D1	Wareley Road	A4
Eastfield Road	D1	Wellington Street	D1
Eastgate	D2	Wentworth Street	B3
East Station Road	C4	Westgate	A1
Embankment Road	C3		
Exchange Street	D2		
Fengate Close	D2		
Field Walk	D1		
Fitzwilliam Street	B1		
Frank Perkins Parkway	D4		
Geneva Street	B1		
Gladstone Street	A1		
Granby Street	C2		
Hawksbill Way	B4		
Hereward Close	D2		
Hereward Road	D2		
King Street	B2		
Laxton Square	C2		
Lea Gardens	A3		
Lincoln Road	B1		
London Road	B4		
Long Causeway	B2		
Manor House Street	B1		
Mayor's Walk	A1		
Midgate	B2		
Morris Street	D1		
Nene Street	D2		

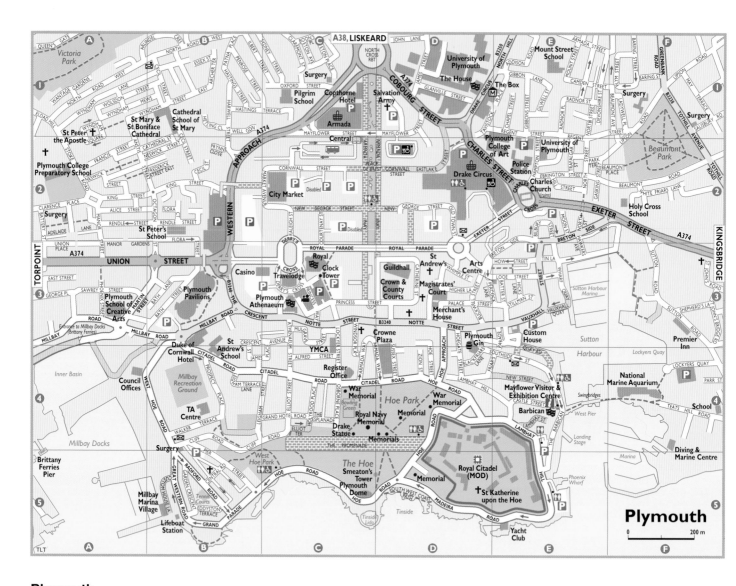

Plymouth

Plymouth is found on atlas page **6 D8**

Addison Road..............E1	Clarence Place A2	Great Western Road..............B5	Mayflower Street D1	Radnor Street E1	West Hoe Road..............A4
Adelaide Lane A2	Cliff Road B4	Greenbank Road F1	May Terrace..............F1	Raleigh Street..............C2	Wharf Quay E3
Alfred Street C4	Cobourg Street D1	Hampton Street..............E2	Millbay Road..............A3	Regent Street E1	Whimple Street..............D3
Alice Street A2	Cornwall Street..............C2	Harwell Street..............B1	Moon Street..............E2	Rendle Street A2	White Friars Lane..............F2
Anstis Street A2	Courtenay Street..............C3	Hastings Street..............B1	Mount Street E1	Royal Parade..............C3	Windsor Place..............C3
Archer Terrace..............B1	Crescent Avenue B3	Hastings Terrace..............B1	Mulgrave Street..............C3	St James Place B4	Wolsdon Street..............A1
Armada Street E1	Custom House Lane..............B5	Hawkers Avenue E2	Neswick Street..............A2	St John's Bridge Road F3	Wyndham Lane..............A1
Armada Way C2	Derry's Cross C3	Hetling Close B1	New George Street C2	St John's Road..............F3	Wyndham Mews..............A1
Armada Way C4	Devonshire Street E1	Hicks Lane E3	New Street..............E4	Salisbury Road F1	Wyndham Square..............A1
Arundel Crescent A1	Drake Circus..............D1	Higher Lane D3	North Cross Roundabout C1	Sawrey Street A3	Wyndham Street East A1
Athenaeum Street..............C3	Eastlake Street..............D2	Hill Street E2	North Hill E1	Shepherd's Lane F3	Zion Street..............D4
Baring Street..............F1	East Street A3	Hoe Approach..............D4	North Road West A1	Southside Street..............D4	
Bath Lane B3	Ebrington Street..............E2	Hoegate Street..............D3	North Street..............E2	South West Coast Path D5	
Bath Street B3	Eddystone Terrace..............B5	Hoe Road C5	Notte Street..............C3	Stillman Street..............E3	
Batter Street E3	Eldad Hill A1	Hoe Street D3	Octagon Street B2	Stoke Road..............A2	
Battery Street A2	Elliot Street C4	Holyrood Place..............C4	Old Town Street D2	Sussex Street..............D3	
Beaumont Avenue F1	Elliot Terrace..............C4	How Street..............E3	Osborne Place C1	Sutton Road..............F3	
Beaumont Place E2	Essex Street B1	Ilbert Street..............B1	Oxford Street C1	Sydney Street B1	
Beaumont Road F2	Eton Avenue C1	James Street D1	Palace Street..............D3	Tavistock Place..............D1	
Bilbury Street..............E2	Eton Place C1	John Lane D1	Park Terrace E2	Teats Hill Road..............F4	
Blackfriars Lane D4	Exeter Street D2	King Street A2	Parr Street F4	The Barbican..............E4	
Boon's Place..............C1	Exeter Street E2	Ladywell Place F1	Patna Place B1	The Crescent..............B3	
Breton Side D3	Flora Court B2	Lambhay Hill D4	Peacock Lane D3	The Esplanade C4	
Buckwell Street D3	Flora Street B2	Lambhay Street..............D4	Penrose Street..............B1	The Promenade C4	
Camden Street..............E1	Francis Street A2	Leigham Street..............B4	Phoenix Street..............A3	Tin Lane E3	
Castle Street..............E4	Frederick Street East B2	Leigham Terrace Lane B4	Pier Street..............B5	Tothill Avenue..............F1	
Cathedral Street..............A2	Friar's Parade D4	Lipson Road F1	Place de Brest C2	Tothill Road..............F2	
Catherine Street D3	Garden Crescent B5	Lockyers Quay F4	Plym Street F1	Trafalgar Street..............E2	
Cecil Street..............B1	Gasking Street E2	Lockyer Street C3	Princess Street..............C3	Union Place..............A3	
Central Road..............B5	George Place A3	Looe Street E3	Princess Way..............C3	Union Street..............A3	
Chapel Street..............E1	Gibbon Lane..............E1	Madeira Road D5	Prospect Place B4	Vauxhall Quay E3	
Charles Cross E2	Gibbons Street E1	Manor Gardens A3	Prynne Close..............B2	Vauxhall Street..............E3	
Charles Street D2	Gilwell Street E1	Manor Street..............A2	Quay Road E4	Walker Terrace B4	
Citadel Road B4	Glanville Street D1	Market Avenue C2	Queen's Gate A1	Wantage Gardens A1	
Citadel Road C4	Grand Hotel Road C4	Martin Street A3	Radford Road B5	Well Garden B1	
Claremont Street C1	Grand Parade B5	Mayflower Street C1	Radnor Place..............E1	Western Approach..............B2	

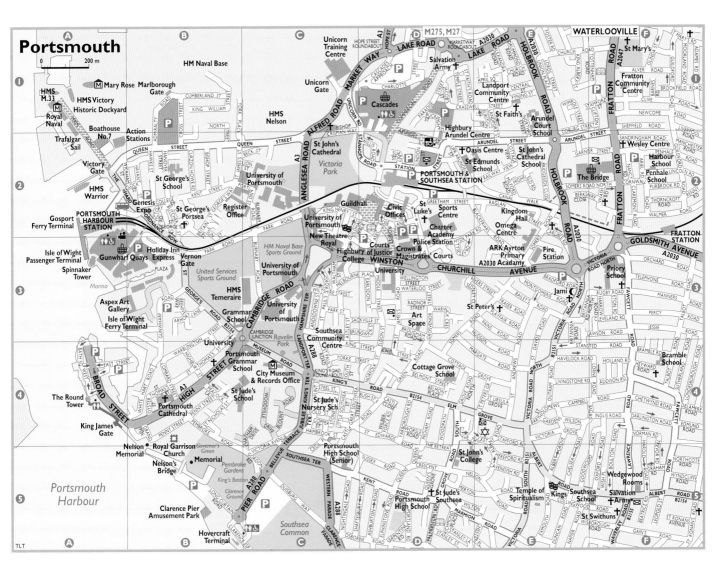

Portsmouth

Portsmouth is found on atlas page **14 H7**

Admiralty Road B2
Albany Road E5
Albert Grove E5
Albert Road E5
Alec Rose Lane D3
Alexandra Road E1
Alfred Road C1
Alver Road F1
Anglesea Road C2
Ariel Road F2
Armory Lane B3
Arundel Street D2
Arundel Street E2
Ashburton Road D5
Bailey's Road E3
Bath Square A4
Bellevue Terrace C5
Belmont Place D4
Bishop Crispian Way C2
Bishop Street B2
Blackfriars Road E2
Blount Road C4
Boulton Road F5
Bramble Road F4
Bridgeside Close E2
Britain Street B2
Broad Street A4
Brookfield Road F1
Brunswick Street C3
Buckingham Street D1
Cambridge Road C3
Campbell Road E4
Canal Walk E2
Carlisle Road E2
Cascades Approach D1
Castle Road C4

Cavendish Road E5
Central Street E1
Charlotte Street D1
Chelsea Road E5
Chester Place E5
Chetwynd Road F4
Churchill Avenue D3
Church Road E1
Claremont Road F2
Clarence Parade C5
Cleveland Road F3
Clive Road F1
Clock Street B2
College Street B2
Collingwood Road E5
Commercial Road D1
Cornwall Road F2
Cottage Grove D4
Cottage View D4
Crasswell Street D1
Cross Street B2
Cumberland Street B1
Curzon Howe Road B1
Darlington Road F4
Drummond Road E1
Duisburg Way C5
Duncan Road E5
Earlsdon Street D3
East Street A4
Eldon Street D4
Elm Grove D4
Elphinstone Road D5
Exmouth Road E5
Fawcett Road F3
Fawcett Road F4
Flint Street C4

Foster Road E1
Fratton Road F2
Gain's Road F5
Garnier Street E2
Goldsmith Avenue F3
Gold Street C4
Goodwood Road E5
Gordon Road C5
Great Southsea Street C4
Green Road D4
Greetham Street D2
Grosvenor Street D3
Grove Road North D4
Grove Road South D5
Guildford Road F1
Guildhall Walk C2
Gunwharf Road B3
Hambrook Street C4
Hampshire Terrace C3
Harold Road F5
Havant Street B2
Havelock Road E4
Hawke Street B2
Hereford Road E5
Highbury Street B4
High Street B4
Holbrook Road E1
Holland Road F4
Hudson Road E3
Hyde Park Road D3
Inglis Road F4
Jessie Road F3
Jubilee Terrace C4
Kent Road D5
Kent Street B2
King Albert Street E1
King Henry I Street C2
King's Road C4
King's Terrace C4
King Street C4
King William Street B1

Lake Road D1
Landport Street E1
Landport Terrace C3
Landsdowne Street C3
Lawrence Road F5
Lawson Road F3
Leopold Street F5
Lincoln Road F2
Little Southsea Street C4
Livingstone Road E4
Lombard Street B4
Londesborough Road F4
Lords Street E1
Lorne Road F4
Main Road A1
Manners Road F3
Margate Road D4
Market Way C1
Marmion Road D5
Mary Rose Street D2
Melbourne Place C3
Merton Road D5
Middle Street D3
Milford Road E2
Montgomerie Road E3
Moorland Road F1
Museum Road C4
Napier Road E5
Nelson Road D5
Newcome Road F1
Nightingale Road C5
Norfolk Street D4
Norman Road F4
Olinda Street F1
Orchard Road F3
Ordnance Row B2
Osborne Road C5
Outram Road D4
Oxford Road F5
Oyster Street B4
Pains Road E3

Palmerston Road D5
Paradise Street D1
Park Road B3
Pelham Road D4
Pembroke Road B4
Penhale Road F2
Penny Street B4
Percy Road F3
Pier Road C5
Playfair Road E3
Portland Road D5
Purbrook Road F2
Queens Crescent D5
Queen Street B2
Raglan Street E2
Railway View E2
Richmond Place D5
Rivers Street D3
Rugby Road F3
Sackville Street C3
St Andrews Road E4
St Bartholomews Gardens E4
St Davids Road E4
St Edwards Road D4
St Faith's Road D1
St George's Road B3
St George's Square B2
St George's Way B2
St James's Road E4
St James's Street B2
St Nicholas Street B4
St Paul's Road C3
St Peters Grove E4
St Thomas's Street B4
Sandringham Road F2
Shaftesbury Road C5
Somers Road D4
Somers Road D4
Somers Road North E2
Southsea Terrace C5
Stafford Road E4

Stamford Street E1
Stanhope Road D2
Stansted Road E4
Station Street D2
Steel Street C4
Stone Street C4
Sussex Road D5
Sutherland Road F4
Talbot Road F4
Telephone Road F3
Temple Street D1
The Hard A2
The Retreat D5
The Thicket D4
Thorncroft Road F2
Tottenham Road F1
Trevor Road F4
Unicorn Road C1
Upper Arundel Street D2
Victoria Avenue C5
Victoria Grove E4
Victoria Road North E4
Victoria Road North F3
Victoria Road South E5
Vivash Road F2
Walmer Road F2
Warblington Street B4
Warwick Crescent D3
Waterloo Street D3
Waverley Road F5
Western Parade C5
West Street A4
White Hart Road B4
Wilson Grove E4
Wiltshire Street C3
Winston Churchill Avenue D3
Wisborough Road E5
Woodpath D4
Woodville Drive D4
Yarborough Road D4
Yorke Street C4

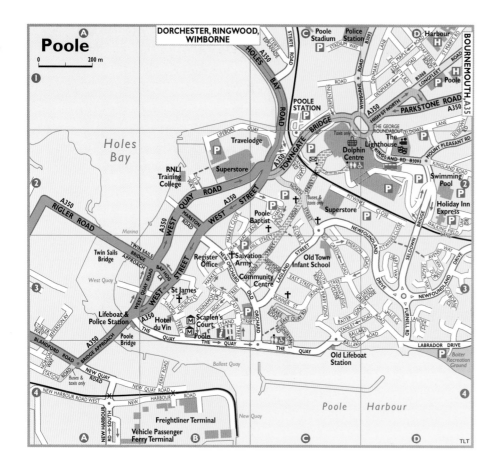

Poole

Poole is found on atlas page **12 H6**

Avenel Way	D3	New Orchard	B3
Baiter Gardens	C3	New Quay Road	A4
Ballard Close	C3	New Street	B3
Ballard Road	C4	North Street	C2
Bay Hog Lane	B3	Norton Way	A4
Blandford Road	A3	Oak Drive	D2
Bridge Approach	A4	Old Orchard	B3
Castle Street	B3	Parkstone Road	D1
Chapel Lane	C2	Perry Gardens	C3
Church Street	B3	Pitwines Close	C2
Cinnamon Lane	B3	Poole Bridge	A3
Colborne Close	D3	Rigler Road	A2
Dear Hay Lane	B3	St Mary's Road	D1
Denmark Lane	D1	Seager Way	D3
Denmark Road	D1	Seldown Bridge	D3
Drake Road	C3	Seldown Lane	D2
Durrell Way	D3	Seldown Road	D2
East Quay Road	C3	Serpentine Road	C1
East Street	C3	Shaftesbury Road	C3
Elizabeth Road	D1	Skinner Street	C3
Emerson Road	C3	Slip Way	B2
Ferry Road	B4	South Road	C3
Fisherman's Road	C3	Stabler Way	A3
Furnell Road	D3	Stadium Way	C1
Globe Lane	C2	Stanley Road	C3
Green Close	D3	Sterte Esplanade	C1
Green Road	C3	Sterte Road	C1
High Street	B3	Strand Street	B3
High Street North	D1	Thames Street	B3
Hill Street	C3	The Quay	B3
Holes Bay Road	C1	Towngate Bridge	C2
Jefferson Avenue	A3	Twin Sails Bridge Approach	A3
Kingland Road	D2	Twin Sails Bridge	C3
Labrador Drive	D4	Vallis Close	D3
Lagland Street	C3	Vanguard Road	C2
Lander Close	D3	Walking Field Lane	D2
Liberty Way	D3	Westons Lane	C3
Lifeboat Quay	B2	West Quay Road	B2
Longfleet Road	D1	West Street	B3
Maple Road	D1	Whatleigh Close	C3
Market Close	B2	Wimborne Road	D1
Market Street	B3		
Marston Road	B2		
Mount Pleasant Road	D2		
Newfoundland Drive	C2		
New Harbour Road	A4		
New Harbour Road South	A4		
New Harbour Road West	A4		

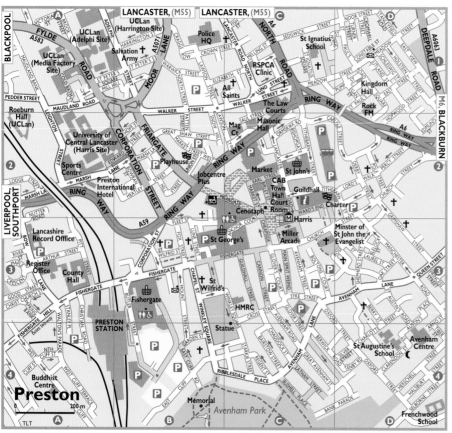

Preston

Preston is found on atlas page **88 G5**

Adelphi Street	A1	Holstein Street	D1
Arthur Street	A3	Hopwood Street	D2
Avenham Lane	C4	Jutland Street	D1
Avenham Road	C3	Lancaster Road	C2
Avenham Street	C3	Lancaster Road North	C1
Berwick Road	C4	Latham Street	C4
Birley Street	C2	Lawson Street	B1
Boltons Court	C3	Leighton Street	A2
Bow Lane	A3	Lund Street	C1
Butler Street	B3	Lune Street	B3
Cannon Street	C3	Main Sprit Weind	C3
Carlisle Street	C2	Manchester Road	D3
Chaddock Street	C4	Market Street	C2
Chapel Street	B3	Market Street West	B2
Charlotte Street	D4	Marsh Lane	A2
Cheapside	C3	Maudland Road	A1
Christ Church Street	A3	Meadow Street	C1
Church Street	C3	Moor Lane	B1
Clarendon Street	D4	Mount Street	B3
Corporation Street	B2	North Road	C1
Corporation Street	B3	Oak Street	D1
Craggs Row	B1	Ormskirk Road	C2
Cross Street	C3	Oxford Street	C3
Crown Street	B1	Pedder Street	A1
Deepdale Road	D1	Percy Street	D2
Derby Street	D2	Pitt Street	A3
Earl Street	C2	Pole Street	C2
East Cliff	B4	Pump Street	D1
East Street	D1	Queen Street	D3
Edmund Street	D2	Ribblesdale Place	B4
Edward Street	A2	Ring Way	B2
Elizabeth Street	B1	Rose Street	D3
Fishergate	B3	St Austin's Road	D3
Fishergate Hill	A4	St Paul's Road	D2
Fleet Street	B3	St Paul's Square	D1
Fox Street	B3	St Peter's Street	B1
Friargate	B2	Sedgwick Street	C1
Friargate	C2	Selborne Street	D4
Fylde Road	A1	Shepherd Street	D3
Glover's Court	C3	Snow Hill	B2
Glover Street	C3	Syke Street	C3
Great Avenham Street	C4	Tithebarn Street	C2
Great Shaw Street	B2	Walker Street	B1
Grimshaw Street	D2	Walton's Parade	A3
Guildhall Street	C3	Ward's End	B3
Harrington Street	B1	Warwick Street	B1
Heatley Street	B2	West Cliff	A4
Herschell Street	D4	Winkley Square	B3

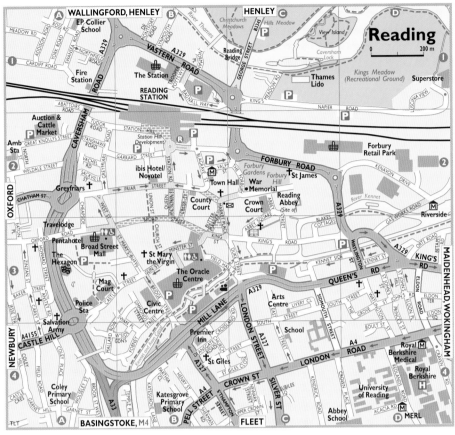

Reading

Reading is found on atlas page **35 K10**

Abbey Square	C3	King's Meadow Road	C1
Abbey Street	C2	King's Road	D3
Addison Road	A1	King Street	B3
Anstey Road	A3	Livery Close	C3
Baker Street	A3	London Road	C4
Blagrave Street	B2	London Street	C3
Blakes Cottages	C3	Mallard Row	A4
Boult Street	D4	Market Place	B2
Bridge Street	B3	Mill Lane	B4
Broad Street	B3	Minster Street	B3
Brook Street West	A4	Napier Road	C1
Buttermarket	B3	Newark Street	C4
Cardiff Road	A1	Northfield Road	A1
Carey Street	A3	Oxford Road	A3
Castle Hill	A4	Parthia Close	B4
Castle Street	A3	Pell Street	B4
Caversham Road	A2	Prince's Street	D3
Chatham Street	A2	Queen's Road	C3
Cheapside	A2	Queen Victoria Street	B2
Church Street	B3	Redlands Road	D4
Church Street	B4	Ross Road	A1
Coley Place	A4	Sackville Street	A2
Craven Road	D4	St Giles Close	B4
Crossland Road	B4	St John's Road	D3
Cross Street	B2	St Mary's Butts	B3
Crown Street	C4	Sidmouth Street	C3
Deansgate Road	B4	Silver Street	C4
Duke Street	C3	Simmonds Street	B3
East Street	C3	Southampton Street	B4
Eldon Road	D3	South Street	C3
Field Road	A4	Station Hill	B2
Fobney Street	B4	Station Road	B2
Forbury Road	C2	Swan Place	B3
Friar Street	B2	Swansea Road	A1
Garnet Street	A4	The Forbury	C2
Garrard Street	B2	Tudor Road	A2
Gas Works Road	D3	Union Street	B2
George Street	C1	Upper Crown Street	C4
Great Knollys Street	A2	Vachel Road	A2
Greyfriars Road	A2	Valpy Street	B2
Gun Street	B3	Vastern Road	B1
Henry Street	B4	Watlington Street	D3
Howard Street	A3	Weldale Street	A2
Katesgrove Lane	B4	West Street	A2
Kenavon Drive	D2	Wolseley Street	A4
Kendrick Road	C4	Yield Hall Place	B3
Kennet Side	C3	York Road	A1
Kennet Street	D3	Zinzan Street	A3

Royal Tunbridge Wells

Royal Tunbridge Wells is found on atlas page **25 N3**

Albert Street	C1	Lansdowne Road	C2
Arundel Road	C4	Lime Hill Road	B1
Bayhall Road	D2	Linden Park Road	A4
Belgrave Road	C1	Little Mount Sion	B4
Berkeley Road	B4	London Road	A2
Boyne Park	A1	Lonsdale Gardens	B2
Buckingham Road	C4	Madeira Park	B4
Calverley Park	C2	Major York's Road	A4
Calverley Park Gardens	D2	Meadow Road	B1
Calverley Road	C2	Molyneux Park Road	A1
Calverley Street	C2	Monson Road	C2
Cambridge Gardens	D4	Monson Way	B2
Cambridge Street	D3	Mount Edgcumbe Road	A3
Camden Hill	D3	Mount Ephraim	A2
Camden Park	D3	Mount Ephraim Road	B1
Camden Road	C1	Mountfield Gardens	C3
Carlton Road	D2	Mountfield Road	C3
Castle Road	A2	Mount Pleasant Avenue	B2
Castle Street	B3	Mount Pleasant Road	B2
Chapel Place	B4	Mount Sion	B4
Christchurch Avenue	B3	Nevill Street	B4
Church Road	A2	Newton Road	B1
Civic Way	B2	Norfolk Road	C4
Claremont Gardens	C4	North Street	D2
Claremont Road	C4	Oakfield Court Road	D3
Clarence Road	B2	Park Street	D3
Crescent Road	C2	Pembury Road	D2
Culverden Street	B1	Poona Road	C4
Dale Street	C1	Prince's Street	D3
Dudley Road	B1	Prospect Road	D3
Eden Road	B4	Rock Villa Road	B1
Eridge Road	A4	Royal Chase	A1
Farmcombe Lane	C4	St James' Road	D1
Farmcombe Road	C4	Sandrock Road	D1
Ferndale	D1	Somerville Gardens	A1
Frant Road	A4	South Green	B3
Frog Lane	B4	Station Approach	B3
Garden Road	C1	Stone Street	D1
Garden Street	C1	Sussex Mews	A4
George Street	D3	Sutherland Road	C3
Goods Station Road	B1	Tunnel Road	C1
Grecian Road	C4	Upper Grosvenor Road	B1
Grosvenor Road	B1	Vale Avenue	B3
Grove Hill Gardens	C3	Vale Road	B3
Grove Hill Road	C3	Victoria Road	C1
Guildford Road	C3	Warwick Park	B4
Hanover Road	B1	Wood Street	C1
High Street	B4	York Road	B2

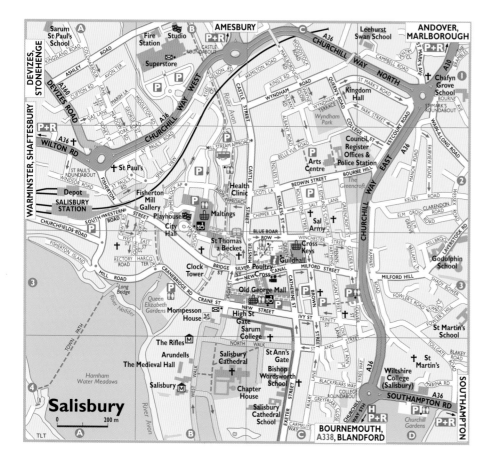

Salisbury

Salisbury is found on atlas page 21 M9

Albany Road	C1	Kingsland Road	A1
Ashley Road	A1	King's Road	C1
Avon Approach	B2	Laverstock Road	D3
Bedwin Street	C2	Malthouse Lane	B3
Belle Vue Road	C2	Manor Road	D2
Blackfriars Way	C4	Marlborough Road	C1
Blue Boar Row	C3	Meadow Road	A1
Bourne Avenue	D1	Middleton Road	A1
Bourne Hill	C2	Milford Hill	D3
Bridge Street	B3	Milford Street	C3
Brown Street	C3	Mill Road	A3
Campbell Road	D1	Minster Street	C3
Castle Street	B1	Nelson Road	B1
Catherine Street	C3	New Canal	B3
Chipper Lane	C2	New Street	B3
Churchfields Road	A2	North Street	B3
Churchill Way East	D3	Park Street	D1
Churchill Way North	C1	Pennyfarthing Street	C3
Churchill Way South	C4	Queen's Road	C1
Churchill Way West	B2	Queen Street	C3
Clarendon Road	D2	Rampart Road	D3
Clifton Road	A1	Rectory Road	A3
Coldharbour Lane	A1	Rollestone Street	C2
College Street	C1	St Ann Street	C4
Cranebridge Road	B3	St Edmund's Church Street	C2
Crane Street	B3	St Mark's Avenue	D1
Devizes Road	A1	St Mark's Road	D1
Dew's Road	A3	St Paul's Road	B2
East Street	B3	Salt Lane	C2
Elm Grove	D2	Scots Lane	C2
Elm Grove Road	D2	Sidney Street	A1
Endless Street	C2	Silver Street	B3
Estcourt Road	D2	Southampton Road	D4
Exeter Street	C4	South Street	A3
Eyres Way	D4	South Western Road	A2
Fairview Road	D2	Spire View	B2
Fisherton Street	A2	Summerlock Approach	B2
Fowler's Road	D3	Tollgate Road	D4
Friary Lane	C4	Trinity Street	C3
Gas Lane	A1	Wain-A-Long Road	D2
George Street	A1	Wessex Road	D2
Gigant Street	C3	West Street	A3
Greencroft Street	C2	Wilton Road	A2
Guilder Lane	C3	Winchester Street	C3
Hamilton Road	C1	Windsor Road	A2
High Street	B3	Woodstock Road	C1
Ivy Street	C3	Wyndham Road	C1
Kelsey Road	D2	York Road	A1

Sheffield

Sheffield is found on atlas page 84 E3

Angel Street	C2	Howard Street	C4
Arundel Gate	C3	Hoyle Street	A1
Arundel Street	C4	King Street	C2
Backfields	B3	Lambert Street	B1
Bailey Street	A2	Leopold Street	B3
Balm Green	B3	Mappin Street	A3
Bank Street	C2	Meetinghouse Lane	C2
Barkers Pool	B3	Mulberry Street	C2
Broad Lane	A2	Newcastle Street	A2
Broad Street	D2	New Street	C2
Brown Street	C4	Norfolk Street	C3
Cambridge Street	B3	North Church Street	B2
Campo Lane	B2	Orchard Street	B3
Carver Street	B3	Paradise Street	B2
Castlegate	C1	Pinstone Street	B3
Castle Street	C2	Pond Hill	C3
Charles Street	B4	Pond Street	C3
Charter Row	B4	Portobello Street	A3
Church Street	B2	Queen Street	B2
Commercial Street	C2	Rockingham Street	A2
Corporation Street	B1	St James Street	B2
Cross Burgess Street	B3	Scargill Croft	C2
Cutlers Gate	D1	Scotland Street	A1
Derek Dooley Way	D1	Sheaf Street	D4
Devonshire Street	A3	Shoreham Street	C4
Division Street	A3	Shrewsbury Road	D4
Dixon Lane	C2	Silver Street	B2
Duke Street	D2	Smithfield	A1
Exchange Street	D2	Snig Hill	C2
Eyre Street	B4	Solly Street	A2
Fig Tree Lane	C2	South Street Park	D3
Fitzwilliam Street	A4	Suffolk Road	C4
Flat Street	C3	Surrey Street	C3
Furnace Hill	B1	Talbot Street	D4
Furnival Gate	B4	Tenter Street	B2
Furnival Road	D1	Townhead Street	B2
Furnival Street	C4	Trafalgar Street	A4
Garden Street	A2	Trippet Lane	B3
George Street	C2	Union Street	B4
Gibralter Street	B1	Vicar Lane	B2
Harmer Lane	C3	Victoria Station Road	D1
Harts Head	C2	Waingate	C2
Hawley Street	B2	Wellington Street	A4
Haymarket	C2	West Bar	B2
High Street	C2	West Bar Green	B2
Holland Street	A3	West Street	A3
Hollis Croft	A2	White Croft	A2
Holly Street	B3	York Street	C2

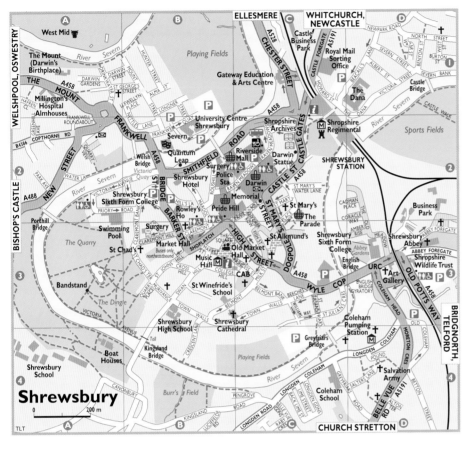

Shrewsbury

Shrewsbury is found on atlas page **56 H2**

Abbey Foregate	D3	Mardol	B2
Albert Street	D1	Market Street	B3
Alma Street	B1	Milk Street	C3
Amber Rise	D3	Moreton Crescent	D4
Barker Street	B2	Mount Street	B1
Beacall's Lane	D1	Murivance	B3
Beeches Lane	C3	Nettles Lane	B1
Belle Vue Gardens	C4	Newpark Road	D1
Belle Vue Road	D4	New Street	A2
Belmont	B3	North Street	D1
Belmont Bank	C3	Old Coleham	D3
Benyon Street	D1	Old Potts Way	D3
Betton Street	D4	Park Avenue	A2
Bridge Street	B2	Pengrove	C4
Burton Street	D1	Pound Close	D4
Butcher Row	C2	Pride Hill	C2
Canonbury	A4	Princess Street	B3
Castle Foregate	C1	Priory Road	A2
Castle Gates	C2	Quarry Place	B3
Castle Street	C2	Quarry View	A2
Chester Street	C1	Raven Meadows	B2
Claremont Bank	B3	Roushill	B2
Claremont Hill	B3	St Chad's Terrace	B3
Claremont Street	B3	St George's Street	A1
Coleham Head	D3	St Johns Hill	B3
College Hill	B3	St Julians Crescent	C3
Copthorne Road	A2	St Julians Friars	C3
Coracle Way	D2	St Mary's Place	C2
Crescent Lane	B4	St Mary's Street	C2
Cross Hill	B3	St Mary's Water Lane	C2
Darwin Gardens	A1	Salters Lane	D4
Darwin Street	A1	Severn Bank	D1
Dogpole	C3	Severn Street	D1
Drinkwater Street	A1	Shoplatch	B3
Fish Street	C3	Smithfield Road	B2
Frankwell	A2	Swan Hill	B3
Frankwell Quay	B2	The Dana	D1
Greenhill Avenue	A2	The Mount	A1
Greyfriars Road	C4	The Old Meadow	D3
High Street	C3	The Square	B3
Hill's Lane	B2	Town Walls	B3
Howard Street	C1	Victoria Avenue	A2
Hunter Street	B1	Victoria Street	D1
Kingsland Road	B4	Water Lane	A2
Lime Street	C4	Water Street	D1
Longden Coleham	C4	West Street	D1
Longden Road	C4	Williams Way	C3
Longner Street	B1	Wyle Cop	C3

Southend-on-Sea

Southend-on-Sea is found on atlas page **38 E4**

Albert Road	C3	Lancaster Gardens	C2
Alexandra Road	A3	Leamington Road	D2
Alexandra Street	A3	London Road	A2
Ambleside Drive	D2	Lucy Road	C4
Ashburnham Road	A2	Luker Road	A2
Baltic Avenue	B3	Marine Parade	C4
Baxter Avenue	A1	Milton Street	B1
Beach Road	D4	Napier Avenue	A2
Boscombe Road	C1	Nelson Street	A3
Bournemouth Park Road	D1	Oban Road	D1
Cambridge Road	B3	Old Southend Road	D3
Capel Terrace	A3	Outing Close	D3
Chancellor Road	B3	Pitmans Close	B2
Cheltenham Road	D2	Pleasant Road	C3
Chichester Road	B1	Portland Avenue	B3
Christchurch Road	D1	Princes Street	A2
Church Road	B3	Prittlewell Square	A3
Clarence Road	A3	Quebec Avenue	B2
Clarence Street	B3	Queen's Road	A2
Clifftown Parade	A4	Queensway	A1
Clifftown Road	A3	Queensway	C3
Coleman Street	B1	Royal Terrace	B4
Cromer Road	C2	Runwell Terrace	A3
Devereux Road	A4	St Ann's Road	B1
Eastern Esplanade	D4	St Leonard's Road	C3
Elmer Approach	A2	Scratton Road	A3
Elmer Avenue	A2	Short Street	B1
Essex Street	D1	Southchurch Avenue	D2
Ferndown Close	D1	Southchurch Road	B2
Fowler Close	D2	Stanier Close	D2
Gordon Place	A2	Stanley Road	C3
Gordon Road	A2	Sutton Road	C1
Grange Gardens	C2	Swanage Road	C1
Grover Street	B3	Toledo Road	C2
Guildford Road	B1	Tylers Avenue	B3
Hamlet Road	A3	Tyrrel Drive	C2
Hartington Place	C4	Victoria Avenue	A1
Hartington Road	C3	Warrior Square East	B2
Hastings Road	C2	Warrior Square North	B2
Hawtree Close	D4	Warrior Square	B2
Herbert Grove	C3	Wesley Road	C3
Heygate Avenue	B3	Western Esplanade	A4
High Street	B2	Weston Road	B3
Hillcrest Road	C2	Whitegate Road	B2
Honiton Road	D2	Wimborne Road	C1
Horace Road	C3	Windermere Road	D2
Kilworth Avenue	C2	Woodgrange Drive	D3
Kursaal Way	D4	York Road	B3

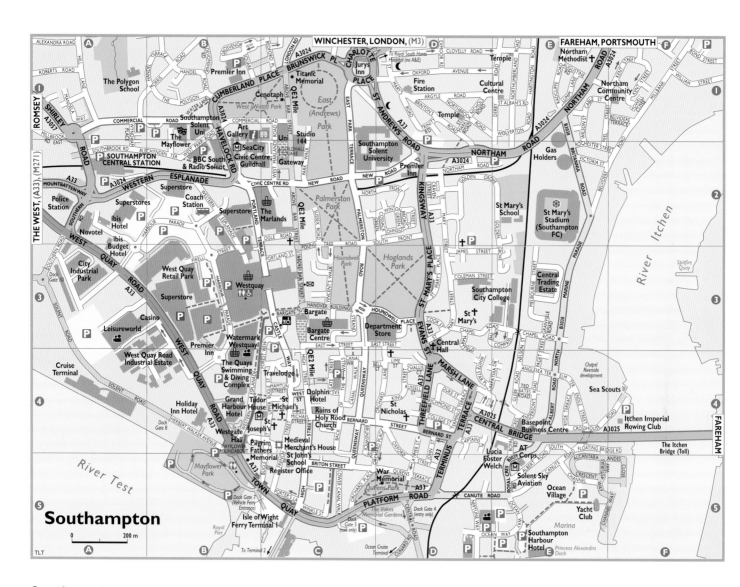

Southampton

Southampton is found on atlas page **14 D4**

Above Bar Street.....................C1
Albert Road North...................E4
Albert Road South...................E5
Alcantara Crescent.................E5
Alexandra Road......................A1
Anderson's Road.....................E4
Andes Close............................F5
Anglesea Terrace....................E4
Argyle Road.............................D1
Asturias Way............................E5
Augustine Road.......................E1
Back Of The Walls...................C4
Bargate Street.........................C3
Bedford Place..........................C1
Bell Street................................D4
Belvidere Road........................E2
Belvidere Terrace....................F1
Bernard Street.........................C4
Blechynden Terrace................B2
Bond Street..............................F1
Brinton's Road.........................D1
Britannia Road.........................E1
Briton Street............................C5
Broad Green.............................D2
Brunswick Place......................C1
Brunswick Square....................C1
Bugle Street.............................C5
Cable Street.............................E1
Canal Walk...............................C4
Canute Road.............................D5
Captains Place.........................D4
Carpathia Drive.......................D4
Castle Way................................C4
Central Bridge..........................D4
Central Road............................D5
Challis Court............................D4

Channel Way............................E5
Chapel Road.............................D3
Charlotte Place........................C1
Civic Centre Road....................B2
Clovelly Road...........................D1
Coleman Street........................D3
College Street..........................D4
Commercial Road....................A1
Cook Street...............................D3
Cossack Green.........................D2
Craven Street...........................D2
Crosshouse Road.....................E4
Cumberland Place....................B1
Cunard Road............................D5
Derby Road...............................E1
Devonshire Road.....................B1
Duke Street..............................D4
Eastgate Street........................C4
East Park Terrace....................C1
East Street................................C3
Elm Terrace.............................E4
Endle Street.............................E4
Evans Street.............................D3
Exmoor Road...........................D1
Floating Bridge Road..............E4
Forest View..............................C4
French Street............................C5
Glebe Road...............................E4
Golden Grove...........................D2
Granville Road.........................E3
Grosvenor Square....................B1
Hamtun Street.........................C5
Handel Road.............................B1
Handel Terrace........................B1
Hanover Buildings...................C3
Harbour Parade.......................B2

Hartington Road......................E1
Havelock Road.........................B1
Herbert Walker Avenue..........B4
High Street...............................C4
Hill Lane...................................A1
Houndwell Place......................D3
Howell Close............................F1
Itchen Bridge...........................F4
James Street............................D3
Johnson Street.........................D2
John Street...............................D5
Kent Street................................F1
King Street................................D4
Kingsway..................................D2
Latimer Street.........................D5
Lime Street...............................D4
London Road............................C1
Lower Canal Walk....................C5
Lumpy Lane..............................E1
Mandela Way...........................A1
Marine Parade.........................E3
Marsh Lane...............................D4
Maryfield..................................D3
Mayflower Roundabout...........B4
Melbourne Street.....................E3
Millbank Street........................F1
Millbrook Road East...............A1
Morris Road..............................B1
Mountbatten Way.....................A2
Nelson Street...........................E4
Neptune Way............................D5
New Road..................................C2
Nichols Road............................D1
Northam Road..........................D2
Northbrook Road......................D1
North Front...............................C2

Northumberland Road.............E1
Ocean Way...............................D5
Ogle Road.................................C2
Orchard Place...........................C5
Oxford Avenue.........................D1
Oxford Street...........................D4
Paget Street.............................D4
Palmerston Road......................C2
Park Walk.................................C2
Peel Street................................E1
Pirelli Street.............................B3
Platform Road..........................C5
Porter's Lane............................C5
Portland Street.........................C3
Portland Terrace......................B2
Pound Tree Road......................C3
Queens Terrace........................D5
Queensway...............................C4
Radcliffe Road..........................E1
Richmond Street......................D4
Roberts Road............................A1
Rochester Street......................E2
Royal Crescent Road...............E5
Russell Street...........................D4
Ryde Terrace............................E4
St Alban's Road........................E1
St Andrews Road......................D1
St Marks Road..........................D1
St Mary's Place........................D3
St Mary's Road.........................D1
St Mary Street..........................D2
St Michael Street.....................C4
Shirley Road.............................A1
Solent Road..............................A3
Southbrook Road......................A2
Southern Road..........................A2

South Front..............................C2
Strand......................................C3
Sussex Road.............................C2
Ted Bates Road........................E4
Terminus Terrace.....................D5
The Compass............................D3
The Polygon.............................B1
Threefield Lane........................D4
Town Quay................................B5
Trinity Road.............................D1
Upper Bugle Street..................C4
Victoria Street..........................E2
Vincent's Walk.........................C3
Water Lane...............................B1
Western Esplanade..................A2
Western Esplanade..................B4
West Marlands Road................C2
West Park Road........................B2
West Quay Road.......................A2
West Street...............................C4
White Star Place......................D4
William Street..........................F1
Wilson Street...........................E1
Winkle Street...........................C5
Winton Street...........................D2
Wolverton Road........................E1
Wyndham Place........................A1

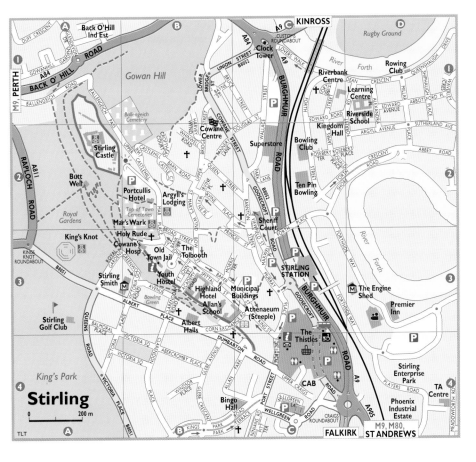

Stirling

Stirling is found on atlas page **133 M9**

Abbey Road	D2
Abbotsford Place	D1
Abercromby Place	B4
Academy Road	B3
Albert Place	A3
Alexandra Place	D1
Allan Park	B4
Argyll Avenue	D2
Back O' Hill Road	A1
Baker Street	B3
Ballengeich Road	A1
Ballengeich Pass	A1
Balmoral Place	A3
Bank Street	B3
Barn Road	B2
Barnton Street	C2
Bayne Street	B1
Bow Street	B3
Broad Street	B3
Bruce Street	B1
Burghmuir Road	C1
Castle Court	B2
Clarendon Place	B4
Clarendon Road	B3
Corn Exchange Road	B3
Cowane Street	B1
Craigs Roundabout	C4
Crofthead Court	B2
Customs Roundabout	C1
Dean Crescent	D1
Douglas Street	C2
Dumbarton Road	B4
Edward Avenue	D1
Edward Road	C1
Forrest Road	D2
Forth Crescent	C2
Forthside Way	C3
Forth Street	C1
Forth Place	C3
Forth View	C1
Glebe Avenue	B4
Glebe Crescent	B4
Glendevon Drive	A1
Goosecroft Road	C2
Gowanhill Gardens	A1
Greenwood Avenue	A3
Harvey Wynd	B1
Irvine Place	B2
James Street	C2
Kings Knot Roundabout	A3
Kings Park Road	B4
King Street	C3
Lovers Walk	C1
Lower Bridge Street	B1
Lower Castlehill	B2
Mar Place	B2
Maxwell Place	C3
Meadowforth Road	D4
Millar Place	D1
Morris Terrace	B3
Murray Place	C3
Ninians Road	C4
Park Lane	C2
Park Terrace	B4
Players Road	D4
Port Street	C4
Princes Street	B3
Queenshaugh Drive	D1
Queens Road	A3
Queen Street	B2
Raploch Road	A2
Ronald Place	C2
Rosebery Place	C2
Rosebery Terrace	C2
Royal Gardens	A3
St John Street	B3
St Mary's Wynd	B2
Shiphaugh Place	D1
Shore Road	C2
Spittal Street	B3
Sutherland Avenue	D2
Tannery Lane	B2
Union Street	B1
Upper Bridge Street	B2
Upper Castlehill	A2
Upper Craigs	C4
Victoria Place	A4
Victoria Road	B3
Victoria Square	A4
Viewfield Street	C2
Wallace Street	C2
Waverley Crescent	D1
Wellgreen Lane	C4
Wellgreen Road	C4
Whinwell Road	B2
Windsor Place	B4

Stockton-on-Tees

Stockton-on-Tees is found on atlas page **104 D7**

1825 Way	B4
Allison Street	B1
Alma Street	B1
Bath Lane	C1
Bedford Street	A1
Bishop Street	B2
Bishopton Lane	A1
Bishopton Road	A1
Bowesfield Lane	A4
Bridge Road	B3
Bridge Road	C4
Bright Street	B2
Britannia Road	A1
Brunswick Street	B3
Bute Street	A2
Church Road	D1
Clarence Row	C1
Corportion Street	A2
Council of Europe Boulevard	C2
Cromwell Avenue	B1
Dixon Street	A2
Dovecot Street	A3
Dugdale Street	D1
Durham Road	A1
Durham Street	A2
Edwards Street	A4
Farrer Street	B1
Finkle Street	B3
Frederick Street	B1
Fudan Way	D3
Gooseport Road	D1
Hartington Road	A3
Harvard Avenue	D3
High Street	B2
Hill Street East	D1
Hume Street	B1
Hutchinson Street	A2
John Street	B2
King Street	B2
Knightport Road	D1
Knowles Street	C2
Laing Street	B1
Leeds Street	B2
Lobdon Street	B2
Lodge Street	B3
Mandale Road	D4
Maritime Road	C1
Massey Road	D3
Melbourne Street	A2
Middle Street	B2
Mill Street West	A2
Nelson Terrace	B2
North Shore Road	D2
Northport Road	D1
Northshore Link	C2
Norton Road	B1
Palmerston Street	A2
Park Road	A4
Park Terrace	C3
Parkfield Road	B4
Parliament Street	B4
Portrack Lane	D1
Prince Regent Street	B3
Princess Avenue	C1
Princeton Drive	D4
Quayside Road	C3
Raddcliffe Crescent	D3
Ramsgate	B3
Riverside	C3
Russell Street	B2
St Paul's Street	A1
Silver Street	B2
Skinner Street	B3
Station Street	D4
Sydney Street	B2
The Square	D2
Thistle Green	C2
Thomas Street	B1
Thompson Street	B1
Tower Street	B4
Union Street East	C1
University Boulevard	C3
Vane Street	B2
Vicarage Street	A1
Wellington Street	A2
West Row	B3
Westbourne Street	A4
Westpoint Road	C3
Wharf Street	B4
William Street	B3
Woodland Street	A4
Worthing Street	A3
Yale Crescent	C4
Yarm Lane	A4
Yarm Road	A4

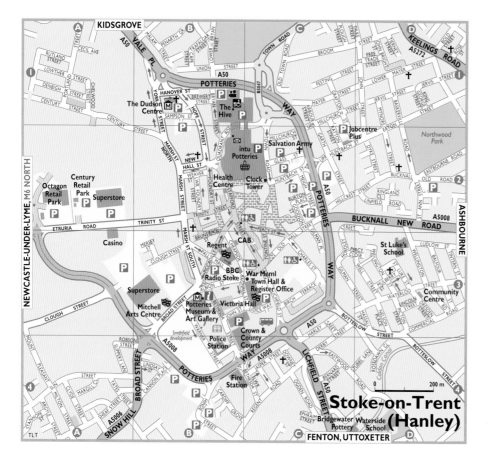

Stoke-on-Trent (Hanley)

Stoke-on-Trent (Hanley) is found on atlas page **70 F5**

Albion Street	B3	Linfield Road	D2
Bagnall Street	B3	Lower Mayer Street	D1
Balfour Street	D3	Lowther Street	A1
Baskerville Road	D1	Ludlow Street	D3
Bathesda Street	B4	Malam Street	B1
Bernard Street	C4	Marsh Street	B2
Bethesda Street	B3	Marsh Street North	B2
Birch Terrace	C3	Marsh Street South	B3
Botteslow Street	C3	Mayer Street	C1
Broad Street	B4	Mersey Street	B3
Broom Street	C1	Milton Street	A4
Brunswick Street	B3	Mount Pleasant	A4
Bryan Street	B1	Mynors Street	D1
Bucknall New Road	C2	New Hall Street	B2
Bucknall Old Road	D2	Ogden Road	C4
Cardiff Grove	B4	Old Hall Street	C3
Century Street	A1	Old Town Road	C1
Charles Street	C3	Pall Mall	B3
Cheapside	B3	Percy Street	C2
Chelwood Street	A1	Piccadilly	B3
Clough Street	A3	Portland Street	A1
Clyde Street	A4	Potteries Way	B1
Commercial Road	D3	Potteries Way	B4
Denbigh Street	A1	Quadrant Road	B2
Derby Street	C4	Regent Road	C4
Dyke Street	D2	Rutland Street	A1
Eastwood Road	C4	St John Street	D1
Eaton Street	D2	St Luke Street	D3
Etruria Road	A2	Sampson Street	B1
Foundry Street	B2	Sheaf Street	A4
Garth Street	C2	Slippery Lane	A4
Gilman Street	C3	Snow Hill	A4
Goodson Street	C2	Stafford Street	B2
Grafton Street	C1	Sun Street	A4
Hanover Street	B1	Tontine Street	C3
Harley Street	C4	Town Road	C2
Hillchurch	C2	Trafalgar Street	B1
Hillcrest Street	C2	Trinity Street	B2
Hinde Street	B4	Union Street	B1
Hope Street	B1	Upper Hillchurch Street	C2
Hordley Street	C3	Upper Huntbach Street	C2
Huntbach Street	C2	Warner Street	B3
Jasper Street	C4	Waterloo Street	D3
Jervis Street	D1	Well Street	D3
John Street	B3	Wellington Road	D3
Keelings Road	D1	Wellington Street	D3
Lichfield Street	C3	Yates Street	A1
Lidice Way	C3	York Street	B1

Stratford-upon-Avon

Stratford-upon-Avon is found on atlas page **47 P3**

Albany Road	A3	New Broad Street	B4
Alcester Road	A2	New Street	B4
Arden Street	B2	Old Red Lion Court	C2
Avenue Road	C1	Old Town	C4
Bancroft Place	C2	Orchard Way	A4
Birmingham Road	B1	Payton Street	C2
Brewery Street	B1	Percy Street	C1
Bridge Foot	D2	Rother Street	B3
Bridge Street	C2	Rowley Crescent	D1
Bridgeway	D2	Ryland Street	B4
Broad Street	B4	St Andrew's Crescent	A3
Brookvale Road	A4	St Gregory's Road	C1
Brunel Way	A2	St Martin's Close	A3
Bull Street	B4	Sanctus Drive	B4
Cedar Close	D1	Sanctus Road	A4
Chapel Lane	C3	Sanctus Street	B4
Chapel Street	C3	Sandfield Road	A4
Cherry Orchard	A4	Scholars Lane	B3
Cherry Street	B4	Seven Meadows Road	A4
Chestnut Walk	B3	Shakespeare Street	B1
Church Street	B3	Sheep Street	C3
Clopton Bridge	D3	Shipston Road	D4
Clopton Road	B1	Shottery Road	A3
College Lane	B4	Shrieves Walk	C3
College Mews	B4	Southern Lane	C3
College Street	B4	Swan's Nest	D3
Ely Gardens	B3	The Willows	A3
Ely Street	B3	Tiddington Road	D3
Evesham Place	B3	Town Square	B2
Evesham Road	A4	Tramway Bridge	D3
Garrick Way	A4	Tyler Street	C2
Great William Street	C1	Union Street	C2
Greenhill Street	B2	Warwick Court	C1
Grove Road	B3	Warwick Crescent	D1
Guild Street	C2	Warwick Road	C2
Henley Street	C2	Waterside	C3
High Street	C3	Welcombe Road	D1
Holtom Street	B4	Wellesbourne Grove	B1
John Street	C2	Western Road	B1
Kendall Avenue	B1	West Street	B4
Lock Close	C2	Willows Drive North	A2
Maidenhead Road	C1	Windsor Street	B2
Mansell Street	B2	Wood Street	B2
Mayfield Avenue	C1		
Meer Street	B2		
Mill Lane	C4		
Mulberry Street	C1		
Narrow Lane	B4		

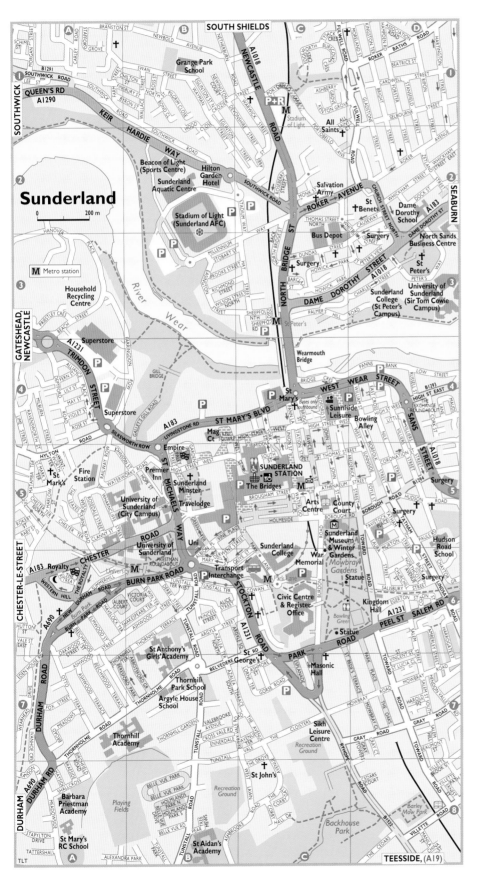

SOUTH SHIELDS

Sunderland

Sunderland

Sunderland is found on atlas page **113 N9**

Abbotsford Green	B7	Milburn Street	A4
Abbs Street	C2	Millennium Way	B3
Albion Place	B6	Monk Street	C2
Alice Street	B6	Moreland Street	D1
Alliance Place	A4	Morgan Street	A1
Amberley Street	D6	Mowbray Road	D7
Argyle Square	B6	Netherburn Road	B1
Argyle Street	B6	Newbold Avenue	B1
Ashbrooke Road	B8	Newcastle Road	C1
Ashmore Street	C7	New Durham Road	A6
Ashwood Street	A7	Nile Street	D4
Ashwood Terrace	A7	Norfolk Street	D5
Association Road	D1	North Bridge Street	C3
Athenaeum Street	C5	Northcote Avenue	D6
Azalea Terrace North	B6	North Street	B1
Azalea Terrace South	B7	Oakwood Street	A6
Back North Bridge Street	C3	Olive Street	B6
Beach Street	A3	Otto Terrace	A7
Bedford Street	C4	Palmer's Hill Road	C3
Beechwood Street	A6	Panns Bank	D4
Beechwood Terrace	A7	Park Lane	C5
Belvedere Road	B7	Park Place	D6
Beresford Park	A7	Park Road	C6
Birchfield Road	A7	Pauls Road	D5
Borough Road	D5	Peel Street	D6
Bridge Crescent	C4	Portobello Lane	C1
Bridge Street	C4	Queen's Road	A1
Briery Vale Road	C7	Railway Row	A5
Bright Street	D1	Ravensworth Street	A4
Brooke Street	B3	Richmond Street	B3
Brougham Street	C5	Ripon Street	D1
Burdon Road	C5	Roker Avenue	C2
Burn Park Road	B6	Roker Baths Road	D1
Cardwell Street	D1	Rosedale Street	A5
Carley Road	A1	Ross Street	B1
Charles Street	D3	Russell Street	D4
Chester Road	A6	Ryhope Road	C7
Churchill Street	D6	St Bede's Terrace	D7
Church Street North	D2	St Mary's Boulevard	B4
Clanny Street	A5	St Michaels Way	B5
Cork Street	D4	St Peter's View	D3
Coronation Street	D5	St Thomas' Street	C5
Cowan Terrace	C6	St Vincent Street	D7
Cross Vale Road	B7	Salem Road	D6
Crozier Street	B1	Salem Street	D6
Dame Dorothy Street	C3	Salem Street South	D7
Deptford Road	A4	Salisbury Street	D6
Derby Street	B6	Sans Street	D4
Derwent Street	B6	Selbourne Street	D1
Devonshire Street	B1	Shakespeare Terrace	A6
Dock Street	D2	Shallcross	A8
Dundas Street	C3	Sheepfolds Road	C3
Durham Road	A7	Silksworth Row	A4
Easington Street	B3	South Street	C5
East Cross Street	D4	Southwick Road	A1
Eden House Road	A7	Southwick Road	C2
Egerton Street	D6	Stadium Way	C2
Eglinton Street	B1	Stansfield Street	D1
Eglinton Street North	B1	Station Street	C4
Elmwood Street	A6	Stobart Street	B3
Ennerdale	B7	Stockton Road	C6
Farm Street	A1	Swan Street	B1
Farringdon Row	B4	Tatham Street	D5
Fawcett Street	C4	Tatham Street Back	D5
Forster Street	D1	The Avenue	C7
Fox Street	A7	The Cloisters	C7
Foyle Street	D5	The Royalty	A6
Frederick Street	D5	Thomas Street North	C2
Fulwell Road	C1	Thornhill Terrace	B6
Galley's Gill Road	B4	Thornholme Road	A7
Gladstone Street	D1	Toward Road	D5
Gorse Road	C7	Trimdon Street	A4
Gray Road	D7	Tunstall Road	B7
Green Terrace	B5	Tunstall Terrace	B6
Hampden Road	D1	Tunstall Terrace West	B6
Hanover Place	A2	Tunstall Vale	B8
Harlow Street	A5	Union Street	C4
Harrogate Street	D6	Valebrooke Avenue	B7
Hartington Street	D1	Villette Road	D8
Havelock Terrace	A6	Villiers Street	D4
Hay Street	C3	Vine Place	B5
Hendon Valley Road	D7	Wallace Street	B1
High Street East	D4	Warwick Street	C1
High Street West	B5	Waterloo Place	C5
Holmeside	C5	Waterworks Road	A5
Hope Street	B5	Wayman Street	B1
Howick Park	C3	Wearhead Drive	A7
Hudson Road	D5	Westbourne Road	A5
Hylton Road	A5	Western Hill	A6
Johnson Street	A5	West Lawn	C8
John Street	C4	West Street	C5
Keir Hardie Way	A1	West Sunniside	D4
Laura Street	D5	West Wear Street	C4
Lindsay Road	D6	Wharncliffe Street	A5
Little Villiers Street	D4	Whickham Street	D2
Livingstone Road	B4	Whickham Street East	D2
Low Street	D4	Whitburn Street	D3
Mary Street	B6	William Street	D4
Mauds Lane	D4	Wilson Street North	B3
Meadowside	A8	York Street	C4
Middle Street	C5	Zetland Street	D2

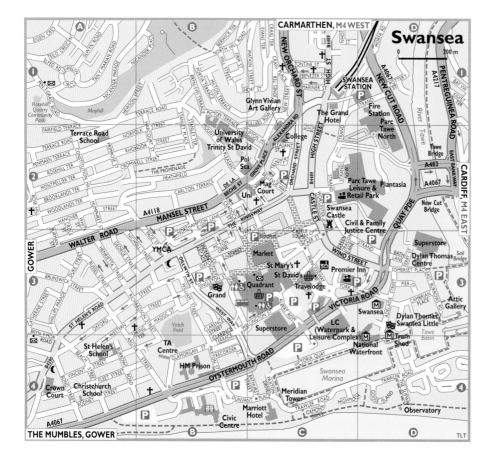

Swansea

Swansea is found on atlas page **29 J6**

Adelaide Street	D3	New Orchard Street	C1
Alexandra Road	C2	New Street	C1
Argyle Street	A4	Nicander Parade	A1
Bath Lane	D3	Nicholl Street	A3
Beach Street	A4	Norfolk Street	A2
Bond Street	A4	North Hill Road	B1
Brunswick Street	A3	Northampton Lane	B2
Burrows Road	A4	Orchard Street	C2
Caer Street	C3	Oxford Street	A3
Carlton Terrace	B2	Oystermouth Road	B4
Castle Street	C2	Page Street	B3
Catherine Street	A3	Park Street	B3
Clarence Street	B3	Paxton Street	B4
Clifton Hill	C2	Pentreguinea Road	D1
Constituion Street	A2	Pen-Y-Graig Road	A1
Cradock Street	B2	Picton Lane	A1
Craig Place	C1	Pier Street	D3
Cromwell Street	A2	Primrose Street	A2
De La Beche Street	B2	Princess Way	C3
Dillwyn Street	B3	Quay Parade	D2
Duke Street	A3	Recorder Street	B4
Dunvant Place	B4	Rhondda Street	A2
East Bank Way	D2	Richardson Street	A3
East Burrows Road	D3	Rodney Street	A4
Ebenezer Street	C1	Rose Hill	A2
Elfed Road	A1	Russel Street	A3
Ferry Street	D3	St Helen's Road	A3
Firm Street	B1	Short Street	B1
Fleet Street	A4	Singleton Street	B3
George Street	A3	Somerset Place	D3
Glamorgan Street	B4	Strand	C1
Green Dragon Lane	C3	Tan Y Marian Road	A1
Grove Place	C2	Teilo Crescent	A1
Hanover Street	A2	Terrace Road	A2
Harcourt Street	B2	The Kingsway	B2
Heathfield	B2	Tontine Street	C1
Henrietta Street	A3	Trawler Road	C4
Hewson Street	A1	Victoria Quay	C4
High Street	C2	Victoria Road	C3
Hill Street	B1	Vincent Street	A4
Humphrey Street	A2	Walter Road	A3
Islwyn Road	A1	Watkin Street	C1
Llewelyn Circle	A1	Wellington Street	C3
Madoc Street	B3	West Way	B3
Mansel Street	B2	Western Street	A4
Mariner Street	C1	William Street	B3
Mount Pleasant	B2	Wind Street	C3
New Cut Road	D1	York Street	C3

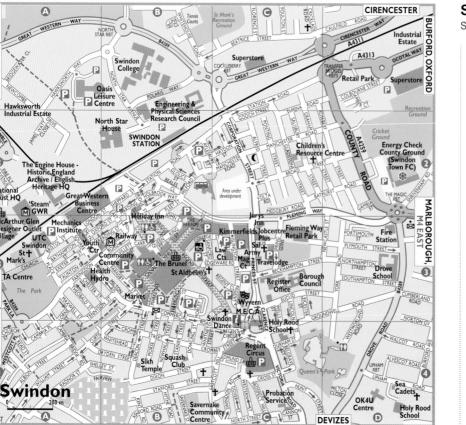

Swindon

Swindon is found on atlas page **33 M8**

Albion Street	A4	Islington Street	C3
Alfred Street	C2	John Street	B3
Ashford Road	B4	King Street	B3
Aylesbury Street	B2	London Street	A3
Bathurst Road	C2	Manchester Road	C2
Beckhampton Street	C3	Market Street	B3
Bridge Street	B2	Maxwell Street	A3
Bristol Street	A3	Medgbury Road	C2
Broad Street	C2	Milford Street	B2
Cambria Bridge Road	A4	Milton Road	B3
Canal Walk	B3	Morley Street	B3
Carr Street	B3	Morse Street	B4
Chester Street	A3	Newcastle Street	D3
Church Place	A3	Newcombe Drive	A1
Cirencester Way	D1	Newhall Street	B4
Clarence Street	C3	Northampton Street	D3
College Street	B3	North Star Avenue	B1
Commercial Road	B3	Ocotal Way	D1
Corporation Street	C2	Park Lane	A3
County Road	D2	Plymouth Street	D3
Crombey Street	B4	Polaris Way	B1
Curtis Street	A4	Ponting Street	C2
Deacon Street	B4	Portsmouth Street	D3
Dixon Street	B4	Princes Street	C3
Dover Street	C4	Prospect Hill	C4
Dowling Street	B4	Queen Street	B3
Drove Road	D4	Radnor Street	A4
Dryden Street	A4	Regent Place	A3
Eastcott Hill	C4	Regent Street	B3
East Street	B2	Rosebery Street	C2
Edgeware Road	B3	Salisbury Street	C2
Elmina Road	C1	Sanford Street	B3
Emlyn Square	A3	Sheppard Street	B2
Euclid Street	C3	Southampton Street	D3
Faringdon Road	A3	Stafford Street	B4
Farnsby Street	B3	Stanier Street	B4
Fire Fly Avenue	A2	Station Road	B2
Fleet Street	B2	Swindon Road	C4
Fleming Way	C3	Tennyson Street	A3
Gladstone Street	C2	Theobald Street	A3
Gooch Street	C2	Victoria Road	C4
Graham Street	C2	Villett Street	B3
Great Western Way	A1	Westcott Place	A4
Groundwell Road	C3	Western Street	C4
Havelock Street	B3	Whitehead Street	B4
Hawksworth Way	A1	Whitney Street	B4
Haydon Street	C2	William Street	A4
Holbrook Way	B2	York Road	D3

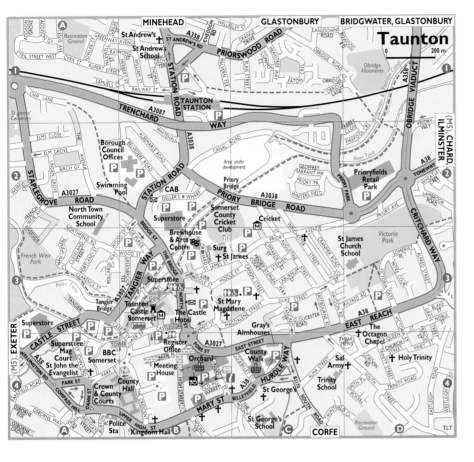

Taunton

Taunton is found on atlas page **18 H10**

Abbey Close	D2	Maxwell Street	A1
Albemarle Road	B2	Middle Street	B3
Alfred Street	D3	Northfield Road	A3
Alma Street	C4	North Street	B3
Belvedere Road	B2	Obridge Road	C1
Billetfield	C4	Obridge Viaduct	D2
Billet Street	C4	Old Pig Market	B4
Bridge Street	B2	Parkfield Road	A4
Canal Road	B2	Park Street	A4
Cann Street	A4	Paul Street	B4
Canon Street	C3	Plais Street	C1
Castle Street	A4	Portland Street	A3
Cheddon Road	B1	Priorswood Road	B1
Chip Lane	A1	Priory Avenue	C3
Church Street	D4	Priory Bridge Road	B2
Clarence Street	A3	Queen Street	D4
Cleveland Street	A3	Railway Street	B1
Compass Hill	A4	Raymond Street	A1
Cranmer Road	C3	Rupert Street	A1
Critchard Way	D2	St Andrew's Road	B1
Cyril Street	A1	St Augustine Street	C3
Deller's Wharf	B2	St James Street	B3
Duke Street	C3	St John's Road	A4
Eastbourne Road	C3	Samuels Court	A1
Eastleigh Road	D4	South Road	C4
East Reach	D3	South Street	D4
East Street	C4	Staplegrove Road	A2
Fore Street	B4	Station Road	B2
Fowler Street	A1	Stephen Street	C3
French Weir Avenue	A2	Stephen Way	C3
Gloucester Road	C3	Tancred Street	C3
Grange Drive	C1	The Avenue	A2
Grays Street	D3	The Bridge	B3
Greenway Avenue	A1	The Crescent	B4
Gyffarde Street	C3	Thomas Street	B1
Hammet Street	B4	Toneway	D2
Haydon Road	C3	Tower Street	B4
Herbert Street	B1	Trenchard Way	B1
High Street	B4	Trinity Street	D4
Hugo Street	C3	Upper High Street	B4
Hurdle Way	C4	Victoria Gate	D3
Laburnum Street	C3	Victoria Street	D4
Lansdowne Road	C1	Viney Street	D4
Leslie Avenue	A1	Wellington Road	A4
Linden Grove	A2	Wilfred Road	C3
Lower Middle Street	B3	William Street	B1
Magdalene Street	B3	Winchester Street	C2
Mary Street	B4	Wood Street	B3

Torquay

Torquay is found on atlas page **7 N6**

Abbey Road	B1	Middle Warbury Road	D1
Alexandra Road	C1	Mill Lane	A1
Alpine Road	C2	Montpellier Road	D3
Ash Hill Road	C1	Morgan Avenue	B1
Avenue Road	A1	Palm Road	B1
Bampfylde Road	A2	Parkhill Road	D4
Beacon Hill	D4	Pembroke Road	C1
Belgrave Road	A1	Pennsylvania Road	D1
Braddons Hill Road East	D3	Pimlico	C2
Braddons Hill Road West	C2	Potters Hill	C1
Braddons Street	D2	Princes Road	C1
Bridge Road	A1	Queen Street	C2
Camden Road	D1	Rathmore Road	A2
Cary Parade	C3	Rock Road	C2
Cary Road	C3	Rosehill Road	D1
Castle Lane	C1	St Efride's Road	A1
Castle Road	C1	St Luke's Road	B2
Cavern Road	D1	St Marychurch Road	C1
Chestnut Avenue	A2	Scarborough Road	B2
Church Lane	A1	Seaway Lane	A4
Church Street	A1	Shedden Hill Road	B3
Cleveland Road	A1	Solbro Road	A3
Croft Hill	B2	South Hill Road	D3
Croft Road	B2	South Street	A1
East Street	A1	Stentiford Hill Road	C2
Ellacombe Road	C1	Strand	D3
Falkland Road	A2	Sutherland Road	D1
Fleet Street	C3	Temperance Street	C2
Grafton Road	D2	The King's Drive	A3
Hennapyn Road	A4	The Terrace	D3
Higher Union Lane	B1	Torbay Road	A4
Hillesdon Road	D2	Tor Church Road	A1
Hoxton Road	D1	Tor Hill Road	B1
Hunsdon Road	D3	Torwood Street	D3
Laburnum Street	A1	Trematon Ave	B1
Lime Avenue	A2	Trinity Hill	D3
Lower Ellacombe		Union Street	B1
Church Road	D1	Upper Braddons Hill	D2
Lower Union Lane	C2	Vanehill Road	D4
Lower Warbury Road	D1	Vansittart Road	A1
Lucius Street	A1	Vaughan Parade	C3
Lymington Road	B1	Victoria Parade	D4
Magdalene Road	B1	Victoria Road	C1
Market Street	C2	Vine Road	A1
Marion View	D3	Walnut Road	A2
Meadfoot Lane	D4	Warberry Road West	C1
Melville Lane	C2	Warren Road	B2
Melville Street	C2	Wellington Road	C1

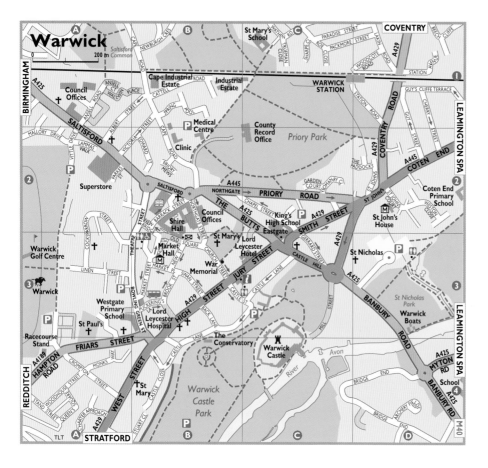

Warwick

Warwick is found on atlas page **59 L11**

Albert Street	A2	Old Square	B3
Ansell Court	A1	Packmore Street	C1
Ansell Road	A1	Paradise Street	C1
Archery Fields	D4	Parkes Street	A2
Back Lane	B3	Priory Mews	B2
Banbury Road	D3	Priory Road	C2
Barrack Street	B2	Puckering's Lane	B3
Beech Cliffe	D1	Queen's Square	A4
Bowling Green Street	B3	Roe Close	C1
Bridge End	D4	St Johns	D2
Brook Street	B3	St Johns Court	D2
Cape Road	B1	Saltisford	C1
Castle Close	B4	Sharpe Close	C1
Castle Hill	C3	Smith Street	C2
Castle Lane	B4	Spring Pool	B1
Castle Street	B3	Stand Street	A4
Cattell Road	B1	Station Avenue	D1
Chapel Street	C2	Station Road	D1
Charter Approach	A4	Stuart Close	B4
Cherry Street	D1	Swan Street	B3
Church Street	B3	Theatre Street	B3
Cocksparrow Street	A3	The Butts	B3
Coten End	D2	The Paddocks	D2
Coventry Road	D2	Trueman Close	D1
Crompton Street	A4	Victoria Street	A2
Edward Street	B2	Vittle Drive	A2
Friars Street	A4	Wallwin Place	A1
Garden Court	C2	Wathen Road	C1
Gerrard Street	C3	Weston Close	A4
Guy's Cliffe Terrace	D1	West Street	A4
Guy Street	D1	Woodcote Road	D1
Hampton Road	A4	Woodhouse Street	A4
High Street	B3	Yeomanry Close	C2
Jury Street	B3		
Lakin Road	D1		
Lammas Walk	A2		
Linen Street	A3		
Mallory Drive	A2		
Market Place	B3		
Market Street	B3		
Mill Street	C3		
Monks Way	A4		
Myton Road	D4		
New Bridge	B2		
Newburgh Crescent	B1		
New Street	B3		
Northgate	B2		
Northgate Street	B2		

Watford

Watford is found on atlas page **50 D11**

Addiscombe Road	B3	Marlborough Road	B3
Albert Road North	B2	Merton Road	B4
Albert Road South	B2	Mildred Avenue	A3
Alexandra Road	A1	Monica Close	D1
Anglian Close	D1	Nascot Street	B1
Beechen Grove	C3	New Road	D4
Brocklesbury Close	D2	New Street	C3
Burton Avenue	A4	Orphanage Road	C1
Cassiobury Drive	A2	Park Avenue	A3
Cassio Road	A3	Peace Prospect	A2
Chester Road	A4	Percy Road	A4
Chester Street	A4	Pretoria Road	A4
Clarendon Road	C1	Prince Street	C2
Cross Street	C2	Queen's Road	C3
Denmark Street	A1	Queen Street	C3
Derby Road	C3	Radlett Road	D2
Duke Street	C2	Raphael Drive	D1
Durban Road East	A4	Reeds Crescent	C1
Durban Road West	A4	Rickmansworth Road	A3
Earl Street	C3	Rosslyn Road	B3
Ebury Road	D2	St Albans Road	B1
Essex Road	A1	St John's Road	B1
Estcourt Road	C2	St Mary's Road	B1
Exchange Road	B3	St Pauls Way	B1
Farraline Road	B4	Shady Lane	D1
Feranley Street	B4	Shaftesbury Road	D2
Francis Road	B3	Smith Street	C4
Franklin Road	B1	Sotheron Road	C1
Gartlet Road	C2	Southsea Avenue	A4
Gaumont Approach	B2	Stanley Road	B4
George Street	C4	Station Road	B1
Gladstone Road	D3	Stephenson Way	B1
Granville Road	A4	Sutton Road	C2
Grosvenor Road	C3	The Avenue	A1
Halsey Road	B2	The Broadway	C4
Harwoods Road	A4	The Crescent	C4
Hempstead Road	A1	The Parade	B2
High Street	C3	Upton Road	B3
Hyde Road	A2	Vicarage Road	B4
Keele Close	C1	Water Lane	D4
King Street	C4	Wellington Road	B3
Lady's Close	C4	Wellstones	B3
Link Road	D1	Westland Road	B1
Loates Lane	C3	West Street	B1
Lord Street	C3	Whippendell Road	A4
Lower High Street	D4	Wiggenhall Road	B4
Malden Road	A1	Woodford Road	C1
Market Street	B4		

Winchester

Winchester is found on atlas page **22 E9**

Alex Terrace	A3	Market Lane	C3
Alison Way	A1	Marston Gate	B1
Andover Road	B1	Merchants Place	B2
Archery Lane	A3	Mews Lane	A3
Bar End Road	D4	Middle Brook Street	C2
Beaufort Road	A4	Minster Lane	B3
Beggar's Lane	D2	Newburgh Street	A2
Blue Ball Hill	D2	North Walls	C1
Bridge Street	D3	Parchment Street	B2
Canon Street	B4	Park Avenue	C2
Canute Road	D4	Romsey Road	A2
Chesil Street	D3	St Clement Street	B2
Chester Road	D2	St Cross Road	A4
Christchurch Road	A4	St George's Street	B2
City Road	B1	St James' Lane	A3
Clifton Hill	A2	St James Terrace	A3
Clifton Road	A1	St James' Villas	A4
Clifton Terrace	A2	St John's Street	D3
Colebrook Street	C3	St Martin's Close	D2
College Street	B4	St Michael's Gardens	B4
College Walk	C4	St Michael's Road	B4
Colson Road	D1	St Paul's Hill	A1
Compton Road	A4	St Peter Street	B2
Cross Street	B2	St Swithun Street	B3
Crowder Terrace	A3	St Thomas Street	B3
Culver Road	B4	Silchester Place	B1
Culverwell Gardens	B4	Silver Hill	C3
Durngate Place	D2	Southgate Street	B3
Durngate Terrace	D2	Staple Gardens	B2
Eastgate Street	D3	Station Road	A1
East Hill	D4	Stockbridge Road	A1
Edgar Road	A4	Sussex Street	A2
Friarsgate	C2	Sutton Gardens	B2
Friary Gardens	B4	Swan Lane	B1
Gladstone Street	A1	Symonds Street	B3
Gordon Road	C1	Tanner Street	C3
Great Minster Street	B3	The Broadway	C3
Highcliffe Road	D4	The Square	B3
High Street	B2	Tower Road	A1
Hyde Abbey Road	B1	Tower Street	A2
Hyde Close	B1	Trafalgar Street	B3
Hyde Street	B1	Union Street	C2
Jewry Street	B2	Upper Brook Street	C2
Kingsgate Street	B4	Upper High Street	A2
Lawn Street	C2	Victoria Road	B1
Little Minster Street	B3	Wales Street	D2
Lower Brook Street	C2	Water Lane	D3
Magdalen Hill	D3	Wharf Hill	D4

Wolverhampton

Wolverhampton is found on atlas page **58 D5**

Bath Avenue	A1	Peel Street	B3
Bath Road	A2	Penn Road	B4
Bell Street	B3	Piper's Row	D2
Berry Street	C2	Pitt Street	B3
Bilston Road	D3	Powlett Street	D4
Bilston Street	C3	Princess Street	C2
Birch Street	B2	Queen Square	B2
Broad Street	C2	Queen Street	C2
Castle Street	C3	Raby Street	D4
Chapel Ash	A3	Raglan Street	A3
Church Lane	B4	Red Lion Street	B2
Church Street	B4	Retreat Street	A4
Clarence Road	B2	Ring Road St Andrews	A2
Clarence Street	B2	Ring Road St Davids	D2
Cleveland Road	D4	Ring Road St Georges	C4
Cleveland Street	B3	Ring Road St Johns	B4
Corn Hill	D2	Ring Road St Marks	B3
Culwell Street	D1	Ring Road St Patricks	C1
Dale Street	A4	Ring Road St Peters	B2
Darlington Street	B3	Russell Street	A4
Dudley Road	C4	St George's Parade	C3
Dudley Street	C2	St John's Square	C4
Fold Street	B3	St Mark's Road	A3
Fryer Street	C2	St Mark's Street	A3
Garrick Street	C3	Salop Street	B3
Graiseley Street	A4	School Street	B3
Great Brickkiln Street	A4	Skinner Street	B3
Great Western Street	C1	Snow Hill	C3
Grimstone Street	D1	Stafford Street	C1
Horseley Fields	D2	Stephenson Street	A3
Hospital Street	D4	Stewart Street	B4
Lansdown Road	A1	Summer Row	B3
Lever Street	C4	Tempest Street	C3
Lichfield Street	C2	Temple Street	B3
Little's Lane	C1	Thomas Street	B4
Long Street	C2	Tower Street	C3
Lord Street	A3	Vicarage Road	D4
Mander Street	A4	Victoria Street	B3
Market Street	C3	Walsall Street	D3
Merridale Street	A4	Warwick Street	D3
Middle Cross	D3	Waterloo Road	B1
Mitre Fold	B2	Wednesfield Road	D1
Molineux Street	B1	Westbury Street	B2
New Hampton Road East	A1	Whitmore Hill	B1
North Street	B2	Whitmore Street	C2
Park Avenue	A1	Worcester Street	B4
Park Road East	B1	Wulfruna Street	C2
Park Road West	A2	Zoar Street	A4

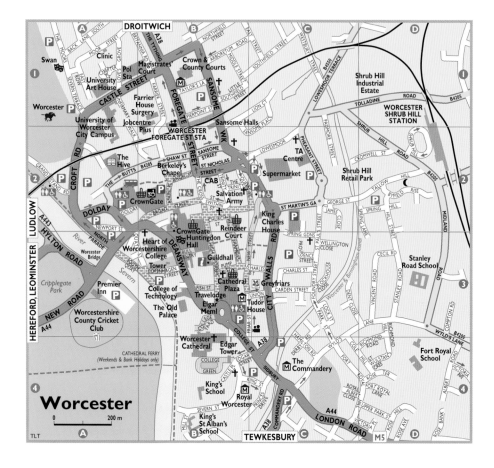

Worcester

Worcester

Worcester is found on atlas page **46 G4**

Albert Road	D4	Middle Street	B1
Angel Street	B2	Midland Road	D2
Arboretum Road	B1	Mill Street	B4
Back Lane South	A1	Moor Street	A1
Blockhouse Close	C3	Newport Street	A2
Britannia Road	A1	New Road	A3
Broad Street	B2	New Street	C3
Byfield Rise	D2	Northfield Street	B1
Carden Street	C3	North Parade	A1
Castle Street	A1	Padmore Street	C3
Cathedral Ferry	A4	Park Street	C3
Cecil Road	D3	Pheasant Street	C2
Charles Street	C3	Pierpoint Street	B1
Charter Place	A1	Providence Street	C3
Church Street	B2	Pump Street	B3
City Walls Road	C3	Quay Street	A3
Cole Hill	C4	Queen Street	B3
College Street	B3	Richmond Road	D4
Commandery Road	C4	Rose Hill	D4
Compton Road	D3	Rose Terrace	D4
Copenhagen Street	B3	St Martin's Gate	C2
Croft Road	A2	St Nicholas Street	B2
Cromwell Street	D2	St Paul's Street	C3
Deansway	B3	St Swithin Street	B2
Dent Close	C3	Sansome Walk	B1
Derby Road	C4	Severn Street	B4
Dolday	A2	Severn Terrace	A1
East Street	B1	Shaw Street	B2
Edgar Street	B4	Shrub Hill Road	D2
Farrier Street	B1	Sidbury	C4
Fish Street	B3	Southfield Street	C1
Foregate Street	B1	Spring Hill	D2
Fort Royal Hill	C4	Stanley Road	D3
Foundry Street	C3	Tallow Hill	D2
Friar Street	C3	Taylor's Lane	B1
George Street	C2	The Butts	A2
Grandstand Road	A2	The Cross	B2
Hamilton Road	C3	The Moors	A1
High Street	B3	The Shambles	B2
Hill Street	D2	The Tything	B1
Hylton Road	A3	Tolladine Road	C1
King Street	B4	Trinity Street	B2
Little Southfield Street	B1	Union Street	C3
Lock Street	C3	Upper Park Street	D4
London Road	C4	Vincent Road	C3
Love's Grove	A1	Wellington Close	C3
Lowesmoor	C2	Westbury Street	C1
Lowesmoor Terrace	C1	Wyld's Lane	C3

York

York

York is found on atlas page **98 C10**

Aldwark	C2	Lower Ousegate	C3
Barbican Road	D4	Lower Priory Street	B3
Bishopgate Street	B4	Low Petergate	C2
Bishophill Senior	B3	Margaret Street	D3
Black Horse Lane	D2	Market Street	C2
Blake Street	B2	Micklegate	A3
Blossom Street	A4	Minster Yard	B1
Bootham	B1	Monkgate	C1
Bridge Street	B3	Museum Street	B2
Buckingham Street	B3	Navigation Road	D3
Cemetery Road	D4	New Street	B2
Church Street	C2	North Street	B2
Clifford Street	C3	Nunnery Lane	A3
College Street	C1	Ogleforth	C1
Colliergate	C2	Palmer Lane	D2
Coney Street	B2	Palmer Street	D2
Coppergate	C3	Paragon Street	D4
Cromwell Road	B4	Parliament Street	C2
Davygate	B2	Pavement	C2
Deangate	C1	Peasholme Green	D2
Dove Street	B4	Percy's Lane	D3
Duncombe Place	B2	Piccadilly	C3
Dundas Street	D2	Price's Lane	B4
Fairfax Street	B3	Priory Street	C3
Fawcett Street	D4	Queen Street	A3
Feasegate	C2	Rougier Street	B2
Fetter Lane	B3	St Andrewgate	C2
Finkle Street	C2	St Denys' Road	D3
Fishergate	D4	St Leonard's Place	B1
Foss Bank	D1	St Martins Lane	B2
Fossgate	C2	St Maurice's Road	C1
Foss Islands Road	D2	St Saviourgate	C2
George Street	D3	St Saviours Place	C2
Gillygate	B1	Scarcroft Road	A4
Goodramgate	C2	Shambles	C2
Hampden Street	B4	Skeldergate	B3
High Ousegate	C3	Spen Lane	C2
High Petergate	B1	Spurriergate	B2
Holgate Road	A4	Station Road	A2
Hope Street	D4	Stonegate	B2
Hungate	D2	Swinegate	C2
Jewbury	D1	The Stonebow	C2
Kent Street	D4	Toft Green	A3
King Street	C3	Tower Street	C3
Kyme Street	B4	Trinity Lane	B3
Lendal	B2	Victor Street	B4
Long Close Lane	D4	Walmgate	D3
Lord Mayor's Walk	C1	Wellington Road	B2

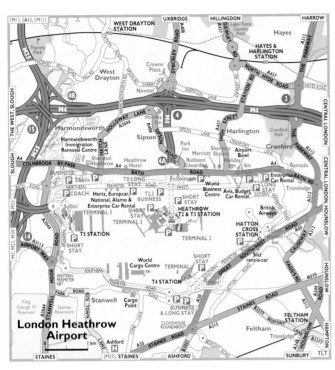

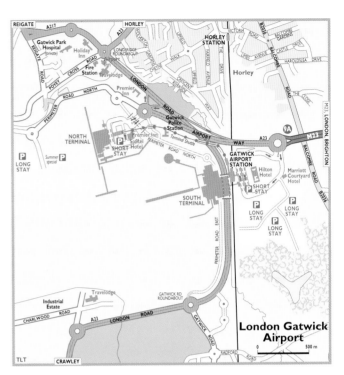

London Heathrow Airport – 17 miles west of central London, M25 junction 14 and M4 junction 4A

Satnav Location: TW6 1EW (Terminal 2), TW6 1QG (T3), TW6 3XA (T4), TW6 2GA (T5)
Information: visit *www.heathrow.com*
Parking: short-stay, long-stay and business parking is available.
Public Transport: coach, bus, rail and London Underground.
There are several 4-star and 3-star hotels within easy reach of the airport.
Car hire facilities are available.

London Gatwick Airport – 29 miles south of central London, M23 junction 9A

Satnav Location: RH6 0NP (South terminal), RH6 0PJ (North terminal)
Information: visit *www.gatwickairport.com*
Parking: short and long-stay parking is available at both the North and South terminals.
Public Transport: coach, bus and rail.
There are several 4-star and 3-star hotels within easy reach of the airport.
Car hire facilities are available.

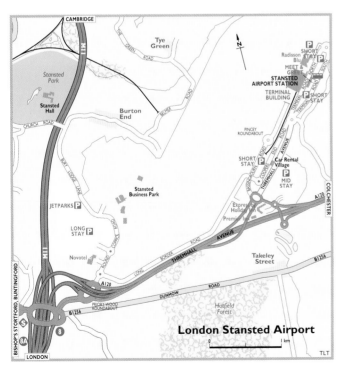

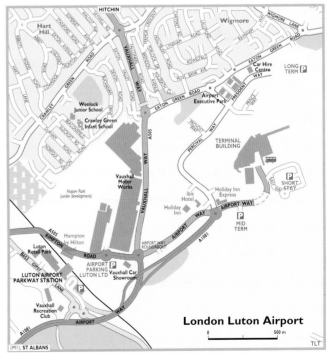

London Stansted Airport – 36 miles north-east of central London, M11 junction 8/8A

Satnav Location: CM24 1RW
Information: visit *www.stanstedairport.com*
Parking: short, mid and long-stay open-air parking is available.
Public Transport: coach, bus and direct rail link to London on the Stansted Express.
There are several hotels within easy reach of the airport.
Car hire facilities are available.

London Luton Airport – 34 miles north of central London

Satnav Location: LU2 9QT
Information: visit *www.london-luton.co.uk*
Parking: short-term, mid-term and long-stay parking is available.
Public Transport: coach, bus and rail.
There are several hotels within easy reach of the airport.
Car hire facilities are available.

London City Airport – 8 miles east of central London

Satnav Location: E16 2PX
Information: visit www.londoncityairport.com
Parking: short and long-stay open-air parking is available.
Public Transport: easy access to the rail network, Docklands Light Railway and the London Underground.
There are 5-star, 4-star and 3-star hotels within easy reach of the airport.
Car hire facilities are available.

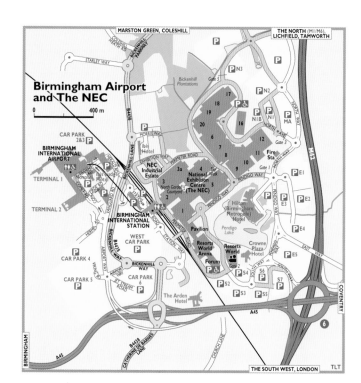

Birmingham Airport – 10 miles east of Birmingham, M42 junction 6

Satnav Location: B26 3QJ
Information: visit www.birminghamairport.co.uk
Parking: short and long-stay parking is available.
Public Transport: Air-Rail Link service operates every 2 minutes to and from Birmingham International Railway Station & Interchange.
There are several 4-star and 3-star hotels within easy reach of the airport.
Car hire facilities are available.

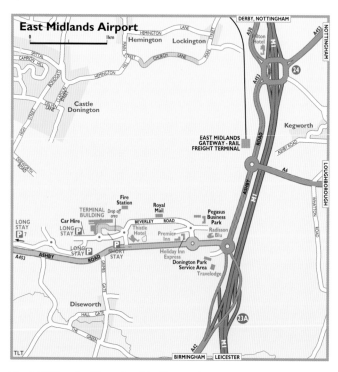

East Midlands Airport – 14 miles south-west of Nottingham, M1 junction 23A/24

Satnav Location: DE74 2SA
Information: visit www.eastmidlandsairport.com
Parking: short and long-stay parking is available.
Public Transport: bus and coach services to major towns and cities in the East Midlands.
There are several 3-star hotels within easy reach of the airport.
Car hire facilities are available.

Manchester Airport – 10 miles south of Manchester, M56 junction 5

Satnav Location: M90 1QX
Information visit www.manchesterairport.co.uk
Parking: short and long-stay parking is available.
Public Transport: coach, bus and rail.
There are several 4-star and 3-star hotels within easy reach of the airport.
Car hire facilities are available.

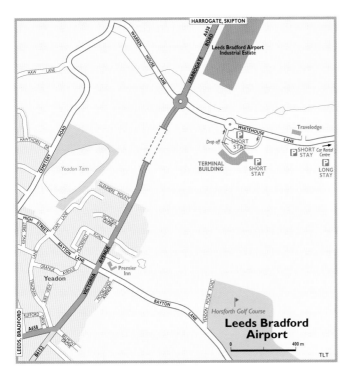

Leeds Bradford Airport – 8 miles north-east of Bradford and 8 miles north-west of Leeds

Satnav Location: LS19 7TU
Information: visit *www.leedsbradfordairport.co.uk*
Parking: short, mid-term and long-stay parking is available.
Public Transport: bus service operates every 30 minutes from Bradford, Leeds and Otley.
There are several 4-star and 3-star hotels within easy reach of the airport.
Car hire facilities are available.

Aberdeen Airport – 7 miles north-west of Aberdeen

Satnav Location: AB21 7DU
Information: visit *www.aberdeenairport.com*
Parking: short and long-stay parking is available.
Public Transport: regular bus service to central Aberdeen.
There are several 4-star and 3-star hotels within easy reach of the airport.
Car hire facilities are available.

Edinburgh Airport – 9 miles west of Edinburgh

Satnav Location: EH12 9DN
Information: visit *www.edinburghairport.com*
Parking: short and long-stay parking is available.
Public Transport: regular bus services to central Edinburgh, Glasgow and Fife and a tram service to Edinburgh.
There are several 4-star and 3-star hotels within easy reach of the airport.
Car hire and valet parking facilities are available.

Glasgow Airport – 10 miles west of Glasgow, M8 junction 28/29

Satnav Location: PA3 2SW
Information: visit *www.glasgowairport.com*
Parking: short and long-stay parking is available.
Public Transport: regular coach services operate direct to central Glasgow.
There are several 3-star hotels within easy reach of the airport.
Car hire facilities are available.

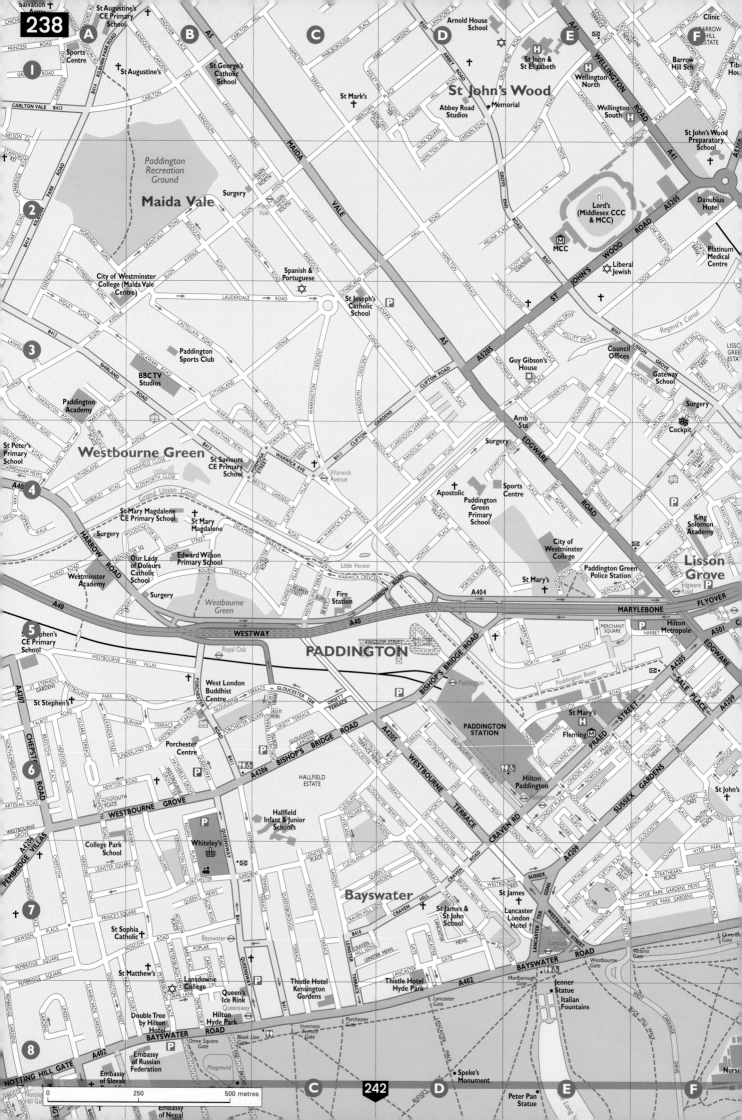

Central London index

This index lists street and station names, and top places of tourist interest shown in red. Names are listed in alphabetical order and written in full, but may be abbreviated on the map. Each entry is followed by its Postcode District and then the page number and grid reference to the square in which the name is found. Names are asterisked (*) in the index where there is insufficient space to show them on the map.

A

Abbey Gardens NW8 238 C1
Abbey Orchard Street SW1P 244 B4
Abbey Road NW8 238 D1
Abbey Street SE1 246 B7
Abchurch Lane EC4N 241 L7
Abercorn Close NW8 238 C1
Abercorn Place NW8 238 C1
Aberdeen Place NW8 238 E3
Aberdour Street SE1 245 M5
Abingdon Road W8 242 A4
Abingdon Street SW1P 244 C3
Abingdon Villas W8 242 A4
Ackroyd Drive E3 247 L1
Acorn Walk SE16 247 K5
Acton Street WC1X 240 E2
Adam and Eve Mews W8 242 A3
Adam's Row W1K 239 K8
Adam Street WC2N 240 D8
Addington Street SE1 244 E3
Addle Hill EC4V 241 H7
Adelina Grove E1 246 F1
Adeline Place WC1B 240 B5
Adler Street E1 246 D2
Admiral Place SE16 247 K5
Admiral Walk W9 238 A4
Adpar Street W2 238 E4
Agar Street WC2N 240 D8
Agdon Street EC1V 241 H3
Agnes Street E14 247 L2
Ainsty Street SE16 247 G6
Air Street W1B 240 A8
Alaska Street SE1 244 F2
Albany Road SE5 245 L8
Albany Street NW1 239 L1
Albemarle Street W1S 239 L8
Albermarle Way EC1V 241 H4
Alberta Street SE17 245 H6
Albert Bridge SW3 243 G8
Albert Embankment SE1 244 D7
Albert Gardens E1 247 H3
Albert Gate SW1X 243 H2
Albert Place W8 242 C3
Albion Gate W2 239 G7
Albion Place EC1M 241 H4
Albion Street SE16 247 G7
Albion Street W2 239 G7
Aldenham Street NW1 240 A1
Aldermanbury EC2V 241 K6
Alderney Mews SE1 245 K4
Alderney Street SW1V 243 L6
Aldersgate Street EC1A 241 J4
Aldford Street W1K 239 J8
Aldgate EC3M 246 B3
Aldgate ⊖ EC3N 246 B3
Aldgate East ⊖ E1 246 C2
Aldgate High Street EC3N 246 B3
Aldgate Square EC3N 246 B3
Aldsworth Close W9 238 B4
Aldwych WC2E 240 E7
Alexander Place SW7 242 F5
Alexander Street W2 238 A6
Alexandra Gate SW7 242 E3
Alfred Mews WC1E 240 B4
Alfred Place WC1E 240 B4
Alfred Road W2 238 A5
Alice Street SE1 245 M4
Alie Street E1 246 C3
Allen Street W8 242 A4
Allhallows Lane EC4R 241 L8
Allington Street SW1E 243 M4
Allitsen Road NW8 238 F1
Allsop Place NW1 239 H4
Alma Square NW8 238 D1
Alpha Place SW3 243 G8
Alsace Road SE17 245 M7
Alscot Road * SE1 246 C8
Alvey Street SE17 245 M6
Ambergate Street SE17 245 H7
Amberley Road W9 238 A4
Ambrosden Avenue SW1P 244 A4
Amelia Street SE17 245 J6
America Square EC3N 246 B3
America Street SE1 245 J2
Ampton Street WC1X 240 E2
Amwell Street EC1R 240 F2
Anchorage Point E14 247 M6
Andover Place NW6 238 B1
Angel ⊖ N1 241 G1
Angela Hooper Place * SW1E 244 A4
Angel Junction N1 241 G1
Angel Lane EC4R 241 L8
Angel Street EC1A 241 J6
Ann Moss Way SE16 246 F8
Ann's Close SW1X 243 J3
Ansdell Street W8 242 B4
Antill Terrace E1 247 H2
Antizan Street E1 246 B2
Apple Tree Yard SW1Y 240 A8
Appold Street EC2A 241 M4
Apsley Gate W1J 243 J2
Apsley House & Wellington Museum W1J 243 K2
Aquinas Street SE1 245 G1
Arbour Square E1 247 H2
Archangel Street SE16 247 J7
Archer Street W1B 240 B7
Arch Street SE1 245 J4
Arden Estate N1 241 M1
Argyle Square WC1H 240 D2
Argyle Street WC1H 240 D2
Argyll Road W8 242 A3
Argyll Street W1F 239 M6
Arlington Street SW1A 243 M1
Arlington Way EC1R 241 G2
Arne Street WC2H 240 D6
Arneway Street SW1P 244 B5
Arnhem Place E14 247 M8
Arnold Estate SE1 246 C7
Arnside Street SE17 245 K8
Artesian Road W11 238 A6
Arthur Street EC4V 241 L7
Artichoke Hill E1W 246 E4
Artillery Lane E1 246 A1
Artillery Row SW1P 244 B4
Arundel Street WC2R 240 F7
Ashbridge Street NW8 238 F4
Ashburn Gardens SW7 242 C5
Ashburn Place SW7 242 C5
Ashby Street EC1V 241 H2
Asher Way E1W 246 D4
Ashfield Street E1 246 E2
Ashford Street N1 241 M2
Ashley Place SW1P 243 M4
Ashmill Street NW1 238 F4
Ashmole Street SW8 244 F8
Ashworth Road W9 238 B2
Assam Street E1 246 C2
Assembly Passage E1 247 G1
Astell Street SW3 243 G6
Aston Street E14 247 K1
Astwood Mews SW7 242 C5
Atherstone Mews SW7 242 D5
Atterbury Street SW1P 244 C6
Attneave Street WC1X 240 F3
Augustus Street NW1 239 L1
Aulton Place SE11 245 G7
Austin Friars EC2N 241 L6
Australia Gate SW1A 243 M3
Austral Street SE11 245 H5
Aveline Street SE11 244 F7
Ave Maria Lane EC1A 241 H6
Avenue Dock Hill SE16 247 J6
Avery Farm Row SW1W 243 K6
Avery Row W1K 239 L7
Aybrook Street W1U 239 J5
Aylesbury Road SE17 245 L7
Aylesbury Street EC1R 241 H4
Aylesford Street SW1V 244 B7
Aylward Street E1 247 G2
Ayres Street SE1 245 K2

B

Babmaes Street SW1Y 240 B8
Bache's Street N1 241 L2
Back Church Lane E1 246 D3
Back Hill EC1R 241 G4
Bacon Grove SE1 246 B8
Bainbridge Street WC1A 240 C6
Bakers Mews W1U 239 J6
Baker's Row EC1R 241 G4
Baker Street NW1 239 H4
Baker Street W1U 239 J5
Baker Street ⊖ NW1 239 H4
Balcombe Street NW1 239 G3
Balderton Street W1K 239 J7
Baldwin's Gardens EC1N 240 F5
Baldwin Street EC1V 241 L2
Bale Road E1 247 J1
Balfe Street N1 240 D1
Balfour Mews W1K 239 K8
Balfour Place W1K 239 J8
Balfour Street SE17 245 K5
Baltic Street East EC1Y 241 J3
Baltic Street West EC1Y 241 J4
Balvaird Place SW1V 244 C7
Bank ⊖ ⊖ EC2R 241 L6
Bank End SE1 245 K1
Bankside SE1 241 J8
Banner Street EC1Y 241 K3
Banqueting House SW1A 244 C2
Banyard Road SE16 246 E8
Barbican ⊖ EC1A 241 J4
Barbican Estate EC2Y 241 J5
Barge House Street SE1 245 G1
Bark Place W2 238 B7
Barkston Gardens SW5 242 B6
Barley Corn Way E14 247 L4
Barlow/Congreve Estate SE17 245 M5
Barlow Place W1J 239 L7
Barlow Street SE17 245 L5
Barnardo Street E1 247 H3
Barnby Street NW1 240 A1
Barnes Street E14 247 J2
Barnham Street SE1 246 A6
Baron's Place SE1 245 G3
Baron Street N1 241 G1
Barrett Street W1U 239 K6
Barrow Hill Estate NW8 238 F1
Barrow Hill Road NW8 238 F1
Barter Street WC1A 240 D5
Bartholomew Close EC1A 241 J5
Bartholomew Lane EC2R 241 L6
Bartholomew Street SE1 245 L5
Bartlett Court EC4A 241 G6
Barton Street SW1P 244 C4
Basil Street SW3 243 H4
Basin Approach E14 247 K3
Basinghall Avenue EC2V 241 K5
Basinghall Street EC2V 241 K5
Bastwick Street EC1V 241 J3
Bateman's Buildings W1D 240 B6
Bateman Street W1D 240 B6
Bath Street EC1V 241 K2
Bath Terrace SE1 245 J4
Bathurst Mews W2 238 E7
Bathurst Street W2 238 E7
Battle Bridge Lane SE1 245 M1
Batty Street E1 246 D2
Bayley Street WC1B 240 B5
Baylis Road SE1 244 F3
Bayswater ⊖ W2 238 B7
Bayswater Road W2 238 E7
Baythorne Street E3 247 L1
Beaconsfield Road SE17 245 M7
Beak Street W1F 240 A7
Bear Gardens SE1 241 J8
Bear Lane SE1 245 H1
Beauchamp Place SW3 243 G4
Beaufort Gardens SW3 243 G4
Beaufort Street SW3 242 E8
Beaumont Place W1T 240 A3
Beaumont Street W1G 239 K4
Beccles Street E14 247 M3
Beckett Street SE1 245 L3
Beckway Street SE17 245 M6
Bedale Street SE1 245 L1
Bedford Avenue WC1B 240 C5
Bedfordbury WC2N 240 C7
Bedford Gardens W8 242 A2
Bedford Place WC1N 240 D4
Bedford Row WC1R 240 E4
Bedford Square WC1B 240 B5
Bedford Street WC2E 240 D7
Bedford Way WC1H 240 C3
Bedlow Close NW8 238 F3
Beech Street EC2Y 241 J4
Beeston Place SW1W 243 L4
Belgrave Mews North * SW1X 243 J3
Belgrave Mews South * SW1X 243 K4
Belgrave Place SW1X 243 J4
Belgrave Road SW1V 243 L5
Belgrave Road SW1V 244 A6
Belgrave Square SW1X 243 J3
Belgrave Street E1 247 J2
Belgrove Street WC1H 240 D2
Bell Lane E1 246 B1
Bell Street NW1 238 F4
Bell Yard WC2A 240 F6
Belvedere Road SE1 244 E2
Benjamin Street EC1M 241 H4
Ben Jonson Road E1 247 J1
Bennett Street SW1A 243 M1
Ben Smith Way SE16 246 D7
Benson Quay E1W 246 F4
Bentinck Mews W1U 239 K6
Bentinck Street W1U 239 K6
Bere Street E1W 247 H3
Bergen Square SE16 247 K8
Berkeley Mews W1H 239 H6
Berkeley Square W1J 239 L8
Berkeley Street W1J 239 L8
Bermondsey ⊖ ⊖ SE16 246 E7
Bermondsey Spa SE16 246 C8
Bermondsey Square SE1 246 A8
Bermondsey Street SE1 246 A6
Bermondsey Wall East SE16 246 E7
Bermondsey Wall Estate SE16 246 D7
Bermondsey Wall West SE16 246 C6
Bernard Street WC1N 240 D4
Berners Mews W1T 240 A5
Berners Place W1F 240 A6
Berners Street W1T 240 A5
Bernhardt Crescent NW8 238 F3
Berryfield Road SE17 245 J6
Berry Street EC1V 241 H3
Berwick Street W1F 240 A6
Bessborough Gardens SW1V 244 C6
Bessborough Street SW1V 244 B6
Betterton Street WC2H 240 D6
Bevenden Street N1 241 L2
Bevin Close SE16 247 J5
Bevington Street SE16 246 D7
Bevin Way WC1X 240 F1
Bevis Marks EC3A 246 A2
Bewley Street E1 246 F3
Bickenhall Street W1U 239 H4
Bidborough Street WC1H 240 C2
Biddulph Road W9 238 B2
Big Ben (Elizabeth Tower) SW1A 244 D3
Bigland Street E1 246 E3
Billiter Square EC3M 246 A3
Billiter Street EC3M 246 A3
Bina Gardens SW5 242 C6
Bingham Place W1U 239 J4
Binney Street W1K 239 K7
Birchfield Street E14 247 M3
Birchin Lane EC3V 241 L7
Birdcage Walk SW1H 244 A3
Birde Lane EC4Y 241 H6
Bird Street W1C 239 K6
Birkenhead Street N1 240 D1
Bishop's Bridge Road W2 238 C6
Bishopsgate EC2M 246 A2
Bishops Square E1 246 B1
Bishop's Terrace SE11 245 G5
Bittern Street SE1 245 J3
Blackall Street EC2A 241 M3
Blackburne's Mews W1K 239 J7
Blackfriars ⇌ ⊖ EC4V 241 H7
Blackfriars Bridge SE1 241 H8
Blacklands Terrace SW3 243 H6
Black Friars Lane EC4V 241 H7
Blackfriars Road SE1 245 H3
Blackhorse Court SE1 245 L4
Black Lion Gate W2 238 B8
Black Prince Road SE11 244 E6
Blackwood Street SE17 245 K6
Blandford Street W1U 239 H5
Blenheim Street W1S 239 L7
Bletchley Street N1 241 K1
Blomfield Mews W2 238 C5
Blomfield Road W9 238 C4
Blomfield Street EC2M 241 M5
Blomfield Villas W2 238 C5
Bloomfield Terrace SW1W 243 J6
Bloomsbury Square WC1A 240 D5
Bloomsbury Street WC1B 240 C5
Bloomsbury Way WC1A 240 C5
Blount Street E14 247 K2
Blue Ball Yard SW1A 243 M1
Bohn Road E1 247 J1
Bolsover Street W1W 239 L4
Bolton Gardens SW5 242 B6
Bolton Street W1J 243 L1
Bond Street ⊖ W1C 239 K6
Bondway SW8 244 D8
Bonhill Street EC2A 241 L4
Bonnington Square SW8 244 E8
Boot Street N1 241 M2
Borough ⊖ SE1 245 K3
Borough High Street SE1 245 K3
Borough Road SE1 245 H3
Boscobel Place SW1W 243 K5
Boscobel Street NW8 238 E4
Boss Street SE1 246 B6
Boston Place NW1 239 G3
Botolph Lane EC3R 241 M7
Boundary Lane SE17 245 K8
Boundary Row SE1 245 G2
Bourdon Street W1K 239 L7
Bourlet Close W1W 239 M5
Bourne Estate EC1N 240 F4
Bourne Street SW1W 243 J6
Bourne Terrace W2 238 B5
Bouverie Place W2 238 F6
Bouverie Street EC4Y 241 G6
Bowland Yard * SW1X 243 J3
Bow Lane EC4M 241 K6
Bowling Green Lane EC1R 241 G3
Bowling Green Place SE1 245 L2
Bowling Green Street SE11 244 F8
Bowling Green Walk N1 241 M2
Bowsell Street WC1N 240 D4
Bow Street WC2E 240 D7
Boyd Street E1 246 D3
Boyfield Street SE1 245 H3
Boyle Street W1S 239 M7
Boyson Road SE17 245 K8
Brackley Street EC1Y 241 J4
Bradenham Close SE17 245 K8
Brad Street SE1 245 G2
Braganza Street SE17 245 H7
Braham Street E1 246 C3
Bramerton Street SW3 242 F7
Bramham Gardens SW5 242 B6
Branch Road E14 247 J3
Brandon Estate SE17 245 H8
Brandon Street SE17 245 K6
Brangton Road SE11 244 F7
Bray Crescent SE16 247 H6
Bray Place SW3 243 H6
Bread Street EC4M 241 K7
Bream's Buildings EC4A 240 F6
Brechin Place SW7 242 D6
Breezer's Hill E1W 246 D4
Brendon Street W1H 239 G5
Bressenden Place SW1W 243 L4
Brettell Street SE17 245 L7
Brewers Green SW1H 244 A3
Brewer Street W1F 240 A7
Brewhouse Lane E1W 246 F6
Brewhouse Walk SE16 247 J5
Brick Court WC2R 240 F7
Brick Lane E1 246 C1
Brick Street W1J 243 K2
Bridewell Place EC4V 241 H7
Bridgeman Street NW8 238 F1
Bridge Place SW1V 243 L5
Bridgeport Place E1W 246 D4
Bridge Street SW1A 244 D3
Bridgewater Street EC2Y 241 J4
Bridgeway Street NW1 240 A1
Bridle Lane W1F 240 A7
Bridstow Place W2 238 A6
Brightlingsea Place E14 247 L4
Brill Place NW1 240 C1
Briset Street EC1M 241 H4
Bristol Gardens W9 238 B4
Britannia Street WC1X 240 E2
Britannia Walk N1 241 L2
Britannia Way N1 241 K1
Britten Street SW3 242 F7
Britton Street EC1M 241 H4
Broadbent Street W1K 239 L7
Broadgate Circle EC2M 241 M5
Broadley Street NW8 238 F4
Broadley Terrace NW1 238 F4
Broadstone Place W1U 239 J5
Broad Walk NW1 239 K1
Broad Walk W2 239 H7
Broadwall SE1 245 G1
Broadway SW1H 244 B4
Broadwick Street W1F 240 A7
Brockham Street SE1 245 K4
Brodlove Lane E1W 247 H3
Bromley Street E1 247 J2
Brompton Place SW3 243 G4
Brompton Road SW3 243 G4
Brompton Road SW7 242 F5
Brompton Square SW3 242 F4
Bronti Close SE17 245 K7
Brook Drive SE11 245 G5
Brooke Street EC1N 240 F5
Brook Gate W2 239 H8
Brook Mews North W2 238 D7
Brook's Mews W1K 239 K7
Brook Street W1K 239 K7
Brook Street W2 238 E7
Brown Heart Gardens W1K 239 K7
Browning Mews W1G 239 K5
Browning Street SE17 245 K6
Brownlow Mews WC1N 240 E3
Brownlow Street WC1V 240 E5
Brown Street W1H 239 G6
Brunel Road SE16 247 G6
Brune Street E1 246 B1
Brunswick Close SE1 246 A6
Brunswick Gardens W8 242 A1
Brunswick Place N1 241 L2
Brunswick Quay SE16 247 J8
Brunswick Square WC1N 240 D3
Brunswick Street WC1N 240 D3
Brunton Place E14 247 K3
Brushfield Street E1 246 B1
Bruton Lane W1J 239 L8
Bruton Place W1J 239 L7
Bruton Street W1J 239 L8
Bryan Road SE16 247 K6
Bryanstone Mews West W1H 239 G5
Bryanston Mews East W1H 239 H5
Bryanston Place W1H 239 G5
Bryanston Square W1H 239 H5
Bryanston Street W1C 239 H7
Buck Hill Walk W2 238 E8
Buckingham Gate SW1E 243 L3
Buckingham Mews SW1E 243 M3
Buckingham Palace SW1A 243 L3
Buckingham Palace Road SW1W 243 L5
Buckingham Place SW1E 243 M4
Buckland Street N1 241 L1
Buckle Street E1 246 C2
Bucknall Street WC2H 240 C6
Buckters Rents SE16 247 J5
Budge's Walk W2 242 D2
Bulleid Way SW1V 243 L5
Bulstrode Street W1U 239 K5
Bunhill Row EC1Y 241 L3
Burdett Estate E14 247 M1
Burdett Road E14 247 L2
Burdett Street SE1 244 F3
Burgess Street E14 247 M1
Burge Street SE1 245 L4
Burlington Arcade W1J 239 M8
Burlington Gardens W1S 239 M8
Burnhouse Place SW1W 243 J6
Burnsall Street SW3 243 G7
Burnside Close SE16 247 J5
Burrell Street SE1 245 H1
Burslem Street E1 246 D3
Burton Grove SE17 245 L7
Burton Street WC1H 240 C3
Burwood Place W2 239 G6
Bury Close SE16 247 H5
Bury Court EC3A 246 A2
Bury Place WC1A 240 D5
Bury Street EC3A 246 A2
Bury Street SW1Y 244 A1
Bury Walk SW3 242 F6
Bushell Street E1W 246 D5
Bush Lane EC4V 241 L7
Butcher Row E14 247 J3
Bute Street SW7 242 E5
Butler Place SW1H 244 B4
Butler's Wharf SE1 246 C6
Buttesland Street N1 241 L2
Byefield Close SE16 247 K6
Bylands Close SE16 247 J5
Byng Place WC1E 240 B4
Byng Street E14 247 M6
Byward Street EC3R 246 A4
Bywater Place SE16 247 K5
Bywater Street SW3 243 G6

C

Cabbell Street NW1 238 F5
Cable Street E1 246 F3
Cadiz Street SE17 245 K7
Cadogan Gardens SW3 243 H5
Cadogan Gate SW1X 243 H5
Cadogan Lane SW1X 243 J4
Cadogan Place SW1X 243 J4
Cadogan Square SW1X 243 H5
Cadogan Street SW3 243 G6
Caledonian Road N1 240 D1
Caledonia Street N1 240 D1
Cale Street SW3 242 F6
Callow Street SW3 242 D7
Calshot Street N1 240 E1
Calthorpe Street WC1X 240 E3
Cambridge Circus WC2H 240 C7
Cambridge Gardens NW6 238 A1
Cambridge Gate NW1 239 L3
Cambridge Road NW6 238 A1
Cambridge Road NW6 238 A2
Cambridge Square W2 238 F6
Cambridge Street SW1V 243 L6
Cambridge Terrace NW1 239 L2
Cambridge Terrace Mews NW1 239 L3
Camdenhurst Street E14 247 K2
Camera Place SW10 242 D8
Camomile Street EC3A 246 A2
Campden Grove W8 242 A2
Campden Hill Road W8 242 A2
Campden Street W8 242 A1
Camperdown Street E1 246 C3
Canada Estate SE16 247 G7
Canada Gate SW1A 243 M3
Canada Street SE16 247 H7
Canada Water ⊖ ⊖ SE16 247 G7
Canada Wharf SE16 247 L5
Canal Street SE5 245 L8
Canary Riverside E14 247 L4
Candle Street E1 247 K1
Canning Place W8 242 C4
Cannon Drive E14 247 M4
Cannon Street EC4N 241 K7
Cannon Street ⇌ ⊖ EC4R 241 K7
Cannon Street Road E1 246 E3
Canon Beck Road SE16 247 G6
Canon Row SW1A 244 D3
Canton Street E14 247 M3
Capeners Close * SW1X 243 J3
Capland Street NW8 238 E3
Capper Street WC1E 240 A4
Capstan Way SE16 247 K5
Carbis Road E14 247 L2
Carburton Street W1W 239 L4
Cardigan Street SE11 244 F6
Cardington Street NW1 240 A2
Carey Street WC2A 240 F6
Carlisle Avenue EC3N 246 B3
Carlisle Lane SE1 244 F4
Carlisle Place SW1P 243 M5
Carlisle Street W1D 240 B6
Carlos Place W1K 239 K7
Carlton Gardens SW1Y 244 B2
Carlton Hill NW6 238 B1
Carlton House Terrace SW1Y 244 B1
Carlton Street W1J 243 L1
Carlton Vale NW6 238 A1
Carlton Vale NW6 238 B1
Carlyle Square SW3 242 F7
Carmelite Street EC4Y 241 G7
Carnaby Street W1F 239 M7
Caroline Place W2 238 B7
Caroline Street E1 247 H3
Caroline Terrace SW1W 243 J5
Carpenter Street W1K 239 K7
Carrington Street W1J 243 L1
Carr Street E14 247 K1
Carteret Street SW1H 244 B3
Carter Lane EC4V 241 H7
Carter Place SE17 245 K7
Carter Street SE17 245 J7
Carthusian Street EC1M 241 J4
Carting Lane WC2R 240 D8
Cartwright Gardens WC1H 240 C2
Cartwright Street E1 246 C4
Casey Close NW8 238 F3
Casson Street E1 246 C1
Castellain Road W9 238 B3
Castlebrook Close SE11 245 G5
Castle Lane SW1E 243 M4
Catesby Street SE17 245 L6
Cathay Street SE16 246 F7
Cathcart Road SW10 242 C8
Cathedral Walk SW1E 243 M4
Catherine Place SW1E 243 M4
Catherine Street WC2E 240 D7
Cato Street W1H 239 G5
Causton Street SW1P 244 B6

Cavell Street E1 246 F1
Cavendish Avenue NW8 238 E1
Cavendish Place W1G 239 L6
Cavendish Square W1G 239 L6
Cavendish Street N1 241 L1
Caversham Street SW3 243 G8
Caxton Street SW1H 244 B4
Cayton Street EC1V 241 K2
Centaur Street SE1 244 F4
Central Street EC1V 241 J2
Chadwell Street EC1R 241 G1
Chadwick Street SW1P 244 B4
Chagford Street NW1 239 H4
Chalton Street NW1 240 B1
Chambers Street SE16 246 D7
Chamber Street E1 246 C3
Chambers Wharf SE16 246 D6
Chancel Street SE1 245 H1
Chancery Lane WC2A 240 F5
Chancery Lane ⊖ WC1V 240 F5
Chandos Place WC2N 240 C8
Chandos Street W1G 239 L5
Chantry Square W8 242 B4
Chapel Market N1 240 F1
Chapel Street NW1 238 F5
Chapel Street SW1X 243 K3
Chaplin Close SE1 245 G3
Chapman Street E1 246 E3
Chapter Road SE17 245 H7
Chapter Street SW1P 244 B6
Chargrove Close SE16 247 H6
Charing Cross ⇌ ⊖ WC2N 244 D1
Charing Cross Road WC2H 240 B6
Charing Cross Road WC2N 240 C7
Charlbert Street NW8 238 F1
Charles II Street SW1Y 240 B8
Charles Square N1 241 M2
Charles Street W1J 243 K1
Charleston Street SE17 245 K6
Charlotte Road EC2A 241 M3
Charlotte Street W1T 240 A4
Charlwood Place SW1V 244 A6
Charlwood Street SW1V 243 M7
Charlwood Street SW1V 244 A6
Charrington Street NW1 240 B1
Charterhouse Square EC1M 241 H4
Charterhouse Street EC1M 241 G5
Chart Street N1 241 L2
Chaseley Street E14 247 J2
Chatham Street SE17 245 L5
Cheapside EC2V 241 K6
Chelsea Bridge SW1W 243 K8
Chelsea Bridge Road SW1W 243 J7
Chelsea Embankment SW3 243 G8
Chelsea Manor Gardens SW3 242 F7
Chelsea Manor Street SW3 243 G7
Chelsea Park Gardens SW3 242 E8
Chelsea Physic Garden SW3 243 H8
Chelsea Square SW3 242 E7
Cheltenham Terrace SW3 243 H6
Chenies Mews WC1E 240 B4
Chenies Street WC1E 240 B4
Cheniston Gardens W8 242 A4
Chepstow Place W2 238 A7
Chepstow Road W2 238 A6
Chequer Street EC1Y 241 K3
Cherbury Street N1 241 L1
Cherry Garden Street SE16 246 E7
Chesham Close SW1X 243 J4
Chesham Place SW1X 243 J4
Chesham Street SW1X 243 J4
Chester Close SW1X 243 K3
Chester Close North NW1 239 L2
Chester Close South NW1 239 L2
Chesterfield Gardens W1J 243 K1
Chesterfield Hill W1J 239 K8
Chesterfield Street W1J 243 K1
Chester Gate NW1 239 L2
Chester Mews SW1X 243 K3
Chester Place NW1 239 L1
Chester Road NW1 239 K2
Chester Row SW1W 243 K5
Chester Square SW1W 243 K5
Chester Square Mews SW1W 243 K4
Chester Street SW1X 243 K4
Chester Terrace NW1 239 L2
Chester Way SE11 245 G6
Cheval Place SW7 243 G4
Cheval Street E14 247 M7
Cheyne Gardens SW3 243 G8
Cheyne Row SW3 242 F8
Cheyne Walk SW3 242 F8
Chicheley Street SE1 244 E2
Chichester Road NW6 238 A1
Chichester Road W2 238 C5
Chichester Street SW1V 244 A7
Chicksand Street E1 246 C1
Chigwell Hill E1W 246 E4
Child's Place SW5 242 A5
Child's Street SW5 242 A5
Chiltern Street W1U 239 J4
Chilworth Mews W2 238 D6
Chilworth Street W2 238 D6
China Hall Mews SE16 247 G8
Chinatown W1D 240 B7
Chippenham Mews W9 238 A4
Chiswell Street EC1Y 241 K4
Chitty Street W1T 240 A4
Christchurch Street SW3 243 G8
Christian Street E1 246 D3
Christina Street EC2A 241 M3
Christopher Close SE16 247 H6
Christopher Street EC2A 241 L4
Chudleigh Street E1 247 H2
Chumleigh Street SE5 245 M8
Churchill Gardens Road SW1V 243 L7
Churchill War Rooms SW1A 244 C3
Church Street NW8 238 F4
Church Way NW1 240 B2
Churchyard Row SE1 245 H5
Churton Place SW1V 244 A6
Churton Street SW1V 244 A6
Circus Road NW8 238 E1
Cirencester Square W2 238 A5
City Garden Row N1 241 J1
City Road EC1V 241 J1
City Road EC1Y 241 L3
City Thameslink ⇌ EC4M 241 H6
Clabon Mews SW1X 243 H5
Clack Street SE16 247 G7
Clanricarde Gardens W2 238 A8
Clarkson Row NW1 239 M1
Claremont Square N1 240 F1
Clarence Gardens NW1 239 L2
Clarence Mews SE16 247 G6
Clarendon Gardens W9 238 D4
Clarendon Gate W2 238 F7
Clarendon Place W2 238 F7
Clarendon Street SW1V 243 L6
Clareville Grove SW7 242 D6
Clareville Street SW7 242 D6
Clarges Mews W1J 243 L1
Clarges Street W1J 243 L1
Clark Street E1 246 F2
Carkson Row NW1 239 M1
Claverton Street SW1V 244 A7
Clave Street E1W 246 F5
Clay Street W1U 239 H5
Clayton Street SE11 244 F8
Cleaver Square SE11 245 G7
Cleaver Street SE11 245 G7
Clegg Street E1W 246 F5
Clemence Street E14 247 L2
Clements Lane EC4N 241 L7
Clement's Road SE16 246 E8
Clenston Mews W1H 239 H6
Clere Street EC2A 241 L3
Clerkenwell Close EC1R 241 G3
Clerkenwell Green EC1R 241 G4
Clerkenwell Road EC1M 241 G4
Cleveland Gardens W2 238 C6
Cleveland Mews W1T 239 M4
Cleveland Place SW1Y 244 A1
Cleveland Row SW1A 244 A2
Cleveland Square W2 238 C6
Cleveland Street W1T 239 M4
Cleveland Terrace W2 238 D6
Clifford Street W1S 239 M7
Clifton Gardens W9 238 C4
Clifton Place SE16 247 G6
Clifton Place W2 238 E7
Clifton Road W9 238 D3
Clifton Street EC2A 241 M3
Clifton Villas W9 238 C4
Clink Street SE1 245 K1
Clipper Close SE16 247 H6
Clipstone Mews W1W 239 M4
Clipstone Street W1W 239 L4
Cliveden Place SW1W 243 J5
Cloak Lane EC4R 241 K7
Cloth Fair EC1A 241 J5
Cloth Street EC1A 241 J5
Cluny Place SE1 246 A8
Cobb Street E1 246 B2
Cobourg Street NW1 240 A2
Coburg Close SW1P 244 A5
Cochrane Mews NW8 238 E1
Cochrane Street NW8 238 E1
Cock Lane EC1A 241 H5
Cockspur Street SW1Y 244 C1
Codling Close * E1W 246 D5
Coin Street SE1 245 G1
Coke Street E1 246 D2
Colbeck Mews SW7 242 C6
Colebrook Row N1 241 H1
Coleherne Road SW10 242 B7
Coleman Street EC2R 241 L6
Cole Street SE1 245 K3
Coley Street WC1X 240 F3
College Hill EC4R 241 K7
College Street EC4R 241 K7
Collett Road SE16 246 D8
Collier Street N1 240 E1
Collingham Gardens SW5 242 B6
Collingham Place SW5 242 B5
Collingham Road SW5 242 B5
Colnbrook Street SE1 245 H4
Colombo Street SE1 245 H1
Colonnade WC1N 240 D4
Coltman Street E14 247 K2
Commercial Road E1 246 D2
Commercial Road E14 247 K3
Commercial Street E1 246 B1
Compton Street EC1V 241 H3
Concert Hall Approach SE1 244 E2
Conder Street E14 247 K2
Conduit Mews W2 238 E6
Conduit Place W2 238 E6
Conduit Street W1S 239 L7
Congreve Street SE17 245 M5
Connaught Close W2 238 F7
Connaught Place W2 239 G7
Connaught Square W2 239 G6
Connaught Street W2 239 G6
Cons Street SE1 245 G2
Constitution Hill SW1A 243 L3
Content Street SE17 245 K5
Conway Street W1T 239 M4
Cookham Crescent SE16 247 H6
Cook's Road SE17 245 H8
Coombs Street N1 241 J1
Cooper's Lane Estate NW1 240 B1
Cooper's Row EC3N 246 B3
Copenhagen Place E14 247 L2
Cope Place W8 242 A4
Copley Court SE17 245 J8
Copley Street E1 247 H2
Copperfield Road E3 247 K1
Copperfield Street SE1 245 J2
Copthall Avenue EC2R 241 L6
Coptic Street WC1A 240 C5
Coral Street SE1 245 G3
Coram Street WC1H 240 C3
Cork Square E1W 246 E5
Cork Street W1S 239 M8
Corlett Street NW1 238 F5
Cornhill EC3V 241 L6
Cornwall Gardens SW7 242 C4
Cornwall Mews South SW7 242 C5
Cornwall Road SE1 244 F1
Cornwall Road SE1 245 G2
Cornwall Street E1 246 E3
Cornwall Terrace Mews NW1 239 H4
Cornwood Drive E1 247 G2
Coronet Street N1 241 M2
Corporation Row EC1R 241 G3
Corsham Street N1 241 L2
Cosser Street SE1 244 F4
Cosway Street NW1 239 G4
Cottage Place SW3 242 F4
Cottesmore Gardens W8 242 B4
Cottons Lane SE1 245 M1
Coulson Street SW3 243 H6
Counter Street SE1 245 M1
County Street SE1 245 K5
Courtenay Square SE11 244 F7
Courtenay Street SE11 244 F6
Courtfield Gardens SW5 242 B5
Courtfield Mews * SW5 242 C5
Courtfield Road SW7 242 C5
Court Street E1 246 E1
Cousin Lane SE1 241 K8
Covent Garden ⊖ WC2E 240 D7
Covent Garden WC2E 240 D7
Coventry Street W1D 240 B8
Cowcross Street EC1M 241 H4
Cowper Street EC2A 241 L3
Crail Row SE17 245 L5
Cramer Street W1U 239 J5
Crampton Street SE17 245 J6
Cranbourn Street WC2H 240 C7
Cranleigh Street NW1 240 A1
Cranley Gardens SW7 242 D6
Cranley Mews SW7 242 D6
Cranley Place SW7 242 E6
Cranston Estate N1 241 L1
Cranwood Street EC1V 241 L2
Craven Hill W2 238 D7
Craven Hill Gardens W2 238 C7
Craven Road W2 238 D7
Craven Street WC2N 244 D1
Craven Terrace W2 238 D7
Crawford Passage EC1R 241 G3
Crawford Place W1H 239 G5
Crawford Street W1H 239 G5
Creechurch Lane EC3A 246 A3
Creed Lane EC4V 241 H7
Cresswell Place SW10 242 D6
Cressy Place E1 247 G1
Crestfield Street WC1H 240 D2
Crimscott Street SE1 246 A8
Crispin Street E1 246 B1
Cromer Street WC1H 240 D2
Crompton Street W2 238 D4
Cromwell Mews * SW7 242 E5
Cromwell Place SW7 242 E5
Cromwell Road SW5 242 B5
Cromwell Road SW7 242 E5
Crondall Court N1 241 M1
Crondall Street N1 241 L1
Cropley Street N1 241 K1
Crosby Row SE1 245 L3
Cross Lane EC3R 246 A4
Crosswall EC3N 246 B3
Crowder Street E1 246 E3
Crucifix Lane SE1 246 A6
Cruikshank Street WC1X 240 F1
Crutched Friars EC3N 246 A3
Cuba Street E14 247 M6
Cubitt Street WC1X 240 E2
Culford Gardens SW3 243 H6
Culling Road SE16 246 F7
Cullum Street EC3M 241 M7
Culross Street W1K 239 J8
Culworth Street NW8 238 F1
Cumberland Gardens WC1X 240 F2
Cumberland Gate W2 239 H7
Cumberland Market NW1 239 L2
Cumberland Street SW1V 243 L6
Cumberland Terrace NW1 239 K1
Cumberland Terrace Mews NW1 239 L1
Cumberland Wharf SE16 247 G6
Cumming Street N1 240 E1
Cundy Street SW1W 243 K6
Cunningham Place NW8 238 E3
Cureton Street SW1P 244 C6
Curlew Street SE1 246 B6
Cursitor Street EC4A 240 F6
Curtain Road EC2A 241 M3
Curtain Road EC2A 241 M4
Curzon Gate W2 243 K2
Curzon Street W1J 243 K1
Cuthbert Street W2 238 E4
Cutler Street EC3A 246 A2
Cynthia Street N1 240 F1
Cypress Place W1T 240 A4
Cyrus Street EC1V 241 H3

D

Dacre Street SW1H 244 B3
Dakin Place E1 247 J1
Dallington Street EC1V 241 H3
Damien Street E1 246 F2
Dane Street WC1R 240 E5
Dansey Place W1D 240 B7
Dante Road SE11 245 H5
Danvers Street SW3 242 F8
D'Arblay Street W1F 240 A6
Dartford Street SE17 245 K8
Dartmouth Street SW1H 244 B3
Darwin Street SE17 245 L5
Date Street SE17 245 K7
Davenant Street E1 246 D1
Daventry Street NW1 238 F4
Davidge Street SE1 245 H3
Davies Mews W1K 239 K7
Davies Street W1K 239 K7
Dawes Street SE17 245 L6
Dawson Place W2 238 A7
Deal Porters Way SE16 247 G8
Deal Street E1 246 D1
Dean Bradley Street SW1P 244 C5
Dean Close SE16 247 H6
Deancross Street E1 246 F3
Deanery Street W1K 243 K1
Dean Farrar Street SW1H 244 B3
Dean Ryle Street SW1P 244 C5
Dean's Buildings SE17 245 L6
Dean Stanley Street SW1P 244 C4
Dean Street W1D 240 B6
Dean's Yard SW1P 244 C4
Decima Street SE1 245 M4
Deck Close SE16 247 J6
Defoe Close SE16 247 K7
Delamere Street W2 238 C5
Delamere Terrace W2 238 B4
De Laune Street SE17 245 H7
Delaware Road W9 238 B3
Dellow Street E1 246 F3
Delverton Road SE17 245 H7
Denbigh Place SW1V 243 M6
Denbigh Street SW1V 243 M6
Denbigh Street SW1V 244 A6
Denman Street W1D 240 B7
Denmark Street WC2H 240 C6
Denny Close SE11 245 G6
Denny Street SE11 245 G6
Denyer Street SW3 243 G5
Derby Gate SW1A 244 D3
Derby Street W1J 243 K1
Dering Street W1S 239 L6
Derry Street W8 242 B3
De Vere Gardens W8 242 C3
Deverell Street SE1 245 L4
Devonport Street E1 247 G3
Devonshire Close W1G 239 K4
Devonshire Mews South W1G 239 K4
Devonshire Mews West W1G 239 K4
Devonshire Place W1G 239 K4
Devonshire Place Mews W1G 239 K4
Devonshire Row EC2M 246 A2
Devonshire Square EC2M 246 A2
Devonshire Street W1G 239 K4
Devonshire Terrace W2 238 D7
De Walden Street W1G 239 K5
Dickens Estate SE16 246 D7
Dickens Square SE1 245 K4
Dilke Street SW3 243 H8
Dingley Place EC1V 241 K2
Dingley Road EC1V 241 J2
Disney Place SE1 245 K2
Distaff Lane EC4V 241 J7
Distin Street SE11 244 F6
Dockhead SE1 246 C7
Dockley Road SE16 246 D8
Dock Street E1 246 D4
Doddington Grove SE17 245 H7
Doddington Place SE17 245 H8
Dodson Street SE1 245 G3
Dod Street E14 247 M2
Dolben Street SE1 245 H2
Dolland Street SE11 244 E7
Dolphin Square SW1V 244 A7
Dolphin Square SW1V 244 B7
Dombey Street WC1N 240 E4
Dominion Drive SE16 247 H7
Dominion Street EC2A 241 L5
Donegal Street N1 240 F1
Dongola Road E1 247 J1
Donne Place SW3 243 G5
Doon Street SE1 244 F1
Dora Street E14 247 L2
Doric Way NW1 240 B2
Dorset Rise EC4Y 241 G7
Dorset Square NW1 239 H4
Dorset Street W1U 239 H5
Doughty Mews WC1N 240 E3
Doughty Street WC1N 240 E3
Douglas Street SW1P 244 B6
Douro Place W8 242 C3
Douthwaite Square * E1W 246 D5
Dovehouse Street SW3 242 E6
Dover Street W1J 243 L1
Dover Street W1S 239 L8
Dowgate Hill EC4R 241 K7
Downfield Close W9 238 B4
Downing Street SW1A 244 C2
Down Street W1J 243 K2
Downtown Road SE16 247 K6
D'Oyley Street SW1X 243 J5
Draco Street SE17 245 J8
Drake Close SE16 247 H6
Draycott Avenue SW3 243 G5
Draycott Place SW3 243 H6
Draycott Terrace SW3 243 H5
Drayson Mews W8 242 A3
Drayton Gardens SW10 242 D6
Druid Street SE1 246 A6
Druid Street SE1 246 B6
Drummond Crescent NW1 240 B2
Drummond Gate * SW1V 244 B6
Drummond Road SE16 246 E8
Drummond Street NW1 240 A3
Drury Lane WC2B 240 D6
Dryden Court SE11 245 G5
Dryden Street WC2B 240 D6
Duchess Mews W1G 239 L5
Duchess Street W1B 239 L5
Duchy Street SE1 245 G1
Duckett Street E1 247 J1
Duck Lane W1F 240 B6
Dufferin Street EC1Y 241 K4
Duke of Wellington Place SW1W 243 K3
Duke of York Square SW3 243 H6
Duke of York Street SW1Y 244 A1
Duke Shore Wharf E14 247 K4
Duke's Lane W8 242 A2
Duke's Place EC3A 246 B2
Duke's Road WC1H 240 C2
Duke Street W1K 239 K7
Duke Street W1U 239 J6
Duke Street Hill SE1 245 L1
Duke Street St James's SW1Y 244 A1
Dunbar Wharf E14 247 L4
Duncannon Street WC2N 240 C8
Duncan Terrace N1 241 H1
Dundee Street E1W 246 E5
Dundee Wharf E14 247 L4
Dunelm Street E1 247 H2
Dunlop Place SE16 246 C8
Dunraven Street W1K 239 H7
Dunster Court EC3R 246 A3
Duplex Ride SW1X 243 H3
Durand's Wharf SE16 247 L6
Durham Row E1 247 J1
Durham Street SE11 244 E7
Durham Terrace W2 238 A6
Dyott Street WC1A 240 C6
Dysart Street EC2A 241 M4

E

Eagle Court EC1M 241 H4
Eagle Street WC1R 240 E5
Eamont Street NW8 239 G1
Eardley Crescent SW5 242 A7
Earlham Street WC2H 240 C7
Earl's Court ⇌ ⊖ SW5 242 A6
Earl's Court Gardens SW5 242 B6
Earl's Court Road SW5 242 A6
Earl's Court Square SW5 242 A6
Earlstoke Street EC1V 241 H2
Earl Street EC2A 241 M4
Earnshaw Street WC2H 240 C6
East Arbour Street E1 247 H2
Eastbourne Mews W2 238 D6
Eastbourne Terrace W2 238 D6
Eastcastle Street W1W 240 A6
Eastcheap EC3M 241 M7
Eastfield Street E14 247 K1
East India Dock Road E14 247 M3
East Lane SE16 246 D6
Easton Street WC1X 240 F3
East Poultry Avenue EC1A 241 H5
East Road N1 241 L2
East Smithfield E1W 246 C4
East Street SE17 245 L6
East Tenter Street E1 246 C3
Eaton Close SW1W 243 J5
Eaton Gate SW1W 243 J5
Eaton Lane SW1W 243 L4
Eaton Mews North SW1W 243 J5
Eaton Mews South SW1W 243 K5
Eaton Mews West SW1W 243 K5
Eaton Place SW1X 243 J4
Eaton Row SW1W 243 K4
Eaton Square SW1W 243 K5
Eaton Terrace SW1W 243 J5
Ebbisham Drive SW8 244 E8
Ebury Bridge SW1W 243 K6
Ebury Bridge Road SW1W 243 K7
Ebury Mews SW1W 243 K5
Ebury Square SW1W 243 K6
Ebury Street SW1W 243 K5
Eccleston Bridge SW1W 243 L5
Eccleston Mews SW1X 243 K4
Eccleston Place SW1W 243 L5
Eccleston Square SW1V 243 L6
Eccleston Street SW1X 243 K4
Edbrooke Road W9 238 A3
Edge Street W8 242 A1
Edgware Road W2 238 F5
Edgware Road ⊖ NW1 238 F5
Edinburgh Gate SW1X 243 H3
Edith Grove SW10 242 C8
Edwards Mews W1H 239 J6
Egerton Crescent SW3 242 F5
Egerton Gardens SW3 242 F5
Egerton Terrace SW3 243 G4
Eglington Court SE17 245 J7
Elba Place SE17 245 K5
Eldon Road W8 242 B4
Eldon Street EC2M 241 L5
Eleanor Close SE16 247 H6
Elephant & Castle SE1 245 J4
Elephant & Castle ⇌ ⊖ SE1 245 J5
Elephant Lane SE16 246 F6
Elephant Road SE17 245 J5
Elf Row E1W 247 G3
Elgar Street SE16 247 K7
Elgin Avenue W9 238 B2
Elgin Mews North W9 238 C2
Elgin Mews South W9 238 C2
Elia Mews N1 241 H1
Elia Street N1 241 H1
Elim Estate SE1 245 M3
Elim Street SE1 245 M3
Elizabeth Bridge SW1V 243 L6
Elizabeth Street SW1W 243 K5
Ellen Street E1 246 D3
Elliott's Row SE11 245 H5
Ellis Street SW1X 243 J5
Elmfield Way W9 238 A4
Elm Park Gardens SW10 242 E7
Elm Park Lane SW3 242 E7
Elm Park Road SW3 242 E8
Elm Place SW7 242 E7
Elms Mews W2 238 D7
Elm Street WC1X 240 F4
Elm Tree Road NW8 238 E2
Elnathan Mews W9 238 B4
Elsa Street E1 247 J1
Elsted Street SE17 245 L6
Elvaston Mews SW7 242 D4
Elvaston Place SW7 242 D4
Elverton Street SW1P 244 B5
Ely Place EC1N 241 G5
Elystan Place SW3 243 G6
Elystan Street SW3 242 F6
Embankment ⊖ WC2N 244 D1
Embankment Gardens SW3 243 H8
Embankment Place WC2N 244 D1
Emba Street SE16 246 D7
Emerald Street WC1N 240 E4
Emerson Street SE1 245 J1
Emery Hill Street SW1P 244 A5
Emery Street SE1 245 G3
Emperor's Gate SW7 242 C5
Empire Square SE1 245 L3
Empress Place SW6 242 A7
Endell Street WC2H 240 C6
Endsleigh Gardens WC1H 240 B3
Endsleigh Place WC1H 240 B3
Endsleigh Street WC1H 240 B3
Enford Street W1H 239 G5
English Grounds SE1 245 M1
Enid Street SE16 246 C8
Ennismore Gardens SW7 242 F3
Ennismore Gardens Mews SW7 242 F3
Ennismore Mews SW7 242 F3
Ennismore Street SW7 242 F4
Ensign Street E1 246 D4
Epworth Street EC2A 241 L3
Erasmus Street SW1P 244 C6
Errol Street EC1Y 241 K4
Essendine Road W9 238 A3
Essex Street WC2R 240 F7
Essex Villas W8 242 A3
Europa Place EC1V 241 J2
Euston ⇌ ⊖ ⊖ NW1 240 B2
Euston Road NW1 240 B3
Euston Square NW1 240 B2
Euston Square ⊖ NW1 240 A3
Euston Street NW1 240 A3
Evelyn Gardens SW7 242 D7
Evelyn Walk N1 241 L1
Eversholt Street NW1 240 A1
Everton Mews NW1 239 M2
Ewer Street SE1 245 J2
Ewhurst Close E1 247 G1
Exchange Square EC2A 241 M4
Exeter Street WC2E 240 D7
Exhibition Road SW7 242 E3
Exmouth Market EC1R 241 G3
Exon Street SE17 245 M6
Exton Street SE1 244 F2
Eyre Street Hill EC1R 240 F4

F

Fairclough Street E1 246 D3
Fair Street SE1 246 B6
Falmouth Road SE1 245 K4
Fann Street EC1M 241 J4
Fanshaw Street N1 241 M1
Farmer Street W8 242 A1
Farm Lane SW6 242 A8
Farm Street W1K 239 K8
Farnham Place SE1 245 J1
Farrance Street E14 247 M3
Farringdon ⇌ ⊖ EC1M 241 G4
Farringdon Lane EC1R 241 G4
Farringdon Road EC1R 240 F3

Farringdon Street EC1M 241 H5
Farrins Rents SE16 247 J5
Farrow Place SE16 247 K7
Farthing Fields * E1W 246 F5
Fashion Street E1 246 B1
Faunce Street SE17 245 H7
Fawcett Street SW10 242 C8
Featherstone Street EC1Y 241 L3
Fenchurch Avenue EC3M 246 A3
Fenchurch Buildings EC3M 246 A3
Fenchurch Place EC3M 246 A3
Fenchurch Street EC3M 246 A3
Fenchurch Street ⇌ EC3M 246 A3
Fendall Street SE1 246 B8
Fenning Street SE1 245 M2
Fentiman Road SW8 244 D8
Fernsbury Street WC1X 240 F2
Fetter Lane EC4A 241 G6
Fieldgate Street E1 246 D2
Fielding Street SE17 245 J7
Field Street WC1X 240 E1
Finborough Road SW10 242 B8
Finch Lane EC3V 241 L6
Finland Street SE16 247 K8
Finsbury Circus EC2M 241 L5
Finsbury Estate EC1R 241 G3
Finsbury Market EC2A 241 M4
Finsbury Square EC2A 241 L4
Finsbury Street EC2Y 241 L4
First Street SW3 243 G5
Fishermans Drive SE16 247 J6
Fisher Street WC1R 240 D5
Fisherton Street NW8 238 E3
Fish Street Hill EC3R 241 L7
Fitzalan Street SE11 244 F5
Fitzhardinge Street W1H 239 J6
Fitzroy Square W1T 239 M4
Fitzroy Street W1T 239 M4
Flamborough Street E14 247 J3
Flank Street E1 246 C4
Flaxman Terrace WC1H 240 C3
Fleet Street EC4A 241 G6
Fleming Road SE17 245 H8
Fletcher Street E1 246 D3
Flint Street SE17 245 L6
Flitcroft Street WC2H 240 C6
Flockton Street SE16 246 D7
Flood Street SW3 243 G7
Flood Walk SW3 243 G7
Floral Street WC2E 240 D7
Foley Street W1W 239 M5
Forbes Street E1 246 D3
Fordham Street E1 246 D2
Ford Square E1 246 F2
Fore Street EC2Y 241 K5
Formosa Street W9 238 C4
Forset Street W1H 239 G6
Forsyth Gardens SE17 245 H8
Fort Street E1 246 B1
Fortune Street EC1Y 241 K4
Forum Magnum Square SE1 244 E3
Foster Lane EC2V 241 J6
Foulis Terrace SW7 242 E6
Foundry Close SE16 247 J5
Fournier Street E1 246 B1
Fowey Close E1W 246 E5
Frampton Street NW8 238 E4
Francis Street SW1P 244 A5
Frankland Close * SE16 246 F8
Franklin's Row SW3 243 H6
Frazier Street SE1 245 G3
Frean Street SE16 246 C8
Frederick Close W2 239 G7
Frederick Street WC1X 240 E2
Frederic Mews * SW1X 243 J3
Freemantle Street SE17 245 M6
Friday Street EC4V 241 J7
Friend Street EC1V 241 H2
Frith Street W1D 240 B6
Fulbourne Street E1 246 E1
Fulford Street SE16 246 F7
Fulham Road SW10 242 D8
Fulham Road SW3 242 F6
Furnival Street EC4A 240 F5
Fynes Street SW1P 244 B5

G

Gabriel's Wharf SE1 245 G1
Gainsford Street SE1 246 B6
Galleon Close SE16 247 G6
Galsworthy Avenue E14 247 K2
Galway Street EC1V 241 K2
Gambia Street SE1 245 H2
Garden Road NW8 238 D1
Garden Row SE1 245 H4
Garden Street E1 247 H1
Garden Terrace * SW1V 244 B6
Garden Walk EC2A 241 M3
Gard Street EC1V 241 J2
Garford Street E14 247 M4
Garnault Place EC1R 241 G3
Garnet Street E1W 246 F4
Garrett Street EC1Y 241 K3
Garrick Street WC2E 240 C7
Garterway SE16 247 H7
Garway Road W2 238 B6
Gaspar Mews SW7 242 C5
Gataker Street * SE16 246 E8
Gate Mews SW7 242 F3
Gateforth Street NW8 238 F3
Gate Mews NW1 239 L3
Gatesborough Street * EC2A 241 M3
Gate Street WC2A 240 E5
Gatliff Road SW1W 243 K7
Gaunt Street SE1 245 J4
Gayfere Street SW1P 244 C4
Gaywood Street SE1 245 H4
Gaza Street SE17 245 H7
Gedling Place SE1 246 C7
Gee Street EC1V 241 J3
George Mathers Road SE11 245 H5
George Row SE16 246 C7
George Street W1H 239 H6
George Yard W1K 239 K7
Geraldine Street SE1 245 H4
Gerald Road SW1W 243 K5
Gerrard Street W1D 240 B7
Gerridge Street SE1 245 G3
Gertrude Street SW10 242 D8
Gibson Road SE11 244 E5
Gilbert Place WC1A 240 C5
Gilbert Road SE11 245 G5
Gilbert Street W1K 239 K7
Gildea Street W1W 239 L5
Gillingham Street SW1V 243 M5
Gill Street E14 247 L3
Gilston Road SW10 242 D7
Giltspur Street EC1A 241 H5
Gladstone Street SE1 245 H4
Glamis Place E1W 247 G4
Glamis Road E1W 247 G4
Glasgow Terrace SW1V 243 M7
Glasshill Street SE1 245 J3
Glasshouse Street W1B 240 A8
Glasshouse Walk SE11 244 D7
Glasshouse Yard EC1 241 J4
Glebe Place SW3 242 F7
Gledhow Road SW5 242 C6
Glentworth Street NW1 239 H4
Globe Pond Road SE16 247 J5
Globe Street SE1 245 K3
Gloucester Court * EC3R 246 A4
Gloucester Gardens W2 238 C6
Gloucester Mews W2 238 D6
Gloucester Mews West W2 238 C6
Gloucester Place NW1 239 H3
Gloucester Place W1U 239 H5
Gloucester Place Mews W1U 239 H5
Gloucester Road SW7 242 C4
Gloucester Road SW7 242 D6
Gloucester Road ⊖ SW7 242 C5
Gloucester Square W2 238 F6
Gloucester Street SW1V 243 M7
Gloucester Terrace W2 238 B5
Gloucester Terrace W2 238 D6
Gloucester Walk W8 242 A2
Gloucester Way EC1R 241 G2
Glyn Street SE11 244 E7
Godfrey Street SW3 243 G6
Goding Street SE11 244 D7
Godliman Street EC4V 241 J7
Godwin Close N1 241 K1
Golden Hinde II SE1 245 L1
Golden Jubilee Bridge WC2N 244 D1
Golden Lane EC1Y 241 J4
Golden Square W1F 240 A7
Golding Street E1 246 E3
Goldney Road W9 238 A4
Goldsmith Street EC2V 241 K6
Gomm Road SE16 247 G8
Goodge Place W1T 240 A5
Goodge Street W1T 240 A5
Goodge Street ⊖ W1T 240 B5
Goodwin Close SE16 246 C8
Gordon Place W8 242 A2
Gordon Square WC1H 240 B3
Gordon Street WC1H 240 B3
Gore Street SW7 242 D4
Goring Street * EC3A 246 A2
Gosfield Street W1W 239 L5
Goslett Yard WC2H 240 B6
Goswell Road EC1V 241 H1
Gough Street WC1X 240 F3
Goulston Street E1 246 B2
Gower Mews WC1E 240 B5
Gower Place NW1 240 A3
Gower Street WC1E 240 B3
Gower's Walk E1 246 D2
Gracechurch Street EC3V 241 M7
Grafton Place NW1 240 B2
Grafton Street W1S 239 L8
Grafton Way W1T 240 A4
Graham Street N1 241 J1
Graham Terrace SW1W 243 J6
Granby Terrace NW1 239 M1
Grand Avenue EC1A 241 H5
Grange Road SE1 246 B8
Grange Walk SE1 246 A8
Grange Yard SE1 246 B8
Grantully Road W9 238 B2
Granville Place W1H 239 J6
Granville Road NW6 238 A1
Granville Square WC1X 240 F2
Grape Street WC2H 240 C6
Gravel Lane E1 246 B2
Gray's Inn Road WC1X 240 D2
Gray's Inn Square WC1R 240 F5
Gray Street SE1 245 G3
Great Castle Street W1G 239 L6
Great Central Street NW1 239 G4
Great Chapel Street W1D 240 B6
Great College Street SW1P 244 C4
Great Cumberland Place W1H 239 H6
Great Dover Street SE1 245 K3
Great Eastern Street EC2A 241 M3
Great George Street SW1P 244 C3
Great Guildford Street SE1 245 J1
Great James Street WC1N 240 E4
Great Marlborough Street W1F 239 M7
Great Maze Pond SE1 245 L2
Great New Portland Street WC2H 240 C7
Greatorex Street E1 246 D1
Great Ormond Street WC1N 240 D4
Great Percy Street WC1X 240 F2
Great Peter Street SW1P 244 B4
Great Portland Street W1W 239 L4
Great Portland Street ⊖ W1W 239 L4
Great Pulteney Street W1F 240 A7
Great Queen Street WC2B 240 D6
Great Russell Street WC1B 240 C5
Great Scotland Yard SW1A 244 C1
Great Smith Street SW1P 244 C4
Great Suffolk Street SE1 245 H2
Great Sutton Street EC1V 241 H4
Great Swan Alley EC2R 241 L6
Great Titchfield Street W1W 239 M4
Great Tower Street EC3M 241 M7
Great Tower Street EC3R 246 A4
Great Winchester Street EC2N 241 L6
Great Windmill Street W1D 240 B7
Greek Street W1D 240 B6
Greenacre Square SE16 247 J6
Green Bank E1W 246 E5
Greenberry Street NW8 238 F1
Greencoat Place SW1P 244 A5
Green Coat Row SW1P 244 A4
Greenfield Road E1 246 D2
Greenham Close SE1 244 F3
Green Park ⊖ W1J 243 M1
Green Street W1K 239 J7
Greenwell Street W1W 239 L4
Greet Street SE1 245 G2
Grenade Street E14 247 L4
Grendon Street NW8 238 F3
Grenville Place SW7 242 C5
Gresham Street EC2V 241 J6
Gresse Street W1T 240 B5
Greville Street EC1N 241 G5
Greycoat Place SW1P 244 B4
Greycoat Street SW1P 244 B4
Grigg's Place SE1 246 A8
Grosvenor Bridge SW8 243 L8
Grosvenor Crescent SW1X 243 J3
Grosvenor Crescent Mews SW1X 243 J3
Grosvenor Gardens SW1W 243 L4
Grosvenor Gardens
Mews East SW1W 243 L4
Grosvenor Gardens
Mews North SW1W 243 L4
Grosvenor Gardens
Mews South * SW1W 243 L4
Grosvenor Gate W2 239 H8
Grosvenor Hill W1K 239 L7
Grosvenor Place SW1X 243 K3
Grosvenor Road SW1V 243 L8
Grosvenor Square W1K 239 J7
Grosvenor Street W1K 239 K7
Grosvenor Terrace SE5 245 J8
Grove End Road NW8 238 D2
Guildhouse Street SW1V 243 M5
Guilford Street WC1N 240 D4
Guinness Square SE1 245 M5
Gulliver Street SE16 247 K8
Gunpowder Square EC4A 241 G6
Gun Street E1 246 B1
Gunthorpe Street E1 246 C2
Gutter Lane EC2V 241 J6
Guy Street SE1 245 L3

H

Haberdasher Street N1 241 L2
Haddonhall Estate SE1 245 M4
Hainton Close E1 246 F3
Halcrow Street * E1 246 F2
Half Moon Street W1J 243 L1
Halford Road SW6 242 A8
Halkin Place SW1X 243 J4
Halkin Street SW1X 243 K3
Hallam Street W1W 239 L5
Halley Street E14 247 K1
Hallfield Estate W2 238 C6
Hall Place W2 238 E4
Hall Road NW8 238 D2
Hall Street EC1V 241 H2
Halpin Place SE17 245 M6
Halsey Street SW3 243 G5
Hamilton Close NW8 238 D2
Hamilton Close SE16 247 K7
Hamilton Gardens NW8 238 D2
Hamilton Place W1J 243 K2
Hamilton Terrace NW8 238 C1
Hamlet Way SE1 245 L3
Hammett Street EC3N 246 B4
Hampden Close NW1 240 B1
Hampden Gurney Street W2 239 H6
Hampstead Road NW1 239 M2
Hampton Street SE17 245 J6
Hanbury Street E1 246 C1
Hand Court WC1V 240 E5
Handel Street WC1N 240 D3
Hankey Place SE1 245 L3
Hannibal Road E1 247 G1
Hanover Square W1S 239 L6
Hanover Street W1S 239 L7
Hans Crescent SW3 243 H3
Hanson Street W1W 239 M4
Hans Place SW1X 243 H4
Hans Road SW3 243 G4
Hans Street SW1X 243 H4
Hanway Place W1T 240 B6
Hanway Street W1T 240 B6
Harbet Road W2 238 F5
Harcourt Street W1H 239 G5
Harcourt Terrace SW10 242 C7
Hardinge Street E1W 247 G3
Hardwick Street EC1R 241 G2
Hardwidge Street SE1 245 M2
Hardy Close SE16 247 H6
Harewood Place W1G 239 L6
Harewood Row NW1 239 G4
Harewood Avenue NW1 239 G4
Harford Street E1 247 J1
Harleyford Road SE11 244 E8
Harley Gardens SW10 242 D7
Harley Place W1G 239 K5
Harley Street W1G 239 K4
Harmsworth Street SE17 245 G7
Harold Estate SE1 246 A8
Harper Road SE1 245 K4
Harpour Street WC1N 240 E4
Harriet Street SW1X 243 H3
Harriet Walk SW1X 243 H3
Harrington Gardens SW7 242 C6
Harrington Road SW7 242 E5
Harrington Square NW1 239 M1
Harrington Street NW1 239 M2
Harrison Street WC1H 240 D2
Harrods SW1X 243 G4
Harrowby Street W1H 239 G6
Harrow Place E1 246 B2
Harrow Road W2 238 A4
Hart Street EC3R 246 A3
Hasker Street SW3 243 G5
Hastings Street WC1H 240 C2
Hatfields SE1 245 G1
Hatherley Grove W2 238 B6
Hatteraick Road SE16 247 G6
Hatton Garden EC1N 241 G4
Hatton Street W2 238 E4
Hatton Wall EC1N 241 G4
Havering Street E1 247 H3
Haverstock Street N1 241 J1
Hawke Place * SE16 247 H6
Haydon Street EC3N 246 B3
Hayes Place NW1 239 G4
Hay Hill W1J 239 L8
Hayles Street SE11 245 H5
Haymarket SW1Y 240 B8
Hayne Street EC1A 241 J4
Hay's Lane SE1 245 M1
Hay's Mews W1J 239 L8
Haywood Place EC1R 241 H3
Headfort Place SW1X 243 K3
Head Street E1 247 H2
Hearnshaw Street E14 247 K2
Hearn Street EC2A 241 M4
Heathcote Street WC1N 240 E3
Heddon Street W1B 239 M7
Heddon Street W1S 240 A7
Hedger Street SE11 245 H5
Heiron Street SE17 245 J8
Hellings Street E1W 246 D5
Helmet Row EC1V 241 K3
Helsinki Square SE16 247 L8
Henderson Drive NW8 238 E3
Heneage Lane EC3A 246 A3
Heneage Street E1 246 C1
Henrietta Place W1G 239 L6
Henrietta Street WC2E 240 D7
Henriques Street E1 246 D2
Henshaw Street SE17 245 L5
Herbal Hill EC1R 241 G4
Herbert Crescent SW1X 243 H4
Herbrand Street WC1H 240 C3
Hercules Road SE1 244 F4
Hereford Road W2 238 A6
Hereford Square SW7 242 D6
Hermitage Street W2 238 E5
Hermitage Wall E1W 246 D5
Hermit Street EC1V 241 H2
Heron Place SE16 247 K5
Heron Quay E14 247 M5
Herrick Street SW1P 244 C6
Hertford Street W1J 243 K2
Hertsmere Road E14 247 M4
Hesper Mews SW5 242 B6
Hessel Street E1 246 E3
Hewett Street EC2A 241 M3
Heygate Street SE17 245 J5
Hide Place SW1P 244 B6
High Holborn WC1V 240 E5
High Street Kensington ⊖ W8 242 A3
Hildyard Road SW6 242 A8
Hilliards Court E1W 246 F5
Hillingdon Street SE17 245 J8
Hill Road NW8 238 D1
Hills Place W1F 239 M6
Hill Street W1J 239 K8
Hinde Street W1U 239 K6
Hind Grove E14 247 M3
Hindgrove Area E14 247 M3
Hithe Grove SE16 247 G8
HMS Belfast SE1 246 A5
Hobart Place SW1W 243 K4
Hobury Street SW10 242 D8
Hogarth Road SW5 242 B6
Holbein Mews SW1W 243 J6
Holbein Place SW1W 243 J6
Holborn EC1N 241 G5
Holborn ⊖ WC2B 240 E5
Holborn Circus EC1N 241 G5
Holborn Viaduct EC1A 241 G5
Holford Street WC1X 240 F2
Holland Street SE1 245 H1
Holland Street W8 242 A3
Hollen Street W1F 240 A6
Holles Street W1C 239 L6
Hollywood Road SW10 242 C8
Holyoak Road SE11 245 H5
Holyrood Street SE1 245 M2
Holyrood Street SE1 246 A6
Holywell Row EC2A 241 M4
Homefield Street * N1 241 M1
Homer Row W1H 239 G5
Homer Street W1H 239 G5
Hooper Street E1 246 D3
Hopetown Street E1 246 C1
Hopkins Street W1F 240 A7
Hopton Street SE1 245 H1
Hopwood Road SE17 245 L8
Hornton Place W8 242 A3
Hornton Street W8 242 A2
Horse & Dolphin Yard W1D 240 B7
Horseferry Road E14 247 J3
Horseferry Road SW1P 244 B4
Horse Guards Avenue SW1A 244 C2
Horse Guards Parade SW1A 244 C2
Horse Guards Road SW1A 244 C2
Horselydown Lane SE1 246 B6
Horsley Street SE17 245 K8
Hosier Lane EC1A 241 H5
Hothfield Place SE16 247 G8
Hotspur Street SE11 244 F6
Houghton Street WC2A 240 E6
Houndsditch EC3A 246 A2
Houses of Parliament SW1A 244 D3
Howick Place SW1E 244 A4
Howland Street W1T 240 A4
Howland Way SE16 247 K7
Howley Place W2 238 D4
Hoxton Square N1 241 M2
Hoxton Street N1 241 M1
Hudson's Place SW1V 243 M5
Hugh Mews SW1V 243 L6
Hugh Street SW1V 243 L5
Hugh Street SW1V 243 L6
Hull Close SE16 247 J6
Hull Street EC1V 241 J2
Hungerford Bridge SE1 244 E1
Hunter Close SE1 245 M4
Hunter Street WC1N 240 D3
Huntley Street WC1E 240 A4
Huntsman Street SE17 245 M6
Huntsworth Mews NW1 239 H3
Hurley Crescent SE16 247 H6
Hutching's Street E14 247 M7
Hutton Street EC4Y 241 G7
Hyde Park W2 243 G1
Hyde Park Corner W1J 243 K2
Hyde Park Corner ⊖ W1J 243 K2
Hyde Park Court SW7 242 D3
Hyde Park Crescent W2 238 F6
Hyde Park Gardens Mews W2 238 F7
Hyde Park Gardens W2 238 F7
Hyde Park Gate SW7 242 C3
Hyde Park Gate SW7 242 D3
Hyde Park Square W2 238 F7
Hyde Park Street W2 238 F7

I

Idol Lane EC3R 241 M7
Ifield Road SW10 242 B8
Iliffe Street SE17 245 J6
Iliffe Yard SE17 245 J6
Imperial College Road SW7 242 D4
Imperial War Museum SE1 245 G4
India Street EC3N 246 B3
Ingestre Place W1F 240 A7
Inglebert Street EC1R 240 F2
Ingram Close SE11 244 E5
Inner Circle NW1 239 J2
Inverness Terrace W2 238 B6
Inverness Terrace Gate W2 238 C8
Invicta Plaza SE1 245 H1
Inville Road SE17 245 L7
Ironmonger Lane EC2V 241 K6
Ironmonger Row EC1V 241 K2
Irving Street WC2N 240 C8
Isambard Place SE16 247 G6
Island Row E14 247 K3
Iverna Court W8 242 A4
Iverna Gardens W8 242 A4
Ives Street SW3 243 G5
Ivor Place NW1 239 G4
Ixworth Place SW3 242 F6

J

Jacob Street SE1 246 C6
Jamaica Gate SE16 246 F8
Jamaica Road SE1 246 C7
Jamaica Road SE16 246 E7
Jamaica Street E1 247 G2
Jamaica Wharf SE1 246 C6
James Street W1U 239 K6
James Street WC2E 240 D7
Jameson Street W8 242 A1
Jamuna Close E14 247 K1
Janeway Street SE16 246 D7
Jardine Road E1W 247 J4
Java Wharf SE1 246 C6
Jay Mews SW7 242 D3
Jermyn Street SW1Y 240 A8
Jerome Crescent NW8 238 F3
Jewery Street EC3N 246 B3
Joan Street SE1 245 G2
Jockey's Fields WC1R 240 E4
Johanna Street SE1 244 F3
John Adam Street WC2N 240 D8
John Carpenter Street EC4Y 241 G7
John Fisher Street E1 246 C4
John Islip Street SW1P 244 C5
John Prince's Street W1G 239 L6
John Roll Way SE16 246 D7
John Ruskin Street SE5 245 J8
John's Mews WC1N 240 E4
Johnson's Place SW1V 244 A7
Johnson Street E1 247 G3
John Street WC1N 240 E4
Joiner Street SE1 245 L1
Jonathan Street SE11 244 E6
Jubilee Place SW3 243 G6
Jubilee Street E1 247 G2
Jubilee Walk W8 242 B1
Judd Street WC1H 240 C2
Junction Mews W2 238 F5
Juxon Street SE11 244 E5

K

Katherine Close SE16 247 H5
Kean Street WC2B 240 E6
Keel Close SE16 247 J6
Keeley Street WC2B 240 E6
Keeton's Road SE16 246 E7
Kell Street SE1 245 H3
Kelso Place W8 242 B4
Kemble Street WC2B 240 E6
Kempsford Gardens SW5 242 A7
Kempsford Road SE11 245 G6
Kendall Place W1U 239 J5
Kendal Street W2 239 G6
Kennet Street E1W 246 D5
Kenning Street SE16 247 G6
Kennings Way SE11 245 G7
Kennington ⊖ SE11 245 H7
Kennington Lane SE11 244 E7
Kennington Oval SE11 244 E8
Kennington Park Gardens SE11 245 G8
Kennington Park Place SE11 245 G7
Kennington Park Road SE11 245 G7
Kennington Road SE1 244 F4
Kennington Road SE11 245 G5
Kennnington Oval SE11 244 F8
Kenrick Place W1U 239 J5
Kensington Church Street W8 242 A1
Kensington Court W8 242 B3
Kensington Gardens W2 242 C1
Kensington Gardens Square W2 238 B6
Kensington Gate W8 242 C4
Kensington Gore SW7 242 D3
Kensington High Street W8 242 A4
Kensington Palace W8 242 B2
Kensington Palace Gardens W8 242 B1
Kensington Palace Gardens W8 242 B2
Kensington Place W8 242 A1
Kensington Road SW7 243 G3
Kensington Road W8 242 B3
Kensington Square W8 242 B3
Kenton Street WC1H 240 C3
Kenway Road SW5 242 A6
Keystone Close N1 240 D1
Keyworth Street SE1 245 H4
Kia Oval (Surrey County
Cricket Ground) SE11 244 F8
Kilburn Park Road NW6 238 A2
Kildare Terrace W2 238 A6
Killick Street N1 240 E1
Kinburn Street SE16 247 H6
Kinder Street E1 246 E2
King & Queen Wharf SE16 247 H5
King and Queen Street SE17 245 K6
King Charles Street SW1A 244 C2
King David Lane E1 247 G3
Kingdom Street W2 238 C5
King Edward Street EC1A 241 J6
King Edward Walk SE1 245 G4
King James Street SE1 245 H3
Kingly Street W1F 239 M7
King's Arms Yard EC2R 241 L6
King's Bench Street SE1 245 H2
Kingscote Street EC4V 241 H7
King's Cross ⇌ N1C 240 D1
King's Cross Road WC1X 240 E2
King's Cross Square N1C 240 D1
King's Cross St Pancras ⊖ N1C 240 D1
Kingsgate Walk * SW1E 244 A4
King's Head Yard SE1 245 L1
King's Mews WC1N 240 E4
Kingsmill Terrace NW8 238 E1
King Square EC1V 241 J2
King's Road SW3 242 E8
King's Scholars Passage SW1P 243 M5
King's Stairs Close SE16 246 F6
King Street WC2E 240 D7
King Street SW1Y 244 A1
King Street EC2V 241 K6

Kingsway WC2B 240 E6
King William Street EC4N 241 L7
Kinnerton Place North * SW1X 243 J3
Kinnerton Place South * SW1X 243 J3
Kinnerton Street SW1X 243 J3
Kinnerton Yard * SW1X 243 J3
Kipling Estate SE1 245 L3
Kipling Street SE1 245 L3
Kirby Estate SE16 246 D7
Kirby Grove SE1 245 M3
Kirby Street EC1N 241 G4
Knaresborough Place SW5 242 B5
Knightrider Street EC4V 241 H7
Knightsbridge SW1X 243 H3
Knightsbridge ⊖ SW3 243 H3
Knox Street W1H 239 H4
Kynance Mews SW7 242 C4
Kynance Place SW7 242 C4

L

Lackington Street EC2A 241 L4
Lafone Street SE1 246 B6
Lagado Mews SE16 247 H5
Lambeth Bridge SW1P 244 D5
Lambeth High Street SE1 244 E5
Lambeth Hill EC4V 241 J7
Lambeth North ⊖ SE1 244 F3
Lambeth Palace Road SE1 244 E4
Lambeth Road SE1 244 F4
Lambeth Walk SE11 244 F5
Lamb's Conduit Street WC1N 240 E4
Lamb's Passage EC1Y 241 K4
Lamb Street E1 246 B1
Lamb Way SE1 246 A7
Lamlash Street SE11 245 H5
Lanark Place W9 238 D3
Lanark Road W9 238 B1
Lancaster Gate W2 238 D7
Lancaster Gate W2 238 D8
Lancaster Gate ⊖ W2 238 E7
Lancaster Mews W2 238 D7
Lancaster Place WC2E 240 E7
Lancaster Street SE1 245 H3
Lancaster Terrace W2 238 E7
Lancaster Walk W2 238 D8
Lancelot Place SW7 243 G3
Lancing Street NW1 240 B2
Lanesborough Place * SW1X 243 J3
Langdale Street E1 246 E3
Langford Place NW8 238 D1
Langham Place W1B 239 L5
Langham Street W1W 239 L5
Langham Street W1W 239 M5
Langley Lane SW8 244 D8
Langley Street WC2H 240 C7
Langton Close WC1X 240 E3
Lanhill Road W9 238 A3
Lansdowne Place SE1 245 L4
Lant Street SE1 245 J3
Larcom Street SE17 245 K6
Lauderdale Road W9 238 B3
Laud Street SE11 244 E7
Launcelot Street SE1 244 F3
Launceston Place W8 242 C4
Laurence Pountney Lane EC4V 241 L7
Lavender Road SE16 247 K5
Lavender Wharf SE16 247 K4
Lavington Street SE1 245 J1
Lawn Lane SW8 244 D8
Lawrence Street SW3 242 F8
Lawrence Wharf SE16 247 L6
Law Street SE1 245 L4
Laxton Place NW1 239 L3
Laystall Street EC1R 240 F4
Leadenhall Street EC3A 246 A3
Leadenhall Street EC3V 241 M6
Leake Street SE1 244 E2
Leather Lane EC1N 241 G4
Leathermarket Street SE1 245 M3
Leeke Street WC1X 240 E2
Lees Place W1K 239 J7
Leicester Square ⊖ WC2H 240 C7
Leicester Square WC2H 240 C7
Leicester Street WC2H 240 B7
Leigh Street WC1H 240 C3
Leinster Gardens W2 238 C6
Leinster Mews W2 238 C7
Leinster Place W2 238 C7
Leinster Square W2 238 A7
Leinster Terrace W2 238 C7
Leman Street E1 246 C3
Lennox Gardens SW1X 243 G4
Lennox Gardens Mews SW1X 243 G5
Leonard Street EC2A 241 L3
Leopold Estate E3 247 M1
Leopold Street E3 247 L1
Leroy Street SE1 245 M5
Lever Street EC1V 241 J2
Lewisham Street SW1H 244 B3
Lexham Gardens W8 242 A5
Lexham Mews W8 242 A5
Lexington Street W1F 240 A7
Leyden Street E1 246 B2
Leydon Close SE16 247 H5
Library Street SE1 245 H3
Lidlington Place NW1 240 A1
Lilestone Street NW8 238 F3
Lilley Close E1W 246 D5
Lillie Road SW6 242 A7
Lillie Yard SW6 242 A7
Limeburner Lane EC4M 241 H6
Lime Close E1W 246 D5
Limehouse Causeway E14 247 L4
Limehouse Link E14 247 L3
Limehouse ⇌ ⊖ E14 247 J3
Limerston Street SW10 242 D8
Lime Street EC3M 241 M7
Lincoln's Inn Fields WC2A 240 E6
Linden Gardens W2 238 A8
Lindley Street E1 246 F1
Lindsay Square SW1V 244 B7
Lindsey Street EC1A 241 H4
Linhope Street NW1 239 G3
Linsey Street SE16 246 D8
Lisle Street WC2H 240 B7
Lisson Green Estate NW8 238 F3
Lisson Grove NW1 239 G4
Lisson Grove NW8 238 F3
Lisson Street NW1 238 F4
Litchfield Street WC2H 240 C7
Little Argyll Street W1F 239 M6
Little Britain EC1A 241 J5
Little Chester Street SW1X 243 K4
Little George Street SW1P 244 C3
Little Marlborough Street W1F 240 A7
Little New Street EC4A 241 G6
Little Portland Street W1G 239 L6
Little Russell Street WC1A 240 C5
Little St James's Street SW1A 243 M2
Little Sanctuary SW1A 244 C3
Little Somerset Street E1 246 B3
Little Titchfield Street W1W 239 M5
Liverpool Grove SE17 245 K7
Liverpool Street EC2M 241 M5
Liverpool Street ⇌ ⊖ EC2M 241 M5
Lizard Street EC1V 241 K3
Llewellyn Street SE16 246 D7
Lloyd Baker Street WC1X 240 F2
Lloyd's Avenue EC3N 246 B3
Lloyd Square WC1X 240 F2
Lloyds Row EC1R 241 G2
Lloyd Street WC1X 240 F2
Locksley Estate E14 247 L2
Locksley Street E14 247 L1
Lockyer Street SE1 245 L3
Lodge Road NW8 238 F3
Loftie Street SE16 246 D7
Logan Place W8 242 A5
Lolesworth Close E1 246 B1
Lollard Street SE11 244 F5
Lollard Street SE11 244 F6
Loman Street SE1 245 J2
Lomas Street E1 246 D1
Lombard Lane EC4Y 241 G6
Lombard Street EC3V 241 L7
London Bridge EC4R 241 L8
London Bridge ⇌ ⊖ SE1 245 L1
London Bridge Street SE1 245 L1
London Dungeon SE1 244 E2
London Eye SE1 244 E2
London Mews W2 238 E6
London Road SE1 245 H4
London Street EC3R 246 A3
London Street W2 238 E6
London Transport Museum WC2E 240 D7
London Wall EC2M 241 K5
London Zoo ZSL NW1 239 J1
Long Acre WC2E 240 D7
Longford Street NW1 239 L3
Long Lane EC1A 241 J5
Long Lane SE1 245 L3
Longmoore Street SW1V 243 M5
Longridge Road SW5 242 A5
Longville Road SE11 245 H5
Long Walk SE1 246 A8
Long Yard WC1N 240 E4
Lord North Street SW1P 244 C4
Lord's Cricket Ground NW8 238 E2
Lorenzo Street WC1X 240 E1
Lorrimore Road SE17 245 J8
Lorrimore Square SE17 245 H8
Lothbury EC2R 241 L6
Loughborough Street SE11 244 F7
Lovat Lane EC3R 241 M7
Love Lane EC2V 241 K6
Lovell Place SE16 247 K7
Lowell Street E14 247 K2
Lower Belgrave Street SW1W 243 K4
Lower Grosvenor Place SW1W 243 L4
Lower James Street W1F 240 A7
Lower John Street W1F 240 A7
Lower Marsh SE1 244 F3
Lower Road SE16 247 G7
Lower Sloane Street SW1W 243 J6
Lower Thames Street EC3R 246 A4
Lower Thames Street EC3R 241 M8
Lowndes Close * SW1X 243 J4
Lowndes Place SW1X 243 J4
Lowndes Square SW1X 243 H3
Lowndes Street SW1X 243 J4
Lucan Place SW3 242 F5
Lucey Road SE16 246 C8
Ludgate Circus EC4M 241 H6
Ludgate Hill EC4M 241 H6
Luke Street EC2A 241 M3
Lukin Street E1 247 G3
Lumley Street W1K 239 K7
Lupus Street SW1V 243 L7
Lupus Street SW1V 244 B7
Luton Street NW8 238 E4
Luxborough Street W1U 239 J4
Lyall Mews SW1X 243 J4
Lyall Street SW1X 243 J4
Lyons Place NW8 238 E3
Lytham Street SE17 245 K7

M

Macclesfield Road EC1V 241 J2
Macclesfield Street * W1D 240 B7
Mace Close E1W 246 E5
Macklin Street WC2B 240 D6
Mackworth Street NW1 239 M2
Macleod Street SE17 245 K7
Madame Tussauds NW1 239 J4
Maddox Street W1S 239 M7
Magdalen Street SE1 245 M2
Magee Street SE11 244 F8
Maguire Street SE1 246 C6
Maida Avenue W9 238 D4
Maida Vale W9 238 C2
Maida Vale ⊖ W9 238 C2
Maiden Lane SE1 245 K1
Maiden Lane WC2E 240 D7
Major Road SE16 246 D7
Makins Street SW3 243 G6
Malet Street WC1E 240 B4
Mallord Street SW3 242 E8
Mallory Street NW8 238 F3
Mallow Street EC1Y 241 L3
Malta Street EC1V 241 H3
Maltby Street SE1 246 B7
Manchester Square W1U 239 J6
Manchester Street W1U 239 J5
Manciple Street SE1 245 L3
Mandeville Place W1U 239 K6
Manette Street W1D 240 B6
Manilla Street E14 247 M6
Manningford Close EC1V 241 H2
Manor Place SE17 245 J7
Manresa Road SW3 242 F7
Mansell Street E1 246 C3
Mansfield Mews W1G 239 L5
Mansfield Street W1G 239 L5
Mansion House ⊖ EC4V 241 K7
Manson Mews SW7 242 D5
Manson Place SW7 242 D6
Mapleleaf Square SE16 247 J6
Maples Place E1 246 F1
Maple Street W1T 239 M4
Marble Arch ⊖ W1C 239 H7
Marchmont Street WC1H 240 C3
Margaret Street W1W 239 L6
Margaretta Terrace SW3 242 F7
Margery Street WC1X 240 F3
Marigold Street SE16 246 E7
Marine Street SE16 246 C7
Market Mews W1J 243 K1
Market Place W1W 239 M6
Markham Square SW3 243 G6
Markham Street SW3 243 G6
Mark Lane EC3R 246 A4
Marlborough Gate W2 238 E7
Marlborough Place NW8 238 C1
Marlborough Road SW1A 244 A2
Marlborough Street SW3 242 F6
Marloes Road W8 242 B4
Marlow Way SE16 247 H6
Maroon Street E14 247 K2
Marshall Street W1F 240 A7
Marshalsea Road SE1 245 K2
Marsham Street SW1P 244 C5
Marsh Wall E14 247 M5
Martha's Buildings EC1V 241 K3
Martha Street E1 246 F3
Martin Lane EC4V 241 L7
Maryland Road W9 238 A4
Marylands Road W9 238 A4
Marylebone ⇌ ⊖ NW1 239 G4
Marylebone Flyover W2 238 E5
Marylebone High Street W1U 239 K5
Marylebone Lane W1U 239 K6
Marylebone Road NW1 239 G4
Marylebone Street W1G 239 K5
Marylee Way SE11 244 F6
Masjid Lane E14 247 M2
Mason Street SE17 245 M5
Massinger Street SE17 245 M6
Masters Street E1 247 J1
Matlock Street E14 247 J2
Matthew Parker Street SW1H 244 C3
Maunsel Street SW1P 244 B5
Mayfair Place W1J 243 L1
Mayflower Street SE16 246 F7
Mayford Estate NW1 240 A1
Maynards Quay E1W 246 F4
May's Court WC2N 240 C8
McAuley Close SE1 244 F4
McLeod's Mews SW7 242 C5
Meadcroft Road SE11 245 G8
Meadcroft Road SE11 245 H8
Meadow Road SW8 244 E8
Meadow Row SE1 245 J5
Mead Row SE1 244 F4
Meakin Estate SE1 245 M4
Mecklenburgh Square WC1N 240 E3
Medway Street SW1P 244 B5
Meeting House Alley E1W 246 E5
Melcombe Place NW1 239 G4
Melcombe Street W1U 239 H4
Melina Place NW8 238 D2
Melior Street SE1 245 M2
Melton Street NW1 240 A2
Memorial Gates SW1W 243 K3
Mepham Street SE1 244 F2
Mercer Street WC2H 240 C7
Merchant Square W2 238 E5
Merlin Street EC1R 240 F2
Mermaid Court SE1 245 K2
Merrick Square SE1 245 K4
Merrington Road SW6 242 A8
Merrow Street SE17 245 L7
Methley Street SE11 245 G7
Meymott Street SE1 245 G2
Micawber Street N1 241 K1
Micklethwaite Road SW6 242 A8
Middlesex Street E1 246 A1
Middlesex Street E1 246 B2
Middle Street EC1A 241 J5
Middle Temple WC2R 240 F7
Middle Temple Lane EC4Y 240 F7
Middleton Drive SE16 247 H6
Midland Road NW1 240 C1
Midship Close SE16 247 H6
Milborne Grove SW10 242 D7
Milcote Street SE1 245 H3
Miles Street SW8 244 D8
Milford Lane WC2R 240 F7
Milk Street EC2V 241 K6
Milk Yard E1W 247 G4
Millbank SW1P 244 D4
Millennium Bridge SE1 241 J8
Millennium Harbour E14 247 M6
Milligan Street E14 247 L4
Millman Mews WC1N 240 E4
Millman Street WC1N 240 E4
Mill Place E14 247 K3
Millstream Road SE1 246 B7
Mill Street SE1 246 C6
Mill Street W1S 239 L7
Milner Street SW3 243 G5
Milton Street EC2Y 241 K4
Milverton Street SE11 245 G7
Mincing Lane EC3M 246 A4
Minera Mews SW1W 243 J5
Minories EC3N 246 B3
Mitchell Street EC1V 241 J3
Mitre Road SE1 245 G2
Mitre Street EC3A 246 A3
Molyneux Street W1H 239 G5
Monck Street SW1P 244 C4
Monkton Street SE11 245 G5
Monkwell Square EC2Y 241 K5
Monmouth Place W2 238 A6
Monmouth Road W2 238 A6
Monmouth Street WC2H 240 C6
Montague Close SE1 245 L1
Montague Place EC3R 240 C5
Montague Street WC1B 240 C5
Montagu Mansions W1U 239 H5
Montagu Mews North W1H 239 H5
Montagu Mews West W1H 239 H6
Montagu Place W1H 239 H5
Montagu Row W1U 239 H5
Montagu Square W1H 239 H5
Montagu Street W1H 239 H6
Montford Place SE11 244 F7
Monthorpe Road E1 246 C1
Montpelier Square SW7 243 G3
Montpelier Street SW7 243 G3
Montpelier Walk SW7 242 G3
Montrose Place SW1X 243 K3
Monument ⊖ EC4R 241 L7
Monument Street EC3R 241 L7
Monument Street EC3R 241 M7
Monza Street E1W 247 G4
Moodkee Street SE16 247 G7
Moore Street SW3 243 H5
Moorfields EC2Y 241 L5
Moorgate EC2R 241 L6
Moorgate ⇌ ⊖ EC2Y 241 L5
Moor Lane EC2Y 241 K5
Moor Street W1D 240 C7
Mora Street EC1V 241 K2
Morecambe Street SE17 245 K6
Moreland Street EC1V 241 H2
More London SE1 246 A5
Moreton Place SW1V 244 A6
Moreton Street SW1V 244 B6
Moreton Terrace SW1V 244 A6
Morgan's Lane SE1 245 M2
Morgan's Lane SE1 246 A5
Morley Street SE1 245 G3
Mornington Crescent NW1 239 M1
Mornington Place NW1 239 L1
Mornington Terrace NW1 239 L1
Morocco Street SE1 246 A7
Morpeth Terrace SW1P 243 M5
Morris Street E1 246 F3
Morshead Road W9 238 A2
Mortimer Market WC1E 240 A4
Mortimer Street W1T 240 A5
Mortimer Street W1W 239 M5
Morton Place SE1 244 F4
Morwell Street WC1B 240 B5
Moscow Place W2 238 B7
Moscow Road W2 238 B7
Mossop Street SW3 243 G5
Motcomb Street SW1X 243 J4
Mount Gate W2 242 E2
Mount Mills EC1V 241 J3
Mount Pleasant WC1X 240 F4
Mount Row W1K 239 K8
Mount Street W1K 239 K8
Mount Street Mews W1K 239 K8
Mount Terrace E1 246 E1
Moxon Street W1U 239 J5
Mulberry Street E1 246 D2
Mulberry Walk SW3 242 E8
Mulready Street NW8 238 F4
Mundy Street N1 241 M2
Munster Square NW1 239 L3
Munton Road SE17 245 K5
Murphy Street SE1 244 F3
Murray Grove N1 241 K1
Musbury Street E1 247 G2
Muscovy Street EC3N 246 A4
Museum of London EC2Y 241 J5
Museum Street WC1A 240 C5
Myddelton Passage EC1R 241 G2
Myddelton Square EC1R 241 G1
Myddelton Street EC1R 241 G3
Myrdle Street E1 246 D2

N

Naoroji Street WC1X 240 F2
Napier Grove N1 241 K1
Narrow Street E14 247 K4
Nash Street NW1 239 L2
Nassau Street W1W 239 M5
Nathaniel Close * E1 246 C2
National Portrait Gallery WC2H 240 C8
Natural History Museum SW7 242 E4
Neal Street WC2H 240 C6
Neathouse Place * SW1V 243 M5
Neckinger SE1 246 C8
Needleman Street SE16 247 H7
Nelson Close NW6 238 A1
Nelson Place N1 241 H1
Nelson's Column WC2N 240 C8
Nelson Square SE1 245 H2
Nelson Street E1 246 E2
Nelson Terrace N1 241 H1
Neptune Street SE16 247 G7
Nesham Street E1W 246 D4
Netherton Grove SW10 242 D8
Netley Street NW1 239 M2
Nevern Place SW5 242 A6
Nevern Square SW5 242 A6
Neville Street SW7 242 E6
Newark Street E1 246 E2
New Atlas Wharf E14 247 M8
New Bond Street W1S 239 L7
New Bond Street W1S 239 L8
New Bridge Street EC4V 241 H6
New Broad Street EC2M 241 M5
New Burlington Street W1S 239 M7
Newburn Street SE11 244 F7
Newbury Street EC1A 241 J5
Newcastle Place W2 238 E5
New Cavendish Street W1G 239 L5
New Change EC4M 241 J6
New Church Road SE5 245 L8
Newcomen Street SE1 245 K2
New Compton Street WC2H 240 C6
Newcourt Street NW8 238 F1
Newell Street E14 247 L3
New Fetter Lane EC4A 241 G6
Newgate Street WC1A 241 H6
New Globe Walk SE1 241 J8
New Goulston Street E1 246 B2
Newham's Row SE1 246 A7
Newington Butts SE1 245 H5
Newington Causeway SE1 245 J4
New Kent Road SE1 245 K5
Newlands Quay E1W 246 F4
Newman Street W1T 240 A5
New North Place EC2A 241 M3
New North Road N1 241 L1
New North Street WC1N 240 D4
New Oxford Street WC1A 240 C6
Newport Street SE11 244 E5
New Quebec Street W1H 239 H6
New Ride SW7 242 E3
New Road E1 246 E2
New Row WC2N 240 C7
New Spring Gardens Walk SE1 244 D7
New Square WC2A 240 F6
New Street EC2M 246 A2
New Street Square EC4A 241 G6
Newton Road W2 238 A6
Newton Street WC2B 240 D5
New Union Street EC2Y 241 K5
Nicholas Lane EC3V 241 L7
Nicholson Street SE1 245 H1
Nightingale Place SW10 242 D8
Nile Street N1 241 K2
Nine Elms Lane SW8 244 C8
Noble Street EC2V 241 J6
Noel Road N1 241 J1
Noel Street W1F 240 A6
Norbiton Road E14 247 L2
Norfolk Crescent W2 239 G6
Norfolk Place W2 238 E6
Norfolk Square W2 238 E6
Norman Street EC1V 241 J3
Norris Street SW1Y 240 B8
Northampton Road EC1R 241 G3
Northampton Square EC1V 241 H2
North Audley Street W1K 239 J7
North Bank NW8 238 F2
Northburgh Street EC1V 241 H3
North Carriage Drive W2 238 F7
Northdown Street N1 240 D1
Northey Street E14 247 K4
North Gower Street NW1 240 A2
Northington Street WC1N 240 E4
North Mews WC1N 240 E4
North Ride W2 239 G7
North Row W1K 239 J7
North Terrace SW3 242 F5
Northumberland Alley EC3N 246 B3
Northumberland Avenue WC2N 244 C1
Northumberland Place W2 238 A6
Northumberland Street WC2N 244 C1
North Wharf Road W2 238 E5
Northwick Terrace NW8 238 D3
Norway Gate SE16 247 K7
Norway Place E14 247 L3
Norwich Street EC4A 240 F5
Nottingham Place W1U 239 J4
Nottingham Street W1U 239 J4
Notting Hill Gate W11 238 A8
Notting Hill Gate ⊖ W11 242 A1
Nugent Terrace NW8 238 D1
Nutford Place W1H 239 G6

O

Oakden Street SE11 245 G5
Oakington Road W9 238 A3
Oak Lane E14 247 L3
Oakley Close EC1V 241 H1
Oakley Gardens SW3 243 G8
Oakley Square NW1 240 A1
Oakley Street SW3 242 F8
Oak Tree Road NW8 238 F2
Oat Lane EC2V 241 J5
Occupation Road SE17 245 J6
Ocean Square E1 247 J1
Ocean Street E1 247 J1
Odessa Street SE16 247 L7
Ogle Street W1W 239 M5
Old Bailey EC4M 241 H6
Old Barrack Yard SW1X 243 J3
Old Bond Street W1S 239 M8
Old Broad Street EC2N 241 M6
Old Brompton Road SW5 242 B6
Old Brompton Road SW7 242 D6
Old Burlington Street W1S 239 M7
Oldbury Place W1U 239 J4
Old Castle Street E1 246 B2
Old Cavendish Street W1G 239 L6
Old Church Road E1 247 H2
Old Church Street SW3 242 E7
Old Compton Street W1D 240 B7
Old Court Place W8 242 B3
Old Gloucester Street WC1N 240 D4
Old Jamaica Road SE16 246 C7
Old Jewry EC2R 241 K6
Old Kent Road SE1 245 M5
Old Marylebone Road NW1 239 G5
Old Montague Street E1 246 C1
Old North Street WC1X 240 E5
Old Paradise Street SE11 244 E5
Old Park Lane W1J 243 K2
Old Pye Street SW1P 244 B4
Old Queen Street SW1H 244 B3
Old Square WC2A 240 F6
Old Street EC1V 241 J3
Old Street ⇌ ⊖ EC1Y 241 L3
Old Street Junction EC1Y 241 L3
Oliver's Yard EC1Y 241 L3
Olney Road SE17 245 J8
O'Meara Street SE1 245 K2
Omega Place N1 240 D1
Onega Gate SE16 247 K8
Ongar Road SW6 242 A8
Onslow Gardens SW7 242 D6
Onslow Square SW7 242 E5
Onslow Square SW7 242 E6
Ontario Street SE1 245 J4
Ontario Way E14 247 M4
Opal Street SE1 245 H6
Orange Place SE16 247 G8
Orange Square SW1W 243 K6
Orange Street E1W 246 D5
Orange Street WC2H 240 B8
Orb Street SE17 245 L6
Orchardson Street NW8 238 E4
Orchard Street W1H 239 J6
Orde Hall Street WC1N 240 E4
Orient Street SE11 245 H5
Orme Court W2 238 B8
Orme Lane W2 238 B8
Orme Square Gate W2 238 B8
Ormond Close WC1N 240 D4
Ormonde Gate SW3 243 H7
Ormond Yard SW1Y 240 A8
Orsett Mews W2 238 C6
Orsett Street SE11 244 E6
Orsett Terrace W2 238 C5
Orton Street E1W 246 D5
Osbert Street SW1V 244 B6
Osborn Street E1 246 C2
Oslo Square SE16 247 K7
Osnaburgh Street NW1 239 L3
Osnaburgh Terrace NW1 239 L3
Ossington Buildings W1U 239 J5
Ossington Street W2 238 A7
Ossulston Street NW1 240 B1
Oswin Street SE11 245 H5
Othello Close SE1 245 H6
Otto Street SE17 245 H8
Outer Circle NW1 239 H3
Outer Circle NW1 239 K1
Oval ⊖ SE11 244 F8

Oval Way SE11 244 E7
Ovington Square SW3 243 G4
Ovington Street SW3 243 G5
Owen Street EC1V 241 G1
Oxendon Street SW1Y 240 B8
Oxford Circus ⊖ W1B 239 M6
Oxford Road NW6 238 A1
Oxford Square W2 238 F6
Oxford Street W1C 239 L6
Oxford Street WC1A 240 A6

P

Pace Place E1 246 E3
Pacific Wharf SE16 247 H5
Paddington ⇌ ⊖ W2 238 D6
Paddington Green W2 238 E5
Paddington Street W1U 239 J5
Pageant Crescent SE16 247 K5
Page Street SW1P 244 B5
Paget Street EC1V 241 H2
Pakenham Street WC1X 240 E3
Palace Avenue W8 242 B2
Palace Court W2 238 A7
Palace Gardens Terrace W8 242 A1
Palace Gate W8 242 C3
Palace Green W8 242 B2
Palace of Westminster SW1A 244 D3
Palace Place SW1E 243 M4
Palace Street SW1E 243 M4
Pall Mall SW1Y 244 A1
Pall Mall East SW1Y 244 B1
Palmer Street SW1H 244 B3
Pancras Lane EC4N 241 K6
Pancras Road N1C 240 C1
Panton Street SW1Y 240 B8
Paradise Street SE16 246 E7
Paradise Walk SW3 243 H8
Pardoner Street SE1 245 L4
Pardon Street EC1V 241 H3
Parfett Street E1 246 D2
Paris Garden SE1 245 G1
Park Crescent W1B 239 K4
Park Crescent Mews West W1G 239 K4
Parker's Row SE1 246 C7
Parker Street WC2B 240 D6
Park Lane W1K 239 H7
Park Lane W2 243 J1
Park Place SW1A 243 M1
Park Place Villas W2 238 D4
Park Road NW1 239 H3
Park Square East NW1 239 L3
Park Square Mews NW1 239 K3
Park Square West NW1 239 K3
Park Street SE1 245 K1
Park Street W1K 239 J7
Park Village East NW1 239 L1
Park Walk SW10 242 D8
Park West Place W2 239 G6
Parliament Street SW1A 244 C2
Parry Street SW8 244 D8
Passmore Street SW1W 243 J6
Paternoster Square 241 J6
Pater Street W8 242 A4
Pattina Walk SE16 247 K5
Paul Street EC2A 241 M3
Paultons Square SW3 242 E8
Paveley Street NW1 239 G3
Pavilion Road SW1X 243 H3
Pavilion Street SW1X 243 H4
Paxton Terrace SW1V 243 L7
Peabody Avenue SW1V 243 L7
Peabody Estate SE1 245 J1
Peacock Street SE17 245 J6
Pearl Street E1W 246 F5
Pearman Street SE1 245 G3
Pear Tree Court EC1R 241 G3
Peartree Lane E1W 247 G4
Pear Tree Street EC1V 241 J3
Peel Street W8 242 A1
Peerless Street EC1V 241 K2
Pelham Crescent SW7 242 F6
Pelham Place SW7 242 F5
Pelham Street SW7 242 F5
Pelier Street SE17 245 K8
Pemberton Row EC4A 241 G6
Pembridge Gardens W2 238 A8
Pembridge Place W2 238 A7
Pembridge Square W2 238 A7
Pembridge Villas W11 238 A7
Pembroke Close SW1X 243 J3
Penang Street E1W 246 F5
Penfold Place NW8 238 F5
Penfold Street NW8 238 E4
Pennant Mews W8 242 B5
Pennington Street E1W 246 D4
Pennyfields E14 247 M4
Penrose Grove SE17 245 J7
Penrose Street SE17 245 J7
Penton Place SE17 245 H6
Penton Rise WC1X 240 E2
Penton Street N1 240 F1
Pentonville Road N1 240 E1
Penywern Road SW5 242 A6
Pepper Street SE1 245 J2
Pepys Street EC3N 246 A4
Percival Street EC1V 241 H3
Percy Circus WC1X 240 F2
Percy Street W1T 240 B5
Perkin's Rents SW1P 244 B4
Perryn Road SE16 246 E7
Petersham Mews SW7 242 D4
Petersham Place SW7 242 C4
Peter Street W1F 240 B7
Peto Place NW1 239 L3
Petticoat Lane E1 246 B2
Petty France SW1H 244 A3
Petty Wales EC3R 246 A4
Petyward SW3 243 G6
Phelp Street SE17 245 L7
Phene Street SW3 243 G8
Phillimore Walk W8 242 A3
Philpot Lane EC3M 241 M7
Philpot Street E1 246 E2
Phipp's Mews SW1W 243 L5
Phipp Street EC2A 241 M3
Phoenix Place WC1X 240 F3
Phoenix Road NW1 240 B1
Phoenix Street WC2H 240 C6
Piccadilly W1J 243 L2
Piccadilly Arcade SW1Y 243 M1
Piccadilly Circus W1B 240 A8
Piccadilly Circus ⊖ W1J 240 B8
Pickard Street EC1V 241 J2
Picton Place W1U 239 K6
Pier Head E1W 246 E6
Pigott Street E14 247 M3
Pilgrimage Street SE1 245 L3
Pimlico ⊖ SW1V 244 B6
Pimlico Road SW1W 243 J6
Pinchin Street E1 246 D3
Pindar Street EC2A 241 M4
Pindock Mews W9 238 B3
Pine Street EC1R 240 F3
Pitfield Street N1 241 M1
Pitsea Street E1 247 H3
Pitt's Head Mews W1J 243 K2
Pitt Street W8 242 A2
Pixley Street E14 247 L2
Platina Street * EC2A 241 L3
Plover Way SE16 247 K8
Plumbers Row E1 246 D2
Plumtree Court EC4A 241 G5
Plympton Street NW8 238 F4
Pocock Street SE1 245 H2
Poland Street W1F 240 A6
Pollen Street W1S 239 L7
Pollitt Drive NW8 238 E3
Polperro Mews SE11 245 G5
Polygon Road NW1 240 B1
Pond Place SW3 242 F6
Ponler Street E1 246 E3
Ponsonby Place SW1P 244 C6
Ponsonby Terrace SW1P 244 C6
Ponton Road SW1V 244 B8
Pont Street SW1X 243 H4
Poolmans Street SE16 247 H6
Pope Street SE1 246 B7
Poplar Place W2 238 B7
Poppin's Court EC4A 241 H6
Porchester Gardens W2 238 B7
Porchester Gate W2 238 C8
Porchester Place W2 239 G6
Porchester Road W2 238 B5
Porchester Square W2 238 B6
Porchester Terrace W2 238 C7
Porchester Terrace North W2 238 C6
Porlock Street SE1 245 L3
Porter Street NW1 239 H4
Porteus Road W2 238 D5
Portland Place W1B 239 L4
Portland Place W1B 239 L5
Portland Square E1W 246 E5
Portland Street SE17 245 L7
Portman Close W1H 239 J6
Portman Mews South W1H 239 J6
Portman Square W1H 239 J6
Portman Street W1H 239 J6
Portpool Lane EC1N 240 F4
Portsea Place W2 239 G6
Portsmouth Street WC2A 240 E6
Portsoken Street E1 246 B3
Portugal Street WC2A 240 E6
Potier Street SE1 245 L4
Potters Fields SE1 246 B6
Pottery Street SE16 246 E7
Poultry EC2V 241 K6
Powis Place WC1N 240 D4
Praed Mews W2 238 E6
Praed Street W2 238 E6
Pratt Walk SE1 244 E5
Premier Place E14 247 M4
Prescot Street E1 246 C3
Preston Close SE1 245 M5
Price's Street SE1 245 H1
Prideaux Place WC1X 240 F2
Primrose Street EC2A 246 A1
Prince Albert Road NW8 238 F1
Prince Consort Road SW7 242 D3
Princelet Street E1 246 C1
Prince of Wales Gate SW7 242 F3
Princes Arcade SW1Y 240 A8
Prince's Gardens SW7 242 E3
Prince's Gate Mews SW7 242 E4
Princes Riverside Road SE16 247 H5
Prince's Square W2 238 A7
Princess Road NW6 238 A1
Princess Street SE1 245 H4
Princes Street W1B 239 L6
Prince's Street EC2R 241 L6
Princeton Street WC1R 240 E5
Prioress Street SE1 245 L4
Priory Green Estate N1 240 E1
Priory Walk SW10 242 D7
Proctor Street WC1V 240 E5
Prospect Place E1W 247 G5
Prospect Street SE16 246 E7
Provident Court W1K 239 J7
Provost Street N1 241 L1
Prusom Street E1W 246 F5
Pudding Lane EC3R 241 M7
Pumphouse Mews E1 246 D3
Purbrook Street SE1 246 A7
Purcell Street N1 241 M1
Purchese Street NW1 240 B1

Q

Quebec Way SE16 247 J7
Queen Anne's Gate SW1H 244 B3
Queen Anne Street W1G 239 K5
Queen Elizabeth Street SE1 246 B6
Queen Mother Gate W2 243 J2
Queensborough Terrace W2 238 C7
Queensburry Place SW7 242 E5
Queen's Gardens W2 238 C7
Queen's Gate SW7 242 D3
Queen's Gate SW7 242 D4
Queen's Gate Gardens SW7 242 D5
Queen's Gate Mews SW7 242 D4
Queen's Gate Place SW7 242 D4
Queen's Gate Place Mews SW7 242 D4
Queen's Gate Terrace SW7 242 C4
Queen's Mews W2 238 B7
Queen Square WC1N 240 D4
Queen's Row SE17 245 K7
Queen Street EC4N 241 K7
Queen Street W1J 243 L1
Queen Street Place EC4R 241 K7
Queen's Walk SE1 246 A5
Queen's Walk SW1A 243 M2
Queensway W2 238 B6
Queensway ⊖ W2 238 B8
Queen Victoria Street EC4V 241 J7
Quick Street N1 241 H1

R

Raby Street E14 247 K2
Radcliffe Road SE1 246 B8
Radcot Street SE11 245 G7
Radnor Mews W2 238 E6
Radnor Place W2 238 F6
Radnor Street EC1V 241 K3
Radnor Walk SW3 243 G7
Railway Approach SE1 245 L1
Railway Avenue SE16 247 G6
Railway Street N1 240 D1
Raine Street E1W 246 F5
Ralston Street SW3 243 H7
Ramillies Place W1F 239 M6
Ramillies Street W1F 239 M6
Rampart Street E1 246 E2
Rampayne Street SW1V 244 B6
Randall Road SE11 244 D6
Randall Row SE11 244 E6
Randolph Avenue W9 238 B1
Randolph Crescent W9 238 C3
Randolph Gardens NW6 238 B1
Randolph Mews W9 238 D4
Randolph Road W9 238 C4
Ranelagh Grove SW1W 243 K6
Ranelagh Road SW1V 244 A7
Rangoon Street * EC3N 246 B3
Ranston Street NW8 238 F4
Raphael Street SW7 243 G3
Ratcliffe Cross Street E1W 247 J3
Ratcliffe Lane E14 247 J3
Rathbone Place W1T 240 B5
Rathbone Street W1T 240 A5
Raven Row E1 246 F1
Ravensdon Street SE11 245 G7
Ravey Street EC2A 241 M3
Rawlings Street SW3 243 G5
Rawstorne Street EC1V 241 H2
Ray Street EC1R 241 G4
Reardon Place E1W 246 E5
Reardon Street E1W 246 E5
Rectory Square E1 247 H1
Redan Place W2 238 B6
Redburn Street SW3 243 G7
Redcastle Close E1W 247 G4
Redcliffe Gardens SW10 242 B7
Redcliffe Mews SW10 242 C7
Redcliffe Place SW10 242 C8
Redcliffe Road SW10 242 D7
Redcliffe Square SW10 242 B7
Redcliffe Street SW10 242 B8
Redcross Way SE1 245 K2
Redesdale Street SW3 243 G7
Redfield Lane SW5 242 A5
Redhill Street NW1 239 L1
Red Lion Row SE5 245 K8
Red Lion Square WC1R 240 E5
Red Lion Street WC2B 240 E5
Redman's Road E1 247 G1
Red Place W1K 239 J7
Redriff Road SE16 247 J8
Reedworth Street SE11 245 G6
Reeves Mews W1K 239 J8
Regal Close E1 246 D1
Regan Way N1 241 M1
Regency Street SW1P 244 B5
Regent Place W1B 240 A7
Regent's Park ⊖ W1B 239 L4
Regent's Park NW1 239 J1
Regent's Park Estate NW1 239 L2
Regent Square WC1H 240 D2
Regent Street SW1Y 240 B8
Regent Street W1S 239 M7
Relton Mews SW7 243 G4
Remington Street N1 241 H1
Remnant Street WC2A 240 E6
Renforth Street SE16 247 G7
Renfrew Road SE11 245 H5
Rennie Street SE1 245 H1
Rephidim Street SE1 245 M4
Repton Street E14 247 K2
Reveley Square SE16 247 K7
Rex Place W1K 239 J8
Rhodeswell Road E14 247 L2
Rich Street E14 247 M3
Rickett Street SW6 242 A8
Ridgemount Street WC1E 240 B4
Ridgemount Gardens WC1E 240 B4
Riding House Street W1W 239 M5
Riley Road SE1 246 B7
Ripley's Believe It or Not! W1J 240 B8
Risborough Street SE1 245 J2
Risdon Street SE16 247 G7
Rissinghill Street N1 240 F1
River Street EC1R 240 F2
Rivington Street EC2A 241 M3
Robert Adam Street W1U 239 J6
Roberts Close SE16 247 J7
Robert Street NW1 239 L2
Rochester Row SW1P 244 A5
Rochester Street SW1P 244 B5
Rockingham Street SE1 245 J4
Rocliffe Street N1 241 H1
Roding Mews E1W 246 D5
Rodmarton Street W1U 239 H5
Rodney Place SE17 245 K5
Rodney Road SE17 245 K5
Rodney Street N1 240 E1
Roger Street WC1N 240 E4
Roland Gardens SW7 242 D6
Roland Way SE17 245 L7
Romford Street E1 246 E2
Romilly Street W1D 240 B7
Romney Street SW1P 244 C5
Rood Lane EC3M 241 M7
Ropemaker Road SE16 247 K7
Ropemaker Street EC2Y 241 L4
Roper Lane SE1 246 B7
Rope Street SE16 247 K8
Rope Walk Gardens E1 246 E2
Rosary Gardens SW7 242 D6
Roscoe Street EC1Y 241 K3
Rose Alley SE1 241 K8
Rosebery Avenue EC1R 240 F3
Rosemoor Street SW3 243 G6
Rose Street WC2E 240 C7
Rossmore Road NW1 239 G3
Rotary Street SE1 245 H3
Rotherhithe ⊖ SE16 247 G6
Rotherhithe Street SE16 247 G6
Rotherhithe Street SE16 247 J4
Rotherhithe Tunnel SE16 247 H5
Rothsay Street SE1 245 M4
Rotten Row W2 242 F2
Rouel Road SE16 246 C8
Roupell Street SE1 245 G2
Royal Albert Hall SW7 242 E3
Royal Avenue SW3 243 H6
Royal Hospital Road SW3 243 H7
Royal Mint Street E1 246 C4
Royal Oak ⊖ W2 238 B5
Royal Oak Yard SE1 246 A7
Royal Opera House WC2E 240 D7
Royal Road SE17 245 H8
Royal Street SE1 244 E3
Rudolph Road NW6 238 A1
Rugby Street WC1N 240 E4
Rum Close E1W 246 F4
Rupack Street SE16 246 F7
Rupert Street W1D 240 B7
Rushworth Street SE1 245 H2
Russell Court SW1A 244 A2
Russell Square WC1B 240 C4
Russell Square ⊖ WC1B 240 D4
Russell Street WC2B 240 D7
Russia Dock Road SE16 247 K6
Rutherford Street SW1P 244 B5
Rutland Gardens SW7 243 G3
Rutland Gate SW7 242 F3
Rutland Mews SW7 242 F4
Rutland Street SW7 242 F4
Ryder Street SW1Y 244 A1

S

Sackville Street W1S 240 A8
Saffron Hill EC1N 241 G4
Saffron Street EC1N 241 G4
Sail Street SE11 244 F5
St Agnes Place SE11 245 G8
St Alban's Grove W8 242 B4
St Alban's Street SW1Y 240 B8
St Alphage Garden EC2Y 241 K5
St Andrews Hill EC4V 241 H7
St Andrew's Place NW1 239 L3
St Andrew Street EC4A 241 G5
St Anne's Court W1F 240 B6
St Ann's Street SW1P 244 C4
St Anselm's Place W1K 239 K7
St Barnabas Street SW1W 243 K6
St Botolph Street EC3N 246 B2
St Bride Street EC4A 241 G6
St Chad's Street WC1H 240 D2
St Clare Street EC3N 246 B3
St Clements Lane WC2A 240 E6
St Cross Street EC1N 241 G4
St Dunstan's Hill EC3R 241 M8
St Dunstan's Lane EC3R 241 M7
St Elmos Road SE16 247 J7
St Ermin's Hill SW1H 244 B3
St George's Circus SE1 245 H3
St George's Drive SW1V 243 M6
St George's Estate E1 246 D3
St George's Lane * EC3R 241 M7
St George's Road SE1 245 G4
St George's Square SW1V 244 B7
St George Street W1S 239 L7
St Giles High Street WC2H 240 C6
St Helen's Place EC3A 241 M6
St James Market * SW1Y 240 B8
St James's Park ⊖ SW1H 244 B3
St James's Park SW1A 244 B3
St James's Place SW1A 243 M2
St James's Road SE16 246 D8
St James's Square SW1Y 244 A1
St James's Street SW1A 243 M1
St James Walk EC1R 241 G3
St John's Lane EC1M 241 H4
St John's Place EC1M 241 H4
St John's Square EC1V 241 H4
St John Street EC1V 241 H2
St John's Wood High Street NW8 238 F1
St John's Wood Road NW8 238 E3
St Katharine's Way E1W 246 C5
St Leonard's Terrace SW3 243 H7
St Loo Avenue SW3 243 G8
St Luke's Close EC1V 241 K3
St Luke's Street SW3 242 F6
St Manningtree E1 246 C2
St Mark Street E1 246 C3
St Martin's Lane WC2N 240 C7
St Martin's le Grand EC1A 241 J6
St Martin's Place WC2N 240 C8
St Mary at Hill EC3R 241 M8
St Mary Axe EC3A 246 A3
St Marychurch Street SE16 246 F7
St Mary's Gardens SE11 245 G5
St Mary's Terrace W2 238 D4
St Mary's Walk SE11 245 G5
St Matthew Street SW1P 244 B4
St Michael's Street W2 238 F6
St Olav's Square SE16 246 F7
St Oswald's Place SE11 244 E7
St Oswulf Street * SW1P 244 C6
St Pancras International ⇌ N1C 240 C1
St Paul's ⊖ EC1A 241 J6
St Paul's Avenue SE16 247 J5
St Paul's Cathedral EC4M 241 J6
St Paul's Churchyard EC4M 241 J6
St Paul's Way E3 247 L1
St Petersburgh Mews W2 238 B7
St Petersburgh Place W2 238 B7
St Saviours Wharf SE1 246 C6
St Stephen's Gardens W2 238 A5
St Swithin's Lane EC4N 241 L7
St Thomas Street SE1 245 L2
St Vincent Street W1U 239 J5
Salamanca Street SE1 244 D6
Salem Road W2 238 B7
Sale Place W2 238 F5
Salisbury Court EC4Y 241 G6
Salisbury Place W1H 239 H4
Salisbury Street NW8 238 F4
Salmon Lane E14 247 J2
Salter Road SE16 247 J5
Salter Street E14 247 M4
Samford Street NW8 238 F4
Sampson Street E1W 246 D5
Sancroft Street SE11 244 F6
Sandland Street WC1R 240 E5
Sandpiper Close SE16 247 L6
Sandwich Street WC1H 240 C2
Sandy's Row E1 246 B1
Sans Walk EC1R 241 G3
Sardinia Street WC2A 240 E6
Savage Gardens EC3N 246 B3
Savile Row W1S 239 M7
Savoy Hill WC2R 240 E8
Savoy Place WC2R 240 D8
Savoy Street WC2E 240 E7
Sawyer Street SE1 245 J2
Scala Street W1T 240 A5
Scandrett Street E1W 246 E5
Scarborough Street E1 246 C3
Scarsdale Villas W8 242 A4
Schooner Close * SE16 247 H6
Science Museum SW7 242 E4
Scoresby Street SE1 245 H2
Scotch House Junction SW1X 243 H3
Scotland Place SW1A 244 C1
Scott Ellis Gardens NW8 238 E2
Scott Lidgett Crescent SE16 246 D7
Scrutton Street EC2A 241 M3
Seaford Street WC1H 240 D2
Seagrave Road SW6 242 A8
Sea Life London Aquarium SE1 244 E3
Searles Road SE1 245 L5
Sebastian Street EC1V 241 H2
Secker Street SE1 244 F2
Sedan Way SE17 245 M6
Sedding Street SW1X 243 J5
Seddon Street WC1X 240 E3
Seething Lane EC3N 246 A4
Sekforde Street EC1R 241 H3
Selfridges W1A 239 J6
Selsey Street E14 247 M1
Selwood Place SW7 242 E6
Semley Place SW1W 243 K6
Senior Street W2 238 B4
Senrab Street E1 247 H2
Serle Street WC2A 240 F6
Serpentine Bridge W2 242 E1
Serpentine Road W2 242 F2
Seth Street SE16 247 G7
Settles Street E1 246 D2
Seven Dials WC2H 240 C6
Seville Street SW1X 243 H3
Sevington Street W9 238 A3
Seward Street EC1V 241 J3
Seymour Mews W1H 239 J6
Seymour Place W1H 239 G5
Seymour Street W1H 239 H6
Seymour Street W2 239 G7
Seymour Walk SW10 242 C7
Shad Thames SE1 246 B6
Shad Thames SE1 246 C6
Shadwell ⊖ ⊖ E1 246 F3
Shadwell Gardens E1 246 F3
Shaftesbury Avenue W1D 240 B7
Shaftesbury Avenue WC2H 240 C6
Shaftesbury Street N1 241 K1
Shakespeare's Globe SE1 241 J8
Shand Street SE1 246 A6
Sharsted Street SE17 245 H7
Shaw Crescent E14 247 K2
Shawfield Street SW3 243 G7
Sheffield Terrace W8 242 A2
Sheldon Square W2 238 D5
Shelmerdine Close E3 247 M1
Shelton Street WC2H 240 D6
Shepherdess Walk N1 241 K1
Shepherd Street W1J 243 K1
Sheraton Street W1F 240 B6
Sherborne Lane EC4N 241 L7
Sherwood Street W1D 240 A7
Ship and Mermaid Row SE1 245 M2
Shipwright Road SE16 247 K7
Shirland Road W9 238 A3
Shoe Lane EC4A 241 G5
Shorter Street EC3N 246 B4
Shorts Gardens WC2H 240 C6
Short Street SE1 245 G2
Shoulder of Mutton Alley E14 247 K4
Shouldham Street W1H 239 G5
Shroton Street NW1 238 F4
Siddons Lane W1H 239 H4
Sidmouth Street WC1N 240 D3
Sidney Square E1 246 F2
Sidney Street E1 246 F1
Silex Street SE1 245 H3
Silk Street EC2Y 241 K4
Silver Walk SE16 247 K5
Silvester Street SE1 245 K3
Singer Street EC2A 241 L3
Sir John Soane's Museum WC2A 240 E5
Sir Simon Milton Square SW1V 243 L4
Skinner Place * SW1W 243 J6
Skinners Lane EC4V 241 K7
Skinner Street EC1R 241 G3
Slippers Place SE16 246 F8
Sloane Avenue SW3 243 G6
Sloane Court East SW3 243 J6
Sloane Court West SW3 243 J6
Sloane Gardens SW1W 243 J6
Sloane Square SW1W 243 J5
Sloane Square ⊖ SW1W 243 J6
Sloane Street SW1X 243 H3
Sloane Terrace SW1X 243 J5
Smeaton Street E1W 246 E5
Smithfield Street EC1A 241 H5
Smith Square SW1P 244 C4
Smith Street SW3 243 G7
Smith Terrace SW3 243 G7
Smithy Street E1 247 G1
Snowden Street EC2A 241 M4
Snow Hill EC1A 241 H5
Snowsfields SE1 245 L2
Soho Square W1D 240 B6
Soho Street W1D 240 B6
Somerford Way SE16 247 K7
Somers Crescent W2 238 F6
Somerset House WC2R 240 E7
Somerstown Estate NW1 240 A1
Sondes Street SE17 245 L7
South & West Africa Gate SW1A 244 A3
Southall Place SE1 245 L3
Southampton Buildings WC2A 240 F5
Southampton Place WC1A 240 D5
Southampton Row WC1B 240 D4
Southampton Street WC2E 240 D7
South Audley Street W1K 239 K8
South Carriage Drive SW1X 243 H3
South Carriage Drive SW7 242 F3
South Eaton Place SW1W 243 J5
Southern Street N1 240 E1
South Kensington ⊖ SW7 242 E4
South Kensington ⊖ SW7 242 E5
South Lambeth Road SW8 244 D8
South Molton Lane W1K 239 K7
South Molton Street W1K 239 K7
South Parade SW3 242 E7
South Place EC2M 241 L5
South Sea Street SE16 247 L8
South Square WC1R 240 F5

South Street W1K 243 J1
South Tenter Street E1 246 C3
South Terrace SW7 242 F5
Southwark ⊖ SE1 245 H2
Southwark Bridge SE1 241 K8
Southwark Bridge Road SE1 245 J3
Southwark Park Road SE16 246 E8
Southwark Street SE1 245 H1
Southwell Gardens SW7 242 C5
South Wharf Road W2 238 E6
Southwick Mews W2 238 F6
Southwick Place W2 238 F6
Southwick Street W2 238 F6
Sovereign Close E1W 246 F4
Sovereign Crescent SE16 247 J4
Spanish Place W1U 239 J5
Spa Road SE16 246 C8
Spear Mews SW5 242 A6
Spelman Street E1 246 C1
Spence Close SE16 247 K7
Spencer Street EC1V 241 H2
Spenser Street SW1E 244 A4
Spert Street E14 247 J4
Spital Square E1 246 A1
Spring Gardens SW1A 244 C1
Spring Street W2 238 E6
Spurgeon Street SE1 245 L4
Spur Road SE1 244 F3
Stables Way SE11 244 F7
Stable Yard Road SW1A 244 A2
Stacey Street WC2H 240 C6
Stafford Place SW1E 243 M3
Stafford Road NW6 238 A2
Stafford Street W1S 239 M8
Stafford Terrace W8 242 A3
Stainer Street SE1 245 L2
Staining Lane EC2V 241 K6
Stainsby Road E14 247 M2
Stalham Street SE16 246 F8
Stamford Street SE1 245 G1
Stanford Place SE1 245 M6
Stanford Road W8 242 B4
Stanford Street * SW1V 244 B6
Stanhope Close * SE16 247 H6
Stanhope Gardens SW7 242 D5
Stanhope Gate W1K 243 K1
Stanhope Mews SW7 242 D5
Stanhope Mews East SW7 242 D5
Stanhope Mews West SW7 242 D5
Stanhope Place W2 239 G7
Stanhope Place Gate W2 239 G7
Stanhope Row W1J 243 K1
Stanhope Street NW1 239 M1
Stanhope Terrace W2 238 E7
Stannary Street SE11 245 G7
Staples Close SE16 247 J5
Staple Street SE1 245 L3
Starcross Street NW1 240 A2
Star Street W2 238 F6
Station Approach SE1 244 F3
Stave Yard Road SE16 247 J5
Stead Street SE17 245 K6
Steedman Street SE17 245 J5
Steel's Lane E1 247 G3
Steeres Way SE16 247 K7
Stephenson Way NW1 240 A3
Stephen Street W1T 240 B5
Stepney Green E1 247 H1
Stepney High Street E1 247 J1
Stepney Way E1 246 E1
Sterling Street SW7 243 G3
Stevedore Street E1W 246 E5
Stevens Street SE1 246 A7
Steward Street * E1 246 B1
Stewart's Grove SW3 242 F6
Stew Lane EC4V 241 J7
Stillington Street SW1P 244 A5
Stockholm Way E1W 246 D5
Stocks Place E14 247 M3
Stone Buildings WC2A 240 F5
Stonecutter Street EC4A 241 G6
Stoney Lane E1 246 B2
Stoney Street SE1 245 K1
Stopford Road SE17 245 J7
Store Street WC1E 240 B5
Storey's Gate SW1H 244 C3
Storks Road SE16 246 D8
Stoughton Close SE11 244 E6
Stourcliffe Street W1H 239 G6
Strafford Street E14 247 M6
Strand WC2R 240 D8
Stratford Place W1C 239 K6
Stratford Road W8 242 A5
Strathearn Place W2 238 F7
Stratton Street W1J 243 L1
Strutton Ground SW1P 244 B4
Strype Street E1 246 B2
Stuart Road NW6 238 A2
Stukeley Street WC2B 240 D6
Sturgeon Road SE17 245 J7
Sturge Street SE1 245 J3
Sturt Street N1 241 K1
Stutfield Street E1 246 D3
Sudley Street N1 241 H1
Sudrey Street SE1 245 J3
Suffolk Lane EC4V 241 L7
Suffolk Street SW1Y 240 B8
Sugar Lane SE16 246 D7
Sugar Quay Walk EC3R 246 A4
Sullivan Road SE11 245 G5
Summercourt Road E1 247 G2
Summers Street EC1R 240 F4
Sumner Place SW7 242 E6
Sumner Street SE1 245 J1
Sunderland Terrace W2 238 A6
Sun Passage SE16 246 D8
Sun Street EC2M 241 M4
Sun Street Passage EC2M 241 M5
Surrendale Place W9 238 A4
Surrey Quays Road SE16 247 H7
Surrey Row SE1 245 H2
Surrey Square SE17 245 M6
Surrey Street WC2E 240 E7
Surrey Water Road SE16 247 H6
Sussex Gardens W2 238 E6
Sussex Mews East W2 238 E7
Sussex Place NW1 239 H3
Sussex Place W2 238 E6
Sussex Square W2 238 E7
Sussex Street SW1V 243 L7
Sutherland Avenue W9 238 A4
Sutherland Row SW1V 243 L7
Sutherland Square SE17 245 J7
Sutherland Street SW1V 243 L7
Sutton Row W1D 240 B6
Sutton Street E1 247 G3
Suttons Way EC1Y 241 K4
Swain Street NW8 238 F3
Swallow Place W1B 239 L6
Swallow Street W1B 240 A8
Swan Lane EC4R 241 L8
Swan Mead SE1 245 M4
Swan Road SE16 247 G6
Swan Street SE1 245 K3
Swan Walk SW3 243 H8
Swedenborg Gardens E1 246 E4
Sweeney Crescent SE1 246 C7
Swinton Street WC1X 240 E2
Sydney Place SW7 242 F6
Sydney Street SW3 242 F6
Symons Street SW3 243 H6

T

Tabard Gardens Estate SE1 245 L3
Tabard Street SE1 245 L3
Tabernacle Street EC2A 241 L3
Tachbrook Street SW1V 244 A6
Talbot Road W2 238 A6
Talbot Square W2 238 E6
Talbot Yard SE1 245 L2
Tallis Street EC4Y 241 G7
Tamworth Street SW6 242 A8
Tanner Street SE1 246 A7
Taplow Street N1 241 K1
Tarling Street E1 246 F3
Tarver Road SE17 245 H7
Tate Britain SW1P 244 C6
Tate Modern SE1 241 J8
Tatum Street SE17 245 M6
Taunton Place NW1 239 G3
Tavistock Place WC1H 240 C3
Tavistock Square WC1H 240 C3
Tavistock Street WC2E 240 D7
Taviton Street WC1H 240 B3
Teak Close SE16 247 K6
Tedworth Square SW3 243 G7
Telford Terrace SW1V 243 M7
Temeraire Street SE16 247 G6
Temple ⊖ WC2R 240 F7
Temple Avenue EC4Y 241 G7
Temple Lane EC4Y 241 G7
Temple Place WC2R 240 F7
Templeton Place SW5 242 A5
Tench Street E1W 246 E5
Tenniel Close W2 238 C7
Tennis Street SE1 245 L2
Tenterden Street W1S 239 L6
Tenterground E1 246 B1
Teredo Street SE16 247 J8
Terminus Place SW1V 243 L4
Thame Road SE16 247 H6
Thanet Street WC1H 240 C2
Thavies Inn EC4A 241 G6
Thayer Street W1U 239 K5
The Arches WC2N 240 D8
The Boltons SW10 242 C7
The British Library NW1 240 C2
The British Museum WC1B 240 C5
The Broad Walk W2 238 B8
The Broad Walk W8 242 C2
The Cut SE1 245 G2
Theed Street SE1 245 G2
The Flower Walk W2 242 D3
The Grange SE1 246 B8
The Highway E1W 246 E4
The Little Boltons SW10 242 C7
The Mall SW1A 244 B2
The Mitre E14 247 L3
The Monument EC3R 241 L7
The National Gallery WC2N 240 C8
Theobald's Road WC1X 240 E4
Theobald Street SE1 245 L5
The Oval (Surrey County Cricket Ground) SE11 244 F8
The Shard SE1 245 L2
The Vale SW3 242 E8
Thirleby Road SW1P 244 A4
Thomas More Street E1W 246 D4
Thomas Road E14 247 M2
Thoresby Street N1 241 K1
Thorney Street SW1P 244 C5
Thornton Place W1H 239 H4
Thrale Street SE1 245 K1
Thrawl Street E1 246 C1
Threadneedle Street EC2R 241 L6
Three Colt Street E14 247 L3
Three Oak Lane SE1 246 B6
Throgmorton Avenue EC2N 241 L6
Throgmorton Street EC2N 241 L6
Thurland Road SE16 246 D8
Thurloe Place SW7 242 F5
Thurloe Square SW7 242 F5
Thurloe Street SW7 242 E5
Thurlow Street SE17 245 M7
Tichbourne Row W2 238 F6
Tiller Road E14 247 M8
Tillman Street E1 246 E3
Tilney Street W1J 243 K1
Timber Pond Road SE16 247 J6
Tinsley Road E1 247 G1
Tinworth Street SE11 244 D6
Tisdall Place SE17 245 L6
Tite Street SW3 243 H8
Tiverton Street SE1 245 J4
Token House Yard EC2R 241 L6
Tolmer's Square NW1 240 A3
Tomlin's Terrace E14 247 K2
Tonbridge Street WC1H 240 D2
Tooley Street SE1 245 L1
Tooley Street SE1 246 B6
Tor Gardens W8 242 A2
Torquay Street W2 238 A5
Torrens Street EC1V 241 G1
Torrington Place E1W 246 D5
Torrington Place WC1E 240 B4
Torrington Square WC1E 240 B4
Tothill Street SW1H 244 B3
Tottenham Court Road W1T 240 A4
Tottenham Court Road ⊖ W1D 240 B6
Tottenham Street W1T 240 A5
Toulmin Street SE1 245 J3
Tower Bridge EC3N 246 B5
Tower Bridge Approach EC3N 246 B5
Tower Bridge Road SE1 246 A7
Tower Bridge Wharf E1W 246 C5
Tower Gateway ⊖ EC3N 246 B4
Tower Hill EC3N 246 B4
Tower Hill ⊖ EC3N 246 B4
Tower of London EC3N 246 B4
Tower Place EC3R 246 A4
Tower Street WC2H 240 C7
Townsend Street SE17 245 M5
Toynbee Street E1 246 B1
Trafalgar Gardens E1 247 H1
Trafalgar Square WC2N 240 C8
Trafalgar Street SE17 245 L7
Transept Street NW1 238 F5
Trebeck Street W1J 243 L1
Trebovir Road SW5 242 A6
Tregunter Road SW10 242 C7
Trenton Road SE16 246 E8
Tresham Crescent NW8 238 F3
Trevor Place SW7 243 G3
Trevor Square SW7 243 G3
Trevor Street SW7 243 G3
Trinidad Street E14 247 M4
Trinity Church Square SE1 245 K3
Trinity Square EC3N 246 B4
Trinity Street SE1 245 K3
Trump Street EC2V 241 K6
Tudor Street EC4Y 241 G7
Tufton Street SW1P 244 C4
Tunnel Road SE16 247 G6
Turks Row SW3 243 J6
Turner's Road E3 247 L2
Turner Street E1 246 E2
Turnmill Street EC1N 241 G4
Turpentine Lane SW1V 243 L7
Turquand Street SE17 245 K6
Tyers Gate SE1 245 M3
Tyers Street SE11 244 E7
Tyers Terrace SE11 244 E7
Tyron Street SW3 243 H6
Tysoe Street EC1R 241 G3

U

Udall Street SW1P 244 A5
Ufford Street SE1 245 G2
Ulster Place NW1 239 K4
Umberston Street E1 246 E2
Undershaft EC3A 246 A2
Underwood Road N1 241 K2
Underwood Street N1 241 K1
Union Street SE1 245 H2
University Street WC1E 240 A4
Upbrook Mews W2 238 D6
Upper Belgrave Street SW1X 243 K4
Upper Berkeley Street W1H 239 H6
Upper Brook Street W1K 239 J7
Upper Cheyne Row SW3 242 F8
Upper Grosvenor Street W1K 239 J8
Upper Ground SE1 244 F1
Upper Harley Street NW1 239 K3
Upper James Street W1F 240 A7
Upper John Street W1F 240 A7
Upper Marsh SE1 244 E3
Upper Montagu Street W1H 239 H5
Upper St Martin's WC2H 240 C7
Upper Tachbrook Street SW1V 244 A5
Upper Thames Street EC4V 241 J7
Upper Wimpole Street W1G 239 K4
Upper Woburn Place WC1H 240 B2
Urlwin Street SE5 245 J8
Uxbridge Street W8 242 A1

V

Valentine Place SE1 245 G3
Vandon Passage SW1H 244 A3
Vandon Street SW1H 244 A4
Varden Street E1 246 E2
Varndell Street NW1 239 M2
Vauban Street SE16 246 C8
Vaughan Street SE16 247 L7
Vaughan Way E1W 246 D5
Vauxhall ⇌ ⊖ SW8 244 D7
Vauxhall Bridge SW1V 244 C7
Vauxhall Bridgefoot SE1 244 D7
Vauxhall Bridge Road SW1V 243 M5
Vauxhall Cross SE1 244 D7
Vauxhall Grove SW8 244 D8
Vauxhall Street SE11 244 E6
Vauxhall Walk SE11 244 E6
Venables Street W2 238 E4
Vere Street W1G 239 K6
Vernon Place WC1A 240 D5
Vernon Rise WC1X 240 E2
Verulam Street WC1X 240 F4
Vestry Street N1 241 L2
Victoria ⇌ ⊖ SW1V 243 L5
Victoria & Albert Museum SW7 242 F4
Victoria Embankment SW1A 244 D2
Victoria Embankment WC2R 240 F7
Victoria Gate W2 238 F7
Victoria Road W8 242 C4
Victoria Square SW1W 243 L4
Victoria Street SW1E 243 L4
Victory Place SE17 245 K5
Victory Way SE16 247 K7
Vigo Street W1S 239 M8
Villa Street SE17 245 L7
Villiers Street WC2N 240 D8
Vincent Close SE16 247 K7
Vincent Square SW1P 244 B5
Vincent Street SW1P 244 B5
Vincent Terrace N1 241 H1
Vince Street EC1V 241 L2
Vine Court E1 246 D1
Vinegar Street E1W 246 E5
Vine Hill EC1R 240 F4
Vine Lane SE1 246 A6
Vine Street EC3N 246 B3
Violet Hill NW8 238 C1
Virgil Street SE1 244 F4
Virginia Street E1W 246 D4
Viscount Street EC2Y 241 J4

W

Wadding Street SE17 245 K6
Wakefield Street WC1H 240 D3
Wakeling Street E14 247 J3
Wakley Street EC1V 241 H2
Walbrook EC4N 241 L7
Walcorde Avenue SE17 245 K6
Walcot Square SE11 245 G5
Walden Street E1 246 E2
Waley Street E1 247 J1
Wallwood Street E14 247 M1
Walnut Tree Walk SE11 244 F5
Walpole Street SW3 243 H6
Walter Terrace E1 247 H2
Walton Place SW3 243 H4
Walton Street SW3 243 G4
Walworth Place SE17 245 K7
Walworth Road SE17 245 J5
Wandsworth Road SW8 244 C8
Wansey Street SE17 245 J6
Wapping ⊖ E1W 246 F5
Wapping High Street E1W 246 E6
Wapping Lane E1W 246 F4
Wapping Wall E1W 247 G5
Warden's Grove SE1 245 J2
Wardour Street W1F 240 B6
Warner Street EC1R 240 F4
Warren Street W1T 239 M4
Warren Street ⊖ NW1 239 M3
Warrington Crescent W9 238 C3
Warrington Gardens W9 238 C4
Warwick Avenue W9 238 B3
Warwick Avenue ⊖ W9 238 C4
Warwick Crescent W2 238 C5
Warwick House Street SW1Y 244 B1
Warwick Lane EC4M 241 H6
Warwick Place W9 238 C4
Warwick Road SW5 242 A6
Warwick Row SW1E 243 L4
Warwick Square SW1V 243 M6
Warwick Street W1B 240 A7
Warwick Way SW1V 243 L6
Waterhouse Square EC1N 241 G5
Waterloo ⇌ ⊖ SE1 244 F2
Waterloo Bridge SE1 244 E1
Waterloo Bridge WC2R 240 E8
Waterloo East ⇌ SE1 245 G2
Waterloo Place SW1Y 244 B1
Waterloo Road SE1 244 F1
Waterloo Road SE1 245 G2
Waterman Way E1W 246 E5
Waterside Close SE16 246 D7
Watling Street EC4N 241 K7
Watney Street E1 246 F3
Watts Street E1W 246 E5
Waveney Close E1W 246 D5
Waverton Street W1J 239 K8
Weavers Lane SE1 246 A6
Webber Row SE1 245 G3
Webber Street SE1 245 H3
Webb Street SE1 246 A8
Webster Road SE16 246 D8
Weigh House Street W1K 239 K7
Welbeck Street W1G 239 K5
Welbeck Way W1G 239 K6
Welland Mews E1W 246 E5
Wellclose Square E1 246 D4
Wellesley Street E1 247 H2
Wellesley Terrace N1 241 K2
Wellington Arch W1J 243 K2
Wellington Square SW3 243 H6
Wellington Place NW8 238 E2
Wellington Road NW8 238 E1
Wellington Street WC2E 240 D7
Wells Mews W1T 240 A5
Wells Street W1T 240 A5
Wells Way SE5 245 M8
Wenlock Road N1 241 K1
Wenlock Street N1 241 K1
Wentworth Street E1 246 B2
Werrington Street NW1 240 A1
Wesley Street W1G 239 K5
West Arbour Street E1 247 G2
Westbourne Crescent W2 238 D7
Westbourne Gardens W2 238 B6
Westbourne Gate W2 238 E7
Westbourne Grove W2 238 A6
Westbourne Grove Terrace W2 238 B6
Westbourne Park Road W2 238 A5
Westbourne Park Villas W2 238 A5
Westbourne Street W2 238 E7
Westbourne Terrace W2 238 D6
Westbourne Terrace Mews W2 238 C6
Westbourne Terrace Road W2 238 C5
West Brompton ⇌ ⊖ ⊖ SW5 242 A7
West Carriage Drive W2 242 E2
Westcott Road SE17 245 H8
West Cromwell Road SW5 242 A5
Western Place SE16 247 G6
Westferry ⊖ E14 247 M4
Westferry Circus E14 247 M5
Westferry Road E14 247 M5
West Gardens E1W 246 F4
Westgate Terrace SW10 242 B7
West Halkin Street SW1X 243 J4
West Harding Street EC4A 241 G6
West India Avenue E14 247 M5
West India Dock Road E14 247 M3
Westland Place N1 241 K2
West Lane SE16 246 E7
Westminster ⊖ SW1A 244 D3
Westminster Abbey SW1P 244 C3
Westminster Bridge SE1 244 D3
Westminster Bridge Road SE1 244 F3
Westmoreland Place SW1V 243 L7
Westmoreland Road SE17 245 K8
Westmoreland Street W1G 239 K5
Westmoreland Terrace SW1V 243 L7
Weston Rise WC1X 240 E1
Weston Street SE1 245 M2
Weston Street SE1 245 M3
Westport Street E1 247 H2
West Poultry Avenue EC1A 241 H5
West Road SW3 243 H7
West Smithfield EC1A 241 H5
West Square SE11 245 H4
West Street WC2H 240 C7
West Tenter Street E1 246 C3
West Warwick Place SW1V 243 M6
Westway W2 238 B5
Wetherby Gardens SW5 242 C6
Weyhill Road E1 246 D2
Weymouth Mews W1G 239 L5
Weymouth Street W1G 239 K5
Wharfdale Road N1 240 D1
Wharfedale Street SW10 242 B7
Wharf Road N1 241 J1
Wharton Street WC1X 240 F2
Wheatley Street W1G 239 K5
Whetstone Park WC2A 240 E5
Whidborne Street WC1H 240 D2
Whiskin Street EC1R 241 G2
Whitcomb Street WC2H 240 B8
Whitechapel ⇌ ⊖ ⊖ E1 246 E1
Whitechapel Estate E1 246 C4
Whitechapel High Street E1 246 C2
Whitechapel Road E1 246 D1
Whitecross Street EC1Y 241 K3
Whitefriars Street EC4Y 241 G6
Whitehall SW1A 244 C2
Whitehall Court SW1A 244 D2
Whitehall Place SW1A 244 D1
White Hart Street SE11 245 G6
White Hart Yard SE1 245 L2
Whitehaven Street NW8 238 F4
Whitehead's Grove SW3 243 G6
White Horse Lane E1 247 H1
Whitehorse Road E1 247 J1
Whitehorse Road E1 247 J3
White Horse Street W1J 243 L1
White Kennett Street E1 246 B2
White Lion Hill EC4V 241 H7
White Lion Street N1 240 F1
White's Grounds SE1 246 A7
White's Row E1 246 B1
White Tower Way E1 247 J1
Whitfield Place W1T 240 A4
Whitfield Street W1T 240 A4
Whitgift Street SE11 244 E5
Whittaker Street SW1W 243 J6
Whittlesey Street SE1 245 G2
Wicker Street E1 246 E3
Wickham Close E1 247 G1
Wickham Street SE11 244 E7
Wicklow Street WC1X 240 E2
Widegate Street E1 246 A1
Widley Road W9 238 A3
Wigmore Place W1G 239 K5
Wigmore Street W1U 239 K6
Wigton Place SE11 245 G7
Wilbraham Place SW1X 243 J5
Wilcox Place * SW1E 244 A4
Wild Court WC2B 240 E6
Wild's Rents SE1 245 M4
Wild Street WC2B 240 D6
Wilfred Street SW1E 243 M4
Wilkes Street E1 246 B1
William IV Street WC2N 240 C8
William Mews SW1X 243 H3
William Road NW1 239 M3
Willow Place SW1P 244 A5
Willow Street EC2A 241 M3
Wilmington Square WC1X 240 F3
Wilmington Street WC1X 240 F2
Wilson Grove SE16 246 E7
Wilson Street EC2A 241 L4
Wilton Crescent SW1X 243 J3
Wilton Mews SW1X 243 K4
Wilton Place SW1X 243 J3
Wilton Road SW1V 243 M5
Wilton Row SW1X 243 J3
Wilton Street SW1X 243 K4
Wimpole Mews W1G 239 K5
Wimpole Street W1G 239 K5
Winchester Street SW1V 243 L6
Winchester Walk SE1 245 K1
Wincott Street SE11 245 G5
Windmill Road SE11 244 F7
Windmill Street W1T 240 B5
Windrose Close SE16 247 H6
Windsor Terrace N1 241 K1
Wine Close E1W 246 F5
Winnett Street W1D 240 B7
Winsland Mews W2 238 E6
Winsland Street W2 238 E6
Winsley Street W1W 240 A6
Winthrop Street E1 246 E1
Woburn Place WC1H 240 C3
Woburn Square WC1H 240 C4
Wodeham Gardens E1 246 E1
Wolfe Crescent SE16 247 H7
Wolseley Street SE1 246 C6
Woodbridge Street EC1R 241 G3
Woodchester Square W9 238 A4
Woodfall Street SW3 243 H7
Woodland Crescent SE16 247 H7
Woodseer Street E1 246 C1
Woods Mews W1K 239 J7
Woods Place SE1 246 A8
Woodstock Street W1C 239 K6
Wood Street EC2V 241 K6
Woolaston Close SE1 245 J5
Wooler Street SE17 245 L7
Wootton Street SE1 245 G2
Worgan Street SE11 244 E6
Worgan Street SE16 247 H8
Wormwood Street EC2M 241 M5
Worship Street EC2A 241 M4
Wren Street WC1X 240 E3
Wright's Lane W8 242 A3
Wyatt Close SE16 247 L7
Wyclif Street EC1V 241 H2
Wymering Road W9 238 A2
Wynard Terrace SE11 244 F7
Wyndham Place W1H 239 H5
Wyndham Street W1H 239 G4
Wynnstay Gardens W8 242 A4
Wynyatt Street EC1V 241 H2
Wythburn Place W1H 239 H6

Y

Yalding Road * SE16 246 C8
Yardley Street WC1X 240 F2
Yeoman's Row SW3 243 G4
York Boulevard WC2N 240 D8
York Bridge NW1 239 J3
York Gate NW1 239 J4
York Road SE1 244 E2
Yorkshire Road E14 247 K3
York Square E14 247 J2
York Street W1H 239 G5
York Street W1U 239 H5
York Terrace East NW1 239 J4
York Terrace West NW1 239 J4
York Way N1 240 D1
Young Street W8 242 B3

Z

Zoar Street SE1 245 J1
ZSL London Zoo NW1 239 J1

This index lists places appearing in the main map section of the atlas in alphabetical order. The reference following each name gives the atlas page number and grid reference of the square in which the place appears. The map shows counties, unitary authorities and administrative areas, together with a list of the abbreviated name forms used in the index. The top 100 places of tourist interest are indexed in red, World Heritage sites in green, motorway service areas in blue, airports in blue *italic* and National Parks in green *italic*.

Scotland

Abers	Aberdeenshire
Ag & B	Argyll and Bute
Angus	Angus
Border	Scottish Borders
C Aber	City of Aberdeen
C Dund	City of Dundee
C Edin	City of Edinburgh
C Glas	City of Glasgow
Clacks	Clackmannanshire (1)
D & G	Dumfries & Galloway
E Ayrs	East Ayrshire
E Duns	East Dunbartonshire (2)
E Loth	East Lothian
E Rens	East Renfrewshire (3)
Falk	Falkirk
Fife	Fife
Highld	Highland
Inver	Inverclyde (4)
Mdloth	Midlothian (5)
Moray	Moray
N Ayrs	North Ayrshire
N Lans	North Lanarkshire (6)
Ork	Orkney Islands
P & K	Perth & Kinross
Rens	Renfrewshire (7)
S Ayrs	South Ayrshire
S Lans	South Lanarkshire
Shet	Shetland Islands
Stirlg	Stirling
W Duns	West Dunbartonshire (8)
W Isls	Western Isles (Na h-Eileanan an Iar)
W Loth	West Lothian

Wales

Blae G	Blaenau Gwent (9)
Brdgnd	Bridgend (10)
Caerph	Caerphilly (11)
Cardif	Cardiff
Carmth	Carmarthenshire
Cerdgn	Ceredigion
Conwy	Conwy
Denbgs	Denbighshire
Flints	Flintshire
Gwynd	Gwynedd
IoA	Isle of Anglesey
Mons	Monmouthshire
Myr Td	Merthyr Tydfil (12)
Neath	Neath Port Talbot (13)
Newpt	Newport (14)
Pembks	Pembrokeshire
Powys	Powys
Rhondd	Rhondda Cynon Taf (15)
Swans	Swansea
Torfn	Torfaen (16)
V Glam	Vale of Glamorgan (17)
Wrexhm	Wrexham

Channel Islands & Isle of Man

Guern	Guernsey
Jersey	Jersey
IoM	Isle of Man

England

BaNES	Bath & N E Somerset (18)
Barns	Barnsley (19)
BCP	Bournemouth, Christchurch and Poole (20)
Bed	Bedford
Birm	Birmingham
Bl w D	Blackburn with Darwen (21)
Bolton	Bolton (22)
Bpool	Blackpool
Br & H	Brighton & Hove (23)
Br For	Bracknell Forest (24)
Bristl	City of Bristol
Bucks	Buckinghamshire
Bury	Bury (25)
C Beds	Central Bedfordshire
C Brad	City of Bradford
C Derb	City of Derby
C KuH	City of Kingston upon Hull
C Leic	City of Leicester
C Nott	City of Nottingham

C Pete	City of Peterborough
C Plym	City of Plymouth
C Port	City of Portsmouth
C Sotn	City of Southampton
C Stke	City of Stoke-on-Trent
C York	City of York
Calder	Calderdale (26)
Cambs	Cambridgeshire
Ches E	Cheshire East
Ches W	Cheshire West and Chester
Cnwll	Cornwall
Covtry	Coventry
Cumb	Cumbria
Darltn	Darlington (27)
Derbys	Derbyshire
Devon	Devon
Donc	Doncaster (28)
Dorset	Dorset
Dudley	Dudley (29)
Dur	Durham
E R Yk	East Riding of Yorkshire
E Susx	East Sussex
Essex	Essex
Gatesd	Gateshead (30)
Gloucs	Gloucestershire
Gt Lon	Greater London
Halton	Halton (31)
Hants	Hampshire
Hartpl	Hartlepool (32)
Herefs	Herefordshire
Herts	Hertfordshire
IoS	Isles of Scilly
IoW	Isle of Wight
Kent	Kent
Kirk	Kirklees (33)
Knows	Knowsley (34)
Lancs	Lancashire
Leeds	Leeds
Leics	Leicestershire
Lincs	Lincolnshire
Lpool	Liverpool
Luton	Luton

M Keyn	Milton Keynes
Manch	Manchester
Medway	Medway
Middsb	Middlesbrough
N Linc	North Lincolnshire
N Som	North Somerset
N Tyne	North Tyneside (35)
N u Ty	Newcastle upon Tyne
N York	North Yorkshire
NE Lin	North East Lincolnshire
Nhants	Northamptonshire
Norfk	Norfolk
Notts	Nottinghamshire
Nthumb	Northumberland
Oldham	Oldham (36)
Oxon	Oxfordshire
R & Cl	Redcar & Cleveland
Readg	Reading
Rochdl	Rochdale (37)
Rothm	Rotherham (38)
Rutlnd	Rutland
S Glos	South Gloucestershire (39)
S on T	Stockton-on-Tees (40)
S Tyne	South Tyneside (41)
Salfd	Salford (42)
Sandw	Sandwell (43)
Sefton	Sefton (44)
Sheff	Sheffield
Shrops	Shropshire
Slough	Slough (45)
Solhll	Solihull (46)
Somset	Somerset
St Hel	St Helens (47)
Staffs	Staffordshire
Sthend	Southend-on-Sea
Stockp	Stockport (48)
Suffk	Suffolk
Sundld	Sunderland
Surrey	Surrey
Swindn	Swindon
Tamesd	Tameside (49)
Thurr	Thurrock (50)
Torbay	Torbay
Traffd	Trafford (51)
W & M	Windsor & Maidenhead (52)
W Berk	West Berkshire
W Susx	West Sussex
Wakefd	Wakefield (53)
Warrtn	Warrington (54)
Warwks	Warwickshire
Wigan	Wigan (55)
Wilts	Wiltshire
Wirral	Wirral (56)
Wokham	Wokingham (57)
Wolves	Wolverhampton (58)
Worcs	Worcestershire
Wrekin	Telford & Wrekin (59)
Wsall	Walsall (60)

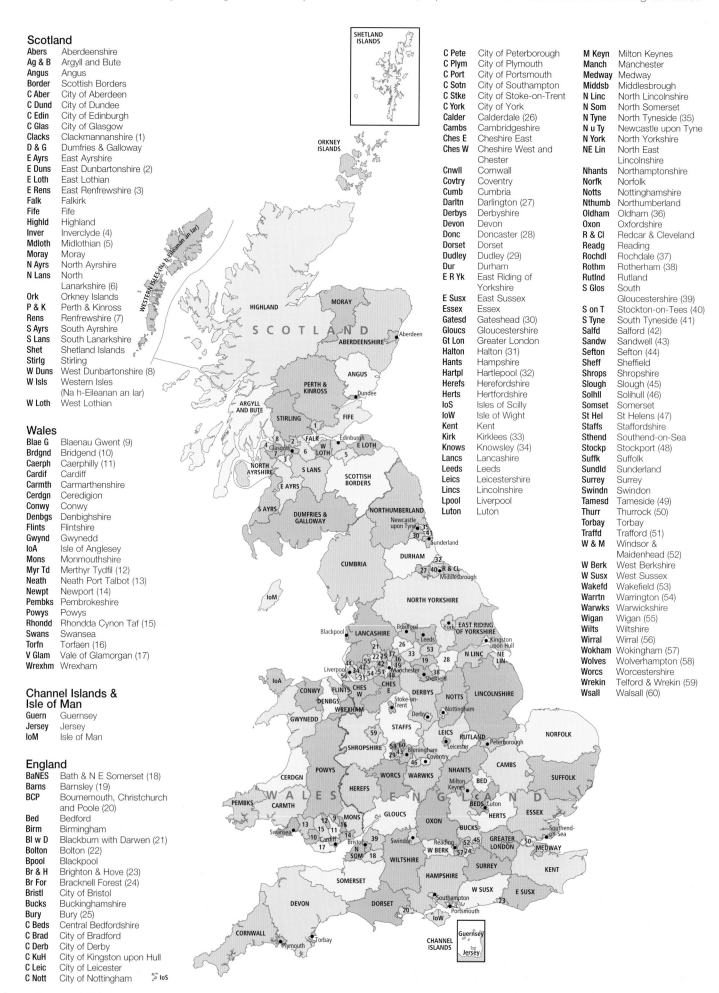

A

Abbas Combe Somset 20 D10
Abberley Worcs 57 P11
Abberley Common Worcs 57 N11
Abberton Essex 52 H8
Abberton Worcs 47 J4
Abberwick Nthumb 119 M8
Abbess Roding Essex 51 N8
Abbey Devon 10 C2
Abbey-Cwm-Hir Powys 55 P10
Abbeydale Sheff 84 D4
Abbey Dore Herefs 45 M8
Abbey Green Staffs 70 H3
Abbey Hill Somset 19 J11
Abbey St Bathans Border 129 K7
Abbeystead Lancs 95 M10
Abbeytown Cumb 110 C10
Abbey Village Lancs 89 J6
Abbey Wood Gt Lon 37 L5
Abbotrule Border 118 B8
Abbots Bickington Devon 16 F9
Abbots Bromley Staffs 71 K10
Abbotsbury Dorset 11 M7
Abbot's Chair Derbys 83 M6
Abbots Deuglie P & K 134 E5
Abbotsham Devon 16 G6
Abbotskerswell Devon 7 M5
Abbots Langley Herts 50 C10
Abbotsleigh Devon 7 L9
Abbots Leigh N Som 31 P10
Abbotsley Cambs 62 B9
Abbots Morton Worcs 47 K3
Abbots Ripton Cambs 62 B5
Abbot's Salford Warwks 47 L4
Abbotstone Hants 22 G8
Abbotswood Hants 22 C10
Abbots Worthy Hants 22 E8
Abbotts Ann Hants 22 B6
Abbott Street Dorset 12 G4
Abcott Shrops 56 F9
Abdon Shrops 57 K7
Abenhall Gloucs 46 C11
Aberaeron Cerdgn 43 J2
Aberaman Rhondd 30 D4
Aberangell Gwynd 55 J2
Aber-arad Carmth 42 F6
Aberarder Highld 147 Q2
Aberargie P & K 134 F4
Aberarth Cerdgn 43 J2
Aberavon Neath 29 K7
Aber-banc Cerdgn 42 G6
Aberbargoed Caerph 30 G4
Aberbeeg Blae G 30 H4
Abercanaid Myr Td 30 E4
Abercarn Caerph 30 H6
Abercastle Pembks 40 G4
Abercegir Powys 55 J4
Aberchalder Lodge Highld 147 J7
Aberchirder Abers 158 F7
Aber Clydach Powys 44 G10
Abercorn W Loth 127 K2
Abercraf Powys 29 M2
Abercregan Neath 29 M5
Abercwmboi Rhondd 30 D5
Abercych Pembks 41 P2
Abercynon Rhondd 30 E6
Aberdalgie P & K 134 D3
Aberdare Rhondd 30 D4
Aberdaron Gwynd 66 B9
Aberdeen C Aber 151 N6
Aberdeen Airport C Aber 151 M5
Aberdesach Gwynd 66 G4
Aberdour Fife 134 F10
Aberdulais Neath 29 L5
Aberdyfi Gwynd 54 E5
Aberedw Powys 44 F5
Abereiddy Pembks 40 E4
Abererch Gwynd 66 F7
Aberfan Myr Td 30 E4
Aberfeldy P & K 141 L8
Aberffraw IoA 78 F11
Aberffrwd Cerdgn 54 F9
Aberford Leeds 91 L3
Aberfoyle Stirlg 132 G7
Abergarw Brdgnd 29 P8
Abergarwed Neath 29 M4
Abergavenny Mons 31 J2
Abergele Conwy 80 C9
Aber-giar Carmth 43 K6
Abergorlech Carmth 43 L8
Abergwesyn Powys 44 B4
Abergwili Carmth 42 H10
Abergwydol Powys 54 H4
Abergwynfi Neath 29 N5
Abergwyngregyn Gwynd 79 M10
Abergynolwyn Gwynd 54 F3
Aberhafesp Powys 55 P6
Aberhosan Powys 55 J5
Aberkenfig Brdgnd 29 N8
Aberlady E Loth 128 D4
Aberlemno Angus 143 J6
Aberllefenni Gwynd 54 H3
Aberllynfi Powys 44 H7
Aberlour, Charlestown of Moray 157 P9
Abermagwr Cerdgn 54 F10
Aber-meurig Cerdgn 43 L3
Abermorddu Flints 69 K3
Abermule Powys 56 B6
Abernant Carmth 42 F10
Abernant Rhondd 30 D4
Abernethy P & K 134 F4
Abernyte P & K 142 D11
Aberporth Cerdgn 42 E4
Abersoch Gwynd 66 E9
Abersychan Torfn 31 J4
Aberthin V Glam 30 D10
Abertillery Blae G 30 H4
Abertridwr Caerph 30 F7
Abertridwr Powys 68 D11
Abertysswg Caerph 30 F3
Aberuthven P & K 134 B4
Aberyscir Powys 44 D9
Aberystwyth Cerdgn 54 D8
Abingdon-on-Thames Oxon 34 E5
Abinger Common Surrey 36 D11
Abinger Hammer Surrey 36 C11
Abington Nhants 60 G8
Abington S Lans 116 C6
Abington Pigotts Cambs 50 H2
Abington Services S Lans 116 C6
Abingworth W Susx 24 D7
Ab Kettleby Leics 73 J6
Ab Lench Worcs 47 K4
Ablington Gloucs 33 M3
Ablington Wilts 21 N5
Abney Derbys 83 Q8
Above Church Staffs 71 J4
Aboyne Abers 150 E8
Abhainn Suidhe W Isls 168 f7
Abram Wigan 82 D4
Abriachan Highld 155 Q10
Abridge Essex 51 L11
Abronhill N Lans 126 D2
Abson S Glos 32 D10
Abthorpe Nhants 48 H5
Aby Lincs 87 M5
Acaster Malbis C York 98 B11
Acaster Selby N York 91 P2
Accrington Lancs 89 M5
Acha Ag & B 136 F5
Achahoish Ag & B 123 N4
Achalader P & K 141 R8
Achaleven Ag & B 138 G11
Acha Mor W Isls 168 i5
Achanalt Highld 155 J5
Achandunie Highld 156 A3
Achany Highld 162 D6
Acharacle Highld 138 B4
Acharn Highld 138 C7
Acharn P & K 141 J9
Achavanich Highld 167 L8
Achduart Highld 160 G6
Achfary Highld 164 G9
A'Chill Highld 144 C6
Achiltibuie Highld 160 G5
Achina Highld 166 B4
Achinhoan Ag & B 120 E8
Achintee Highld 154 B9
Achintraid Highld 153 Q10
Achmelvich Highld 160 H2
Achmore Highld 153 R11
Achmore W Isls 168 i5
Achnacarnin Highld 164 B10
Achnacarry Highld 146 F10
Achnacloich Highld 145 J6
Achnaconeran Highld 147 L4
Achnacroish Ag & B 138 F9
Achnadrish House Ag & B 137 M5
Achnafauld P & K 141 L10
Achnagarron Highld 156 B3
Achnaha Highld 137 M2
Achnahaird Highld 160 G4
Achnahannet Highld 148 H2
Achnairn Highld 162 D4
Achnalea Highld 138 F5
Achnamara Ag & B 130 F10
Achnasheen Highld 154 G6
Achnashellach Highld 154 D8
Achnastank Moray 157 P11
Achosnich Highld 137 L2
Achranich Highld 138 C8
Achreamie Highld 166 H3
Achriabhach Highld 139 L4
Achriesgill Highld 164 G6
Achtoty Highld 165 Q4
Achurch Nhants 61 M4
Achvaich Highld 162 G8
Achvarasdal Highld 166 G4
Ackergill Highld 167 Q6
Acklam Middsb 104 E7
Acklam N York 98 F8
Ackleton Shrops 57 P5
Acklington Nthumb 119 P10
Ackton Wakefd 91 L6
Ackworth Moor Top Wakefd 91 L7
Acle Norfk 77 N9
Acock's Green Birm 58 H8
Acol Kent 39 P8
Acomb C York 98 B10
Acomb Nthumb 112 D7
Acombe Somset 10 D2
Aconbury Herefs 45 Q8
Acre Lancs 89 M6
Acrefair Wrexhm 69 J6
Acton Ches E 70 A4
Acton Dorset 12 G9
Acton Gt Lon 36 F4
Acton Shrops 56 E8
Acton Staffs 70 E6
Acton Suffk 52 E2
Acton Worcs 58 B11
Acton Wrexhm 69 K4
Acton Beauchamp Herefs 46 C4
Acton Bridge Ches W 82 C9
Acton Burnell Shrops 57 J4
Acton Green Herefs 46 C4
Acton Pigott Shrops 57 J4
Acton Round Shrops 57 L5
Acton Scott Shrops 56 H7
Acton Trussell Staffs 70 G11
Acton Turville S Glos 32 F8
Adbaston Staffs 70 D9
Adber Dorset 19 Q10
Adbolton Notts 72 F3
Adderbury Oxon 48 E7
Adderley Shrops 70 B7
Adderstone Nthumb 119 M4
Addiewell W Loth 126 H5
Addingham C Brad 96 G11
Addington Bucks 49 K9
Addington Gt Lon 37 J8
Addington Kent 37 Q9
Addiscombe Gt Lon 36 H7
Addlestone Surrey 36 C8
Addlestonemoor Surrey 36 C7
Addlethorpe Lincs 87 P7
Adeney Wrekin 70 B11
Adeyfield Herts 50 C9
Adfa Powys 55 P4
Adforton Herefs 56 G10
Adisham Kent 39 M11
Adlestrop Gloucs 47 P9
Adlingfleet E R Yk 92 D6
Adlington Ches E 83 K8
Adlington Lancs 89 J8
Admaston Staffs 71 J10
Admaston Wrekin 57 L2
Admington Warwks 47 P5
Adpar Cerdgn 42 F6
Adsborough Somset 19 J9
Adscombe Somset 18 G7
Adstock Bucks 49 K8
Adstone Nhants 48 G4
Adswood Stockp 83 J7
Adversane W Susx 24 C6
Advie Highld 157 L11
Adwalton Leeds 90 G5
Adwell Oxon 35 J5
Adwick le Street Donc 91 N9
Adwick upon Dearne Donc 91 M10
Ae D & G 109 L3
Ae Bridgend D & G 109 M3
Afan Forest Park Neath 29 N5
Affetside Bury 89 M8
Affleck Abers 158 E9
Affpuddle Dorset 12 D6
Affric Lodge Highld 146 F3
Afon-wen Flints 80 G10
Afon Wen Gwynd 66 G7
Afton Devon 7 L6
Afton IoW 13 P7
Agglethorpe N York 96 G3
Aigburth Lpool 81 M7
Aike E R Yk 99 L11
Aiketgate Cumb 111 J11
Aikhead Cumb 110 D11
Aikton Cumb 110 E10
Ailby Lincs 87 M5
Ailey Herefs 45 L5
Ailsworth C Pete 74 B11
Ainderby Quernhow N York 97 M4
Ainderby Steeple N York 97 M2
Aingers Green Essex 53 K7
Ainsdale Sefton 88 C8
Ainsdale-on-Sea Sefton 88 B8
Ainstable Cumb 111 K11
Ainsworth Bury 89 M8
Ainthorpe N York 105 K9
Aintree Sefton 81 M5
Ainville W Loth 127 L5
Aird Ag & B 130 F7
Aird D & G 106 E5
Aird W Isls 168 k4
Àird a' Mhulaidh W Isls 168 g6
Aird Asaig W Isls 168 g7
Aird Dhubh Highld 153 N9
Airdeny Ag & B 131 K2
Aird of Kinloch Ag & B 137 N10
Aird of Sleat Highld 145 J7
Airdrie N Lans 126 D4
Airdriehill N Lans 126 D4
Airds of Kells D & G 108 E6
Àird Uig W Isls 168 f4
Airidh a bhruaich W Isls 168 h6
Airieland D & G 108 G9
Airlie Angus 142 E7
Airmyn E R Yk 92 B6
Airntully P & K 141 Q10
Airor Highld 145 M6
Airth Falk 133 Q10
Airton N York 96 D9
Aisby Lincs 73 Q3
Aisby Lincs 85 Q2
Aisgill Cumb 102 E11
Aish Devon 6 H6
Aish Devon 7 L7
Aisholt Somset 18 G7
Aiskew N York 97 L3
Aislaby N York 98 F3
Aislaby N York 105 N9
Aislaby S on T 104 D8
Aisthorpe Lincs 86 B4
Aith Shet 169 q8
Akeld Nthumb 119 J5
Akeley Bucks 49 K7
Akenham Suffk 53 L2
Albaston Cnwll 5 Q7
Alberbury Shrops 56 F2
Albourne W Susx 24 G7
Albourne Green W Susx 24 G7
Albrighton Shrops 57 Q4
Albrighton Shrops 69 N11
Alburgh Norfk 65 K4
Albury Herts 51 K6
Albury Oxon 35 J3
Albury Surrey 36 B11
Albury End Herts 51 K6
Albury Heath Surrey 36 C11
Alby Hill Norfk 76 H5
Alcaig Highld 155 Q6
Alcaston Shrops 56 H7
Alcester Warwks 47 L3
Alcester Lane End Birm 58 G8
Alciston E Susx 25 M9
Alcombe Somset 18 C5
Alcombe Wilts 32 F11
Alconbury Cambs 61 Q5
Alconbury Weston Cambs 61 Q5
Aldborough N York 97 P7
Aldborough Norfk 76 H5
Aldbourne Wilts 33 Q9
Aldbrough E R Yk 93 M3
Aldbrough St John N York 103 P8
Aldbury Herts 35 Q2
Aldcliffe Lancs 95 K8
Aldclune P & K 141 L5
Aldeburgh Suffk 65 P10
Aldeby Norfk 65 N3
Aldenham Herts 50 D11
Alderbury Wilts 21 N9
Aldercar Derbys 84 F11
Alderford Norfk 76 G8
Alderholt Dorset 13 K2
Alderley Gloucs 32 E6
Alderley Edge Ches E 82 H9
Aldermans Green Covtry 59 N8
Aldermaston W Berk 34 G11
Alderminster Warwks 47 P5
Alder Moor Staffs 71 N9
Aldersey Green Ches W 69 N3
Aldershot Hants 23 N4
Alderton Gloucs 47 K8
Alderton Nhants 49 K5
Alderton Shrops 69 N10
Alderton Suffk 53 P3
Alderton Wilts 32 F8
Alderwasley Derbys 71 Q4
Aldfield N York 97 L7
Aldford Ches W 69 M3
Aldgate Rutlnd 73 P10
Aldham Essex 52 F6
Aldham Suffk 52 J2
Aldingbourne W Susx 15 P5
Aldingham Cumb 94 F6
Aldington Kent 27 J4
Aldington Worcs 47 L6
Aldington Corner Kent 27 J4
Aldivalloch Moray 150 B2
Aldochlay Ag & B 132 D9
Aldon Shrops 56 G9
Aldoth Cumb 109 P11
Aldreth Cambs 62 F6
Aldridge Wsall 58 G4
Aldringham Suffk 65 N9
Aldro N York 98 G8
Aldsworth Gloucs 33 N3
Aldsworth W Susx 15 L5
Aldunie Moray 150 B2
Aldwark Derbys 84 B9
Aldwark N York 97 Q8
Aldwick W Susx 15 P7
Aldwincle Nhants 61 M4
Aldworth W Berk 34 G9
Alexandria W Duns 125 K2
Aley Somset 18 G7
Alfardisworthy Devon 16 D9
Alfington Devon 10 C5
Alfold Surrey 24 B4
Alfold Bars W Susx 24 B4
Alfold Crossways Surrey 24 B3
Alford Abers 150 F4
Alford Lincs 87 N5
Alford Somset 20 B8
Alfreton Derbys 84 F9
Alfrick Worcs 46 D4
Alfrick Pound Worcs 46 D4
Alfriston E Susx 25 M10
Algarkirk Lincs 74 E3
Alhampton Somset 20 B8
Alkborough N Linc 92 E6
Alkerton Gloucs 32 E3
Alkerton Oxon 48 C6
Alkham Kent 27 N3
Alkington Shrops 69 P7
Alkmonton Derbys 71 M7
Allaleigh Devon 7 L8
Allanaquoich Abers 149 L9
Allanbank N Lans 126 E6
Allanton Border 129 M9
Allanton N Lans 126 E6
Allanton S Lans 126 C7
Allaston Gloucs 32 B4
Allbrook Hants 22 E10
All Cannings Wilts 21 L2
Allendale Nthumb 112 B9
Allen End Warwks 59 J5
Allenheads Nthumb 112 C11
Allensford Dur 112 G10
Allen's Green Herts 51 L7
Allensmore Herefs 45 P7
Allenton C Derb 72 B4
Aller Devon 17 P6
Aller Somset 19 M9
Allerby Cumb 100 E3
Allercombe Devon 9 P6
Aller Cross Devon 17 N6
Allerford Somset 18 B5
Allerston N York 98 H4
Allerthorpe E R Yk 98 F11
Allerton C Brad 90 E4
Allerton Highld 156 D4
Allerton Lpool 81 M7
Allerton Bywater Leeds 91 L5
Allerton Mauleverer N York 97 P9
Allesley Covtry 59 M8
Allestree C Derb 72 A3
Allet Common Cnwll 3 K4
Allexton Leics 73 L10
Allgreave Ches E 83 L11
Allhallows Medway 38 D6
Allhallows-on-Sea Medway 38 D6
Alligin Shuas Highld 153 Q6
Allimore Green Staffs 70 F11
Allington Dorset 11 K6
Allington Kent 38 C10
Allington Lincs 73 M2
Allington Wilts 21 L2
Allington Wilts 21 P7
Allington Wilts 32 G9
Allithwaite Cumb 94 H5
Alloa Clacks 133 P9
Allonby Cumb 100 E2
Allostock Ches W 82 F10
Alloway S Ayrs 114 F4
Allowenshay Somset 10 H2
All Saints South Elmham Suffk 65 L5
Allscott Shrops 57 N5
Allscott Wrekin 57 L2
All Stretton Shrops 56 H5
Alltami Flints 81 K11
Alltchaorunn Highld 139 M7
Alltmawr Powys 44 F5
Alltwalis Carmth 42 H8
Alltwen Neath 29 K4
Alltyblaca Cerdgn 43 K5
Allweston Dorset 11 P2
Allwood Green Suffk 64 E7
Almeley Herefs 45 L4
Almeley Wooton Herefs 45 L4
Almer Dorset 12 F5
Almholme Donc 91 P9
Almington Staffs 70 C8
Almodington W Susx 15 M7
Almondbank P & K 134 D2
Almondbury Kirk 90 F8
Almondsbury S Glos 32 B8
Alne N York 97 Q7
Alness Highld 156 B4
Alnham Nthumb 119 J8
Alnmouth Nthumb 119 P8
Alnwick Nthumb 119 N8
Alperton Gt Lon 36 E4
Alphamstone Essex 52 E4
Alpheton Suffk 64 B11
Alphington Devon 9 M6
Alpington Norfk 77 K11
Alport Derbys 84 B8
Alpraham Ches E 69 Q3
Alresford Essex 53 J7
Alrewas Staffs 59 J2
Alsager Ches E 70 D3
Alsagers Bank Staffs 70 D5
Alsop en le Dale Derbys 71 M4
Alston Cumb 111 P11
Alston Devon 10 G4
Alstone Gloucs 47 J8
Alstone Somset 19 K5
Alstonefield Staffs 71 L3
Alston Sutton Somset 19 M4
Alswear Devon 17 N7
Alt Oldham 83 K4
Altandhu Highld 160 F4
Altarnun Cnwll 5 L5
Altass Highld 162 C6
Altcreich Ag & B 138 B10
Altgaltraig Ag & B 124 C3
Altham Lancs 89 M4
Althorne Essex 38 F2
Althorpe N Linc 92 D9
Altnabreac Station Highld 166 H7
Altnaharra Highld 165 N9
Altofts Wakefd 91 K6
Alton Derbys 84 E8
Alton Hants 23 K7
Alton Staffs 71 K6
Alton Wilts 21 N5
Alton Barnes Wilts 21 M2
Alton Pancras Dorset 11 Q4
Alton Priors Wilts 21 M2
Alton Towers Staffs 71 K6
Altrincham Traffd 82 G7
Altskeith Hotel Stirlg 132 F7
Alva Clacks 133 P8
Alvanley Ches W 81 P10
Alvaston C Derb 72 B4
Alvechurch Worcs 58 F10
Alvecote Warwks 59 K4
Alvediston Wilts 21 J10
Alveley Shrops 57 P8
Alverdiscott Devon 17 J6
Alverstoke Hants 14 H7
Alverstone IoW 14 G9
Alverthorpe Wakefd 91 J6
Alverton Notts 73 K2
Alves Moray 157 L5
Alvescot Oxon 33 Q4
Alveston S Glos 32 B7
Alveston Warwks 47 P3
Alvingham Lincs 87 L2
Alvington Gloucs 32 B4
Alwalton C Pete 74 B11
Alwinton Nthumb 118 H9
Alwoodley Leeds 90 H2
Alwoodley Gates Leeds 91 J2
Alyth P & K 142 C8
Am Bàgh a Tuath W Isls 168 c17
Ambergate Derbys 84 D10
Amber Hill Lincs 86 H11
Amberley Gloucs 32 G4
Amberley W Susx 24 B8
Amber Row Derbys 84 E9
Amberstone E Susx 25 N8
Amble Nthumb 119 Q10
Amblecote Dudley 58 C7
Ambler Thorn C Brad 90 D5
Ambleside Cumb 101 L10
Ambleston Pembks 41 K5
Ambrosden Oxon 48 H11
Amcotts N Linc 92 E8
America Cambs 62 F5
Amersham Bucks 35 Q5
Amersham Common Bucks 35 Q5
Amersham Old Town Bucks 35 Q5
Amersham on the Hill Bucks 35 Q5
Amerton Staffs 70 H9
Amesbury Wilts 21 N6
Amhuinnsuidhe W Isls 168 f7
Amington Staffs 59 K4
Amisfield D & G 109 M4
Amlwch IoA 78 G6
Ammanford Carmth 28 H2
Amotherby N York 98 E6
Ampfield Hants 22 D10
Ampleforth N York 98 B5
Ampney Crucis Gloucs 33 L4
Ampney St Mary Gloucs 33 L4
Ampney St Peter Gloucs 33 L4
Amport Hants 22 B6
Ampthill C Beds 50 B3
Ampton Suffk 64 B7
Amroth Pembks 41 N9
Amulree P & K 141 L10
Amwell Herts 50 E8
Anaheilt Highld 138 E5
Ancaster Lincs 73 P2
Ancells Farm Hants 23 M3
Anchor Shrops 56 B7
Ancroft Nthumb 129 P11
Ancrum Border 118 B6
Ancton W Susx 15 Q6
Anderby Lincs 87 P5
Anderby Creek Lincs 87 Q5
Andersea Somset 19 K8
Andersfield Somset 18 H8
Anderson Dorset 12 E5
Anderton Ches W 82 D9
Anderton Cnwll 6 C8
Andover Hants 22 C5
Andoversford Gloucs 47 K11
Andreas IoM 80 f2
Anelog Gwynd 66 B9
Anerley Gt Lon 36 H7
Anfield Lpool 81 M6
Angarrack Cnwll 2 F6
Angarrick Cnwll 3 K6
Angelbank Shrops 57 K9
Angersleigh Somset 18 G11
Angerton Cumb 110 D9
Angle Pembks 40 G10
Anglesey IoA 78 G8
Anglesey Abbey Cambs 62 H8
Angmering W Susx 24 C10
Angram N York 97 R11
Angram N York 102 G11
Angrouse Cnwll 2 H10
Anick Nthumb 112 D7
Ankerville Highld 156 E3
Ankle Hill Leics 73 K7
Anlaby E R Yk 92 H5
Anmer Norfk 75 P5
Anmore Hants 15 J4
Annan D & G 110 C7
Annandale Water Services D & G 109 P2
Annaside Cumb 94 B3
Annat Highld 154 A7
Annathill N Lans 126 C3
Anna Valley Hants 22 C6
Annbank S Ayrs 114 H3
Anne Hathaway's Cottage Warwks 47 N4
Annesley Notts 84 H10
Annesley Woodhouse Notts 84 G10
Annfield Plain Dur 113 J10
Anniesland C Glas 125 N4
Annitsford N Tyne 113 L6
Annscroft Shrops 56 H3
Ansdell Lancs 88 C5
Ansford Somset 20 B8
Ansley Warwks 59 M6

Anslow Staffs 71 N9
Anslow Gate Staffs 71 M10
Anslow Lees Staffs 71 N10
Ansteadbrook Surrey 23 P8
Anstey Hants 23 K6
Anstey Herts 51 K4
Anstey Leics 72 F9
Anstruther Fife 135 P7
Ansty W Susx 24 G6
Ansty Warwks 59 P8
Ansty Wilts 21 J9
Ansty Cross Dorset 12 C4
Anthill Common Hants 14 H4
Anthonys Surrey 36 B8
Anthorn Cumb 110 C9
Antingham Norfk 77 K5
An t-Ob W Isls 168 f9
Antonine Wall 126 E2
Anton's Gowt Lincs 87 K11
Antony Cnwll 5 Q11
Antrobus Ches W 82 D9
Anvil Corner Devon 16 F11
Anvil Green Kent 27 K2
Anwick Lincs 86 F10
Anwoth D & G 108 C9
Aperfield Gt Lon 37 K9
Apes Dale Worcs 58 E10
Apethorpe Nhants 73 Q11
Apeton Staffs 70 F11
Apley Lincs 86 F5
Apperknowle Derbys 84 E5
Apperley Gloucs 46 G9
Apperley Bridge C Brad 90 F3
Apperley Dene Nthumb 112 G9
Appersett N York 96 C2
Appin Ag & B 138 G8
Appleby N Linc 92 G8
Appleby-in-Westmorland Cumb 102 C6
Appleby Magna Leics 59 M3
Appleby Parva Leics 59 M3
Appleby Street Herts 50 H10
Applecross Highld 153 N9
Appledore Devon 9 Q2
Appledore Devon 16 H5
Appledore Kent 26 G6
Appledore Heath Kent 26 G5
Appleford Oxon 34 F6
Applegarth Town D & G 109 P4
Applehaigh Wakefd 91 K8
Appleshaw Hants 22 B5
Applethwaite Cumb 101 J5
Appleton Halton 81 Q7
Appleton Oxon 34 D4
Appleton Warrtn 82 D8
Appleton-le-Moors N York 98 E3
Appleton-le-Street N York 98 E6
Appleton Roebuck N York 91 P2
Appleton Thorn Warrtn 82 D8
Appleton Wiske N York 104 C10
Appletreehall Border 117 Q7
Appletreewick N York 96 G8
Appley Somset 18 E10
Appley Bridge Lancs 88 G9
Apse Heath IoW 14 G10
Apsley End C Beds 50 D4
Apuldram W Susx 15 M6
Arabella Highld 156 E2
Arbirlot Angus 143 L9
Arborfield Wokham 35 L11
Arborfield Cross Wokham 35 L11
Arborfield Green Wokham 35 L11
Arbourthorne Sheff 84 E3
Arbroath Angus 143 L9
Arbuthnott Abers 143 P2
Arcadia Kent 26 E4
Archddu Carmth 28 D4
Archdeacon Newton Darltn 103 Q7
Archencarroch W Duns 132 E11
Archiestown Moray 157 N9
Archirondel Jersey 11 c1
Arclid Ches E 70 D2
Ardallie Abers 159 P10
Ardanaiseig Hotel Ag & B 131 M3
Ardaneaskan Highld 153 Q10
Ardarroch Highld 153 Q10
Ardbeg Ag & B 122 F10
Ardbeg Ag & B 124 D4
Ardbeg Ag & B 131 P11
Ardcharnich Highld 161 K9
Ardchiavaig Ag & B 137 K12
Ardchonnell Ag & B 131 K5
Ardchronie Highld 162 E9
Ardchullarie More Stirlg 132 H5
Arddarroch Ag & B 131 Q9
Arddleen Powys 69 J11
Ard Dorch Highld 145 J2
Ardechive Highld 146 E9
Ardeer N Ayrs 124 H9
Ardeley Herts 50 H5
Ardelve Highld 145 Q2
Arden Ag & B 132 D11
Ardens Grafton Warwks 47 M4
Ardentallen Ag & B 130 G3
Ardentinny Ag & B 131 P10
Ardentraive Ag & B 124 C3
Ardeonaig Stirlg 140 G10
Ardersier Highld 156 D7
Ardessie Highld 160 H9
Ardfern Ag & B 130 G7
Ardfernal Ag & B 123 J5
Ardgartan Ag & B 132 B7
Ardgay Highld 162 D8
Ardgour Highld 139 J5
Ardgowan Inver 124 G3
Ardhallow Ag & B 124 F3
Ardhasig W Isls 168 g7
Ardheslaig Highld 153 P6
Ardindrean Highld 161 K9
Ardingly W Susx 24 H5
Ardington Oxon 34 D7
Ardington Wick Oxon 34 D7
Ardlamont Ag & B 124 B4
Ardleigh Essex 53 J6
Ardleigh Heath Essex 52 H5
Ardler P & K 142 D9
Ardley Oxon 48 F9
Ardley End Essex 51 M8
Ardlui Ag & B 132 C4
Ardlussa Ag & B 130 C10
Ardmair Highld 161 J7
Ardmaleish Ag & B 124 D4
Ardminish Ag & B 123 K10
Ardmolich Highld 138 C3
Ardmore Ag & B 125 J2
Ardmore Highld 162 G9
Ardnadam Ag & B 131 P11
Ardnagrask Highld 155 P8
Ardnamurchan Highld 137 P2
Ardnarff Highld 154 A10
Ardnastang Highld 138 E5
Ardpatrick Ag & B 123 N8
Ardrishaig Ag & B 130 H10
Ardross Highld 155 R3
Ardrossan N Ayrs 124 G9
Ardsley Barns 91 K9
Ardsley East Leeds 91 J5
Ardslignish Highld 137 P3
Ardtalla Ag & B 122 G9
Ardtoe Highld 138 A3
Arduaine Ag & B 130 F5
Ardullie Highld 155 Q5
Ardvasar Highld 145 K7
Ardvorlich P & K 133 J3
Ardvourlie W Isls 168 g6
Ardwell D & G 106 F8
Ardwick Manch 83 J5
Areley Kings Worcs 57 P10
Arevegaig Highld 138 B4
Arford Hants 23 M7
Arglam E R Yk 92 C3
Argoed Caerph 30 G5
Argoed Shrops 69 K10
Argoed Mill Powys 44 D2
Argos Hill E Susx 25 N5
Argyll Forest Park Ag & B 131 Q7
Aribruach W Isls 168 h6
Aridhglas Ag & B 137 J11
Arileod Ag & B 136 F5
Arinagour Ag & B 136 G4
Ariogan Ag & B 130 H2
Arisaig Highld 145 L10
Arisaig House Highld 145 L11
Arkendale N York 97 N8
Arkesden Essex 51 L4
Arkholme Lancs 95 M6
Arkleby Cumb 100 F3
Arkleton D & G 110 G2
Arkle Town N York 103 K10
Arkley Gt Lon 50 F11
Arksey Donc 91 P9
Arkwright Town Derbys 84 F6
Arle Gloucs 46 H10
Arlecdon Cumb 100 D7
Arlescote Warwks 48 C5
Arlesey C Beds 50 E3
Arleston Wrekin 57 M2
Arley Ches E 82 E8
Arley Warwks 59 L6
Arlingham Gloucs 32 D2
Arlington Devon 17 L3
Arlington E Susx 25 M9
Arlington Gloucs 33 M3
Arlington Beccott Devon 17 L3
Armadale Highld 145 K7
Armadale Highld 166 C4
Armadale W Loth 126 G4
Armaside Cumb 100 G5
Armathwaite Cumb 111 K11
Arminghall Norfk 77 K11
Armitage Staffs 71 K11
Armitage Bridge Kirk 90 E8
Armley Leeds 90 H4
Armscote Warwks 47 P6
Armshead Staffs 70 G5
Armston Nhants 61 N3
Armthorpe Donc 91 Q10
Arnabost Ag & B 136 G3
Arnaby Cumb 94 D4
Arncliffe N York 96 D6
Arncliffe Cote N York 96 D6
Arncroach Fife 135 N6
Arndilly House Moray 157 P8
Arne Dorset 12 G7
Arnesby Leics 60 D2
Arngask P & K 134 E5
Arnisdale Highld 145 P5
Arnish Highld 153 K8
Arniston Mdloth 127 Q5
Arnol W Isls 168 i3
Arnold E R Yk 93 K2
Arnold Notts 85 J11
Arnprior Stirlg 133 J9
Arnside Cumb 95 K5
Aros Ag & B 137 P6
Arowry Wrexhm 69 N7
Arrad Foot Cumb 94 G4
Arram E R Yk 92 H2
Arran N Ayrs 120 H4
Arrathorne N York 97 K2
Arreton IoW 14 F9
Arrina Highld 153 N6
Arrington Cambs 62 D10
Arrochar Ag & B 132 B7
Arrow Warwks 47 L3
Arrowfield Top Worcs 58 F10
Arscott Shrops 56 G3
Artafallie Highld 156 A8
Arthington Leeds 90 H2
Arthingworth Nhants 60 G4
Arthog Gwynd 54 E2
Arthrath Abers 159 N10
Arthursdale Leeds 91 K3
Artrochie Abers 159 P11
Arundel W Susx 24 B9
Asby Cumb 100 E6
Ascog Ag & B 124 E5
Ascot W & M 35 P11
Ascott Warwks 48 B8
Ascott Earl Oxon 48 B11
Ascott-under-Wychwood Oxon 48 B11
Asenby N York 97 N5
Asfordby Leics 73 J7
Asfordby Hill Leics 73 J7
Asgarby Lincs 86 F11
Asgarby Lincs 87 K7
Ash Devon 7 L9
Ash Devon 17 J10
Ash Dorset 12 E2
Ash Kent 37 P8
Ash Kent 39 N10
Ash Somset 19 J10
Ash Somset 19 N10
Ash Surrey 23 P4
Ashampstead W Berk 34 G9
Ashampstead Green W Berk 34 G9
Ashbocking Suffk 64 H11
Ashbourne Derbys 71 M5
Ashbrittle Somset 18 E10
Ashburnham Place E Susx 25 Q8
Ashburton Devon 7 K4
Ashbury Devon 8 D5
Ashbury Oxon 33 Q7
Ashby N Linc 92 E9
Ashby by Partney Lincs 87 M7
Ashby cum Fenby NE Lin 93 N10
Ashby de la Launde Lincs 86 E9
Ashby-de-la-Zouch Leics 72 B7
Ashby Folville Leics 73 J8
Ashby Magna Leics 60 C2
Ashby Parva Leics 60 B3
Ashby Puerorum Lincs 87 K6
Ashby St Ledgers Nhants 60 C7
Ashby St Mary Norfk 77 L11
Ashchurch Gloucs 46 H8
Ashcombe Devon 9 M9
Ashcombe N Som 19 K2
Ashcott Somset 19 M7
Ashdon Essex 51 N2
Ashdown Forest E Susx 25 L4
Ashe Hants 22 F4
Asheldham Essex 52 G11
Ashen Essex 52 B3
Ashendon Bucks 35 K2
Asheridge Bucks 35 P4
Ashfield Hants 22 C11
Ashfield Herefs 46 A10
Ashfield Stirlg 133 M7
Ashfield cum Thorpe Suffk 65 J9
Ashfield Green Suffk 63 N9
Ashfield Green Suffk 65 K7
Ashfold Crossways W Susx 24 F5
Ashford Devon 6 H9
Ashford Devon 17 J4
Ashford Kent 26 H3
Ashford Surrey 36 C6
Ashford Bowdler Shrops 57 J10
Ashford Carbonell Shrops 57 J10
Ashford Hill Hants 22 G2
Ashford in the Water Derbys 83 Q11
Ashgill S Lans 126 D7
Ash Green Surrey 23 P5
Ash Green Warwks 59 M8
Ashill Devon 10 B2
Ashill Norfk 76 B11
Ashill Somset 19 K11
Ashingdon Essex 38 E3
Ashington BCP 12 H5
Ashington Nthumb 113 L3
Ashington Somset 19 Q10
Ashington W Susx 24 D7
Ashkirk Border 117 P6
Ashlett Hants 14 E6
Ashleworth Gloucs 46 F9
Ashleworth Quay Gloucs 46 F9
Ashley Cambs 63 L8
Ashley Ches E 82 G8
Ashley Devon 17 M9
Ashley Dorset 13 K4
Ashley Gloucs 32 H6
Ashley Hants 13 N5
Ashley Hants 22 C8
Ashley Kent 27 P2
Ashley Nhants 60 G2
Ashley Staffs 70 D7
Ashley Wilts 32 F11
Ashley Green Bucks 35 Q3
Ashleyhay Derbys 71 P4
Ashley Heath Dorset 13 K4
Ashley Moor Herefs 56 H11
Ash Magna Shrops 69 Q7
Ashmansworth Hants 22 D3
Ashmansworthy Devon 16 E8
Ashmead Green Gloucs 32 E5
Ashmill Devon 5 P2
Ash Mill Devon 17 P7
Ashmore Dorset 20 H11
Ashmore Green W Berk 34 F11
Ashorne Warwks 48 B3
Ashover Derbys 84 D8
Ashover Hay Derbys 84 D8
Ashow Warwks 59 M10
Ash Parva Shrops 69 Q7
Ashperton Herefs 46 B6
Ashprington Devon 7 L7
Ash Priors Somset 18 G9
Ashreigney Devon 17 L9
Ash Street Suffk 52 H2
Ashtead Surrey 36 E9
Ash Thomas Devon 9 P2
Ashton C Pete 74 B9
Ashton Ches W 81 Q11
Ashton Cnwll 2 G8
Ashton Devon 9 L8
Ashton Hants 22 F11
Ashton Herefs 45 Q2
Ashton Inver 124 G2
Ashton Nhants 49 L5
Ashton Nhants 61 N3
Ashton Somset 19 M5
Ashton Common Wilts 20 G3
Ashton Hill Wilts 20 H3
Ashton-in-Makerfield Wigan 82 C5
Ashton Keynes Wilts 33 K6
Ashton under Hill Worcs 47 J7
Ashton-under-Lyne Tamesd 83 K5
Ashton upon Mersey Traffd 82 G6
Ashton Vale Bristl 31 Q10
Ashurst Hants 13 P2
Ashurst Kent 25 M3
Ashurst Lancs 88 F9
Ashurst W Susx 24 E7
Ashurstwood W Susx 25 K3
Ash Vale Surrey 23 N4
Ashwater Devon 5 P2
Ashwell Herts 50 G3
Ashwell Rutlnd 73 M8
Ashwell Somset 19 L11
Ashwell End Herts 50 G2
Ashwellthorpe Norfk 64 G2
Ashwick Somset 20 B5
Ashwicken Norfk 75 P7
Ashwood Staffs 58 C7
Askam in Furness Cumb 94 E5
Askern Donc 91 P8
Askerswell Dorset 11 L6
Askett Bucks 35 M3
Askham Cumb 101 P6
Askham Notts 85 M6
Askham Bryan C York 98 B11
Askham Richard C York 98 A11
Asknish Ag & B 131 J9
Askrigg N York 96 D2
Askwith N York 97 J11
Aslackby Lincs 74 A4
Aslacton Norfk 64 H3
Aslockton Notts 73 J3
Asney Somset 19 N7
Aspall Suffk 64 H9
Aspatria Cumb 100 F2
Aspenden Herts 51 J5
Aspenshaw Derbys 83 M7
Asperton Lincs 74 E3
Aspley Staffs 70 E8
Aspley Guise C Beds 49 P7
Aspley Heath C Beds 49 P8
Aspley Heath Warwks 58 G10
Aspull Wigan 89 J9
Aspull Common Wigan 82 D5
Asselby E R Yk 92 B5
Asserby Lincs 87 N5
Asserby Turn Lincs 87 N5
Assington Suffk 52 F4
Assington Green Suffk 63 N10
Astbury Ches E 70 E2
Astcote Nhants 49 J4
Asterby Lincs 87 J5
Asterley Shrops 56 F3
Asterton Shrops 56 F6
Asthall Oxon 33 Q2
Asthall Leigh Oxon 34 B2
Astle Highld 162 G8
Astley Shrops 69 P11
Astley Warwks 59 M7
Astley Wigan 82 F4
Astley Worcs 57 P11
Astley Abbots Shrops 57 N5
Astley Bridge Bolton 89 L8
Astley Cross Worcs 57 Q11
Astley Green Wigan 82 F5
Aston Birm 58 G7
Aston Ches E 69 R5
Aston Ches W 82 C9
Aston Derbys 83 Q8
Aston Flints 81 L11
Aston Herefs 45 P2
Aston Herts 50 G6
Aston Oxon 34 B4
Aston Rothm 84 G3
Aston Shrops 57 Q6
Aston Shrops 69 P9
Aston Staffs 70 D6
Aston Staffs 70 F10
Aston Wokham 35 L8
Aston Wrekin 57 L3
Aston Abbotts Bucks 49 M10
Aston Botterell Shrops 57 L8
Aston-by-Stone Staffs 70 G8
Aston Cantlow Warwks 47 M2
Aston Clinton Bucks 35 N2
Aston Crews Herefs 46 C10
Aston Cross Gloucs 46 H8
Aston End Herts 50 G6
Aston-Eyre Shrops 57 M6
Aston Fields Worcs 58 E11
Aston Flamville Leics 59 Q6
Aston Heath Ches W 82 C9
Aston Ingham Herefs 46 C10
Aston juxta Mondrum Ches E 70 A3
Aston le Walls Nhants 48 E4
Aston Magna Gloucs 47 N7
Aston Munslow Shrops 57 J7
Aston-on-Carrant Gloucs 46 H8
Aston on Clun Shrops 56 F8
Aston Pigott Shrops 56 E3
Aston Rogers Shrops 56 E3
Aston Rowant Oxon 35 K5
Aston Sandford Bucks 35 L3
Aston Somerville Worcs 47 K7
Aston-sub-Edge Gloucs 47 M6
Aston Tirrold Oxon 34 G7
Aston-upon-Trent Derbys 72 C5
Aston Upthorpe Oxon 34 G7
Astrop Nhants 48 F7
Astrope Herts 35 N2
Astwick C Beds 50 F3
Astwith Derbys 84 F8
Astwood M Keyn 49 Q5
Astwood Worcs 58 D11
Astwood Bank Worcs 47 K2
Aswarby Lincs 73 R3
Aswardby Lincs 87 L6
Atcham Shrops 57 J3
Atch Lench Worcs 47 K4
Athelhampton Dorset 12 C6
Athelington Suffk 65 J7
Athelney Somset 19 K9
Athelstaneford E Loth 128 E4
Atherfield Green IoW 14 E11
Atherington Devon 17 K7
Atherington W Susx 24 B10
Atherstone Somset 19 L11
Atherstone Warwks 59 M5
Atherstone on Stour Warwks 47 P4
Atherton Wigan 82 E4
Atley Hill N York 103 Q10
Atlow Derbys 71 N5
Attadale Highld 154 B10
Attenborough Notts 72 E4
Atterby Lincs 86 C2
Attercliffe Sheff 84 E3
Atterley Shrops 57 L5
Atterton Leics 72 B11
Attingham Park Shrops 57 J2
Attleborough Norfk 64 E2
Attleborough Warwks 59 N6
Attlebridge Norfk 76 G8
Attleton Green Suffk 63 M10
Atwick E R Yk 99 P10
Atworth Wilts 32 G11
Auberrow Herefs 45 P5
Aubourn Lincs 86 B8
Auchbreck Moray 149 N2
Auchedly Abers 159 L11
Auchenblae Abers 143 N2
Auchenbowie Stirlg 133 M10
Auchencairn D & G 108 G10
Auchencairn D & G 109 L4
Auchencairn N Ayrs 121 K6
Auchencrow Border 129 M7
Auchendinny Mdloth 127 P5
Auchengray S Lans 126 H7
Auchenhalrig Moray 157 R5
Auchenheath S Lans 126 E9
Auchenhessnane D & G 115 R8
Auchenlochan Ag & B 124 B3
Auchenmade N Ayrs 125 K8
Auchenmalg D & G 106 H7
Auchentiber N Ayrs 125 K8
Auchindrain Ag & B 131 L7
Auchindrean Highld 161 K10
Auchininna Abers 158 G8
Auchinleck E Ayrs 115 L3
Auchinloch N Lans 126 B3
Auchinstarry N Lans 126 C2
Auchintore Highld 139 K3
Auchiries Abers 159 Q10
Auchlean Highld 148 F8
Auchlee Abers 151 M8
Auchleven Abers 150 G3
Auchlochan S Lans 126 E10
Auchlossan Abers 150 F7
Auchlyne Stirlg 132 G2
Auchmillan E Ayrs 115 K2
Auchmithie Angus 143 M9
Auchmuirbridge Fife 134 G7
Auchnacree Angus 142 H5
Auchnagatt Abers 159 M9
Auchnarrow Moray 149 N3
Auchnotteroch D & G 106 C5
Auchroisk Moray 157 Q7
Auchterarder P & K 133 Q5
Auchteraw Highld 147 K6
Auchterblair Highld 148 G3
Auchtercairn Highld 153 Q2
Auchterderran Fife 134 G8
Auchterhouse Angus 142 E10
Auchterless Abers 158 H9
Auchtermuchty Fife 134 G5
Auchterneed Highld 155 N6
Auchtertool Fife 134 G9
Auchtertyre Highld 145 P2
Auchtubh Stirlg 132 H3
Auckengill Highld 167 Q4
Auckley Donc 91 Q10
Audenshaw Tamesd 83 K5
Audlem Ches E 70 B6
Audley Staffs 70 D4
Audley End Essex 51 M3
Audley End Essex 52 D4
Audley End Suffk 64 B11
Audley End House & Gardens Essex 51 M3
Audmore Staffs 70 E10
Audnam Dudley 58 C7
Aughertree Cumb 101 J3
Aughton E R Yk 92 B3
Aughton Lancs 88 D9
Aughton Lancs 95 M7
Aughton Rothm 84 G3
Aughton Wilts 21 P3
Aughton Park Lancs 88 E9
Auldearn Highld 156 G6
Aulden Herefs 45 P4
Auldgirth D & G 109 K3
Auldhouse S Lans 125 Q7
Ault a' chruinn Highld 146 A3
Aultbea Highld 160 D9
Aultgrishin Highld 160 A9
Aultguish Inn Highld 155 L3
Ault Hucknall Derbys 84 G7
Aultmore Moray 158 B7
Aultnagoire Highld 147 N3
Aultnamain Highld 162 F10
Aunby Lincs 73 Q8
Aunk Devon 9 P4
Aunsby Lincs 73 Q3
Aust S Glos 31 Q7
Austendike Lincs 74 E6
Austerfield Donc 85 L2
Austerlands Oldham 90 B9
Austhorpe Leeds 91 K4
Austonley Kirk 90 E9
Austrey Warwks 59 L3
Austwick N York 95 R7
Authorpe Lincs 87 L4
Authorpe Row Lincs 87 P6
Avebury Wilts 33 M11
Avebury Wilts 33 M11
Avebury Trusloe Wilts 33 L11
Aveley Thurr 37 N4
Avening Gloucs 32 G5
Averham Notts 85 N10
Aveton Gifford Devon 6 H9
Aviemore Highld 148 F5
Avington W Berk 34 C11
Avoch Highld 156 C6
Avon Hants 13 K5
Avonbridge Falk 126 G3
Avon Dassett Warwks 48 D4
Avonmouth Bristl 31 P9
Avonwick Devon 7 J7
Awbridge Hants 22 B10
Awkley S Glos 31 Q7
Awliscombe Devon 10 C4
Awre Gloucs 32 D3
Awsworth Notts 72 D2
Axborough Worcs 58 C9
Axbridge Somset 19 M4
Axford Hants 22 H6
Axford Wilts 33 P10
Axmansford Hants 22 G2
Axminster Devon 10 F5
Axmouth Devon 10 F6
Axton Flints 80 G8
Aycliffe Dur 103 Q6
Aydon Nthumb 112 F7
Aylburton Gloucs 32 B4
Ayle Nthumb 111 P11
Aylesbeare Devon 9 P6
Aylesbury Bucks 35 M2
Aylesby NE Lin 93 M9
Aylesford Kent 38 B10
Aylesham Kent 39 M11
Aylestone C Leic 72 F10
Aylestone Park C Leic 72 F10
Aylmerton Norfk 76 H4
Aylsham Norfk 76 H6
Aylton Herefs 46 C7
Aylworth Gloucs 47 M10
Aymestrey Herefs 56 G11
Aynho Nhants 48 F8
Ayot Green Herts 50 F8
Ayot St Lawrence Herts 50 E7
Ayot St Peter Herts 50 F7
Ayr S Ayrs 114 F3
Aysgarth N York 96 F3
Ayshford Devon 18 D11
Ayside Cumb 94 H4
Ayston Rutlnd 73 M10

Aythorpe Roding Essex 51 N7
Ayton Border 129 N7
Azerley N York 97 L6

B

Babbacombe Torbay 7 N5
Babbington Notts 72 D2
Babbinswood Shrops 69 K9
Babbs Green Herts 51 J7
Babcary Somset 19 Q9
Babel Carmth 44 A7
Babel Green Suffk 63 M11
Babell Flints 80 H10
Babeny Devon 8 G9
Bablock Hythe Oxon 34 D4
Babraham Cambs 62 H10
Babworth Notts 85 L4
Bachau IoA 78 G8
Bache Shrops 56 H8
Bacheldre Powys 56 C6
Bachelor's Bump E Susx 26 D9
Backaland Ork 169 e3
Backbarrow Cumb 94 H4
Backe Carmth 41 Q7
Backfolds Abers 159 P7
Backford Ches W 81 M10
Backford Cross Ches W 81 M10
Backies Highld 163 J6
Back of Keppoch Highld 145 L10
Back o' th' Brook Staffs 71 K4
Back Street Suffk 63 M9
Backwell N Som 31 N11
Backworth N Tyne 113 M6
Bacon's End Solhll 59 J7
Baconsthorpe Norfk 76 G4
Bacton Herefs 45 M8
Bacton Norfk 77 L5
Bacton Suffk 64 F8
Bacton Green Suffk 64 E8
Bacup Lancs 89 P6
Badachro Highld 153 P3
Badanloch Highld 166 C10
Badbury Swindn 33 N8
Badby Nhants 60 C9
Badcall Highld 164 F5
Badcaul Highld 160 G8
Baddeley Edge C Stke 70 G4
Baddeley Green C Stke 70 G4
Baddesley Clinton Warwks 59 K10
Baddesley Ensor Warwks 59 L5
Baddidarrach Highld 160 H2
Baddinsgill Border 127 L7
Badenscoth Abers 158 G10
Badentarbet Highld 160 G5
Badenyon Abers 149 Q4
Badersfield Norfk 77 K7
Badgall Cnwll 5 L4
Badgeney Cambs 74 H11
Badger Shrops 57 P5
Badger's Cross Cnwll 2 D7
Badgers Mount Kent 37 L8
Badgeworth Gloucs 46 H11
Badgworth Somset 19 L4
Badharlick Cnwll 5 M4
Badicaul Highld 145 N2
Badingham Suffk 65 L8
Badlesmere Kent 38 H11
Badlieu Border 116 F7
Badlipster Highld 167 M7
Badluarach Highld 160 F8
Badninish Highld 162 H8
Badrallach Highld 160 H8
Badsey Worcs 47 L6
Badshot Lea Surrey 23 N5
Badsworth Wakefd 91 M8
Badwell Ash Suffk 64 D8
Badwell Green Suffk 64 E8
Bagber Dorset 12 C2
Bagby N York 97 Q4
Bag Enderby Lincs 87 L6
Bagendon Gloucs 33 K3
Bagginswood Shrops 57 M8
Baggrow Cumb 100 G2
Bàgh a' Chaisteil W Isls 168 b18
Bagham Kent 39 J11
Bagillt Flints 81 J9
Baginton Warwks 59 M10
Baglan Neath 29 K6
Bagley Leeds 90 G3
Bagley Shrops 69 M9
Bagley Somset 19 N5
Bagmore Hants 23 J6
Bagnall Staffs 70 G4
Bagnor W Berk 34 E11
Bagshot Surrey 23 P2
Bagshot Wilts 34 B11
Bagstone S Glos 32 C7
Bagthorpe Notts 84 G10
Bagworth Leics 72 C9
Bagwy Llydiart Herefs 45 N9
Baildon C Brad 90 F3
Baildon Green C Brad 90 E3
Baile Ailein W Isls 168 h5
Baile a' Mhanaich W Isls 168 c12
Baile Mòr Ag & B 136 H11
Bailey Green Hants 23 J9
Baileyhead Cumb 111 K5
Bailiff Bridge Calder 90 E5
Baillieston C Glas 126 B5
Bailrigg Lancs 95 K9
Bainbridge N York 96 D2
Bainshole Abers 158 F10
Bainton C Pete 74 A9
Bainton E R Yk 99 K10
Bainton Oxon 48 G9
Baintown Fife 135 K7
Bairnkine Border 118 C7
Baker's End Herts 51 J7
Baker Street Thurr 37 P4
Bakewell Derbys 84 B7
Bala Gwynd 68 B7
Balallan W Isls 168 h5
Balbeg Highld 155 M11
Balbeggie P & K 134 F2
Balblair Highld 155 P8
Balblair Highld 156 C4
Balby Donc 91 P10
Balcary D & G 108 H11
Balchraggan Highld 155 P9
Balchreick Highld 164 E4
Balcombe W Susx 24 H4
Balcombe Lane W Susx 24 H4
Balcomie Links Fife 135 Q6
Baldersby N York 97 N5
Baldersby St James N York 97 N5
Balderstone Lancs 89 J4
Balderstone Rochdl 89 Q8
Balderton Notts 85 P10
Baldhu Cnwll 3 K5
Baldinnie Fife 135 L5
Baldinnies P & K 134 C4
Baldock Herts 50 F4
Baldock Services Herts 50 F3
Baldovie C Dund 142 H11
Baldrine IoM 80 f5
Baldslow E Susx 26 D9
Baldwin IoM 80 e5
Baldwinholme Cumb 110 F10
Baldwin's Gate Staffs 70 D7
Baldwin's Hill W Susx 25 J3
Bale Norfk 76 E4
Baledgarno P & K 142 D11
Balemartine Ag & B 136 B7
Balerno C Edin 127 M4
Balfarg Fife 134 H7
Balfield Angus 143 J4
Balfour Ork 169 d5
Balfron Stirlg 132 G10
Balgaveny Abers 158 G9
Balgonar Fife 134 C9
Balgowan D & G 106 F9
Balgowan Highld 147 Q9
Balgown Highld 152 F4
Balgracie D & G 106 C5
Balgray S Lans 116 B6
Balham Gt Lon 36 G6
Balhary P & K 142 D8
Balholmie P & K 142 A10
Baligill Highld 166 E3
Balintore Angus 142 D6
Balintore Highld 156 F2
Balintraid Highld 156 C3
Balivanich W Isls 168 c12
Balk N York 97 Q4
Balkeerie Angus 142 E9
Balkholme E R Yk 92 C5
Ballabeg IoM 80 c7
Ballachulish Highld 139 K6
Ballafesson IoM 80 b7
Ballajora IoM 80 g3
Ballakilpheric IoM 80 b7
Ballamodha IoM 80 c7
Ballanlay Ag & B 124 C5
Ballantrae S Ayrs 114 A11
Ballards Gore Essex 38 F3
Ballards Green Warwks 59 L6
Ballasalla IoM 80 c7
Ballater Abers 150 B8
Ballaugh IoM 80 d3
Ballchraggan Highld 156 D2
Ballencrieff E Loth 128 D4
Ballevullin Ag & B 136 B6
Ball Green C Stke 70 F4
Ball Haye Green Staffs 70 H3
Ball Hill Hants 22 D2
Ballidon Derbys 71 N4
Balliekine N Ayrs 120 G4
Balliemore Ag & B 131 N8
Balligmorrie S Ayrs 114 D9
Ballimore Stirlg 132 G4
Ballindalloch Moray 157 M10
Ballindean P & K 134 H2
Ballingdon Suffk 52 E3
Ballinger Common Bucks 35 P4
Ballingham Herefs 46 A8
Ballingry Fife 134 F8
Ballinluig P & K 141 N7
Ballinshoe Angus 142 G7
Ballintuim P & K 141 R6
Balloch Highld 156 C8
Balloch N Lans 126 C3
Balloch P & K 133 N4
Balloch S Ayrs 114 F8
Balloch W Duns 132 D11
Balls Cross W Susx 23 Q9
Balls Green E Susx 25 L3
Ball's Green Gloucs 32 G5
Ballygown Ag & B 137 L7
Ballygrant Ag & B 122 E6
Ballyhaugh Ag & B 136 F4
Balmacara Highld 145 P2
Balmaclellan D & G 108 E5
Balmae D & G 108 E12
Balmaha Stirlg 132 E9
Balmalcolm Fife 135 J6
Balmangan D & G 108 D11
Balmedie Abers 151 P4
Balmer Heath Shrops 69 M8
Balmerino Fife 135 K3
Balmerlawn Hants 13 P4
Balmichael N Ayrs 120 H5
Balmore E Duns 125 P3
Balmuchy Highld 163 K11
Balmule Fife 134 G10
Balmullo Fife 135 L3
Balnacoil Highld 163 J4
Balnacra Highld 154 C8
Balnacroft Abers 149 P9
Balnafoich Highld 156 B10
Balnaguard P & K 141 M7
Balnahard Ag & B 137 M9
Balnain Highld 155 M11
Balnakeil Highld 165 J3
Balne N York 91 P7
Balquharn P & K 141 P10
Balquhidder Stirlg 132 G3
Balsall Common Solhll 59 K9
Balsall Heath Birm 58 G8
Balsall Street Solhll 59 K9
Balscote Oxon 48 C6
Balsham Cambs 63 J10
Baltasound Shet 169 t3
Balterley Staffs 70 D4
Balterley Green Staffs 70 D4
Balterley Heath Staffs 70 C4
Baltersan D & G 107 M5
Balthangie Abers 159 K7
Baltonsborough Somset 19 P8
Balvicar Ag & B 130 F4
Balvraid Highld 145 P4
Balvraid Highld 156 E11
Balwest Cnwll 2 F7
Bamber Bridge Lancs 88 H5
Bamber's Green Essex 51 N6
Bamburgh Nthumb 119 N4
Bamburgh Castle Nthumb 119 N3
Bamford Derbys 84 B4
Bamford Rochdl 89 P8
Bampton Cumb 101 P7
Bampton Devon 18 C10
Bampton Oxon 34 B4
Bampton Grange Cumb 101 P7
Banavie Highld 139 L2
Banbury Oxon 48 E6
Bancffosfelen Carmth 28 E2
Banchory Abers 150 H8
Banchory-Devenick Abers 151 N7
Bancycapel Carmth 28 D2
Bancyfelin Carmth 42 F11
Banc-y-ffordd Carmth 42 H7
Bandirran P & K 142 C11
Bandrake Head Cumb 94 G3
Banff Abers 158 G5
Bangor Gwynd 79 K10
Bangor-on-Dee Wrexhm 69 L5
Bangors Cnwll 5 L2
Bangor's Green Lancs 88 D9
Bangrove Suffk 64 C7
Banham Norfk 64 F4
Bank Hants 13 N3
Bankend D & G 109 M7
Bankfoot P & K 141 Q10
Bankglen E Ayrs 115 L5
Bank Ground Cumb 101 K11
Bankhead C Aber 151 N6
Bankhead S Lans 116 D2
Bank Newton N York 96 D10
Banknock Falk 126 D2
Banks Cumb 111 L8
Banks Lancs 88 D6
Banks Green Worcs 58 E11
Bankshill D & G 110 C4
Bank Street Worcs 46 B2
Bank Top Calder 90 E6
Bank Top Lancs 88 G9
Banningham Norfk 77 J6
Bannister Green Essex 51 Q6
Bannockburn Stirlg 133 N9
Banstead Surrey 36 G9
Bantham Devon 6 H10
Banton N Lans 126 C2
Banwell N Som 19 L3
Bapchild Kent 38 F9
Bapton Wilts 21 J7
Barabhas W Isls 168 i3
Barassie S Ayrs 125 J11
Barbaraville Highld 156 C3
Barber Booth Derbys 83 P8
Barber Green Cumb 94 H4
Barbieston S Ayrs 114 H4
Barbon Cumb 95 N4
Barbridge Ches E 69 R3
Barbrook Devon 17 N2
Barby Nhants 60 B6
Barcaldine Ag & B 138 H9
Barcheston Warwks 47 Q7
Barclose Cumb 110 H8
Barcombe E Susx 25 K8
Barcombe Cross E Susx 25 K7
Barcroft C Brad 90 C3
Barden N York 96 H2
Barden Park Kent 37 N11
Bardfield End Green Essex 51 P4
Bardfield Saling Essex 51 Q5
Bardney Lincs 86 F7
Bardon Leics 72 C8
Bardon Mill Nthumb 111 Q8
Bardowie E Duns 125 P3
Bardown E Susx 25 Q5
Bardrainney Inver 125 J3
Bardsea Cumb 94 G6
Bardsey Leeds 91 K2
Bardsey Island Gwynd 66 A10
Bardsley Oldham 83 K4
Bardwell Suffk 64 C7
Bare Lancs 95 K8
Bareppa Cnwll 3 K8
Barfad D & G 107 K4
Barford Norfk 76 G10
Barford Warwks 47 Q2
Barford St John Oxon 48 D8
Barford St Martin Wilts 21 L8
Barford St Michael Oxon 48 D8
Barfrestone Kent 39 N11
Bargate Derbys 84 E11
Bargeddie N Lans 126 B5
Bargoed Caerph 30 G5
Bargrennan D & G 107 L2
Barham Cambs 61 P5
Barham Kent 39 M11
Barham Suffk 64 G11
Bar Hill Cambs 62 E8
Barholm Lincs 74 A8
Barkby Leics 72 G9
Barkby Thorpe Leics 72 G9
Barkers Green Shrops 69 P9
Barkestone-le-Vale Leics 73 K4
Barkham Wokham 35 L11
Barking Gt Lon 37 K4
Barking Suffk 64 F11
Barkingside Gt Lon 37 K3
Barking Tye Suffk 64 F11
Barkisland Calder 90 D7
Barkla Shop Cnwll 3 J3
Barkston Lincs 73 N2
Barkston Ash N York 91 M3
Barkway Herts 51 J3
Barlanark C Glas 126 B5
Barlaston Staffs 70 F7
Barlavington W Susx 23 Q11
Barlborough Derbys 84 G5
Barlby N York 91 Q4
Barlestone Leics 72 C9
Barley Herts 51 K3
Barley Lancs 89 N2
Barleycroft End Herts 51 K5
Barley Hole Rothm 91 K11
Barleythorpe Rutlnd 73 L9
Barling Essex 38 F4
Barlings Lincs 86 E6
Barlochan D & G 108 H9
Barlow Derbys 84 D6
Barlow Gatesd 113 J8
Barlow N York 91 Q5
Barmby Moor E R Yk 98 F11
Barmby on the Marsh E R Yk 92 A5
Barmer Norfk 75 R4
Barming Heath Kent 38 B10
Barmollack Ag & B 120 F3
Barmouth Gwynd 67 L11
Barmpton Darltn 104 B7
Barmston E R Yk 99 P9
Barnaby Green Suffk 65 P5
Barnacarry Ag & B 131 L9
Barnack C Pete 74 A9
Barnacle Warwks 59 N8
Barnard Castle Dur 103 L7
Barnard Gate Oxon 34 D2
Barnardiston Suffk 63 M11
Barnbarroch D & G 108 H9
Barnburgh Donc 91 M10
Barnby Suffk 65 P4
Barnby Dun Donc 91 Q9
Barnby in the Willows Notts 85 Q10
Barnby Moor Notts 85 L4
Barncorkrie D & G 106 E10
Barnehurst Gt Lon 37 L5
Barnes Gt Lon 36 F5
Barnes Street Kent 37 P11
Barnet Gt Lon 50 F11
Barnetby le Wold N Linc 93 J9
Barnet Gate Gt Lon 50 F11
Barney Norfk 76 D5
Barnham Suffk 64 B6
Barnham W Susx 15 Q6
Barnham Broom Norfk 76 F10
Barnhead Angus 143 M6
Barnhill C Dund 142 H11
Barnhill Ches W 69 N4
Barnhill Moray 157 L6
Barnhills D & G 106 C3
Barningham Dur 103 L8
Barningham Suffk 64 D6
Barnoldby le Beck NE Lin 93 M10
Barnoldswick Lancs 96 C11
Barnsdale Bar Donc 91 N8
Barns Green W Susx 24 D5
Barnsley Barns 91 J9
Barnsley Gloucs 33 L4
Barnsole Kent 39 N10
Barnstaple Devon 17 K5
Barnston Essex 51 P7
Barnston Wirral 81 K8
Barnstone Notts 73 J3
Barnt Green Worcs 58 F10
Barnton C Edin 127 M3
Barnton Ches W 82 D10
Barnwell All Saints Nhants 61 M4
Barnwell St Andrew Nhants 61 N4
Barnwood Gloucs 46 G11
Baron's Cross Herefs 45 P3
Baronwood Cumb 101 P2
Barr S Ayrs 114 E9
Barra W Isls 168 b17
Barra Airport W Isls 168 c17
Barrachan D & G 107 L8
Barraigh W Isls 168 b17
Barrananaoil Ag & B 130 G6
Barrapoll Ag & B 136 A7
Barras Cumb 102 F8
Barrasford Nthumb 112 D6
Barregarrow IoM 80 d4
Barrets Green Ches E 69 Q3
Barrhead E Rens 125 M6
Barrhill S Ayrs 114 D11
Barrington Cambs 62 E11
Barrington Somset 19 L11
Barripper Cnwll 2 G6
Barrmill N Ayrs 125 K7
Barrock Highld 167 N2
Barrow Gloucs 46 G10
Barrow Lancs 89 L3
Barrow Rutlnd 73 M7
Barrow Shrops 57 M4
Barrow Somset 20 D8
Barrow Suffk 63 N8
Barroway Drove Norfk 75 L10
Barrow Bridge Bolton 89 K8
Barrow Burn Nthumb 118 G8
Barrowby Lincs 73 M3
Barrowden Rutlnd 73 N10
Barrowford Lancs 89 P3
Barrow Gurney N Som 31 P11
Barrow Haven N Linc 93 J6
Barrow Hill Derbys 84 F5
Barrow-in-Furness Cumb 94 E7
Barrow Island Cumb 94 D7
Barrow Nook Lancs 81 N4
Barrow's Green Ches E 70 B3
Barrow Street Wilts 20 F8
Barrow-upon-Humber N Linc 93 J6
Barrow upon Soar Leics 72 F7
Barrow upon Trent Derbys 72 B5
Barrow Vale BaNES 20 B2
Barry Angus 143 J11
Barry V Glam 30 F11
Barry Island V Glam 30 F11
Barsby Leics 72 H8
Barsham Suffk 65 M4
Barston Solhll 59 K9
Bartestree Herefs 45 R6
Barthol Chapel Abers 159 K11
Bartholomew Green Essex 52 B7
Barthomley Ches E 70 D4
Bartley Hants 13 P2
Bartley Green Birm 58 F8
Bartlow Cambs 63 J11
Barton Cambs 62 F9
Barton Ches W 69 M4
Barton Gloucs 47 L9
Barton Herefs 45 K3
Barton Lancs 88 D9
Barton Lancs 88 G3
Barton N York 103 P9
Barton Oxon 34 G3
Barton Torbay 7 N5
Barton Warwks 47 M4
Barton Bendish Norfk 75 P9
Barton End Gloucs 32 F5
Barton Green Staffs 71 M11
Barton Hartshorn Bucks 48 H8
Barton Hill N York 98 E8
Barton in Fabis Notts 72 E4
Barton in the Beans Leics 72 B9
Barton-le-Clay C Beds 50 C4
Barton-le-Street N York 98 E6
Barton-le-Willows N York 98 E8
Barton Mills Suffk 63 M6
Barton-on-Sea Hants 13 M6
Barton-on-the-Heath Warwks 47 Q8
Barton Park Services N York 103 P9
Barton St David Somset 19 P8
Barton Seagrave Nhants 61 J5
Barton Stacey Hants 22 D6
Barton Town Devon 17 M3
Barton Turf Norfk 77 M7
Barton-under-Needwood Staffs 71 M11
Barton-upon-Humber N Linc 92 H6
Barton upon Irwell Salfd 82 G5
Barton Waterside N Linc 92 H6
Barugh Barns 91 J9
Barugh Green Barns 91 J9
Barvas W Isls 168 i3
Barway Cambs 63 J5
Barwell Leics 72 C11
Barwick Devon 17 K10
Barwick Herts 51 J7
Barwick Somset 11 M2
Barwick in Elmet Leeds 91 L3
Baschurch Shrops 69 M10
Bascote Warwks 48 D2
Bascote Heath Warwks 48 C2
Base Green Suffk 64 E9
Basford Green Staffs 70 H4
Bashall Eaves Lancs 89 K2
Bashall Town Lancs 89 L2
Bashley Hants 13 M5
Basildon Essex 38 B4
Basingstoke Hants 22 H4
Baslow Derbys 84 C6
Bason Bridge Somset 19 K5
Bassaleg Newpt 31 J7
Bassendean Border 128 G10
Bassenthwaite Cumb 100 H4
Bassett C Sotn 22 D11
Bassingbourn-cum-Kneesworth Cambs 50 H2
Bassingfield Notts 72 G3
Bassingham Lincs 86 B9
Bassingthorpe Lincs 73 P5
Bassus Green Herts 50 H5
Basted Kent 37 P9
Baston Lincs 74 B8
Bastwick Norfk 77 N8
Batch Somset 19 K3
Batchworth Herts 36 C2
Batchworth Heath Herts 36 C2
Batcombe Dorset 11 N4
Batcombe Somset 20 C7
Bate Heath Ches E 82 E9
Batford Herts 50 D7
Bath BaNES 20 D2
Bath BaNES 20 E2
Bathampton BaNES 32 E11
Bathealton Somset 18 E10
Batheaston BaNES 32 E11
Bathford BaNES 32 E11
Bathgate W Loth 126 H4
Bathley Notts 85 N9
Bathpool Cnwll 5 M7
Bathpool Somset 19 J9
Bath Side Essex 53 N5
Bathville W Loth 126 G4
Bathway Somset 19 Q4
Batley Kirk 90 G6
Batsford Gloucs 47 N8
Batson Devon 7 J11
Battersby N York 104 G9
Battersea Gt Lon 36 G5
Battisborough Cross Devon 6 F9
Battisford Suffk 64 F11
Battisford Tye Suffk 64 E11
Battle E Susx 26 C8
Battle Powys 44 E8
Battleborough Somset 19 K4
Battledown Gloucs 47 J10
Battledykes Angus 142 H6
Battlefield Shrops 69 P11
Battlesbridge Essex 38 C3
Battlesden C Beds 49 Q9
Battleton Somset 18 B9
Battlies Green Suffk 64 C9
Battram Leics 72 C9
Battramsley Cross Hants 13 P5
Batt's Corner Hants 23 M6
Baughton Worcs 46 G6
Baughurst Hants 22 G2
Baulds Abers 150 G9
Baulking Oxon 34 B6
Baumber Lincs 86 H6
Baunton Gloucs 33 K4
Baveney Wood Shrops 57 M9
Baverstock Wilts 21 K8
Bawburgh Norfk 76 H10
Bawdeswell Norfk 76 E7
Bawdrip Somset 19 K7
Bawdsey Suffk 53 P3
Bawsey Norfk 75 N6
Bawtry Donc 85 K2
Baxenden Lancs 89 M5
Baxterley Warwks 59 L5
Baxter's Green Suffk 63 N9
Bay Highld 152 D7
Bayble W Isls 168 k4
Baybridge Hants 22 F10
Baybridge Nthumb 112 E10
Baycliff Cumb 94 F6
Baydon Wilts 33 Q9
Bayford Herts 50 H9
Bayford Somset 20 D9
Bayhead W Isls 168 c11
Bay Horse Lancs 95 K10
Bayley's Hill Kent 37 M10
Baylham Suffk 64 G11
Baynard's Green Oxon 48 F9
Baysdale Abbey N York 104 H9
Baysham Herefs 45 R9
Bayston Hill Shrops 56 H3
Baythorne End Essex 52 B3
Bayton Worcs 57 M10
Bayton Common Worcs 57 N10
Bayworth Oxon 34 E4
Beach S Glos 32 D10
Beachampton Bucks 49 L7
Beachamwell Norfk 75 Q9
Beachley Gloucs 31 Q6
Beachy Head E Susx 25 N11
Beacon Devon 10 D3
Beacon End Essex 52 G7
Beacon Hill Kent 26 D5
Beacon Hill Notts 85 P10
Beacon Hill Surrey 23 N7
Beacon's Bottom Bucks 35 L5
Beaconsfield Bucks 35 P6
Beaconsfield Services Bucks 35 Q7
Beadlam N York 98 D4
Beadlow C Beds 50 D3

Beadnell Nthumb 119 P5
Beaford Devon 17 K8
Beal N York 91 N5
Beal Nthumb 119 L2
Bealbury Cnwll 5 P8
Bealsmill Cnwll 5 P6
Beam Hill Staffs 71 N9
Beamhurst Staffs 71 K7
Beaminster Dorset 11 K4
Beamish Dur 113 K10
Beamish Museum Dur 113 K10
Beamsley N York 96 G10
Bean Kent 37 N6
Beanacre Wilts 32 H11
Beanley Nthumb 119 L7
Beardon Devon 8 D8
Beardwood Bl w D 89 K5
Beare Devon 9 N4
Beare Green Surrey 24 E2
Bearley Warwks 47 N2
Bearley Cross Warwks 47 N2
Bearpark Dur 103 P2
Bearsden E Duns 125 N3
Bearsted Kent 38 D10
Bearstone Shrops 70 C7
Bearwood BCP 12 H5
Bearwood Birm 58 F7
Bearwood Herefs 45 M3
Beattock D & G 116 F10
Beauchamp Roding Essex 51 N9
Beauchief Sheff 84 D4
Beaudesert Warwks 59 J11
Beaufort Blae G 30 G2
Beaulieu Hants 14 C6
Beaulieu Road Station Hants 13 P3
Beauly Highld 155 P8
Beaumaris IoA 79 L9
Beaumaris Castle IoA 79 L9
Beaumont Cumb 110 F9
Beaumont Essex 53 L7
Beaumont Jersey 11 b2
Beaumont Hill Darltn 103 Q7
Beaumont Leys C Leic 72 F9
Beausale Warwks 59 K10
Beauworth Hants 22 G9
Beaworthy Devon 8 C5
Beazley End Essex 52 B6
Bebington Wirral 81 L8
Bebside Nthumb 113 L4
Beccles Suffk 65 N4
Becconsall Lancs 88 F6
Beckbury Shrops 57 P4
Beckenham Gt Lon 37 J7
Beckermet Cumb 100 D9
Beckett End Norfk 75 Q11
Beckfoot Cumb 94 D3
Beckfoot Cumb 100 G10
Beck Foot Cumb 102 B11
Beckfoot Cumb 109 N11
Beckford Worcs 47 J7
Beckhampton Wilts 33 L11
Beck Hole N York 105 M10
Beckingham Lincs 85 Q10
Beckingham Notts 85 N3
Beckington Somset 20 F4
Beckjay Shrops 56 F9
Beckley E Susx 26 E7
Beckley Hants 13 M5
Beckley Oxon 34 G2
Beck Row Suffk 63 L5
Becks C Brad 96 F11
Beck Side Cumb 94 E4
Beck Side Cumb 94 H4
Beckton Gt Lon 37 K4
Beckwithshaw N York 97 L10
Becontree Gt Lon 37 L3
Becquet Vincent Jersey 11 b1
Bedale N York 97 L3
Bedburn Dur 103 L4
Bedchester Dorset 20 G11
Beddau Rhondd 30 E7
Beddgelert Gwynd 67 K5
Beddingham E Susx 25 K9
Beddington Gt Lon 36 H7
Beddington Corner Gt Lon 36 G7
Bedfield Suffk 65 J8
Bedfield Little Green Suffk 65 J8
Bedford Bed 61 M11
Bedgebury Cross Kent 26 B5
Bedgrove Bucks 35 M2
Bedham W Susx 24 B6
Bedhampton Hants 15 K5
Bedingfield Suffk 64 H8
Bedingfield Green Suffk 64 H8
Bedlam N York 97 L8
Bedlington Nthumb 113 L4
Bedlinog Myr Td 30 E4
Bedminster Bristl 31 Q10
Bedminster Down Bristl 31 Q10
Bedmond Herts 50 C10
Bednall Staffs 70 H11
Bedrule Border 118 B7
Bedstone Shrops 56 F9
Bedwas Caerph 30 G7
Bedwellty Caerph 30 G4
Bedworth Warwks 59 N7
Bedworth Woodlands Warwks 59 M7
Beeby Leics 72 H9
Beech Hants 23 J7
Beech Staffs 70 F7
Beech Hill W Berk 23 J2
Beechingstoke Wilts 21 L3
Beedon W Berk 34 E9
Beedon Hill W Berk 34 E9
Beeford E R Yk 99 N10
Beeley Derbys 84 C7
Beelsby NE Lin 93 M10
Beenham W Berk 34 G11
Beenham's Heath W & M 35 M9
Beeny Cnwll 5 J3
Beer Devon 10 E7
Beer Somset 19 M8
Beercrocombe Somset 19 K10
Beer Hackett Dorset 11 N2
Beesands Devon 7 L10
Beesby Lincs 87 N4
Beeson Devon 7 L10
Beeston C Beds 61 Q11
Beeston Ches W 69 P3
Beeston Leeds 90 H4
Beeston Norfk 76 C8
Beeston Notts 72 E3
Beeston Regis Norfk 76 H3
Beeswing D & G 109 J7
Beetham Cumb 95 K5
Beetham Somset 10 F2
Beetley Norfk 76 D8
Began Cardif 30 H8
Begbroke Oxon 34 E2
Begdale Cambs 75 J9
Begelly Pembks 41 M9
Beggarington Hill Leeds 90 H6
Beggar's Bush Powys 45 K2
Beguildy Powys 56 B9
Beighton Norfk 77 M10
Beighton Sheff 84 F4
Beinn Na Faoghla W Isls 168 d12
Beith N Ayrs 125 K7
Bekesbourne Kent 39 L10
Bekesbourne Hill Kent 39 L10
Belaugh Norfk 77 K8
Belbroughton Worcs 58 D9
Belchalwell Dorset 12 C3
Belchalwell Street Dorset 12 C3
Belchamp Otten Essex 52 D3
Belchamp St Paul Essex 52 C3
Belchamp Walter Essex 52 D3
Belchford Lincs 87 J5
Belford Nthumb 119 M4
Belgrave C Leic 72 F9
Belhaven E Loth 128 H4
Belhelvie Abers 151 N4
Belhinnie Abers 150 D2
Bellabeg Abers 150 B5
Bellamore Herefs 45 M6
Bellanoch Ag & B 130 F9
Bellasize E R Yk 92 D5
Bellaty Angus 142 C6
Bell Bar Herts 50 G9
Bell Busk N York 96 D9
Belleau Lincs 87 M5
Bell End Worcs 58 D9
Bellerby N York 96 H2
Bellever Devon 8 G9
Belle Vue Cumb 110 G9
Belle Vue Wakefd 91 J7
Bellfield S Lans 126 E11
Bell Heath Worcs 58 D9
Bell Hill Hants 23 K10
Bellingdon Bucks 35 P3
Bellingham Nthumb 112 B4
Belloch Ag & B 120 C4
Bellochantuy Ag & B 120 C5
Bell o' th' Hill Ches W 69 P5
Bellows Cross Dorset 13 J2
Bells Cross Suffk 64 H11
Bellshill N Lans 126 C5
Bellshill Nthumb 119 M4
Bellside N Lans 126 E6
Bellsquarry W Loth 127 K4
Bells Yew Green E Susx 25 P3
Belluton BaNES 20 B2
Belmaduthy Highld 156 A6
Belmesthorpe Rutlnd 73 Q8
Belmont Bl w D 89 K7
Belmont Gt Lon 36 G8
Belmont S Ayrs 114 F4
Belmont Shet 169 s3
Belnacraig Abers 150 B4
Belowda Cnwll 4 F9
Belper Derbys 84 D11
Belper Lane End Derbys 84 D11
Belph Derbys 84 H5
Belsay Nthumb 112 G5
Belses Border 117 R5
Belsford Devon 7 K7
Belsize Herts 50 B10
Belstead Suffk 53 K3
Belstone Devon 8 F6
Belthorn Bl w D 89 L6
Beltinge Kent 39 L8
Beltingham Nthumb 111 Q8
Beltoft N Linc 92 D9
Belton Leics 72 C6
Belton Lincs 73 N3
Belton N Linc 92 C9
Belton Norfk 77 P11
Belton House Lincs 73 N3
Belton in Rutland Rutlnd 73 L10
Beltring Kent 37 Q11
Belvedere Gt Lon 37 L5
Belvoir Leics 73 L4
Bembridge IoW 14 H9
Bemerton Wilts 21 M8
Bempton E R Yk 99 P6
Benacre Suffk 65 Q5
Benbecula W Isls 168 d12
Benbecula Airport W Isls 168 c12
Benbuie D & G 115 P8
Benderloch Ag & B 138 G10
Benenden Kent 26 D5
Benfieldside Dur 112 G10
Bengates Norfk 77 L6
Bengeo Herts 50 H8
Bengeworth Worcs 47 K6
Benhall Green Suffk 65 M9
Benhall Street Suffk 65 M9
Benholm Abers 143 Q4
Beningbrough N York 98 A9
Benington Herts 50 G6
Benington Lincs 87 L11
Benington Sea End Lincs 87 M11
Benllech IoA 79 J8
Benmore Ag & B 131 N10
Bennacott Cnwll 5 M3
Bennan N Ayrs 121 J7
Bennet Head Cumb 101 M6
Bennetland E R Yk 92 D5
Bennett End Bucks 35 L5
Ben Nevis Highld 139 M3
Benniworth Lincs 86 H4
Benover Kent 26 B2
Ben Rhydding C Brad 96 H11
Benslie N Ayrs 125 J9
Benson Oxon 34 H6
Bentfield Green Essex 51 M5
Benthall Shrops 57 M4
Bentham Gloucs 46 H11
Benthoul C Aber 151 L7
Bentlawnt Shrops 56 E4
Bentley Donc 91 P9
Bentley E R Yk 92 H3
Bentley Hants 23 L6
Bentley Suffk 53 K4
Bentley Warwks 59 L5
Bentley Heath Herts 50 G11
Bentley Heath Solhll 59 J9
Benton Devon 17 M4
Bentpath D & G 110 F2
Bentwichen Devon 17 N5
Bentworth Hants 23 J6
Benvie Angus 142 E11
Benville Dorset 11 L4
Benwick Cambs 62 D2
Beoley Worcs 58 G11
Beoraidbeg Highld 145 L9
Bepton W Susx 23 N11
Berden Essex 51 L5
Berea Pembks 40 E4
Bere Alston Devon 6 C5
Bere Ferrers Devon 6 D6
Berepper Cnwll 2 H9
Bere Regis Dorset 12 D6
Bergh Apton Norfk 77 L11
Berhill Somset 19 M7
Berinsfield Oxon 34 G5
Berkeley Gloucs 32 C5
Berkeley Heath Gloucs 32 C5
Berkeley Road Gloucs 32 D4
Berkhamsted Herts 35 Q3
Berkley Somset 20 F5
Berkswell Solhll 59 K9
Bermondsey Gt Lon 36 H5
Bermuda Warwks 59 N7
Bernera Highld 145 P3
Bernisdale Highld 152 G7
Berrick Prior Oxon 34 H6
Berrick Salome Oxon 34 H6
Berriedale Highld 163 Q2
Berrier Cumb 101 L5
Berriew Powys 56 B4
Berrington Nthumb 119 K2
Berrington Shrops 57 J3
Berrington Worcs 57 K11
Berrington Green Worcs 57 K11
Berrow Somset 19 J4
Berrow Worcs 46 E8
Berrow Green Worcs 46 D3
Berry Brow Kirk 90 E8
Berry Cross Devon 16 H9
Berry Down Cross Devon 17 K3
Berryfields Bucks 49 L11
Berry Hill Gloucs 31 Q2
Berry Hill Pembks 41 L2
Berryhillock Moray 158 D5
Berryhillock Moray 158 D7
Berrynarbor Devon 17 K2
Berry Pomeroy Devon 7 L6
Berry's Green Gt Lon 37 K9
Bersham Wrexhm 69 K5
Bersted W Susx 15 P6
Berthengam Flints 80 G9
Berwick E Susx 25 M9
Berwick Bassett Wilts 33 L10
Berwick Hill Nthumb 113 J5
Berwick St James Wilts 21 L7
Berwick St John Wilts 20 H10
Berwick St Leonard Wilts 20 H8
Berwick Station E Susx 25 M9
Berwick-upon-Tweed Nthumb 129 P9
Bescaby Leics 73 L5
Bescar Lancs 88 D8
Besford Shrops 69 Q9
Besford Worcs 46 H6
Bessacarr Donc 91 Q10
Bessels Leigh Oxon 34 E4
Besses o' th' Barn Bury 89 N9
Bessingby E R Yk 99 P7
Bessingham Norfk 76 H4
Bestbeech Hill E Susx 25 P4
Besthorpe Norfk 64 F2
Besthorpe Notts 85 P8
Bestwood Village Notts 85 J11
Beswick E R Yk 99 L11
Betchcott Shrops 56 G5
Betchworth Surrey 36 F10
Bethania Cerdgn 43 L2
Bethania Gwynd 67 N6
Bethel Gwynd 68 C7
Bethel Gwynd 79 J11
Bethel IoA 78 F10
Bethel Powys 68 F10
Bethersden Kent 26 F3
Bethesda Gwynd 79 L11
Bethesda Pembks 41 L7
Bethlehem Carmth 43 N9
Bethnal Green Gt Lon 36 H4
Betley Staffs 70 D5
Betsham Kent 37 P6
Betteshanger Kent 39 P11
Bettiscombe Dorset 10 H4
Bettisfield Wrexhm 69 N7
Betton Shrops 70 B7
Betton Strange Shrops 57 J3
Bettws Brdgnd 29 P7
Bettws Newpt 31 J6
Bettws Cedewain Powys 55 Q5
Bettws Ifan Cerdgn 42 F5
Bettws-Newydd Mons 31 L3
Bettyhill Highld 166 B4
Betws Carmth 28 H2
Betws Bledrws Cerdgn 43 L4
Betws Garmon Gwynd 67 J3
Betws Gwerfil Goch Denbgs 68 D5
Betws-y-Coed Conwy 67 P3
Betws-yn-Rhos Conwy 80 C10
Beulah Cerdgn 42 E5
Beulah Powys 44 C4
Bevendean Br & H 24 H9
Bevercotes Notts 85 L6
Beverley E R Yk 92 H3
Beverston Gloucs 32 G6
Bevington Gloucs 32 C5
Bewaldeth Cumb 100 H4
Bewcastle Cumb 111 L6
Bewdley Worcs 57 P9
Bewerley N York 97 J7
Bewholme E R Yk 99 P11
Bewlbridge Kent 25 Q4
Bexhill-on-Sea E Susx 26 B10
Bexley Gt Lon 37 L6
Bexleyheath Gt Lon 37 L5
Bexleyhill W Susx 23 P9
Bexon Kent 38 E10
Bexwell Norfk 75 M10
Beyton Suffk 64 C9
Beyton Green Suffk 64 C9
Bhaltos W Isls 168 f4
Bhatarsaigh W Isls 168 b18
Bibstone S Glos 32 C6
Bibury Gloucs 33 M3
Bicester Oxon 48 G10
Bickenhill Solhll 59 J8
Bicker Lincs 74 D3
Bicker Bar Lincs 74 D3
Bicker Gauntlet Lincs 74 D3
Bickershaw Wigan 82 D4
Bickerstaffe Lancs 81 N4
Bickerton Ches E 69 P4
Bickerton Devon 7 L11
Bickerton N York 97 Q10
Bickerton Nthumb 119 J10
Bickford Staffs 58 C2
Bickington Devon 7 L4
Bickington Devon 17 J5
Bickleigh Devon 6 E6
Bickleigh Devon 9 M3
Bickleton Devon 17 J5
Bickley Ches W 69 P5
Bickley Gt Lon 37 K7
Bickley N York 99 J2
Bickley Worcs 57 L10
Bickley Moss Ches W 69 P5
Bicknacre Essex 52 C11
Bicknoller Somset 18 F7
Bicknor Kent 38 E10
Bickton Hants 13 K2
Bicton Herefs 45 P2
Bicton Shrops 56 D8
Bicton Shrops 69 M11
Bidborough Kent 25 N2
Bidden Hants 23 K5
Biddenden Kent 26 E4
Biddenden Green Kent 26 E3
Biddenham Bed 61 M10
Biddestone Wilts 32 G10
Biddisham Somset 19 L4
Biddlesden Bucks 48 H7
Biddlestone Nthumb 119 J9
Biddulph Staffs 70 F3
Biddulph Moor Staffs 70 G3
Bideford Devon 16 H6
Bidford-on-Avon Warwks 47 M4
Bidston Wirral 81 K6
Bielby E R Yk 92 C2
Bieldside C Aber 151 M7
Bierley IoW 14 F11
Bierton Bucks 49 M11
Big Balcraig D & G 107 L9
Bigbury Devon 6 H9
Bigbury-on-Sea Devon 6 H10
Bigby Lincs 93 J9
Biggar Cumb 94 D7
Biggar S Lans 116 E3
Biggin Derbys 71 M3
Biggin Derbys 71 P5
Biggin N York 91 N4
Biggin Hill Gt Lon 37 K9
Biggleswade C Beds 50 E2
Bigholms D & G 110 F4
Bighouse Highld 166 E4
Bighton Hants 22 H8
Biglands Cumb 110 E10
Bignor W Susx 15 Q4
Bigrigg Cumb 100 D8
Big Sand Highld 160 B11
Bigton Shet 169 q11
Bilborough C Nott 72 E2
Bilbrook Somset 18 D6
Bilbrook Staffs 58 C4
Bilbrough N York 98 A11
Bilbster Highld 167 N6
Bildershaw Dur 103 P6
Bildeston Suffk 52 G2
Billacott Cnwll 5 M3
Billericay Essex 37 Q2
Billesdon Leics 73 J10
Billesley Warwks 47 M3
Billingborough Lincs 74 B4
Billinge St Hel 82 B4
Billingford Norfk 64 H6
Billingford Norfk 76 E7
Billingham S on T 104 E6
Billinghay Lincs 86 G10
Billingley Barns 91 L10
Billingshurst W Susx 24 C5
Billingsley Shrops 57 N8
Billington C Beds 49 P10
Billington Lancs 89 L3
Billington Staffs 70 F10
Billockby Norfk 77 N9
Billy Row Dur 103 N3
Bilsborrow Lancs 88 G3
Bilsby Lincs 87 N5
Bilsham W Susx 15 Q6
Bilsington Kent 26 H5
Bilsthorpe Notts 85 K8
Bilsthorpe Moor Notts 85 L8
Bilston Mdloth 127 P5
Bilston Wolves 58 E5
Bilstone Leics 72 B9
Bilting Kent 27 J2
Bilton E R Yk 93 L4
Bilton N York 97 M9
Bilton Nthumb 119 P8
Bilton Warwks 59 Q10
Bilton Banks Nthumb 119 P8
Bilton-in-Ainsty N York 97 Q11
Binbrook Lincs 86 H2
Binchester Blocks Dur 103 P4
Bincombe Dorset 11 P8
Binegar Somset 20 B5
Bines Green W Susx 24 E7
Binfield Br For 35 M10
Binfield Heath Oxon 35 K9
Bingfield Nthumb 112 E6
Bingham Notts 73 J3
Bingham's Melcombe Dorset 12 C4
Bingley C Brad 90 E3
Bings Heath Shrops 69 P11
Binham Norfk 76 D4
Binley Covtry 59 N9
Binley Hants 22 D4
Binley Woods Warwks 59 N9
Binnegar Dorset 12 E7
Binniehill Falk 126 F3
Binscombe Surrey 23 Q5
Binsey Oxon 34 E3
Binstead IoW 14 G8
Binsted Hants 23 L6
Binsted W Susx 15 Q5
Binton Warwks 47 M4
Bintree Norfk 76 E7
Binweston Shrops 56 E4
Birch Essex 52 F8
Birch Rochdl 89 P9
Bircham Newton Norfk 75 Q4
Bircham Tofts Norfk 75 Q4
Birchanger Essex 51 M6
Birchanger Green Services Essex 51 M6
Birch Cross Staffs 71 L8
Birchencliffe Kirk 90 E7
Bircher Herefs 56 H11
Birchett's Green E Susx 25 Q4
Birchfield Birm 58 G6
Birch Green Essex 52 F8
Birch Green Herts 50 G8
Birch Green Worcs 46 G5
Birchgrove Cardif 30 G9
Birchgrove Swans 29 K5
Birchgrove W Susx 25 K5
Birch Heath Ches W 69 P2
Birch Hill Ches W 81 Q10
Birchington Kent 39 P8
Birchington-on-Sea Kent 39 N8
Birchley Heath Warwks 59 L6
Birchmoor Warwks 59 L4
Birchmoor Green C Beds 49 Q8
Birchover Derbys 84 B8
Birch Services Rochdl 89 N9
Birch Vale Derbys 83 M7
Birchwood Lincs 86 B7
Birch Wood Somset 10 E2
Birchwood Warrtn 82 E6
Bircotes Notts 85 K2
Birdbrook Essex 52 B3
Birdforth N York 97 Q5
Birdham W Susx 15 M6
Birdingbury Warwks 59 P11
Birdlip Gloucs 32 H2
Birdoswald Cumb 111 M7
Birdsall N York 98 G7
Birds Edge Kirk 90 G9
Birds Green Essex 51 N9
Birdsgreen Shrops 57 P7
Birdsmoorgate Dorset 10 H4
Bird Street Suffk 64 E11
Birdwell Barns 91 J10
Birdwood Gloucs 46 D11
Birgham Border 118 E3
Birichin Highld 162 H8
Birkacre Lancs 88 H8
Birkby N York 104 B10
Birkdale Sefton 88 C8
Birkenbog Abers 158 D4
Birkenhead Wirral 81 L7
Birkenhead (Queensway) Tunnel Lpool 81 L7
Birkenhills Abers 158 H8
Birkenshaw Kirk 90 G5
Birkhall Abers 149 Q9
Birkhill Angus 142 F11
Birkhill D & G 117 J7
Birkholme Lincs 73 P6
Birkin N York 91 N5
Birks Leeds 90 H5
Birkshaw Nthumb 111 Q7
Birley Herefs 45 P4
Birley Carr Sheff 84 D2
Birling Kent 37 Q8
Birling Nthumb 119 P9
Birling Gap E Susx 25 N11
Birlingham Worcs 46 H6
Birmingham Birm 58 G7
Birmingham Airport Solhll 59 J8
Birnam P & K 141 P9
Birness Abers 159 N11
Birse Abers 150 F8
Birsemore Abers 150 E8
Birstall Kirk 90 G5
Birstall Leics 72 F9
Birstwith N York 97 K9
Birthorpe Lincs 74 B4
Birtley Gatesd 113 L9
Birtley Herefs 56 F11
Birtley Nthumb 112 C5
Birts Street Worcs 46 E7
Bisbrooke Rutlnd 73 M11
Biscathorpe Lincs 86 H4
Biscovey Cnwll 3 R3
Bisham W & M 35 M7
Bishampton Worcs 47 J4
Bish Mill Devon 17 N6
Bishop Auckland Dur 103 P5
Bishopbridge Lincs 86 D2
Bishopbriggs E Duns 125 Q3
Bishop Burton E R Yk 92 G3
Bishop Middleham Dur 104 B4
Bishopmill Moray 157 N5
Bishop Monkton N York 97 M7
Bishop Norton Lincs 86 C2
Bishopsbourne Kent 39 L11
Bishops Cannings Wilts 21 K2
Bishop's Castle Shrops 56 E7
Bishop's Caundle Dorset 11 P2
Bishop's Cleeve Gloucs 47 J9
Bishop's Frome Herefs 46 C5
Bishops Gate Surrey 35 Q10
Bishop's Green Essex 51 P7
Bishop's Green Hants 22 F2
Bishop's Hull Somset 18 H10
Bishop's Itchington Warwks 48 C3
Bishops Lydeard Somset 18 G9
Bishop's Norton Gloucs 46 F10
Bishop's Nympton Devon 17 P7
Bishop's Offley Staffs 70 D9
Bishop's Stortford Herts 51 L6
Bishop's Sutton Hants 22 H8
Bishop's Tachbrook Warwks 48 B2
Bishop's Tawton Devon 17 K6
Bishopsteignton Devon 7 N4
Bishopstoke Hants 22 E11
Bishopston Swans 28 G7
Bishopstone Bucks 35 M2
Bishopstone E Susx 25 L10
Bishopstone Herefs 45 N6
Bishopstone Kent 39 M8
Bishopstone Swindn 33 P8
Bishopstone Wilts 21 L9
Bishopstrow Wilts 20 G6
Bishop Sutton BaNES 19 Q3
Bishop's Waltham Hants 22 G11
Bishopswood Somset 10 F2
Bishop's Wood Staffs 58 B3
Bishopsworth Bristl 31 Q11
Bishop Thornton N York 97 L8
Bishopthorpe C York 98 B11
Bishopton Darltn 104 C6
Bishopton Rens 125 L3
Bishopton Warwks 47 N3

Bishop Wilton E R Yk 98 F9
Bishton Newpt 31 L7
Bishton Staffs 71 J10
Bisley Gloucs 32 H3
Bisley Surrey 23 Q3
Bisley Camp Surrey 23 P3
Bispham Bpool 88 C2
Bispham Green Lancs 88 F8
Bissoe Cnwll 3 K5
Bisterne Hants 13 K4
Bitchet Green Kent 37 N10
Bitchfield Lincs 73 P5
Bittadon Devon 17 J3
Bittaford Devon 6 H7
Bittering Norfk 76 C8
Bitterley Shrops 57 K9
Bitterne C Sotn 14 E4
Bitteswell Leics 60 B3
Bitton S Glos 32 C11
Bix Oxon 35 K8
Bixter Shet 169 q8
Blaby Leics 72 F11
Blackadder Border 129 L9
Blackawton Devon 7 L8
Blackbeck Cumb 100 D9
Blackborough Devon 10 B3
Blackborough End Norfk 75 N7
Black Bourton Oxon 33 Q4
Blackboys E Susx 25 M6
Blackbrook Derbys 84 D11
Blackbrook St Hel 82 B5
Blackbrook Staffs 70 D7
Blackbrook Surrey 36 E11
Blackburn Abers 151 L5
Blackburn Bl w D 89 K5
Blackburn Rothm 84 E2
Blackburn W Loth 126 H4
Blackburn with Darwen Services Bl w D 89 K6
Black Callerton N u Ty 113 J7
Black Carr Norfk 64 F2
Black Corner W Susx 24 G3
Blackcraig E Ayrs 115 M6
Black Crofts Ag & B 138 G11
Black Cross Cnwll 4 E9
Blackden Heath Ches E 82 G10
Blackdog Abers 151 P5
Black Dog Devon 9 K3
Blackdown Devon 8 D9
Blackdown Dorset 10 H4
Blackdyke Cumb 109 P10
Blacker Barns 91 J9
Blacker Hill Barns 91 K10
Blackfen Gt Lon 37 L6
Blackfield Hants 14 D6
Blackford Cumb 110 G8
Blackford P & K 133 P6
Blackford Somset 19 M5
Blackford Somset 20 C9
Blackfordby Leics 72 A7
Blackgang IoW 14 E11
Blackhall C Edin 127 N3
Blackhall Colliery Dur 104 E3
Blackhall Mill Gatesd 112 H9
Blackhall Rocks Dur 104 E3
Blackhaugh Border 117 N3
Blackheath Essex 52 H7
Blackheath Gt Lon 37 J5
Blackheath Sandw 58 E7
Blackheath Suffk 65 N7
Blackheath Surrey 36 B11
Black Heddon Nthumb 112 G5
Blackhill Abers 159 Q6
Blackhill Abers 159 Q9
Blackhill Dur 112 G10
Blackhill of Clackriach Abers 159 M8
Blackhorse Devon 9 N6
Blackjack Lincs 74 E3
Blackland Wilts 33 K11
Black Lane Ends Lancs 89 Q2
Blacklaw D & G 116 E9
Blackley Manch 83 J4
Blacklunans P & K 142 A5
Blackmarstone Herefs 45 Q7
Blackmill Brdgnd 29 P7
Blackmoor Hants 23 L8
Black Moor Leeds 90 H3
Blackmoor N Som 19 N2
Blackmoorfoot Kirk 90 D8
Blackmoor Gate Devon 17 L3
Blackmore Essex 51 P10
Blackmore End Essex 52 B5
Blackmore End Herts 50 E7
Black Mountains 45 K9
Blackness Falk 127 K2
Blacknest Hants 23 L6
Blacknest W & M 35 Q11
Black Notley Essex 52 C7
Blacko Lancs 89 P2
Black Pill Swans 28 H6
Blackpool Bpool 88 C3
Blackpool Devon 7 L4
Blackpool Devon 7 M9
Blackpool Gate Cumb 111 K5
Blackpool Zoo Bpool 88 C3
Blackridge W Loth 126 F4
Blackrock Cnwll 2 H7
Blackrock Mons 30 H2
Blackrod Bolton 89 J8
Blacksboat Moray 157 M10
Blackshaw D & G 109 M7
Blackshaw Head Calder 90 B5
Blacksmith's Green Suffk 64 G8
Blacksnape Bl w D 89 L6
Blackstone W Susx 24 F7
Black Street Suffk 65 Q4
Black Tar Pembks 41 J9
Blackthorn Oxon 48 H11
Blackthorpe Suffk 64 C9
Blacktoft E R Yk 92 D6
Blacktop C Aber 151 M7
Black Torrington Devon 8 C3
Blackwall Derbys 71 P5
Blackwall Tunnel Gt Lon 37 J4
Blackwater Cnwll 3 J4
Blackwater Hants 23 M3
Blackwater IoW 14 F9
Blackwater Somset 19 J11
Blackwaterfoot N Ayrs 120 H6
Blackwell Cumb 110 H10
Blackwell Darltn 103 Q8
Blackwell Derbys 83 P10
Blackwell Derbys 84 F9
Blackwell Warwks 47 P6
Blackwell Worcs 58 E10
Blackwellsend Green Gloucs 46 E9
Blackwood Caerph 30 G5
Blackwood D & G 109 K3
Blackwood S Lans 126 D9
Blackwood Hill Staffs 70 G3
Blacon Ches W 81 M11
Bladbean Kent 27 L2
Bladnoch D & G 107 M7
Bladon Oxon 34 E2
Bladon Somset 19 M10
Blaenannerch Cerdgn 42 D5
Blaenau Ffestiniog Gwynd 67 N5
Blaenavon Torfn 31 J3
Blaenavon Industrial Landscape Torfn 30 H3
Blaencwm Rhondd 29 P5
Blaen Dyryn Powys 44 C7
Blaenffos Pembks 41 N3
Blaengarw Brdgnd 29 P6
Blaengeuffordd Cerdgn 54 E8
Blaengwrach Neath 29 N3
Blaengwynfi Neath 29 N5
Blaenllechau Rhondd 30 D5
Blaenpennal Cerdgn 43 M2
Blaenplwyf Cerdgn 54 D9
Blaenporth Cerdgn 42 E5
Blaenrhondda Rhondd 29 P5
Blaenwaun Carmth 41 P5
Blaen-y-coed Carmth 42 F9
Blaen-y-cwm Blae G 30 F2
Blaenycwm Cerdgn 55 J9
Blagdon N Som 19 P3
Blagdon Somset 18 H11
Blagdon Torbay 7 M6
Blagdon Hill Somset 18 H11
Blagill Cumb 111 P11
Blaguegate Lancs 88 F9
Blaich Highld 139 J2
Blain Highld 138 B4
Blaina Blae G 30 H3
Blair Atholl P & K 141 L4
Blair Drummond Stirlg 133 L8
Blairgowrie P & K 142 B8
Blairhall Fife 134 B10
Blairingone P & K 134 B8
Blairlogie Stirlg 133 N8
Blairmore Ag & B 131 P11
Blairmore Highld 164 E5
Blair's Ferry Ag & B 124 B4
Blaisdon Gloucs 46 D11
Blakebrook Worcs 57 Q9
Blakedown Worcs 58 C9
Blake End Essex 52 B7
Blakeley Lane Staffs 70 H5
Blakemere Ches W 82 C10
Blakemere Herefs 45 M6
Blakemore Devon 7 K6
Blakenall Heath Wsall 58 F4
Blakeney Gloucs 32 C3
Blakeney Norfk 76 E3
Blakenhall Ches E 70 C5
Blakenhall Wolves 58 D5
Blakeshall Worcs 58 B8
Blakesley Nhants 48 H4
Blanchland Nthumb 112 E10
Blandford Camp Dorset 12 F3
Blandford Forum Dorset 12 E3
Blandford St Mary Dorset 12 E3
Bland Hill N York 97 K10
Blanefield Stirlg 125 N2
Blankney Lincs 86 E8
Blantyre S Lans 126 B6
Blàr a' Chaorainn Highld 139 L4
Blarghour Ag & B 131 K5
Blargie Highld 147 Q9
Blarmachfoldach Highld 139 K4
Blashford Hants 13 L3
Blaston Leics 73 L11
Blatherwycke Nhants 73 P11
Blawith Cumb 94 F3
Blawquhairn D & G 108 D4
Blaxhall Suffk 65 M10
Blaxton Donc 91 R10
Blaydon Gatesd 113 J8
Bleadney Somset 19 N5
Bleadon N Som 19 K3
Bleak Street Somset 20 E8
Blean Kent 39 K9
Bleasby Lincs 86 F4
Bleasby Notts 85 M11
Bleasdale Lancs 95 M11
Bleatarn Cumb 102 D8
Bleathwood Herefs 57 K10
Blebocraigs Fife 135 L4
Bleddfa Powys 56 C11
Bledington Gloucs 47 P10
Bledlow Bucks 35 L4
Bledlow Ridge Bucks 35 L5
Bleet Wilts 20 G3
Blegbie E Loth 128 D7
Blencarn Cumb 102 B4
Blencogo Cumb 110 C11
Blendworth Hants 15 K4
Blenheim Palace Oxon 48 D11
Blennerhasset Cumb 100 G2
Bletchingdon Oxon 48 F11
Bletchingley Surrey 36 H10
Bletchley M Keyn 49 N8
Bletchley Shrops 69 R8
Bletchley Park Museum M Keyn 49 N8
Bletherston Pembks 41 L6
Bletsoe Bed 61 M9
Blewbury Oxon 34 F7
Blickling Norfk 76 H6
Blidworth Notts 85 J9
Blidworth Bottoms Notts 85 J10
Blindburn Nthumb 118 F8
Blindcrake Cumb 100 F4
Blindley Heath Surrey 37 J11
Blisland Cnwll 5 J7
Blissford Hants 13 L2
Bliss Gate Worcs 57 N10
Blisworth Nhants 49 K4
Blithbury Staffs 71 K11
Blitterlees Cumb 109 P10
Blockley Gloucs 47 N7
Blofield Norfk 77 L10
Blofield Heath Norfk 77 L9
Blo Norton Norfk 64 E6
Bloomfield Border 118 A6
Blore Staffs 70 C8
Blore Staffs 71 L5
Blounce Hants 23 K5
Blounts Green Staffs 71 K8
Blowick Sefton 88 D7
Bloxham Oxon 48 D7
Bloxholm Lincs 86 E10
Bloxwich Wsall 58 E4
Bloxworth Dorset 12 E6
Blubberhouses N York 97 J9
Blue Anchor Cnwll 4 E10
Blue Anchor Somset 18 D6
Blue Bell Hill Kent 38 B9
Blue John Cavern Derbys 83 P8
Blundellsands Sefton 81 L5
Blundeston Suffk 65 Q2
Blunham C Beds 61 Q10
Blunsdon St Andrew Swindn 33 M7
Bluntington Worcs 58 D10
Bluntisham Cambs 62 E6
Blunts Cnwll 5 N9
Blunts Green Warwks 58 H11
Blurton C Stke 70 F6
Blyborough Lincs 86 B2
Blyford Suffk 65 N6
Blymhill Staffs 57 Q2
Blymhill Lawn Staffs 57 Q2
Blyth Notts 85 K3
Blyth Nthumb 113 M4
Blyth Bridge Border 127 L8
Blythburgh Suffk 65 N6
Blythe Border 128 F10
Blythe Bridge Staffs 70 H6
Blythe End Warwks 59 K6
Blythe Marsh Staffs 70 H6
Blyth Services Notts 85 K3
Blyton Lincs 85 Q2
Boarhills Fife 135 P5
Boarhunt Hants 14 H5
Boarley Kent 38 C10
Boarsgreave Lancs 89 N6
Boarshead E Susx 25 M4
Boar's Head Wigan 88 H9
Boars Hill Oxon 34 E4
Boarstall Bucks 34 H2
Boasley Cross Devon 8 D6
Boath Highld 155 Q3
Boat of Garten Highld 148 G4
Bobbing Kent 38 E8
Bobbington Staffs 57 Q6
Bobbingworth Essex 51 M9
Bocaddon Cnwll 5 K10
Bocking Essex 52 C7
Bocking Churchstreet Essex 52 C6
Bockleton Worcs 46 A2
Boconnoc Cnwll 5 J9
Boddam Abers 159 R9
Boddam Shet 169 q12
Boddington Gloucs 46 G9
Bodedern IoA 78 E8
Bodelwyddan Denbgs 80 E9
Bodenham Herefs 45 Q4
Bodenham Wilts 21 N9
Bodenham Moor Herefs 45 Q4
Bodewryd IoA 78 G6
Bodfari Denbgs 80 F10
Bodffordd IoA 78 G9
Bodham Norfk 76 G3
Bodiam E Susx 26 C6
Bodicote Oxon 48 E7
Bodieve Cnwll 4 F7
Bodinnick Cnwll 5 J11
Bodle Street Green E Susx 25 Q8
Bodmin Cnwll 4 H8
Bodmin Moor Cnwll 5 K6
Bodney Norfk 64 A2
Bodorgan IoA 78 F11
Bodsham Kent 27 K2
Boduan Gwynd 66 E7
Bodwen Cnwll 4 G9
Bodymoor Heath Warwks 59 J5
Bogallan Highld 156 A7
Bogbrae Abers 159 P10
Bogend S Ayrs 125 L11
Boggs Holdings E Loth 128 C5
Boghall Mdloth 127 N4
Boghall W Loth 126 H4
Boghead S Lans 126 D9
Bogmoor Moray 157 R5
Bogmuir Abers 143 L3
Bogniebrae Abers 158 E8
Bognor Regis W Susx 15 P7
Bogroy Highld 148 G3
Bogue D & G 108 D4
Bohetherick Cnwll 5 Q8
Bohortha Cnwll 3 M7
Bohuntine Highld 146 H11
Bojewyan Cnwll 2 B7
Bokiddick Cnwll 4 H9
Bolam Dur 103 N6
Bolam Nthumb 112 H4
Bolberry Devon 6 H11
Bold Heath St Hel 82 B7
Boldmere Birm 58 H6
Boldon Colliery S Tyne 113 M8
Boldre Hants 13 P5
Boldron Dur 103 K8
Bole Notts 85 N3
Bolehill Derbys 84 C9
Bole Hill Derbys 84 D6
Bolenowe Cnwll 2 H6
Bolham Devon 18 C11
Bolham Water Devon 10 D2
Bolingey Cnwll 3 K3
Bollington Ches E 83 K9
Bollington Cross Ches E 83 K9
Bollow Gloucs 32 D2
Bolney W Susx 24 G6
Bolnhurst Bed 61 N9
Bolnore W Susx 24 H6
Bolshan Angus 143 L7
Bolsover Derbys 84 G6
Bolster Moor Kirk 90 D7
Bolsterstone Sheff 90 H11
Boltby N York 97 Q3
Boltenstone Abers 150 C5
Bolter End Bucks 35 L6
Bolton Bolton 89 L9
Bolton Cumb 102 B6
Bolton E Loth 128 E6
Bolton E R Yk 98 F10
Bolton Nthumb 119 M8
Bolton Abbey N York 96 G10
Bolton Bridge N York 96 G10
Bolton-by-Bowland Lancs 96 A11
Boltonfellend Cumb 111 J7
Boltongate Cumb 100 H2
Bolton-le-Sands Lancs 95 K7
Bolton Low Houses Cumb 100 H2
Bolton New Houses Cumb 100 H2
Bolton-on-Swale N York 103 Q11
Bolton Percy N York 91 N2
Bolton Town End Lancs 95 K7
Bolton upon Dearne Barns 91 M10
Bolventor Cnwll 5 K6
Bomarsund Nthumb 113 L4
Bomere Heath Shrops 69 N11
Bonar Bridge Highld 162 E8
Bonawe Ag & B 139 J11
Bonby N Linc 92 H7
Boncath Pembks 41 P3
Bonchester Bridge Border 118 A8
Bonchurch IoW 14 G11
Bondleigh Devon 8 G4
Bonds Lancs 88 F2
Bonehill Devon 8 H9
Bonehill Staffs 59 J4
Bo'ness Falk 134 C11
Boney Hay Staffs 58 F2
Bonhill W Duns 125 K2
Boningale Shrops 57 Q4
Bonjedward Border 118 C6
Bonkle N Lans 126 E6
Bonnington Angus 143 K10
Bonnington Kent 27 J4
Bonnybank Fife 135 K7
Bonnybridge Falk 126 E2
Bonnykelly Abers 159 L7
Bonnyrigg Mdloth 127 Q4
Bonnyton Angus 142 E10
Bonsall Derbys 84 C9
Bonshaw Tower D & G 110 D6
Bont Mons 45 M11
Bontddu Gwynd 67 M11
Bont-Dolgadfan Powys 55 K4
Bont-goch Cerdgn 54 F7
Bonthorpe Lincs 87 N6
Bontnewydd Cerdgn 54 E11
Bontnewydd Gwynd 66 H3
Bontuchel Denbgs 68 E3
Bonvilston V Glam 30 E10
Bonwm Denbgs 68 F6
Bon-y-maen Swans 29 J5
Boode Devon 17 J4
Booker Bucks 35 M6
Booley Shrops 69 Q9
Boon Border 128 F10
Boon Hill Staffs 70 E4
Boorley Green Hants 14 F4
Boosbeck R & Cl 105 J7
Boose's Green Essex 52 D5
Boot Cumb 100 G10
Booth Calder 90 C5
Boothby Graffoe Lincs 86 C9
Boothby Pagnell Lincs 73 P4
Boothferry E R Yk 92 B5
Booth Green Ches E 83 K8
Boothstown Salfd 82 F4
Booth Town Calder 90 D5
Boothville Nhants 60 G8
Bootle Cumb 94 C3
Bootle Sefton 81 L5
Boots Green Ches W 82 G10
Boot Street Suffk 53 M2
Booze N York 103 K10
Boraston Shrops 57 L11
Bordeaux Guern 10 c1
Borden Kent 38 E9
Borden W Susx 23 M10
Border Cumb 110 C10
Bordley N York 96 D7
Boreham Essex 52 C10
Boreham Wilts 20 G6
Boreham Street E Susx 25 Q8
Borehamwood Herts 50 E11
Boreland D & G 110 C2
Boreraig Highld 152 B7
Boreton Shrops 57 J3
Borgh W Isls 168 b17
Borgh W Isls 168 j2
Borgie Highld 165 Q5
Borgue D & G 108 D11
Borgue Highld 167 K11
Borley Essex 52 D3
Borley Green Essex 52 D3
Borley Green Suffk 64 D9
Borneskitaig Highld 152 F3
Borness D & G 108 D11
Boroughbridge N York 97 N7
Borough Green Kent 37 P9
Borras Head Wrexhm 69 L4
Borrowash Derbys 72 C4
Borrowby N York 97 P3
Borrowby N York 105 L7
Borrowdale Cumb 101 J7
Borrowstoun Falk 134 B11
Borstal Medway 38 B8
Borth Cerdgn 54 E6
Borthwick Mdloth 128 B8
Borthwickbrae Border 117 N8
Borthwickshiels Border 117 N7
Borth-y-Gest Gwynd 67 K7
Borve Highld 152 G8
Borve W Isls 168 b17
Borve W Isls 168 f8
Borve W Isls 168 j2
Borwick Lancs 95 L6
Borwick Lodge Cumb 101 K11
Borwick Rails Cumb 94 D5
Bosavern Cnwll 2 B7
Bosbury Herefs 46 C6
Boscarne Cnwll 4 G8
Boscastle Cnwll 4 H3
Boscombe BCP 13 K6
Boscombe Wilts 21 P7
Boscoppa Cnwll 3 Q3
Bosham W Susx 15 M6
Bosham Hoe W Susx 15 M6
Bosherston Pembks 41 J12
Boskednan Cnwll 2 C7
Boskenna Cnwll 2 C9
Bosley Ches E 83 K11
Bosoughan Cnwll 4 D9
Bossall N York 98 E8
Bossiney Cnwll 4 H4
Bossingham Kent 27 L2
Bossington Somset 18 A5
Bostock Green Ches W 82 E11
Boston Lincs 74 F2
Boston Spa Leeds 97 P11
Boswarthan Cnwll 2 C7
Boswinger Cnwll 3 P5
Botallack Cnwll 2 B7
Botany Bay Gt Lon 50 G11
Botcheston Leics 72 D10
Botesdale Suffk 64 E6
Bothal Nthumb 113 K3
Bothampstead W Berk 34 F9
Bothamsall Notts 85 L6
Bothel Cumb 100 G3
Bothenhampton Dorset 11 K6
Bothwell S Lans 126 C6
Bothwell Services S Lans 126 C6
Botley Bucks 35 Q4
Botley Hants 14 F4
Botley Oxon 34 E3
Botolph Claydon Bucks 49 K10
Botolphs W Susx 24 E9
Botolph's Bridge Kent 27 K5
Bottesford Leics 73 L3
Bottesford N Linc 92 E9
Bottisham Cambs 62 H8
Bottomcraig Fife 135 K3
Bottom of Hutton Lancs 88 F5
Bottom o' th' Moor Bolton 89 K8
Bottoms Calder 89 Q6
Bottoms Cnwll 2 B9
Botts Green Warwks 59 K6
Botusfleming Cnwll 5 Q9
Botwnnog Gwynd 66 D8
Bough Beech Kent 37 L11
Boughrood Powys 44 G7
Boughspring Gloucs 31 Q5
Boughton Nhants 60 G7
Boughton Norfk 75 P10
Boughton Notts 85 L7
Boughton Aluph Kent 26 H2
Boughton End C Beds 49 Q7
Boughton Green Kent 38 C11
Boughton Malherbe Kent 26 E2
Boughton Monchelsea Kent 38 C11
Boughton Street Kent 39 J10
Boulby R & Cl 105 L7
Boulder Clough Calder 90 C6
Bouldnor IoW 14 C9
Bouldon Shrops 57 J7
Boulmer Nthumb 119 Q8
Boulston Pembks 41 J8
Boultham Lincs 86 C7
Boundary Staffs 70 H6
Bourn Cambs 62 D9
Bournbrook Birm 58 F8
Bourne Lincs 74 A6
Bournebridge Essex 37 M2
Bourne End Bed 61 M8
Bourne End Bucks 35 N7
Bourne End C Beds 49 Q6
Bourne End Herts 50 B9
Bournemouth BCP 13 J6
Bournemouth Airport BCP 13 K5
Bournes Green Gloucs 32 H4
Bournes Green Sthend 38 F4
Bournheath Worcs 58 E10
Bournmoor Dur 113 M10
Bournstream Gloucs 32 D6
Bournville Birm 58 F8
Bourton Dorset 20 E8
Bourton N Som 19 L2
Bourton Oxon 33 P7
Bourton Shrops 57 K5
Bourton Wilts 21 K2
Bourton on Dunsmore Warwks 59 P10
Bourton-on-the-Hill Gloucs 47 N8
Bourton-on-the-Water Gloucs 47 N10
Bousd Ag & B 136 H3
Boustead Hill Cumb 110 E9
Bouth Cumb 94 G3
Bouthwaite N York 96 H6
Bouts Worcs 47 K3
Boveney Bucks 35 P9
Boveridge Dorset 13 J2
Bovey Tracey Devon 9 K9
Bovingdon Herts 50 B10
Bovingdon Green Bucks 35 M7
Bovinger Essex 51 M9
Bovington Dorset 12 D7
Bovington Camp Dorset 12 D7
Bow Cumb 110 F9
Bow Devon 7 L7
Bow Devon 8 H4
Bow Gt Lon 37 J4
Bow Ork 169 c7
Bowbank Dur 102 H6
Bow Brickhill M Keyn 49 P8
Bowbridge Gloucs 32 G3
Bowburn Dur 104 B3
Bowcombe IoW 14 E9
Bowd Devon 10 C6
Bowden Border 117 R4
Bowden Devon 7 L9
Bowden Hill Wilts 32 H11
Bowdon Traffd 82 G7
Bower Highld 167 M4
Bowerchalke Wilts 21 K10
Bowerhill Wilts 20 H2
Bower Hinton Somset 19 N11
Bower House Tye Suffk 52 G3
Bowermadden Highld 167 M4
Bowers Staffs 70 E7
Bowers Gifford Essex 38 C4
Bowershall Fife 134 D9
Bower's Row Leeds 91 L5
Bowes Dur 103 J8
Bowgreave Lancs 88 F2
Bowhouse D & G 109 M7
Bowithick Cnwll 5 K5
Bowker's Green Lancs 81 N4
Bowland Border 117 P2
Bowland Bridge Cumb 95 J3
Bowley Herefs 45 Q4
Bowley Town Herefs 45 Q4
Bowlhead Green Surrey 23 P7
Bowling C Brad 90 F4
Bowling W Duns 125 L3
Bowling Bank Wrexhm 69 L5
Bowling Green Worcs 46 F4
Bowmanstead Cumb 101 K11
Bowmore Ag & B 122 D8
Bowness-on-Solway Cumb 110 D8
Bowness-on-Windermere Cumb 101 M11
Bow of Fife Fife 135 J5
Bowriefauld Angus 143 J8
Bowscale Cumb 101 L4
Bowsden Nthumb 119 J2
Bowston Cumb 101 N11

Bow Street Cerdgn 54 E7
Bow Street Norfk 64 E2
Bowthorpe Norfk 76 H10
Box Gloucs 32 G4
Box Wilts 32 F11
Boxbush Gloucs 32 D2
Boxbush Gloucs 46 C10
Box End Bed 61 M11
Boxford Suffk 52 G3
Boxford W Berk 34 D10
Boxgrove W Susx 15 P5
Box Hill Surrey 36 E10
Boxley Kent 38 C10
Boxmoor Herts 50 B9
Box's Shop Cnwll 16 C11
Boxted Essex 52 G5
Boxted Essex 52 H5
Boxted Suffk 64 A11
Boxted Cross Essex 52 H5
Boxwell Gloucs 32 F6
Boxworth Cambs 62 D8
Boyden End Suffk 63 M9
Boyden Gate Kent 39 M8
Boylestone Derbys 71 M7
Boyndie Abers 158 F5
Boyndlie Abers 159 M5
Boynton E R Yk 99 N7
Boysack Angus 143 L8
Boys Hill Dorset 11 P2
Boythorpe Derbys 84 E7
Boyton Cnwll 5 N3
Boyton Suffk 53 Q2
Boyton Wilts 21 J7
Boyton Cross Essex 51 P9
Boyton End Suffk 52 B3
Bozeat Nhants 61 K9
Braaid IoM 80 d6
Brabling Green Suffk 65 K9
Brabourne Kent 27 K3
Brabourne Lees Kent 27 J3
Brabstermire Highld 167 P3
Bracadale Highld 152 F10
Braceborough Lincs 74 A8
Bracebridge Heath Lincs 86 C7
Bracebridge Low Fields Lincs 86 C7
Braceby Lincs 73 Q3
Bracewell Lancs 96 C11
Brackenfield Derbys 84 E9
Brackenhirst N Lans 126 C4
Brackenthwaite Cumb 110 E11
Brackenthwaite N York 97 L10
Brackla Brdgnd 29 P9
Bracklesham W Susx 15 M7
Brackletter Highld 146 F11
Brackley Nhants 48 G7
Brackley Hatch Nhants 48 H6
Bracknell Br For 35 N11
Braco P & K 133 N6
Bracobrae Moray 158 D7
Bracon Ash Norfk 64 H2
Bracora Highld 145 M9
Bracorina Highld 145 M9
Bradaford Devon 5 P3
Bradbourne Derbys 71 N4
Bradbury Dur 104 B5
Bradden Nhants 48 H5
Braddock Cnwll 5 K9
Bradeley C Stke 70 F4
Bradenham Bucks 35 M5
Bradenstoke Wilts 33 K9
Bradfield Devon 9 Q3
Bradfield Essex 53 K5
Bradfield Norfk 77 K5
Bradfield Sheff 84 C2
Bradfield W Berk 34 H10
Bradfield Combust Suffk 64 B10
Bradfield Green Ches E 70 B3
Bradfield Heath Essex 53 K5
Bradfield St Clare Suffk 64 C10
Bradfield St George Suffk 64 C10
Bradford C Brad 90 F4
Bradford Cnwll 5 J6
Bradford Devon 16 G10
Bradford Nthumb 112 G5
Bradford Nthumb 119 N4
Bradford Abbas Dorset 11 M2
Bradford Leigh Wilts 20 F2
Bradford-on-Avon Wilts 20 F2
Bradford-on-Tone Somset 18 G10
Bradford Peverell Dorset 11 P6
Bradiford Devon 17 K5
Brading IoW 14 H9
Bradley Ches W 69 P5
Bradley Derbys 71 N5
Bradley Hants 22 H6
Bradley Kirk 90 F6
Bradley N York 96 F4
Bradley NE Lin 93 M9
Bradley Staffs 70 F11
Bradley Wolves 58 E5
Bradley Worcs 47 J2
Bradley Wrexhm 69 K4
Bradley Green Somset 19 J7
Bradley Green Warwks 59 L4
Bradley Green Worcs 47 J2
Bradley in the Moors Staffs 71 K6
Bradley Stoke S Glos 32 B8
Bradmore Notts 72 F4
Bradney Somset 19 K7
Bradninch Devon 9 N4
Bradninch Devon 17 L5
Bradnop Staffs 71 J3
Bradnor Green Herefs 45 K3
Bradpole Dorset 11 K6
Bradshaw Bolton 89 L8
Bradshaw Calder 90 D5
Bradshaw Kirk 90 D8
Bradstone Devon 5 P5
Bradwall Green Ches E 70 D2
Bradwell Derbys 83 Q8
Bradwell Devon 17 J3
Bradwell Essex 52 D7
Bradwell M Keyn 49 M6
Bradwell Norfk 77 Q11
Bradwell-on-Sea Essex 52 H10
Bradwell Waterside Essex 52 G10
Bradworthy Devon 16 E9
Brae Highld 156 B5
Brae Shet 169 q7
Braeface Falk 133 M11
Braehead Angus 143 M7
Braehead D & G 107 M7
Braehead S Lans 126 H7
Braeintra Highld 153 R11
Braemar Abers 149 M9
Braemore Highld 161 K11
Braemore Highld 167 J11
Brae Roy Lodge Highld 147 J9
Braeside Inver 124 G3
Braes of Coul Angus 142 D6
Braes of Enzie Moray 158 A6
Braeswick Ork 169 f3
Braevallich Ag & B 131 K6
Braewick Shet 169 p6
Brafferton Darltn 103 Q6
Brafferton N York 97 P6
Brafield-on-the-Green Nhants 60 H9
Bragar W Isls 168 h3
Bragbury End Herts 50 G6
Braidwood S Lans 126 E8
Brailsford Derbys 71 P6
Brailsford Green Derbys 71 P6
Brain's Green Gloucs 32 C3
Braintree Essex 52 C7
Braiseworth Suffk 64 G7
Braishfield Hants 22 C9
Braithwaite C Brad 90 C2
Braithwaite Cumb 100 H6
Braithwell Donc 84 H2
Braken Hill Wakefd 91 L7
Bramber W Susx 24 E8
Brambridge Hants 22 E10
Bramcote Notts 72 E3
Bramcote Warwks 59 P7
Bramdean Hants 22 H9
Bramerton Norfk 77 K11
Bramfield Herts 50 G7
Bramfield Suffk 65 M7
Bramford Suffk 53 K2
Bramhall Stockp 83 J8
Bramham Leeds 91 L2
Bramhope Leeds 90 H2
Bramley Hants 23 J3
Bramley Leeds 90 G3
Bramley Rothm 84 G2
Bramley Surrey 24 B2
Bramley Corner Hants 22 H3
Bramley Green Hants 23 J3
Bramley Head N York 96 H9
Bramling Kent 39 M10
Brampford Speke Devon 9 M5
Brampton Cambs 62 B6
Brampton Cumb 102 C6
Brampton Cumb 111 K8
Brampton Lincs 85 P5
Brampton Norfk 77 J7
Brampton Rothm 91 L10
Brampton Suffk 65 N5
Brampton Abbotts Herefs 46 B9
Brampton Ash Nhants 60 G3
Brampton Bryan Herefs 56 F10
Brampton-en-le-Morthen Rothm 84 G3
Bramshall Staffs 71 K8
Bramshaw Hants 21 Q11
Bramshill Hants 23 K2
Bramshott Hants 23 M8
Bramwell Somset 19 M9
Branault Highld 137 N2
Brancaster Norfk 75 Q2
Brancaster Staithe Norfk 75 Q2
Brancepeth Dur 103 P3
Branchill Moray 157 K7
Brand End Lincs 87 L11
Branderburgh Moray 157 N3
Brandesburton E R Yk 99 N11
Brandeston Suffk 65 J9
Brand Green Gloucs 46 D9
Brandis Corner Devon 16 G11
Brandiston Norfk 76 G7
Brandon Dur 103 P2
Brandon Lincs 86 B11
Brandon Nthumb 119 K7
Brandon Suffk 63 N3
Brandon Warwks 59 P9
Brandon Bank Norfk 63 K3
Brandon Creek Norfk 63 K2
Brandon Parva Norfk 76 F10
Brandsby N York 98 B6
Brandy Wharf Lincs 92 H11
Brane Cnwll 2 C8
Bran End Essex 51 Q5
Branksome BCP 12 H6
Branksome Park BCP 13 J6
Bransbury Hants 22 D6
Bransby Lincs 85 Q5
Branscombe Devon 10 D7
Bransford Worcs 46 E4
Bransgore Hants 13 L5
Bransholme C KuH 93 K4
Bransley Shrops 57 M9
Branson's Cross Worcs 58 G10
Branston Leics 73 L5
Branston Lincs 86 D7
Branston Staffs 71 N10
Branston Booths Lincs 86 E7
Branstone IoW 14 G10
Brant Broughton Lincs 86 B10
Brantham Suffk 53 K5
Branthwaite Cumb 100 E6
Branthwaite Cumb 101 J3
Brantingham E R Yk 92 F5
Branton Donc 91 Q10
Branton Nthumb 119 K7
Branton Green N York 97 P8
Branxton Nthumb 118 G3
Brassey Green Ches W 69 P2
Brassington Derbys 71 N4
Brasted Kent 37 L9
Brasted Chart Kent 37 L10
Brathens Abers 150 H8
Bratoft Lincs 87 N8
Brattleby Lincs 86 B4
Bratton Somset 18 B5
Bratton Wilts 20 H4
Bratton Wrekin 57 L2
Bratton Clovelly Devon 8 C6
Bratton Fleming Devon 17 L4
Bratton Seymour Somset 20 C9
Braughing Herts 51 J5
Braughing Friars Herts 51 K6
Braunston Nhants 60 B7
Braunston Rutlnd 73 L9
Braunstone Town Leics 72 F10
Braunton Devon 16 H4
Brawby N York 98 E5
Brawl Highld 166 D3
Braworth N York 104 F9
Bray W & M 35 P9
Braybrooke Nhants 60 G4
Braydon Wilts 33 L7
Braydon Brook Wilts 33 J6
Braydon Side Wilts 33 K7
Brayford Devon 17 M5
Bray's Hill E Susx 25 Q8
Bray Shop Cnwll 5 N7
Braystones Cumb 100 D9
Braythorn N York 97 K11
Brayton N York 91 Q4
Braywick W & M 35 N9
Braywoodside W & M 35 N9
Brazacott Cnwll 5 M3
Breach Kent 27 L2
Breach Kent 38 D8
Breachwood Green Herts 50 E6
Breacleit W Isls 168 g4
Breaclete W Isls 168 g4
Breaden Heath Shrops 69 M7
Breadsall Derbys 72 B3
Breadstone Gloucs 32 D4
Breadward Herefs 45 K4
Breage Cnwll 2 G8
Breakachy Highld 155 N9
Breakish Highld 145 L3
Brealangwell Lodge Highld 162 C8
Bream Gloucs 32 B3
Breamore Hants 21 N11
Brean Somset 19 J3
Breanais W Isls 168 e5
Brearley Calder 90 C5
Brearton N York 97 M8
Breascleit W Isls 168 h4
Breasclete W Isls 168 h4
Breaston Derbys 72 D4
Brechfa Carmth 43 K8
Brechin Angus 143 L5
Breckles Norfk 64 D3
Brecon Powys 44 E9
Brecon Beacons National Park 44 E10
Bredbury Stockp 83 K6
Brede E Susx 26 D8
Bredenbury Herefs 46 B3
Bredfield Suffk 65 K11
Bredgar Kent 38 E9
Bredhurst Kent 38 C9
Bredon Worcs 46 H7
Bredon's Hardwick Worcs 46 H7
Bredon's Norton Worcs 46 H7
Bredwardine Herefs 45 L6
Breedon on the Hill Leics 72 C6
Breich W Loth 126 H5
Breightmet Bolton 89 L9
Breighton E R Yk 92 B4
Breinton Herefs 45 P7
Bremhill Wilts 33 J10
Bremridge Devon 17 M6
Brenchley Kent 25 Q2
Brendon Devon 16 F10
Brendon Devon 17 P2
Brendon Hill Somset 18 D8
Brenfield Ag & B 123 P3
Brenish W Isls 168 e5
Brenkley N u Ty 113 K5
Brent Cross Gt Lon 36 F3
Brent Eleigh Suffk 52 F2
Brentford Gt Lon 36 E5
Brentingby Leics 73 K7
Brent Knoll Somset 19 K4
Brent Mill Devon 6 H7
Brent Pelham Herts 51 K4
Brentwood Essex 37 N2
Brenzett Kent 26 H6
Brenzett Green Kent 26 H6
Brereton Staffs 71 K11
Brereton Green Ches E 70 D2
Brereton Heath Ches E 82 H11
Brereton Hill Staffs 71 K11
Bressay Shet 169 s9
Bressingham Norfk 64 F5
Bressingham Common Norfk 64 F5
Bretby Derbys 71 P10
Bretford Warwks 59 P9
Bretforton Worcs 47 L6
Bretherton Lancs 88 F6
Brettabister Shet 169 r8
Brettenham Norfk 64 C5
Brettenham Suffk 64 D11
Bretton C Pete 74 C10
Bretton Derbys 84 B5
Bretton Flints 69 L2
Brewers End Essex 51 N6
Brewer Street Surrey 36 H10
Brewood Staffs 58 C3
Briantspuddle Dorset 12 D6
Brick End Essex 51 N5
Brickendon Herts 50 H9
Bricket Wood Herts 50 D10
Brick Houses Sheff 84 D4
Brickkiln Green Essex 52 B5
Bricklehampton Worcs 47 J6
Bride IoM 80 f1
Bridekirk Cumb 100 F4
Bridell Pembks 41 N2
Bridestowe Devon 8 D7
Brideswell Abers 158 E10
Bridford Devon 9 K7
Bridge Kent 39 L11
Bridge End Cumb 94 D4
Bridge End Cumb 110 G11
Bridge End Devon 6 H9
Bridge End Dur 103 K3
Bridge End Essex 51 Q4
Bridge End Lincs 74 B3
Bridgefoot Angus 142 F10
Bridgefoot Cumb 100 E5
Bridge Green Essex 51 L3
Bridgehampton Somset 19 Q10
Bridge Hewick N York 97 M6
Bridgehill Dur 112 G10
Bridgehouse Gate N York 97 J7
Bridgemary Hants 14 G6
Bridgemere Ches E 70 C5
Bridgend Abers 158 D10
Bridgend Ag & B 120 E4
Bridgend Ag & B 122 D7
Bridgend Angus 143 J4
Bridgend Brdgnd 29 P9
Bridgend Cerdgn 42 C5
Bridgend Cumb 101 M8
Bridgend D & G 116 F9
Bridgend Devon 6 F9
Bridgend Fife 135 K5
Bridgend Moray 158 A11
Bridgend P & K 134 E3
Bridgend W Loth 127 J2
Bridgend of Lintrathen Angus 142 D7
Bridge of Alford Abers 150 F4
Bridge of Allan Stirlg 133 M8
Bridge of Avon Moray 149 M4
Bridge of Avon Moray 157 M10
Bridge of Balgie P & K 140 E8
Bridge of Brewlands Angus 142 B5
Bridge of Brown Highld 149 L3
Bridge of Cally P & K 142 A7
Bridge of Canny Abers 150 H8
Bridge of Craigisla Angus 142 D7
Bridge of Dee D & G 108 F9
Bridge of Don C Aber 151 N6
Bridge of Dye Abers 150 H10
Bridge of Earn P & K 134 E4
Bridge of Ericht P & K 140 D6
Bridge of Feugh Abers 151 J8
Bridge of Gairn Abers 150 B8
Bridge of Gaur P & K 140 D6
Bridge of Marnoch Abers 158 E7
Bridge of Muchalls Abers 151 M9
Bridge of Orchy Ag & B 139 P10
Bridge of Tilt P & K 141 L4
Bridge of Tynet Moray 158 A5
Bridge of Walls Shet 169 p8
Bridge of Weir Rens 125 K4
Bridge Reeve Devon 17 M9
Bridgerule Devon 16 D11
Bridges Shrops 56 F5
Bridge Sollers Herefs 45 N6
Bridge Street Suffk 52 E2
Bridgetown Cnwll 5 N4
Bridgetown Somset 18 B8
Bridge Trafford Ches W 81 P10
Bridge Yate S Glos 32 C10
Bridgham Norfk 64 D4
Bridgnorth Shrops 57 N6
Bridgwater Somset 19 J7
Bridgwater Services Somset 19 K8
Bridlington E R Yk 99 P7
Bridport Dorset 11 K6
Bridstow Herefs 46 A10
Brierfield Lancs 89 N3
Brierley Barns 91 L8
Brierley Gloucs 46 B11
Brierley Herefs 45 P3
Brierley Hill Dudley 58 D7
Brierlow Bar Derbys 83 N11
Brierton Hartpl 104 E4
Briery Cumb 101 J6
Brigg N Linc 92 H9
Briggate Norfk 77 L6
Briggswath N York 105 N9
Brigham Cumb 100 E4
Brigham Cumb 101 J6
Brigham E R Yk 99 M10
Brighouse Calder 90 E6
Brighstone IoW 14 D10
Brightgate Derbys 84 C9
Brighthampton Oxon 34 C4
Brightholmlee Sheff 90 H11
Brightley Devon 8 F5
Brightling E Susx 25 Q6
Brightlingsea Essex 53 J8
Brighton Br & H 24 H10
Brighton Cnwll 3 N3
Brighton City Airport W Susx 24 E9
Brighton le Sands Sefton 81 L5
Brightons Falk 126 G2
Brightwalton W Berk 34 D9
Brightwalton Green W Berk 34 D9
Brightwalton Holt W Berk 34 D9
Brightwell Suffk 53 N3
Brightwell Baldwin Oxon 35 J5
Brightwell-cum-Sotwell Oxon 34 G6
Brightwell Upperton Oxon 35 J6
Brignall Dur 103 L8
Brig o'Turk Stirlg 132 G6
Brigsley NE Lin 93 N10
Brigsteer Cumb 95 K3
Brigstock Nhants 61 K3
Brill Bucks 35 J2
Brill Cnwll 3 J8
Brilley Herefs 45 K5
Brimfield Herefs 57 J11
Brimfield Cross Herefs 57 J11
Brimington Derbys 84 F6
Brimley Devon 9 K9
Brimpsfield Gloucs 32 H2
Brimpton W Berk 22 G2
Brimpton Common W Berk 22 G2
Brimscombe Gloucs 32 G4
Brimstage Wirral 81 L8
Brincliffe Sheff 84 D4
Brind E R Yk 92 B4
Brindham Somset 19 P7
Brindister Shet 169 p8
Brindle Lancs 88 H6
Brindley Ches E 69 Q4
Brineton Staffs 57 Q2
Bringhurst Leics 60 H2
Bringsty Common Herefs 46 D3
Brington Cambs 61 N5
Brininghám Norfk 76 E5
Brinkely Notts 85 M10
Brinkhill Lincs 87 L6
Brinkley Cambs 63 K10
Brinklow Warwks 59 P9
Brinkworth Wilts 33 K8
Brinscall Lancs 89 J6
Brinscombe Somset 19 M4
Brinsea N Som 19 M2
Brinsley Notts 84 G11
Brinsop Herefs 45 N6
Brinsworth Rothm 84 F3
Brinton Norfk 76 E4
Brinyan Ork 169 d4
Brisco Cumb 110 H10
Brisley Norfk 76 C7
Brislington Bristl 32 B10
Brissenden Green Kent 26 F4
Bristol Bristl 31 Q10
Bristol Airport N Som 31 P11
Bristol Zoo Gardens Bristl 31 Q10
Briston Norfk 76 F5
Brisworthy Devon 6 F5
Britannia Lancs 89 P6
Britford Wilts 21 N9
Brithdir Caerph 30 F4
Brithdir Gwynd 67 P11
British Legion Village Kent 38 B10
Briton Ferry Neath 29 K6
Britwell Salome Oxon 35 J6
Brixham Torbay 7 N7
Brixton Devon 6 F8
Brixton Gt Lon 36 H5
Brixton Deverill Wilts 20 G7
Brixworth Nhants 60 F6
Brize Norton Oxon 33 Q3
Brize Norton Airport Oxon 33 Q3
Broad Alley Worcs 58 C11
Broad Blunsdon Swindn 33 M6
Broadbottom Tamesd 83 L6
Broadbridge W Susx 15 M5
Broadbridge Heath W Susx 24 D4
Broad Campden Gloucs 47 N7
Broad Carr Calder 90 D7
Broad Chalke Wilts 21 K9
Broad Clough Lancs 89 P6
Broadclyst Devon 9 N5
Broadfield Inver 125 J3
Broadfield Pembks 41 M10
Broadford Highld 145 K3
Broad Ford Kent 26 B4
Broadford Bridge W Susx 24 C6
Broadgairhill Border 117 J8
Broadgrass Green Suffk 64 D9
Broad Green Cambs 63 L8
Broad Green Essex 52 E7
Broad Green Worcs 46 E3
Broad Green Worcs 58 E10
Broadhaugh Border 129 M9
Broad Haven Pembks 40 G8
Broadheath Traffd 82 G7
Broadheath Worcs 57 M11
Broadhembury Devon 10 C4
Broadhempston Devon 7 L5
Broad Hill Cambs 63 J5
Broad Hinton Wilts 33 M9
Broadholme Lincs 85 Q6
Broadland Row E Susx 26 D8
Broadlay Carmth 28 C3
Broad Layings Hants 22 D2
Broadley Essex 51 K9
Broadley Lancs 89 P7
Broadley Moray 158 A5
Broadley Common Essex 51 K9
Broad Marston Worcs 47 M5
Broadmayne Dorset 12 B7
Broad Meadow Staffs 70 E5
Broadmere Hants 22 H5
Broadmoor Gloucs 46 B11
Broadmoor Pembks 41 L9
Broadnymett Devon 8 H4
Broad Oak Carmth 43 L10
Broad Oak Cumb 94 C2
Broadoak Dorset 11 J5
Broad Oak E Susx 25 P6
Broad Oak E Susx 26 D8
Broadoak Gloucs 32 C2
Broad Oak Hants 23 L4
Broad Oak Herefs 45 P10
Broad Oak Kent 39 L9
Broad Oak St Hel 82 B5
Broadoak Wrexhm 69 L3
Broad Road Suffk 65 K6
Broadsands Torbay 7 M7
Broad's Green Essex 51 Q8
Broadstairs Kent 39 Q8
Broadstone BCP 12 H5
Broadstone Mons 31 P4
Broadstone Shrops 57 J7
Broad Street E Susx 26 E8
Broad Street Essex 51 N7
Broad Street Kent 27 K3
Broad Street Kent 38 D10
Broad Street Medway 38 C7
Broad Street Wilts 21 M3
Broad Street Green Essex 52 E10
Broad Town Wilts 33 L9
Broadwas Worcs 46 E3
Broadwater Herts 50 F6
Broadwater W Susx 24 D10
Broadwaters Worcs 58 B9
Broadway Carmth 28 C3
Broadway Carmth 41 Q8
Broadway Pembks 40 G8
Broadway Somset 19 K11
Broadway Suffk 65 M6
Broadway Worcs 47 L7
Broadwell Gloucs 31 Q2
Broadwell Gloucs 47 P9
Broadwell Oxon 33 Q4
Broadwell Warwks 59 Q11
Broadwey Dorset 11 P8
Broadwindsor Dorset 11 J4
Broadwood Kelly Devon 8 F3
Broadwoodwidger Devon 5 Q4
Brobury Herefs 45 L6
Brochel Highld 153 K8
Brochroy Ag & B 139 J11
Brock Lancs 88 G2
Brockamin Worcs 46 E4
Brockbridge Hants 22 H11
Brockdish Norfk 65 J6
Brockencote Worcs 58 C10
Brockenhurst Hants 13 P4
Brocketsbrae S Lans 126 E10
Brockford Green Suffk 64 G8
Brockford Street Suffk 64 G8
Brockhall Nhants 60 D8
Brockham Surrey 36 E11
Brockhampton Gloucs 46 H9
Brockhampton Gloucs 47 K10
Brockhampton Hants 15 K5
Brockhampton Herefs 46 A8
Brockhampton Green Dorset 11 Q3
Brockholes Kirk 90 F8
Brockhurst Derbys 84 D8
Brockhurst Warwks 59 Q8
Brocklebank Cumb 101 K2
Brocklesby Lincs 93 K8
Brockley N Som 31 N11
Brockley Suffk 64 A7
Brockley Green Suffk 63 M11
Brockley Green Suffk 64 A11
Brockleymoor Cumb 101 N3
Brockmoor Dudley 58 D7
Brockscombe Devon 8 C5
Brock's Green Hants 22 F2
Brockton Shrops 56 E4
Brockton Shrops 56 E7

Brockton Shrops 57 K6
Brockton Shrops 57 N4
Brockton Staffs 70 E8
Brockweir Gloucs 31 P4
Brockwood Park Hants 22 H9
Brockworth Gloucs 46 G11
Brocton Cnwll 4 G8
Brocton Staffs 70 H11
Brodick N Ayrs 121 K4
Brodie Moray 156 H6
Brodsworth Donc 91 N9
Brogaig Highld 152 H4
Brogborough C Beds 49 Q7
Brokenborough Wilts 32 H7
Broken Cross Ches E 83 J10
Broken Cross Ches W 82 E10
Brokerswood Wilts 20 F4
Bromborough Wirral 81 M8
Brome Suffk 64 G6
Brome Street Suffk 64 H6
Bromeswell Suffk 65 L11
Bromfield Cumb 110 C11
Bromfield Shrops 56 H9
Bromham Bed 61 M10
Bromham Wilts 33 J11
Bromley Barns 91 J11
Bromley Dudley 58 D7
Bromley Gt Lon 37 K7
Bromley Shrops 57 N5
Bromley Common Gt Lon 37 K7
Bromley Cross Bolton 89 L8
Bromley Cross Essex 53 J6
Bromley Green Kent 26 G4
Bromlow Shrops 56 E4
Brompton Medway 38 C8
Brompton N York 104 C11
Brompton-by-Sawdon N York 99 J4
Brompton-on-Swale N York 103 P11
Brompton Ralph Somset 18 E8
Brompton Regis Somset 18 C8
Bromsash Herefs 46 C10
Bromsberrow Gloucs 46 D8
Bromsberrow Heath Gloucs 46 D8
Bromsgrove Worcs 58 E10
Bromstead Heath Staffs 70 D11
Bromyard Herefs 46 C4
Bromyard Downs Herefs 46 C3
Bronaber Gwynd 67 N8
Bronant Cerdgn 54 E11
Broncroft Shrops 57 J7
Brongest Cerdgn 42 F5
Bronington Wrexhm 69 N7
Bronllys Powys 44 G8
Bronwydd Carmth 42 H10
Bronydd Powys 45 J5
Bronygarth Shrops 69 J7
Brook Carmth 41 Q9
Brook Hants 13 N2
Brook Hants 22 B9
Brook IoW 14 C10
Brook Kent 27 J3
Brook Surrey 23 P7
Brook Surrey 36 C11
Brooke Norfk 65 K2
Brooke Rutlnd 73 L9
Brookenby Lincs 93 M11
Brook End Bed 61 N8
Brook End C Beds 61 Q11
Brook End Cambs 61 N6
Brook End M Keyn 49 P6
Brookfield Rens 125 L5
Brookhampton Oxon 34 H5
Brookhampton Somset 20 B9
Brook Hill Hants 13 N2
Brook House Denbgs 80 F11
Brookhouse Lancs 95 L8
Brookhouse Rothm 84 H3
Brookhouse Green Ches E 70 E2
Brookhouses Derbys 83 M7
Brookland Kent 26 G6
Brooklands Traffd 82 G6
Brookmans Park Herts 50 F10
Brooks Powys 55 Q5
Brooksby Leics 72 H7
Brooks End Kent 39 N8
Brooks Green W Susx 24 D6
Brook Street Essex 37 N2
Brook Street Kent 26 F5
Brook Street Suffk 52 D2
Brook Street W Susx 24 H5
Brookthorpe Gloucs 32 F2
Brookville Norfk 75 P11
Brookwood Surrey 23 Q3
Broom C Beds 50 E2
Broom Rothm 84 F2
Broom Warwks 47 L4
Broombank Worcs 57 M10
Broome Norfk 65 M3
Broome Shrops 56 G8
Broome Worcs 58 D9
Broomedge Warrtn 82 F7
Broome Park Nthumb 119 M8
Broomer's Corner W Susx 24 D6
Broomershill W Susx 24 C7
Broomfield Essex 52 B9
Broomfield Kent 38 D11
Broomfield Kent 39 L8
Broomfield Somset 18 H8
Broomfields Shrops 69 M11
Broomfleet E R Yk 92 E5
Broom Green Norfk 76 D7
Broomhall W & M 35 Q11
Broomhaugh Nthumb 112 F8
Broom Hill Barns 91 L10
Broom Hill Dorset 12 H4
Broom Hill Notts 84 H11
Broomhill Nthumb 119 P10
Broom Hill Worcs 58 D9
Broomhill Green Ches E 70 A5
Broomley Nthumb 112 F8
Broompark Dur 103 P2
Broom's Green Gloucs 46 D8
Broomsthorpe Norfk 76 A6
Broom Street Kent 38 H9
Brora Highld 163 L6
Broseley Shrops 57 M4
Brotherhouse Bar Lincs 74 E8
Brotherlee Dur 102 H3
Brothertoft Lincs 87 J11
Brotherton N York 91 M5
Brotton R & Cl 105 J7
Broubster Highld 166 H5
Brough Cumb 102 E8
Brough Derbys 83 Q8
Brough E R Yk 92 F5
Brough Highld 167 M2
Brough Notts 85 P9
Brough Shet 169 s7
Broughall Shrops 69 Q6
Brough Lodge Shet 169 s4
Brough Sowerby Cumb 102 E8
Broughton Border 116 G3
Broughton Bucks 35 M2
Broughton Cambs 62 C5
Broughton Flints 69 K2
Broughton Hants 22 B8
Broughton Lancs 88 G4
Broughton M Keyn 49 N7
Broughton N Linc 92 G9
Broughton N York 96 D10
Broughton N York 98 F6
Broughton Nhants 60 H5
Broughton Oxon 48 D7
Broughton Salfd 82 H4
Broughton Staffs 70 D8
Broughton V Glam 29 P10
Broughton Astley Leics 60 B2
Broughton Beck Cumb 94 F4
Broughton Gifford Wilts 20 G2
Broughton Green Worcs 47 J2
Broughton Hackett Worcs 46 H4
Broughton-in-Furness Cumb 94 E3
Broughton Mains D & G 107 N8
Broughton Mills Cumb 94 E2
Broughton Moor Cumb 100 E4
Broughton Poggs Oxon 33 P4
Broughton Tower Cumb 94 E3
Broughty Ferry C Dund 142 H11
Brough with St Giles N York 103 P11
Brow End Cumb 94 F6
Brownber Cumb 102 D9
Brown Candover Hants 22 G7
Brown Edge Lancs 88 D8
Brown Edge Staffs 70 G4
Brown Heath Ches W 69 N2
Brownheath Shrops 69 N9
Brownhill Abers 159 L9
Brownhills Fife 135 N4
Brownhills Wsall 58 F3
Brownieside Nthumb 119 N6
Browninghill Green Hants 22 G3
Brown Lees Staffs 70 F3
Brownlow Heath Ches E 70 E2
Brownrigg Cumb 100 D6
Brownrigg Cumb 110 C10
Brownsea Island Dorset 12 H7
Brown's Green Birm 58 G6
Brownsham Devon 16 D6
Browns Hill Gloucs 32 G4
Brownsover Warwks 60 B5
Brownston Devon 6 H8
Brown Street Suffk 64 F9
Brow-of-the-Hill Norfk 75 N7
Browston Green Norfk 77 P11
Broxa N York 99 J2
Broxbourne Herts 51 J9
Broxburn E Loth 128 H4
Broxburn W Loth 127 K3
Broxfield Nthumb 119 P7
Broxted Essex 51 N5
Broxton Ches W 69 N4
Broyle Side E Susx 25 L8
Bruan Highld 167 P9
Bruar P & K 141 K4
Bruchag Ag & B 124 E6
Bruera Ches W 69 M2
Bruern Abbey Oxon 47 Q10
Bruichladdich Ag & B 122 C7
Bruisyard Suffk 65 L8
Bruisyard Street Suffk 65 L8
Brumby N Linc 92 E9
Brund Staffs 71 L2
Brundall Norfk 77 L10
Brundish Suffk 65 K8
Brundish Street Suffk 65 K7
Brunery Highld 138 C3
Brunnion Cnwll 2 E6
Brunslow Shrops 56 F8
Brunswick Village N u Ty 113 K6
Bruntcliffe Leeds 90 H5
Brunthwaite C Brad 96 G11
Bruntingthorpe Leics 60 D3
Brunton Fife 135 J3
Brunton Nthumb 119 P6
Brunton Wilts 21 P3
Brushford Devon 17 M10
Brushford Somset 18 B9
Bruton Somset 20 C7
Bryan's Green Worcs 58 C11
Bryanston Dorset 12 E3
Bryant's Bottom Bucks 35 N5
Brydekirk D & G 110 C6
Bryher IoS 2 b2
Brymbo Wrexhm 69 J4
Brympton Somset 19 P11
Bryn Carmth 28 F4
Bryn Ches W 82 D10
Bryn Neath 29 M6
Bryn Shrops 56 D7
Bryn Wigan 82 C4
Brynamman Carmth 29 K2
Brynberian Pembks 41 M3
Brynbryddan Neath 29 L6
Bryn Bwbach Gwynd 67 L7
Bryncae Rhondd 30 C8
Bryncethin Brdgnd 29 P8
Bryncir Gwynd 66 H6
Bryn-côch Neath 29 K5
Bryncroes Gwynd 66 C8
Bryncrug Gwynd 54 E4
Bryn Du IoA 78 E10
Bryn-Eden Gwynd 67 N9
Bryneglwys Denbgs 68 F5
Brynfields Wrexhm 69 K6
Brynford Flints 80 H10
Bryn Gates Wigan 82 C4
Bryn Golau Rhondd 30 D7
Bryngwran IoA 78 F9
Bryngwyn Mons 31 L3
Bryngwyn Powys 44 H5
Bryn-Henllan Pembks 41 K3
Brynhoffnant Cerdgn 42 F4
Bryning Lancs 88 E5
Brynithel Blae G 30 H4
Brynmawr Blae G 30 G2
Bryn-mawr Gwynd 66 C8
Brynmenyn Brdgnd 29 P8
Brynmill Swans 28 H6
Brynna Rhondd 30 C8
Bryn-penarth Powys 55 Q4
Brynrefail Gwynd 67 K2
Brynrefail IoA 78 H7
Brynsadler Rhondd 30 D8
Bryn Saith Marchog Denbgs 68 E4
Brynsiencyn IoA 78 H11
Brynteg IoA 78 H8
Bryn-y-bal Flints 69 J2
Bryn-y-Maen Conwy 79 Q9
Bryn-yr-Eos Wrexhm 69 J6
Bualintur Highld 144 F3
Buarth-draw Flints 80 H9
Bubbenhall Warwks 59 N10
Bubwith E R Yk 92 B3
Buccleuch Border 117 L8
Buchanan Smithy Stirlg 132 F10
Buchanhaven Abers 159 R8
Buchanty P & K 133 Q2
Buchany Stirlg 133 L7
Buchlyvie Stirlg 132 H9
Buckabank Cumb 110 G11
Buckden Cambs 61 Q7
Buckden N York 96 D5
Buckenham Norfk 77 M10
Buckerell Devon 10 C4
Buckfast Devon 7 J5
Buckfastleigh Devon 7 J5
Buckhaven Fife 135 K8
Buckholt Mons 45 Q11
Buckhorn Devon 5 P2
Buckhorn Weston Dorset 20 E10
Buckhurst Hill Essex 37 K2
Buckie Moray 158 B4
Buckingham Bucks 49 J8
Buckland Bucks 35 N2
Buckland Devon 6 H10
Buckland Gloucs 47 L7
Buckland Hants 13 P5
Buckland Herts 51 J4
Buckland Kent 27 P3
Buckland Oxon 34 B5
Buckland Surrey 36 F10
Buckland Brewer Devon 16 G7
Buckland Common Bucks 35 P3
Buckland Dinham Somset 20 E4
Buckland Filleigh Devon 16 H10
Buckland in the Moor Devon 7 J4
Buckland Monachorum Devon 6 D5
Buckland Newton Dorset 11 P3
Buckland Ripers Dorset 11 P8
Buckland St Mary Somset 10 F2
Buckland-Tout-Saints Devon 7 K9
Bucklebury W Berk 34 G10
Bucklers Hard Hants 14 D6
Bucklesham Suffk 53 M3
Buckley Flints 69 J2
Buckley Green Warwks 59 J11
Bucklow Hill Ches E 82 F8
Buckminster Leics 73 M6
Bucknall C Stke 70 G5
Bucknall Lincs 86 G7
Bucknell Oxon 48 G9
Bucknell Shrops 56 F10
Buckpool Moray 158 B4
Bucksburn C Aber 151 M6
Buck's Cross Devon 16 F7
Bucks Green W Susx 24 C4
Buckshaw Village Lancs 88 H6
Bucks Hill Herts 50 C10
Bucks Horn Oak Hants 23 M6
Buck's Mills Devon 16 F7
Buckton E R Yk 99 P6
Buckton Herefs 56 F10
Buckton Nthumb 119 L3
Buckworth Cambs 61 P5
Budby Notts 85 K7
Buddileigh Staffs 70 C5
Bude Cnwll 16 C10
Budge's Shop Cnwll 5 N10
Budlake Devon 9 N4
Budle Nthumb 119 N3
Budleigh Salterton Devon 9 Q8
Budlett's Common E Susx 25 L6
Budock Water Cnwll 3 K7
Buerton Ches E 70 B6
Bugbrooke Nhants 60 E9
Bugford Devon 7 L8
Buglawton Ches E 70 F2
Bugle Cnwll 4 G10
Bugley Dorset 20 E10
Bugthorpe E R Yk 98 F9
Buildwas Shrops 57 L4
Builth Road Powys 44 E4
Builth Wells Powys 44 E4
Bulbourne Herts 35 P2
Bulbridge Wilts 21 L8
Bulby Lincs 73 R5
Bulford Wilts 21 N6
Bulford Camp Wilts 21 N6
Bulkeley Ches E 69 P4
Bulkington Warwks 59 N7
Bulkington Wilts 20 H3
Bulkworthy Devon 16 F9
Bullamoor N York 97 N2
Bull Bay IoA 78 G6
Bullbridge Derbys 84 E10
Bullbrook Br For 35 N11
Bullen's Green Herts 50 F9
Bulley Gloucs 46 E11
Bullgill Cumb 100 E3
Bullinghope Herefs 45 Q7
Bullington Hants 22 E6
Bullington Lincs 86 E5
Bullockstone Kent 39 L8
Bull's Green Herts 50 G7
Bull's Green Norfk 65 N3
Bulmer Essex 52 D3
Bulmer N York 98 D7
Bulmer Tye Essex 52 D4
Bulphan Thurr 37 P3
Bulstone Devon 10 D7
Bulstrode Herts 50 B10
Bulverhythe E Susx 26 C10
Bulwark Abers 159 M8
Bulwell C Nott 72 E2
Bulwick Nhants 61 L2
Bumble's Green Essex 51 K9
Bunacaimb Highld 145 L10
Bunarkaig Highld 146 F10
Bunbury Ches E 69 Q3
Bunbury Heath Ches E 69 Q3
Bunchrew Highld 155 R8
Buncton W Susx 24 D8
Bundalloch Highld 145 Q2
Bunessan Ag & B 137 K11
Bungay Suffk 65 L4
Bunker's Hill Lincs 87 J10
Bunnahabhain Ag & B 122 F5
Bunny Notts 72 F5
Buntait Highld 155 M11
Buntingford Herts 51 J5
Bunwell Norfk 64 G3
Bunwell Hill Norfk 64 G3
Bupton Derbys 71 N7
Burbage Derbys 83 M10
Burbage Leics 59 P6
Burbage Wilts 21 P2
Burcher Herefs 45 L2
Burchett's Green W & M 35 M8
Burcombe Wilts 21 L8
Burcot Oxon 34 G5
Burcot Worcs 58 E10
Burcote Shrops 57 N5
Burcott Bucks 49 M11
Burcott Bucks 49 N10
Burdale N York 98 H8
Bures Essex 52 F5
Burford Oxon 33 Q2
Burford Shrops 57 K11
Burg Ag & B 137 K6
Burgate Suffk 64 F6
Burgates Hants 23 L9
Burge End Herts 50 D4
Burgess Hill W Susx 24 H7
Burgh Suffk 65 J11
Burgh by Sands Cumb 110 F9
Burgh Castle Norfk 77 P10
Burghclere Hants 22 E2
Burghead Moray 157 L4
Burghfield W Berk 35 J11
Burghfield Common W Berk 35 J11
Burgh Heath Surrey 36 F9
Burgh Hill E Susx 26 B6
Burghill Herefs 45 P6
Burgh Island Devon 6 G10
Burgh le Marsh Lincs 87 P7
Burgh next Aylsham Norfk 77 J6
Burgh on Bain Lincs 86 H3
Burgh St Margaret Norfk 77 N9
Burgh St Peter Norfk 65 P3
Burghwallis Donc 91 N8
Burham Kent 38 B9
Buriton Hants 23 K11
Burland Ches E 69 R4
Burlawn Cnwll 4 F7
Burleigh Gloucs 32 G4
Burlescombe Devon 18 E11
Burleston Dorset 12 C6
Burlestone Devon 7 L9
Burley Hants 13 M4
Burley Rutlnd 73 M8
Burley Shrops 56 H8
Burleydam Ches E 69 R6
Burley Gate Herefs 46 A5
Burley in Wharfedale C Brad 97 J11
Burley Lawn Hants 13 M4
Burley Street Hants 13 M4
Burley Wood Head C Brad 90 F2
Burlingham Green Norfk 77 M9
Burlingjobb Powys 45 K3
Burlington Shrops 57 P2
Burlton Shrops 69 N9
Burmarsh Kent 27 K5
Burmington Warwks 47 Q7
Burn N York 91 P5
Burnage Manch 83 J6
Burnaston Derbys 71 P8
Burnbanks Cumb 101 P7
Burnbrae N Lans 126 F6
Burn Bridge N York 97 L10
Burnby E R Yk 98 G11
Burn Cross Sheff 91 J11
Burndell W Susx 15 Q6
Burnden Bolton 89 L9
Burnedge Rochdl 89 Q8
Burneside Cumb 101 P11
Burneston N York 97 M4
Burnett BaNES 32 C11
Burnfoot Border 117 N8
Burnfoot Border 117 Q7
Burnfoot D & G 109 L2
Burnfoot D & G 110 F3
Burnfoot D & G 117 M11
Burnfoot P & K 134 B7
Burnham Bucks 35 P8
Burnham N Linc 93 J7
Burnham Deepdale Norfk 75 R2
Burnham Green Herts 50 G7
Burnham Market Norfk 76 A3
Burnham Norton Norfk 76 A3
Burnham-on-Crouch Essex 38 F2
Burnham-on-Sea Somset 19 K5
Burnham Overy Norfk 76 A3
Burnham Overy Staithe Norfk 76 A3
Burnham Thorpe Norfk 76 B3
Burnhead D & G 116 B11
Burnhervie Abers 151 J4
Burnhill Green Staffs 57 P4
Burnhope Dur 113 J11
Burnhouse N Ayrs 125 K7
Burniston N York 99 L2
Burnley Lancs 89 N4
Burnmouth Border 129 P7
Burn Naze Lancs 88 C2
Burn of Cambus Stirlg 133 L7
Burnopfield Dur 113 J9
Burnrigg Cumb 111 J9
Burnsall N York 96 F8
Burnside Angus 142 G6
Burnside Angus 143 J7
Burnside Fife 134 F6
Burnside Moray 157 M4
Burnside W Loth 127 K2
Burnside of Duntrune Angus 142 G11
Burntcommon Surrey 36 B10
Burntheath Derbys 71 N8
Burnt Heath Essex 53 J6
Burnt Hill W Berk 34 G10
Burnthouse Cnwll 3 K6
Burnt Houses Dur 103 M6
Burntisland Fife 134 G10
Burnt Oak E Susx 25 M5
Burnton E Ayrs 115 J6
Burntwood Flints 69 J2
Burntwood Staffs 58 G3
Burntwood Green Staffs 58 G3
Burnt Yates N York 97 L8
Burnworthy Somset 18 G11
Burpham Surrey 36 B10
Burpham W Susx 24 B9
Burradon N Tyne 113 L6
Burradon Nthumb 119 J9
Burrafirth Shet 169 t2
Burras Cnwll 2 H7
Burraton Cnwll 5 Q8
Burravoe Shet 169 s5
Burrells Cumb 102 C7
Burrelton P & K 142 C10
Burridge Devon 10 G3
Burridge Devon 17 K4
Burridge Hants 14 F4
Burrill N York 97 K3
Burringham N Linc 92 D9
Burrington Devon 17 L8
Burrington Herefs 56 G10
Burrington N Som 19 N3
Burrough End Cambs 63 K9
Burrough Green Cambs 63 K9
Burrough on the Hill Leics 73 K8
Burrow Lancs 95 N6
Burrow Somset 18 B6
Burrow Bridge Somset 19 L8
Burrowhill Surrey 23 Q2
Burrows Cross Surrey 36 C11
Burry Swans 28 E6
Burry Green Swans 28 E6
Burry Port Carmth 28 D4
Burscough Lancs 88 E8
Burscough Bridge Lancs 88 E8
Bursea E R Yk 92 D4
Burshill E R Yk 99 M11
Bursledon Hants 14 E5
Burslem C Stke 70 F5
Burstall Suffk 53 J3
Burstock Dorset 11 J4
Burston Norfk 64 G5
Burston Staffs 70 G8
Burstow Surrey 24 H2
Burstwick E R Yk 93 M5
Burtersett N York 96 C3
Burtholme Cumb 111 K8
Burthorpe Green Suffk 63 N8
Burthwaite Cumb 110 H11
Burthy Cnwll 4 E10
Burtle Hill Somset 19 L6
Burtoft Lincs 74 E3
Burton BCP 13 L6
Burton Ches W 69 P2
Burton Ches W 81 L10
Burton Dorset 11 P6
Burton Nthumb 119 N4
Burton Pembks 41 J9
Burton Somset 11 L2
Burton Somset 18 G6
Burton Wilts 20 F8
Burton Wilts 32 F9
Burton Agnes E R Yk 99 N8
Burton Bradstock Dorset 11 K7
Burton-by-Lincoln Lincs 86 C6
Burton Coggles Lincs 73 P5
Burton Dassett Warwks 48 C4
Burton End Essex 51 M6
Burton End Suffk 63 L11
Burton Fleming E R Yk 99 M6
Burton Green Warwks 59 L9
Burton Green Wrexhm 69 K3
Burton Hastings Warwks 59 P7
Burton-in-Kendal Cumb 95 L5
Burton-in-Kendal Services Cumb 95 L5
Burton in Lonsdale N York 95 P6
Burton Joyce Notts 72 G2
Burton Latimer Nhants 61 K6
Burton Lazars Leics 73 K7
Burton Leonard N York 97 M8
Burton on the Wolds Leics 72 F6
Burton Overy Leics 72 H11
Burton Pedwardine Lincs 74 B2
Burton Pidsea E R Yk 93 M4
Burton Salmon N York 91 M5
Burton's Green Essex 52 D6
Burton upon Stather N Linc 92 E7
Burton upon Trent Staffs 71 N10
Burton Waters Lincs 86 B6
Burtonwood Warrtn 82 C6
Burtonwood Services Warrtn 82 C6
Burwardsley Ches W 69 P3
Burwarton Shrops 57 L7
Burwash E Susx 25 Q6
Burwash Common E Susx 25 P6
Burwash Weald E Susx 25 Q6
Burwell Cambs 63 J7
Burwell Lincs 87 L5
Burwen IoA 78 G6
Burwick Ork 169 d8
Bury Bury 89 N8
Bury Cambs 62 C4
Bury Somset 18 B9
Bury W Susx 24 B8
Bury End C Beds 50 D3
Bury Green Herts 51 L6
Bury St Edmunds Suffk 64 B9
Burythorpe N York 98 F8
Busby E Rens 125 P6
Busby Stoop N York 97 N4
Buscot Oxon 33 P5
Bush Abers 143 P4
Bush Cnwll 16 C10
Bush Bank Herefs 45 P4
Bushbury Wolves 58 D4
Bushby Leics 72 H10
Bushey Herts 50 D11
Bushey Heath Herts 36 D2
Bush Green Norfk 65 J4
Bush Green Suffk 64 C10
Bush Hill Park Gt Lon 50 H11
Bushley Worcs 46 G8
Bushley Green Worcs 46 G8
Bushmead Bed 61 P8
Bushmoor Shrops 56 G7
Bushton Wilts 33 L9
Busk Cumb 102 B2
Buslingthorpe Lincs 86 E3
Bussage Gloucs 32 G4
Bussex Somset 19 L7
Butcher's Cross E Susx 25 N5
Butcombe N Som 19 P2
Bute Ag & B 124 C4

Butleigh Somset 19 P8
Butleigh Wootton Somset 19 P7
Butler's Cross Bucks 35 M3
Butler's Hill Notts 84 H11
Butlers Marston Warwks 48 B4
Butley Suffk 65 M11
Butley High Corner Suffk 53 Q2
Buttercrambe N York 98 E9
Butterdean Border 129 K7
Butterknowle Dur 103 M5
Butterleigh Devon 9 N3
Butterley Derbys 84 F10
Buttermere Cumb 100 G7
Buttermere Wilts 22 B2
Butters Green Staffs 70 E4
Buttershaw C Brad 90 E5
Butterstone P & K 141 Q8
Butterton Staffs 70 E2
Butterton Staffs 71 K3
Butterwick Dur 104 C4
Butterwick Lincs 87 L11
Butterwick N York 98 E5
Butterwick N York 99 K6
Butt Green Ches E 70 B4
Buttington Powys 56 C3
Buttonbridge Shrops 57 N9
Buttonoak Shrops 57 P9
Buttsash Hants 14 D5
Buttsbear Cross Cnwll 16 D11
Butt's Green Essex 52 C11
Buxhall Suffk 64 E10
Buxhall Fen Street Suffk 64 E10
Buxted E Susx 25 L6
Buxton Derbys 83 N10
Buxton Norfk 77 J7
Buxton Heath Norfk 76 H7
Buxworth Derbys 83 M8
Bwlch Powys 44 H10
Bwlchgwyn Wrexhm 69 J4
Bwlchllan Cerdgn 43 L3
Bwlchnewydd Carmth 42 G10
Bwlchtocyn Gwynd 66 E9
Bwlch-y-cibau Powys 68 G11
Bwlch-y-Ddar Powys 68 G10
Bwlchyfadfa Cerdgn 42 H5
Bwlch-y-ffridd Powys 55 P5
Bwlch-y-groes Pembks 41 P3
Bwlchymyrdd Swans 28 G5
Bwlch-y-sarnau Powys 55 N10
Byermoor Gatesd 113 J9
Byers Green Dur 103 P4
Byfield Nhants 48 F4
Byfleet Surrey 36 C8
Byford Herefs 45 M6
Bygrave Herts 50 G3
Byker N u Ty 113 L8
Byland Abbey N York 98 A5
Bylaugh Norfk 76 E8
Bylchau Conwy 68 C2
Byley Ches W 82 F11
Bynea Carmth 28 F5
Byrness Nthumb 118 E10
Bystock Devon 9 P8
Bythorn Cambs 61 N5
Byton Herefs 45 M2
Bywell Nthumb 112 F8
Byworth W Susx 23 Q10

C

Cabbacott Devon 16 G7
Cabourne Lincs 93 K10
Cabrach Ag & B 122 G7
Cabrach Moray 150 B2
Cabus Lancs 95 K11
Cackle Street E Susx 25 L5
Cackle Street E Susx 25 Q7
Cackle Street E Susx 26 D8
Cadbury Devon 9 M3
Cadbury Barton Devon 17 M8
Cadbury World Birm 58 F8
Cadder E Duns 125 Q3
Caddington C Beds 50 C7
Caddonfoot Border 117 P3
Cadeby Donc 91 N10
Cadeby Leics 72 C10
Cadeleigh Devon 9 M3
Cade Street E Susx 25 P6
Cadgwith Cnwll 3 J11
Cadham Fife 134 H7
Cadishead Salfd 82 F6
Cadle Swans 28 H5
Cadley Lancs 88 G4
Cadley Wilts 21 P4
Cadley Wilts 33 P11
Cadmore End Bucks 35 L6
Cadnam Hants 13 P2
Cadney N Linc 92 H10
Cadole Flints 68 H2
Cadoxton V Glam 30 F11
Cadoxton Juxta-Neath Neath 29 L5
Cadwst Denbgs 68 D7
Caeathro Gwynd 67 J2
Caehopkin Powys 29 M2
Caenby Lincs 86 C3
Caerau Brdgnd 29 N6
Caerau Cardif 30 F9
Cae'r-bont Powys 29 M2
Cae'r bryn Carmth 28 G2
Caerdeon Gwynd 67 M11
Caer Farchell Pembks 40 E5
Caergeiliog IoA 78 E9
Caergwrle Flints 69 K3
Caerhun Conwy 79 P10
Caerlanrig Border 117 M10
Caerleon Newpt 31 K6
Caernarfon Gwynd 66 H2
Caernarfon Castle Gwynd 66 H2
Caerphilly Caerph 30 G7
Caersws Powys 55 N6
Caerwedros Cerdgn 42 G3
Caerwent Mons 31 N6
Caerwys Flints 80 G10
Caerynwch Gwynd 67 P11
Caggle Street Mons 45 M11
Caim IoA 79 L8
Caio Carmth 43 N7
Cairinis W Isls 168 d11
Cairnbaan Ag & B 130 G9
Cairnbulg Abers 159 P4
Cairncross Border 129 M7
Cairncurran Inver 125 J3
Cairndow Ag & B 131 P5
Cairneyhill Fife 134 C10
Cairngarroch D & G 106 E8
Cairngorms National Park 149 K7
Cairnie Abers 158 C9
Cairnorrie Abers 159 L9
Cairnryan D & G 106 E4
Cairnty Moray 157 Q7
Caister-on-Sea Norfk 77 Q9
Caistor Lincs 93 K10
Caistor St Edmund Norfk 77 J11
Cakebole Worcs 58 C10
Cake Street Norfk 64 F3
Calais Street Suffk 52 G4
Calanais W Isls 168 h4
Calbourne IoW 14 D9
Calceby Lincs 87 L5
Calcoed Flints 80 H10
Calcot Gloucs 33 L2
Calcot W Berk 35 J10
Calcot Row W Berk 35 J10
Calcots Moray 157 P5
Calcott Kent 39 L9
Calcott Shrops 56 G2
Calcutt N York 97 M9
Calcutt Wilts 33 M6
Caldbeck Cumb 101 K2
Caldbergh N York 96 G3
Caldecote Cambs 61 P3
Caldecote Cambs 62 D9
Caldecote Herts 50 F3
Caldecote Nhants 49 J4
Caldecote Highfields Cambs 62 E9
Caldecott Nhants 61 L7
Caldecott Oxon 34 E5
Caldecott Rutlnd 61 J2
Caldecotte M Keyn 49 N7
Calder Cumb 100 D10
Calderbank N Lans 126 D5
Calder Bridge Cumb 100 D9
Calderbrook Rochdl 89 Q7
Caldercruix N Lans 126 E4
Calder Grove Wakefd 91 J7
Caldermill S Lans 126 B9
Caldermore Rochdl 89 Q7
Calder Vale Lancs 95 L11
Calderwood S Lans 126 B6
Caldey Island Pembks 41 M11
Caldicot Mons 31 N7
Caldmore Wsall 58 F5
Caldwell N York 103 N8
Caldy Wirral 81 J7
Caledfwlch Carmth 43 N9
Calenick Cnwll 3 L5
Calf of Man IoM 80 a8
Calford Green Suffk 63 M11
Calfsound Ork 169 e3
Calgary Ag & B 137 K5
Califer Moray 157 K6
California Falk 126 G2
California Norfk 77 Q8
California Cross Devon 7 J8
Calke Derbys 72 B6
Calke Abbey Derbys 72 B6
Callakille Highld 153 M6
Callander Stirlg 133 J6
Callanish W Isls 168 h4
Callaughton Shrops 57 L5
Callerton N u Ty 113 J7
Callestick Cnwll 3 K3
Calligarry Highld 145 K7
Callington Cnwll 5 P8
Callingwood Staffs 71 M10
Callow Herefs 45 P8
Callow End Worcs 46 F4
Callow Hill Wilts 33 K8
Callow Hill Worcs 47 K2
Callow Hill Worcs 57 N10
Callows Grave Worcs 57 K11
Calmore Hants 13 P2
Calmsden Gloucs 33 K3
Calne Wilts 33 J10
Calow Derbys 84 F6
Calshot Hants 14 E6
Calstock Cnwll 6 C5
Calstone Wellington Wilts 33 K11
Calthorpe Norfk 76 H5
Calthorpe Street Norfk 77 N6
Calthwaite Cumb 101 N2
Calton N York 96 D9
Calton Staffs 71 L5
Calveley Ches E 69 Q3
Calver Derbys 84 B6
Calverhall Shrops 69 R7
Calver Hill Herefs 45 M5
Calverleigh Devon 9 M2
Calverley Leeds 90 G3
Calver Sough Derbys 84 B6
Calvert Bucks 49 J10
Calverton M Keyn 49 L7
Calverton Notts 85 K11
Calvine P & K 141 K4
Calvo Cumb 109 P10
Calzeat Border 116 G3
Cam Gloucs 32 E5
Camasachoirce Highld 138 D5
Camasine Highld 138 D5
Camas Luinie Highld 146 A2
Camastianavaig Highld 153 J10
Camault Muir Highld 155 P9
Camber E Susx 26 G8
Camberley Surrey 23 N2
Camberwell Gt Lon 36 H5
Camblesforth N York 91 Q5
Cambo Nthumb 112 F3
Cambois Nthumb 113 M4
Camborne Cnwll 2 G5
Camborne & Redruth Mining District Cnwll 2 G5
Cambourne Cambs 62 D9
Cambridge Cambs 62 G9
Cambridge Gloucs 32 D4
Cambridge Airport Cambs 62 G9
Cambrose Cnwll 2 H4
Cambus Clacks 133 P9
Cambusavie Highld 162 H7
Cambusbarron Stirlg 133 M9
Cambuskenneth Stirlg 133 N9
Cambuslang S Lans 125 Q5
Cambus o' May Abers 150 C8
Cambuswallace S Lans 116 E3
Camden Town Gt Lon 36 G4
Cameley BaNES 20 B3
Camelford Cnwll 5 J5
Camelon Falk 133 P11
Camerory Highld 157 J11
Camer's Green Worcs 46 E7
Camerton BaNES 20 C3
Camerton Cumb 100 D4
Camghouran P & K 140 E6
Camieston Border 117 R4
Cammachmore Abers 151 N8
Cammeringham Lincs 86 B4
Camore Highld 162 H9
Campbeltown Ag & B 120 D7
Campbeltown Airport Ag & B 120 C7
Camperdown N Tyne 113 L6
Cample D & G 109 J2
Campmuir P & K 142 C10
Camps W Loth 127 K4
Campsall Donc 91 N8
Campsea Ash Suffk 65 L10
Camps End Cambs 51 P2
Campton C Beds 50 D3
Camptown Border 118 C8
Camrose Pembks 40 H6
Camserney P & K 141 K8
Camusnagaul Highld 139 K3
Camusnagaul Highld 160 H9
Camusteel Highld 153 N9
Camusterrach Highld 153 N9
Canada Hants 21 Q11
Canal Foot Cumb 94 G5
Canaston Bridge Pembks 41 L7
Candacraig Abers 149 Q8
Candlesby Lincs 87 N7
Candle Street Suffk 64 E7
Candover Green Shrops 57 J3
Candy Mill Border 116 F2
Cane End Oxon 35 J9
Canewdon Essex 38 F3
Canford Bottom Dorset 12 H4
Canford Cliffs BCP 13 J7
Canford Heath BCP 12 H6
Canford Magna BCP 12 H5
Canhams Green Suffk 64 F8
Canisbay Highld 167 P2
Canklow Rothm 84 F2
Canley Covtry 59 M9
Cann Dorset 20 G10
Canna Highld 144 B6
Cann Common Dorset 20 G10
Cannich Highld 155 K11
Cannington Somset 19 J7
Canning Town Gt Lon 37 K4
Cannock Staffs 58 E2
Cannock Chase Staffs 70 H11
Cannock Wood Staffs 58 F2
Cannon Bridge Herefs 45 N6
Canonbie D & G 110 G5
Canon Frome Herefs 46 B6
Canon Pyon Herefs 45 P5
Canons Ashby Nhants 48 G4
Canonstown Cnwll 2 E6
Canterbury Kent 39 K10
Canterbury Cathedral Kent 39 L10
Cantley Norfk 77 M11
Cantlop Shrops 57 J3
Canton Cardif 30 G9
Cantraywood Highld 156 D8
Cantsfield Lancs 95 N6
Canvey Island Essex 38 C5
Canwick Lincs 86 C7
Canworthy Water Cnwll 5 L3
Caol Highld 139 L2
Caolas Scalpaigh W Isls 168 h8
Caoles Ag & B 136 D6
Caonich Highld 146 D9
Capel Kent 25 P2
Capel Surrey 24 E2
Capel Bangor Cerdgn 54 F8
Capel Betws Lleucu Cerdgn 43 M3
Capel Coch IoA 78 H8
Capel Curig Conwy 67 N3
Capel Cynon Cerdgn 42 G5
Capel Dewi Carmth 43 J10
Capel Dewi Cerdgn 43 J6
Capel-Dewi Cerdgn 54 E8
Capel Garmon Conwy 67 Q3
Capel Green Suffk 53 Q2
Capel Gwyn Carmth 43 J10
Capel Gwyn IoA 78 E9
Capel Gwynfe Carmth 43 P10
Capel Hendre Carmth 28 G2
Capel Isaac Carmth 43 L9
Capel Iwan Carmth 41 Q3
Capel-le-Ferne Kent 27 N4
Capelles Guern 10 c1
Capel Llanilltern Cardif 30 E9
Capel Mawr IoA 78 G10
Capel Parc IoA 78 G7
Capel St Andrew Suffk 53 Q2
Capel St Mary Suffk 53 J4
Capel Seion Cerdgn 54 E9
Capel Trisant Cerdgn 54 G9
Capeluchaf Gwynd 66 G5
Capelulo Conwy 79 N9
Capel-y-ffin Powys 45 K8
Capel-y-graig Gwynd 79 J11
Capenhurst Ches W 81 M10
Capernwray Lancs 95 L6
Cape Wrath Highld 164 G1
Capheaton Nthumb 112 F4
Caplaw E Rens 125 L6
Capon's Green Suffk 65 K8
Cappercleuch Border 117 J6
Capstone Medway 38 C8
Capton Devon 7 L8
Capton Somset 18 E7
Caputh P & K 141 Q9
Caradon Mining District Cnwll 5 M7
Caradon Town Cnwll 5 M7
Carbeth Inn Stirlg 125 N2
Carbis Cnwll 4 G10
Carbis Bay Cnwll 2 E6
Carbost Highld 152 F11
Carbost Highld 152 G8
Carbrook Sheff 84 E3
Carbrooke Norfk 76 C11
Carburton Notts 85 K6
Carclaze Cnwll 3 Q3
Car Colston Notts 73 J2
Carcroft Donc 91 N9
Cardenden Fife 134 G8
Cardeston Shrops 56 F2
Cardewlees Cumb 110 G10
Cardhu Moray 157 M9
Cardiff Cardif 30 G9
Cardiff Airport V Glam 30 E11
Cardiff Gate Services Cardif 30 H8
Cardiff West Services Cardif 30 E9
Cardigan Cerdgn 42 C5
Cardinal's Green Cambs 63 K11
Cardington Bed 61 N11
Cardington Shrops 57 J5
Cardinham Cnwll 5 J8
Cardrain D & G 106 F11
Cardrona Border 117 L3
Cardross Ag & B 125 J2
Cardryne D & G 106 F11
Cardurnock Cumb 110 C9
Careby Lincs 73 Q7
Careston Angus 143 J5
Carew Pembks 41 K10
Carew Cheriton Pembks 41 K10
Carew Newton Pembks 41 K10
Carey Herefs 45 R8
Carfin N Lans 126 D6
Carfraemill Border 128 E9
Cargate Green Norfk 77 M9
Cargenbridge D & G 109 L6
Cargill P & K 142 B10
Cargo Cumb 110 G9
Cargreen Cnwll 6 C6
Cargurrel Cnwll 3 M6
Carham Nthumb 118 E3
Carhampton Somset 18 D6
Carharrack Cnwll 3 J5
Carie P & K 140 F6
Carinish W Isls 168 d11
Carisbrooke IoW 14 E9
Cark Cumb 94 H5
Carkeel Cnwll 5 Q9
Càrlabhagh W Isls 168 h3
Carland Cross Cnwll 3 M3
Carlbury Darltn 103 P7
Carlby Lincs 73 Q8
Carlcroft Nthumb 118 F8
Carlecotes Barns 83 Q4
Carleen Cnwll 2 G7
Carlesmoor N York 97 K6
Carleton Cumb 100 D9
Carleton Cumb 101 P5
Carleton Cumb 110 H10
Carleton Lancs 88 C3
Carleton Wakefd 91 M6
Carleton Forehoe Norfk 76 F10
Carleton-in-Craven N York 96 E11
Carleton Rode Norfk 64 G3
Carleton St Peter Norfk 77 L11
Carlidnack Cnwll 3 K8
Carlincraig Abers 158 G9
Carlingcott BaNES 20 C3
Carlin How R & Cl 105 K7
Carlisle Cumb 110 H9
Carlisle Airport Cumb 111 J8
Carloggas Cnwll 4 D8
Carlops Border 127 M6
Carloway W Isls 168 h3
Carlton Barns 91 K8
Carlton Bed 61 L9
Carlton Cambs 63 K10
Carlton Leeds 91 J5
Carlton Leics 72 B10
Carlton N York 91 Q6
Carlton N York 96 G4
Carlton N York 98 C3
Carlton Notts 72 G2
Carlton S on T 104 C6
Carlton Suffk 65 M9
Carlton Colville Suffk 65 Q4
Carlton Curlieu Leics 72 H11
Carlton Green Cambs 63 K10
Carlton Husthwaite N York 97 Q5
Carlton-in-Cleveland N York 104 F10
Carlton in Lindrick Notts 85 J4
Carlton-le-Moorland Lincs 86 B9
Carlton Miniott N York 97 N4
Carlton-on-Trent Notts 85 N8
Carlton Scroop Lincs 86 B11
Carluke S Lans 126 E7
Carlyon Bay Cnwll 3 R3
Carmacoup S Lans 115 Q2
Carmarthen Carmth 42 H10
Carmel Carmth 43 L11
Carmel Flints 80 H9
Carmel Gwynd 66 H4
Carmichael S Lans 116 C3
Carmunnock C Glas 125 P6
Carmyle C Glas 125 Q5
Carmyllie Angus 143 J9
Carnaby E R Yk 99 N7
Carnbee Fife 135 N6
Carnbo P & K 134 D7
Carn Brea Cnwll 2 H5
Carnbrogie Abers 151 M2
Carndu Highld 145 Q2
Carnduff S Lans 126 B8
Carne Cnwll 3 K9
Carne Cnwll 3 N6
Carne Cnwll 4 F10
Carnell E Ayrs 125 M11
Carnewas Cnwll 4 D8
Carnforth Lancs 95 K6
Carn-gorm Highld 146 B3
Carnhedryn Pembks 40 F5
Carnhell Green Cnwll 2 G6
Carnie Abers 151 L6
Carnkie Cnwll 2 H5
Carnkie Cnwll 3 J7
Carnkiet Cnwll 3 K3
Carno Powys 55 M5
Carnock Fife 134 C10
Carnon Downs Cnwll 3 K5
Carnousie Abers 158 G7
Carnoustie Angus 143 K11
Carnsmerry Cnwll 4 G10
Carnwath S Lans 126 H8
Carnyorth Cnwll 2 B7
Carol Green Solhll 59 L9
Carpalla Cnwll 3 P3
Carperby N York 96 F3
Carr Rothm 84 H2
Carradale Ag & B 120 F4
Carrbridge Highld 148 G3
Carrbrook Tamesd 83 L4
Carrefour Jersey 11 b1
Carreglefn IoA 78 F7
Carr Gate Wakefd 91 J6
Carrhouse N Linc 92 C9
Carrick Ag & B 131 J10
Carrick Castle Ag & B 131 P9
Carriden Falk 134 C11
Carrington Lincs 87 K9
Carrington Mdloth 127 Q5
Carrington Traffd 82 F6
Carrog Conwy 67 P5
Carrog Denbgs 68 F6
Carron Falk 133 P11
Carron Moray 157 N9
Carronbridge D & G 116 B11
Carron Bridge Stirlg 133 L11
Carronshore Falk 133 P11
Carrow Hill Mons 31 M6
Carr Shield Nthumb 112 B11
Carrutherstown D & G 109 P6
Carruth House Inver 125 K4
Carr Vale Derbys 84 G7
Carrville Dur 104 B2
Carsaig Ag & B 137 N11
Carseriggan D & G 107 K4
Carsethorn D & G 109 L9
Carshalton Gt Lon 36 G8
Carsington Derbys 71 P4
Carskey Ag & B 120 C10
Carsluith D & G 107 N7
Carsphairn D & G 115 L9
Carstairs S Lans 126 G8
Carstairs Junction S Lans 126 H8
Carswell Marsh Oxon 34 B5
Carter's Clay Hants 22 B10
Carters Green Essex 51 M8
Carterton Oxon 33 Q3
Carterway Heads Nthumb 112 F10
Carthew Cnwll 4 G10
Carthorpe N York 97 M4
Cartington Nthumb 119 K10
Cartland S Lans 126 F8
Cartledge Derbys 84 D5
Cartmel Cumb 94 H5
Cartmel Fell Cumb 95 J3
Carway Carmth 28 E3
Carwinley Cumb 110 H6
Cashe's Green Gloucs 32 F3
Cashmoor Dorset 12 G2
Cassington Oxon 34 E2
Cassop Dur 104 B3
Castallack Cnwll 2 D8
Castel Guern 10 b2
Castell Conwy 79 P11
Castell-y-bwch Torfn 31 J6
Casterton Cumb 95 N5
Castle Cnwll 4 H10
Castle Acre Norfk 75 R7
Castle Ashby Nhants 61 J9
Castlebay W Isls 168 b18
Castle Bolton N York 96 F2
Castle Bromwich Solhll 58 H7
Castle Bytham Lincs 73 P7
Castlebythe Pembks 41 K5
Castle Caereinion Powys 56 B3
Castle Camps Cambs 51 P2
Castle Carrock Cumb 111 K9
Castlecary Falk 126 D2
Castle Cary Somset 20 B8
Castle Combe Wilts 32 F9
Castle Donington Leics 72 C5
Castle Douglas D & G 108 G8
Castle Eaton Swindn 33 M5
Castle Eden Dur 104 D3
Castle End C Pete 74 B9
Castleford Wakefd 91 L5
Castle Frome Herefs 46 C5
Castle Gate Cnwll 2 D7
Castle Green Cumb 95 L2
Castle Green Surrey 23 Q2
Castle Gresley Derbys 71 P11
Castle Hedingham Essex 52 C4
Castlehill Border 117 J3
Castlehill Highld 167 L3
Castle Hill Kent 25 Q2
Castle Hill Suffk 53 K2
Castlehill W Duns 125 K2
Castle Howard N York 98 E6
Castle Kennedy D & G 106 F6
Castle Lachlan Ag & B 131 L8
Castlemartin Pembks 40 H11
Castlemilk C Glas 125 P6
Castle Morris Pembks 40 H4
Castlemorton Worcs 46 E7
Castlemorton Common Worcs 46 E7
Castle O'er D & G 110 D2
Castle Rising Norfk 75 N6
Castleside Dur 112 G11
Castle Stuart Highld 156 C8
Castlethorpe M Keyn 49 M6
Castlethorpe N Linc 92 G9
Castleton Ag & B 130 H11
Castleton Border 111 K3
Castleton Derbys 83 Q8
Castleton N York 105 J9
Castleton Newpt 31 J8
Castleton Rochdl 89 P8
Castletown Ches W 69 M4
Castletown Dorset 11 P10
Castletown Highld 167 L3
Castletown IoM 80 c8
Castletown Sundld 113 N9
Castley N York 97 L11
Caston Norfk 64 D2
Castor C Pete 74 B11
Caswell Bay Swans 28 G7
Catacol N Ayrs 123 R10
Cat and Fiddle Derbys 83 M10
Catbrain S Glos 31 Q8
Catbrook Mons 31 P4
Catch Flints 81 J10
Catchall Cnwll 2 C8
Catchem's Corner Solhll 59 L9
Catchgate Dur 113 J10
Catcliffe Rothm 84 F3
Catcomb Wilts 33 K9
Catcott Somset 19 L7
Catcott Burtle Somset 19 M6
Caterham Surrey 36 H9
Catfield Norfk 77 M7
Catfield Common Norfk 77 N7
Catford Gt Lon 37 J6
Catforth Lancs 88 F3
Cathcart C Glas 125 P5
Cathedine Powys 44 G9
Catherine-de-Barnes Solhll 59 J8
Catherine Slack C Brad 90 D5
Catherington Hants 15 J4
Catherston Leweston Dorset 10 H6
Catherton Shrops 57 M9

Catisfield Hants 14 G5
Catley Herefs 46 C6
Catley Lane Head Rochdl 89 P7
Catlodge Highld 147 Q9
Catlow Lancs 89 P3
Catlowdy Cumb 111 J5
Catmere End Essex 51 L3
Catmore W Berk 34 E8
Caton Devon 7 K4
Caton Lancs 95 L8
Caton Green Lancs 95 M7
Cator Court Devon 8 G9
Catrine E Ayrs 115 K2
Cat's Ash Newpt 31 L6
Catsfield E Susx 26 B9
Catsfield Stream E Susx 26 B9
Catsgore Somset 19 P9
Catsham Somset 19 Q8
Catshill Worcs 58 E10
Catstree Shrops 57 N5
Cattadale Ag & B 120 C9
Cattal N York 97 P10
Cattawade Suffk 53 K5
Catterall Lancs 88 F2
Catteralslane Shrops 69 Q6
Catterick N York 103 P11
Catterick Bridge N York 103 P11
Catterick Garrison N York 103 N11
Catterlen Cumb 101 N4
Catterline Abers 143 R2
Catterton N York 97 R11
Catteshall Surrey 23 Q6
Catthorpe Leics 60 C5
Cattishall Suffk 64 B8
Cattistock Dorset 11 M5
Catton N York 97 N5
Catton Nthumb 112 B9
Catwick E R Yk 99 N11
Catworth Cambs 61 N6
Caudle Green Gloucs 32 H2
Caulcott C Beds 50 B2
Caulcott Oxon 48 F10
Cauldcots Angus 143 M8
Cauldhame Stirlg 133 J9
Cauldmill Border 117 Q7
Cauldon Staffs 71 K5
Cauldon Lowe Staffs 71 K5
Cauldwell Derbys 71 P11
Caulkerbush D & G 109 K9
Caulside D & G 110 H4
Caundle Marsh Dorset 11 P2
Caunsall Worcs 58 C8
Caunton Notts 85 M8
Causeway Hants 23 K10
Causeway End Cumb 95 K3
Causeway End D & G 107 M6
Causeway End Essex 51 Q7
Causewayend S Lans 116 E3
Causewayhead Cumb 109 P10
Causewayhead Stirlg 133 N8
Causeyend Abers 151 N4
Causey Park Nthumb 113 J2
Causey Park Bridge Nthumb 113 J2
Cavendish Suffk 63 P11
Cavenham Suffk 63 N6
Caversfield Oxon 48 G9
Caversham Readg 35 K10
Caverswall Staffs 70 H6
Caverton Mill Border 118 D5
Cavil E R Yk 92 C4
Cawdor Highld 156 E7
Cawkwell Lincs 87 J5
Cawood N York 91 P3
Cawsand Cnwll 6 C8
Cawston Norfk 76 G7
Cawston Warwks 59 Q10
Cawthorn N York 98 F3
Cawthorne Barns 90 H9
Cawton N York 98 C5
Caxton Cambs 62 D9
Caxton End Cambs 62 D9
Caxton Gibbet Cambs 62 C8
Caynham Shrops 57 K10
Caythorpe Lincs 86 B11
Caythorpe Notts 85 L11
Cayton N York 99 M4
Ceannabeinne Highld 165 K3
Ceann a Bhaigh W Isls 168 c11
Ceannacroc Lodge Highld 146 G5
Cearsiadar W Isls 168 i6
Ceciliford Mons 31 P4
Cefn Newpt 31 J7
Cefn Berain Conwy 80 D11
Cefn-brith Conwy 68 B4
Cefn-bryn-brain Carmth 29 K2
Cefn Byrle Powys 29 M2
Cefn Canel Powys 68 H8
Cefn Coch Powys 68 F9
Cefn-coed-y-cymmer Myr Td 30 D3
Cefn Cribwr Brdgnd 29 N8
Cefn Cross Brdgnd 29 N8
Cefn-ddwysarn Gwynd 68 C7
Cefn-Einion Shrops 56 D7
Cefneithin Carmth 28 G2
Cefngorwydd Powys 44 C5
Cefn-mawr Wrexhm 69 J6
Cefnpennar Rhondd 30 D4
Cefn-y-bedd Flints 69 K3
Cefn-y-pant Carmth 41 N5
Ceint IoA 78 H9
Cellan Cerdgn 43 M5
Cellardyke Fife 135 P7
Cellarhead Staffs 70 H5
Celleron Cumb 101 N5
Celynen Caerph 30 H5
Cemaes IoA 78 F6
Cemmaes Powys 55 J3
Cemmaes Road Powys 55 J4
Cenarth Cerdgn 41 Q2
Cerbyd Pembks 40 F5
Ceres Fife 135 L5
Cerne Abbas Dorset 11 P4
Cerney Wick Gloucs 33 L5
Cerrigceinwen IoA 78 G10
Cerrigydrudion Conwy 68 C5
Cess Norfk 77 N8
Ceunant Gwynd 67 J2
Chaceley Gloucs 46 G8
Chacewater Cnwll 3 K5
Chackmore Bucks 49 J7
Chacombe Nhants 48 E6
Chadbury Worcs 47 K5
Chadderton Oldham 89 Q9
Chadderton Fold Oldham 89 Q9
Chaddesden C Derb 72 B3
Chaddesley Corbett Worcs 58 C10
Chaddlehanger Devon 8 C9
Chaddleworth W Berk 34 D9
Chadlington Oxon 48 B10
Chadshunt Warwks 48 B4
Chadwell Leics 73 K6
Chadwell Shrops 57 P2
Chadwell End Bed 61 N7
Chadwell Heath Gt Lon 37 L3
Chadwell St Mary Thurr 37 P5
Chadwick Worcs 58 B11
Chadwick End Solhll 59 K10
Chadwick Green St Hel 82 B5
Chaffcombe Somset 10 H2
Chafford Hundred Thurr 37 P5
Chagford Devon 8 H7
Chailey E Susx 25 J7
Chainbridge Cambs 74 H10
Chainhurst Kent 26 B2
Chalbury Dorset 12 H3
Chalbury Common Dorset 12 H3
Chaldon Surrey 36 H9
Chaldon Herring Dorset 12 C8
Chale IoW 14 E11
Chale Green IoW 14 E11
Chalfont Common Bucks 36 B2
Chalfont St Giles Bucks 35 Q6
Chalfont St Peter Bucks 36 B2
Chalford Gloucs 32 G4
Chalford Oxon 35 K4
Chalford Wilts 20 G4
Chalgrave C Beds 50 B5
Chalgrove Oxon 34 H5
Chalk Kent 37 Q6
Chalk End Essex 51 P8
Chalkhouse Green Oxon 35 K9
Chalkway Somset 10 H3
Chalkwell Kent 38 E9
Challaborough Devon 6 H10
Challacombe Devon 17 M3
Challoch D & G 107 L4
Challock Kent 38 H11
Chalmington Dorset 11 M4
Chalton C Beds 50 B5
Chalton C Beds 61 P10
Chalton Hants 23 K11
Chalvey Slough 35 Q9
Chalvington E Susx 25 M9
Chambers Green Kent 26 F3
Chandler's Cross Herts 50 C11
Chandlers Cross Worcs 46 E7
Chandler's Ford Hants 22 D11
Channel's End Bed 61 P9
Channel Tunnel Terminal Kent 27 L4
Chantry Somset 20 D5
Chantry Suffk 53 K3
Chapel Cumb 100 H4
Chapel Fife 134 H9
Chapel Allerton Leeds 91 J3
Chapel Allerton Somset 19 M4
Chapel Amble Cnwll 4 F6
Chapel Brampton Nhants 60 F7
Chapelbridge Cambs 62 C2
Chapel Chorlton Staffs 70 E7
Chapel Cross E Susx 25 P6
Chapel End Bed 61 P9
Chapel End C Beds 50 C2
Chapel End Cambs 61 P4
Chapel End Warwks 59 M6
Chapelend Way Essex 52 B4
Chapel-en-le-Frith Derbys 83 N8
Chapel Field Bury 89 M9
Chapelgate Lincs 74 H6
Chapel Green Warwks 48 E2
Chapel Green Warwks 59 L7
Chapel Haddlesey N York 91 P5
Chapelhall N Lans 126 D5
Chapel Hill Abers 159 Q10
Chapel Hill Lincs 86 H10
Chapel Hill Mons 31 P5
Chapel Hill N York 97 M11
Chapelhope Border 117 J7
Chapelknowe D & G 110 F6
Chapel Lawn Shrops 56 E9
Chapel-le-Dale N York 95 Q5
Chapel Leigh Somset 18 F9
Chapel Milton Derbys 83 N8
Chapel of Garioch Abers 151 J3
Chapel Rossan D & G 106 F9
Chapel Row E Susx 25 P8
Chapel Row Essex 52 C11
Chapel Row W Berk 34 G11
Chapels Cumb 94 E4
Chapel St Leonards Lincs 87 Q6
Chapel Stile Cumb 101 K9
Chapelton Abers 151 M9
Chapelton Angus 143 L8
Chapelton Devon 17 K6
Chapelton S Lans 126 B8
Chapeltown Bl w D 89 L7
Chapel Town Cnwll 4 D10
Chapeltown Moray 149 N3
Chapeltown Sheff 91 K11
Chapmanslade Wilts 20 F5
Chapmans Well Devon 5 P3
Chapmore End Herts 50 H7
Chappel Essex 52 E6
Charaton Cnwll 5 N8
Chard Somset 10 G3
Chard Junction Somset 10 G4
Chardleigh Green Somset 10 G2
Chardstock Devon 10 G4
Charfield S Glos 32 D6
Chargrove Gloucs 46 H11
Charing Kent 26 G2
Charing Heath Kent 26 F2
Charing Hill Kent 38 G11
Charingworth Gloucs 47 N7
Charlbury Oxon 48 C11
Charlcombe BaNES 32 D11
Charlcutt Wilts 33 J9
Charlecote Warwks 47 Q3
Charlemont Sandw 58 F6
Charles Devon 17 M5
Charleshill Surrey 23 N6
Charleston Angus 142 F8
Charlestown C Aber 151 N7
Charlestown C Brad 90 F3
Charlestown Calder 90 B5
Charlestown Cnwll 3 Q3
Charlestown Cnwll 3 Q3
Charlestown Derbys 83 M6
Charlestown Dorset 11 P9
Charlestown Fife 134 D11
Charlestown Highld 153 Q3
Charlestown Highld 156 A8
Charlestown Salfd 82 H4
Charlestown of Aberlour Moray 157 P9
Charles Tye Suffk 64 E11
Charlesworth Derbys 83 M6
Charlinch Somset 18 H7
Charlottetown Fife 134 H5
Charlton Gt Lon 37 K5
Charlton Hants 22 C5
Charlton Herts 50 E5
Charlton Nhants 48 F7
Charlton Nthumb 112 B4
Charlton Oxon 34 D7
Charlton Somset 19 J9
Charlton Somset 20 B6
Charlton Somset 20 C4
Charlton Surrey 36 C7
Charlton W Susx 15 N4
Charlton Wilts 20 H10
Charlton Wilts 33 J7
Charlton Worcs 47 K5
Charlton Worcs 58 B10
Charlton Wrekin 57 K2
Charlton Abbots Gloucs 47 K10
Charlton Adam Somset 19 P9
Charlton All Saints Wilts 21 N10
Charlton Down Dorset 11 P5
Charlton Hill Shrops 57 K3
Charlton Horethorne Somset 20 C10
Charlton Kings Gloucs 47 J10
Charlton Mackrell Somset 19 P9
Charlton Marshall Dorset 12 F4
Charlton Musgrove Somset 20 D9
Charlton-on-Otmoor Oxon 48 G11
Charlton on the Hill Dorset 12 E4
Charlton St Peter Wilts 21 M3
Charlwood Hants 23 J8
Charlwood Surrey 24 F2
Charminster Dorset 11 P6
Charmouth Dorset 10 H6
Charndon Bucks 49 J10
Charney Bassett Oxon 34 C6
Charnock Green Lancs 88 H7
Charnock Richard Lancs 88 H7
Charnock Richard Services Lancs 88 G7
Charsfield Suffk 65 K10
Chart Corner Kent 38 C11
Charter Alley Hants 22 G3
Charterhall Border 129 K10
Charterhouse Somset 19 N3
Chartershall Stirlg 133 M9
Charterville Allotments Oxon 34 B2
Chartham Kent 39 K11
Chartham Hatch Kent 39 K10
Chart Hill Kent 26 C2
Chartridge Bucks 35 P4
Chart Sutton Kent 26 D2
Chartway Street Kent 38 D11
Charvil Wokham 35 L9
Charwelton Nhants 60 B9
Chase Terrace Staffs 58 F3
Chasetown Staffs 58 F3
Chastleton Oxon 47 P9
Chasty Devon 16 E11
Chatburn Lancs 89 M2
Chatcull Staffs 70 D8
Chatham Caerph 30 H7
Chatham Medway 38 C8
Chatham Green Essex 52 B8
Chathill Nthumb 119 N5
Chatley Worcs 46 G2
Chatsworth House Derbys 84 C6
Chattenden Medway 38 C7
Chatter End Essex 51 L5
Chatteris Cambs 62 E3
Chatterton Lancs 89 M7
Chattisham Suffk 53 J3
Chatto Border 118 E7
Chatton Nthumb 119 L5
Chaul End C Beds 50 C6
Chawleigh Devon 17 N9
Chawley Oxon 34 E4
Chawston Bed 61 Q9
Chawton Hants 23 K7
Chaxhill Gloucs 32 D2
Chazey Heath Oxon 35 J9
Cheadle Staffs 71 J6
Cheadle Stockp 83 J7
Cheadle Heath Stockp 83 J7
Cheadle Hulme Stockp 83 J7
Cheam Gt Lon 36 F8
Cheapside W & M 35 P11
Chearsley Bucks 35 K2
Chebsey Staffs 70 F9
Checkendon Oxon 35 J8
Checkley Ches E 70 C5
Checkley Herefs 46 A7
Checkley Staffs 71 J7
Checkley Green Ches E 70 C5
Chedburgh Suffk 63 N9
Cheddar Somset 19 N4
Cheddington Bucks 49 P11
Cheddleton Staffs 70 H4
Cheddleton Heath Staffs 70 H4
Cheddon Fitzpaine Somset 18 H9
Chedglow Wilts 32 H6
Chedgrave Norfk 65 M2
Chedington Dorset 11 K3
Chediston Suffk 65 M6
Chediston Green Suffk 65 M6
Chedworth Gloucs 33 L2
Chedzoy Somset 19 K7
Cheeseman's Green Kent 26 H4
Cheetham Hill Manch 82 H4
Cheldon Devon 8 H2
Chelford Ches E 82 H10
Chellaston C Derb 72 B4
Chellington Bed 61 L9
Chelmarsh Shrops 57 N7
Chelmick Shrops 56 H6
Chelmondiston Suffk 53 M4
Chelmorton Derbys 83 P11
Chelmsford Essex 52 B10
Chelmsley Wood Solhll 59 J7
Chelsea Gt Lon 36 G5
Chelsfield Gt Lon 37 L8
Chelsham Surrey 37 J9
Chelston Somset 18 G10
Chelsworth Suffk 52 G2
Cheltenham Gloucs 46 H10
Chelveston Nhants 61 L7
Chelvey N Som 31 N11
Chelwood BaNES 20 B2
Chelwood Common E Susx 25 K5
Chelwood Gate E Susx 25 K4
Chelworth Wilts 33 J6
Chelworth Lower Green Wilts 33 L6
Chelworth Upper Green Wilts 33 L6
Cheney Longville Shrops 56 G8
Chenies Bucks 50 B11
Chepstow Mons 31 P6
Chequerbent Bolton 89 K9
Chequers Corner Norfk 75 J9
Cherhill Wilts 33 K10
Cherington Gloucs 32 H5
Cherington Warwks 47 Q7
Cheriton Devon 17 N2
Cheriton Hants 22 G9
Cheriton Kent 27 M4
Cheriton Pembks 41 J11
Cheriton Swans 28 E6
Cheriton Bishop Devon 9 J6
Cheriton Fitzpaine Devon 9 L3
Cherrington Wrekin 70 B11
Cherry Burton E R Yk 92 G2
Cherry Hinton Cambs 62 G9
Cherry Orchard Worcs 46 G4
Cherry Willingham Lincs 86 D6
Chertsey Surrey 36 B7
Cherwell Valley Services Oxon 48 F9
Cheselbourne Dorset 12 C5
Chesham Bucks 35 Q4
Chesham Bury 89 N8
Chesham Bois Bucks 35 Q5
Cheshunt Herts 51 J10
Chesil Beach Dorset 11 N9
Chesley Kent 38 E9
Cheslyn Hay Staffs 58 E3
Chessetts Wood Warwks 59 J10
Chessington Gt Lon 36 E8
Chessington World of Adventures Gt Lon 36 E8
Chester Ches W 81 N11
Chesterblade Somset 20 C6
Chesterfield Derbys 84 E6
Chesterfield Staffs 58 G3
Chesterhill Mdloth 128 B7
Chester-le-Street Dur 113 L10
Chester Moor Dur 113 L11
Chesters Border 118 B6
Chesters Border 118 B8
Chester Services Ches W 81 P9
Chesterton Cambs 62 G8
Chesterton Cambs 74 B11
Chesterton Gloucs 33 K4
Chesterton Oxon 48 G10
Chesterton Shrops 57 P5
Chesterton Staffs 70 E5
Chesterton Green Warwks 48 C3
Chesterwood Nthumb 112 B7
Chester Zoo Ches W 81 N10
Chestfield Kent 39 K8
Chestnut Street Kent 38 E9
Cheston Devon 6 H7
Cheswardine Shrops 70 C8
Cheswick Nthumb 129 Q10
Cheswick Green Solhll 58 H9
Chetnole Dorset 11 N3
Chettiscombe Devon 9 N2
Chettisham Cambs 62 H4
Chettle Dorset 12 G2
Chetton Shrops 57 M6
Chetwode Bucks 48 H9
Chetwynd Wrekin 70 C10
Chetwynd Aston Wrekin 70 D11
Cheveley Cambs 63 L8
Chevening Kent 37 L9
Cheverton IoW 14 E10
Chevington Suffk 63 N9
Cheviot Hills 118 E9
Chevithorne Devon 18 C11
Chew Magna BaNES 19 Q2
Chew Moor Bolton 89 K9
Chew Stoke BaNES 19 Q2
Chewton Keynsham BaNES 32 C11
Chewton Mendip Somset 19 Q4
Chichacott Devon 8 F5
Chicheley M Keyn 49 P5
Chichester W Susx 15 N6
Chickerell Dorset 11 N8
Chickering Suffk 65 J6
Chicklade Wilts 20 H8
Chicksands C Beds 50 D3
Chickward Herefs 45 K4
Chidden Hants 23 J11
Chiddingfold Surrey 23 Q7
Chiddingly E Susx 25 M8
Chiddingstone Kent 25 M2
Chiddingstone Causeway Kent 37 M11
Chiddingstone Hoath Kent 25 L2
Chideock Dorset 11 J6
Chidham W Susx 15 L6
Chidswell Kirk 90 H6
Chieveley W Berk 34 E10
Chieveley Services W Berk 34 E10
Chignall St James Essex 51 Q8
Chignall Smealy Essex 51 Q8
Chigwell Essex 37 K2
Chigwell Row Essex 37 L2
Chilbolton Hants 22 C6
Chilcomb Hants 22 F9
Chilcombe Dorset 11 L6
Chilcompton Somset 20 B4
Chilcote Leics 59 L2
Childer Thornton Ches W 81 M9
Child Okeford Dorset 12 D2
Childrey Oxon 34 C7
Child's Ercall Shrops 70 B9
Childswickham Worcs 47 L7
Childwall Lpool 81 N7
Childwick Bury Herts 50 D8
Childwick Green Herts 50 D8
Chilfrome Dorset 11 M5
Chilgrove W Susx 15 M4
Chilham Kent 39 J11
Chilla Devon 8 B4
Chillaton Devon 8 B8
Chillenden Kent 39 N11
Chillerton IoW 14 E10
Chillesford Suffk 65 M11
Chillingham Nthumb 119 L5
Chillington Devon 7 K10
Chillington Somset 10 H2
Chilmark Wilts 21 J8
Chilmington Green Kent 26 G3
Chilson Oxon 48 B11
Chilsworthy Cnwll 5 Q7
Chilsworthy Devon 16 E10
Chiltern Green C Beds 50 D7
Chiltern Hills 35 L5
Chilthorne Domer Somset 19 P11
Chilton Bucks 35 J2
Chilton Devon 9 L4
Chilton Dur 103 Q5
Chilton Kent 27 N3
Chilton Oxon 34 E7
Chilton Suffk 52 E3
Chilton Candover Hants 22 G6
Chilton Cantelo Somset 19 Q10
Chilton Foliat Wilts 34 B10
Chilton Polden Somset 19 L6
Chilton Street Suffk 63 N11
Chilton Trinity Somset 19 J7
Chilwell Notts 72 E3
Chilworth Hants 22 D11
Chilworth Surrey 36 B11
Chimney Oxon 34 C4
Chineham Hants 23 J3
Chingford Gt Lon 37 J2
Chinley Derbys 83 M8
Chinnor Oxon 35 L4
Chipchase Castle Nthumb 112 C5
Chipnall Shrops 70 C8
Chippenham Cambs 63 L7
Chippenham Wilts 32 H10
Chipperfield Herts 50 B10
Chipping Herts 51 J4
Chipping Lancs 89 J2
Chipping Campden Gloucs 47 N7
Chipping Hill Essex 52 D8
Chipping Norton Oxon 48 B9
Chipping Ongar Essex 51 N10
Chipping Sodbury S Glos 32 D8
Chipping Warden Nhants 48 E5
Chipshop Devon 8 B9
Chipstable Somset 18 D9
Chipstead Kent 37 M9
Chipstead Surrey 36 G9
Chirbury Shrops 56 D5
Chirk Wrexhm 69 J7
Chirnside Border 129 M8
Chirnsidebridge Border 129 M8
Chirton Wilts 21 L3
Chisbury Wilts 33 Q11
Chiselborough Somset 11 K2
Chiseldon Swindn 33 N8
Chiselhampton Oxon 34 G5
Chisholme Border 117 N8
Chislehurst Gt Lon 37 K6
Chislet Kent 39 M9
Chisley Calder 90 C5
Chiswell Green Herts 50 D10
Chiswick Gt Lon 36 F5
Chiswick End Cambs 62 E11
Chisworth Derbys 83 L6
Chitcombe E Susx 26 D7
Chithurst W Susx 23 M10
Chittering Cambs 62 G7
Chitterne Wilts 21 J6
Chittlehamholt Devon 17 M7
Chittlehampton Devon 17 L6
Chittoe Wilts 33 J11
Chivelstone Devon 7 K11
Chivenor Devon 17 J5
Chiverton Cross Cnwll 3 J4
Chlenry D & G 106 F5
Chobham Surrey 23 Q2
Cholderton Wilts 21 P6
Cholesbury Bucks 35 P3
Chollerford Nthumb 112 D6
Chollerton Nthumb 112 D6
Cholmondeston Ches E 70 A3
Cholsey Oxon 34 G7
Cholstrey Herefs 45 P3
Chop Gate N York 104 G11
Choppington Nthumb 113 L4
Chopwell Gatesd 112 H9
Chorley Ches E 69 Q4
Chorley Lancs 88 H7
Chorley Shrops 57 M8
Chorley Staffs 58 G2
Chorleywood Herts 50 B11
Chorleywood West Herts 50 B11
Chorlton Ches E 70 C4
Chorlton-cum-Hardy Manch 82 H6
Chorlton Lane Ches W 69 N5
Choulton Shrops 56 F7
Chowley Ches W 69 N3
Chrishall Essex 51 K3
Chrisswell Inver 124 G3
Christchurch BCP 13 L6
Christchurch Cambs 75 J11
Christchurch Gloucs 31 Q2
Christchurch Newpt 31 K7
Christian Malford Wilts 33 J9
Christleton Ches W 81 N11
Christmas Common Oxon 35 K6
Christmas Pie Surrey 23 P5
Christon N Som 19 L3
Christon Bank Nthumb 119 P6
Christow Devon 9 K7
Christ's Hospital W Susx 24 D5
Chuck Hatch E Susx 25 L4
Chudleigh Devon 9 L9
Chudleigh Knighton Devon 9 K9
Chulmleigh Devon 17 M9
Chunal Derbys 83 M6
Church Lancs 89 L5
Churcham Gloucs 46 E11
Church Aston Wrekin 70 C11
Church Brampton Nhants 60 F7
Church Brough Cumb 102 E8
Church Broughton Derbys 71 N8
Church Cove Cnwll 3 J11
Church Crookham Hants 23 M4
Churchdown Gloucs 46 G11
Church Eaton Staffs 70 E11
Church End Bed 61 N9
Church End Bed 61 P9
Church End Bucks 35 K3
Church End C Beds 49 Q10
Church End C Beds 49 Q8
Church End C Beds 50 B4
Church End C Beds 50 B7
Church End C Beds 50 E3

Church End C Beds 61 Q10
Church End Cambs 61 N6
Church End Cambs 62 B4
Church End Cambs 62 D5
Churchend Essex 38 H3
Church End Essex 51 P6
Church End Essex 52 B6
Church End Essex 52 B8
Church End Gloucs 46 G7
Church End Gt Lon 36 F2
Church End Herts 50 D8
Church End Herts 50 G4
Church End Herts 51 K6
Church End Lincs 74 D4
Church End Lincs 93 R11
Church End Warwks 59 K6
Church End Warwks 59 L6
Church Enstone Oxon 48 C9
Church Fenton N York 91 N3
Churchfield Sandw 58 F6
Churchgate Herts 50 H10
Churchgate Street Essex 51 L8
Church Green Devon 10 D5
Church Gresley Derbys 71 P11
Church Hanborough Oxon 34 D2
Church Hill Staffs 58 F2
Church Houses N York 105 J11
Churchill Devon 10 F4
Churchill Devon 17 K3
Churchill N Som 19 M3
Churchill Oxon 47 Q10
Churchill Worcs 46 H4
Churchill Worcs 58 C9
Churchinford Somset 10 E2
Church Knowle Dorset 12 F8
Church Laneham Notts 85 P5
Church Langton Leics 60 F2
Church Lawford Warwks 59 Q9
Church Lawton Ches E 70 E3
Church Leigh Staffs 71 J7
Church Lench Worcs 47 K4
Church Mayfield Staffs 71 M6
Church Minshull Ches E 70 B2
Church Norton W Susx 15 N7
Churchover Warwks 60 B4
Church Preen Shrops 57 J5
Church Pulverbatch Shrops 56 G4
Churchstanton Somset 10 D2
Churchstoke Powys 56 D6
Churchstow Devon 7 J9
Church Stowe Nhants 60 D9
Church Street Essex 52 C3
Church Street Kent 38 B7
Church Street Suffk 65 P5
Church Stretton Shrops 56 H6
Churchthorpe Lincs 93 P11
Churchtown Bpool 88 C2
Churchtown Cnwll 4 H6
Churchtown Derbys 84 C8
Churchtown Devon 17 M3
Churchtown IoM 80 f3
Churchtown Lancs 88 F2
Church Town N Linc 92 C9
Churchtown Sefton 88 D7
Church Village Rhondd 30 E7
Church Warsop Notts 85 J7
Church Wilne Derbys 72 C4
Churnsike Lodge Nthumb 111 N5
Churston Ferrers Torbay 7 N7
Churt Surrey 23 N7
Churton Ches W 69 M3
Churwell Leeds 90 H5
Chwilog Gwynd 66 G7
Chyandour Cnwll 2 D7
Chyanvounder Cnwll 2 H9
Chyeowling Cnwll 3 K5
Chyvarloe Cnwll 2 H9
Cil Powys 56 B4
Cilcain Flints 80 H11
Cilcennin Cerdgn 43 K2
Cilcewydd Powys 56 C4
Cilfrew Neath 29 L4
Cilfynydd Rhondd 30 E6
Cilgerran Pembks 41 N2
Cilgwyn Carmth 43 P9
Cilgwyn Gwynd 66 H4
Ciliau-Aeron Cerdgn 43 K3
Cilmaengwyn Neath 29 K3
Cilmery Powys 44 E4
Cilrhedyn Pembks 41 Q4
Cilsan Carmth 43 L10
Ciltalgarth Gwynd 68 A6
Cilycwm Carmth 43 Q7
Cimla Neath 29 L5
Cinderford Gloucs 32 C2
Cinder Hill Wolves 58 D6
Cippenham Slough 35 Q8
Cirencester Gloucs 33 K4
Citadilla N York 103 P11
City Gt Lon 36 H4
City V Glam 30 C9
City Airport Gt Lon 37 K4
City Dulas IoA 78 H7
Clabhach Ag & B 136 F4
Clachaig Ag & B 131 N11
Clachaig Inn Highld 139 L6
Clachan Ag & B 123 N8
Clachan Ag & B 130 F4
Clachan Ag & B 131 M7
Clachan Ag & B 138 F9
Clachan Highld 153 J10
Clachan-a-Luib W Isls 168 d11
Clachan Mor Ag & B 136 B6
Clachan na Luib W Isls 168 d11
Clachan of Campsie E Duns 125 Q2
Clachan-Seil Ag & B 130 F4
Clachnaharry Highld 156 A8
Clachtoll Highld 164 B11
Clackavoid P & K 142 A5
Clacket Lane Services Surrey 37 K10
Clackmannan Clacks 133 Q9
Clackmannanshire Bridge Fife 133 Q10
Clackmarras Moray 157 N6
Clacton-on-Sea Essex 53 L8
Cladich Ag & B 131 M3
Cladswell Worcs 47 L3
Claggan Highld 138 C8
Claigan Highld 152 C7
Clandown BaNES 20 C3
Clanfield Hants 23 J11
Clanfield Oxon 33 Q4
Clannaborough Devon 8 H4
Clanville Hants 22 B5
Clanville Somset 20 B8
Claonaig Ag & B 123 Q8
Clapgate Dorset 12 H4
Clapgate Herts 51 K6
Clapham Bed 61 M10
Clapham Devon 9 L7
Clapham Gt Lon 36 G5
Clapham N York 95 Q7
Clapham W Susx 24 C9
Clapham Green Bed 61 M10
Clap Hill Kent 27 J4
Clappersgate Cumb 101 L10
Clapton Somset 11 J3
Clapton Somset 20 B4
Clapton-in-Gordano N Som 31 N10
Clapton-on-the-Hill Gloucs 47 N11
Clapworthy Devon 17 M7
Clarach Cerdgn 54 E8
Claravale Gatesd 112 H8
Clarbeston Pembks 41 L6
Clarbeston Road Pembks 41 K6
Clarborough Notts 85 M4
Clare Suffk 63 N11
Clarebrand D & G 108 G7
Clarencefield D & G 109 N7
Clarewood Nthumb 112 F7
Clarilaw Border 117 Q7
Clark's Green Surrey 24 E3
Clarkston E Rens 125 P6
Clashmore Highld 162 G9
Clashmore Highld 164 B10
Clashnessie Highld 164 C10
Clashnoir Moray 149 N3
Clathy P & K 134 B3
Clathymore P & K 134 C3
Clatt Abers 150 E2
Clatter Powys 55 M6
Clatterford End Essex 51 P8
Clatworthy Somset 18 E8
Claughton Lancs 88 G2
Claughton Lancs 95 M7
Claughton Wirral 81 L7
Clavelshay Somset 19 J8
Claverdon Warwks 59 J11
Claverham N Som 31 N11
Clavering Essex 51 L4
Claverley Shrops 57 P6
Claverton BaNES 20 E2
Claverton Down BaNES 20 E2
Clawdd-coch V Glam 30 E9
Clawdd-newydd Denbgs 68 E4
Clawthorpe Cumb 95 L5
Clawton Devon 5 P2
Claxby Lincs 86 F2
Claxby Lincs 87 N6
Claxton N York 98 D9
Claxton Norfk 77 L11
Claybrooke Magna Leics 59 Q7
Clay Common Suffk 65 P5
Clay Coton Nhants 60 C5
Clay Cross Derbys 84 E8
Claydon Oxon 48 E5
Claydon Suffk 53 K2
Clay End Herts 50 H6
Claygate D & G 110 G5
Claygate Kent 26 B3
Claygate Surrey 36 E8
Claygate Cross Kent 37 P9
Clayhall Gt Lon 37 K2
Clayhanger Devon 18 D10
Clayhanger Wsall 58 F4
Clayhidon Devon 18 G11
Clayhill E Susx 26 D7
Clayhill Hants 13 P3
Clayhithe Cambs 62 H8
Clayock Highld 167 L5
Claypit Hill Cambs 62 E10
Claypits Gloucs 32 E3
Claypole Lincs 85 P11
Claythorpe Lincs 87 M5
Clayton C Brad 90 E4
Clayton Donc 91 M9
Clayton W Susx 24 G8
Clayton Green Lancs 88 H6
Clayton-le-Moors Lancs 89 M4
Clayton-le-Woods Lancs 88 H6
Clayton West Kirk 90 H8
Clayworth Notts 85 M3
Cleadale Highld 144 G10
Cleadon S Tyne 113 N8
Clearbrook Devon 6 E5
Clearwell Gloucs 31 Q3
Cleasby N York 103 Q8
Cleat Ork 169 d8
Cleatlam Dur 103 M7
Cleator Cumb 100 D8
Cleator Moor Cumb 100 D7
Cleckheaton Kirk 90 F5
Cleedownton Shrops 57 K8
Cleehill Shrops 57 K9
Cleekhimin N Lans 126 D6
Clee St Margaret Shrops 57 K8
Cleestanton Shrops 57 K9
Cleethorpes NE Lin 93 P9
Cleeton St Mary Shrops 57 L9
Cleeve N Som 31 N11
Cleeve Oxon 34 H8
Cleeve Hill Gloucs 47 J9
Cleeve Prior Worcs 47 L5
Cleghornie E Loth 128 F3
Clehonger Herefs 45 N7
Cleish P & K 134 D8
Cleland N Lans 126 D6
Clement's End C Beds 50 B8
Clement Street Kent 37 M6
Clenamacrie Ag & B 131 J2
Clench Common Wilts 33 N11
Clenchwarton Norfk 75 L6
Clenerty Abers 159 J5
Clent Worcs 58 D9
Cleobury Mortimer Shrops 57 M9
Cleobury North Shrops 57 L7
Cleongart Ag & B 120 C5
Clephanton Highld 156 E7
Clerkhill D & G 117 K11
Cleuch-head D & G 115 R7
Clevancy Wilts 33 L9
Clevedon N Som 31 M10
Cleveley Oxon 48 C10
Cleveleys Lancs 88 C2
Cleverton Wilts 33 J7
Clewer Somset 19 M4
Cley next the Sea Norfk 76 E3
Cliburn Cumb 101 Q6
Cliddesden Hants 22 H5
Cliff Warwks 59 K5
Cliffe Lancs 89 L4
Cliffe Medway 38 B6
Cliffe N York 91 R4
Cliffe N York 103 P7
Cliff End E Susx 26 E9
Cliffe Woods Medway 38 B7
Clifford Herefs 45 J5
Clifford Leeds 91 L2
Clifford Chambers Warwks 47 N4
Clifford's Mesne Gloucs 46 D10
Cliffsend Kent 39 P9
Clifton Bristl 31 Q10
Clifton C Beds 50 E3
Clifton C Nott 72 E4
Clifton C York 98 B10
Clifton Calder 90 F6
Clifton Cumb 101 P5
Clifton Derbys 71 M6
Clifton Devon 17 L3
Clifton Donc 91 N11
Clifton Lancs 88 F4
Clifton N York 97 J11
Clifton Nthumb 113 K4
Clifton Oxon 48 E8
Clifton Salfd 82 G4
Clifton Worcs 46 F5
Clifton Campville Staffs 59 L2
Clifton Hampden Oxon 34 F5
Clifton Reynes M Keyn 49 P4
Clifton upon Dunsmore Warwks 60 B5
Clifton upon Teme Worcs 46 D2
Cliftonville Kent 39 Q7
Climping W Susx 15 Q6
Clink Somset 20 E5
Clint N York 97 L9
Clinterty C Aber 151 L5
Clint Green Norfk 76 E9
Clintmains Border 118 B4
Clipiau Gwynd 55 J2
Clippesby Norfk 77 N9
Clipsham Rutlnd 73 P7
Clipston Nhants 60 F4
Clipston Notts 72 G4
Clipstone C Beds 49 P9
Clipstone Notts 85 J8
Clitheroe Lancs 89 L2
Clive Shrops 69 P10
Cliveden Bucks 35 P7
Clixby Lincs 93 J10
Cloatley Wilts 33 J6
Clocaenog Denbgs 68 E4
Clochan Moray 158 B5
Clock Face St Hel 82 B6
Cloddiau Powys 56 C3
Clodock Herefs 45 L9
Cloford Somset 20 D6
Clola Abers 159 P9
Clophill C Beds 50 C3
Clopton Nhants 61 N4
Clopton Suffk 65 J11
Clopton Corner Suffk 65 J11
Clopton Green Suffk 63 N10
Clopton Green Suffk 64 D10
Clos du Valle Guern 10 c1
Closeburn D & G 109 J2
Closeburnmill D & G 109 K2
Closeclark IoM 80 c6
Closworth Somset 11 M2
Clothall Herts 50 G4
Clotton Ches W 69 P2
Cloudesley Bush Warwks 59 Q7
Clouds Herefs 46 A7
Clough Oldham 89 Q9
Clough Foot Calder 89 Q6
Clough Head Calder 90 D7
Cloughton N York 99 L2
Cloughton Newlands N York 105 R11
Clousta Shet 169 q8
Clova Angus 142 E3
Clovelly Devon 16 E7
Clovenfords Border 117 P3
Clovulin Highld 139 J5
Clow Bridge Lancs 89 N5
Clowne Derbys 84 G5
Clows Top Worcs 57 N10
Cloy Wrexhm 69 L6
Cluanie Inn Highld 146 D5
Cluanie Lodge Highld 146 D5
Clubworthy Cnwll 5 M3
Clugston D & G 107 L6
Clun Shrops 56 E8
Clunas Highld 156 F8
Clunbury Shrops 56 F8
Clunderwen Carmth 41 M7
Clune Highld 148 D2
Clunes Highld 146 F10
Clungunford Shrops 56 F9
Clunie P & K 141 R9
Clunton Shrops 56 E8
Cluny Fife 134 G8
Clutton BaNES 20 B3
Clutton Ches W 69 N4
Clutton Hill BaNES 20 B3
Clwt-y-bont Gwynd 67 K2
Clydach Mons 30 H2
Clydach Swans 29 J4
Clydach Vale Rhondd 30 C6
Clydebank W Duns 125 M3
Clydey Pembks 41 Q3
Clyffe Pypard Wilts 33 L9
Clynder Ag & B 131 Q11
Clyne Neath 29 M4
Clynnog Fawr Gwynd 66 G5
Clyro Powys 45 J6
Clyst Honiton Devon 9 N6
Clyst Hydon Devon 9 P4
Clyst St George Devon 9 N7
Clyst St Lawrence Devon 9 P4
Clyst St Mary Devon 9 N6
Cnoc W Isls 168 j4
Cnwch Coch Cerdgn 54 F10
Coad's Green Cnwll 5 M6
Coal Aston Derbys 84 E5
Coalbrookvale Blae G 30 G3
Coalburn S Lans 126 E11
Coalburns Gatesd 112 H8
Coaley Gloucs 32 E4
Coalhill Essex 38 C2
Coalmoor Wrekin 57 M3
Coalpit Heath S Glos 32 C8
Coal Pool Wsall 58 F5
Coalport Wrekin 57 M4
Coalsnaughton Clacks 133 Q8
Coal Street Suffk 65 J7
Coaltown of Balgonie Fife 134 H8
Coaltown of Wemyss Fife 135 J8
Coalville Leics 72 C8
Coanwood Nthumb 111 N9
Coat Somset 19 N10
Coatbridge N Lans 126 C4
Coatdyke N Lans 126 C4
Coate Swindn 33 N8
Coate Wilts 21 K2
Coates Cambs 74 F11
Coates Gloucs 33 J4
Coates Lincs 86 B4
Coates Notts 85 P4
Coates W Susx 23 Q11
Coatham R & Cl 104 G5
Coatham Mundeville Darltn 103 Q6
Cobbaton Devon 17 L6
Coberley Gloucs 47 J11
Cobhall Common Herefs 45 P7
Cobham Kent 37 Q7
Cobham Surrey 36 D8
Cobham Services Surrey 36 D9
Coblers Green Essex 51 Q7
Cobley Dorset 21 K10
Cobnash Herefs 45 P2
Cobo Guern 10 b1
Cobridge C Stke 70 F5
Coburby Abers 159 M5
Cock Alley Derbys 84 F6
Cockayne N York 104 H11
Cockayne Hatley C Beds 62 C11
Cock Bank Wrexhm 69 L5
Cock Bevington Warwks 47 L4
Cock Bridge Abers 149 P6
Cockburnspath Border 129 K5
Cock Clarks Essex 52 D11
Cock & End Suffk 63 M10
Cockenzie and Port Seton E Loth 128 C4
Cocker Bar Lancs 88 G6
Cocker Brook Lancs 89 L5
Cockerham Lancs 95 K10
Cockermouth Cumb 100 F4
Cockernhoe Herts 50 D6
Cockersdale Leeds 90 G5
Cockett Swans 28 H6
Cockfield Dur 103 M6
Cockfield Suffk 64 C11
Cockfosters Gt Lon 50 G11
Cock Green Essex 51 Q7
Cocking W Susx 23 N11
Cocking Causeway W Susx 23 N11
Cockington Torbay 7 M6
Cocklake Somset 19 M5
Cockley Beck Cumb 100 H10
Cockley Cley Norfk 75 Q10
Cock Marling E Susx 26 E8
Cockpole Green Wokham 35 L8
Cocks Cnwll 3 K3
Cockshutford Shrops 57 K7
Cockshutt Shrops 69 M9
Cock Street Kent 38 C11
Cockthorpe Norfk 76 D3
Cockwells Cnwll 2 E7
Cockwood Devon 9 N8
Cockwood Somset 18 H6
Cockyard Derbys 83 M9
Cockyard Herefs 45 N8
Coddenham Suffk 64 G11
Coddington Ches W 69 N3
Coddington Herefs 46 D6
Coddington Notts 85 P10
Codford St Mary Wilts 21 J7
Codford St Peter Wilts 21 J7
Codicote Herts 50 F7
Codmore Hill W Susx 24 C6
Codnor Derbys 84 F11
Codrington S Glos 32 D9
Codsall Staffs 58 C4
Codsall Wood Staffs 58 B4
Coedely Rhondd 30 D7
Coed Hirwaun Neath 29 M8
Coedkernew Newpt 31 J8
Coed Morgan Mons 31 L2
Coedpoeth Wrexhm 69 J4
Coed Talon Flints 69 J3
Coedway Powys 69 K11
Coed-y-Bryn Cerdgn 42 G5
Coed-y-caerau Newpt 31 L6
Coed-y-Cwm Rhondd 30 E6
Coed-y-paen Mons 31 K5
Coed-yr-ynys Powys 44 H10
Coed Ystumgwern Gwynd 67 K10
Coelbren Powys 29 N2
Coffinswell Devon 7 M5
Coffle End Bed 61 M9
Cofton Devon 9 N8
Cofton Hackett Worcs 58 F9
Cogan V Glam 30 G10
Cogenhoe Nhants 60 H8
Cogges Oxon 34 C3
Coggeshall Essex 52 E7
Coggin's Mill E Susx 25 N5
Coignafearn Highld 148 C4
Coilacriech Abers 149 Q8
Coilantogle Stirlg 132 H6
Coillore Highld 152 F10
Coity Brdgnd 29 P8
Col W Isls 168 j4
Colaboll Highld 162 D4
Colan Cnwll 4 D9
Colaton Raleigh Devon 10 B7
Colbost Highld 152 C8
Colburn N York 103 N11
Colby Cumb 102 C6
Colby IoM 80 b7
Colby Norfk 77 J5
Colchester Essex 52 G6
Colchester Zoo Essex 52 G7
Cold Ash W Berk 34 F11
Cold Ashby Nhants 60 E5
Cold Ashton S Glos 32 E10
Cold Aston Gloucs 47 M11
Coldbackie Highld 165 P4
Coldbeck Cumb 102 D10
Cold Blow Pembks 41 M8
Cold Brayfield M Keyn 49 P4
Cold Cotes N York 95 Q6
Coldean Br & H 24 H9
Coldeast Devon 7 L4
Colden Calder 90 B5
Colden Common Hants 22 E10
Coldfair Green Suffk 65 N9
Coldham Cambs 74 H10
Cold Hanworth Lincs 86 D4
Coldharbour Cnwll 3 K4
Coldharbour Devon 9 Q2
Coldharbour Gloucs 31 Q4
Cold Harbour Herts 50 D7
Cold Harbour Oxon 34 H9
Coldharbour Surrey 24 D2
Cold Hatton Wrekin 70 A10
Cold Hatton Heath Wrekin 70 A10
Cold Hesledon Dur 113 P11
Cold Hiendley Wakefd 91 K8
Cold Higham Nhants 49 J4
Coldingham Border 129 N6
Cold Kirby N York 98 A4
Coldmeece Staffs 70 F8
Cold Newton Leics 73 J9
Cold Northcott Cnwll 5 L4
Cold Norton Essex 52 E11
Cold Overton Leics 73 L8
Coldred Kent 27 N2
Coldridge Devon 17 M10
Coldstream Border 118 F3
Coldwaltham W Susx 24 B7
Coldwell Herefs 45 N7
Coldwells Abers 159 N10
Cold Weston Shrops 57 K8
Cole Somset 20 C8
Colebatch Shrops 56 E7
Colebrook C Plym 6 E7
Colebrook Devon 9 P3
Colebrooke Devon 9 J5
Coleby Lincs 86 C8
Coleby N Linc 92 E7
Cole End Warwks 59 K7
Coleford Devon 9 J4
Coleford Gloucs 31 Q2
Coleford Somset 20 C5
Coleford Water Somset 18 F8
Colegate End Norfk 64 H4
Cole Green Herts 50 G8
Cole Green Herts 51 K4
Cole Henley Hants 22 E4
Colehill Dorset 12 H4
Coleman Green Herts 50 E8
Coleman's Hatch E Susx 25 K4
Colemere Shrops 69 M8
Colemore Hants 23 K8
Colemore Green Shrops 57 N5
Colenden P & K 134 E2
Coleorton Leics 72 C7
Colerne Wilts 32 F10
Colesbourne Gloucs 33 K2
Cole's Cross Devon 7 K9
Coles Cross Dorset 10 H4
Colesden Bed 61 P9
Coles Green Suffk 53 K3
Coleshill Bucks 35 P5
Coleshill Oxon 33 P6
Coleshill Warwks 59 K7
Colestocks Devon 10 B4
Coley BaNES 19 Q3
Colgate W Susx 24 F4
Colinsburgh Fife 135 M7
Colinton C Edin 127 N4
Colintraive Ag & B 124 C3
Colkirk Norfk 76 C6
Coll Ag & B 136 G4
Coll W Isls 168 j4
Collace P & K 142 C11
Collafirth Shet 169 q5
Coll Airport Ag & B 136 F4
Collaton Devon 7 J11
Collaton St Mary Torbay 7 M6
College of Roseisle Moray 157 L4
College Town Br For 23 N2
Collessie Fife 134 H5
Colleton Mills Devon 17 M8
Collier Row Gt Lon 37 M2
Collier's End Herts 51 J6
Collier's Green E Susx 26 C7
Colliers Green Kent 26 C4
Collier Street Kent 26 B2
Colliery Row Sundld 113 M11
Collieston Abers 151 Q2
Collin D & G 109 M5
Collingbourne Ducis Wilts 21 P4
Collingbourne Kingston Wilts 21 P3
Collingham Leeds 97 N11
Collingham Notts 85 P8
Collington Herefs 46 B2
Collingtree Nhants 60 G9
Collins Green Warrtn 82 C6
Collins Green Worcs 46 D3
Colliston Angus 143 L8
Colliton Devon 10 B4
Collyweston Nhants 73 P10
Colmonell S Ayrs 114 B10
Colmworth Bed 61 P9
Colnabaichin Abers 149 P6
Colnbrook Slough 36 B5
Colne Cambs 62 E5
Colne Lancs 89 P3
Colne Bridge Kirk 90 F6
Colne Edge Lancs 89 P2
Colne Engaine Essex 52 D5
Colney Norfk 76 H10
Colney Heath Herts 50 F9
Colney Street Herts 50 E10
Coln Rogers Gloucs 33 L3
Coln St Aldwyns Gloucs 33 M3
Coln St Dennis Gloucs 33 L2
Colonsay Ag & B 136 b2
Colonsay Airport Ag & B 136 b3
Colpy Abers 158 F11
Colquhar Border 117 L2
Colquite Cnwll 4 H7
Colscott Devon 16 F9
Colsterdale N York 96 H4
Colsterworth Lincs 73 N6
Colston Bassett Notts 73 J4
Coltfield Moray 157 L5
Colt Hill Hants 23 L4
Coltishall Norfk 77 K8
Colton Cumb 94 G3
Colton Leeds 91 K4
Colton N York 91 N2
Colton Norfk 76 G10
Colton Staffs 71 J10
Colt's Hill Kent 25 P2
Columbjohn Devon 9 N5
Colva Powys 45 J4
Colvend D & G 109 J10
Colwall Herefs 46 E6
Colwell Nthumb 112 E5

Colwich Staffs 71 J10
Colwick Notts 72 G2
Colwinston V Glam 29 P9
Colworth W Susx 15 P6
Colwyn Bay Conwy 80 B9
Colyford Devon 10 F6
Colyton Devon 10 E6
Combe Devon 7 J11
Combe Herefs 45 L2
Combe Oxon 48 D11
Combe W Berk 22 C2
Combe Almer Dorset 12 G5
Combe Common Surrey 23 P7
Combe Down BaNES 20 E2
Combe Fishacre Devon 7 L5
Combe Florey Somset 18 G8
Combe Hay BaNES 20 D3
Combeinteignhead Devon 7 N4
Combe Martin Devon 17 K2
Combe Raleigh Devon 10 D4
Comberbach Ches W 82 D9
Comberford Staffs 59 J3
Comberton Cambs 62 E9
Comberton Herefs 56 H11
Combe St Nicholas Somset 10 G2
Combpyne Devon 10 F6
Combridge Staffs 71 K7
Combrook Warwks 48 B4
Combs Derbys 83 M9
Combs Suffk 64 E10
Combs Ford Suffk 64 E10
Combwich Somset 19 J6
Comers Abers 150 H6
Comhampton Worcs 58 B11
Commercial End Cambs 63 J8
Commins Coch Powys 55 J4
Commondale N York 105 J8
Common Edge Bpool 88 C4
Common End Cumb 100 D6
Common Moor Cnwll 5 L8
Common Platt Wilts 33 M7
Commonside Ches W 82 B10
Commonside Derbys 71 N6
Common Side Derbys 84 D5
Commonwood Shrops 69 N9
Commonwood Wrexhm 69 L4
Compass Somset 19 J8
Compstall Stockp 83 L6
Compstonend D & G 108 E10
Compton Devon 7 M6
Compton Hants 22 B9
Compton Hants 22 E9
Compton Staffs 57 Q8
Compton Surrey 23 Q5
Compton W Berk 34 F8
Compton W Susx 15 L4
Compton Wilts 21 M4
Compton Abbas Dorset 20 G11
Compton Abdale Gloucs 47 L11
Compton Bassett Wilts 33 K10
Compton Beauchamp Oxon 33 Q7
Compton Bishop Somset 19 L3
Compton Chamberlayne
Wilts 21 K9
Compton Dando BaNES 20 B2
Compton Dundon Somset 19 N8
Compton Durville Somset 19 M11
Compton Greenfield S Glos 31 Q8
Compton Martin BaNES 19 P3
Compton Pauncefoot
Somset 20 B9
Compton Valence Dorset 11 M6
Comrie Fife 134 C10
Comrie P & K 133 M3
Conaglen House Highld 139 J4
Conchra Highld 145 Q2
Concraigie P & K 141 Q9
Conder Green Lancs 95 K9
Conderton Worcs 47 J7
Condicote Gloucs 47 N9
Condorrat N Lans 126 C3
Condover Shrops 56 H3
Coney Hill Gloucs 46 G11
Coneyhurst Common
W Susx 24 D6
Coneysthorpe N York 98 E6
Coneythorpe N York 97 N9
Coney Weston Suffk 64 D6
Conford Hants 23 M8
Congdon's Shop Cnwll 5 M6
Congerstone Leics 72 B9
Congham Norfk 75 P6
Congleton Ches E 70 F2
Congl-y-wal Gwynd 67 N6
Congresbury N Som 19 M2
Congreve Staffs 58 D2
Conheath D & G 109 L7
Conicavel Moray 156 H7
Coningsby Lincs 86 H9
Conington Cambs 61 Q3
Conington Cambs 62 D7
Conisbrough Donc 91 N11
Conisholme Lincs 93 R11
Coniston Cumb 101 K11
Coniston E R Yk 93 L3
Coniston Cold N York 96 D10
Conistone N York 96 E7
Connah's Quay Flints 81 K11
Connel Ag & B 138 G11
Connel Park E Ayrs 115 M5
Connor Downs Cnwll 2 F6
Conon Bridge Highld 155 P6
Cononley N York 96 E11
Consall Staffs 70 H5
Consett Dur 112 H10
Constable Burton N York 97 J2
Constable Lee Lancs 89 N6
Constantine Cnwll 3 J8
Constantine Bay Cnwll 4 D7
Contin Highld 155 N6
Conwy Conwy 79 P9
Conwy Castle Conwy 79 P9
Conyer Kent 38 G9
Conyer's Green Suffk 64 B8
Cooden E Susx 26 B10
Cookbury Devon 16 G10
Cookbury Wick Devon 16 F10
Cookham W & M 35 N7
Cookham Dean W & M 35 N7
Cookham Rise W & M 35 N7
Cookhill Worcs 47 L3
Cookley Suffk 65 L6
Cookley Worcs 58 B8
Cookley Green Oxon 35 J6
Cookney Abers 151 M9
Cooksbridge E Susx 25 K8
Cooksey Green Worcs 58 D11
Cook's Green Essex 53 L8
Cooks Green Suffk 64 D11
Cookshill Staffs 70 G6
Cooksland Cnwll 4 H8
Cooksmill Green Essex 51 P9
Cookson Green Ches W 82 C10
Coolham W Susx 24 D6
Cooling Medway 38 C6
Cooling Street Medway 38 B7
Coombe Cnwll 2 G5
Coombe Cnwll 3 L5
Coombe Cnwll 3 N3
Coombe Devon 7 N4
Coombe Devon 9 K8
Coombe Devon 10 C6
Coombe Gloucs 32 E6
Coombe Hants 23 J10
Coombe Wilts 21 M4
Coombe Bissett Wilts 21 M9
Coombe Cellars Devon 7 N4
Coombe Cross Hants 23 J10
Coombe Hill Gloucs 46 G9
Coombe Keynes Dorset 12 D8
Coombe Pafford Torbay 7 N5
Coombes W Susx 24 E9
Coombes-Moor Herefs 45 M2
Coombe Street Somset 20 E8
Coombeswood Dudley 58 E7
Coopersale Common Essex 51 L10
Coopersale Street Essex 51 L10
Cooper's Corner Kent 37 L11
Coopers Green E Susx 25 L6
Coopers Green Herts 50 E9
Cooper Street Kent 39 P9
Cooper Turning Bolton 89 J9
Cootham W Susx 24 C8
Copdock Suffk 53 K3
Copford Green Essex 52 F7
Copgrove N York 97 M8
Copister Shet 169 r6
Cople Bed 61 P11
Copley Calder 90 D6
Copley Dur 103 L5
Copley Tamesd 83 L5
Coplow Dale Derbys 83 Q9
Copmanthorpe C York 98 B11
Copmere End Staffs 70 E9
Copp Lancs 88 E3
Coppathorne Cnwll 16 C11
Coppenhall Staffs 70 G11
Coppenhall Moss Ches E 70 C3
Copperhouse Cnwll 2 F6
Coppicegate Shrops 57 N8
Coppingford Cambs 61 Q5
Coppins Corner Kent 26 F2
Copplestone Devon 9 J4
Coppull Lancs 88 H8
Coppull Moor Lancs 88 H8
Copsale W Susx 24 E6
Copster Green Lancs 89 K4
Copston Magna Warwks 59 Q7
Cop Street Kent 39 N9
Copthall Green Essex 51 K10
Copt Heath Solhll 59 J9
Copt Hewick N York 97 M6
Copthorne Cnwll 5 M3
Copthorne W Susx 24 H3
Copt Oak Leics 72 D8
Copy's Green Norfk 76 C4
Copythorne Hants 13 P2
Coram Street Suffk 52 H3
Corbets Tey Gt Lon 37 N3
Corbière Jersey 11 a2
Corbridge Nthumb 112 E8
Corby Nhants 61 J3
Corby Glen Lincs 73 Q6
Corby Hill Cumb 111 J9
Cordon N Ayrs 121 K5
Cordwell Derbys 84 D5
Coreley Shrops 57 L10
Cores End Bucks 35 P7
Corfe Somset 18 H11
Corfe Castle Dorset 12 G8
Corfe Mullen Dorset 12 G5
Corfton Shrops 56 H7
Corgarff Abers 149 P6
Corhampton Hants 22 H10
Corks Pond Kent 25 Q2
Corlae D & G 115 N8
Corley Warwks 59 M7
Corley Ash Warwks 59 L7
Corley Moor Warwks 59 L8
Corley Services Warwks 59 M7
Cormuir Angus 142 E4
Cornard Tye Suffk 52 F3
Corndon Devon 8 G7
Corner Row Lancs 88 E4
Corney Cumb 94 C2
Cornforth Dur 104 B4
Cornhill Abers 158 E6
Cornhill-on-Tweed Nthumb 118 G3
Cornholme Calder 89 Q5
Cornish Hall End Essex 51 Q3
Cornoigmore Ag & B 136 B6
Cornriggs Dur 102 F2
Cornsay Dur 103 M2
Cornsay Colliery Dur 103 N2
Corntown Highld 155 Q6
Corntown V Glam 29 P9
Cornwall Airport Newquay
Cnwll 4 D9
Cornwell Oxon 47 Q9
Cornwood Devon 6 G7
Cornworthy Devon 7 L7
Corpach Highld 139 K2
Corpusty Norfk 76 G6
Corrachree Abers 150 D7
Corran Highld 139 J5
Corran Highld 145 P6
Corrany IoM 80 g4
Corrie D & G 110 D3
Corrie N Ayrs 121 K3
Corriecravie N Ayrs 120 H7
Corriegills N Ayrs 121 K4
Corriegour Lodge Hotel
Highld 146 H9
Corriemoille Highld 155 L5
Corrimony Highld 155 L11
Corringham Lincs 85 Q2
Corringham Thurr 38 B5
Corris Gwynd 54 H3
Corris Uchaf Gwynd 54 G3
Corrow Ag & B 131 P7
Corry Highld 145 K3
Corscombe Devon 8 F5
Corscombe Dorset 11 L3
Corse Gloucs 46 E9
Corse Lawn Gloucs 46 F8
Corsham Wilts 32 G10
Corsindae Abers 150 H6
Corsley Wilts 20 F5
Corsley Heath Wilts 20 F5
Corsock D & G 108 G5
Corston BaNES 32 C11
Corston Wilts 32 H8
Corstorphine C Edin 127 M3
Cors-y-Gedol Gwynd 67 L10
Cortachy Angus 142 F6
Corton Suffk 65 Q2
Corton Wilts 20 H6
Corton Denham Somset 20 B10
Coruanan Highld 139 K4
Corwen Denbgs 68 E6
Coryates Dorset 11 N7
Coryton Devon 8 C8
Coryton Thurr 38 B5
Cosby Leics 72 E11
Coseley Dudley 58 D6
Cosford Shrops 57 Q3
Cosgrove Nhants 49 L6
Cosham C Port 15 J5
Cosheston Pembks 41 K10
Coshieville P & K 141 J8
Cossall Notts 72 D2
Cossall Marsh Notts 72 D2
Cossington Leics 72 G8
Cossington Somset 19 L6
Costessey Norfk 76 H9
Costock Notts 72 F5
Coston Leics 73 L6
Coston Norfk 76 F10
Cote Oxon 34 C4
Cote Somset 19 K6
Cotebrook Ches W 82 C11
Cotehill Cumb 111 J10
Cotes Cumb 95 K3
Cotes Leics 72 F6
Cotes Staffs 70 E8
Cotesbach Leics 60 B4
Cotes Heath Staffs 70 E8
Cotford St Luke Somset 18 G9
Cotgrave Notts 72 G3
Cothal Abers 151 M4
Cotham Notts 85 N11
Cothelstone Somset 18 G8
Cotherstone Dur 103 K7
Cothill Oxon 34 E5
Cotleigh Devon 10 E4
Cotmanhay Derbys 72 D2
Coton Cambs 62 F9
Coton Nhants 60 E6
Coton Shrops 69 P8
Coton Staffs 59 J4
Coton Staffs 70 E10
Coton Staffs 70 H8
Coton Clanford Staffs 70 F10
Coton Hayes Staffs 70 H8
Coton Hill Shrops 56 H2
Coton in the Clay Staffs 71 M9
Coton in the Elms Derbys 71 N11
Coton Park Derbys 71 P11
Cotswolds 33 J3
Cotswold Wildlife Park &
Gardens Oxon 33 P3
Cott Devon 7 K6
Cottam E R Yk 99 K7
Cottam Lancs 88 G4
Cottam Notts 85 P5
Cottenham Cambs 62 F7
Cotterdale N York 96 B2
Cottered Herts 50 H5
Cotteridge Birm 58 F8
Cotterstock Nhants 61 M2
Cottesbrooke Nhants 60 F6
Cottesmore Rutlnd 73 N8
Cottingham E R Yk 92 H4
Cottingham Nhants 60 H2
Cottingley C Brad 90 E3
Cottisford Oxon 48 G8
Cotton Suffk 64 F8
Cotton End Bed 61 N11
Cotton Tree Lancs 89 Q3
Cottown Abers 150 E2
Cottown Abers 151 K4
Cottown of Gight Abers 159 K9
Cotts Devon 6 C5
Cotwall Wrekin 69 R11
Cotwalton Staffs 70 G8
Couch's Mill Cnwll 5 J10
Coughton Herefs 46 A10
Coughton Warwks 47 L2
Coulaghailtro Ag & B 123 M6
Coulags Highld 154 C9
Coulderton Cumb 100 C9
Coull Abers 150 E7
Coulport Ag & B 131 Q10
Coulsdon Gt Lon 36 G9
Coulston Wilts 21 J4
Coulter S Lans 116 E4
Coultershaw Bridge W Susx 23 Q11
Coultings Somset 18 H6
Coulton N York 98 C6
Coultra Fife 135 K3
Cound Shrops 57 K3
Coundlane Shrops 57 K4
Coundon Dur 103 P5
Coundon Grange Dur 103 P5
Countersett N York 96 D3
Countess Wilts 21 N6
Countess Cross Essex 52 E5
Countess Wear Devon 9 M7
Countesthorpe Leics 72 F11
Countisbury Devon 17 N2
Coupar Angus P & K 142 C10
Coup Green Lancs 88 H5
Coupland Cumb 102 D7
Coupland Nthumb 118 H4
Cour Ag & B 123 P10
Court-at-Street Kent 27 J4
Courteachan Highld 145 L8
Courteenhall Nhants 49 L4
Court Henry Carmth 43 L10
Courtsend Essex 38 H3
Courtway Somset 18 H8
Cousland Mdloth 128 B6
Cousley Wood E Susx 25 Q4
Cove Ag & B 131 Q11
Cove Border 129 K5
Cove Devon 18 C11
Cove Hants 23 N3
Cove Highld 160 C8
Cove Bay C Aber 151 P7
Cove Bottom Suffk 65 P6
Covehithe Suffk 65 Q5
Coven Staffs 58 D3
Coveney Cambs 62 G4
Covenham St
Bartholomew Lincs 87 K2
Covenham St Mary Lincs 87 K2
Coven Heath Staffs 58 D3
Coventry Covtry 59 M9
Coverack Cnwll 3 K10
Coverack Bridges Cnwll 2 H7
Coverham N York 96 H3
Covington Cambs 61 N6
Covington S Lans 116 D3
Cowan Bridge Lancs 95 N5
Cowbeech E Susx 25 P8
Cowbit Lincs 74 E7
Cowbridge V Glam 30 C10
Cowdale Derbys 83 N10
Cowden Kent 25 L2
Cowdenbeath Fife 134 F9
Cowden Pound Kent 25 L2
Cowden Station Kent 25 L2
Cowers Lane Derbys 71 Q5
Cowes IoW 14 E7
Cowesby N York 97 Q3
Cowesfield Green Wilts 21 Q10
Cowfold W Susx 24 F6
Cowgill Cumb 95 R3
Cow Green Suffk 64 F8
Cowhill S Glos 32 B6
Cowie Stirlg 133 N10
Cowlam E R Yk 99 K7
Cowley Devon 9 M5
Cowley Gloucs 33 J2
Cowley Gt Lon 36 C4
Cowley Oxon 34 F4
Cowling Lancs 88 H7
Cowling N York 90 B2
Cowling N York 97 K3
Cowlinge Suffk 63 M10
Cowmes Kirk 90 F7
Cowpe Lancs 89 N6
Cowpen Nthumb 113 L4
Cowpen Bewley S on T 104 E6
Cowplain Hants 15 J4
Cowshill Dur 102 G2
Cowslip Green N Som 19 N2
Cowthorpe N York 97 P10
Coxall Herefs 56 F10
Coxbank Ches E 70 B6
Coxbench Derbys 72 B2
Coxbridge Somset 19 P7
Cox Common Suffk 65 N5
Coxford Cnwll 5 K2
Coxford Norfk 76 B6
Coxgreen Staffs 57 Q7
Coxheath Kent 38 B11
Coxhoe Dur 104 B3
Coxley Somset 19 P6
Coxley Wakefd 90 H7
Coxley Wick Somset 19 P6
Coxpark Cnwll 5 Q7
Coxtie Green Essex 51 N11
Coxwold N York 98 A5
Coychurch Brdgnd 29 P9
Coylton S Ayrs 114 H4
Coylumbridge Highld 148 G5
Coytrahen Brdgnd 29 N7
Crabbs Cross Worcs 58 F11
Crab Orchard Dorset 13 J3
Crabtree W Susx 24 F5
Crabtree Green Wrexhm 69 K6
Crackenthorpe Cumb 102 C6
Crackington Haven Cnwll 5 J2
Crackley Staffs 70 E4
Crackley Warwks 59 L10
Crackleybank Shrops 57 P2
Crackpot N York 103 J11
Cracoe N York 96 E8
Craddock Devon 10 B2
Cradle End Herts 51 L6
Cradley Dudley 58 D7
Cradley Herefs 46 D5
Cradley Heath Sandw 58 D7
Cradoc Powys 44 E8
Crafthole Cnwll 5 P11
Crafton Bucks 49 N11
Crag Foot Lancs 95 K6
Craggan Highld 149 J2
Cragganmore Moray 157 M10
Cragg Hill Leeds 90 G3
Cragg Vale Calder 90 C6
Craghead Dur 113 K10
Cragside House & Garden
Nthumb 119 L10
Crai Powys 44 B10
Craibstone Moray 158 C6
Craichie Angus 143 J8
Craig Angus 143 M6
Craig Highld 154 D8
Craigbank E Ayrs 115 L5
Craigburn Border 127 N7
Craig-cefn-parc Swans 29 J4
Craigcleuch D & G 110 F3
Craigdam Abers 159 K11
Craigdhu Ag & B 130 G6
Craigearn Abers 151 J5
Craigellachie Moray 157 P9
Craigend P & K 134 E3
Craigend Rens 125 M3
Craigendoran Ag & B 132 C11
Craigends Rens 125 L4
Craighlaw D & G 107 K5
Craighouse Ag & B 122 H6
Craigie P & K 141 R9
Craigie S Ayrs 125 L11
Craigiefold Abers 159 M4
Craigley D & G 108 G9
Craig Llangiwg Neath 29 K4
Craiglockhart C Edin 127 N3
Craigmillar C Edin 127 Q3
Craignant Shrops 69 J7
Craigneston D & G 115 Q10
Craigneuk N Lans 126 D4
Craigneuk N Lans 126 D6
Craignure Ag & B 138 C10
Craigo Angus 143 M5
Craig Penllyn V Glam 30 C9
Craigrothie Fife 135 K5
Craigruie Stirlg 132 F3
Craig's End Essex 52 B4
Craigton Angus 143 J10
Craigton C Aber 151 L7
Craigton E Rens 125 M7
Craigton of Airlie Angus 142 E7
Craig-y-Duke Neath 29 K4
Craig-y-nos Powys 44 A11
Craik Border 117 L9
Crail Fife 135 Q6
Crailing Border 118 C6
Craiselound N Linc 92 C11
Crakehall N York 97 K3
Crakehill N York 97 P6
Crakemarsh Staffs 71 K7
Crambe N York 98 E8
Cramlington Nthumb 113 L5
Cramond C Edin 127 M2
Cramond Bridge C Edin 127 M2
Crampmoor Hants 22 C10
Cranage Ches E 82 G11
Cranberry Staffs 70 E7
Cranborne Dorset 13 J2
Cranbourne Br For 35 P10
Cranbrook Devon 9 N6
Cranbrook Kent 26 C4
Cranbrook Common Kent 26 C4
Crane Moor Barns 91 J10
Crane's Corner Norfk 76 C9
Cranfield C Beds 49 Q6
Cranford Devon 16 E7
Cranford Gt Lon 36 D5
Cranford St Andrew Nhants 61 K5
Cranford St John Nhants 61 K5
Cranham Gloucs 32 G2
Cranham Gt Lon 37 N3
Cranhill Warwks 47 M4
Crank St Hel 81 Q5
Cranleigh Surrey 24 C3
Cranmer Green Suffk 64 E7
Cranmore IoW 14 C8
Cranmore Somset 20 C6
Cranoe Leics 73 K11
Cransford Suffk 65 L9
Cranshaws Border 128 H7
Cranstal IoM 80 g1
Cranswick E R Yk 99 L10
Crantock Cnwll 4 B9
Cranwell Lincs 86 D11
Cranwich Norfk 63 N2
Cranworth Norfk 76 D11
Craobh Haven Ag & B 130 F6
Crapstone Devon 6 E5
Crarae Ag & B 131 K8
Crask Inn Highld 162 C2
Crask of Aigas Highld 155 N9
Craster Nthumb 119 Q7
Craswall Herefs 45 K7
Crateford Staffs 58 D3
Cratfield Suffk 65 L6
Crathes Abers 151 K8
Crathie Abers 149 P8
Crathie Highld 147 P9
Crathorne N York 104 D9
Craven Arms Shrops 56 G8
Crawcrook Gatesd 112 H8
Crawford Lancs 81 P4
Crawford S Lans 116 D6
Crawfordjohn S Lans 116 B6
Crawley Hants 22 D8
Crawley Oxon 34 B2
Crawley W Susx 24 G3
Crawley Down W Susx 24 H3
Crawleyside Dur 103 J2
Crawshawbooth Lancs 89 N5
Crawton Abers 143 R2
Craxe's Green Essex 52 F8
Cray N York 96 D5
Crayford Gt Lon 37 M5
Crayke N York 98 B6
Craymere Beck Norfk 76 F5
Crays Hill Essex 38 B3
Cray's Pond Oxon 34 H8
Craythorne Staffs 71 N9
Craze Lowman Devon 9 N2
Crazies Hill Wokham 35 L8
Creacombe Devon 17 Q8
Creagan Inn Ag & B 138 H9
Creag Ghoraidh W Isls 168 c13
Creagorry W Isls 168 c13
Creaguaineach Lodge
Highld 139 Q4
Creamore Bank Shrops 69 P8
Creaton Nhants 60 F6
Creca D & G 110 D6
Credenhill Herefs 45 P6
Crediton Devon 9 K4
Creebank D & G 107 K2
Creebridge D & G 107 M4
Creech Dorset 12 F8
Creech Heathfield Somset 19 J9
Creech St Michael Somset 19 J9
Creed Cnwll 3 N4
Creekmoor BCP 12 H6
Creekmouth Gt Lon 37 L4
Creeksea Essex 38 F2
Creeting St Mary Suffk 64 F10
Creeton Lincs 73 Q6
Creetown D & G 107 N6
Cregneash IoM 80 a8
Creg ny Baa IoM 80 e5
Cregrina Powys 44 G4
Creich Fife 135 J3
Creigiau Cardif 30 E8
Cremyll Cnwll 6 D8
Cressage Shrops 57 K4
Cressbrook Derbys 83 Q10
Cresselly Pembks 41 L9
Cressex Bucks 35 M6
Cressing Essex 52 C7
Cresswell Nthumb 113 L2
Cresswell Pembks 41 L9
Cresswell Staffs 70 H7
Creswell Derbys 84 H6
Creswell Green Staffs 58 G2
Cretingham Suffk 65 J9
Cretshengan Ag & B 123 M6
Crewe Ches E 70 C3
Crewe-by-Farndon Ches W 69 M4
Crewe Green Ches E 70 C3
Crew Green Powys 69 K11
Crewkerne Somset 11 J3
Crews Hill Station Gt Lon 50 H10
Crewton C Derb 72 B4
Crianlarich Stirlg 132 D2
Cribyn Cerdgn 43 K4

Criccieth Gwynd 66 H7
Crich Derbys 84 D10
Crich Carr Derbys 84 D10
Crichton Mdloth 128 B7
Crick Mons 31 N6
Crick Nhants 60 C6
Crickadarn Powys 44 F6
Cricket St Thomas Somset 10 H3
Crickheath Shrops 69 J10
Crickhowell Powys 45 J11
Cricklade Wilts 33 L6
Cricklewood Gt Lon 36 F3
Cridling Stubbs N York 91 N6
Crieff P & K 133 P3
Criggan Cnwll 4 G9
Criggion Powys 69 J11
Crigglestone Wakefd 91 J7
Crimble Rochdl 89 P8
Crimond Abers 159 Q6
Crimplesham Norfk 75 N10
Crimscote Warwks 47 P5
Crinaglack Highld 155 M9
Crinan Ag & B 130 F9
Crindledyke N Lans 126 E6
Cringleford Norfk 76 H10
Cringles C Brad 96 F11
Crinow Pembks 41 M8
Cripplesease Cnwll 2 E6
Cripplestyle Dorset 13 J2
Cripp's Corner E Susx 26 C7
Croachy Highld 148 B2
Croanford Cnwll 4 G7
Crockenhill Kent 37 M7
Crocker End Oxon 35 K7
Crockerhill W Susx 15 P5
Crockernwell Devon 9 J6
Crocker's Ash Herefs 45 Q11
Crockerton Wilts 20 G6
Crocketford D & G 108 H6
Crockey Hill C York 98 C11
Crockham Hill Kent 37 K10
Crockhurst Street Kent 37 P11
Crockleford Heath Essex 52 H6
Crock Street Somset 10 G2
Croeserw Neath 29 N5
Croes-goch Pembks 40 F4
Croes-lan Cerdgn 42 G6
Croesor Gwynd 67 L6
Croesyceiliog Carmth 42 H11
Croesyceiliog Torfn 31 K5
Croes-y-mwyalch Torfn 31 K6
Croes-y-pant Mons 31 K4
Croft Leics 72 E11
Croft Lincs 87 P8
Croft Warrtn 82 D6
Croftamie Stirlg 132 F10
Croft Mitchell Cnwll 2 H6
Crofton Cumb 110 F10
Crofton Wakefd 91 K7
Crofton Wilts 21 Q2
Croft-on-Tees N York 103 Q9
Croftown Highld 161 K10
Crofts Moray 157 P7
Crofts Bank Traffd 82 G5
Crofts of Dipple Moray 157 Q6
Crofts of Savoch Abers 159 P5
Crofty Swans 28 F6
Crogen Gwynd 68 D7
Croggan Ag & B 130 E2
Croglin Cumb 111 L11
Croick Highld 162 B8
Cromarty Highld 156 D4
Crombie Fife 134 D11
Cromdale Highld 149 K2
Cromer Herts 50 G5
Cromer Norfk 77 J3
Cromford Derbys 84 C9
Cromhall S Glos 32 C6
Cromhall Common S Glos 32 C7
Cromor W Isls 168 j5
Crompton Fold Oldham 89 Q9
Cromwell Notts 85 N8
Cronberry E Ayrs 115 M3
Crondall Hants 23 L5
Cronkbourne IoM 80 e6
Cronk-y-Voddy IoM 80 d4
Cronton Knows 81 P7
Crook Cumb 101 N11
Crook Dur 103 N3
Crookdake Cumb 100 G2
Crooke Wigan 88 H9
Crooked End Gloucs 46 B11
Crookedholm E Ayrs 125 M10
Crooked Soley Wilts 34 B10
Crookes Sheff 84 D3
Crookhall Dur 112 H10
Crookham Nthumb 118 H3
Crookham W Berk 22 F2
Crookham Village Hants 23 L4
Crook Inn Border 116 G5
Crooklands Cumb 95 L4
Crook of Devon P & K 134 C7
Cropper Derbys 71 N7
Cropredy Oxon 48 E5
Cropston Leics 72 F8
Cropthorne Worcs 47 J5
Cropton N York 98 F3
Cropwell Bishop Notts 72 H3
Cropwell Butler Notts 72 H3
Cros W Isls 168 k1
Crosbost W Isls 168 i5
Crosby Cumb 100 E3
Crosby IoM 80 d6
Crosby N Linc 92 E8
Crosby Sefton 81 L5
Crosby Garret Cumb 102 D9
Crosby Ravensworth Cumb 102 B8
Crosby Villa Cumb 100 E3
Croscombe Somset 19 Q6
Crosemere Shrops 69 M9
Crosland Edge Kirk 90 E8
Crosland Hill Kirk 90 E8
Cross Somset 19 M4
Crossaig Ag & B 123 P9
Crossapol Ag & B 136 B7
Cross Ash Mons 45 N11
Cross-at-Hand Kent 26 C2
Crossbost W Isls 168 i5
Crossbush W Susx 24 B9
Crosscanonby Cumb 100 E3
Cross Coombe Cnwll 3 J3
Crossdale Street Norfk 77 J4
Cross End Bed 61 N9
Cross End Essex 52 E5
Crossens Sefton 88 D6
Cross Flatts C Brad 90 E2
Crossford Fife 134 D10
Crossford S Lans 126 E8
Crossgate Cnwll 5 N4
Crossgate Lincs 74 D5
Crossgate Staffs 70 G7
Crossgatehall E Loth 128 B6
Crossgates E Ayrs 125 K9
Crossgates Fife 134 E10
Cross Gates Leeds 91 K4
Crossgates N York 99 L4
Crossgates Powys 44 F2
Crossgill Lancs 95 M8
Cross Green Devon 5 P4
Cross Green Leeds 91 J4
Cross Green Staffs 58 D3
Cross Green Suffk 64 A11
Cross Green Suffk 64 B10
Cross Green Suffk 64 D11
Cross Hands Carmth 28 G2
Crosshands Carmth 41 N6
Crosshands E Ayrs 125 M11
Cross Hands Pembks 41 L8
Cross Hill Derbys 84 F11
Crosshill Fife 134 F8
Crosshill S Ayrs 114 F6
Cross Hills N York 96 F11
Crosshouse E Ayrs 125 K10
Cross Houses Shrops 57 J3
Cross Houses Shrops 57 M6
Cross in Hand E Susx 25 N6
Cross Inn Cerdgn 42 G3
Cross Inn Cerdgn 43 K2
Cross Inn Pembks 41 M9
Cross Inn Rhondd 30 E8
Cross Keys Ag & B 132 C10
Crosskeys Caerph 30 H6
Cross Keys Wilts 32 G10
Crosskirk Highld 166 H3
Crosslands Cumb 94 G3
Cross Lane IoW 14 F9
Cross Lane Head Shrops 57 N5
Cross Lanes Cnwll 2 H9
Cross Lanes Cnwll 3 K5
Cross Lanes N York 98 A8
Crosslanes Shrops 69 K11
Cross Lanes Wrexhm 69 L5
Crosslee Rens 125 L4
Crossley Kirk 90 G6
Crossmichael D & G 108 F7
Cross Oak Powys 44 G10
Cross of Jackston Abers 158 H11
Cross o' th' hands Derbys 71 P5
Crosspost W Susx 24 G6
Crossroads Abers 150 F6
Crossroads Abers 151 K9
Cross Roads C Brad 90 D3
Cross Street Suffk 64 H6
Crosston Angus 143 J6
Cross Town Ches E 82 G9
Crossway Mons 45 N11
Crossway Powys 44 F3
Crossway Green Mons 31 P6
Crossway Green Worcs 58 B11
Crossways Dorset 12 C7
Crosswell Pembks 41 M3
Crosthwaite Cumb 95 J2
Croston Lancs 88 F7
Crostwick Norfk 77 K8
Crostwight Norfk 77 L6
Crouch Kent 37 P9
Crouch Kent 39 J10
Crouch End Gt Lon 36 H3
Croucheston Wilts 21 L9
Crouch Hill Dorset 11 Q2
Crough House Green Kent 37 K11
Croughton Nhants 48 F8
Crovie Abers 159 K4
Crow Hants 13 L4
Crowan Cnwll 2 G7
Crowborough E Susx 25 M4
Crowborough Warren E Susx 25 M4
Crowcombe Somset 18 F7
Crowdecote Derbys 83 P11
Crowden Derbys 83 N5
Crowden Devon 8 C5
Crowdhill Hants 22 E10
Crowdleham Kent 37 N9
Crow Edge Barns 83 Q4
Crowell Oxon 35 K5
Crow End Cambs 62 D9
Crowfield Nhants 48 H6
Crowfield Suffk 64 G10
Crowfield Green Suffk 64 G10
Crowgate Street Norfk 77 L7
Crow Green Essex 51 N11
Crowhill E Loth 129 J5
Crow Hill Herefs 46 B9
Crowhole Derbys 84 D5
Crowhurst E Susx 26 C9
Crowhurst Surrey 37 J11
Crowhurst Lane End Surrey 37 J11
Crowland Lincs 74 D8
Crowland Suffk 64 E7
Crowlas Cnwll 2 E7
Crowle N Linc 92 C8
Crowle Worcs 46 H3
Crowle Green Worcs 46 H3
Crowmarsh Gifford Oxon 34 H7
Crown Corner Suffk 65 K7
Crownhill C Plym 6 D7
Crownpits Surrey 23 Q6
Crownthorpe Norfk 76 F11
Crowntown Cnwll 2 G7
Crows-an-Wra Cnwll 2 B8
Crow's Green Essex 51 Q5
Crowshill Norfk 76 D10
Crow's Nest Cnwll 5 M8
Crowsnest Shrops 56 F4
Crowthorne Wokham 23 M2
Crowton Ches W 82 C10
Croxall Staffs 59 J2
Croxby Lincs 93 L11
Croxdale Dur 103 Q3
Croxden Staffs 71 K7
Croxley Green Herts 50 C11
Croxteth Lpool 81 N5
Croxton Cambs 62 B8
Croxton N Linc 93 J8
Croxton Norfk 64 B4
Croxton Norfk 76 D5
Croxton Staffs 70 D8
Croxtonbank Staffs 70 D8
Croxton Green Ches E 69 Q4
Croxton Kerrial Leics 73 L5
Croy Highld 156 D8
Croy N Lans 126 C2
Croyde Devon 16 G4
Croyde Bay Devon 16 G4
Croydon Cambs 62 D11
Croydon Gt Lon 36 H7
Crubenmore Highld 148 B9
Cruckmeole Shrops 56 G3
Cruckton Shrops 56 G2
Cruden Bay Abers 159 Q10
Crudgington Wrekin 70 A11
Crudie Abers 159 J6
Crudwell Wilts 33 J6
Cruft Devon 8 D5
Crûg Powys 56 B10
Crugmeer Cnwll 4 E6
Crugybar Carmth 43 N7
Crug-y-byddar Powys 56 B8
Crumlin Caerph 30 H5
Crumplehorn Cnwll 5 L11
Crumpsall Manch 82 H4
Crundale Kent 27 J2
Crundale Pembks 41 J7
Crunwere Pembks 41 N8
Cruwys Morchard Devon 9 L2
Crux Easton Hants 22 D3
Cruxton Dorset 11 N5
Crwbin Carmth 28 E2
Cryers Hill Bucks 35 N5
Crymych Pembks 41 N4
Crynant Neath 29 L4
Crystal Palace Gt Lon 36 H6
Cuaig Highld 153 N6
Cuan Ag & B 130 F5
Cubbington Warwks 59 M11
Cubert Cnwll 4 B10
Cubley Barns 90 G10
Cublington Bucks 49 M10
Cublington Herefs 45 N7
Cuckfield W Susx 24 H5
Cucklington Somset 20 E9
Cuckney Notts 85 J6
Cuckoo Bridge Lincs 74 D6
Cuckoo's Corner Hants 23 K6
Cuckoo's Nest Ches W 69 L2
Cuddesdon Oxon 34 G4
Cuddington Bucks 35 K2
Cuddington Ches W 82 C10
Cuddington Heath Ches W 69 N5
Cuddy Hill Lancs 88 F3
Cudham Gt Lon 37 K9
Cudliptown Devon 8 D9
Cudnell BCP 13 J5
Cudworth Barns 91 K9
Cudworth Somset 10 H2
Cuerdley Cross Warrtn 82 B7
Cufaude Hants 23 J3
Cuffley Herts 50 H10
Cuil Highld 138 H6
Culbokie Highld 155 R6
Culbone Somset 17 Q2
Culburnie Highld 155 N9
Culcabock Highld 156 B9
Culcharry Highld 156 F7
Culcheth Warrtn 82 E6
Culdrain Abers 158 D11
Culduie Highld 153 N9
Culford Suffk 64 A7
Culgaith Cumb 102 B5
Culham Oxon 34 F5
Culkein Highld 164 B10
Culkein Drumbeg Highld 164 D10
Culkerton Gloucs 32 H5
Cullen Moray 158 D4
Cullercoats N Tyne 113 N6
Cullerlie Abers 151 K7
Cullicudden Highld 156 A5
Cullingworth C Brad 90 D3
Cuillin Hills Highld 144 G3
Cullipool Ag & B 130 E5
Cullivoe Shet 169 s3
Culloden Highld 156 C8
Cullompton Devon 9 P3
Cullompton Services Devon 9 P3
Culm Davy Devon 18 F11
Culmington Shrops 56 H8
Culmstock Devon 10 C2
Culnacraig Highld 160 H6
Culnaightrie D & G 108 G10
Culnaknock Highld 153 J5
Culpho Suffk 53 M2
Culrain Highld 162 D8
Culross Fife 134 B10
Culroy S Ayrs 114 F5
Culsalmond Abers 158 G11
Culscadden D & G 107 N8
Culshabbin D & G 107 K7
Culswick Shet 169 p9
Cultercullen Abers 151 N3
Cults C Aber 151 M7
Culverstone Green Kent 37 P8
Culverthorpe Lincs 73 Q2
Culworth Nhants 48 F5
Culzean Castle & Country Park S Ayrs 114 D5
Cumbernauld N Lans 126 D3
Cumbernauld Village N Lans 126 D2
Cumberworth Lincs 87 P6
Cumdivock Cumb 110 F11
Cuminestown Abers 159 K7
Cumledge Border 129 K8
Cummersdale Cumb 110 G10
Cummertrees D & G 109 P7
Cummingston Moray 157 L4
Cumnock E Ayrs 115 L3
Cumnor Oxon 34 E4
Cumrew Cumb 111 L10
Cumrue D & G 109 N3
Cumwhinton Cumb 111 J10
Cumwhitton Cumb 111 K10
Cundall N York 97 P6
Cunninghamhead N Ayrs 125 K9
Cunningsburgh Shet 169 r10
Cupar Fife 135 K5
Cupar Muir Fife 135 K5
Curbar Derbys 84 C6
Curbridge Hants 14 F4
Curbridge Oxon 34 B3
Curdridge Hants 14 F4
Curdworth Warwks 59 J6
Curland Somset 19 J11
Curridge W Berk 34 E10
Currie C Edin 127 M4
Curry Mallet Somset 19 K10
Curry Rivel Somset 19 L9
Curteis Corner Kent 26 E4
Curtisden Green Kent 26 B3
Curtisknowle Devon 7 J8
Cury Cnwll 2 H9
Cushnie Abers 150 E5
Cushuish Somset 18 G8
Cusop Herefs 45 J6
Cusworth Donc 91 N10
Cutcloy D & G 107 N11
Cutcombe Somset 18 B7
Cutgate Rochdl 89 P8
Cuthill Highld 162 H9
Cutiau Gwynd 67 L11
Cutler's Green Essex 51 N4
Cutmadoc Cnwll 4 H9
Cutmere Cnwll 5 N9
Cutnall Green Worcs 58 C11
Cutsdean Gloucs 47 L8
Cutsyke Wakefd 91 L6
Cutthorpe Derbys 84 D6
Cuttivett Cnwll 5 P9
Cuxham Oxon 35 J5
Cuxton Medway 38 B8
Cuxwold Lincs 93 L10
Cwm Blae G 30 G3
Cwm Denbgs 80 F9
Cwmafan Neath 29 L6
Cwmaman Rhondd 30 D5
Cwmann Carmth 43 L5
Cwmavon Torfn 31 J3
Cwmbach Carmth 28 E4
Cwmbach Carmth 41 Q5
Cwmbâch Powys 44 H7
Cwmbach Rhondd 30 D4
Cwmbach Llechrhyd Powys 44 E4
Cwmbelan Powys 55 L8
Cwmbran Torfn 31 J6
Cwmbrwyno Cerdgn 54 G8
Cwm Capel Carmth 28 E4
Cwmcarn Caerph 30 H6
Cwmcarvan Mons 31 N3
Cwm-celyn Blae G 30 H3
Cwm-Cewydd Gwynd 55 K2
Cwm-cou Cerdgn 41 Q2
Cwm Crawnon Powys 44 G11
Cwmdare Rhondd 30 C4
Cwmdu Carmth 43 M8
Cwmdu Powys 44 H10
Cwmdu Swans 28 H6
Cwmduad Carmth 42 G8
Cwm Dulais Swans 28 H4
Cwmdwr Carmth 43 P8
Cwmfelin Brdgnd 29 N7
Cwmfelin Myr Td 30 E4
Cwmfelin Boeth Carmth 41 N7
Cwmfelinfach Caerph 30 G6
Cwmfelin Mynach Carmth 41 P6
Cwmffrwd Carmth 42 H11
Cwmgiedd Powys 29 L2
Cwmgorse Carmth 29 K2
Cwm Gwaun Pembks 41 K4
Cwmgwili Carmth 28 G2
Cwmgwrach Neath 29 N4
Cwmhiraeth Carmth 42 F7
Cwm-Ifor Carmth 43 N9
Cwm Irfon Powys 44 B5
Cwmisfael Carmth 43 J11
Cwm Llinau Powys 55 J3
Cwmllynfell Neath 29 K2
Cwmmawr Carmth 28 F2
Cwm Morgan Carmth 41 Q4
Cwmparc Rhondd 29 P5
Cwmpengraig Carmth 42 G7
Cwm Penmachno Conwy 67 P5
Cwmpennar Rhondd 30 D4
Cwmrhos Powys 44 H10
Cwmrhydyceirw Swans 29 J5
Cwmsychbant Cerdgn 43 J5
Cwmtillery Blae G 30 H3
Cwm-twrch Isaf Powys 29 L2
Cwm-twrch Uchaf Powys 29 L2
Cwm-y-glo Carmth 28 G2
Cwm-y-glo Gwynd 67 K2
Cwmyoy Mons 45 K10
Cwmystwyth Cerdgn 54 H10
Cwrt Gwynd 54 F5
Cwrt-newydd Cerdgn 43 J5
Cwrt-y-gollen Powys 45 J11
Cyfarthfa Castle Museum Myr Td 30 D3
Cyffylliog Denbgs 68 E3
Cyfronydd Powys 55 Q3
Cylibebyll Neath 29 K4
Cymau Flints 69 J3
Cymmer Neath 29 N5
Cymmer Rhondd 30 D6
Cynghordy Carmth 43 R6
Cynheidre Carmth 28 E3
Cynonville Neath 29 M5
Cynwyd Denbgs 68 E6
Cynwyl Elfed Carmth 42 G9

D

Daccombe Devon 7 N5
Dacre Cumb 101 N5
Dacre N York 97 J8
Dacre Banks N York 97 J8
Daddry Shield Dur 102 G3
Dadford Bucks 49 J7
Dadlington Leics 72 C11
Dafen Carmth 28 F4
Daffy Green Norfk 76 D10
Dagenham Gt Lon 37 M4
Daglingworth Gloucs 33 J3
Dagnall Bucks 49 Q11
Dagworth Suffk 64 E9
Dail bho Dheas W Isls 168 j1
Dailly S Ayrs 114 E7
Dainton Devon 7 M5
Dairsie Fife 135 L4
Daisy Hill Bolton 82 E4
Daisy Hill Leeds 90 H5
Dalabrog W Isls 168 c15
Dalavich Ag & B 131 K5
Dalbeattie D & G 108 H8
Dalbury Derbys 71 P8
Dalby IoM 80 b6
Dalby Lincs 87 M7
Dalby N York 98 C6
Dalcapon P & K 141 N7
Dalchalm Highld 163 L5
Dalchreichart Highld 146 H5
Dalchruin P & K 133 L4
Dalcrue P & K 134 C2
Dalderby Lincs 87 J7
Dalditch Devon 9 P8
Dale Cumb 101 P2
Dale Derbys 72 C3
Dale Pembks 40 F9
Dale Bottom Cumb 101 J6
Dale End Derbys 84 B8
Dale End N York 96 E11
Dale Hill E Susx 26 B5
Dalehouse N York 105 L7
Dalelia Highld 138 C4
Dalgarven N Ayrs 124 H8
Dalgety Bay Fife 134 F11
Dalgig E Ayrs 115 L5
Dalginross P & K 133 M3
Dalguise P & K 141 N8
Dalhalvaig Highld 166 E6
Dalham Suffk 63 M8
Daliburgh W Isls 168 c15
Dalkeith Mdloth 127 Q4
Dallas Moray 157 L7
Dallinghoo Suffk 65 K10
Dallington E Susx 25 Q7
Dallington Nhants 60 F8
Dallow N York 97 J6
Dalmally Ag & B 131 P2
Dalmary Stirlg 132 G8
Dalmellington E Ayrs 115 J6
Dalmeny C Edin 127 L2
Dalmore Highld 156 B4
Dalmuir W Duns 125 M3
Dalnabreck Highld 138 C4
Dalnacardoch P & K 140 H3
Dalnahaitnach Highld 148 F4
Dalnaspidal P & K 140 F3
Dalnawillan Lodge Highld 166 H8
Daloist P & K 141 J6
Dalqueich P & K 134 D7
Dalquhairn S Ayrs 114 F8
Dalreavoch Highld 162 H5
Dalry N Ayrs 124 H8
Dalrymple E Ayrs 114 G5
Dalserf S Lans 126 D7
Dalsmeran Ag & B 120 B9
Dalston Cumb 110 G10
Dalston Gt Lon 36 H4
Dalswinton D & G 109 K3
Dalton Cumb 95 L5
Dalton D & G 109 P6
Dalton Lancs 88 F9
Dalton N York 97 P5
Dalton N York 103 M9
Dalton Nthumb 112 H6
Dalton Rothm 84 G2
Dalton-in-Furness Cumb 94 E6
Dalton-le-Dale Dur 113 P11
Dalton Magna Rothm 84 G2
Dalton-on-Tees N York 103 Q9
Dalton Parva Rothm 84 G2
Dalton Piercy Hartpl 104 E4
Dalveich Stirlg 133 J3
Dalwhinnie Highld 147 Q11
Dalwood Devon 10 E4
Damask Green Herts 50 G5
Damerham Hants 21 M11
Damgate Norfk 77 N10
Dam Green Norfk 64 E4
Damnaglaur D & G 106 F10
Danaway Kent 38 E9
Danbury Essex 52 C10
Danby N York 105 K9
Danby Bottom N York 105 J10
Danby Wiske N York 104 B11
Dandaleith Moray 157 P8
Danderhall Mdloth 127 Q4
Danebridge Ches E 83 L11
Dane End Herts 50 H6
Danegate E Susx 25 N4
Danehill E Susx 25 K5
Dane Hills C Leic 72 F10
Danemoor Green Norfk 76 F10
Danesford Shrops 57 N6
Danesmoor Derbys 84 F8
Dane Street Kent 39 J11
Daniel's Water Kent 26 G3
Danshillock Abers 158 H6
Danskine E Loth 128 F6
Danthorpe E R Yk 93 N4
Danzey Green Warwks 58 H11
Dapple Heath Staffs 71 J9
Darby Green Hants 23 M2
Darcy Lever Bolton 89 L9
Dardy Powys 45 J11
Darenth Kent 37 N6
Daresbury Halton 82 C8
Darfield Barns 91 L10
Darfoulds Notts 85 J5
Dargate Kent 39 J9
Dargavel Rens 125 L3
Darite Cnwll 5 M8
Darland Medway 38 C8
Darland Wrexhm 69 L3
Darlaston Wsall 58 E5
Darlaston Green Wsall 58 E5
Darley N York 97 K9
Darley Abbey C Derb 72 B3
Darley Bridge Derbys 84 C8
Darley Dale Derbys 84 C8
Darley Green Solhll 59 J10
Darleyhall Herts 50 D6
Darley Head N York 97 J9
Darlingscott Warwks 47 P6
Darlington Darltn 103 Q8
Darliston Shrops 69 Q8
Darlton Notts 85 N6
Darnford Staffs 58 H3
Darnick Border 117 Q4
Darowen Powys 55 J4
Darra Abers 158 H8
Darracott Devon 16 C8
Darracott Devon 16 H4
Darras Hall Nthumb 113 J6
Darrington Wakefd 91 M7
Darsham Suffk 65 N8
Darshill Somset 20 B6
Dartford Kent 37 M6
Dartford Crossing Kent 37 N5
Dartington Devon 7 K6
Dartmeet Devon 6 H4
Dartmoor National Park Devon 8 G9
Dartmouth Devon 7 M8

- Darton Barns 91 J8
- Darvel E Ayrs 125 P10
- Darwell Hole E Susx 25 Q7
- Darwen Bl w D 89 K6
- Datchet W & M 35 Q9
- Datchworth Herts 50 G7
- Datchworth Green Herts 50 G7
- Daubhill Bolton 89 L9
- Daugh of Kinermony Moray 157 N9
- Dauntsey Wilts 33 J8
- Dava Highld 157 J10
- Davenham Ches W 82 E10
- Davenport Stockp 83 K7
- Davenport Green Ches E 82 H9
- Davenport Green Traffd 82 H7
- Daventry Nhants 60 C8
- Davidson's Mains C Edin 127 N2
- Davidstow Cnwll 5 K4
- David Street Kent 37 P8
- Davington D & G 117 J10
- Davington Hill Kent 38 H9
- Daviot Abers 151 J2
- Daviot Highld 156 C10
- Daviot House Highld 156 C9
- Davis's Town E Susx 25 M7
- Davoch of Grange Moray 158 C7
- Davyhulme Traffd 82 G5
- Daw End Wsall 58 F4
- Dawesgreen Surrey 36 F11
- Dawley Wrekin 57 M3
- Dawlish Devon 9 N9
- Dawlish Warren Devon 9 N9
- Dawn Conwy 80 B10
- Daws Green Somset 18 G10
- Daws Heath Essex 38 D4
- Daw's House Cnwll 5 N5
- Dawsmere Lincs 74 H4
- Daybrook Notts 85 J11
- Day Green Ches E 70 D3
- Dayhills Staffs 70 H8
- Dayhouse Bank Worcs 58 E9
- Daylesford Gloucs 47 P9
- Ddol Flints 80 G10
- Ddol-Cownwy Powys 68 D11
- Deal Kent 39 Q11
- Dean Cumb 100 E5
- Dean Devon 7 J6
- Dean Devon 17 L2
- Dean Devon 17 N2
- Dean Dorset 21 J11
- Dean Hants 22 D8
- Dean Hants 22 G11
- Dean Lancs 89 P5
- Dean Oxon 48 B10
- Dean Somset 20 C6
- Dean Bottom Kent 37 N7
- Deanburnhaugh Border 117 M8
- Deancombe Devon 7 J6
- Dean Court Oxon 34 E3
- Deane Bolton 89 K9
- Deane Hants 22 F4
- Dean End Dorset 21 J11
- Dean Head Barns 90 H10
- Deanhead Kirk 90 C7
- Deanland Dorset 21 J11
- Deanlane End W Susx 15 K4
- Dean Prior Devon 7 J6
- Deanraw Nthumb 112 B8
- Dean Row Ches E 83 J8
- Deans W Loth 127 J4
- Deanscales Cumb 100 E5
- Deanshanger Nhants 49 L7
- Deanshaugh Moray 157 R7
- Deanston Stirlg 133 L7
- Dean Street Kent 38 B11
- Dearham Cumb 100 E3
- Dearnley Rochdl 89 Q7
- Debach Suffk 65 J11
- Debden Essex 51 K11
- Debden Essex 51 N4
- Debden Green Essex 51 N4
- Debenham Suffk 64 H9
- Deblin's Green Worcs 46 F5
- Dechmont W Loth 127 J3
- Dechmont Road W Loth 127 J4
- Deddington Oxon 48 E8
- Dedham Essex 53 J5
- Dedham Heath Essex 53 J5
- Dedworth W & M 35 P9
- Deene Nhants 61 K2
- Deenethorpe Nhants 61 L2
- Deepcar Sheff 90 H11
- Deepcut Surrey 23 P3
- Deepdale Cumb 95 Q4
- Deepdale N York 96 C5
- Deeping Gate C Pete 74 B9
- Deeping St James Lincs 74 C9
- Deeping St Nicholas Lincs 74 D7
- Deerhurst Gloucs 46 G8
- Deerhurst Walton Gloucs 46 G9
- Deerton Street Kent 38 G9
- Defford Worcs 46 H6
- Defynnog Powys 44 C9
- Deganwy Conwy 79 P9
- Degnish Ag & B 130 F5
- Deighton C York 91 Q2
- Deighton N York 104 C10
- Deiniolen Gwynd 67 K2
- Delabole Cnwll 4 H5
- Delamere Ches W 82 C11
- Delfrigs Abers 151 P3
- Delley Devon 17 J7
- Delliefure Highld 157 K11
- Dell Quay W Susx 15 M6
- Delly End Oxon 34 C2
- Delnabo Moray 149 M4
- Delny Highld 156 C3
- Delph Oldham 90 B9
- Delves Dur 112 H11
- Delvin End Essex 52 C4
- Dembleby Lincs 73 Q3
- Demelza Cnwll 4 F9
- Denaby Donc 91 M11
- Denaby Main Donc 91 M11
- Denbies Surrey 36 D10
- Denbigh Denbgs 80 F11
- Denbrae Fife 135 K4
- Denbury Devon 7 L5
- Denby Derbys 84 E11
- Denby Bottles Derbys 84 E11
- Denby Dale Kirk 90 G9
- Denchworth Oxon 34 C6
- Dendron Cumb 94 E6
- Denel End C Beds 50 B3
- Denfield P & K 134 B4
- Denford Nhants 61 L5
- Dengie Essex 52 G11
- Denham Bucks 36 B3
- Denham Suffk 63 N8
- Denham Suffk 64 H7
- Denham End Suffk 63 N8
- Denham Green Bucks 36 B3
- Denham Green Suffk 64 H7
- Denhead Abers 159 N7
- Denhead Fife 135 M5
- Denhead of Gray C Dund 142 F11
- Denholm Border 117 R7
- Denholme C Brad 90 D4
- Denholme Clough C Brad 90 D4
- Denio Gwynd 66 F7
- Denmead Hants 15 J4
- Denmore C Aber 151 N5
- Denne Park W Susx 24 E5
- Dennington Suffk 65 K8
- Denny Falk 133 N11
- Dennyloanhead Falk 133 N11
- Den of Lindores Fife 134 H4
- Denshaw Oldham 90 B8
- Denside Abers 151 L8
- Densole Kent 27 M3
- Denston Suffk 63 N10
- Denstone Staffs 71 K6
- Denstroude Kent 39 K9
- Dent Cumb 95 Q3
- Denton Cambs 61 Q3
- Denton Darltn 103 P7
- Denton E Susx 25 L10
- Denton Kent 27 M2
- Denton Kent 37 Q6
- Denton Lincs 73 M4
- Denton N York 96 H11
- Denton Nhants 60 H9
- Denton Norfk 65 K4
- Denton Oxon 34 G4
- Denton Tamesd 83 K5
- Denver Norfk 75 M10
- Denwick Nthumb 119 P8
- Deopham Norfk 76 E11
- Deopham Green Norfk 64 E2
- Depden Suffk 63 N9
- Depden Green Suffk 63 N9
- Deptford Gt Lon 37 J5
- Deptford Wilts 21 K7
- Derby C Derb 72 B3
- Derby Devon 17 K5
- Derbyhaven IoM 80 c8
- Derculich P & K 141 L7
- Dereham Norfk 76 D9
- Deri Caerph 30 F4
- Derril Devon 16 E11
- Derringstone Kent 27 M2
- Derrington Staffs 70 F10
- Derriton Devon 16 E11
- Derry Hill Wilts 33 J10
- Derrythorpe N Linc 92 D9
- Dersingham Norfk 75 N4
- Dervaig Ag & B 137 L5
- Derwen Denbgs 68 E4
- Derwenlas Powys 54 G5
- Derwent Valley Mills Derbys 84 D9
- Derwent Water Cumb 101 J6
- Derwydd Carmth 43 M11
- Desborough Nhants 60 H4
- Desford Leics 72 D10
- Deskford Moray 158 D5
- Detchant Nthumb 119 L3
- Detling Kent 38 C10
- Deuxhill Shrops 57 M7
- Devauden Mons 31 N5
- Devil's Bridge Cerdgn 54 G9
- Devitts Green Warwks 59 L6
- Devizes Wilts 21 K2
- Devonport C Plym 6 D8
- Devonside Clacks 133 Q8
- Devoran Cnwll 3 K6
- Devoran & Perran Cnwll 3 K6
- Dewarton Mdloth 128 B7
- Dewlish Dorset 12 C5
- Dewsbury Kirk 90 G6
- Dewsbury Moor Kirk 90 G6
- Deytheur Powys 68 H11
- Dial N Som 31 P11
- Dial Green W Susx 23 P9
- Dial Post W Susx 24 E7
- Dibberford Dorset 11 K4
- Dibden Hants 14 D5
- Dibden Purlieu Hants 14 D5
- Dickens Heath Solhll 58 H9
- Dickleburgh Norfk 64 H5
- Didbrook Gloucs 47 L8
- Didcot Oxon 34 F6
- Diddington Cambs 61 Q7
- Diddlebury Shrops 57 J7
- Didley Herefs 45 P8
- Didling W Susx 23 M11
- Didmarton Gloucs 32 F7
- Didsbury Manch 82 H6
- Didworthy Devon 6 H6
- Digby Lincs 86 E10
- Digg Highld 152 H4
- Diggle Oldham 90 C9
- Digmoor Lancs 88 F9
- Digswell Herts 50 F7
- Digswell Water Herts 50 G8
- Dihewyd Cerdgn 43 J3
- Dilham Norfk 77 L6
- Dilhorne Staffs 70 H6
- Dill Hall Lancs 89 M5
- Dillington Cambs 61 P7
- Dilston Nthumb 112 E8
- Dilton Wilts 20 G5
- Dilton Marsh Wilts 20 F5
- Dilwyn Herefs 45 N4
- Dimple Bolton 89 L7
- Dimple Derbys 84 C8
- Dinas Carmth 41 Q4
- Dinas Cnwll 4 E7
- Dinas Gwynd 66 D7
- Dinas Gwynd 66 H3
- Dinas Rhondd 30 D6
- Dinas Cross Pembks 41 K3
- Dinas Dinlle Gwynd 66 G3
- Dinas-Mawddwy Gwynd 67 R11
- Dinas Powys V Glam 30 G10
- Dinder Somset 19 Q6
- Dinedor Herefs 45 Q7
- Dingestow Mons 31 N2
- Dingle Lpool 81 M7
- Dingleden Kent 26 D5
- Dingley Nhants 60 G3
- Dingwall Highld 155 P6
- Dinmael Conwy 68 D6
- Dinnet Abers 150 D8
- Dinnington N u Ty 113 K6
- Dinnington Rothm 84 H3
- Dinnington Somset 11 J2
- Dinorwic Gwynd 67 K2
- Dinton Bucks 35 L2
- Dinton Wilts 21 K8
- Dinwoodie D & G 109 P2
- Dinworthy Devon 16 E8
- Dipford Somset 18 H10
- Dipley Hants 23 K3
- Dippen Ag & B 120 F4
- Dippenhall Surrey 23 M5
- Dippermill Devon 8 B3
- Dippertown Devon 8 B8
- Dippin N Ayrs 121 K7
- Dipple Moray 157 Q6
- Dipple S Ayrs 114 D7
- Diptford Devon 7 J7
- Dipton Dur 113 J10
- Diptonmill Nthumb 112 D8
- Dirleton E Loth 128 E3
- Dirt Pot Nthumb 112 C11
- Discoed Powys 45 K2
- Diseworth Leics 72 D6
- Dishforth N York 97 N6
- Disley Ches E 83 L8
- Diss Norfk 64 G5
- Disserth Powys 44 E3
- Distington Cumb 100 D6
- Ditchampton Wilts 21 L8
- Ditcheat Somset 20 B7
- Ditchingham Norfk 65 L3
- Ditchling E Susx 24 H7
- Ditherington Shrops 57 J2
- Ditteridge Wilts 32 F11
- Dittisham Devon 7 M7
- Ditton Kent 38 B10
- Ditton Green Cambs 63 L9
- Ditton Priors Shrops 57 L7
- Dixton Gloucs 47 J8
- Dixton Mons 31 P2
- Dizzard Cnwll 5 K2
- Dobcross Oldham 90 B9
- Dobwalls Cnwll 5 L8
- Doccombe Devon 9 J7
- Dochgarroch Highld 155 R9
- Dockenfield Surrey 23 M6
- Docker Lancs 95 M6
- Docking Norfk 75 Q3
- Docklow Herefs 45 R3
- Dockray Cumb 101 L6
- Dockray Cumb 110 E11
- Dodbrooke Devon 7 J10
- Doddinghurst Essex 51 N11
- Doddington Cambs 62 F2
- Doddington Kent 38 F10
- Doddington Lincs 85 Q6
- Doddington Nthumb 119 J4
- Doddington Shrops 57 L9
- Doddiscombsleigh Devon 9 L7
- Dodd's Green Ches E 69 R6
- Doddshill Norfk 75 N4
- Doddy Cross Cnwll 5 N9
- Dodford Nhants 60 D8
- Dodford Worcs 58 D10
- Dodington S Glos 32 E8
- Dodington Somset 18 G6
- Dodleston Ches W 69 L2
- Dodscott Devon 17 J8
- Dodside E Rens 125 N7
- Dod's Leigh Staffs 71 J8
- Dodworth Barns 91 J9
- Dodworth Bottom Barns 91 J10
- Dodworth Green Barns 91 J10
- Doe Bank Birm 58 H5
- Doe Lea Derbys 84 G7
- Dogdyke Lincs 86 H9
- Dogley Lane Kirk 90 F8
- Dogmersfield Hants 23 L4
- Dogridge Wilts 33 L7
- Dogsthorpe C Pete 74 C10
- Dog Village Devon 9 N5
- Dolanog Powys 55 P2
- Dolau Powys 55 Q11
- Dolaucothi Carmth 43 N6
- Dolbenmaen Gwynd 67 J6
- Doley Staffs 70 C9
- Dolfach Powys 55 L4
- Dol-fôr Powys 55 J3
- Dolfor Powys 55 Q7
- Dolgarrog Conwy 79 P11
- Dolgellau Gwynd 67 N11
- Dolgoch Gwynd 54 F4
- Dol-gran Carmth 42 H8
- Doll Highld 163 K6
- Dollar Clacks 134 B8
- Dollarfield Clacks 134 B8
- Dolley Green Powys 56 D11
- Dollwen Cerdgn 54 F8
- Dolphin Flints 80 H10
- Dolphinholme Lancs 95 L10
- Dolphinton S Lans 127 L8
- Dolton Devon 17 K9
- Dolwen Conwy 80 B10
- Dolwyddelan Conwy 67 N4
- Dolybont Cerdgn 54 E7
- Dolyhir Powys 45 J3
- Domgay Powys 69 J11
- Donaldson's Lodge Nthumb 118 G2
- Doncaster Donc 91 P10
- Doncaster Carr Donc 91 P10
- Doncaster North Services Donc 91 R8
- *Doncaster Sheffield Airport* Donc 91 R11
- Donhead St Andrew Wilts 20 H10
- Donhead St Mary Wilts 20 H10
- Donibristle Fife 134 F10
- Doniford Somset 18 E6
- Donington Lincs 74 D3
- Donington on Bain Lincs 86 H4
- Donington Park Services Leics 72 D5
- Donington Southing Lincs 74 D4
- Donisthorpe Leics 59 M2
- Donkey Street Kent 27 K5
- Donkey Town Surrey 23 P2
- Donnington Gloucs 47 N9
- Donnington Herefs 46 D8
- Donnington Shrops 57 K3
- Donnington W Berk 34 E11
- Donnington W Susx 15 N6
- Donnington Wrekin 57 N2
- Donnington Wood Wrekin 57 N2
- Donyatt Somset 10 G2
- Doomsday Green W Susx 24 E5
- Doonfoot S Ayrs 114 F4
- Dora's Green Hants 23 M5
- Dorback Lodge Highld 149 K4
- Dorchester Dorset 11 P6
- Dorchester-on-Thames Oxon 34 G6
- Dordon Warwks 59 L4
- Dore Sheff 84 D4
- Dores Highld 155 Q11
- Dorking Surrey 36 E11
- Dorking Tye Suffk 52 F4
- Dormansland Surrey 25 K2
- Dormans Park Surrey 25 J2
- Dormington Herefs 46 A6
- Dormston Worcs 47 J3
- Dorn Gloucs 47 P8
- Dorney Bucks 35 P9
- Dornie Highld 145 Q2
- Dornoch Highld 162 H9
- Dornock D & G 110 D7
- Dorrery Highld 167 J6
- Dorridge Solhll 59 J10
- Dorrington Lincs 86 E10
- Dorrington Shrops 56 H4
- Dorrington Shrops 70 C6
- Dorsington Warwks 47 M5
- Dorstone Herefs 45 L6
- Dorton Bucks 35 J2
- Dosthill Staffs 59 K5
- Dothan IoA 78 F10
- Dottery Dorset 11 K5
- Doublebois Cnwll 5 K9
- Doughton Gloucs 32 G6
- Douglas IoM 80 e6
- Douglas S Lans 116 A4
- Douglas and Angus C Dund 142 G11
- Douglas Pier Ag & B 131 P8
- Douglastown Angus 142 G8
- Douglas Water S Lans 116 B3
- Douglas West S Lans 126 E11
- Doulting Somset 20 B6
- Dounby Ork 169 b4
- Doune Highld 161 Q6
- Doune Stirlg 133 L7
- Dounepark S Ayrs 114 C8
- Dounie Highld 162 D8
- Dousland Devon 6 E5
- Dovaston Shrops 69 L10
- Dove Dale Derbys 71 L4
- Dove Green Notts 84 G10
- Dove Holes Derbys 83 N9
- Dovenby Cumb 100 E4
- Dover Kent 27 P3
- Dover Wigan 82 D4
- Dover Castle Kent 27 P3
- Dovercourt Essex 53 M5
- Doverdale Worcs 58 C11
- Doveridge Derbys 71 L8
- Doversgreen Surrey 36 G11
- Dowally P & K 141 P8
- Dowbridge Lancs 88 E4
- Dowdeswell Gloucs 47 K11
- Dowlais Myr Td 30 E3
- Dowland Devon 17 K9
- Dowlish Ford Somset 10 H2
- Dowlish Wake Somset 10 H2
- Down Ampney Gloucs 33 L5
- Downderry Cnwll 5 N11
- Downe Gt Lon 37 K8
- Downend Gloucs 32 F5
- Downend IoW 14 F9
- Downend S Glos 32 C9
- Downend W Berk 34 E9
- Downfield C Dund 142 F11
- Downgate Cnwll 5 M7
- Downgate Cnwll 5 P7
- Downham Essex 38 B2
- Downham Gt Lon 37 J6
- Downham Lancs 89 M2
- Downham Market Norfk 75 M10
- Down Hatherley Gloucs 46 G10
- Downhead Somset 19 Q9
- Downhead Somset 20 C5
- Downhill Cnwll 4 D8
- Downhill P & K 134 D2
- Downholland Cross Lancs 88 D9
- Downholme N York 103 M11
- Downicarey Devon 5 P3
- Downies Abers 151 N9
- Downing Flints 80 H9
- Downley Bucks 35 M5
- Down St Mary Devon 8 H4
- Downside Somset 20 B4
- Downside Somset 20 B6
- Downside Surrey 36 D9
- Down Thomas Devon 6 E8
- Downton Hants 13 N6
- Downton Wilts 21 N10
- Dowsby Lincs 74 B5
- Dowsdale Lincs 74 E8
- Doxey Staffs 70 F10
- Doxford Nthumb 119 N6
- Doynton S Glos 32 D10
- Draethen Caerph 30 H7
- Draffan S Lans 126 D8
- Dragonby N Linc 92 F8
- Dragons Green W Susx 24 D6
- Drakeholes Notts 85 M2
- Drakelow Worcs 57 Q8
- Drakemyre N Ayrs 124 H7
- Drakes Broughton Worcs 46 H5
- Drakewalls Cnwll 6 C4
- Draughton N York 96 F10
- Draughton Nhants 60 G5
- Drax N York 92 A5
- Drax Hales N York 91 R5
- Draycote Warwks 59 P10
- Draycot Foliat Swindn 33 N9
- Draycott Derbys 72 C4
- Draycott Gloucs 47 N7
- Draycott Shrops 57 Q6
- Draycott Somset 19 N4
- Draycott Somset 19 Q10
- Draycott Worcs 46 G5
- Draycott in the Clay Staffs 71 M9
- Draycott in the Moors Staffs 70 H6
- Drayford Devon 9 J2
- Drayton C Port 15 J5
- Drayton Leics 60 H2
- Drayton Lincs 74 D3
- Drayton Norfk 76 H9
- Drayton Oxon 34 E6
- Drayton Oxon 48 D6
- Drayton Somset 19 M10
- Drayton Worcs 58 D9
- Drayton Bassett Staffs 59 J4
- Drayton Beauchamp Bucks 35 P2
- Drayton Manor Park Staffs 59 J4
- Drayton Parslow Bucks 49 M9
- Drayton St Leonard Oxon 34 G5
- Drebley N York 96 G9
- Dreemskerry IoM 80 g3
- Dreen Hill Pembks 40 H8
- Drefach Carmth 28 F2
- Drefach Carmth 42 G7
- Drefach Cerdgn 43 J5
- Drefelin Carmth 42 G7
- Dreghorn N Ayrs 125 K10
- Drellingore Kent 27 M3
- Drem E Loth 128 E4
- Dresden C Stke 70 G6
- Drewsteignton Devon 8 H6
- Driby Lincs 87 L6
- Driffield E R Yk 99 L9
- Driffield Gloucs 33 L5
- Driffield Cross Roads Gloucs 33 L5
- Drift Cnwll 2 C8
- Drigg Cumb 100 E11
- Drighlington Leeds 90 G5
- Drimnin Highld 137 P5
- Drimpton Dorset 11 J4
- Drimsallie Highld 138 H2
- Dringhouses C York 98 B11
- Drinkstone Suffk 64 D9
- Drinkstone Green Suffk 64 D9
- Drive End Dorset 11 M3
- Driver's End Herts 50 F6
- Drointon Staffs 71 J9
- Droitwich Spa Worcs 46 G2
- Dron P & K 134 E4
- Dronfield Derbys 84 E5
- Dronfield Woodhouse Derbys 84 D5
- Drongan E Ayrs 114 H4
- Dronley Angus 142 E10
- Droop Dorset 12 C3
- Dropping Well Rothm 84 E2
- Droxford Hants 22 H11
- Droylsden Tamesd 83 K5
- Druid Denbgs 68 D6
- Druidston Pembks 40 G7
- Druimarbin Highld 139 K3
- Druimavuic Ag & B 139 J8
- Druimdrishaig Ag & B 123 M5
- Druimindarroch Highld 145 L11
- Drum Ag & B 124 A2
- Drum P & K 134 C7
- Drumalbin S Lans 116 C3
- Drumbeg Highld 164 D10
- Drumblade Abers 158 E9
- Drumbreddon D & G 106 E9
- Drumbuie Highld 153 P11
- Drumburgh Cumb 110 E9
- Drumburn D & G 109 J10
- Drumburn D & G 109 L8
- Drumchapel C Glas 125 N3
- Drumchastle P & K 140 G6
- Drumclog S Lans 125 Q10
- Drumeldrie Fife 135 L7
- Drumelzier Border 116 G4
- Drumfearn Highld 145 L4
- Drumfrennie Abers 151 J8
- Drumgley Angus 142 G7
- Drumguish Highld 148 D7
- Drumin Moray 157 M11
- Drumjohn D & G 115 K8
- Drumlamford S Ayrs 107 J2
- Drumlasie Abers 150 G6
- Drumleaning Cumb 110 E10
- Drumlemble Ag & B 120 C8
- Drumlithie Abers 151 K11
- Drummoddie D & G 107 L8
- Drummore D & G 106 F10
- Drummuir Moray 158 A9
- Drumnadrochit Highld 155 P11
- Drumnagorrach Moray 158 D7
- Drumpark D & G 109 J5
- Drumrunie Highld 161 K5
- Drumshang S Ayrs 114 E5
- Drumuie Highld 152 H8
- Drumuillie Highld 148 G3
- Drumvaich Stirlg 133 K7
- Drumzie P & K 134 E6
- Druridge Nthumb 119 Q11
- Drury Flints 69 J2
- Drws-y-coed Gwynd 67 J4
- Drybeck Cumb 102 C7
- Drybridge Moray 158 B5
- Drybridge N Ayrs 125 K10
- Drybrook Gloucs 46 B11
- Dryburgh Border 118 A4
- Dry Doddington Lincs 85 Q11
- Dry Drayton Cambs 62 E8
- Drymen Stirlg 132 F10
- Drymuir Abers 159 M8
- Drynoch Highld 152 G11
- Dry Sandford Oxon 34 E4
- Dryslwyn Carmth 43 L10
- Dry Street Essex 37 Q3
- Dryton Shrops 57 K3
- Dubford Abers 159 J5
- Dublin Suffk 64 H8
- Duchally Highld 161 P3
- Duck End Bed 50 C2
- Duck End Cambs 62 B8
- Duck End Essex 51 Q4
- Duck End Essex 51 Q5
- Duckend Green Essex 52 B7
- Duckington Ches W 69 N4
- Ducklington Oxon 34 C3
- Duck's Cross Bed 61 P9
- Duddenhoe End Essex 51 L3
- Duddingston C Edin 127 P3
- Duddington Nhants 73 P10
- Duddlestone Somset 18 H10
- Duddleswell E Susx 25 L5
- Duddlewick Shrops 57 M8
- Duddo Nthumb 118 H2
- Duddon Ches W 69 P2
- Duddon Bridge Cumb 94 D3
- Duddon Common Ches W 81 Q11
- Dudleston Shrops 69 K7
- Dudleston Heath Shrops 69 L7
- Dudley Dudley 58 D6

Dudley N Tyne 113 L6
Dudley Hill C Brad 90 F4
Dudley Port Sandw 58 E6
Dudnill Shrops 57 L10
Dudsbury Dorset 13 J5
Dudswell Herts 35 Q3
Duffield Derbys 72 A2
Duffryn Neath 29 M5
Dufftown Moray 157 Q9
Duffus Moray 157 M4
Dufton Cumb 102 C5
Duggleby N York 98 H7
Duirinish Highld 153 P11
Duisdalemore Highld 145 M5
Duisky Highld 139 J2
Dukestown Blae G 30 F2
Duke Street Suffk 53 J3
Dukinfield Tamesd 83 K5
Dulas IoA 78 H7
Dulcote Somset 19 Q6
Dulford Devon 9 Q3
Dull P & K 141 K8
Dullatur N Lans 126 C2
Dullingham Cambs 63 K9
Dullingham Ley Cambs 63 K9
Dulnain Bridge Highld 148 H3
Duloe Bed 61 Q8
Duloe Cnwll 5 L10
Dulsie Bridge Highld 156 G9
Dulverton Somset 18 B9
Dulwich Gt Lon 36 H6
Dumbarton W Duns 125 L2
Dumbleton Gloucs 47 K7
Dumfries D & G 109 L5
Dumgoyne Stirlg 132 G11
Dummer Hants 22 G5
Dumpton Kent 39 Q8
Dun Angus 143 M6
Dunalastair P & K 140 H6
Dunan Ag & B 124 F3
Dunan Highld 145 J2
Dunan P & K 140 C6
Dunaverty Ag & B 120 C10
Dunball Somset 19 K6
Dunbar E Loth 128 H4
Dunbeath Highld 167 L11
Dunbeg Ag & B 138 F11
Dunblane Stirlg 133 M7
Dunbog Fife 134 H4
Dunbridge Hants 22 B9
Duncanston Highld 155 Q6
Duncanstone Abers 150 F2
Dunchideock Devon 9 L7
Dunchurch Warwks 59 Q10
Duncote Nhants 49 J4
Duncow D & G 109 L4
Duncrievie P & K 134 E6
Duncton W Susx 23 Q11
Dundee C Dund 142 G11
Dundee Airport C Dund 135 K2
Dundon Somset 19 N8
Dundonald S Ayrs 125 K11
Dundonnell Highld 160 H9
Dundraw Cumb 110 D11
Dundreggan Highld 147 J5
Dundrennan D & G 108 F11
Dundry N Som 31 Q11
Dunecht Abers 151 K6
Dunfermline Fife 134 D10
Dunfield Gloucs 33 M5
Dunford Bridge Barns 83 Q4
Dungate Kent 38 F10
Dungavel S Lans 126 B10
Dunge Wilts 20 G4
Dungeness Kent 27 J8
Dungworth Sheff 84 C3
Dunham Massey Traffd 82 F7
Dunham-on-the-Hill Ches W 81 P10
Dunham-on-Trent Notts 85 P6
Dunhampstead Worcs 46 H2
Dunhampton Worcs 58 B11
Dunham Town Traffd 82 F7
Dunham Woodhouses Traffd 82 F7
Dunholme Lincs 86 D5
Dunino Fife 135 N5
Dunipace Falk 133 N11
Dunkeld P & K 141 P9
Dunkerton BaNES 20 D3
Dunkeswell Devon 10 C3
Dunkeswick N York 97 M11
Dunkirk Ches W 81 M10
Dunkirk Kent 39 J10
Dunkirk S Glos 32 E7
Dunkirk Wilts 21 J2
Dunk's Green Kent 37 P10
Dunlappie Angus 143 K4
Dunley Hants 22 E4
Dunley Worcs 57 P11
Dunlop E Ayrs 125 L8
Dunmaglass Highld 147 P3
Dunmere Cnwll 4 G8
Dunmore Falk 133 P10
Dunnet Highld 167 M2
Dunnichen Angus 143 J8
Dunning P & K 134 C5
Dunnington C York 98 D10
Dunnington E R Yk 99 P10
Dunnington Warwks 47 L4
Dunnockshaw Lancs 89 N5
Dunn Street Kent 38 C9
Dunoon Ag & B 124 F2
Dunphail Moray 157 J8
Dunragit D & G 106 G6
Duns Border 129 K9
Dunsa Derbys 84 B6
Dunsby Lincs 74 B5
Dunscar Bolton 89 L8
Dunscore D & G 109 J4
Dunscroft Donc 91 Q9
Dunsdale R & Cl 104 H7
Dunsden Green Oxon 35 K9
Dunsdon Devon 16 E10
Dunsfold Surrey 24 B3
Dunsford Devon 9 K7
Dunshalt Fife 134 G5
Dunshillock Abers 159 N8
Dunsill Notts 84 G8
Dunsley N York 105 N8
Dunsley Staffs 58 C8
Dunsmore Bucks 35 N3
Dunsop Bridge Lancs 95 P11
Dunstable C Beds 50 B6
Dunstall Staffs 71 M10
Dunstall Common Worcs 46 G6
Dunstall Green Suffk 63 M8
Dunstan Nthumb 119 P7
Dunstan Steads Nthumb 119 P6
Dunster Somset 18 C6
Duns Tew Oxon 48 E9
Dunston Gatesd 113 K8
Dunston Lincs 86 E8
Dunston Norfk 77 J11
Dunston Staffs 70 G11
Dunstone Devon 6 F8
Dunstone Devon 8 H9
Dunston Heath Staffs 70 G11
Dunsville Donc 91 Q9
Dunswell E R Yk 93 J3
Dunsyre S Lans 127 K8
Dunterton Devon 5 P6
Dunthrop Oxon 48 C9
Duntisbourne Abbots Gloucs 33 J3
Duntisbourne Leer Gloucs 33 J3
Duntisbourne Rouse Gloucs 33 J3
Duntish Dorset 11 P3
Duntocher W Duns 125 M3
Dunton Bucks 49 M10
Dunton C Beds 50 F2
Dunton Norfk 76 B5
Dunton Bassett Leics 60 B2
Dunton Green Kent 37 M9
Dunton Wayletts Essex 37 Q2
Duntulm Highld 152 G3
Dunure S Ayrs 114 E4
Dunvant Swans 28 G6
Dunvegan Highld 152 D8
Dunwich Suffk 65 P7
Dunwood Staffs 70 G3
Durdar Cumb 110 H10
Durgan Cnwll 3 K8
Durham Dur 103 Q2
Durham Cathedral Dur 103 Q2
Durham Services Dur 104 B3
Durham Tees Valley Airport S on T 104 C8
Durisdeer D & G 116 B10
Durisdeermill D & G 116 B10
Durkar Wakefd 91 J7
Durleigh Somset 19 J7
Durley Hants 22 F11
Durley Wilts 21 P2
Durley Street Hants 22 F11
Durlock Kent 39 N10
Durlock Kent 39 P9
Durlow Common Herefs 46 B7
Durn Rochdl 89 Q7
Durness Highld 165 K3
Durno Abers 151 J2
Duror Highld 138 H6
Durran Ag & B 131 K6
Durrington W Susx 24 D9
Durrington Wilts 21 N6
Durris Abers 151 K8
Dursley Gloucs 32 E5
Dursley Cross Gloucs 46 C10
Durston Somset 19 J9
Durweston Dorset 12 E3
Duston Nhants 60 F8
Duthil Highld 148 G3
Dutlas Powys 56 C9
Duton Hill Essex 51 P5
Dutson Cnwll 5 N4
Dutton Ches W 82 C9
Duxford Cambs 62 G11
Duxford Oxon 34 C5
Duxford IWM Cambs 62 G11
Dwygyfylchi Conwy 79 N9
Dwyran IoA 78 G11
Dyce C Aber 151 M5
Dyer's End Essex 52 B4
Dyfatty Carmth 28 E4
Dyffrydan Gwynd 54 F2
Dyffryn Brdgnd 29 N6
Dyffryn Myr Td 30 E4
Dyffryn V Glam 30 E10
Dyffryn Ardudwy Gwynd 67 K10
Dyffryn Castell Cerdgn 54 H8
Dyffryn Cellwen Neath 29 N2
Dyke Lincs 74 B6
Dyke Moray 156 H6
Dykehead Angus 142 C7
Dykehead Angus 142 F6
Dykehead N Lans 126 F6
Dykehead Stirlg 132 H8
Dykelands Abers 143 N4
Dykends Angus 142 D6
Dykeside Abers 158 H9
Dylife Powys 55 K6
Dymchurch Kent 27 K6
Dymock Gloucs 46 D8
Dyrham S Glos 32 D9
Dysart Fife 135 J9
Dyserth Denbgs 80 F9

E

Eachway Worcs 58 E9
Eachwick Nthumb 112 H6
Eagland Hill Lancs 95 J11
Eagle Lincs 85 Q7
Eagle Barnsdale Lincs 85 Q7
Eagle Moor Lincs 85 Q7
Eaglescliffe S on T 104 D7
Eaglesfield Cumb 100 E5
Eaglesfield D & G 110 D6
Eaglesham E Rens 125 P7
Eagley Bolton 89 L8
Eairy IoM 80 c6
Eakring Notts 85 L8
Ealand N Linc 92 C8
Ealing Gt Lon 36 E4
Eals Nthumb 111 N9
Eamont Bridge Cumb 101 P5
Earby Lancs 96 D11
Earcroft Bl w D 89 K6
Eardington Shrops 57 N6
Eardisland Herefs 45 N3
Eardisley Herefs 45 L5
Eardiston Shrops 69 L9
Eardiston Worcs 57 M11
Earith Cambs 62 E5
Earle Nthumb 119 J5
Earlestown St Hel 82 C5
Earley Wokham 35 K10
Earlham Norfk 76 H10
Earlish Highld 152 F5
Earls Barton Nhants 61 J8
Earls Colne Essex 52 E6
Earls Common Worcs 47 J3
Earl's Croome Worcs 46 G6
Earlsditton Shrops 57 L9
Earlsdon Covtry 59 M9
Earl's Down E Susx 25 P7
Earlsferry Fife 135 M7
Earlsfield Gt Lon 36 G6
Earlsford Abers 159 K11
Earl's Green Suffk 64 E8
Earlsheaton Kirk 90 H6
Earl Shilton Leics 72 D11
Earl Soham Suffk 65 J9
Earl Sterndale Derbys 83 N11
Earlston Border 117 R3
Earlston E Ayrs 125 L10
Earl Stonham Suffk 64 G10
Earlswood Surrey 36 G11
Earlswood Warwks 58 H10
Earlswood Common Mons 31 N6
Earnley W Susx 15 M7
Earnshaw Bridge Lancs 88 G6
Earsdon N Tyne 113 M6
Earsdon Nthumb 113 J2
Earsham Norfk 65 L4
Earswick C York 98 C9
Eartham W Susx 15 P5
Earthcott S Glos 32 C7
Easby N York 104 G9
Easdale Ag & B 130 E4
Easebourne W Susx 23 P10
Easenhall Warwks 59 Q9
Eashing Surrey 23 P6
Easington Bucks 35 J2
Easington Dur 104 D2
Easington E R Yk 93 Q7
Easington Nthumb 119 M4
Easington Oxon 35 J5
Easington R & Cl 105 K7
Easington Colliery Dur 104 D2
Easington Lane Sundld 113 N11
Easingwold N York 98 A7
Easole Street Kent 39 N11
Eassie and Nevay Angus 142 E9
East Aberthaw V Glam 30 D11
East Allington Devon 7 K9
East Anstey Devon 17 R6
East Anton Hants 22 C5
East Appleton N York 103 P11
East Ashey IoW 14 G9
East Ashling W Susx 15 M5
East Aston Hants 22 D5
East Ayton N York 99 K3
East Balsdon Cnwll 5 M2
East Bank Blae G 30 H3
East Barkwith Lincs 86 G4
East Barming Kent 38 B11
East Barnby N York 105 M8
East Barnet Gt Lon 50 G11
East Barns E Loth 129 J4
East Barsham Norfk 76 C5
East Beckham Norfk 76 H4
East Bedfont Gt Lon 36 C6
East Bergholt Suffk 53 J5
East Bierley Kirk 90 F5
East Bilney Norfk 76 D8
East Blatchington E Susx 25 L10
East Bloxworth Dorset 12 E6
East Boldon S Tyne 113 N8
East Boldre Hants 14 C6
East Bolton Nthumb 119 M7
Eastbourne Darltn 104 B8
Eastbourne E Susx 25 P11
East Bower Somset 19 K7
East Bradenham Norfk 76 C10
East Brent Somset 19 K4
Eastbridge Suffk 65 P8
East Bridgford Notts 72 H2
East Briscoe Dur 103 J7
Eastbrook V Glam 30 G10
East Buckland Devon 17 M5
East Budleigh Devon 9 Q8
Eastburn C Brad 90 C2
Eastburn E R Yk 99 K9
East Burnham Bucks 35 Q8
East Burton Dorset 12 D7
Eastbury W Berk 34 B9
East Butsfield Dur 112 H11
East Butterwick N Linc 92 D9
Eastby N York 96 F10
East Calder W Loth 127 K4
East Carleton Norfk 76 H11
East Carlton Leeds 90 G2
East Carlton Nhants 60 H3
East Chaldon Dorset 12 C8
East Challow Oxon 34 C7
East Charleton Devon 7 K10
East Chelborough Dorset 11 M3
East Chiltington E Susx 25 J7
East Chinnock Somset 11 K2
East Chisenbury Wilts 21 M4
East Cholderton Hants 21 Q5
Eastchurch Kent 38 G7
East Clandon Surrey 36 C10
East Claydon Bucks 49 K9
East Clevedon N Som 31 M10
East Coker Somset 11 L2
Eastcombe Gloucs 32 G4
Eastcombe Somset 18 G8
East Compton Somset 20 B6
East Cornworthy Devon 7 L7
East Cote Cumb 109 P9
Eastcote Gt Lon 36 D3
Eastcote Nhants 49 J4
Eastcote Solhll 59 J9
Eastcott Cnwll 16 D8
Eastcott Wilts 21 K3
East Cottingwith E R Yk 92 B2
Eastcourt Wilts 21 P2
Eastcourt Wilts 33 J6
East Cowes IoW 14 F7
East Cowick E R Yk 91 R6
East Cowton N York 104 B10
East Cramlington Nthumb 113 L5
East Cranmore Somset 20 C6
East Creech Dorset 12 F8
East Curthwaite Cumb 110 F11
East Dean E Susx 25 N11
East Dean Gloucs 46 C10
East Dean Hants 21 Q9
East Dean W Susx 15 P4
Eastdown Devon 7 L9
East Down Devon 17 L3
East Drayton Notts 85 N5
East Dulwich Gt Lon 36 H5
East Dundry N Som 31 Q11
East Ella C KuH 93 J5
East End Bed 61 P9
East End C Beds 49 Q6
East End E R Yk 93 L4
East End E R Yk 93 N5
Eastend Essex 38 F3
East End Essex 51 K8
East End Hants 14 C7
East End Hants 22 D2
East End Herts 51 L5
East End Kent 26 D4
East End Kent 38 G7
East End M Keyn 49 P6
East End Oxon 48 C11
East End Somset 20 C5
East End Suffk 53 K4
Easter Balmoral Abers 149 P9
Easter Compton S Glos 31 Q8
Easter Dalziel Highld 156 D7
Eastergate W Susx 15 P5
Easterhouse C Glas 126 B4
Easter Howgate Mdloth 127 N5
Easter Kinkell Highld 155 Q6
Easter Moniack Highld 155 Q9
Eastern Green Covtry 59 L9
Easter Ord Abers 151 L7
Easter Pitkierie Fife 135 P6
Easter Skeld Shet 169 q9
Easter Softlaw Border 118 E4
Easterton Wilts 21 K4
Eastertown Somset 19 K4
East Everleigh Wilts 21 P4
East Farleigh Kent 38 B11
East Farndon Nhants 60 F4
East Ferry Lincs 92 D11
Eastfield N Lans 126 F5
Eastfield N York 99 L4
East Firsby Lincs 86 D3
East Fortune E Loth 128 E4
East Garforth Leeds 91 L4
East Garston W Berk 34 C9
Eastgate Dur 103 J3
Eastgate Lincs 74 B7
Eastgate Norfk 76 G7
East Ginge Oxon 34 D7
East Goscote Leics 72 G8
East Grafton Wilts 21 Q2
East Green Suffk 65 N8
East Grimstead Wilts 21 P9
East Grinstead W Susx 25 J3
East Guldeford E Susx 26 F7
East Haddon Nhants 60 E7
East Hagbourne Oxon 34 F7
East Halton N Linc 93 K7
East Ham Gt Lon 37 K4
Eastham Wirral 81 M8
Eastham Ferry Wirral 81 M8
Easthampton Herefs 45 N2
East Hanney Oxon 34 D6
East Hanningfield Essex 52 C11
East Hardwick Wakefd 91 M7
East Harling Norfk 64 D4
East Harlsey N York 104 D11
East Harnham Wilts 21 M9
East Harptree BaNES 19 Q3
East Hartford Nthumb 113 L5
East Harting W Susx 23 L11
East Hatch Wilts 20 H9
East Hatley Cambs 62 C10
East Hauxwell N York 97 J2
East Haven Angus 143 K10
Eastheath Wokham 35 L11
East Heckington Lincs 74 C2
East Hedleyhope Dur 103 N2
East Helmsdale Highld 163 N3
East Hendred Oxon 34 E7
East Heslerton N York 99 J5
East Hewish N Som 19 M2
East Hoathly E Susx 25 M7
East Holme Dorset 12 E7
East Hope Dur 103 K9
Easthope Shrops 57 K5
Easthorpe Essex 52 F7
Easthorpe Notts 85 M10
East Horrington Somset 19 Q5
East Horsley Surrey 36 C10
East Horton Nthumb 119 K4
East Howe BCP 13 J5
East Huntington C York 98 C9
East Huntspill Somset 19 K5
East Hyde C Beds 50 D7
East Ilkerton Devon 17 N2
East Ilsley W Berk 34 E8
Eastington Devon 8 H3
Eastington Gloucs 32 E3
Eastington Gloucs 33 M2
East Keal Lincs 87 L8
East Kennett Wilts 33 M11
East Keswick Leeds 91 K2
East Kilbride S Lans 125 Q7
East Kimber Devon 8 C5
East Kirkby Lincs 87 K8
East Knighton Dorset 12 D7
East Knowstone Devon 17 Q7
East Knoyle Wilts 20 G8
East Lambrook Somset 19 M11
Eastlands D & G 108 H6
East Langdon Kent 27 P2
East Langton Leics 60 F2
East Lavant W Susx 15 N5
East Lavington W Susx 23 P11
East Layton N York 103 N9
Eastleach Martin Gloucs 33 P4
Eastleach Turville Gloucs 33 N3
East Leake Notts 72 F5
East Learmouth Nthumb 118 G3
East Leigh Devon 6 H8
East Leigh Devon 7 K7
East Leigh Devon 8 G3
Eastleigh Devon 16 H6
Eastleigh Hants 22 E11
East Lexham Norfk 76 B8
Eastling Kent 38 G10
East Linton E Loth 128 F4
East Liss Hants 23 L9
East Lockinge Oxon 34 D7
East Lound N Linc 92 C11
East Lulworth Dorset 12 E8
East Lutton N York 99 J7
East Lydeard Somset 18 G9
East Lydford Somset 19 Q8
East Malling Kent 38 B10
East Malling Heath Kent 37 Q9
East Marden W Susx 15 M4
East Markham Notts 85 M6
East Martin Hants 21 L11
East Marton N York 96 D10
East Meon Hants 23 J10
East Mere Devon 18 C11
East Mersea Essex 52 H9
East Midlands Airport Leics 72 D5
East Molesey Surrey 36 D7
Eastmoor Norfk 75 P10
East Morden Dorset 12 F6
East Morton C Brad 90 D2
East Morton D & G 116 B10
East Ness N York 98 D5
East Newton E R Yk 93 N3
Eastney C Port 15 J7
Eastnor Herefs 46 D7
East Norton Leics 73 K10
Eastoft N Linc 92 D7
East Ogwell Devon 7 L4
Easton Cambs 61 P6
Easton Cumb 110 E9
Easton Devon 8 H7
Easton Dorset 11 P10
Easton Hants 22 F8
Easton Lincs 73 N5
Easton Norfk 76 G9
Easton Somset 19 P5
Easton Suffk 65 K10
Easton W Berk 34 D10
Easton Wilts 32 G10
Easton Grey Wilts 32 G7
Easton-in-Gordano N Som 31 P9
Easton Maudit Nhants 61 J9
Easton-on-the-Hill Nhants 73 Q10
Easton Royal Wilts 21 P2
East Orchard Dorset 20 F11
East Ord Nthumb 129 P9
East Panson Devon 5 P3
East Parley BCP 13 J5
East Peckham Kent 37 Q11
East Pennard Somset 19 Q7
East Perry Cambs 61 Q7
East Portlemouth Devon 7 K11
East Prawle Devon 7 K11
East Preston W Susx 24 C10
East Pulham Dorset 11 Q3
East Putford Devon 16 F8
East Quantoxhead Somset 18 F6
East Rainham Medway 38 D8
East Rainton Sundld 113 M11
East Ravendale NE Lin 93 M11
East Raynham Norfk 76 B6
Eastrea Cambs 74 E11
Eastriggs D & G 110 D7
East Rigton Leeds 91 K2
Eastrington E R Yk 92 C5
East Rolstone N Som 19 L2
Eastrop Swindn 33 P6
East Rounton N York 104 D10
East Rudham Norfk 76 A6
East Runton Norfk 76 H3
East Ruston Norfk 77 L6
Eastry Kent 39 P11
East Saltoun E Loth 128 D6
Eastshaw W Susx 23 N10
East Sheen Gt Lon 36 F6
East Shefford W Berk 34 C10
East Sleekburn Nthumb 113 L4
East Somerton Norfk 77 P8
East Stockwith Lincs 85 N2
East Stoke Dorset 12 E7
East Stoke Notts 85 N11
East Stour Dorset 20 F10
East Stour Common Dorset 20 F10
East Stourmouth Kent 39 N9
East Stowford Devon 17 L6
East Stratton Hants 22 F6
East Studdal Kent 27 P2
East Sutton Kent 26 D2
East Taphouse Cnwll 5 K9
East-the-Water Devon 16 H6
East Thirston Nthumb 119 N10
East Tilbury Thurr 37 Q5
East Tilbury Village Thurr 37 Q5
East Tisted Hants 23 K8
East Torrington Lincs 86 F4
East Tuddenham Norfk 76 F9
East Tytherley Hants 21 Q9
East Tytherton Wilts 33 J10
East Village Devon 9 K3
Eastville Bristl 32 B10
Eastville Lincs 87 M9
East Wall Shrops 57 J6
East Walton Norfk 75 P7
East Water Somset 19 P4
East Week Devon 8 G6
Eastwell Leics 73 K5
East Wellow Hants 22 B10
East Wemyss Fife 135 J8
East Whitburn W Loth 126 H4
Eastwick Herts 51 K8
East Wickham Gt Lon 37 L5
East Williamston Pembks 41 L10
East Winch Norfk 75 N7
East Winterslow Wilts 21 P8
East Wittering W Susx 15 L7
East Witton N York 96 H3
Eastwood Notts 84 G11
Eastwood Sthend 38 D4
East Woodburn Nthumb 112 D3
Eastwood End Cambs 62 F2
East Woodhay Hants 22 D2
East Woodlands Somset 20 E6
East Worldham Hants 23 L7
East Wretham Norfk 64 C3
East Youlstone Devon 16 D8
Eathorpe Warwks 59 N11
Eaton Ches E 83 J11
Eaton Ches W 69 Q2
Eaton Leics 73 K5
Eaton Norfk 77 J10
Eaton Notts 85 M5
Eaton Oxon 34 D4
Eaton Shrops 56 F7
Eaton Shrops 57 J7
Eaton Bishop Herefs 45 N7
Eaton Bray C Beds 49 Q10
Eaton Constantine Shrops 57 K3
Eaton Ford Cambs 61 Q9
Eaton Green C Beds 49 Q10
Eaton Hastings Oxon 33 Q5
Eaton Mascott Shrops 57 J3
Eaton Socon Cambs 61 Q9

Eaton upon Tern Shrops 70 B10
Eaves Brow Warrtn 82 D6
Eaves Green Solhll 59 L8
Ebberston N York 98 H4
Ebbesborne Wake Wilts 21 J10
Ebbw Vale Blae G 30 G3
Ebchester Dur 112 H9
Ebdon N Som 19 L2
Ebford Devon 9 N7
Ebley Gloucs 32 F3
Ebnal Ches W 69 N5
Ebnall Herefs 45 P3
Ebrington Gloucs 47 N6
Ebsworthy Devon 8 D6
Ecchinswell Hants 22 E3
Ecclaw Border 129 K6
Ecclefechan D & G 110 C6
Eccles Border 118 E2
Eccles Kent 38 B9
Eccles Salfd 82 G5
Ecclesall Sheff 84 D4
Ecclesfield Sheff 84 E2
Eccles Green Herefs 45 M5
Eccleshall Staffs 70 E9
Eccleshill C Brad 90 F3
Ecclesmachan W Loth 127 K3
Eccles on Sea Norfk 77 N6
Eccles Road Norfk 64 E4
Eccleston Ches W 69 M2
Eccleston Lancs 88 G7
Eccleston St Hel 81 P5
Eccleston Green Lancs 88 G7
Echt Abers 151 J6
Eckford Border 118 D5
Eckington Derbys 84 F5
Eckington Worcs 46 H6
Ecton Nhants 60 H8
Ecton Staffs 71 K3
Edale Derbys 83 P7
Eday Ork 169 e3
Eday Airport Ork 169 e3
Edburton W Susx 24 F8
Edderside Cumb 109 P11
Edderton Highld 162 G10
Eddington Kent 39 L8
Eddleston Border 127 N8
Eddlewood S Lans 126 C7
Edenbridge Kent 37 K11
Edenfield Lancs 89 N7
Edenhall Cumb 101 Q4
Edenham Lincs 73 R6
Eden Mount Cumb 95 J5
Eden Park Gt Lon 37 J7
Eden Project Cnwll 3 Q3
Edensor Derbys 84 B7
Edentaggart Ag & B 132 C9
Edenthorpe Donc 91 Q9
Edern Gwynd 66 D7
Edgarley Somset 19 P7
Edgbaston Birm 58 G8
Edgcombe Cnwll 3 J7
Edgcott Bucks 49 J10
Edgcott Somset 17 Q4
Edge Gloucs 32 F3
Edge Shrops 56 F3
Edgebolton Shrops 69 Q10
Edge End Gloucs 31 Q2
Edgefield Norfk 76 F5
Edgefield Green Norfk 76 F5
Edgefold Bolton 89 L9
Edge Green Ches W 69 N4
Edgehill Warwks 48 C5
Edgerley Shrops 69 L11
Edgerton Kirk 90 E7
Edgeside Lancs 89 N6
Edgeworth Gloucs 32 H3
Edgeworthy Devon 9 K2
Edginswell Torbay 7 M5
Edgiock Worcs 47 K2
Edgmond Wrekin 70 C11
Edgmond Marsh Wrekin 70 C10
Edgton Shrops 56 F7
Edgware Gt Lon 36 E2
Edgworth Bl w D 89 L7
Edinbane Highld 152 E7
Edinburgh C Edin 127 P3
Edinburgh Airport C Edin 127 L3
Edinburgh Castle C Edin 127 P3
Edinburgh Old & New Town C Edin 127 P3
Edinburgh Royal Botanic Gardens C Edin 127 N2
Edinburgh Zoo RZSS C Edin 127 N3
Edingale Staffs 59 K2
Edingham D & G 108 H8
Edingley Notts 85 L9
Edingthorpe Norfk 77 L5
Edingthorpe Green Norfk 77 L5
Edington Border 129 M9
Edington Nthumb 113 J4
Edington Somset 19 L7
Edington Wilts 20 H4
Edington Burtle Somset 19 L6
Edingworth Somset 19 L4
Edistone Devon 16 D7
Edithmead Somset 19 K5
Edith Weston Rutlnd 73 N9
Edlesborough Bucks 49 Q11
Edlingham Nthumb 119 M9
Edlington Lincs 86 H6
Edmond Castle Cumb 111 J9
Edmondsham Dorset 13 J2
Edmondsley Dur 113 K11
Edmondthorpe Leics 73 M7
Edmonton Cnwll 4 F7
Edmonton Gt Lon 36 H2
Edmundbyers Dur 112 F10
Ednam Border 118 D3
Ednaston Derbys 71 N6
Edney Common Essex 51 Q10
Edradynate P & K 141 L7
Edrom Border 129 L8
Edstaston Shrops 69 P8
Edstone Warwks 47 N2
Edvin Loach Herefs 46 C3
Edwalton Notts 72 F3
Edwardstone Suffk 52 F3
Edwardsville Myr Td 30 E5
Edwinsford Carmth 43 M8
Edwinstowe Notts 85 K7
Edworth C Beds 50 F2
Edwyn Ralph Herefs 46 B3
Edzell Angus 143 L4
Edzell Woods Abers 143 L4
Efail-fach Neath 29 L5
Efail Isaf Rhondd 30 E8
Efailnewydd Gwynd 66 F7
Efail-Rhyd Powys 68 G9
Efailwen Carmth 41 M5
Efenechtyd Denbgs 68 F3
Effgill D & G 110 F2
Effingham Surrey 36 D10
Effingham Junction Surrey 36 D9
Efflinch Staffs 71 M11
Efford Devon 9 L4
Egbury Hants 22 D4
Egdean W Susx 23 Q10
Egerton Bolton 89 L8
Egerton Kent 26 F2
Egerton Forstal Kent 26 E2
Eggborough N York 91 P6
Eggbuckland C Plym 6 E7
Eggesford Devon 17 M9
Eggington C Beds 49 Q9
Egginton Derbys 71 P9
Egglescliffe S on T 104 D8
Eggleston Dur 103 J6
Egham Surrey 36 B6
Egham Wick Surrey 35 Q10
Egleton Rutlnd 73 M9
Eglingham Nthumb 119 M7
Egloshayle Cnwll 4 G7
Egloskerry Cnwll 5 M4
Eglwysbach Conwy 79 Q10
Eglwys-Brewis V Glam 30 D11
Eglwys Cross Wrexhm 69 N6
Eglwys Fach Cerdgn 54 F5
Eglwyswrw Pembks 41 M3
Egmanton Notts 85 M7
Egremont Cumb 100 D8
Egremont Wirral 81 L6
Egton N York 105 M9
Egton Bridge N York 105 M10
Egypt Bucks 35 Q7
Egypt Hants 22 E6
Eigg Highld 144 G10
Eight Ash Green Essex 52 F6
Eilanreach Highld 145 P4
Eilean Donan Castle Highld 145 Q2
Eisgein W Isls 168 i6
Eishken W Isls 168 i6
Eisteddfa Gurig Cerdgn 54 H8
Elan Valley Powys 55 K11
Elan Village Powys 44 C2
Elberton S Glos 32 B7
Elbridge W Susx 15 P6
Elburton C Plym 6 E8
Elcombe Swindn 33 M8
Elcot W Berk 34 C11
Eldernell Cambs 74 F11
Eldersfield Worcs 46 E8
Elderslie Rens 125 L5
Elder Street Essex 51 N4
Eldon Dur 103 P5
Eldwick C Brad 90 E2
Elerch Cerdgn 54 F7
Elfhill Abers 151 L10
Elford Nthumb 119 N4
Elford Staffs 59 J2
Elgin Moray 157 N5
Elgol Highld 144 H5
Elham Kent 27 L3
Elie Fife 135 M7
Elilaw Nthumb 119 J9
Elim IoA 78 F8
Eling Hants 14 C4
Elkesley Notts 85 L5
Elkstone Gloucs 33 J2
Ella Abers 158 F6
Ellacombe Torbay 7 N6
Elland Calder 90 E6
Elland Lower Edge Calder 90 E6
Ellary Ag & B 123 M4
Ellastone Staffs 71 L6
Ellel Lancs 95 K9
Ellemford Border 129 J7
Ellenabeich Ag & B 130 E4
Ellenborough Cumb 100 D3
Ellenbrook Salfd 82 F4
Ellenhall Staffs 70 E9
Ellen's Green Surrey 24 C3
Ellerbeck N York 104 D11
Ellerby N York 105 L8
Ellerdine Heath Wrekin 69 R10
Ellerhayes Devon 9 N4
Elleric Ag & B 139 J8
Ellerker E R Yk 92 F5
Ellers N York 90 C2
Ellerton E R Yk 92 B3
Ellerton N York 103 Q11
Ellerton Shrops 70 C9
Ellesborough Bucks 35 M3
Ellesmere Shrops 69 L8
Ellesmere Port Ches W 81 N9
Ellingham Hants 13 K3
Ellingham Norfk 65 M3
Ellingham Nthumb 119 N5
Ellingstring N York 97 J4
Ellington Cambs 61 Q6
Ellington Nthumb 113 L2
Ellington Thorpe Cambs 61 Q6
Elliots Green Somset 20 E5
Ellisfield Hants 22 H5
Ellishader Highld 153 J4
Ellistown Leics 72 C8
Ellon Abers 159 N11
Ellonby Cumb 101 M3
Ellough Suffk 65 N4
Elloughton E R Yk 92 F5
Ellwood Gloucs 31 Q3
Elm Cambs 75 J9
Elmbridge Worcs 58 D11
Elmdon Essex 51 L3
Elmdon Solhll 59 J8
Elmdon Heath Solhll 59 J8
Elmer W Susx 15 Q6
Elmers End Gt Lon 37 J7
Elmer's Green Lancs 88 G9
Elmesthorpe Leics 72 D11
Elm Green Essex 52 C10
Elmhurst Staffs 58 H2
Elmley Castle Worcs 47 J6
Elmley Lovett Worcs 58 C11
Elmore Gloucs 46 E11
Elmore Back Gloucs 46 E11
Elm Park Gt Lon 37 M3
Elmscott Devon 16 C7
Elmsett Suffk 53 J2
Elms Green Worcs 57 N11
Elmstead Heath Essex 53 J7
Elmstead Market Essex 53 J7
Elmstead Row Essex 53 J7
Elmsted Kent 27 K3
Elmstone Kent 39 N9
Elmstone Hardwicke Gloucs 46 H9
Elmswell E R Yk 99 K9
Elmswell Suffk 64 D9
Elmton Derbys 84 H6
Elphin Highld 161 L4
Elphinstone E Loth 128 B6
Elrick Abers 151 L6
Elrig D & G 107 K8
Elrington Nthumb 112 C8
Elsdon Nthumb 112 D2
Elsecar Barns 91 K11
Elsenham Essex 51 M5
Elsfield Oxon 34 F2
Elsham N Linc 92 H8
Elsing Norfk 76 F8
Elslack N York 96 D11
Elson Hants 14 H6
Elson Shrops 69 L7
Elsrickle S Lans 116 F2
Elstead Surrey 23 P6
Elsted W Susx 23 M11
Elsthorpe Lincs 73 R6
Elstob Dur 104 B6
Elston Lancs 88 H4
Elston Notts 85 N11
Elston Wilts 21 L6
Elstone Devon 17 M8
Elstow Bed 61 N11
Elstree Herts 50 E11
Elstronwick E R Yk 93 M4
Elswick Lancs 88 E3
Elswick N u Ty 113 K8
Elsworth Cambs 62 D8
Elterwater Cumb 101 K10
Eltham Gt Lon 37 K6
Eltisley Cambs 62 C9
Elton Bury 89 M8
Elton Cambs 61 N2
Elton Ches W 81 P9
Elton Derbys 84 B8
Elton Gloucs 32 D2
Elton Herefs 56 H10
Elton S on T 104 D7
Elton Green Ches W 81 P10
Elton-on-the-Hill Notts 73 K3
Eltringham Nthumb 112 G8
Elvanfoot S Lans 116 D7
Elvaston Derbys 72 C4
Elveden Suffk 63 P4
Elvetham Heath Hants 23 M3
Elvingston E Loth 128 D5
Elvington C York 98 E11
Elvington Kent 39 N11
Elwell Devon 17 M5
Elwick Hartpl 104 E4
Elwick Nthumb 119 M3
Elworth Ches E 70 C2
Elworthy Somset 18 E8
Ely Cambs 62 H4
Ely Cardif 30 F9
Emberton M Keyn 49 N5
Embleton Cumb 100 G4
Embleton Dur 104 D5
Embleton Nthumb 119 P6
Embo Highld 163 J8
Emborough Somset 20 B4
Embo Street Highld 163 J8
Embsay N York 96 F10
Emery Down Hants 13 N3
Emley Kirk 90 G8
Emley Moor Kirk 90 G8
Emmbrook Wokham 35 M11
Emmer Green Readg 35 K9
Emmett Carr Derbys 84 G5
Emmington Oxon 35 K4
Emneth Norfk 75 J9
Emneth Hungate Norfk 75 K9
Empingham Rutlnd 73 N9
Empshott Hants 23 L8
Empshott Green Hants 23 K8
Emsworth Hants 15 K5
Enborne W Berk 34 D11
Enborne Row W Berk 22 D2
Enchmarsh Shrops 57 J5
Enderby Leics 72 E11
Endmoor Cumb 95 L4
Endon Staffs 70 G4
Endon Bank Staffs 70 G4
Enfield Gt Lon 51 J11
Enfield Lock Gt Lon 51 J11
Enfield Wash Gt Lon 51 J11
Enford Wilts 21 M4
Engine Common S Glos 32 C8
England's Gate Herefs 45 Q4
Englefield W Berk 34 H10
Englefield Green Surrey 35 Q10
Engleseabrook Ches E 70 D4
English Bicknor Gloucs 46 A11
Englishcombe BaNES 20 D2
English Frankton Shrops 69 N9
Engollan Cnwll 4 D7
Enham Alamein Hants 22 C5
Enmore Somset 18 H7
Enmore Green Dorset 20 G10
Ennerdale Bridge Cumb 100 E7
Enniscaven Cnwll 4 F10
Enochdhu P & K 141 Q5
Ensay Ag & B 137 K6
Ensbury BCP 13 J5
Ensdon Shrops 69 M11
Ensis Devon 17 K6
Enson Staffs 70 G9
Enstone Oxon 48 C10
Enterkinfoot D & G 116 B10
Enterpen N York 104 E9
Enville Staffs 58 B7
Eòlaigearraidh W Isls 168 c17
Eoligarry W Isls 168 c17
Epney Gloucs 32 E2
Epperstone Notts 85 L11
Epping Essex 51 L10
Epping Green Essex 51 K9
Epping Green Herts 50 G9
Epping Upland Essex 51 K10
Eppleby N York 103 N8
Eppleworth E R Yk 92 H4
Epsom Surrey 36 F8
Epwell Oxon 48 C6
Epworth N Linc 92 C10
Epworth Turbary N Linc 92 C10
Erbistock Wrexhm 69 L6
Erdington Birm 58 H6
Eridge Green E Susx 25 N3
Eridge Station E Susx 25 M4
Erines Ag & B 123 Q4
Eriska Ag & B 138 G9
Eriskay W Isls 168 c17
Eriswell Suffk 63 M5
Erith Gt Lon 37 M5
Erlestoke Wilts 21 J4
Ermington Devon 6 G8
Erpingham Norfk 76 H5
Erriottwood Kent 38 F10
Errogie Highld 147 P3
Errol P & K 134 G3
Erskine Rens 125 M3
Erskine Bridge Rens 125 M3
Ervie D & G 106 D4
Erwarton Suffk 53 M5
Erwood Powys 44 F6
Eryholme N York 104 B9
Eryrys Denbgs 68 H3
Escalls Cnwll 2 B8
Escomb Dur 103 N4
Escott Somset 18 E7
Escrick N York 91 Q2
Esgair Carmth 42 G9
Esgair Cerdgn 54 D11
Esgairgeiliog Powys 54 H3
Esgerdawe Carmth 43 M6
Esgyryn Conwy 79 Q9
Esh Dur 103 N2
Esher Surrey 36 D8
Esholt C Brad 90 F2
Eshott Nthumb 119 P11
Eshton N York 96 D9
Esh Winning Dur 103 N2
Eskadale Highld 155 N9
Eskbank Mdloth 127 Q4
Eskdale Green Cumb 100 F10
Eskdalemuir D & G 117 K11
Eske E R Yk 93 J2
Eskham Lincs 93 Q11
Eskholme Donc 91 Q7
Esperley Lane Ends Dur 103 M6
Esprick Lancs 88 E3
Essendine Rutlnd 73 Q8
Essendon Herts 50 G9
Essich Highld 156 A10
Essington Staffs 58 E4
Esslemont Abers 151 N2
Eston R & Cl 104 F7
Etal Nthumb 118 H3
Etchilhampton Wilts 21 K2
Etchingham E Susx 26 B6
Etchinghill Kent 27 L4
Etchinghill Staffs 71 J11
Etchingwood E Susx 25 M6
Etling Green Norfk 76 E9
Etloe Gloucs 32 C3
Eton W & M 35 Q9
Eton Wick W & M 35 P9
Etruria C Stke 70 F5
Etteridge Highld 148 B9
Ettersgill Dur 102 G5
Ettiley Heath Ches E 70 C2
Ettingshall Wolves 58 D5
Ettington Warwks 47 Q5
Etton C Pete 74 B9
Etton E R Yk 92 G2
Ettrick Border 117 K8
Ettrickbridge Border 117 M6
Ettrickhill Border 117 K8
Etwall Derbys 71 P8
Eudon George Shrops 57 M7
Euston Suffk 64 B6
Euximoor Drove Cambs 75 J11
Euxton Lancs 88 H7
Evancoyd Powys 45 K2
Evanton Highld 155 R4
Evedon Lincs 86 E11
Evelith Shrops 57 N3
Evelix Highld 162 H8
Evenjobb Powys 45 K2
Evenley Nhants 48 G8
Evenlode Gloucs 47 P9
Evenwood Dur 103 N6
Evenwood Gate Dur 103 N6
Evercreech Somset 20 B7
Everingham E R Yk 92 D2
Everleigh Wilts 21 P4
Everley N York 99 K3
Eversholt C Beds 49 Q8
Evershot Dorset 11 M4
Eversley Hants 23 L2
Eversley Cross Hants 23 L2
Everthorpe E R Yk 92 F4
Everton C Beds 62 B10
Everton Hants 13 N6
Everton Lpool 81 L6
Everton Notts 85 L2
Evertown D & G 110 G5
Evesbatch Herefs 46 C5
Evesham Worcs 47 K6
Evington C Leic 72 G10
Ewden Village Sheff 90 H11
Ewell Surrey 36 F8
Ewell Minnis Kent 27 N3
Ewelme Oxon 34 H6
Ewen Gloucs 33 K5
Ewenny V Glam 29 P9
Ewerby Lincs 86 F11
Ewerby Thorpe Lincs 86 F11
Ewhurst Surrey 24 C2
Ewhurst Green E Susx 26 C7
Ewhurst Green Surrey 24 C3
Ewloe Flints 81 L11
Ewloe Green Flints 81 K11
Ewood Bl w D 89 K5
Ewood Bridge Lancs 89 M6
Eworthy Devon 8 B5
Ewshot Hants 23 M5
Ewyas Harold Herefs 45 M9
Exbourne Devon 8 F4
Exbury Hants 14 D6
Exceat E Susx 25 M11
Exebridge Somset 18 B10
Exelby N York 97 L3
Exeter Devon 9 M6
Exeter Airport Devon 9 N6
Exeter Services Devon 9 N6
Exford Somset 17 R4
Exfordsgreen Shrops 56 H3
Exhall Warwks 47 M3
Exhall Warwks 59 N7
Exlade Street Oxon 35 J8
Exley Head C Brad 90 C2
Exminster Devon 9 M7
Exmoor National Park 17 R4
Exmouth Devon 9 P8
Exning Suffk 63 K7
Exted Kent 27 L3
Exton Devon 9 N7
Exton Hants 22 H10
Exton Rutlnd 73 N8
Exton Somset 18 B8
Exwick Devon 9 M6
Eyam Derbys 84 B5
Eydon Nhants 48 F5
Eye C Pete 74 D10
Eye Herefs 45 P2
Eye Suffk 64 G7
Eye Green C Pete 74 D10
Eyemouth Border 129 N7
Eyeworth C Beds 62 C11
Eyhorne Street Kent 38 D11
Eyke Suffk 65 L11
Eynesbury Cambs 61 Q9
Eynsford Kent 37 M7
Eynsham Oxon 34 D3
Eype Dorset 11 J6
Eyre Highld 152 G7
Eythorne Kent 27 N2
Eyton Herefs 45 P2
Eyton Shrops 56 F2
Eyton Shrops 56 F7
Eyton Shrops 69 M10
Eyton Wrexhm 69 L6
Eyton on Severn Shrops 57 K3
Eyton upon the Weald Moors Wrekin 57 M2

F

Faccombe Hants 22 C3
Faceby N York 104 E10
Fachwen Powys 68 D11
Facit Lancs 89 P7
Fackley Notts 84 G8
Faddiley Ches E 69 Q4
Fadmoor N York 98 D3
Faerdre Swans 29 J4
Faifley W Duns 125 M3
Failand N Som 31 P10
Failford S Ayrs 115 J2
Failsworth Oldham 83 J4
Fairbourne Gwynd 54 E2
Fairburn N York 91 M5
Fairfield Derbys 83 N10
Fairfield Kent 26 G6
Fairfield Worcs 58 D9
Fairfield Park Herts 50 F4
Fairford Gloucs 33 N4
Fairford Park Gloucs 33 N4
Fairgirth D & G 109 J9
Fair Green Norfk 75 N7
Fairhaven Lancs 88 C5
Fair Isle Shet 169 t14
Fair Isle Airport Shet 169 t14
Fairlands Surrey 23 Q4
Fairlie N Ayrs 124 G7
Fairlight E Susx 26 E9
Fairlight Cove E Susx 26 E9
Fairmile Devon 10 B5
Fairmile Surrey 36 D8
Fairnilee Border 117 P4
Fair Oak Hants 22 E11
Fairoak Staffs 70 D8
Fair Oak Green Hants 23 J2
Fairseat Kent 37 P8
Fairstead Essex 52 C8
Fairstead Norfk 75 M6
Fairstead Norfk 77 K7
Fairwarp E Susx 25 L5
Fairwater Cardif 30 F9
Fairy Cross Devon 16 G7
Fakenham Norfk 76 C6
Fakenham Magna Suffk 64 C6
Fala Mdloth 128 C7
Fala Dam Mdloth 128 C7
Falcut Nhants 48 G6
Faldingworth Lincs 86 E4
Faldouët Jersey 11 c2
Falfield S Glos 32 C6
Falkenham Suffk 53 N4
Falkirk Falk 133 P11
Falkirk Wheel Falk 133 P11
Falkland Fife 134 H6
Fallburn S Lans 116 D3
Fallgate Derbys 84 E8
Fallin Stirlg 133 N9
Fallodon Nthumb 119 N6
Fallowfield Manch 83 J6
Fallowfield Nthumb 112 D7
Falmer E Susx 25 J9
Falmouth Cnwll 3 L7
Falnash Border 117 M9
Falsgrave N York 99 L3
Falstone Nthumb 111 P3
Fanagmore Highld 164 E7
Fancott C Beds 50 B5
Fanellan Highld 155 N9
Fangdale Beck N York 98 B2
Fangfoss E R Yk 98 F10
Fanmore Ag & B 137 L7
Fannich Lodge Highld 154 H4
Fans Border 118 B2
Far Bletchley M Keyn 49 N8
Farcet Cambs 62 B2
Far Cotton Nhants 60 G9
Farden Shrops 57 K9
Fareham Hants 14 G5
Farewell Staffs 58 G2
Far Forest Worcs 57 N9
Farforth Lincs 87 K5
Far Green Gloucs 32 E4
Faringdon Oxon 33 Q5
Farington Lancs 88 G5
Farlam Cumb 111 L9
Farleigh N Som 31 P11
Farleigh Surrey 37 J8
Farleigh Hungerford Somset 20 F3
Farleigh Wallop Hants 22 H5
Farlesthorpe Lincs 87 N6
Farleton Cumb 95 L4
Farleton Lancs 95 M7
Farley Derbys 84 C8
Farley Staffs 71 K6
Farley Wilts 21 P9

Farley Green Suffk 63 M10
Farley Green Surrey 36 C11
Farley Hill Wokham 23 K2
Farleys End Gloucs 32 E2
Farlington C Port 15 J5
Farlington N York 98 C7
Farlow Shrops 57 L8
Farmborough BaNES 20 C2
Farmbridge End Essex 51 P8
Farmcote Gloucs 47 L9
Farmcote Shrops 57 P6
Farmington Gloucs 47 M11
Farmoor Oxon 34 E3
Far Moor Wigan 82 B4
Farms Common Cnwll 2 H7
Farm Town Leics 72 B7
Farmtown Moray 158 D7
Farnah Green Derbys 84 D11
Farnborough Gt Lon 37 K8
Farnborough Hants 23 N4
Farnborough W Berk 34 D8
Farnborough Warwks 48 D5
Farnborough Park Hants 23 N3
Farncombe Surrey 23 Q6
Farndish Bed 61 K8
Farndon Ches W 69 M4
Farndon Notts 85 N10
Farne Islands Nthumb 119 P3
Farnell Angus 143 L6
Farnham Dorset 21 J11
Farnham Essex 51 L6
Farnham N York 97 M8
Farnham Suffk 65 M9
Farnham Surrey 23 M5
Farnham Common Bucks 35 Q7
Farnham Green Essex 51 L5
Farnham Royal Bucks 35 Q8
Farningham Kent 37 M7
Farnley Leeds 90 H4
Farnley N York 97 K11
Farnley Tyas Kirk 90 F8
Farnsfield Notts 85 K9
Farnworth Bolton 89 L9
Farnworth Halton 81 Q7
Far Oakridge Gloucs 32 H4
Farr Highld 148 E7
Farr Highld 156 B11
Farr Highld 166 B4
Farraline Highld 147 P3
Farringdon Devon 9 P6
Farrington Gurney BaNES 20 B3
Far Sawrey Cumb 101 L11
Farsley Leeds 90 G3
Farther Howegreen Essex 52 D11
Farthing Green Kent 26 D2
Farthinghoe Nhants 48 F7
Farthingloe Kent 27 N3
Farthingstone Nhants 48 H4
Farthing Street Gt Lon 37 K8
Fartown Kirk 90 F7
Farway Devon 10 D5
Fasnacloich Ag & B 139 J8
Fasnakyle Highld 147 J2
Fassfern Highld 139 J2
Fatfield Sundld 113 M10
Faugh Cumb 111 K10
Fauld Staffs 71 M9
Fauldhouse W Loth 126 G5
Faulkbourne Essex 52 C8
Faulkland Somset 20 D4
Fauls Shrops 69 Q8
Faversham Kent 38 H9
Fawdington N York 97 P6
Fawdon N u Ty 113 K7
Fawdon Nthumb 119 K7
Fawfieldhead Staffs 71 K2
Fawkham Green Kent 37 N7
Fawler Oxon 48 C11
Fawley Bucks 35 L7
Fawley Hants 14 E6
Fawley W Berk 34 C8
Fawley Chapel Herefs 46 A9
Fawnog Flints 81 J11
Fawsley Nhants 60 C9
Faxfleet E R Yk 92 E6
Faygate W Susx 24 F4
Fazakerley Lpool 81 M5
Fazeley Staffs 59 K4
Fearby N York 97 J4
Fearn Highld 156 E2
Fearnan P & K 140 H9
Fearnbeg Highld 153 N6
Fearnhead Warrtn 82 D6
Fearnmore Highld 153 N5
Fearnoch Ag & B 124 A2
Featherstone Staffs 58 D3
Featherstone Wakefd 91 L7
Feckenham Worcs 47 K2
Feering Essex 52 E7
Feetham N York 103 J11
Feizor N York 96 A7
Felbridge Surrey 25 J3
Felbrigg Norfk 77 J4
Felcourt Surrey 25 J2
Felden Herts 50 B10
Felindre Carmth 42 G7
Felindre Carmth 43 L10
Felindre Carmth 43 P9
Felindre Cerdgn 43 L3
Felindre Powys 44 H10
Felindre Powys 56 B8
Felindre Swans 28 H4
Felindre Farchog Pembks 41 M3
Felinfach Cerdgn 43 K3
Felinfach Powys 44 F8
Felinfoel Carmth 28 F4
Felingwm Isaf Carmth 43 K10
Felingwm Uchaf Carmth 43 K10
Felin-newydd Powys 44 G7
Felixkirk N York 97 Q4
Felixstowe Suffk 53 P5
Felixstowe Ferry Suffk 53 P4
Felkington Nthumb 118 H2
Felkirk Wakefd 91 K8
Felling Gatesd 113 L8
Fell Lane C Brad 90 C2
Fell Side Cumb 101 K3
Felmersham Bed 61 L9
Felmingham Norfk 77 K6
Felpham W Susx 15 P7
Felsham Suffk 64 C10
Felsted Essex 51 Q6
Feltham Gt Lon 36 D6
Felthamhill Surrey 36 C6
Felthorpe Norfk 76 H8
Felton Herefs 46 A5
Felton N Som 31 P11
Felton Nthumb 119 N10
Felton Butler Shrops 69 L11
Feltwell Norfk 63 M2
Fenay Bridge Kirk 90 F7
Fence Lancs 89 N3
Fence Rothm 84 F3
Fence Houses Sundld 113 M11
Fencott Oxon 48 G11
Fendike Corner Lincs 87 N8
Fen Ditton Cambs 62 G8
Fen Drayton Cambs 62 D7
Fen End Lincs 74 D6
Fen End Solhll 59 K10
Fenham Nthumb 119 L2
Feniscliffe Bl w D 89 K5
Feniscowles Bl w D 89 J5
Feniton Devon 10 C5
Fenn Green Shrops 57 P8
Fenn Street Medway 38 C6
Fenny Bentley Derbys 71 M5
Fenny Bridges Devon 10 C5
Fenny Compton Warwks 48 D4
Fenny Drayton Leics 72 B11
Fenny Stratford M Keyn 49 N8
Fenrother Nthumb 113 J2
Fenstanton Cambs 62 D7
Fenstead End Suffk 63 P10
Fen Street Norfk 64 D2
Fen Street Suffk 64 H9
Fenton C Stke 70 F6
Fenton Cambs 62 D5
Fenton Cumb 111 K9
Fenton Lincs 85 P5
Fenton Lincs 85 Q10
Fenton Notts 85 N4
Fenton Nthumb 119 J4
Fenton Barns E Loth 128 E3
Fenwick Donc 91 P7
Fenwick E Ayrs 125 M9
Fenwick Nthumb 112 G6
Fenwick Nthumb 119 L2
Feock Cnwll 3 L6
Feolin Ferry Ag & B 122 F6
Fergushill N Ayrs 125 J9
Feriniquarrie Highld 152 B7
Fermain Bay Guern 10 c2
Fern Angus 142 H5
Ferndale Rhondd 30 C5
Ferndown Dorset 13 J4
Ferness Highld 156 H8
Fernham Oxon 33 Q6
Fernhill Heath Worcs 46 G3
Fernhurst W Susx 23 N9
Fernie Fife 135 J4
Ferniegair S Lans 126 C7
Fernilea Highld 152 F11
Fernilee Derbys 83 M9
Fernwood Notts 85 P10
Ferrensby N York 97 N8
Ferriby Sluice N Linc 92 G6
Ferrindonald Highld 145 L6
Ferring W Susx 24 C10
Ferrybridge Wakefd 91 M6
Ferrybridge Services
Wakefd 91 M6
Ferryden Angus 143 N6
Ferryhill Dur 103 Q4
Ferryhill Station Dur 103 Q4
Ferry Point Highld 162 G9
Ferryside Carmth 28 C2
Ferrytown Highld 162 G9
Fersfield Norfk 64 F5
Fersit Highld 139 R2
Feshiebridge Highld 148 F7
Fetcham Surrey 36 D9
Fetlar Shet 169 t4
Fetterangus Abers 159 N7
Fettercairn Abers 143 M3
Fewcott Oxon 48 F9
Fewston N York 97 J10
Ffairfach Carmth 43 M10
Ffair Rhos Cerdgn 54 G11
Ffald-y-Brenin Carmth 43 M6
Ffarmers Carmth 43 N6
Ffawyddog Powys 45 J11
Ffestiniog Gwynd 67 N6
Ffestiniog Railway Gwynd 67 M6
Ffordd-las Denbgs 68 F2
Fforest Carmth 28 G4
Fforest Gôch Neath 29 K4
Ffostrasol Cerdgn 42 G5
Ffrith Flints 69 J3
Ffynnonddewi Cerdgn 42 G4
Ffynnongroyw Flints 80 G8
Ffynnon-oer Cerdgn 43 K4
Fickleshole Surrey 37 J8
Fiddington Gloucs 46 H8
Fiddington Somset 18 H6
Fiddleford Dorset 12 D2
Fiddlers Green Cnwll 4 C10
Fiddlers Hamlet Essex 51 L10
Field Staffs 71 J8
Field Broughton Cumb 94 H4
Field Dalling Norfk 76 E4
Fieldhead Cumb 101 N3
Field Head Leics 72 D9
Fifehead Magdalen Dorset 20 E10
Fifehead Neville Dorset 12 C2
Fifehead St Quintin Dorset 12 C2
Fife Keith Moray 158 B7
Fifield Oxon 47 P11
Fifield W & M 35 P9
Fifield Wilts 21 M4
Figheldean Wilts 21 N5
Filands Wilts 32 H7
Filby Norfk 77 P9
Filey N York 99 N4
Filgrave M Keyn 49 N5
Filkins Oxon 33 P4
Filleigh Devon 8 H2
Filleigh Devon 17 M6
Fillingham Lincs 86 B3
Fillongley Warwks 59 L7
Filmore Hill Hants 23 J9
Filton S Glos 32 B9
Fimber E R Yk 98 H8
Finavon Angus 142 H6
Fincham Norfk 75 N9
Finchampstead Wokham 23 L2
Fincharn Ag & B 131 J7
Finchdean Hants 15 K4
Finchingfield Essex 51 Q4
Finchley Gt Lon 36 G2
Findern Derbys 71 Q8
Findhorn Moray 157 J5
Findhorn Bridge Highld 148 E2
Findochty Moray 158 C4
Findo Gask P & K 134 C4
Findon Abers 151 N8
Findon W Susx 24 D9
Findon Mains Highld 155 R5
Findrack House Abers 150 G7
Finedon Nhants 61 K6
Fingal Street Suffk 65 J8
Fingask P & K 134 F4
Fingest Bucks 35 L6
Finghall N York 97 J3
Fingland Cumb 110 E9
Fingland D & G 115 Q4
Finglesham Kent 39 P11
Fingringhoe Essex 52 H7
Finkle Green Essex 52 B3
Finkle Street Barns 91 J11
Finlarig Stirlg 140 E11
Finmere Oxon 48 H8
Finnart P & K 140 D6
Finningham Suffk 64 F8
Finningley Donc 91 R11
Finsbay W Isls 168 f9
Finstall Worcs 58 E10
Finsthwaite Cumb 94 H3
Finstock Oxon 48 C11
Finstown Ork 169 c5
Fintry Abers 159 J7
Fintry Stirlg 133 J10
Finzean Abers 150 G9
Fionnphort Ag & B 137 J11
Fionnsbhagh W Isls 168 f9
Firbank Cumb 95 N2
Firbeck Rothm 85 J3
Firby N York 97 L3
Firby N York 98 E7
Firgrove Rochdl 89 Q8
Firle E Susx 25 L9
Firsby Lincs 87 N8
Firsdown Wilts 21 P8
Fir Tree Dur 103 M4
Fishbourne IoW 14 G8
Fishbourne W Susx 15 M6
Fishbourne Roman Palace
W Susx 15 M6
Fishburn Dur 104 C4
Fishcross Clacks 133 P8
Fisher W Susx 15 N6
Fisherford Abers 158 G10
Fisherrow E Loth 127 Q3
Fisher's Pond Hants 22 E10
Fisher's Row Lancs 95 J11
Fisherstreet W Susx 23 P8
Fisherton Highld 156 C7
Fisherton S Ayrs 114 E4
Fisherton de la Mere Wilts 21 K7
Fisherwick Staffs 59 J3
Fishery Estate W & M 35 N8
Fishguard Pembks 41 J3
Fishlake Donc 91 R8
Fishleigh Devon 8 D3
Fishmere End Lincs 74 E3
Fishnish Pier Ag & B 138 B9
Fishpond Bottom Dorset 10 H5
Fishponds Bristl 32 B9
Fishtoft Lincs 74 G2
Fishtoft Drove Lincs 87 K11
Fishwick Lancs 88 H5
Fiskavaig Highld 152 E11
Fiskerton Lincs 86 D6
Fiskerton Notts 85 M10
Fitling E R Yk 93 N4
Fittleton Wilts 21 M5
Fittleworth W Susx 24 B7
Fitton End Cambs 74 H8
Fitz Shrops 69 M11
Fitzhead Somset 18 F9
Fitzroy Somset 18 G9
Fitzwilliam Wakefd 91 L7
Five Ash Down E Susx 25 L6
Five Ashes E Susx 25 N5
Five Bells Somset 18 E6
Five Bridges Herefs 46 B5
Fivecrosses Ches W 82 B9
Fivehead Somset 19 L10
Fivelanes Cnwll 5 L5
Five Lanes Mons 31 M6
Five Oak Green Kent 37 P11
Five Oaks Jersey 11 c2
Five Oaks W Susx 24 C5
Five Roads Carmth 28 E3
Five Wents Kent 38 D11
Flack's Green Essex 52 C9
Flackwell Heath Bucks 35 N7
Fladbury Worcs 47 J5
Fladdabister Shet 169 r10
Flagg Derbys 83 P11
Flamborough E R Yk 99 Q6
Flamborough Head E R Yk 99 R6
Flamingo Land Theme
Park N York 98 F5
Flamstead Herts 50 C8
Flamstead End Herts 50 H10
Flansham W Susx 15 Q6
Flanshaw Wakefd 91 J6
Flappit Spring C Brad 90 D3
Flasby N York 96 D9
Flash Staffs 83 M11
Flashader Highld 152 E7
Flaunden Herts 50 B10
Flawborough Notts 73 K2
Flawith N York 97 Q7
Flax Bourton N Som 31 P11
Flaxby N York 97 N9
Flaxley Gloucs 46 C11
Flaxmere Ches W 82 C10
Flaxpool Somset 18 F7
Flaxton N York 98 D8
Fleckney Leics 60 D2
Flecknoe Warwks 60 B8
Fledborough Notts 85 P6
Fleet Dorset 11 N8
Fleet Hants 15 K6
Fleet Hants 23 M4
Fleet Lincs 74 G6
Fleetend Hants 14 F5
Fleet Hargate Lincs 74 G6
Fleet Services Hants 23 L3
Fleetwood Lancs 94 G11
Fleggburgh Norfk 77 N9
Flemingston V Glam 30 D11
Flemington S Lans 126 B6
Flempton Suffk 63 P7
Fletchersbridge Cnwll 5 J8
Fletcher's Green Kent 37 M11
Fletchertown Cumb 100 H2
Fletching E Susx 25 K6
Fleur-de-lis Caerph 30 G5
Flexbury Cnwll 16 C10
Flexford Surrey 23 P4
Flimby Cumb 100 D4
Flimwell E Susx 26 B5
Flint Flints 81 J10
Flintham Notts 85 M11
Flint Mountain Flints 81 J10
Flinton E R Yk 93 M3
Flint's Green Solhll 59 L8
Flishinghurst Kent 26 C4
Flitcham Norfk 75 P5
Flitton C Beds 50 C3
Flitwick C Beds 50 B4
Flixborough N Linc 92 E8
Flixborough Stather N Linc 92 E8
Flixton N York 99 L5
Flixton Suffk 65 L4
Flixton Traffd 82 F6
Flockton Kirk 90 G8
Flockton Green Kirk 90 H7
Flodden Nthumb 118 H3
Flodigarry Highld 152 H3
Flookburgh Cumb 94 H5
Flordon Norfk 64 H2
Flore Nhants 60 D8
Flotterton Nthumb 119 J10
Flowers Green E Susx 25 P8
Flowton Suffk 53 J2
Flushdyke Wakefd 90 H6
Flushing Cnwll 3 L7
Fluxton Devon 10 B6
Flyford Flavell Worcs 47 J3
Fobbing Thurr 38 B5
Fochabers Moray 157 Q6
Fochriw Caerph 30 F3
Fockerby N Linc 92 D7
Foddington Somset 19 Q9
Foel Powys 55 M2
Foelgastell Carmth 28 F2
Foel y Dyffryn Brdgnd 29 N6
Foggathorpe E R Yk 92 C3
Fogo Border 129 K10
Fogwatt Moray 157 N6
Foindle Highld 164 E7
Folda Angus 142 B5
Fole Staffs 71 J7
Foleshill Covtry 59 N8
Folke Dorset 11 P2
Folkestone Kent 27 M4
Folkingham Lincs 73 R4
Folkington E Susx 25 N10
Folksworth Cambs 61 P3
Folkton N York 99 M5
Folla Rule Abers 158 H11
Follifoot N York 97 M10
Folly Gate Devon 8 E5
Folly Hill Surrey 23 M5
Fonmon V Glam 30 D11
Fonthill Bishop Wilts 20 H8
Fonthill Gifford Wilts 20 H8
Fontmell Magna Dorset 20 G11
Fontmell Parva Dorset 12 D2
Fontwell W Susx 15 P5
Font-y-gary V Glam 30 E11
Foolow Derbys 83 Q9
Foots Cray Gt Lon 37 L6
Forbestown Abers 150 B5
Forcett N York 103 N8
Ford Ag & B 130 H7
Ford Bucks 35 L3
Ford Derbys 84 F4
Ford Devon 6 G8
Ford Devon 7 K10
Ford Devon 16 G7
Ford Gloucs 47 L9
Ford Nthumb 118 H3
Ford Shrops 56 G2
Ford Somset 18 E9
Ford Somset 19 Q4
Ford Staffs 71 K4
Ford W Susx 15 Q6
Ford Wilts 21 N8
Ford Wilts 32 F9
Forda Devon 8 D6
Fordcombe Kent 25 M2
Fordell Fife 134 F10
Forden Powys 56 C4
Ford End Essex 51 Q7
Forder Green Devon 7 K5
Ford Green Lancs 95 K11
Fordham Cambs 63 K6
Fordham Essex 52 F6
Fordham Norfk 75 M11
Fordham Heath Essex 52 F6
Ford Heath Shrops 56 G2
Fordingbridge Hants 13 K2
Fordon E R Yk 99 L5
Fordoun Abers 143 N2
Ford's Green Suffk 64 F8
Fordstreet Essex 52 F6
Ford Street Somset 18 G11
Fordton Devon 9 K5
Fordwells Oxon 34 B2
Fordwich Kent 39 L10
Fordyce Abers 158 E5
Forebridge Staffs 70 G10
Foremark Derbys 72 A5
Forest Guern 10 b2
Forest N York 103 Q10
Forest Becks Lancs 96 A10
Forestburn Gate Nthumb 119 L11
Forest Chapel Ches E 83 L10
Forest Coal Pit Mons 45 K10
Forest Gate Gt Lon 37 K3
Forest Green Surrey 24 D2
Forest Hall N Tyne 113 L7
Forest Head Cumb 111 L9
Forest Hill Gt Lon 37 J6
Forest Hill Oxon 34 G3
Forest-in-Teesdale Dur 102 G4
Forest Lane Head N York 97 M9
Forest Mill Clacks 134 B9
Forest of Bowland Lancs 95 N10
Forest of Dean Gloucs 32 B2
Forest Row E Susx 25 K4
Forest Side IoW 14 E9
Forestside W Susx 15 L4
Forest Town Notts 85 J8
Forfar Angus 142 H7
Forgandenny P & K 134 D4
Forge Powys 54 H5
Forge Hammer Torfn 31 J5
Forge Side Torfn 30 H3
Forgie Moray 158 A7
Forgieside Moray 158 B7
Forgue Abers 158 F8
Forhill Worcs 58 G9
Formby Sefton 88 C9
Forncett End Norfk 64 G3
Forncett St Mary Norfk 64 H3
Forncett St Peter Norfk 64 H3
Fornham All Saints Suffk 64 A8
Fornham St Martin Suffk 64 B8
Fornighty Highld 156 G7
Forres Moray 157 J6
Forsbrook Staffs 70 H6
Forse Highld 167 M10
Forshaw Heath Warwks 58 G10
Forsinard Highld 166 E8
Forss Highld 166 H3
Forston Dorset 11 P5
Fort Augustus Highld 147 K6
Forteviot P & K 134 D4
Forth S Lans 126 G7
Forthampton Gloucs 46 G8
Fort Hommet Guern 10 b1
Forth Rail Bridge C Edin 127 L2
Forth Road Bridge Fife 127 L2
Fortingall P & K 140 H8
Forton Hants 22 D6
Forton Lancs 95 K10
Forton Shrops 69 M11
Forton Somset 10 G3
Forton Staffs 70 D10
Fort Richmond Guern 10 b2
Fortrie Abers 158 G8
Fortrose Highld 156 C6
Fortuneswell Dorset 11 P10
Fort William Highld 139 L3
Forty Green Bucks 35 P6
Forty Hill Gt Lon 50 H11
Forward Green Suffk 64 G10
Fosbury Wilts 22 B3
Foscot Oxon 47 P10
Foscote Nhants 49 J5
Fosdyke Lincs 74 F4
Fosdyke Bridge Lincs 74 F4
Foss P & K 141 J6
Fossebridge Gloucs 33 L2
Foss-y-ffin Cerdgn 42 H2
Fosterhouses Donc 91 R8
Foster Street Essex 51 L9
Foston Derbys 71 M8
Foston Leics 60 D2
Foston Lincs 73 M2
Foston N York 98 D7
Foston on the Wolds E R Yk 99 N9
Fotherby Lincs 87 K2
Fothergill Cumb 100 D4
Fotheringhay Nhants 61 N2
Foula Shet 169 k10
Foula Airport Shet 169 k10
Foulbridge Cumb 110 H11
Foulby Wakefd 91 K7
Foulden Border 129 N8
Foulden Norfk 75 Q11
Foul End Warwks 59 K6
Foul Mile E Susx 25 P7
Foulness Island Essex 38 G3
Foulridge Lancs 89 P2
Foulsham Norfk 76 E7
Fountainhall Border 128 C10
Four Ashes Solhll 59 J9
Four Ashes Staffs 57 Q7
Four Ashes Staffs 58 D3
Four Ashes Suffk 64 E7
Four Cabots Guern 10 b2
Four Crosses Powys 69 J11
Four Crosses Staffs 58 E3
Four Elms Kent 37 L11
Four Foot Somset 19 Q8
Four Forks Somset 18 H7
Four Gates Bolton 89 J9
Four Gotes Cambs 75 J7
Four Lane End Barns 90 H10
Four Lane Ends Ches W 69 Q2
Four Lanes Cnwll 2 H6
Fourlanes End Ches E 70 E3
Four Marks Hants 23 J7
Four Mile Bridge IoA 78 D9
Four Oaks Birm 58 H5
Four Oaks E Susx 26 E7
Four Oaks Gloucs 46 C9
Four Oaks Solhll 59 K8
Fourpenny Highld 163 J8
Four Points W Berk 34 G9
Four Roads Carmth 28 D3
Four Shire Stone Warwks 47 P8
Fourstones Nthumb 112 C7
Four Throws Kent 26 C6
Four Wents Kent 37 P10
Fovant Wilts 21 K9
Foveran Abers 151 P3
Fowey Cnwll 5 J11
Fowley Common Warrtn 82 E5
Fowlhall Kent 37 Q11
Fowlis Angus 142 E11
Fowlis Wester P & K 133 Q3
Fowlmere Cambs 62 F11
Fownhope Herefs 46 A8
Foxbar Rens 125 M5
Foxcombe Devon 8 C7
Fox Corner Surrey 23 Q4
Foxcote Gloucs 47 K11
Foxcote Somset 20 D3
Foxdale IoM 80 c6
Foxearth Essex 52 D3
Foxendown Kent 37 P7
Foxfield Cumb 94 E3
Foxham Wilts 33 J9
Fox Hatch Essex 51 N11
Foxhills Hants 13 P2
Foxhole Cnwll 3 P3
Foxholes N York 99 L6
Foxhunt Green E Susx 25 M7
Foxley Nhants 48 H4
Foxley Norfk 76 E7
Foxley Wilts 32 G7
Foxlydiate Worcs 58 F11
Fox Street Essex 52 H6
Foxt Staffs 71 J5
Foxton Cambs 62 F11
Foxton Dur 104 C6
Foxton Leics 60 F3

Foxton N York 104 D11
Foxup N York 96 C5
Foxwist Green Ches W 82 D11
Foxwood Shrops 57 L9
Foy Herefs 46 A9
Foyers Highld 147 M3
Foynesfield Highld 156 F7
Fraddam Cnwll 2 F7
Fraddon Cnwll 4 E10
Fradley Staffs 59 J2
Fradswell Staffs 70 H8
Fraisthorpe E R Yk 99 P8
Framfield E Susx 25 L6
Framingham Earl Norfk 77 K11
Framingham Pigot Norfk 77 K11
Framlingham Suffk 65 K9
Frampton Dorset 11 N5
Frampton Lincs 74 F3
Frampton Cotterell S Glos 32 C8
Frampton Mansell Gloucs 32 H4
Frampton-on-Severn Gloucs 32 D3
Frampton West End Lincs 74 F2
Framsden Suffk 64 H10
Framwellgate Moor Dur 103 Q2
Franche Worcs 57 Q9
Frandley Ches W 82 D9
Frankaborough Devon 5 P3
Frankby Wirral 81 J7
Frankfort Norfk 77 L7
Franklands Gate Herefs 45 Q5
Frankley Worcs 58 E8
Frankley Services Worcs 58 E8
Franksbridge Powys 44 G3
Frankton Warwks 59 P10
Frant E Susx 25 N3
Fraserburgh Abers 159 N4
Frating Essex 53 J7
Frating Green Essex 53 J7
Fratton C Port 15 J6
Freathy Cnwll 5 P11
Freckenham Suffk 63 L6
Freckleton Lancs 88 E5
Freebirch Derbys 84 D6
Freeby Leics 73 L6
Freefolk Hants 22 E5
Freehay Staffs 71 J6
Freeland Oxon 34 D2
Freethorpe Norfk 77 N10
Freethorpe Common Norfk 77 N11
Freiston Lincs 74 G2
Fremington Devon 17 J5
Fremington N York 103 K11
Frenchay S Glos 32 B9
Frenchbeer Devon 8 G7
French Street Kent 37 L10
Frenich P & K 141 K6
Frensham Surrey 23 M6
Freshfield Sefton 88 B9
Freshford Wilts 20 E2
Freshwater IoW 13 P7
Freshwater Bay IoW 13 P7
Freshwater East Pembks 41 K11
Fressingfield Suffk 65 K6
Freston Suffk 53 L4
Freswick Highld 167 Q3
Fretherne Gloucs 32 D2
Frettenham Norfk 77 J8
Freuchie Fife 134 H6
Freystrop Pembks 41 J8
Friar Park Sandw 58 F6
Friar's Gate E Susx 25 L4
Friars' Hill N York 98 E3
Friar Waddon Dorset 11 N7
Friday Bridge Cambs 75 J10
Friday Street Suffk 65 J10
Friday Street Suffk 65 L11
Friday Street Suffk 65 M9
Friday Street Surrey 36 D11
Fridaythorpe E R Yk 98 H9
Friden Derbys 71 M2
Friendly Calder 90 D6
Friern Barnet Gt Lon 36 G2
Friesthorpe Lincs 86 E4
Frieston Lincs 86 B11
Frieth Bucks 35 L6
Friezeland Notts 84 G10
Frilford Oxon 34 D5
Frilsham W Berk 34 F10
Frimley Surrey 23 N3
Frimley Green Surrey 23 N3
Frindsbury Medway 38 B8
Fring Norfk 75 P4
Fringford Oxon 48 H9
Frinsted Kent 38 E10
Frinton-on-Sea Essex 53 M7
Friockheim Angus 143 K8
Friog Gwynd 67 M11
Frisby on the Wreake Leics 72 H7
Friskney Lincs 87 N9
Friskney Eaudike Lincs 87 N9
Friston E Susx 25 N11
Friston Suffk 65 N9
Fritchley Derbys 84 E10
Fritham Hants 13 M2
Frith Bank Lincs 87 K11
Frith Common Worcs 57 M11
Frithelstock Devon 16 H8
Frithelstock Stone Devon 16 H8
Frithend Hants 23 M7
Frithsden Herts 50 B9
Frithville Lincs 87 K10
Frittenden Kent 26 D3
Frittiscombe Devon 7 L10
Fritton Norfk 65 J3
Fritton Norfk 77 P11
Fritwell Oxon 48 F9
Frizinghall C Brad 90 E3
Frizington Cumb 100 D7
Frocester Gloucs 32 E4
Frodesley Shrops 57 J4
Frodsham Ches W 81 Q9
Frogden Border 118 E5
Frog End Cambs 62 E11
Frog End Cambs 62 H9
Froggatt Derbys 84 B5
Froghall Staffs 71 J5
Frogham Hants 13 L2
Frogham Kent 39 N11
Frogmore Devon 7 K10
Frognall Lincs 74 C8
Frogpool Cnwll 3 K5
Frog Pool Worcs 57 P11
Frogwell Cnwll 5 N8
Frolesworth Leics 60 B2
Frome Somset 20 E5
Frome St Quintin Dorset 11 M4
Fromes Hill Herefs 46 C5
Fron Gwynd 66 F7
Fron Gwynd 67 J4
Fron Powys 56 B5
Fron Powys 56 C4
Froncysyllte Wrexhm 69 J6
Fron-goch Gwynd 68 B7
Fron Isaf Wrexhm 69 J6
Frostenden Suffk 65 P5
Frosterley Dur 103 K3
Froxfield C Beds 49 Q8
Froxfield Wilts 33 Q11
Froxfield Green Hants 23 K9
Fryern Hill Hants 22 D10
Fryerning Essex 51 P10
Fryton N York 98 D6
Fuinary Highld 137 Q6
Fulbeck Lincs 86 B10
Fulbourn Cambs 62 H9
Fulbrook Oxon 33 Q2
Fulflood Hants 22 E8
Fulford C York 98 C11
Fulford Somset 18 H9
Fulford Staffs 70 H7
Fulham Gt Lon 36 G5
Fulking W Susx 24 F8
Fullaford Devon 17 M4
Fullarton N Ayrs 125 J10
Fuller's End Essex 51 M5
Fuller's Moor Ches W 69 N4
Fuller Street Essex 52 B8
Fuller Street Kent 37 N9
Fullerton Hants 22 C7
Fulletby Lincs 87 J6
Fullready Warwks 47 Q5
Full Sutton E R Yk 98 E9
Fullwood E Ayrs 125 L7
Fulmer Bucks 35 Q7
Fulmodeston Norfk 76 D5
Fulnetby Lincs 86 E5
Fulney Lincs 74 E6
Fulstone Kirk 90 F9
Fulstow Lincs 93 P11
Fulwell Oxon 48 C10
Fulwell Sundld 113 N9
Fulwood Lancs 88 G4
Fulwood Notts 84 G9
Fulwood Sheff 84 D3
Fulwood Somset 18 H10
Fundenhall Norfk 64 H2
Funtington W Susx 15 M5
Funtley Hants 14 G5
Funtullich P & K 133 M2
Furley Devon 10 F4
Furnace Ag & B 131 L7
Furnace Carmth 28 F4
Furnace Cerdgn 54 F5
Furnace End Warwks 59 K6
Furner's Green E Susx 25 K5
Furness Vale Derbys 83 M8
Furneux Pelham Herts 51 K5
Further Quarter Kent 26 E4
Furtho Nhants 49 L6
Furzehill Devon 17 N2
Furzehill Dorset 12 H4
Furzehills Lincs 87 J6
Furzeley Corner Hants 15 J4
Furze Platt W & M 35 N8
Furzley Hants 21 Q11
Fyfett Somset 10 E2
Fyfield Essex 51 N9
Fyfield Hants 21 Q5
Fyfield Oxon 34 D5
Fyfield Wilts 21 N2
Fyfield Wilts 33 M11
Fyfield Bavant Wilts 21 K9
Fylingthorpe N York 105 P10
Fyning W Susx 23 M10
Fyvie Abers 159 J10

G

Gabroc Hill E Ayrs 125 M7
Gaddesby Leics 72 H8
Gaddesden Row Herts 50 C8
Gadfa IoA 78 H7
Gadgirth S Ayrs 114 H3
Gadlas Shrops 69 L7
Gaer Powys 44 H10
Gaerllwyd Mons 31 M5
Gaerwen IoA 78 H10
Gagingwell Oxon 48 D9
Gailes N Ayrs 125 J10
Gailey Staffs 58 D2
Gainford Dur 103 N7
Gainsborough Lincs 85 P3
Gainsford End Essex 52 B4
Gairloch Highld 153 Q2
Gairlochy Highld 146 F11
Gairneybridge P & K 134 E8
Gaisgill Cumb 102 B9
Gaitsgill Cumb 110 G11
Galashiels Border 117 P3
Galgate Lancs 95 K9
Galhampton Somset 20 B9
Gallanachbeg Ag & B 130 G2
Gallanachmore Ag & B 130 G2
Gallantry Bank Ches E 69 P4
Gallatown Fife 134 H9
Galley Common Warwks 59 M6
Galleywood Essex 52 B11
Gallovie Highld 147 P10
Galloway Forest Park 114 H10
Gallowfauld Angus 142 G9
Gallowhill P & K 142 B10
Gallows Green Essex 52 F6
Gallows Green Worcs 46 H2
Gallowstree Common Oxon 35 J8
Galltair Highld 145 P3
Gallt-y-foel Gwynd 67 K2
Gally Hill Hants 23 M4
Gallypot Street E Susx 25 L3
Galmisdale Highld 144 G11
Galmpton Devon 6 H10
Galmpton Torbay 7 M7
Galphay N York 97 L6
Galston E Ayrs 125 N10
Gamballs Green Staffs 83 M11
Gamblesby Cumb 102 B3
Gambles Green Essex 52 C9
Gamelsby Cumb 110 E10
Gamesley Derbys 83 M6
Gamlingay Cambs 62 B10
Gamlingay Cinques Cambs 62 B10
Gamlingay Great Heath Cambs 62 B10
Gammersgill N York 96 G4
Gamrie Abers 159 J5
Gamston Notts 72 F3
Gamston Notts 85 M5
Ganarew Herefs 45 Q11
Ganavan Bay Ag & B 138 F11
Gang Cnwll 5 N8
Ganllwyd Gwynd 67 N10
Gannachy Angus 143 K3
Ganstead E R Yk 93 K4
Ganthorpe N York 98 D6
Ganton N York 99 K5
Ganwick Corner Herts 50 G11
Gappah Devon 9 L9
Garbity Moray 157 Q7
Garboldisham Norfk 64 E5
Garbole Highld 148 D3
Garchory Abers 149 Q5
Garden City Flints 81 L11
Gardeners Green Wokham 35 M11
Gardenstown Abers 159 K5
Garden Village Sheff 90 H11
Garderhouse Shet 169 q9
Gardham E R Yk 92 G2
Gare Hill Somset 20 E6
Garelochhead Ag & B 131 Q9
Garford Oxon 34 D5
Garforth Leeds 91 L4
Gargrave N York 96 D10
Gargunnock Stirlg 133 L9
Garlic Street Norfk 65 J5
Garlieston D & G 107 N8
Garlinge Kent 39 P8
Garlinge Green Kent 39 K11
Garlogie Abers 151 K6
Garmond Abers 159 K7
Garmouth Moray 157 Q5
Garmston Shrops 57 L3
Garnant Carmth 29 J2
Garndolbenmaen Gwynd 66 H6
Garnett Bridge Cumb 101 P11
Garnfadryn Gwynd 66 D8
Garnswllt Swans 28 H3
Garn-yr-erw Torfn 30 H3
Garrabost W Isls 168 k4
Garrallan E Ayrs 115 K4
Garras Cnwll 3 J9
Garreg Gwynd 67 L6
Garrigill Cumb 102 D2
Garriston N York 97 J2
Garroch D & G 108 C4
Garrochtrie D & G 106 F10
Garrochty Ag & B 124 D7
Garros Highld 152 H5
Garsdale Cumb 95 Q3
Garsdale Head Cumb 96 A2
Garsdon Wilts 33 J7
Garshall Green Staffs 70 H8
Garsington Oxon 34 G4
Garstang Lancs 95 K11
Garston Herts 50 D10
Garston Lpool 81 N8
Garswood St Hel 82 C5
Gartachossan Ag & B 122 D7
Gartcosh N Lans 126 B4
Garth Brdgnd 29 N6
Garth Mons 31 K6
Garth Powys 44 D5
Garth Powys 56 D10
Garth Wrexhm 69 J6
Garthamlock C Glas 126 B4
Garthbrengy Powys 44 E8
Gartheli Cerdgn 43 L3
Garthmyl Powys 56 B5
Garthorpe Leics 73 L6
Garthorpe N Linc 92 D7
Garth Row Cumb 101 P11
Garths Cumb 95 L3
Gartly Abers 158 D11
Gartmore Stirlg 132 G8
Gartness N Lans 126 D5
Gartness Stirlg 132 G10
Gartocharn W Duns 132 E10
Garton E R Yk 93 N3
Garton-on-the-Wolds E R Yk 99 K9
Gartymore Highld 163 N4
Garva Bridge Highld 147 N9
Garvald Border 127 L8
Garvald E Loth 128 F5
Garvan Highld 138 H2
Garvard Ag & B 136 b3
Garve Highld 155 L5
Garvellachs Ag & B 130 D5
Garvestone Norfk 76 E10
Garvock Inver 124 H3
Garway Herefs 45 P10
Garway Common Herefs 45 P10
Garway Hill Herefs 45 N9
Garynahine W Isls 168 h4
Garyvard W Isls 168 i6
Gasper Wilts 20 E8
Gastard Wilts 32 G11
Gasthorpe Norfk 64 D5
Gaston Green Essex 51 L7
Gatcombe IoW 14 E9
Gatebeck Cumb 95 L3
Gate Burton Lincs 85 P4
Gateford Notts 85 J4
Gateforth N York 91 P5
Gatehead E Ayrs 125 K10
Gate Helmsley N York 98 D9
Gatehouse Nthumb 111 Q3
Gatehouse of Fleet D & G 108 C9
Gateley Norfk 76 D7
Gatenby N York 97 M3
Gatesgarth Cumb 100 G7
Gateshaw Border 118 E6
Gateshead Gatesd 113 L8
Gates Heath Ches W 69 N2
Gateside Angus 142 G9
Gateside E Rens 125 M6
Gateside Fife 134 F6
Gateside N Ayrs 125 K7
Gateslack D & G 116 B10
Gathurst Wigan 88 G9
Gatley Stockp 82 H7
Gatton Surrey 36 G10
Gattonside Border 117 Q3
Gatwick Airport W Susx 24 G2
Gaufron Powys 55 M11
Gaulby Leics 72 H10
Gauldry Fife 135 K3
Gauldswell P & K 142 C7
Gaulkthorn Lancs 89 M5
Gaultree Norfk 75 J9
Gaunton's Bank Ches E 69 Q5
Gaunt's Common Dorset 12 H3
Gaunt's End Essex 51 N5
Gautby Lincs 86 G6
Gavinton Border 129 K9
Gawber Barns 91 J9
Gawcott Bucks 49 J8
Gawsworth Ches E 83 J11
Gawthorpe Wakefd 90 H6
Gawthrop Cumb 95 P3
Gawthwaite Cumb 94 F4
Gay Bowers Essex 52 C11
Gaydon Warwks 48 C4
Gayhurst M Keyn 49 M5
Gayle N York 96 C3
Gayles N York 103 M9
Gay Street W Susx 24 C6
Gayton Nhants 49 K4
Gayton Norfk 75 P7
Gayton Staffs 70 H9
Gayton Wirral 81 K8
Gayton le Marsh Lincs 87 M4
Gayton Thorpe Norfk 75 P7
Gaywood Norfk 75 M6
Gazeley Suffk 63 M8
Gear Cnwll 3 J9
Gearraidh Bhaird W Isls 168 i6
Gearraidh na h-Aibhne W Isls 168 h4
Geary Highld 152 D5
Gedding Suffk 64 C10
Geddington Nhants 61 J4
Gedling Notts 72 G2
Gedney Lincs 74 H6
Gedney Broadgate Lincs 74 H6
Gedney Drove End Lincs 75 J5
Gedney Dyke Lincs 74 H5
Gedney Hill Lincs 74 F8
Gee Cross Tamesd 83 L6
Geeston Rutlnd 73 P10
Geldeston Norfk 65 M3
Gelli Rhondd 30 C6
Gelli Torfn 31 J6
Gellifor Denbgs 68 F2
Gelligaer Caerph 30 F5
Gelligroes Caerph 30 G6
Gelligron Neath 29 K4
Gellilydan Gwynd 67 M7
Gellinudd Neath 29 K4
Gelly Pembks 41 L7
Gellyburn P & K 141 Q10
Gellywen Carmth 41 Q6
Gelston D & G 108 G9
Gelston Lincs 86 B11
Gembling E R Yk 99 N9
Gentleshaw Staffs 58 G2
Georgefield D & G 110 E2
George Green Bucks 35 Q8
Georgeham Devon 16 H4
Georgemas Junction Station Highld 167 L5
George Nympton Devon 17 N7
Georgetown Blae G 30 G3
Georgia Cnwll 2 D6
Georth Ork 169 c4
Gerlan Gwynd 79 L11
Germansweek Devon 8 B6
Germoe Cnwll 2 F8
Gerrans Cnwll 3 M6
Gerrards Cross Bucks 36 B3
Gerrick R & Cl 105 K8
Gestingthorpe Essex 52 D4
Geuffordd Powys 56 C2
Gib Hill Ches W 82 D9
Gibraltar Lincs 87 Q9
Gibsmere Notts 85 M11
Giddeahall Wilts 32 G10
Giddy Green Dorset 12 D7
Gidea Park Gt Lon 37 M2
Gidleigh Devon 8 G7
Giffnock E Rens 125 P6
Gifford E Loth 128 E6
Giffordtown Fife 134 H5
Giggleswick N York 96 B8
Gigha Ag & B 123 K10
Gilberdyke E R Yk 92 D5
Gilbert's End Worcs 46 F6
Gilbert Street Hants 22 H8
Gilchriston E Loth 128 D6
Gilcrux Cumb 100 F3
Gildersome Leeds 90 G5
Gildingwells Rothm 85 J3
Gilesgate Moor Dur 103 Q2
Gileston V Glam 30 D11
Gilfach Caerph 30 G5
Gilfach Goch Brdgnd 30 C6
Gilfachrheda Cerdgn 42 H3
Gilgarran Cumb 100 D6
Gill Cumb 101 M5
Gillamoor N York 98 D3
Gillan Cnwll 3 K8
Gillen Highld 152 D6
Gillesbie D & G 110 C2
Gilling East N York 98 C5
Gillingham Dorset 20 F9
Gillingham Medway 38 C8
Gillingham Norfk 65 N3
Gilling West N York 103 N9
Gillock Highld 167 M5
Gillow Heath Staffs 70 F3
Gills Highld 167 P2
Gill's Green Kent 26 C5
Gilmanscleuch Border 117 L6
Gilmerton C Edin 127 P4
Gilmerton P & K 133 P3
Gilmonby Dur 103 J8
Gilmorton Leics 60 C3
Gilsland Nthumb 111 M7
Gilson Warwks 59 J7
Gilstead C Brad 90 E3
Gilston Border 128 C8
Gilston Herts 51 K8
Gilston Park Herts 51 K8
Giltbrook Notts 84 G11
Gilwern Mons 30 H2
Gimingham Norfk 77 K4
Ginclough Ches E 83 L9
Gingers Green E Susx 25 P8
Gipping Suffk 64 F9
Gipsey Bridge Lincs 87 J11
Girdle Toll N Ayrs 125 J9
Girlington C Brad 90 E4
Girlsta Shet 169 r8
Girsby N York 104 C9
Girtford C Beds 61 Q11
Girthon D & G 108 D10
Girton Cambs 62 F8
Girton Notts 85 P7
Girvan S Ayrs 114 C8
Gisburn Lancs 96 B11
Gisleham Suffk 65 Q4
Gislingham Suffk 64 F7
Gissing Norfk 64 G4
Gittisham Devon 10 C5
Gladestry Powys 45 J3
Gladsmuir E Loth 128 D5
Glais Swans 29 K4
Glaisdale N York 105 L9
Glamis Angus 142 F8
Glanaber Gwynd 67 L4
Glanaman Carmth 29 J2
Glandford Norfk 76 E3
Glan-Duar Carmth 43 K6
Glandwr Pembks 41 N5
Glan-Dwyfach Gwynd 66 H6
Glandyfi Cerdgn 54 F5
Glangrwyney Powys 45 J11
Glanllynfi Brdgnd 29 N6
Glanmule Powys 56 B6
Glanrhyd Pembks 41 M2
Glan-rhyd Powys 29 L3
Glanton Nthumb 119 L8
Glanton Pike Nthumb 119 L8
Glanvilles Wootton Dorset 11 P3
Glan-y-don Flints 80 H9
Glan-y-llyn Rhondd 30 F8
Glan-y-nant Powys 55 L8
Glan-yr-afon Gwynd 68 B6
Glan-yr-afon Gwynd 68 D6
Glan-yr-afon IoA 79 L8
Glan-yr-afon Swans 28 H3
Glan-y-wern Gwynd 67 L8
Glapthorn Nhants 61 M2
Glapwell Derbys 84 G7
Glasbury Powys 44 H7
Glascoed Denbgs 80 D10
Glascoed Mons 31 K4
Glascote Staffs 59 K4
Glascwm Powys 44 H4
Glasfryn Conwy 68 B4
Glasgow C Glas 125 P4
Glasgow Airport Rens 125 M4
Glasgow Prestwick Airport S Ayrs 114 G2
Glasgow Science Centre C Glas 125 P4
Glasinfryn Gwynd 79 K11
Glasnacardoch Bay Highld 145 L8
Glasnakille Highld 144 H5
Glasphein Highld 152 B8
Glaspwll Powys 54 G5
Glassenbury Kent 26 C4
Glassford S Lans 126 C8
Glass Houghton Wakefd 91 L6
Glasshouse Gloucs 46 D10
Glasshouse Hill Gloucs 46 D10
Glasshouses N York 97 J8
Glasslaw Abers 159 L6
Glasson Cumb 110 E8
Glasson Lancs 95 J9
Glassonby Cumb 101 Q3
Glasterlaw Angus 143 K7
Glaston Rutlnd 73 M10
Glastonbury Somset 19 P7
Glatton Cambs 61 Q3
Glazebrook Warrtn 82 E6
Glazebury Warrtn 82 E5
Glazeley Shrops 57 N7
Gleadless Sheff 84 E4
Gleadsmoss Ches E 82 H11
Gleaston Cumb 94 F6
Glebe Highld 147 N4
Gledhow Leeds 91 J3
Gledpark D & G 108 D10
Gledrid Shrops 69 K7
Glemsford Suffk 52 D2
Glenallachie Moray 157 P9
Glenancross Highld 145 L9
Glenaros House Ag & B 137 P7
Glen Auldyn IoM 80 f3
Glenbarr Ag & B 120 C4
Glenbarry Abers 158 E7
Glenbeg Highld 137 P3
Glenbervie Abers 151 K11
Glenboig N Lans 126 C4
Glenborrodale Highld 137 Q3
Glenbranter Ag & B 131 N8
Glenbreck Border 116 F6
Glenbrittle Highld 144 F3
Glenbuck E Ayrs 115 P2
Glencally Angus 142 F5
Glencaple D & G 109 L7
Glencarse P & K 134 F3
Glencoe Highld 139 L6
Glencothe Border 116 F5
Glencraig Fife 134 F9
Glencrosh D & G 115 Q10
Glendale Highld 152 B8
Glendaruel Ag & B 131 K11
Glendevon P & K 134 B7
Glendoe Lodge Highld 147 L6
Glendoick P & K 134 G3
Glenduckie Fife 134 H4
Glenegedale Ag & B 122 D9
Glenelg Highld 145 P4
Glenerney Moray 157 J8
Glenfarg P & K 134 E5
Glenfield Leics 72 E9
Glenfinnan Highld 145 R11
Glenfintaig Lodge Highld 146 G10
Glenfoot P & K 134 F4
Glenfyne Lodge Ag & B 131 Q4
Glengarnock N Ayrs 125 J7
Glengolly Highld 167 K3
Glengorm Castle Ag & B 137 L4
Glengrasco Highld 152 G9
Glenholm Border 116 G4
Glenhoul D & G 115 M10
Glenisla Angus 142 C5
Glenkin Ag & B 131 N11
Glenkindie Abers 150 C5
Glenlivet Moray 149 M2
Glenlochar D & G 108 F8
Glenlomond P & K 134 F7

Glenluce D & G 106 G6
Glenmassen Ag & B 131 N10
Glenmavis N Lans 126 D4
Glen Maye IoM 80 b6
Glen Mona IoM 80 g4
Glenmore Highld 152 G9
Glenmore Lodge Highld 148 H6
Glen Nevis House Highld 139 L3
Glenochil Clacks 133 P8
Glen Parva Leics 72 F11
Glenquiech Angus 142 G5
Glenralloch Ag & B 123 Q6
Glenridding Cumb 101 L7
Glenrothes Fife 134 H7
Glenshero Lodge Highld 147 P9
Glenstriven Ag & B 124 D2
Glentham Lincs 86 D2
Glentrool D & G 107 L2
Glen Trool Lodge D & G 114 H11
Glentruim Highld 148 B9
Glentworth Lincs 86 B3
Glenuig Highld 138 B2
Glenvarragill Highld 152 H10
Glen Vine IoM 80 d6
Glenwhilly D & G 106 G3
Glespin S Lans 115 R2
Glewstone Herefs 45 R10
Glinton C Pete 74 C9
Glooston Leics 73 K11
Glossop Derbys 83 M6
Gloster Hill Nthumb 119 Q10
Gloucester Gloucs 46 F11
Gloucester Services Gloucs 32 F2
Gloucestershire Airport Gloucs 46 G10
Glusburn N York 96 F11
Glutt Lodge Highld 166 H9
Gluvian Cnwll 4 E9
Glympton Oxon 48 D10
Glynarthen Cerdgn 42 F5
Glyn Ceiriog Wrexhm 68 H7
Glyncoch Rhondd 30 E6
Glyncorrwg Neath 29 N5
Glynde E Susx 25 L9
Glyndebourne E Susx 25 L8
Glyndyfrdwy Denbgs 68 F6
Glynneath Neath 29 N3
Glyntaff Rhondd 30 E7
Glyntawe Powys 44 A11
Glynteg Carmth 42 G7
Gnosall Staffs 70 E10
Gnosall Heath Staffs 70 E10
Goadby Leics 73 K11
Goadby Marwood Leics 73 K5
Goatacre Wilts 33 K9
Goatham Green E Susx 26 D7
Goathill Dorset 20 C11
Goathland N York 105 M10
Goathurst Somset 19 J8
Goathurst Common Kent 37 L10
Goat Lees Kent 26 H2
Gobowen Shrops 69 K8
Godalming Surrey 23 Q6
Goddard's Corner Suffk 65 K8
Goddard's Green Kent 26 D5
Goddards Green W Susx 24 G6
Godden Green Kent 37 N9
Godford Cross Devon 10 C4
Godington Oxon 48 H9
Godley Tamesd 83 L5
Godmanchester Cambs 62 B6
Godmanstone Dorset 11 P5
Godmersham Kent 39 J11
Godney Somset 19 N6
Godolphin Cross Cnwll 2 G7
Godre'r-graig Neath 29 L3
Godshill Hants 21 N11
Godshill IoW 14 F10
Godstone Staffs 71 J8
Godstone Surrey 37 J10
Godsworthy Devon 8 D9
Godwinscroft Hants 13 L5
Goetre Mons 31 K3
Goff's Oak Herts 50 H10
Gogar C Edin 127 M3
Goginan Cerdgn 54 F8
Golan Gwynd 67 J6
Golant Cnwll 5 J11
Golberdon Cnwll 5 N7
Golborne Wigan 82 D5
Golcar Kirk 90 D7
Goldcliff Newpt 31 L8
Golden Cross E Susx 25 M8
Golden Green Kent 37 P11
Golden Grove Carmth 43 L11
Goldenhill C Stke 70 F4
Golden Hill Pembks 41 J10
Golden Pot Hants 23 K6
Golden Valley Derbys 84 F10
Golders Green Gt Lon 36 F3
Goldfinch Bottom W Berk 22 F2
Goldhanger Essex 52 F10
Gold Hill Cambs 62 H2
Gold Hill Dorset 12 D2
Golding Shrops 57 J4
Goldington Bed 61 N10
Goldsborough N York 97 N9
Goldsborough N York 105 M8
Golds Green Sandw 58 E6
Goldsithney Cnwll 2 E7
Goldstone Kent 39 N9
Goldstone Shrops 70 C9
Goldthorpe Barns 91 M10
Goldworthy Devon 16 F7
Golford Kent 26 C4
Golford Green Kent 26 C4
Gollanfield Highld 156 E7
Gollinglith Foot N York 96 H4
Golly Wrexhm 69 K3
Golsoncott Somset 18 D7
Golspie Highld 163 J6
Gomeldon Wilts 21 N7
Gomersal Kirk 90 G5
Gomshall Surrey 36 C11
Gonalston Notts 85 L11
Gonerby Hill Foot Lincs 73 N3
Gonfirth Shet 169 q7
Goodameavy Devon 6 E6
Good Easter Essex 51 P8
Gooderstone Norfk 75 Q10
Goodleigh Devon 17 L5
Goodmanham E R Yk 92 E2
Goodmayes Gt Lon 37 L3
Goodnestone Kent 38 H9
Goodnestone Kent 39 N11
Goodrich Herefs 45 R11
Goodrington Torbay 7 M7
Goodshaw Lancs 89 N5
Goodshaw Fold Lancs 89 N5
Goodstone Devon 7 K4
Goodwick Pembks 40 H3
Goodwood W Susx 15 N5
Goodworth Clatford Hants 22 C6
Goodyers End Warwks 59 M7
Goole E R Yk 92 B6
Goole Fields E R Yk 92 C6
Goom's Hill Worcs 47 K4
Goonbell Cnwll 3 J4
Goonhavern Cnwll 3 K3
Goonvrea Cnwll 3 J4
Goosecruives Abers 151 K11
Gooseford Devon 8 G6
Goose Green Essex 53 K6
Goose Green Kent 26 D4
Goose Green Kent 37 P10
Goose Green S Glos 32 C10
Goose Green W Susx 24 D7
Goose Green Wigan 82 C4
Gooseham Cnwll 16 C8
Gooseham Mill Cnwll 16 C8
Goosehill Green Worcs 46 H2
Goose Pool Herefs 45 P7
Goosey Oxon 34 C6
Goosnargh Lancs 88 H3
Goostrey Ches E 82 G10
Gordano Services N Som 31 P9
Gorddinog Conwy 79 M10
Gordon Border 118 B2
Gordon Arms Hotel Border 117 L5
Gordonstown Abers 158 E6
Gordonstown Abers 158 H10
Gore Powys 45 K3
Gorebridge Mdloth 127 Q5
Gorefield Cambs 74 H8
Gore Pit Essex 52 E8
Gores Wilts 21 M3
Gore Street Kent 39 N8
Gorey Jersey 11 c2
Goring Oxon 34 H8
Goring-by-Sea W Susx 24 D10
Goring Heath Oxon 35 J9
Gorleston on Sea Norfk 77 Q11
Gorrachie Abers 158 H6
Gorran Churchtown Cnwll 3 P5
Gorran Haven Cnwll 3 Q5
Gorran High Lanes Cnwll 3 P5
Gorrig Cerdgn 42 H6
Gors Cerdgn 54 E9
Gorsedd Flints 80 H9
Gorse Hill Swindn 33 N7
Gorseinon Swans 28 G5
Gorseybank Derbys 71 P4
Gorsgoch Cerdgn 43 J4
Gorslas Carmth 28 G2
Gorsley Gloucs 46 C9
Gorsley Common Herefs 46 C9
Gorstage Ches W 82 D10
Gorstan Highld 155 L5
Gorstella Ches W 69 L2
Gorsten Ag & B 138 C11
Gorst Hill Worcs 57 N10
Gorsty Hill Staffs 71 L9
Gorthleck Highld 147 N3
Gorton Manch 83 J5
Gosbeck Suffk 64 H10
Gosberton Lincs 74 D4
Gosberton Clough Lincs 74 C5
Gosfield Essex 52 C6
Gosford Devon 10 C5
Gosford Oxon 34 E2
Gosforth Cumb 100 E10
Gosforth N u Ty 113 K7
Gosling Street Somset 19 P8
Gosmore Herts 50 E5
Gospel End Staffs 58 C6
Gospel Green W Susx 23 P8
Gosport Hants 14 H7
Gossard's Green C Beds 49 Q6
Gossington Gloucs 32 D4
Goswick Nthumb 119 L2
Gotham Notts 72 E4
Gotherington Gloucs 47 J9
Gotton Somset 18 H9
Goudhurst Kent 26 B4
Goulceby Lincs 87 J5
Gourdas Abers 159 J9
Gourdie C Dund 142 F11
Gourdon Abers 143 Q3
Gourock Inver 124 G2
Govan C Glas 125 N4
Goveton Devon 7 K9
Govilon Mons 31 J2
Gowdall E R Yk 91 Q6
Gower Highld 155 P6
Gower Swans 28 F6
Gowerton Swans 28 G5
Gowkhall Fife 134 D10
Gowthorpe E R Yk 98 F10
Goxhill E R Yk 93 L2
Goxhill N Linc 93 K6
Goytre Neath 29 L7
Grabhair W Isls 168 i6
Graby Lincs 74 A5
Grade Cnwll 3 J11
Gradeley Green Ches E 69 Q4
Graffham W Susx 23 P11
Grafham Cambs 61 Q7
Grafham Surrey 24 B2
Grafton Herefs 45 P7
Grafton N York 97 P8
Grafton Oxon 33 Q4
Grafton Shrops 69 M11
Grafton Worcs 46 A2
Grafton Worcs 47 J7
Grafton Flyford Worcs 47 J3
Grafton Regis Nhants 49 L5
Grafton Underwood Nhants 61 K4
Grafty Green Kent 26 E2
Graianrhyd Denbgs 68 H3
Graig Conwy 79 Q10
Graig Denbgs 80 F10
Graigfechan Denbgs 68 F4
Grain Medway 38 E6
Grains Bar Oldham 90 B9
Grainsby Lincs 93 N11
Grainthorpe Lincs 93 Q11
Grampound Cnwll 3 N4
Grampound Road Cnwll 3 N3
Gramsdal W Isls 168 d12
Gramsdale W Isls 168 d12
Granborough Bucks 49 L9
Granby Notts 73 K3
Grandborough Warwks 59 Q11
Grand Chemins Jersey 11 c2
Grandes Rocques Guern 10 b1
Grandtully P & K 141 M7
Grange Cumb 101 J7
Grange Medway 38 C8
Grange P & K 134 H2
Grange Wirral 81 J7
Grange Crossroads Moray 158 C7
Grange Hall Moray 157 K5
Grangehall S Lans 116 D2
Grange Hill Essex 37 K2
Grangemill Derbys 84 B9
Grange Moor Kirk 90 G7
Grangemouth Falk 133 Q11
Grange of Lindores Fife 134 H4
Grange-over-Sands Cumb 95 J5
Grangepans Falk 134 C11
Grange Park Nhants 60 G9
Grangetown R & Cl 104 F6
Grangetown Sundld 113 P10
Grange Villa Dur 113 K10
Gransmoor E R Yk 99 N9
Gransmore Green Essex 51 Q6
Granston Pembks 40 G4
Grantchester Cambs 62 F9
Grantham Lincs 73 N3
Granton C Edin 127 N2
Grantown-on-Spey Highld 149 J2
Grantsfield Herefs 45 Q2
Grantshouse Border 129 L6
Grappenhall Warrtn 82 D7
Grasby Lincs 93 J10
Grasmere Cumb 101 K9
Grasscroft Oldham 83 L4
Grassendale Lpool 81 M7
Grassgarth Cumb 101 K2
Grass Green Essex 52 B4
Grassington N York 96 F8
Grassmoor Derbys 84 F7
Grassthorpe Notts 85 N7
Grateley Hants 21 Q6
Gratwich Staffs 71 J8
Graveley Cambs 62 C8
Graveley Herts 50 F5
Gravelly Hill Birm 58 H6
Gravelsbank Shrops 56 E4
Graveney Kent 39 J9
Gravesend Kent 37 Q6
Gravir W Isls 168 i6
Grayingham Lincs 92 F11
Grayrigg Cumb 101 Q11
Grays Thurr 37 P5
Grayshott Hants 23 N7
Grayson Green Cumb 100 C5
Grayswood Surrey 23 P8
Graythorpe Hartpl 104 F5
Grazeley Wokham 35 J11
Greasbrough Rothm 91 L11
Greasby Wirral 81 K7
Greasley Notts 84 G11
Great Abington Cambs 62 H11
Great Addington Nhants 61 L5
Great Alne Warwks 47 M3
Great Altcar Lancs 88 C9
Great Amwell Herts 51 J8
Great Asby Cumb 102 C8
Great Ashfield Suffk 64 D8
Great Ayton N York 104 G8
Great Baddow Essex 52 B11
Great Badminton S Glos 32 F8
Great Bardfield Essex 51 Q4
Great Barford Bed 61 P10
Great Barr Sandw 58 F5
Great Barrington Gloucs 33 P2
Great Barrow Ches W 81 P11
Great Barton Suffk 64 B8
Great Barugh N York 98 E5
Great Bavington Nthumb 112 E4
Great Bealings Suffk 53 M2
Great Bedwyn Wilts 21 Q2
Great Bentley Essex 53 K7
Great Billing Nhants 60 H8
Great Bircham Norfk 75 Q4
Great Blakenham Suffk 64 G11
Great Blencow Cumb 101 N4
Great Bolas Wrekin 70 A10
Great Bookham Surrey 36 D10
Great Bosullow Cnwll 2 C7
Great Bourton Oxon 48 E5
Great Bowden Leics 60 F3
Great Bradley Suffk 63 L10
Great Braxted Essex 52 E9
Great Bricett Suffk 64 E11
Great Brickhill Bucks 49 P8
Great Bridgeford Staffs 70 F9
Great Brington Nhants 60 E7
Great Bromley Essex 53 J6
Great Broughton Cumb 100 E4
Great Broughton N York 104 F9
Great Budworth Ches W 82 E9
Great Burdon Darltn 104 B7
Great Burstead Essex 37 Q2
Great Busby N York 104 F9
Great Canfield Essex 51 N7
Great Carlton Lincs 87 M3
Great Casterton Rutlnd 73 Q9
Great Chalfield Wilts 20 G2
Great Chart Kent 26 G3
Great Chatwell Staffs 57 P2
Great Chell C Stke 70 F4
Great Chesterford Essex 51 M2
Great Cheverell Wilts 21 J4
Great Chishill Cambs 51 K3
Great Clacton Essex 53 L8
Great Cliffe Wakefd 91 J7
Great Clifton Cumb 100 D5
Great Coates NE Lin 93 M9
Great Comberton Worcs 47 J6
Great Comp Kent 37 P9
Great Corby Cumb 111 J10
Great Cornard Suffk 52 E3
Great Cowden E R Yk 93 M2
Great Coxwell Oxon 33 Q6
Great Cransley Nhants 60 H5
Great Cressingham Norfk 76 B11
Great Crosthwaite Cumb 101 J6
Great Cubley Derbys 71 M7
Great Cumbrae Island N Ayrs 124 F6
Great Dalby Leics 73 J8
Great Denham Bed 61 M11
Great Doddington Nhants 61 J8
Great Doward Herefs 45 Q11
Great Dunham Norfk 76 B9
Great Dunmow Essex 51 P6
Great Durnford Wilts 21 M7
Great Easton Essex 51 P5
Great Easton Leics 60 H2
Great Eccleston Lancs 88 E2
Great Edstone N York 98 E4
Great Ellingham Norfk 64 E2
Great Elm Somset 20 D5
Great Everdon Nhants 60 C9
Great Eversden Cambs 62 E10
Great Fencote N York 97 L2
Greatfield Wilts 33 L7
Great Finborough Suffk 64 E10
Greatford Lincs 74 A8
Great Fransham Norfk 76 B9
Great Gaddesden Herts 50 B8
Greatgate Staffs 71 K7
Great Gidding Cambs 61 P4
Great Givendale E R Yk 98 G10
Great Glemham Suffk 65 L9
Great Glen Leics 72 H11
Great Gonerby Lincs 73 M3
Great Gransden Cambs 62 C9
Great Green Cambs 50 G2
Great Green Norfk 65 K4
Great Green Suffk 64 C10
Great Green Suffk 64 C8
Great Habton N York 98 F5
Great Hale Lincs 74 B2
Great Hallingbury Essex 51 M7
Greatham Hants 23 L8
Greatham Hartpl 104 E5
Greatham W Susx 24 B7
Great Hampden Bucks 35 M4
Great Harrowden Nhants 61 J6
Great Harwood Lancs 89 L4
Great Haseley Oxon 34 H4
Great Hatfield E R Yk 93 L2
Great Haywood Staffs 70 H10
Great Heck N York 91 P6
Great Henny Essex 52 E4
Great Hinton Wilts 20 H3
Great Hockham Norfk 64 D3
Great Holland Essex 53 M8
Great Hollands Br For 35 N11
Great Horkesley Essex 52 G5
Great Hormead Herts 51 K5
Great Horton C Brad 90 E4
Great Horwood Bucks 49 L8
Great Houghton Barns 91 L9
Great Houghton Nhants 60 G9
Great Hucklow Derbys 83 Q9
Great Kelk E R Yk 99 N9
Great Kimble Bucks 35 M3
Great Kingshill Bucks 35 N5
Great Langdale Cumb 101 J9
Great Langton N York 103 Q11
Great Leighs Essex 52 B8
Great Limber Lincs 93 K9
Great Linford M Keyn 49 N6
Great Livermere Suffk 64 B7
Great Longstone Derbys 84 B6
Great Lumley Dur 113 L11
Great Lyth Shrops 56 H3
Great Malvern Worcs 46 E5
Great Maplestead Essex 52 D5
Great Marton Bpool 88 C3
Great Massingham Norfk 75 Q6
Great Melton Norfk 76 G10
Great Meols Wirral 81 J6
Great Milton Oxon 34 H4
Great Missenden Bucks 35 N4
Great Mitton Lancs 89 L3
Great Mongeham Kent 39 Q11
Great Moulton Norfk 64 H3
Great Munden Herts 51 J6
Great Musgrave Cumb 102 E8
Great Ness Shrops 69 L11
Great Notley Essex 52 B7
Great Oak Mons 31 L2
Great Oakley Essex 53 L6
Great Oakley Nhants 61 J3
Great Offley Herts 50 D5
Great Ormside Cumb 102 D7
Great Orton Cumb 110 F10
Great Ouseburn N York 97 P8
Great Oxendon Nhants 60 F4
Great Oxney Green Essex 51 Q9
Great Palgrave Norfk 76 A9
Great Park N u Ty 113 K6
Great Parndon Essex 51 K9
Great Pattenden Kent 26 B3
Great Paxton Cambs 62 B8
Great Plumpton Lancs 88 D4
Great Plumstead Norfk 77 L9
Great Ponton Lincs 73 N4
Great Potheridge Devon 17 J9
Great Preston Leeds 91 L5
Great Purston Nhants 48 F7
Great Raveley Cambs 62 C4
Great Rissington Gloucs 47 N11
Great Rollright Oxon 48 B8
Great Ryburgh Norfk 76 D6
Great Ryle Nthumb 119 K8
Great Ryton Shrops 56 H4
Great Saling Essex 51 Q5
Great Salkeld Cumb 101 Q3
Great Sampford Essex 51 P3
Great Saredon Staffs 58 E3
Great Saughall Ches W 81 M11
Great Saxham Suffk 63 N8
Great Shefford W Berk 34 C9
Great Shelford Cambs 62 G10
Great Smeaton N York 104 B10
Great Snoring Norfk 76 C5
Great Somerford Wilts 33 J8
Great Soudley Shrops 70 C9
Great Stainton Darltn 104 B6
Great Stambridge Essex 38 E3
Great Staughton Cambs 61 P8
Great Steeping Lincs 87 M8
Great Stoke S Glos 32 B8
Great Stonar Kent 39 P10
Greatstone-on-Sea Kent 27 J7
Great Strickland Cumb 101 Q6
Great Stukeley Cambs 62 B6
Great Sturton Lincs 86 H5
Great Sutton Ches W 81 M9
Great Sutton Shrops 57 J8
Great Swinburne Nthumb 112 D5
Great Tew Oxon 48 D9
Great Tey Essex 52 E6
Great Thurlow Suffk 63 L10
Great Torrington Devon 16 H8
Great Tosson Nthumb 119 K10
Great Totham Essex 52 E9
Great Totham Essex 52 E9
Great Tows Lincs 86 H2
Great Urswick Cumb 94 F6
Great Wakering Essex 38 F4
Great Waldingfield Suffk 52 F3
Great Walsingham Norfk 76 C4
Great Waltham Essex 51 Q8
Great Warford Ches E 82 H9
Great Warley Essex 37 N2
Great Washbourne Gloucs 47 J8
Great Weeke Devon 8 H7
Great Welnetham Suffk 64 B10
Great Wenham Suffk 53 J4
Great Whittington Nthumb 112 F6
Great Wigborough Essex 52 G8
Great Wilbraham Cambs 63 J9
Great Wilne Derbys 72 C4
Great Wishford Wilts 21 L7
Great Witchingham Norfk 76 G7
Great Witcombe Gloucs 32 H2
Great Witley Worcs 57 P11
Great Wolford Warwks 47 Q8
Greatworth Nhants 48 G6
Great Wratting Suffk 63 L11
Great Wymondley Herts 50 F5
Great Wyrley Staffs 58 E3
Great Wytheford Shrops 69 Q11
Great Yarmouth Norfk 77 Q10
Great Yeldham Essex 52 C4
Grebby Lincs 87 M7
Greeba IoM 80 d5
Green Denbgs 80 F11
Green Bank Cumb 94 H4
Greenbottom Cnwll 3 K4
Greenburn W Loth 126 G5
Greencroft Hall Dur 113 J11
Green Cross Surrey 23 N7
Green Down Somset 19 Q4
Green End Bed 61 M11
Green End Bed 61 N8
Green End Bed 61 P10
Green End Bed 61 P8
Green End Cambs 61 Q4
Green End Cambs 62 B6
Green End Cambs 62 E9
Green End Cambs 62 G7
Green End Cambs 62 G8
Green End Herts 50 G4
Green End Herts 50 H4
Green End Herts 50 H6
Greenend Oxon 48 B10
Green End Warwks 59 L7
Greenfield Ag & B 131 Q9
Greenfield C Beds 50 C4
Greenfield Flints 80 H9
Greenfield Highld 146 G7
Greenfield Oldham 83 L4
Greenfield Oxon 35 K6
Greenford Gt Lon 36 D4
Greengairs N Lans 126 D3
Greengates C Brad 90 F3
Greengill Cumb 100 F3
Greenhalgh Lancs 88 E3
Greenham Somset 18 E10
Greenham W Berk 34 E11
Green Hammerton N York 97 Q9
Greenhaugh Nthumb 111 Q3
Green Head Cumb 110 G11
Greenhead Nthumb 111 N7
Green Heath Staffs 58 E2
Greenheys Salfd 82 F4
Greenhill D & G 109 P5
Greenhill Falk 126 E2
Greenhill Herefs 46 D5
Greenhill Kent 39 L8
Greenhill S Lans 116 C4
Green Hill Wilts 33 L7
Greenhillocks Derbys 84 F11
Greenhills S Lans 125 Q7
Greenhithe Kent 37 N5
Greenholm E Ayrs 125 N10
Greenholme Cumb 101 Q9
Greenhouse Border 117 R6
Greenhow Hill N York 96 H8
Greenland Highld 167 M3
Greenland Sheff 84 E3
Greenlands Bucks 35 L7
Green Lane Devon 9 J9
Green Lane Worcs 47 L2
Greenlaw Border 129 J10
Greenlea D & G 109 M5
Greenloaning P & K 133 N6
Green Moor Barns 90 H11
Greenmount Bury 89 M8
Green Oak E R Yk 92 D5
Greenock Inver 124 H2
Greenodd Cumb 94 G4
Green Ore Somset 19 Q4
Green Quarter Cumb 101 N10
Greensgate Norfk 76 G8
Greenshields S Lans 116 E2
Greenside Gatesd 112 H8
Greenside Kirk 90 F7
Greens Norton Nhants 49 J5
Greenstead Green Essex 52 D6
Greensted Essex 51 M10
Green Street E Susx 26 C9
Green Street Gloucs 46 G11
Green Street Herts 50 E11
Green Street Herts 51 L6
Green Street Worcs 46 G5
Green Street Green Gt Lon 37 L8
Green Street Green Kent 37 N6
Greenstreet Green Suffk 52 H2
Green Tye Herts 51 K7
Greenway Gloucs 46 D8
Greenway Somset 19 K10
Greenway V Glam 30 E10
Greenway Worcs 57 N10
Greenwich Gt Lon 37 J5
Greenwich Maritime Gt Lon 37 J5
Greet Gloucs 47 K8
Greete Shrops 57 K10
Greetham Lincs 87 K6
Greetham Rutlnd 73 N8
Greetland Calder 90 D6
Gregson Lane Lancs 88 H5
Greinton Somset 19 M7
Grenaby IoM 80 c7
Grendon Nhants 61 J8
Grendon Warwks 59 L5
Grendon Green Herefs 46 A3

Grendon Underwood Bucks 49 J10
Grenofen Devon 6 D4
Grenoside Sheff 84 D2
Greosabhagh W Isls 168 g8
Gresford Wrexhm 69 K4
Gresham Norfk 76 H4
Greshornish Highld 152 E7
Gressenhall Norfk 76 D8
Gressenhall Green Norfk 76 D8
Gressingham Lancs 95 M7
Gresty Green Ches E 70 C4
Greta Bridge Dur 103 L8
Gretna D & G 110 F7
Gretna Green D & G 110 F7
Gretna Services D & G 110 F7
Gretton Gloucs 47 K8
Gretton Nhants 61 J2
Gretton Shrops 57 J5
Grewelthorpe N York 97 K5
Grey Friars Suffk 65 P7
Greygarth N York 97 J6
Grey Green N Linc 92 C9
Greylake Somset 19 L8
Greylees Lincs 73 Q2
Greyrigg D & G 109 N3
Greys Green Oxon 35 K8
Greysouthen Cumb 100 E5
Greystoke Cumb 101 M4
Greystone Angus 143 J9
Greywell Hants 23 K4
Gribb Dorset 10 H4
Gribthorpe E R Yk 92 C3
Griff Warwks 59 N7
Griffithstown Torfn 31 J5
Griffydam Leics 72 C7
Griggs Green Hants 23 M8
Grimeford Village Lancs 89 J8
Grimesthorpe Sheff 84 E3
Grimethorpe Barns 91 L9
Grimley Worcs 46 F2
Grimmet S Ayrs 114 F5
Grimoldby Lincs 87 L3
Grimpo Shrops 69 L9
Grimsargh Lancs 88 H4
Grimsby NE Lin 93 N8
Grimscote Nhants 49 J4
Grimscott Cnwll 16 D10
Grimshader W Isls 168 j5
Grimshaw Bl w D 89 L6
Grimshaw Green Lancs 88 F8
Grimsthorpe Lincs 73 Q6
Grimston E R Yk 93 N3
Grimston Leics 72 H6
Grimston Norfk 75 P6
Grimstone Dorset 11 N6
Grimstone End Suffk 64 C8
Grinacombe Moor Devon 5 Q3
Grindale E R Yk 99 N6
Grindle Shrops 57 P4
Grindleford Derbys 84 B5
Grindleton Lancs 95 R11
Grindley Brook Shrops 69 P6
Grindlow Derbys 83 Q9
Grindon Nthumb 118 H2
Grindon S on T 104 C5
Grindon Staffs 71 K4
Grindon Hill Nthumb 112 B7
Grindonrigg Nthumb 118 H2
Gringley on the Hill Notts 85 M2
Grinsdale Cumb 110 G9
Grinshill Shrops 69 P10
Grinton N York 103 K11
Griomaisiader W Isls 168 j5
Grishipoll Ag & B 136 F4
Grisling Common E Susx 25 K6
Gristhorpe N York 99 M4
Griston Norfk 64 C2
Gritley Ork 169 e6
Grittenham Wilts 33 K8
Grittleton Wilts 32 G8
Grizebeck Cumb 94 E4
Grizedale Cumb 94 G2
Groby Leics 72 E9
Groes Conwy 68 D2
Groes-faen Rhondd 30 E8
Groesffordd Gwynd 66 D7
Groesffordd Powys 44 F9
Groesffordd Marli Denbgs 80 E10
Groeslon Gwynd 66 H3
Groeslon Gwynd 67 J2
Groes-lwyd Powys 56 C2
Groes-Wen Caerph 30 F7
Grogarry W Isls 168 c14
Grogport Ag & B 120 F3
Groigearraidh W Isls 168 c14
Gromford Suffk 65 M10
Gronant Flints 80 F8
Groombridge E Susx 25 M3
Grosebay W Isls 168 g8
Grosmont Mons 45 N10
Grosmont N York 105 M9
Groton Suffk 52 G3
Grotton Oldham 83 L4
Grouville Jersey 11 c2
Grove Bucks 49 P10
Grove Dorset 11 P10
Grove Kent 39 M9
Grove Notts 85 M5
Grove Oxon 34 D6
Grove Pembks 41 J10
Grove Green Kent 38 C10
Grovenhurst Kent 26 B3
Grove Park Gt Lon 37 K6
Grovesend S Glos 32 C7
Grovesend Swans 28 G4
Grubb Street Kent 37 N7
Gruinard Highld 160 E9
Gruinart Ag & B 122 C6
Grula Highld 144 E2
Gruline Ag & B 137 N7
Grumbla Cnwll 2 C8
Grundisburgh Suffk 65 J11
Gruting Shet 169 p9
Grutness Shet 169 r12
Gualachulain Highld 139 L8
Guanockgate Lincs 74 G8
Guardbridge Fife 135 M4
Guarlford Worcs 46 F5
Guay P & K 141 P8
Guernsey Guern 10 b2
Guernsey Airport Guern 10 b2
Guestling Green E Susx 26 E9
Guestling Thorn E Susx 26 E8
Guestwick Norfk 76 F6
Guide Bridge Tamesd 83 K5
Guide Post Nthumb 113 L3
Guilden Morden Cambs 50 G2
Guilden Sutton Ches W 81 N11
Guildford Surrey 23 Q5
Guildstead Kent 38 D9
Guildtown P & K 142 A11
Guilsborough Nhants 60 E6
Guilsfield Powys 56 C2
Guilton Kent 39 N10
Guiltreehill S Ayrs 114 G5
Guineaford Devon 17 K4
Guisborough R & Cl 104 H7
Guiseley Leeds 90 F2
Guist Norfk 76 E6
Guiting Power Gloucs 47 L10
Gullane E Loth 128 D3
Gulling Green Suffk 64 A10
Gulval Cnwll 2 D7
Gulworthy Devon 6 D4
Gumfreston Pembks 41 M10
Gumley Leics 60 E3
Gummow's Shop Cnwll 4 D10
Gunby E R Yk 92 B3
Gunby Lincs 73 N6
Gunby Lincs 87 N7
Gundleton Hants 22 H8
Gun Green Kent 26 C5
Gun Hill E Susx 25 N8
Gun Hill Warwks 59 L7
Gunn Devon 17 L5
Gunnerside N York 103 J11
Gunnerton Nthumb 112 D6
Gunness N Linc 92 D8
Gunnislake Cnwll 6 C4
Gunnista Shet 169 s9
Gunthorpe C Pete 74 C10
Gunthorpe N Linc 92 D11
Gunthorpe Norfk 76 E5
Gunthorpe Notts 72 H2
Gunton Suffk 65 Q2
Gunwalloe Cnwll 2 H9
Gupworthy Somset 18 C8
Gurnard IoW 14 E7
Gurnett Ches E 83 K10
Gurney Slade Somset 20 B5
Gurnos Powys 29 L3
Gushmere Kent 38 H10
Gussage All Saints Dorset 12 H2
Gussage St Andrew Dorset 12 G2
Gussage St Michael Dorset 12 G2
Guston Kent 27 P3
Gutcher Shet 169 s4
Guthrie Angus 143 K7
Guyhirn Cambs 74 H10
Guyhirn Gull Cambs 74 G10
Guy's Marsh Dorset 20 F10
Guyzance Nthumb 119 P10
Gwaenysgor Flints 80 F8
Gwalchmai IoA 78 F9
Gwastadnant Gwynd 67 L3
Gwaun-Cae-Gurwen Carmth 29 J2
Gwbert on Sea Cerdgn 42 C4
Gwealavellan Cnwll 2 G5
Gweek Cnwll 3 J8
Gwehelog Mons 31 L4
Gwenddwr Powys 44 F6
Gwennap Cnwll 3 J5
Gwennap Mining District Cnwll 3 K5
Gwenter Cnwll 3 J10
Gwernaffield Flints 81 J11
Gwernesney Mons 31 M4
Gwernogle Carmth 43 K8
Gwernymynydd Flints 68 H2
Gwersyllt Wrexhm 69 K4
Gwespyr Flints 80 G8
Gwindra Cnwll 3 P3
Gwinear Cnwll 2 F6
Gwithian Cnwll 2 F5
Gwredog IoA 78 G7
Gwrhay Caerph 30 G5
Gwyddelwern Denbgs 68 E5
Gwyddgrug Carmth 43 J7
Gwynfryn Wrexhm 69 J4
Gwystre Powys 55 P11
Gwytherin Conwy 68 A2
Gyfelia Wrexhm 69 K5
Gyrn Goch Gwynd 66 G5

H

Habberley Shrops 56 F4
Habberley Worcs 57 Q9
Habergham Lancs 89 N4
Habertoft Lincs 87 P7
Habin W Susx 23 M10
Habrough NE Lin 93 K8
Hacconby Lincs 74 B5
Haceby Lincs 73 Q3
Hacheston Suffk 65 L10
Hackbridge Gt Lon 36 G7
Hackenthorpe Sheff 84 F4
Hackford Norfk 76 F11
Hackforth N York 97 K2
Hack Green Ches E 70 A5
Hackland Ork 169 c4
Hackleton Nhants 60 H9
Hacklinge Kent 39 P11
Hackman's Gate Worcs 58 C9
Hackness N York 99 K2
Hackness Somset 19 K5
Hackney Gt Lon 36 H4
Hackthorn Lincs 86 C4
Hackthorpe Cumb 101 P6
Hacton Gt Lon 37 N3
Hadden Border 118 E3
Haddenham Bucks 35 K3
Haddenham Cambs 62 G5
Haddington E Loth 128 E5
Haddington Lincs 86 B8
Haddiscoe Norfk 65 N2
Haddo Abers 159 K10
Haddon Cambs 61 P2
Hade Edge Kirk 83 P4
Hadfield Derbys 83 M5
Hadham Cross Herts 51 K7
Hadham Ford Herts 51 K6
Hadleigh Essex 38 D4
Hadleigh Suffk 52 H3
Hadleigh Heath Suffk 52 G3
Hadley Worcs 46 G2
Hadley Wrekin 57 M2
Hadley End Staffs 71 L10
Hadley Wood Gt Lon 50 G11
Hadlow Kent 37 P10
Hadlow Down E Susx 25 M6
Hadnall Shrops 69 P10
Hadrian's Wall 112 E7
Hadstock Essex 51 N2
Hadston Nthumb 119 Q11
Hadzor Worcs 46 H2
Haffenden Quarter Kent 26 E3
Hafodunos Conwy 80 B11
Hafod-y-bwch Wrexhm 69 K5
Hafod-y-coed Blae G 30 H4
Hafodyrynys Caerph 30 H5
Haggate Lancs 89 P3
Haggbeck Cumb 111 J6
Haggersta Shet 169 q9
Haggerston Nthumb 119 K2
Haggington Hill Devon 17 K2
Haggs Falk 126 D2
Hagley Herefs 45 R6
Hagley Worcs 58 D8
Hagmore Green Suffk 52 G4
Hagnaby Lincs 87 K8
Hagnaby Lincs 87 N5
Hagworthingham Lincs 87 K7
Haigh Wigan 89 J9
Haighton Green Lancs 88 H4
Haile Cumb 100 D9
Hailes Gloucs 47 K8
Hailey Herts 51 J8
Hailey Oxon 34 C2
Hailey Oxon 34 H7
Hailsham E Susx 25 N9
Hail Weston Cambs 61 Q8
Hainault Gt Lon 37 L2
Haine Kent 39 Q8
Hainford Norfk 77 J8
Hainton Lincs 86 G4
Hainworth C Brad 90 D3
Haisthorpe E R Yk 99 N8
Hakin Pembks 40 G9
Halam Notts 85 L10
Halbeath Fife 134 E10
Halberton Devon 9 P2
Halcro Highld 167 M4
Hale Cumb 95 L5
Hale Halton 81 P8
Hale Hants 21 N11
Hale Somset 20 D9
Hale Surrey 23 M5
Hale Traffd 82 G7
Hale Bank Halton 81 P8
Hale Barns Traffd 82 G7
Hale Green E Susx 25 N8
Hale Nook Lancs 88 D2
Hales Norfk 65 M2
Hales Staffs 70 C8
Halesgate Lincs 74 F5
Hales Green Derbys 71 M6
Halesowen Dudley 58 E8
Hales Place Kent 39 K10
Hale Street Kent 37 Q11
Halesville Essex 38 F3
Halesworth Suffk 65 M6
Halewood Knows 81 P7
Halford Devon 7 L4
Halford Shrops 56 G8
Halford Warwks 47 Q5
Halfpenny Cumb 95 L3
Halfpenny Green Staffs 58 B6
Halfpenny Houses N York 97 K4
Halfway Carmth 43 M8
Halfway Carmth 44 A8
Halfway Sheff 84 F4
Halfway W Berk 34 D11
Halfway Bridge W Susx 23 P10
Halfway House Shrops 56 E2
Halfway Houses Kent 38 F7
Halifax Calder 90 D5
Halket E Ayrs 125 L7
Halkirk Highld 167 K5
Halkyn Flints 81 J10
Hall E Rens 125 L7
Hallam Fields Derbys 72 D2
Halland E Susx 25 L7
Hallaton Leics 73 K11
Hallatrow BaNES 20 B3
Hallbankgate Cumb 111 L9
Hallbeck Cumb 95 N3
Hall Cliffe Wakefd 90 H7
Hall Cross Lancs 88 E4
Hall Dunnerdale Cumb 100 H11
Hallen S Glos 31 Q8
Hall End Bed 61 M11
Hall End C Beds 50 C3
Hallfield Gate Derbys 84 E9
Hallgarth Dur 104 B2
Hallglen Falk 126 F2
Hall Green Birm 58 H8
Hallin Highld 152 D6
Halling Medway 38 B9
Hallington Lincs 87 K3
Hallington Nthumb 112 E5
Halliwell Bolton 89 K8
Halloughton Notts 85 L10
Hallow Worcs 46 F3
Hallow Heath Worcs 46 F3
Hallsands Devon 7 L11
Hall's Green Essex 51 K9
Hall's Green Herts 50 G5
Hallthwaites Cumb 94 D3
Hallworthy Cnwll 5 K4
Hallyne Border 116 H2
Halmer End Staffs 70 D5
Halmond's Frome Herefs 46 C5
Halmore Gloucs 32 D4
Halnaker W Susx 15 P5
Halsall Lancs 88 D8
Halse Nhants 48 G6
Halse Somset 18 F9
Halsetown Cnwll 2 E6
Halsham E R Yk 93 N5
Halsinger Devon 17 J4
Halstead Essex 52 D5
Halstead Kent 37 L8
Halstead Leics 73 K9
Halstock Dorset 11 L3
Halsway Somset 18 F7
Haltcliff Bridge Cumb 101 L3
Haltham Lincs 86 H8
Haltoft End Lincs 87 L11
Halton Bucks 35 N3
Halton Halton 82 B8
Halton Lancs 95 L8
Halton Leeds 91 K4
Halton Nthumb 112 E7
Halton Wrexhm 69 K7
Halton East N York 96 F10
Halton Fenside Lincs 87 M8
Halton Gill N York 96 C5
Halton Green Lancs 95 L7
Halton Holegate Lincs 87 M7
Halton Lea Gate Nthumb 111 M9
Halton Quay Cnwll 5 Q8
Halton Shields Nthumb 112 F7
Halton West N York 96 B10
Haltwhistle Nthumb 111 P8
Halvana Cnwll 5 L6
Halvergate Norfk 77 N10
Halwell Devon 7 K8
Halwill Devon 8 B5
Halwill Junction Devon 8 B4
Ham Devon 10 E4
Ham Gloucs 32 C5
Ham Gloucs 47 J10
Ham Gt Lon 36 E6
Ham Kent 39 P11
Ham Somset 19 J9
Ham Somset 20 C5
Ham Wilts 22 B2
Hambleden Bucks 35 L7
Hambledon Hants 14 H4
Hambledon Surrey 23 Q7
Hamble-le-Rice Hants 14 E5
Hambleton Lancs 88 D2
Hambleton N York 91 P4
Hambleton Moss Side Lancs 88 D2
Hambridge Somset 19 L10
Hambrook S Glos 32 B9
Hambrook W Susx 15 L5
Ham Common Dorset 20 F9
Hameringham Lincs 87 K7
Hamerton Cambs 61 P5
Ham Green Herefs 46 E6
Ham Green Kent 26 E6
Ham Green Kent 38 D8
Ham Green N Som 31 P9
Ham Green Worcs 47 K2
Ham Hill Kent 37 Q8
Hamilton S Lans 126 C6
Hamilton Services S Lans 126 C6
Hamlet Dorset 11 M3
Hamlins E Susx 25 N9
Hammerpot W Susx 24 C9
Hammersmith Gt Lon 36 F5
Hammerwich Staffs 58 G3
Hammerwood E Susx 25 K3
Hammond Street Herts 50 H10
Hammoon Dorset 12 D2
Hamnavoe Shet 169 q10
Hampden Park E Susx 25 P10
Hamperden End Essex 51 N4
Hampnett Gloucs 47 L11
Hampole Donc 91 N8
Hampreston Dorset 13 J5
Hampsfield Cumb 95 J4
Hampson Green Lancs 95 K10
Hampstead Gt Lon 36 G3
Hampstead Norreys W Berk 34 F9
Hampsthwaite N York 97 L9
Hampton C Pete 61 Q2
Hampton Devon 10 F5
Hampton Gt Lon 36 D7
Hampton Kent 39 L8
Hampton Shrops 57 N7
Hampton Swindn 33 N6
Hampton Worcs 47 K6
Hampton Bishop Herefs 45 R7
Hampton Court Palace Gt Lon 36 E7
Hampton Fields Gloucs 32 G5
Hampton Green Ches W 69 P5
Hampton Heath Ches W 69 P5
Hampton-in-Arden Solhll 59 K8
Hampton Loade Shrops 57 N7
Hampton Lovett Worcs 58 C11
Hampton Lucy Warwks 47 Q3
Hampton Magna Warwks 59 L11
Hampton on the Hill Warwks 47 Q2
Hampton Poyle Oxon 48 F11
Hampton Wick Gt Lon 36 E7
Hamptworth Wilts 21 P11
Hamrow Norfk 76 C7
Hamsey E Susx 25 K8
Hamsey Green Surrey 37 J9
Hamstall Ridware Staffs 71 L11
Hamstead Birm 58 G6
Hamstead IoW 14 D8
Hamstead Marshall W Berk 34 D11
Hamsterley Dur 103 M4
Hamsterley Dur 112 H9
Hamstreet Kent 26 H5
Ham Street Somset 19 Q8
Hamwood N Som 19 L3
Hamworthy BCP 12 G6
Hanbury Staffs 71 M9
Hanbury Worcs 47 J2
Hanby Lincs 73 Q4
Hanchet End Suffk 63 K11
Hanchurch Staffs 70 E6
Handa Island Highld 164 D7
Handale R & Cl 105 K7
Hand and Pen Devon 9 P5
Handbridge Ches W 81 N11
Handcross W Susx 24 G5
Handforth Ches E 83 J8
Hand Green Ches W 69 P2
Handley Ches W 69 N3
Handley Derbys 84 E8
Handley Green Essex 51 Q10
Handsacre Staffs 71 K11
Handsworth Birm 58 F7
Handsworth Sheff 84 F3
Handy Cross Bucks 35 N6
Hanford C Stke 70 F6
Hanford Dorset 12 D2
Hanging Heaton Kirk 90 H6
Hanging Houghton Nhants 60 G6
Hanging Langford Wilts 21 K7
Hangleton Br & H 24 G9
Hangleton W Susx 24 C10
Hanham S Glos 32 B10
Hankelow Ches E 70 B5
Hankerton Wilts 33 J6
Hankham E Susx 25 P9
Hanley C Stke 70 F5
Hanley Castle Worcs 46 F6
Hanley Child Worcs 57 M11
Hanley Swan Worcs 46 F6
Hanley William Worcs 57 M11
Hanlith N York 96 C8
Hanmer Wrexhm 69 N7
Hannaford Devon 17 L6
Hannah Lincs 87 N5
Hannington Hants 22 F3
Hannington Nhants 60 H6
Hannington Swindn 33 N6
Hannington Wick Swindn 33 N5
Hanscombe End C Beds 50 D4
Hanslope M Keyn 49 M5
Hanthorpe Lincs 74 A6
Hanwell Gt Lon 36 E5
Hanwell Oxon 48 D6
Hanwood Shrops 56 G3
Hanworth Gt Lon 36 D6
Hanworth Norfk 76 H4
Happendon S Lans 116 B4
Happendon Services S Lans 116 B4
Happisburgh Norfk 77 M5
Happisburgh Common Norfk 77 M6
Hapsford Ches W 81 P10
Hapton Lancs 89 M4
Hapton Norfk 64 H2
Harberton Devon 7 K7
Harbertonford Devon 7 K7
Harbledown Kent 39 K10
Harborne Birm 58 F8
Harborough Magna Warwks 59 Q9
Harbottle Nthumb 118 H10
Harbourneford Devon 7 J6
Harbours Hill Worcs 58 E11
Harbridge Hants 13 K2
Harbridge Green Hants 13 K2
Harbury Warwks 48 C3
Harby Leics 73 J4
Harby Notts 85 Q6
Harcombe Devon 9 L8
Harcombe Devon 10 D6
Harcombe Bottom Devon 10 G5
Harden C Brad 90 D3
Harden Wsall 58 F4
Hardendale Cumb 101 Q8
Hardenhuish Wilts 32 H10
Hardgate Abers 151 K7
Hardgate D & G 108 H7
Hardgate N York 97 L8
Hardgate W Duns 125 N3
Hardham W Susx 24 B7
Hardhorn Lancs 88 D3
Hardingham Norfk 76 E11
Hardingstone Nhants 60 G9
Hardington Somset 20 D4
Hardington Mandeville Somset 11 L2
Hardington Marsh Somset 11 L3
Hardington Moor Somset 11 L2
Hardisworthy Devon 16 C7
Hardley Hants 14 D6
Hardley Street Norfk 77 M11
Hardmead M Keyn 49 P5
Hardraw N York 96 C2
Hardsough Lancs 89 M6
Hardstoft Derbys 84 F8
Hardway Hants 14 H6
Hardway Somset 20 D8
Hardwick Bucks 49 M11
Hardwick Cambs 62 E9
Hardwick Nhants 60 H7
Hardwick Norfk 65 J4
Hardwick Oxon 34 C3
Hardwick Oxon 48 G9
Hardwick Rothm 84 G3
Hardwick Wsall 58 G5
Hardwicke Gloucs 32 E2
Hardwicke Gloucs 46 H9
Hardwick Hall Derbys 84 G8
Hardwick Village Notts 85 K5
Hardy's Green Essex 52 F7
Harebeating E Susx 25 N8
Hareby Lincs 87 K7
Hare Croft C Brad 90 D3
Harefield Gt Lon 36 C2
Hare Green Essex 53 K6
Hare Hatch Wokham 35 M9
Harehill Derbys 71 M7
Harehills Leeds 91 J4
Harehope Nthumb 119 L6
Harelaw Border 117 Q6
Harelaw D & G 110 H5
Harelaw Dur 113 J10
Hareplain Kent 26 D4
Haresceugh Cumb 102 B2
Harescombe Gloucs 32 F2
Haresfield Gloucs 32 F2
Harestock Hants 22 E8
Hare Street Essex 51 K9
Hare Street Essex 51 M10
Hare Street Herts 51 J5
Harewood Leeds 97 M11
Harewood End Herefs 45 Q9
Harford Devon 6 G7
Hargate Norfk 64 G3
Hargatewall Derbys 83 P9
Hargrave Ches W 69 N2
Hargrave Nhants 61 M6
Hargrave Suffk 63 N9
Harker Cumb 110 G8
Harkstead Suffk 53 L5
Harlaston Staffs 59 K2
Harlaxton Lincs 73 M4
Harlech Gwynd 67 K8
Harlech Castle Gwynd 67 K8
Harlescott Shrops 69 N11
Harlesden Gt Lon 36 F4
Harlesthorpe Derbys 84 G5
Harleston Devon 7 K9
Harleston Norfk 65 J5
Harleston Suffk 64 E9
Harlestone Nhants 60 F8
Harle Syke Lancs 89 P3
Harley Rothm 91 K11
Harley Shrops 57 K4
Harlington C Beds 50 B4
Harlington Donc 91 M10
Harlington Gt Lon 36 C5
Harlosh Highld 152 D9
Harlow Essex 51 K8
Harlow Carr RHS N York 97 L10
Harlow Hill Nthumb 112 G7
Harlthorpe E R Yk 92 B3
Harlton Cambs 62 E10
Harlyn Cnwll 4 D6

- Harman's Cross Dorset 12 G8
- Harmby N York 96 H3
- Harmer Green Herts 50 G7
- Harmer Hill Shrops 69 N10
- Harmondsworth Gt Lon 36 C5
- Harmston Lincs 86 C8
- Harnage Shrops 57 K4
- Harnham Nthumb 112 G4
- Harnhill Gloucs 33 L4
- Harold Hill Gt Lon 37 M2
- Haroldston West Pembks 40 G7
- Haroldswick Shet 169 t2
- Harold Wood Gt Lon 37 N2
- Harome N York 98 C4
- Harpenden Herts 50 D8
- Harpford Devon 10 B6
- Harpham E R Yk 99 M8
- Harpley Norfk 75 Q5
- Harpley Worcs 46 C2
- Harpole Nhants 60 E8
- Harpsdale Highld 167 K5
- Harpsden Oxon 35 L8
- Harpswell Lincs 86 B3
- Harpurhey Manch 83 J4
- Harpur Hill Derbys 83 N10
- Harraby Cumb 110 H10
- Harracott Devon 17 K6
- Harrapool Highld 145 L3
- Harrietfield P & K 134 B2
- Harrietsham Kent 38 E11
- Harringay Gt Lon 36 H3
- Harrington Cumb 100 C5
- Harrington Lincs 87 L6
- Harrington Nhants 60 G4
- Harringworth Nhants 73 N11
- Harris W Isls 168 f8
- Harriseahead Staffs 70 F3
- Harriston Cumb 100 G2
- Harrogate N York 97 M9
- Harrold Bed 61 K9
- Harrop Dale Oldham 90 C9
- Harrow Gt Lon 36 E3
- Harrowbarrow Cnwll 5 Q7
- Harrowden Bed 61 N11
- Harrowgate Village Darltn 103 Q7
- Harrow Green Suffk 64 B11
- Harrow Hill Gloucs 46 C11
- Harrow on the Hill Gt Lon 36 E3
- Harrow Weald Gt Lon 36 E2
- Harston Cambs 62 F10
- Harston Leics 73 L4
- Harswell E R Yk 92 D2
- Hart Hartpl 104 E3
- Hartburn Nthumb 112 G3
- Hartburn S on T 104 D7
- Hartest Suffk 64 A11
- Hartfield E Susx 25 L3
- Hartford Cambs 62 C6
- Hartford Ches W 82 D10
- Hartford Somset 18 C9
- Hartfordbridge Hants 23 L3
- Hartford End Essex 51 Q7
- Hartforth N York 103 N9
- Hartgrove Dorset 20 F11
- Harthill Ches W 69 N3
- Harthill N Lans 126 G5
- Harthill Rothm 84 G4
- Harthope D & G 116 E8
- Hartington Derbys 71 L2
- Hartington Nthumb 112 F3
- Hartland Devon 16 D7
- Hartland Quay Devon 16 C7
- Hartlebury Worcs 58 B10
- Hartlepool Hartpl 104 F4
- Hartley Cumb 102 E9
- Hartley Kent 26 C5
- Hartley Kent 37 P7
- Hartley Nthumb 113 M5
- Hartley Green Kent 37 P7
- Hartley Green Staffs 70 H9
- Hartley Wespall Hants 23 J3
- Hartley Wintney Hants 23 L3
- Hartlip Kent 38 D9
- Hartoft End N York 98 E2
- Harton N York 98 E8
- Harton S Tyne 113 N7
- Harton Shrops 56 H7
- Hartpury Gloucs 46 E10
- Hartshead Kirk 90 F6
- Hartshead Moor Services Calder 90 F6
- Hartshill C Stke 70 F5
- Hartshill Warwks 59 M6
- Hartshorne Derbys 71 Q10
- Hartside Nthumb 119 J7
- Hartsop Cumb 101 M8
- Hart Station Hartpl 104 E3
- Hartswell Somset 18 E9
- Hartwell Nhants 49 L4
- Hartwith N York 97 K8
- Hartwood N Lans 126 E6
- Hartwoodmyres Border 117 N6
- Harvel Kent 37 Q8
- Harvington Worcs 47 L5
- Harvington Worcs 58 C10
- Harwell Notts 85 L2
- Harwell Oxon 34 E7
- Harwich Essex 53 N5
- Harwood Bolton 89 L8
- Harwood Dur 102 F4
- Harwood Nthumb 112 F2
- Harwood Dale N York 105 Q11
- Harwood Lee Bolton 89 L8
- Harworth Notts 85 K2
- Hasbury Dudley 58 E8
- Hascombe Surrey 24 B3
- Haselbech Nhants 60 F5
- Haselbury Plucknett Somset 11 K2
- Haseley Warwks 59 K11
- Haseley Green Warwks 59 K11
- Haseley Knob Warwks 59 K10
- Haselor Warwks 47 M3
- Hasfield Gloucs 46 F9
- Hasguard Pembks 40 G9
- Hasholme E R Yk 92 D4
- Haskayne Lancs 88 D9
- Hasketon Suffk 65 J11
- Hasland Derbys 84 E7
- Haslemere Surrey 23 P8
- Haslingden Lancs 89 M6
- Haslingfield Cambs 62 F10
- Haslington Ches E 70 C3
- Hassall Ches E 70 D3
- Hassall Green Ches E 70 D3
- Hassell Street Kent 27 J2
- Hassingham Norfk 77 M10
- Hassness Cumb 100 G7
- Hassocks W Susx 24 H7
- Hassop Derbys 84 B6
- Haste Hill Surrey 23 P8
- Haster Highld 167 P6
- Hasthorpe Lincs 87 N7
- Hastingleigh Kent 27 J2
- Hastings E Susx 26 D10
- Hastings Somset 19 K11
- Hastingwood Essex 51 L9
- Hastoe Herts 35 P3
- Haswell Dur 104 C2
- Haswell Plough Dur 104 C2
- Hatch C Beds 61 Q11
- Hatch Beauchamp Somset 19 K10
- Hatch End Bed 61 N8
- Hatch End Gt Lon 36 D2
- Hatchet Gate Hants 14 C6
- Hatching Green Herts 50 D8
- Hatchmere Ches W 82 C10
- Hatcliffe NE Lin 93 M10
- Hatfield Donc 91 R9
- Hatfield Herefs 46 A3
- Hatfield Herts 50 F9
- Hatfield Worcs 46 G4
- Hatfield Broad Oak Essex 51 M7
- Hatfield Heath Essex 51 M7
- Hatfield Peverel Essex 52 C9
- Hatfield Woodhouse Donc 92 A9
- Hatford Oxon 34 B6
- Hatherden Hants 22 B4
- Hatherleigh Devon 8 D4
- Hathern Leics 72 E6
- Hatherop Gloucs 33 N3
- Hathersage Derbys 84 B4
- Hathersage Booths Derbys 84 B4
- Hatherton Ches E 70 B5
- Hatherton Staffs 58 E2
- Hatley St George Cambs 62 C10
- Hatt Cnwll 5 Q9
- Hattersley Tamesd 83 L6
- Hattingley Hants 22 H7
- Hatton Abers 159 Q10
- Hatton Angus 142 H9
- Hatton Derbys 71 N8
- Hatton Gt Lon 36 C5
- Hatton Lincs 86 G5
- Hatton Shrops 56 H6
- Hatton Warrtn 82 C8
- Hatton Warwks 59 K11
- Hatton Heath Ches W 69 N2
- Hatton of Fintray Abers 151 L4
- Haugh E Ayrs 115 J2
- Haugh Lincs 87 M5
- Haugh Rochdl 89 Q8
- Haugham Lincs 87 K4
- Haughhead E Duns 125 Q2
- Haugh Head Nthumb 119 K5
- Haughley Suffk 64 E9
- Haughley Green Suffk 64 E9
- Haugh of Glass Moray 158 B10
- Haugh of Urr D & G 108 H7
- Haughs of Kinnaird Angus 143 L6
- Haughton Ches E 69 Q3
- Haughton Notts 85 L6
- Haughton Powys 69 K11
- Haughton Shrops 57 M5
- Haughton Shrops 57 N3
- Haughton Shrops 69 L9
- Haughton Shrops 69 Q11
- Haughton Staffs 70 F10
- Haughton Green Tamesd 83 K6
- Haughton le Skerne Darltn 104 B7
- Haultwick Herts 50 H6
- Haunton Staffs 59 K2
- Hautes Croix Jersey 11 b1
- Hauxton Cambs 62 F10
- Havannah Ches E 70 F2
- Havant Hants 15 K5
- Haven Herefs 45 N4
- Haven Bank Lincs 86 H10
- Haven Side E R Yk 93 L5
- Havenstreet IoW 14 G8
- Havercroft Wakefd 91 K8
- Haverfordwest Pembks 41 J7
- Haverhill Suffk 63 L11
- Haverigg Cumb 94 D5
- Havering-atte-Bower Gt Lon 37 M2
- Haversham M Keyn 49 M6
- Haverthwaite Cumb 94 G4
- Haverton Hill S on T 104 E6
- Havyatt N Som 19 N2
- Havyatt Somset 19 P7
- Hawarden Flints 81 L11
- Hawbridge Worcs 46 H5
- Hawbush Green Essex 52 C7
- Hawcoat Cumb 94 E6
- Hawen Cerdgn 42 F5
- Hawes N York 96 C3
- Hawe's Green Norfk 65 J2
- Hawford Worcs 46 F2
- Hawick Border 117 Q8
- Hawkchurch Devon 10 G4
- Hawkedon Suffk 63 N10
- Hawkenbury Kent 26 D2
- Hawkeridge Wilts 20 G4
- Hawkerland Devon 9 Q7
- Hawker's Cove Cnwll 4 E6
- Hawkesbury S Glos 32 E7
- Hawkesbury Warwks 59 N8
- Hawkesbury Upton S Glos 32 E7
- Hawkes End Covtry 59 L8
- Hawk Green Stockp 83 L7
- Hawkhill Nthumb 119 P8
- Hawkhurst Kent 26 C5
- Hawkhurst Common E Susx 25 M7
- Hawkinge Kent 27 M4
- Hawkley Hants 23 K9
- Hawkley Wigan 82 C4
- Hawkridge Somset 17 R5
- Hawksdale Cumb 110 G11
- Hawkshaw Bury 89 M7
- Hawkshead Cumb 101 L11
- Hawkshead Hill Cumb 101 K11
- Hawksland S Lans 116 A3
- Hawkspur Green Essex 51 Q4
- Hawkstone Shrops 69 Q8
- Hawkswick N York 96 E6
- Hawksworth Leeds 90 F2
- Hawksworth Notts 73 K2
- Hawkwell Essex 38 E3
- Hawkwell Nthumb 112 G6
- Hawley Hants 23 N3
- Hawley Kent 37 M6
- Hawling Gloucs 47 L10
- Hawnby N York 98 A3
- Haworth C Brad 90 C3
- Hawridge Bucks 35 P3
- Hawstead Suffk 64 B10
- Hawstead Green Suffk 64 B10
- Hawthorn Dur 113 P11
- Hawthorn Hants 23 J8
- Hawthorn Rhondd 30 E7
- Hawthorn Hill Br For 35 N10
- Hawthorn Hill Lincs 86 H9
- Hawthorpe Lincs 73 Q5
- Hawton Notts 85 N10
- Haxby C York 98 C9
- Haxby Gates C York 98 C9
- Haxey N Linc 92 C11
- Haxey Carr N Linc 92 C10
- Haxted Surrey 37 K11
- Haxton Wilts 21 M5
- Hay Cnwll 3 P3
- Hay Cnwll 4 F7
- Haydock St Hel 82 C5
- Haydon BaNES 20 C4
- Haydon Dorset 20 C11
- Haydon Somset 19 J10
- Haydon Bridge Nthumb 112 B8
- Haydon Wick Swindn 33 M7
- Haye Cnwll 5 P7
- Hayes Gt Lon 36 C4
- Hayes Gt Lon 37 K7
- Hayes End Gt Lon 36 C4
- Hayfield Ag & B 131 M3
- Hayfield Derbys 83 M7
- Hayfield Green Donc 91 R11
- Haygate Wrekin 57 L2
- Hay Green Norfk 75 K7
- Hayhillock Angus 143 J9
- Hayle Cnwll 2 F6
- Hayle Port Cnwll 2 F6
- Hayley Green Dudley 58 E8
- Hayling Island Hants 15 K6
- Haymoor Green Ches E 70 B4
- Hayne Devon 9 J7
- Hayne Devon 18 C11
- Haynes C Beds 50 C2
- Haynes Church End C Beds 50 C2
- Haynes West End C Beds 50 C2
- Hay-on-Wye Powys 45 J6
- Hayscastle Pembks 40 G5
- Hayscastle Cross Pembks 40 H5
- Haysden Kent 37 N11
- Hay Street Herts 51 J5
- Hayton Cumb 100 F2
- Hayton Cumb 111 K9
- Hayton E R Yk 98 G11
- Hayton Notts 85 M4
- Hayton's Bent Shrops 57 J8
- Haytor Vale Devon 9 J9
- Haytown Devon 16 F9
- Haywards Heath W Susx 24 H6
- Haywood Donc 91 P8
- Haywood Herefs 45 P8
- Haywood Oaks Notts 85 K9
- Hazards Green E Susx 25 Q8
- Hazelbank S Lans 126 E8
- Hazelbury Bryan Dorset 12 B3
- Hazeleigh Essex 52 D11
- Hazeley Hants 23 K3
- Hazelford Notts 85 M11
- Hazel Grove Stockp 83 K7
- Hazelhurst Tamesd 83 L4
- Hazelslade Staffs 58 F2
- Hazel Street Kent 25 Q3
- Hazel Stub Suffk 51 Q2
- Hazelton Walls Fife 135 J3
- Hazelwood Derbys 84 D11
- Hazlemere Bucks 35 N5
- Hazlerigg N u Ty 113 K6
- Hazles Staffs 71 J5
- Hazleton Gloucs 47 L11
- Heacham Norfk 75 N3
- Headbourne Worthy Hants 22 E8
- Headbrook Herefs 45 K3
- Headcorn Kent 26 D3
- Headingley Leeds 90 H3
- Headington Oxon 34 F3
- Headlam Dur 103 N7
- Headlesscross N Lans 126 G6
- Headless Cross Worcs 58 F11
- Headley Hants 22 F2
- Headley Hants 23 M7
- Headley Surrey 36 F10
- Headley Down Hants 23 M7
- Headley Heath Worcs 58 G9
- Headon Devon 16 F11
- Headon Notts 85 M5
- Heads Nook Cumb 111 K10
- Heage Derbys 84 E10
- Healaugh N York 97 R11
- Healaugh N York 103 K11
- Heald Green Stockp 82 H7
- Heale Devon 17 L2
- Heale Somset 18 H10
- Heale Somset 19 L9
- Healey N York 97 J4
- Healey Nthumb 112 F9
- Healey Rochdl 89 P7
- Healey Wakefd 90 H7
- Healeyfield Dur 112 G11
- Healing NE Lin 93 M8
- Heamoor Cnwll 2 D7
- Heanor Derbys 84 F11
- Heanton Punchardon Devon 17 J4
- Heapham Lincs 85 Q3
- Hearn Hants 23 M7
- Heart of Scotland Services N Lans 126 G5
- Hearts Delight Kent 38 E9
- Heasley Mill Devon 17 N5
- Heaste Highld 145 K4
- Heath Derbys 84 F7
- Heath Wakefd 91 K6
- Heath and Reach C Beds 49 P9
- Heath Common W Susx 24 D7
- Heathcote Derbys 71 L2
- Heathcote Shrops 70 B9
- Heath End Bucks 35 N5
- Heath End Hants 22 D2
- Heath End Leics 72 B6
- Heath End Warwks 47 P2
- Heather Leics 72 B8
- Heathfield Cambs 62 G11
- Heathfield Devon 9 K9
- Heathfield E Susx 25 N6
- Heathfield N York 96 H7
- Heathfield Somset 18 G9
- Heathfield Village Oxon 48 F11
- Heath Green Worcs 58 G10
- Heath Hall D & G 109 L5
- Heath Hayes & Wimblebury Staffs 58 F2
- Heath Hill Shrops 57 P2
- Heath House Somset 19 M5
- Heathrow Airport Gt Lon 36 C5
- Heathstock Devon 10 E4
- Heathton Shrops 57 Q6
- Heath Town Wolves 58 D5
- Heathwaite N York 104 E10
- Heatley Staffs 71 K9
- Heatley Warrtn 82 F7
- Heaton Bolton 89 K9
- Heaton C Brad 90 E3
- Heaton Lancs 95 J8
- Heaton N u Ty 113 L7
- Heaton Staffs 70 H2
- Heaton Chapel Stockp 83 J6
- Heaton Mersey Stockp 83 J6
- Heaton Norris Stockp 83 J6
- Heaton's Bridge Lancs 88 E8
- Heaverham Kent 37 N9
- Heaviley Stockp 83 K7
- Heavitree Devon 9 M6
- Hebburn S Tyne 113 M8
- Hebden N York 96 F8
- Hebden Bridge Calder 90 B5
- Hebden Green Ches W 82 D11
- Hebing End Herts 50 H6
- Hebron Carmth 41 N5
- Hebron IoA 78 H8
- Hebron Nthumb 113 J3
- Heckfield Hants 23 K2
- Heckfield Green Suffk 64 H6
- Heckfordbridge Essex 52 F7
- Heckington Lincs 74 B2
- Heckmondwike Kirk 90 G6
- Heddington Wilts 33 J11
- Heddon-on-the-Wall Nthumb 112 H7
- Hedenham Norfk 65 L3
- Hedge End Hants 14 E4
- Hedgerley Bucks 35 Q7
- Hedgerley Green Bucks 35 Q7
- Hedging Somset 19 K9
- Hedley on the Hill Nthumb 112 G9
- Hednesford Staffs 58 E2
- Hedon E R Yk 93 L5
- Hedsor Bucks 35 P7
- Heeley Sheff 84 E4
- Hegdon Hill Herefs 46 A4
- Heglibister Shet 169 q8
- Heighington Darltn 103 P6
- Heighington Lincs 86 D7
- Heightington Worcs 57 P10
- Heiton Border 118 D4
- Hele Devon 7 J4
- Hele Devon 9 N4
- Hele Devon 17 J2
- Hele Somset 18 G10
- Helebridge Cnwll 16 C11
- Hele Lane Devon 9 J2
- Helensburgh Ag & B 132 B11
- Helenton S Ayrs 125 K11
- Helford Cnwll 3 K8
- Helford Passage Cnwll 3 K8
- Helhoughton Norfk 76 B6
- Helions Bumpstead Essex 51 Q2
- Hellaby Rothm 84 H2
- Helland Cnwll 4 H7
- Hellandbridge Cnwll 4 H7
- Hell Corner W Berk 22 C2
- Hellescott Cnwll 5 M4
- Hellesdon Norfk 77 J9
- Hellesveor Cnwll 2 E5
- Hellidon Nhants 60 B9
- Hellifield N York 96 C9
- Hellingly E Susx 25 N8
- Hellington Norfk 77 L11
- Helm Nthumb 119 N11
- Helmdon Nhants 48 G6
- Helme Kirk 90 D8
- Helmingham Suffk 64 H10
- Helmington Row Dur 103 N3
- Helmsdale Highld 163 N3
- Helmshore Lancs 89 M6
- Helmsley N York 98 C4
- Helperby N York 97 P7
- Helperthorpe N York 99 K6
- Helpringham Lincs 74 B2
- Helpston C Pete 74 B9
- Helsby Ches W 81 P9
- Helsey Lincs 87 P6
- Helston Cnwll 2 H8
- Helstone Cnwll 4 H5
- Helton Cumb 101 P6
- Helwith N York 103 L10
- Helwith Bridge N York 96 B7
- Hemblington Norfk 77 L9
- Hembridge Somset 19 Q7
- Hemel Hempstead Herts 50 C9
- Hemerdon Devon 6 F7
- Hemingbrough N York 91 R4
- Hemingby Lincs 86 H6
- Hemingfield Barns 91 K10
- Hemingford Abbots Cambs 62 C6
- Hemingford Grey Cambs 62 C6
- Hemingstone Suffk 64 G11
- Hemington Leics 72 D5
- Hemington Nhants 61 N3
- Hemington Somset 20 D4
- Hemley Suffk 53 N3
- Hemlington Middsb 104 F8
- Hempholme E R Yk 99 M10
- Hempnall Norfk 65 J3
- Hempnall Green Norfk 65 J3
- Hempriggs Moray 157 L5
- Hempstead Essex 51 P3
- Hempstead Medway 38 C9
- Hempstead Norfk 76 G4
- Hempstead Norfk 77 N6
- Hempsted Gloucs 46 F11
- Hempton Norfk 76 C6
- Hempton Oxon 48 D8
- Hemsby Norfk 77 P8
- Hemswell Lincs 86 B2
- Hemswell Cliff Lincs 86 B3
- Hemsworth Wakefd 91 L8
- Hemyock Devon 10 C2
- Henbury Bristl 31 Q9
- Henbury Ches E 83 J10
- Hendham Devon 7 J8
- Hendomen Powys 56 C5
- Hendon Gt Lon 36 F3
- Hendon Sundld 113 P9
- Hendra Cnwll 3 J6
- Hendra Cnwll 4 G6
- Hendre Brdgnd 29 P8
- Hendre Flints 80 H11
- Hendy Carmth 28 G4
- Heneglwys IoA 78 G9
- Henfield W Susx 24 F7
- Henford Devon 5 P3
- Henfynyw Cerdgn 43 J2
- Henghurst Kent 26 G4
- Hengoed Caerph 30 G6
- Hengoed Powys 45 J4
- Hengoed Shrops 69 J8
- Hengrave Suffk 63 P7
- Henham Essex 51 M5
- Heniarth Powys 55 Q3
- Henlade Somset 19 J10
- Henley Dorset 11 P4
- Henley Gloucs 46 H11
- Henley Shrops 56 H7
- Henley Shrops 57 J9
- Henley Somset 19 M8
- Henley Suffk 64 H11
- Henley W Susx 23 N9
- Henley Green Covtry 59 N8
- Henley-in-Arden Warwks 59 J11
- Henley-on-Thames Oxon 35 L8
- Henley Park Surrey 23 P4
- Henley's Down E Susx 26 B9
- Henley Street Kent 37 Q7
- Henllan Cerdgn 42 G6
- Henllan Denbgs 80 E11
- Henllan Amgoed Carmth 41 N7
- Henllys Torfn 31 J6
- Henlow C Beds 50 E3
- Hennock Devon 9 K8
- Henny Street Essex 52 E4
- Henryd Conwy 79 P10
- Henry's Moat (Castell Hendre) Pembks 41 K5
- Hensall N York 91 P6
- Henshaw Nthumb 111 Q8
- Hensingham Cumb 100 C7
- Henstead Suffk 65 P4
- Hensting Hants 22 E10
- Henstridge Somset 20 D11
- Henstridge Ash Somset 20 D10
- Henstridge Marsh Somset 20 D10
- Henton Oxon 35 L4
- Henton Somset 19 N5
- Henwick Worcs 46 F3
- Henwood Cnwll 5 M7
- Henwood Oxon 34 E4
- Heolgerrig Myr Td 30 D3
- Heol-las Swans 29 J5
- Heol Senni Powys 44 C10
- Heol-y-Cyw Brdgnd 29 P8
- Hepburn Nthumb 119 L6
- Hepple Nthumb 119 J10
- Hepscott Nthumb 113 K4
- Heptonstall Calder 90 B5
- Hepworth Kirk 90 F9
- Hepworth Suffk 64 D7
- Herbrandston Pembks 40 G9
- Hereford Herefs 45 Q7
- Hereson Kent 39 Q8
- Heribusta Highld 152 F3
- Heriot Border 128 C9
- Hermiston C Edin 127 M3
- Hermitage Border 117 Q11
- Hermitage Dorset 11 P3
- Hermitage W Berk 34 F10
- Hermitage W Susx 15 L5
- Hermit Hill Barns 91 J10
- Hermon Carmth 42 G8
- Hermon IoA 78 F11
- Hermon Pembks 41 P4
- Herne Kent 39 L8
- Herne Bay Kent 39 L8
- Herne Common Kent 39 L8
- Herne Hill Gt Lon 36 H6
- Herne Pound Kent 37 Q10
- Herner Devon 17 K6
- Hernhill Kent 39 J9
- Herodsfoot Cnwll 5 L9
- Heronden Kent 39 N11
- Herongate Essex 37 P2
- Heronsford S Ayrs 114 B11
- Heronsgate Herts 36 B2
- Herriard Hants 23 J5
- Herringfleet Suffk 65 P2
- Herring's Green Bed 50 C2
- Herringswell Suffk 63 M6
- Herringthorpe Rothm 84 F2
- Herrington Sundld 113 N10
- Hersden Kent 39 M9
- Hersham Cnwll 16 D10
- Hersham Surrey 36 D8
- Herstmonceux E Susx 25 P8
- Herston Dorset 12 H9
- Herston Ork 169 d7
- Hertford Herts 50 H8
- Hertford Heath Herts 51 J8
- Hertingfordbury Herts 50 H8
- Hesketh Bank Lancs 88 E6
- Hesketh Lane Lancs 89 J2
- Hesket Newmarket Cumb 101 K3
- Heskin Green Lancs 88 G7
- Hesleden Dur 104 D3
- Hesleden N York 96 C6
- Hesley Donc 85 K2
- Hesleyside Nthumb 112 B4
- Heslington C York 98 C10
- Hessay C York 97 R10
- Hessenford Cnwll 5 N10
- Hessett Suffk 64 C9
- Hessle E R Yk 92 H5
- Hessle Wakefd 91 L7
- Hest Bank Lancs 95 K7
- Hestley Green Suffk 64 H8
- Heston Gt Lon 36 D5
- Heston Services Gt Lon 36 D5
- Hestwall Ork 169 b5
- Heswall Wirral 81 K8
- Hethe Oxon 48 G9
- Hethersett Norfk 76 G11
- Hethersgill Cumb 111 J7
- Hetherside Cumb 110 H7
- Hetherson Green Ches W 69 P4
- Hethpool Nthumb 118 G5
- Hett Dur 103 Q3

Hetton N York 96 E9
Hetton-le-Hole Sundld 113 N11
Hetton Steads Nthumb 119 K3
Heugh Nthumb 112 G6
Heughhead Abers 150 B5
Heugh Head Border 129 M7
Heveningham Suffk 65 L7
Hever Kent 37 L11
Heversham Cumb 95 K4
Hevingham Norfk 76 H7
Hewas Water Cnwll 3 P4
Hewelsfield Gloucs 31 Q4
Hewenden C Brad 90 D3
Hewish N Som 19 M2
Hewish Somset 11 J3
Hewood Dorset 10 H4
Hexham Nthumb 112 D8
Hextable Kent 37 M6
Hexthorpe Donc 91 P10
Hexton Herts 50 D4
Hexworthy Cnwll 5 P5
Hexworthy Devon 6 H4
Hey Lancs 89 P2
Heybridge Essex 51 P11
Heybridge Essex 52 E10
Heybridge Basin Essex 52 E10
Heybrook Bay Devon 6 D9
Heydon Cambs 51 K3
Heydon Norfk 76 G6
Heydour Lincs 73 Q3
Hey Houses Lancs 88 C5
Heylipoll Ag & B 136 B7
Heylor Shet 169 p5
Heyrod Tamesd 83 L5
Heysham Lancs 95 J8
Heyshaw N York 97 J8
Heyshott W Susx 23 N11
Heyside Oldham 89 Q9
Heytesbury Wilts 20 H6
Heythrop Oxon 48 C9
Heywood Rochdl 89 P8
Heywood Wilts 20 G4
Hibaldstow N Linc 92 G10
Hickleton Donc 91 M9
Hickling Norfk 77 N7
Hickling Notts 72 H5
Hickling Green Norfk 77 N7
Hickling Heath Norfk 77 N7
Hickling Pastures Notts 72 H5
Hickmans Green Kent 39 J10
Hicks Forstal Kent 39 L9
Hickstead W Susx 24 G6
Hidcote Bartrim Gloucs 47 N6
Hidcote Boyce Gloucs 47 N6
High Ackworth Wakefd 91 L7
Higham Barns 91 J9
Higham Derbys 84 E9
Higham Kent 37 P11
Higham Kent 38 B7
Higham Lancs 89 N3
Higham Suffk 52 H4
Higham Suffk 63 M7
Higham Dykes Nthumb 112 H5
Higham Ferrers Nhants 61 L7
Higham Gobion C Beds 50 D4
Higham Hill Gt Lon 37 J2
Higham on the Hill Leics 72 B11
Highampton Devon 8 C4
Highams Park Gt Lon 37 J2
High Angerton Nthumb 112 G3
High Ardwell D & G 106 E8
High Auldgirth D & G 109 K3
High Bankhill Cumb 101 Q2
High Beach Essex 51 K11
High Bentham N York 95 P7
High Bewaldeth Cumb 100 H4
High Bickington Devon 17 L7
High Biggins Cumb 95 N5
High Birkwith N York 96 B5
High Blantyre S Lans 126 B6
High Bonnybridge Falk 126 E2
High Borrans Cumb 101 M10
High Bradley N York 96 F11
High Bray Devon 17 M5
Highbridge Hants 22 E10
Highbridge Somset 19 K5
Highbrook W Susx 25 J4
High Brooms Kent 25 N2
High Bullen Devon 17 J7
Highburton Kirk 90 F8
Highbury Gt Lon 36 H3
Highbury Somset 20 C5
High Buston Nthumb 119 P9
High Callerton Nthumb 113 J6
High Casterton Cumb 95 N5
High Catton E R Yk 98 E10
Highclere Hants 22 D3
Highcliffe BCP 13 M6
High Close Dur 103 N7
High Cogges Oxon 34 C3
High Common Norfk 76 D10
High Coniscliffe Darltn 103 P7
High Crosby Cumb 111 J9
High Cross Cnwll 3 J8
High Cross E Ayrs 125 L8
High Cross Hants 23 K9
High Cross Herts 51 J7
Highcross Lancs 88 C3
High Cross W Susx 24 F7
High Cross Warwks 59 K11
High Drummore D & G 106 F10
High Dubmire Sundld 113 M11
High Easter Essex 51 P8
High Eggborough N York 91 P6
High Ellington N York 97 J4
Higher Alham Somset 20 C6
Higher Ansty Dorset 12 C4
Higher Ballam Lancs 88 D4
Higher Bartle Lancs 88 G4
Higher Berry End C Beds 49 Q8
Higher Bockhampton Dorset 12 B6
Higher Brixham Torbay 7 N8
Higher Burrowton Devon 9 P5
Higher Burwardsley Ches W 69 P3
High Ercall Wrekin 69 Q11
Higher Chillington Somset 10 H2
Higher Clovelly Devon 16 E7
Highercombe Somset 18 B8
Higher Coombe Dorset 11 L6
Higher Disley Ches E 83 L8
Higher Folds Wigan 82 E4
Higherford Lancs 89 P2
Higher Gabwell Devon 7 N5
Higher Halstock Leigh Dorset 11 L3
Higher Harpers Lancs 89 N3
Higher Heysham Lancs 95 J8
Higher Hurdsfield Ches E 83 K10
Higher Irlam Salfd 82 F5
Higher Kingcombe Dorset 11 L5
Higher Kinnerton Flints 69 K2
Higher Marston Ches W 82 E9
Higher Muddiford Devon 17 K4
Higher Nyland Dorset 20 D10
Higher Ogden Rochdl 90 B8
Higher Pentire Cnwll 2 H8
Higher Penwortham Lancs 88 G5
Higher Prestacott Devon 5 P2
Higher Studfold N York 96 B6
Higher Town Cnwll 3 L5
Higher Town Cnwll 4 G9
Higher Town IoS 2 c1
Higher Tregantle Cnwll 5 Q11
Higher Walton Lancs 88 H5
Higher Walton Warrtn 82 C7
Higher Wambrook Somset 10 F3
Higher Waterston Dorset 11 Q5
Higher Whatcombe Dorset 12 D4
Higher Wheelton Lancs 89 J6
Higher Whitley Ches W 82 D8
Higher Wincham Ches W 82 E9
Higher Wraxhall Dorset 11 M4
Higher Wych Ches W 69 N6
High Etherley Dur 103 N5
High Ferry Lincs 87 L11
Highfield E R Yk 92 B3
Highfield Gatesd 112 H9
Highfield N Ayrs 125 J7
Highfields Donc 91 N9
High Flats Kirk 90 G9
High Garrett Essex 52 C6
Highgate E Susx 25 K4
Highgate Gt Lon 36 G3
Highgate Kent 26 C5
High Grange Dur 103 N4
High Grantley N York 97 K7
High Green Cumb 101 M10
High Green Kirk 90 G8
High Green Norfk 64 H4
High Green Norfk 76 G10
High Green Sheff 91 J11
High Green Shrops 57 N8
High Green Suffk 64 B9
High Green Worcs 46 G5
Highgreen Manor Nthumb 112 B2
High Halden Kent 26 E4
High Halstow Medway 38 C6
High Ham Somset 19 M8
High Harrington Cumb 100 D5
High Harrogate N York 97 M9
High Haswell Dur 104 C2
High Hatton Shrops 69 R10
High Hauxley Nthumb 119 Q10
High Hawsker N York 105 P9
High Hesket Cumb 101 N2
High Hoyland Barns 90 H9
High Hunsley E R Yk 92 G3
High Hurstwood E Susx 25 L5
High Hutton N York 98 F7
High Ireby Cumb 100 H3
High Kelling Norfk 76 G3
High Kilburn N York 97 R5
High Killerby N York 99 M4
High Knipe Cumb 101 P7
High Lands Dur 103 M5
Highlane Ches E 83 J11
Highlane Derbys 84 F4
High Lane Stockp 83 L7
High Lanes Cnwll 2 F6
High Laver Essex 51 M9
Highlaws Cumb 109 P11
Highleadon Gloucs 46 E10
High Legh Ches E 82 F8
Highleigh W Susx 15 M7
High Leven S on T 104 E8
Highley Shrops 57 N8
High Littleton BaNES 20 B3
High Lorton Cumb 100 G5
High Marishes N York 98 G5
High Marnham Notts 85 P6
High Melton Donc 91 N10
High Mickley Nthumb 112 G8
Highmoor Cumb 110 E11
Highmoor Oxon 35 K8
Highmoor Cross Oxon 35 K8
Highmoor Hill Mons 31 N7
High Moorsley Sundld 113 M11
Highnam Gloucs 46 E11
Highnam Green Gloucs 46 E10
High Newport Sundld 113 N10
High Newton Cumb 95 J4
High Nibthwaite Cumb 94 F3
High Offley Staffs 70 D9
High Ongar Essex 51 N10
High Onn Staffs 70 E11
High Park Corner Essex 52 H7
High Pennyvenie E Ayrs 115 J6
High Post Wilts 21 N7
Highridge N Som 31 Q11
High Roding Essex 51 P7
High Row Cumb 101 L3
High Row Cumb 101 L6
High Salter Lancs 95 N8
High Salvington W Susx 24 D9
High Scales Cumb 110 C11
High Seaton Cumb 100 D4
High Shaw N York 96 C2
High Side Cumb 100 H4
High Spen Gatesd 112 H9
Highstead Kent 39 M8
Highsted Kent 38 F9
High Stoop Dur 103 M2
High Street Cnwll 3 P3
High Street Kent 26 B5
Highstreet Kent 39 J9
High Street Suffk 65 N10
High Street Suffk 65 N7
Highstreet Green Essex 52 C5
Highstreet Green Surrey 23 Q7
Hightae D & G 109 N5
Highter's Heath Birm 58 G9
High Throston Hartpl 104 E4
Hightown Ches E 70 F2
Hightown Hants 13 L4
Hightown Sefton 81 L4
High Town Staffs 58 E2
Hightown Green Suffk 64 D10
High Toynton Lincs 87 J7
High Trewhitt Nthumb 119 K9
High Urpeth Dur 113 K10
High Valleyfield Fife 134 C10
High Warden Nthumb 112 D7
Highway Herefs 45 P5
Highway Wilts 33 K10
Highweek Devon 7 L4
High Westwood Dur 112 H9
Highwood Essex 51 P10
Highwood Staffs 71 K8
Highwood Hill Gt Lon 36 F2
High Woolaston Gloucs 31 Q5
High Worsall N York 104 C9
Highworth Swindn 33 P6
High Wray Cumb 101 L11
High Wych Herts 51 L8
High Wycombe Bucks 35 N6
Hilborough Norfk 75 R10
Hilcote Derbys 84 G9
Hilcott Wilts 21 M3
Hildenborough Kent 37 N11
Hilden Park Kent 37 N11
Hildersham Cambs 62 H11
Hilderstone Staffs 70 H8
Hilderthorpe E R Yk 99 P7
Hilfield Dorset 11 N3
Hilgay Norfk 75 M11
Hill S Glos 32 B5
Hill Warwks 59 Q11
Hillam N York 91 N5
Hillbeck Cumb 102 E7
Hillborough Kent 39 M8
Hill Brow Hants 23 L9
Hillbutts Dorset 12 G4
Hill Chorlton Staffs 70 D7
Hillclifflane Derbys 71 P5
Hill Common Norfk 77 N7
Hill Common Somset 18 F9
Hill Deverill Wilts 20 G6
Hilldyke Lincs 87 K11
Hill End Dur 103 K3
Hill End Fife 134 C8
Hillend Fife 134 E11
Hill End Gloucs 46 H7
Hillend Mdloth 127 P4
Hillend N Lans 126 E4
Hillend Swans 28 D6
Hillersland Gloucs 31 Q2
Hillerton Devon 8 H5
Hillesden Bucks 49 J9
Hillesley Gloucs 32 E7
Hillfarrance Somset 18 G10
Hill Green Kent 38 D9
Hillgrove W Susx 23 P9
Hillhampton Herefs 46 A5
Hillhead Abers 158 E10
Hillhead Devon 7 N8
Hill Head Hants 14 F6
Hillhead S Lans 116 D2
Hillhead of Cocklaw Abers 159 Q9
Hilliard's Cross Staffs 59 J2
Hilliclay Highld 167 L4
Hillingdon Gt Lon 36 C4
Hillington C Glas 125 N5
Hillington Norfk 75 P5
Hillis Corner IoW 14 E8
Hillmorton Warwks 60 B6
Hillock Vale Lancs 89 M5
Hill of Beath Fife 134 F9
Hill of Fearn Highld 163 J11
Hillowton D & G 108 G8
Hillpool Worcs 58 C9
Hillpound Hants 22 G11
Hill Ridware Staffs 71 K11
Hillside Abers 151 N8
Hillside Angus 143 N5
Hillside Devon 7 J6
Hill Side Kirk 90 F7
Hill Side Worcs 46 E2
Hills Town Derbys 84 G7
Hillstreet Hants 22 B11
Hillswick Shet 169 p6
Hill Top Dur 103 J6
Hill Top Hants 14 D6
Hill Top Kirk 90 D8
Hill Top Rothm 84 E2
Hill Top Sandw 58 E6
Hill Top Wakefd 91 J7
Hillwell Shet 169 q12
Hilmarton Wilts 33 K9
Hilperton Wilts 20 G3
Hilperton Marsh Wilts 20 G3
Hilsea C Port 15 J6
Hilston E R Yk 93 N4
Hiltingbury Hants 22 D10
Hilton Border 129 M9
Hilton Cambs 62 C7
Hilton Cumb 102 D6
Hilton Derbys 71 N8
Hilton Dorset 12 C4
Hilton Dur 103 N6
Hilton Highld 156 F2
Hilton S on T 104 E8
Hilton Shrops 57 P5
Hilton Park Services Staffs 58 E4
Himbleton Worcs 46 H3
Himley Staffs 58 C6
Hincaster Cumb 95 L4
Hinchley Wood Surrey 36 E7
Hinckley Leics 59 P6
Hinderclay Suffk 64 E6
Hinderwell N York 105 L7
Hindford Shrops 69 K8
Hindhead Surrey 23 N7
Hindhead Tunnel Surrey 23 N7
Hindle Fold Lancs 89 L4
Hindley Nthumb 112 F9
Hindley Wigan 82 D4
Hindley Green Wigan 82 D4
Hindlip Worcs 46 G3
Hindolveston Norfk 76 E6
Hindon Wilts 20 H8
Hindringham Norfk 76 D4
Hingham Norfk 76 E11
Hinksford Staffs 58 C7
Hinstock Shrops 70 B9
Hintlesham Suffk 53 J3
Hinton Gloucs 32 C4
Hinton Hants 13 M5
Hinton Herefs 45 L7
Hinton S Glos 32 D9
Hinton Shrops 56 G3
Hinton Shrops 57 M8
Hinton Admiral Hants 13 M5
Hinton Ampner Hants 22 H9
Hinton Blewett BaNES 19 Q3
Hinton Charterhouse BaNES 20 E3
Hinton Cross Worcs 47 K6
Hinton-in-the-Hedges Nhants 48 G7
Hinton Marsh Hants 22 G9
Hinton Martell Dorset 12 H3
Hinton on the Green Worcs 47 K6
Hinton Parva Swindn 33 P8
Hinton St George Somset 11 J2
Hinton St Mary Dorset 20 E11
Hinton Waldrist Oxon 34 C5
Hints Shrops 57 L10
Hints Staffs 59 J4
Hinwick Bed 61 K8
Hinxhill Kent 26 H3
Hinxton Cambs 62 G11
Hinxworth Herts 50 F2
Hipperholme Calder 90 E5
Hipsburn Nthumb 119 P8
Hipswell N York 103 N11
Hirn Abers 151 J7
Hirnant Powys 68 D10
Hirst Nthumb 113 L3
Hirst Courtney N York 91 Q6
Hirwaen Denbgs 68 F2
Hirwaun Rhondd 30 C3
Hiscott Devon 17 J6
Histon Cambs 62 F8
Hitcham Suffk 64 D11
Hitcham Causeway Suffk 64 D11
Hitcham Street Suffk 64 D11
Hitchin Herts 50 E5
Hither Green Gt Lon 37 J6
Hittisleigh Devon 8 H5
Hive E R Yk 92 D4
Hixon Staffs 71 J9
Hoaden Kent 39 N10
Hoar Cross Staffs 71 L10
Hoarwithy Herefs 45 Q9
Hoath Kent 39 M9
Hoathly Kent 25 Q3
Hobarris Shrops 56 E9
Hobbles Green Suffk 63 M10
Hobbs Cross Essex 51 L11
Hobbs Cross Essex 51 L8
Hobkirk Border 118 A8
Hobland Hall Norfk 77 Q11
Hobsick Notts 84 G11
Hobson Dur 113 J9
Hoby Leics 72 H7
Hoccombe Somset 18 F9
Hockering Norfk 76 F9
Hockerton Notts 85 M9
Hockley Ches E 83 K8
Hockley Covtry 59 L9
Hockley Essex 38 D3
Hockley Staffs 59 K4
Hockley Heath Solhll 59 J10
Hockliffe C Beds 49 Q9
Hockwold cum Wilton Norfk 63 M3
Hockworthy Devon 18 D11
Hoddesdon Herts 51 J9
Hoddlesden Bl w D 89 L6
Hoddom Cross D & G 110 C6
Hoddom Mains D & G 110 C6
Hodgehill Ches E 82 H11
Hodgeston Pembks 41 K11
Hodnet Shrops 69 R9
Hodsock Notts 85 K3
Hodsoll Street Kent 37 P8
Hodson Swindn 33 N8
Hodthorpe Derbys 84 H5
Hoe Hants 22 G11
Hoe Norfk 76 D8
Hoe Benham W Berk 34 D11
Hoe Gate Hants 14 H4
Hoff Cumb 102 C7
Hogben's Hill Kent 38 H10
Hoggards Green Suffk 64 B10
Hoggeston Bucks 49 M10
Hoggrill's End Warwks 59 K6
Hog Hill E Susx 26 E8
Hoghton Lancs 89 J5
Hoghton Bottoms Lancs 89 J5
Hognaston Derbys 71 N4
Hogsthorpe Lincs 87 P6
Holbeach Lincs 74 G6
Holbeach Bank Lincs 74 G5
Holbeach Clough Lincs 74 G5
Holbeach Drove Lincs 74 F8
Holbeach Hurn Lincs 74 G5
Holbeach St Johns Lincs 74 G7
Holbeach St Mark's Lincs 74 G4
Holbeach St Matthew Lincs 74 H4
Holbeck Notts 84 H6
Holbeck Woodhouse Notts 84 H6
Holberrow Green Worcs 47 K3
Holbeton Devon 6 G8
Holborn Gt Lon 36 H4
Holborough Kent 37 Q8
Holbrook Derbys 72 B2
Holbrook Sheff 84 F4
Holbrook Suffk 53 L4
Holbrook Moor Derbys 84 E11
Holbrooks Covtry 59 M8
Holburn Nthumb 119 K3
Holbury Hants 14 D6
Holcombe Devon 7 P4
Holcombe Somset 20 C5
Holcombe Rogus Devon 18 E11
Holcot Nhants 60 G7
Holden Lancs 96 A11
Holdenby Nhants 60 E7
Holden Gate Calder 89 P6
Holder's Green Essex 51 P5
Holdgate Shrops 57 K7
Holdingham Lincs 86 E11
Holditch Dorset 10 G4
Holdsworth Calder 90 D5
Holehouse Derbys 83 M6
Hole-in-the-Wall Herefs 46 B9
Holemoor Devon 16 G10
Hole Street W Susx 24 D8
Holford Somset 18 G6
Holgate C York 98 B10
Holker Cumb 94 H5
Holkham Norfk 76 B3
Hollacombe Devon 16 F11
Holland Fen Lincs 86 H11
Holland Lees Lancs 88 G9
Holland-on-Sea Essex 53 L8
Hollandstoun Ork 169 g1
Hollee D & G 110 E7
Hollesley Suffk 53 Q3
Hollicombe Torbay 7 M6
Hollingbourne Kent 38 D10
Hollingbury Br & H 24 H9
Hollingdon Bucks 49 N9
Hollingrove E Susx 25 Q6
Hollingthorpe Leeds 91 K4
Hollington Derbys 71 N7
Hollington Staffs 71 K7
Hollingworth Tamesd 83 M5
Hollins Bury 89 N9
Hollins Derbys 84 D6
Hollins Staffs 70 H5
Hollinsclough Staffs 83 N11
Hollins End Sheff 84 E4
Hollins Green Warrtn 82 E6
Hollins Lane Lancs 95 K10
Hollinswood Wrekin 57 N3
Hollinwood Shrops 69 P7
Hollocombe Devon 17 L9
Holloway Derbys 84 D9
Holloway Gt Lon 36 H3
Holloway Wilts 20 G8
Hollowell Nhants 60 E6
Hollowmoor Heath Ches W 81 P11
Hollows D & G 110 G5
Hollybush Caerph 30 G4
Hollybush E Ayrs 114 G4
Hollybush Herefs 46 E7
Holly End Norfk 75 J9
Holly Green Worcs 46 G6
Hollyhurst Ches E 69 Q6
Hollym E R Yk 93 P5
Hollywood Worcs 58 G9
Holmbridge Kirk 90 E9
Holmbury St Mary Surrey 24 D2
Holmbush Cnwll 3 Q3
Holmcroft Staffs 70 G10
Holme Cambs 61 Q3
Holme Cumb 95 L5
Holme Kirk 90 E9
Holme N Linc 92 F9
Holme N York 97 N4
Holme Notts 85 P9
Holme Chapel Lancs 89 P5
Holme Green N York 91 P2
Holme Hale Norfk 76 B10
Holme Lacy Herefs 45 R7
Holme Marsh Herefs 45 L4
Holme next the Sea Norfk 75 P2
Holme on the Wolds E R Yk 99 K11
Holme Pierrepont Notts 72 G3
Holmer Herefs 45 Q6
Holmer Green Bucks 35 P5
Holme St Cuthbert Cumb 109 P11
Holmes Chapel Ches E 82 G11
Holmesfield Derbys 84 D5
Holmes Hill E Susx 25 M8
Holmeswood Lancs 88 E7
Holmethorpe Surrey 36 G10
Holme upon Spalding Moor E R Yk 92 D3
Holmewood Derbys 84 F7
Holmfield Calder 90 D5
Holmfirth Kirk 90 E9
Holmhead E Ayrs 115 L3
Holmpton E R Yk 93 Q6
Holmrook Cumb 100 E11
Holmshurst E Susx 25 P5
Holmside Dur 113 K11
Holmwrangle Cumb 111 K11
Holne Devon 7 J5
Holnest Dorset 11 P3
Holnicote Somset 18 B5
Holsworthy Devon 16 E11
Holsworthy Beacon Devon 16 F10
Holt Dorset 12 H4
Holt Norfk 76 F4
Holt Wilts 20 G2
Holt Worcs 46 F2
Holt Wrexhm 69 M4
Holtby C York 98 D10
Holt End Worcs 58 G11
Holt Fleet Worcs 46 F2
Holt Green Lancs 88 D9
Holt Heath Dorset 13 J4
Holt Heath Worcs 46 F2
Holton Oxon 34 H3
Holton Somset 20 C9
Holton Suffk 65 N6
Holton cum Beckering Lincs 86 F4
Holton Heath Dorset 12 F6
Holton Hill E Susx 25 Q5
Holton le Clay Lincs 93 N10
Holton le Moor Lincs 93 J11
Holton St Mary Suffk 53 J4
Holt Street Kent 39 N11
Holtye E Susx 25 L3
Holway Flints 80 H9
Holwell Dorset 11 P2
Holwell Herts 50 E4
Holwell Leics 73 J6
Holwell Oxon 33 P3
Holwick Dur 102 H5
Holworth Dorset 12 C8
Holybourne Hants 23 K6
Holy Cross Worcs 58 D9
Holyfield Essex 51 J10
Holyhead IoA 78 C8
Holy Island IoA 78 D8
Holy Island Nthumb 119 M2
Holy Island Nthumb 119 M2
Holymoorside Derbys 84 D7
Holyport W & M 35 N9
Holystone Nthumb 119 J10
Holytown N Lans 126 D5
Holywell C Beds 50 B7
Holywell Cambs 62 D6
Holywell Cnwll 4 B10
Holywell Dorset 11 M4
Holywell Flints 80 H9
Holywell Nthumb 113 M6
Holywell Warwks 59 K11
Holywell Green Calder 90 D7
Holywell Lake Somset 18 F10
Holywell Row Suffk 63 M5
Holywood D & G 109 K4
Holywood Village D & G 109 L5
Homer Shrops 57 L4
Homer Green Sefton 81 L4
Homersfield Suffk 65 K4
Homescales Cumb 95 M3
Hom Green Herefs 46 A10
Homington Wilts 21 M9
Honeyborough Pembks 40 H9
Honeybourne Worcs 47 M6
Honeychurch Devon 8 F4
Honey Hill Kent 39 K9

Honeystreet Wilts 21 M2
Honey Tye Suffk 52 G4
Honiley Warwks 59 K10
Honing Norfk 77 L6
Honingham Norfk 76 G9
Honington Lincs 73 N2
Honington Suffk 64 C7
Honington Warwks 47 Q6
Honiton Devon 10 D4
Honley Kirk 90 E8
Honnington Wrekin 70 C11
Hoo Kent 39 N9
Hoobrook Worcs 58 B10
Hood Green Barns 91 J10
Hood Hill Rothm 91 K11
Hooe C Plym 6 E8
Hooe E Susx 25 Q8
Hoo End Herts 50 E6
Hoo Green Ches E 82 F8
Hoohill Bpool 88 C3
Hook Cambs 62 F2
Hook Devon 10 G3
Hook E R Yk 92 C5
Hook Gt Lon 36 E8
Hook Hants 14 F5
Hook Hants 23 K4
Hook Pembks 41 J8
Hook Wilts 33 L8
Hook-a-Gate Shrops 56 H3
Hook Bank Worcs 46 F6
Hooke Dorset 11 L4
Hook End Essex 51 N10
Hookgate Staffs 70 C7
Hook Green Kent 25 Q3
Hook Green Kent 37 P6
Hook Norton Oxon 48 C8
Hook Street Gloucs 32 C5
Hook Street Wilts 33 L8
Hookway Devon 9 L5
Hookwood Surrey 24 G2
Hooley Surrey 36 G9
Hooley Bridge Rochdl 89 P8
Hoo Meavy Devon 6 E5
Hoo St Werburgh Medway 38 C7
Hooton Ches W 81 M9
Hooton Levitt Rothm 84 H2
Hooton Pagnell Donc 91 M9
Hooton Roberts Rothm 91 M11
Hopcrofts Holt Oxon 48 E9
Hope Derbys 83 Q8
Hope Devon 6 H10
Hope Flints 69 K3
Hope Powys 56 D3
Hope Shrops 56 E4
Hope Staffs 71 L4
Hope Bagot Shrops 57 K10
Hope Bowdler Shrops 56 H6
Hope End Green Essex 51 N6
Hopehouse Border 117 K7
Hopeman Moray 157 L4
Hope Mansell Herefs 46 B11
Hopesay Shrops 56 F8
Hopetown Wakefd 91 K6
Hope under Dinmore Herefs 45 Q4
Hopgrove C York 98 C10
Hopperton N York 97 P9
Hop Pole Lincs 74 C8
Hopsford Warwks 59 P8
Hopstone Shrops 57 P6
Hopton Derbys 71 P4
Hopton Shrops 69 L10
Hopton Staffs 70 G9
Hopton Suffk 64 D6
Hopton Cangeford Shrops 57 J8
Hopton Castle Shrops 56 F9
Hoptonheath Shrops 56 F9
Hopton on Sea Norfk 65 Q2
Hopton Wafers Shrops 57 L9
Hopwas Staffs 59 J4
Hopwood Rochdl 89 P9
Hopwood Worcs 58 F9
Hopwood Park Services Worcs 58 F10
Horam E Susx 25 N7
Horbling Lincs 74 B3
Horbury Wakefd 90 H7
Horcott Gloucs 33 N4
Horden Dur 104 D2
Horderley Shrops 56 G7
Hordle Hants 13 N5
Hordley Shrops 69 L8
Horeb Carmth 28 E3
Horeb Cerdgn 42 G6
Horfield Bristl 31 Q9
Horham Suffk 65 J7
Horkesley Heath Essex 52 G6
Horkstow N Linc 92 G7
Horley Oxon 48 D6
Horley Surrey 24 G2
Hornblotton Green Somset 19 Q8
Hornby Lancs 95 M7
Hornby N York 97 K2
Hornby N York 104 C9
Horncastle Lincs 87 J7
Hornchurch Gt Lon 37 M3
Horncliffe Nthumb 129 N10
Horndean Border 129 N10
Horndean Hants 15 K4
Horndon Devon 8 D8
Horndon on the Hill Thurr 37 Q4
Horne Surrey 24 H2
Horner Somset 18 B5
Horne Row Essex 52 C11
Horners Green Suffk 52 G3
Horney Common E Susx 25 L5
Horn Hill Bucks 36 B2
Horning Norfk 77 L8
Horninghold Leics 73 L11
Horninglow Staffs 71 N9
Horningsea Cambs 62 G8
Horningsham Wilts 20 F6
Horningtoft Norfk 76 C7
Horningtops Cnwll 5 M9
Hornsbury Somset 10 G2
Hornsby Cumb 111 K10
Hornsbygate Cumb 111 K10
Horns Cross Devon 16 F7
Horns Cross E Susx 26 D7
Hornsea E R Yk 99 P11
Hornsey Gt Lon 36 H3
Horn's Green Gt Lon 37 L9
Horn Street Kent 27 L4
Hornton Oxon 48 C5
Horpit Swindn 33 P8
Horra Shet 169 r4
Horrabridge Devon 6 E5
Horringer Suffk 64 A9
Horringford IoW 14 F9
Horrocks Fold Bolton 89 L8
Horrocksford Lancs 89 M2
Horsacott Devon 17 J5
Horsebridge Devon 5 Q6
Horsebridge E Susx 25 N8
Horsebridge Hants 22 B8
Horsebridge Shrops 56 F3
Horsebridge Staffs 70 H4
Horsebrook Staffs 58 C2
Horsecastle N Som 31 M11
Horsedown Cnwll 2 G7
Horsehay Wrekin 57 M3
Horseheath Cambs 63 K11
Horsehouse N York 96 F4
Horsell Surrey 23 Q3
Horseman's Green Wrexhm 69 M6
Horsenden Bucks 35 L4
Horsey Norfk 77 P7
Horsey Somset 19 K7
Horsey Corner Norfk 77 P7
Horsford Norfk 76 H8
Horsforth Leeds 90 G3
Horsham W Susx 24 E4
Horsham Worcs 46 D3
Horsham St Faith Norfk 77 J8
Horsington Lincs 86 G7
Horsington Somset 20 D10
Horsley Derbys 72 B2
Horsley Gloucs 32 F5
Horsley Nthumb 112 G7
Horsley Nthumb 118 F11
Horsley Cross Essex 53 K6
Horsleycross Street Essex 53 K6
Horsley-Gate Derbys 84 D5
Horsleyhill Border 117 Q7
Horsley's Green Bucks 35 L6
Horsley Woodhouse Derbys 72 B2
Horsmonden Kent 26 B3
Horspath Oxon 34 G3
Horstead Norfk 77 K8
Horsted Keynes W Susx 25 J5
Horton Bucks 49 P11
Horton Dorset 12 H3
Horton Lancs 96 C10
Horton Nhants 49 M4
Horton S Glos 32 E8
Horton Shrops 69 N9
Horton Somset 10 G2
Horton Staffs 70 G3
Horton Surrey 36 E8
Horton Swans 28 E7
Horton W & M 36 B5
Horton Wilts 21 K2
Horton Wrekin 57 M2
Horton Cross Somset 19 K11
Horton-cum-Studley Oxon 34 G2
Horton Green Ches W 69 N5
Horton Heath Hants 22 E11
Horton-in-Ribblesdale N York 96 B6
Horton Kirby Kent 37 N7
Horwich Bolton 89 J8
Horwich End Derbys 83 M8
Horwood Devon 17 J6
Hoscar Lancs 88 F8
Hoscote Border 117 M8
Hose Leics 73 J5
Hosey Hill Kent 37 L10
Hosh P & K 133 P3
Hoswick Shet 169 r11
Hotham E R Yk 92 E4
Hothfield Kent 26 G3
Hoton Leics 72 F6
Hott Nthumb 111 Q3
Hough Ches E 70 C4
Hough Ches E 83 J9
Hougham Lincs 73 M2
Hough End Leeds 90 G4
Hough Green Halton 81 P7
Hough-on-the-Hill Lincs 86 B11
Houghton Cambs 62 C6
Houghton Cumb 110 H9
Houghton Hants 22 B8
Houghton Nthumb 112 H7
Houghton Pembks 41 J9
Houghton W Susx 24 B8
Houghton Conquest C Beds 50 B2
Houghton Gate Dur 113 M10
Houghton Green E Susx 26 F7
Houghton Green Warrtn 82 D6
Houghton le Side Darltn 103 P6
Houghton-le-Spring Sundld 113 M11
Houghton on the Hill Leics 72 H10
Houghton Regis C Beds 50 B6
Houghton St Giles Norfk 76 C4
Hound Green Hants 23 K3
Houndslow Border 128 G10
Houndsmoor Somset 18 F9
Houndwood Border 129 L7
Hounslow Gt Lon 36 D5
Househill Highld 156 F6
Houses Hill Kirk 90 F7
Housieside Abers 151 M2
Houston Rens 125 L4
Houstry Highld 167 L10
Houton Ork 169 c6
Hove Br & H 24 G10
Hove Edge Calder 90 E6
Hoveringham Notts 85 L11
Hoveton Norfk 77 L8
Hovingham N York 98 D5
Howbrook Barns 91 J11
How Caple Herefs 46 B8
Howden E R Yk 92 B5
Howden-le-Wear Dur 103 N4
Howe Highld 167 P4
Howe IoM 80 a8
Howe N York 97 N4
Howe Norfk 65 K2
Howe Bridge Wigan 82 E4
Howe Green Essex 52 B11
Howegreen Essex 52 D11
Howell Lincs 86 F11
How End C Beds 50 B2
Howe of Teuchar Abers 159 J8
Howes D & G 110 C7
Howe Street Essex 51 Q4
Howe Street Essex 51 Q8
Howey Powys 44 F3
Howgate Cumb 100 C6
Howgate Mdloth 127 N6
Howgill Lancs 96 B11
Howick Nthumb 119 Q7
Howle Wrekin 70 B10
Howle Hill Herefs 46 B10
Howlett End Essex 51 N4
Howley Somset 10 F3
How Mill Cumb 111 K9
Howmore W Isls 168 c14
Hownam Border 118 E7
Howrigg Cumb 110 F11
Howsham N Linc 92 H10
Howsham N York 98 E8
Howtel Nthumb 118 G4
Howt Green Kent 38 E8
Howton Herefs 45 N9
Howtown Cumb 101 M7
How Wood Herts 50 D10
Howwood Rens 125 K5
Hoxa Ork 169 d7
Hoxne Suffk 64 H6
Hoy Ork 169 b7
Hoylake Wirral 81 J7
Hoyland Barns 91 K10
Hoyland Common Barns 91 K10
Hoylandswaine Barns 90 H10
Hoyle W Susx 23 P11
Hoyle Mill Barns 91 K9
Hubberholme N York 96 D5
Hubberston Pembks 40 G9
Hubbert's Bridge Lincs 74 E2
Huby N York 97 L11
Huby N York 98 B7
Huccaby Devon 6 H4
Hucclecote Gloucs 46 G11
Hucking Kent 38 D10
Hucknall Notts 84 H11
Huddersfield Kirk 90 E7
Huddington Worcs 46 H3
Hudnall Herts 50 B8
Hudswell N York 103 M10
Huggate E R Yk 98 H9
Hugglescote Leics 72 C8
Hughenden Valley Bucks 35 N5
Hughley Shrops 57 K5
Hugh Town IoS 2 c2
Huish Devon 17 J9
Huish Wilts 21 M2
Huish Champflower Somset 18 E9
Huish Episcopi Somset 19 M9
Hùisinis W Isls 168 e6
Huisinish W Isls 168 e6
Hulcote C Beds 49 P7
Hulcote Nhants 49 K5
Hulcott Bucks 49 N11
Hulham Devon 9 P8
Hulland Derbys 71 N5
Hulland Ward Derbys 71 P5
Hullavington Wilts 32 G8
Hull Bridge E R Yk 93 J2
Hullbridge Essex 38 D2
Hull, Kingston upon C KuH 93 J5
Hulme Manch 82 H5
Hulme Staffs 70 G5
Hulme Warrtn 82 D6
Hulme End Staffs 71 L3
Hulme Walfield Ches E 82 H11
Hulse Heath Ches E 82 F8
Hulton Lane Ends Bolton 89 K9
Hulverstone IoW 14 C10
Hulver Street Norfk 76 C9
Hulver Street Suffk 65 P4
Humber Devon 9 L9
Humber Herefs 45 Q3
Humber Bridge N Linc 92 H6
Humberside Airport N Linc 93 J8
Humberston NE Lin 93 P9
Humberstone C Leic 72 G9
Humberton N York 97 P7
Humbie E Loth 128 D7
Humbleton E R Yk 93 M4
Humbleton Nthumb 119 J5
Humby Lincs 73 Q4
Hume Border 118 D2
Humshaugh Nthumb 112 D6
Huna Highld 167 Q2
Huncoat Lancs 89 M4
Huncote Leics 72 E11
Hundalee Border 118 B7
Hundall Derbys 84 E5
Hunderthwaite Dur 103 J6
Hundleby Lincs 87 L7
Hundle Houses Lincs 86 H10
Hundleton Pembks 41 J10
Hundon Suffk 63 M11
Hundred End Lancs 88 E6
Hundred House Powys 44 G4
Hungarton Leics 72 H9
Hungerford Hants 13 L2
Hungerford Somset 18 D6
Hungerford W Berk 34 B11
Hungerford Newtown W Berk 34 C10
Hunger Hill Bolton 89 K9
Hunger Hill Lancs 88 G8
Hungerstone Herefs 45 N7
Hungerton Lincs 73 M5
Hungryhatton Shrops 70 B9
Hunmanby N York 99 M5
Hunningham Warwks 59 N11
Hunnington Worcs 58 E8
Hunsbury Hill Nhants 60 F9
Hunsdon Herts 51 K8
Hunsingore N York 97 P10
Hunslet Leeds 91 J4
Hunsonby Cumb 101 Q3
Hunstanton Norfk 75 N2
Hunstanworth Dur 112 D11
Hunsterson Ches E 70 B5
Hunston Suffk 64 D8
Hunston W Susx 15 N6
Hunston Green Suffk 64 D8
Hunstrete BaNES 20 B2
Hunsworth Kirk 90 F5
Hunt End Worcs 47 K2
Hunter's Inn Devon 17 M2
Hunter's Quay Ag & B 124 F2
Huntham Somset 19 K9
Hunthill Lodge Angus 142 H3
Huntingdon Cambs 62 B6
Huntingfield Suffk 65 L7
Huntingford Dorset 20 F9
Huntington C York 98 C9
Huntington Ches W 69 M2
Huntington E Loth 128 D5
Huntington Herefs 45 K4
Huntington Herefs 45 P6
Huntington Staffs 58 E2
Huntingtowerfield P & K 134 D2
Huntley Gloucs 46 D11
Huntly Abers 158 D10
Hunton Hants 22 E6
Hunton Kent 26 B2
Hunton N York 97 J2
Hunton Bridge Herts 50 C10
Hunt's Corner Norfk 64 F4
Huntscott Somset 18 B6
Hunt's Cross Lpool 81 N7
Hunts Green Bucks 35 N4
Hunts Green Warwks 59 J5
Huntsham Devon 18 D10
Huntshaw Devon 17 J7
Huntshaw Cross Devon 17 J7
Huntspill Somset 19 K5
Huntstile Somset 19 J8
Huntworth Somset 19 K8
Hunwick Dur 103 N4
Hunworth Norfk 76 F4
Hurcott Somset 19 L11
Hurdcott Wilts 21 N8
Hurdsfield Ches E 83 K10
Hurley W & M 35 M8
Hurley Warwks 59 K5
Hurley Bottom W & M 35 M8
Hurley Common Warwks 59 K5
Hurlford E Ayrs 125 M10
Hurlston Green Lancs 88 D8
Hurn BCP 13 K5
Hurn's End Lincs 87 M11
Hursley Hants 22 D9
Hurst Dorset 12 C6
Hurst N York 103 K10
Hurst Somset 19 N11
Hurst Wokham 35 L10
Hurstbourne Priors Hants 22 D5
Hurstbourne Tarrant Hants 22 C4
Hurst Green E Susx 26 B6
Hurst Green Essex 53 J8
Hurst Green Lancs 89 K3
Hurst Green Surrey 37 K10
Hurst Hill Dudley 58 D6
Hurstley Herefs 45 M5
Hurstpierpoint W Susx 24 G7
Hurst Wickham W Susx 24 G7
Hurstwood Lancs 89 P4
Hurtiso Ork 169 e6
Hurtmore Surrey 23 P5
Hurworth Burn Dur 104 D4
Hurworth-on-Tees Darltn 104 B9
Hurworth Place Darltn 103 Q9
Hury Dur 103 J7
Husbands Bosworth Leics 60 D4
Husborne Crawley C Beds 49 Q7
Husthwaite N York 97 R6
Hutcherleigh Devon 7 K8
Hut Green N York 91 P6
Huthwaite Notts 84 G9
Huttoft Lincs 87 P5
Hutton Border 129 N9
Hutton Cumb 101 M5
Hutton E R Yk 99 L10
Hutton Essex 37 P2
Hutton Lancs 88 F5
Hutton N Som 19 L3
Hutton Bonville N York 104 B10
Hutton Buscel N York 99 K4
Hutton Conyers N York 97 M6
Hutton Cranswick E R Yk 99 L10
Hutton End Cumb 101 N3
Hutton Hang N York 97 J3
Hutton Henry Dur 104 D3
Hutton-le-Hole N York 98 E2
Hutton Lowcross R & Cl 104 G8
Hutton Magna Dur 103 M8
Hutton Mulgrave N York 105 M9
Hutton Roof Cumb 95 M5
Hutton Roof Cumb 101 L4
Hutton Rudby N York 104 E9
Hutton Sessay N York 97 Q5
Hutton Wandesley N York 97 R10
Huxham Devon 9 M5
Huxham Green Somset 19 Q7
Huxley Ches W 69 P2
Huyton Knows 81 N6
Hycemoor Cumb 94 B3
Hyde Gloucs 32 G4
Hyde Hants 13 L2
Hyde Tamesd 83 K6
Hyde Heath Bucks 35 P4
Hyde Lea Staffs 70 G11
Hydestile Surrey 23 Q6
Hykeham Moor Lincs 86 B7
Hylands House & Park Essex 51 Q10
Hyndford Bridge S Lans 116 C2
Hynish Ag & B 136 B8
Hyssington Powys 56 E6
Hystfield Gloucs 32 C5
Hythe Essex 52 H6
Hythe Hants 14 D5
Hythe Kent 27 L5
Hythe Somset 19 M4
Hythe End W & M 36 B6
Hyton Cumb 94 B3

I

Ibberton Dorset 12 C3
Ible Derbys 84 B9
Ibsley Hants 13 L3
Ibstock Leics 72 C9
Ibstone Bucks 35 L6
Ibthorpe Hants 22 C4
Iburndale N York 105 N9
Ibworth Hants 22 G4
Icelton N Som 31 L11
Ichrachan Ag & B 139 J11
Ickburgh Norfk 75 R11
Ickenham Gt Lon 36 C3
Ickford Bucks 34 H3
Ickham Kent 39 M10
Ickleford Herts 50 E4
Icklesham E Susx 26 E8
Ickleton Cambs 51 L2
Icklingham Suffk 63 N6
Ickornshaw N York 90 B2
Ickwell Green C Beds 61 Q11
Icomb Gloucs 47 P10
Idbury Oxon 47 P11
Iddesleigh Devon 17 K10
Ide Devon 9 L6
Ideford Devon 9 L9
Ide Hill Kent 37 L10
Iden E Susx 26 F7
Iden Green Kent 26 B4
Iden Green Kent 26 D5
Idle C Brad 90 F3
Idless Cnwll 3 L4
Idlicote Warwks 47 Q6
Idmiston Wilts 21 N7
Idole Carmth 42 H11
Idridgehay Derbys 71 P5
Idrigill Highld 152 F5
Idstone Oxon 33 Q8
Iffley Oxon 34 F4
Ifield W Susx 24 G3
Ifold W Susx 24 B4
Iford BCP 13 K6
Iford E Susx 25 K9
Ifton Mons 31 N7
Ifton Heath Shrops 69 K7
Ightfield Shrops 69 Q7
Ightham Kent 37 N9
Iken Suffk 65 N10
Ilam Staffs 71 L4
Ilchester Somset 19 P10
Ilderton Nthumb 119 K6
Ilford Gt Lon 37 K3
Ilford Somset 19 L11
Ilfracombe Devon 17 J2
Ilkeston Derbys 72 D2
Ilketshall St Andrew Suffk 65 M4
Ilketshall St John Suffk 65 M4
Ilketshall St Lawrence Suffk 65 M5
Ilketshall St Margaret Suffk 65 L4
Ilkley C Brad 96 H11
Illand Cnwll 5 M6
Illey Dudley 58 E8
Illidge Green Ches E 70 D2
Illingworth Calder 90 D5
Illogan Cnwll 2 H5
Illston on the Hill Leics 73 J11
Ilmer Bucks 35 L3
Ilmington Warwks 47 P6
Ilminster Somset 10 H2
Ilsington Devon 9 J9
Ilsington Dorset 12 C6
Ilston Swans 28 G6
Ilton N York 97 J5
Ilton Somset 19 L11
Imachar N Ayrs 120 G3
Immingham NE Lin 93 L8
Immingham Dock NE Lin 93 L7
Impington Cambs 62 F8
Ince Ches W 81 P9
Ince Blundell Sefton 81 L4
Ince-in-Makerfield Wigan 82 C4
Inchbae Lodge Hotel Highld 155 M4
Inchbare Angus 143 L4
Inchberry Moray 157 Q6
Incheril Highld 154 D5
Inchinnan Rens 125 M4
Inchlaggan Highld 146 F7
Inchmichael P & K 134 G2
Inchmore Highld 155 Q8
Inchnadamph Highld 161 M2
Inchture P & K 134 H2
Inchvuilt Highld 154 H10
Inchyra P & K 134 F3
Indian Queens Cnwll 4 E10
Ingatestone Essex 51 P11
Ingbirchworth Barns 90 G9
Ingerthorpe N York 97 L7
Ingestre Staffs 70 H10
Ingham Lincs 86 B4
Ingham Norfk 77 M6
Ingham Suffk 64 B7
Ingham Corner Norfk 77 M6
Ingleborough Norfk 75 J7
Ingleby Derbys 72 A5
Ingleby Arncliffe N York 104 D10
Ingleby Barwick S on T 104 D8
Ingleby Cross N York 104 E10
Ingleby Greenhow N York 104 G9
Ingleigh Green Devon 8 F3
Inglesbatch BaNES 20 D2
Inglesham Swindn 33 P5
Ingleston D & G 109 L7
Ingleton Dur 103 N6
Ingleton N York 95 P6
Inglewhite Lancs 88 G3
Ingmanthorpe N York 97 P10
Ingoe Nthumb 112 F6
Ingol Lancs 88 G4
Ingoldisthorpe Norfk 75 N4
Ingoldmells Lincs 87 Q7
Ingoldsby Lincs 73 Q5
Ingram Nthumb 119 K7
Ingrave Essex 37 P2
Ingrow C Brad 90 D3
Ings Cumb 101 M11
Ingst S Glos 31 Q7
Ingthorpe Rutlnd 73 P9
Ingworth Norfk 76 H6
Inkberrow Worcs 47 K3
Inkerman Dur 103 M3
Inkhorn Abers 159 M10
Inkpen W Berk 22 C2
Inkstack Highld 167 N2
Inmarsh Wilts 20 H2
Innellan Ag & B 124 F3
Innerleithen Border 117 L3
Innerleven Fife 135 K7
Innermessan D & G 106 E5
Innerwick E Loth 129 J5
Innesmill Moray 157 P5
Innsworth Gloucs 46 G10
Insch Abers 150 G2
Insh Highld 148 E7
Inskip Lancs 88 F3
Inskip Moss Side Lancs 88 F3
Instow Devon 16 H5
Insworke Cnwll 6 C8
Intake Sheff 84 E4
Inver Abers 149 N9
Inver Highld 163 K10
Inver P & K 141 P9
Inverailort Highld 145 N11
Inveralligin Highld 153 Q6
Inverallochy Abers 159 P4
Inveran Highld 162 D7
Inveraray Ag & B 131 M6
Inverarish Highld 153 K10
Inverarity Angus 142 H9
Inverarnan Stirlg 132 C4

Inverasdale Highld 160 C10
Inverbeg Ag & B 132 C8
Inverbervie Abers 143 Q3
Inverboyndie Abers 158 G5
Invercreran House Hotel Ag & B 139 J8
Inverdruie Highld 148 F5
Inveresk E Loth 127 Q3
Inveresragan Ag & B 138 H10
Inverey Abers 149 K10
Inverfarigaig Highld 147 N3
Inverfolla Ag & B 138 H9
Invergarry Highld 147 J7
Invergeldie P & K 133 L2
Invergloy Highld 146 G10
Invergordon Highld 156 C4
Invergowrie P & K 142 E11
Inverguseran Highld 145 M6
Inverhadden P & K 140 G6
Inverie Highld 145 N7
Inverinan Ag & B 131 K4
Inverinate Highld 145 R3
Inverkeilor Angus 143 M8
Inverkeithing Fife 134 E11
Inverkeithny Abers 158 F8
Inverkip Inver 124 G3
Inverkirkaig Highld 160 H3
Inverlael Highld 161 K9
Inverlair Highld 139 Q2
Inverliever Lodge Ag & B 130 H6
Inverlochy Ag & B 131 P2
Invermark Angus 150 C11
Invermoriston Highld 147 L4
Invernaver Highld 166 B4
Inverneill Ag & B 123 P3
Inverness Highld 156 B8
Inverness Airport Highld 156 D7
Invernettie Abers 159 R9
Invernoaden Ag & B 131 N8
Inveroran Hotel Ag & B 139 P9
Inverquharity Angus 142 G6
Inverquhomery Abers 159 P8
Inverroy Highld 146 H11
Inversanda Highld 138 G6
Invershiel Highld 146 A4
Invershin Highld 162 D7
Invershore Highld 167 M9
Inversnaid Hotel Stirlg 132 C6
Inverugie Abers 159 Q8
Inveruglas Ag & B 132 C6
Inveruglass Highld 148 E7
Inverurie Abers 151 K3
Inwardleigh Devon 8 E5
Inworth Essex 52 E8
Iochdar W Isls 168 c13
Iona Ag & B 136 H10
Iping W Susx 23 N10
iPort Logistics Park Donc 91 Q11
Ipplepen Devon 7 L5
Ipsden Oxon 34 H7
Ipstones Staffs 71 J5
Ipswich Suffk 53 L3
Irby Wirral 81 K8
Irby in the Marsh Lincs 87 N8
Irby upon Humber NE Lin 93 L10
Irchester Nhants 61 K7
Ireby Cumb 100 H3
Ireby Lancs 95 P5
Ireland C Beds 50 D2
Ireleth Cumb 94 E5
Ireshopeburn Dur 102 G3
Ireton Wood Derbys 71 P5
Irlam Salfd 82 F6
Irnham Lincs 73 Q5
Iron Acton S Glos 32 C8
Iron Bridge Cambs 75 J11
Ironbridge Wrekin 57 M4
Ironbridge Gorge Wrekin 57 M4
Iron Cross Warwks 47 L4
Ironmacannie D & G 108 E5
Irons Bottom Surrey 36 F11
Ironville Derbys 84 F10
Irstead Norfk 77 M7
Irthington Cumb 111 J8
Irthlingborough Nhants 61 K6
Irton N York 99 L4
Irvine N Ayrs 125 J10
Isauld Highld 166 G3
Isbister Shet 169 q4
Isbister Shet 169 s7
Isfield E Susx 25 K7
Isham Nhants 61 J6
Isington Hants 23 L6
Islandpool Worcs 58 C8
Islay Ag & B 122 E4
Islay Airport Ag & B 122 D9
Isle Abbotts Somset 19 L10
Isle Brewers Somset 19 L10
Isleham Cambs 63 K6
Isle of Dogs Gt Lon 37 J5
Isle of Grain Medway 38 E6
Isle of Lewis W Isls 168 i4
Isle of Man IoM 80 e4
Isle of Man Ronaldsway Airport IoM 80 c8
Isle of Mull Ag & B 137 Q8
Isle of Purbeck Dorset 12 H8
Isle of Sheppey Kent 38 G8
Isle of Skye Highld 152 G10
Isle of Thanet Kent 39 P8
Isle of Walney Cumb 94 D7
Isle of Whithorn D & G 107 N10
Isle of Wight IoW 14 F9
Isleornsay Highld 145 M5
Isles of Scilly IoS 2 c2
Isles of Scilly St Mary's Airport IoS 2 c2
Islesteps D & G 109 L6
Islet Village Guern 10 c1
Isleworth Gt Lon 36 E5
Isley Walton Leics 72 C6
Islibhig W Isls 168 f5
Islington Gt Lon 36 H4
Islip Nhants 61 L5
Islip Oxon 34 F2
Islivig W Isls 168 f5
Isombridge Wrekin 57 L2
Istead Rise Kent 37 P6
Itchen Abbas Hants 22 F8
Itchen Stoke Hants 22 G8
Itchingfield W Susx 24 D5
Itchington S Glos 32 C7
Itteringham Norfk 76 G5
Itton Devon 8 G5
Itton Mons 31 N5
Itton Common Mons 31 N5
Ivegill Cumb 101 M2
Ivelet N York 102 H11
Iver Bucks 36 B4
Iver Heath Bucks 36 B4
Iveston Dur 112 H10
Ivinghoe Bucks 49 P11
Ivinghoe Aston Bucks 49 Q11
Ivington Herefs 45 P3
Ivington Green Herefs 45 P3
Ivybridge Devon 6 G7
Ivychurch Kent 26 H6
Ivy Cross Dorset 20 G10
Ivy Hatch Kent 37 N10
Ivy Todd Norfk 76 B10
Iwade Kent 38 F8
Iwerne Courtney Dorset 12 E2
Iwerne Minster Dorset 12 E2
Ixworth Suffk 64 C7
Ixworth Thorpe Suffk 64 C7

J

Jack Green Lancs 88 H5
Jack Hill N York 97 J10
Jack-in-the-Green Devon 9 P5
Jack's Bush Hants 21 Q7
Jacksdale Notts 84 F10
Jackson Bridge Kirk 90 F9
Jackton S Lans 125 P7
Jacobstow Cnwll 5 K2
Jacobstowe Devon 8 E4
Jacobs Well Surrey 23 Q4
Jameston Pembks 41 L11
Jamestown Highld 155 N6
Jamestown W Duns 132 D11
Janetstown Highld 167 L10
Janetstown Highld 167 Q6
Jardine Hall D & G 109 P3
Jarrow S Tyne 113 M8
Jarvis Brook E Susx 25 M5
Jasper's Green Essex 52 B6
Jawcraig Falk 126 E2
Jaywick Essex 53 L9
Jealott's Hill Br For 35 N10
Jeater Houses N York 97 P2
Jedburgh Border 118 B6
Jeffreyston Pembks 41 L9
Jemimaville Highld 156 C4
Jerbourg Guern 10 c2
Jersey Jersey 11 b1
Jersey Airport Jersey 11 a2
Jersey Marine Neath 29 K6
Jerusalem Lincs 86 B6
Jesmond N u Ty 113 L7
Jevington E Susx 25 N10
Jingle Street Mons 31 N2
Jockey End Herts 50 B8
Jodrell Bank Ches E 82 G10
Johnby Cumb 101 M4
John Lennon Airport Lpool 81 N8
John o' Groats Highld 167 Q2
Johns Cross E Susx 26 B7
Johnshaven Abers 143 P4
Johnson Street Norfk 77 M8
Johnston Pembks 40 H8
Johnstone D & G 117 J10
Johnstone Rens 125 L5
Johnstonebridge D & G 109 P2
Johnstown Carmth 42 G11
Johnstown Wrexhm 69 K5
Joppa C Edin 127 Q3
Joppa Cerdgn 54 D11
Joppa S Ayrs 114 H4
Jordans Bucks 35 Q6
Jordanston Pembks 40 H4
Jordanthorpe Sheff 84 E4
Joyden's Wood Kent 37 M6
Jubilee Corner Kent 26 D2
Jump Barns 91 K10
Jumper's Town E Susx 25 L4
Juniper Nthumb 112 D9
Juniper Green C Edin 127 M4
Jura Ag & B 122 H3
Jurassic Coast Devon 10 G7
Jurby IoM 80 e2
Jurston Devon 8 G8

K

Kaber Cumb 102 E8
Kaimend S Lans 126 H8
Kames Ag & B 124 B3
Kames E Ayrs 115 N2
Kea Cnwll 3 L5
Keadby N Linc 92 D8
Keal Cotes Lincs 87 L8
Kearby Town End N York 97 M11
Kearsley Bolton 82 G4
Kearsley Nthumb 112 F5
Kearsney Kent 27 N3
Kearstwick Cumb 95 N5
Kearton N York 103 J11
Keasden N York 95 Q7
Keaton Devon 6 G8
Keckwick Halton 82 C8
Keddington Lincs 87 K3
Keddington Corner Lincs 87 L3
Kedington Suffk 63 M11
Kedleston Derbys 71 Q6
Keelby Lincs 93 L8
Keele Staffs 70 E5
Keele Services Staffs 70 E6
Keele University Staffs 70 E5
Keeley Green Bed 61 M11
Keelham C Brad 90 D4
Keeres Green Essex 51 N8
Keeston Pembks 40 H7
Keevil Wilts 20 H3
Kegworth Leics 72 D5
Kehelland Cnwll 2 G5
Keig Abers 150 G4
Keighley C Brad 90 D2
Keilarsbrae Clacks 133 P9
Keillour P & K 134 B2
Keiloch Abers 149 M9
Keils Ag & B 122 H6
Keinton Mandeville Somset 19 P8
Keir Mill D & G 109 J2
Keirsleywell Row Nthumb 111 Q10
Keisby Lincs 73 Q5
Keisley Cumb 102 D6
Keiss Highld 167 P4
Keith Moray 158 B7
Keithick P & K 142 C10
Keithock Angus 143 L5
Keithtown Highld 155 P6
Kelbrook Lancs 89 Q2
Kelby Lincs 73 Q2
Keld Cumb 101 Q8
Keld N York 102 G10
Keld Head N York 98 F4
Keldholme N York 98 E3
Kelfield N Linc 92 D10
Kelfield N York 91 P3
Kelham Notts 85 N9
Kelhead D & G 109 P7
Kellacott Devon 5 Q4
Kellamergh Lancs 88 E5
Kellas Angus 142 H10
Kellas Moray 157 M7
Kellaton Devon 7 L11
Kelleth Cumb 102 C9
Kelling Norfk 76 F3
Kellington N York 91 P6
Kelloe Dur 104 B3
Kelloholm D & G 115 P5
Kells Cumb 100 C7
Kelly Devon 5 P5
Kelly Bray Cnwll 5 P7
Kelmarsh Nhants 60 F5
Kelmscott Oxon 33 P5
Kelsale Suffk 65 M8
Kelsall Ches W 81 Q11
Kelshall Herts 50 H3
Kelsick Cumb 110 C10
Kelso Border 118 D4
Kelstedge Derbys 84 D8
Kelstern Lincs 86 H3
Kelsterton Flints 81 K10
Kelston BaNES 32 D11
Keltneyburn P & K 141 J8
Kelton D & G 109 L6
Kelty Fife 134 E9
Kelvedon Essex 52 E8
Kelvedon Hatch Essex 51 N11
Kelynack Cnwll 2 B8
Kemacott Devon 17 M2
Kemback Fife 135 L5
Kemberton Shrops 57 N4
Kemble Gloucs 33 J5
Kemble Wick Gloucs 33 J5
Kemerton Worcs 47 J7
Kemeys Commander Mons 31 K4
Kemnay Abers 151 J4
Kempe's Corner Kent 26 H2
Kempley Gloucs 46 C9
Kempley Green Gloucs 46 C9
Kempsey Worcs 46 F5
Kempsford Gloucs 33 N5
Kemps Green Warwks 58 H10
Kempshott Hants 22 H4
Kempston Bed 61 M11
Kempston Hardwick Bed 50 B2
Kempton Shrops 56 F8
Kemp Town Br & H 24 H10
Kemsing Kent 37 N9
Kemsley Kent 38 F8
Kemsley Street Kent 38 D9
Kenardington Kent 26 G5
Kenchester Herefs 45 N6
Kencot Oxon 33 Q4
Kendal Cumb 95 L2
Kenderchurch Herefs 45 N9
Kendleshire S Glos 32 C9
Kenfig Brdgnd 29 M8
Kenfig Hill Brdgnd 29 M8
Kenilworth Warwks 59 L10
Kenley Gt Lon 36 H8
Kenley Shrops 57 K4
Kenmore Highld 153 P6
Kenmore P & K 141 J8
Kenn Devon 9 M7
Kenn N Som 31 M11
Kennacraig Ag & B 123 P7
Kennall Vale Cnwll 3 J6
Kennards House Cnwll 5 M5
Kenneggy Cnwll 2 F8
Kennerleigh Devon 9 K3
Kennet Clacks 133 Q9
Kennethmont Abers 150 E2
Kennett Cambs 63 L7
Kennford Devon 9 M7
Kenninghall Norfk 64 E4
Kennington Kent 26 H2
Kennington Oxon 34 F4
Kennoway Fife 135 K7
Kenny Somset 19 K11
Kenny Hill Suffk 63 L5
Kennythorpe N York 98 F7
Kenovay Ag & B 136 B6
Kensaleyre Highld 152 G7
Kensington Gt Lon 36 G5
Kensington Palace Gt Lon 36 G4
Kensworth Common C Beds 50 B7
Kentallen Highld 139 J6
Kentchurch Herefs 45 N9
Kentford Suffk 63 M7
Kent Green Ches E 70 E3
Kentisbeare Devon 9 Q3
Kentisbury Devon 17 L3
Kentisbury Ford Devon 17 L3
Kentish Town Gt Lon 36 G4
Kentmere Cumb 101 N10
Kenton Devon 9 N8
Kenton Gt Lon 36 E3
Kenton N u Ty 113 K7
Kenton Suffk 64 H8
Kenton Bankfoot N u Ty 113 K7
Kentra Highld 138 B4
Kents Bank Cumb 94 H5
Kent's Green Gloucs 46 D10
Kent's Oak Hants 22 B10
Kent Street E Susx 26 C8
Kent Street Kent 37 Q10
Kenwick Shrops 69 M8
Kenwyn Cnwll 3 L4
Kenyon Warrtn 82 D5
Keoldale Highld 165 J3
Keppoch Highld 145 Q3
Kepwick N York 97 Q2
Keresley Covtry 59 M8
Kermincham Ches E 82 H11
Kernborough Devon 7 K10
Kerne Bridge Herefs 46 A11
Kerrera Ag & B 130 G2
Kerridge Ches E 83 K9
Kerridge-end Ches E 83 K9
Kerris Cnwll 2 C8
Kerry Powys 55 Q6
Kerrycroy Ag & B 124 E5
Kersall Notts 85 M8
Kersbrook Devon 9 Q8
Kerscott Devon 17 L6
Kersey Suffk 52 H3
Kersey Tye Suffk 52 G3
Kersey Upland Suffk 52 G3
Kershader W Isls 168 i6
Kershopefoot Cumb 111 J4
Kersoe Worcs 47 J6
Kerswell Devon 10 B3
Kerswell Green Worcs 46 G5
Kerthen Wood Cnwll 2 F7
Kesgrave Suffk 53 M2
Kessingland Suffk 65 Q4
Kessingland Beach Suffk 65 Q4
Kestle Cnwll 3 P4
Kestle Mill Cnwll 4 C10
Keston Gt Lon 37 K8
Keswick Cumb 101 J6
Keswick Norfk 77 J11
Ketsby Lincs 87 L5
Kettering Nhants 61 J5
Ketteringham Norfk 76 H11
Kettins P & K 142 C10
Kettlebaston Suffk 64 D11
Kettlebridge Fife 135 J6
Kettlebrook Staffs 59 K4
Kettleburgh Suffk 65 K9
Kettle Green Herts 51 K7
Kettleholm D & G 109 P5
Kettleness N York 105 M7
Kettleshulme Ches E 83 L9
Kettlesing N York 97 K9
Kettlesing Bottom N York 97 K9
Kettlestone Norfk 76 D5
Kettlethorpe Lincs 85 P5
Kettletoft Ork 169 f3
Kettlewell N York 96 E6
Ketton Rutlnd 73 P10
Kew Gt Lon 36 E5
Kew Royal Botanic Gardens Gt Lon 36 E5
Kewstoke N Som 19 K2
Kexbrough Barns 91 J9
Kexby C York 98 E10
Kexby Lincs 85 Q3
Key Green Ches E 70 F2
Key Green N York 105 M10
Keyham Leics 72 H9
Keyhaven Hants 13 P6
Keyingham E R Yk 93 M5
Keymer W Susx 24 H7
Keynsham BaNES 32 C11
Keysoe Bed 61 N8
Keysoe Row Bed 61 N8
Keyston Cambs 61 M5
Key Street Kent 38 E9
Keyworth Notts 72 G4
Kibbear Somset 18 H10
Kibblesworth Gatesd 113 K9
Kibworth Beauchamp Leics 60 E2
Kibworth Harcourt Leics 60 E2
Kidbrooke Gt Lon 37 K5
Kidburngill Cumb 100 E6
Kiddemore Green Staffs 58 C3
Kidderminster Worcs 58 B9
Kiddington Oxon 48 D10
Kidd's Moor Norfk 76 G11
Kidlington Oxon 34 E2
Kidmore End Oxon 35 J9
Kidsdale D & G 107 M10
Kidsgrove Staffs 70 E4
Kidstones N York 96 E4
Kidwelly Carmth 28 D3
Kiel Crofts Ag & B 138 G10
Kielder Nthumb 111 M2
Kielder Forest 111 M3
Kiells Ag & B 122 F6
Kilbarchan Rens 125 L5
Kilbeg Highld 145 L6
Kilberry Ag & B 123 M7
Kilbirnie N Ayrs 125 J7
Kilbride Ag & B 123 M4
Kilbride Ag & B 124 C4
Kilbuiack Moray 157 K5
Kilburn Derbys 84 E11
Kilburn Gt Lon 36 F4
Kilburn N York 97 R5
Kilby Leics 72 G11
Kilchamaig Ag & B 123 P7
Kilchattan Ag & B 124 E7
Kilchattan Ag & B 136 b2
Kilcheran Ag & B 138 E10
Kilchoan Highld 137 M3
Kilchoman Ag & B 122 B7
Kilchrenan Ag & B 131 L3
Kilconquhar Fife 135 M7
Kilcot Gloucs 46 C9
Kilcoy Highld 155 Q7
Kilcreggan Ag & B 131 Q11
Kildale N York 104 H9
Kildalloig Ag & B 120 E8
Kildary Highld 156 D3
Kildavaig Ag & B 124 B4
Kildavanan Ag & B 124 C4
Kildonan Highld 163 L2
Kildonan N Ayrs 121 K7
Kildonan Lodge Highld 163 L2
Kildonnan Highld 144 G10
Kildrochet House D & G 106 E6
Kildrummy Abers 150 D4
Kildwick N York 96 F11
Kilfinan Ag & B 124 A2
Kilfinnan Highld 146 H8
Kilford Denbgs 80 F11
Kilgetty Pembks 41 M9
Kilgrammie S Ayrs 114 E7
Kilgwrrwg Common Mons 31 N5
Kilham E R Yk 99 M8
Kilham Nthumb 118 G4
Kilkenneth Ag & B 136 A7
Kilkenzie Ag & B 120 C7
Kilkerran Ag & B 120 D8
Kilkhampton Cnwll 16 D9
Killamarsh Derbys 84 G4
Killay Swans 28 H6
Killearn Stirlg 132 G10
Killen Highld 156 B6
Killerby Darltn 103 N7
Killerton Devon 9 N4
Killichonan P & K 140 D6
Killiechonate Highld 146 G11
Killiechronan Ag & B 137 N7
Killiecrankie P & K 141 M5
Killilan Highld 154 B11
Killimster Highld 167 P5
Killin Stirlg 140 E11
Killinghall N York 97 L9
Killington Cumb 95 N3
Killington Devon 17 M2
Killington Lake Services Cumb 95 M2
Killingworth N Tyne 113 L6
Killiow Cnwll 3 L5
Killochyett Border 128 D10
Kilmacolm Inver 125 K3
Kilmahog Stirlg 133 J6
Kilmahumaig Ag & B 130 F9
Kilmaluag Highld 152 G3
Kilmany Fife 135 K3
Kilmarnock E Ayrs 125 L10
Kilmartin Ag & B 130 G8
Kilmaurs E Ayrs 125 L9
Kilmelford Ag & B 130 H5
Kilmersdon Somset 20 C4
Kilmeston Hants 22 G9
Kilmichael Ag & B 120 C7
Kilmichael Glassary Ag & B 130 H9
Kilmichael of Inverlussa Ag & B 130 F10
Kilmington Devon 10 F5
Kilmington Wilts 20 E7
Kilmington Common Wilts 20 E7
Kilmington Street Wilts 20 E7
Kilmorack Highld 155 N9
Kilmore Ag & B 130 H2
Kilmore Highld 145 L6
Kilmory Ag & B 123 M5
Kilmory Highld 137 N2
Kilmory N Ayrs 121 J7
Kilmuir Highld 152 D8
Kilmuir Highld 152 F3
Kilmuir Highld 156 B8
Kilmuir Highld 156 D3
Kilmun Ag & B 131 P11
Kilnave Ag & B 122 C5
Kilncadzow S Lans 126 F8
Kilndown Kent 26 B4
Kiln Green Wokham 35 M9
Kilnhill Cumb 100 H4
Kilnhouses Ches W 82 D11
Kilnhurst Rothm 91 M11
Kilninver Ag & B 130 G3
Kiln Pit Hill Nthumb 112 F9
Kilnsea E R Yk 93 R7
Kilnsey N York 96 E7
Kilnwick E R Yk 99 K11
Kilnwick Percy E R Yk 98 G11
Kiloran Ag & B 136 b2
Kilpatrick N Ayrs 120 H6
Kilpeck Herefs 45 N8
Kilpin E R Yk 92 C5
Kilpin Pike E R Yk 92 C5
Kilrenny Fife 135 P7
Kilsby Nhants 60 C6
Kilspindie P & K 134 G2
Kilstay D & G 106 F10
Kilsyth N Lans 126 C2
Kiltarlity Highld 155 P9
Kilton R & Cl 105 K7
Kilton Somset 18 G6
Kilton Thorpe R & Cl 105 J7
Kilvaxter Highld 152 F4
Kilve Somset 18 F6
Kilvington Notts 73 L2
Kilwinning N Ayrs 125 J9
Kimberley Norfk 76 F11
Kimberley Notts 72 D2
Kimberworth Rothm 84 F2
Kimblesworth Dur 113 L11
Kimble Wick Bucks 35 M3
Kimbolton Cambs 61 P7
Kimbolton Herefs 45 Q2
Kimcote Leics 60 C3
Kimmeridge Dorset 12 F9
Kimmerston Nthumb 119 J3
Kimpton Hants 21 Q5
Kimpton Herts 50 E7
Kimworthy Devon 16 E9
Kinbrace Highld 166 E10
Kinbuck Stirlg 133 M6
Kincaple Fife 135 M4
Kincardine Fife 133 Q10
Kincardine Highld 162 E9
Kincardine Bridge Fife 133 Q10
Kincardine O'Neil Abers 150 F8
Kinclaven P & K 142 B10
Kincorth C Aber 151 N7
Kincorth House Moray 157 J5
Kincraig Highld 148 E6
Kincraigie P & K 141 N8
Kindallachan P & K 141 N8
Kinerarach Ag & B 123 L9
Kineton Gloucs 47 L9
Kineton Warwks 48 B4
Kinfauns P & K 134 F3
Kingarth Ag & B 124 D6
Kingcausie Abers 151 M8
Kingcoed Mons 31 M3
Kingerby Lincs 86 E2
Kingford Devon 16 D10
Kingham Oxon 47 Q10
Kingholm Quay D & G 109 L6
Kinghorn Fife 134 H10
Kinglassie Fife 134 G8
Kingoodie P & K 135 J2
King's Acre Herefs 45 P6
Kingsand Cnwll 6 C8
Kingsash Bucks 35 N3
Kingsbarns Fife 135 P5
Kingsbridge Devon 7 J10
Kingsbridge Somset 18 C7
Kings Bridge Swans 28 G5
King's Bromley Staffs 71 L11
Kingsburgh Highld 152 F6
Kingsbury Gt Lon 36 E3
Kingsbury Warwks 59 K5
Kingsbury Episcopi Somset 19 M10
King's Caple Herefs 45 R9
Kingsclere Hants 22 F3
King's Cliffe Nhants 73 Q11
Kings Clipstone Notts 85 K8
Kingscote Gloucs 32 F5
Kingscott Devon 17 J8
King's Coughton Warwks 47 L3

Kingscross N Ayrs 121 K6
Kingsdon Somset 19 P9
Kingsdown Kent 27 Q2
Kingsdown Swindn 33 N7
Kingsdown Wilts 32 F11
Kingseat Abers 151 N4
Kingseat Fife 134 E9
Kingsey Bucks 35 K3
Kingsfold W Susx 24 E3
Kingsford C Aber 151 M6
Kingsford E Ayrs 125 L8
Kingsford Worcs 57 Q8
Kingsgate Kent 39 Q7
Kings Green Gloucs 46 E8
Kingshall Street Suffk 64 C9
Kingsheanton Devon 17 K4
King's Heath Birm 58 G8
Kings Hill Kent 37 Q9
King's Hill Wsall 58 E5
Kings House Hotel Highld 139 P7
Kingshurst Solhll 59 J7
Kingside Hill Cumb 110 C10
Kingskerswell Devon 7 M5
Kingskettle Fife 135 J6
Kingsland Dorset 11 K5
Kingsland Herefs 45 N2
Kingsland IoA 78 D8
Kings Langley Herts 50 C10
Kingsley Ches W 82 C10
Kingsley Hants 23 L7
Kingsley Staffs 71 J5
Kingsley Green W Susx 23 N8
Kingsley Holt Staffs 71 J5
Kingsley Park Nhants 60 G8
Kingslow Shrops 57 P5
King's Lynn Norfk 75 M6
Kings Meaburn Cumb 102 B6
Kingsmead Hants 14 G4
King's Mills Guern 10 b2
King's Moss St Hel 81 Q4
Kingsmuir Angus 142 H8
Kings Muir Border 117 K3
Kingsmuir Fife 135 N6
Kings Newnham Warwks 59 Q9
King's Newton Derbys 72 B5
Kingsnorth Kent 26 H4
King's Norton Birm 58 G9
King's Norton Leics 72 H10
Kings Nympton Devon 17 M8
King's Pyon Herefs 45 N4
Kings Ripton Cambs 62 C5
King's Somborne Hants 22 C8
King's Stag Dorset 11 Q2
King's Stanley Gloucs 32 F4
King's Sutton Nhants 48 E7
Kingstanding Birm 58 G6
Kingsteignton Devon 7 M4
King Sterndale Derbys 83 N10
Kingsthorne Herefs 45 P8
Kingsthorpe Nhants 60 G8
Kingston Cambs 62 D9
Kingston Cnwll 5 P6
Kingston Devon 6 G9
Kingston Devon 9 Q7
Kingston Dorset 12 C3
Kingston Dorset 12 G9
Kingston E Loth 128 E3
Kingston Hants 13 K4
Kingston IoW 14 E10
Kingston Kent 39 L11
Kingston W Susx 24 C10
Kingston Bagpuize Oxon 34 D5
Kingston Blount Oxon 35 K5
Kingston Deverill Wilts 20 F7
Kingstone Herefs 45 N7
Kingstone Somset 10 H2
Kingstone Staffs 71 K9
Kingstone Winslow Oxon 33 Q7
Kingston Lacy House & Gardens Dorset 12 G4
Kingston Lisle Oxon 34 B7
Kingston near Lewes E Susx 25 J9
Kingston on Soar Notts 72 E5
Kingston on Spey Moray 157 Q4
Kingston Russell Dorset 11 M6
Kingston St Mary Somset 18 H9
Kingston Seymour N Som 31 M11
Kingston Stert Oxon 35 K4
Kingston upon Hull C KuH 93 J5
Kingston upon Thames Gt Lon 36 E7
Kingstown Cumb 110 G9
King's Walden Herts 50 E6
Kingswear Devon 7 M8
Kingswells C Aber 151 M6
Kings Weston Bristl 31 P9
Kingswinford Dudley 58 C7
Kingswood Bucks 49 J11
Kingswood Gloucs 32 D6
Kingswood Kent 38 D11
Kingswood Powys 56 C4
Kingswood S Glos 32 B10
Kingswood Somset 18 F7
Kingswood Surrey 36 F9
Kingswood Warwks 59 J10
Kingswood Brook Warwks 59 J10
Kingswood Common Herefs 45 K4
Kingswood Common Staffs 58 B4
Kings Worthy Hants 22 E8
Kingthorpe Lincs 86 F5
Kington Herefs 45 K3
Kington S Glos 32 B6
Kington Worcs 47 J3
Kington Langley Wilts 32 H9
Kington Magna Dorset 20 E10
Kington St Michael Wilts 32 H9
Kingussie Highld 148 D7
Kingweston Somset 19 P8
Kinharrachie Abers 159 M11
Kinharvie D & G 109 K7
Kinkell Bridge P & K 133 Q4
Kinknockie Abers 159 P9
Kinleith C Edin 127 M4
Kinlet Shrops 57 N8
Kinloch Highld 144 F8
Kinloch Highld 164 H10
Kinloch Highld 165 N6
Kinloch P & K 142 A9
Kinlochard Stirlg 132 F7
Kinlochbervie Highld 164 F5
Kinlocheil Highld 138 H2
Kinlochewe Highld 154 D5
Kinloch Hourn Highld 146 B6
Kinlochlaggan Highld 147 N10
Kinlochleven Highld 139 M5
Kinlochmoidart Highld 138 C3
Kinlochnanuagh Highld 145 M11
Kinloch Rannoch P & K 140 G6
Kinloss Moray 157 K5
Kinmel Bay Conwy 80 D8
Kinmuck Abers 151 L4
Kinmundy Abers 151 M4
Kinnabus Ag & B 122 C11
Kinnadie Abers 159 N9
Kinnaird P & K 141 N6
Kinneff Abers 143 Q2
Kinnelhead D & G 116 E10
Kinnell Angus 143 L7
Kinnerley Shrops 69 K10
Kinnersley Herefs 45 L5
Kinnersley Worcs 46 G6
Kinnerton Powys 45 J2
Kinnerton Shrops 56 F5
Kinnerton Green Flints 69 K2
Kinnesswood P & K 134 F7
Kinninvie Dur 103 L6
Kinnordy Angus 142 F6
Kinoulton Notts 72 H4
Kinross P & K 134 E7
Kinrossie P & K 142 B11
Kinross Services P & K 134 E7
Kinsbourne Green Herts 50 D7
Kinsey Heath Ches E 70 B6
Kinsham Herefs 56 F11
Kinsham Worcs 46 H7
Kinsley Wakefd 91 L8
Kinson BCP 13 J5
Kintail Highld 146 B4
Kintbury W Berk 34 C11
Kintessack Moray 157 J5
Kintillo P & K 134 E4
Kinton Herefs 56 G10
Kinton Shrops 69 L11
Kintore Abers 151 K4
Kintour Ag & B 122 G9
Kintra Ag & B 122 D10
Kintra Ag & B 137 J10
Kintraw Ag & B 130 G7
Kintyre Ag & B 120 D4
Kinveachy Highld 148 G4
Kinver Staffs 58 B8
Kiplin N York 103 Q11
Kippax Leeds 91 L4
Kippen Stirlg 133 J9
Kippford D & G 108 H10
Kipping's Cross Kent 25 P2
Kirbister Ork 169 c6
Kirby Bedon Norfk 77 K10
Kirby Bellars Leics 73 J7
Kirby Cane Norfk 65 M3
Kirby Corner Covtry 59 L9
Kirby Cross Essex 53 M7
Kirby Fields Leics 72 E10
Kirby Green Norfk 65 M3
Kirby Grindalythe N York 99 J7
Kirby Hill N York 97 N7
Kirby Hill N York 103 M9
Kirby Knowle N York 97 Q3
Kirby-le-Soken Essex 53 M7
Kirby Misperton N York 98 F5
Kirby Muxloe Leics 72 E10
Kirby Sigston N York 97 P2
Kirby Underdale E R Yk 98 G9
Kirby Wiske N York 97 N4
Kirdford W Susx 24 B5
Kirk Highld 167 N5
Kirkabister Shet 169 r10
Kirkandrews D & G 108 D11
Kirkandrews upon Eden Cumb 110 G9
Kirkbampton Cumb 110 F9
Kirkbean D & G 109 L9
Kirk Bramwith Donc 91 Q8
Kirkbride Cumb 110 D9
Kirkbridge N York 97 L2
Kirkbuddo Angus 143 J9
Kirkburn Border 117 K3
Kirkburn E R Yk 99 K9
Kirkburton Kirk 90 F8
Kirkby Knows 81 N5
Kirkby Lincs 86 E2
Kirkby N York 104 F9
Kirkby Fleetham N York 97 L2
Kirkby Green Lincs 86 E9
Kirkby-in-Ashfield Notts 84 H9
Kirkby-in-Furness Cumb 94 E4
Kirkby la Thorpe Lincs 86 E11
Kirkby Lonsdale Cumb 95 N5
Kirkby Malham N York 96 C8
Kirkby Mallory Leics 72 D10
Kirkby Malzeard N York 97 K6
Kirkby Mills N York 98 E3
Kirkbymoorside N York 98 D3
Kirkby on Bain Lincs 86 H8
Kirkby Overblow N York 97 M11
Kirkby Stephen Cumb 102 E9
Kirkby Thore Cumb 102 B5
Kirkby Underwood Lincs 73 R5
Kirkby Wharf N York 91 N2
Kirkby Woodhouse Notts 84 G10
Kirkcaldy Fife 134 H9
Kirkcambeck Cumb 111 K7
Kirkchrist D & G 108 E10
Kirkcolm D & G 106 D4
Kirkconnel D & G 115 P5
Kirkconnell D & G 109 L7
Kirkcowan D & G 107 K5
Kirkcudbright D & G 108 E10
Kirkdale Lpool 81 L6
Kirk Deighton N York 97 N10
Kirk Ella E R Yk 92 H5
Kirkfieldbank S Lans 116 B2
Kirkgunzeon D & G 109 J7
Kirk Hallam Derbys 72 D2
Kirkham Lancs 88 E4
Kirkham N York 98 E7
Kirkhamgate Wakefd 90 H6
Kirk Hammerton N York 97 Q9
Kirkharle Nthumb 112 F4
Kirkhaugh Nthumb 111 N11
Kirkheaton Kirk 90 F7
Kirkheaton Nthumb 112 F5
Kirkhill Highld 155 Q8
Kirkhope S Lans 116 D9
Kirkhouse Cumb 111 L9
Kirkhouse Green Donc 91 Q8
Kirkibost Highld 145 J4
Kirkinch P & K 142 E9
Kirkinner D & G 107 M7
Kirkintilloch E Duns 126 B3
Kirk Ireton Derbys 71 P4
Kirkland Cumb 100 E7
Kirkland Cumb 102 B4
Kirkland D & G 109 M3
Kirkland D & G 115 P5
Kirkland D & G 115 R9
Kirkland Guards Cumb 100 G2
Kirk Langley Derbys 71 P7
Kirkleatham R & Cl 104 G6
Kirklevington S on T 104 D9
Kirkley Suffk 65 Q3
Kirklington N York 97 M4
Kirklington Notts 85 L9
Kirklinton Cumb 110 H7
Kirkliston C Edin 127 L3
Kirkmabreck D & G 107 N6
Kirkmaiden D & G 106 F10
Kirk Merrington Dur 103 Q4
Kirk Michael IoM 80 d3
Kirkmichael P & K 141 Q6
Kirkmichael S Ayrs 114 F6
Kirkmuirhill S Lans 126 D9
Kirknewton Nthumb 118 H4
Kirknewton W Loth 127 L4
Kirkney Abers 158 D11
Kirk of Shotts N Lans 126 E5
Kirkoswald Cumb 101 Q2
Kirkoswald S Ayrs 114 D6
Kirkpatrick D & G 109 K2
Kirkpatrick Durham D & G 108 G6
Kirkpatrick-Fleming D & G 110 E6
Kirk Sandall Donc 91 Q9
Kirksanton Cumb 94 C4
Kirk Smeaton N York 91 N7
Kirkstall Leeds 90 H3
Kirkstead Lincs 86 G8
Kirkstile Abers 158 D10
Kirkstile D & G 110 G2
Kirkstone Pass Inn Cumb 101 M9
Kirkstyle Highld 167 P2
Kirkthorpe Wakefd 91 K6
Kirkton Abers 150 G2
Kirkton D & G 109 L4
Kirkton Fife 135 K2
Kirkton Highld 145 P2
Kirkton Highld 154 B9
Kirkton P & K 134 B4
Kirkton Manor Border 117 J3
Kirkton of Airlie Angus 142 E7
Kirkton of Auchterhouse Angus 142 E10
Kirkton of Barevan Highld 156 E8
Kirkton of Collace P & K 142 B11
Kirkton of Glenbuchat Abers 150 B4
Kirkton of Kingoldrum Angus 142 E6
Kirkton of Lethendy P & K 142 A9
Kirkton of Logie Buchan Abers 151 P2
Kirkton of Maryculter Abers 151 M8
Kirkton of Menmuir Angus 143 J5
Kirkton of Monikie Angus 143 J10
Kirkton of Rayne Abers 158 G11
Kirkton of Skene Abers 151 L6
Kirkton of Tealing Angus 142 G10
Kirkton of Tough Abers 150 G5
Kirktown Abers 159 N4
Kirktown Abers 159 Q7
Kirktown of Alvah Abers 158 G5
Kirktown of Bourtie Abers 151 L2
Kirktown of Fetteresso Abers 151 M10
Kirktown of Mortlach Moray 157 Q10
Kirktown of Slains Abers 151 Q2
Kirkurd Border 116 G2
Kirkwall Ork 169 d5
Kirkwall Airport Ork 169 d6
Kirkwhelpington Nthumb 112 E4
Kirk Yetholm Border 118 F5
Kirmington N Linc 93 K8
Kirmond le Mire Lincs 86 G2
Kirn Ag & B 124 F2
Kirriemuir Angus 142 F7
Kirstead Green Norfk 65 K2
Kirtlebridge D & G 110 D6
Kirtling Cambs 63 L9
Kirtling Green Cambs 63 L9
Kirtlington Oxon 48 E11
Kirtomy Highld 166 B4
Kirton Lincs 74 F3
Kirton Notts 85 L7
Kirton Suffk 53 N3
Kirton End Lincs 74 E2
Kirtonhill W Duns 125 K2
Kirton Holme Lincs 74 E2
Kirton in Lindsey N Linc 92 F11
Kirwaugh D & G 107 M7
Kishorn Highld 153 Q10
Kislingbury Nhants 60 E9
Kitebrook Warwks 47 P8
Kite Green Warwks 59 J11
Kites Hardwick Warwks 59 Q11
Kitleigh Cnwll 5 L2
Kitt Green Wigan 88 G9
Kittisford Somset 18 E10
Kittle Swans 28 G7
Kitt's Green Birm 59 J7
Kittybrewster C Aber 151 N6
Kitwood Hants 23 J8
Kivernoll Herefs 45 P8
Kiveton Park Rothm 84 G4
Knaith Lincs 85 P4
Knaith Park Lincs 85 P3
Knap Corner Dorset 20 F10
Knaphill Surrey 23 Q3
Knapp Somset 19 K9
Knapp Hill Hants 22 D10
Knapthorpe Notts 85 M9
Knapton C York 98 B10
Knapton N York 98 H5
Knapton Norfk 77 L5
Knapton Green Herefs 45 N4
Knapwell Cambs 62 D8
Knaresborough N York 97 N9
Knarsdale Nthumb 111 N10
Knaven Abers 159 L9
Knayton N York 97 P3
Knebworth Herts 50 G6
Knedlington E R Yk 92 B5
Kneesall Notts 85 M8
Kneeton Notts 85 M11
Knelston Swans 28 E7
Knenhall Staffs 70 G7
Knettishall Suffk 64 D5
Knightacott Devon 17 M4
Knightcote Warwks 48 D4
Knightley Staffs 70 E9
Knightley Dale Staffs 70 E10
Knighton BCP 12 H5
Knighton C Leic 72 G10
Knighton Devon 6 E9
Knighton Dorset 11 N2
Knighton Powys 56 D10
Knighton Somset 18 G6
Knighton Staffs 70 C6
Knighton Staffs 70 D9
Knighton Wilts 33 Q10
Knighton on Teme Worcs 57 L11
Knightsbridge Gloucs 46 G9
Knightsmill Cnwll 4 H5
Knightwick Worcs 46 D3
Knill Herefs 45 K2
Knipoch Ag & B 130 G3
Knipton Leics 73 L4
Knitsley Dur 112 H11
Kniveton Derbys 71 N4
Knock Cumb 102 C5
Knock Highld 145 L6
Knock Moray 158 D7
Knock W Isls 168 j4
Knockally Highld 167 K11
Knockan Highld 161 L4
Knockando Moray 157 M9
Knockbain Highld 155 Q9
Knockbain Highld 156 A6
Knock Castle N Ayrs 124 F5
Knockdee Highld 167 L4
Knockdow Ag & B 124 E3
Knockdown Wilts 32 F7
Knockeen S Ayrs 114 F8
Knockenkelly N Ayrs 121 K6
Knockentiber E Ayrs 125 L10
Knockhall Kent 37 N6
Knockholt Kent 37 L9
Knockholt Pound Kent 37 L9
Knockin Shrops 69 K10
Knockinlaw E Ayrs 125 L10
Knockmill Kent 37 N8
Knocknain D & G 106 C5
Knockrome Ag & B 123 J5
Knocksharry IoM 80 c4
Knocksheen D & G 108 C4
Knockvennie Smithy D & G 108 G6
Knodishall Suffk 65 N9
Knodishall Common Suffk 65 N9
Knole Somset 19 N9
Knole Park S Glos 31 Q8
Knolls Green Ches E 82 H9
Knolton Wrexhm 69 L7
Knook Wilts 20 H6
Knossington Leics 73 L9
Knott End-on-Sea Lancs 94 H11
Knotting Bed 61 M8
Knotting Green Bed 61 M8
Knottingley Wakefd 91 N6
Knotty Ash Lpool 81 N6
Knotty Green Bucks 35 P6
Knowbury Shrops 57 K9
Knowe D & G 107 K3
Knowehead D & G 115 M9
Knoweside S Ayrs 114 E5
Knowle Bristl 32 B10
Knowle Devon 9 J4
Knowle Devon 9 P3
Knowle Devon 9 Q8
Knowle Devon 16 H4
Knowle Shrops 57 K10
Knowle Solhll 59 J9
Knowle Somset 18 C6
Knowle Cross Devon 9 P5
Knowlefield Cumb 110 H9
Knowle Green Lancs 89 J3
Knowle Hill Surrey 35 Q11
Knowle St Giles Somset 10 G2
Knowle Village Hants 14 G5
Knowle Wood Calder 89 Q6
Knowl Green Essex 52 C3
Knowl Hill W & M 35 M9
Knowlton Dorset 12 H3
Knowlton Kent 39 N11
Knowsley Knows 81 N5
Knowsley Safari Park Knows 81 P6
Knowstone Devon 17 Q7
Knox N York 97 L9
Knox Bridge Kent 26 C3
Knoydart Highld 145 P7
Knucklas Powys 56 D10
Knuston Nhants 61 K7
Knutsford Ches E 82 G9
Knutsford Services Ches E 82 F9
Knutton Staffs 70 E5
Krumlin Calder 90 D7
Kuggar Cnwll 3 J10
Kyleakin Highld 145 N2
Kyle of Lochalsh Highld 145 N2
Kylerhea Highld 145 N3
Kylesku Highld 164 F10
Kylesmorar Highld 145 P9
Kyles Scalpay W Isls 168 h8
Kylestrome Highld 164 F10
Kynaston Herefs 46 B7
Kynaston Shrops 69 L10
Kynnersley Wrekin 70 B11
Kyre Green Worcs 46 B2
Kyre Park Worcs 46 B2
Kyrewood Worcs 57 K11
Kyrle Somset 18 E10

L

La Bellieuse Guern 10 b2
Lacasaigh W Isls 168 i5
Lacasdal W Isls 168 j4
Laceby NE Lin 93 M9
Lacey Green Bucks 35 M4
Lach Dennis Ches W 82 F10
Lackenby R & Cl 104 G7
Lackford Suffk 63 N6
Lackford Green Suffk 63 N6
Lacock Wilts 32 H11
Ladbroke Warwks 48 D3
Ladderedge Staffs 70 H4
Laddingford Kent 37 Q11
Lade Bank Lincs 87 L10
Ladock Cnwll 3 M3
Lady Ork 169 f2
Ladybank Fife 135 J6
Ladycross Cnwll 5 N4
Ladygill S Lans 116 C5
Lady Hall Cumb 94 D3
Ladykirk Border 129 M10
Ladyridge Herefs 46 A8
Lady's Green Suffk 63 N9
Ladywood Birm 58 G7
Ladywood Worcs 46 G2
La Fontenelle Guern 10 c1
La Fosse Guern 10 b2
Lag D & G 109 J3
Laga Highld 138 A5
Lagavulin Ag & B 122 F10
Lagg N Ayrs 121 J7
Laggan Highld 146 H8
Laggan Highld 147 Q9
Lagganlia Highld 148 F7
La Greve Guern 10 c1
La Grève de Lecq Jersey 11 a1
La Hougue Bie Jersey 11 c2
La Houguette Guern 10 b2
Laid Highld 165 K5
Laide Highld 160 E8
Laig Highld 144 G10
Laigh Clunch E Ayrs 125 M8
Laigh Fenwick E Ayrs 125 M9
Laigh Glenmuir E Ayrs 115 M3
Laighstonehall S Lans 126 C7
Laindon Essex 37 Q3
Lairg Highld 162 D5
Laisterdyke C Brad 90 F4
Laithes Cumb 101 N4
Lake Devon 8 D7
Lake Devon 17 K5
Lake IoW 14 G10
Lake Wilts 21 M7
Lake District Cumb 100 H8
Lake District National Park Cumb 100 H8
Lakenheath Suffk 63 M4
Laker's Green Surrey 24 B3
Lakes End Norfk 75 K11
Lakeside Cumb 94 H3
Laleham Surrey 36 C7
Laleston Brdgnd 29 N9
Lamanva Cnwll 3 K7
Lamarsh Essex 52 E4
Lamas Norfk 77 J7
Lambden Border 118 D2
Lamberhurst Kent 25 Q3
Lamberhurst Down Kent 25 Q3
Lamberton Border 129 P8
Lambeth Gt Lon 36 H5
Lambfair Green Suffk 63 M10
Lambley Notts 85 K11
Lambley Nthumb 111 N9
Lambourn W Berk 34 B9
Lambourne End Essex 37 L2
Lambourn Woodlands W Berk 34 B9
Lamb Roe Lancs 89 L3
Lambs Green W Susx 24 F3
Lambston Pembks 40 H7
Lamellion Cnwll 5 L9
Lamerton Devon 8 C9
Lamesley Gatesd 113 L9
Lamington S Lans 116 D4
Lamlash N Ayrs 121 K5
Lamonby Cumb 101 M3
Lamorick Cnwll 4 G9
Lamorna Cnwll 2 C9
Lamorran Cnwll 3 M5
Lampen Cnwll 5 K8
Lampeter Cerdgn 43 L5
Lampeter Velfrey Pembks 41 N8
Lamphey Pembks 41 K10
Lamplugh Cumb 100 E6
Lamport Nhants 60 G6
Lamyatt Somset 20 C7
Lana Devon 5 N2
Lana Devon 16 E10
Lanark S Lans 116 B2
Lancaster Lancs 95 K8
Lancaster Services Lancs 95 L10
Lancaut Gloucs 31 P5
Lanchester Dur 113 J11
Lancing W Susx 24 E10
L'Ancresse Guern 10 c1
Landbeach Cambs 62 G7
Landcross Devon 16 H7
Landerberry Abers 151 J7
Landford Wilts 21 Q11
Land-hallow Highld 167 L10
Landimore Swans 28 E6
Landkey Devon 17 K5
Landore Swans 29 J5
Landrake Cnwll 5 P9
Landscove Devon 7 K5
Land's End Cnwll 2 A8
Land's End Airport Cnwll 2 B8
Landshipping Pembks 41 K8
Landue Cnwll 5 P6
Landulph Cnwll 6 C6
Landwade Suffk 63 K7
Lane Cnwll 4 C9
Laneast Cnwll 5 L5
Lane Bottom Lancs 89 P3
Lane End Bucks 35 M6
Lane End Cnwll 4 G8
Lane End Hants 22 G9
Lane End Kent 37 N6
Lane End Lancs 96 C11
Lane End Warrtn 82 E6
Lane End Wilts 20 F5
Lane Ends Derbys 71 N8
Lane Ends Lancs 89 M4
Lane Ends N York 90 B2
Lane Green Staffs 58 C4
Laneham Notts 85 P5
Lanehead Dur 102 F2
Lane Head Dur 103 M8
Lanehead Nthumb 111 Q3
Lane Head Wigan 82 D5
Lane Head Wsall 58 E4
Lane Heads Lancs 88 E3
Lanercost Cumb 111 L8
Laneshaw Bridge Lancs 89 Q2
Lane Side Lancs 89 M6
Langaford Devon 5 Q2
Langal Highld 138 C4
Langaller Somset 19 J9
Langar Notts 73 J4
Langbank Rens 125 K3
Langbar N York 96 G10
Langbaurgh N York 104 G8

Langcliffe N York 96 B8
Langdale End N York 99 J2
Langdon Cnwll 5 N4
Langdon Beck Dur 102 G4
Langdown Hants 14 D5
Langdyke Fife 135 J7
Langenhoe Essex 52 H8
Langford C Beds 50 E2
Langford Devon 9 P4
Langford Essex 52 D10
Langford N Som 19 N2
Langford Notts 85 P9
Langford Oxon 33 P4
Langford Budville Somset 18 F10
Langham Dorset 20 E9
Langham Essex 52 H5
Langham Norfk 76 E3
Langham Rutlnd 73 L8
Langham Suffk 64 D8
Langho Lancs 89 L4
Langholm D & G 110 G4
Langland Swans 28 H7
Langlee Border 117 Q3
Langley Ches E 83 K10
Langley Derbys 84 F11
Langley Gloucs 47 K9
Langley Hants 14 D6
Langley Herts 50 F6
Langley Kent 38 D11
Langley Nthumb 112 B8
Langley Oxon 47 Q11
Langley Rochdl 89 P9
Langley Slough 36 B5
Langley Somset 18 E9
Langley W Susx 23 M9
Langley Warwks 47 N2
Langley Burrell Wilts 32 H9
Langley Castle Nthumb 112 B8
Langley Common Derbys 71 P7
Langley Green Derbys 71 P7
Langley Green Essex 52 E7
Langley Green Warwks 47 N2
Langley Heath Kent 38 D11
Langley Lower Green Essex 51 K4
Langley Marsh Somset 18 E9
Langley Mill Derbys 84 F11
Langley Moor Dur 103 Q2
Langley Park Dur 113 K11
Langley Street Norfk 77 M11
Langley Upper Green Essex 51 K4
Langley Vale Surrey 36 F9
Langney E Susx 25 P10
Langold Notts 85 J3
Langore Cnwll 5 M4
Langport Somset 19 M9
Langrick Lincs 87 J11
Langridge BaNES 32 D11
Langridgeford Devon 17 K7
Langrigg Cumb 110 C11
Langrish Hants 23 K10
Langsett Barns 90 G10
Langside P & K 133 M5
Langstone Hants 15 K6
Langstone Newpt 31 L7
Langthorne N York 97 K2
Langthorpe N York 97 N7
Langthwaite N York 103 K10
Langtoft E R Yk 99 L7
Langtoft Lincs 74 B8
Langton Dur 103 N7
Langton Lincs 86 H7
Langton Lincs 87 L6
Langton N York 98 F7
Langton by Wragby Lincs 86 F5
Langton Green Kent 25 M3
Langton Green Suffk 64 G7
Langton Herring Dorset 11 N8
Langton Long Blandford Dorset 12 F3
Langton Matravers Dorset 12 H9
Langtree Devon 16 H8
Langtree Week Devon 16 H8
Langwathby Cumb 101 Q4
Langwell House Highld 163 Q2
Langwith Derbys 84 H7
Langwith Junction Derbys 84 H7
Langworth Lincs 86 E5
Lanhydrock House & Gardens Cnwll 4 H9
Lanivet Cnwll 4 G9
Lanjeth Cnwll 3 P3
Lank Cnwll 4 H6
Lanlivery Cnwll 4 H10
Lanner Cnwll 3 J6
Lanoy Cnwll 5 M6
Lanreath Cnwll 5 K10
Lansallos Cnwll 5 K11
Lanteglos Cnwll 4 H5
Lanteglos Highway Cnwll 5 J11
Lanton Border 118 B6
Lanton Nthumb 118 H4
La Passee Guern 10 b1
Lapford Devon 8 H3
Laphroaig Ag & B 122 E10
Lapley Staffs 58 C2
La Pulente Jersey 11 a2
Lapworth Warwks 59 J10
Larachbeg Highld 138 B8
Larbert Falk 133 P11
Larbreck Lancs 88 E2
Largie Abers 158 F11
Largiemore Ag & B 131 J10
Largoward Fife 135 M6
Largs N Ayrs 124 G6
Largybeg N Ayrs 121 K7
Largymore N Ayrs 121 K7
Larkbeare Devon 9 Q5
Larkfield Inver 124 G2
Larkfield Kent 38 B10
Larkhall S Lans 126 D7
Larkhill Wilts 21 M6
Larling Norfk 64 D4
La Rocque Jersey 11 c2
La Rousaillerie Guern 10 b1
Lartington Dur 103 K7
Lasborough Gloucs 32 F6
Lasham Hants 23 J6
Lashbrook Devon 8 B3
Lashbrook Devon 16 G10
Lashenden Kent 26 D3
Lask Edge Staffs 70 G3
Lasswade Mdloth 127 Q4
Lastingham N York 98 E2
Latcham Somset 19 M5
Latchford Herts 51 J6
Latchford Oxon 35 J4
Latchford Warrtn 82 D7
Latchingdon Essex 52 E11
Latchley Cnwll 5 Q7
Lately Common Warrtn 82 E5
Lathbury M Keyn 49 N6
Latheron Highld 167 M10
Latheronwheel Highld 167 L10
Lathom Lancs 88 F8
Lathones Fife 135 M6
Latimer Bucks 50 B11
Latteridge S Glos 32 C8
Lattiford Somset 20 C9
Latton Wilts 33 L5
Lauder Border 128 E10
Laugharne Carmth 28 B2
Laughterton Lincs 85 P5
Laughton E Susx 25 L8
Laughton Leics 60 E3
Laughton Lincs 74 A4
Laughton Lincs 92 D11
Laughton-en-le-Morthen Rothm 84 H3
Launcells Cnwll 16 C10
Launcells Cross Cnwll 16 D10
Launceston Cnwll 5 N5
Launton Oxon 48 H10
Laurencekirk Abers 143 N3
Laurieston D & G 108 E8
Laurieston Falk 126 G2
Lavendon M Keyn 49 P4
Lavenham Suffk 52 F2
Lavernock V Glam 30 G11
Laversdale Cumb 111 J8
Laverstock Wilts 21 N8
Laverstoke Hants 22 E5
Laverton Gloucs 47 L7
Laverton N York 97 K6
Laverton Somset 20 E4
La Villette Guern 10 b2
Lavister Wrexhm 69 L3
Law S Lans 126 E7
Lawers P & K 140 G10
Lawford Essex 53 J5
Lawford Somset 18 F7
Law Hill S Lans 126 E7
Lawhitton Cnwll 5 P5
Lawkland N York 95 R7
Lawkland Green N York 96 A7
Lawley Wrekin 57 M3
Lawnhead Staffs 70 E9
Lawrence Weston Bristl 31 P9
Lawrenny Pembks 41 K9
Lawshall Suffk 64 B11
Lawshall Green Suffk 64 B11
Lawton Herefs 45 N3
Laxay W Isls 168 i5
Laxdale W Isls 168 j4
Laxey IoM 80 f5
Laxfield Suffk 65 K7
Laxford Bridge Highld 164 F7
Laxo Shet 169 r7
Laxton E R Yk 92 C5
Laxton Nhants 73 P11
Laxton Notts 85 M7
Laycock C Brad 90 C2
Layer Breton Essex 52 F8
Layer-de-la-Haye Essex 52 G7
Layer Marney Essex 52 F8
Layham Suffk 52 H3
Layland's Green W Berk 34 C11
Laymore Dorset 10 H4
Layter's Green Bucks 35 Q6
Laytham E R Yk 92 B3
Laythes Cumb 110 D9
Lazenby R & Cl 104 G7
Lazonby Cumb 101 P3
Lea Derbys 84 D9
Lea Herefs 46 C10
Lea Lincs 85 P3
Lea Shrops 56 F7
Lea Shrops 56 G3
Lea Wilts 33 J7
Leachkin Highld 156 A8
Leadburn Border 127 N6
Leadenham Lincs 86 B10
Leaden Roding Essex 51 N8
Leadgate Cumb 102 D2
Leadgate Dur 112 H10
Leadgate Nthumb 112 H9
Leadhills S Lans 116 B7
Leadingcross Green Kent 38 E11
Leadmill Derbys 84 B4
Leafield Oxon 48 B11
Leagrave Luton 50 C6
Leahead Ches W 70 B2
Lea Heath Staffs 71 J9
Leake N York 97 P2
Leake Common Side Lincs 87 L10
Lealholm N York 105 L9
Lealholm Side N York 105 L9
Lealt Highld 153 J5
Leam Derbys 84 B5
Lea Marston Warwks 59 K6
Leamington Hastings Warwks 59 P11
Leamington Spa Warwks 59 M11
Leamside Dur 113 M11
Leap Cross E Susx 25 N8
Leasgill Cumb 95 K4
Leasingham Lincs 86 E11
Leasingthorne Dur 103 Q4
Leatherhead Surrey 36 E9
Leathley N York 97 K11
Leaton Shrops 69 N11
Leaton Wrekin 57 L2
Lea Town Lancs 88 F4
Leaveland Kent 38 H11
Leavenheath Suffk 52 G4
Leavening N York 98 F8
Leaves Green Gt Lon 37 K8
Lea Yeat Cumb 95 R3
Lebberston N York 99 M4
Le Bigard Guern 10 b2
Le Bourg Guern 10 b2
Le Bourg Jersey 11 c2
Lechlade on Thames Gloucs 33 P5
Lecht Gruinart Ag & B 122 C6
Leck Lancs 95 N5
Leckbuie P & K 140 H9
Leckford Hants 22 C7
Leckhampstead Bucks 49 K7
Leckhampstead W Berk 34 D9
Leckhampstead Thicket W Berk 34 D9
Leckhampton Gloucs 46 H11
Leckmelm Highld 161 K9
Leckwith V Glam 30 G10
Leconfield E R Yk 92 H2
Ledaig Ag & B 138 G10
Ledburn Bucks 49 P10
Ledbury Herefs 46 D7
Leddington Gloucs 46 C8
Ledgemoor Herefs 45 N4
Ledicot Herefs 45 N2
Ledmore Highld 161 L4
Ledsham Ches W 81 M10
Ledsham Leeds 91 M5
Ledston Leeds 91 L5
Ledstone Devon 7 J9
Ledston Luck Leeds 91 L4
Ledwell Oxon 48 D9
Lee Devon 16 H2
Lee Gt Lon 37 J5
Lee Hants 22 C11
Lee Shrops 69 M8
Leebotwood Shrops 56 H5
Lee Brockhurst Shrops 69 P9
Leece Cumb 94 E7
Lee Chapel Essex 37 Q3
Lee Clump Bucks 35 P4
Lee Common Bucks 35 P4
Leeds Kent 38 D11
Leeds Leeds 90 H4
Leeds Bradford Airport Leeds 90 G2
Leeds Castle Kent 38 D11
Leedstown Cnwll 2 G7
Lee Green Ches E 70 B2
Leek Staffs 70 H3
Leek Wootton Warwks 59 L11
Lee Mill Devon 6 F7
Leeming C Brad 90 C4
Leeming N York 97 L3
Leeming Bar N York 97 L3
Lee Moor Devon 6 F6
Lee-on-the-Solent Hants 14 G6
Lees C Brad 90 C3
Lees Derbys 71 P7
Lees Oldham 83 L4
Lees Green Derbys 71 P7
Leesthorpe Leics 73 K8
Leeswood Flints 69 J2
Leetown P & K 134 G3
Leftwich Ches W 82 E10
Legar Powys 45 J11
Legbourne Lincs 87 L4
Legburthwaite Cumb 101 K7
Legerwood Border 118 A2
Legoland W & M 35 P10
Le Gron Guern 10 b2
Legsby Lincs 86 F3
Le Haguais Jersey 11 c2
Le Hocq Jersey 11 c2
Leicester C Leic 72 F10
Leicester Forest East Leics 72 E10
Leicester Forest East Services Leics 72 E10
Leigh Devon 17 N9
Leigh Dorset 11 N3
Leigh Gloucs 46 G9
Leigh Kent 37 M11
Leigh Shrops 56 E4
Leigh Surrey 36 F11
Leigh Wigan 82 E5
Leigh Wilts 33 L6
Leigh Worcs 46 E4
Leigh Beck Essex 38 D5
Leigh Delamere Wilts 32 G9
Leigh Delamere Services Wilts 32 G9
Leigh Green Kent 26 F5
Leigh Knoweglass S Lans 125 Q7
Leighland Chapel Somset 18 D7
Leigh-on-Sea Sthend 38 D4
Leigh Park Dorset 12 H5
Leigh Park Hants 15 K5
Leigh Sinton Worcs 46 E4
Leighswood Wsall 58 G4
Leighterton Gloucs 32 F6
Leighton N York 97 J5
Leighton Powys 56 C3
Leighton Shrops 57 L3
Leighton Somset 20 D6
Leighton Bromswold Cambs 61 P5
Leighton Buzzard C Beds 49 P9
Leigh upon Mendip Somset 20 C5
Leigh Woods N Som 31 Q10
Leinthall Earls Herefs 56 G11
Leinthall Starkes Herefs 56 G11
Leintwardine Herefs 56 G10
Leire Leics 60 B3
Leiston Suffk 65 N9
Leith C Edin 127 P2
Leitholm Border 118 E2
Lelant Cnwll 2 E6
Lelley E R Yk 93 M4
Lem Hill Worcs 57 N9
Lempitlaw Border 118 E4
Lemreway W Isls 168 i6
Lemsford Herts 50 F8
Lenchwick Worcs 47 K5
Lendalfoot S Ayrs 114 B9
Lendrick Stirlg 132 H6
Lendrum Terrace Abers 159 R9
Lenham Kent 38 E11
Lenham Heath Kent 26 F2
Lenie Highld 147 N2
Lennel Border 118 G2
Lennox Plunton D & G 108 D10
Lennoxtown E Duns 125 Q2
Lent Bucks 35 P8
Lenton C Nott 72 F3
Lenton Lincs 73 Q4
Lenwade Norfk 76 F8
Lenzie E Duns 126 B3
Leochel-Cushnie Abers 150 E5
Leomansley Staffs 58 H3
Leominster Herefs 45 P3
Leonard Stanley Gloucs 32 F4
Leoville Jersey 11 a1
Lepe Hants 14 D7
Lephin Highld 152 B8
Leppington N York 98 F8
Lepton Kirk 90 G7
Lerags Ag & B 130 H2
L'Erée Guern 10 a2
Lerryn Cnwll 5 J10
Lerwick Shet 169 r9
Les Arquêts Guern 10 b2
Lesbury Nthumb 119 P8
Les Hubits Guern 10 c2
Leslie Abers 150 F3
Leslie Fife 134 H7
Les Lohiers Guern 10 b2
Lesmahagow S Lans 126 E10
Les Murchez Guern 10 b2
Lesnewth Cnwll 5 J3
Les Nicolles Guern 10 b2
Les Quartiers Guern 10 c1
Les Quennevais Jersey 11 a2
Les Sages Guern 10 b2
Lessingham Norfk 77 M6
Lessonhall Cumb 110 D10
Lestowder Cnwll 3 K9
Les Villets Guern 10 b2
Leswalt D & G 106 D5
L'Etacq Jersey 11 a1
Letchmore Heath Herts 50 E11
Letchworth Garden City Herts 50 F4
Letcombe Bassett Oxon 34 C8
Letcombe Regis Oxon 34 C7
Letham Angus 143 J8
Letham Border 118 C9
Letham Falk 133 P10
Letham Fife 135 J5
Letham Grange Angus 143 L8
Lethenty Abers 150 F3
Lethenty Abers 159 K9
Letheringham Suffk 65 K10
Letheringsett Norfk 76 F4
Lettaford Devon 8 H8
Letterewe Highld 154 C3
Letterfearn Highld 145 Q3
Letterfinlay Lodge Hotel Highld 146 H9
Lettermorar Highld 145 M10
Letters Highld 161 K9
Lettershaw S Lans 116 B6
Letterston Pembks 40 H5
Lettoch Highld 149 J4
Lettoch Highld 157 L11
Letton Herefs 45 L5
Letton Herefs 56 F10
Lett's Green Kent 37 L9
Letty Green Herts 50 G8
Letwell Rothm 85 J3
Leuchars Fife 135 M3
Leumrabhagh W Isls 168 i6
Leurbost W Isls 168 i5
Levalsa Meor Cnwll 3 Q4
Levedale Staffs 70 F11
Level's Green Essex 51 L6
Leven E R Yk 99 N11
Leven Fife 135 K7
Levens Cumb 95 K3
Levens Green Herts 51 J6
Levenshulme Manch 83 J6
Levenwick Shet 169 r11
Leverburgh W Isls 168 f9
Leverington Cambs 74 H8
Leverstock Green Herts 50 C9
Leverton Lincs 87 M11
Le Villocq Guern 10 b1
Levington Suffk 53 M4
Levisham N York 98 G2
Lew Oxon 34 B3
Lewannick Cnwll 5 M5
Lewdown Devon 8 C7
Lewes E Susx 25 K8
Leweston Pembks 40 H6
Lewisham Gt Lon 37 J6
Lewiston Highld 147 N2
Lewistown Brdgnd 29 P7
Lewis Wych Herefs 45 L3
Lewknor Oxon 35 K5
Leworthy Devon 16 E11
Leworthy Devon 17 M4
Lewson Street Kent 38 G9
Lewth Lancs 88 F3
Lewtrenchard Devon 8 C7
Lexden Essex 52 G6
Lexworthy Somset 19 J7
Ley Cnwll 5 K8
Leybourne Kent 37 Q9
Leyburn N York 96 H2
Leycett Staffs 70 D5
Leygreen Herts 50 E6
Ley Hill Bucks 35 Q4
Leyland Lancs 88 G6
Leyland Green St Hel 82 C4
Leylodge Abers 151 K5
Leys Abers 159 P7
Leys P & K 142 D10
Leysdown-on-Sea Kent 38 H7
Leysmill Angus 143 L8
Leys of Cossans Angus 142 F8
Leysters Herefs 45 R2
Leyton Gt Lon 37 J3
Leytonstone Gt Lon 37 J3
Lezant Cnwll 5 N6
Lezerea Cnwll 2 H7
Lhanbryde Moray 157 P5
Libanus Powys 44 D9
Libberton S Lans 116 D2
Libbery Worcs 47 J3
Liberton C Edin 127 P4
Lichfield Staffs 58 H3
Lickey Worcs 58 E9
Lickey End Worcs 58 E10
Lickey Rock Worcs 58 E10
Lickfold W Susx 23 P9
Liddaton Green Devon 8 C8
Liddesdale Highld 138 D6
Liddington Swindn 33 P8
Lidgate Derbys 84 D5
Lidgate Suffk 63 M9
Lidget Donc 91 R10
Lidgett Notts 85 K7
Lidham Hill E Susx 26 D8
Lidlington C Beds 49 Q7
Lidsey W Susx 15 P6
Lidsing Kent 38 C9
Liff Angus 142 E11
Lifford Birm 58 G8
Lifton Devon 5 P4
Liftondown Devon 5 P4
Lighthorne Warwks 48 B3
Lighthorne Heath Warwks 48 C3
Lightwater Surrey 23 P2
Lightwater Valley Theme Park N York 97 L5
Lightwood C Stke 70 G6
Lightwood Green Ches E 70 A6
Lightwood Green Wrexhm 69 L6
Lilbourne Nhants 60 C5
Lilburn Tower Nthumb 119 K6
Lilleshall Wrekin 70 C11
Lilley Herts 50 D5
Lilley W Berk 34 D9
Lilliesleaf Border 117 Q5
Lillingstone Dayrell Bucks 49 K7
Lillingstone Lovell Bucks 49 K6
Lillington Dorset 11 N2
Lilliput BCP 12 H7
Lilstock Somset 18 G5
Lilyhurst Shrops 57 N2
Limbrick Lancs 89 J7
Limbury Luton 50 C6
Limebrook Herefs 56 F11
Limefield Bury 89 N8
Limekilnburn S Lans 126 C7
Limekilns Fife 134 D11
Limerigg Falk 126 F3
Limerstone IoW 14 D10
Limestone Brae Nthumb 111 Q11
Lime Street Worcs 46 F8
Limington Somset 19 P10
Limmerhaugh E Ayrs 115 M2
Limpenhoe Norfk 77 M11
Limpley Stoke Wilts 20 E2
Limpsfield Surrey 37 K10
Limpsfield Chart Surrey 37 K10
Linby Notts 84 H10
Linchmere W Susx 23 N8
Lincluden D & G 109 L5
Lincoln Lincs 86 C6
Lincomb Worcs 57 Q11
Lincombe Devon 7 J10
Lincombe Devon 16 H2
Lindale Cumb 95 J4
Lindal in Furness Cumb 94 E5
Lindfield W Susx 24 H5
Lindford Hants 23 M7
Lindley Kirk 90 E7
Lindley N York 97 K11
Lindores Fife 134 H4
Lindow End Ches E 82 H9
Lindridge Worcs 57 M11
Lindsell Essex 51 P5
Lindsey Suffk 52 G2
Lindsey Tye Suffk 52 G2
Liney Somset 19 L7
Linford Hants 13 L3
Linford Thurr 37 Q5
Lingbob C Brad 90 D3
Lingdale R & Cl 105 J7
Lingen Herefs 56 F11
Lingfield Surrey 25 J2
Lingwood Norfk 77 M10
Liniclate W Isls 168 c13
Linicro Highld 152 F4
Linkend Worcs 46 F8
Linkenholt Hants 22 C3
Linkhill Kent 26 D6
Linkinhorne Cnwll 5 N7
Linktown Fife 134 H9
Linkwood Moray 157 N5
Linley Shrops 56 F6
Linley Green Herefs 46 C4
Linleygreen Shrops 57 M5
Linlithgow W Loth 126 H2
Linshiels Nthumb 118 G9
Linsidemore Highld 162 C7
Linslade C Beds 49 P9
Linstead Parva Suffk 65 L6
Linstock Cumb 110 H9
Linthurst Worcs 58 E10
Linthwaite Kirk 90 E8
Lintlaw Border 129 L8
Lintmill Moray 158 D4
Linton Border 118 E5
Linton Cambs 63 J11
Linton Derbys 71 P11
Linton Herefs 46 C9
Linton Kent 38 C11
Linton Leeds 97 N11
Linton N York 96 E8
Linton Nthumb 113 L2
Linton Heath Derbys 71 P11
Linton Hill Herefs 46 C10
Linton-on-Ouse N York 97 Q8
Linwood Hants 13 L3
Linwood Lincs 86 F3
Linwood Rens 125 L5
Lionacleit W Isls 168 c13
Lional W Isls 168 k1
Lions Green E Susx 25 N7
Liphook Hants 23 M8
Lipley Shrops 70 C8
Liscard Wirral 81 K6
Liscombe Somset 18 A8
Liskeard Cnwll 5 M9
Lismore Ag & B 138 E9
Liss Hants 23 L9
Lissett E R Yk 99 N9
Liss Forest Hants 23 L9
Lissington Lincs 86 F4
Liston Essex 52 E3
Lisvane Cardif 30 G8
Liswerry Newpt 31 K7
Litcham Norfk 76 B8
Litchborough Nhants 48 H4
Litchfield Hants 22 E4
Litherland Sefton 81 L5
Litlington Cambs 50 H2
Litlington E Susx 25 M10
Little Abington Cambs 62 H11
Little Addington Nhants 61 L6
Little Airies D & G 107 M8
Little Almshoe Herts 50 F5
Little Alne Warwks 47 M2
Little Altcar Sefton 88 C9
Little Amwell Herts 51 J8
Little Asby Cumb 102 C9
Little Aston Staffs 58 G5
Little Atherfield IoW 14 E11
Little Ayton N York 104 G8
Little Baddow Essex 52 C10
Little Badminton S Glos 32 F8
Little Bampton Cumb 110 E9
Little Bardfield Essex 51 Q4
Little Barford Bed 61 Q9
Little Barningham Norfk 76 G5
Little Barrington Gloucs 33 P2
Little Barrow Ches W 81 P11
Little Barugh N York 98 F5
Little Bavington Nthumb 112 E5
Little Bealings Suffk 53 M2

Littlebeck N York 105 N10
Little Bedwyn Wilts 33 Q11
Little Bentley Essex 53 K6
Little Berkhamsted Herts 50 G9
Little Billing Nhants 60 H8
Little Billington C Beds 49 P10
Little Birch Herefs 45 Q8
Little Bispham Bpool 88 C2
Little Blakenham Suffk 53 K2
Little Blencow Cumb 101 N4
Little Bloxwich Wsall 58 F4
Little Bognor W Susx 24 B6
Little Bolehill Derbys 71 P4
Little Bollington Ches E 82 F7
Little Bookham Surrey 36 D10
Littleborough Devon 9 K2
Littleborough Notts 85 P4
Littleborough Rochdl 89 Q7
Littlebourne Kent 39 M10
Little Bourton Oxon 48 E6
Little Bowden Leics 60 F3
Little Bradley Suffk 63 L10
Little Brampton Herefs 45 L2
Little Brampton Shrops 56 F8
Little Braxted Essex 52 D9
Little Brechin Angus 143 K5
Littlebredy Dorset 11 M7
Little Brickhill M Keyn 49 P8
Little Bridgeford Staffs 70 F9
Little Brington Nhants 60 E8
Little Bromley Essex 53 J6
Little Broughton Cumb 100 E4
Little Budworth Ches W 82 C11
Littleburn Highld 156 A7
Little Burstead Essex 37 Q2
Littlebury Essex 51 M3
Littlebury Green Essex 51 L3
Little Bytham Lincs 73 Q7
Little Canfield Essex 51 N6
Little Carlton Lincs 87 L3
Little Carlton Notts 85 N9
Little Casterton Rutlnd 73 Q9
Little Catwick E R Yk 93 K2
Little Catworth Cambs 61 P6
Little Cawthorpe Lincs 87 L4
Little Chalfont Bucks 35 Q5
Little Chart Kent 26 F2
Little Chesterford Essex 51 M2
Little Cheveney Kent 26 B3
Little Cheverell Wilts 21 J4
Little Chishill Cambs 51 K3
Little Clacton Essex 53 L8
Little Clanfield Oxon 33 Q4
Little Clifton Cumb 100 E5
Little Coates NE Lin 93 M9
Little Comberton Worcs 47 J6
Little Common E Susx 26 B10
Little Comp Kent 37 P9
Little Compton Warwks 47 Q8
Little Corby Cumb 111 J9
Little Cornard Suffk 52 F4
Littlecott Wilts 21 M4
Little Cowarne Herefs 46 B4
Little Coxwell Oxon 33 Q6
Little Crakehall N York 97 K2
Little Cransley Nhants 60 H5
Little Cressingham Norfk 76 B11
Little Crosby Sefton 81 L4
Little Crosthwaite Cumb 100 H5
Little Cubley Derbys 71 M7
Little Dalby Leics 73 K8
Littledean Gloucs 32 C2
Little Dewchurch Herefs 45 Q8
Little Ditton Cambs 63 L9
Little Doward Herefs 45 Q11
Littledown Hants 22 B3
Little Downham Cambs 62 H4
Little Driffield E R Yk 99 L9
Little Dunham Norfk 76 B9
Little Dunkeld P & K 141 P9
Little Dunmow Essex 51 Q6
Little Durnford Wilts 21 M8
Little Easton Essex 51 P6
Little Eaton Derbys 72 B2
Little Ellingham Norfk 64 E2
Little Elm Somset 20 D5
Little Everdon Nhants 60 C9
Little Eversden Cambs 62 E10
Little Faringdon Oxon 33 P4
Little Fencote N York 97 L2
Little Fenton N York 91 N3
Littleferry Highld 163 J7
Little Fransham Norfk 76 C9
Little Gaddesden Herts 35 Q2
Little Garway Herefs 45 N10
Little Gidding Cambs 61 P4
Little Glemham Suffk 65 L10
Little Gorsley Herefs 46 C10
Little Gransden Cambs 62 C9
Little Green Notts 73 J2
Little Green Somset 20 D5
Little Grimsby Lincs 87 K2
Little Gringley Notts 85 M4
Little Habton N York 98 E5
Little Hadham Herts 51 K6
Little Hale Lincs 74 B2
Little Hallam Derbys 72 D2
Little Hallingbury Essex 51 M7
Littleham Devon 9 P8
Littleham Devon 16 G7
Little Hampden Bucks 35 N4
Littlehampton W Susx 24 B10
Little Hanford Dorset 12 D2
Little Harrowden Nhants 61 J6
Little Haseley Oxon 34 H4
Little Hatfield E R Yk 93 L2
Little Hautbois Norfk 77 K7
Little Haven Pembks 40 G8
Littlehaven W Susx 24 E4
Little Hay Staffs 58 H4
Little Hayfield Derbys 83 M7
Little Haywood Staffs 71 J10
Little Heath Staffs 70 F11
Little Heath W Berk 35 J10
Littlehempston Devon 7 L6
Little Hereford Herefs 57 K11
Little Horkesley Essex 52 G5
Little Hormead Herts 51 K5
Little Horsted E Susx 25 L7
Little Horton C Brad 90 F4
Little Horton Wilts 21 K2
Little Horwood Bucks 49 L8
Little Houghton Barns 91 L9
Little Houghton Nhants 60 H9
Littlehoughton Nthumb 119 P7
Little Hucklow Derbys 83 Q9
Little Hulton Salfd 82 F4
Little Hungerford W Berk 34 F10
Little Hutton N York 97 Q5
Little Irchester Nhants 61 K7
Little Kelk E R Yk 99 M9
Little Keyford Somset 20 E5
Little Kimble Bucks 35 M3
Little Kineton Warwks 48 B4
Little Kingshill Bucks 35 N5
Little Knox D & G 108 H8
Little Langdale Cumb 101 K10
Little Langford Wilts 21 K7
Little Laver Essex 51 M9
Little Leigh Ches W 82 D9
Little Leighs Essex 52 B8
Little Lever Bolton 89 M9
Little Linford M Keyn 49 M6
Little Load Somset 19 N10
Little London Bucks 34 H2
Little London Cambs 74 H11
Little London E Susx 25 N6
Little London Essex 51 L5
Little London Essex 51 Q3
Little London Gloucs 46 D11
Little London Hants 22 C5
Little London Hants 22 H3
Little London Leeds 90 G3
Little London Lincs 74 D6
Little London Lincs 74 H6
Little London Lincs 87 K6
Little London Norfk 75 L6
Little London Powys 55 N7
Little Longstone Derbys 83 Q10
Little Madeley Staffs 70 D5
Little Malvern Worcs 46 E6
Little Mancot Flints 81 L11
Little Maplestead Essex 52 D5
Little Marcle Herefs 46 C7
Little Marland Devon 17 J9
Little Marlow Bucks 35 N7
Little Massingham Norfk 75 Q6
Little Melton Norfk 76 H10
Littlemill Abers 149 Q8
Littlemill Highld 156 G7
Little Mill Mons 31 K4
Little Milton Oxon 34 H4
Little Missenden Bucks 35 P5
Little Mongeham Kent 39 P11
Littlemoor Derbys 84 E8
Little Moor Somset 19 K8
Littlemore Oxon 34 F4
Little Musgrave Cumb 102 E8
Little Ness Shrops 69 M11
Little Neston Ches W 81 K9
Little Newcastle Pembks 41 J5
Little Newsham Dur 103 M7
Little Norton Somset 19 N11
Little Oakley Essex 53 M6
Little Oakley Nhants 61 J3
Little Odell Bed 61 L9
Little Offley Herts 50 D5
Little Ormside Cumb 102 D7
Little Orton Cumb 110 G9
Little Ouse Cambs 63 K3
Little Ouseburn N York 97 P8
Littleover C Derb 72 A4
Little Oxendon Nhants 60 F4
Little Packington Warwks 59 K8
Little Pattenden Kent 26 B2
Little Paxton Cambs 61 Q8
Little Petherick Cnwll 4 E7
Little Plumpton Lancs 88 D4
Little Plumstead Norfk 77 L9
Little Ponton Lincs 73 N4
Littleport Cambs 63 J3
Littleport Bridge Cambs 63 J3
Little Posbrook Hants 14 F6
Little Potheridge Devon 17 J9
Little Preston Leeds 91 K4
Little Preston Nhants 48 G4
Littler Ches W 82 D11
Little Raveley Cambs 62 C5
Little Reedness E R Yk 92 D6
Little Ribston N York 97 N10
Little Rissington Gloucs 47 N11
Little Rollright Oxon 47 Q8
Little Rowsley Derbys 84 C7
Little Ryburgh Norfk 76 D6
Little Ryle Nthumb 119 K8
Little Ryton Shrops 56 H4
Little Salkeld Cumb 101 Q3
Little Sampford Essex 51 Q4
Little Sandhurst Br For 23 M2
Little Saredon Staffs 58 D3
Little Saughall Ches W 81 M11
Little Saxham Suffk 63 P8
Little Scatwell Highld 155 L6
Little Shelford Cambs 62 G10
Little Shrewley Warwks 59 K11
Little Silver Devon 9 M3
Little Singleton Lancs 88 D3
Little Skipwith N York 91 R3
Little Smeaton N York 91 N7
Little Snoring Norfk 76 D5
Little Sodbury S Glos 32 E8
Little Sodbury End S Glos 32 D8
Little Somborne Hants 22 C8
Little Somerford Wilts 33 J8
Little Soudley Shrops 70 C9
Little Stainforth N York 96 B7
Little Stainton Darltn 104 B6
Little Stanion Nhants 61 J3
Little Stanney Ches W 81 N10
Little Staughton Bed 61 P8
Little Steeping Lincs 87 M8
Little Stoke Staffs 70 G8
Littlestone-on-Sea Kent 27 J7
Little Stonham Suffk 64 G9
Little Stretton Leics 72 H10
Little Stretton Shrops 56 G6
Little Strickland Cumb 101 Q7
Little Stukeley Cambs 62 B5
Little Sugnall Staffs 70 E8
Little Sutton Ches W 81 M9
Little Sutton Shrops 57 J8
Little Swinburne Nthumb 112 D5
Little Sypland D & G 108 F10
Little Tew Oxon 48 C9
Little Tey Essex 52 E7
Little Thetford Cambs 62 H5
Little Thirkleby N York 97 Q5
Little Thornage Norfk 76 F4
Little Thornton Lancs 88 D2
Little Thorpe Dur 104 D2
Littlethorpe Leics 72 E11
Littlethorpe N York 97 M7
Little Thurlow Suffk 63 L10
Little Thurlow Green Suffk 63 L10
Little Thurrock Thurr 37 P5
Littleton Angus 142 E7
Littleton BaNES 19 Q2
Littleton Ches W 81 N11
Littleton D & G 108 D9
Littleton Dorset 12 E4
Littleton Hants 22 E8
Littleton Somset 19 N8
Littleton Surrey 23 Q5
Littleton Surrey 36 C7
Littleton Drew Wilts 32 F8
Littleton-on-Severn S Glos 31 Q7
Littleton Pannell Wilts 21 K4
Little Torrington Devon 16 H8
Little Totham Essex 52 E9
Little Town Cumb 100 H7
Littletown Dur 104 B2
Little Town Lancs 89 K3
Little Town Warrtn 82 D6
Little Twycross Leics 72 A9
Little Urswick Cumb 94 F6
Little Wakering Essex 38 F4
Little Walden Essex 51 M2
Little Waldingfield Suffk 52 F2
Little Walsingham Norfk 76 C4
Little Waltham Essex 52 B9
Little Warley Essex 37 P2
Little Washbourne Gloucs 47 J8
Little Weighton E R Yk 92 G4
Little Welnetham Suffk 64 B10
Little Welton Lincs 87 K3
Little Wenham Suffk 53 J4
Little Wenlock Wrekin 57 L3
Little Weston Somset 20 B9
Little Whitefield IoW 14 G9
Little Whittingham Green Suffk 65 K6
Little Whittington Nthumb 112 E7
Littlewick Green W & M 35 M9
Little Wilbraham Cambs 62 H9
Littlewindsor Dorset 11 J4
Little Witcombe Gloucs 46 H11
Little Witley Worcs 46 E2
Little Wittenham Oxon 34 G6
Little Wolford Warwks 47 Q7
Littlewood Staffs 58 E3
Little Woodcote Gt Lon 36 G8
Littleworth Bucks 49 N10
Littleworth Oxon 34 B5
Littleworth Staffs 58 F2
Littleworth Staffs 70 G10
Littleworth W Susx 24 E6
Littleworth Worcs 46 G4
Littleworth Worcs 47 J2
Littleworth Common Bucks 35 P7
Little Wratting Suffk 63 L11
Little Wymington Bed 61 L8
Little Wymondley Herts 50 F5
Little Wyrley Staffs 58 F3
Little Wytheford Shrops 69 Q11
Little Yeldham Essex 52 C4
Littley Green Essex 51 Q7
Litton Derbys 83 Q9
Litton N York 96 D6
Litton Somset 19 Q4
Litton Cheney Dorset 11 L6
Liurbost W Isls 168 i5
Liverpool Lpool 81 L6
Liverpool Maritime Mercantile City Lpool 81 L7
Liversedge Kirk 90 F6
Liverton Devon 9 K9
Liverton R & Cl 105 K7
Liverton Mines R & Cl 105 K7
Liverton Street Kent 38 E11
Livingston W Loth 127 K4
Livingston Village W Loth 127 J4
Lixwm Flints 80 H10
Lizard Cnwll 3 J11
Llaingoch IoA 78 C8
Llaithddu Powys 55 P8
Llan Powys 55 K4
Llanaber Gwynd 67 L11
Llanaelhaearn Gwynd 66 F6
Llanafan Cerdgn 54 F10
Llanafan-Fawr Powys 44 D3
Llanafan-fechan Powys 44 D4
Llanallgo IoA 79 J7
Llanarmon Gwynd 66 G7
Llanarmon Dyffryn Ceiriog Wrexhm 68 G8
Llanarmon-yn-Ial Denbgs 68 G3
Llanarth Cerdgn 42 H3
Llanarth Mons 31 L2
Llanarthne Carmth 43 K11
Llanasa Flints 80 G8
Llanbabo IoA 78 F7
Llanbadarn Fawr Cerdgn 54 E8
Llanbadarn Fynydd Powys 55 P9
Llanbadarn-y-garreg Powys 44 G5
Llanbadoc Mons 31 L5
Llanbadrig IoA 78 F6
Llanbeder Newpt 31 L6
Llanbedr Gwynd 67 K9
Llanbedr Powys 44 G5
Llanbedr Powys 45 J10
Llanbedr-Dyffryn-Clwyd Denbgs 68 F3
Llanbedrgoch IoA 79 J8
Llanbedrog Gwynd 66 E8
Llanbedr-y-Cennin Conwy 79 P11
Llanberis Gwynd 67 K2
Llanbethêry V Glam 30 D11
Llanbister Powys 55 Q10
Llanblethian V Glam 30 C10
Llanboidy Carmth 41 P6
Llanbradach Caerph 30 F6
Llanbrynmair Powys 55 K4
Llancadle V Glam 30 D11
Llancarfan V Glam 30 D10
Llancayo Mons 31 L4
Llancloudy Herefs 45 P10
Llancynfelyn Cerdgn 54 E6
Llandaff Cardif 30 G9
Llandanwg Gwynd 67 K9
Llandarcy Neath 29 K5
Llandawke Carmth 41 Q8
Llanddaniel Fab IoA 78 H10
Llanddarog Carmth 43 K11
Llanddeiniol Cerdgn 54 D10
Llanddeiniolen Gwynd 79 J11
Llandderfel Gwynd 68 C7
Llanddeusant Carmth 43 Q10
Llanddeusant IoA 78 E7
Llanddew Powys 44 F8
Llanddewi Swans 28 E7
Llanddewi Brefi Cerdgn 43 N3
Llanddewi'r Cwm Powys 44 E5
Llanddewi Rhydderch Mons 31 L2
Llanddewi Velfrey Pembks 41 M7
Llanddewi Ystradenni Powys 55 Q11
Llanddoged Conwy 67 Q2
Llanddona IoA 79 K9
Llanddowror Carmth 41 Q8
Llanddulas Conwy 80 C9
Llanddwywe Gwynd 67 K10
Llanddyfnan IoA 79 J9
Llandecwyn Gwynd 67 L7
Llandefaelog Powys 44 E8
Llandefaelog-Tre'r-Graig Powys 44 G9
Llandefalle Powys 44 G7
Llandegfan IoA 79 K10
Llandegla Denbgs 68 G4
Llandegley Powys 44 G2
Llandegveth Mons 31 K5
Llandegwning Gwynd 66 D9
Llandeilo Carmth 43 M10
Llandeilo Graban Powys 44 F6
Llandeilo'r Fan Powys 44 B8
Llandeloy Pembks 40 G5
Llandenny Mons 31 M4
Llandevaud Newpt 31 M6
Llandevenny Mons 31 M7
Llandinabo Herefs 45 Q9
Llandinam Powys 55 N7
Llandissilio Pembks 41 M6
Llandogo Mons 31 P4
Llandough V Glam 30 C10
Llandough V Glam 30 G10
Llandovery Carmth 43 Q8
Llandow V Glam 29 P10
Llandre Carmth 43 N6
Llandre Cerdgn 54 E7
Llandre Isaf Pembks 41 M5
Llandrillo Denbgs 68 D7
Llandrillo-yn-Rhos Conwy 79 Q8
Llandrindod Wells Powys 44 F2
Llandrinio Powys 69 J11
Llandudno Conwy 79 P8
Llandudno Junction Conwy 79 P9
Llandulas Powys 44 B6
Llandwrog Gwynd 66 H3
Llandybie Carmth 43 M11
Llandyfaelog Carmth 28 D2
Llandyfan Carmth 43 M11
Llandyfriog Cerdgn 42 F6
Llandyfrydog IoA 78 G7
Llandygai Gwynd 79 K10
Llandygwydd Cerdgn 41 P2
Llandynan Denbgs 68 G5
Llandyrnog Denbgs 80 G11
Llandyssil Powys 56 B5
Llandysul Cerdgn 42 H6
Llanedeyrn Cardif 30 H8
Llanedi Carmth 28 G3
Llaneglwys Powys 44 F7
Llanegryn Gwynd 54 E3
Llanegwad Carmth 43 K10
Llaneilian IoA 78 H6
Llanelian-yn-Rhôs Conwy 80 B9
Llanelidan Denbgs 68 F4
Llanelieu Powys 44 H8
Llanellen Mons 31 K2
Llanelli Carmth 28 F4
Llanelltyd Gwynd 67 N11
Llanelly Mons 30 H2
Llanelly Hill Mons 30 H2
Llanelwedd Powys 44 E4
Llanenddwyn Gwynd 67 K10
Llanengan Gwynd 66 D9
Llanerch Gwynd 68 A11
Llanerch Powys 56 E6
Llanerchymedd IoA 78 G8
Llanerfyl Powys 55 N3
Llanfachraeth IoA 78 E8
Llanfachreth Gwynd 67 P10
Llanfaelog IoA 78 E10
Llanfaelrhys Gwynd 66 C9
Llanfaenor Mons 45 N11
Llanfaes IoA 79 L9
Llanfaes Powys 44 E9
Llanfaethlu IoA 78 E7
Llanfair Gwynd 67 K9
Llanfair Caereinion Powys 55 Q3
Llanfair Clydogau Cerdgn 43 M4
Llanfair Dyffryn Clwyd Denbgs 68 F3
Llanfairfechan Conwy 79 M10
Llanfair Kilgeddin Mons 31 L3
Llanfair-Nant-Gwyn Pembks 41 N3
Llanfairpwllgwyngyll IoA 79 J10
Llanfair Talhaiarn Conwy 80 C10
Llanfair Waterdine Shrops 56 C9
Llanfairynghornwy IoA 78 E6
Llanfair-yn-Neubwll IoA 78 E9
Llanfallteg Carmth 41 N6
Llanfallteg West Carmth 41 M7
Llanfarian Cerdgn 54 D9
Llanfechain Powys 68 G10
Llanfechell IoA 78 F6
Llanferres Denbgs 68 G2
Llanfflewyn IoA 78 F7
Llanfigael IoA 78 E8
Llanfihangel-ar-arth Carmth 43 J7
Llanfihangel Glyn Myfyr Conwy 68 C5
Llanfihangel Nant Bran Powys 44 C8
Llanfihangel-nant-Melan Powys 44 H3
Llanfihangel Rhydithon Powys 56 B11
Llanfihangel Rogiet Mons 31 N7
Llanfihangel Tal-y-llyn Powys 44 G9
Llanfihangel-uwch-Gwili Carmth 43 J10
Llanfihangel-y-Creuddyn Cerdgn 54 F9
Llanfihangel-yng-Ngwynfa Powys 68 E11
Llanfihangel yn Nhowyn IoA 78 E9
Llanfihangel-y-pennant Gwynd 54 F3
Llanfihangel-y-pennant Gwynd 67 J6
Llanfihangel-y-traethau Gwynd 67 K8
Llanfilo Powys 44 G8
Llanfoist Mons 31 J2
Llanfor Gwynd 68 B7
Llanfrechfa Torfn 31 K6
Llanfrothen Gwynd 67 L6
Llanfrynach Powys 44 F9
Llanfwrog Denbgs 68 F3
Llanfwrog IoA 78 E8
Llanfyllin Powys 68 F11
Llanfynydd Carmth 43 L9
Llanfynydd Flints 69 J3
Llanfyrnach Pembks 41 P4
Llangadfan Powys 55 N2
Llangadog Carmth 28 D3
Llangadog Carmth 43 P9
Llangadwaladr IoA 78 F11
Llangadwaladr Powys 68 G8
Llangaffo IoA 78 G11
Llangain Carmth 42 G11
Llangammarch Wells Powys 44 C5
Llangan V Glam 30 C9
Llangarron Herefs 45 Q10
Llangasty-Talyllyn Powys 44 G9
Llangathen Carmth 43 L10
Llangattock Powys 45 J11
Llangattock Lingoed Mons 45 M10
Llangattock-Vibon-Avel Mons 45 P11
Llangedwyn Powys 68 G10
Llangefni IoA 78 H9
Llangeinor Brdgnd 29 P7
Llangeitho Cerdgn 43 M3
Llangeler Carmth 42 G7
Llangelynin Gwynd 54 D3
Llangendeirne Carmth 28 E2
Llangennech Carmth 28 G4
Llangennith Swans 28 D6
Llangenny Powys 45 J11
Llangernyw Conwy 80 B11
Llangian Gwynd 66 D9
Llangiwg Neath 29 K3
Llangloffan Pembks 40 H4
Llanglydwen Carmth 41 N5
Llangoed IoA 79 L9
Llangoedmor Cerdgn 42 D5
Llangollen Denbgs 68 H6
Llangolman Pembks 41 M5
Llangors Powys 44 G9
Llangorwen Cerdgn 54 E8
Llangovan Mons 31 N3
Llangower Gwynd 68 B8
Llangrannog Cerdgn 42 F4
Llangristiolus IoA 78 G10
Llangrove Herefs 45 Q11
Llangua Mons 45 M9
Llangunllo Powys 56 C10
Llangunnor Carmth 42 H10
Llangurig Powys 55 L9
Llangwm Conwy 68 C6
Llangwm Mons 31 M5
Llangwm Pembks 41 J9
Llangwnnadl Gwynd 66 C8
Llangwyfan Denbgs 80 G11
Llangwyllog IoA 78 G9
Llangwyryfon Cerdgn 54 D10
Llangybi Cerdgn 43 M4
Llangybi Gwynd 66 G6
Llangybi Mons 31 L5
Llangyfelach Swans 28 H5
Llangynhafal Denbgs 68 F2
Llangynidr Powys 44 H11
Llangynin Carmth 41 Q7
Llangynllo Cerdgn 42 G6
Llangynog Carmth 28 B2
Llangynog Powys 68 E9
Llangynwyd Brdgnd 29 N7
Llanhamlach Powys 44 F9
Llanharan Rhondd 30 D8
Llanharry Rhondd 30 D8
Llanhennock Mons 31 L6
Llanhilleth Blae G 30 H4
Llanidan IoA 78 H11
Llanidloes Powys 55 M8
Llaniestyn Gwynd 66 D8
Llanigon Powys 45 J7
Llanilar Cerdgn 54 E9
Llanilid Rhondd 30 C8
Llanina Cerdgn 42 H3
Llanio Cerdgn 43 M3
Llanishen Cardif 30 G8
Llanishen Mons 31 N4
Llanllechid Gwynd 79 L11
Llanlleonfel Powys 44 C4
Llanllowell Mons 31 L5
Llanllugan Powys 55 P4
Llanllwch Carmth 42 G11
Llanllwchaiarn Powys 55 Q6
Llanllwni Carmth 43 J7
Llanllyfni Gwynd 66 H4
Llanmadoc Swans 28 D6
Llanmaes V Glam 30 C11
Llanmartin Newpt 31 L7
Llanmerewig Powys 56 B6
Llanmihangel V Glam 30 C10
Llanmiloe Carmth 41 P9
Llanmorlais Swans 28 F6
Llannefydd Conwy 80 D10
Llannon Carmth 28 F3
Llannor Gwynd 66 F7
Llanon Cerdgn 54 C11
Llanover Mons 31 K3
Llanpumsaint Carmth 42 H9
Llanrhaeadr-ym-Mochnant Powys 68 F9
Llanrhian Pembks 40 F4
Llanrhidian Swans 28 E6
Llanrhos Conwy 79 P8
Llanrhychwyn Conwy 67 P2
Llanrhyddlad IoA 78 E7
Llanrhystud Cerdgn 54 C11
Llanrothal Herefs 45 P11
Llanrug Gwynd 67 J2
Llanrumney Cardif 30 H8
Llanrwst Conwy 67 Q2
Llansadurnen Carmth 41 Q8
Llansadwrn Carmth 43 N8
Llansadwrn IoA 79 K9
Llansaint Carmth 28 C3
Llansamlet Swans 29 J5

Llansanffraid Glan Conwy Conwy 79 Q9
Llansannan Conwy 80 C11
Llansannor V Glam 30 C9
Llansantffraed Powys 44 G10
Llansantffraed-Cwmdeuddwr Powys 55 M11
Llansantffraed-in-Elvel Powys 44 F4
Llansantffraid Cerdgn 54 C11
Llansantffraid-ym-Mechain Powys 68 H10
Llansawel Carmth 43 M7
Llansilin Powys 68 H9
Llansoy Mons 31 M4
Llanspyddid Powys 44 E9
Llanstadwell Pembks 40 H10
Llansteffan Carmth 28 C2
Llanstephan Powys 44 G6
Llantarnam Torfn 31 K6
Llanteg Pembks 41 N8
Llanthewy Skirrid Mons 45 L11
Llanthony Mons 45 K9
Llantilio-Crossenny Mons 31 L2
Llantilio Pertholey Mons 45 L11
Llantood Pembks 41 N2
Llantrisant IoA 78 F8
Llantrisant Mons 31 L5
Llantrisant Rhondd 30 D8
Llantrithyd V Glam 30 D10
Llantwit Fardre Rhondd 30 E7
Llantwit Major V Glam 30 C11
Llantysilio Denbgs 68 G6
Llanuwchllyn Gwynd 68 A8
Llanvaches Newpt 31 M6
Llanvair Discoed Mons 31 M6
Llanvapley Mons 31 L2
Llanvetherine Mons 45 M11
Llanveynoe Herefs 45 L8
Llanvihangel Crucorney Mons 45 L10
Llanvihangel Gobion Mons 31 K3
Llanvihangel-Ystern-Llewern Mons 31 M2
Llanwarne Herefs 45 Q9
Llanwddyn Powys 68 D11
Llanwenarth Mons 31 J2
Llanwenog Cerdgn 43 J5
Llanwern Newpt 31 L7
Llanwinio Carmth 41 Q5
Llanwnda Gwynd 66 H3
Llanwnda Pembks 40 H3
Llanwnnen Cerdgn 43 K5
Llanwnog Powys 55 N6
Llanwonno Rhondd 30 D5
Llanwrda Carmth 43 P8
Llanwrin Powys 54 H4
Llanwrthwl Powys 44 D2
Llanwrtyd Powys 44 B5
Llanwrtyd Wells Powys 44 B5
Llanwyddelan Powys 55 P4
Llanyblodwel Shrops 68 H10
Llanybri Carmth 28 B2
Llanybydder Carmth 43 K6
Llanycefn Pembks 41 L6
Llanychaer Pembks 41 J3
Llanycil Gwynd 68 B8
Llanycrwys Carmth 43 M5
Llanymawddwy Gwynd 68 B11
Llanymynech Powys 69 J10
Llanynghenedl IoA 78 E8
Llanynys Denbgs 68 F2
Llan-y-pwll Wrexhm 69 L4
Llanyre Powys 44 E2
Llanystumdwy Gwynd 66 H7
Llanywern Powys 44 G9
Llawhaden Pembks 41 L7
Llawnt Shrops 68 H8
Llawryglyn Powys 55 L6
Llay Wrexhm 69 K3
Llechcynfarwy IoA 78 F8
Llechfaen Powys 44 F9
Llechrhyd Caerph 30 F3
Llechryd Cerdgn 41 P2
Llechylched IoA 78 E9
Lledrod Cerdgn 54 E10
Lleyn Peninsula Gwynd 66 E7
Llidiardau Gwynd 68 A7
Llidiartnenog Carmth 43 K7
Llidiart-y-parc Denbgs 68 F6
Llithfaen Gwynd 66 F6
Lloc Flints 80 G9
Llowes Powys 44 H6
Llwydcoed Rhondd 30 C4
Llwydiarth Powys 68 D11
Llwyn Denbgs 68 E2
Llwyncelyn Cerdgn 42 H3
Llwyndafydd Cerdgn 42 G3
Llwynderw Powys 56 C4
Llwyn-drain Pembks 41 Q4
Llwyn-du Mons 45 K11
Llwyndyrys Gwynd 66 F6
Llwyngwril Gwynd 54 D3
Llwynhendy Carmth 28 F5
Llwynmawr Wrexhm 68 H7
Llwyn-on Myr Td 30 D2
Llwyn-y-brain Carmth 41 N8
Llwyn-y-groes Cerdgn 43 L3
Llwynypia Rhondd 30 C6
Llynclys Shrops 69 J10
Llynfaes IoA 78 G9
Llyn-y-pandy Flints 81 J11
Llysfaen Conwy 80 B9
Llyswen Cerdgn 43 J2
Llyswen Powys 44 G7
Llysworney V Glam 30 C10
Llys-y-frân Pembks 41 K6
Llywel Powys 44 B8
Load Brook Sheff 84 C3
Loan Falk 126 H2
Loanend Nthumb 129 N9
Loanhead Mdloth 127 P4
Loaningfoot D & G 109 L9
Loans S Ayrs 125 J11
Lobb Devon 16 H4
Lobhillcross Devon 8 C7
Lochailort Highld 145 N11
Lochaline Highld 138 B9
Lochans D & G 106 E6
Locharbriggs D & G 109 L4
Lochavich Ag & B 131 J4
Lochawe Ag & B 131 N2
Loch Baghasdail W Isls 168 c16
Lochboisdale W Isls 168 c16
Lochbuie Ag & B 137 Q10
Lochcarron Highld 154 A10
Lochdon Ag & B 138 C11
Lochdonhead Ag & B 138 C11
Lochead Ag & B 123 N4
Lochearnhead Stirlg 132 H3
Lochee C Dund 142 F11
Locheilside Station Highld 138 H2
Lochend Highld 155 Q10
Locheport W Isls 168 d11
Loch Euphoirt W Isls 168 d11
Lochfoot D & G 109 J6
Lochgair Ag & B 131 J9
Lochgelly Fife 134 F9
Lochgilphead Ag & B 130 H10
Lochgoilhead Ag & B 131 Q7
Lochieheads Fife 134 H5
Lochill Moray 157 P5
Lochindorb Lodge Highld 156 H10
Lochinver Highld 160 H2
Loch Lomond and The Trossachs National Park 132 E5
Loch Loyal Lodge Highld 165 P7
Lochluichart Highld 155 K5
Lochmaben D & G 109 N4
Lochmaddy W Isls 168 e11
Loch nam Madadh W Isls 168 e11
Loch Ness Highld 147 N2
Lochore Fife 134 F8
Lochranza N Ayrs 124 A7
Loch Sgioport W Isls 168 d14
Lochside Abers 143 N5
Lochside D & G 109 L5
Lochside Highld 156 E7
Lochskipport W Isls 168 d14
Lochslin Highld 163 J10
Lochton S Ayrs 107 J2
Lochty Angus 143 J5
Lochty Fife 135 N6
Lochuisge Highld 138 D6
Lochwinnoch Rens 125 K6
Lochwood D & G 116 F11
Lockengate Cnwll 4 G9
Lockerbie D & G 109 P4
Lockeridge Wilts 33 M11
Lockerley Hants 22 B9
Locking N Som 19 L3
Locking Stumps Warrtn 82 D6
Lockington E R Yk 99 K11
Lockington Leics 72 D5
Lockleywood Shrops 70 B9
Locksbottom Gt Lon 37 K7
Locksgreen IoW 14 D8
Locks Heath Hants 14 F5
Lockton N York 98 G3
Loddington Leics 73 K10
Loddington Nhants 60 H5
Loddiswell Devon 7 J9
Loddon Norfk 65 M2
Lode Cambs 62 H8
Lode Heath Solhll 59 J8
Loders Dorset 11 K6
Lodsworth W Susx 23 P10
Lofthouse Leeds 91 J5
Lofthouse N York 96 H6
Lofthouse Gate Wakefd 91 J6
Loftus R & Cl 105 K7
Logan E Ayrs 115 L3
Loganbeck Cumb 94 D2
Loganlea W Loth 126 H5
Loggerheads Staffs 70 C7
Logie Angus 143 M5
Logie Fife 135 L3
Logie Moray 157 J7
Logie Coldstone Abers 150 C7
Logie Newton Abers 158 G10
Logie Pert Angus 143 M5
Logierait P & K 141 N7
Logierieve Abers 151 N2
Login Carmth 41 N6
Lolworth Cambs 62 E8
Lonbain Highld 153 M7
Londesborough E R Yk 98 H11
London Gt Lon 36 H4
London Apprentice Cnwll 3 Q4
London Beach Kent 26 E4
London Colney Herts 50 E10
Londonderry N York 97 M3
London End Nhants 61 K7
London Gateway Services Gt Lon 36 E2
London Gatwick Airport W Susx 24 G2
London Heathrow Airport Gt Lon 36 C5
London Luton Airport Luton 50 D6
London Oxford Airport Oxon 48 E11
London Southend Airport Essex 38 E4
London Stansted Airport Essex 51 N6
Londonthorpe Lincs 73 P3
London Zoo ZSL Gt Lon 36 G4
Londubh Highld 160 D10
Lonemore Highld 153 P2
Long Ashton N Som 31 P10
Long Bank Worcs 57 P10
Long Bennington Lincs 73 L2
Longbenton N Tyne 113 L7
Longborough Gloucs 47 N9
Long Bredy Dorset 11 M6
Longbridge Birm 58 F9
Longbridge Warwks 47 Q2
Longbridge Deverill Wilts 20 G6
Long Buckby Nhants 60 D7
Longburgh Cumb 110 F9
Longburton Dorset 11 N2
Long Cause Devon 7 K6
Long Clawson Leics 73 J5
Longcliffe Derbys 84 B9
Longcombe Devon 7 L7
Long Common Hants 14 F4
Long Compton Staffs 70 F10
Long Compton Warwks 47 Q8
Longcot Oxon 33 Q6
Long Crendon Bucks 35 J3
Long Crichel Dorset 12 G2
Longcroft Cumb 110 D9
Longcross Surrey 35 Q11
Longden Shrops 56 G3
Longden Common Shrops 56 G3
Long Ditton Surrey 36 E7
Longdon Staffs 58 G2
Longdon Worcs 46 F7
Longdon Green Staffs 58 G2
Longdon Heath Worcs 46 F7
Longdon upon Tern Wrekin 69 R11
Longdown Devon 9 L6
Longdowns Cnwll 3 J7
Long Drax N York 92 A5
Long Duckmanton Derbys 84 F6
Long Eaton Derbys 72 D4
Longfield Kent 37 P7
Longford Covtry 59 N8
Longford Derbys 71 N7
Longford Gloucs 46 F10
Longford Gt Lon 36 C5
Longford Kent 37 M9
Longford Shrops 70 A8
Longford Wrekin 70 C11
Longforgan P & K 134 H2
Longformacus Border 128 H8
Longframlington Nthumb 119 M10
Long Green Ches W 81 P10
Long Green Worcs 46 F8
Longham Dorset 13 J5
Longham Norfk 76 C8
Long Hanborough Oxon 34 D2
Longhaven Abers 159 R10
Long Hedges Lincs 87 L11
Longhirst Nthumb 113 K3
Longhope Gloucs 46 C11
Longhope Ork 169 c7
Longhorsley Nthumb 112 H2
Longhoughton Nthumb 119 P7
Long Itchington Warwks 59 P11
Longlands Cumb 101 J3
Longlane Derbys 71 N7
Long Lawford Warwks 59 Q9
Longleat Safari & Adventure Park Wilts 20 F6
Longlevens Gloucs 46 G11
Longley Calder 90 D6
Longley Kirk 90 E9
Longley Green Worcs 46 D4
Longleys P & K 142 D9
Long Load Somset 19 N10
Longmanhill Abers 158 H5
Long Marston Herts 49 N11
Long Marston N York 97 R10
Long Marston Warwks 47 N5
Long Marton Cumb 102 C6
Long Meadowend Shrops 56 G8
Long Melford Suffk 52 E2
Longmoor Camp Hants 23 L8
Longmorn Moray 157 N6
Longmoss Ches E 83 J10
Long Newnton Gloucs 32 H6
Longnewton Border 118 A5
Long Newton E Loth 128 E7
Longnewton S on T 104 C7
Longney Gloucs 32 E2
Longniddry E Loth 128 C4
Longnor Shrops 56 H4
Longnor Staffs 71 K2
Longparish Hants 22 D5
Longpark Cumb 110 H8
Long Preston N York 96 B9
Longridge Lancs 89 J3
Longridge Staffs 70 G11
Longridge W Loth 126 G5
Longriggend N Lans 126 E3
Long Riston E R Yk 93 K2
Longrock Cnwll 2 E7
Longsdon Staffs 70 H4
Longshaw Wigan 82 B4
Longside Abers 159 P8
Long Sight Oldham 89 Q9
Longslow Shrops 70 B7
Longstanton Cambs 62 E7
Longstock Hants 22 C7
Longstone Pembks 41 M9
Longstowe Cambs 62 D10
Long Stratton Norfk 64 H3
Long Street M Keyn 49 L5
Longstreet Wilts 21 M4
Long Sutton Hants 23 K5
Long Sutton Lincs 74 H6
Long Sutton Somset 19 N9
Longthorpe C Pete 74 C11
Long Thurlow Suffk 64 E8
Longthwaite Cumb 101 M6
Longton C Stke 70 G6
Longton Lancs 88 F5
Longtown Cumb 110 G7
Longtown Herefs 45 L9
Longueville Jersey 11 c2
Longville in the Dale Shrops 57 J6
Long Waste Wrekin 69 R11
Long Whatton Leics 72 D6
Longwick Bucks 35 L3
Long Wittenham Oxon 34 F6
Longwitton Nthumb 112 G3
Longwood D & G 108 F8
Longwood Shrops 57 L3
Longworth Oxon 34 C5
Longyester E Loth 128 E7
Lôn-las Swans 29 K5
Lonmay Abers 159 P6
Lonmore Highld 152 D8
Looe Cnwll 5 M11
Loose Kent 38 C11
Loosebeare Devon 8 H3
Loosegate Lincs 74 F5
Loosley Row Bucks 35 M4
Lootcherbrae Abers 158 F7
Lopcombe Corner Wilts 21 Q7
Lopen Somset 11 J2
Loppington Shrops 69 N9
Lorbottle Nthumb 119 K9
Lordington W Susx 15 L5
Lordsbridge Norfk 75 L8
Lordshill C Sotn 22 C11
Lords Wood Medway 38 C9
Lornty P & K 142 B8
Loscoe Derbys 84 F11
Loscombe Dorset 11 K5
Losgaintir W Isls 168 f8
Lossiemouth Moray 157 N3
Lostford Shrops 69 R8
Lostock Gralam Ches W 82 E10
Lostock Green Ches W 82 E10
Lostock Hall Lancs 88 G5
Lostock Hall Fold Bolton 89 K9
Lostock Junction Bolton 89 K9
Lostwithiel Cnwll 5 J10
Lothbeg Highld 163 L4
Lothersdale N York 96 E11
Lothmore Highld 163 M4
Loudwater Bucks 35 P6
Loughborough Leics 72 E7
Loughor Swans 28 G5
Loughton Essex 51 K11
Loughton M Keyn 49 M7
Loughton Shrops 57 L8
Lound Lincs 73 R7
Lound Notts 85 L3
Lound Suffk 65 Q2
Lounston Devon 9 J9
Lount Leics 72 B7
Louth Lincs 87 K3
Loveclough Lancs 89 N5
Lovedean Hants 15 J4
Lover Wilts 21 P10
Loversall Donc 91 P11
Loves Green Essex 51 P10
Lovesome Hill N York 104 C11
Loveston Pembks 41 L9
Lovington Somset 19 Q8
Low Ackworth Wakefd 91 M7
Low Angerton Nthumb 112 G4
Lowbands Gloucs 46 E8
Low Barbeth D & G 106 D4
Low Barlings Lincs 86 E6
Low Bell End N York 105 K11
Low Bentham N York 95 N7
Low Biggins Cumb 95 N5
Low Borrowbridge Cumb 102 B10
Low Bradfield Sheff 84 C2
Low Bradley N York 96 F11
Low Braithwaite Cumb 101 M2
Low Burnham N Linc 92 C10
Low Buston Nthumb 119 P9
Lowca Cumb 100 C6
Low Catton E R Yk 98 E10
Low Coniscliffe Darltn 103 Q8
Low Crosby Cumb 110 H9
Lowdham Notts 85 L11
Low Dinsdale Darltn 104 B8
Lowe Shrops 69 N8
Lowe Hill Staffs 70 H3
Low Ellington N York 97 K4
Lower Aisholt Somset 18 H7
Lower Ansty Dorset 12 C4
Lower Apperley Gloucs 46 G9
Lower Arboll Highld 163 K10
Lower Arncott Oxon 48 H11
Lower Ashton Devon 9 K8
Lower Assendon Oxon 35 K8
Lower Badcall Highld 164 E8
Lower Ballam Lancs 88 D4
Lower Bartle Lancs 88 F4
Lower Basildon W Berk 34 H9
Lower Bearwood Herefs 45 M3
Lower Beeding W Susx 24 F5
Lower Benefield Nhants 61 L3
Lower Bentley Worcs 58 E11
Lower Beobridge Shrops 57 P6
Lower Birchwood Derbys 84 F10
Lower Boddington Nhants 48 E4
Lower Boscaswell Cnwll 2 B7
Lower Bourne Surrey 23 M6
Lower Brailes Warwks 48 B7
Lower Breakish Highld 145 L3
Lower Bredbury Stockp 83 K6
Lower Broadheath Worcs 46 F3
Lower Broxwood Herefs 45 M4
Lower Buckenhill Herefs 46 B8
Lower Bullingham Herefs 45 Q7
Lower Burgate Hants 21 N11
Lower Burrowton Devon 9 P5
Lower Burton Herefs 45 N3
Lower Caldecote C Beds 61 Q11
Lower Cam Gloucs 32 D4
Lower Canada N Som 19 L3
Lower Catesby Nhants 60 B9
Lower Chapel Powys 44 E7
Lower Chicksgrove Wilts 21 J9
Lower Chute Wilts 22 B4
Lower Clapton Gt Lon 36 H3
Lower Clent Worcs 58 D9
Lower Common Hants 23 L2
Lower Creedy Devon 9 K4
Lower Crossings Derbys 83 M8
Lower Cumberworth Kirk 90 G9
Lower Darwen Bl w D 89 K5
Lower Dean Bed 61 N7
Lower Denby Kirk 90 G9
Lower Diabaig Highld 153 P5
Lower Dicker E Susx 25 N8
Lower Dinchope Shrops 56 H8
Lower Down Shrops 56 E8
Lower Dunsforth N York 97 P8
Lower Egleton Herefs 46 B5
Lower Elkstone Staffs 71 K3
Lower Ellastone Staffs 71 L6
Lower End Bucks 35 J3
Lower End M Keyn 49 P7
Lower End Nhants 60 H9
Lower End Nhants 61 J8
Lower Everleigh Wilts 21 N4
Lower Exbury Hants 14 D7
Lower Eythorne Kent 27 N2
Lower Failand N Som 31 P10
Lower Farringdon Hants 23 K7
Lower Feltham Gt Lon 36 C6
Lower Fittleworth W Susx 24 B7
Lower Foxdale IoM 80 c6
Lower Frankton Shrops 69 L8
Lower Freystrop Pembks 41 J8
Lower Froyle Hants 23 L6
Lower Gabwell Devon 7 N5
Lower Gledfield Highld 162 D8
Lower Godney Somset 19 N6
Lower Gornal Dudley 58 D6
Lower Gravenhurst C Beds 50 D3
Lower Green Herts 50 E4
Lower Green Herts 51 K4
Lower Green Kent 25 N2
Lower Green Kent 25 P2
Lower Green Norfk 76 D4
Lower Green Staffs 58 D3
Lower Green Suffk 63 M7
Lower Hacheston Suffk 65 L10
Lower Halstock Leigh Dorset 11 L3
Lower Halstow Kent 38 E8
Lower Hamworthy BCP 12 G6
Lower Hardres Kent 39 L11
Lower Harpton Herefs 45 K2
Lower Hartlip Kent 38 D9
Lower Hartshay Derbys 84 E10
Lower Hartwell Bucks 35 L2
Lower Hatton Staffs 70 E7
Lower Hawthwaite Cumb 94 E3
Lower Hergest Herefs 45 K3
Lower Heyford Oxon 48 E10
Lower Heysham Lancs 95 J8
Lower Higham Kent 38 B7
Lower Holbrook Suffk 53 L4
Lower Hordley Shrops 69 L9
Lower Horncroft W Susx 24 B7
Lowerhouse Lancs 89 N4
Lower Houses Kirk 90 F7
Lower Howsell Worcs 46 E5
Lower Irlam Salfd 82 F6
Lower Kilburn Derbys 72 B2
Lower Kilcott Gloucs 32 E7
Lower Killeyan Ag & B 122 C11
Lower Kingcombe Dorset 11 M5
Lower Kingswood Surrey 36 F10
Lower Kinnerton Ches W 69 K2
Lower Langford N Som 19 N2
Lower Largo Fife 135 L7
Lower Leigh Staffs 71 J7
Lower Lemington Gloucs 47 P8
Lower Llanfadog Powys 55 M11
Lower Lovacott Devon 17 J6
Lower Loxhore Devon 17 L4
Lower Lydbrook Gloucs 46 A11
Lower Lye Herefs 56 G11
Lower Machen Newpt 30 H7
Lower Maes-coed Herefs 45 L8
Lower Mannington Dorset 13 J4
Lower Marston Somset 20 E6
Lower Meend Gloucs 31 Q4
Lower Merridge Somset 18 H8
Lower Middleton Cheney Nhants 48 F6
Lower Milton Somset 19 P5
Lower Moor Worcs 47 J5
Lower Morton S Glos 32 B6
Lower Nazeing Essex 51 J9
Lower Norton Warwks 47 P2
Lower Nyland Dorset 20 E10
Lower Penarth V Glam 30 G11
Lower Penn Staffs 58 C5
Lower Pennington Hants 13 P6
Lower Penwortham Lancs 88 G5
Lower Peover Ches E 82 F10
Lower Place Rochdl 89 Q8
Lower Pollicott Bucks 35 K2
Lower Quinton Warwks 47 N5
Lower Rainham Medway 38 D8
Lower Raydon Suffk 52 H4
Lower Roadwater Somset 18 D7
Lower Salter Lancs 95 N8
Lower Seagry Wilts 33 J8
Lower Sheering Essex 51 L8
Lower Shelton C Beds 49 Q6
Lower Shiplake Oxon 35 L9
Lower Shuckburgh Warwks 48 E2
Lower Slaughter Gloucs 47 N10
Lower Soothill Kirk 90 H6
Lower Soudley Gloucs 32 C3
Lower Standen Kent 27 M3
Lower Stanton St Quintin Wilts 32 H8
Lower Stoke Medway 38 D6
Lower Stondon C Beds 50 E3
Lower Stone Gloucs 32 C6
Lower Stonnall Staffs 58 G4
Lower Stow Bedon Norfk 64 D3
Lower Street Dorset 12 D5
Lower Street E Susx 26 B9
Lower Street Norfk 77 K4
Lower Street Suffk 63 N10
Lower Street Suffk 64 G11
Lower Stretton Warrtn 82 D8
Lower Stroud Dorset 11 K5
Lower Sundon C Beds 50 C5
Lower Swanwick Hants 14 E5
Lower Swell Gloucs 47 N9
Lower Tadmarton Oxon 48 D7
Lower Tale Devon 9 Q4
Lower Tasburgh Norfk 64 H2
Lower Tean Staffs 71 J7
Lower Thurlton Norfk 65 N2
Lower Town Cnwll 2 H8
Lower Town Devon 7 J4
Lower Town Herefs 46 B6
Lower Town Pembks 41 J3
Lower Trebullett Cnwll 5 N6
Lower Treluswell Cnwll 3 K6
Lower Tysoe Warwks 48 B5
Lower Ufford Suffk 65 K11
Lower Upcott Devon 9 L8
Lower Upham Hants 22 F11
Lower Upnor Medway 38 C7
Lower Vexford Somset 18 F7
Lower Walton Warrtn 82 D7
Lower Waterston Dorset 12 B5
Lower Weare Somset 19 M4
Lower Weedon Nhants 60 D9
Lower Welson Herefs 45 K4
Lower Westmancote Worcs 46 H7
Lower Whatcombe Dorset 12 D4
Lower Whatley Somset 20 D5
Lower Whitley Ches W 82 D9
Lower Wick Gloucs 32 D5
Lower Wick Worcs 46 F4
Lower Wield Hants 22 H6
Lower Willingdon E Susx 25 N10
Lower Withington Ches E 82 H11
Lower Woodend Bucks 35 M7
Lower Woodford Wilts 21 M7
Lower Wraxhall Dorset 11 M4
Lower Wyche Worcs 46 E6
Lower Wyke C Brad 90 F5
Lowesby Leics 73 J9
Lowestoft Suffk 65 Q3
Loweswater Cumb 100 F6
Low Fell Gatesd 113 L9
Lowfield Heath W Susx 24 G3
Low Gartachorrans Stirlg 132 F10
Low Gate Nthumb 112 D8
Low Gettbridge Cumb 111 K9
Lowgill Cumb 102 B11
Lowgill Lancs 95 P8
Low Grantley N York 97 K6
Low Green N York 97 K9
Low Habberley Worcs 57 Q9
Low Ham Somset 19 M9
Low Harrogate N York 97 L9
Low Hawsker N York 105 P9
Low Hesket Cumb 111 J11
Low Hutton N York 98 F7
Lowick Cumb 94 F3
Lowick Nhants 61 L4

Lowick Nthumb 119 K3
Lowick Bridge Cumb 94 F3
Lowick Green Cumb 94 F3
Low Knipe Cumb 101 P7
Low Laithe N York 97 J8
Lowlands Dur 103 M5
Lowlands Torfn 31 J5
Low Langton Lincs 86 G5
Low Leighton Derbys 83 M7
Low Lorton Cumb 100 G5
Low Marishes N York 98 G5
Low Marnham Notts 85 P7
Low Middleton Nthumb 119 M3
Low Mill N York 105 J11
Low Moor C Brad 90 F5
Low Moorsley Sundld 113 M11
Low Moresby Cumb 100 C6
Low Newton Cumb 95 J4
Low Row Cumb 100 G2
Low Row Cumb 101 L3
Low Row Cumb 111 L8
Low Row N York 103 J11
Low Salchrie D & G 106 D4
Low Santon N Linc 92 F8
Lowsonford Warwks 59 J11
Low Street Norfk 77 L7
Low Street Thurr 37 Q5
Low Tharston Norfk 64 H2
Lowther Cumb 101 P6
Lowthorpe E R Yk 99 M8
Lowton Devon 8 G4
Lowton Somset 18 G11
Lowton Wigan 82 D5
Lowton Common Wigan 82 D5
Lowton St Mary's Wigan 82 D5
Low Torry Fife 134 C10
Low Toynton Lincs 87 J6
Low Valley Barns 91 L10
Low Wood Cumb 94 G4
Low Worsall N York 104 C9
Low Wray Cumb 101 L10
Loxbeare Devon 18 B11
Loxhill Surrey 24 B3
Loxhore Devon 17 L4
Loxhore Cott Devon 17 L4
Loxley Warwks 47 Q4
Loxley Green Staffs 71 K8
Loxter Herefs 46 D6
Loxton N Som 19 L3
Loxwood W Susx 24 B4
Lubenham Leics 60 F3
Lucasgate Lincs 87 M11
Lucas Green Surrey 23 P2
Luccombe Somset 18 B6
Luccombe Village IoW 14 G11
Lucker Nthumb 119 N4
Luckett Cnwll 5 P7
Lucking Street Essex 52 D5
Luckington Wilts 32 F8
Lucklawhill Fife 135 L3
Lucknam Wilts 32 F10
Luckwell Bridge Somset 18 B7
Lucton Herefs 45 N2
Lucy Cross N York 103 P8
Ludag W Isls 168 c16
Ludborough Lincs 93 N11
Ludbrook Devon 6 H8
Ludchurch Pembks 41 M8
Luddenden Calder 90 C5
Luddenden Foot Calder 90 C5
Luddenham Court Kent 38 G9
Luddesdown Kent 37 Q7
Luddington N Linc 92 D7
Luddington Warwks 47 N4
Luddington in the Brook Nhants 61 P4
Ludford Lincs 86 G3
Ludford Shrops 57 J10
Ludgershall Bucks 49 J11
Ludgershall Wilts 21 Q4
Ludgvan Cnwll 2 E7
Ludham Norfk 77 M8
Ludlow Shrops 57 J9
Ludney Somset 10 H2
Ludwell Wilts 20 H10
Ludworth Dur 104 C2
Luffenhall Herts 50 G5
Luffincott Devon 5 N3
Luffness E Loth 128 D4
Lugar E Ayrs 115 L3
Luggate Burn E Loth 128 F5
Lugg Green Herefs 45 N2
Luggiebank N Lans 126 D3
Lugton E Ayrs 125 L7
Lugwardine Herefs 45 R6
Luib Highld 145 J2
Luing Ag & B 130 E5
Lulham Herefs 45 N6
Lullington Derbys 59 K2
Lullington E Susx 25 M10
Lullington Somset 20 E4
Lulsgate Bottom N Som 31 P11
Lulsley Worcs 46 D3
Lulworth Camp Dorset 12 D8
Lumb Calder 90 C6
Lumb Lancs 89 N6
Lumbutts Calder 90 B6
Lumby N York 91 M4
Lumphanan Abers 150 F7
Lumphinnans Fife 134 F9
Lumsden Abers 150 D3
Lunan Angus 143 M7
Lunanhead Angus 142 H7
Luncarty P & K 134 D2
Lund E R Yk 99 K11
Lund N York 91 R4
Lundie Angus 142 D10
Lundin Links Fife 135 L7
Lundin Mill Fife 135 L7
Lundy Devon 16 A2
Lundy Green Norfk 65 J3
Lunga Ag & B 130 E6
Lunna Shet 169 r7
Lunsford Kent 37 Q9
Lunsford's Cross E Susx 26 B9
Lunt Sefton 81 L4
Luntley Herefs 45 M3
Luppitt Devon 10 D3
Lupridge Devon 7 J8
Lupset Wakefd 91 J7
Lupton Cumb 95 M4
Lurgashall W Susx 23 P9
Lurley Devon 18 B11
Lusby Lincs 87 K7
Luscombe Devon 7 K7
Luson Devon 6 G8
Luss Ag & B 132 D9
Lussagiven Ag & B 130 C10
Lusta Highld 152 D6
Lustleigh Devon 9 J8
Luston Herefs 45 P2
Luthermuir Abers 143 M4
Luthrie Fife 135 J4
Lutley Dudley 58 D8
Luton Devon 9 M9
Luton Devon 10 B4
Luton Luton 50 C6
Luton Medway 38 C8
Luton Airport Luton 50 D6
Lutterworth Leics 60 B4
Lutton Devon 6 F7
Lutton Devon 6 H6
Lutton Lincs 74 H5
Lutton Nhants 61 P3
Luxborough Somset 18 C7
Luxulyan Cnwll 4 H10
Luxulyan Valley Cnwll 4 H10
Luzley Tamesd 83 L4
Lybster Highld 167 M9
Lydbury North Shrops 56 E7
Lydcott Devon 17 M4
Lydd Kent 26 H7
Lydd Airport Kent 27 J7
Lydden Kent 27 N2
Lydden Kent 39 Q8
Lyddington Rutlnd 73 M11
Lydd-on-Sea Kent 27 J8
Lydeard St Lawrence Somset 18 F8
Lyde Green Hants 23 K3
Lydford Devon 8 D7
Lydford on Fosse Somset 19 Q8
Lydgate Calder 89 Q5
Lydgate Rochdl 90 B7
Lydham Shrops 56 E6
Lydiard Green Wilts 33 L7
Lydiard Millicent Wilts 33 L7
Lydiard Tregoze Swindn 33 M8
Lydiate Sefton 81 M4
Lydiate Ash Worcs 58 E9
Lydlinch Dorset 12 B2
Lydney Gloucs 32 B4
Lydstep Pembks 41 L11
Lye Dudley 58 D8
Lye Cross N Som 19 N2
Lye Green Bucks 35 Q4
Lye Green E Susx 25 M4
Lye Green Warwks 59 J11
Lye Head Worcs 57 P10
Lye's Green Wilts 20 F5
Lyford Oxon 34 C6
Lymbridge Green Kent 27 K3
Lyme Regis Dorset 10 G6
Lyminge Kent 27 L3
Lymington Hants 13 P5
Lyminster W Susx 24 B10
Lymm Warrtn 82 E7
Lymm Services Warrtn 82 E8
Lympne Kent 27 K4
Lympsham Somset 19 K4
Lympstone Devon 9 N8
Lynbridge Devon 17 N2
Lynchat Highld 148 D7
Lynch Green Norfk 76 H10
Lyndhurst Hants 13 P3
Lyndon Rutlnd 73 N10
Lyndon Green Birm 58 H7
Lyne Border 117 J2
Lyne Surrey 36 B7
Lyneal Shrops 69 M8
Lyne Down Herefs 46 B8
Lyneham Devon 9 L9
Lyneham Oxon 47 Q10
Lyneham Wilts 33 K9
Lyneholmford Cumb 111 K6
Lynemouth Nthumb 113 L2
Lyne of Skene Abers 151 K5
Lynesack Dur 103 L5
Lyness Ork 169 c7
Lyng Norfk 76 F8
Lyng Somset 19 K9
Lynmouth Devon 17 N2
Lynn Staffs 58 G4
Lynn Wrekin 70 D11
Lynsted Kent 38 F9
Lynstone Cnwll 16 C10
Lynton Devon 17 N2
Lynton Cross Devon 17 J3
Lyon's Gate Dorset 11 P3
Lyonshall Herefs 45 L3
Lytchett Matravers Dorset 12 F5
Lytchett Minster Dorset 12 G6
Lyth Highld 167 N4
Lytham Lancs 88 D5
Lytham St Annes Lancs 88 C5
Lythbank Shrops 56 H3
Lythe N York 105 M8
Lythmore Highld 167 J3

M

Mabe Burnthouse Cnwll 3 K7
Mablethorpe Lincs 87 P4
Macclesfield Ches E 83 K10
Macduff Abers 158 H5
Macharioch Ag & B 120 D10
Machen Caerph 30 H7
Machrie N Ayrs 120 G5
Machrihanish Ag & B 120 B7
Machrins Ag & B 136 b3
Machynlleth Powys 54 G4
Machynys Carmth 28 F5
Mackworth Derbys 71 Q7
Macmerry E Loth 128 C5
Maddaford Devon 8 D6
Madderty P & K 134 B3
Maddington Wilts 21 L6
Maddiston Falk 126 G2
Madehurst W Susx 15 Q4
Madeley Staffs 70 D6
Madeley Wrekin 57 M4
Madeley Heath Staffs 70 D5
Madford Devon 10 C2
Madingley Cambs 62 E8
Madley Herefs 45 N7
Madresfield Worcs 46 F5
Madron Cnwll 2 D7
Maenaddwyn IoA 78 H8
Maenan Conwy 79 P11
Maenclochog Pembks 41 L5
Maendy V Glam 30 D9
Maenporth Cnwll 3 K8
Maentwrog Gwynd 67 M6
Maen-y-groes Cerdgn 42 G3
Maer Cnwll 16 C10
Maer Staffs 70 D7
Maerdy Carmth 43 N9
Maerdy Conwy 68 D6
Maerdy Rhondd 30 C5
Maesbrook Shrops 69 K10
Maesbury Shrops 69 K9
Maesbury Marsh Shrops 69 K9
Maes-glas Newpt 31 J7
Maesgwynne Carmth 41 P6
Maeshafn Denbgs 68 H2
Maesllyn Cerdgn 42 G6
Maesmynis Powys 44 E5
Maesmynis Powys 44 E5
Maesteg Brdgnd 29 N6
Maesybont Carmth 43 L11
Maesycwmmer Caerph 30 G6
Magdalen Laver Essex 51 M9
Maggieknockater Moray 157 Q8
Maggots End Essex 51 L5
Magham Down E Susx 25 P8
Maghull Sefton 81 M4
Magna Park Leics 60 B4
Magor Mons 31 M7
Magor Services Mons 31 M7
Maidenbower W Susx 24 G3
Maiden Bradley Wilts 20 F7
Maidencombe Torbay 7 N5
Maidenhayne Devon 10 F5
Maiden Head N Som 31 Q11
Maidenhead W & M 35 N8
Maiden Law Dur 113 J11
Maiden Newton Dorset 11 M5
Maidens S Ayrs 114 D6
Maiden's Green Br For 35 P10
Maidenwell Lincs 87 K5
Maiden Wells Pembks 41 J11
Maidford Nhants 48 H4
Maids Moreton Bucks 49 K7
Maidstone Kent 38 C10
Maidstone Services Kent 38 D10
Maidwell Nhants 60 F5
Mail Shet 169 r9
Maindee Newpt 31 K7
Mainland Ork 169 d6
Mainland Shet 169 r8
Mainsforth Dur 104 B4
Mains of Balhall Angus 143 J5
Mains of Balnakettle Abers 143 L3
Mains of Dalvey Highld 157 L11
Mains of Haulkerton Abers 143 N3
Mains of Lesmoir Abers 150 D2
Mains of Melgunds Angus 143 J6
Mainsriddle D & G 109 K9
Mainstone Shrops 56 D7
Maisemore Gloucs 46 F10
Major's Green Worcs 58 H9
Makeney Derbys 72 B2
Malborough Devon 7 J11
Malcoff Derbys 83 N8
Malden Rushett Gt Lon 36 E8
Maldon Essex 52 E10
Malham N York 96 D8
Maligar Highld 152 H5
Mallaig Highld 145 L8
Mallaigvaig Highld 145 L8
Malleny Mills C Edin 127 M4
Mallows Green Essex 51 L5
Malltraeth IoA 78 G11
Mallwyd Gwynd 55 K2
Malmesbury Wilts 32 H7
Malmsmead Devon 17 P2
Malpas Ches W 69 N5
Malpas Cnwll 3 L5
Malpas Newpt 31 K6
Malshanger Hants 22 G4
Malswick Gloucs 46 D10
Maltby Lincs 87 K4
Maltby Rothm 84 H2
Maltby S on T 104 E8
Maltby le Marsh Lincs 87 N4
Malting Green Essex 52 G7
Maltman's Hill Kent 26 F3
Malton N York 98 F6
Malvern Worcs 46 E5
Malvern Hills 46 E6
Malvern Link Worcs 46 E5
Malvern Wells Worcs 46 E6
Mamble Worcs 57 M10
Mamhilad Mons 31 K4
Manaccan Cnwll 3 K9
Manafon Powys 55 Q4
Manais W Isls 168 g9
Manaton Devon 9 J8
Manby Lincs 87 L3
Mancetter Warwks 59 M5
Manchester Manch 82 H5
Manchester Airport Manch 82 H8
Mancot Flints 81 L11
Mandally Highld 146 H7
Manea Cambs 62 G3
Maney Birm 58 H5
Manfield N York 103 P8
Mangersta W Isls 168 f4
Mangerton Dorset 11 K5
Mangotsfield S Glos 32 C9
Mangrove Green Herts 50 D6
Mangurstadh W Isls 168 f4
Manhay Cnwll 2 H7
Manish W Isls 168 g9
Mankinholes Calder 90 B6
Manley Ches W 81 Q10
Manmoel Caerph 30 G4
Mannal Ag & B 136 B7
Manningford Bohune Wilts 21 M3
Manningford Bruce Wilts 21 M3
Manningham C Brad 90 E3
Mannings Heath W Susx 24 F5
Mannington Dorset 13 J3
Manningtree Essex 53 K5
Mannofield C Aber 151 N7
Manorbier Pembks 41 L11
Manorbier Newton Pembks 41 K10
Manordeilo Carmth 43 N9
Manorhill Border 118 C4
Manorowen Pembks 40 H3
Manor Park Gt Lon 37 K3
Mansell Gamage Herefs 45 M6
Mansell Lacy Herefs 45 N5
Mansergh Cumb 95 N4
Mansfield E Ayrs 115 M5
Mansfield Notts 84 H8
Mansfield Woodhouse Notts 84 H8
Mansriggs Cumb 94 F4
Manston Dorset 20 F11
Manston Kent 39 P8
Manston Leeds 91 K4
Manswood Dorset 12 G3
Manthorpe Lincs 73 N3
Manthorpe Lincs 73 R7
Manton N Linc 92 F10
Manton Notts 85 K5
Manton Rutlnd 73 M10
Manton Wilts 33 N11
Manuden Essex 51 L5
Manwood Green Essex 51 M8
Maperton Somset 20 C9
Maplebeck Notts 85 M8
Maple Cross Herts 36 B2
Mapledurham Oxon 35 J9
Mapledurwell Hants 23 J4
Maplehurst W Susx 24 E6
Maplescombe Kent 37 N8
Mapleton Derbys 71 M5
Mapleton Kent 37 L11
Mapperley Derbys 72 C2
Mapperley Park C Nott 72 F2
Mapperton Dorset 11 L5
Mappleborough Green Warwks 58 G11
Mappleton E R Yk 93 M2
Mapplewell Barns 91 J8
Mappowder Dorset 12 B3
Marazanvose Cnwll 3 K3
Marazion Cnwll 2 E7
Marbhig W Isls 168 j6
Marbury Ches E 69 Q5
March Cambs 74 H11
March S Lans 116 D8
Marcham Oxon 34 E5
Marchamley Shrops 69 Q9
Marchamley Wood Shrops 69 Q8
Marchington Staffs 71 L8
Marchington Woodlands Staffs 71 L9
Marchros Gwynd 66 E9
Marchwiel Wrexhm 69 L5
Marchwood Hants 14 C4
Marcross V Glam 29 P11
Marden Herefs 45 Q5
Marden Kent 26 B3
Marden Wilts 21 L3
Marden Ash Essex 51 N10
Marden Beech Kent 26 B3
Marden's Hill E Susx 25 M4
Marden Thorn Kent 26 C3
Mardlebury Herts 50 G7
Mardy Mons 45 L11
Marefield Leics 73 J9
Mareham le Fen Lincs 87 J8
Mareham on the Hill Lincs 87 J7
Marehay Derbys 84 E11
Marehill W Susx 24 C7
Maresfield E Susx 25 L6
Marfleet C KuH 93 K5
Marford Wrexhm 69 L3
Margam Neath 29 L7
Margaret Marsh Dorset 20 F11
Margaret Roding Essex 51 N8
Margaretting Essex 51 Q10
Margaretting Tye Essex 51 Q10
Margate Kent 39 Q7
Margnaheglish N Ayrs 121 K5
Margrie D & G 108 C10
Margrove Park R & Cl 105 J7
Marham Norfk 75 P9
Marhamchurch Cnwll 16 C11
Marholm C Pete 74 B10
Marian-glas IoA 79 J8
Mariansleigh Devon 17 N7
Marine Town Kent 38 F7
Marionburgh Abers 151 J6
Marishader Highld 152 H5
Maristow Devon 6 D6
Marjoriebanks D & G 109 N4
Mark Somset 19 L5
Markbeech Kent 25 L2
Markby Lincs 87 N5
Mark Causeway Somset 19 L5
Mark Cross E Susx 25 N4
Markeaton C Derb 72 A3
Market Bosworth Leics 72 C10
Market Deeping Lincs 74 B8
Market Drayton Shrops 70 B8
Market Harborough Leics 60 F3
Market Lavington Wilts 21 K4
Market Overton Rutlnd 73 M7
Market Rasen Lincs 86 F3
Market Stainton Lincs 86 H5
Market Warsop Notts 85 J7
Market Weighton E R Yk 92 E2
Market Weston Suffk 64 D6
Markfield Leics 72 D9
Markham Caerph 30 G4
Markham Moor Notts 85 M6
Markinch Fife 134 H7
Markington N York 97 L7
Markle E Loth 128 F4
Marksbury BaNES 20 C2
Mark's Corner IoW 14 E8
Marks Tey Essex 52 F7
Markwell Cnwll 5 P10
Markyate Herts 50 C7
Marlborough Wilts 33 N11
Marlbrook Herefs 45 Q4
Marlbrook Worcs 58 E10
Marlcliff Warwks 47 L4
Marldon Devon 7 M6
Marle Green E Susx 25 N7
Marlesford Suffk 65 L10
Marley Kent 39 L11
Marley Kent 39 P11
Marley Green Ches E 69 Q5
Marley Hill Gatesd 113 K9
Marlingford Norfk 76 G10
Marloes Pembks 40 E9
Marlow Bucks 35 M7
Marlow Herefs 56 G9
Marlow Bottom Bucks 35 M7
Marlpit Hill Kent 37 K11
Marlpits E Susx 25 L5
Marlpits E Susx 26 B9
Marlpool Derbys 84 F11
Marnhull Dorset 20 E11
Marple Stockp 83 L7
Marple Bridge Stockp 83 L7
Marr Donc 91 N9
Marrick N York 103 L11
Marros Carmth 41 P9
Marsden Kirk 90 C8
Marsden S Tyne 113 N8
Marsden Height Lancs 89 P3
Marsett N York 96 D3
Marsh Bucks 35 M3
Marsh C Brad 90 C3
Marsh Devon 10 F2
Marshall's Heath Herts 50 E8
Marshalswick Herts 50 E9
Marsham Norfk 76 H7
Marsh Baldon Oxon 34 G5
Marsh Benham W Berk 34 D11
Marshborough Kent 39 P10
Marshbrook Shrops 56 G7
Marshchapel Lincs 93 Q11
Marsh Farm Luton 50 C5
Marshfield Newpt 31 J8
Marshfield S Glos 32 E10
Marshgate Cnwll 5 K3
Marsh Gibbon Bucks 48 H10
Marsh Green Devon 9 P6
Marsh Green Kent 25 K2
Marsh Green Wrekin 57 L2
Marshland St James Norfk 75 K9
Marsh Lane Derbys 84 F5
Marsh Lane Gloucs 31 Q3
Marshside Sefton 88 D7
Marsh Street Somset 18 C6
Marshwood Dorset 10 H5
Marske N York 103 M10
Marske-by-the-Sea R & Cl 104 H6
Marsland Green Wigan 82 E5
Marston Ches W 82 E9
Marston Herefs 45 M3
Marston Lincs 73 M2
Marston Oxon 34 F3
Marston Staffs 58 B2
Marston Staffs 70 G9
Marston Warwks 59 K6
Marston Wilts 21 J3
Marston Green Solhll 59 J7
Marston Jabbet Warwks 59 N7
Marston Magna Somset 19 Q10
Marston Meysey Wilts 33 M5
Marston Montgomery Derbys 71 L7
Marston Moretaine C Beds 49 Q6
Marston on Dove Derbys 71 N9
Marston St Lawrence Nhants 48 F6
Marston Stannett Herefs 45 R3
Marston Trussell Nhants 60 E3
Marstow Herefs 45 R11
Marsworth Bucks 35 P2
Marten Wilts 21 Q2
Marthall Ches E 82 G9
Martham Norfk 77 P8
Martin Hants 21 L11
Martin Kent 27 P2
Martin Lincs 86 F9
Martin Lincs 86 H7
Martindale Cumb 101 M7
Martin Dales Lincs 86 G8
Martin Drove End Hants 21 L10
Martinhoe Devon 17 M2
Martin Hussingtree Worcs 46 G2
Martinscroft Warrtn 82 E7
Martinstown Dorset 11 N7
Martlesham Suffk 53 M2
Martlesham Heath Suffk 53 M2
Martletwy Pembks 41 K8
Martley Worcs 46 E2
Martock Somset 19 N11
Marton Ches E 83 J11
Marton Ches W 82 D11
Marton Cumb 94 E5
Marton E R Yk 93 L3
Marton E R Yk 99 Q7
Marton Lincs 85 P4
Marton Middsb 104 F7
Marton N York 97 P8
Marton N York 98 E4
Marton Shrops 56 D4
Marton Warwks 59 P11
Marton-le-Moor N York 97 N6
Martyr's Green Surrey 36 C9
Martyr Worthy Hants 22 F8
Marvig W Isls 168 j6
Marwell Wildlife Hants 22 F10
Marwick Ork 169 b4
Marwood Devon 17 J4
Marybank Highld 155 N7
Maryburgh Highld 155 P6
Marygold Border 129 L8
Maryhill C Glas 125 P4
Marykirk Abers 143 M4
Maryland Mons 31 P3
Marylebone Gt Lon 36 G4
Marylebone Wigan 88 H9
Marypark Moray 157 M10
Maryport Cumb 100 D3
Maryport D & G 106 F11
Marystow Devon 8 B8
Mary Tavy Devon 8 D9
Maryton Angus 143 M6
Marywell Abers 150 F8
Marywell Abers 151 N8
Marywell Angus 143 M9
Masham N York 97 K4
Mashbury Essex 51 Q8
Mason N u Ty 113 K6
Masongill N York 95 P5
Mastin Moor Derbys 84 G5
Matching Essex 51 M8
Matching Green Essex 51 M8
Matching Tye Essex 51 M8
Matfen Nthumb 112 F6
Matfield Kent 25 Q2
Mathern Mons 31 P6
Mathon Herefs 46 D5
Mathry Pembks 40 G4
Matlask Norfk 76 H5
Matlock Derbys 84 D9
Matlock Bank Derbys 84 D8
Matlock Bath Derbys 84 C9
Matlock Dale Derbys 84 C9
Matson Gloucs 46 G11
Matterdale End Cumb 101 L6
Mattersey Notts 85 L3
Mattersey Thorpe Notts 85 L3

Mattingley Hants 23 K3
Mattishall Norfk 76 F9
Mattishall Burgh Norfk 76 F9
Mauchline E Ayrs 115 J2
Maud Abers 159 M8
Maufant Jersey 11 c1
Maugersbury Gloucs 47 P9
Maughold IoM 80 g3
Mauld Highld 155 M10
Maulden C Beds 50 C3
Maulds Meaburn Cumb 102 B7
Maunby N York 97 N3
Maund Bryan Herefs 45 R4
Maundown Somset 18 E9
Mautby Norfk 77 P9
Mavesyn Ridware Staffs 71 K11
Mavis Enderby Lincs 87 L7
Mawbray Cumb 109 N11
Mawdesley Lancs 88 F8
Mawdlam Brdgnd 29 M8
Mawgan Cnwll 3 J8
Mawgan Porth Cnwll 4 D8
Maw Green Ches E 70 C3
Mawla Cnwll 3 J4
Mawnan Cnwll 3 K8
Mawnan Smith Cnwll 3 K8
Mawsley Nhants 60 H5
Mawthorpe Lincs 87 N6
Maxey C Pete 74 B9
Maxstoke Warwks 59 K7
Maxted Street Kent 27 K3
Maxton Border 118 B4
Maxton Kent 27 P3
Maxwelltown D & G 109 L5
Maxworthy Cnwll 5 M3
Mayals Swans 28 H7
May Bank Staffs 70 F5
Maybole S Ayrs 114 E6
Maybury Surrey 36 B9
Mayes Green Surrey 24 D3
Mayfield E Susx 25 N5
Mayfield Mdloth 128 B7
Mayfield Staffs 71 M5
Mayford Surrey 23 Q3
May Hill Gloucs 46 D10
Mayland Essex 52 F11
Maylandsea Essex 52 F11
Maynard's Green E Susx 25 N7
Maypole Birm 58 G9
Maypole Kent 39 M9
Maypole Mons 45 P11
Maypole Green Norfk 65 N2
Maypole Green Suffk 64 C10
Maypole Green Suffk 65 K8
May's Green Oxon 35 K8
May's Green Surrey 36 C9
Mead Devon 16 C8
Meadgate BaNES 20 C3
Meadle Bucks 35 M3
Meadowfield Dur 103 P3
Meadowtown Shrops 56 E4
Meadwell Devon 5 Q5
Meaford Staffs 70 F7
Mealabost W Isls 168 j4
Meal Bank Cumb 101 P11
Mealrigg Cumb 109 P11
Mealsgate Cumb 100 H2
Meanwood Leeds 90 H3
Mearbeck N York 96 B8
Meare Somset 19 N6
Meare Green Somset 19 J10
Meare Green Somset 19 K9
Mearns E Rens 125 N6
Mears Ashby Nhants 60 H7
Measham Leics 72 A8
Meath Green Surrey 24 G2
Meathop Cumb 95 J4
Meaux E R Yk 93 J3
Meavaig W Isls 168 f4
Meavy Devon 6 E5
Medbourne Leics 60 H2
Medburn Nthumb 112 H6
Meddon Devon 16 D8
Meden Vale Notts 85 J7
Medlam Lincs 87 K9
Medlar Lancs 88 E3
Medmenham Bucks 35 M8
Medomsley Dur 112 H10
Medstead Hants 23 J7
Medway Services Medway 38 D9
Meerbrook Staffs 70 H2
Meer Common Herefs 45 M4
Meesden Herts 51 K4
Meeson Wrekin 70 A10
Meeth Devon 17 J10
Meeting Green Suffk 63 M9
Meeting House Hill Norfk 77 L6
Meidrim Carmth 41 Q6
Meifod Powys 56 B2
Meigle P & K 142 D9
Meikle Carco D & G 115 Q5
Meikle Earnock S Lans 126 C7
Meikle Kilmory Ag & B 124 D5
Meikle Obney P & K 141 P10
Meikleour P & K 142 B10
Meikle Wartle Abers 158 H11
Meinciau Carmth 28 E2
Meir C Stke 70 G6
Meir Heath Staffs 70 G6
Melbost W Isls 168 j4
Melbourn Cambs 51 J2
Melbourne Derbys 72 B5
Melbourne E R Yk 92 C2
Melbur Cnwll 3 N3
Melbury Devon 16 F8
Melbury Abbas Dorset 20 G10
Melbury Bubb Dorset 11 M3
Melbury Osmond Dorset 11 M3
Melbury Sampford Dorset 11 M3
Melchbourne Bed 61 M7
Melcombe Bingham Dorset 12 C4
Meldon Devon 8 E6
Meldon Nthumb 112 H4
Meldon Park Nthumb 112 H3
Meldreth Cambs 62 E11
Meldrum Stirlg 133 L8
Melfort Ag & B 130 G5
Meliden Denbgs 80 F8
Melinau Pembks 41 N8
Melin-byrhedyn Powys 55 J5
Melincourt Neath 29 M4
Melin-y-coed Conwy 67 Q2
Melin-y-ddol Powys 55 P3
Melin-y-wig Denbgs 68 D5
Melkinthorpe Cumb 101 Q5
Melkridge Nthumb 111 P8
Melksham Wilts 20 H2
Mellangoose Cnwll 2 H8
Mell Green W Berk 34 E9
Mellguards Cumb 110 H11
Melling Lancs 95 M6
Melling Sefton 81 M4
Melling Mount Sefton 81 N4
Mellis Suffk 64 F7
Mellon Charles Highld 160 C8
Mellon Udrigle Highld 160 D7
Mellor Lancs 89 K4
Mellor Stockp 83 L7
Mellor Brook Lancs 89 J4
Mells Somset 20 D5
Mells Suffk 65 N6
Melmerby Cumb 102 B3
Melmerby N York 96 G3
Melmerby N York 97 M5
Melness Highld 165 N4
Melon Green Suffk 64 A10
Melplash Dorset 11 K5
Melrose Border 117 Q4
Melsetter Ork 169 b8
Melsonby N York 103 N9
Meltham Kirk 90 E8
Meltham Mills Kirk 90 E8
Melton E R Yk 92 G5
Melton Suffk 65 K11
Meltonby E R Yk 98 F10
Melton Constable Norfk 76 E5
Melton Mowbray Leics 73 K7
Melton Ross N Linc 93 J8
Melvaig Highld 160 A9
Melverley Shrops 69 K11
Melverley Green Shrops 69 K11
Melvich Highld 166 E4
Membury Devon 10 F4
Membury Services W Berk 34 B9
Memsie Abers 159 N5
Memus Angus 142 G6
Menabilly Cnwll 4 H11
Menagissey Cnwll 3 J4
Menai Bridge IoA 79 K10
Mendham Suffk 65 K5
Mendip Hills 19 P4
Mendlesham Suffk 64 G8
Mendlesham Green Suffk 64 F9
Menheniot Cnwll 5 M9
Menithwood Worcs 57 N11
Menna Cnwll 3 N3
Mennock D & G 115 R6
Menston C Brad 90 F2
Menstrie Clacks 133 P8
Menthorpe N York 92 B4
Mentmore Bucks 49 P11
Meoble Highld 145 N10
Meole Brace Shrops 56 H2
Meonstoke Hants 22 H11
Meopham Kent 37 P7
Meopham Green Kent 37 P7
Meopham Station Kent 37 P7
Mepal Cambs 62 F4
Meppershall C Beds 50 D3
Merbach Herefs 45 L5
Mere Ches E 82 F8
Mere Wilts 20 F8
Mere Brow Lancs 88 E7
Mereclough Lancs 89 P4
Mere Green Birm 58 H5
Mere Green Worcs 47 J2
Mere Heath Ches W 82 E10
Meresborough Medway 38 D9
Mereworth Kent 37 Q10
Meriden Solhll 59 K8
Merkadale Highld 152 F11
Merley BCP 12 H5
Merlin's Bridge Pembks 40 H8
Merrington Shrops 69 N10
Merrion Pembks 40 H11
Merriott Somset 11 J2
Merrivale Devon 8 D9
Merrow Surrey 36 B10
Merry Field Hill Dorset 12 H4
Merry Hill Herts 36 D2
Merryhill Wolves 58 C5
Merry Lees Leics 72 D9
Merrymeet Cnwll 5 M8
Mersea Island Essex 52 H8
Mersey Crossing Halton 81 Q8
Mersham Kent 27 J3
Merstham Surrey 36 G10
Merston W Susx 15 N6
Merstone IoW 14 F9
Merther Cnwll 3 M5
Merthyr Carmth 42 G10
Merthyr Cynog Powys 44 D7
Merthyr Dyfan V Glam 30 F11
Merthyr Mawr Brdgnd 29 N9
Merthyr Tydfil Myr Td 30 D3
Merthyr Vale Myr Td 30 E5
Merton Devon 17 J9
Merton Gt Lon 36 G6
Merton Norfk 64 C2
Merton Oxon 48 G11
Meshaw Devon 17 P8
Messing Essex 52 E8
Messingham N Linc 92 E10
Metfield Suffk 65 K5
Metherell Cnwll 5 Q8
Metheringham Lincs 86 E8
Methil Fife 135 K8
Methilhill Fife 135 K7
Methley Leeds 91 K5
Methley Junction Leeds 91 K5
Methlick Abers 159 L10
Methven P & K 134 C2
Methwold Norfk 63 M2
Methwold Hythe Norfk 63 M2
Mettingham Suffk 65 M4
Metton Norfk 76 J4
Mevagissey Cnwll 3 Q5
Mexborough Donc 91 M10
Mey Highld 167 N2
Meysey Hampton Gloucs 33 M4
Miabhaig W Isls 168 f4
Michaelchurch Herefs 45 Q9
Michaelchurch Escley Herefs 45 L8
Michaelchurch-on-Arrow Powys 45 J4
Michaelstone-y-Fedw Newpt 30 H8
Michaelston-le-Pit V Glam 30 G10
Michaelstow Cnwll 4 H6
Michaelwood Services Gloucs 32 D5
Michelcombe Devon 6 H5
Micheldever Hants 22 F7
Micheldever Station Hants 22 F6
Michelmersh Hants 22 B9
Mickfield Suffk 64 G9
Micklebring Donc 84 H2
Mickleby N York 105 M8
Micklefield Leeds 91 L4
Micklefield Green Herts 50 B11
Mickleham Surrey 36 E10
Mickleover C Derb 71 Q8
Micklethwaite C Brad 90 E2
Micklethwaite Cumb 110 E10
Mickleton Dur 103 J6
Mickleton Gloucs 47 N6
Mickletown Leeds 91 L5
Mickle Trafford Ches W 81 N11
Mickley Derbys 84 D5
Mickley N York 97 L5
Mickley Green Suffk 64 A10
Mickley Square Nthumb 112 G8
Mid Ardlaw Abers 159 M5
Midbea Ork 169 d2
Mid Beltie Abers 150 G7
Mid Bockhampton BCP 13 L5
Mid Calder W Loth 127 K4
Mid Clyth Highld 167 N9
Mid Culbeuchly Abers 158 G5
Middle Assendon Oxon 35 K7
Middle Aston Oxon 48 E9
Middle Barton Oxon 48 D9
Middlebie D & G 110 D5
Middlebridge P & K 141 L4
Middle Chinnock Somset 11 K2
Middle Claydon Bucks 49 K9
Middlecliffe Barns 91 L9
Middlecott Devon 8 H7
Middle Duntisbourne Gloucs 33 J3
Middleham N York 96 H3
Middle Handley Derbys 84 F5
Middle Harling Norfk 64 D4
Middlehill Cnwll 5 M8
Middlehill Wilts 32 F11
Middlehope Shrops 56 H7
Middle Kames Ag & B 131 J10
Middle Littleton Worcs 47 L5
Middle Madeley Staffs 70 D5
Middle Maes-coed Herefs 45 L8
Middlemarsh Dorset 11 P3
Middle Mayfield Staffs 71 L6
Middle Mill Pembks 40 F5
Middlemoor Devon 6 D4
Middle Quarter Kent 26 E4
Middle Rasen Lincs 86 E3
Middle Rocombe Devon 7 N5
Middle Salter Lancs 95 N8
Middlesbrough Middsb 104 E7
Middlesceugh Cumb 101 M2
Middleshaw Cumb 95 M3
Middlesmoor N York 96 G6
Middle Stoford Somset 18 G10
Middle Stoke Medway 38 D6
Middlestone Dur 103 Q4
Middlestone Moor Dur 103 P4
Middle Stoughton Somset 19 M5
Middlestown Wakefd 90 H7
Middle Street Gloucs 32 E4
Middle Taphouse Cnwll 5 K9
Middlethird Border 118 C2
Middleton Ag & B 136 A7
Middleton Cumb 95 N3
Middleton Derbys 71 M2
Middleton Derbys 84 C9
Middleton Essex 52 E4
Middleton Hants 22 D6
Middleton Herefs 57 J11
Middleton Lancs 95 J9
Middleton Leeds 91 J5
Middleton N York 96 H11
Middleton N York 98 F3
Middleton Nhants 60 H3
Middleton Norfk 75 N7
Middleton Nthumb 112 G4
Middleton Nthumb 119 M3
Middleton P & K 134 E6
Middleton Rochdl 89 P9
Middleton Shrops 57 J9
Middleton Shrops 69 K9
Middleton Suffk 65 N8
Middleton Swans 28 D7
Middleton Warwks 59 J5
Middleton Cheney Nhants 48 E6
Middleton Green Staffs 70 H7
Middleton Hall Nthumb 119 J5
Middleton-in-Teesdale Dur 102 H5
Middleton Moor Suffk 65 N8
Middleton One Row Darltn 104 C8
Middleton-on-Leven N York 104 E9
Middleton-on-Sea W Susx 15 Q6
Middleton on the Hill Herefs 45 Q2
Middleton on the Wolds E R Yk 99 J11
Middleton Park C Aber 151 N5
Middleton Priors Shrops 57 L6
Middleton Quernhow N York 97 M5
Middleton St George Darltn 104 B8
Middleton Scriven Shrops 57 M7
Middleton Stoney Oxon 48 F10
Middleton Tyas N York 103 P9
Middletown Cumb 100 C9
Middle Town IoS 2 b3
Middletown N Som 31 N10
Middletown Powys 56 E2
Middle Tysoe Warwks 48 B6
Middle Wallop Hants 21 Q7
Middlewich Ches E 82 F11
Middle Winterslow Wilts 21 P8
Middlewood Cnwll 5 M6
Middlewood Herefs 45 K6
Middle Woodford Wilts 21 M7
Middlewood Green Suffk 64 F9
Middle Yard Gloucs 32 F4
Middlezoy Somset 19 L8
Middridge Dur 103 P5
Midford BaNES 20 E2
Midge Hall Lancs 88 G6
Midgeholme Cumb 111 M9
Midgham W Berk 34 G11
Midgley Calder 90 C5
Midgley Wakefd 90 H8
Mid Holmwood Surrey 36 E11
Midhopestones Sheff 90 G11
Midhurst W Susx 23 N10
Mid Lavant W Susx 15 N5
Midlem Border 117 Q5
Mid Mains Highld 155 M10
Midney Somset 19 N9
Midpark Ag & B 124 C6
Midsomer Norton BaNES 20 C4
Midtown Highld 165 N4
Midville Lincs 87 L9
Midway Ches E 83 K8
Mid Yell Shet 169 s4
Migdale Highld 162 E8
Migvie Abers 150 C6
Milborne Port Somset 20 C11
Milborne St Andrew Dorset 12 D5
Milborne Wick Somset 20 C10
Milbourne Nthumb 112 H5
Milbourne Wilts 33 J7
Milburn Cumb 102 C5
Milbury Heath S Glos 32 C6
Milby N York 97 P7
Milcombe Oxon 48 D8
Milden Suffk 52 G2
Mildenhall Suffk 63 M6
Mildenhall Wilts 33 P11
Milebrook Powys 56 E10
Milebush Kent 26 C2
Mile Elm Wilts 33 J11
Mile End Essex 52 G6
Mile End Gloucs 31 Q2
Mile End Suffk 65 L4
Mileham Norfk 76 C8
Mile Oak Br & H 24 F9
Mile Oak Kent 25 Q2
Mile Oak Staffs 59 J4
Miles Hope Herefs 45 R2
Milesmark Fife 134 D10
Miles Platting Manch 83 J5
Mile Town Kent 38 F7
Milfield Nthumb 118 H4
Milford Derbys 84 E11
Milford Devon 16 C7
Milford Powys 55 P6
Milford Staffs 70 H10
Milford Surrey 23 P6
Milford Haven Pembks 40 H9
Milford on Sea Hants 13 N6
Milkwall Gloucs 31 Q3
Millais Jersey 11 a1
Milland W Susx 23 M9
Milland Marsh W Susx 23 M9
Mill Bank Calder 90 C6
Millbeck Cumb 101 J5
Millbreck Abers 159 P9
Millbridge Surrey 23 M6
Millbrook C Beds 50 B3
Millbrook C Sotn 14 C4
Millbrook Cnwll 6 C8
Millbrook Jersey 11 b2
Millbrook Tamesd 83 L5
Mill Brow Stockp 83 L7
Millbuie Abers 151 K6
Millbuie Highld 155 Q7
Millcombe Devon 7 L9
Mill Common Norfk 77 L11
Mill Common Suffk 65 N5
Millcorner E Susx 26 D7
Millcraig Highld 156 B3
Mill Cross Devon 7 J6
Milldale Staffs 71 L4
Mill End Bucks 35 L7
Millend Gloucs 32 D5
Mill End Herts 50 H4
Millerhill Mdloth 127 Q4
Miller's Dale Derbys 83 P10
Millers Green Derbys 71 P4
Miller's Green Essex 51 N9
Millerston C Glas 125 Q4
Millgate Lancs 89 P7
Mill Green Cambs 63 K11
Mill Green Essex 51 P10
Mill Green Herts 50 F8
Mill Green Lincs 74 D6
Mill Green Norfk 64 G5
Millgreen Shrops 70 B9
Mill Green Staffs 58 G4
Mill Green Staffs 71 K10
Mill Green Suffk 52 G3
Mill Green Suffk 64 D10
Mill Green Suffk 64 G9
Mill Green Suffk 65 L9
Millhalf Herefs 45 K5
Millhayes Devon 10 E4
Millhead Lancs 95 K6
Millheugh S Lans 126 C7
Mill Hill E Susx 25 P9
Mill Hill Gt Lon 36 F2
Millhouse Ag & B 124 B3
Millhouse Cumb 101 L3
Millhousebridge D & G 109 P3
Millhouse Green Barns 90 G10
Millhouses Barns 91 L10
Millhouses Sheff 84 D4
Milliken Park Rens 125 L5
Millin Cross Pembks 41 J8
Millington E R Yk 98 G10
Mill Lane Hants 23 L4
Millmeece Staffs 70 E8
Millness Cumb 95 L4
Mill of Drummond P & K 133 N4
Mill of Haldane W Duns 132 D11
Millom Cumb 94 D4
Millook Cnwll 5 K2
Millpool Cnwll 2 F7
Millpool Cnwll 5 J7
Millport N Ayrs 124 F7
Mill Side Cumb 95 J4
Mill Street Kent 37 Q9
Mill Street Norfk 76 F8
Mill Street Suffk 64 F7
Millthorpe Derbys 84 D5
Millthrop Cumb 95 P2
Milltimber C Aber 151 M7
Milltown Abers 149 P6
Milltown Abers 150 D4
Milltown Cnwll 5 J10
Milltown D & G 110 F5
Milltown Derbys 84 E8
Milltown Devon 17 K4
Milltown Highld 153 N9
Milltown of Auchindoun Moray 157 R9
Milltown of Campfield Abers 150 H7
Milltown of Edinvillie Moray 157 P9
Milltown of Learney Abers 150 G7
Milltown of Rothiemay Moray 158 E8
Milnathort P & K 134 E7
Milngavie E Duns 125 P3
Milnrow Rochdl 89 Q8
Milnthorpe Cumb 95 K4
Milnthorpe Wakefd 91 J7
Milovaig Highld 152 B8
Milson Shrops 57 L10
Milstead Kent 38 F10
Milston Wilts 21 N5
Milthorpe Lincs 74 B4
Milthorpe Nhants 48 G5
Milton C Stke 70 G4
Milton Cambs 62 G8
Milton Cumb 111 L8
Milton D & G 106 H7
Milton D & G 108 H6
Milton Derbys 71 Q9
Milton Highld 155 N11
Milton Highld 155 Q8
Milton Highld 156 D3
Milton Highld 167 P6
Milton Inver 125 K4
Milton Kent 37 Q6
Milton Moray 149 M4
Milton Moray 158 D5
Milton N Som 19 K2
Milton Newpt 31 L7
Milton Notts 85 M6
Milton Oxon 34 E6
Milton Oxon 48 E7
Milton P & K 141 Q5
Milton Pembks 41 K10
Milton Somset 19 N10
Milton Stirlg 132 G7
Milton W Duns 125 L3
Milton Abbas Dorset 12 D4
Milton Abbot Devon 5 Q6
Milton Bridge Mdloth 127 P5
Milton Bryan C Beds 49 Q8
Milton Clevedon Somset 20 C7
Milton Combe Devon 6 D5
Milton Common Oxon 35 J4
Milton Damerel Devon 16 F9
Milton End Gloucs 32 D2
Milton End Gloucs 33 M4
Milton Ernest Bed 61 M9
Milton Green Ches W 69 N3
Milton Hill Oxon 34 E6
Milton Keynes M Keyn 49 N7
Milton Lilbourne Wilts 21 N2
Milton Malsor Nhants 60 F9
Milton Morenish P & K 140 F10
Milton of Auchinhove Abers 150 F7
Milton of Balgonie Fife 135 J7
Milton of Buchanan Stirlg 132 E9
Milton of Campsie E Duns 126 B2
Milton of Finavon Angus 142 H6
Milton of Leys Highld 156 B9
Milton of Murtle C Aber 151 M7
Milton on Stour Dorset 20 E9
Milton Regis Kent 38 F9
Milton Street E Susx 25 M10
Milton-under-Wychwood Oxon 47 Q11
Milverton Somset 18 F9
Milverton Warwks 59 M11
Milwich Staffs 70 H8
Milwr Flints 80 H10
Minard Ag & B 131 K8
Minchington Dorset 12 G2
Minchinhampton Gloucs 32 G4
Mindrum Nthumb 118 F4
Minehead Somset 18 C5
Minera Wrexhm 69 J4
Minety Wilts 33 K6
Minffordd Gwynd 67 K7
Mingarrypark Highld 138 B4
Miningsby Lincs 87 K8
Minions Cnwll 5 M7
Minishant S Ayrs 114 F5
Minllyn Gwynd 55 K2
Minnigaff D & G 107 M4
Minnonie Abers 159 J5
Minshull Vernon Ches E 70 B2
Minskip N York 97 N8
Minstead Hants 13 N2
Minsted W Susx 23 N10
Minster Kent 39 P9
Minsterley Shrops 56 F3
Minster Lovell Oxon 34 B2
Minster-on-Sea Kent 38 G7
Minsterworth Gloucs 46 E11
Minterne Magna Dorset 11 P4
Minterne Parva Dorset 11 P4
Minting Lincs 86 G6
Mintlaw Abers 159 N8
Minto Border 117 R6
Minton Shrops 56 G6
Minwear Pembks 41 K8
Minworth Birm 59 J6
Mirehouse Cumb 100 C7
Mireland Highld 167 P4
Mirfield Kirk 90 G7
Miserden Gloucs 32 H3
Miskin Rhondd 30 D5
Miskin Rhondd 30 D8
Misson Notts 85 L2
Misterton Leics 60 C4
Misterton Notts 85 N2
Misterton Somset 11 K3
Mistley Essex 53 K5
Mistley Heath Essex 53 K5
Mitcham Gt Lon 36 G7
Mitcheldean Gloucs 46 C11
Mitchell Cnwll 3 M3
Mitchellslacks D & G 116 D11
Mitchel Troy Mons 31 N2
Mitford Nthumb 113 J3
Mithian Cnwll 3 J3
Mitton Staffs 70 F11
Mixbury Oxon 48 H8
Mixenden Calder 90 D5
Moats Tye Suffk 64 E10
Mobberley Ches E 82 G9
Mobberley Staffs 71 J6
Moccas Herefs 45 M6
Mochdre Conwy 79 Q9
Mochdre Powys 55 P7
Mochrum D & G 107 K8
Mockbeggar Hants 13 L3
Mockbeggar Kent 26 B2

Mockerkin Cumb 100 E6
Modbury Devon 6 H8
Moddershall Staffs 70 G7
Moelfre IoA 79 J7
Moelfre Powys 68 G9
Moel Tryfan Gwynd 67 J3
Moffat D & G 116 F9
Mogador Surrey 36 F10
Moggerhanger C Beds 61 P11
Moira Leics 71 Q11
Molash Kent 38 H11
Mol-chlach Highld 144 G5
Mold Flints 68 H2
Moldgreen Kirk 90 F7
Molehill Green Essex 51 N6
Molehill Green Essex 52 B7
Molescroft E R Yk 92 H2
Molesden Nthumb 112 H4
Molesworth Cambs 61 N5
Moll Highld 153 K11
Molland Devon 17 Q6
Mollington Ches W 81 M10
Mollington Oxon 48 D5
Mollinsburn N Lans 126 C3
Monachty Cerdgn 43 K2
Mondynes Abers 143 P2
Monewden Suffk 65 J10
Moneydie P & K 134 D2
Moneyrow Green W & M 35 N9
Moniaive D & G 115 Q9
Monifieth Angus 142 H11
Monikie Angus 142 H10
Monimail Fife 134 H5
Monington Pembks 41 M2
Monk Bretton Barns 91 K9
Monken Hadley Gt Lon 50 F11
Monk Fryston N York 91 N5
Monkhide Herefs 46 B6
Monkhill Cumb 110 F9
Monkhopton Shrops 57 L6
Monkland Herefs 45 P3
Monkleigh Devon 16 H7
Monknash V Glam 29 P10
Monkokehampton Devon 8 E3
Monkseaton N Tyne 113 M6
Monks Eleigh Suffk 52 G2
Monk's Gate W Susx 24 F5
Monks Heath Ches E 82 H10
Monk Sherborne Hants 22 H3
Monks Horton Kent 27 K3
Monksilver Somset 18 E7
Monks Kirby Warwks 59 Q8
Monk Soham Suffk 65 J8
Monkspath Solhll 58 H9
Monks Risborough Bucks 35 M4
Monksthorpe Lincs 87 M7
Monk Street Essex 51 P5
Monkswood Mons 31 K4
Monkton Devon 10 D4
Monkton Kent 39 N9
Monkton S Ayrs 114 G2
Monkton S Tyne 113 M8
Monkton V Glam 29 P10
Monkton Combe BaNES 20 E2
Monkton Deverill Wilts 20 G7
Monkton Farleigh Wilts 32 F11
Monkton Heathfield Somset 19 J9
Monkton Up Wimborne Dorset 12 H2
Monkton Wyld Dorset 10 G5
Monkwearmouth Sundld 113 N9
Monkwood Hants 23 J8
Monmore Green Wolves 58 D5
Monmouth Mons 31 P2
Monnington on Wye Herefs 45 M6
Monreith D & G 107 L9
Montacute Somset 19 N11
Montcliffe Bolton 89 K8
Montford Shrops 56 G2
Montford Bridge Shrops 69 M11
Montgarrie Abers 150 F4
Montgomery Powys 56 C5
Monton Salfd 82 G5
Montrose Angus 143 N6
Mont Saint Guern 10 b2
Monxton Hants 22 B6
Monyash Derbys 83 Q11
Monymusk Abers 150 H4
Monzie P & K 133 P2
Moodiesburn N Lans 126 B3
Moonzie Fife 135 J4
Moor Allerton Leeds 91 J3
Moorbath Dorset 11 J5
Moorby Lincs 87 J8
Moorcot Herefs 45 M3
Moor Crichel Dorset 12 G3
Moordown BCP 13 J6
Moore Halton 82 C8
Moor End C Beds 49 Q10
Moor End Calder 90 D5
Moor End Devon 17 M10
Moorend Gloucs 32 D4
Moor End Lancs 88 D2
Moor End N York 91 Q3
Moorends Donc 92 A7
Moorgreen Hants 22 E11
Moor Green Herts 50 H5
Moorgreen Notts 84 G11
Moorhall Derbys 84 D6
Moorhampton Herefs 45 M5
Moorhead C Brad 90 E3
Moor Head Leeds 90 G5
Moorhouse Cumb 110 E10
Moorhouse Cumb 110 F9
Moorhouse Donc 91 M8
Moorhouse Notts 85 N7
Moorhouse Bank Surrey 37 K10
Moorland Somset 19 K8
Moorlinch Somset 19 L7
Moor Monkton N York 97 R9
Moor Row Cumb 100 D8
Moor Row Cumb 110 D11
Moorsholm R & Cl 105 J8
Moorside Dorset 20 E11
Moorside Dur 112 G11
Moor Side Lancs 88 E4
Moor Side Lancs 88 F3
Moorside Leeds 90 G3
Moor Side Lincs 87 J9
Moorside Oldham 89 Q9
Moorstock Kent 27 K4
Moor Street Birm 58 E8
Moor Street Medway 38 D8
Moorswater Cnwll 5 L9
Moorthorpe Wakefd 91 M8
Moortown Devon 6 E4
Moortown Hants 13 L4
Moortown IoW 14 D10
Moortown Leeds 90 H3
Moortown Lincs 93 J11
Moortown Wrekin 69 R11
Morangie Highld 162 H10
Morar Highld 145 L9
Morborne Cambs 61 P2
Morchard Bishop Devon 9 J3
Morchard Road Devon 9 J3
Morcombelake Dorset 11 J6
Morcott Rutlnd 73 N10
Morda Shrops 69 J9
Morden Dorset 12 F5
Morden Gt Lon 36 G7
Mordiford Herefs 45 R7
Mordon Dur 104 B5
More Shrops 56 E6
Morebath Devon 18 C9
Morebattle Border 118 E6
Morecambe Lancs 95 J8
Moredon Swindn 33 M7
Morefield Highld 161 J7
Morehall Kent 27 M4
Moreleigh Devon 7 K8
Morenish P & K 140 F10
Moresby Parks Cumb 100 C7
Morestead Hants 22 F9
Moreton Dorset 12 D7
Moreton Essex 51 M9
Moreton Herefs 45 Q2
Moreton Oxon 35 J4
Moreton Staffs 70 D11
Moreton Staffs 71 L9
Moreton Wirral 81 K7
Moreton Corbet Shrops 69 Q10
Moretonhampstead Devon 9 J7
Moreton-in-Marsh Gloucs 47 P8
Moreton Jeffries Herefs 46 B5
Moretonmill Shrops 69 Q10
Moreton Morrell Warwks 48 B3
Moreton on Lugg Herefs 45 Q5
Moreton Paddox Warwks 48 B4
Moreton Pinkney Nhants 48 G5
Moreton Say Shrops 70 A8
Moreton Valence Gloucs 32 E3
Morfa Cerdgn 42 F4
Morfa Bychan Gwynd 67 J7
Morfa Dinlle Gwynd 66 G3
Morfa Glas Neath 29 N3
Morfa Nefyn Gwynd 66 D6
Morganstown Cardif 30 F8
Morgan's Vale Wilts 21 N10
Morham E Loth 128 F5
Moriah Cerdgn 54 E9
Morland Cumb 102 B6
Morley Ches E 82 H8
Morley Derbys 72 B2
Morley Dur 103 M5
Morley Leeds 90 H5
Morley Green Ches E 82 H8
Morley St Botolph Norfk 64 F2
Mornick Cnwll 5 N7
Morningside C Edin 127 N3
Morningside N Lans 126 E6
Morningthorpe Norfk 65 J3
Morpeth Nthumb 113 J3
Morphie Abers 143 N5
Morrey Staffs 71 L11
Morridge Side Staffs 71 J4
Morriston Swans 29 J5
Morston Norfk 76 E3
Mortehoe Devon 16 H2
Morthen Rothm 84 G3
Mortimer W Berk 23 J2
Mortimer Common W Berk 35 J11
Mortimer's Cross Herefs 45 N2
Mortimer West End Hants 22 H2
Mortlake Gt Lon 36 F5
Morton Cumb 101 N3
Morton Cumb 110 G10
Morton Derbys 84 F8
Morton IoW 14 H9
Morton Lincs 74 A6
Morton Lincs 85 P2
Morton Lincs 85 Q8
Morton Notts 85 M10
Morton Shrops 69 J10
Morton-on-Swale N York 97 M2
Morton on the Hill Norfk 76 G8
Morton Tinmouth Dur 103 N6
Morvah Cnwll 2 C6
Morval Cnwll 5 M10
Morvich Highld 146 B3
Morville Shrops 57 M6
Morville Heath Shrops 57 M6
Morwenstow Cnwll 16 C8
Mosborough Sheff 84 F4
Moscow E Ayrs 125 M9
Mose Shrops 57 P6
Mosedale Cumb 101 L4
Moseley Birm 58 G8
Moseley Wolves 58 D5
Moseley Worcs 46 F3
Moses Gate Bolton 89 L9
Moss Ag & B 136 B7
Moss Donc 91 P8
Moss Wrexhm 69 K4
Mossat Abers 150 D4
Mossbank Shet 169 r6
Moss Bank St Hel 81 Q5
Mossbay Cumb 100 C5
Mossblown S Ayrs 114 H3
Mossbrow Traffd 82 F7
Mossburnford Border 118 C7
Mossdale D & G 108 E6
Mossdale E Ayrs 115 J7
Moss Edge Lancs 88 E2
Moss End Ches E 82 E9
Mossend N Lans 126 C5
Mosser Mains Cumb 100 F5
Mossley Ches E 70 F2
Mossley Tamesd 83 L4
Mosspaul Hotel Border 117 M11
Moss Side Cumb 110 C10
Moss-side Highld 156 F6
Moss Side Lancs 88 D4
Moss Side Sefton 81 M4
Mosstodloch Moray 157 Q6
Mossyard D & G 107 P7
Mossy Lea Lancs 88 G8
Mosterton Dorset 11 K3
Moston Manch 83 J4
Moston Shrops 69 Q9
Moston Green Ches E 70 C2
Mostyn Flints 80 H8
Motcombe Dorset 20 G9
Mothecombe Devon 6 G9
Motherby Cumb 101 M5
Motherwell N Lans 126 C6
Motspur Park Gt Lon 36 F7
Mottingham Gt Lon 37 K6
Mottisfont Hants 22 B9
Mottisfont Hants 22 B9
Mottistone IoW 14 D10
Mottram in Longdendale Tamesd 83 L5
Mottram St Andrew Ches E 83 J9
Mouilpied Guern 10 b2
Mouldsworth Ches W 81 Q10
Moulin P & K 141 M6
Moulsecoomb Br & H 24 H9
Moulsford Oxon 34 G8
Moulsoe M Keyn 49 P6
Moultavie Highld 156 A3
Moulton Ches W 82 E11
Moulton Lincs 74 F6
Moulton N York 103 P10
Moulton Nhants 60 G7
Moulton Suffk 63 L8
Moulton V Glam 30 E11
Moulton Chapel Lincs 74 E7
Moulton St Mary Norfk 77 M10
Moulton Seas End Lincs 74 F5
Mount Cnwll 4 B10
Mount Cnwll 5 J8
Mount Kirk 90 D7
Mountain C Brad 90 D4
Mountain Ash Rhondd 30 D5
Mountain Cross Border 127 M8
Mountain Street Kent 39 J11
Mount Ambrose Cnwll 3 J5
Mount Bures Essex 52 F5
Mountfield E Susx 26 B7
Mountgerald Highld 155 Q5
Mount Hawke Cnwll 3 J4
Mount Hermon Cnwll 2 H10
Mountjoy Cnwll 4 D9
Mount Lothian Mdloth 127 P6
Mountnessing Essex 51 P11
Mounton Mons 31 P6
Mount Pleasant Ches E 70 E3
Mount Pleasant Derbys 71 P11
Mount Pleasant Derbys 84 D11
Mount Pleasant Dur 103 Q4
Mount Pleasant E R Yk 93 N3
Mount Pleasant E Susx 25 K7
Mount Pleasant Norfk 64 D3
Mount Pleasant Suffk 63 M11
Mount Pleasant Worcs 47 K2
Mountsorrel Leics 72 F8
Mount Sorrel Wilts 21 K10
Mount Tabor Calder 90 D5
Mousehole Cnwll 2 D8
Mouswald D & G 109 N6
Mow Cop Ches E 70 F3
Mowhaugh Border 118 F6
Mowmacre Hill C Leic 72 F9
Mowsley Leics 60 D3
Moy Highld 147 L11
Moy Highld 156 D11
Moyle Highld 145 Q4
Moylegrove Pembks 41 M2
Muasdale Ag & B 120 C3
Muchalls Abers 151 N9
Much Birch Herefs 45 Q8
Much Cowarne Herefs 46 B5
Much Dewchurch Herefs 45 P8
Muchelney Somset 19 M10
Muchelney Ham Somset 19 M10
Much Hadham Herts 51 K7
Much Hoole Lancs 88 F6
Much Hoole Town Lancs 88 F6
Muchlarnick Cnwll 5 L10
Much Marcle Herefs 46 C8
Much Wenlock Shrops 57 L5
Muck Highld 144 F12
Mucking Thurr 37 Q4
Muckleburgh Collection Norfk 76 G3
Muckleford Dorset 11 N6
Mucklestone Staffs 70 C7
Muckley Shrops 57 L5
Muckton Lincs 87 L4
Muddiford Devon 17 K4
Muddles Green E Susx 25 M8
Mudeford BCP 13 L6
Mudford Somset 19 Q11
Mudford Sock Somset 19 Q11
Mudgley Somset 19 N5
Mud Row Kent 38 H7
Mugdock Stirlg 125 P2
Mugeary Highld 152 G10
Mugginton Derbys 71 P6
Muggintonlane End Derbys 71 P6
Muggleswick Dur 112 F11
Muirden Abers 158 H7
Muirdrum Angus 143 K10
Muiresk Abers 158 G8
Muirhead Angus 142 E11
Muirhead Fife 134 H6
Muirhead N Lans 126 B4
Muirhouses Falk 134 C11
Muirkirk E Ayrs 115 N2
Muirmill Stirlg 133 L11
Muir of Fowlis Abers 150 F5
Muir of Miltonduff Moray 157 M6
Muir of Ord Highld 155 P7
Muirshearlich Highld 146 E11
Muirtack Abers 159 N10
Muirton P & K 133 Q5
Muirton Mains Highld 155 N7
Muirton of Ardblair P & K 142 B9
Muker N York 102 H11
Mulbarton Norfk 76 H11
Mulben Moray 157 R7
Mulfra Cnwll 2 D7
Mull Ag & B 137 Q9
Mullacott Cross Devon 17 J3
Mullion Cnwll 2 H10
Mullion Cove Cnwll 2 H10
Mumby Lincs 87 P6
Munderfield Row Herefs 46 B4
Munderfield Stocks Herefs 46 C4
Mundesley Norfk 77 L4
Mundford Norfk 63 P2
Mundham Norfk 65 L2
Mundon Hill Essex 52 E11
Mundy Bois Kent 26 F2
Mungrisdale Cumb 101 L4
Munlochy Highld 156 A7
Munnoch N Ayrs 124 H8
Munsley Herefs 46 C6
Munslow Shrops 57 J7
Murchington Devon 8 G7
Murcot Worcs 47 L6
Murcott Oxon 48 G11
Murcott Wilts 33 J6
Murkle Highld 167 L3
Murlaggan Highld 146 C9
Murrell Green Hants 23 K3
Murroes Angus 142 H10
Murrow Cambs 74 G9
Mursley Bucks 49 M9
Murston Kent 38 F9
Murthill Angus 142 H6
Murthly P & K 141 R10
Murton C York 98 C10
Murton Cumb 102 D6
Murton Dur 113 N11
Murton N Tyne 113 M6
Murton Nthumb 129 P10
Murton Swans 28 G7
Musbury Devon 10 F6
Muscoates N York 98 D5
Musselburgh E Loth 127 Q3
Muston Leics 73 L3
Muston N York 99 M5
Mustow Green Worcs 58 C10
Muswell Hill Gt Lon 36 G3
Mutehill D & G 108 E11
Mutford Suffk 65 P4
Muthill P & K 133 P4
Mutterton Devon 9 P3
Muxton Wrekin 57 N2
Mybster Highld 167 L6
Myddfai Carmth 43 Q8
Myddle Shrops 69 N10
Mydroilyn Cerdgn 43 J3
Myerscough Lancs 88 F3
Mylor Cnwll 3 L6
Mylor Bridge Cnwll 3 L6
Mynachlog ddu Pembks 41 M4
Myndd-llan Flints 80 H10
Myndtown Shrops 56 F7
Mynydd Bach Cerdgn 54 G9
Mynydd-bach Mons 31 N6
Mynydd-Bach Swans 29 J5
Mynyddgarreg Carmth 28 D3
Mynydd Isa Flints 69 J2
Mynydd Llandygai Gwynd 79 L11
Mynytho Gwynd 66 E8
Myrebird Abers 151 J8
Myredykes Border 118 A11
Mytchett Surrey 23 N3
Mytholm Calder 90 B5
Mytholmroyd Calder 90 C5
Mythop Lancs 88 D4
Myton-on-Swale N York 97 P7

N

Naast Highld 160 C10
Nab's Head Lancs 89 J5
Na Buirgh W Isls 168 f8
Naburn C York 98 B11
Naccolt Kent 27 J3
Nackington Kent 39 L11
Nacton Suffk 53 M3
Nafferton E R Yk 99 M9
Nag's Head Gloucs 32 G5
Nailbridge Gloucs 46 B11
Nailsbourne Somset 18 H9
Nailsea N Som 31 N10
Nailstone Leics 72 C9
Nailsworth Gloucs 32 F5
Nairn Highld 156 F6
Nalderswood Surrey 36 F11
Nancegollan Cnwll 2 G7
Nancledra Cnwll 2 D6
Nanhoron Gwynd 66 D8
Nannerch Flints 80 H11
Nanpantan Leics 72 E7
Nanpean Cnwll 4 F10
Nanquidno Cnwll 2 B8
Nanstallon Cnwll 4 G8
Nant-ddu Powys 30 D2
Nanternis Cerdgn 42 G3
Nantgaredig Carmth 43 J10
Nantgarw Rhondd 30 F7
Nant-glas Powys 55 M11
Nantglyn Denbgs 68 D2
Nantgwyn Powys 55 M9
Nant Gwynant Gwynd 67 L4
Nantlle Gwynd 67 J4
Nantmawr Shrops 69 J10
Nantmel Powys 55 N11
Nantmor Gwynd 67 L5
Nant Peris Gwynd 67 L3
Nantwich Ches E 70 B4
Nant-y-Bwch Blae G 30 F2
Nantycaws Carmth 43 J11
Nant-y-derry Mons 31 K3
Nantyffyllon Brdgnd 29 N6
Nantyglo Blae G 30 G2
Nant-y-gollen Shrops 68 H9
Nant-y-moel Brdgnd 29 P6
Nant-y-pandy Conwy 79 M10
Naphill Bucks 35 M5
Napleton Worcs 46 G5
Nappa N York 96 C10
Napton on the Hill Warwks 48 E2
Narberth Pembks 41 M8
Narborough Leics 72 E11
Narborough Norfk 75 P8
Narkurs Cnwll 5 N10
Nasareth Gwynd 66 H5
Naseby Nhants 60 E5
Nash Bucks 49 L8
Nash Gt Lon 37 K8
Nash Herefs 45 L2
Nash Newpt 31 K8
Nash Shrops 57 L10
Nash End Worcs 57 P8
Nashes Green Hants 23 J5
Nash Lee Bucks 35 M3
Nash Street Kent 37 P7
Nassington Nhants 73 R11
Nastend Gloucs 32 E3
Nasty Herts 51 J6
Nateby Cumb 102 E9
Nateby Lancs 88 F2
National Memorial Arboretum Staffs 59 J2
National Motor Museum (Beaulieu) Hants 14 C6
National Space Centre C Leic 72 F9
Natland Cumb 95 L3
Naughton Suffk 52 H2
Naunton Gloucs 47 M10
Naunton Worcs 46 G7
Naunton Beauchamp Worcs 47 J4
Navenby Lincs 86 C9
Navestock Essex 51 M11
Navestock Side Essex 51 N11
Navidale Highld 163 N3
Navity Highld 156 D5
Nawton N York 98 D4
Nayland Suffk 52 G5
Nazeing Essex 51 K9
Nazeing Gate Essex 51 K9
Neacroft Hants 13 L5
Neal's Green Warwks 59 M8
Neap Shet 169 s8
Near Cotton Staffs 71 K5
Near Sawrey Cumb 101 L11
Neasden Gt Lon 36 F3
Neasham Darltn 104 B8
Neath Neath 29 L5
Neatham Hants 23 K6
Neatishead Norfk 77 L7
Nebo Cerdgn 54 C11
Nebo Conwy 67 Q3
Nebo Gwynd 66 H4
Nebo IoA 78 H6
Necton Norfk 76 B10
Nedd Highld 164 D10
Nedderton Nthumb 113 K4
Nedging Suffk 52 G2
Nedging Tye Suffk 52 H2
Needham Norfk 65 J5
Needham Market Suffk 64 F10
Needham Street Suffk 63 M7
Needingworth Cambs 62 D6
Neen Savage Shrops 57 M9
Neen Sollars Shrops 57 M10
Neenton Shrops 57 L7
Nefyn Gwynd 66 E6
Neilston E Rens 125 M6
Nelson Caerph 30 F5
Nelson Lancs 89 P3
Nemphlar S Lans 116 B2
Nempnett Thrubwell BaNES 19 P2
Nenthall Cumb 111 Q11
Nenthead Cumb 102 E2
Nenthorn Border 118 C3
Neopardy Devon 9 J5
Nep Town W Susx 24 F7
Nerabus Ag & B 122 B8
Nercwys Flints 68 H2
Nerston S Lans 125 Q6
Nesbit Nthumb 119 J4
Nesfield N York 96 G11
Ness Ches W 81 L9
Nesscliffe Shrops 69 L11
Neston Ches W 81 K9
Neston Wilts 32 G11
Netchwood Shrops 57 L6
Nether Abington S Lans 116 C6
Nether Alderley Ches E 82 H9
Netheravon Wilts 21 M5
Nether Blainslie Border 117 Q2
Netherbrae Abers 159 J6
Nether Broughton Leics 72 H5
Netherburn S Lans 126 D8
Netherbury Dorset 11 K5
Netherby Cumb 110 G6
Netherby N York 97 M11
Nether Cerne Dorset 11 P5
Nethercleuch D & G 109 P3
Nether Compton Dorset 19 Q11
Nethercote Warwks 60 B8
Nethercott Devon 5 P2
Nethercott Devon 16 H4
Nether Crimond Abers 151 L3
Nether Dallachy Moray 157 R5
Netherend Gloucs 31 Q4
Nether Exe Devon 9 M4
Netherfield E Susx 26 B8
Netherfield Leics 72 F7
Netherfield Notts 72 G2
Nether Fingland S Lans 116 C8
Nethergate N Linc 92 C11
Nethergate Norfk 76 F6
Netherhampton Wilts 21 M9
Nether Handley Derbys 84 F5
Nether Handwick Angus 142 F9
Nether Haugh Rothm 91 L11
Netherhay Dorset 11 J3
Nether Headon Notts 85 M5
Nether Heage Derbys 84 E10
Nether Heyford Nhants 60 E9
Nether Kellet Lancs 95 L7
Nether Kinmundy Abers 159 Q9
Netherland Green Staffs 71 L8
Nether Langwith Notts 84 H6
Netherlaw D & G 108 F12
Netherley Abers 151 M9
Nethermill D & G 109 M3
Nethermuir Abers 159 M9
Netherne-on-the-Hill Surrey 36 G9
Netheroyd Hill Kirk 90 E7
Nether Padley Derbys 84 B5
Nether Poppleton C York 98 B10
Nether Row Cumb 101 K3
Netherseal Derbys 59 L2
Nether Silton N York 97 Q2
Nether Skyborry Shrops 56 D10
Nether Stowey Somset 18 G7
Nether Street Essex 51 N8
Netherstreet Wilts 21 J2
Netherthong Kirk 90 E9
Netherthorpe Derbys 84 F6
Netherton Angus 143 J6
Netherton Devon 7 M4
Netherton Dudley 58 D7
Netherton Hants 22 C3
Netherton Herefs 45 Q9
Netherton Kirk 90 E8
Netherton N Lans 126 D7
Netherton Nthumb 119 J9
Netherton Oxon 34 D5
Netherton P & K 142 A7
Netherton Sefton 81 M5
Netherton Shrops 57 N8

Netherton Stirlg 125 P2
Netherton Wakefd 90 H7
Netherton Worcs 47 J6
Nethertown Cumb 100 C9
Nethertown Highld 167 Q1
Nethertown Lancs 89 L3
Nethertown Staffs 71 L11
Netherurd Border 116 G2
Nether Wallop Hants 22 B7
Nether Wasdale Cumb 100 F10
Nether Welton Cumb 110 G11
Nether Westcote Gloucs 47 P10
Nether Whitacre Warwks 59 K6
Nether Whitecleuch S Lans 116 A7
Nether Winchendon Bucks 35 K2
Netherwitton Nthumb 112 G2
Nethy Bridge Highld 149 J3
Netley Hants 14 E5
Netley Marsh Hants 13 P2
Nettlebed Oxon 35 J7
Nettlebridge Somset 20 B5
Nettlecombe Dorset 11 L5
Nettlecombe IoW 14 F11
Nettleden Herts 50 B8
Nettleham Lincs 86 D5
Nettlestead Kent 37 Q10
Nettlestead Green Kent 37 Q10
Nettlestone IoW 14 H8
Nettlesworth Dur 113 L11
Nettleton Lincs 93 K10
Nettleton Wilts 32 F9
Nettleton Shrub Wilts 32 F9
Netton Devon 6 F9
Netton Wilts 21 M7
Neuadd Carmth 43 P10
Neuadd-ddu Powys 55 L9
Nevendon Essex 38 C3
Nevern Pembks 41 L2
Nevill Holt Leics 60 H2
New Abbey D & G 109 L7
New Aberdour Abers 159 L5
New Addington Gt Lon 37 J8
Newall Leeds 97 J11
New Alresford Hants 22 G8
New Alyth P & K 142 C8
Newark C Pete 74 D10
Newark Ork 169 g2
Newark-on-Trent Notts 85 N10
New Arram E R Yk 92 H2
Newarthill N Lans 126 D6
New Ash Green Kent 37 P7
New Balderton Notts 85 P10
Newbarn Kent 27 L3
New Barn Kent 37 P7
New Barnet Gt Lon 50 G11
New Barton Nhants 61 J8
Newbattle Mdloth 127 Q4
New Bewick Nthumb 119 L6
Newbie D & G 110 C7
Newbiggin Cumb 94 B2
Newbiggin Cumb 94 F7
Newbiggin Cumb 101 N5
Newbiggin Cumb 102 B5
Newbiggin Cumb 111 L11
Newbiggin Dur 102 H5
Newbiggin Dur 112 H11
Newbiggin N York 96 E2
Newbiggin N York 96 F3
Newbiggin-by-the-Sea
Nthumb 113 M3
Newbigging Angus 142 D9
Newbigging Angus 142 G10
Newbigging Angus 142 H10
Newbigging S Lans 127 J8
Newbiggin-on-Lune Cumb 102 D10
New Bilton Warwks 59 Q9
Newbold Derbys 84 E6
Newbold Leics 72 C7
Newbold on Avon Warwks 59 Q9
Newbold on Stour Warwks 47 P5
Newbold Pacey Warwks 47 Q3
Newbold Revel Warwks 59 Q8
Newbold Verdon Leics 72 C10
New Bolingbroke Lincs 87 K9
Newborough C Pete 74 D9
Newborough IoA 78 G11
Newborough Staffs 71 L9
Newbottle Nhants 48 F7
Newbottle Sundld 113 M10
New Boultham Lincs 86 C6
Newbourne Suffk 53 N3
New Bradwell M Keyn 49 M6
New Brampton Derbys 84 E6
New Brancepeth Dur 103 P2
Newbridge C Edin 127 L3
Newbridge Caerph 30 H5
Newbridge Cerdgn 43 K3
Newbridge Cnwll 2 C7
Newbridge Cnwll 3 K5
Newbridge D & G 109 K5
Newbridge Hants 21 Q11
Newbridge IoW 14 D9
New Bridge N York 98 G3
Newbridge Oxon 34 D4
Newbridge Wrexhm 69 J6
Newbridge Green Worcs 46 F7
Newbridge-on-Usk Mons 31 L6
Newbridge-on-Wye Powys 44 E3
New Brighton Flints 81 K11
New Brighton Wirral 81 L6
New Brinsley Notts 84 G10
New Brotton R & Cl 105 J6
Newbrough Nthumb 112 C7
New Broughton Wrexhm 69 K4
New Buckenham Norfk 64 F3
Newbuildings Devon 9 J4
Newburgh Abers 151 P2
Newburgh Abers 159 N6
Newburgh Fife 134 G4
Newburgh Lancs 88 F8
Newburn N u Ty 113 J7
New Bury Bolton 82 F4
Newbury Somset 20 C5
Newbury W Berk 34 E11
Newbury Wilts 20 F6
Newbury Park Gt Lon 37 K3
Newby Cumb 101 Q6
Newby Lancs 96 B11
Newby N York 95 Q7
Newby N York 99 L2
Newby N York 104 F8
Newby Bridge Cumb 94 H3
Newby Cross Cumb 110 G10
Newby East Cumb 111 J9
Newby Head Cumb 101 Q6
New Byth Abers 159 K7
Newby West Cumb 110 G10
Newby Wiske N York 97 N3
Newcastle Mons 45 N11
Newcastle Shrops 56 D8
Newcastle Airport Nthumb 113 J6
Newcastle Emlyn Carmth 42 F6
Newcastleton Border 111 J3
Newcastle-under-Lyme
Staffs 70 E5
Newcastle upon Tyne N u Ty 113 K8
Newchapel Pembks 41 P3
Newchapel Staffs 70 F4
Newchapel Surrey 25 J2
Newchurch Blae G 30 G2
Newchurch Herefs 45 M4
Newchurch IoW 14 G9
Newchurch Kent 27 J5
Newchurch Mons 31 N5
Newchurch Powys 45 J4
Newchurch Staffs 71 L10
Newchurch in Pendle Lancs 89 N3
New Costessey Norfk 76 H9
New Cowper Cumb 109 P11
Newcraighall C Edin 127 Q3
New Crofton Wakefd 91 K7
New Cross Cerdgn 54 E9
New Cross Gt Lon 37 J5
New Cross Somset 19 M11
New Cumnock E Ayrs 115 M5
New Cut E Susx 26 D8
New Deer Abers 159 L8
New Delaval Nthumb 113 L5
New Delph Oldham 90 B9
New Denham Bucks 36 B4
Newdigate Surrey 24 E2
New Duston Nhants 60 F8
New Earswick C York 98 C9
New Eastwood Notts 84 G11
New Edlington Donc 91 N11
New Elgin Moray 157 N5
New Ellerby E R Yk 93 L3
Newell Green Br For 35 N10
New Eltham Gt Lon 37 K6
New End Worcs 47 L2
Newenden Kent 26 D6
New England C Pete 74 C10
New England Essex 52 B3
Newent Gloucs 46 D9
New Farnley Leeds 90 H4
New Ferry Wirral 81 L7
Newfield Dur 103 P4
Newfield Dur 113 K10
Newfield Highld 156 D2
New Fletton C Pete 74 C11
New Forest National Park 13 N3
Newfound Hants 22 G4
New Fryston Wakefd 91 M5
Newgale Pembks 40 G6
New Galloway D & G 108 D5
Newgate Norfk 76 E3
Newgate Street Herts 50 H9
New Gilston Fife 135 L6
New Grimsby IoS 2 b1
Newhall Ches E 69 R5
Newhall Derbys 71 P10
Newham Nthumb 119 N5
New Hartley Nthumb 113 M5
Newhaven C Edin 127 P2
Newhaven Derbys 71 M2
Newhaven E Susx 25 K10
New Haw Surrey 36 C8
New Hedges Pembks 41 M10
New Herrington Sundld 113 M10
Newhey Rochdl 89 Q8
New Holkham Norfk 76 B4
New Holland N Linc 93 J6
Newholm N York 105 N8
New Houghton Derbys 84 G7
New Houghton Norfk 75 Q5
Newhouse N Lans 126 D5
New Houses N York 96 B6
New Houses Wigan 82 C4
New Hutton Cumb 95 M2
New Hythe Kent 38 B10
Newick E Susx 25 K6
Newingreen Kent 27 K4
Newington Kent 27 L4
Newington Kent 38 E9
Newington Oxon 34 H5
Newington Shrops 56 G8
Newington Bagpath Gloucs 32 F6
New Inn Carmth 43 J7
New Inn Torfn 31 K5
New Invention Shrops 56 D9
New Lakenham Norfk 77 J10
New Lanark S Lans 116 B2
New Lanark Village S Lans 116 B2
Newland C KuH 93 J4
Newland Cumb 94 G5
Newland E R Yk 92 D5
Newland Gloucs 31 Q3
Newland N York 92 A6
Newland Oxon 34 C3
Newland Somset 17 Q4
Newland Worcs 46 E5
Newlandrig Mdloth 128 B7
Newlands Border 111 K2
Newlands Cumb 101 K3
Newlands Nthumb 112 G9
Newlands of Dundurcas
Moray 157 P7
New Lane Lancs 88 E8
New Lane End Warrtn 82 D6
New Langholm D & G 110 G4
New Leake Lincs 87 M9
New Leeds Abers 159 N7
New Lodge Barns 91 K9
New Longton Lancs 88 G5
New Luce D & G 106 G5
Newlyn Cnwll 2 D8
Newmachar Abers 151 M4
Newmains N Lans 126 E6
New Malden Gt Lon 36 F7
Newman's End Essex 51 M8
Newman's Green Suffk 52 E3
Newmarket Suffk 63 K8
Newmarket W Isls 168 j4
New Marske R & Cl 104 H6
New Marston Oxon 34 F3
New Marton Shrops 69 K8
New Mill Abers 151 K11
Newmill Border 117 P8
New Mill Cnwll 2 D7
New Mill Herts 35 P2
New Mill Kirk 90 F9
Newmill Moray 158 B7
Newmillerdam Wakefd 91 J7
Newmill of Inshewan Angus 142 G5
Newmills C Edin 127 M4
New Mills Cnwll 3 M3
New Mills Derbys 83 M7
Newmills Fife 134 C10
Newmills Mons 31 P3
New Mills Powys 55 P4
Newmiln P & K 142 A11
Newmilns E Ayrs 125 N10
New Milton Hants 13 M5
New Mistley Essex 53 K5
New Moat Pembks 41 L5
Newnes Shrops 69 L8
Newney Green Essex 51 Q9
Newnham Hants 23 K4
Newnham Herts 50 F3
Newnham Kent 38 G10
Newnham Nhants 60 C9
Newnham Bridge Worcs 57 L11
Newnham on Severn Gloucs 32 C2
New Ollerton Notts 85 L7
New Oscott Birm 58 G6
New Pitsligo Abers 159 L6
New Polzeath Cnwll 4 E6
Newport Cnwll 5 N4
Newport Dorset 12 E5
Newport E R Yk 92 E4
Newport Essex 51 M4
Newport Gloucs 32 D5
Newport Highld 163 Q2
Newport IoW 14 F9
Newport Newpt 31 K7
Newport Norfk 77 Q8
Newport Pembks 41 L3
Newport Wrekin 70 C11
Newport-on-Tay Fife 135 L2
Newport Pagnell M Keyn 49 N6
Newport Pagnell Services
M Keyn 49 N6
Newpound Common W Susx 24 C5
New Prestwick S Ayrs 114 F3
New Quay Cerdgn 42 G3
Newquay Cnwll 4 C9
New Quay Essex 52 H7
Newquay Zoo Cnwll 4 C9
New Rackheath Norfk 77 K9
New Radnor Powys 45 J2
New Rent Cumb 101 N3
New Ridley Nthumb 112 G9
New Road Side N York 90 B2
New Romney Kent 27 J7
New Rossington Donc 91 Q11
New Row Cerdgn 54 G10
New Row Lancs 89 J3
New Sauchie Clacks 133 P9
Newsbank Ches E 82 H11
Newseat Abers 158 H11
Newsham Lancs 88 G3
Newsham N York 97 N4
Newsham N York 103 M8
Newsham Nthumb 113 M5
New Sharlston Wakefd 91 K7
Newsholme E R Yk 92 B5
Newsholme Lancs 96 B10
New Shoreston Nthumb 119 N4
New Silksworth Sundld 113 N10
New Skelton R & Cl 105 J7
Newsome Kirk 90 F8
New Somerby Lincs 73 N3
New Springs Wigan 88 H9
Newstead Border 117 R4
Newstead Notts 84 H10
Newstead Nthumb 119 N5
New Stevenston N Lans 126 D6
New Street Herefs 45 L3
New Swanington Leics 72 C7
Newthorpe N York 91 M4
Newthorpe Notts 84 G11
New Thundersley Essex 38 C4
Newtimber W Susx 24 G8
Newtoft Lincs 86 D3
Newton Ag & B 131 L8
Newton Border 118 B6
Newton Brdgnd 29 M9
Newton C Beds 50 F2
Newton Cambs 62 F11
Newton Cambs 74 H8
Newton Cardif 30 H9
Newton Ches W 69 P3
Newton Ches W 81 N11
Newton Ches W 82 B9
Newton Cumb 94 E6
Newton Derbys 84 F9
Newton Herefs 45 L8
Newton Herefs 45 Q4
Newton Herefs 56 F11
Newton Highld 155 Q7
Newton Highld 156 C8
Newton Highld 156 D4
Newton Highld 167 P7
Newton Lancs 88 C3
Newton Lancs 95 M6
Newton Lincs 73 Q3
Newton Mdloth 127 Q4
Newton Moray 157 M5
Newton Moray 157 Q5
Newton N York 98 H6
Newton Nhants 61 J4
Newton Norfk 76 A8
Newton Notts 72 H2
Newton Nthumb 112 F8
Newton Nthumb 118 H9
Newton S Lans 116 C4
Newton S Lans 126 B5
Newton Sandw 58 F6
Newton Shrops 69 M8
Newton Somset 18 F7
Newton Staffs 71 J9
Newton Suffk 52 F3
Newton W Loth 127 K2
Newton Warwks 60 B5
Newton Wilts 21 P10
Newton Abbot Devon 7 M4
Newton Arlosh Cumb 110 D9
Newton Aycliffe Dur 103 Q6
Newton Bewley Hartpl 104 E5
Newton Blossomville
M Keyn 49 P4
Newton Bromswold Nhants 61 L7
Newton Burgoland Leics 72 B9
Newton-by-the-Sea
Nthumb 119 P5
Newton by Toft Lincs 86 D3
Newton Ferrers Devon 6 F9
Newton Ferry W Isls 168 d10
Newton Flotman Norfk 65 J2
Newtongrange Mdloth 127 Q5
Newton Green Mons 31 P6
Newton Harcourt Leics 72 G11
Newton Heath Manch 83 J4
Newtonhill Abers 151 N9
Newton Hill Wakefd 91 J6
Newton-in-Bowland Lancs 95 P10
Newton Kyme N York 91 M2
Newton-le-Willows N York 97 K3
Newton-le-Willows St Hel 82 C5
Newtonloan Mdloth 127 Q5
Newton Longville Bucks 49 M8
Newton Mearns E Rens 125 N6
Newtonmill Angus 143 L5
Newtonmore Highld 148 C8
Newton Morrell N York 103 P9
Newton Mountain Pembks 41 J9
Newton Mulgrave N York 105 L7
Newton of Balcanquhal
P & K 134 F5
Newton of Balcormo Fife 135 N7
Newton-on-Ouse N York 97 R9
Newton-on-Rawcliffe
N York 98 G2
Newton on the Hill Shrops 69 N10
Newton-on-the-Moor
Nthumb 119 N9
Newton on Trent Lincs 85 P6
Newton Poppleford Devon 10 B7
Newton Purcell Oxon 48 H8
Newton Regis Warwks 59 L3
Newton Reigny Cumb 101 N4
Newton St Cyres Devon 9 L5
Newton St Faith Norfk 77 J8
Newton St Loe BaNES 20 D2
Newton St Petrock Devon 16 G9
Newton Solney Derbys 71 P9
Newton Stacey Hants 22 D6
Newton Stewart D & G 107 M4
Newton Tony Wilts 21 P6
Newton Tracey Devon 17 J6
Newton under Roseberry
R & Cl 104 G8
Newton Underwood Nthumb 112 H3
Newton upon Derwent
E R Yk 98 E11
Newton Valence Hants 23 K8
Newton Wamphray D & G 109 P2
Newton with Scales Lancs 88 F4
Newtown BCP 12 H6
Newtown Blae G 30 G3
Newtown Ches W 82 B9
Newtown Cnwll 2 F8
Newtown Cnwll 5 M6
Newtown Cumb 101 P6
Newtown Cumb 109 P11
Newtown Cumb 110 G8
Newtown Cumb 111 K8
Newtown D & G 115 Q5
Newtown Derbys 83 L8
Newtown Devon 9 Q5
Newtown Devon 17 P6
Newtown Dorset 11 K4
New Town Dorset 12 G3
New Town Dorset 21 J11
New Town Dorset 21 J11
New Town E Susx 25 L6
Newtown Gloucs 32 C4
Newtown Hants 13 N2
Newtown Hants 14 H4
Newtown Hants 22 E2
Newtown Herefs 45 P3
Newtown Herefs 45 Q8
Newtown Herefs 46 B5
Newtown Highld 147 K7
Newtown IoW 14 D8
New Town Nhants 61 L5
Newtown Nthumb 119 J4
Newtown Nthumb 119 K10
Newtown Nthumb 119 K5
Newtown Powys 55 Q6
Newtown Rhondd 30 E5
Newtown Shrops 69 M10
Newtown Shrops 69 N8
Newtown Somset 10 F2
Newtown Staffs 58 E4
Newtown Staffs 70 G2
Newtown Wigan 82 C4
Newtown Wilts 20 H9
Newtown Wilts 21 Q2
New Town Wilts 33 Q10
Newtown Worcs 46 G3
Newtown Worcs 58 D9
Newtown-in-St Martin
Cnwll 3 J9
Newtown Linford Leics 72 E9
Newtown of Beltrees Rens 125 K6
Newtown St Boswells
Border 117 R4
Newtown Unthank Leics 72 D10
New Tredegar Caerph 30 F4
New Trows S Lans 126 E10
New Tupton Derbys 84 E7
Newtyle Angus 142 D9
New Walsoken Cambs 75 J9
New Waltham NE Lin 93 N10
New Whittington Derbys 84 E5
New Winton E Loth 128 C5
New Yatt Oxon 34 C2
Newyears Green Gt Lon 36 C3
Newyork Ag & B 131 K5
New York Lincs 86 H9
New York N Tyne 113 M6
New York N York 97 J8
Nextend Herefs 45 L3
Neyland Pembks 41 J9
Niarbyl IoM 80 b6
Nibley Gloucs 32 C3
Nibley S Glos 32 C8
Nibley Green Gloucs 32 D5
Nicholashayne Devon 18 F11
Nicholaston Swans 28 F7
Nickies Hill Cumb 111 K7
Nidd N York 97 M8
Nigg C Aber 151 N7
Nigg Highld 156 E3
Nigg Ferry Highld 156 D4
Nimlet BaNES 32 D10
Ninebanks Nthumb 111 Q10
Nine Elms Swindn 33 M7
Nine Wells Pembks 40 E6
Ninfield E Susx 26 B9
Ningwood IoW 14 C9
Nisbet Border 118 C5
Nisbet Hill Border 129 K9
Niton IoW 14 F11
Nitshill C Glas 125 N5
Noah's Ark Kent 37 N9
Noak Bridge Essex 37 Q2
Noak Hill Gt Lon 37 M2
Noblethorpe Barns 90 H9
Nobold Shrops 56 H2
Nobottle Nhants 60 E8
Nocton Lincs 86 E8
Nogdam End Norfk 77 M11
Noke Oxon 34 F2
Nolton Pembks 40 G7
Nolton Haven Pembks 40 G7
No Man's Heath Ches W 69 P5
No Man's Heath Warwks 59 L3
No Man's Land Cnwll 5 M10
Nomansland Devon 9 K2
Nomansland Wilts 21 Q11
Noneley Shrops 69 N9
Nonington Kent 39 N11
Nook Cumb 95 L4
Nook Cumb 111 J5
Norbiton Gt Lon 36 E7
Norbreck Bpool 88 C2
Norbridge Herefs 46 D6
Norbury Ches E 69 Q5
Norbury Derbys 71 L6
Norbury Gt Lon 36 H7
Norbury Shrops 56 F6
Norbury Staffs 70 D10
Norbury Common Ches E 69 Q5
Norbury Junction Staffs 70 D10
Norchard Worcs 58 B11
Norcott Brook Ches W 82 D8
Norcross Lancs 88 C2
Nordelph Norfk 75 L10
Norden Rochdl 89 P8
Nordley Shrops 57 M5
Norfolk Broads Norfk 77 P10
Norham Nthumb 129 N10
Norland Town Calder 90 D6
Norley Ches W 82 C10
Norleywood Hants 14 C7
Norlington E Susx 25 K8
Normanby Lincs 86 C3
Normanby N Linc 92 E7
Normanby N York 98 E4
Normanby R & Cl 104 F7
Normanby le Wold Lincs 93 K11
Norman Cross Cambs 61 Q2
Normandy Surrey 23 P4
Normans Bay E Susx 25 Q9
Norman's Green Devon 9 Q4
Normanton C Derb 72 A4
Normanton Leics 73 L2
Normanton Notts 85 M10
Normanton Rutlnd 73 N9
Normanton Wakefd 91 K6
Normanton Wilts 21 M6
Normanton le Heath Leics 72 B8
Normanton on Cliffe Lincs 86 B11
Normanton on Soar Notts 72 E6
Normanton on the Wolds
Notts 72 G4
Normanton on Trent Notts 85 N7
Normoss Lancs 88 C3
Norney Surrey 23 P6
Norrington Common Wilts 20 G2
Norris Green Cnwll 5 Q8
Norris Green Lpool 81 M6
Norris Hill Leics 72 A7
Norristhorpe Kirk 90 G6
Northacre Norfk 64 D2
Northall Bucks 49 Q10
Northallerton N York 97 N2
Northall Green Norfk 76 D9
Northam C Sotn 14 D4
Northam Devon 16 H6
Northampton Nhants 60 G8
Northampton Worcs 58 B11
Northampton Services
Nhants 60 F9
North Anston Rothm 84 H4
North Ascot Br For 35 P11
North Aston Oxon 48 E9
Northaw Herts 50 G10
Northay Somset 10 F2
North Baddesley Hants 22 C10
North Ballachulish Highld 139 K5
North Barrow Somset 20 B9
North Barsham Norfk 76 C4
Northbay W Isls 168 c17
North Benfleet Essex 38 C4
North Berwick E Loth 128 E3
North Bitchburn Dur 103 N4
North Blyth Nthumb 113 M4
North Boarhunt Hants 14 H4
North Bockhampton BCP 13 L5
Northborough C Pete 74 C9
Northbourne Kent 39 P11
North Bovey Devon 8 H8
North Bradley Wilts 20 G3
North Brentor Devon 8 C8
North Brewham Somset 20 D7
North Bridge Surrey 23 Q7
Northbridge Street E Susx 26 B7
Northbrook Hants 22 F7
Northbrook Oxon 48 E10
North Brook End Cambs 50 G2
North Buckland Devon 16 H3
North Burlingham Norfk 77 M10
North Cadbury Somset 20 B9
North Carlton Lincs 86 B5
North Carlton Notts 85 J4
North Cave E R Yk 92 E4
North Cerney Gloucs 33 K3
North Chailey E Susx 25 J6
Northchapel W Susx 23 Q9
North Charford Hants 21 N11
North Charlton Nthumb 119 N6
North Cheam Gt Lon 36 F7
North Cheriton Somset 20 C9
North Chideock Dorset 11 J6
Northchurch Herts 35 Q3
North Cliffe E R Yk 92 E3
North Clifton Notts 85 P6
North Close Dur 103 Q4
North Cockerington Lincs 87 L2
North Connel Ag & B 138 G11
North Cornelly Brdgnd 29 M8
North Corner Cnwll 3 K10

North Cotes Lincs 93 P10
Northcott Devon 5 N3
Northcott Devon 10 B2
Northcott Devon 10 C3
North Country Cnwll 2 H5
Northcourt Oxon 34 E5
North Cove Suffk 65 P4
North Cowton N York 103 Q10
North Crawley M Keyn 49 P6
North Cray Gt Lon 37 L6
North Creake Norfk 76 B4
North Curry Somset 19 K9
North Dalton E R Yk 99 J10
North Deighton N York 97 N10
Northdown Kent 39 Q7
North Downs 38 F10
North Duffield N York 92 A3
Northedge Derbys 84 E7
North Elham Kent 27 L3
North Elkington Lincs 87 J2
North Elmham Norfk 76 D7
North Elmsall Wakefd 91 M8
Northend Bucks 35 K6
North End C Port 15 J6
North End Cumb 110 F9
North End Dorset 20 F9
North End E R Yk 93 L2
North End E R Yk 93 N4
North End Essex 51 Q7
North End Hants 21 M11
North End Hants 22 G9
North End Leics 72 F7
North End Lincs 74 D2
North End Lincs 87 M3
North End Lincs 92 H11
North End Lincs 93 P10
North End N Linc 93 K6
North End N Som 31 M11
North End Nhants 61 L7
North End Norfk 64 D3
North End Nthumb 119 M10
North End Sefton 81 L4
North End W Susx 15 Q6
North End W Susx 24 D9
Northend Warwks 48 C4
Northenden Manch 82 H7
Northend Woods Bucks 35 P7
North Erradale Highld 160 A10
North Evington C Leic 72 G10
North Fambridge Essex 38 E2
North Featherstone Wakefd 91 L6
North Ferriby E R Yk 92 G5
Northfield Birm 58 F9
Northfield C Aber 151 N6
Northfield E R Yk 92 H5
Northfields Lincs 73 Q9
Northfleet Kent 37 P6
North Frodingham E R Yk 99 N10
North Gorley Hants 13 L2
North Green Norfk 65 J4
North Green Suffk 65 L9
North Green Suffk 65 M8
North Greetwell Lincs 86 D6
North Grimston N York 98 G7
North Halling Medway 38 B8
North Haven Shet 169 t14
North Hayling Hants 15 K6
North Hazelrigg Nthumb 119 L4
North Heasley Devon 17 N5
North Heath W Susx 24 C6
North Hele Devon 18 D10
North Hill Cnwll 5 M6
North Hillingdon Gt Lon 36 C4
North Hinksey Village Oxon 34 E3
North Holmwood Surrey 36 E11
North Huish Devon 7 J7
North Hykeham Lincs 86 B7
Northiam E Susx 26 D7
Northill C Beds 61 P11
Northington Gloucs 32 D3
Northington Hants 22 G7
North Kelsey Lincs 92 H10
North Kessock Highld 156 B8
North Killingholme N Linc 93 K7
North Kilvington N York 97 P3
North Kilworth Leics 60 D4
North Kingston Hants 13 L4
North Kyme Lincs 86 G10
North Lancing W Susx 24 E9
North Landing E R Yk 99 Q6
Northlands Lincs 87 K10
Northleach Gloucs 33 M2
North Lee Bucks 35 M3
North Lees N York 97 L6
Northleigh Devon 10 D5
Northleigh Devon 17 L5
North Leigh Kent 27 K2
North Leigh Oxon 34 C2
North Leverton with Habblesthorpe Notts 85 N4
Northlew Devon 8 D5
North Littleton Worcs 47 L5
Northload Bridge Somset 19 N7
North Lopham Norfk 64 E5
North Luffenham Rutlnd 73 N10
North Marden W Susx 23 M11
North Marston Bucks 49 L10
North Middleton Mdloth 128 B8
North Middleton Nthumb 119 J6
North Millbrex Abers 159 K9
North Milmain D & G 106 E7
North Molton Devon 17 N6
Northmoor Oxon 34 D4
North Moreton Oxon 34 G7
Northmuir Angus 142 F6
North Mundham W Susx 15 N6
North Muskham Notts 85 N9
North Newbald E R Yk 92 F3
North Newington Oxon 48 D6
North Newnton Wilts 21 M3
North Newton Somset 19 K8
Northney Hants 15 K6
North Nibley Gloucs 32 D5
North Oakley Hants 22 F4
North Ockendon Gt Lon 37 N3
Northolt Gt Lon 36 D4
Northolt Airport Gt Lon 36 C3
Northop Flints 81 J11
Northop Hall Flints 81 K11
North Ormesby Middsb 104 F7
North Ormsby Lincs 87 J2
Northorpe Kirk 90 G6
Northorpe Lincs 74 A7
Northorpe Lincs 74 D3
Northorpe Lincs 92 E11
North Otterington N York 97 N3
Northover Somset 19 N7
Northover Somset 19 P10
North Owersby Lincs 86 E2
Northowram Calder 90 E5
North Perrott Somset 11 K3
North Petherton Somset 19 J8
North Petherwin Cnwll 5 M4
North Pickenham Norfk 76 B10
North Piddle Worcs 47 J4
North Poorton Dorset 11 L5
Northport Dorset 12 F7
North Poulner Hants 13 L3
North Queensferry Fife 134 E11
North Radworthy Devon 17 P5
North Rauceby Lincs 86 D11
Northrepps Norfk 77 J4
North Reston Lincs 87 L4
North Rigton N York 97 L11
North Ripley Hants 13 L5
North Rode Ches E 83 J11
North Ronaldsay Ork 169 g1
North Ronaldsay Airport Ork 169 g1
North Row Cumb 100 H4
North Runcton Norfk 75 M7
North Scale Cumb 94 D7
North Scarle Lincs 85 P7
North Seaton Nthumb 113 L3
North Seaton Colliery Nthumb 113 L3
North Shian Ag & B 138 G9
North Shields N Tyne 113 N7
North Shoebury Sthend 38 F4
North Shore Bpool 88 C3
North Side C Pete 74 E11
North Side Cumb 100 C5
North Skelton R & Cl 105 J7
North Somercotes Lincs 93 R11
North Stainley N York 97 L5
North Stainmore Cumb 102 F7
North Stifford Thurr 37 P4
North Stoke BaNES 32 D11
North Stoke Oxon 34 H7
North Stoke W Susx 24 B8
Northstowe Cambs 62 F7
North Street Cambs 63 J7
North Street Hants 21 N11
North Street Hants 22 H8
North Street Kent 38 H10
North Street Medway 38 D7
North Street W Berk 34 H10
North Sunderland Nthumb 119 P4
North Tamerton Cnwll 5 N2
North Tawton Devon 8 G4
North Third Stirlg 133 M10
North Thoresby Lincs 93 N11
North Togston Nthumb 119 P10
North Tolsta W Isls 168 k3
Northton W Isls 168 e9
North Town Devon 17 J10
North Town Somset 19 Q6
North Town W & M 35 N8
North Tuddenham Norfk 76 F9
North Uist W Isls 168 c10
Northumberland National Park Nthumb 111 Q4
North Walbottle N u Ty 113 J7
North Walsham Norfk 77 K5
North Waltham Hants 22 G5
North Warnborough Hants 23 K4
Northway Somset 18 F9
North Weald Bassett Essex 51 L10
North Wheatley Notts 85 N3
North Whilborough Devon 7 M5
Northwich Ches W 82 E10
North Wick BaNES 31 Q11
Northwick S Glos 31 Q7
Northwick Somset 19 L5
Northwick Worcs 46 F3
North Widcombe BaNES 19 Q3
North Willingham Lincs 86 G3
North Wingfield Derbys 84 F7
North Witham Lincs 73 N6
Northwold Norfk 75 Q11
Northwood C Stke 70 F5
Northwood Derbys 84 C8
Northwood Gt Lon 36 C2
Northwood IoW 14 E8
Northwood Shrops 69 N8
Northwood Green Gloucs 46 D11
North Wootton Dorset 11 P2
North Wootton Norfk 75 M6
North Wootton Somset 19 Q6
North Wraxall Wilts 32 F9
North Wroughton Swindn 33 M8
North York Moors National Park 105 K10
Norton Donc 91 N7
Norton E Susx 25 L10
Norton Gloucs 46 G10
Norton Halton 82 C8
Norton Hants 22 E6
Norton Herts 50 F4
Norton IoW 13 P7
Norton Mons 45 N10
Norton N Som 19 K2
Norton Nhants 60 C8
Norton Notts 85 J6
Norton Powys 56 E11
Norton S on T 104 D6
Norton Sheff 84 E4
Norton Shrops 56 H8
Norton Shrops 57 K3
Norton Shrops 57 L8
Norton Shrops 57 N4
Norton Suffk 64 D8
Norton Swans 28 H7
Norton W Susx 15 P5
Norton Wilts 32 G8
Norton Worcs 46 G4
Norton Worcs 47 K5
Norton Bavant Wilts 20 H6
Norton Bridge Staffs 70 F8
Norton Canes Staffs 58 F3
Norton Canes Services Staffs 58 F3
Norton Canon Herefs 45 M5
Norton Corner Norfk 76 F6
Norton Disney Lincs 85 Q9
Norton Ferris Wilts 20 E7
Norton Fitzwarren Somset 18 G9
Norton Green IoW 13 P7
Norton Hawkfield BaNES 19 Q2
Norton Heath Essex 51 P10
Norton in Hales Shrops 70 C7
Norton-Juxta-Twycross Leics 59 M3
Norton-le-Clay N York 97 P6
Norton-le-Moors C Stke 70 F4
Norton Lindsey Warwks 47 P2
Norton Little Green Suffk 64 D8
Norton Malreward BaNES 20 B2
Norton Mandeville Essex 51 N10
Norton-on-Derwent N York 98 F6
Norton St Philip Somset 20 E3
Norton Subcourse Norfk 65 N2
Norton sub Hamdon Somset 19 N11
Norton Wood Herefs 45 M5
Norwell Notts 85 N8
Norwell Woodhouse Notts 85 M8
Norwich Norfk 77 J10
Norwich Airport Norfk 77 J9
Norwick Shet 169 t2
Norwood Clacks 133 P9
Norwood Derbys 84 G4
Norwood Kent 27 J5
Norwood End Essex 51 N9
Norwood Green Calder 90 E5
Norwood Green Gt Lon 36 D5
Norwood Hill Surrey 24 F2
Norwoodside Cambs 74 H11
Noseley Leics 73 J11
Noss Mayo Devon 6 F9
Nosterfield N York 97 L4
Nosterfield End Cambs 51 P2
Nostie Highld 145 Q2
Notgrove Gloucs 47 M10
Nottage Brdgnd 29 M9
Notter Cnwll 5 P9
Nottingham C Nott 72 F3
Nottington Dorset 11 P8
Notton Wakefd 91 J8
Notton Wilts 32 H11
Nounsley Essex 52 C9
Noutard's Green Worcs 57 Q11
Nowton Suffk 64 B9
Nox Shrops 56 G2
Nuffield Oxon 35 J7
Nunburnholme E R Yk 98 G11
Nuncargate Notts 84 H10
Nunclose Cumb 111 J11
Nuneaton Warwks 59 N6
Nuneham Courtenay Oxon 34 G5
Nunhead Gt Lon 36 H5
Nunkeeling E R Yk 99 N11
Nun Monkton N York 97 R9
Nunney Somset 20 D5
Nunney Catch Somset 20 D6
Nunnington Herefs 45 R6
Nunnington N York 98 D5
Nunsthorpe NE Lin 93 N9
Nunthorpe C York 98 C10
Nunthorpe Middsb 104 F8
Nunthorpe Village Middsb 104 F8
Nunton Wilts 21 N9
Nunwick N York 97 M6
Nunwick Nthumb 112 C6
Nupdown S Glos 32 B5
Nup End Bucks 49 N11
Nupend Gloucs 32 E3
Nuptown Br For 35 N10
Nursling Hants 22 C11
Nursted Hants 23 L10
Nursteed Wilts 21 K2
Nurton Staffs 58 B5
Nutbourne W Susx 15 L5
Nutbourne W Susx 24 C7
Nutfield Surrey 36 H10
Nuthall Notts 72 E2
Nuthampstead Herts 51 K4
Nuthurst W Susx 24 E5
Nutley E Susx 25 K5
Nutley Hants 22 H6
Nuttall Bury 89 M7
Nutwell Donc 91 Q10
Nybster Highld 167 Q4
Nyetimber W Susx 15 N7
Nyewood W Susx 23 M10
Nymans W Susx 24 G5
Nymet Rowland Devon 17 N10
Nymet Tracey Devon 8 H4
Nympsfield Gloucs 32 F4
Nynehead Somset 18 F10
Nythe Somset 19 M8
Nyton W Susx 15 P5

O

Oadby Leics 72 G10
Oad Street Kent 38 E9
Oakall Green Worcs 46 F2
Oakamoor Staffs 71 J6
Oakbank W Loth 127 K4
Oak Cross Devon 8 D5
Oakdale Caerph 30 G5
Oake Somset 18 G9
Oaken Staffs 58 C4
Oakenclough Lancs 95 L11
Oakengates Wrekin 57 N2
Oakenholt Flints 81 K10
Oakenshaw Dur 103 N3
Oakenshaw Kirk 90 F5
Oakerthorpe Derbys 84 E10
Oakford Cerdgn 43 J3
Oakford Devon 18 B10
Oakfordbridge Devon 18 B10
Oakgrove Ches E 83 K11
Oakham Rutlnd 73 M9
Oakhanger Ches E 70 D4
Oakhanger Hants 23 L7
Oakhill Somset 20 B5
Oakhurst Kent 37 N10
Oakington Cambs 62 F8
Oaklands Powys 44 E4
Oakle Street Gloucs 46 E11
Oakley BCP 12 H5
Oakley Bed 61 M10
Oakley Bucks 34 H2
Oakley Fife 134 C10
Oakley Hants 22 G4
Oakley Oxon 35 L4
Oakley Suffk 64 H6
Oakley Green W & M 35 P9
Oakley Park Powys 55 M7
Oakridge Lynch Gloucs 32 H4
Oaks Lancs 89 K4
Oaks Shrops 56 G4
Oaksey Wilts 33 J6
Oaks Green Derbys 71 M8
Oakshaw Ford Cumb 111 K5
Oakshott Hants 23 K9
Oakthorpe Leics 59 M2
Oak Tree Darltn 104 C8
Oakwood C Derb 72 B3
Oakwood Nthumb 112 D7
Oakworth C Brad 90 C3
Oare Kent 38 H9
Oare Somset 17 P2
Oare Wilts 21 N2
Oasby Lincs 73 Q3
Oath Somset 19 L9
Oathlaw Angus 142 H6
Oatlands Park Surrey 36 C7
Oban Ag & B 130 H2
Oban Airport Ag & B 138 G10
Obley Shrops 56 E9
Obney P & K 141 P10
Oborne Dorset 20 C11
Obthorpe Lincs 74 A8
Occold Suffk 64 H7
Occumster Highld 167 N9
Ochiltree E Ayrs 115 K3
Ockbrook Derbys 72 C3
Ocker Hill Sandw 58 E6
Ockeridge Worcs 46 E2
Ockham Surrey 36 C9
Ockle Highld 137 P1
Ockley Surrey 24 D2
Ocle Pychard Herefs 46 A5
Octon E R Yk 99 L7
Odcombe Somset 19 P11
Odd Down BaNES 20 D2
Oddendale Cumb 101 Q8
Oddingley Worcs 46 H3
Oddington Gloucs 47 P9
Oddington Oxon 48 G11
Odell Bed 61 L9
Odham Devon 8 C4
Odiham Hants 23 K4
Odsal C Brad 90 F5
Odsey Cambs 50 G3
Odstock Wilts 21 M9
Odstone Leics 72 B9
Offchurch Warwks 59 N11
Offenham Worcs 47 L5
Offerton Stockp 83 K7
Offerton Sundld 113 M9
Offham E Susx 25 K8
Offham Kent 37 Q9
Offham W Susx 24 B9
Offleymarsh Staffs 70 D9
Offord Cluny Cambs 62 B7
Offord D'Arcy Cambs 62 B7
Offton Suffk 53 J2
Offwell Devon 10 D5
Ogbourne Maizey Wilts 33 N10
Ogbourne St Andrew Wilts 33 N10
Ogbourne St George Wilts 33 P10
Ogden Calder 90 D4
Ogle Nthumb 112 H5
Oglet Lpool 81 N8
Ogmore V Glam 29 N9
Ogmore-by-Sea V Glam 29 N9
Ogmore Vale Brdgnd 29 P6
Ogwen Bank Gwynd 79 L11
Okeford Fitzpaine Dorset 12 D2
Okehampton Devon 8 E5
Oker Side Derbys 84 C8
Okewood Hill Surrey 24 D3
Olchard Devon 9 L9
Old Nhants 60 G6
Old Aberdeen C Aber 151 N6
Old Alresford Hants 22 G8
Oldany Highld 164 C10
Old Auchenbrack D & G 115 Q8
Old Basford C Nott 72 F2
Old Basing Hants 23 J4
Old Beetley Norfk 76 D8
Oldberrow Warwks 58 H11
Old Bewick Nthumb 119 L6
Old Bolingbroke Lincs 87 L7
Old Bramhope Leeds 90 G2
Old Brampton Derbys 84 D6
Old Bridge of Urr D & G 108 G7
Old Buckenham Norfk 64 F3
Old Burghclere Hants 22 E3
Oldbury Kent 37 N9
Oldbury Sandw 58 E7
Oldbury Shrops 57 N6
Oldbury Warwks 59 M6
Oldbury Naite S Glos 32 B6
Oldbury-on-Severn S Glos 32 B6
Oldbury on the Hill Gloucs 32 F7
Old Byland N York 98 B3
Old Cantley Donc 91 Q10
Old Cassop Dur 104 B3
Oldcastle Mons 45 L10
Oldcastle Heath Ches W 69 N5
Old Catton Norfk 77 J9
Old Churchstoke Powys 56 D6
Old Clee NE Lin 93 N9
Old Cleeve Somset 18 D6
Old Colwyn Conwy 80 B9
Oldcotes Notts 85 J3
Old Coulsdon Gt Lon 36 H9
Old Dailly S Ayrs 114 D8
Old Dalby Leics 72 H6
Old Dam Derbys 83 P9
Old Deer Abers 159 N8
Old Ditch Somset 19 P5
Old Edlington Donc 91 N11
Old Eldon Dur 103 P5
Old Ellerby E R Yk 93 L3
Old Felixstowe Suffk 53 P4
Oldfield C Brad 90 C3
Oldfield Worcs 46 F2
Old Fletton C Pete 74 C11
Oldford Somset 20 E4
Old Forge Herefs 45 R11
Old Furnace Herefs 45 P10
Old Glossop Derbys 83 M6
Old Goole E R Yk 92 B6
Old Grimsby IoS 2 b1
Old Hall Green Herts 51 J6
Oldhall Green Suffk 64 B10
Old Hall Street Norfk 77 L5
Oldham Oldham 83 K4
Oldhamstocks E Loth 129 J5
Old Harlow Essex 51 L8
Old Heath Essex 52 H7
Old Hunstanton Norfk 75 N2
Old Hurst Cambs 62 D5
Old Hutton Cumb 95 M3
Old Inns Services N Lans 126 D2
Old Kea Cnwll 3 L5
Old Kilpatrick W Duns 125 M3
Old Knebworth Herts 50 F6
Old Lakenham Norfk 77 J10
Oldland S Glos 32 C10
Old Langho Lancs 89 L3
Old Laxey IoM 80 f5
Old Leake Lincs 87 M10
Old Malton N York 98 F6
Oldmeldrum Abers 151 L2
Oldmill Cnwll 5 P7
Old Milverton Warwks 59 L11
Oldmixon N Som 19 K3
Old Newton Suffk 64 F9
Old Oxted Surrey 37 J10
Old Portlethen Abers 151 N8
Old Quarrington Dur 104 B3
Old Radford C Nott 72 F2
Old Radnor Powys 45 K3
Old Rayne Abers 150 H2
Old Romney Kent 26 H7
Old Shoreham W Susx 24 F9
Oldshoremore Highld 164 F5
Old Soar Kent 37 P10
Old Sodbury S Glos 32 E8
Old Somerby Lincs 73 P4
Oldstead N York 98 A5
Old Stratford Nhants 49 L6
Old Struan P & K 141 K4
Old Swarland Nthumb 119 N10
Old Swinford Dudley 58 D8
Old Tebay Cumb 102 B9
Old Thirsk N York 97 P4
Old Town Calder 90 C5
Old Town Cumb 95 M4
Old Town Cumb 101 N2
Old Town E Susx 25 N11
Old Town IoS 2 c2
Old Trafford Traffd 82 H5
Old Tupton Derbys 84 E7
Oldwall Cumb 111 J8
Oldwalls Swans 28 E6
Old Warden C Beds 50 D2
Oldways End Somset 17 R7
Old Weston Cambs 61 N5
Old Wick Highld 167 Q7
Old Windsor W & M 35 Q10
Old Wives Lees Kent 39 J11
Old Woking Surrey 36 B9
Old Wolverton M Keyn 49 M6
Old Woodhall Lincs 86 H7
Old Woods Shrops 69 N10
Olgrinmore Highld 167 J6
Olive Green Staffs 71 L11
Oliver's Battery Hants 22 E9
Ollaberry Shet 169 q5
Ollach Highld 153 J10
Ollerton Ches E 82 G9
Ollerton Notts 85 L7
Ollerton Shrops 70 A9
Olmarch Cerdgn 43 M3
Olmstead Green Cambs 51 P2
Olney M Keyn 49 N4
Olrig House Highld 167 L3
Olton Solhll 58 H8
Olveston S Glos 32 B7
Ombersley Worcs 46 F2
Ompton Notts 85 L7
Once Brewed Nthumb 111 P7
Onchan IoM 80 e6
Onecote Staffs 71 J3
Onehouse Suffk 64 E10
Onen Mons 31 M2
Ongar Street Herefs 56 F11
Onibury Shrops 56 H9
Onich Highld 139 J5
Onllwyn Neath 29 M2
Onneley Staffs 70 D6
Onslow Green Essex 51 Q7
Onslow Village Surrey 23 Q5
Onston Ches W 82 C10
Openwoodgate Derbys 84 E11
Opinan Highld 153 N3
Orbliston Moray 157 Q6
Orbost Highld 152 D9
Orby Lincs 87 N7
Orchard Portman Somset 18 H10
Orcheston Wilts 21 L5
Orcop Herefs 45 P9
Orcop Hill Herefs 45 P9
Ord Abers 158 F6
Ordhead Abers 150 H5
Ordie Abers 150 D7
Ordiequish Moray 157 Q6
Ordley Nthumb 112 D9
Ordsall Notts 85 M5
Ore E Susx 26 D9
Oreleton Common Herefs 56 H11
Oreton Shrops 57 M8
Orford Suffk 65 N11
Orford Warrtn 82 D6
Organford Dorset 12 F6
Orgreave Staffs 71 L11
Orkney Islands Ork 169 d6
Orkney Neolithic Ork 169 c5
Orlestone Kent 26 H5
Orleton Herefs 56 H11
Orleton Worcs 57 N11
Orlingbury Nhants 61 J6
Ormathwaite Cumb 101 J5
Ormesby R & Cl 104 F7
Ormesby St Margaret Norfk 77 P9
Ormesby St Michael Norfk 77 P9
Ormiscaig Highld 160 D8
Ormiston E Loth 128 C6
Ormsaigmore Highld 137 M3
Ormsary Ag & B 123 M5
Ormskirk Lancs 88 E9
Ornsby Hill Dur 113 J11
Oronsay Ag & B 136 b4
Orphir Ork 169 c6
Orpington Gt Lon 37 L7
Orrell Sefton 81 L5
Orrell Wigan 82 B4
Orrell Post Wigan 88 G9
Orrisdale IoM 80 d3
Orroland D & G 108 G11
Orsett Thurr 37 P4
Orsett Heath Thurr 37 P4
Orslow Staffs 70 E11
Orston Notts 73 K2
Orthwaite Cumb 101 J4
Ortner Lancs 95 L10

Orton Cumb 102 B9
Orton Nhants 60 H5
Orton Staffs 58 C5
Orton Longueville C Pete 74 C11
Orton-on-the-Hill Leics 59 M4
Orton Rigg Cumb 110 F10
Orton Waterville C Pete 74 C11
Orwell Cambs 62 E10
Osbaldeston Lancs 89 J4
Osbaldeston Green Lancs 89 J4
Osbaldwick C York 98 C10
Osbaston Leics 72 C10
Osbaston Shrops 69 K10
Osborne IoW 14 F8
Osborne House IoW 14 F8
Osbournby Lincs 73 R3
Oscroft Ches W 81 Q11
Ose Highld 152 E9
Osgathorpe Leics 72 C7
Osgodby Lincs 86 E2
Osgodby N York 91 Q4
Osgodby N York 99 M4
Oskaig Highld 153 J10
Oskamull Ag & B 137 M7
Osmaston Derbys 71 M6
Osmington Dorset 11 Q8
Osmington Mills Dorset 12 B8
Osmondthorpe Leeds 91 J4
Osmotherley N York 104 E11
Osney Oxon 34 E3
Ospringe Kent 38 H9
Ossett Wakefd 90 H6
Ossington Notts 85 N8
Ostend Essex 38 F2
Osterley Gt Lon 36 E5
Oswaldkirk N York 98 C5
Oswaldtwistle Lancs 89 L5
Oswestry Shrops 69 J9
Otford Kent 37 M9
Otham Kent 38 C11
Otham Hole Kent 38 D11
Othery Somset 19 L8
Otley Leeds 97 K11
Otley Suffk 65 J10
Otley Green Suffk 65 J10
Otterbourne Hants 22 E10
Otterburn N York 96 C9
Otterburn Nthumb 112 C2
Otter Ferry Ag & B 131 J11
Otterham Cnwll 5 K3
Otterhampton Somset 18 H6
Otterham Quay Kent 38 D8
Otterham Station Cnwll 5 K4
Otternish W Isls 168 e10
Ottershaw Surrey 36 B8
Otterswick Shet 169 s5
Otterton Devon 10 B7
Otterwood Hants 14 D6
Ottery St Mary Devon 10 C5
Ottinge Kent 27 L3
Ottringham E R Yk 93 N6
Oughterby Cumb 110 E9
Oughtershaw N York 96 C4
Oughterside Cumb 100 F2
Oughtibridge Sheff 84 D2
Oughtrington Warrtn 82 E7
Oulston N York 98 A6
Oulton Cumb 110 D10
Oulton Leeds 91 K5
Oulton Norfk 76 G6
Oulton Staffs 70 D10
Oulton Staffs 70 G7
Oulton Suffk 65 Q3
Oulton Broad Suffk 65 Q3
Oulton Street Norfk 76 H6
Oundle Nhants 61 M3
Ounsdale Staffs 58 C6
Our Dynamic Earth C Edin 127 P3
Ousby Cumb 102 B4
Ousden Suffk 63 M9
Ousefleet E R Yk 92 D6
Ouston Dur 113 L10
Outchester Nthumb 119 M4
Out Elmstead Kent 39 M11
Outgate Cumb 101 L11
Outhgill Cumb 102 E10
Outhill Warwks 58 H11
Outlands Staffs 70 D8
Outlane Kirk 90 D7
Out Newton E R Yk 93 Q6
Out Rawcliffe Lancs 88 E2
Out Skerries Shet 169 t6
Outwell Norfk 75 K10
Outwick Hants 21 M11
Outwood Surrey 36 H11
Outwood Wakefd 91 J6
Outwood Gate Bury 89 M9
Outwoods Leics 72 C7
Outwoods Staffs 70 D11
Ouzlewell Green Leeds 91 J5
Ovenden Calder 90 D5
Over Cambs 62 E6
Over Ches W 82 D11
Over Gloucs 46 F11
Over S Glos 31 Q8
Over Burrows Derbys 71 P7
Overbury Worcs 47 J7
Overcombe Dorset 11 P8
Over Compton Dorset 19 Q11
Over End Cambs 61 N2
Overgreen Derbys 84 D6
Over Green Warwks 59 J6
Over Haddon Derbys 84 B7
Over Kellet Lancs 95 L7
Over Kiddington Oxon 48 D10
Overleigh Somset 19 N7
Overley Staffs 71 M11
Over Monnow Mons 31 P2
Over Norton Oxon 48 B9
Over Peover Ches E 82 G10
Overpool Ches W 81 M9
Overscaig Highld 161 Q2
Overseal Derbys 71 P11
Over Silton N York 97 P2
Oversland Kent 39 J10
Oversley Green Warwks 47 L3
Overstone Nhants 60 G7
Over Stowey Somset 18 G7
Overstrand Norfk 77 J3
Over Stratton Somset 19 M11
Overstreet Wilts 21 L7
Over Tabley Ches E 82 F9
Overthorpe Nhants 48 E6
Overton C Aber 151 M5
Overton Ches W 81 Q9
Overton Hants 22 F5
Overton Lancs 95 J9
Overton N York 98 B9
Overton Shrops 57 J10
Overton Swans 28 E7
Overton Wakefd 90 H7
Overton Wrexhm 69 L6
Overton Bridge Wrexhm 69 L6
Overton Green Ches E 70 E2
Overtown Lancs 89 P5
Overtown Lancs 95 N5
Overtown N Lans 126 E7
Overtown Swindn 33 N9
Overtown Wakefd 91 K7
Over Wallop Hants 21 Q7
Over Whitacre Warwks 59 L6
Over Woodhouse Derbys 84 G6
Over Worton Oxon 48 D9
Overy Oxon 34 G6
Oving Bucks 49 L10
Oving W Susx 15 P6
Ovingdean Br & H 25 J10
Ovingham Nthumb 112 G8
Ovington Dur 103 M8
Ovington Essex 52 C3
Ovington Hants 22 G8
Ovington Norfk 76 C11
Ovington Nthumb 112 G8
Ower Hants 14 E6
Ower Hants 22 B11
Owermoigne Dorset 12 C7
Owlbury Shrops 56 E6
Owlerton Sheff 84 D3
Owlpen Gloucs 32 E5
Owl's Green Suffk 65 K8
Owlsmoor Br For 23 M2
Owlswick Bucks 35 L3
Owmby Lincs 86 D3
Owmby Lincs 93 J10
Owslebury Hants 22 F10
Owston Donc 91 P8
Owston Leics 73 K9
Owston Ferry N Linc 92 D10
Owstwick E R Yk 93 N4
Owthorne E R Yk 93 P5
Owthorpe Notts 72 H4
Owton Manor Hartpl 104 E5
Oxborough Norfk 75 P10
Oxbridge Dorset 11 K5
Oxcombe Lincs 87 K5
Oxcroft Derbys 84 G6
Oxen End Essex 51 Q5
Oxenholme Cumb 95 L3
Oxenhope C Brad 90 C4
Oxen Park Cumb 94 G3
Oxenpill Somset 19 M6
Oxenton Gloucs 47 J8
Oxenwood Wilts 22 B3
Oxford Oxon 34 F3
Oxford Airport Oxon 48 E11
Oxford Services Oxon 34 H4
Oxhey Herts 50 D11
Oxhill Dur 113 J10
Oxhill Warwks 48 B5
Oxley Wolves 58 D4
Oxley Green Essex 52 F9
Oxley's Green E Susx 25 Q6
Oxlode Cambs 62 G3
Oxnam Border 118 C7
Oxnead Norfk 77 J7
Oxshott Surrey 36 D8
Oxshott Heath Surrey 36 D8
Oxspring Barns 90 H10
Oxted Surrey 37 J10
Oxton Border 128 D9
Oxton N York 91 N2
Oxton Notts 85 K10
Oxton Wirral 81 L7
Oxwich Swans 28 E7
Oxwich Green Swans 28 E7
Oxwick Norfk 76 C6
Oykel Bridge Highld 161 P6
Oyne Abers 150 H2
Oystermouth Swans 28 H7
Ozleworth Gloucs 32 E6

P

Pabail W Isls 168 k4
Packers Hill Dorset 11 Q2
Packington Leics 72 B8
Packmoor C Stke 70 F4
Packmores Warwks 59 L11
Padanaram Angus 142 G7
Padbury Bucks 49 K8
Paddington Gt Lon 36 G4
Paddington Warrtn 82 D7
Paddlesworth Kent 27 L4
Paddlesworth Kent 37 Q8
Paddock Wood Kent 25 Q2
Paddolgreen Shrops 69 P8
Padfield Derbys 83 M5
Padgate Warrtn 82 D7
Padhams Green Essex 51 P11
Padiham Lancs 89 M4
Padside N York 97 J9
Padstow Cnwll 4 E6
Padworth W Berk 34 H11
Page Bank Dur 103 P3
Pagham W Susx 15 N7
Paglesham Essex 38 F3
Paignton Torbay 7 M6
Pailton Warwks 59 Q8
Paine's Cross E Susx 25 P6
Painleyhill Staffs 71 J8
Painscastle Powys 44 H5
Painshawfield Nthumb 112 G8
Painsthorpe E R Yk 98 G9
Painswick Gloucs 32 G3
Painter's Forstal Kent 38 G10
Paisley Rens 125 M5
Pakefield Suffk 65 Q3
Pakenham Suffk 64 C8
Pale Gwynd 68 C7
Pale Green Essex 51 Q2
Palestine Hants 21 Q6
Paley Street W & M 35 N9
Palfrey Wsall 58 F5
Palgrave Suffk 64 G6
Pallington Dorset 12 C6
Palmersbridge Cnwll 5 K6
Palmers Green Gt Lon 36 H2
Palmerston E Ayrs 115 K4
Palmerstown V Glam 30 F11
Palnackie D & G 108 H9
Palnure D & G 107 N5
Palterton Derbys 84 G7
Pamber End Hants 22 H3
Pamber Green Hants 22 H3
Pamber Heath Hants 22 H2
Pamington Gloucs 46 H8
Pamphill Dorset 12 G4
Pampisford Cambs 62 G11
Panborough Somset 19 N5
Panbride Angus 143 K10
Pancrasweek Devon 16 D10
Pancross V Glam 30 D11
Pandy Caerph 30 G7
Pandy Gwynd 54 E4
Pandy Gwynd 68 A9
Pandy Mons 45 L10
Pandy Powys 55 L4
Pandy Wrexhm 68 G7
Pandy'r Capel Denbgs 68 E4
Pandy Tudur Conwy 67 R2
Panfield Essex 52 B6
Pangbourne W Berk 34 H9
Pangdean W Susx 24 G8
Panks Bridge Herefs 46 B5
Pannal N York 97 M10
Pannal Ash N York 97 L10
Pant Shrops 69 J10
Pantasaph Flints 80 H9
Panteg Pembks 40 H4
Pantersbridge Cnwll 5 K8
Pant-ffrwyth Brdgnd 29 P8
Pant Glas Gwynd 66 H5
Pantglas Powys 54 H5
Pant-Gwyn Carmth 43 L9
Pant-lasau Swans 29 J4
Pant Mawr Powys 55 J8
Panton Lincs 86 G5
Pant-pastynog Denbgs 68 D2
Pantperthog Gwynd 54 G4
Pant-y-dwr Powys 55 M10
Pant-y-ffridd Powys 56 B4
Pantyffynnon Carmth 28 H2
Pantygaseg Torfn 31 J5
Pantygelli Mons 45 L11
Pant-y-gog Brdgnd 29 P6
Pantymenyn Carmth 41 M5
Pant-y-mwyn Flints 68 G2
Panxworth Norfk 77 M9
Papa Stour Shet 169 n7
Papa Stour Airport Shet 169 n8
Papa Westray Ork 169 d1
Papa Westray Airport Ork 169 d1
Papcastle Cumb 100 F4
Papigoe Highld 167 Q6
Papple E Loth 128 F5
Papplewick Notts 84 H10
Papworth Everard Cambs 62 C8
Papworth St Agnes Cambs 62 C8
Par Cnwll 3 R3
Paramour Street Kent 39 N9
Parbold Lancs 88 F8
Parbrook Somset 19 Q7
Parbrook W Susx 24 C5
Parc Gwynd 68 A8
Parcllyn Cerdgn 42 D4
Parc Seymour Newpt 31 M6
Pardshaw Cumb 100 E6
Parham Suffk 65 L9
Park D & G 109 K2
Park Nthumb 111 N8
Park Bottom Cnwll 2 H5
Park Bridge Tamesd 83 K4
Park Corner E Susx 25 M3
Park Corner Oxon 35 J7
Park Corner W & M 35 N8
Park End Bed 49 Q4
Parkend Gloucs 32 B3
Park End Nthumb 112 C5
Parker's Green Kent 37 P11
Parkeston Essex 53 M5
Parkeston Quay Essex 53 M5
Park Farm Kent 26 H4
Parkgate Ches W 81 K9
Parkgate Cumb 110 D11
Parkgate D & G 109 M3
Parkgate E Susx 26 B9
Parkgate Essex 51 Q5
Park Gate Hants 14 F5
Parkgate Kent 26 E5
Parkgate Kent 37 M8
Park Gate Leeds 90 F2
Parkgate Surrey 24 F2
Park Gate Worcs 58 D10
Park Green Essex 51 L5
Park Green Suffk 64 G9
Parkhall W Duns 125 M3
Parkham Devon 16 F7
Parkham Ash Devon 16 F7
Park Head Derbys 84 E10
Park Hill Gloucs 31 Q5
Parkhouse Mons 31 P4
Parkmill Swans 28 F7
Park Royal Gt Lon 36 E4
Parkside Dur 113 P11
Parkside N Lans 126 E6
Parkside Wrexhm 69 L3
Parkstone BCP 12 H6
Park Street Herts 50 D10
Park Street W Susx 24 D4
Parkway Herefs 46 D7
Parley Green BCP 13 K5
Parmoor Bucks 35 L7
Parracombe Devon 17 M2
Parrog Pembks 41 L3
Parsonby Cumb 100 F3
Parson Cross Sheff 84 D2
Parson Drove Cambs 74 G9
Parson's Heath Essex 52 H6
Parson's Hill Derbys 71 P9
Partick C Glas 125 N4
Partington Traffd 82 F6
Partney Lincs 87 M7
Parton Cumb 100 C6
Partridge Green W Susx 24 E7
Partrishow Powys 45 K10
Parwich Derbys 71 M4
Paslow Wood Common Essex 51 N10
Passenham Nhants 49 L7
Passfield Hants 23 M8
Passingford Bridge Essex 51 M11
Paston C Pete 74 C10
Paston Norfk 77 L5
Pasturefields Staffs 70 H10
Patchacott Devon 8 C5
Patcham Br & H 24 H9
Patchetts Green Herts 50 D11
Patching W Susx 24 C9
Patchole Devon 17 L3
Patchway S Glos 32 B8
Pateley Bridge N York 97 J7
Paternoster Heath Essex 52 F8
Pathe Somset 19 L8
Pathhead Fife 134 H9
Pathhead Mdloth 128 B7
Pathlow Warwks 47 N3
Path of Condie P & K 134 D5
Patmore Heath Herts 51 K5
Patna E Ayrs 114 H5
Patney Wilts 21 L3
Patrick IoM 80 b5
Patrick Brompton N York 97 K2
Patricroft Salfd 82 G5
Patrington E R Yk 93 P6
Patrington Haven E R Yk 93 P6
Patrixbourne Kent 39 L10
Patterdale Cumb 101 L7
Pattingham Staffs 57 Q5
Pattishall Nhants 49 J4
Pattiswick Green Essex 52 D7
Patton Shrops 57 K5
Patton Bridge Cumb 101 Q11
Paul Cnwll 2 D8
Paulerspury Nhants 49 K5
Paull E R Yk 93 L5
Paulton BaNES 20 C3
Paultons Park Hants 22 B11
Paunton Herefs 46 C4
Pauperhaugh Nthumb 119 M11
Pave Lane Wrekin 70 D11
Pavenham Bed 61 L9
Pawlett Somset 19 J6
Pawston Nthumb 118 G4
Paxford Gloucs 47 N7
Paxton Border 129 N9
Payden Street Kent 38 F11
Payhembury Devon 10 B4
Paynter's Lane End Cnwll 2 H5
Paythorne Lancs 96 B10
Paytoe Herefs 56 G10
Peacehaven E Susx 25 K10
Peak Dale Derbys 83 N9
Peak District National Park 83 Q6
Peak Forest Derbys 83 P9
Peak Hill Lincs 74 E7
Peakirk C Pete 74 C9
Pearson's Green Kent 25 Q2
Peartree Green Herefs 46 A8
Peasedown St John BaNES 20 D3
Peasehill Derbys 84 F11
Peaseland Green Norfk 76 F8
Peasemore W Berk 34 E9
Peasenhall Suffk 65 M8
Pease Pottage W Susx 24 G4
Pease Pottage Services W Susx 24 G4
Peaslake Surrey 24 C2
Peasley Cross St Hel 81 Q6
Peasmarsh E Susx 26 E7
Peasmarsh Somset 10 G2
Peasmarsh Surrey 23 Q5
Peathill Abers 159 M4
Peat Inn Fife 135 M6
Peatling Magna Leics 60 C2
Peatling Parva Leics 60 C3
Peaton Shrops 57 J7
Pebmarsh Essex 52 E5
Pebsham E Susx 26 C10
Pebworth Worcs 47 M5
Pecket Well Calder 90 B5
Peckforton Ches E 69 P3
Peckham Gt Lon 36 H5
Peckleton Leics 72 D10
Pedairffordd Powys 68 F10
Pedlinge Kent 27 K4
Pedmore Dudley 58 D8
Pedwell Somset 19 M7
Peebles Border 117 K2
Peel IoM 80 b5
Peel Lancs 88 D4
Peel Common Hants 14 G6
Peene Kent 27 L4
Peening Quarter Kent 26 E6
Peggs Green Leics 72 C7
Pegsdon C Beds 50 D4
Pegswood Nthumb 113 K3
Pegwell Kent 39 Q9
Peinchorran Highld 153 J11
Peinlich Highld 152 G6
Pelcomb Pembks 40 H7
Pelcomb Bridge Pembks 40 H7
Pelcomb Cross Pembks 40 H7
Peldon Essex 52 G8
Pell Green E Susx 25 P4
Pelsall Wsall 58 F4
Pelsall Wood Wsall 58 F4
Pelton Dur 113 L10
Pelton Fell Dur 113 L10
Pelutho Cumb 109 P11
Pelynt Cnwll 5 L10
Pemberton Carmth 28 F4
Pemberton Wigan 82 C4
Pembles Cross Kent 26 E2
Pembrey Carmth 28 D4
Pembridge Herefs 45 M3
Pembroke Pembks 41 J10
Pembroke Dock Pembks 41 J10
Pembrokeshire Coast National Park Pembks 40 F6
Pembury Kent 25 P2
Pen-allt Herefs 45 R9
Penallt Mons 31 P2
Penally Pembks 41 M11
Penare Cnwll 3 P5
Penarth V Glam 30 G10
Penblewin Pembks 41 M7
Pen-bont Rhydybeddau Cerdgn 54 F8
Penbryn Cerdgn 42 E4
Pencader Carmth 42 H7
Pencaenewydd Gwynd 66 G6
Pencaitland E Loth 128 C6
Pencarnisiog IoA 78 F10
Pencarreg Carmth 43 K5
Pencarrow Cnwll 5 J5
Pencelli Powys 44 F9
Penclawdd Swans 28 F5
Pencoed Brdgnd 30 C8
Pencombe Herefs 46 A4
Pencoyd Herefs 45 Q9
Pencraig Herefs 45 R10
Pencraig Powys 68 D9
Pendeen Cnwll 2 B7
Penderyn Rhondd 29 P3
Pendine Carmth 41 P9
Pendlebury Salfd 82 G4
Pendleton Lancs 89 M3
Pendock Worcs 46 E8
Pendoggett Cnwll 4 G6
Pendomer Somset 11 L2
Pendoylan V Glam 30 E9
Penegoes Powys 54 H4
Penelewey Cnwll 3 L5
Pen-ffordd Pembks 41 L6
Pengam Caerph 30 G5
Pengam Cardif 30 H9
Penge Gt Lon 37 J6
Pengelly Cnwll 4 H5
Pengenffordd Powys 44 H9
Pengorffwysfa IoA 78 H6
Pengover Green Cnwll 5 M8
Pen-groes-oped Mons 31 K3
Pengwern Denbgs 80 E9
Penhale Cnwll 2 H10
Penhale Cnwll 4 E10
Penhale Cnwll 4 H9
Penhale Cnwll 5 Q11
Penhallow Cnwll 3 K3
Penhalurick Cnwll 3 J6
Penhalvean Cnwll 3 J6
Penhill Swindn 33 N7
Penhow Newpt 31 M6
Penhurst E Susx 25 Q7
Peniarth Gwynd 54 E3
Penicuik Mdloth 127 N6
Peniel Carmth 42 H10
Peniel Denbgs 68 D2
Penifiler Highld 152 H9
Peninver Ag & B 120 E7
Penisarwaun Gwynd 67 K2
Penistone Barns 90 G10
Penjerrick Cnwll 3 K7
Penketh Warrtn 82 C7
Penkill S Ayrs 114 D8
Penkridge Staffs 58 D2
Penlean Cnwll 5 L2
Penleigh Wilts 20 G4
Penley Wrexhm 69 M6
Penllergaer Swans 28 H5
Pen-llyn IoA 78 F8
Penllyn V Glam 30 C9
Pen-lôn IoA 78 G11
Penmachno Conwy 67 P4
Penmaen Caerph 30 G5
Penmaen Swans 28 F7
Penmaenan Conwy 79 N9
Penmaenmawr Conwy 79 N9
Penmaenpool Gwynd 67 M11
Penmark V Glam 30 E11
Penmon IoA 79 L8
Penmorfa Gwynd 67 J6
Penmynydd IoA 79 J10
Penn Bucks 35 P6
Penn Wolves 58 C5
Pennal Gwynd 54 F4
Pennan Abers 159 K4
Pennant Cerdgn 43 K2
Pennant Denbgs 68 D8
Pennant Powys 55 K5
Pennant-Melangell Powys 68 D9
Pennar Pembks 41 J10
Pennard Swans 28 G7
Pennerley Shrops 56 F5
Pennicott Devon 9 L4
Pennines 90 B3
Pennington Cumb 94 F5
Pennington Hants 13 P5
Pennington Green Wigan 89 J9
Pennorth Powys 44 G9
Penn Street Bucks 35 P5
Pennsylvania S Glos 32 D10
Penny Bridge Cumb 94 G4
Pennycross Ag & B 137 N10
Pennygate Norfk 77 L7
Pennyghael Ag & B 137 N10
Pennyglen S Ayrs 114 E5
Penny Green Derbys 84 H5
Penny Hill Lincs 74 G5
Pennymoor Devon 9 L2
Pennywell Sundld 113 N9
Penparc Cerdgn 42 D5
Penparcau Cerdgn 54 D8
Penpedairheol Caerph 30 F5
Penpedairheol Mons 31 K4
Penpergwm Mons 31 K2
Penperlleni Mons 31 K4
Penpethy Cnwll 4 H4
Penpillick Cnwll 4 H10
Penpol Cnwll 3 L6
Penpoll Cnwll 5 J11
Penponds Cnwll 2 G6
Penpont Cnwll 4 H7
Penpont D & G 108 H2
Penpont Powys 44 D9
Penquit Devon 6 G8
Penrest Cnwll 5 N6
Penrherber Carmth 41 Q3
Pen-rhiw Pembks 41 P2
Penrhiwceiber Rhondd 30 E5
Pen Rhiwfawr Neath 29 K2
Penrhiwllan Cerdgn 42 G6
Penrhiw-pal Cerdgn 42 F5
Penrhos Gwynd 66 E8
Penrhos IoA 78 D8
Penrhos Mons 31 M2
Penrhos Powys 29 M2
Penrhos garnedd Gwynd 79 K10
Penrhyn Bay Conwy 79 Q8
Penrhyn-coch Cerdgn 54 E8
Penrhyndeudraeth Gwynd 67 L7
Penrhyn-side Conwy 79 Q8
Penrhys Rhondd 30 D6
Penrice Swans 28 E7
Penrioch N Ayrs 120 G3
Penrith Cumb 101 P4
Penrose Cnwll 4 D7
Penruddock Cumb 101 M5
Penryn Cnwll 3 K7
Pensarn Conwy 80 D9
Pensax Worcs 57 N11
Pensby Wirral 81 K8
Penselwood Somset 20 E8

Pensford BaNES 20 B2
Pensham Worcs 46 H6
Penshaw Sundld 113 M10
Penshurst Kent 25 M2
Penshurst Station Kent 37 M11
Pensilva Cnwll 5 M7
Pensnett Dudley 58 D7
Penstone Devon 9 J4
Penstrowed Powys 55 P6
Pentewan Cnwll 3 Q4
Pentir Gwynd 79 K11
Pentire Cnwll 4 B9
Pentlepoir Pembks 41 M9
Pentlow Essex 63 P11
Pentlow Street Essex 63 P11
Pentney Norfk 75 P8
Pentonbridge Cumb 110 H5
Penton Grafton Hants 22 B5
Penton Mewsey Hants 22 B5
Pentraeth IoA 79 J9
Pentre Denbgs 68 E2
Pentre Flints 81 L11
Pentre Mons 31 K3
Pentre Mons 31 M4
Pentre Powys 55 P7
Pentre Powys 56 B7
Pentre Powys 56 D6
Pentre Rhondd 30 C5
Pentre Shrops 69 L11
Pentre Wrexhm 69 J6
Pentre-bâch Cerdgn 43 L5
Pentre Bach Flints 81 J9
Pentrebach Myr Td 30 E4
Pentre-bach Powys 44 C8
Pentrebeirdd Powys 56 B2
Pentre Berw IoA 78 H10
Pentre-bont Conwy 67 N4
Pentre-cagel Carmth 42 F6
Pentrecelyn Denbgs 68 F4
Pentre-celyn Powys 55 K3
Pentre-chwyth Swans 29 J6
Pentre-clawdd Shrops 69 J8
Pentre-cwrt Carmth 42 G7
Pentredwr Denbgs 68 G5
Pentrefelin Gwynd 67 J7
Pentrefelin IoA 78 G6
Pentre Ffwrndan Flints 81 K10
Pentrefoelas Conwy 67 R4
Pentregalar Pembks 41 N4
Pentregat Cerdgn 42 G4
Pentre-Gwenlais Carmth 43 M11
Pentre Gwynfryn Gwynd 67 K9
Pentre Halkyn Flints 81 J10
Pentre Hodrey Shrops 56 E9
Pentre Isaf Conwy 80 D10
Pentre Llanrhaeadr Denbgs 68 E2
Pentre Llifior Powys 56 B5
Pentre-llwyn-llwyd Powys 44 D4
Pentre-llyn Cerdgn 54 E9
Pentre-llyn-cymmer Conwy 68 C4
Pentre-Maw Powys 55 K4
Pentre Meyrick V Glam 30 C9
Pentre-piod Torfn 31 J4
Pentre-poeth Newpt 31 J7
Pentre'rbryn Cerdgn 42 G4
Pentre'r-felin Cerdgn 43 M5
Pentre'r Felin Conwy 79 Q11
Pentre'r-felin Powys 44 C8
Pentre Saron Denbgs 68 D2
Pentre-tafarn-y-fedw Conwy 67 Q2
Pentre ty gwyn Carmth 43 R7
Pentrich Derbys 84 E10
Pentridge Dorset 21 K11
Pen-twyn Caerph 30 H4
Pen-twyn Mons 31 P3
Pen-twyn Torfn 31 J4
Pentwynmaur Caerph 30 G5
Pentyrch Cardif 30 F8
Penwithick Cnwll 4 G10
Penwood Hants 22 D2
Penwyllt Powys 44 B11
Penybanc Carmth 43 M10
Penybont Powys 44 G2
Pen-y-bont Powys 68 H10
Penybontfawr Powys 68 E10
Pen-y-bryn Pembks 41 N2
Pen-y-cae Powys 29 M2
Penycae Wrexhm 69 J5
Pen-y-cae-mawr Mons 31 M5
Penycaerau Gwynd 66 B9
Pen-y-cefn Flints 80 G9
Pen-y-clawdd Mons 31 N3
Pen-y-coedcae Rhondd 30 E7
Penycwn Pembks 40 G6
Pen-y-fai Brdgnd 29 N8
Pen-y-felin Flints 80 H11
Penyffordd Flints 69 K2
Pen-y-ffordd Flints 80 G8
Penyffridd Gwynd 67 J3
Pen-y-garn Cerdgn 54 E7
Pen-y-Garnedd Powys 68 F10
Pen-y-graig Gwynd 66 C8
Penygraig Rhondd 30 D6
Penygroes Carmth 28 G2
Penygroes Gwynd 66 H4
Penygroeslon Gwynd 66 C8
Pen-y-Gwryd Gwynd 67 M3
Pen-y-lan V Glam 30 C9
Pen-y-Mynydd Carmth 28 E4
Penymynydd Flints 69 K2
Pen-y-pass Gwynd 67 L3
Pen-yr-Heol Mons 31 M2
Penysarn IoA 78 H6
Pen-y-stryt Denbgs 68 H4
Penywaun Rhondd 30 C4
Penzance Cnwll 2 D7
Peopleton Worcs 46 H4
Peover Heath Ches E 82 G10
Peper Harow Surrey 23 P6
Peplow Shrops 70 A10
Pepper's Green Essex 51 P8
Pepperstock C Beds 50 C7
Perceton N Ayrs 125 K9
Percyhorner Abers 159 N4
Perelle Guern 10 b2
Perham Down Wilts 21 Q5
Periton Somset 18 C5
Perivale Gt Lon 36 E4
Perkins Village Devon 9 P6
Perkinsville Dur 113 L10
Perlethorpe Notts 85 K6
Perranarworthal Cnwll 3 K6
Perranporth Cnwll 3 K3
Perranuthnoe Cnwll 2 E8
Perranwell Cnwll 3 K3
Perranwell Cnwll 3 K6
Perran Wharf Cnwll 3 K6
Perranzabuloe Cnwll 3 K3
Perrott's Brook Gloucs 33 K3
Perry Birm 58 G6
Perry Barr Birm 58 G6
Perry Green Essex 52 D7
Perry Green Herts 51 K7
Perry Green Wilts 33 J7
Perrystone Hill Herefs 46 B9
Perry Street Somset 10 G3
Pershall Staffs 70 E9
Pershore Worcs 46 H5
Pertenhall Bed 61 N7
Perth P & K 134 E3
Perthy Shrops 69 L8
Perton Herefs 46 A6
Perton Staffs 58 C5
Pertwood Wilts 20 G7
Peterborough C Pete 74 C11
Peterborough Services Cambs 61 P2
Peterchurch Herefs 45 L7
Peterculter C Aber 151 L7
Peterhead Abers 159 R8
Peterlee Dur 104 D2
Petersfield Hants 23 K10
Peter's Green Herts 50 D7
Petersham Gt Lon 36 E6
Peters Marland Devon 16 H9
Peterstone Wentlooge Newpt 31 J9
Peterston-super-Ely V Glam 30 E9
Peterstow Herefs 45 R10
Peters Village Kent 38 B9
Peter Tavy Devon 8 D9
Petham Kent 39 K11
Petherwin Gate Cnwll 5 M4
Petrockstow Devon 17 J10
Petsoe End M Keyn 49 N5
Pet Street Kent 27 J2
Pett E Susx 26 E9
Pettaugh Suffk 64 H10
Pett Bottom Kent 39 L11
Petterden Angus 142 G10
Pettinain S Lans 116 D2
Pettistree Suffk 65 L10
Petton Devon 18 D10
Petton Shrops 69 M9
Petts Wood Gt Lon 37 L7
Pettycur Fife 134 H10
Petty France S Glos 32 E7
Pettymuk Abers 151 N3
Petworth W Susx 23 Q10
Pevensey E Susx 25 P9
Pevensey Bay E Susx 25 Q10
Pewsey Wilts 21 N2
Pewsham Wilts 32 H10
Pheasant's Hill Bucks 35 L7
Phepson Worcs 46 H3
Philadelphia Sundld 113 M10
Philham Devon 16 D7
Philiphaugh Border 117 N5
Phillack Cnwll 2 F6
Philleigh Cnwll 3 M6
Philpot End Essex 51 P7
Philpstoun W Loth 127 K2
Phocle Green Herefs 46 B9
Phoenix Green Hants 23 L3
Pibsbury Somset 19 M9
Pica Cumb 100 D6
Piccadilly Warwks 59 K5
Piccotts End Herts 50 B9
Pickburn Donc 91 N9
Pickering N York 98 F4
Picket Piece Hants 22 C5
Picket Post Hants 13 L3
Picket Twenty Hants 22 C5
Pickford Covtry 59 L8
Pickford Green Covtry 59 L8
Pickhill N York 97 M4
Picklescott Shrops 56 G5
Pickmere Ches E 82 E9
Pickney Somset 18 G9
Pickstock Wrekin 70 C10
Pickup Bank Bl w D 89 L6
Pickwell Devon 16 H3
Pickwell Leics 73 K8
Pickwick Wilts 32 G10
Pickworth Lincs 73 Q4
Pickworth Rutlnd 73 P8
Picton Ches W 81 N10
Picton Flints 80 G8
Picton N York 104 D9
Piddinghoe E Susx 25 K10
Piddington Bucks 35 M6
Piddington Nhants 49 M4
Piddington Oxon 48 H11
Piddlehinton Dorset 11 Q5
Piddletrenthide Dorset 11 Q5
Pidley Cambs 62 D5
Piercebridge Darltn 103 P7
Pierowall Ork 169 d2
Piff's Elm Gloucs 46 H9
Pigdon Nthumb 113 J3
Pigeon Green Warwks 47 P2
Pig Oak Dorset 12 H4
Pig Street Herefs 45 M5
Pikehall Derbys 71 M3
Pilford Dorset 12 H4
Pilgrims Hatch Essex 51 N11
Pilham Lincs 85 Q2
Pill N Som 31 P9
Pillaton Cnwll 5 P9
Pillatonmill Cnwll 5 P9
Pillerton Hersey Warwks 47 Q5
Pillerton Priors Warwks 47 Q5
Pilleth Powys 56 D11
Pilley Barns 91 J10
Pilley Hants 13 P5
Pilley Bailey Hants 13 P5
Pillgwenlly Newpt 31 K7
Pillhead Devon 16 H6
Pilling Lancs 95 J11
Pilling Lane Lancs 94 H11
Pilning S Glos 31 Q7
Pilot Inn Kent 27 J8
Pilsbury Derbys 71 L2
Pilsdon Dorset 11 J5
Pilsgate C Pete 73 R9
Pilsley Derbys 84 B6
Pilsley Derbys 84 F8
Pilson Green Norfk 77 M9
Piltdown E Susx 25 K6
Pilton Devon 17 K5
Pilton Nhants 61 M4
Pilton Rutlnd 73 N10
Pilton Somset 19 Q6
Pilton Green Swans 28 D7
Pimbo Lancs 81 P4
Pimlico Herts 50 C9
Pimlico Lancs 89 L2
Pimlico Nhants 48 H6
Pimperne Dorset 12 F3
Pinchbeck Lincs 74 D5
Pinchbeck Bars Lincs 74 C5
Pincheon Green Donc 91 R7
Pinchinthorpe R & Cl 104 G8
Pincock Lancs 88 G7
Pinfold Lancs 88 D8
Pinford End Suffk 64 A10
Pinged Carmth 28 D4
Pingewood W Berk 35 J11
Pin Green Herts 50 G5
Pinhoe Devon 9 N6
Pinkett's Booth Covtry 59 L8
Pinkney Wilts 32 G7
Pinkneys Green W & M 35 N8
Pinley Covtry 59 N9
Pinley Green Warwks 59 K11
Pin Mill Suffk 53 M4
Pinminnoch S Ayrs 114 C9
Pinmore S Ayrs 114 D9
Pinn Devon 10 C7
Pinner Gt Lon 36 D3
Pinner Green Gt Lon 36 D2
Pinsley Green Ches E 69 Q5
Pinvin Worcs 47 J5
Pinwherry S Ayrs 114 D10
Pinxton Derbys 84 G10
Pipe and Lyde Herefs 45 Q6
Pipe Aston Herefs 56 H10
Pipe Gate Shrops 70 C6
Pipehill Staffs 58 G3
Piperdam Angus 142 D11
Piperhill Highld 156 F7
Pipers Pool Cnwll 5 M5
Pipewell Nhants 60 H3
Pippacott Devon 17 J4
Pippin Street Lancs 88 H6
Pipton Powys 44 H7
Pirbright Surrey 23 P3
Pirbright Camp Surrey 23 P3
Pirnie Border 118 C5
Pirnmill N Ayrs 120 G3
Pirton Herts 50 D4
Pirton Worcs 46 G5
Pisgah Cerdgn 54 F9
Pishill Oxon 35 K7
Pistyll Gwynd 66 E6
Pitblae Abers 159 N5
Pitcairngreen P & K 134 D2
Pitcalnie Highld 156 E3
Pitcaple Abers 151 J2
Pitcarity Angus 142 E4
Pitchcombe Gloucs 32 G3
Pitchcott Bucks 49 L10
Pitcher Row Lincs 74 E4
Pitchford Shrops 57 J4
Pitch Green Bucks 35 L4
Pitch Place Surrey 23 N7
Pitch Place Surrey 23 Q4
Pitchroy Moray 157 M10
Pitcombe Somset 20 C8
Pitcot V Glam 29 N10
Pitcox E Loth 128 G5
Pitfichie Abers 150 H4
Pitglassie Abers 158 G9
Pitgrudy Highld 162 H8
Pitlessie Fife 135 J6
Pitlochry P & K 141 M6
Pitmachie Abers 150 H2
Pitmain Highld 148 C7
Pitmedden Abers 151 M2
Pitmedden Garden Abers 151 M2
Pitminster Somset 18 H11
Pitmuies Angus 143 K8
Pitmunie Abers 150 H5
Pitney Somset 19 N9
Pitroddie P & K 134 G2
Pitscottie Fife 135 L5
Pitsea Essex 38 B4
Pitses Oldham 83 K4
Pitsford Nhants 60 G7
Pitstone Bucks 49 P11
Pitt Devon 18 D11
Pitt Hants 22 E9
Pittarrow Abers 143 N3
Pitt Court Gloucs 32 D5
Pittenweem Fife 135 P7
Pitteuchar Fife 134 H8
Pittington Dur 104 B2
Pittodrie House Hotel Abers 150 H3
Pitton Wilts 21 P8
Pitt's Wood Kent 37 P11
Pittulie Abers 159 N4
Pityme Cnwll 4 F6
Pity Me Dur 113 L11
Pivington Kent 26 F2
Pixey Green Suffk 65 J6
Pixham Surrey 36 E10
Plains N Lans 126 D4
Plain Street Cnwll 4 F6
Plaish Shrops 57 J5
Plaistow Gt Lon 37 K4
Plaistow W Susx 24 B4
Plaitford Hants 21 Q11
Plank Lane Wigan 82 D5
Plas Cymyran IoA 78 D9
Plastow Green Hants 22 F2
Platt Bridge Wigan 82 D4
Platt Lane Shrops 69 P7
Platts Heath Kent 38 E11
Plawsworth Dur 113 L11
Plaxtol Kent 37 P10
Playden E Susx 26 F7
Playford Suffk 53 M2
Play Hatch Oxon 35 K9
Playing Place Cnwll 3 L5
Playley Green Gloucs 46 E8
Plealey Shrops 56 G3
Plean Stirlg 133 N10
Pleasance Fife 134 G5
Pleasington Bl w D 89 J5
Pleasley Derbys 84 H8
Pleasleyhill Notts 84 H8
Pleasurewood Hills Suffk 65 Q2
Pleck Dorset 11 Q2
Pledgdon Green Essex 51 N5
Pledwick Wakefd 91 J7
Pleinheaume Guern 10 b1
Plemont Jersey 11 a1
Plemstall Ches W 81 P10
Plenmeller Nthumb 111 P8
Pleshey Essex 51 Q8
Plockton Highld 153 Q11
Plowden Shrops 56 F7
Plox Green Shrops 56 F4
Pluckley Kent 26 F2
Pluckley Station Kent 26 F3
Pluckley Thorne Kent 26 F3
Plucks Gutter Kent 39 N9
Plumbland Cumb 100 G3
Plumgarths Cumb 95 K2
Plumley Ches E 82 F10
Plump Hill Gloucs 46 C11
Plumpton Cumb 94 G5
Plumpton Cumb 101 N3
Plumpton E Susx 25 J8
Plumpton Nhants 48 G5
Plumpton End Nhants 49 K6
Plumpton Green E Susx 25 J7
Plumpton Head Cumb 101 P3
Plumstead Gt Lon 37 K5
Plumstead Norfk 76 G5
Plumstead Green Norfk 76 G4
Plumtree Notts 72 G4
Plumtree Green Kent 26 D2
Plungar Leics 73 K4
Plurenden Kent 26 F4
Plush Dorset 11 Q4
Plusha Cnwll 5 M5
Plushabridge Cnwll 5 N7
Plwmp Cerdgn 42 G4
Plymouth C Plym 6 D8
Plympton C Plym 6 E7
Plymstock C Plym 6 E8
Plymtree Devon 9 Q4
Pockley N York 98 C3
Pocklington E R Yk 98 G11
Pode Hole Lincs 74 D6
Podimore Somset 19 P10
Podington Bed 61 K8
Podmore Staffs 70 D7
Point Clear Essex 53 K9
Pointon Lincs 74 B4
Pokesdown BCP 13 K6
Polbain Highld 160 F4
Polbathic Cnwll 5 N10
Polbeth W Loth 127 J5
Polbrock Cnwll 4 G8
Poldark Mine Cnwll 2 H7
Polebrook Nhants 61 N3
Pole Elm Worcs 46 F4
Polegate E Susx 25 N10
Pole Moor Kirk 90 D7
Polesden Lacey Surrey 36 D10
Polesworth Warwks 59 L4
Polgigga Cnwll 2 B9
Polglass Highld 160 G5
Polgooth Cnwll 3 P3
Polgown D & G 115 P7
Poling W Susx 24 B10
Poling Corner W Susx 24 B9
Polkerris Cnwll 4 H11
Pollard Street Norfk 77 L5
Pollington E R Yk 91 Q7
Polloch Highld 138 D4
Pollokshaws C Glas 125 P5
Pollokshields C Glas 125 P5
Polmassick Cnwll 3 P4
Polmear Cnwll 4 H11
Polmont Falk 126 G2
Polnish Highld 145 N11
Polperro Cnwll 5 L11
Polruan Cnwll 5 J11
Polsham Somset 19 P6
Polstead Suffk 52 G4
Polstead Heath Suffk 52 G3
Poltalloch Ag & B 130 G8
Poltescoe Cnwll 3 J10
Poltimore Devon 9 N5
Polton Mdloth 127 P5
Polwarth Border 129 J9
Polyphant Cnwll 5 M5
Polzeath Cnwll 4 E6
Pomathorn Mdloth 127 N6
Pomeroy Derbys 83 P11
Ponde Powys 44 G7
Pondersbridge Cambs 62 C2
Ponders End Gt Lon 51 J11
Ponsanooth Cnwll 3 K6
Ponsonby Cumb 100 E9
Ponsongath Cnwll 3 K10
Ponsworthy Devon 7 J4
Pont Abraham Services Carmth 28 G3
Pontac Jersey 11 c2
Pontamman Carmth 28 H2
Pontantwn Carmth 28 D2
Pontardawe Neath 29 K4
Pontarddulais Swans 28 G4
Pont-ar-gothi Carmth 43 K10
Pont-ar-Hydfer Powys 44 B9
Pont-ar-llechau Carmth 43 P10
Pontarsais Carmth 42 H9
Pontblyddyn Flints 69 J2
Pont Cyfyng Conwy 67 N3
Pontcysyllte Aqueduct Wrexhm 69 J6
Pont Dolgarrog Conwy 79 P11
Pontdolgoch Powys 55 N6
Pont-Ebbw Newpt 31 J7
Pontefract Wakefd 91 M6
Ponteland Nthumb 113 J6
Ponterwyd Cerdgn 54 G8
Pontesbury Shrops 56 F3
Pontesbury Hill Shrops 56 F3
Pontesford Shrops 56 G3
Pontfadog Wrexhm 68 H7
Pontfaen Pembks 41 K4
Pont-faen Powys 44 D8
Pontgarreg Cerdgn 42 F4
Pontgarreg Pembks 41 M2
Ponthenri Carmth 28 E3
Ponthir Torfn 31 K6
Ponthirwaun Cerdgn 42 E5
Pontllanfraith Caerph 30 G5
Pontlliw Swans 28 H4
Pontllyfni Gwynd 66 G4
Pontlottyn Caerph 30 F3
Pont Morlais Carmth 28 F3
Pontnêddféchan Neath 29 P3
Pontnewydd Torfn 31 J5
Pontnewynydd Torfn 31 J4
Pont Pen-y-benglog Gwynd 67 M2
Pontrhydfendigaid Cerdgn 54 G11
Pont Rhyd-sarn Gwynd 67 R9
Pont Rhyd-y-cyff Brdgnd 29 N7
Pont-rhyd-y-fen Neath 29 L6
Pontrhydygroes Cerdgn 54 G10
Pontrhydyrun Torfn 31 J5
Pontrilas Herefs 45 M9
Pont Robert Powys 55 Q2
Pont-rug Gwynd 67 J2
Ponts Green E Susx 25 Q7
Pontshaen Cerdgn 42 H5
Pontshill Herefs 46 B10
Pontsticill Myr Td 30 E2
Pont Walby Neath 29 N3
Pontwelly Carmth 42 H6
Pontyates Carmth 28 E3
Pontyberem Carmth 28 F2
Pont-y-blew Wrexhm 69 K7
Pontybodkin Flints 69 J3
Pontyclun Rhondd 30 D8
Pontycymer Brdgnd 29 P6
Pontyglasier Pembks 41 M3
Pontygwaith Rhondd 30 D6
Pontygynon Pembks 41 M3
Pontymister Caerph 30 H6
Pont-y-pant Conwy 67 P4
Pontypool Torfn 31 J4
Pontypridd Rhondd 30 E7
Pont-yr-hafod Pembks 40 H5
Pont-yr-Rhyl Brdgnd 29 P7
Pontywaun Caerph 30 H6
Pool Cnwll 2 H5
Pool IoS 2 b2
Poole BCP 12 H6
Poole Keynes Gloucs 33 J5
Poolewe Highld 160 D10
Pooley Bridge Cumb 101 N6
Pooley Street Norfk 64 F5
Poolfold Staffs 70 F3
Pool Head Herefs 45 R4
Poolhill Gloucs 46 D9
Pool in Wharfedale Leeds 97 K11
Pool of Muckhart Clacks 134 C7
Pool Quay Powys 56 D2
Pool Street Essex 52 C4
Pooting's Kent 37 L11
Popham Hants 22 G6
Poplar Gt Lon 37 J4
Poplar Street Suffk 65 N8
Porchfield IoW 14 D8
Poringland Norfk 77 K11
Porkellis Cnwll 2 H7
Porlock Somset 18 A5
Porlock Weir Somset 17 R2
Portachoillan Ag & B 123 N8
Port-an-Eorna Highld 153 P11
Port Appin Ag & B 138 G8
Port Askaig Ag & B 122 F6
Portavadie Ag & B 124 A4
Port Bannatyne Ag & B 124 D4
Portbury N Som 31 P9
Port Carlisle Cumb 110 D8
Port Charlotte Ag & B 122 C8
Portchester Hants 14 H5
Port Clarence S on T 104 E6
Port Driseach Ag & B 124 B3
Port Ellen Ag & B 122 E10
Port Elphinstone Abers 151 K3
Portencalzie D & G 106 D3
Portencross N Ayrs 124 F8
Port Erin IoM 80 a8
Portesham Dorset 11 N7
Portessie Moray 158 B4
Port e Vullen IoM 80 g3
Port Eynon Swans 28 E7
Portfield Gate Pembks 40 H7
Portgate Devon 5 Q4
Port Gaverne Cnwll 4 G5
Port Glasgow Inver 125 J3
Portgordon Moray 158 A5
Portgower Highld 163 N4
Porth Cnwll 4 C9
Porth Rhondd 30 D6
Porthallow Cnwll 3 K9
Porthallow Cnwll 5 L11
Porthcawl Brdgnd 29 M9
Porthcothan Cnwll 4 D7
Porthcurno Cnwll 2 B9
Porthdinllaen Gwynd 66 D6
Port Henderson Highld 153 P3
Porthgain Pembks 40 F4
Porthgwarra Cnwll 2 B9
Porthill Staffs 70 E5
Porthkea Cnwll 3 L5
Porthkerry V Glam 30 E11
Porthleven Cnwll 2 G8
Porthmadog Gwynd 67 K7
Porthmeor Cnwll 2 C6
Porth Navas Cnwll 3 K8
Porthoustock Cnwll 3 P5
Porthoustock Cnwll 3 L9
Porthpean Cnwll 3 Q3
Porthtowan Cnwll 2 H4
Porthwgan Wrexhm 69 L5
Porthyrhyd Carmth 43 K11
Porth-y-Waen Shrops 69 J10
Portincaple Ag & B 131 Q9
Portinfer Jersey 11 a1
Portington E R Yk 92 C4
Portinnisherrich Ag & B 131 K5
Portinscale Cumb 101 J6
Port Isaac Cnwll 4 F5
Portishead N Som 31 N9
Portknockie Moray 158 C4
Portland Dorset 11 P10
Portlethen Abers 151 N8
Portling D & G 109 J10
Portloe Cnwll 3 N6
Port Logan D & G 106 E9
Portlooe Cnwll 5 L11
Portmahomack Highld 163 L10
Portmeirion Gwynd 67 K7
Portmellon Cnwll 3 Q5
Port Mòr Highld 144 F12
Portmore Hants 13 P5
Port Mulgrave N York 105 L7
Portnacroish Ag & B 138 G8
Portnaguran W Isls 168 k4
Portnahaven Ag & B 122 A9
Portnalong Highld 152 E11
Port nan Giuran W Isls 168 k4
Port nan Long W Isls 168 d10
Port Nis W Isls 168 k1

Portobello C Edin 127 Q3
Portobello Gatesd 113 L9
Portobello Wolves 58 E5
Port of Menteith Stirlg 132 H7
Port of Ness W Isls 168 k1
Porton Wilts 21 N7
Portontown Devon 5 Q6
Portpatrick D & G 106 C7
Port Quin Cnwll 4 F5
Port Ramsay Ag & B 138 F8
Portreath Cnwll 2 H4
Portreath Harbour Cnwll 2 H4
Portree Highld 152 H9
Port Righ Ag & B 120 F4
Port St Mary IoM 80 b8
Portscatho Cnwll 3 M6
Portsea C Port 14 H6
Portskerra Highld 166 E3
Portskewett Mons 31 N7
Portslade Br & H 24 G9
Portslade-by-Sea Br & H 24 G9
Portslogan D & G 106 C6
Portsmouth C Port 14 H7
Portsmouth Calder 89 Q5
Portsmouth Arms Devon 17 L8
Portsmouth Dockyard C Port 14 H6
Port Soderick IoM 80 d7
Port Solent C Port 14 H5
Portsonachan Hotel Ag & B 131 L3
Portsoy Abers 158 E4
Port Sunlight Wirral 81 L8
Portswood C Sotn 14 D4
Port Talbot Neath 29 L7
Port Tennant Swans 29 J6
Portuairk Highld 137 L2
Portway Herefs 45 P6
Portway Herefs 45 P7
Portway Sandw 58 E7
Portway Worcs 58 G10
Port Wemyss Ag & B 122 A9
Port William D & G 107 K9
Portwrinkle Cnwll 5 P11
Portyerrock D & G 107 N10
Posbury Devon 9 K5
Posenhall Shrops 57 M4
Poslingford Suffk 63 N11
Posso Border 117 J4
Postbridge Devon 8 G9
Postcombe Oxon 35 K4
Post Green Dorset 12 G6
Postling Kent 27 K4
Postwick Norfk 77 K10
Potarch Abers 150 G8
Potsgrove C Beds 49 Q8
Potten End Herts 50 B9
Potten Street Kent 39 N8
Potter Brompton N York 99 K5
Pottergate Street Norfk 64 H3
Potterhanworth Lincs 86 E7
Potterhanworth Booths Lincs 86 E7
Potter Heigham Norfk 77 N8
Potterne Wilts 21 J3
Potterne Wick Wilts 21 J3
Potter Row Bucks 35 P4
Potters Bar Herts 50 F10
Potters Brook Lancs 95 K10
Potter's Cross Staffs 58 B8
Potters Crouch Herts 50 D9
Potter's Forstal Kent 26 E2
Potters Green Covtry 59 N8
Potter's Green E Susx 25 M6
Potter's Green Herts 51 J6
Pottersheath Herts 50 F7
Potters Marston Leics 72 D11
Potter Somersal Derbys 71 L7
Potterspury Nhants 49 L6
Potter Street Essex 51 L9
Potterton Abers 151 N4
Potterton Leeds 91 L3
Potthorpe Norfk 76 C7
Pottle Street Wilts 20 F6
Potto N York 104 E10
Potton C Beds 62 B11
Pott Row Norfk 75 P6
Pott's Green Essex 52 F7
Pott Shrigley Ches E 83 K9
Poughill Cnwll 16 C10
Poughill Devon 9 L3
Poulner Hants 13 L3
Poulshot Wilts 21 J3
Poulton Gloucs 33 L4
Poulton Wirral 81 L6
Poulton-le-Fylde Lancs 88 C3
Poulton Priory Gloucs 33 L5
Pound Bank Worcs 57 N10
Poundbury Dorset 11 P6
Poundffald Swans 28 G6
Poundgate E Susx 25 L5
Pound Green E Susx 25 M6
Pound Green Suffk 63 M10
Pound Green Worcs 57 P9
Pound Hill W Susx 24 G3
Poundon Bucks 48 H9
Poundsbridge Kent 25 M2
Poundsgate Devon 7 J4
Poundstock Cnwll 5 L2
Pound Street Hants 22 E2
Pounsley E Susx 25 M6
Pouton D & G 107 N8
Pouy Street Suffk 65 M7
Povey Cross Surrey 24 G2
Powburn Nthumb 119 L7
Powderham Devon 9 N8
Powerstock Dorset 11 L5
Powfoot D & G 109 P7
Pow Green Herefs 46 D6
Powhill Cumb 110 D9
Powick Worcs 46 F4
Powmill P & K 134 C8
Poxwell Dorset 12 B8
Poyle Slough 36 B5
Poynings W Susx 24 G8
Poyntington Dorset 20 C10
Poynton Ches E 83 K8
Poynton Wrekin 69 Q11
Poynton Green Wrekin 69 Q11
Poyston Cross Pembks 41 J7
Poystreet Green Suffk 64 D10
Praa Sands Cnwll 2 F8
Pratt's Bottom Gt Lon 37 L8
Praze-an-Beeble Cnwll 2 G6
Predannack Wollas Cnwll 2 H10
Prees Shrops 69 Q8
Preesall Lancs 94 H11
Prees Green Shrops 69 Q8
Preesgweene Shrops 69 J7
Prees Heath Shrops 69 Q7
Prees Higher Heath Shrops 69 Q7
Prees Lower Heath Shrops 69 Q8
Prendwick Nthumb 119 K8
Pren-gwyn Cerdgn 42 H6
Prenteg Gwynd 67 K6
Prenton Wirral 81 L7
Prescot Knows 81 P6
Prescott Devon 10 B2
Prescott Shrops 57 M8
Prescott Shrops 69 M10
Presnerb Angus 142 B4
Pressen Nthumb 118 F3
Prestatyn Denbgs 80 F8
Prestbury Ches E 83 J9
Prestbury Gloucs 47 J10
Presteigne Powys 45 L2
Prestleigh Somset 20 B6
Prestolee Bolton 89 M9
Preston Border 129 K8
Preston Br & H 24 H9
Preston Devon 7 M4
Preston Dorset 11 Q8
Preston E R Yk 93 L4
Preston Gloucs 33 K4
Preston Herts 50 E6
Preston Kent 38 H9
Preston Kent 39 M9
Preston Lancs 88 G5
Preston Nthumb 119 N5
Preston Rutlnd 73 M10
Preston Shrops 57 J2
Preston Somset 18 E7
Preston Torbay 7 M6
Preston Wilts 33 K9
Preston Wilts 33 Q10
Preston Bagot Warwks 59 J11
Preston Bissett Bucks 49 J9
Preston Bowyer Somset 18 F9
Preston Brockhurst Shrops 69 P10
Preston Brook Halton 82 C8
Preston Candover Hants 22 H6
Preston Capes Nhants 48 G4
Preston Crowmarsh Oxon 34 H6
Preston Deanery Nhants 60 G9
Preston Green Warwks 59 J11
Preston Gubbals Shrops 69 N11
Preston Montford Shrops 56 G2
Preston on Stour Warwks 47 P5
Preston on Tees S on T 104 D7
Preston on the Hill Halton 82 C8
Preston on Wye Herefs 45 M6
Prestonpans E Loth 128 B5
Preston Patrick Cumb 95 L4
Preston Plucknett Somset 19 P11
Preston St Mary Suffk 64 C11
Preston Street Kent 39 N9
Preston-under-Scar N York 96 G2
Preston upon the Weald Moors Wrekin 70 B11
Preston Wynne Herefs 45 R5
Prestwich Bury 82 H4
Prestwick Nthumb 113 J6
Prestwick S Ayrs 114 G2
Prestwick Airport S Ayrs 114 G2
Prestwood Bucks 35 N4
Prestwood Staffs 58 C7
Price Town Brdgnd 29 P6
Prickwillow Cambs 63 J4
Priddy Somset 19 P4
Priestacott Devon 8 B3
Priestcliffe Derbys 83 P10
Priestcliffe Ditch Derbys 83 P10
Priest Hutton Lancs 95 L6
Priestland E Ayrs 125 P10
Priestley Green Calder 90 E5
Priest Weston Shrops 56 D5
Priestwood Green Kent 37 Q8
Primethorpe Leics 60 B2
Primrose Green Norfk 76 F8
Primrosehill Border 129 K8
Primrose Hill Cambs 62 E3
Primrose Hill Derbys 84 F9
Primrose Hill Dudley 58 D7
Primrose Hill Lancs 88 D9
Primsidemill Border 118 F5
Prince of Wales Bridge Mons 31 P7
Princes Gate Pembks 41 M8
Princes Risborough Bucks 35 M4
Princethorpe Warwks 59 P10
Princetown Devon 6 F4
Prinsted W Susx 15 L5
Prion Denbgs 68 E2
Prior Rigg Cumb 111 J7
Priors Halton Shrops 56 H9
Priors Hardwick Warwks 48 E3
Priorslee Wrekin 57 N2
Priors Marston Warwks 48 E3
Priors Norton Gloucs 46 G10
Priory Wood Herefs 45 K5
Prisk V Glam 30 D9
Priston BaNES 20 C2
Pristow Green Norfk 64 G4
Prittlewell Sthend 38 E4
Privett Hants 23 J9
Prixford Devon 17 K4
Probus Cnwll 3 M4
Prora E Loth 128 E4
Prospect Cumb 100 F2
Prospidnick Cnwll 2 G7
Protstonhill Abers 159 K5
Prudhoe Nthumb 112 G8
Prussia Cove Cnwll 2 F8
Pubil P & K 140 C9
Publow BaNES 20 B2
Puckeridge Herts 51 J6
Puckington Somset 19 L11
Pucklechurch S Glos 32 C9
Puckrup Gloucs 46 G7
Puddinglake Ches W 82 F11
Puddington Ches W 81 L10
Puddington Devon 9 K2
Puddledock Norfk 64 F3
Puddletown Dorset 12 C6
Pudleston Herefs 45 R3
Pudsey Leeds 90 G4
Pulborough W Susx 24 B7
Puleston Wrekin 70 C10
Pulford Ches W 69 L3
Pulham Dorset 11 Q3
Pulham Market Norfk 64 H4
Pulham St Mary Norfk 65 J4
Pullens Green S Glos 32 B6
Pulloxhill C Beds 50 C4
Pulverbatch Shrops 56 G4
Pumpherston W Loth 127 K4
Pumsaint Carmth 43 N6
Puncheston Pembks 41 K5
Puncknowle Dorset 11 L7
Punnett's Town E Susx 25 P6
Purbrook Hants 15 J5
Purfleet Thurr 37 N5
Puriton Somset 19 K6
Purleigh Essex 52 D11
Purley Gt Lon 36 H8
Purley on Thames W Berk 35 J9
Purlogue Shrops 56 D9
Purlpit Wilts 32 G11
Purls Bridge Cambs 62 G3
Purse Caundle Dorset 20 C11
Purshull Green Worcs 58 C10
Purslow Shrops 56 F8
Purston Jaglin Wakefd 91 L7
Purtington Somset 10 H3
Purton Gloucs 32 C3
Purton Gloucs 32 C4
Purton Wilts 33 L7
Purton Stoke Wilts 33 L6
Pury End Nhants 49 K5
Pusey Oxon 34 C5
Putley Herefs 46 B7
Putley Green Herefs 46 B7
Putloe Gloucs 32 E3
Putney Gt Lon 36 F6
Putsborough Devon 16 G3
Puttenham Herts 35 N2
Puttenham Surrey 23 P5
Puttock End Essex 52 D3
Putton Dorset 11 N8
Putts Corner Devon 10 C5
Puxley Nhants 49 L6
Puxton N Som 19 M2
Pwll Carmth 28 E4
Pwllcrochan Pembks 40 H10
Pwll-du Mons 30 H2
Pwll-glas Denbgs 68 F4
Pwllgloyw Powys 44 E8
Pwllheli Gwynd 66 F7
Pwllmeyric Mons 31 P6
Pwll-trap Carmth 41 Q7
Pwll-y-glaw Neath 29 L6
Pydew Conwy 79 Q9
Pye Bridge Derbys 84 F10
Pyecombe W Susx 24 G8
Pye Corner Newpt 31 K7
Pye Green Staffs 58 E2
Pyle Brdgnd 29 M8
Pyleigh Somset 18 F8
Pylle Somset 20 B7
Pymoor Cambs 62 G3
Pymore Dorset 11 K6
Pyrford Surrey 36 B9
Pyrton Oxon 35 J5
Pytchley Nhants 61 J6
Pyworthy Devon 16 E11

Q

Quabbs Shrops 56 C8
Quadring Lincs 74 D4
Quadring Eaudike Lincs 74 D4
Quainton Bucks 49 K10
Quaker's Yard Myr Td 30 E5
Quaking Houses Dur 113 J10
Quantock Hills Somset 18 G7
Quarff Shet 169 r10
Quarley Hants 21 Q6
Quarndon Derbys 72 A2
Quarr Hill IoW 14 G8
Quarrier's Village Inver 125 K4
Quarrington Lincs 73 R2
Quarrington Hill Dur 104 B3
Quarrybank Ches W 82 C11
Quarry Bank Dudley 58 D7
Quarrywood Moray 157 M5
Quarter N Ayrs 124 F5
Quarter S Lans 126 C7
Quatford Shrops 57 N6
Quatt Shrops 57 P7
Quebec Dur 103 N2
Quedgeley Gloucs 32 F2
Queen Adelaide Cambs 63 J4
Queenborough Kent 38 F7
Queen Camel Somset 19 Q10
Queen Charlton BaNES 32 B11
Queen Dart Devon 17 Q8
Queen Elizabeth Forest Park Stirlg 132 G7
Queenhill Worcs 46 G7
Queen Oak Dorset 20 E8
Queen's Bower IoW 14 G10
Queensbury C Brad 90 E4
Queensferry Flints 81 L11
Queensferry Crossing Fife 134 E11
Queen's Head Shrops 69 K9
Queen's Hills Norfk 76 H9
Queenslie C Glas 126 B4
Queen's Park Bed 61 M11
Queen's Park Nhants 60 G8
Queen Street Kent 37 Q11
Queen Street Wilts 33 K7
Queenzieburn N Lans 126 B2
Quendon Essex 51 M4
Queniborough Leics 72 G8
Quenington Gloucs 33 M4
Quernmore Lancs 95 L9
Queslett Birm 58 G6
Quethiock Cnwll 5 N9
Quick's Green W Berk 34 G9
Quidenham Norfk 64 E4
Quidhampton Hants 22 F4
Quidhampton Wilts 21 M8
Quina Brook Shrops 69 P8
Quinbury End Nhants 48 H4
Quinton Dudley 58 E8
Quinton Nhants 49 L4
Quinton Green Nhants 49 L4
Quintrell Downs Cnwll 4 C9
Quixhall Staffs 71 L6
Quixwood Border 129 K7
Quoditch Devon 5 Q2
Quoig P & K 133 N3
Quorn Leics 72 F7
Quothquan S Lans 116 D3
Quoyburray Ork 169 e6
Quoyloo Ork 169 b4

R

Raasay Highld 153 K9
Rabbit's Cross Kent 26 C2
Rableyheath Herts 50 F7
Raby Cumb 110 C10
Raby Wirral 81 L9
Rachan Mill Border 116 G4
Rachub Gwynd 79 L11
Rackenford Devon 17 R8
Rackham W Susx 24 B8
Rackheath Norfk 77 K9
Racks D & G 109 M6
Rackwick Ork 169 b7
Radbourne Derbys 71 P7
Radcliffe Bury 89 M9
Radcliffe Nthumb 119 Q10
Radcliffe on Trent Notts 72 G3
Radclive Bucks 49 J8
Radcot Oxon 33 Q5
Raddery Highld 156 C6
Raddington Somset 18 D9
Radernie Fife 135 M6
Radford Covtry 59 M8
Radford Semele Warwks 48 B2
Radlet Somset 18 H7
Radlett Herts 50 E10
Radley Devon 17 N7
Radley Oxon 34 F5
Radley W Berk 34 C11
Radley Green Essex 51 P9
Radmore Green Ches E 69 Q3
Radnage Bucks 35 L5
Radstock BaNES 20 C4
Radstone Nhants 48 G6
Radway Warwks 48 C5
Radwell Bed 61 M9
Radwell Herts 50 F3
Radwinter Essex 51 P3
Radwinter End Essex 51 P3
Radyr Cardif 30 F8
RAF College (Cranwell) Lincs 86 D11
Rafford Moray 157 K6
RAF Museum Cosford Shrops 57 P3
RAF Museum Hendon Gt Lon 36 F2
Ragdale Leics 72 H7
Ragdon Shrops 56 H6
Raginnis Cnwll 2 D8
Raglan Mons 31 M3
Ragnall Notts 85 P6
Raigbeg Highld 148 E2
Rainbow Hill Worcs 46 G3
Rainford St Hel 81 P4
Rainham Gt Lon 37 M4
Rainham Medway 38 D8
Rainhill St Hel 81 P6
Rainhill Stoops St Hel 81 Q6
Rainow Ches E 83 K9
Rainsough Bury 82 H4
Rainton N York 97 N5
Rainworth Notts 85 J9
Raisbeck Cumb 102 B9
Raise Cumb 111 P11
Raisthorpe N York 98 H8
Rait P & K 134 G2
Raithby Lincs 87 K4
Raithby Lincs 87 L7
Raithwaite N York 105 N8
Rake Hants 23 M9
Rakewood Rochdl 89 Q8
Ralia Highld 148 C8
Ram Carmth 43 L5
Ramasaig Highld 152 B9
Rame Cnwll 3 J7
Rame Cnwll 6 C9
Ram Hill S Glos 32 C9
Ram Lane Kent 26 G2
Rampisham Dorset 11 M4
Rampside Cumb 94 E7
Rampton Cambs 62 F7
Rampton Notts 85 P5
Ramsbottom Bury 89 M7
Ramsbury Wilts 33 Q10
Ramscraigs Highld 167 K11
Ramsdean Hants 23 K10
Ramsdell Hants 22 G3
Ramsden Oxon 48 C11
Ramsden Worcs 46 H5
Ramsden Bellhouse Essex 38 B3
Ramsden Heath Essex 38 B2
Ramsey Cambs 62 C3
Ramsey Essex 53 M5
Ramsey IoM 80 g3
Ramsey Forty Foot Cambs 62 D3
Ramsey Heights Cambs 62 B4
Ramsey Island Essex 52 F10
Ramsey Island Pembks 40 D6
Ramsey Mereside Cambs 62 C3
Ramsey St Mary's Cambs 62 C3
Ramsgate Kent 39 Q8
Ramsgill N York 96 H6
Ramshaw Dur 103 M5
Ramshaw Dur 112 E11
Ramsholt Suffk 53 P3
Ramshope Nthumb 118 D10
Ramshorn Staffs 71 K5
Ramsley Devon 8 G6
Ramsnest Common Surrey 23 P8
Ranby Lincs 86 H5
Ranby Notts 85 L4
Rand Lincs 86 F5
Randwick Gloucs 32 F3
Ranfurly Rens 125 K4
Rangemore Staffs 71 M10
Rangeworthy S Glos 32 C7
Rankinston E Ayrs 115 J5
Ranksborough Rutlnd 73 L8
Rank's Green Essex 52 B8
Rannoch Station P & K 140 B6
Ranscombe Somset 18 B6
Ranskill Notts 85 L3
Ranton Staffs 70 F10
Ranton Green Staffs 70 E10
Ranworth Norfk 77 M9
Raploch Stirlg 133 M9
Rapness Ork 169 e2
Rapps Somset 19 K11
Rascarrel D & G 108 G11
Rashfield Ag & B 131 N11
Rashwood Worcs 58 D11
Raskelf N York 97 Q6
Rassau Blae G 30 G2
Rastrick Calder 90 E6
Ratagan Highld 145 R4
Ratby Leics 72 E9
Ratcliffe Culey Leics 72 A11
Ratcliffe on Soar Notts 72 D5
Ratcliffe on the Wreake Leics 72 G8
Rathen Abers 159 N5
Rathillet Fife 135 K3
Rathmell N York 96 B9
Ratho C Edin 127 L3
Ratho Station C Edin 127 L3
Rathven Moray 158 B4
Ratlake Hants 22 D10
Ratley Warwks 48 C5
Ratling Kent 39 M11
Ratlinghope Shrops 56 G5
Rattar Highld 167 N2
Ratten Row Cumb 101 K2
Ratten Row Cumb 110 G11
Ratten Row Lancs 88 E2
Rattery Devon 7 J6
Rattlesden Suffk 64 D10
Ratton Village E Susx 25 N10
Rattray P & K 142 B8
Raughton Cumb 110 G11
Raughton Head Cumb 110 G11
Raunds Nhants 61 L6
Ravenfield Rothm 91 M11
Ravenglass Cumb 100 E11
Ravenhills Green Worcs 46 D4
Raveningham Norfk 65 M2
Ravenscar N York 105 Q10
Ravenscraig N Lans 126 D6
Ravensdale IoM 80 e3
Ravensden Bed 61 N10
Ravenseat N York 102 G10
Ravenshead Notts 85 J10
Ravensmoor Ches E 69 R4
Ravensthorpe Kirk 90 G6
Ravensthorpe Nhants 60 E6
Ravenstone Leics 72 C8
Ravenstone M Keyn 49 M4
Ravenstonedale Cumb 102 D10
Ravenstruther S Lans 126 G8
Ravensworth N York 103 M9
Raw N York 105 P9
Rawcliffe C York 98 B10
Rawcliffe E R Yk 92 A6
Rawcliffe Bridge E R Yk 92 A6
Rawdon Leeds 90 G3
Rawling Street Kent 38 F10
Rawmarsh Rothm 91 L11
Rawnsley Staffs 58 F2
Rawreth Essex 38 C3
Rawridge Devon 10 E3
Rawtenstall Lancs 89 N6
Raydon Suffk 52 H4
Raylees Nthumb 112 D2
Rayleigh Essex 38 D3
Raymond's Hill Devon 10 G5
Rayne Essex 52 B7
Raynes Park Gt Lon 36 F7
Reach Cambs 63 J7
Read Lancs 89 M4
Reading Readg 35 K10
Reading Services W Berk 35 J11
Reading Street Kent 26 F5
Reading Street Kent 39 Q8
Reagill Cumb 102 B7
Realwa Cnwll 2 G6
Rearquhar Highld 162 G8
Rearsby Leics 72 H8
Rease Heath Ches E 70 A4
Reay Highld 166 G4
Reculver Kent 39 M8
Red Ball Devon 18 E11
Redberth Pembks 41 L10
Redbourn Herts 50 D8
Redbourne N Linc 92 G11
Redbrook Gloucs 31 P3
Redbrook Wrexhm 69 P6
Redbrook Street Kent 26 F4
Redburn Highld 156 G8
Redburn Nthumb 111 Q8
Redcar R & Cl 104 H6
Redcastle D & G 108 H7
Redcastle Highld 155 Q8
Red Dial Cumb 110 E11
Redding Falk 126 G2
Reddingmuirhead Falk 126 G2
Reddish Stockp 83 J6
Redditch Worcs 58 F11
Rede Suffk 63 P9
Redenhall Norfk 65 K5
Redenham Hants 22 B5
Redesmouth Nthumb 112 C4
Redford Abers 143 P3
Redford Angus 143 K9
Redford W Susx 23 N9
Redfordgreen Border 117 M7
Redgate Rhondd 30 D7
Redgorton P & K 134 D2
Redgrave Suffk 64 E6
Redhill Abers 151 K7
Red Hill BCP 13 J5
Redhill Herts 50 H4
Redhill N Som 19 N2
Redhill Surrey 36 G10
Red Hill Warwks 47 M3
Redisham Suffk 65 N5
Redland Bristl 31 Q9
Redland Ork 169 c4
Redlingfield Suffk 64 H7
Redlingfield Green Suffk 64 H7
Red Lodge Suffk 63 L6
Red Lumb Rochdl 89 N7
Redlynch Somset 20 D8
Redlynch Wilts 21 P10
Redmain Cumb 100 F4
Redmarley Worcs 57 P11
Redmarley D'Abitot Gloucs 46 E8
Redmarshall S on T 104 C6
Redmile Leics 73 K3
Redmire N York 96 F2
Redmyre Abers 143 P2
Rednal Birm 58 F9
Rednal Shrops 69 L9
Redpath Border 118 A3

Redpoint Highld 153 N4
Red Post Cnwll 16 D10
Red Rock Wigan 88 H9
Red Roses Carmth 41 P8
Red Row Nthumb 119 Q11
Redruth Cnwll 2 H5
Redstocks Wilts 20 H2
Redstone P & K 142 B11
Redstone Cross Pembks 41 M7
Red Street Staffs 70 E4
Redvales Bury 89 N9
Red Wharf Bay IoA 79 J8
Redwick Newpt 31 M8
Redwick S Glos 31 P7
Redworth Darltn 103 P6
Reed Herts 51 J3
Reedham Norfk 77 N11
Reedness E R Yk 92 C6
Reeds Beck Lincs 86 H7
Reeds Holme Lancs 89 N6
Reepham Lincs 86 D6
Reepham Norfk 76 G7
Reeth N York 103 K11
Reeves Green Solhll 59 L9
Regaby IoM 80 f2
Regil N Som 19 P2
Reiff Highld 160 F4
Reigate Surrey 36 G10
Reighton N York 99 N5
Reinigeadal W Isls 168 h7
Reisque Abers 151 M4
Reiss Highld 167 P6
Rejerrah Cnwll 4 B10
Releath Cnwll 2 H7
Relubbus Cnwll 2 F7
Relugas Moray 156 H8
Remenham Wokham 35 L8
Remenham Hill Wokham 35 L8
Rempstone Notts 72 F6
Rendcomb Gloucs 33 K3
Rendham Suffk 65 L9
Rendlesham Suffk 65 L11
Renfrew Rens 125 N4
Renhold Bed 61 N10
Renishaw Derbys 84 G5
Rennington Nthumb 119 P7
Renton W Duns 125 K2
Renwick Cumb 101 Q2
Repps Norfk 77 N8
Repton Derbys 71 Q9
Reraig Highld 145 P2
Resaurie Highld 156 C8
Rescassa Cnwll 3 P5
Rescorla Cnwll 3 P4
Resipole Burn Highld 138 C5
Reskadinnick Cnwll 2 G5
Resolis Highld 156 B4
Resolven Neath 29 M4
Rest and be thankful Ag & B 131 Q6
Reston Border 129 M7
Restronguet Cnwll 3 L6
Reswallie Angus 143 J7
Reterth Cnwll 4 E9
Retford Notts 85 M4
Retire Cnwll 4 G9
Rettendon Essex 38 C2
Retyn Cnwll 4 D10
Revesby Lincs 87 J8
Rew Devon 7 J11
Rew Devon 7 K4
Rewe Devon 9 M5
Rew Street IoW 14 E8
Rexon Devon 5 Q4
Reydon Suffk 65 P6
Reymerston Norfk 76 E10
Reynalton Pembks 41 L9
Reynoldston Swans 28 E7
Rezare Cnwll 5 P6
Rhadyr Mons 31 L4
Rhandirmwyn Carmth 43 Q6
Rhayader Powys 55 M11
Rheindown Highld 155 P8
Rhenigidale W Isls 168 h7
Rhes-y-cae Flints 80 H10
Rhewl Denbgs 68 F2
Rhewl Denbgs 68 G6
Rhewl Mostyn Flints 80 H8
Rhicarn Highld 164 C11
Rhiconich Highld 164 G6
Rhicullen Highld 156 B3
Rhigos Rhondd 29 P3
Rhives Highld 163 J6
Rhiwbina Cardif 30 G8
Rhiwbryfdir Gwynd 67 M5
Rhiwderyn Newpt 31 J7
Rhiwen Gwynd 67 K2
Rhiwinder Rhondd 30 D7
Rhiwlas Gwynd 68 B7
Rhiwlas Gwynd 79 K11
Rhiwlas Powys 68 G8
Rhiwsaeson Rhondd 30 E8
Rhode Somset 19 J8
Rhoden Green Kent 37 Q11
Rhodesia Notts 85 J5
Rhodes Minnis Kent 27 L3
Rhodiad-y-brenin Pembks 40 E5
Rhonehouse D & G 108 F9
Rhoose V Glam 30 E11
Rhos Carmth 42 G7
Rhos Denbgs 68 F2
Rhos Neath 29 K4
Rhosaman Carmth 29 K2
Rhosbeirio IoA 78 F6
Rhoscefnhir IoA 79 J9
Rhoscolyn IoA 78 D9
Rhoscrowther Pembks 40 H10
Rhosesmor Flints 81 J11
Rhos-fawr Gwynd 66 F7
Rhosgadfan Gwynd 67 J3
Rhosgoch IoA 78 G7
Rhosgoch Powys 44 H5
Rhos Haminiog Cerdgn 43 K2
Rhoshill Pembks 41 N2
Rhoshirwaun Gwynd 66 C9
Rhoslan Gwynd 66 H6
Rhoslefain Gwynd 54 D3
Rhosllanerchrugog Wrexhm 69 J5
Rhôs Lligwy IoA 78 H7
Rhosmaen Carmth 43 M10
Rhosmeirch IoA 78 H9
Rhosneigr IoA 78 E10
Rhosnesni Wrexhm 69 L4
Rhôs-on-Sea Conwy 79 Q8
Rhosrobin Wrexhm 69 K4
Rhossili Swans 28 D7
Rhostrehwfa IoA 78 G10
Rhostryfan Gwynd 66 H3
Rhostyllen Wrexhm 69 K5
Rhosybol IoA 78 G7
Rhos-y-brithdir Powys 68 F10
Rhosygadfa Shrops 69 K8
Rhos-y-garth Cerdgn 54 E10
Rhos-y-gwaliau Gwynd 68 B8
Rhos-y-llan Gwynd 66 C7
Rhosymedre Wrexhm 69 J6
Rhos-y-meirch Powys 56 D11
Rhu Ag & B 132 B11
Rhuallt Denbgs 80 F9
Rhubodach Ag & B 124 C3
Rhuddall Heath Ches W 69 Q2
Rhuddlan Cerdgn 43 J6
Rhuddlan Denbgs 80 E9
Rhulen Powys 44 G5
Rhunahaorine Ag & B 123 M10
Rhyd Gwynd 67 L6
Rhydargaeau Carmth 42 H9
Rhydcymerau Carmth 43 L7
Rhydd Worcs 46 F5
Rhyd-Ddu Gwynd 67 K4
Rhydding Neath 29 K5
Rhydgaled Conwy 68 C2
Rhydlanfair Conwy 67 Q4
Rhydlewis Cerdgn 42 F5
Rhydlios Gwynd 66 B9
Rhydlydan Conwy 68 A4
Rhydowen Cerdgn 42 H5
Rhydroser Cerdgn 54 D11
Rhydspence Herefs 45 J5
Rhydtalog Flints 68 H4
Rhyd-uchaf Gwynd 68 B7
Rhyd-y-clafdy Gwynd 66 E8
Rhydycroesau Shrops 68 H8
Rhydyfelin Cerdgn 54 D9
Rhydyfelin Rhondd 30 E7
Rhyd-y-foel Conwy 80 C9
Rhydyfro Neath 29 K3
Rhyd-y-groes Gwynd 79 K11
Rhydymain Gwynd 67 Q10
Rhyd-y-meirch Mons 31 K3
Rhydymwyn Flints 81 J11
Rhyd-y-pennau Cerdgn 54 E7
Rhyd-yr-onnen Gwynd 54 E4
Rhyd-y-sarn Gwynd 67 M6
Rhyl Denbgs 80 E8
Rhymney Caerph 30 F3
Rhynd P & K 134 F3
Rhynie Abers 150 D2
Rhynie Highld 163 J11
Ribbesford Worcs 57 P10
Ribbleton Lancs 88 H4
Ribby Lancs 88 E4
Ribchester Lancs 89 K3
Riber Derbys 84 D9
Riby Lincs 93 L9
Riccall N York 91 Q3
Riccarton Border 111 K2
Riccarton E Ayrs 125 L10
Richards Castle Herefs 56 H11
Richings Park Bucks 36 B5
Richmond Gt Lon 36 E6
Richmond N York 103 N10
Richmond Sheff 84 F3
Rich's Holford Somset 18 F8
Rickerscote Staffs 70 G10
Rickford N Som 19 N3
Rickham Devon 7 K11
Rickinghall Suffk 64 E6
Rickling Essex 51 L4
Rickling Green Essex 51 M5
Rickmansworth Herts 36 C2
Riddell Border 117 Q6
Riddings Derbys 84 F10
Riddlecombe Devon 17 L9
Riddlesden C Brad 90 D2
Ridge BaNES 19 Q3
Ridge Dorset 12 F7
Ridge Herts 50 F10
Ridge Wilts 21 J8
Ridgebourne Powys 44 F2
Ridge Green Surrey 36 H11
Ridge Lane Warwks 59 L6
Ridge Row Kent 27 M3
Ridgeway Derbys 84 F4
Ridgeway Worcs 47 K2
Ridgeway Cross Herefs 46 D5
Ridgewell Essex 52 B3
Ridgewood E Susx 25 L7
Ridgmont C Beds 49 Q7
Riding Mill Nthumb 112 F8
Ridley Kent 37 P8
Ridley Nthumb 111 Q8
Ridley Green Ches E 69 Q4
Ridlington Norfk 77 L5
Ridlington Rutlnd 73 L10
Ridlington Street Norfk 77 L5
Ridsdale Nthumb 112 D4
Rievaulx N York 98 B3
Rigg D & G 110 E7
Riggend N Lans 126 D3
Righoul Highld 156 F7
Rigmadon Park Cumb 95 N4
Rigsby Lincs 87 M5
Rigside S Lans 116 B3
Riley Green Lancs 89 J5
Rileyhill Staffs 58 H2
Rilla Mill Cnwll 5 M7
Rillaton Cnwll 5 M7
Rillington N York 98 H6
Rimington Lancs 96 B11
Rimpton Somset 20 B10
Rimswell E R Yk 93 P5
Rinaston Pembks 41 J5
Rindleford Shrops 57 N5
Ringford D & G 108 E9
Ringinglow Sheff 84 C4
Ringland Norfk 76 G9
Ringles Cross E Susx 25 L6
Ringlestone Kent 38 E10
Ringley Bolton 89 M9
Ringmer E Susx 25 K8
Ringmore Devon 6 H9
Ringmore Devon 7 N4
Ringorm Moray 157 P9
Ring's End Cambs 74 G10
Ringsfield Suffk 65 N4
Ringsfield Corner Suffk 65 N4
Ringshall Herts 35 Q2
Ringshall Suffk 64 E11
Ringshall Stocks Suffk 64 F11
Ringstead Nhants 61 L5
Ringstead Norfk 75 P2
Ringwood Hants 13 L3
Ringwould Kent 27 Q2
Rinmore Abers 150 C4
Rinsey Cnwll 2 F8
Rinsey Croft Cnwll 2 G8
Ripe E Susx 25 M8
Ripley Derbys 84 E10
Ripley Hants 13 L5
Ripley N York 97 L8
Ripley Surrey 36 C9
Riplingham E R Yk 92 G4
Riplington Hants 23 J10
Ripon N York 97 M6
Rippingale Lincs 74 A5
Ripple Kent 39 Q11
Ripple Worcs 46 G7
Ripponden Calder 90 C7
Risabus Ag & B 122 D11
Risbury Herefs 45 Q4
Risby N Linc 92 F8
Risby Suffk 63 P7
Risca Caerph 30 H6
Rise E R Yk 93 L2
Riseden E Susx 25 P4
Riseden Kent 26 B4
Risegate Lincs 74 D5
Riseholme Lincs 86 C5
Risehow Cumb 100 D4
Riseley Bed 61 M8
Riseley Wokham 23 K2
Rishangles Suffk 64 H8
Rishton Lancs 89 L4
Rishworth Calder 90 C7
Rising Bridge Lancs 89 M5
Risley Derbys 72 D3
Risley Warrtn 82 E6
Risplith N York 97 K7
Rivar Wilts 22 B2
Rivenhall End Essex 52 D8
River Kent 27 N3
River W Susx 23 P10
River Bank Cambs 62 H7
Riverford Highld 155 P7
Riverhead Kent 37 M9
Rivers Corner Dorset 12 C2
Rivington Lancs 89 J8
Rivington Services Lancs 89 J8
Roachill Devon 17 R7
Roade Nhants 49 L4
Road Green Norfk 65 K3
Roadhead Cumb 111 K6
Roadmeetings S Lans 126 F8
Roadside E Ayrs 115 L4
Roadside Highld 167 L4
Roadwater Somset 18 D7
Roag Highld 152 D9
Roa Island Cumb 94 E7
Roan of Craigoch S Ayrs 114 E7
Roast Green Essex 51 L4
Roath Cardif 30 G9
Roberton Border 117 N8
Roberton S Lans 116 C5
Robertsbridge E Susx 26 B7
Roberttown Kirk 90 F6
Robeston Wathen Pembks 41 L7
Robgill Tower D & G 110 D6
Robin Hill Staffs 70 G3
Robin Hood Lancs 88 G8
Robin Hood Leeds 91 J5
Robinhood End Essex 52 B4
Robin Hood's Bay N York 105 Q9
Roborough Devon 6 E6
Roborough Devon 17 K8
Robroyston C Glas 125 Q4
Roby Knows 81 N6
Roby Mill Lancs 88 G9
Rocester Staffs 71 L7
Roch Pembks 40 G6
Rochdale Rochdl 89 P8
Roche Cnwll 4 F9
Rochester Medway 38 B8
Rochester Nthumb 118 F11
Rochford Essex 38 E3
Rochford Worcs 57 L11
Roch Gate Pembks 40 G6
Rock Cnwll 4 E6
Rock Neath 29 L6
Rock Nthumb 119 P6
Rock W Susx 24 D8
Rock Worcs 57 N10
Rockbeare Devon 9 P6
Rockbourne Hants 21 M11
Rockcliffe Cumb 110 G8
Rockcliffe D & G 108 H10
Rockcliffe Cross Cumb 110 F8
Rock End Staffs 70 F3
Rockend Torbay 7 N6
Rock Ferry Wirral 81 L7
Rockfield Highld 163 L10
Rockfield Mons 31 N2
Rockford Devon 17 P2
Rockford Hants 13 L3
Rockgreen Shrops 57 J9
Rockhampton S Glos 32 C6
Rockhead Cnwll 4 H5
Rockhill Shrops 56 D9
Rock Hill Worcs 58 E11
Rockingham Nhants 61 J2
Rockland All Saints Norfk 64 D2
Rockland St Mary Norfk 77 L11
Rockland St Peter Norfk 64 D2
Rockley Notts 85 M6
Rockley Wilts 33 N10
Rockliffe Lancs 89 P6
Rockville Ag & B 131 Q9
Rockwell End Bucks 35 L7
Rockwell Green Somset 18 F10
Rodborough Gloucs 32 F4
Rodbourne Swindn 33 M7
Rodbourne Wilts 32 H8
Rodd Herefs 45 L2
Roddam Nthumb 119 K6
Rodden Dorset 11 N8
Roddymoor Dur 103 N3
Rode Somset 20 F4
Rode Heath Ches E 70 E3
Rode Heath Ches E 83 J11
Rodel W Isls 168 f9
Roden Wrekin 69 Q11
Rodhuish Somset 18 D7
Rodington Wrekin 57 K2
Rodington Heath Wrekin 57 K2
Rodley Gloucs 32 D2
Rodley Leeds 90 G3
Rodmarton Gloucs 32 H5
Rodmell E Susx 25 K9
Rodmersham Kent 38 F9
Rodmersham Green Kent 38 F9
Rodney Stoke Somset 19 N5
Rodsley Derbys 71 N6
Rodway Somset 19 J6
Roecliffe N York 97 N7
Roe Cross Tamesd 83 L5
Roe Green Herts 50 F9
Roe Green Herts 50 H4
Roe Green Salfd 82 F4
Roehampton Gt Lon 36 F6
Roffey W Susx 24 E4
Rogart Highld 162 G6
Rogate W Susx 23 M10
Roger Ground Cumb 101 L11
Rogerstone Newpt 31 J7
Roghadal W Isls 168 f9
Rogiet Mons 31 N7
Roke Oxon 34 H6
Roker Sundld 113 P9
Rollesby Norfk 77 N8
Rolleston Leics 73 J10
Rolleston Notts 85 M10
Rollestone Wilts 21 L5
Rolleston on Dove Staffs 71 N9
Rolston E R Yk 93 M2
Rolstone N Som 19 L2
Rolvenden Kent 26 D5
Rolvenden Layne Kent 26 E5
Romaldkirk Dur 103 J6
Romanby N York 97 N2
Romanno Bridge Border 127 M8
Romansleigh Devon 17 N7
Romden Castle Kent 26 E3
Romesdal Highld 152 G7
Romford Dorset 13 J3
Romford Gt Lon 37 M3
Romiley Stockp 83 K6
Romney Street Kent 37 N8
Romsey Cambs 62 G9
Romsey Hants 22 C10
Romsley Shrops 57 P8
Romsley Worcs 58 E8
Rona Highld 153 L6
Ronachan Ag & B 123 M9
Rood Ashton Wilts 20 G3
Rookhope Dur 102 H2
Rookley IoW 14 F10
Rookley Green IoW 14 F10
Rooks Bridge Somset 19 L4
Rooks Nest Somset 18 E8
Rookwith N York 97 K3
Roos E R Yk 93 N4
Roose Cumb 94 E7
Roosebeck Cumb 94 F7
Roothams Green Bed 61 N9
Ropley Hants 22 H8
Ropley Dean Hants 22 H8
Ropley Soke Hants 23 J8
Ropsley Lincs 73 P4
Rora Abers 159 Q7
Rorrington Shrops 56 E4
Rosarie Moray 158 A7
Rose Cnwll 3 K3
Roseacre Lancs 88 E3
Rose Ash Devon 17 P7
Rosebank S Lans 126 E8
Rosebush Pembks 41 L5
Rosecare Cnwll 5 K2
Rosecliston Cnwll 4 C10
Rosedale Abbey N York 105 K11
Rose Green Essex 52 F6
Rose Green Suffk 52 F4
Rose Green Suffk 52 G3
Rose Green W Susx 15 P7
Rosehall Highld 162 B6
Rosehearty Abers 159 M4
Rose Hill E Susx 25 L7
Rose Hill Lancs 89 N4
Rosehill Shrops 69 N11
Roseisle Moray 157 L4
Roselands E Susx 25 P10
Rosemarket Pembks 41 J9
Rosemarkie Highld 156 C6
Rosemary Lane Devon 10 D2
Rosemount P & K 142 B9
Rosenannon Cnwll 4 F8
Rosenithon Cnwll 3 L9
Roser's Cross E Susx 25 M6
Rosevean Cnwll 4 G10
Rosevine Cnwll 3 M6
Rosewarne Cnwll 2 G6
Rosewell Mdloth 127 P5
Roseworth S on T 104 D6
Roseworthy Cnwll 2 G6
Rosgill Cumb 101 P7
Roskestal Cnwll 2 B9
Roskhill Highld 152 D9
Roskorwell Cnwll 3 K9
Rosley Cumb 110 F11
Roslin Mdloth 127 P5
Rosliston Derbys 71 N11
Rosneath Ag & B 132 B11
Ross D & G 108 D12
Ross Nthumb 119 M3
Rossett Wrexhm 69 L3
Rossett Green N York 97 L10
Rossington Donc 91 Q11
Ross-on-Wye Herefs 46 A10
Roster Highld 167 N9
Rostherne Ches E 82 F8
Rosthwaite Cumb 101 J8
Roston Derbys 71 L6
Rosudgeon Cnwll 2 F8
Rosyth Fife 134 E11
Rothbury Nthumb 119 L10
Rotherby Leics 72 H7
Rotherfield E Susx 25 N5
Rotherfield Greys Oxon 35 K8
Rotherfield Peppard Oxon 35 K8
Rotherham Rothm 84 F2
Rothersthorpe Nhants 60 F9
Rotherwick Hants 23 K3
Rothes Moray 157 P8
Rothesay Ag & B 124 D5
Rothiebrisbane Abers 158 H10
Rothiemurchus Lodge Highld 148 H6
Rothienorman Abers 158 H10
Rothley Leics 72 F8
Rothley Nthumb 112 F3
Rothmaise Abers 158 G11
Rothwell Leeds 91 J5
Rothwell Lincs 93 K11
Rothwell Nhants 60 H4
Rotsea E R Yk 99 M10
Rottal Lodge Angus 142 F4
Rottingdean Br & H 25 J10
Rottington Cumb 100 C8
Roucan D & G 109 M5
Roud IoW 14 F10
Rougham Norfk 76 A7
Rougham Suffk 64 C9
Rough Close Staffs 70 G7
Rough Common Kent 39 K10
Roughlee Lancs 89 N2
Roughpark Abers 149 Q5
Roughton Lincs 86 H8
Roughton Norfk 77 J4
Roughton Shrops 57 P6
Roughway Kent 37 P10
Roundbush Essex 52 E11
Round Bush Herts 50 D11
Roundbush Green Essex 51 N8
Round Green Luton 50 D6
Roundham Somset 11 J3
Roundhay Leeds 91 J3
Rounds Green Sandw 58 E7
Round Street Kent 37 Q7
Roundstreet Common W Susx 24 C5
Roundswell Devon 17 J5
Roundway Wilts 21 K2
Roundyhill Angus 142 F7
Rousay Ork 169 c3
Rousdon Devon 10 F6
Rousham Oxon 48 E10
Rous Lench Worcs 47 K4
Routenburn N Ayrs 124 F5
Routh E R Yk 93 J2
Rout's Green Bucks 35 L5
Row Cnwll 4 H6
Row Cumb 95 K3
Row Cumb 102 B4
Rowanburn D & G 110 H5
Rowardennan Stirlg 132 D8
Rowarth Derbys 83 M7
Row Ash Hants 14 F4
Rowberrow Somset 19 N3
Rowborough IoW 14 E10
Rowde Wilts 21 J2
Rowden Devon 8 F5
Rowen Conwy 79 P10
Rowfield Derbys 71 M5
Rowfoot Nthumb 111 N8
Rowford Somset 18 H9
Row Green Essex 52 B7
Rowhedge Essex 52 H7
Rowhook W Susx 24 D4
Rowington Warwks 59 K11
Rowland Derbys 84 B6
Rowland's Castle Hants 15 K4
Rowlands Gill Gatesd 113 J9
Rowledge Surrey 23 M6
Rowley Dur 112 G11
Rowley E R Yk 92 G4
Rowley Shrops 56 E3
Rowley Hill Kirk 90 F8
Rowley Regis Sandw 58 E7
Rowlstone Herefs 45 M9
Rowly Surrey 24 B2
Rowner Hants 14 G6
Rowney Green Worcs 58 F10
Rownhams Hants 22 C11
Rownhams Services Hants 22 C11
Rowrah Cumb 100 E7
Rowsham Bucks 49 M11
Rowsley Derbys 84 C7
Rowstock Oxon 34 E7
Rowston Lincs 86 E9
Rowthorne Derbys 84 G8
Rowton Ches W 69 M2
Rowton Shrops 56 F2
Rowton Shrops 69 L11
Rowton Wrekin 69 R11
Row Town Surrey 36 B8
Roxburgh Border 118 C4
Roxby N Linc 92 F7
Roxby N York 105 L7
Roxton Bed 61 Q10
Roxwell Essex 51 P9
Royal Leamington Spa Warwks 59 M11
Royal Oak Darltn 103 P6
Royal Oak Lancs 81 N4
Royal's Green Ches E 69 R6
Royal Sutton Coldfield Birm 58 H5
Royal Tunbridge Wells Kent 25 N3
Royal Wootton Bassett Wilts 33 L8
Royal Yacht Britannia C Edin 127 P2
Roy Bridge Highld 146 H11
Roydhouse Kirk 90 G8
Roydon Essex 51 K8
Roydon Norfk 64 G5
Roydon Norfk 75 P6
Roydon Hamlet Essex 51 K9
Royston Barns 91 K8
Royston Herts 51 J2
Royton Oldham 89 Q9
Rozel Jersey 11 c1
Ruabon Wrexhm 69 K6
Ruaig Ag & B 136 D6
Ruan High Lanes Cnwll 3 N6
Ruan Lanihorne Cnwll 3 M5
Ruan Major Cnwll 3 J10
Ruan Minor Cnwll 3 J10
Ruardean Gloucs 46 B11
Ruardean Hill Gloucs 46 B11
Ruardean Woodside Gloucs 46 B11
Rubery Birm 58 E9
Rubha Ban W Isls 168 c16
Ruckcroft Cumb 101 P2
Ruckhall Herefs 45 P7
Ruckinge Kent 26 H5
Ruckland Lincs 87 K5
Ruckley Shrops 57 J4
Rudbaxton Pembks 41 J6
Rudby N York 104 E9
Rudchester Nthumb 112 H7
Ruddington Notts 72 F4
Ruddle Gloucs 32 C2
Ruddlemoor Cnwll 3 Q3
Rudford Gloucs 46 E10
Rudge Somset 20 F4
Rudgeway S Glos 32 B7

Rudgwick W Susx 24 C4
Rudhall Herefs 46 B9
Rudheath Ches W 82 E10
Rudheath Woods Ches E 82 F10
Rudley Green Essex 52 D11
Rudloe Wilts 32 F10
Rudry Caerph 30 H7
Rudston E R Yk 99 M7
Rudyard Staffs 70 H3
Ruecastle Border 118 B6
Rufford Lancs 88 F7
Rufford Abbey Notts 85 K8
Rufforth C York 98 A10
Rug Denbgs 68 E6
Rugby Warwks 60 B5
Rugeley Staffs 71 J11
Ruigh'riabhach Highld 160 G7
Ruisgarry W Isls 168 e9
Ruishton Somset 19 J9
Ruisigearraidh W Isls 168 e9
Ruislip Gt Lon 36 C3
Rùm Highld 144 E8
Rumbach Moray 158 A7
Rumbling Bridge P & K 134 C8
Rumburgh Suffk 65 L5
Rumby Hill Dur 103 N4
Rumford Cnwll 4 D7
Rumford Falk 126 G2
Rumney Cardif 30 H9
Rumwell Somset 18 G10
Runcorn Halton 81 Q8
Runcton W Susx 15 N6
Runcton Holme Norfk 75 M9
Runfold Surrey 23 N5
Runhall Norfk 76 F10
Runham Norfk 77 P9
Runham Norfk 77 Q10
Runnington Somset 18 F10
Runsell Green Essex 52 C10
Runshaw Moor Lancs 88 G7
Runswick N York 105 M7
Runtaleave Angus 142 D4
Runwell Essex 38 C3
Ruscombe Wokham 35 L9
Rushall Herefs 46 B7
Rushall Norfk 64 H5
Rushall Wilts 21 M3
Rushall Wsall 58 F4
Rushbrooke Suffk 64 B9
Rushbury Shrops 57 J6
Rushden Herts 50 H4
Rushden Nhants 61 L7
Rushenden Kent 38 F7
Rusher's Cross E Susx 25 P5
Rushford Devon 8 C9
Rushford Norfk 64 C5
Rush Green Essex 53 L8
Rush Green Gt Lon 37 M3
Rush Green Herts 50 F6
Rush Green Warrtn 82 E7
Rushlake Green E Susx 25 P7
Rushmere Suffk 65 P4
Rushmere St Andrew Suffk 53 L2
Rushmoor Surrey 23 N6
Rushock Herefs 45 L3
Rushock Worcs 58 C10
Rusholme Manch 83 J6
Rushton Ches W 69 Q2
Rushton Nhants 60 H4
Rushton Shrops 57 L3
Rushton Spencer Staffs 70 G2
Rushwick Worcs 46 F4
Rushyford Dur 103 Q5
Ruskie Stirlg 133 J7
Ruskington Lincs 86 E10
Rusland Cross Cumb 94 G3
Rusper W Susx 24 F3
Ruspidge Gloucs 32 C2
Russell Green Essex 52 B9
Russell's Water Oxon 35 K7
Russel's Green Suffk 65 K7
Russ Hill Surrey 24 F2
Rusthall Kent 25 N3
Rustington W Susx 24 B10
Ruston N York 99 K4
Ruston Parva E R Yk 99 M8
Ruswarp N York 105 N9
Ruthall Shrops 57 K6
Rutherford Border 118 B4
Rutherglen S Lans 125 Q5
Ruthernbridge Cnwll 4 G8
Ruthin Denbgs 68 F3
Ruthrieston C Aber 151 N7
Ruthven Abers 158 D8
Ruthven Angus 142 D8
Ruthven Highld 148 D8
Ruthven Highld 156 E11
Ruthvoes Cnwll 4 E9
Ruthwaite Cumb 100 H3
Ruthwell D & G 109 N7
Ruxley Corner Gt Lon 37 L6
Ruxton Green Herefs 45 Q11
Ruyton-XI-Towns Shrops 69 L10
Ryal Nthumb 112 F6
Ryall Dorset 11 J5
Ryall Worcs 46 G6
Ryarsh Kent 37 Q8
Rycote Oxon 35 J3
Rydal Cumb 101 L9
Ryde IoW 14 G8
Rye E Susx 26 F7
Ryebank Shrops 69 P8
Ryeford Herefs 46 B10
Rye Foreign E Susx 26 E7
Rye Harbour E Susx 26 F8
Ryehill E R Yk 93 M5
Ryeish Green Wokham 35 K11
Rye Street Worcs 46 E7
Ryhall Rutlnd 73 Q8
Ryhill Wakefd 91 K8
Ryhope Sundld 113 P10
Rylah Derbys 84 G7
Ryland Lincs 86 D5
Rylands Notts 72 E3
Rylstone N York 96 E9
Ryme Intrinseca Dorset 11 M2
Ryther N York 91 P3
Ryton Gatesd 113 J8
Ryton N York 98 F5
Ryton Shrops 57 P4
Ryton Warwks 59 P7
Ryton-on-Dunsmore Warwks 59 N10
Ryton Woodside Gatesd 112 H8
RZSS Edinburgh Zoo C Edin 127 N3

S

Sabden Lancs 89 M3
Sabine's Green Essex 51 M11
Sacombe Herts 50 H7
Sacombe Green Herts 50 H7
Sacriston Dur 113 K11
Sadberge Darltn 104 B7
Saddell Ag & B 120 E5
Saddington Leics 60 E2
Saddlebow Norfk 75 M7
Saddlescombe W Susx 24 G8
Sadgill Cumb 101 N9
Saffron Walden Essex 51 M3
Sageston Pembks 41 L10
Saham Hills Norfk 76 C11
Saham Toney Norfk 76 B11
Saighton Ches W 69 M2
St Abbs Border 129 N6
St Agnes Border 128 H7
St Agnes Cnwll 3 J3
St Agnes IoS 2 b3
St Agnes Mining District Cnwll 3 J4
St Albans Herts 50 D9
St Allen Cnwll 3 L3
St Andrew Guern 10 b2
St Andrews Fife 135 N4
St Andrews Botanic Garden Fife 135 N4
St Andrews Major V Glam 30 F10
St Andrews Well Dorset 11 K6
St Anne's Lancs 88 C5
St Ann's D & G 109 N2
St Ann's Chapel Cnwll 5 Q7
St Ann's Chapel Devon 6 H9
St Anthony-in-Meneage Cnwll 3 K8
St Anthony's Hill E Susx 25 P10
St Arvans Mons 31 P5
St Asaph Denbgs 80 E10
St Athan V Glam 30 D11
St Aubin Jersey 11 b2
St Austell Cnwll 3 Q3
St Bees Cumb 100 C8
St Blazey Cnwll 3 R3
St Blazey Gate Cnwll 3 R3
St Boswells Border 118 A4
St Brelade Jersey 11 a2
St Brelade's Bay Jersey 11 a2
St Breock Cnwll 4 F7
St Breward Cnwll 4 H6
St Briavels Gloucs 31 Q4
St Brides Pembks 40 F8
St Bride's Major V Glam 29 N10
St Brides Netherwent Mons 31 M7
St Brides-super-Ely V Glam 30 E9
St Brides Wentlooge Newpt 31 J8
St Budeaux C Plym 6 D7
Saintbury Gloucs 47 M7
St Buryan Cnwll 2 C8
St Catherine BaNES 32 E11
St Catherines Ag & B 131 N6
St Chloe Gloucs 32 F4
St Clears Carmth 41 Q7
St Cleer Cnwll 5 L8
St Clement Cnwll 3 M5
St Clement Jersey 11 c2
St Clether Cnwll 5 L5
St Colmac Ag & B 124 C4
St Columb Major Cnwll 4 E9
St Columb Minor Cnwll 4 C9
St Columb Road Cnwll 4 E10
St Combs Abers 159 Q5
St Cross South Elmham Suffk 65 K5
St Cyrus Abers 143 N5
St David's P & K 133 Q3
St Davids Pembks 40 E5
St Davids Cathedral Pembks 40 E5
St Day Cnwll 3 J5
St Decumans Somset 18 E6
St Dennis Cnwll 4 F10
St Devereux Herefs 45 N8
St Dogmaels Pembks 42 C5
St Dogwells Pembks 41 J5
St Dominick Cnwll 5 Q8
St Donats V Glam 29 P11
St Edith's Marsh Wilts 21 J2
St Endellion Cnwll 4 F6
St Enoder Cnwll 4 D10
St Erme Cnwll 3 L4
St Erney Cnwll 5 P10
St Erth Cnwll 2 F6
St Erth Praze Cnwll 2 F6
St Ervan Cnwll 4 D7
St Eval Cnwll 4 D8
St Ewe Cnwll 3 P4
St Fagans Cardif 30 F9
St Fagans: National History Museum Cardif 30 F9
St Fergus Abers 159 Q7
St Fillans P & K 133 K3
St Florence Pembks 41 L10
St Gennys Cnwll 5 J2
St George Conwy 80 D9
St Georges N Som 19 L2
St George's V Glam 30 F9
St George's Hill Surrey 36 C8
St Germans Cnwll 5 P10
St Giles in the Wood Devon 17 J8
St Giles-on-the-Heath Devon 5 P3
St Gluvia's Cnwll 3 K7
St Harmon Powys 55 M10
St Helen Auckland Dur 103 N5
St Helens Cumb 100 D4
St Helen's E Susx 26 D9
St Helens IoW 14 H9
St Helens St Hel 81 Q5
St Helier Gt Lon 36 G7
St Helier Jersey 11 b2
St Hilary Cnwll 2 E7
St Hilary V Glam 30 D10
Saint Hill Devon 10 B3
Saint Hill W Susx 25 J3
St Illtyd Blae G 30 H4
St Ippolyts Herts 50 E5
St Ishmael's Pembks 40 F9
St Issey Cnwll 4 E7
St Ive Cnwll 5 N8
St Ive Cross Cnwll 5 N8
St Ives Cambs 62 D6
St Ives Cnwll 2 E5
St Ives Dorset 13 K4
St James Norfk 77 K7
St James's End Nhants 60 F8
St James South Elmham Suffk 65 L5
St Jidgey Cnwll 4 E8
St John Cnwll 5 Q11
St John Jersey 11 b1
St Johns Dur 103 L4
St John's E Susx 25 M4
St John's IoM 80 c5
St John's Kent 37 M9
St Johns Surrey 23 Q3
St Johns Worcs 46 F4
St John's Chapel Devon 17 J6
St John's Chapel Dur 102 G3
St John's Fen End Norfk 75 K8
St John's Highway Norfk 75 K8
St John's Kirk S Lans 116 D3
St John's Town of Dalry D & G 108 D4
St John's Wood Gt Lon 36 G4
St Judes IoM 80 e2
St Just Cnwll 2 B7
St Just-in-Roseland Cnwll 3 L6
St Just Mining District Cnwll 2 B7
St Katherines Abers 159 J11
St Keverne Cnwll 3 K9
St Kew Cnwll 4 G6
St Kew Highway Cnwll 4 G6
St Keyne Cnwll 5 L9
St Lawrence Cnwll 4 G8
St Lawrence Essex 52 G11
St Lawrence IoW 14 F11
St Lawrence Jersey 11 b1
St Lawrence Kent 39 Q8
St Leonards Bucks 35 P3
St Leonards Dorset 13 K4
St Leonards E Susx 26 D10
St Leonard's Street Kent 37 Q9
St Levan Cnwll 2 B9
St Lythans V Glam 30 F10
St Mabyn Cnwll 4 G7
St Madoes P & K 134 F3
St Margarets Herefs 45 M8
St Margarets Herts 51 J8
St Margaret's at Cliffe Kent 27 Q3
St Margaret's Hope Ork 169 d7
St Margaret South Elmham Suffk 65 L5
St Marks IoM 80 c7
St Martin Cnwll 3 J9
St Martin Cnwll 5 M10
St Martin Guern 10 b2
St Martin Jersey 11 c1
St Martin's IoS 2 c1
St Martin's P & K 142 B11
St Martin's Shrops 69 K7
St Martin's Moor Shrops 69 K7
St Mary Jersey 11 a1
St Mary Bourne Hants 22 D4
St Marychurch Torbay 7 N5
St Mary Church V Glam 30 D10
St Mary Cray Gt Lon 37 L7
St Mary Hill V Glam 30 C9
St Mary in the Marsh Kent 27 J6
St Mary's IoS 2 c2
St Mary's Ork 169 d6
St Mary's Bay Kent 27 J6
St Mary's Hoo Medway 38 D6
St Mary's Platt Kent 37 P9
St Maughans Mons 45 P11
St Maughans Green Mons 45 P11
St Mawes Cnwll 3 L7
St Mawgan Cnwll 4 D8
St Mellion Cnwll 5 P8
St Mellons Cardif 30 H8
St Merryn Cnwll 4 D7
St Mewan Cnwll 3 P3
St Michael Caerhays Cnwll 3 P5
St Michael Church Somset 19 K8
St Michael Penkevil Cnwll 3 M5
St Michaels Kent 26 E4
St Michaels Worcs 57 K11
St Michael's Mount Cnwll 2 E8
St Michael's on Wyre Lancs 88 F2
St Michael South Elmham Suffk 65 L5
St Minver Cnwll 4 F6
St Monans Fife 135 N7
St Neot Cnwll 5 K8
St Neots Cambs 61 Q8
St Newlyn East Cnwll 4 C10
St Nicholas Pembks 40 H3
St Nicholas V Glam 30 E10
St Nicholas-at-Wade Kent 39 N8
St Ninians Stirlg 133 M9
St Olaves Norfk 65 P2
St Osyth Essex 53 K8
St Ouen Jersey 11 a1
St Owen's Cross Herefs 45 Q10
St Paul's Cray Gt Lon 37 L7
St Paul's Walden Herts 50 E6
St Peter Jersey 11 a1
St Peter Port Guern 10 c2
St Peter's Guern 10 b2
St Peter's Kent 39 Q8
St Peter's Hill Cambs 62 B6
St Petrox Pembks 41 J11
St Pinnock Cnwll 5 L9
St Quivox S Ayrs 114 G3
St Ruan Cnwll 3 J10
St Sampson Guern 10 c1
St Saviour Guern 10 b2
St Saviour Jersey 11 b2
St Stephen Cnwll 3 N3
St Stephens Cnwll 5 N4
St Stephens Cnwll 5 Q10
St Teath Cnwll 4 H5
St Thomas Devon 9 M6
St Margaret's Bay Kent 27 Q3
St Tudy Cnwll 4 H6
St Twynnells Pembks 41 J11
St Veep Cnwll 5 J10
St Vigeans Angus 143 L9
St Wenn Cnwll 4 F9
St Weonards Herefs 45 P10
St Winnow Cnwll 5 J10
St y-Nyll V Glam 30 E9
Salcombe Devon 7 J11
Salcombe Regis Devon 10 D7
Salcott-cum-Virley Essex 52 F9
Sale Traffd 82 G6
Saleby Lincs 87 N5
Sale Green Worcs 46 H3
Salehurst E Susx 26 C7
Salem Carmth 43 M9
Salem Cerdgn 54 F8
Salen Ag & B 137 P7
Salen Highld 138 B5
Salesbury Lancs 89 K4
Salford C Beds 49 P7
Salford Oxon 47 Q9
Salford Salfd 82 H5
Salford Priors Warwks 47 L4
Salfords Surrey 36 G11
Salhouse Norfk 77 L9
Saline Fife 134 C9
Salisbury Wilts 21 M8
Salisbury Plain Wilts 21 L6
Salkeld Dykes Cumb 101 P3
Salle Norfk 76 G7
Salmonby Lincs 87 K6
Salperton Gloucs 47 L10
Salph End Bed 61 N10
Salsburgh N Lans 126 E5
Salt Staffs 70 H9
Salta Cumb 109 N11
Saltaire C Brad 90 E3
Saltaire C Brad 90 E3
Saltash Cnwll 6 C7
Saltburn Highld 156 C3
Saltburn-by-the-Sea R & Cl 105 J6
Saltby Leics 73 M5
Salt Coates Cumb 110 C10
Saltcoats Cumb 100 E11
Saltcoats N Ayrs 124 G9
Saltcotes Lancs 88 D5
Saltdean Br & H 25 J10
Salterbeck Cumb 100 C5
Salterforth Lancs 96 C11
Salterswall Ches W 82 D11
Salterton Wilts 21 M7
Saltfleet Lincs 87 N2
Saltfleetby All Saints Lincs 87 N2
Saltfleetby St Clement Lincs 87 N2
Saltfleetby St Peter Lincs 87 M3
Saltford BaNES 32 C11
Salthouse Norfk 76 F3
Saltley Birm 58 H7
Saltmarsh Newpt 31 K8
Saltmarshe E R Yk 92 C6
Saltney Flints 69 L2
Salton N York 98 E5
Saltrens Devon 16 H7
Saltwick Nthumb 113 J4
Saltwood Kent 27 L4
Salvington W Susx 24 D9
Salwarpe Worcs 46 G2
Salway Ash Dorset 11 K5
Sambourne Warwks 47 L2
Sambrook Wrekin 70 C10
Samlesbury Lancs 88 H4
Samlesbury Bottoms Lancs 89 J5
Sampford Arundel Somset 18 F11
Sampford Brett Somset 18 E6
Sampford Courtenay Devon 8 F4
Sampford Moor Somset 18 F11
Sampford Peverell Devon 9 P2
Sampford Spiney Devon 6 E4
Samsonlane Ork 169 f4
Samson's Corner Essex 53 J8
Samuelston E Loth 128 D5
Sanaigmore Ag & B 122 B5
Sancreed Cnwll 2 C8
Sancton E R Yk 92 E3
Sand Somset 19 M5
Sandaig Highld 145 M7
Sandale Cumb 100 H2
Sandal Magna Wakefd 91 J7
Sanday Ork 169 f2
Sanday Airport Ork 169 f2
Sandbach Ches E 70 D2
Sandbach Services Ches E 70 D2
Sandbank Ag & B 131 P11
Sandbanks BCP 12 H7
Sandend Abers 158 E4
Sanderstead Gt Lon 36 H8
Sandford Cumb 102 D7
Sandford Devon 9 K4
Sandford Dorset 12 F7
Sandford Hants 13 L4
Sandford IoW 14 F10
Sandford N Som 19 M3
Sandford S Lans 126 C9
Sandford Shrops 69 K10
Sandford Shrops 69 Q8
Sandford-on-Thames Oxon 34 F4
Sandford Orcas Dorset 20 B10
Sandford St Martin Oxon 48 D9
Sandgate Kent 27 M4
Sandhaven Abers 159 N4
Sandhead D & G 106 E8
Sandhill Rothm 91 L11
Sandhills Dorset 11 M4
Sandhills Dorset 11 P2
Sand Hills Leeds 91 K3
Sandhills Oxon 34 G3
Sandhills Surrey 23 P7
Sandhoe Nthumb 112 E7
Sandhole Ag & B 131 L8
Sand Hole E R Yk 92 D3
Sandholme E R Yk 92 D4
Sandholme Lincs 74 F3
Sandhurst Br For 23 M2
Sandhurst Gloucs 46 F10
Sandhurst Kent 26 D6
Sandhurst Cross Kent 26 C6
Sandhutton N York 97 N4
Sand Hutton N York 98 D9
Sandiacre Derbys 72 D3
Sandilands Lincs 87 P4
Sandiway Ches W 82 D10
Sandleheath Hants 21 M11
Sandleigh Oxon 34 E4
Sandley Dorset 20 E10
Sandling Kent 38 C10
Sandlow Green Ches E 82 G11
Sandness Shet 169 n8
Sandon Essex 52 B11
Sandon Herts 50 H4
Sandon Staffs 70 G9
Sandon Bank Staffs 70 G9
Sandown IoW 14 G10
Sandplace Cnwll 5 M10
Sandridge Herts 50 E8
Sandridge Wilts 32 H11
Sandringham Norfk 75 N5
Sands Bucks 35 M6
Sandsend N York 105 N8
Sand Side Cumb 94 E4
Sandside Cumb 95 K4
Sandtoft N Linc 92 B9
Sandway Kent 38 E11
Sandwich Kent 39 P10
Sandwich Bay Kent 39 Q10
Sandwick Cumb 101 M7
Sandwick Shet 169 r11
Sandwick W Isls 168 j4
Sandwith Cumb 100 C8
Sandwith Newtown Cumb 100 C8
Sandy C Beds 61 Q11
Sandy Bank Lincs 87 J9
Sandycroft Flints 81 L11
Sandy Cross E Susx 25 N6
Sandy Cross Herefs 46 C3
Sandyford D & G 110 D2
Sandygate Devon 7 M4
Sandygate IoM 80 e2
Sandy Haven Pembks 40 G9
Sandyhills D & G 109 J9
Sandylands Lancs 95 J8
Sandy Lane C Brad 90 E3
Sandylane Staffs 70 C7
Sandylane Swans 28 G7
Sandy Lane Wilts 33 J11
Sandy Lane Wrexhm 69 M6
Sandy Park Devon 8 H7
Sandysike Cumb 110 G7
Sandyway Herefs 45 P9
Sangobeg Highld 165 K3
Sangomore Highld 165 K3
Sankey Bridges Warrtn 82 C7
Sankyn's Green Worcs 57 P11
Sanna Highld 137 L2
Sanndabhaig W Isls 168 j4
Sannox N Ayrs 124 C8
Sanquhar D & G 115 Q6
Santon Cumb 100 F10
Santon IoM 80 d7
Santon Bridge Cumb 100 F10
Santon Downham Suffk 63 P3
Sapcote Leics 59 Q6
Sapey Common Herefs 46 D2
Sapiston Suffk 64 C6
Sapley Cambs 62 B6
Sapperton Derbys 71 M8
Sapperton Gloucs 32 H4
Sapperton Lincs 73 Q4
Saracen's Head Lincs 74 F5
Sarclet Highld 167 P8
Sarisbury Hants 14 F5
Sarn Brdgnd 29 P8
Sarn Powys 56 C6
Sarnau Carmth 42 F11
Sarnau Cerdgn 42 F4
Sarnau Gwynd 68 C7
Sarnau Powys 44 E8
Sarnau Powys 68 H11
Sarn Bach Gwynd 66 E9
Sarnesfield Herefs 45 M4
Sarn Mellteyrn Gwynd 66 C8
Sarn Park Services Brdgnd 29 P8
Sarn-wen Powys 69 J11
Saron Carmth 28 H2
Saron Carmth 42 G7
Saron Gwynd 66 H3
Saron Gwynd 79 J11
Sarratt Herts 50 B11
Sarre Kent 39 N8
Sarsden Oxon 47 Q10
Sarson Hants 22 B6
Satley Dur 103 M2
Satmar Kent 27 N4
Satron N York 102 H11
Satterleigh Devon 17 M7
Satterthwaite Cumb 94 G2
Satwell Oxon 35 K8
Sauchen Abers 151 J5
Saucher P & K 142 B11
Sauchieburn Abers 143 M4
Saul Gloucs 32 D3
Saundby Notts 85 N3
Saundersfoot Pembks 41 M10
Saunderton Bucks 35 L4
Saunderton Station Bucks 35 M5
Saunton Devon 16 H4
Sausthorpe Lincs 87 L7
Saverley Green Staffs 70 H7
Savile Town Kirk 90 G6
Sawbridge Warwks 60 B7
Sawbridgeworth Herts 51 L8
Sawdon N York 99 J4
Sawley Derbys 72 D4
Sawley Lancs 96 A11
Sawley N York 97 K7
Sawston Cambs 62 G11
Sawtry Cambs 61 Q4
Saxby Leics 73 L7
Saxby Lincs 86 D3
Saxby All Saints N Linc 92 G7
Saxelbye Leics 72 H6
Saxham Street Suffk 64 F9
Saxilby Lincs 85 Q5
Saxlingham Norfk 76 E4
Saxlingham Green Norfk 65 J2
Saxlingham Nethergate Norfk 65 J2
Saxlingham Thorpe Norfk 65 J2
Saxmundham Suffk 65 M9
Saxondale Notts 72 H3
Saxon Street Cambs 63 L9
Saxtead Suffk 65 K8
Saxtead Green Suffk 65 K9
Saxtead Little Green Suffk 65 J8
Saxthorpe Norfk 76 G5
Saxton N York 91 M3
Sayers Common W Susx 24 G7
Scackleton N York 98 C6
Scadabay W Isls 168 g8
Scadabhagh W Isls 168 g8
Scafell Pike Cumb 100 H9
Scaftworth Notts 85 L2
Scagglethorpe N York 98 G6
Scalasaig Ag & B 136 b3
Scalby E R Yk 92 D5
Scalby N York 99 L2
Scald End Bed 61 M9
Scaldwell Nhants 60 G6
Scaleby Cumb 110 H8
Scalebyhill Cumb 110 H8
Scale Houses Cumb 111 L11
Scales Cumb 94 F6
Scales Cumb 101 K5

Scalesceugh Cumb 110 H11
Scalford Leics 73 K6
Scaling N York 105 K8
Scaling Dam R & Cl 105 K8
Scalloway Shet 169 r10
Scalpay Highld 153 L11
Scalpay W Isls 168 h8
Scamblesby Lincs 87 J5
Scammonden Kirk 90 D7
Scamodale Highld 138 E3
Scampston N York 98 H5
Scampton Lincs 86 C5
Scaniport Highld 156 A10
Scapegoat Hill Kirk 90 D7
Scarba Ag & B 130 D7
Scarborough N York 99 L3
Scarcewater Cnwll 3 N3
Scarcliffe Derbys 84 G7
Scarcroft Leeds 91 K2
Scarfskerry Highld 167 N2
Scargill Dur 103 L8
Scarinish Ag & B 136 C7
Scarisbrick Lancs 88 D8
Scarness Cumb 100 H4
Scarning Norfk 76 D9
Scarrington Notts 73 J2
Scarth Hill Lancs 88 E9
Scarthingwell N York 91 M3
Scartho NE Lin 93 N9
Scatsta Airport Shet 169 q6
Scaur D & G 108 H10
Scawby N Linc 92 G9
Scawsby Donc 91 N10
Scawthorpe Donc 91 P9
Scawton N York 98 A4
Scayne's Hill W Susx 25 J6
Scethrog Powys 44 G9
Scholar Green Ches E 70 E3
Scholes Kirk 90 F5
Scholes Kirk 90 F9
Scholes Leeds 91 K3
Scholes Rothm 91 K11
Scholes Wigan 88 H9
School Aycliffe Dur 103 Q6
School Green C Brad 90 E4
School Green Ches W 70 A2
Schoolgreen Wokham 35 K11
School House Dorset 10 H4
Scissett Kirk 90 G8
Scleddau Pembks 40 H4
Scofton Notts 85 K4
Scole Norfk 64 H6
Scone P & K 134 E2
Sconser Highld 153 J11
Scoonie Fife 135 K7
Scopwick Lincs 86 E9
Scoraig Highld 160 G7
Scorborough E R Yk 99 L11
Scorrier Cnwll 3 J5
Scorriton Devon 7 J5
Scorton Lancs 95 L11
Scorton N York 103 Q10
Sco Ruston Norfk 77 K7
Scotby Cumb 110 H9
Scotch Corner N York 103 P9
Scotch Corner Rest Area N York 103 P9
Scotforth Lancs 95 K9
Scot Hay Staffs 70 D5
Scothern Lincs 86 D5
Scotland Lincs 73 Q4
Scotland Gate Nthumb 113 L4
Scotlandwell P & K 134 F7
Scot Lane End Bolton 89 J9
Scotscalder Station Highld 167 J5
Scotsdike Cumb 110 G6
Scot's Gap Nthumb 112 F3
Scotsmill Abers 150 F4
Scotstoun C Glas 125 N4
Scotswood N u Ty 113 K8
Scotter Lincs 92 E10
Scotterthorpe Lincs 92 E10
Scottish Seabird Centre E Loth 128 F2
Scottish Wool Centre Stirlg 132 G7
Scottlethorpe Lincs 73 R6
Scotton Lincs 92 E11
Scotton N York 97 M9
Scotton N York 103 N11
Scottow Norfk 77 K7
Scott Willoughby Lincs 73 R3
Scoulton Norfk 76 D11
Scounslow Green Staffs 71 K9
Scourie Highld 164 E8
Scourie More Highld 164 D8
Scousburgh Shet 169 q12
Scouthead Oldham 90 B9
Scrabster Highld 167 K2
Scraesburgh Border 118 C7
Scrafield Lincs 87 K7
Scrainwood Nthumb 119 J9
Scrane End Lincs 74 G2
Scraptoft Leics 72 G9
Scratby Norfk 77 Q8
Scrayingham N York 98 E9
Scrays E Susx 26 C8
Scredington Lincs 74 A2
Scremby Lincs 87 M7
Scremerston Nthumb 129 Q10
Screveton Notts 73 J2
Scrivelsby Lincs 87 J7
Scriven N York 97 M9
Scrooby Notts 85 L2
Scropton Derbys 71 M8
Scrub Hill Lincs 86 H9
Scruton N York 97 L2
Scuggate Cumb 110 H6
Scullomie Highld 165 P4
Sculthorpe Norfk 76 B5
Scunthorpe N Linc 92 E8
Scurlage Swans 28 E7
Sea Somset 10 G2
Seaborough Dorset 11 J3
Seabridge Staffs 70 E6
Seabrook Kent 27 L4
Seaburn Sundld 113 P9
Seacombe Wirral 81 L6
Seacroft Leeds 91 K3
Seacroft Lincs 87 Q8
Seadyke Lincs 74 F3
Seafield W Loth 127 J4
Seaford E Susx 25 L11
Seaforth Sefton 81 L5
Seagrave Leics 72 G7
Seagry Heath Wilts 33 J8
Seaham Dur 113 P11
Seahouses Nthumb 119 P4
Seal Kent 37 N9
Sealand Flints 81 M11
Seale Surrey 23 N5
Seamer N York 99 L4
Seamer N York 104 E8
Seamill N Ayrs 124 G8
Sea Palling Norfk 77 N6
Searby Lincs 93 J9
Seasalter Kent 39 J9
Seascale Cumb 100 D10
Seathwaite Cumb 100 H11
Seathwaite Cumb 100 H8
Seatle Cumb 94 H4
Seatoller Cumb 100 H8
Seaton Cnwll 5 N11
Seaton Cumb 100 D4
Seaton Devon 10 E6
Seaton Dur 113 N11
Seaton E R Yk 99 P11
Seaton Kent 39 M10
Seaton Nthumb 113 M5
Seaton Rutlnd 73 N11
Seaton Burn N Tyne 113 K6
Seaton Carew Hartpl 104 F5
Seaton Delaval Nthumb 113 M5
Seaton Ross E R Yk 92 C2
Seaton Sluice Nthumb 113 M5
Seatown Dorset 11 J6
Seave Green N York 104 G10
Seaview IoW 14 H8
Seaville Cumb 110 C10
Seavington St Mary Somset 11 J2
Seavington St Michael Somset 19 M11
Sebastopol Torfn 31 J5
Sebergham Cumb 101 L2
Seckington Warwks 59 L3
Second Severn Crossing Mons 31 P7
Sedbergh Cumb 95 P2
Sedbury Gloucs 31 P6
Sedbusk N York 96 C2
Sedgeberrow Worcs 47 K7
Sedgebrook Lincs 73 M3
Sedge Fen Suffk 63 L4
Sedgefield Dur 104 C5
Sedgeford Norfk 75 P3
Sedgehill Wilts 20 G9
Sedgemoor Services Somset 19 L4
Sedgley Dudley 58 D6
Sedgley Park Bury 82 H4
Sedgwick Cumb 95 L3
Sedlescombe E Susx 26 C8
Sedrup Bucks 35 M2
Seed Kent 38 F10
Seend Wilts 20 H2
Seend Cleeve Wilts 20 H2
Seer Green Bucks 35 Q6
Seething Norfk 65 L2
Sefton Sefton 81 M4
Seghill Nthumb 113 L6
Seighford Staffs 70 F9
Seion Gwynd 79 J11
Seisdon Staffs 58 B5
Selattyn Shrops 69 J8
Selborne Hants 23 K8
Selby N York 91 Q4
Selham W Susx 23 P10
Selhurst Gt Lon 36 H7
Selkirk Border 117 P5
Sellack Herefs 45 R9
Sellafield Station Cumb 100 D10
Sellafirth Shet 169 s4
Sellan Cnwll 2 C7
Sellick's Green Somset 18 H11
Sellindge Kent 27 J4
Selling Kent 38 H10
Sells Green Wilts 20 H2
Selly Oak Birm 58 F8
Selmeston E Susx 25 M9
Selsdon Gt Lon 37 J8
Selsey W Susx 15 N8
Selsfield Common W Susx 24 H4
Selside Cumb 101 P11
Selside N York 96 A5
Selsley Gloucs 32 F4
Selsted Kent 27 M3
Selston Notts 84 G10
Selworthy Somset 18 B5
Semer Suffk 52 G2
Semington Wilts 20 G2
Semley Wilts 20 G9
Sempringham Lincs 74 B4
Send Surrey 36 B9
Send Marsh Surrey 36 B9
Senghenydd Caerph 30 F6
Sennen Cnwll 2 B8
Sennen Cove Cnwll 2 B8
Sennybridge Powys 44 C9
Serlby Notts 85 K3
Sessay N York 97 Q5
Setchey Norfk 75 M8
Setley Hants 13 P4
Seton Mains E Loth 128 C4
Settle N York 96 B8
Settrington N York 98 G6
Seven Ash Somset 18 G8
Sevenhampton Gloucs 47 K10
Sevenhampton Swindn 33 P6
Seven Kings Gt Lon 37 L3
Sevenoaks Kent 37 M9
Sevenoaks Weald Kent 37 M10
Seven Sisters Neath 29 M3
Seven Springs Gloucs 47 J11
Seven Star Green Essex 52 F6
Severn Beach S Glos 31 P8
Severn Bridge S Glos 31 Q6
Severn Stoke Worcs 46 G6
Severn View Services S Glos 31 Q7
Sevick End Bed 61 N10
Sevington Kent 26 H3
Sewards End Essex 51 N3
Sewardstonebury Essex 51 J11
Sewell C Beds 49 Q10
Sewerby E R Yk 99 P7
Seworgan Cnwll 3 J7
Sewstern Leics 73 M6
Sexhow N York 104 E9
Sgalpaigh W Isls 168 h8
Sgiogarstaigh W Isls 168 k1
Shabbington Bucks 35 J3
Shackerley Shrops 57 Q3
Shackerstone Leics 72 B9
Shacklecross Derbys 72 C4
Shackleford Surrey 23 P5
Shade Calder 89 Q6
Shader W Isls 168 i2
Shadforth Dur 104 B2
Shadingfield Suffk 65 N5
Shadoxhurst Kent 26 G4
Shadwell Leeds 91 J3
Shadwell Norfk 64 C5
Shaftenhoe End Herts 51 K3
Shaftesbury Dorset 20 G10
Shaftholme Donc 91 P9
Shafton Barns 91 K8
Shafton Two Gates Barns 91 K8
Shakerley Wigan 82 E4
Shalbourne Wilts 22 B2
Shalcombe IoW 14 C9
Shalden Hants 23 J6
Shalden Green Hants 23 K6
Shaldon Devon 7 N4
Shalfleet IoW 14 D9
Shalford Essex 52 B6
Shalford Surrey 36 B11
Shalford Green Essex 52 B6
Shallowford Staffs 70 F9
Shalmsford Street Kent 39 J11
Shalstone Bucks 48 H7
Shamley Green Surrey 24 B2
Shandford Angus 142 H5
Shandon Ag & B 132 B10
Shandwick Highld 156 F2
Shangton Leics 73 J11
Shankhouse Nthumb 113 L5
Shanklin IoW 14 G10
Shantron Ag & B 132 C10
Shap Cumb 101 Q7
Shapinsay Ork 169 e5
Shapwick Dorset 12 F4
Shapwick Somset 19 M7
Shard End Birm 59 J7
Shardlow Derbys 72 C4
Shareshill Staffs 58 D3
Sharlston Wakefd 91 K7
Sharlston Common Wakefd 91 K7
Sharman's Cross Solhll 58 H9
Sharnal Street Medway 38 C7
Sharnbrook Bed 61 L9
Sharneyford Lancs 89 P6
Sharnford Leics 59 Q6
Sharnhill Green Dorset 11 Q3
Sharoe Green Lancs 88 G4
Sharow N York 97 M6
Sharpenhoe C Beds 50 C4
Sharperton Nthumb 119 J10
Sharp Green Norfk 77 M7
Sharpness Gloucs 32 C4
Sharpthorne W Susx 25 J4
Sharptor Cnwll 5 M7
Sharpway Gate Worcs 58 E11
Sharrington Norfk 76 E4
Shatterford Worcs 57 P8
Shatterling Kent 39 N10
Shatton Derbys 84 B4
Shaugh Prior Devon 6 E6
Shave Cross Dorset 11 J5
Shavington Ches E 70 B4
Shaw C Brad 90 C3
Shaw Oldham 89 Q9
Shaw Swindn 33 M7
Shaw W Berk 34 E11
Shaw Wilts 32 G11
Shawbirch Wrekin 57 L2
Shawbost W Isls 168 h3
Shawbury Shrops 69 Q10
Shawclough Rochdl 89 P8
Shaw Common Gloucs 46 C9
Shawdon Hill Nthumb 119 L8
Shawell Leics 60 B4
Shawford Hants 22 E9
Shawforth Lancs 89 P6
Shaw Green Herts 50 H4
Shaw Green Lancs 88 G7
Shaw Green N York 97 L10
Shawhead D & G 109 J5
Shaw Mills N York 97 L8
Shawsburn S Lans 126 D7
Shear Cross Wilts 20 G6
Shearington D & G 109 M7
Shearsby Leics 60 D2
Shearston Somset 19 J8
Shebbear Devon 16 G10
Shebdon Staffs 70 D9
Shebster Highld 166 H4
Shedfield Hants 14 G4
Sheen Staffs 71 L2
Sheepbridge Derbys 84 E6
Sheep Hill Dur 113 J9
Sheepridge Kirk 90 F7
Sheepscar Leeds 91 J4
Sheepscombe Gloucs 32 G2
Sheepstor Devon 6 F5
Sheepwash Devon 8 C3
Sheepwash Nthumb 113 L3
Sheepway N Som 31 N9
Sheepy Magna Leics 72 A10
Sheepy Parva Leics 72 A10
Sheering Essex 51 M8
Sheerness Kent 38 F7
Sheerwater Surrey 36 B8
Sheet Hants 23 L10
Sheffield Cnwll 2 D8
Sheffield Sheff 84 E3
Sheffield Bottom W Berk 34 H11
Sheffield Green E Susx 25 K5
Sheffield Park E Susx 25 K6
Shefford C Beds 50 D3
Shefford Woodlands W Berk 34 C10
Sheigra Highld 164 E4
Sheinton Shrops 57 L4
Shelderton Shrops 56 G9
Sheldon Birm 58 J8
Sheldon Derbys 83 Q11
Sheldon Devon 10 C3
Sheldwich Kent 38 H10
Sheldwich Lees Kent 38 H10
Shelf Calder 90 E5
Shelfanger Norfk 64 G5
Shelfield Warwks 47 M2
Shelfield Wsall 58 F4
Shelfield Green Warwks 47 M2
Shelford Notts 72 H2
Shelford Warwks 59 P7
Shellacres Nthumb 118 G2
Shelley Essex 51 N9
Shelley Kirk 90 G8
Shelley Suffk 52 H4
Shelley Far Bank Kirk 90 G8
Shellingford Oxon 34 B6
Shellow Bowells Essex 51 P9
Shelsley Beauchamp Worcs 46 D2
Shelsley Walsh Worcs 46 D2
Shelton Bed 61 M7
Shelton Norfk 65 J3
Shelton Notts 73 K2
Shelton Shrops 56 H2
Shelton Green Norfk 65 J3
Shelton Lock C Derb 72 B4
Shelton Under Harley Staffs 70 E7
Shelve Shrops 56 E5
Shelwick Herefs 45 Q6
Shenfield Essex 51 P11
Shenington Oxon 48 C6
Shenley Herts 50 E10
Shenley Brook End M Keyn 49 M7
Shenleybury Herts 50 E10
Shenley Church End M Keyn 49 M7
Shenmore Herefs 45 M7
Shennanton D & G 107 K5
Shenstone Staffs 58 H4
Shenstone Worcs 58 C10
Shenstone Woodend Staffs 58 H4
Shenton Leics 72 B11
Shenval Moray 149 N2
Shepeau Stow Lincs 74 F8
Shephall Herts 50 G6
Shepherd's Bush Gt Lon 36 F4
Shepherd's Green Oxon 35 K8
Shepherds Patch Gloucs 32 D4
Shepherdswell Kent 27 N2
Shepley Kirk 90 F9
Shepperdine S Glos 32 B5
Shepperton Surrey 36 C7
Shepperton Green Surrey 36 C7
Shepreth Cambs 62 E11
Shepshed Leics 72 D7
Shepton Beauchamp Somset 19 M11
Shepton Mallet Somset 20 B6
Shepton Montague Somset 20 C8
Shepway Kent 38 C11
Sheraton Dur 104 D3
Sherborne Dorset 20 B11
Sherborne Gloucs 33 N2
Sherborne Somset 19 Q3
Sherborne St John Hants 22 H3
Sherbourne Warwks 47 Q2
Sherburn Dur 104 B2
Sherburn N York 99 K5
Sherburn Hill Dur 104 B2
Sherburn in Elmet N York 91 M4
Shere Surrey 36 C11
Shereford Norfk 76 B6
Sherfield English Hants 21 Q10
Sherfield on Loddon Hants 23 J3
Sherfin Lancs 89 M5
Sherford Devon 7 K10
Sherford Dorset 12 F6
Sheriffhales Shrops 57 P2
Sheriff Hutton N York 98 D7
Sheringham Norfk 76 H3
Sherington M Keyn 49 N5
Shermanbury W Susx 24 F7
Shernborne Norfk 75 P4
Sherrington Wilts 21 J7
Sherston Wilts 32 G7
Sherwood C Nott 72 F2
Sherwood Forest Notts 85 K8
Shetland Islands Shet 169 r8
Shettleston C Glas 125 Q5
Shevington Wigan 88 G9
Shevington Moor Wigan 88 G8
Shevington Vale Wigan 88 G9
Sheviock Cnwll 5 P10
Shibden Head C Brad 90 D5
Shide IoW 14 F9
Shidlaw Nthumb 118 F3
Shiel Bridge Highld 146 A4
Shieldaig Highld 153 Q7
Shieldhill D & G 109 M3
Shieldhill Falk 126 F2
Shieldhill House Hotel S Lans 116 E2
Shields N Lans 126 D6
Shielfoot Highld 138 B3
Shielhill Angus 142 G6
Shielhill Inver 124 G3
Shifford Oxon 34 C4
Shifnal Shrops 57 N3
Shilbottle Nthumb 119 N9
Shildon Dur 103 P5
Shillford E Rens 125 M6
Shillingford Devon 18 C10
Shillingford Oxon 34 G6
Shillingford Abbot Devon 9 M7
Shillingford St George Devon 9 M7
Shillingstone Dorset 12 D2
Shillington C Beds 50 D4
Shillmoor Nthumb 118 G9
Shilton Oxon 33 Q3
Shilton Warwks 59 P8
Shimpling Norfk 64 H5
Shimpling Suffk 64 B11
Shimpling Street Suffk 64 B11
Shincliffe Dur 103 Q2
Shiney Row Sundld 113 M10
Shinfield Wokham 35 K11
Shingay Cambs 62 D11
Shingle Street Suffk 53 Q3
Shinnersbridge Devon 7 K6
Shinness Highld 162 C4
Shipbourne Kent 37 N10
Shipdham Norfk 76 D10
Shipham Somset 19 M3
Shiphay Torbay 7 M5
Shiplake Oxon 35 L9
Shiplake Row Oxon 35 K9
Shiplate N Som 19 L3
Shipley C Brad 90 F3
Shipley Derbys 72 C2
Shipley Shrops 57 Q5
Shipley W Susx 24 D6
Shipley Bridge Surrey 24 H2
Shipley Hatch Kent 26 H4
Shipmeadow Suffk 65 M3
Shippea Hill Station Cambs 63 K4
Shippon Oxon 34 E5
Shipston-on-Stour Warwks 47 Q6
Shipton Bucks 49 L9
Shipton Gloucs 47 K11
Shipton N York 98 B9
Shipton Shrops 57 K6
Shipton Bellinger Hants 21 P5
Shipton Gorge Dorset 11 K6
Shipton Green W Susx 15 M7
Shipton Moyne Gloucs 32 G7
Shipton-on-Cherwell Oxon 48 E11
Shiptonthorpe E R Yk 92 E2
Shipton-under-Wychwood Oxon 47 Q11
Shirburn Oxon 35 J5
Shirdley Hill Lancs 88 D8
Shire Cumb 102 B3
Shirebrook Derbys 84 H7
Shiregreen Sheff 84 E2
Shirehampton Bristl 31 P9
Shiremoor N Tyne 113 M6
Shirenewton Mons 31 N6
Shire Oak Wsall 58 G4
Shireoaks Notts 85 J4
Shirkoak Kent 26 F4
Shirland Derbys 84 F9
Shirlett Shrops 57 L5
Shirley C Sotn 14 D4
Shirley Derbys 71 N6
Shirley Gt Lon 37 J7
Shirley Solhll 58 H9
Shirl Heath Herefs 45 N3
Shirrell Heath Hants 14 G4
Shirwell Devon 17 L4
Shiskine N Ayrs 120 H6
Shittlehope Dur 103 K3
Shobdon Herefs 45 N2
Shobley Hants 13 L3
Shobrooke Devon 9 L4
Shoby Leics 72 H6
Shocklach Ches W 69 M5
Shocklach Green Ches W 69 M5
Shoeburyness Sthend 38 F4
Sholden Kent 39 Q11
Sholing C Sotn 14 E4
Shoot Hill Shrops 56 G2
Shop Cnwll 4 D7
Shop Cnwll 16 C9
Shopwyke W Susx 15 N5
Shore Rochdl 89 Q7
Shoreditch Gt Lon 36 H4
Shoreditch Somset 18 H10
Shoreham Kent 37 M8
Shoreham-by-Sea W Susx 24 F9
Shoreswood Nthumb 129 N10
Shorley Hants 22 G9
Shorncote Gloucs 33 K5
Shorne Kent 37 Q6
Shortacross Cnwll 5 M10
Shortbridge E Susx 25 L6
Shortfield Common Surrey 23 M6
Shortgate E Susx 25 L7
Short Heath Birm 58 G6
Shortheath Hants 23 L7
Short Heath Wsall 58 E4
Shortlanesend Cnwll 3 L4
Shortlees E Ayrs 125 L10
Shortstown Bed 61 N11
Shorwell IoW 14 E10
Shoscombe BaNES 20 D3
Shotesham Norfk 65 J2
Shotgate Essex 38 C3
Shotley Suffk 53 M4
Shotley Bridge Dur 112 G10
Shotleyfield Nthumb 112 G10
Shotley Gate Suffk 53 M5
Shotley Street Suffk 53 M4
Shottenden Kent 38 H11
Shottermill Surrey 23 N8
Shottery Warwks 47 N4
Shotteswell Warwks 48 D5
Shottisham Suffk 53 P3
Shottle Derbys 71 Q5
Shottlegate Derbys 71 Q5
Shotton Dur 104 C5
Shotton Dur 104 D3
Shotton Flints 81 L11
Shotton Nthumb 113 K5
Shotton Nthumb 118 F4
Shotton Colliery Dur 104 C2
Shotts N Lans 126 F6
Shotwick Ches W 81 L10
Shougle Moray 157 N6
Shouldham Norfk 75 N9
Shouldham Thorpe Norfk 75 N9
Shoulton Worcs 46 F3
Shover's Green E Susx 25 Q4
Shraleybrook Staffs 70 D5
Shrawardine Shrops 69 L11
Shrawley Worcs 57 Q11
Shreding Green Bucks 36 B4
Shrewley Warwks 59 K11
Shrewsbury Shrops 56 H2
Shrewton Wilts 21 L6
Shripney W Susx 15 P6
Shrivenham Oxon 33 P7
Shropham Norfk 64 D3
Shroton Dorset 12 E2
Shrub End Essex 52 G7
Shucknall Herefs 46 A6
Shudy Camps Cambs 51 P2
Shuna Ag & B 130 F6
Shurdington Gloucs 46 H11
Shurlock Row W & M 35 M10
Shurnock Worcs 47 K2
Shurrery Highld 166 H5
Shurrery Lodge Highld 166 H5
Shurton Somset 18 H6
Shustoke Warwks 59 K6
Shute Devon 9 L4
Shute Devon 10 F5
Shutford Oxon 48 C6
Shut Heath Staffs 70 F10
Shuthonger Gloucs 46 G7
Shutlanger Nhants 49 K5
Shutterton Devon 9 N9
Shutt Green Staffs 58 C3
Shuttington Warwks 59 L3
Shuttlewood Derbys 84 G6
Shuttleworth Bury 89 N7
Siabost W Isls 168 h3
Siadar W Isls 168 i2
Sibbertoft Nhants 60 E4
Sibdon Carwood Shrops 56 G8
Sibford Ferris Oxon 48 C7
Sibford Gower Oxon 48 C7
Sible Hedingham Essex 52 C5
Sibley's Green Essex 51 P5

Siblyback Cnwll 5 L7
Sibsey Lincs 87 L10
Sibsey Fenside Lincs 87 K10
Sibson Cambs 74 A11
Sibson Leics 72 B10
Sibster Highld 167 P6
Sibthorpe Notts 85 M6
Sibthorpe Notts 85 N11
Sibton Suffk 65 M8
Sicklesmere Suffk 64 B9
Sicklinghall N York 97 N11
Sidbrook Somset 19 J9
Sidbury Devon 10 C6
Sidbury Shrops 57 M7
Sid Cop Barns 91 K9
Sidcot N Som 19 M3
Sidcup Gt Lon 37 L6
Siddick Cumb 100 D4
Siddington Ches E 82 H10
Siddington Gloucs 33 K5
Sidemoor Worcs 58 E10
Sidestrand Norfk 77 K4
Sidford Devon 10 C6
Sidlesham W Susx 15 N7
Sidlesham Common W Susx 15 N7
Sidley E Susx 26 B10
Sidmouth Devon 10 C7
Siefton Shrops 56 H8
Sigford Devon 7 K4
Sigglesthorne E R Yk 99 P11
Sigingstone V Glam 30 C10
Signet Oxon 33 P2
Silchester Hants 22 H2
Sileby Leics 72 G7
Silecroft Cumb 94 C4
Silfield Norfk 64 G2
Silian Cerdgn 43 L4
Silkstead Hants 22 D10
Silkstone Barns 90 H9
Silkstone Common Barns 90 H10
Silk Willoughby Lincs 73 R2
Silloth Cumb 109 P10
Silpho N York 99 K2
Silsden C Brad 96 F11
Silsoe C Beds 50 C3
Silton Dorset 20 E9
Silverburn Mdloth 127 N5
Silverdale Lancs 95 K6
Silverdale Staffs 70 E5
Silver End Essex 52 D8
Silverford Abers 159 J5
Silvergate Norfk 76 H6
Silverlace Green Suffk 65 L9
Silverley's Green Suffk 65 K6
Silverstone Nhants 49 J6
Silver Street Kent 38 E9
Silver Street Somset 19 P8
Silverton Devon 9 N4
Silverwell Cnwll 3 J4
Silvington Shrops 57 L9
Simister Bury 89 N9
Simmondley Derbys 83 M6
Simonburn Nthumb 112 C6
Simonsbath Somset 17 P4
Simonsburrow Devon 18 F11
Simonstone Lancs 89 M4
Simonstone N York 96 C2
Simprim Border 129 L11
Simpson M Keyn 49 N7
Simpson Cross Pembks 40 G7
Sinclair's Hill Border 129 L9
Sinclairston E Ayrs 115 J4
Sinderby N York 97 M4
Sinderhope Nthumb 112 B10
Sinderland Green Traffd 82 F7
Sindlesham Wokham 35 L11
Sinfin C Derb 72 A4
Singleborough Bucks 49 L8
Single Street Gt Lon 37 K9
Singleton Kent 26 H3
Singleton Lancs 88 D3
Singleton W Susx 15 N4
Singlewell Kent 37 Q6
Sinkhurst Green Kent 26 D3
Sinnarhard Abers 150 D5
Sinnington N York 98 E3
Sinope Leics 72 C7
Sinton Worcs 46 F2
Sinton Worcs 46 F2
Sinton Green Worcs 46 F2
Sipson Gt Lon 36 C5
Sirhowy Blae G 30 F2
Sissinghurst Kent 26 C4
Siston S Glos 32 C9
Sitcott Devon 5 P3
Sithney Cnwll 2 G8
Sithney Common Cnwll 2 G8
Sithney Green Cnwll 2 G8
Sittingbourne Kent 38 F9
Six Ashes Shrops 57 P7
Six Bells Blae G 30 H4
Six Hills Leics 72 G6
Sixhills Lincs 86 G3
Six Mile Bottom Cambs 63 J9
Sixmile Cottages Kent 27 K3
Sixpenny Handley Dorset 21 J11
Six Rues Jersey 11 b1
Sizewell Suffk 65 P9
Skaill Ork 169 e6
Skara Brae Ork 169 b5
Skares E Ayrs 115 K4
Skateraw Abers 151 N9
Skateraw E Loth 129 J5
Skeabost Highld 152 G8
Skeeby N York 103 N10
Skeffington Leics 73 J10
Skeffling E R Yk 93 Q7
Skegby Notts 84 G8
Skegby Notts 85 N7
Skegness Lincs 87 Q8
Skelbo Highld 162 H7
Skelbo Street Highld 162 H8
Skelbrooke Donc 91 N8
Skeldyke Lincs 74 F3
Skellingthorpe Lincs 86 B6
Skellorn Green Ches E 83 K8
Skellow Donc 91 N8
Skelmanthorpe Kirk 90 G8
Skelmersdale Lancs 88 F9
Skelmorlie N Ayrs 124 F4
Skelpick Highld 166 B5
Skelston D & G 108 H3
Skelton C York 98 B9
Skelton Cumb 101 M3
Skelton E R Yk 92 C5
Skelton N York 103 L10
Skelton R & Cl 105 J7
Skelton on Ure N York 97 N7
Skelwith Bridge Cumb 101 K10
Skendleby Lincs 87 M7
Skene House Abers 151 K5
Skenfrith Mons 45 P10
Skerne E R Yk 99 L9
Skerray Highld 165 Q4
Skerricha Highld 164 F6
Skerton Lancs 95 K8
Sketchley Leics 59 P6
Sketty Swans 28 H6
Skewen Neath 29 K5
Skewsby N York 98 C6
Skeyton Norfk 77 J6
Skeyton Corner Norfk 77 K6
Skiall Highld 166 H3
Skidbrooke Lincs 87 M2
Skidbrooke North End Lincs 93 R11
Skidby E R Yk 92 H4
Skigersta W Isls 168 k1
Skilgate Somset 18 C9
Skillington Lincs 73 M5
Skinburness Cumb 109 P9
Skinflats Falk 133 Q11
Skinidin Highld 152 C8
Skinners Green W Berk 34 D11
Skinningrove R & Cl 105 K7
Skipness Ag & B 123 R8
Skipper's Bridge D & G 110 G4
Skiprigg Cumb 110 G11
Skipsea E R Yk 99 P10
Skipsea Brough E R Yk 99 P10
Skipton N York 96 E10
Skipton-on-Swale N York 97 N5
Skipwith N York 91 R3
Skirlaugh E R Yk 93 K3
Skirling Border 116 F3
Skirmett Bucks 35 L6
Skirpenbeck E R Yk 98 E9
Skirwith Cumb 102 B4
Skirwith N York 95 Q6
Skirza Highld 167 Q3
Skitby Cumb 110 H7
Skittle Green Bucks 35 L4
Skokholm Island Pembks 40 D10
Skomer Island Pembks 40 D9
Skulamus Highld 145 L3
Skyborry Green Shrops 56 D10
Skye Green Essex 52 E7
Skye of Curr Highld 148 H3
Skyreholme N York 96 G8
Slack Calder 90 B5
Slackcote Oldham 90 B9
Slack Head Cumb 95 K5
Slackholme End Lincs 87 P6
Slacks of Cairnbanno Abers 159 K8
Slad Gloucs 32 G3
Slade Devon 10 C3
Slade Devon 17 J2
Slade Devon 17 Q6
Slade End Oxon 34 G6
Slade Green Gt Lon 37 M5
Slade Heath Staffs 58 D3
Slade Hooton Rothm 84 H3
Sladesbridge Cnwll 4 G7
Slades Green Worcs 46 F8
Slaggyford Nthumb 111 N10
Slaidburn Lancs 95 Q10
Slaithwaite Kirk 90 D8
Slaley Derbys 84 C9
Slaley Nthumb 112 E9
Slamannan Falk 126 F3
Slapton Bucks 49 P10
Slapton Devon 7 L9
Slapton Nhants 48 H5
Slattocks Rochdl 89 P9
Slaugham W Susx 24 G5
Slaughterford Wilts 32 F10
Slawston Leics 60 G2
Sleaford Hants 23 M7
Sleaford Lincs 86 E11
Sleagill Cumb 101 Q7
Sleap Shrops 69 N9
Sleapford Wrekin 70 A11
Sleapshyde Herts 50 E9
Sleasdairidh Highld 162 E7
Slebech Pembks 41 K7
Sledge Green Worcs 46 F8
Sledmere E R Yk 99 J8
Sleetbeck Cumb 111 K5
Sleight Dorset 12 G5
Sleightholme Dur 103 J8
Sleights N York 105 N9
Slepe Dorset 12 F6
Slickly Highld 167 N3
Sliddery N Ayrs 120 H7
Sligachan Highld 144 G2
Sligrachan Ag & B 131 P9
Slimbridge Gloucs 32 D4
Slindon Staffs 70 E8
Slindon W Susx 15 Q5
Slinfold W Susx 24 D4
Sling Gloucs 31 Q3
Sling Gwynd 79 L11
Slingsby N York 98 D6
Slip End C Beds 50 C7
Slip End Herts 50 G3
Slipton Nhants 61 L5
Slitting Mill Staffs 71 J11
Slockavullin Ag & B 130 G8
Sloley Norfk 77 K7
Sloncombe Devon 8 H7
Sloothby Lincs 87 N6
Slough Slough 35 Q9
Slough Green Somset 19 J11
Slough Green W Susx 24 G5
Slumbay Highld 154 A10
Slyfield Green Surrey 23 Q4
Slyne Lancs 95 K7
Smailholm Border 118 B3
Smallbridge Rochdl 89 Q7
Smallbrook Devon 9 L5
Smallbrook Gloucs 31 Q4
Smallburgh Norfk 77 L7
Smallburn E Ayrs 115 N2
Smalldale Derbys 83 N9
Smalldale Derbys 83 Q8
Small Dole W Susx 24 F8
Smalley Derbys 72 C2
Smalley Common Derbys 72 C2
Smalley Green Derbys 72 C2
Smallfield Surrey 24 H2
Small Heath Birm 58 H7
Small Hythe Kent 26 E5
Smallridge Devon 10 G4
Smallthorne C Stke 70 F4
Smallways N York 103 M8
Smallwood Ches E 70 E2
Small Wood Hey Lancs 94 H11
Smallworth Norfk 64 E5
Smannell Hants 22 C5
Smardale Cumb 102 D9
Smarden Kent 26 E3
Smarden Bell Kent 26 E3
Smart's Hill Kent 25 M2
Smeafield Nthumb 119 L3
Smeatharpe Devon 10 D2
Smeeth Kent 27 J4
Smeeton Westerby Leics 60 E2
Smelthouses N York 97 J8
Smerral Highld 167 L10
Smestow Staffs 58 C6
Smethwick Sandw 58 F7
Smethwick Green Ches E 70 E2
Smirisary Highld 138 A2
Smisby Derbys 72 A7
Smith End Green Worcs 46 E4
Smithfield Cumb 110 H7
Smith Green Lancs 95 K9
Smithies Barns 91 J9
Smithincott Devon 9 Q2
Smith's End Herts 51 K3
Smith's Green Essex 51 N6
Smith's Green Essex 51 Q2
Smithstown Highld 160 B11
Smithton Highld 156 C8
Smithy Bridge Rochdl 89 Q7
Smithy Green Ches E 82 F10
Smithy Green Stockp 83 J7
Smithy Houses Derbys 84 E11
Smockington Leics 59 Q7
Smoo Highld 165 K3
Smythe's Green Essex 52 F8
Snade D & G 108 H3
Snailbeach Shrops 56 F4
Snailwell Cambs 63 K7
Snainton N York 99 J4
Snaith E R Yk 91 Q6
Snake Pass Inn Derbys 83 P6
Snape N York 97 L4
Snape Suffk 65 M10
Snape Green Lancs 88 D8
Snape Street Suffk 65 M10
Snaresbrook Gt Lon 37 K3
Snarestone Leics 72 A9
Snarford Lincs 86 D4
Snargate Kent 26 G6
Snave Kent 26 H6
Sneachill Worcs 46 H4
Snead Powys 56 E6
Sneath Common Norfk 64 H4
Sneaton N York 105 N9
Sneatonthorpe N York 105 P9
Snelland Lincs 86 E4
Snelson Ches E 82 H10
Snelston Derbys 71 M6
Snetterton Norfk 64 D3
Snettisham Norfk 75 N4
Snibston Leics 72 C8
Snig's End Gloucs 46 E9
Snitter Nthumb 119 K10
Snitterby Lincs 86 C2
Snitterfield Warwks 47 P3
Snitterton Derbys 84 C8
Snitton Shrops 57 K9
Snoadhill Kent 26 F3
Snodhill Herefs 45 L6
Snodland Kent 38 B9
Snoll Hatch Kent 37 Q11
Snowden Hill Barns 90 H10
Snowdon Gwynd 67 L4
Snowdon Kent 39 M11
Snowdonia National Park 67 Q9
Snow End Herts 51 K4
Snowshill Gloucs 47 L8
Snow Street Norfk 64 F5
Soake Hants 15 J4
Soar Cardif 30 E8
Soar Devon 7 J11
Soar Powys 44 D8
Soay Highld 144 F5
Soberton Hants 22 H11
Soberton Heath Hants 14 H4
Sockbridge Cumb 101 N5
Sockburn Darltn 104 B9
Sodom Denbgs 80 F10
Sodylt Bank Shrops 69 K7
Soham Cambs 63 J6
Soham Cotes Cambs 63 J5
Solas W Isls 168 d10
Solbury Pembks 40 G8
Soldon Devon 16 E9
Soldon Cross Devon 16 E9
Soldridge Hants 23 J7
Sole Street Kent 27 J2
Sole Street Kent 37 Q7
Solihull Solhll 59 J9
Sollers Dilwyn Herefs 45 N3
Sollers Hope Herefs 46 B8
Sollom Lancs 88 F7
Solva Pembks 40 F6
Solwaybank D & G 110 F5
Somerby Leics 73 K8
Somerby Lincs 93 J9
Somercotes Derbys 84 F10
Somerford BCP 13 L6
Somerford Keynes Gloucs 33 K5
Somerley W Susx 15 M7
Somerleyton Suffk 65 P2
Somersal Herbert Derbys 71 L7
Somersby Lincs 87 K6
Somersham Cambs 62 E5
Somersham Suffk 53 J2
Somerton Oxon 48 E9
Somerton Somset 19 N9
Somerton Suffk 63 P10
Somerwood Shrops 57 K2
Sompting W Susx 24 E9
Sompting Abbotts W Susx 24 E9
Sonning Wokham 35 L9
Sonning Common Oxon 35 K8
Sonning Eye Oxon 35 K9
Sontley Wrexhm 69 K5
Sopley Hants 13 L5
Sopwell Herts 50 E9
Sopworth Wilts 32 F7
Sorbie D & G 107 M8
Sordale Highld 167 K4
Sorisdale Ag & B 136 H3
Sorn E Ayrs 115 L2
Sornhill E Ayrs 125 N11
Sortat Highld 167 N4
Sotby Lincs 86 H5
Sots Hole Lincs 86 F8
Sotterley Suffk 65 N5
Soughton Flints 81 J11
Soulbury Bucks 49 N9
Soulby Cumb 101 N5
Soulby Cumb 102 D8
Souldern Oxon 48 F8
Souldrop Bed 61 L8
Sound Ches E 70 A5
Sound Muir Moray 157 R7
Soundwell S Glos 32 C9
Sourton Devon 8 D6
Soutergate Cumb 94 E4
South Acre Norfk 75 R8
South Alkham Kent 27 M3
Southall Gt Lon 36 D5
South Allington Devon 7 K11
South Alloa Falk 133 P9
Southam Gloucs 47 J9
Southam Warwks 48 D2
South Ambersham W Susx 23 P10
Southampton C Sotn 14 D4
Southampton Airport Hants 22 E11
South Anston Rothm 84 H4
South Ascot W & M 35 P11
South Ashford Kent 26 H3
South Baddesley Hants 14 C7
South Ballachulish Highld 139 K6
South Bank C York 98 B10
South Bank R & Cl 104 F6
South Barrow Somset 20 B9
South Beddington Gt Lon 36 G8
South Beer Cnwll 5 N3
South Benfleet Essex 38 C4
South Bockhampton BCP 13 L5
Southborough Gt Lon 37 K7
Southborough Kent 25 N2
Southbourne BCP 13 K6
Southbourne W Susx 15 L5
South Bowood Dorset 11 J5
South Bramwith Donc 91 Q8
South Brent Devon 6 H6
South Brewham Somset 20 D7
South Broomhill Nthumb 119 P11
Southburgh Norfk 76 E10
South Burlingham Norfk 77 M10
Southburn E R Yk 99 K10
South Cadbury Somset 20 B9
South Carlton Lincs 86 B5
South Carlton Notts 85 J4
South Cave E R Yk 92 F4
South Cerney Gloucs 33 K5
South Chailey E Susx 25 J7
South Chard Somset 10 G3
South Charlton Nthumb 119 N6
South Cheriton Somset 20 C10
South Church Dur 103 P5
Southchurch Sthend 38 F4
South Cleatlam Dur 103 M7
South Cliffe E R Yk 92 E3
South Clifton Notts 85 P6
South Cockerington Lincs 87 L3
South Cornelly Brdgnd 29 M8
Southcott Cnwll 5 K2
Southcott Devon 8 D5
Southcott Devon 9 J8
Southcott Devon 16 G8
Southcott Wilts 21 N3
Southcourt Bucks 35 M2
South Cove Suffk 65 P5
South Creake Norfk 76 B4
South Crosland Kirk 90 E8
South Croxton Leics 72 H8
South Dalton E R Yk 99 K11
South Darenth Kent 37 N7
South Dell W Isls 168 j1
South Downs National Park 25 J9
South Duffield N York 92 A4
South Earlswood Surrey 36 G11
Southease E Susx 25 K9
South Elkington Lincs 87 J3
South Elmsall Wakefd 91 M8
Southend Ag & B 120 C10
South End E R Yk 93 Q7
South End Hants 21 M11
South End Herefs 46 D6
South End N Linc 93 K6
South End Norfk 64 D3
Southend Wilts 33 N10
Southend Airport Essex 38 E4
Southend-on-Sea Sthend 38 E4
Southernby Cumb 101 L3
Southernden Kent 26 E2
Southerndown V Glam 29 N10
Southerness D & G 109 L10
South Erradale Highld 153 N3
Southerton Devon 10 B6
Southery Norfk 63 K2
South Fambridge Essex 38 E3
South Fawley W Berk 34 C8
South Ferriby N Linc 92 G6
South Field E R Yk 92 H5
Southfield Falk 126 E3
Southfleet Kent 37 P6
Southford IoW 14 F11
Southgate Gt Lon 36 G2
Southgate Norfk 75 N4
Southgate Norfk 76 B4
Southgate Norfk 76 G7
Southgate Swans 28 G7
South Godstone Surrey 37 J11
South Gorley Hants 13 L2
South Gosforth N u Ty 113 K7
South Green Essex 37 Q2
South Green Essex 52 H8
South Green Kent 38 E9
South Green Norfk 76 F9
South Green Suffk 64 H6
South Gyle C Edin 127 M3
South Hanningfield Essex 38 B2
South Harting W Susx 23 L11
South Hayling Hants 15 K7
South Hazelrigg Nthumb 119 L4
South Heath Bucks 35 P4
South Heighton E Susx 25 K10
South Hetton Dur 113 N11
South Hiendley Wakefd 91 K8
South Hill Cnwll 5 N7
South Hill Somset 19 N9
South Hinksey Oxon 34 F4
South Hole Devon 16 C7
South Holmwood Surrey 24 E2
South Hornchurch Gt Lon 37 M4
South Horrington Somset 19 Q5
South Huish Devon 6 H10
South Hykeham Lincs 86 B8
South Hylton Sundld 113 N9
Southill C Beds 50 E2
Southington Hants 22 F5
South Kelsey Lincs 92 H11
South Kessock Highld 156 B8
South Killingholme N Linc 93 K7
South Kilvington N York 97 P4
South Kilworth Leics 60 D4
South Kirkby Wakefd 91 L8
South Knighton Devon 7 L4
South Kyme Lincs 86 G11
Southleigh Devon 10 E6
South Leigh Oxon 34 C3
South Leverton Notts 85 N4
South Littleton Worcs 47 L5
South Lopham Norfk 64 E5
South Luffenham Rutlnd 73 N10
South Lynn Norfk 75 M7
South Malling E Susx 25 K8
South Marston Swindn 33 N7
South Merstham Surrey 36 G10
South Middleton Nthumb 119 J6
South Milford N York 91 M4
South Milton Devon 6 J10
South Mimms Herts 50 F10
South Mimms Services Herts 50 F10
Southminster Essex 38 G2
South Molton Devon 17 N6
South Moor Dur 113 J10
Southmoor Oxon 34 C5
South Moreton Oxon 34 G7
Southmuir Angus 142 F7
South Mundham W Susx 15 N6
South Muskham Notts 85 N9
South Newbald E R Yk 92 F3
South Newington Oxon 48 D8
South Newton Wilts 21 L8
South Normanton Derbys 84 F9
South Norwood Gt Lon 36 H7
South Nutfield Surrey 36 H11
South Ockendon Thurr 37 N4
Southoe Cambs 61 Q8
Southolt Suffk 64 H8
South Ormsby Lincs 87 L5
Southorpe C Pete 74 A10
South Ossett Wakefd 90 H7
South Otterington N York 97 N3
Southover Dorset 11 N6
Southover E Susx 25 Q5
South Owersby Lincs 86 E2
Southowram Calder 90 E6
South Park Surrey 36 F11
South Perrott Dorset 11 K3
South Petherton Somset 19 M11
South Petherwin Cnwll 5 N5
South Pickenham Norfk 76 B11
South Pill Cnwll 5 Q10
South Pool Devon 7 K10
South Poorton Dorset 11 L5
Southport Sefton 88 C7
South Queensferry C Edin 127 L2
South Radworthy Devon 17 N5
South Rauceby Lincs 86 D11
South Raynham Norfk 76 B7
South Reddish Stockp 83 J6
Southrepps Norfk 77 K4
South Reston Lincs 87 M4
Southrey Lincs 86 F7
South Ronaldsay Ork 169 d8
Southrop Gloucs 33 N4
Southrope Hants 23 J6
South Runcton Norfk 75 M9
South Scarle Notts 85 P8
Southsea C Port 15 J7
Southsea Wrexhm 69 K4
South Shian Ag & B 138 G9
South Shields S Tyne 113 N7
South Shore Bpool 88 C4
Southside Dur 103 M5
South Somercotes Lincs 87 M2
South Stainley N York 97 M8
South Stifford Thurr 37 N5
South Stoke BaNES 20 D2
South Stoke Oxon 34 G8
South Stoke W Susx 24 B9
South Stour Kent 26 H4
South Street Kent 37 P8
South Street Kent 39 J10
South Street Kent 39 K8
South Tarbrax S Lans 127 J7
South Tawton Devon 8 G6
South Tehidy Cnwll 2 H5
South Thoresby Lincs 87 M5
South Thorpe Dur 103 M8
South Town Hants 23 J7
Southtown Norfk 77 Q10
Southtown Somset 19 K11
South Uist W Isls 168 d14
Southwaite Cumb 110 H11
Southwaite Services Cumb 110 H11
South Walsham Norfk 77 M9
Southwark Gt Lon 36 H5
South Warnborough Hants 23 K5
Southwater W Susx 24 E5
Southwater Street W Susx 24 E5
Southway C Plym 6 D6
Southway Somset 19 P6
South Weald Essex 37 N2
Southwell Dorset 11 P10
Southwell Notts 85 L10
South Weston Oxon 35 K5
South Wheatley Cnwll 5 L3
South Wheatley Notts 85 N3
Southwick Hants 14 H5
Southwick Nhants 61 M2
Southwick Somset 19 L5
Southwick Sundld 113 N9
Southwick W Susx 24 F9
Southwick Wilts 20 F3
South Widcombe BaNES 19 Q3
South Wigston Leics 72 F11
South Willesborough Kent 26 H3
South Willingham Lincs 86 G4
South Wingate Dur 104 D4
South Wingfield Derbys 84 E9
South Witham Lincs 73 N7
Southwold Suffk 65 Q6

South Wonston Hants 22 E7
Southwood Norfk 77 M10
Southwood Somset 19 Q8
South Woodham Ferrers Essex 38 D2
South Wootton Norfk 75 M6
South Wraxall Wilts 20 F2
South Zeal Devon 8 G6
Sovereign Harbour E Susx 25 P10
Sowerby Calder 90 C6
Sowerby N York 97 P4
Sowerby Bridge Calder 90 D6
Sowerby Row Cumb 101 L2
Sower Carr Lancs 88 D2
Sowerhill Somset 18 A10
Sowhill Torfn 31 J4
Sowley Green Suffk 63 M10
Sowood Calder 90 D7
Sowton Devon 6 E5
Sowton Devon 9 N6
Soyland Town Calder 90 C6
Spa Common Norfk 77 K5
Spain's End Essex 51 Q3
Spalding Lincs 74 D6
Spaldington E R Yk 92 C4
Spaldwick Cambs 61 P6
Spalford Notts 85 P7
Spanby Lincs 74 A3
Spanish Green Hants 23 J3
Sparham Norfk 76 F8
Sparhamill Norfk 76 F8
Spark Bridge Cumb 94 G4
Sparket Cumb 101 M5
Sparkford Somset 20 B9
Sparkhill Birm 58 H8
Sparkwell Devon 6 F7
Sparrow Green Norfk 76 C9
Sparrowpit Derbys 83 N8
Sparrows Green E Susx 25 P4
Sparsholt Hants 22 D8
Sparsholt Oxon 34 B7
Spartylea Nthumb 112 C11
Spath Staffs 71 K7
Spaunton N York 98 E3
Spaxton Somset 18 H7
Spean Bridge Highld 146 G11
Spear Hill W Susx 24 D7
Spearywell Hants 22 B9
Speen Bucks 35 M5
Speen W Berk 34 E11
Speeton N York 99 P6
Speke Lpool 81 N8
Speldhurst Kent 25 N2
Spellbrook Herts 51 L7
Spelmonden Kent 26 B4
Spelsbury Oxon 48 B10
Spen Kirk 90 F5
Spencers Wood Wokham 35 K11
Spen Green Ches E 70 E2
Spennithorne N York 96 H3
Spennymoor Dur 103 Q4
Spernall Warwks 47 L2
Spetchley Worcs 46 G4
Spetisbury Dorset 12 F4
Spexhall Suffk 65 M5
Spey Bay Moray 157 R4
Speybridge Highld 149 J2
Speyview Moray 157 P9
Spilsby Lincs 87 M7
Spindlestone Nthumb 119 N4
Spinkhill Derbys 84 G5
Spinningdale Highld 162 F9
Spion Kop Notts 85 J7
Spirthill Wilts 33 J9
Spital Wirral 81 L8
Spital Hill Donc 85 K2
Spital in the Street Lincs 86 C2
Spithurst E Susx 25 K7
Spittal E Loth 128 D4
Spittal E R Yk 98 F10
Spittal Highld 167 L6
Spittal Nthumb 129 Q9
Spittal Pembks 41 J6
Spittalfield P & K 141 R9
Spittal of Glenmuick Abers 149 Q10
Spittal of Glenshee P & K 141 R4
Spittal-on-Rule Border 118 A7
Spixworth Norfk 77 J8
Splatt Cnwll 4 E6
Splatt Cnwll 5 L4
Splatt Devon 8 F3
Splayne's Green E Susx 25 K6
Splott Cardif 30 H9
Spofforth N York 97 N10
Spondon C Derb 72 C3
Spon Green Flints 69 J2
Spooner Row Norfk 64 F2
Sporle Norfk 76 A9
Spott E Loth 128 H4
Spottiswoode Border 128 G10
Spratton Nhants 60 F7
Spreakley Surrey 23 M6
Spreyton Devon 8 G5
Spriddlestone Devon 6 E8
Spridlington Lincs 86 D4
Springburn C Glas 125 Q4
Springfield D & G 110 F7
Springfield Essex 52 B10
Springfield Fife 135 J5
Springhill Staffs 58 E4
Springhill Staffs 58 G3
Springholm D & G 108 H6
Springside N Ayrs 125 K10
Springthorpe Lincs 85 Q3
Spring Vale Barns 90 H10
Springwell Sundld 113 L9
Sproatley E R Yk 93 L4
Sproston Green Ches W 82 F11
Sprotbrough Donc 91 N10
Sproughton Suffk 53 K3
Sprouston Border 118 E3
Sprowston Norfk 77 K9
Sproxton Leics 73 M6
Sproxton N York 98 C4
Spunhill Shrops 69 M8
Spurstow Ches E 69 Q3
Spyway Dorset 11 L6
Square and Compass Pembks 40 F4
Stableford Shrops 57 P5
Stableford Staffs 70 E7
Stacey Bank Sheff 84 C2
Stackhouse N York 96 B7
Stackpole Pembks 41 J11
Stackpole Elidor Pembks 41 J11
Stacksford Norfk 64 F3
Stacksteads Lancs 89 P6
Staddiscombe C Plym 6 E8
Staddlethorpe E R Yk 92 D5
Staden Derbys 83 N10
Stadhampton Oxon 34 H5
Stadhlaigearraidh W Isls 168 c14
Staffield Cumb 101 P2
Staffin Highld 152 H4
Stafford Staffs 70 G10
Stafford Services (northbound) Staffs 70 F8
Stafford Services (southbound) Staffs 70 F8
Stagsden Bed 49 Q5
Stainborough Barns 91 J10
Stainburn Cumb 100 D5
Stainburn N York 97 L11
Stainby Lincs 73 N6
Staincross Barns 91 J8
Staindrop Dur 103 M6
Staines-upon-Thames Surrey 36 B6
Stainfield Lincs 74 A6
Stainfield Lincs 86 F6
Stainforth Donc 91 Q8
Stainforth N York 96 B7
Staining Lancs 88 C3
Stainland Calder 90 D7
Stainsacre N York 105 P9
Stainsby Derbys 84 G7
Stainton Cumb 95 L3
Stainton Cumb 101 N5
Stainton Cumb 110 G9
Stainton Donc 85 J2
Stainton Dur 103 L7
Stainton Middsb 104 E8
Stainton N York 103 M11
Stainton by Langworth Lincs 86 E5
Staintondale N York 105 Q11
Stainton le Vale Lincs 86 G2
Stainton with Adgarley Cumb 94 E6
Stair Cumb 100 H6
Stair E Ayrs 114 H3
Stairfoot Barns 91 K9
Stairhaven D & G 106 H7
Staithes N York 105 L7
Stakeford Nthumb 113 L3
Stake Pool Lancs 95 J11
Stakes Hants 15 J5
Stalbridge Dorset 20 D11
Stalbridge Weston Dorset 20 D11
Stalham Norfk 77 M6
Stalham Green Norfk 77 M7
Stalisfield Green Kent 38 G11
Stalland Common Norfk 64 E2
Stallen Dorset 20 B11
Stallingborough NE Lin 93 L8
Stalling Busk N York 96 D3
Stallington Staffs 70 G7
Stalmine Lancs 94 H11
Stalmine Moss Side Lancs 94 H11
Stalybridge Tamesd 83 L5
Stambourne Essex 52 B4
Stambourne Green Essex 51 Q3
Stamford Lincs 73 Q9
Stamford Nthumb 119 P7
Stamford Bridge Ches W 81 P11
Stamford Bridge E R Yk 98 E9
Stamfordham Nthumb 112 G6
Stamford Hill Gt Lon 36 H3
Stanah Lancs 88 D2
Stanborough Herts 50 F8
Stanbridge C Beds 49 Q10
Stanbridge Dorset 12 H4
Stanbury C Brad 90 C3
Stand Bury 89 M9
Stand N Lans 126 D4
Standburn Falk 126 G3
Standeford Staffs 58 D3
Standen Kent 26 E3
Standen Street Kent 26 D5
Standerwick Somset 20 F4
Standford Hants 23 M8
Standingstone Cumb 100 E4
Standish Gloucs 32 E3
Standish Wigan 88 H8
Standish Lower Ground Wigan 88 H9
Standlake Oxon 34 C4
Standon Hants 22 D9
Standon Herts 51 J6
Standon Staffs 70 E7
Standon Green End Herts 51 J7
Standwell Green Suffk 64 G8
Stane N Lans 126 F6
Stanfield Norfk 76 C7
Stanford C Beds 50 E2
Stanford Kent 27 K4
Stanford Shrops 56 E2
Stanford Bishop Herefs 46 C4
Stanford Bridge Worcs 57 N11
Stanford Bridge Wrekin 70 C10
Stanford Dingley W Berk 34 G10
Stanford in the Vale Oxon 34 B6
Stanford le Hope Thurr 37 Q4
Stanford on Avon Nhants 60 C5
Stanford on Soar Notts 72 E6
Stanford on Teme Worcs 57 N11
Stanford Rivers Essex 51 M10
Stanfree Derbys 84 G6
Stanghow R & Cl 105 J7
Stanground C Pete 74 D11
Stanhill Lancs 89 L5
Stanhoe Norfk 75 R3
Stanhope Border 116 G5
Stanhope Dur 103 J3
Stanhope Kent 26 H3
Stanhope Bretby Derbys 71 P10
Stanion Nhants 61 K3
Stanklin Worcs 58 C10
Stanley Derbys 72 C2
Stanley Dur 113 J10
Stanley Notts 84 G8
Stanley P & K 141 R11
Stanley Shrops 57 N8
Stanley Staffs 70 G4
Stanley Wakefd 91 J6
Stanley Common Derbys 72 C2
Stanley Crook Dur 103 N3
Stanley Ferry Wakefd 91 K6
Stanley Gate Lancs 88 E9
Stanley Moor Staffs 70 G4
Stanley Pontlarge Gloucs 47 K8
Stanmer Br & H 24 H9
Stanmore Gt Lon 36 E2
Stanmore Hants 22 E9
Stanmore W Berk 34 E9
Stannersburn Nthumb 111 P3
Stanningfield Suffk 64 B10
Stanningley Leeds 90 G4
Stannington Nthumb 113 K5
Stannington Sheff 84 C3
Stannington Station Nthumb 113 K4
Stansbatch Herefs 45 L2
Stansfield Suffk 63 N10
Stanshope Staffs 71 L4
Stanstead Suffk 52 D2
Stanstead Abbotts Herts 51 J8
Stansted Kent 37 P8
Stansted Airport Essex 51 N6
Stansted Mountfitchet Essex 51 M5
Stanton Derbys 71 P11
Stanton Gloucs 47 L8
Stanton Mons 45 L10
Stanton Nthumb 112 H2
Stanton Staffs 71 L5
Stanton Suffk 64 D7
Stanton by Bridge Derbys 72 B5
Stanton by Dale Derbys 72 D3
Stanton Drew BaNES 19 Q2
Stanton Fitzwarren Swindn 33 N6
Stanton Harcourt Oxon 34 D3
Stanton Hill Notts 84 G8
Stanton in Peak Derbys 84 B8
Stanton Lacy Shrops 56 H9
Stanton Lees Derbys 84 C8
Stanton Long Shrops 57 K6
Stanton-on-the-Wolds Notts 72 G4
Stanton Prior BaNES 20 C2
Stanton St Bernard Wilts 21 L2
Stanton St John Oxon 34 G3
Stanton St Quintin Wilts 32 H9
Stanton Street Suffk 64 D8
Stanton under Bardon Leics 72 D8
Stanton upon Hine Heath Shrops 69 Q10
Stanton Wick BaNES 20 B2
Stantway Gloucs 32 D2
Stanwardine in the Field Shrops 69 M10
Stanwardine in the Wood Shrops 69 M9
Stanway Essex 52 F7
Stanway Gloucs 47 L8
Stanway Green Essex 52 G7
Stanway Green Suffk 65 J7
Stanwell Surrey 36 C6
Stanwell Moor Surrey 36 B6
Stanwick Nhants 61 L6
Stanwick St John N York 103 N8
Stanwix Cumb 110 H9
Staoinebrig W Isls 168 c14
Stape N York 98 F2
Stapehill Dorset 13 J4
Stapeley Ches E 70 B5
Stapenhill Staffs 71 P10
Staple Kent 39 N10
Staple Cross Devon 18 D10
Staplecross E Susx 26 C7
Staplefield W Susx 24 G5
Staple Fitzpaine Somset 19 J11
Stapleford Cambs 62 G10
Stapleford Herts 50 H7
Stapleford Leics 73 L7
Stapleford Lincs 85 Q9
Stapleford Notts 72 D3
Stapleford Wilts 21 L7
Stapleford Abbotts Essex 37 M2
Stapleford Tawney Essex 51 M11
Staplegrove Somset 18 H9
Staplehay Somset 18 H10
Staple Hill Worcs 58 E10
Staplehurst Kent 26 C3
Staplers IoW 14 F9
Staplestreet Kent 39 J9
Stapleton Cumb 111 K6
Stapleton Herefs 56 E11
Stapleton Leics 72 C11
Stapleton N York 103 Q8
Stapleton Shrops 56 H4
Stapleton Somset 19 N10
Stapley Somset 10 D2
Staploe Bed 61 Q8
Staplow Herefs 46 C6
Star Fife 135 J7
Star IoA 79 J10
Star Pembks 41 P4
Star Somset 19 M3
Starbeck N York 97 M9
Starbotton N York 96 E6
Starcross Devon 9 N8
Stareton Warwks 59 M10
Starkholmes Derbys 84 D9
Starlings Green Essex 51 L4
Starr's Green E Susx 26 C8
Starston Norfk 65 J5
Start Devon 7 L10
Startforth Dur 103 K7
Startley Wilts 32 H8
Statenborough Kent 39 P10
Statham Warrtn 82 E7
Stathe Somset 19 L9
Stathern Leics 73 K4
Station Town Dur 104 D3
Staughton Green Cambs 61 P7
Staughton Highway Cambs 61 P8
Staunton Gloucs 31 Q2
Staunton Gloucs 46 E9
Staunton in the Vale Notts 73 L2
Staunton on Arrow Herefs 45 M2
Staunton on Wye Herefs 45 M6
Staveley Cumb 101 N11
Staveley Derbys 84 F6
Staveley N York 97 N8
Staveley-in-Cartmel Cumb 94 H3
Staverton Devon 7 K6
Staverton Gloucs 46 G10
Staverton Nhants 60 B8
Staverton Wilts 20 G2
Staverton Bridge Gloucs 46 G10
Stawell Somset 19 L7
Stawley Somset 18 E10
Staxigoe Highld 167 Q6
Staxton N York 99 L5
Staylittle Cerdgn 54 E7
Staylittle Powys 55 K6
Staynall Lancs 88 D2
Staythorpe Notts 85 N10
Stead C Brad 96 H11
Stean N York 96 G6
Stearsby N York 98 C6
Steart Somset 19 J5
Stebbing Essex 51 Q6
Stebbing Green Essex 51 Q6
Stechford Birm 58 H7
Stede Quarter Kent 26 E4
Stedham W Susx 23 N10
Steel Nthumb 112 D9
Steel Cross E Susx 25 M4
Steelend Fife 134 C9
Steele Road Border 111 K2
Steel Green Cumb 94 D5
Steel Heath Shrops 69 P7
Steen's Bridge Herefs 45 Q3
Steep Hants 23 K9
Steephill IoW 14 F11
Steep Lane Calder 90 C6
Steeple Dorset 12 F8
Steeple Essex 52 F11
Steeple Ashton Wilts 20 H3
Steeple Aston Oxon 48 E9
Steeple Barton Oxon 48 D10
Steeple Bumpstead Essex 51 Q2
Steeple Claydon Bucks 49 K9
Steeple Gidding Cambs 61 P4
Steeple Langford Wilts 21 K7
Steeple Morden Cambs 50 G2
Steep Marsh Hants 23 L9
Steeton C Brad 90 C2
Stein Highld 152 D6
Stella Gatesd 113 J8
Stelling Minnis Kent 27 K2
Stembridge Somset 19 M10
Stenalees Cnwll 4 G10
Stenhouse D & G 115 R9
Stenhousemuir Falk 133 P11
Stenigot Lincs 86 H4
Stenscholl Highld 152 H4
Stenson Fields Derbys 72 A4
Stenton E Loth 128 G5
Steornabhagh W Isls 168 j4
Stepaside Pembks 41 M9
Stepford D & G 109 J4
Stepney Gt Lon 37 J4
Stepping Hill Stockp 83 K7
Steppingley C Beds 50 B3
Stepps N Lans 126 B4
Sternfield Suffk 65 M9
Stert Wilts 21 K3
Stetchworth Cambs 63 K9
Stevenage Herts 50 F5
Steven's Crouch E Susx 26 B8
Stevenston N Ayrs 124 H9
Steventon Hants 22 F5
Steventon Oxon 34 E6
Steventon End Essex 51 N2
Stevington Bed 49 Q4
Stewartby Bed 50 B2
Stewartfield S Lans 125 Q6
Stewarton Ag & B 120 C8
Stewarton E Ayrs 125 L8
Stewkley Bucks 49 N9
Stewley Somset 19 K11
Stewton Lincs 87 L3
Steyne Cross IoW 14 H9
Steyning W Susx 24 E8
Steynton Pembks 40 H9
Stibb Cnwll 16 C9
Stibbard Norfk 76 D6
Stibb Cross Devon 16 G9
Stibb Green Wilts 21 P2
Stibbington Cambs 74 A11
Stichill Border 118 D3
Sticker Cnwll 3 P3
Stickford Lincs 87 L8
Sticklepath Devon 8 F6
Sticklepath Somset 18 D7
Stickling Green Essex 51 L4
Stickney Lincs 87 K9
Stiffkey Norfk 76 D3
Stifford Clays Thurr 37 P4
Stifford's Bridge Herefs 46 D5
Stiff Street Kent 38 E9
Stile Bridge Kent 26 C2
Stileway Somset 19 N6
Stilligarry W Isls 168 c14
Stillingfleet N York 91 P2
Stillington N York 98 B7
Stillington S on T 104 C6
Stilton Cambs 61 Q3
Stinchcombe Gloucs 32 D5
Stinsford Dorset 11 Q6
Stiperstones Shrops 56 F4
Stirchley Birm 58 G8
Stirchley Wrekin 57 M3
Stirling Abers 159 R9
Stirling Stirlg 133 M9
Stirling Castle Stirlg 133 M9
Stirling Services Stirlg 133 N10
Stirtloe Cambs 61 Q7
Stirton N York 96 E10
Stisted Essex 52 D7
Stitchcombe Wilts 33 P11
Stithians Cnwll 3 J6
Stivichall Covtry 59 M9
Stixwould Lincs 86 G7
St Michaels Fife 135 L3
Stoak Ches W 81 N10
Stobo Border 116 H3
Stoborough Dorset 12 F7
Stoborough Green Dorset 12 F7
Stobs Castle Border 117 Q9
Stobswood Nthumb 119 P11
Stock Essex 51 Q11
Stock N Som 19 N2
Stockbridge Hants 22 C7
Stockbriggs S Lans 126 D10
Stockbury Kent 38 D9
Stockcross W Berk 34 D11
Stockdalewath Cumb 110 G11
Stocker's Hill Kent 38 G11
Stockerston Leics 73 L11
Stock Green Worcs 47 J3
Stocking Herefs 46 B8
Stockingford Warwks 59 M6
Stocking Pelham Herts 51 L5
Stockland Devon 10 E4
Stockland Bristol Somset 18 H6
Stockland Green Kent 25 N2
Stockleigh English Devon 9 L3
Stockleigh Pomeroy Devon 9 L4
Stockley Wilts 33 J11
Stockley Hill Herefs 45 M7
Stocklinch Somset 19 L11
Stockmoor Herefs 45 M4
Stockport Stockp 83 J6
Stocksbridge Sheff 90 H11
Stocksfield Nthumb 112 G8
Stockton Herefs 45 Q2
Stockton Norfk 65 M3
Stockton Shrops 56 D4
Stockton Shrops 57 N5
Stockton Warwks 48 D2
Stockton Wilts 21 J7
Stockton Wrekin 70 D11
Stockton Brook Staffs 70 G4
Stockton Heath Warrtn 82 D7
Stockton-on-Tees S on T 104 D7
Stockton on Teme Worcs 57 N11
Stockton on the Forest C York 98 D9
Stockwell Gloucs 32 H2
Stockwell End Wolves 58 C4
Stockwell Heath Staffs 71 K10
Stockwood Bristl 32 B11
Stockwood Dorset 11 M3
Stock Wood Worcs 47 K3
Stodday Lancs 95 K9
Stodmarsh Kent 39 M9
Stody Norfk 76 F4
Stoer Highld 164 B11
Stoford Somset 11 M2
Stoford Wilts 21 L7
Stogumber Somset 18 E7
Stogursey Somset 18 H6
Stoke Covtry 59 N9
Stoke Devon 16 C7
Stoke Hants 15 K6
Stoke Hants 22 D4
Stoke Medway 38 D7
Stoke Abbott Dorset 11 K4
Stoke Albany Nhants 60 H3
Stoke Ash Suffk 64 G7
Stoke Bardolph Notts 72 G2
Stoke Bliss Worcs 46 C2
Stoke Bruerne Nhants 49 K5
Stoke-by-Clare Suffk 52 B3
Stoke-by-Nayland Suffk 52 G4
Stoke Canon Devon 9 M5
Stoke Charity Hants 22 E7
Stoke Climsland Cnwll 5 P7
Stoke Cross Herefs 46 B4
Stoke D'Abernon Surrey 36 D9
Stoke Doyle Nhants 61 M3
Stoke Dry Rutlnd 73 M11
Stoke Edith Herefs 46 B6
Stoke End Warwks 59 J5
Stoke Farthing Wilts 21 L9
Stoke Ferry Norfk 75 P10
Stoke Fleming Devon 7 M9
Stokeford Dorset 12 E7
Stoke Gabriel Devon 7 M7
Stoke Gifford S Glos 32 B9
Stoke Golding Leics 72 B11
Stoke Goldington M Keyn 49 M5
Stoke Green Bucks 35 Q8
Stokeham Notts 85 N5
Stoke Hammond Bucks 49 N9
Stoke Heath Shrops 70 B9
Stoke Heath Worcs 58 D11
Stoke Holy Cross Norfk 77 J11
Stokeinteignhead Devon 7 N4
Stoke Lacy Herefs 46 B5
Stoke Lyne Oxon 48 G9
Stoke Mandeville Bucks 35 M2
Stokenchurch Bucks 35 L5
Stoke Newington Gt Lon 36 H3
Stokenham Devon 7 L10
Stoke-on-Trent C Stke 70 F5
Stoke Orchard Gloucs 46 H9
Stoke Poges Bucks 35 Q8
Stoke Pound Worcs 58 E11
Stoke Prior Herefs 45 Q3
Stoke Prior Worcs 58 D11
Stoke Rivers Devon 17 L4
Stoke Rochford Lincs 73 N5
Stoke Row Oxon 35 J8
Stoke St Gregory Somset 19 K9
Stoke St Mary Somset 19 J10
Stoke St Michael Somset 20 C5
Stoke St Milborough Shrops 57 K8
Stokesay Shrops 56 G8
Stokesby Norfk 77 N9
Stokesley N York 104 F9
Stoke sub Hamdon Somset 19 N11
Stoke Talmage Oxon 35 J5
Stoke Trister Somset 20 D9
Stoke upon Tern Shrops 70 A9
Stoke-upon-Trent C Stke 70 F5
Stoke Wake Dorset 12 C3
Stoke Wharf Worcs 58 E11
Stolford Somset 18 H5
Stondon Massey Essex 51 N10
Stone Bucks 35 L2
Stone Gloucs 32 C5
Stone Kent 37 N6
Stone Rothm 85 J3
Stone Somset 19 Q8
Stone Staffs 70 G8
Stone Worcs 58 C9
Stonea Cambs 62 G2
Stone Allerton Somset 19 L4
Ston Easton Somset 20 B4
Stonebridge N Som 19 L3
Stonebridge Norfk 64 C3
Stonebridge Warwks 59 K8
Stone Bridge Corner C Pete 74 E10
Stonebroom Derbys 84 F9
Stone Chair Calder 90 E5
Stone Cross E Susx 25 M5
Stone Cross E Susx 25 P10
Stone Cross E Susx 25 P4
Stone Cross Kent 25 M3
Stone Cross Kent 26 H4
Stone Cross Kent 39 P10
Stonecross Green Suffk 63 P9
Stonecrouch Kent 26 B5
Stone-edge-Batch N Som 31 N10
Stoneferry C KuH 93 K4
Stonefield Castle Hotel Ag & B 123 Q5
Stonegate E Susx 25 Q5
Stonegate N York 105 L9
Stonegrave N York 98 D5
Stonehall Worcs 46 G5

Stonehaugh Nthumb 111 Q5
Stonehaven Abers 151 M10
Stonehenge Wilts 21 M6
Stone Hill Donc 92 A9
Stonehouse C Plym 6 D8
Stone House Cumb 95 R3
Stonehouse Gloucs 32 F3
Stonehouse Nthumb 111 N9
Stonehouse S Lans 126 D8
Stone in Oxney Kent 26 F6
Stoneleigh Warwks 59 M10
Stoneley Green Ches E 69 R4
Stonely Cambs 61 P7
Stoner Hill Hants 23 K9
Stonesby Leics 73 L6
Stonesfield Oxon 48 C11
Stones Green Essex 53 L6
Stone Street Kent 37 N10
Stone Street Suffk 52 G4
Stone Street Suffk 52 H3
Stone Street Suffk 65 M5
Stonestreet Green Kent 27 J4
Stonethwaite Cumb 101 J8
Stonewells Moray 157 P4
Stonewood Kent 37 N6
Stoneybridge W Isls 168 c14
Stoneybridge Worcs 58 D9
Stoneyburn W Loth 126 H5
Stoney Cross Hants 13 N2
Stoneygate C Leic 72 G10
Stoneyhills Essex 38 G2
Stoneykirk D & G 106 E7
Stoney Middleton Derbys 84 B5
Stoney Stanton Leics 59 Q6
Stoney Stoke Somset 20 D8
Stoney Stratton Somset 20 C7
Stoney Stretton Shrops 56 F3
Stoneywood C Aber 151 M5
Stoneywood Falk 133 M11
Stonham Aspal Suffk 64 G10
Stonnall Staffs 58 G4
Stonor Oxon 35 K7
Stonton Wyville Leics 73 J11
Stony Cross Herefs 46 D5
Stony Cross Herefs 57 J11
Stonyford Hants 22 B11
Stony Houghton Derbys 84 G7
Stony Stratford M Keyn 49 L6
Stonywell Staffs 58 G2
Stoodleigh Devon 17 M5
Stoodleigh Devon 18 B11
Stop 24 Services Kent 27 K4
Stopham W Susx 24 B7
Stopsley Luton 50 D6
Stoptide Cnwll 4 E6
Storeton Wirral 81 L8
Storeyard Green Herefs 46 D6
Storey Arms Powys 44 D10
Stornoway W Isls 168 j4
Stornoway Airport W Isls 168 j4
Storridge Herefs 46 E5
Storrington W Susx 24 C8
Storth Cumb 95 K5
Storwood E R Yk 92 B2
Stotfield Moray 157 N3
Stotfold C Beds 50 F3
Stottesdon Shrops 57 M8
Stoughton Leics 72 G10
Stoughton Surrey 23 Q4
Stoughton W Susx 15 M4
Stoulton Worcs 46 H5
Stourbridge Dudley 58 C8
Stourhead Wilts 20 E8
Stourpaine Dorset 12 E3
Stourport-on-Severn Worcs 57 Q10
Stour Provost Dorset 20 E10
Stour Row Dorset 20 F10
Stourton Leeds 91 J4
Stourton Staffs 58 C8
Stourton Warwks 47 Q7
Stourton Wilts 20 E8
Stourton Caundle Dorset 20 D11
Stout Somset 19 M8
Stove Shet 169 r11
Stoven Suffk 65 N5
Stow Border 117 P2
Stow Lincs 85 Q4
Stow Bardolph Norfk 75 M9
Stow Bedon Norfk 64 D2
Stowbridge Norfk 75 M9
Stow-cum-Quy Cambs 62 H8
Stowe Gloucs 31 Q3
Stowe Shrops 56 E10
Stowe by Chartley Staffs 71 J9
Stowehill Nhants 60 D9
Stowell Somset 20 C10
Stowey BaNES 19 Q3
Stowford Devon 8 B5
Stowford Devon 8 B7
Stowford Devon 10 C7
Stowford Devon 17 M3
Stowlangtoft Suffk 64 D8
Stow Longa Cambs 61 P6
Stow Maries Essex 38 D2
Stowmarket Suffk 64 E10
Stow-on-the-Wold Gloucs 47 N9
Stowting Kent 27 K3
Stowting Common Kent 27 K3
Stowupland Suffk 64 F9
Straanruie Highld 148 H4
Strachan Abers 150 H9
Strachur Ag & B 131 M7
Stradbroke Suffk 65 J7
Stradbrook Wilts 20 H4
Stradishall Suffk 63 N10
Stradsett Norfk 75 N9
Stragglethorpe Lincs 86 B10
Stragglethorpe Notts 72 H3
Straight Soley Wilts 34 B10
Straiton Mdloth 127 P4
Straiton S Ayrs 114 G7
Straloch Abers 151 M3
Straloch P & K 141 P5
Stramshall Staffs 71 K7
Strang IoM 80 e6
Strangeways Salfd 82 H5
Strangford Herefs 46 A9
Stranraer D & G 106 E5
Strata Florida Cerdgn 54 G11
Stratfield Mortimer W Berk 23 J2
Stratfield Saye Hants 23 J2
Stratfield Turgis Hants 23 J3
Stratford C Beds 61 Q11
Stratford Gt Lon 37 J4
Stratford St Andrew Suffk 65 M9
Stratford St Mary Suffk 52 H5
Stratford sub Castle Wilts 21 M8
Stratford Tony Wilts 21 L9
Stratford-upon-Avon Warwks 47 P3
Strath Highld 160 B11
Strathan Highld 160 H2
Strathan Highld 165 N4
Strathaven S Lans 126 C9
Strathblane Stirlg 125 P2
Strathcanaird Highld 161 K6
Strathcarron Highld 154 B9
Strathcoil Ag & B 138 B11
Strathdon Abers 150 B5
Strathkinness Fife 135 M4
Strathloanhead W Loth 126 G3
Strathmashie House Highld 147 P9
Strathmiglo Fife 134 G6
Strathpeffer Highld 155 N6
Strathtay P & K 141 M7
Strathwhillan N Ayrs 121 K4
Strathy Highld 166 D4
Strathy Inn Highld 166 D3
Strathyre Stirlg 132 H4
Stratton Cnwll 16 C10
Stratton Dorset 11 P6
Stratton Gloucs 33 K4
Stratton Audley Oxon 48 H9
Stratton-on-the-Fosse Somset 20 C4
Stratton St Margaret Swindn 33 N7
Stratton St Michael Norfk 65 J3
Stratton Strawless Norfk 77 J7
Stream Somset 18 E7
Streat E Susx 25 J7
Streatham Gt Lon 36 H6
Streatley C Beds 50 C5
Streatley W Berk 34 G8
Street Devon 10 D7
Street Lancs 95 L10
Street N York 105 K10
Street Somset 19 N7
Street Ashton Warwks 59 Q8
Street Dinas Shrops 69 K7
Street End E Susx 25 P6
Street End Kent 39 K11
Street End W Susx 15 N7
Street Gate Gatesd 113 K9
Streethay Staffs 58 H2
Street Houses N York 98 A11
Streetlam N York 104 B11
Street Lane Derbys 84 E11
Streetly Wsall 58 G5
Streetly End Cambs 63 K11
Street on the Fosse Somset 20 B7
Strefford Shrops 56 G7
Strelitz P & K 142 B10
Strelley Notts 72 E2
Strensall C York 98 C8
Strensham Worcs 46 H6
Strensham Services (northbound) Worcs 46 G6
Strensham Services (southbound) Worcs 46 H6
Stretcholt Somset 19 J6
Strete Devon 7 L9
Stretford Herefs 45 N3
Stretford Herefs 45 Q3
Stretford Traffd 82 G6
Strethall Essex 51 L3
Stretham Cambs 62 H6
Strettington W Susx 15 N5
Stretton Ches W 69 M4
Stretton Derbys 84 E8
Stretton Rutlnd 73 N7
Stretton Staffs 58 C2
Stretton Staffs 71 P9
Stretton Warrtn 82 D8
Stretton en le Field Leics 59 M2
Stretton Grandison Herefs 46 B6
Stretton-on-Dunsmore Warwks 59 P10
Stretton on Fosse Warwks 47 P7
Stretton Sugwas Herefs 45 P6
Stretton under Fosse Warwks 59 Q8
Stretton Westwood Shrops 57 K5
Strichen Abers 159 M6
Strines Stockp 83 L7
Stringston Somset 18 G6
Strixton Nhants 61 K8
Stroat Gloucs 31 Q5
Strollamus Highld 145 J2
Stroma Highld 167 Q1
Stromeferry Highld 153 R11
Stromness Ork 169 b6
Stronaba Highld 146 G11
Stronachlachar Stirlg 132 E5
Stronafian Ag & B 131 L11
Stronchrubie Highld 161 L3
Strone Ag & B 131 P11
Strone Highld 146 E11
Strone Highld 147 N2
Stronmilchan Ag & B 131 P2
Stronsay Ork 169 f4
Stronsay Airport Ork 169 f4
Strontian Highld 138 E5
Strood Kent 26 E5
Strood Medway 38 B8
Strood Green Surrey 36 F11
Strood Green W Susx 24 B6
Stroud Gloucs 32 G3
Stroud Hants 23 K10
Stroude Surrey 36 B7
Stroud Green Essex 38 E3
Stroud Green Gloucs 32 F3
Stroxton Lincs 73 N4
Struan Highld 152 E10
Struan P & K 141 K4
Strubby Lincs 87 N4
Strumpshaw Norfk 77 L10
Strutherhill S Lans 126 D8
Struthers Fife 135 K6
Struy Highld 155 M9
Stryd-y-Facsen IoA 78 E8
Stryt-issa Wrexhm 69 J5
Stuartfield Abers 159 N8
Stubbers Green Wsall 58 F4
Stubbington Hants 14 G6
Stubbins Lancs 89 M7
Stubbs Green Norfk 65 K2
Stubhampton Dorset 12 F2
Stubley Derbys 84 D5
Stubshaw Cross Wigan 82 C5
Stubton Lincs 85 Q11
Stuckton Hants 13 L2
Studfold N York 96 B7
Stud Green W & M 35 N9
Studham C Beds 50 B7
Studholme Cumb 110 E9
Studland Dorset 12 H8
Studley Warwks 47 L2
Studley Wilts 33 J10
Studley Common Warwks 47 L2
Studley Roger N York 97 L7
Studley Royal N York 97 L6
Studley Royal Park & Fountains Abbey N York 97 L7
Stuntney Cambs 63 J5
Stunts Green E Susx 25 P8
Sturbridge Staffs 70 E8
Sturgate Lincs 85 Q3
Sturmer Essex 51 Q2
Sturminster Common Dorset 12 C2
Sturminster Marshall Dorset 12 G4
Sturminster Newton Dorset 12 C2
Sturry Kent 39 L9
Sturton N Linc 92 G10
Sturton by Stow Lincs 85 Q4
Sturton le Steeple Notts 85 N4
Stuston Suffk 64 G6
Stutton N York 91 M2
Stutton Suffk 53 L5
Styal Ches E 82 H8
Stydd Lancs 89 K3
Stynie Moray 157 Q5
Styrrup Notts 85 K2
Succoth Ag & B 132 B6
Suckley Worcs 46 D4
Suckley Green Worcs 46 D4
Sudborough Nhants 61 L4
Sudbourne Suffk 65 N11
Sudbrook Lincs 73 P2
Sudbrook Mons 31 P7
Sudbrooke Lincs 86 D5
Sudbury Derbys 71 M8
Sudbury Gt Lon 36 E3
Sudbury Suffk 52 E3
Sudden Rochdl 89 P8
Sudgrove Gloucs 32 H3
Suffield N York 99 K2
Suffield Norfk 77 J5
Sugdon Wrekin 69 R11
Sugnall Staffs 70 D8
Sugwas Pool Herefs 45 P6
Suisnish Highld 145 J4
Sulby IoM 80 e3
Sulgrave Nhants 48 G6
Sulham W Berk 34 H10
Sulhamstead W Berk 34 H11
Sulhamstead Abbots W Berk 34 H11
Sulhamstead Bannister W Berk 34 H11
Sullington W Susx 24 C8
Sullom Shet 169 q6
Sullom Voe Shet 169 r6
Sully V Glam 30 G11
Sumburgh Airport Shet 169 q12
Summerbridge N York 97 K8
Summercourt Cnwll 4 D10
Summerfield Norfk 75 Q3
Summerfield Worcs 58 B10
Summer Heath Bucks 35 K6
Summerhill Pembks 41 N9
Summerhill Staffs 58 G3
Summer Hill Wrexhm 69 K4
Summerhouse Darltn 103 P7
Summerlands Cumb 95 L3
Summerley Derbys 84 E5
Summersdale W Susx 15 N5
Summerseat Bury 89 M8
Summertown Oxon 34 F3
Summit Oldham 89 Q9
Summit Rochdl 89 Q7
Sunbiggin Cumb 102 C9
Sunbury-on-Thames Surrey 36 D7
Sundaywell D & G 108 H4
Sunderland Ag & B 122 B7
Sunderland Cumb 100 G3
Sunderland Lancs 95 J9
Sunderland Sundld 113 N9
Sunderland Bridge Dur 103 Q3
Sundhope Border 117 L5
Sundon Park Luton 50 C5
Sundridge Kent 37 L9
Sunk Island E R Yk 93 N7
Sunningdale W & M 35 Q11
Sunninghill W & M 35 P11
Sunningwell Oxon 34 E4
Sunniside Dur 103 M3
Sunniside Gatesd 113 K9
Sunny Brow Dur 103 N4
Sunnyhill C Derb 72 A4
Sunnyhurst Bl w D 89 K6
Sunnylaw Stirlg 133 M8
Sunnymead Oxon 34 F3
Sunton Wilts 21 P4
Surbiton Gt Lon 36 E7
Surfleet Lincs 74 E5
Surfleet Seas End Lincs 74 E5
Surlingham Norfk 77 L10
Surrex Essex 52 E7
Sustead Norfk 76 H4
Susworth Lincs 92 D10
Sutcombe Devon 16 E9
Sutcombemill Devon 16 E9
Suton Norfk 64 F2
Sutterby Lincs 87 L6
Sutterton Lincs 74 E3
Sutton C Beds 62 B11
Sutton C Pete 74 A11
Sutton Cambs 62 F5
Sutton Devon 7 J10
Sutton Devon 8 H4
Sutton Donc 91 P8
Sutton E Susx 25 L11
Sutton Gt Lon 36 G8
Sutton Kent 27 P2
Sutton N York 91 M5
Sutton Norfk 77 M7
Sutton Notts 73 K3
Sutton Oxon 34 D3
Sutton Pembks 40 H7
Sutton Shrops 57 J2
Sutton Shrops 57 N7
Sutton Shrops 69 L9
Sutton Shrops 70 B8
Sutton St Hel 82 B6
Sutton Staffs 70 D10
Sutton Suffk 53 P2
Sutton W Susx 23 Q11
Sutton Abinger Surrey 36 D11
Sutton-at-Hone Kent 37 N7
Sutton Bassett Nhants 60 G2
Sutton Benger Wilts 32 H9
Sutton Bingham Somset 11 L2
Sutton Bonington Notts 72 E6
Sutton Bridge Lincs 75 J6
Sutton Cheney Leics 72 C10
Sutton Coldfield Birm 58 H5
Sutton Courtenay Oxon 34 F6
Sutton Crosses Lincs 74 H6
Sutton cum Lound Notts 85 L4
Sutton Fields Notts 72 D5
Sutton Green Surrey 36 B10
Sutton Green Wrexhm 69 M5
Sutton Howgrave N York 97 M5
Sutton-in-Ashfield Notts 84 G9
Sutton-in-Craven N York 90 C2
Sutton in the Elms Leics 60 B2
Sutton Lane Ends Ches E 83 K10
Sutton Maddock Shrops 57 N4
Sutton Mallet Somset 19 L7
Sutton Mandeville Wilts 21 J9
Sutton Manor St Hel 81 Q6
Sutton Marsh Herefs 45 R6
Sutton Montis Somset 20 B10
Sutton-on-Hull C KuH 93 K4
Sutton on Sea Lincs 87 P4
Sutton-on-the-Forest N York 98 B8
Sutton on the Hill Derbys 71 N8
Sutton on Trent Notts 85 N7
Sutton Poyntz Dorset 11 Q8
Sutton St Edmund Lincs 74 G8
Sutton St James Lincs 74 G7
Sutton St Nicholas Herefs 45 Q5
Sutton Scotney Hants 22 E7
Sutton Street Kent 38 D10
Sutton-under-Brailes Warwks 48 B7
Sutton-under-Whitestonecliffe N York 97 Q4
Sutton upon Derwent E R Yk 98 E11
Sutton Valence Kent 26 D2
Sutton Veny Wilts 20 H6
Sutton Waldron Dorset 20 G11
Sutton Weaver Ches W 82 B9
Sutton Wick BaNES 19 Q3
Sutton Wick Oxon 34 E6
Swaby Lincs 87 L5
Swadlincote Derbys 71 P11
Swaffham Norfk 75 R9
Swaffham Bulbeck Cambs 63 J8
Swaffham Prior Cambs 63 J8
Swafield Norfk 77 K5
Swainby N York 104 E10
Swainshill Herefs 45 P6
Swainsthorpe Norfk 77 J11
Swainswick BaNES 32 E11
Swalcliffe Oxon 48 C7
Swalecliffe Kent 39 K8
Swallow Lincs 93 L10
Swallow Beck Lincs 86 B7
Swallowcliffe Wilts 21 J9
Swallowfield Wokham 23 K2
Swallownest Rothm 84 G3
Swallows Cross Essex 51 P11
Swampton Hants 22 D4
Swanage Dorset 12 H9
Swanbourne Bucks 49 M9
Swanbridge V Glam 30 G11
Swancote Shrops 57 N6
Swan Green Ches W 82 F10
Swanland E R Yk 92 G5
Swanley Kent 37 M7
Swanley Village Kent 37 M7
Swanmore Hants 22 G11
Swannington Leics 72 C7
Swannington Norfk 76 G8
Swanpool Lincs 86 C7
Swanscombe Kent 37 P6
Swansea Swans 29 J6
Swansea Airport Swans 28 G6
Swansea West Services Swans 28 H5
Swan Street Essex 52 E6
Swanton Abbot Norfk 77 K6
Swanton Morley Norfk 76 E8
Swanton Novers Norfk 76 E5
Swanton Street Kent 38 E10
Swan Valley Nhants 60 F9
Swan Village Sandw 58 E6
Swanwick Derbys 84 F10
Swanwick Hants 14 F5
Swarby Lincs 73 Q2
Swardeston Norfk 77 J11
Swarkestone Derbys 72 B5
Swarland Nthumb 119 N10
Swarraton Hants 22 G7
Swartha C Brad 96 G11
Swarthmoor Cumb 94 F5
Swaton Lincs 74 B3
Swavesey Cambs 62 E7
Sway Hants 13 N5
Swayfield Lincs 73 P6
Swaythling C Sotn 22 D11
Sweet Green Worcs 46 B2
Sweetham Devon 9 L5
Sweethaws E Susx 25 M5
Sweetlands Corner Kent 26 C2
Sweets Cnwll 5 K2
Sweetshouse Cnwll 4 H9
Swefling Suffk 65 L9
Swepstone Leics 72 B8
Swerford Oxon 48 C8
Swettenham Ches E 82 H11
Swffryd Blae G 30 H5
Swift's Green Kent 26 E3
Swilland Suffk 64 H11
Swillbrook Lancs 88 F4
Swillington Leeds 91 K4
Swimbridge Devon 17 L5
Swimbridge Newland Devon 17 L5
Swinbrook Oxon 33 Q2
Swincliffe Kirk 90 G5
Swincliffe N York 97 K9
Swincombe Devon 17 M3
Swindale Cumb 101 P8
Swinden N York 96 C10
Swinderby Lincs 85 Q8
Swindon Gloucs 46 H9
Swindon Nthumb 119 J11
Swindon Staffs 58 C6
Swindon Swindn 33 M8
Swine E R Yk 93 K3
Swinefleet E R Yk 92 C6
Swineford S Glos 32 C11
Swineshead Bed 61 N7
Swineshead Lincs 74 D2
Swineshead Bridge Lincs 74 D2
Swiney Highld 167 M9
Swinford Leics 60 C5
Swinford Oxon 34 D3
Swingfield Minnis Kent 27 M3
Swingfield Street Kent 27 M3
Swingleton Green Suffk 52 G2
Swinhoe Nthumb 119 P5
Swinhope Lincs 93 M11
Swinithwaite N York 96 F3
Swinmore Common Herefs 46 C6
Swinscoe Staffs 71 L5
Swinside Cumb 100 H6
Swinstead Lincs 73 Q6
Swinthorpe Lincs 86 E4
Swinton Border 129 L10
Swinton N York 97 K5
Swinton N York 98 F6
Swinton Rothm 91 M11
Swinton Salfd 82 G4
Swithland Leics 72 F8
Swordale Highld 155 Q4
Swordland Highld 145 N9
Swordly Highld 166 B4
Sworton Heath Ches E 82 E8
Swyddffynnon Cerdgn 54 F11
Swyncombe Oxon 35 J6
Swynnerton Staffs 70 F7
Swyre Dorset 11 L7
Sycharth Powys 68 H9
Sychnant Powys 55 M9
Sychtyn Powys 55 M3
Sydallt Wrexhm 69 K3
Syde Gloucs 33 J2
Sydenham Gt Lon 37 J6
Sydenham Oxon 35 K4
Sydenham Damerel Devon 5 Q6
Sydenhurst Surrey 23 Q8
Syderstone Norfk 76 A5
Sydling St Nicholas Dorset 11 N5
Sydmonton Hants 22 E3
Sydnal Lane Shrops 57 Q3
Syerston Notts 85 M11
Syke Rochdl 89 P7
Sykehouse Donc 91 Q7
Syleham Suffk 65 J6
Sylen Carmth 28 F3
Symbister Shet 169 s7
Symington S Ayrs 125 K11
Symington S Lans 116 D3
Symondsbury Dorset 11 J6
Symonds Yat (East) Herefs 45 R11
Symonds Yat (West) Herefs 45 R11
Sympson Green C Brad 90 F3
Synderford Dorset 10 H4
Synod Inn Cerdgn 42 H4
Syre Highld 165 Q8
Syreford Gloucs 47 K10
Syresham Nhants 48 H6
Syston Leics 72 G8
Syston Lincs 73 N2
Sytchampton Worcs 58 B11
Sywell Nhants 60 H7

T

Tabley Hill Ches E 82 F9
Tackley Oxon 48 E11
Tacolneston Norfk 64 G2
Tadcaster N York 91 M2
Taddington Derbys 83 P10
Taddington Gloucs 47 L8
Taddiport Devon 16 H8
Tadley Hants 22 H2
Tadlow Cambs 62 C11
Tadmarton Oxon 48 C7
Tadwick BaNES 32 D10
Tadworth Surrey 36 F9
Tafarnaubach Blae G 30 F2
Tafarn-y-bwlch Pembks 41 L4
Tafarn-y-Gelyn Denbgs 68 G2
Taff's Well Rhondd 30 F8
Tafolwern Powys 55 K4
Taibach Neath 29 L7
Tain Highld 162 H10
Tain Highld 167 M3
Tai'n Lôn Gwynd 66 G4
Tairbeart W Isls 168 g7
Tai'r Bull Powys 44 D9
Tairgwaith Neath 29 K2
Takeley Essex 51 N6
Takeley Street Essex 51 M6
Talachddu Powys 44 F8
Talacre Flints 80 G8
Talaton Devon 9 Q5
Talbenny Pembks 40 F8
Talbot Green Rhondd 30 D8
Talbot Village BCP 13 J6
Taleford Devon 10 B5
Talerddig Powys 55 L4
Talgarreg Cerdgn 42 H4
Talgarth Powys 44 H8
Talisker Highld 152 E11
Talke Staffs 70 E4
Talke Pits Staffs 70 E4
Talkin Cumb 111 L9
Talladale Highld 154 B3
Talla Linnfoots Border 116 G6
Tallaminnock S Ayrs 114 H8
Tallarn Green Wrexhm 69 M6
Tallentire Cumb 100 F3
Talley Carmth 43 M8
Tallington Lincs 74 A9
Tallwrn Wrexhm 69 J5
Talmine Highld 165 N4
Talog Carmth 42 F9
Talsarn Cerdgn 43 K3
Talsarnau Gwynd 67 L7
Talskiddy Cnwll 4 E8
Talwrn IoA 78 H9
Talwrn Wrexhm 69 L5
Tal-y-bont Cerdgn 54 F7
Tal-y-bont Conwy 79 P11
Tal-y-bont Gwynd 67 K10
Tal-y-bont Gwynd 79 L10
Talybont-on-Usk Powys 44 G10
Tal-y-Cafn Conwy 79 P10

Tal-y-coed Mons 45 N11
Tal-y-garn Rhondd 30 D9
Tal-y-llyn Gwynd 54 G3
Talysarn Gwynd 66 H4
Tal-y-Waun Torfn 31 J4
Talywern Powys 55 J4
Tamar Valley Mining District Devon 6 C5
Tamer Lane End Wigan 82 D4
Tamerton Foliot C Plym 6 D6
Tamworth Staffs 59 K4
Tamworth Green Lincs 74 G2
Tamworth Services Warwks 59 K4
Tancred N York 97 Q9
Tancredston Pembks 40 G5
Tandridge Surrey 37 J10
Tanfield Dur 113 J9
Tanfield Lea Dur 113 J10
Tangasdale W Isls 168 b17
Tangiers Pembks 41 J7
Tangley Hants 22 B4
Tangmere W Susx 15 P5
Tan Hill N York 102 G9
Tankerness Ork 169 e6
Tankersley Barns 91 J11
Tankerton Kent 39 K8
Tannach Highld 167 P7
Tannachie Abers 151 K11
Tannadice Angus 142 H6
Tanner's Green Worcs 58 G10
Tannington Suffk 65 J8
Tannochside N Lans 126 C5
Tansley Derbys 84 D9
Tansor Nhants 61 N2
Tantobie Dur 113 J10
Tanton N York 104 F8
Tanwood Worcs 58 D10
Tanworth in Arden Warwks 58 H10
Tan-y-Bwlch Gwynd 67 M6
Tan-y-fron Conwy 68 C2
Tan-y-fron Wrexhm 69 J4
Tan-y-grisiau Gwynd 67 M5
Tan-y-groes Cerdgn 42 E5
Taobh Tuath W Isls 168 e9
Taplow Bucks 35 P8
Tarbert Ag & B 123 L9
Tarbert Ag & B 123 Q6
Tarbert W Isls 168 g7
Tarbet Ag & B 132 C7
Tarbet Highld 145 N9
Tarbet Highld 164 E7
Tarbock Green Knows 81 P7
Tarbolton S Ayrs 114 H2
Tarbrax S Lans 127 J6
Tardebigge Worcs 58 E11
Tarfside Angus 142 H2
Tarland Abers 150 D7
Tarleton Lancs 88 F6
Tarlscough Lancs 88 E8
Tarlton Gloucs 33 J5
Tarnock Somset 19 L4
Tarns Cumb 109 P11
Tarnside Cumb 95 J2
Tarporley Ches W 69 Q2
Tarr Somset 17 R5
Tarrant Crawford Dorset 12 F4
Tarrant Gunville Dorset 12 F2
Tarrant Hinton Dorset 12 F2
Tarrant Keyneston Dorset 12 F4
Tarrant Launceston Dorset 12 F3
Tarrant Monkton Dorset 12 F3
Tarrant Rawston Dorset 12 F3
Tarrant Rushton Dorset 12 F3
Tarring Neville E Susx 25 K10
Tarrington Herefs 46 B6
Tarskavaig Highld 145 J5
Tarves Abers 159 L11
Tarvin Ches W 81 P11
Tarvin Sands Ches W 81 P11
Tasburgh Norfk 65 J2
Tasley Shrops 57 M6
Taston Oxon 48 C10
Tatenhill Staffs 71 N10
Tathall End M Keyn 49 M5
Tatham Lancs 95 N7
Tathwell Lincs 87 K4
Tatsfield Surrey 37 K9
Tattenhall Ches W 69 N3
Tatterford Norfk 76 B6
Tattersett Norfk 76 A6
Tattershall Lincs 86 H9
Tattershall Bridge Lincs 86 G9
Tattershall Thorpe Lincs 86 H9
Tattingstone Suffk 53 K4
Tattingstone White Horse Suffk 53 K4
Tatton Park Ches E 82 F8
Tatworth Somset 10 G3
Tauchers Moray 157 R8
Taunton Somset 18 H10
Taunton Deane Services Somset 18 G10
Taverham Norfk 76 H9
Taverners Green Essex 51 N7
Tavernspite Pembks 41 N8
Tavistock Devon 6 D4
Tavistock Devon 6 D4
Taw Green Devon 8 G5
Tawstock Devon 17 K6
Taxal Derbys 83 M9
Tay Bridge C Dund 135 L2
Taychreggan Hotel Ag & B 131 L3
Tay Forest Park P & K 141 J5
Tayinloan Ag & B 123 L10
Taynton Gloucs 46 D10
Taynton Oxon 33 P2
Taynuilt Ag & B 139 J11
Tayport Fife 135 M2
Tayvallich Ag & B 130 E10
Tealby Lincs 86 G2
Tealing Angus 142 G10
Team Valley Gatesd 113 K9
Teangue Highld 145 L6
Teanord Highld 155 Q5
Tebay Cumb 102 B10
Tebay Services Cumb 102 B9
Tebworth C Beds 49 Q9
Tedburn St Mary Devon 9 K6
Teddington Gloucs 47 J8
Teddington Gt Lon 36 E6
Tedstone Delamere Herefs 46 C3
Tedstone Wafer Herefs 46 C3
Teesport R & Cl 104 F6
Teesside Park S on T 104 E7
Teeton Nhants 60 E6
Teffont Evias Wilts 21 J8
Teffont Magna Wilts 21 J8
Tegryn Pembks 41 P4
Teigh Rutlnd 73 M7
Teigncombe Devon 8 G7
Teigngrace Devon 7 M4
Teignmouth Devon 7 N4
Teindside Border 117 N9
Telford Wrekin 57 M3
Telford Services Shrops 57 N3
Tellisford Somset 20 F3
Telscombe E Susx 25 K10
Telscombe Cliffs E Susx 25 K10
Tempar P & K 140 G6
Templand D & G 109 N3
Temple Cnwll 5 J7
Temple Mdloth 127 Q6
Temple Balsall Solhll 59 K9
Temple Bar Cerdgn 43 K4
Temple Cloud BaNES 20 B3
Templecombe Somset 20 D10
Temple End Suffk 63 L10
Temple Ewell Kent 27 N3
Temple Grafton Warwks 47 M3
Temple Guiting Gloucs 47 L9
Temple Herdewyke Warwks 48 C4
Temple Hirst N York 91 Q6
Temple Normanton Derbys 84 F7
Temple of Fiddes Abers 151 L11
Temple Sowerby Cumb 102 B5
Templeton Devon 9 L2
Templeton Pembks 41 M8
Templetown Dur 112 H10
Tempsford C Beds 61 Q10
Tenbury Wells Worcs 57 K11
Tenby Pembks 41 M10
Tendring Essex 53 K7
Tendring Green Essex 53 K6
Tendring Heath Essex 53 K6
Ten Mile Bank Norfk 75 L11
Tenpenny Heath Essex 53 J7
Tenterden Kent 26 E5
Terling Essex 52 C8
Tern Wrekin 69 R11
Ternhill Shrops 70 A8
Terregles D & G 109 K5
Terrington N York 98 D6
Terrington St Clement Norfk 75 L6
Terrington St John Norfk 75 K8
Terry's Green Warwks 58 H10
Teston Kent 38 B11
Testwood Hants 14 C4
Tetbury Gloucs 32 G6
Tetbury Upton Gloucs 32 G5
Tetchill Shrops 69 L8
Tetcott Devon 5 N2
Tetford Lincs 87 K6
Tetney Lincs 93 P10
Tetney Lock Lincs 93 P10
Tetsworth Oxon 35 J4
Tettenhall Wolves 58 C4
Tettenhall Wood Wolves 58 C5
Teversal Notts 84 G8
Teversham Cambs 62 G9
Teviothead Border 117 N9
Tewin Herts 50 G8
Tewin Wood Herts 50 G7
Tewkesbury Gloucs 46 G8
Teynham Kent 38 G9
Thackley C Brad 90 F3
Thackthwaite Cumb 100 F6
Thackthwaite Cumb 101 M5
Thainstone Abers 151 K4
Thakeham W Susx 24 D7
Thame Oxon 35 K3
Thames Ditton Surrey 36 E7
Thamesmead Gt Lon 37 L4
Thamesport Medway 38 E7
Thanington Kent 39 K10
Thankerton S Lans 116 D3
Tharston Norfk 64 H3
Thatcham W Berk 34 F11
Thatto Heath St Hel 81 Q6
Thaxted Essex 51 P4
Theakston N York 97 M3
Thealby N Linc 92 E7
Theale Somset 19 N5
Theale W Berk 34 H10
Thearne E R Yk 93 J3
The Bank Ches E 70 E3
The Beeches Gloucs 33 K4
Theberton Suffk 65 N8
The Blythe Staffs 71 J9
The Bog Shrops 56 F5
The Bourne Worcs 47 J3
The Braes Highld 153 J11
The Bratch Staffs 58 C6
The Broad Herefs 45 P2
The Broads 77 P10
The Brunt E Loth 128 H5
The Bryn Mons 31 K3
The Bungalow IoM 80 e4
The Burf Worcs 57 Q11
The Camp Gloucs 32 H3
The Chequer Wrexhm 69 N6
The City Bed 61 P9
The City Bucks 35 L5
The Common Oxon 47 Q9
The Common Wilts 21 P8
The Common Wilts 33 K7
The Corner Kent 26 B3
The Cronk IoM 80 d2
Theddingworth Leics 60 E3
Theddlethorpe All Saints Lincs 87 N3
Theddlethorpe St Helen Lincs 87 N3
The Deep C KuH 93 J5
The Den N Ayrs 125 J7
The Forge Herefs 45 L3
The Forstal Kent 26 H4
The Fouralls Shrops 70 B8
The Green Cumb 94 D4
The Green Essex 52 C8
The Green N York 105 L9
The Green Wilts 20 G8
The Grove Worcs 46 G6
The Haven W Susx 24 C4
The Haw Gloucs 46 F9
The Headland Hartpl 104 F4
The Hendre Mons 31 N2
The Hill Cumb 94 D4
The Holt Wokham 35 M9
The Hundred Herefs 45 Q2
Thelbridge Cross Devon 9 J2
The Leacon Kent 26 G5
The Lee Bucks 35 P4
The Lhen IoM 80 e1
Thelnetham Suffk 64 E6
The Lochs Moray 157 Q5
Thelveton Norfk 64 H5
Thelwall Warrtn 82 E7
The Marsh Powys 56 E5
Themelthorpe Norfk 76 F7
The Middles Dur 113 K10
The Moor Kent 26 C6
The Mumbles Swans 28 H7
The Murray S Lans 125 Q7
The Mythe Gloucs 46 G8
The Narth Mons 31 P3
The Neuk Abers 151 J8
Thenford Nhants 48 F6
Theobald's Green Wilts 33 K11
The Quarry Gloucs 32 D5
The Quarter Kent 26 E3
The Reddings Gloucs 46 H10
Therfield Herts 50 H3
The Rhôs Powys 44 H8
The Ross P & K 133 M3
The Sands Surrey 23 N5
The Shoe Wilts 32 F10
The Smithies Shrops 57 M5
The Spring Warwks 59 L10
The Square Torfn 31 J5
The Stair Kent 37 P11
The Stocks Kent 26 F6
The Straits Hants 23 L7
The Strand Wilts 20 H3
Thetford Norfk 64 B5
Thetford Forest Park 63 P3
Thethwaite Cumb 101 L2
The Towans Cnwll 2 F6
The Vauld Herefs 45 Q5
The Wyke Shrops 57 N3
Theydon Bois Essex 51 K11
Theydon Mount Essex 51 L11
Thicket Priory N York 92 A2
Thickwood Wilts 32 F10
Thimbleby Lincs 86 H6
Thimbleby N York 104 D11
Thingwall Wirral 81 K8
Thirkleby N York 97 Q5
Thirlby N York 97 Q4
Thirlestane Border 128 F10
Thirn N York 97 K3
Thirsk N York 97 P4
Thirtleby E R Yk 93 L4
Thistleton Lancs 88 E3
Thistleton Rutlnd 73 N7
Thistley Green Suffk 63 L5
Thixendale N York 98 G8
Thockrington Nthumb 112 E5
Tholomas Drove Cambs 74 H9
Tholthorpe N York 97 Q7
Thomas Chapel Pembks 41 M9
Thomas Close Cumb 101 M2
Thomastown Abers 158 E10
Thompson Norfk 64 C2
Thong Kent 37 Q6
Thongsbridge Kirk 90 F9
Thoralby N York 96 F3
Thoresby Notts 85 K6
Thoresthorpe Lincs 87 N5
Thoresway Lincs 93 L11
Thorganby Lincs 93 M11
Thorganby N York 92 A2
Thorgill N York 105 K11
Thorington Suffk 65 N7
Thorington Street Suffk 52 H4
Thorlby N York 96 E10
Thorley Herts 51 L7
Thorley IoW 14 C9
Thorley Houses Herts 51 L6
Thorley Street IoW 14 C9
Thormanby N York 97 Q6
Thornaby-on-Tees S on T 104 E7
Thornage Norfk 76 F4
Thornborough Bucks 49 K8
Thornborough N York 97 L5
Thornbury C Brad 90 F4
Thornbury Devon 16 G10
Thornbury Herefs 46 B3
Thornbury S Glos 32 B6
Thornby Cumb 110 E10
Thornby Nhants 60 E5
Thorncliff Staffs 71 J3
Thorncombe Dorset 10 H4
Thorncombe Street Surrey 23 Q6
Thorncott Green C Beds 61 Q11
Thorncross IoW 14 D10
Thorndon Suffk 64 G8
Thorndon Cross Devon 8 D6
Thorne Donc 92 A8
Thorne Coffin Somset 19 P11
Thornecroft Devon 7 K5
Thornehillhead Devon 16 G8
Thorner Leeds 91 K2
Thornes Staffs 58 G4
Thornes Wakefd 91 J7
Thorne St Margaret Somset 18 F10
Thorney Bucks 36 B5
Thorney C Pete 74 E10
Thorney Notts 85 Q6
Thorney Somset 19 M10
Thorney Hill Hants 13 M5
Thorney Island W Susx 15 L6
Thorney Toll Cambs 74 F10
Thornfalcon Somset 19 J10
Thornford Dorset 11 N2
Thorngrafton Nthumb 111 Q7
Thorngrove Somset 19 L8
Thorngumbald E R Yk 93 M5
Thornham Norfk 75 P2
Thornham Magna Suffk 64 G7
Thornham Parva Suffk 64 G7
Thornhaugh C Pete 73 R10
Thornhill C Sotn 14 E4
Thornhill Caerph 30 G8
Thornhill Cumb 100 D9
Thornhill D & G 116 B11
Thornhill Derbys 83 Q8
Thornhill Kirk 90 H7
Thornhill Stirlg 133 K7
Thornhill Lees Kirk 90 G7
Thornhills Calder 90 F6
Thornholme E R Yk 99 N8
Thornicombe Dorset 12 E4
Thornington Nthumb 118 G4
Thornley Dur 103 M3
Thornley Dur 104 C3
Thornley Gate Nthumb 112 B9
Thornliebank E Rens 125 P6
Thorns Suffk 63 M9
Thornsett Derbys 83 M7
Thorns Green Ches E 82 G8
Thornthwaite Cumb 100 H5
Thornthwaite N York 97 J9
Thornton Angus 142 F8
Thornton Bucks 49 K7
Thornton C Brad 90 D4
Thornton E R Yk 98 F11
Thornton Fife 134 H8
Thornton Lancs 88 C2
Thornton Leics 72 D9
Thornton Lincs 86 H7
Thornton Middsb 104 E8
Thornton Nthumb 129 P10
Thornton Pembks 40 H9
Thornton Sefton 81 L4
Thornton Curtis N Linc 93 J7
Thorntonhall S Lans 125 P6
Thornton Heath Gt Lon 36 H7
Thornton Hough Wirral 81 L8
Thornton-in-Craven N York 96 D11
Thornton in Lonsdale N York 95 P6
Thornton-le-Beans N York 97 N2
Thornton-le-Clay N York 98 D7
Thornton-le-Dale N York 98 G4
Thornton le Moor Lincs 92 H11
Thornton-le-Moor N York 97 N3
Thornton-le-Moors Ches W 81 N10
Thornton-le-Street N York 97 P3
Thorntonloch E Loth 129 K5
Thornton Rust N York 96 E3
Thornton Steward N York 97 J3
Thornton Watlass N York 97 K3
Thornwood Common Essex 51 L10
Thornydykes Border 128 G10
Thornythwaite Cumb 101 L6
Thoroton Notts 73 K2
Thorp Arch Leeds 97 P11
Thorpe Derbys 71 M4
Thorpe E R Yk 99 K11
Thorpe Lincs 87 N4
Thorpe N York 96 F8
Thorpe Norfk 65 N2
Thorpe Notts 85 N11
Thorpe Surrey 36 B7
Thorpe Abbotts Norfk 64 H6
Thorpe Acre Leics 72 E7
Thorpe Arnold Leics 73 K6
Thorpe Audlin Wakefd 91 M7
Thorpe Bassett N York 98 H6
Thorpe Bay Sthend 38 F4
Thorpe by Water Rutlnd 73 M11
Thorpe Common Rothm 91 K11
Thorpe Constantine Staffs 59 L3
Thorpe End Norfk 77 K9
Thorpe Green Essex 53 L7
Thorpe Green Lancs 88 H6
Thorpe Green Suffk 64 C11
Thorpe Hesley Rothm 91 K11
Thorpe in Balne Donc 91 P8
Thorpe Langton Leics 60 F2
Thorpe Larches Dur 104 C5
Thorpe Lea Surrey 36 B6
Thorpe le Fallows Lincs 86 B4
Thorpe-le-Soken Essex 53 L7
Thorpe le Street E R Yk 92 D2
Thorpe Malsor Nhants 60 H5
Thorpe Mandeville Nhants 48 F6
Thorpe Market Norfk 77 J4
Thorpe Marriot Norfk 76 H8
Thorpe Morieux Suffk 64 C11
Thorpeness Suffk 65 P10
Thorpe on the Hill Leeds 91 J5
Thorpe on the Hill Lincs 86 B7
Thorpe Park Surrey 36 B7
Thorpe St Andrew Norfk 77 K10
Thorpe St Peter Lincs 87 N8
Thorpe Salvin Rothm 84 H4
Thorpe Satchville Leics 73 J8
Thorpe Thewles S on T 104 C6
Thorpe Tilney Lincs 86 F9
Thorpe Underwood N York 97 Q9
Thorpe Underwood Nhants 60 G4
Thorpe Waterville Nhants 61 M4
Thorpe Willoughby N York 91 P4
Thorpland Norfk 75 M9
Thorrington Essex 53 J8
Thorverton Devon 9 M4
Thrales End C Beds 50 D7
Thrandeston Suffk 64 G6
Thrapston Nhants 61 L5
Threapland Cumb 100 G3
Threapland N York 96 E8
Threapwood Ches W 69 M6
Threapwood Staffs 71 J6
Threapwood Head Staffs 71 J6
Threave S Ayrs 114 F6
Three Ashes Herefs 45 Q10
Three Bridges W Susx 24 G3
Three Burrows Cnwll 3 K4
Three Chimneys Kent 26 D4
Three Cocks Powys 44 H7
Three Crosses Swans 28 G6
Three Cups Corner E Susx 25 P6
Three Gates Worcs 46 C2
Threehammer Common Norfk 77 L8
Three Hammers Cnwll 5 L4
Three Holes Norfk 75 K10
Threekingham Lincs 74 A3
Three Leg Cross E Susx 25 Q4
Three Legged Cross Dorset 13 J3
Three Mile Cross Wokham 35 K11
Threemilestone Cnwll 3 K4
Threemiletown W Loth 127 K2
Three Oaks E Susx 26 D9
Threlkeld Cumb 101 K5
Threshers Bush Essex 51 L9
Threshfield N York 96 E8
Thrigby Norfk 77 P9
Thringarth Dur 102 H6
Thringstone Leics 72 C7
Thrintoft N York 97 M2
Thriplow Cambs 62 F11
Throapham Rothm 84 H3
Throckenhalt Lincs 74 G9
Throcking Herts 50 H4
Throckley N u Ty 113 J7
Throckmorton Worcs 47 J4
Throop BCP 13 K5
Throop Dorset 12 D6
Throphill Nthumb 112 H3
Thropton Nthumb 119 K10
Throsk Stirlg 133 P9
Througham Gloucs 32 H3
Throughgate D & G 109 J4
Throwleigh Devon 8 G6
Throwley Kent 38 G10
Throwley Forstal Kent 38 G11
Thrumpton Notts 72 E4
Thrumpton Notts 85 M4
Thrumster Highld 167 P7
Thrunscoe NE Lin 93 P9
Thrunton Nthumb 119 L8
Thrup Oxon 33 Q5
Thrupp Gloucs 32 G4
Thrupp Oxon 48 E11
Thrushelton Devon 8 B7
Thrussington Leics 72 H7
Thruxton Hants 21 Q5
Thruxton Herefs 45 N8
Thrybergh Rothm 91 M11
Thulston Derbys 72 C4
Thundersley Essex 38 C4
Thurcaston Leics 72 F8
Thurcroft Rothm 84 G3
Thurdon Cnwll 16 D9
Thurgarton Norfk 76 H5
Thurgarton Notts 85 L11
Thurgoland Barns 90 H10
Thurlaston Leics 72 E11
Thurlaston Warwks 59 Q10
Thurlbear Somset 19 J10
Thurlby Lincs 74 A7
Thurlby Lincs 86 B8
Thurlby Lincs 87 N5
Thurleigh Bed 61 N9
Thurlestone Devon 6 H10
Thurloxton Somset 19 J8
Thurlstone Barns 90 G10
Thurlton Norfk 65 N2
Thurlwood Ches E 70 E3
Thurmaston Leics 72 G9
Thurnby Leics 72 G10
Thurne Norfk 77 N8
Thurnham Kent 38 D10
Thurning Nhants 61 N4
Thurning Norfk 76 F6
Thurnscoe Barns 91 M9
Thurrock Services Thurr 37 N5
Thursby Cumb 110 F10
Thursden Lancs 89 Q4
Thursford Norfk 76 D5
Thursley Surrey 23 P7
Thurso Highld 167 K3
Thurstaston Wirral 81 J8
Thurston Suffk 64 C8
Thurston Clough Oldham 90 B9
Thurstonfield Cumb 110 F9
Thurstonland Kirk 90 F8
Thurston Planch Suffk 64 C9
Thurton Norfk 77 L11
Thurvaston Derbys 71 N7
Thuxton Norfk 76 E10
Thwaite N York 102 G11
Thwaite Suffk 64 G8
Thwaite Head Cumb 94 G2
Thwaites C Brad 90 D2
Thwaite St Mary Norfk 65 L2
Thwaites Brow C Brad 90 D2
Thwing E R Yk 99 L6
Tibbermore P & K 134 C3
Tibbers D & G 116 B11
Tibberton Gloucs 46 E10
Tibberton Worcs 46 H3
Tibberton Wrekin 70 B10
Tibenham Norfk 64 G4
Tibshelf Derbys 84 F8
Tibshelf Services Derbys 84 F8
Tibthorpe E R Yk 99 K9
Ticehurst E Susx 25 Q4
Tichborne Hants 22 G8
Tickencote Rutlnd 73 P9
Tickenham N Som 31 N10
Tickford End M Keyn 49 N6
Tickhill Donc 85 J2
Ticklerton Shrops 56 H6
Ticknall Derbys 72 B6
Tickton E R Yk 93 J2
Tidbury Green Solhll 58 H9
Tidcombe Wilts 21 Q3
Tiddington Oxon 34 H4
Tiddington Warwks 47 P3
Tiddleywink Wilts 32 G9
Tidebrook E Susx 25 P4
Tideford Cnwll 5 P10
Tideford Cross Cnwll 5 N9
Tidenham Gloucs 31 Q5
Tideswell Derbys 83 Q9
Tidmarsh W Berk 34 H10
Tidmington Warwks 47 Q7
Tidpit Hants 21 L11
Tidworth Wilts 21 P5
Tiers Cross Pembks 40 H8
Tiffield Nhants 49 K4
Tigerton Angus 143 J5
Tigh a' Ghearraidh W Isls 168 c10
Tigharry W Isls 168 c10
Tighnabruaich Ag & B 124 B3
Tigley Devon 7 K6
Tilbrook Cambs 61 N7
Tilbury Thurr 37 P5
Tilbury Dock Thurr 37 P5
Tilbury Green Essex 52 B3
Tilbury Juxta Clare Essex 52 C3
Tile Cross Birm 59 J7
Tile Hill Covtry 59 L9
Tilehouse Green Solhll 59 J9
Tilehurst Readg 35 J10
Tilford Surrey 23 N6
Tilgate W Susx 24 G4
Tilgate Forest Row W Susx 24 G4
Tilham Street Somset 19 Q7
Tillers Green Gloucs 46 C8
Tillicoultry Clacks 133 Q8
Tillietudlem S Lans 126 E8
Tillingham Essex 52 G11
Tillington Herefs 45 P6
Tillington W Susx 23 Q10
Tillington Common Herefs 45 P5
Tillybirloch Abers 150 H6
Tillyfourie Abers 150 G5
Tillygreig Abers 151 M3
Tillyrie P & K 134 E6
Tilmanstone Kent 39 P11
Tilney All Saints Norfk 75 L7

Tilney High End Norfk 75 L7
Tilney St Lawrence Norfk 75 K8
Tilshead Wilts 21 K5
Tilstock Shrops 69 P7
Tilston Ches W 69 N4
Tilstone Bank Ches W 69 Q3
Tilstone Fearnall Ches W 69 Q2
Tilsworth C Beds 49 Q10
Tilton on the Hill Leics 73 J9
Tiltups End Gloucs 32 F5
Tilty Essex 51 N5
Timberland Lincs 86 F9
Timbersbrook Ches E 70 F2
Timberscombe Somset 18 C6
Timble N York 97 J10
Timewell Devon 18 C9
Timpanheck D & G 110 F6
Timperley Traffd 82 G7
Timsbury BaNES 20 C3
Timsbury Hants 22 B10
Timsgarry W Isls 168 f4
Timsgearraidh W Isls 168 f4
Timworth Suffk 64 B8
Timworth Green Suffk 64 B8
Tincleton Dorset 12 C6
Tindale Cumb 111 M9
Tingewick Bucks 49 J8
Tingley Leeds 90 H5
Tingrith C Beds 50 B4
Tingwall Airport Shet 169 r9
Tingwall Ork 169 d4
Tinhay Devon 5 P4
Tinker's Hill Hants 22 D5
Tinkersley Derbys 84 C8
Tinsley Sheff 84 F2
Tinsley Green W Susx 24 G3
Tintagel Cnwll 4 H4
Tintern Mons 31 P4
Tintinhull Somset 19 N11
Tintwistle Derbys 83 M5
Tinwald D & G 109 M4
Tinwell RutInd 73 Q9
Tippacott Devon 17 P2
Tipp's End Norfk 75 K11
Tiptoe Hants 13 N5
Tipton Sandw 58 E6
Tipton Green Sandw 58 E6
Tipton St John Devon 10 B6
Tiptree Essex 52 E8
Tiptree Heath Essex 52 E8
Tirabad Powys 44 B6
Tircoed Swans 28 H4
Tiree Ag & B 136 C7
Tiree Airport Ag & B 136 C7
Tiretigan Ag & B 123 M7
Tirley Gloucs 46 F9
Tiroran Ag & B 137 M10
Tirphil Caerph 30 F4
Tirril Cumb 101 P5
Tir-y-fron Flints 69 J3
Tisbury Wilts 20 H9
Tisman's Common W Susx 24 C4
Tissington Derbys 71 M4
Titchberry Devon 16 C6
Titchfield Hants 14 F5
Titchfield Common Hants 14 F5
Titchmarsh Nhants 61 M5
Titchwell Norfk 75 Q2
Tithby Notts 72 H3
Titley Herefs 45 L2
Titmore Green Herts 50 F5
Titsey Surrey 37 K10
Titson Cnwll 16 C11
Tittensor Staffs 70 F7
Tittleshall Norfk 76 B7
Titton Worcs 58 B11
Tiverton Ches W 69 Q2
Tiverton Devon 9 N2
Tivetshall St Margaret Norfk 64 H4
Tivetshall St Mary Norfk 64 H4
Tivington Somset 18 B5
Tivy Dale Barns 90 H9
Tixall Staffs 70 H10
Tixover RutInd 73 P10
Toab Shet 169 q12
Toadhole Derbys 84 E9
Toadmoor Derbys 84 D10
Tobermory Ag & B 137 N4
Toberonochy Ag & B 130 E6
Tobha Mòr W Isls 168 c14
Tocher Abers 158 G11
Tochieneal Moray 158 D4
Tockenham Wilts 33 K9
Tockenham Wick Wilts 33 K8
Tocketts R & Cl 104 H7
Tockholes Bl w D 89 K6
Tockington S Glos 32 B7
Tockwith N York 97 Q10
Todber Dorset 20 E11
Todburn Nthumb 119 M11
Toddington C Beds 50 B5
Toddington Gloucs 47 K8
Toddington Services C Beds 50 B5
Todds Green Herts 50 F5
Todenham Gloucs 47 P7
Todhills Angus 142 G10
Todhills Cumb 110 G8
Todhills Dur 103 P4
Todhills Rest Area Cumb 110 G8
Todmorden Calder 89 Q6
Todwick Rothm 84 G4
Toft Cambs 62 E9
Toft Ches E 82 G9
Toft Lincs 73 R7
Toft Shet 169 r6
Toft Warwks 59 Q10
Toft Hill Dur 103 N5
Toft Hill Lincs 86 H8
Toft Monks Norfk 65 N3
Toft next Newton Lincs 86 D3
Toftrees Norfk 76 B6
Toftwood Norfk 76 D9
Togston Nthumb 119 P10
Tokavaig Highld 145 K5
Tokers Green Oxon 35 K9
Tolastadh bho Thuath W Isls 168 k3
Toldish Cnwll 4 E10
Tolland Somset 18 F8
Tollard Farnham Dorset 21 J11
Tollard Royal Wilts 20 H11
Toll Bar Donc 91 P9
Tollbar End Covtry 59 N9
Toller Fratrum Dorset 11 M5
Toller Porcorum Dorset 11 M5
Tollerton N York 97 R8
Tollerton Notts 72 G4
Toller Whelme Dorset 11 L4
Tollesbury Essex 52 G9
Tolleshunt D'Arcy Essex 52 F9
Tolleshunt Knights Essex 52 F9
Tolleshunt Major Essex 52 F9
Tollingham E R Yk 92 D3
Toll of Birness Abers 159 P11
Tolpuddle Dorset 12 C6
Tolworth Gt Lon 36 E7
Tomatin Highld 148 E2
Tomchrasky Highld 146 H5
Tomdoun Highld 146 F7
Tomich Highld 147 J2
Tomich Highld 155 P8
Tomich Highld 156 B3
Tomich Highld 162 E5
Tomintoul Moray 149 M4
Tomlow Warwks 48 E2
Tomnacross Highld 155 P9
Tomnavoulin Moray 149 N2
Tompkin Staffs 70 G4
Ton Mons 31 K4
Ton Mons 31 L5
Tonbridge Kent 37 N11
Tondu Brdgnd 29 N8
Tonedale Somset 18 F10
Tonfanau Gwynd 54 D4
Tong C Brad 90 G4
Tong Kent 38 G10
Tong Shrops 57 P3
Tong W Isls 168 j4
Tonge Leics 72 C6
Tong Green Kent 38 G11
Tongham Surrey 23 N5
Tongland D & G 108 E10
Tong Norton Shrops 57 P3
Tongue Highld 165 N5
Tongue End Lincs 74 C7
Tongwynlais Cardif 30 F8
Tonmawr Neath 29 M5
Tonna Neath 29 L5
Ton-teg Rhondd 30 E7
Tonwell Herts 50 H7
Tonypandy Rhondd 30 C6
Tonyrefail Rhondd 30 D7
Toot Baldon Oxon 34 G4
Toot Hill Essex 51 M10
Toothill Hants 22 C11
Toothill Swindn 33 M8
Tooting Gt Lon 36 G6
Tooting Bec Gt Lon 36 G6
Topcliffe N York 97 N5
Topcroft Norfk 65 K3
Topcroft Street Norfk 65 K3
Top End Bed 61 M8
Topham Donc 91 Q7
Top of Hebers Rochdl 89 P9
Toppesfield Essex 52 B4
Toprow Norfk 64 H2
Topsham Devon 9 N7
Top-y-rhos Flints 69 J3
Torbeg N Ayrs 120 G6
Torboll Highld 162 H7
Torbreck Highld 156 A9
Torbryan Devon 7 L5
Torcastle Highld 139 L2
Torcross Devon 7 L10
Tore Highld 155 R7
Torfrey Cnwll 5 J11
Torinturk Ag & B 123 P7
Torksey Lincs 85 P5
Torlundy Highld 139 L2
Tormarton S Glos 32 E9
Tormore N Ayrs 120 G5
Tornagrain Highld 156 D7
Tornaveen Abers 150 G6
Torness Highld 147 P2
Toronto Dur 103 N4
Torpenhow Cumb 100 H3
Torphichen W Loth 126 H3
Torphins Abers 150 G7
Torpoint Cnwll 6 C7
Torquay Torbay 7 N6
Torquhan Border 128 C10
Torr Devon 6 F8
Torran Highld 153 K8
Torrance E Duns 125 Q3
Torranyard N Ayrs 125 K9
Torre Somset 18 D7
Torridon Highld 154 B6
Torridon House Highld 153 R6
Torrin Highld 145 J3
Torrisdale Ag & B 120 E4
Torrisdale Highld 165 Q4
Torrish Highld 163 M3
Torrisholme Lancs 95 K8
Torrobull Highld 162 D6
Torry C Aber 151 N6
Torryburn Fife 134 C10
Torteval Guern 10 a2
Torthorwald D & G 109 M5
Tortington W Susx 24 B10
Torton Worcs 58 B10
Tortworth S Glos 32 D6
Torvaig Highld 152 H9
Torver Cumb 94 F2
Torwood Falk 133 N11
Torwoodlee Border 117 P3
Torworth Notts 85 L3
Tosberry Devon 16 D7
Toscaig Highld 153 N10
Toseland Cambs 62 B8
Tosside Lancs 95 R9
Tostock Suffk 64 D9
Totaig Highld 152 C7
Tote Highld 152 G8
Tote Highld 153 J5
Tote Hill W Susx 23 N10
Totford Hants 22 G7
Tothill Lincs 87 M4
Totland IoW 13 P7
Totley Sheff 84 D5
Totley Brook Sheff 84 D4
Totnes Devon 7 L6
Toton Notts 72 E4
Totronald Ag & B 136 F4
Totscore Highld 152 F4
Tottenham Gt Lon 36 H2
Tottenhill Norfk 75 M8
Totteridge Gt Lon 36 F2
Totternhoe C Beds 49 Q10
Tottington Bury 89 M8
Tottleworth Lancs 89 L4
Totton Hants 14 C4
Touchen End W & M 35 N9
Toulston N York 91 M2
Toulton Somset 18 G8
Toulvaddie Highld 163 K10
Tovil Kent 38 C11
Towan Cnwll 3 Q4
Towan Cnwll 4 D7
Toward Ag & B 124 E4
Toward Quay Ag & B 124 E4
Towcester Nhants 49 J5
Towednack Cnwll 2 D6
Tower of London Gt Lon 36 H4
Towersey Oxon 35 K3
Towie Abers 150 C5
Tow Law Dur 103 M3
Town End Cambs 74 H11
Town End Cumb 95 J4
Town End Cumb 101 K9
Town End Cumb 102 B5
Townend W Duns 125 K2
Towngate Cumb 111 K11
Towngate Lincs 74 B8
Town Green Lancs 88 E9
Town Green Norfk 77 M9
Townhead Barns 83 Q4
Townhead Cumb 100 E3
Town Head Cumb 101 M10
Townhead Cumb 102 B4
Townhead D & G 109 M3
Town Head N York 96 B9
Townhead of Greenlaw D & G 108 F8
Townhill Fife 134 E10
Town Kelloe Dur 104 C3
Townlake Devon 5 Q7
Town Lane Wigan 82 E5
Town Littleworth E Susx 25 K7
Town of Lowton Wigan 82 D5
Town Row E Susx 25 N4
Towns End Hants 22 G3
Townsend Somset 10 H2
Townshend Cnwll 2 F7
Town Street Suffk 63 N3
Townwell S Glos 32 D6
Town Yetholm Border 118 F5
Towthorpe C York 98 C9
Towthorpe E R Yk 98 H8
Towton N York 91 M3
Towyn Conwy 80 D9
Toxteth Lpool 81 M7
Toynton All Saints Lincs 87 L8
Toynton Fen Side Lincs 87 L8
Toynton St Peter Lincs 87 M8
Toy's Hill Kent 37 L10
Trabboch E Ayrs 114 H3
Trabbochburn E Ayrs 115 J3
Traboe Cnwll 3 J9
Tracebridge Somset 18 E10
Tradespark Highld 156 F6
Trafford Park Traffd 82 G5
Trallong Powys 44 D9
Tranent E Loth 128 C5
Tranmere Wirral 81 L7
Trantelbeg Highld 166 E6
Trantlemore Highld 166 E6
Tranwell Nthumb 113 J4
Trap Carmth 43 N11
Traprain E Loth 128 F4
Trap's Green Warwks 58 H11
Trapshill W Berk 22 C2
Traquair Border 117 L4
Trash Green W Berk 35 J11
Trawden Lancs 89 Q3
Trawscoed Cerdgn 54 F10
Trawsfynydd Gwynd 67 N7
Trealaw Rhondd 30 D6
Treales Lancs 88 E4
Trearddur Bay IoA 78 D9
Treator Cnwll 4 E6
Tre Aubrey V Glam 30 D10
Trebanog Rhondd 30 D6
Trebanos Neath 29 K4
Trebartha Cnwll 5 M6
Trebarwith Cnwll 4 H4
Trebeath Cnwll 5 M4
Trebetherick Cnwll 4 E6
Treborough Somset 18 D7
Trebudannon Cnwll 4 D9
Trebullett Cnwll 5 N6
Treburgett Cnwll 4 H6
Treburley Cnwll 5 P6
Treburrick Cnwll 4 D7
Trebyan Cnwll 4 H9
Trecastle Powys 44 B9
Trecogo Cnwll 5 N5
Trecott Devon 8 F4
Trecwn Pembks 41 J4
Trecynon Rhondd 30 C4
Tredaule Cnwll 5 L5
Tredavoe Cnwll 2 D8
Tredegar Blae G 30 F3
Tredethy Cnwll 4 H7
Tredington Gloucs 46 H9
Tredington Warwks 47 Q6
Tredinnick Cnwll 4 E7
Tredinnick Cnwll 4 G10
Tredinnick Cnwll 5 K8
Tredinnick Cnwll 5 L10
Tredinnick Cnwll 5 M10
Tredomen Powys 44 G8
Tredrissi Pembks 41 L2
Tredrizzick Cnwll 4 F6
Tredunnock Mons 31 L6
Tredustan Powys 44 G8
Treen Cnwll 2 B9
Treen Cnwll 2 C6
Treesmill Cnwll 4 H10
Treeton Rothm 84 F3
Trefasser Pembks 40 G3
Trefdraeth IoA 78 G10
Trefecca Powys 44 G8
Trefeglwys Powys 55 M6
Trefenter Cerdgn 54 E11
Treffgarne Pembks 41 J6
Treffgarne Owen Pembks 40 G5
Treffynnon Pembks 40 G5
Trefil Blae G 30 F2
Trefilan Cerdgn 43 K3
Trefin Pembks 40 F4
Treflach Wood Shrops 69 J9
Trefnannau Powys 68 H11
Trefnant Denbgs 80 F10
Trefonen Shrops 69 J9
Trefor Gwynd 66 F5
Trefor IoA 78 F8
Treforest Rhondd 30 E7
Trefrew Cnwll 5 J5
Trefriw Conwy 67 P2
Tregadillett Cnwll 5 M5
Tre-gagle Mons 31 P3
Tregaian IoA 78 H8
Tregare Mons 31 M2
Tregarne Cnwll 3 K9
Tregaron Cerdgn 43 N3
Tregarth Gwynd 79 L11
Tregaswith Cnwll 4 D9
Tregatta Cnwll 4 H4
Tregawne Cnwll 4 G8
Tregeare Cnwll 5 L4
Tregeiriog Wrexhm 68 G8
Tregele IoA 78 F6
Tregellist Cnwll 4 G6
Tregenna Cnwll 3 M5
Tregeseal Cnwll 2 B7
Tregew Cnwll 3 L7
Tre-Gibbon Rhondd 30 C3
Tregidden Cnwll 3 K9
Tregiskey Cnwll 3 Q4
Treglemais Pembks 40 F5
Tregole Cnwll 5 K2
Tregolls Cnwll 3 J6
Tregonce Cnwll 4 E7
Tregonetha Cnwll 4 F9
Tregonning & Gwinear Mining District Cnwll 2 F7
Tregony Cnwll 3 N5
Tregoodwell Cnwll 5 J5
Tregorrick Cnwll 3 Q3
Tregoss Cnwll 4 F9
Tregoyd Powys 44 H7
Tregrehan Mills Cnwll 3 Q3
Tre-groes Cerdgn 42 H6
Tregullon Cnwll 4 H9
Tregunna Cnwll 4 F7
Tregunnon Cnwll 5 L5
Tregurrian Cnwll 4 D8
Tregynon Powys 55 P5
Tre-gynwr Carmth 42 H11
Trehafod Rhondd 30 D6
Trehan Cnwll 5 Q10
Treharris Myr Td 30 E5
Treharrock Cnwll 4 G6
Trehemborne Cnwll 4 D7
Treherbert Carmth 43 L5
Treherbert Rhondd 29 P5
Trehunist Cnwll 5 N9
Trekenner Cnwll 5 N6
Treknow Cnwll 4 H4
Trelan Cnwll 3 J10
Trelash Cnwll 5 K3
Trelassick Cnwll 3 M3
Trelawne Cnwll 5 L11
Trelawnyd Flints 80 F9
Treleague Cnwll 3 K9
Treleaver Cnwll 3 K10
Trelech Carmth 41 Q4
Trelech a'r Betws Carmth 42 F9
Treleddyd-fawr Pembks 40 E5
Trelew Cnwll 3 L6
Trelewis Myr Td 30 F5
Treligga Cnwll 4 G5
Trelights Cnwll 4 F6
Trelill Cnwll 4 G6
Trelinnoe Cnwll 5 N5
Trelion Cnwll 3 N3
Trelissick Cnwll 3 L6
Trellech Mons 31 P3
Trelleck Grange Mons 31 N4
Trelogan Flints 80 G8
Trelow Cnwll 4 E8
Trelowarren Cnwll 3 J9
Trelowia Cnwll 5 M10
Treluggan Cnwll 3 M6
Trelystan Powys 56 D4
Tremadog Gwynd 67 K7
Tremail Cnwll 5 K4
Tremain Cerdgn 42 D5
Tremaine Cnwll 5 L4
Tremar Cnwll 5 M8
Trematon Cnwll 5 P10
Trembraze Cnwll 5 M8
Tremeirchion Denbgs 80 F10
Tremethick Cross Cnwll 2 C7
Tremore Cnwll 4 G9
Tre-Mostyn Flints 80 G9
Trenance Cnwll 3 L9
Trenance Cnwll 4 D8
Trenance Cnwll 4 E7
Trenarren Cnwll 3 Q4
Trench Wrekin 57 M2
Trench Green Oxon 35 J9
Trendeal Cnwll 3 M3
Trendrine Cnwll 2 D6
Treneague Cnwll 4 F7
Trenear Cnwll 2 H7
Treneglos Cnwll 5 L4
Trenerth Cnwll 2 G6
Trenewan Cnwll 5 K11
Trenewth Cnwll 4 H6
Trengune Cnwll 5 K3
Treninnick Cnwll 4 C9
Trenowah Cnwll 4 B10
Trenoweth Cnwll 3 K7
Trent Dorset 19 Q11
Trentham C Stke 70 F6
Trentishoe Devon 17 L2
Trentlock Derbys 72 D4
Trent Port Lincs 85 P4
Trent Vale C Stke 70 F6
Trenwheal Cnwll 2 G7
Treoes V Glam 29 P9
Treorchy Rhondd 30 C5
Trequite Cnwll 4 G6
Tre'r-ddol Cerdgn 54 F6
Trerhyngyll V Glam 30 D9
Trerulefoot Cnwll 5 N10
Tresaith Cerdgn 42 E4
Tresawle Cnwll 3 M4
Tresco IoS 2 b2
Trescott Staffs 58 C5
Trescowe Cnwll 2 F7
Tresean Cnwll 4 B10
Tresham Gloucs 32 E6
Treshnish Isles Ag & B 136 G7
Tresillian Cnwll 3 M4
Tresinney Cnwll 5 J5
Treskinnick Cross Cnwll 5 L2
Tresmeer Cnwll 5 L4
Tresparrett Cnwll 5 J3
Tressait P & K 141 K5
Tresta Shet 169 q8
Tresta Shet 169 t4
Treswell Notts 85 N5
Treswithian Cnwll 2 G5
Tre Taliesin Cerdgn 54 F6
Trethevey Cnwll 4 H4
Trethewey Cnwll 2 B9
Trethomas Caerph 30 G7
Trethosa Cnwll 3 N3
Trethurgy Cnwll 4 G10
Tretio Pembks 40 E5
Tretire Herefs 45 Q10
Tretower Powys 44 H10
Treuddyn Flints 69 J3
Trevadlock Cnwll 5 M6
Trevalga Cnwll 4 H3
Trevalyn Wrexhm 69 L3
Trevanger Cnwll 4 F6
Trevanson Cnwll 4 F7
Trevarrack Cnwll 2 D7
Trevarren Cnwll 4 E9
Trevarrian Cnwll 4 D8
Trevarrick Cnwll 3 P5
Trevarth Cnwll 3 J5
Trevaughan Carmth 41 P7
Tre-vaughan Carmth 42 G10
Treveal Cnwll 2 D5
Treveal Cnwll 4 B10
Treveighan Cnwll 4 H6
Trevellas Downs Cnwll 3 J3
Trevelmond Cnwll 5 L9
Trevemper Cnwll 4 C10
Treveor Cnwll 3 P5
Treverbyn Cnwll 3 M4
Treverbyn Cnwll 4 G10
Treverva Cnwll 3 K7
Trevescan Cnwll 2 B9
Trevethin Torfn 31 J4
Trevia Cnwll 4 H5
Trevigro Cnwll 5 N8
Trevilla Cnwll 3 L6
Trevilson Cnwll 4 C10
Treviscoe Cnwll 4 E10
Treviskey Cnwll 3 N5
Trevithick Cnwll 3 P4
Trevithick Cnwll 4 D9
Trevoll Cnwll 4 C10
Trevone Cnwll 4 D6
Trevor Wrexhm 69 J6
Trevorgans Cnwll 2 C8
Trevorrick Cnwll 4 E7
Trevose Cnwll 4 D6
Trew Cnwll 2 G8
Trewalder Cnwll 4 H5
Trewalkin Powys 44 H8
Trewarmett Cnwll 4 H4
Trewassa Cnwll 5 J4
Trewavas Cnwll 2 F8
Trewavas Mining District Cnwll 2 F8
Treween Cnwll 5 L5
Trewellard Cnwll 2 B7
Trewen Cnwll 5 M5
Trewennack Cnwll 2 H8
Trewent Pembks 41 K11
Trewern Powys 56 D2
Trewetha Cnwll 4 G5
Trewethern Cnwll 4 G6
Trewidland Cnwll 5 M10
Trewillis Cnwll 3 K10
Trewint Cnwll 5 L5
Trewint Cnwll 5 M9
Trewithian Cnwll 3 M6
Trewoodloe Cnwll 5 N7
Trewoon Cnwll 2 H10
Trewoon Cnwll 3 P3
Treworga Cnwll 3 M5
Treworgan Cnwll 3 L4
Treworlas Cnwll 3 M6
Treworld Cnwll 5 J3
Treworthal Cnwll 3 M6
Tre-wyn Mons 45 L10
Treyarnon Cnwll 4 D7
Treyford W Susx 23 M11
Trickett's Cross Dorset 13 J4
Triermain Cumb 111 L7
Triffleton Pembks 41 J6
Trillacott Cnwll 5 M4
Trimdon Dur 104 C4
Trimdon Colliery Dur 104 C3
Trimdon Grange Dur 104 C3
Trimingham Norfk 77 K4
Trimley Lower Street Suffk 53 N4
Trimley St Martin Suffk 53 N4
Trimley St Mary Suffk 53 N4
Trimpley Worcs 57 P9
Trimsaran Carmth 28 E4
Trims Green Herts 51 L7
Trimstone Devon 17 J3
Trinafour P & K 140 H5
Trinant Caerph 30 H5
Tring Herts 35 P2
Tringford Herts 35 P2
Tring Wharf Herts 35 P2
Trinity Angus 143 L5
Trinity Jersey 11 b1
Trinity Gask P & K 134 B4
Triscombe Somset 18 G7
Trislaig Highld 139 K3
Trispen Cnwll 3 L3
Tritlington Nthumb 113 K2
Troan Cnwll 4 D10
Trochry P & K 141 N9
Troedrhiwfuwch Caerph 30 F4
Troedyraur Cerdgn 42 F5
Troedyrhiw Myr Td 30 E4
Trofarth Conwy 80 B10
Trois Bois Jersey 11 b1
Troon Cnwll 2 H6
Troon S Ayrs 125 J11
Tropical World Roundhay Park Leeds 91 J3
Trossachs Stirlg 132 G6
Trossachs Pier Stirlg 132 F6
Troston Suffk 64 B7
Troswell Cnwll 5 M3
Trotshill Worcs 46 G3
Trottiscliffe Kent 37 P8
Trotton W Susx 23 M10
Troughend Nthumb 112 C2
Trough Gate Lancs 89 P6
Troutbeck Cumb 101 L5
Troutbeck Cumb 101 M10
Troutbeck Bridge Cumb 101 M10
Troway Derbys 84 E5
Trowbridge Wilts 20 G3

Trowell Notts 72 D3
Trowell Services Notts 72 D2
Trowle Common Wilts 20 F3
Trowley Bottom Herts 50 C8
Trowse Newton Norfk 77 J10
Troy Leeds 90 G3
Trudoxhill Somset 20 D6
Trull Somset 18 H10
Trumfleet Donc 91 Q8
Trumpan Highld 152 C5
Trumpet Herefs 46 C7
Trumpington Cambs 62 F10
Trumpsgreen Surrey 35 Q11
Trunch Norfk 77 K5
Trunnah Lancs 88 C2
Truro Cnwll 3 L5
Truscott Cnwll 5 M4
Trusham Devon 9 L8
Trusley Derbys 71 P7
Trusthorpe Lincs 87 P4
Trysull Staffs 58 C6
Tubney Oxon 34 D5
Tuckenhay Devon 7 L7
Tuckhill Shrops 57 P7
Tuckingmill Cnwll 2 H5
Tuckingmill Wilts 20 H9
Tuckton BCP 13 K6
Tucoyse Cnwll 3 P4
Tuddenham Suffk 53 L2
Tuddenham Suffk 63 M6
Tudeley Kent 37 P11
Tudhoe Dur 103 Q3
Tudorville Herefs 46 A10
Tudweiliog Gwynd 66 C7
Tuesley Surrey 23 Q6
Tuffley Gloucs 32 F2
Tufton Hants 22 E5
Tufton Pembks 41 K5
Tugby Leics 73 K10
Tugford Shrops 57 K7
Tughall Nthumb 119 P5
Tullibody Clacks 133 P8
Tullich Abers 150 B8
Tullich Highld 147 Q2
Tullich Highld 156 F2
Tulliemet P & K 141 P7
Tulloch Abers 159 K11
Tullochgorm Ag & B 131 K8
Tulloch Station Highld 147 K11
Tullymurdoch P & K 142 B7
Tullynessle Abers 150 F4
Tulse Hill Gt Lon 36 H6
Tumble Carmth 28 F2
Tumbler's Green Essex 52 D6
Tumby Lincs 86 H9
Tumby Woodside Lincs 87 J9
Tummel Bridge P & K 141 J6
Tunbridge Wells Kent 25 N3
Tundergarth D & G 110 C4
Tunga W Isls 168 j4
Tungate Norfk 77 K6
Tunley BaNES 20 C3
Tunstall C Stke 70 F4
Tunstall E R Yk 93 P4
Tunstall Kent 38 E9
Tunstall Lancs 95 N6
Tunstall N York 103 P11
Tunstall Norfk 77 N10
Tunstall Staffs 70 D9
Tunstall Suffk 65 M10
Tunstall Sundld 113 N10
Tunstead Derbys 83 P10
Tunstead Norfk 77 K7
Tunstead Milton Derbys 83 M8
Tunworth Hants 23 J5
Tupsley Herefs 45 Q6
Turgis Green Hants 23 J3
Turkdean Gloucs 47 M11
Tur Langton Leics 60 F2
Turleigh Wilts 20 F2
Turleygreen Shrops 57 P7
Turn Lancs 89 N7
Turnastone Herefs 45 M7
Turnberry S Ayrs 114 D6
Turnchapel C Plym 6 D8
Turnditch Derbys 71 P5
Turner Green Lancs 89 J4
Turner's Green E Susx 25 P7
Turner's Green Warwks 59 J11
Turners Hill W Susx 24 H3
Turners Puddle Dorset 12 D6
Turnford Herts 51 J10
Turnhouse C Edin 127 M3
Turnworth Dorset 12 D3
Turriff Abers 158 H7
Turton Bottoms Bl w D 89 L7
Turves Cambs 74 F11
Turvey Bed 49 P4
Turville Bucks 35 L6
Turville Heath Bucks 35 K6
Turweston Bucks 48 H7
Tushielaw Inn Border 117 L7
Tutbury Staffs 71 N9
Tutnall Worcs 58 E10
Tutshill Gloucs 31 P6
Tuttington Norfk 77 J6
Tutwell Cnwll 5 P6
Tuxford Notts 85 M6
Twatt Ork 169 b4
Twatt Shet 169 q8
Twechar E Duns 126 B2
Tweedbank Border 117 Q4
Tweedmouth Nthumb 129 P9
Tweedsmuir Border 116 G6
Twelveheads Cnwll 3 K5
Twelve Oaks E Susx 25 Q6
Twemlow Green Ches E 82 G11
Twenty Lincs 74 C6
Twerton BaNES 20 D2
Twickenham Gt Lon 36 E6
Twigworth Gloucs 46 F10
Twineham W Susx 24 G7
Twineham Green W Susx 24 G6
Twinhoe BaNES 20 E3
Twinstead Essex 52 E4
Twitchen Devon 17 P5
Twitchen Shrops 56 F9
Twitham Kent 39 N10
Two Bridges Devon 6 G4
Two Dales Derbys 84 C8
Two Gates Staffs 59 K4
Two Mile Ash W Susx 24 D5
Two Mile Oak Cross Devon 7 L5
Two Pots Devon 17 J3
Two Waters Herts 50 C9
Twycross Leics 72 A10
Twycross Zoo Leics 59 M3
Twyford Bucks 49 J9
Twyford Hants 22 E10
Twyford Leics 73 J8
Twyford Lincs 73 N6
Twyford Norfk 76 E7
Twyford Wokham 35 L9
Twyford Common Herefs 45 Q7
Twyn-carno Caerph 30 F3
Twynholm D & G 108 E10
Twyning Green Gloucs 46 H7
Twynllanan Carmth 43 Q10
Twyn-yr-Odyn V Glam 30 F10
Twyn-y-Sheriff Mons 31 M3
Twywell Nhants 61 L5
Tyberton Herefs 45 M7
Tyburn Birm 58 H6
Tycroes Carmth 28 H2
Ty Croes IoA 78 E10
Tycrwyn Powys 68 F11
Tydd Gote Lincs 75 J7
Tydd St Giles Cambs 74 H7
Tydd St Mary Lincs 74 H7
Tye Hants 15 K6
Tye Green Essex 51 M6
Tye Green Essex 51 N3
Tye Green Essex 52 C7
Tyersal C Brad 90 F4
Tyldesley Wigan 82 E4
Tyler Hill Kent 39 K9
Tylers Green Bucks 35 P6
Tyler's Green Essex 51 M9
Tylers Green Surrey 37 J10
Tylorstown Rhondd 30 D5
Tylwch Powys 55 M8
Ty-nant Conwy 68 C6
Ty-nant Gwynd 68 B9
Tyndrum Stirlg 139 Q11
Ty'n-dwr Denbgs 68 H6
Tyneham Dorset 12 E8
Tynemouth N Tyne 113 N7
Tyne Tunnel S Tyne 113 M7
Tynewydd Rhondd 29 P5
Tyninghame E Loth 128 G4
Tynron D & G 115 R9
Ty'n-y-bryn Rhondd 30 D7
Ty'n-y-coedcae Caerph 30 G7
Tynygongl IoA 79 J8
Tynygraig Cerdgn 54 F11
Ty'n-y-Groes Conwy 79 P10
Tyn-y-nant Rhondd 30 E7
Tyrie Abers 159 M5
Tyringham M Keyn 49 N5
Tyseley Birm 58 H8
Tythegston Brdgnd 29 N9
Tytherington Ches E 83 K9
Tytherington S Glos 32 C7
Tytherington Somset 20 E6
Tytherington Wilts 20 H6
Tytherleigh Devon 10 G4
Tytherton Lucas Wilts 32 H10
Tyttenhanger Herts 50 E9
Tywardreath Cnwll 4 H11
Tywardreath Highway Cnwll 4 H10
Tywyn Conwy 79 P9
Tywyn Gwynd 54 D4

U

Ubbeston Green Suffk 65 L7
Ubley BaNES 19 P3
Uckerby N York 103 P10
Uckfield E Susx 25 L6
Uckinghall Worcs 46 G7
Uckington Gloucs 46 H10
Uckington Shrops 57 K2
Uddingston S Lans 126 B5
Uddington S Lans 116 B4
Udimore E Susx 26 E8
Udny Green Abers 151 M2
Udny Station Abers 151 N3
Uffcott Wilts 33 M9
Uffculme Devon 9 Q2
Uffington Lincs 73 R9
Uffington Oxon 34 B7
Uffington Shrops 57 J2
Ufford C Pete 74 A10
Ufford Suffk 65 K11
Ufton Warwks 48 C2
Ufton Nervet W Berk 34 H11
Ugadale Ag & B 120 E6
Ugborough Devon 6 H7
Uggeshall Suffk 65 N5
Ugglebarnby N York 105 N9
Ughill Sheff 84 C2
Ugley Essex 51 M5
Ugley Green Essex 51 M5
Ugthorpe N York 105 L8
Uibhist A Deas W Isls 168 d14
Uibhist A Tuath W Isls 168 c10
Uig Ag & B 136 F5
Uig Highld 152 B7
Uig Highld 152 F5
Uig W Isls 168 f4
Uigshader Highld 152 G8
Uisken Ag & B 137 K12
Ulbster Highld 167 P8
Ulcat Row Cumb 101 M6
Ulceby Lincs 87 M6
Ulceby N Linc 93 K8
Ulceby Skitter N Linc 93 K7
Ulcombe Kent 26 D2
Uldale Cumb 100 H3
Uley Gloucs 32 E5
Ulgham Nthumb 113 K2
Ullapool Highld 161 J8
Ullenhall Warwks 58 H11
Ullenwood Gloucs 46 H11
Ulleskelf N York 91 N3
Ullesthorpe Leics 60 B3
Ulley Rothm 84 G3
Ullingswick Herefs 46 A5
Ullinish Lodge Hotel Highld 152 E10
Ullock Cumb 100 E6
Ullswater Cumb 101 M6
Ullswater Steamers Cumb 101 L7
Ulnes Walton Lancs 88 G7
Ulpha Cumb 94 D2
Ulpha Cumb 95 K4
Ulrome E R Yk 99 P9
Ulsta Shet 169 r5
Ulting Wick Essex 52 D10
Ulva Ag & B 137 K7
Ulverley Green Solhll 58 H8
Ulverston Cumb 94 F5
Ulwell Dorset 12 H8
Ulzieside D & G 115 Q6
Umberleigh Devon 17 L7
Unapool Highld 164 F10
Underbarrow Cumb 95 K2
Under Burnmouth Border 111 J4
Undercliffe C Brad 90 F4
Underdale Shrops 57 J2
Underling Green Kent 26 C2
Underriver Kent 37 N10
Underwood Newpt 31 L7
Underwood Notts 84 G10
Undley Suffk 63 L4
Undy Mons 31 M7
Union Mills IoM 80 e6
Union Street E Susx 26 B5
Unst Shet 169 s3
Unstone Derbys 84 E5
Unstone Green Derbys 84 E5
Unthank Cumb 101 N3
Unthank Cumb 102 B2
Unthank Cumb 110 G11
Unthank Derbys 84 D5
Unthank Nthumb 129 P10
Upavon Wilts 21 M4
Up Cerne Dorset 11 P4
Upchurch Kent 38 D8
Upcott Devon 17 P6
Upcott Herefs 45 L4
Upend Cambs 63 M9
Up Exe Devon 9 M4
Upgate Norfk 76 G8
Upgate Street Norfk 64 F3
Upgate Street Norfk 65 K3
Uphall Dorset 11 M4
Uphall W Loth 127 K3
Upham Devon 9 L3
Upham Hants 22 F10
Uphampton Herefs 45 M2
Uphampton Worcs 46 F2
Uphill N Som 19 K3
Up Holland Lancs 88 G9
Uplawmoor E Rens 125 L6
Upleadon Gloucs 46 E9
Upleatham R & Cl 104 H7
Uplees Kent 38 H9
Uploders Dorset 11 L6
Uplowman Devon 18 D11
Uplyme Devon 10 G6
Up Marden W Susx 15 L4
Upminster Gt Lon 37 N3
Up Mudford Somset 19 Q11
Up Nately Hants 23 J4
Upottery Devon 10 E3
Upper Affcot Shrops 56 G7
Upper Arley Worcs 57 P8
Upper Arncott Oxon 48 H11
Upper Astrop Nhants 48 F7
Upper Badcall Highld 164 E8
Upper Basildon W Berk 34 G9
Upper Batley Kirk 90 G5
Upper Beeding W Susx 24 E8
Upper Benefield Nhants 61 L3
Upper Bentley Worcs 58 E11
Upper Bighouse Highld 166 E5
Upper Birchwood Derbys 84 F9
Upper Boat Rhondd 30 F7
Upper Boddington Nhants 48 E4
Upper Borth Cerdgn 54 E7
Upper Brailes Warwks 48 B7
Upper Breinton Herefs 45 P6
Upper Broadheath Worcs 46 F3
Upper Broughton Notts 72 H5
Upper Bucklebury W Berk 34 F11
Upper Burgate Hants 21 N11
Upper Bush Medway 37 Q7
Upperby Cumb 110 H10
Upper Caldecote C Beds 61 Q11
Upper Canada N Som 19 L3
Upper Canterton Hants 13 N2
Upper Catesby Nhants 60 B9
Upper Catshill Worcs 58 E10
Upper Chapel Powys 44 E6
Upper Cheddon Somset 18 H9
Upper Chicksgrove Wilts 21 J9
Upper Chute Wilts 21 Q4
Upper Clapton Gt Lon 36 H3
Upper Clatford Hants 22 C6
Upper Coberley Gloucs 47 J11
Upper Cotton Staffs 71 K5
Upper Cound Shrops 57 K3
Upper Cudworth Barns 91 K9
Upper Cumberworth Kirk 90 G9
Upper Dallachy Moray 157 R5
Upper Deal Kent 39 Q11
Upper Dean Bed 61 M7
Upper Denby Kirk 90 G9
Upper Denton Cumb 111 M7
Upper Dicker E Susx 25 N9
Upper Dinchope Shrops 56 H8
Upper Dounreay Highld 166 H3
Upper Dovercourt Essex 53 M5
Upper Drumbane Stirlg 133 K6
Upper Dunsforth N York 97 P8
Upper Eashing Surrey 23 Q6
Upper Eathie Highld 156 D5
Upper Egleton Herefs 46 B6
Upper Elkstone Staffs 71 K3
Upper Ellastone Staffs 71 L6
Upper End Derbys 83 N9
Upper Enham Hants 22 C4
Upper Farmcote Shrops 57 P6
Upper Farringdon Hants 23 K7
Upper Framilode Gloucs 32 E2
Upper Froyle Hants 23 L6
Upperglen Highld 152 E7
Upper Godney Somset 19 N6
Upper Gravenhurst C Beds 50 D3
Upper Green Mons 45 M11
Upper Green Suffk 63 M8
Upper Green W Berk 22 C2
Upper Grove Common Herefs 45 R9
Upper Hackney Derbys 84 C8
Upper Hale Surrey 23 M5
Upper Halliford Surrey 36 C7
Upper Halling Medway 37 Q8
Upper Hambleton Rutlnd 73 N9
Upper Harbledown Kent 39 K10
Upper Hardres Court Kent 39 L11
Upper Hardwick Herefs 45 N3
Upper Hartfield E Susx 25 L4
Upper Hartshay Derbys 84 E10
Upper Hatherley Gloucs 46 H10
Upper Hatton Staffs 70 E7
Upper Haugh Rothm 91 L11
Upper Hayton Shrops 57 J8
Upper Heaton Kirk 90 F7
Upper Helmsley N York 98 D9
Upper Hergest Herefs 45 K4
Upper Heyford Nhants 60 E9
Upper Heyford Oxon 48 E9
Upper Hill Herefs 45 P4
Upper Hockenden Kent 37 M7
Upper Hopton Kirk 90 F7
Upper Howsell Worcs 46 E5
Upper Hulme Staffs 71 J2
Upper Ifold Surrey 24 B4
Upper Inglesham Swindn 33 P5
Upper Kilcott Gloucs 32 E7
Upper Killay Swans 28 G6
Upper Kinchrackine Ag & B 131 P2
Upper Knockando Moray 157 M9
Upper Lambourn W Berk 34 B8
Upper Landywood Staffs 58 E3
Upper Langford N Som 19 N3
Upper Langwith Derbys 84 H7
Upper Largo Fife 135 L7
Upper Leigh Staffs 71 J7
Upper Littleton N Som 19 Q2
Upper Lochton Abers 150 H8
Upper Longdon Staffs 58 G2
Upper Ludstone Shrops 57 Q5
Upper Lybster Highld 167 N9
Upper Lydbrook Gloucs 46 B11
Upper Lyde Herefs 45 P6
Upper Lye Herefs 56 F11
Upper Maes-coed Herefs 45 L8
Upper Midhope Sheff 90 G11
Uppermill Oldham 90 B9
Upper Milton Worcs 57 Q10
Upper Minety Wilts 33 K6
Upper Moor Worcs 47 J5
Upper Moor Side Leeds 90 G4
Upper Mulben Moray 157 R7
Upper Netchwood Shrops 57 L6
Upper Nobut Staffs 71 J7
Upper Norwood W Susx 23 P11
Upper Padley Derbys 84 B5
Upper Pennington Hants 13 P5
Upper Pollicott Bucks 35 K2
Upper Poppleton C York 98 B10
Upper Quinton Warwks 47 N5
Upper Ratley Hants 22 B10
Upper Rissington Gloucs 47 P11
Upper Rochford Worcs 57 L11
Upper Ruscoe D & G 108 C8
Upper Sapey Herefs 46 C2
Upper Saxondale Notts 72 H3
Upper Seagry Wilts 32 H8
Upper Shelton C Beds 49 Q6
Upper Sheringham Norfk 76 G3
Upper Skelmorlie N Ayrs 124 G4
Upper Slaughter Gloucs 47 N10
Upper Soudley Gloucs 32 C2
Upper Spond Herefs 45 L4
Upper Standen Kent 27 M3
Upper Staploe Bed 61 P9
Upper Stoke Norfk 77 K11
Upper Stondon C Beds 50 E3
Upper Stowe Nhants 60 D9
Upper Street Hants 21 N11
Upper Street Norfk 64 H6
Upper Street Norfk 77 L8
Upper Street Norfk 77 M8
Upper Street Suffk 53 K5
Upper Street Suffk 63 N10
Upper Street Suffk 64 G11
Upper Strensham Worcs 46 G7
Upper Sundon C Beds 50 B5
Upper Swell Gloucs 47 N9
Upper Tankersley Barns 91 J11
Upper Tean Staffs 71 J7
Upperthong Kirk 90 E9
Upperthorpe Derbys 84 G4
Upperthorpe N Linc 92 C10
Upper Threapwood Ches W 69 M5
Upperton W Susx 23 Q10
Upper Town Derbys 71 N4
Uppertown Derbys 84 D8
Upper Town Dur 103 L3
Upper Town Herefs 46 A5
Uppertown Highld 167 Q1
Upper Town N Som 31 P11
Upper Town Suffk 64 C8
Upper Tumble Carmth 28 F2
Upper Tysoe Warwks 48 B6
Upper Ufford Suffk 65 K11
Upperup Gloucs 33 K5
Upper Upham Wilts 33 P9
Upper Upnor Medway 38 C7
Upper Victoria Angus 143 J10
Upper Vobster Somset 20 D5
Upper Wardington Oxon 48 E5
Upper Weald M Keyn 49 M7
Upper Weedon Nhants 60 D9
Upper Welland Worcs 46 E6
Upper Wellingham E Susx 25 K8
Upper Weston BaNES 32 D11
Upper Weybread Suffk 65 J6
Upper Wick Worcs 46 F4
Upper Wield Hants 22 H7
Upper Winchendon Bucks 35 K2
Upperwood Derbys 84 C9
Upper Woodford Wilts 21 M7
Upper Wootton Hants 22 G4
Upper Wraxall Wilts 32 F10
Upper Wyche Worcs 46 E6
Uppincott Devon 9 M3
Uppingham Rutlnd 73 M11
Uppington Dorset 12 H3
Uppington Shrops 57 K3
Upsall N York 97 Q3
Upsettlington Border 129 M10
Upshire Essex 51 K10
Up Somborne Hants 22 C8
Upstreet Kent 39 M9
Up Sydling Dorset 11 N4
Upthorpe Suffk 64 D7
Upton Bucks 35 L2
Upton C Pete 74 B10
Upton Cambs 61 Q5
Upton Ches W 81 N11
Upton Cnwll 5 M7
Upton Cnwll 16 C11
Upton Cumb 101 K3
Upton Devon 7 J10
Upton Devon 10 B4
Upton Dorset 12 B8
Upton Dorset 12 G6
Upton E R Yk 99 N10
Upton Halton 81 P7
Upton Hants 22 C11
Upton Hants 22 C3
Upton Leics 72 B11
Upton Lincs 85 Q3
Upton Nhants 60 F9
Upton Norfk 77 M9
Upton Notts 85 M10
Upton Notts 85 M5
Upton Oxon 33 P2
Upton Oxon 34 F7
Upton Pembks 41 K10
Upton R & Cl 105 K7
Upton Slough 35 Q9
Upton Somset 18 C9
Upton Somset 19 N9
Upton Wakefd 91 M8
Upton Warwks 47 M3
Upton Wilts 20 G8
Upton Wirral 81 K7
Upton Bishop Herefs 46 C9
Upton Cheyney S Glos 32 C10
Upton Cressett Shrops 57 M6
Upton Crews Herefs 46 B9
Upton Cross Cnwll 5 M7
Upton End C Beds 50 D4
Upton Grey Hants 23 J5
Upton Heath Ches W 81 N11
Upton Hellions Devon 9 K4
Upton Lovell Wilts 20 H6
Upton Magna Shrops 57 K2
Upton Noble Somset 20 D7
Upton Pyne Devon 9 M5
Upton St Leonards Gloucs 46 G11
Upton Scudamore Wilts 20 G5
Upton Snodsbury Worcs 46 H4
Upton Towans Cnwll 2 F5
Upton-upon-Severn Worcs 46 G6
Upton Warren Worcs 58 D11
Upwaltham W Susx 15 P4
Upware Cambs 62 H6
Upwell Norfk 75 J10
Upwey Dorset 11 P7
Upwick Green Herts 51 L6
Upwood Cambs 62 C4
Urchfont Wilts 21 K3
Urdimarsh Herefs 45 Q5
Ure Bank N York 97 M6
Urlay Nook S on T 104 D8
Urmston Traffd 82 G6
Urpeth Dur 113 L10
Urquhart Moray 157 P5
Urquhart Castle Highld 147 N2
Urra N York 104 G10
Urray Highld 155 P7
Usan Angus 143 N7
Ushaw Moor Dur 103 P2
Usk Mons 31 L4
Usselby Lincs 86 E2
Usworth Sundld 113 M9
Utkinton Ches W 82 B11
Utley C Brad 90 D2
Uton Devon 9 K5
Utterby Lincs 87 K2
Uttoxeter Staffs 71 K8
Uwchmynydd Gwynd 66 B9
Uxbridge Gt Lon 36 C4
Uyeasound Shet 169 s3
Uzmaston Pembks 41 J8

V

Vale Guern 10 c1
Valley IoA 78 D9
Valley End Surrey 23 Q2
Valley Truckle Cnwll 4 H5
Valtos Highld 153 J5
Valtos W Isls 168 f4
Vange Essex 38 B4
Varteg Torfn 31 J3
Vatsetter Shet 169 s5
Vatten Highld 152 D9
Vaynor Myr Td 30 D2
Vazon Bay Guern 10 b2
Veensgarth Shet 169 r9
Velindre Powys 44 H7
Vellow Somset 18 E7
Velly Devon 16 D7
Venngreen Devon 16 F9
Vennington Shrops 56 E3
Venn Ottery Devon 10 B6
Venny Tedburn Devon 9 K5
Venterdon Cnwll 5 P7
Ventnor IoW 14 G11
Venton Devon 6 F7
Vernham Dean Hants 22 B3
Vernham Street Hants 22 B3
Vernolds Common Shrops 56 H8
Verwood Dorset 13 J3
Veryan Cnwll 3 N6
Veryan Green Cnwll 3 N5
Vicarage Devon 10 E7
Vickerstown Cumb 94 D7
Victoria Barns 90 F9
Victoria Blae G 30 G3
Victoria Cnwll 4 F9
Vidlin Shet 169 r7
Viewfield Moray 157 P5
Viewpark N Lans 126 C5
Vigo Kent 37 P8
Village de Putron Guern 10 c2
Ville la Bas Jersey 11 a1
Villiaze Guern 10 b2
Vinehall Street E Susx 26 C7
Vines Cross E Susx 25 N7
Virginia Water Surrey 36 B7
Virginstow Devon 5 P3
Vobster Somset 20 D5
Voe Shet 169 r7
Vowchurch Herefs 45 M7
Vulcan Village St Hel 82 C6

W

Waberthwaite Cumb 94 C2
Wackerfield Dur 103 N6
Wacton Norfk 64 H3

Wadborough Worcs 46 H5
Waddesdon Bucks 49 K11
Waddesdon Manor Bucks 49 K11
Waddeton Devon 7 M7
Waddicar Sefton 81 M5
Waddingham Lincs 92 G11
Waddington Lancs 89 L2
Waddington Lincs 86 C8
Waddon Devon 9 L9
Waddon Dorset 11 N7
Waddon Gt Lon 36 H8
Wadebridge Cnwll 4 F7
Wadeford Somset 10 G2
Wadenhoe Nhants 61 M4
Wadesmill Herts 51 J7
Wadhurst E Susx 25 P4
Wadshelf Derbys 84 D6
Wadswick Wilts 32 F11
Wadworth Donc 91 P11
Waen Denbgs 68 C2
Waen Denbgs 80 G11
Waen Powys 68 H11
Waen Fach Powys 68 H11
Waen-pentir Gwynd 79 K11
Waen-wen Gwynd 79 K11
Wagbeach Shrops 56 F4
Wainfelin Torfn 31 J4
Wainfleet All Saints Lincs 87 N9
Wainfleet Bank Lincs 87 N9
Wainfleet St Mary Lincs 87 N9
Wainford Norfk 65 L3
Wainhouse Corner Cnwll 5 K2
Wainscott Medway 38 B7
Wain's Hill N Som 31 L10
Wainstalls Calder 90 C5
Waitby Cumb 102 E9
Waithe Lincs 93 N10
Wakefield Wakefd 91 J6
Wake Green Birm 58 G8
Wakehurst Place W Susx 24 H4
Wakerley Nhants 73 P11
Wakes Colne Essex 52 E6
Walberswick Suffk 65 P7
Walberton W Susx 15 Q5
Walbottle N u Ty 113 J7
Walbutt D & G 108 F7
Walby Cumb 110 H8
Walcombe Somset 19 Q5
Walcot Lincs 73 R3
Walcot N Linc 92 E6
Walcot Shrops 56 E7
Walcot Shrops 57 K2
Walcot Swindn 33 N8
Walcote Leics 60 C4
Walcote Warwks 47 M3
Walcot Green Norfk 64 G5
Walcott Lincs 86 F9
Walcott Norfk 77 M5
Walden N York 96 F4
Walden Head N York 96 E4
Walden Stubbs N York 91 P7
Walderslade Medway 38 C9
Walderton W Susx 15 L4
Walditch Dorset 11 K6
Waldley Derbys 71 L7
Waldridge Dur 113 L11
Waldringfield Suffk 53 N2
Waldron E Susx 25 M7
Wales Rothm 84 G4
Wales Somset 19 Q10
Walesby Lincs 86 F2
Walesby Notts 85 L6
Walford Herefs 46 A10
Walford Herefs 56 F10
Walford Shrops 69 M10
Walford Staffs 70 E8
Walford Heath Shrops 69 M11
Walgherton Ches E 70 B5
Walgrave Nhants 60 H6
Walhampton Hants 13 P5
Walkden Salfd 82 F4
Walker N u Ty 113 L8
Walkerburn Border 117 M3
Walker Fold Lancs 89 K2
Walkeringham Notts 85 N2
Walkerith Lincs 85 N2
Walkern Herts 50 G5
Walker's Green Herefs 45 Q5
Walker's Heath Birm 58 G9
Walkerton Fife 134 G7
Walkford BCP 13 M6
Walkhampton Devon 6 E5
Walkington E R Yk 92 G3
Walkley Sheff 84 D3
Walk Mill Lancs 89 P5
Walkwood Worcs 47 K2
Wall Nthumb 112 D7
Wall Staffs 58 H3
Wallacetown S Ayrs 114 E7
Wallacetown S Ayrs 114 F3
Wallands Park E Susx 25 K8
Wallasey Wirral 81 K6
Wallasey (Kingsway) Tunnel Wirral 81 L6
Wall End Cumb 94 E4
Wall End Herefs 45 N3
Wallend Medway 38 E6
Waller's Green Herefs 46 C7
Wallhead Cumb 111 J8
Wall Heath Dudley 58 C7
Wall Houses Nthumb 112 F7
Wallingford Oxon 34 H7
Wallington Gt Lon 36 G8
Wallington Hants 14 G5
Wallington Herts 50 G4
Wallington Heath Wsall 58 E4
Wallis Pembks 41 K5
Wallisdown BCP 13 J6
Walliswood Surrey 24 D3
Walls Shet 169 p9
Wallsend N Tyne 113 L7
Wallthwaite Cumb 101 L5
Wall under Haywood Shrops 57 J6
Wallyford E Loth 128 B5
Walmer Kent 39 Q11
Walmer Bridge Lancs 88 F6
Walmersley Bury 89 N8
Walmestone Kent 39 N10
Walmley Birm 58 H6
Walmley Ash Birm 58 H6
Walmsgate Lincs 87 L5
Walney Cumb 94 D7
Walpole Somset 19 K6
Walpole Suffk 65 M7
Walpole Cross Keys Norfk 75 K7
Walpole Highway Norfk 75 K8
Walpole St Andrew Norfk 75 K7
Walpole St Peter Norfk 75 K7
Walrow Somset 19 K5
Walsall Wsall 58 F5
Walsall Wood Wsall 58 F4
Walsden Calder 89 Q6
Walsgrave on Sowe Covtry 59 N8
Walsham le Willows Suffk 64 E7
Walshaw Bury 89 M8
Walshford N York 97 P10
Walsoken Norfk 75 J8
Walston S Lans 127 K8
Walsworth Herts 50 E4
Walter's Ash Bucks 35 M5
Walters Green Kent 25 M2
Walterston V Glam 30 E10
Walterstone Herefs 45 L9
Waltham Kent 27 K2
Waltham NE Lin 93 N10
Waltham Abbey Essex 51 J10
Waltham Chase Hants 14 G4
Waltham Cross Herts 51 J10
Waltham on the Wolds Leics 73 L6
Waltham St Lawrence W & M 35 M9
Waltham's Cross Essex 51 Q4
Walthamstow Gt Lon 37 J3
Walton C Pete 74 C10
Walton Cumb 111 K8
Walton Derbys 84 E7
Walton Leeds 97 P11
Walton Leics 60 C3
Walton M Keyn 49 N7
Walton Powys 45 K3
Walton Shrops 56 H9
Walton Somset 19 N7
Walton Staffs 70 F8
Walton Staffs 70 F9
Walton Suffk 53 N4
Walton W Susx 15 M6
Walton Wakefd 91 K7
Walton Warwks 47 Q4
Walton Wrekin 69 Q11
Walton Cardiff Gloucs 46 H8
Walton East Pembks 41 K6
Walton Elm Dorset 20 E11
Walton Grounds Nhants 48 F8
Walton Highway Norfk 75 J8
Walton-in-Gordano N Som 31 M10
Walton-le-Dale Lancs 88 H5
Walton-on-Thames Surrey 36 D7
Walton-on-the-Hill Staffs 70 H10
Walton-on-the-Hill Surrey 36 F9
Walton-on-the-Naze Essex 53 N7
Walton on the Wolds Leics 72 F7
Walton-on-Trent Derbys 71 N11
Walton Park N Som 31 M10
Walton West Pembks 40 G8
Walwen Flints 80 G9
Walwen Flints 80 H10
Walwen Flints 81 J9
Walwick Nthumb 112 D6
Walworth Darltn 103 P7
Walworth Gt Lon 36 H5
Walworth Gate Darltn 103 P6
Walwyn's Castle Pembks 40 G8
Wambrook Somset 10 F3
Wampool Cumb 110 D10
Wanborough Surrey 23 P5
Wanborough Swindn 33 P8
Wandon End Herts 50 D6
Wandsworth Gt Lon 36 G6
Wangford Suffk 65 P6
Wanlip Leics 72 F8
Wanlockhead D & G 116 B8
Wannock E Susx 25 N10
Wansford C Pete 73 R11
Wansford E R Yk 99 M9
Wanshurst Green Kent 26 C2
Wanstead Gt Lon 37 K3
Wanstrow Somset 20 D6
Wanswell Gloucs 32 C4
Wantage Oxon 34 C7
Wants Green Worcs 46 E3
Wapley S Glos 32 D9
Wappenbury Warwks 59 N11
Wappenham Nhants 48 H5
Warbleton E Susx 25 P7
Warborough Oxon 34 G6
Warboys Cambs 62 D4
Warbreck Bpool 88 C3
Warbstow Cnwll 5 L3
Warburton Traffd 82 F7
Warcop Cumb 102 D7
Warden Kent 38 H7
Warden Nthumb 112 D7
Ward End Birm 58 H7
Warden Street C Beds 50 D2
Ward Green Suffk 64 E9
Ward Green Cross Lancs 89 J3
Wardhedges C Beds 50 C3
Wardington Oxon 48 E5
Wardle Ches E 69 R3
Wardle Rochdl 89 Q7
Wardley Gatesd 113 M8
Wardley Rutlnd 73 L10
Wardley Salfd 82 G4
Wardlow Derbys 83 Q10
Wardsend Ches E 83 K8
Wardy Hill Cambs 62 G4
Ware Herts 51 J8
Wareham Dorset 12 F7
Warehorne Kent 26 G5
Warenford Nthumb 119 M5
Waren Mill Nthumb 119 M4
Warenton Nthumb 119 M4
Wareside Herts 51 J7
Waresley Cambs 62 C10
Waresley Worcs 58 B10
Ware Street Kent 38 C10
Warfield Br For 35 N10
Warfleet Devon 7 M8
Wargate Lincs 74 D4
Wargrave Wokham 35 L9
Warham Herefs 45 P7
Warham Norfk 76 D3
Wark Nthumb 112 C5
Wark Nthumb 118 F3
Warkleigh Devon 17 L7
Warkton Nhants 61 J5
Warkworth Nhants 48 E6
Warkworth Nthumb 119 P9
Warlaby N York 97 M2
Warland Calder 89 Q6
Warleggan Cnwll 5 K8
Warleigh BaNES 20 E2
Warley Town Calder 90 D6
Warlingham Surrey 37 J9
Warmbrook Derbys 71 P4
Warmfield Wakefd 91 K6
Warmingham Ches E 70 C2
Warmington Nhants 61 N2
Warmington Warwks 48 D5
Warminster Wilts 20 G5
Warmley S Glos 32 C10
Warmsworth Donc 91 N10
Warmwell Dorset 12 C7
Warndon Worcs 46 G3
Warner Bros. Studio Tour Herts 50 C10
Warnford Hants 22 H10
Warnham W Susx 24 E4
Warnham Court W Susx 24 E4
Warningcamp W Susx 24 B9
Warninglid W Susx 24 F5
Warren Ches E 83 J10
Warren Pembks 40 H11
Warrenby R & Cl 104 G5
Warrenhill S Lans 116 C3
Warren Row W & M 35 M8
Warren's Green Herts 50 G5
Warren Street Kent 38 F11
Warrington M Keyn 49 N4
Warrington Warrtn 82 D7
Warriston C Edin 127 P2
Warsash Hants 14 E5
Warslow Staffs 71 K3
Warsop Vale Notts 84 H7
Warter E R Yk 98 H10
Warthermaske N York 97 K5
Warthill N York 98 D9
Wartling E Susx 25 Q9
Wartnaby Leics 73 J6
Warton Lancs 88 E5
Warton Lancs 95 K6
Warton Nthumb 119 K10
Warton Warwks 59 L4
Warwick Warwks 59 L11
Warwick Bridge Cumb 111 J9
Warwick Castle Warwks 47 Q2
Warwick-on-Eden Cumb 111 J9
Warwick Services Warwks 48 B3
Warwicksland Cumb 111 J5
Wasbister Ork 169 c3
Wasdale Head Cumb 100 G9
Wash Derbys 83 N8
Washall Green Herts 51 K4
Washaway Cnwll 4 G8
Washbourne Devon 7 K8
Washbrook Somset 19 M4
Washbrook Suffk 53 K3
Washfield Devon 18 B11
Washfold N York 103 L10
Washford Somset 18 E6
Washford Pyne Devon 9 K2
Washingborough Lincs 86 D6
Washington Sundld 113 M9
Washington W Susx 24 D8
Washington Services Gatesd 113 L9
Washwood Heath Birm 58 H7
Wasing W Berk 22 G2
Waskerley Dur 112 F11
Wasperton Warwks 47 Q3
Wasps Nest Lincs 86 E8
Wass N York 98 B5
Wast Water Cumb 100 G9
Watchet Somset 18 E6
Watchfield Oxon 33 P6
Watchfield Somset 19 K5
Watchgate Cumb 101 P11
Watchill Cumb 100 G2
Watcombe Torbay 7 N5
Watendlath Cumb 101 J7
Water Devon 9 J8
Water Lancs 89 N5
Waterbeach Cambs 62 G7
Waterbeach W Susx 15 N5
Waterbeck D & G 110 D5
Waterden Norfk 76 B4
Water Eaton Oxon 34 F2
Water Eaton Staffs 58 D2
Water End Bed 61 P10
Water End Bed 61 P11
Water End C Beds 50 C3
Waterend Cumb 100 F6
Water End E R Yk 92 C3
Water End Essex 51 N2
Water End Herts 50 B8
Water End Herts 50 F10
Waterfall Staffs 71 K4
Waterfoot Ag & B 120 F4
Waterfoot E Rens 125 P6
Waterford Herts 50 H8
Water Fryston Wakefd 91 M5
Watergate Cnwll 5 J5
Waterhead Cumb 101 L10
Waterheads Border 127 N7
Waterhouses Dur 103 N2
Waterhouses Staffs 71 K4
Wateringbury Kent 37 Q10
Waterlane Gloucs 32 H4
Waterloo Cnwll 5 J7
Waterloo Derbys 84 F8
Waterloo Herefs 45 L5
Waterloo Highld 145 L3
Waterloo N Lans 126 E7
Waterloo Norfk 77 J8
Waterloo P & K 141 Q10
Waterloo Pembks 41 J10
Waterloo Sefton 81 L5
Waterloo Cross Devon 9 Q2
Waterloo Port Gwynd 66 H2
Waterlooville Hants 15 J5
Watermead Bucks 49 M11
Watermillock Cumb 101 M6
Water Newton Cambs 74 B11
Water Orton Warwks 59 J6
Waterperry Oxon 34 H3
Waterrow Somset 18 E9
Watersfield W Susx 24 B7
Waterside Bl w D 89 L6
Waterside Bucks 35 Q4
Waterside Cumb 110 D11
Waterside Donc 91 R8
Waterside E Ayrs 114 H6
Waterside E Ayrs 125 M9
Waterside E Duns 126 B3
Water's Nook Bolton 89 K9
Waterstein Highld 152 A8
Waterstock Oxon 34 H3
Waterston Pembks 40 H9
Water Stratford Bucks 49 J8
Water Street Neath 29 M8
Waters Upton Wrekin 70 A11
Water Yeat Cumb 94 F3
Watford Herts 50 D11
Watford Nhants 60 D7
Watford Gap Services Nhants 60 D7
Wath N York 96 H7
Wath N York 97 M5
Wath upon Dearne Rothm 91 L10
Watlington Norfk 75 M8
Watlington Oxon 35 J6
Watnall Notts 84 H11
Watten Highld 167 M6
Wattisfield Suffk 64 E7
Wattisham Suffk 64 E11
Watton Dorset 11 K6
Watton E R Yk 99 L10
Watton Norfk 76 C11
Watton-at-Stone Herts 50 H7
Watton Green Norfk 76 C11
Wattons Green Essex 51 M11
Wattston N Lans 126 D3
Wattstown Rhondd 30 D6
Wattsville Caerph 30 H6
Wauldby E R Yk 92 G5
Waulkmill Abers 150 G9
Waunarlwydd Swans 28 H5
Waunfawr Cerdgn 54 E8
Waunfawr Gwynd 67 J3
Waungron Swans 28 G4
Waunlwyd Blae G 30 G3
Wavendon M Keyn 49 P7
Waverbridge Cumb 110 D11
Waverton Ches W 69 N2
Waverton Cumb 110 D11
Wawne E R Yk 93 J3
Waxham Norfk 77 N6
Waxholme E R Yk 93 P5
Way Kent 39 P8
Waye Devon 7 K4
Wayford Somset 11 J3
Waytown Dorset 11 K5
Way Village Devon 9 L2
Way Wick N Som 19 L2
Weacombe Somset 18 F6
Weald Oxon 34 B4
Wealdstone Gt Lon 36 E3
Weardley Leeds 90 H2
Weare Somset 19 M4
Weare Giffard Devon 16 H7
Wearhead Dur 102 G3
Wearne Somset 19 M9
Weasdale Cumb 102 C10
Weasenham All Saints Norfk 76 A7
Weasenham St Peter Norfk 76 B7
Weaste Salfd 82 H5
Weatheroak Hill Worcs 58 G10
Weaverham Ches W 82 D10
Weaverslake Staffs 71 L11
Weaverthorpe N York 99 K6
Webbington Somset 19 L3
Webb's Heath S Glos 32 C10
Webheath Worcs 58 F11
Webton Herefs 45 N7
Wedderlairs Abers 159 L11
Wedding Hall Fold N York 96 D11
Weddington Kent 39 N10
Weddington Warwks 59 N6
Wedhampton Wilts 21 L3
Wedmore Somset 19 M5
Wednesbury Sandw 58 E5
Wednesfield Wolves 58 D4
Weecar Notts 85 P7
Weedon Bucks 49 M11
Weedon Bec Nhants 60 D9
Weedon Lois Nhants 48 H5
Weeford Staffs 58 H4
Week Devon 7 K6
Week Devon 17 K6
Week Devon 17 N8
Weeke Devon 9 J3
Weeke Hants 22 E8
Weekley Nhants 61 J4
Week St Mary Cnwll 5 L2
Weel E R Yk 93 J3
Weeley Essex 53 K7
Weeley Heath Essex 53 L7
Weem P & K 141 K8
Weeping Cross Staffs 70 G10
Weethley Warwks 47 L3
Weeting Norfk 63 N3
Weeton E R Yk 93 Q6
Weeton Lancs 88 D4
Weeton N York 97 L11
Weetwood Leeds 90 H3
Weir Lancs 89 P5
Weirbrook Shrops 69 K10
Weir Quay Devon 6 C5
Weisdale Shet 169 q8
Welborne Norfk 76 F9
Welbourn Lincs 86 C10
Welburn N York 98 E7
Welbury N York 104 C10
Welby Lincs 73 P3
Welches Dam Cambs 62 G3
Welcombe Devon 16 C8
Weldon Nhants 61 K3
Weldon Bridge Nthumb 119 M11
Welford Nhants 60 D4
Welford W Berk 34 D10
Welford-on-Avon Warwks 47 M4
Welham Leics 60 G2
Welham Notts 85 M4
Welham Bridge E R Yk 92 C4
Welham Green Herts 50 F9
Well Hants 23 L5
Well Lincs 87 M6
Well N York 97 L4
Welland Worcs 46 E6
Wellbank Angus 142 H10
Well End Bucks 35 N7
Well End Herts 50 F11
Wellesbourne Warwks 47 Q3
Wellesbourne Mountford Warwks 47 Q3
Well Head Herts 50 E5
Well Hill Kent 37 L8
Wellhouse W Berk 34 F10
Welling Gt Lon 37 L5
Wellingborough Nhants 61 J7
Wellingham Norfk 76 B7
Wellingore Lincs 86 C9
Wellington Cumb 100 E10
Wellington Herefs 45 P5
Wellington Somset 18 F10
Wellington Wrekin 57 M2
Wellington Heath Herefs 46 D6
Wellington Marsh Herefs 45 P5
Wellow BaNES 20 D3
Wellow IoW 14 C9
Wellow Notts 85 L7
Wellpond Green Herts 51 K6
Wells Somset 19 P5
Wellsborough Leics 72 B10
Wells Green Ches E 70 B4
Wells Head C Brad 90 D4
Wells-next-the-Sea Norfk 76 C3
Wellstye Green Essex 51 P7
Well Town Devon 9 M3
Welltree P & K 134 B3
Wellwood Fife 134 D10
Welney Norfk 62 H2
Welshampton Shrops 69 M7
Welsh Bicknor Herefs 46 A11
Welsh End Shrops 69 P7
Welsh Frankton Shrops 69 L8
Welsh Hook Pembks 40 H5
Welsh Newton Herefs 45 Q11
Welshpool Powys 56 C3
Welsh St Donats V Glam 30 D9
Welton Cumb 101 L2
Welton E R Yk 92 G5
Welton Lincs 86 D5
Welton Nhants 60 C7
Welton le Marsh Lincs 87 N7
Welton le Wold Lincs 87 J3
Welwick E R Yk 93 P6
Welwyn Herts 50 F7
Welwyn Garden City Herts 50 F8
Wem Shrops 69 P9
Wembdon Somset 19 J7
Wembley Gt Lon 36 E3
Wembury Devon 6 E9
Wembworthy Devon 17 M10
Wemyss Bay Inver 124 F4
Wenallt Cerdgn 54 F10
Wendens Ambo Essex 51 M3
Wendlebury Oxon 48 G11
Wendling Norfk 76 C9
Wendover Bucks 35 N3
Wendron Cnwll 2 H7
Wendron Mining District Cnwll 2 H7
Wendy Cambs 62 D11
Wenfordbridge Cnwll 4 H6
Wenhaston Suffk 65 N6
Wennington Cambs 62 B5
Wennington Gt Lon 37 M4
Wennington Lancs 95 N7
Wensley Derbys 84 C8
Wensley N York 96 G3
Wentbridge Wakefd 91 M7
Wentnor Shrops 56 F6
Wentworth Cambs 62 G5
Wentworth Rothm 91 K11
Wentworth Castle Barns 91 J10
Wenvoe V Glam 30 F10
Weobley Herefs 45 N4
Weobley Marsh Herefs 45 N4
Wepham W Susx 24 B9
Wereham Norfk 75 N10
Wergs Wolves 58 C4
Wern Gwynd 67 J7
Wern Powys 44 G11
Wern Powys 56 D2
Wern Shrops 69 J8
Werneth Low Tamesd 83 L6
Wernffrwd Swans 28 F6
Wern-y-gaer Flints 81 J11
Werrington C Pete 74 C10
Werrington Cnwll 5 N4
Werrington Staffs 70 G5
Wervin Ches W 81 N10
Wesham Lancs 88 E4
Wessington Derbys 84 E9
West Aberthaw V Glam 30 D11
West Acre Norfk 75 Q7
West Allerdean Nthumb 129 P10
West Alvington Devon 7 J10
West Amesbury Wilts 21 M6
West Anstey Devon 17 R6
West Appleton N York 97 K2
West Ashby Lincs 87 J6
West Ashling W Susx 15 M5
West Ashton Wilts 20 G3
West Auckland Dur 103 N5
West Ayton N York 99 K4
West Bagborough Somset 18 G8
West Bank Blae G 30 H3
West Bank Halton 81 Q8
West Barkwith Lincs 86 G4
West Barnby N York 105 M8
West Barns E Loth 128 H4
West Barsham Norfk 76 C5
West Bay Dorset 11 K6
West Beckham Norfk 76 G4
West Bedfont Surrey 36 C6
Westbere Kent 39 L9
West Bergholt Essex 52 G6
West Bexington Dorset 11 L7
West Bilney Norfk 75 P7
West Blatchington Br & H 24 G9
West Boldon S Tyne 113 N8
Westborough Lincs 73 M2
Westbourne BCP 13 J6
Westbourne W Susx 15 L5
West Bourton Dorset 20 E9
West Bowling C Brad 90 F4
West Brabourne Kent 27 J3
West Bradenham Norfk 76 C10
West Bradford Lancs 89 L2
West Bradley Somset 19 Q7
West Bretton Wakefd 90 H8
West Bridgford Notts 72 F3
West Briscoe Dur 103 J7
West Bromwich Sandw 58 F6
Westbrook Kent 39 P7
Westbrook W Berk 34 D10
Westbrook Wilts 33 J11
West Buckland Devon 17 M5
West Buckland Somset 18 G10
West Burrafirth Shet 169 p8
West Burton N York 96 F3

West Burton W Susx 15 Q4
Westbury Bucks 48 H7
Westbury Shrops 56 F3
Westbury Wilts 20 G4
Westbury Leigh Wilts 20 G5
Westbury-on-Severn Gloucs 32 D2
Westbury-on-Trym Bristl 31 Q9
Westbury-sub-Mendip Somset 19 P5
West Butsfield Dur 103 M2
West Butterwick N Linc 92 D9
Westby Lancs 88 D4
West Byfleet Surrey 36 B8
West Cairngaan D & G 106 F11
West Caister Norfk 77 Q9
West Calder W Loth 127 J5
West Camel Somset 19 Q10
West Chaldon Dorset 12 C8
West Challow Oxon 34 C7
West Charleton Devon 7 K10
West Chelborough Dorset 11 L3
West Chevington Nthumb 119 P11
West Chiltington W Susx 24 C7
West Chinnock Somset 11 K2
West Chisenbury Wilts 21 M4
West Clandon Surrey 36 B10
West Cliffe Kent 27 P3
Westcliff-on-Sea Sthend 38 E4
West Coker Somset 11 L2
Westcombe Devon 7 K6
Westcombe Somset 20 C7
West Compton Somset 19 Q6
West Compton Abbas Dorset 11 M6
Westcote Gloucs 47 P10
Westcote Barton Oxon 48 D9
Westcott Bucks 49 K11
Westcott Devon 9 P4
Westcott Surrey 36 D11
West Cottingwith N York 92 A2
Westcourt Wilts 21 P2
West Cowick E R Yk 91 Q6
West Cross Swans 28 H7
West Curry Cnwll 5 M3
West Curthwaite Cumb 110 F11
Westdean E Susx 25 M11
West Dean W Susx 15 N4
West Dean Wilts 21 Q9
West Deeping Lincs 74 B9
West Derby Lpool 81 M6
West Dereham Norfk 75 N10
West Ditchburn Nthumb 119 M6
West Down Devon 17 J3
Westdown Camp Wilts 21 K5
Westdowns Cnwll 4 H5
West Drayton Gt Lon 36 C5
West Drayton Notts 85 M6
West Dunnet Highld 167 M2
Wested Kent 37 M7
West Ella E R Yk 92 H5
West End Bed 49 Q4
West End Br For 35 N10
West End Caerph 30 H5
West End Cambs 62 D7
West End Cumb 110 F9
West End E R Yk 92 F4
West End E R Yk 93 L4
West End E R Yk 93 N5
Westend Gloucs 32 E3
West End Hants 14 E4
West End Hants 22 H7
West End Herts 50 G9
West End Herts 50 H9
West End Lancs 89 L5
West End Leeds 90 G3
West End Lincs 93 Q11
West End N Som 31 N11
West End N York 91 N2
West End Norfk 76 C10
West End Norfk 77 Q9
West End Oxon 34 G7
West End S Glos 32 D7
West End Somset 20 C8
West End Surrey 23 P2
West End Surrey 36 D8
West End W & M 35 M9
West End W Susx 24 F7
West End Wilts 20 H10
West End Wilts 21 J10
West End Wilts 33 J9
West End Green Hants 23 J2
Westend Town Nthumb 111 Q7
Westenhanger Kent 27 K4
Wester Aberchalder Highld 147 P3
Westerdale Highld 167 K6
Westerdale N York 105 J9
Westerfield Suffk 53 L2
Westergate W Susx 15 P5
Westerham Kent 37 K10
Westerhope N u Ty 113 J7
Westerland Devon 7 M6
Westerleigh S Glos 32 C9
Western Isles W Isls 168 f8
Wester Ochiltree W Loth 127 J3
Wester Pitkierie Fife 135 P6
Wester Ross Highld 160 F11
Westerton W Susx 15 N5
Westerton of Rossie Angus 143 M7
Westerwick Shet 169 p9
West Ewell Surrey 36 F8
West Farleigh Kent 38 B11
West Farndon Nhants 48 F4
West Felton Shrops 69 K9
Westfield BaNES 20 C4
Westfield Cumb 100 C5
Westfield E Susx 26 D8
Westfield Highld 167 J4
Westfield N Lans 126 C3
Westfield Norfk 76 D10
Westfield W Loth 126 G3
Westfields Dorset 12 B3
Westfields Herefs 45 P6
Westfields of Rattray P & K 142 B8
Westfield Sole Kent 38 C9
West Flotmanby N York 99 M5
Westford Somset 18 F10
Westgate Dur 102 H3
Westgate N Linc 92 C9
Westgate Norfk 76 D3
Westgate Hill C Brad 90 G5
Westgate-on-Sea Kent 39 P7
Westgate Street Norfk 76 H7
West Ginge Oxon 34 D7
West Grafton Wilts 21 P2
West Green Hants 23 K3
West Grimstead Wilts 21 P9
West Grinstead W Susx 24 E6
West Haddlesey N York 91 P5
West Haddon Nhants 60 D6
West Hagbourne Oxon 34 F7
West Hagley Worcs 58 D8
Westhall Suffk 65 N5
West Hallam Derbys 72 C2
West Hallam Common Derbys 72 C2
West Halton N Linc 92 F6
Westham Dorset 11 P9
Westham E Susx 25 P10
West Ham Gt Lon 37 J4
Westham Somset 19 M5
Westhampnett W Susx 15 N5
West Handley Derbys 84 E5
West Hanney Oxon 34 D6
West Hanningfield Essex 38 B2
West Harnham Wilts 21 M9
West Harptree BaNES 19 Q3
West Harting W Susx 23 L10
West Hatch Somset 19 J10
West Hatch Wilts 20 H9
West Haven Angus 143 K10
Westhay Somset 19 M6
Westhead Lancs 88 E9
West Head Norfk 75 L9
West Heath Birm 58 F9
West Heath Hants 22 G3
West Helmsdale Highld 163 N3
West Hendred Oxon 34 D7
West Heslerton N York 99 J5
West Hewish N Som 19 L2
Westhide Herefs 46 A6
Westhill Abers 151 L6
West Hill Devon 9 Q6
Westhill Highld 156 C9
West Hoathly W Susx 25 J4
West Holme Dorset 12 E7
Westholme Somset 19 Q6
Westhope Herefs 45 P4
Westhope Shrops 56 H7
West Horndon Essex 37 P3
Westhorp Nhants 48 F4
Westhorpe Lincs 74 D4
Westhorpe Suffk 64 E8
West Horrington Somset 19 Q5
West Horsley Surrey 36 C10
West Horton Nthumb 119 K4
West Hougham Kent 27 N3
Westhoughton Bolton 89 K9
Westhouse N York 95 P6
Westhouses Derbys 84 F9
West Howe BCP 13 J5
West Howetown Somset 18 B8
Westhumble Surrey 36 E10
West Huntingtower P & K 134 D3
West Huntspill Somset 19 K6
West Hyde C Beds 50 D7
West Hyde Herts 36 B2
West Hythe Kent 27 K5
West Ilkerton Devon 17 N2
West Ilsley W Berk 34 E8
West Itchenor W Susx 15 L6
West Keal Lincs 87 L8
West Kennett Wilts 33 M11
West Kilbride N Ayrs 124 G8
West Kingsdown Kent 37 N8
West Kington Wilts 32 F9
West Kirby Wirral 81 J7
West Knapton N York 98 H5
West Knighton Dorset 12 B7
West Knoyle Wilts 20 G8
West Kyloe Nthumb 119 L2
Westlake Devon 6 G8
West Lambrook Somset 19 M11
Westland Green Herts 51 K6
West Langdon Kent 27 P2
West Lavington W Susx 23 N10
West Lavington Wilts 21 K4
West Layton N York 103 M8
West Leake Notts 72 E5
West Learmouth Nthumb 118 F3
West Lees N York 104 E10
West Leigh Devon 8 G3
Westleigh Devon 16 H6
Westleigh Devon 18 E11
West Leigh Somset 18 F8
Westleton Suffk 65 N8
West Lexham Norfk 76 A8
Westley Shrops 56 F3
Westley Suffk 63 P8
Westley Waterless Cambs 63 K9
West Lilling N York 98 C8
Westlington Bucks 35 L2
West Linton Border 127 M7
Westlinton Cumb 110 G8
West Littleton S Glos 32 E9
West Lockinge Oxon 34 D7
West Lulworth Dorset 12 D8
West Lutton N York 99 J7
West Lydford Somset 19 Q8
West Lyn Devon 17 N2
West Lyng Somset 19 K9
West Lynn Norfk 75 M6
West Malling Kent 37 Q9
West Malvern Worcs 46 E5
West Marden W Susx 15 L4
West Markham Notts 85 M6
Westmarsh Kent 39 N9
West Marsh NE Lin 93 N9
West Marton N York 96 C10
West Melbury Dorset 20 G10
West Melton Rothm 91 L10
West Meon Hants 22 H10
West Meon Hut Hants 23 J9
West Meon Woodlands Hants 22 H9
West Mersea Essex 52 H9
Westmeston E Susx 24 H8
West Mickley Nthumb 112 G8
West Midland Safari Park Worcs 57 Q9
Westmill Herts 50 H7
Westmill Herts 51 J5
West Milton Dorset 11 L5
Westminster Gt Lon 36 G5
Westminster Abbey & Palace Gt Lon 36 G5
West Molesey Surrey 36 D7
West Monkton Somset 19 J9
West Moors Dorset 13 J4
West Morden Dorset 12 F5
West Morriston Border 118 B2
West Morton C Brad 90 D2
West Mudford Somset 19 Q10
Westmuir Angus 142 F7
West Ness N York 98 D5
West Newbiggin Darltn 104 C7
Westnewton Cumb 100 F2
West Newton E R Yk 93 M3
West Newton Norfk 75 N5
West Newton Somset 19 J9
West Norwood Gt Lon 36 H6
Westoe S Tyne 113 N7
West Ogwell Devon 7 L4
Weston BaNES 32 D11
Weston Ches E 70 C4
Weston Devon 10 C4
Weston Devon 10 D7
Weston Dorset 11 P10
Weston Halton 81 Q8
Weston Hants 23 K10
Weston Herefs 45 M3
Weston Herts 50 G4
Weston Lincs 74 E6
Weston N York 97 J11
Weston Nhants 48 G5
Weston Notts 85 N7
Weston Shrops 56 E10
Weston Shrops 57 L6
Weston Shrops 69 J9
Weston Staffs 70 H9
Weston Suffk 65 N4
Weston W Berk 34 C10
Weston Beggard Herefs 46 A6
Westonbirt Gloucs 32 G7
Weston by Welland Nhants 60 G2
Weston Colley Hants 22 F7
Weston Colville Cambs 63 K10
Weston Corbett Hants 23 J5
Weston Coyney C Stke 70 G6
Weston Favell Nhants 60 G8
Weston Green Cambs 63 K10
Weston Heath Shrops 57 P2
Weston Hills Lincs 74 E6
Weston in Arden Warwks 59 N7
Westoning C Beds 50 B4
Weston-in-Gordano N Som 31 M10
Westoning Woodend C Beds 50 B4
Weston Jones Staffs 70 D10
Weston Longville Norfk 76 G8
Weston Lullingfields Shrops 69 M10
Weston-on-Avon Warwks 47 N4
Weston-on-the-Green Oxon 48 F11
Weston Park Staffs 57 Q2
Weston Patrick Hants 23 J5
Weston Rhyn Shrops 69 J7
Weston-sub-Edge Gloucs 47 M6
Weston-super-Mare N Som 19 K2
Weston Turville Bucks 35 N2
Weston-under-Lizard Staffs 57 Q2
Weston under Penyard Herefs 46 B10
Weston-under-Redcastle Shrops 69 Q9
Weston under Wetherley Warwks 59 N11
Weston Underwood Derbys 71 P6
Weston Underwood M Keyn 49 N4
Weston-upon-Trent Derbys 72 C5
Westonzoyland Somset 19 L8
West Orchard Dorset 20 F11
West Overton Wilts 33 M11
Westow N York 98 F7
West Panson Devon 5 N3
West Park Abers 151 K8
West Parley Dorset 13 J5
West Peckham Kent 37 P10
West Peeke Devon 5 N3
West Pelton Dur 113 K10
West Pennard Somset 19 P7
West Pentire Cnwll 4 B9
West Perry Cambs 61 P7
West Pinchbeck Lincs 74 D6
West Porlock Somset 17 R2
Westport Somset 19 L10
West Pulham Dorset 11 Q3
West Putford Devon 16 F8
West Quantoxhead Somset 18 F6
Westquarter Falk 126 G2
Westra V Glam 30 F10
West Raddon Devon 9 L4
West Rainton Dur 113 M11
West Rasen Lincs 86 E3
West Ravendale NE Lin 93 M11
Westray Ork 169 d2
Westray Airport Ork 169 d1
West Raynham Norfk 76 B6
West Retford Notts 85 L4
Westridge Green W Berk 34 G9
Westrigg W Loth 126 G4
Westrop Swindn 33 P6
West Rounton N York 104 D10
West Row Suffk 63 L5
West Rudham Norfk 75 R5
West Runton Norfk 76 H3
Westruther Border 128 G10
Westry Cambs 74 H11
West Saltoun E Loth 128 D6
West Sandford Devon 9 K4
West Sandwick Shet 169 r5
West Scrafton N York 96 G4
West Sleekburn Nthumb 113 L4
West Somerton Norfk 77 P7
West Stafford Dorset 11 Q7
West Stockwith Notts 92 C11
West Stoke W Susx 15 M5
West Stonesdale N York 102 G10
West Stoughton Somset 19 M5
West Stour Dorset 20 E10
West Stourmouth Kent 39 N9
West Stow Suffk 63 P6
West Stowell Wilts 21 M2
West Stratton Hants 22 F6
West Street Kent 38 F11
West Street Kent 39 P11
West Street Medway 38 B6
West Street Suffk 64 D7
West Tanfield N York 97 L5
West Taphouse Cnwll 5 J9
West Tarbert Ag & B 123 Q6
West Tarring W Susx 24 D10
West Thirston Nthumb 119 N11
West Thorney W Susx 15 L6
Westthorpe Derbys 84 G5
West Thorpe Notts 72 G5
West Thurrock Thurr 37 N5
West Tilbury Thurr 37 Q5
West Tisted Hants 23 J9
West Torrington Lincs 86 F4
West Town BaNES 19 P2
West Town Hants 15 K7
West Town Herefs 45 N2
West Town N Som 31 N11
West Town Somset 19 P7
West Town Somset 20 D6
West Tytherley Hants 21 Q9
West Walton Norfk 75 J8
Westward Cumb 101 J2
Westward Ho! Devon 16 G6
Westwell Kent 26 G2
Westwell Oxon 33 P3
Westwell Leacon Kent 26 G2
West Wellow Hants 21 Q11
West Wembury Devon 6 E9
West Wemyss Fife 135 J9
Westwick Cambs 62 F7
Westwick Dur 103 L7
West Wick N Som 19 L2
Westwick Norfk 77 K6
West Wickham Cambs 63 K11
West Wickham Gt Lon 37 J7
West Williamston Pembks 41 K9
West Winch Norfk 75 M7
West Winterslow Wilts 21 P8
West Wittering W Susx 15 L7
West Witton N York 96 G3
Westwood Devon 9 P5
Westwood Kent 37 P6
Westwood Kent 39 Q8
Westwood Notts 84 G10
Westwood Nthumb 111 Q7
Westwood Wilts 20 F3
West Woodburn Nthumb 112 C3
West Woodhay W Berk 22 C2
Westwood Heath Covtry 59 L9
West Woodlands Somset 20 E6
Westwoodside N Linc 92 B10
West Worldham Hants 23 K7
West Worthing W Susx 24 D10
West Wratting Cambs 63 K10
West Wycombe Bucks 35 M6
West Wylam Nthumb 112 H8
West Yatton Wilts 32 G9
West Yoke Kent 37 P7
West Youlstone Cnwll 16 D8
Wetham Green Kent 38 D8
Wetheral Cumb 111 J10
Wetherby Leeds 97 P11
Wetherby Services N York 97 P10
Wetherden Suffk 64 E9
Wetheringsett Suffk 64 G8
Wethersfield Essex 52 B5
Wetherup Street Suffk 64 G9
Wetley Rocks Staffs 70 H5
Wettenhall Ches E 69 R2
Wetton Staffs 71 L3
Wetwang E R Yk 99 J9
Wetwood Staffs 70 D8
Wexcombe Wilts 21 Q3
Wexham Slough 35 Q8
Wexham Street Bucks 35 Q8
Weybourne Norfk 76 G3
Weybourne Surrey 23 N5
Weybread Suffk 65 J5
Weybread Street Suffk 65 J6
Weybridge Surrey 36 C8
Weycroft Devon 10 G5
Weydale Highld 167 L4
Weyhill Hants 22 B5
Weymouth Dorset 11 P9
Whaddon Bucks 49 M8
Whaddon Cambs 62 E11
Whaddon Gloucs 32 F2
Whaddon Wilts 20 G2
Whaddon Wilts 21 N9
Whale Cumb 101 P6
Whaley Derbys 84 H6
Whaley Bridge Derbys 83 M8
Whaley Thorns Derbys 84 H6
Whaligoe Highld 167 P8
Whalley Lancs 89 L3
Whalley Banks Lancs 89 L3
Whalsay Shet 169 s7
Whalton Nthumb 112 H4
Whaplode Lincs 74 F6
Whaplode Drove Lincs 74 F8
Wharf Warwks 48 D4
Wharfe N York 96 A7
Wharles Lancs 88 E3
Wharley End C Beds 49 P6
Wharncliffe Side Sheff 84 C2
Wharram-le-Street N York 98 H7
Wharton Ches W 82 E11
Wharton Herefs 45 Q3
Whashton N York 103 N9
Whasset Cumb 95 L4
Whatcote Warwks 47 Q6
Whateley Warwks 59 K5
Whatfield Suffk 52 H2
Whatley Somset 10 H3
Whatley Somset 20 D5
Whatley's End S Glos 32 C8
Whatlington E Susx 26 C8
Whatsole Street Kent 27 K3
Whatstandwell Derbys 84 D10
Whatton-in-the-Vale Notts 73 J3
Whauphill D & G 107 M8
Whaw N York 103 J10
Wheal Peevor Cnwll 3 J5
Wheal Rose Cnwll 3 J5
Wheatacre Norfk 65 P3
Wheatfield Oxon 35 J5
Wheathampstead Herts 50 E8
Wheathill Shrops 57 L8
Wheathill Somset 19 Q8
Wheatley Calder 90 D5
Wheatley Hants 23 L6
Wheatley Oxon 34 G3
Wheatley Hill Dur 104 C3
Wheatley Hills Donc 91 P10
Wheatley Lane Lancs 89 N3
Wheaton Aston Staffs 58 C2
Wheddon Cross Somset 18 B7
Wheelbarrow Town Kent 27 K2
Wheeler End Bucks 35 M6
Wheeler's Green Wokham 35 L10
Wheelerstreet Surrey 23 P6
Wheelock Ches E 70 D3
Wheelock Heath Ches E 70 D3
Wheelton Lancs 89 J6
Wheldale Wakefd 91 M5
Wheldrake C York 92 A2
Whelford Gloucs 33 N5
Whelpley Hill Bucks 35 Q4
Whelpo Cumb 101 K3
Whelston Flints 81 J9
Whempstead Herts 50 H6
Whenby N York 98 C7
Whepstead Suffk 64 A10
Wherstead Suffk 53 L3
Wherwell Hants 22 C6
Wheston Derbys 83 P9
Whetsted Kent 37 Q11
Whetstone Gt Lon 36 G2
Whetstone Leics 72 F11
Wheyrigg Cumb 110 C11
Whicham Cumb 94 C4
Whichford Warwks 48 B8
Whickham Gatesd 113 K8
Whiddon Devon 8 C5
Whiddon Down Devon 8 G6
Whigstreet Angus 142 H9
Whilton Nhants 60 D8
Whimble Devon 16 F11
Whimple Devon 9 P5
Whimpwell Green Norfk 77 M6
Whinburgh Norfk 76 E10
Whin Lane End Lancs 88 D2
Whinnieliggate D & G 108 F10
Whinnow Cumb 110 F10
Whinnyfold Abers 159 Q11
Whinny Hill S on T 104 C7
Whippingham IoW 14 F8
Whipsnade C Beds 50 B7
Whipsnade Zoo ZSL C Beds 50 B7
Whipton Devon 9 M6
Whirlow Sheff 84 D4
Whisby Lincs 86 B7
Whissendine Rutlnd 73 L8
Whissonsett Norfk 76 C7
Whistlefield Ag & B 131 Q9
Whistlefield Inn Ag & B 131 N9
Whistley Green Wokham 35 L10
Whiston Knows 81 P6
Whiston Nhants 60 H8
Whiston Rothm 84 F3
Whiston Staffs 58 C2
Whiston Staffs 71 J5
Whiston Cross Shrops 57 P4
Whiston Eaves Staffs 71 J5
Whitacre Fields Warwks 59 L6
Whitbeck Cumb 94 C4
Whitbourne Herefs 46 D3
Whitburn S Tyne 113 P8
Whitburn W Loth 126 G5
Whitby Ches W 81 M9
Whitby N York 105 N8
Whitbyheath Ches W 81 M10
Whitchester Border 129 J8
Whitchurch BaNES 32 B11
Whitchurch Bucks 49 M10
Whitchurch Cardif 30 G9
Whitchurch Devon 6 D4
Whitchurch Hants 22 E5
Whitchurch Herefs 45 R11
Whitchurch Oxon 34 H9
Whitchurch Pembks 40 F5
Whitchurch Shrops 69 P6
Whitchurch Canonicorum Dorset 10 H5
Whitchurch Hill Oxon 34 H9
Whitcombe Dorset 11 Q7
Whitcot Shrops 56 F6
Whitcott Keysett Shrops 56 D8
Whiteacre Kent 27 K2
Whiteacre Heath Warwks 59 K6
Whiteash Green Essex 52 C5
White Ball Somset 18 F11
Whitebridge Highld 147 M4
Whitebrook Mons 31 P3
Whitebushes Surrey 36 G11
Whitecairns Abers 151 N4
Whitechapel Gt Lon 36 H4
White Chapel Lancs 88 H2
Whitechurch Pembks 41 N3
Whitecliff Gloucs 31 Q3
White Colne Essex 52 E6
White Coppice Lancs 89 J7
Whitecraig E Loth 127 Q3
Whitecroft Gloucs 32 B3
Whitecrook D & G 106 G6
Whitecross Cnwll 2 E7
White Cross Cnwll 2 H9
Whitecross Cnwll 4 F7
Whitecross Falk 126 H2
White End Worcs 46 E8
Whiteface Highld 162 G9
Whitefarland N Ayrs 120 G3
Whitefaulds S Ayrs 114 E6
Whitefield Bury 89 N9
Whitefield Devon 17 N4
Whitefield Somset 18 E9
Whitefield Lane End Knows 81 P7
Whiteford Abers 151 J2
Whitegate Ches W 82 D11
Whitehall Hants 23 K4
Whitehall Ork 169 f4
Whitehall W Susx 24 D6
Whitehaven Cumb 100 C7
Whitehill Kent 38 H10
Whitehill Leics 72 C8
Whitehill and Bordon Hants 23 L8
Whitehills Abers 158 G4
Whitehouse Abers 150 G5
Whitehouse Ag & B 123 P7
Whitehouse Common Birm 58 H5
Whitekirk E Loth 128 F3
White Kirkley Dur 103 K3
White Lackington Dorset 11 Q5
Whitelackington Somset 19 L11
White Ladies Aston Worcs 46 H4
Whiteleaf Bucks 35 M4
White-le-Head Dur 113 J10
Whiteley Hants 14 F5
Whiteley Bank IoW 14 G10
Whiteley Green Ches E 83 K9
Whiteley Village Surrey 36 C8
Whitemans Green W Susx 24 H5
White Mill Carmth 43 J10
Whitemire Moray 156 H7
Whitemoor C Nott 72 E2
Whitemoor Cnwll 4 F10
Whitemoor Derbys 84 E11
Whitemoor Staffs 70 F2
Whiteness Shet 169 q9
White Notley Essex 52 C8

Whiteoak Green Oxon 34 B2
White Ox Mead BaNES 20 D3
Whiteparish Wilts 21 P10
White Pit Lincs 87 L5
Whiterashes Abers 151 M3
White Roding Essex 51 N8
Whiterow Highld 167 Q7
Whiterow Moray 157 J6
Whiteshill Gloucs 32 F3
Whitesmith E Susx 25 M8
White Stake Lancs 88 G5
Whitestaunton Somset 10 F2
Whitestone Devon 9 L6
White Stone Herefs 45 R6
Whitestone Cross Devon 9 L6
Whitestreet Green Suffk 52 G4
Whitewall Corner N York 98 F7
White Waltham W & M 35 M9
Whiteway BaNES 20 D2
Whiteway Gloucs 32 H2
Whitewell Lancs 95 P11
Whiteworks Devon 6 G4
Whitfield C Dund 142 G11
Whitfield Kent 27 P2
Whitfield Nhants 48 H7
Whitfield Nthumb 111 Q9
Whitfield S Glos 32 C6
Whitfield Hall Nthumb 111 Q9
Whitford Devon 10 F5
Whitford Flints 80 G9
Whitgift E R Yk 92 D6
Whitgreave Staffs 70 G9
Whithorn D & G 107 M9
Whiting Bay N Ayrs 121 K6
Whitkirk Leeds 91 K4
Whitland Carmth 41 N7
Whitlaw Border 117 Q8
Whitletts S Ayrs 114 G3
Whitley N York 91 P6
Whitley Readg 35 K10
Whitley Sheff 84 D2
Whitley Wilts 32 G11
Whitley Bay N Tyne 113 N6
Whitley Chapel Nthumb 112 D9
Whitley Heath Staffs 70 E9
Whitley Lower Kirk 90 G7
Whitley Row Kent 37 L10
Whitlock's End Solhll 58 H9
Whitminster Gloucs 32 E3
Whitmore Dorset 13 J3
Whitmore Staffs 70 E6
Whitnage Devon 18 D11
Whitnash Warwks 48 B2
Whitney-on-Wye Herefs 45 K5
Whitrigg Cumb 100 H3
Whitrigg Cumb 110 D9
Whitrigglees Cumb 110 D9
Whitsbury Hants 21 M11
Whitsome Border 129 M9
Whitson Newpt 31 L8
Whitstable Kent 39 K8
Whitstone Cnwll 5 M2
Whittingham Nthumb 119 L8
Whittingslow Shrops 56 G7
Whittington Derbys 84 E5
Whittington Gloucs 47 K10
Whittington Lancs 95 N5
Whittington Norfk 75 P11
Whittington Shrops 69 K8
Whittington Staffs 58 C8
Whittington Staffs 59 J3
Whittington Warwks 59 L5
Whittington Worcs 46 G4
Whittington Moor Derbys 84 E6
Whittlebury Nhants 49 J6
Whittle-le-Woods Lancs 88 H6
Whittlesey Cambs 74 E11
Whittlesford Cambs 62 G11
Whittlestone Head Bl w D 89 L7
Whitton N Linc 92 F6
Whitton Nthumb 119 L10
Whitton Powys 56 D11
Whitton S on T 104 C6
Whitton Shrops 57 K10
Whitton Suffk 53 K2
Whittonditch Wilts 33 Q10
Whittonstall Nthumb 112 G9
Whitway Hants 22 E3
Whitwell Derbys 84 H5
Whitwell Herts 50 E6
Whitwell IoW 14 F11
Whitwell N York 103 Q11
Whitwell Rutlnd 73 N9
Whitwell-on-the-Hill N York 98 E7
Whitwell Street Norfk 76 G7
Whitwick Leics 72 C7
Whitwood Wakefd 91 L6
Whitworth Lancs 89 P7
Whixall Shrops 69 P8
Whixley N York 97 P9
Whorlton Dur 103 M8
Whorlton N York 104 E10
Whyle Herefs 45 R2
Whyteleafe Surrey 36 H9
Wibdon Gloucs 31 Q5
Wibsey C Brad 90 E4
Wibtoft Warwks 59 Q7
Wichenford Worcs 46 E2
Wichling Kent 38 F10
Wick BCP 13 L6
Wick Devon 10 D4
Wick Highld 167 Q6
Wick S Glos 32 D10
Wick Somset 18 H6
Wick Somset 19 M9
Wick V Glam 29 P10
Wick W Susx 24 B10
Wick Wilts 21 N10
Wick Worcs 47 J5
Wicken Cambs 63 J6
Wicken Nhants 49 K7
Wicken Bonhunt Essex 51 L4
Wickenby Lincs 86 E4
Wick End Bed 49 Q4
Wicken Green Village Norfk 76 A5
Wickersley Rothm 84 G2
Wicker Street Green Suffk 52 G3
Wickford Essex 38 B3
Wickham Hants 14 G4
Wickham W Berk 34 C10
Wickham Bishops Essex 52 D9
Wickhambreaux Kent 39 M10
Wickhambrook Suffk 63 N10
Wickhamford Worcs 47 L6
Wickham Green Suffk 64 F8
Wickham Green W Berk 34 D10
Wickham Heath W Berk 34 D11
Wickham Market Suffk 65 L10
Wickhampton Norfk 77 N10
Wickham St Paul Essex 52 D4
Wickham Skeith Suffk 64 F8
Wickham Street Suffk 63 N10
Wickham Street Suffk 64 F8
Wickhurst Green W Susx 24 D4
Wick John o' Groats Airport Highld 167 Q6
Wicklewood Norfk 76 F11
Wickmere Norfk 76 H5
Wick St Lawrence N Som 31 L11
Wicksteed Park Nhants 61 J5
Wickstreet E Susx 25 M9
Wickwar S Glos 32 D7
Widdington Essex 51 M4
Widdop Calder 89 Q4
Widdrington Nthumb 119 Q11
Widdrington Station Nthumb 113 K2
Widecombe in the Moor Devon 8 H9
Widegates Cnwll 5 M10
Widemouth Bay Cnwll 16 C11
Wide Open N Tyne 113 K6
Widford Essex 51 Q10
Widford Herts 51 K7
Widham Wilts 33 L7
Widley Hants 15 J5
Widmer End Bucks 35 N5
Widmerpool Notts 72 G5
Widmore Gt Lon 37 K7
Widnes Halton 81 Q7
Widworthy Devon 10 E5
Wigan Wigan 88 H9
Wigborough Somset 19 M11
Wiggaton Devon 10 C6
Wiggenhall St Germans Norfk 75 L8
Wiggenhall St Mary Magdalen Norfk 75 L8
Wiggenhall St Mary the Virgin Norfk 75 L8
Wiggenhall St Peter Norfk 75 M8
Wiggens Green Essex 51 Q2
Wiggenstall Staffs 71 K2
Wiggington Shrops 69 K7
Wigginton C York 98 C9
Wigginton Herts 35 P2
Wigginton Oxon 48 C8
Wigginton Staffs 59 K3
Wigginton Bottom Herts 35 P3
Wigglesworth N York 96 B9
Wiggonby Cumb 110 E10
Wiggonholt W Susx 24 C7
Wighill N York 97 Q11
Wighton Norfk 76 C4
Wightwick Wolves 58 C5
Wigley Derbys 84 D6
Wigley Hants 22 B11
Wigmore Herefs 56 G11
Wigmore Medway 38 C9
Wigsley Notts 85 Q6
Wigsthorpe Nhants 61 M4
Wigston Leics 72 G11
Wigston Fields Leics 72 G10
Wigston Parva Leics 59 Q7
Wigthorpe Notts 85 J4
Wigtoft Lincs 74 E3
Wigton Cumb 110 E11
Wigtown D & G 107 M6
Wigtwizzle Sheff 90 G11
Wike Leeds 91 J2
Wilbarston Nhants 60 H3
Wilberfoss E R Yk 98 E10
Wilburton Cambs 62 G5
Wilby Nhants 61 J7
Wilby Norfk 64 E4
Wilby Suffk 65 J7
Wilcot Wilts 21 M2
Wilcott Shrops 69 L11
Wilcrick Newpt 31 M7
Wilday Green Derbys 84 D6
Wildboarclough Ches E 83 L11
Wilden Bed 61 N9
Wilden Worcs 58 B10
Wilde Street Suffk 63 M5
Wildhern Hants 22 C4
Wildhill Herts 50 G9
Wildmanbridge S Lans 126 E7
Wildmill Brdgnd 29 P8
Wildmoor Hants 23 J3
Wildmoor Worcs 58 E9
Wildsworth Lincs 92 D11
Wilford C Nott 72 F3
Wilkesley Ches E 70 A6
Wilkhaven Highld 163 L9
Wilkieston W Loth 127 L4
Wilkin's Green Herts 50 E9
Wilksby Lincs 87 J8
Willand Devon 9 P2
Willards Hill E Susx 26 B7
Willaston Ches E 70 B4
Willaston Ches W 81 L9
Willen M Keyn 49 N6
Willenhall Covtry 59 N9
Willenhall Wsall 58 E5
Willerby E R Yk 92 H4
Willerby N York 99 L5
Willersey Gloucs 47 M7
Willersley Herefs 45 L5
Willesborough Kent 26 H3
Willesborough Lees Kent 26 H3
Willesden Gt Lon 36 F4
Willesleigh Devon 17 L5
Willesley Wilts 32 G7
Willett Somset 18 F8
Willey Shrops 57 M5
Willey Warwks 59 Q8
Willey Green Surrey 23 P4
Williamscot Oxon 48 E5
Williamstown Rhondd 30 D6
Willian Herts 50 F4
Willicote Warwks 47 N5
Willingale Essex 51 N9
Willingdon E Susx 25 N10
Willingham Cambs 62 F6
Willingham by Stow Lincs 85 Q4
Willingham Green Cambs 63 K10
Willingham St Mary Suffk 65 N5
Willington Bed 61 P10
Willington Derbys 71 P9
Willington Dur 103 N3
Willington Kent 38 C11
Willington N Tyne 113 M7
Willington Warwks 47 Q7
Willington Corner Ches W 82 B11
Willitoft E R Yk 92 B4
Williton Somset 18 E6
Willoughby Lincs 87 N6
Willoughby Warwks 60 B7
Willoughby Hills Lincs 87 L11
Willoughby-on-the-Wolds Notts 72 G5
Willoughby Waterleys Leics 60 C2
Willoughton Lincs 86 B2
Willow Green Ches W 82 D9
Willows Green Essex 52 B8
Willsbridge S Glos 32 C10
Willsworthy Devon 8 D8
Willtown Somset 19 L10
Wilmcote Warwks 47 N3
Wilmington BaNES 20 C2
Wilmington Devon 10 E5
Wilmington E Susx 25 M10
Wilmington Kent 37 M6
Wilmslow Ches E 82 H8
Wilnecote Staffs 59 K4
Wilpshire Lancs 89 K4
Wilsden C Brad 90 D3
Wilsford Lincs 73 Q2
Wilsford Wilts 21 M3
Wilsford Wilts 21 M7
Wilsham Devon 17 P2
Wilshaw Kirk 90 E9
Wilsill N York 97 J8
Wilsley Green Kent 26 C4
Wilsley Pound Kent 26 C4
Wilson Herefs 45 R10
Wilson Leics 72 C6
Wilsontown S Lans 126 G6
Wilstead Bed 50 C2
Wilsthorpe Lincs 74 A8
Wilstone Herts 35 P2
Wilstone Green Herts 35 P2
Wilton Cumb 100 D8
Wilton Herefs 46 A10
Wilton N York 98 H4
Wilton R & Cl 104 G7
Wilton Wilts 21 L8
Wilton Wilts 21 Q2
Wilton Dean Border 117 P8
Wimbish Essex 51 N3
Wimbish Green Essex 51 P3
Wimbledon Gt Lon 36 F6
Wimblington Cambs 62 F2
Wimboldsley Ches W 70 B2
Wimborne Minster Dorset 12 H5
Wimborne St Giles Dorset 12 H2
Wimbotsham Norfk 75 M9
Wimpole Cambs 62 E11
Wimpstone Warwks 47 P5
Wincanton Somset 20 D9
Winceby Lincs 87 K7
Wincham Ches W 82 E9
Winchburgh W Loth 127 K3
Winchcombe Gloucs 47 K9
Winchelsea E Susx 26 F8
Winchelsea Beach E Susx 26 F8
Winchester Hants 22 E9
Winchester Services Hants 22 F7
Winchet Hill Kent 26 B3
Winchfield Hants 23 L4
Winchmore Hill Bucks 35 P5
Winchmore Hill Gt Lon 36 H2
Wincle Ches E 83 L11
Wincobank Sheff 84 E2
Winder Cumb 100 D7
Windermere Cumb 101 M11
Windermere Jetty Cumb 101 M11
Winderton Warwks 48 B6
Windhill Highld 155 P8
Windlehurst Stockp 83 L7
Windlesham Surrey 23 P2
Windmill Cnwll 4 D7
Windmill Derbys 83 Q9
Windmill Hill E Susx 25 P8
Windmill Hill Somset 19 K11
Windrush Gloucs 33 N2
Windsole Abers 158 E5
Windsor W & M 35 Q9
Windsor Castle W & M 35 Q9
Windsoredge Gloucs 32 F4
Windsor Green Suffk 64 B11
Windygates Fife 135 J7
Windyharbour Ches E 82 H10
Windy Hill Wrexhm 69 K4
Wineham W Susx 24 F6
Winestead E R Yk 93 N6
Winewall Lancs 89 Q2
Winfarthing Norfk 64 G4
Winford IoW 14 G10
Winford N Som 19 P2
Winforton Herefs 45 K5
Winfrith Newburgh Dorset 12 D8
Wing Bucks 49 N10
Wing Rutlnd 73 M10
Wingate Dur 104 D3
Wingates Bolton 89 K9
Wingates Nthumb 119 L11
Wingerworth Derbys 84 E7
Wingfield C Beds 50 B5
Wingfield Suffk 65 J6
Wingfield Wilts 20 F3
Wingfield Green Suffk 65 J6
Wingham Kent 39 M10
Wingland Lincs 75 J6
Wingmore Kent 27 L2
Wingrave Bucks 49 N11
Winkburn Notts 85 M9
Winkfield Br For 35 P10
Winkfield Row Br For 35 N10
Winkhill Staffs 71 K4
Winkhurst Green Kent 37 L11
Winkleigh Devon 17 L10
Winksley N York 97 L6
Winkton BCP 13 L5
Winlaton Gatesd 113 J8
Winlaton Mill Gatesd 113 J8
Winless Highld 167 P6
Winllan Powys 68 H10
Winmarleigh Lancs 95 K11
Winnall Hants 22 E9
Winnersh Wokham 35 L10
Winnington Ches W 82 D10
Winscales Cumb 100 D5
Winscombe N Som 19 M3
Winsford Ches W 82 E11
Winsford Somset 18 B8
Winsham Devon 17 J4
Winsham Somset 10 H3
Winshill Staffs 71 P10
Winshwen Swans 29 J5
Winskill Cumb 101 Q4
Winslade Hants 23 J5
Winsley Wilts 20 E2
Winslow Bucks 49 L9
Winson Gloucs 33 L3
Winsor Hants 13 P2
Winster Cumb 95 J2
Winster Derbys 84 B8
Winston Dur 103 M7
Winston Suffk 64 H9
Winstone Gloucs 33 J3
Winswell Devon 16 H9
Winterborne Came Dorset 11 Q7
Winterborne Clenston Dorset 12 D4
Winterborne Herringston Dorset 11 P7
Winterborne Houghton Dorset 12 D4
Winterborne Kingston Dorset 12 E5
Winterborne Monkton Dorset 11 P7
Winterborne Stickland Dorset 12 D4
Winterborne Tomson Dorset 12 E5
Winterborne Whitechurch Dorset 12 D4
Winterborne Zelston Dorset 12 E5
Winterbourne S Glos 32 B8
Winterbourne W Berk 34 E10
Winterbourne Abbas Dorset 11 N6
Winterbourne Bassett Wilts 33 L10
Winterbourne Dauntsey Wilts 21 N8
Winterbourne Earls Wilts 21 N8
Winterbourne Gunner Wilts 21 N7
Winterbourne Monkton Wilts 33 L10
Winterbourne Steepleton Dorset 11 N7
Winterbourne Stoke Wilts 21 L6
Winterbrook Oxon 34 H7
Winterburn N York 96 D9
Winteringham N Linc 92 F6
Winterley Ches E 70 C3
Wintersett Wakefd 91 K7
Winterslow Wilts 21 P8
Winterton N Linc 92 F7
Winterton-on-Sea Norfk 77 P8
Winthorpe Lincs 87 Q7
Winthorpe Notts 85 P9
Winton BCP 13 J6
Winton Cumb 102 E8
Winton E Susx 25 M10
Winton N York 104 D11
Wintringham N York 98 H6
Winwick Cambs 61 P4
Winwick Nhants 60 D6
Winwick Warrtn 82 D6
Wirksworth Derbys 71 P4
Wirral 81 K7
Wirswall Ches E 69 P6
Wisbech Cambs 75 J9
Wisbech St Mary Cambs 74 H9
Wisborough Green W Susx 24 C5
Wiseman's Bridge Pembks 41 M9
Wiseton Notts 85 M3
Wishanger Gloucs 32 H3
Wishaw N Lans 126 D6
Wishaw Warwks 59 J6
Wisley Surrey 36 C9
Wisley Garden RHS Surrey 36 C9
Wispington Lincs 86 H6
Wissenden Kent 26 F3
Wissett Suffk 65 M6
Wissington Norfk 75 N11
Wissington Suffk 52 G5
Wistanstow Shrops 56 G7
Wistanswick Shrops 70 B9
Wistaston Ches E 70 B4
Wistaston Green Ches E 70 B4
Wisterfield Ches E 82 H10
Wiston Pembks 41 K7
Wiston S Lans 116 D4
Wiston W Susx 24 D8
Wistow Cambs 62 C4
Wistow Leics 72 G11
Wistow N York 91 P3
Wiswell Lancs 89 L3
Witcham Cambs 62 G4
Witchampton Dorset 12 G3
Witchford Cambs 62 H5
Witcombe Somset 19 N10
Witham Essex 52 D9
Witham Friary Somset 20 D6
Witham on the Hill Lincs 73 R7
Witham St Hughs Lincs 85 Q8
Withcall Lincs 87 J4
Withdean Br & H 24 H9
Witherenden Hill E Susx 25 P5
Witheridge Devon 9 K2
Witherley Leics 72 A11
Withern Lincs 87 M4
Withernsea E R Yk 93 P5
Withernwick E R Yk 93 L2
Withersdale Street Suffk 65 K5
Withersfield Suffk 63 L11
Witherslack Cumb 95 J4
Withiel Cnwll 4 F8
Withiel Florey Somset 18 C8
Withielgoose Cnwll 4 G8
Withington Gloucs 47 K11
Withington Herefs 45 R6
Withington Manch 82 H6
Withington Shrops 57 K2
Withington Staffs 71 J7
Withington Green Ches E 82 H10
Withington Marsh Herefs 45 R6
Withleigh Devon 9 M2
Withnell Lancs 89 J6
Withnell Fold Lancs 89 J6
Withybed Green Worcs 58 F10
Withybrook Warwks 59 P8
Withycombe Somset 18 D6
Withyham E Susx 25 L3
Withy Mills BaNES 20 C3
Withypool Somset 17 Q4
Withywood Bristl 31 Q11
Witley Surrey 23 P7
Witnesham Suffk 64 H11
Witney Oxon 34 C2
Wittering C Pete 73 R10
Wittersham Kent 26 F6
Witton Birm 58 G6
Witton Norfk 77 L10
Witton Norfk 77 L5
Witton Gilbert Dur 113 K11
Witton Green Norfk 77 N11
Witton le Wear Dur 103 M4
Witton Park Dur 103 N4
Wiveliscombe Somset 18 E9
Wivelrod Hants 23 J7
Wivelsfield E Susx 24 H6
Wivelsfield Green E Susx 25 J7
Wivelsfield Station W Susx 24 H7
Wivenhoe Essex 52 H7
Wivenhoe Cross Essex 52 H7
Wiveton Norfk 76 E3
Wix Essex 53 L6
Wixams Bed 50 C2
Wixford Warwks 47 L4
Wix Green Essex 53 L6
Wixhill Shrops 69 Q9
Wixoe Suffk 52 B3
Woburn C Beds 49 P8
Woburn Safari Park C Beds 49 Q8
Woburn Sands M Keyn 49 P7
Wokefield Park W Berk 35 J11
Woking Surrey 36 B9
Wokingham Wokham 35 M11
Wolborough Devon 7 M4
Woldingham Surrey 37 J9
Wold Newton E R Yk 99 L6
Wold Newton NE Lin 93 M11
Wolfclyde S Lans 116 E3
Wolferlow Herefs 46 C2
Wolferton Norfk 75 N5
Wolfhampcote Warwks 60 B7
Wolfhill P & K 142 B11
Wolf Hills Nthumb 111 P9
Wolf's Castle Pembks 41 J5
Wolfsdale Pembks 40 H6
Wollaston Dudley 58 C8
Wollaston Nhants 61 K8
Wollaston Shrops 56 E2
Wollaton C Nott 72 E3
Wollaton Hall & Park C Nott 72 E3
Wolleigh Devon 9 K8
Wollerton Shrops 69 R8
Wollescote Dudley 58 D8
Wolseley Bridge Staffs 71 J10
Wolsingham Dur 103 L3
Wolstanton Staffs 70 F5
Wolstenholme Rochdl 89 N8
Wolston Warwks 59 P9
Wolsty Cumb 109 P10
Wolvercote Oxon 34 E2
Wolverhampton Wolves 58 D5
Wolverhampton Halfpenny Green Airport Staffs 58 B6
Wolverley Shrops 69 N8
Wolverley Worcs 58 B9
Wolverton Hants 22 G3
Wolverton Kent 27 N3
Wolverton M Keyn 49 M6
Wolverton Warwks 47 P2
Wolverton Wilts 20 E8
Wolverton Common Hants 22 G3
Wolvesnewton Mons 31 N5
Wolvey Warwks 59 P7
Wolvey Heath Warwks 59 P7
Wolviston S on T 104 E5
Wombleton N York 98 D4
Wombourne Staffs 58 C6
Wombwell Barns 91 L10
Womenswold Kent 39 M11
Womersley N York 91 N7
Wonastow Mons 31 N2
Wonersh Surrey 36 B11
Wonford Devon 9 M6
Wonson Devon 8 G7
Wonston Dorset 12 B3
Wonston Hants 22 E7
Wooburn Bucks 35 P7
Wooburn Green Bucks 35 P7
Wooburn Moor Bucks 35 P7
Woodacott Devon 16 F10
Woodale N York 96 F5
Woodall Rothm 84 G4
Woodall Services Rothm 84 G4
Woodbank Ches W 81 M10
Woodbastwick Norfk 77 L8
Woodbeck Notts 85 N5
Wood Bevington Warwks 47 L4
Woodborough Notts 85 K11
Woodborough Wilts 21 M3
Woodbridge Devon 10 D5
Woodbridge Dorset 20 G11
Woodbridge Suffk 53 N2
Wood Burcote Nhants 49 J5
Woodbury Devon 9 P7
Woodbury Salterton Devon 9 P7
Woodchester Gloucs 32 F4
Woodchurch Kent 26 F5
Woodchurch Wirral 81 K7
Woodcombe Somset 18 C5
Woodcote Gt Lon 36 G8
Woodcote Oxon 34 H8
Woodcote Wrekin 70 D11
Woodcote Green Worcs 58 D10
Woodcott Hants 22 D4
Woodcroft Gloucs 31 P5
Woodcutts Dorset 21 J11
Wood Dalling Norfk 76 F6
Woodditton Cambs 63 L9
Woodeaton Oxon 34 F2
Wood Eaton Staffs 70 E11
Wooden Pembks 41 M9
Wood End Bed 61 M11
Wood End Bed 61 N7
Wood End C Beds 49 Q6
Wood End Cambs 62 E5
Wood End Gt Lon 36 D4
Wood End Herts 50 H5
Woodend Highld 138 D5
Woodend Nhants 48 H5
Woodend Staffs 71 M9
Woodend W Loth 126 G4
Woodend W Susx 15 M5
Wood End Warwks 58 H10
Wood End Warwks 59 K5
Wood End Warwks 59 L7
Wood End Wolves 58 D4

Wood Enderby Lincs 87 J8
Woodend Green Essex 51 N5
Woodfalls Wilts 21 N10
Woodford Cnwll 16 C9
Woodford Devon 7 K8
Woodford Gloucs 32 C5
Woodford Gt Lon 37 K2
Woodford Nhants 61 L5
Woodford Stockp 83 J8
Woodford Bridge Gt Lon 37 K2
Woodford Green Gt Lon 37 K2
Woodford Halse Nhants 48 F4
Woodford Wells Gt Lon 37 K2
Woodgate Birm 58 E8
Woodgate Devon 18 F11
Woodgate Norfk 76 B8
Woodgate Norfk 76 E8
Woodgate W Susx 15 P6
Woodgate Worcs 58 E11
Wood Green Gt Lon 36 H2
Woodgreen Hants 21 N11
Woodgreen Oxon 34 C2
Woodhall N York 96 E2
Woodhall Hill Leeds 90 G3
Woodhall Spa Lincs 86 G8
Woodham Bucks 49 K11
Woodham Dur 103 Q5
Woodham Surrey 36 B8
Woodham Ferrers Essex 38 C2
Woodham Mortimer Essex 52 D11
Woodham Walter Essex 52 D10
Wood Hayes Wolves 58 D4
Woodhead Abers 159 J10
Woodhill Shrops 57 N8
Woodhill Somset 19 L9
Woodhorn Nthumb 113 L3
Woodhorn Demesne Nthumb 113 M3
Woodhouse Leeds 90 H4
Woodhouse Leics 72 E8
Woodhouse Sheff 84 F4
Woodhouse Wakefd 91 K6
Woodhouse Eaves Leics 72 E8
Woodhouse Green Staffs 70 G2
Woodhouselee Mdloth 127 N5
Woodhouselees D & G 110 G6
Woodhouse Mill Sheff 84 F3
Woodhouses Cumb 110 F10
Woodhouses Oldham 83 K4
Woodhouses Staffs 58 G3
Woodhouses Staffs 71 M11
Woodhuish Devon 7 N8
Woodhurst Cambs 62 D5
Woodingdean Br & H 25 J9
Woodkirk Leeds 90 H5
Woodland Abers 151 M3
Woodland Devon 6 G7
Woodland Devon 7 K5
Woodland Dur 103 L5
Woodland Kent 27 K3
Woodland S Ayrs 114 C8
Woodland Head Devon 9 J5
Woodlands Abers 151 K8
Woodlands Donc 91 N9
Woodlands Dorset 13 J3
Woodlands Hants 13 P2
Woodlands Kent 37 N8
Woodlands N York 97 M10
Woodlands Somset 18 G6
Woodlands Park W & M 35 N9
Woodlands St Mary W Berk 34 B9
Woodland Street Somset 19 P7
Woodland View Sheff 84 D3
Wood Lane Shrops 69 M8
Wood Lane Staffs 70 E5
Woodleigh Devon 7 J9
Woodlesford Leeds 91 K5
Woodley Stockp 83 K6
Woodley Wokham 35 L10
Woodmancote Gloucs 32 E5
Woodmancote Gloucs 33 K3
Woodmancote Gloucs 47 J9
Woodmancote W Susx 15 L5
Woodmancote W Susx 24 F8
Woodmancote Worcs 46 H6
Woodmancott Hants 22 G6
Woodmansey E R Yk 93 J3
Woodmansgreen W Susx 23 N9
Woodmansterne Surrey 36 G9
Woodmanton Devon 9 P7
Woodmarsh Wilts 20 G3
Woodmill Staffs 71 L10
Woodminton Wilts 21 K10
Woodnesborough Kent 39 P10
Woodnewton Nhants 61 M2
Woodnook Notts 84 G10
Wood Norton Norfk 76 E6
Woodplumpton Lancs 88 F4
Woodrising Norfk 76 D11
Wood Row Leeds 91 K5
Woodrow Worcs 58 C9
Wood's Corner E Susx 25 Q7
Woods Eaves Herefs 45 K5
Woodseaves Shrops 70 B8
Woodseaves Staffs 70 D9
Woodsend Wilts 33 P9
Woodsetts Rothm 84 H4
Woodsford Dorset 12 C6
Wood's Green E Susx 25 P4
Woodside Br For 35 P10
Woodside Cumb 100 D4
Woodside Essex 51 L10
Woodside Fife 135 L6
Woodside Gt Lon 36 H7
Woodside Hants 13 P6
Woodside Herts 50 F9
Woodside P & K 142 C10
Woodside Green Kent 38 F11
Woodstock Oxon 48 D11
Woodstock Pembks 41 K5
Woodston C Pete 74 C11
Wood Street Norfk 77 M7
Wood Street Village Surrey 23 Q4
Woodthorpe Derbys 84 G6
Woodthorpe Leics 72 E7
Woodthorpe Lincs 87 M4
Woodton Norfk 65 K3
Woodtown Devon 16 G7
Woodvale Sefton 88 C8
Woodville Derbys 71 Q11
Woodwall Green Staffs 70 D8
Wood Walton Cambs 62 B4
Woodyates Dorset 21 K11
Woody Bay Devon 17 M2
Woofferton Shrops 57 J11
Wookey Somset 19 P5
Wookey Hole Somset 19 P5
Wool Dorset 12 D7
Woolacombe Devon 16 H3
Woolage Green Kent 27 M2
Woolage Village Kent 39 M11
Woolaston Gloucs 31 Q5
Woolaston Common Gloucs 31 Q4
Woolavington Somset 19 K6
Woolbeding W Susx 23 N10
Woolbrook Devon 10 C7
Woolcotts Somset 18 C8
Wooldale Kirk 90 F9
Wooler Nthumb 119 J5
Woolfardisworthy Devon 9 K3
Woolfardisworthy Devon 16 E7
Woolfold Bury 89 M8
Woolfords S Lans 127 J6
Woolhampton W Berk 34 G11
Woolhope Herefs 46 B7
Woolland Dorset 12 C3
Woollard BaNES 20 B2
Woollensbrook Herts 51 J9
Woolley BaNES 32 D11
Woolley Cambs 61 Q6
Woolley Cnwll 16 D8
Woolley Derbys 84 E8
Woolley Wakefd 91 J8
Woolley Bridge Derbys 83 M6
Woolley Edge Services Wakefd 91 J8
Woolley Green W & M 35 M8
Woolmere Green Worcs 47 J2
Woolmer Green Herts 50 G7
Woolmerston Somset 19 J8
Woolminstone Somset 11 J3
Woolpack Kent 26 E4
Woolpit Suffk 64 D9
Woolpit Green Suffk 64 D9
Woolscott Warwks 60 B7
Woolsgrove Devon 9 J4
Woolsington N u Ty 113 J6
Woolstaston Shrops 56 H5
Woolsthorpe by Belvoir Lincs 73 L4
Woolsthorpe-by-Colsterworth Lincs 73 N6
Woolston C Sotn 14 D4
Woolston Devon 7 J10
Woolston Devon 7 J8
Woolston Shrops 56 G7
Woolston Shrops 69 K10
Woolston Somset 18 E7
Woolston Somset 20 C9
Woolston Warrtn 82 D7
Woolstone Gloucs 47 J8
Woolstone M Keyn 49 N7
Woolstone Oxon 33 Q7
Woolston Green Devon 7 K5
Woolton Lpool 81 N7
Woolton Hill Hants 22 D2
Woolverstone Suffk 53 L4
Woolverton Somset 20 E4
Woolwich Gt Lon 37 K5
Woonton Herefs 45 M4
Woonton Herefs 45 R2
Wooperton Nthumb 119 K6
Woore Shrops 70 C6
Wootten Green Suffk 65 J7
Wootton Bed 50 B2
Wootton Hants 13 M5
Wootton Herefs 45 L4
Wootton IoW 14 F8
Wootton Kent 27 M2
Wootton N Linc 93 J7
Wootton Nhants 60 G9
Wootton Oxon 34 E4
Wootton Oxon 48 D11
Wootton Shrops 69 K9
Wootton Staffs 70 E9
Wootton Staffs 71 L6
Wootton Bassett Wilts 33 L8
Wootton Bridge IoW 14 F8
Wootton Broadmead Bed 50 B2
Wootton Common IoW 14 F8
Wootton Courtenay Somset 18 B6
Wootton Fitzpaine Dorset 10 H5
Wootton Rivers Wilts 21 N2
Wootton St Lawrence Hants 22 G4
Wootton Wawen Warwks 47 N2
Worcester Worcs 46 G4
Worcester Park Gt Lon 36 F7
Wordsley Dudley 58 C7
Worfield Shrops 57 P5
Worgret Dorset 12 F7
Workhouse End Bed 61 P10
Workhouse Green Suffk 52 F4
Workington Cumb 100 D5
Worksop Notts 85 J5
Worlaby Lincs 87 K5
Worlaby N Linc 92 H8
Worlds End Bucks 35 N3
Worlds End Hants 14 H4
World's End W Berk 34 E9
Worlds End W Susx 24 H6
Worle N Som 19 L2
Worleston Ches E 70 B3
Worlingham Suffk 65 N4
Worlington Devon 9 J2
Worlington Suffk 63 L6
Worlingworth Suffk 65 J8
Wormald Green N York 97 M7
Wormbridge Herefs 45 N8
Wormegay Norfk 75 N8
Wormelow Tump Herefs 45 P8
Wormhill Derbys 83 P10
Wormhill Herefs 45 N7
Wormingford Essex 52 F5
Worminghall Bucks 34 H3
Wormington Gloucs 47 K7
Worminster Somset 19 Q6
Wormit Fife 135 L2
Wormleighton Warwks 48 E4
Wormley Herts 51 J9
Wormley Surrey 23 P7
Wormleybury Herts 51 J9
Wormley Hill Donc 91 R7
Wormshill Kent 38 E10
Wormsley Herefs 45 N5
Worplesdon Surrey 23 Q4
Worrall Sheff 84 D2
Worrall Hill Gloucs 32 B2
Worsbrough Barns 91 K10
Worsbrough Bridge Barns 91 K10
Worsbrough Dale Barns 91 K10
Worsley Salfd 82 G4
Worstead Norfk 77 L6
Worsthorne Lancs 89 P4
Worston Devon 6 F8
Worston Lancs 89 M2
Worth Kent 39 P10
Worth Somset 19 P5
Worth W Susx 24 H3
Wortham Suffk 64 F6
Worthen Shrops 56 E4
Worthenbury Wrexhm 69 M5
Worthing Norfk 76 D8
Worthing W Susx 24 D10
Worthington Leics 72 C6
Worth Matravers Dorset 12 G9
Worthybrook Mons 31 N2
Worting Hants 22 G4
Wortley Barns 91 J11
Wortley Gloucs 32 E6
Wortley Leeds 90 H4
Worton N York 96 E3
Worton Wilts 21 J3
Wortwell Norfk 65 K5
Wotherton Shrops 56 D4
Wothorpe C Pete 73 Q9
Wotter Devon 6 F6
Wotton Surrey 36 D11
Wotton-under-Edge Gloucs 32 E6
Wotton Underwood Bucks 49 J11
Woughton on the Green M Keyn 49 N7
Wouldham Kent 38 B9
Woundale Shrops 57 P6
Wrabness Essex 53 L5
Wrafton Devon 16 H4
Wragby Lincs 86 F5
Wragby Wakefd 91 L7
Wramplingham Norfk 76 G10
Wrangaton Devon 6 H7
Wrangbrook Wakefd 91 M8
Wrangle Lincs 87 M10
Wrangle Common Lincs 87 M10
Wrangle Lowgate Lincs 87 M10
Wrangway Somset 18 F11
Wrantage Somset 19 K10
Wrawby N Linc 92 H9
Wraxall N Som 31 N10
Wraxall Somset 20 B7
Wray Lancs 95 N7
Wray Castle Cumb 101 L10
Wraysbury W & M 36 B6
Wrayton Lancs 95 N6
Wrea Green Lancs 88 D4
Wreaks End Cumb 94 E3
Wreay Cumb 101 M6
Wreay Cumb 110 H11
Wrecclesham Surrey 23 M6
Wrekenton Gatesd 113 L9
Wrelton N York 98 F3
Wrenbury Ches E 69 Q5
Wrench Green N York 99 K3
Wreningham Norfk 64 H2
Wrentham Suffk 65 P5
Wrenthorpe Wakefd 91 J6
Wrentnall Shrops 56 G4
Wressle E R Yk 92 B4
Wressle N Linc 92 G9
Wrestlingworth C Beds 62 C11
Wretton Norfk 75 N10
Wrexham Wrexhm 69 K4
Wrexham Industrial Estate Wrexhm 69 L4
Wribbenhall Worcs 57 P9
Wrickton Shrops 57 L7
Wrightington Bar Lancs 88 G8
Wright's Green Essex 51 M7
Wrinehill Staffs 70 D5
Wrington N Som 19 N2
Writhlington BaNES 20 C4
Writtle Essex 51 Q9
Wrockwardine Wrekin 57 L2
Wroot N Linc 92 B10
Wrose C Brad 90 F3
Wrotham Kent 37 P9
Wrotham Heath Kent 37 P9
Wrottesley Staffs 58 B4
Wroughton Swindn 33 M8
Wroxall IoW 14 G11
Wroxall Warwks 59 K10
Wroxeter Shrops 57 K3
Wroxham Norfk 77 L8
Wroxton Oxon 48 D6
Wyaston Derbys 71 M6
Wyatt's Green Essex 51 N11
Wyberton Lincs 74 F2
Wyboston Bed 61 Q9
Wybunbury Ches E 70 B5
Wychbold Worcs 58 D11
Wych Cross E Susx 25 K4
Wychnor Staffs 71 M11
Wychwood Ches E 70 C4
Wyck Hants 23 L7
Wyck Rissington Gloucs 47 N10
Wycliffe Dur 103 M8
Wycoller Lancs 89 Q3
Wycomb Leics 73 K6
Wycombe Marsh Bucks 35 N6
Wyddial Herts 51 J4
Wye Kent 27 J2
Wyesham Mons 31 P2
Wyfordby Leics 73 K7
Wyke C Brad 90 F5
Wyke Devon 9 L5
Wyke Devon 10 F5
Wyke Dorset 20 E9
Wyke Shrops 57 L4
Wyke Surrey 23 P4
Wyke Champflower Somset 20 C8
Wykeham N York 99 K4
Wyken Covtry 59 N8
Wyken Shrops 57 P5
Wyke Regis Dorset 11 P9
Wykey Shrops 69 L10
Wykin Leics 72 C11
Wylam Nthumb 112 H8
Wylde Green Birm 58 H6
Wylye Wilts 21 K7
Wymeswold Leics 72 G6
Wymington Bed 61 L8
Wymondham Leics 73 L7
Wymondham Norfk 76 G11
Wyndham Brdgnd 29 P6
Wynford Eagle Dorset 11 M5
Wynyard Park S on T 104 D5
Wynyard Village S on T 104 D5
Wyre Piddle Worcs 47 J5
Wysall Notts 72 G5
Wyson Herefs 57 J11
Wythall Worcs 58 G9
Wytham Oxon 34 E3
Wythburn Cumb 101 K8
Wythenshawe Manch 82 H7
Wythop Mill Cumb 100 G5
Wyton Cambs 62 C6
Wyton E R Yk 93 L4
Wyverstone Suffk 64 E8
Wyverstone Street Suffk 64 E8
Wyville Lincs 73 M5

Y

Yaddlethorpe N Linc 92 E9
Yafford IoW 14 D10
Yafforth N York 97 M2
Yalberton Torbay 7 M7
Yalding Kent 37 Q10
Yanwath Cumb 101 P5
Yanworth Gloucs 33 L2
Yapham E R Yk 98 F10
Yapton W Susx 15 Q6
Yarborough N Som 19 L3
Yarbridge IoW 14 H9
Yarburgh Lincs 87 L2
Yarcombe Devon 10 E3
Yard Devon 17 P7
Yardley Birm 58 H7
Yardley Gobion Nhants 49 L6
Yardley Hastings Nhants 61 J9
Yardley Wood Birm 58 H9
Yardro Powys 45 J3
Yarford Somset 18 H9
Yarkhill Herefs 46 B6
Yarley Somset 19 P6
Yarlington Somset 20 C9
Yarm S on T 104 D8
Yarmouth IoW 14 C9
Yarnacott Devon 17 L5
Yarnbrook Wilts 20 G4
Yarner Devon 9 J9
Yarnfield Staffs 70 F8
Yarnscombe Devon 17 K7
Yarnton Oxon 34 E2
Yarpole Herefs 45 P2
Yarrow Border 117 M5
Yarrow Somset 19 L5
Yarrow Feus Border 117 L5
Yarrowford Border 117 N4
Yarsop Herefs 45 N5
Yarwell Nhants 73 R11
Yate S Glos 32 D8
Yateley Hants 23 M2
Yatesbury Wilts 33 L10
Yattendon W Berk 34 G10
Yatton Herefs 56 G11
Yatton N Som 31 M11
Yatton Keynell Wilts 32 G9
Yaverland IoW 14 H9
Yawl Devon 10 G6
Yawthorpe Lincs 85 Q2
Yaxham Norfk 76 E9
Yaxley Cambs 61 Q2
Yaxley Suffk 64 G7
Yazor Herefs 45 N5
Yeading Gt Lon 36 D4
Yeadon Leeds 90 G2
Yealand Conyers Lancs 95 L6
Yealand Redmayne Lancs 95 L5
Yealand Storrs Lancs 95 K5
Yealmbridge Devon 6 F8
Yealmpton Devon 6 F8
Yearby R & Cl 104 G6
Yearngill Cumb 100 F2
Yearsley N York 98 B6
Yeaton Shrops 69 M11
Yeaveley Derbys 71 M6
Yeavering Nthumb 118 H4
Yedingham N York 98 H5
Yelford Oxon 34 C4
Yell Shet 169 r5
Yelland Devon 16 H5
Yelling Cambs 62 C8
Yelvertoft Nhants 60 C5
Yelverton Devon 6 E5
Yelverton Norfk 77 K11
Yenston Somset 20 D10
Yeoford Devon 9 J5
Yeolmbridge Cnwll 5 N4
Yeo Mill Devon 17 Q6
Yeo Vale Devon 16 G7
Yeovil Somset 19 Q11
Yeovil Marsh Somset 19 P11
Yeovilton Somset 19 P10
Yerbeston Pembks 41 L9
Yesnaby Ork 169 b5
Yetlington Nthumb 119 K9
Yetminster Dorset 11 M2
Yetson Devon 7 L7
Yettington Devon 9 Q7
Yetts o'Muckhart Clacks 134 C7
Yews Green C Brad 90 D4
Yew Tree Sandw 58 F5
Y Felinheli Gwynd 79 J11
Y Ferwig Cerdgn 42 C5
Y Ffôr Gwynd 66 F7
Yielden Bed 61 M7
Yieldingtree Worcs 58 C9
Yieldshields S Lans 126 F7
Yiewsley Gt Lon 36 C4
Y Nant Wrexhm 69 J4
Ynysboeth Rhondd 30 E5
Ynysddu Caerph 30 G6
Ynysforgan Swans 29 J5
Ynyshir Rhondd 30 D6
Ynyslas Cerdgn 54 E6
Ynysmaerdy Rhondd 30 D8
Ynysmeudwy Neath 29 K3
Ynystawe Swans 29 J4
Ynyswen Powys 29 M2
Ynyswen Rhondd 30 C5
Ynysybwl Rhondd 30 E6
Ynysymaengwyn Gwynd 54 D4
Yockenthwaite N York 96 D5
Yockleton Shrops 56 F2
Yokefleet E R Yk 92 D6
Yoker C Glas 125 N4
York C York 98 C10
York Lancs 89 L4
Yorkletts Kent 39 J9
Yorkley Gloucs 32 B3
Yorkshire Dales National Park 96 C5
York Town Surrey 23 N2
Yorton Heath Shrops 69 P10
Youlgreave Derbys 84 B8
Youlthorpe E R Yk 98 F9
Youlton N York 97 Q8
Youngsbury Herts 51 J7
Young's End Essex 52 B8
Yoxall Staffs 71 L11
Yoxford Suffk 65 M8
Y Rhiw Gwynd 66 C9
Ysbyty Cynfyn Cerdgn 54 H9
Ysbyty Ifan Conwy 67 Q5
Ysbyty Ystwyth Cerdgn 54 G10
Ysceifiog Flints 80 H10
Ysgubor-y-Coed Cerdgn 54 F5
Ystalyfera Neath 29 L3
Ystrad Rhondd 30 C5
Ystrad Aeron Cerdgn 43 K3
Ystradfellte Powys 29 P2
Ystrad Ffin Carmth 43 Q5
Ystradgynlais Powys 29 L2
Ystrad Meurig Cerdgn 54 G11
Ystrad Mynach Caerph 30 F6
Ystradowen V Glam 30 D9
Ystumtuen Cerdgn 54 G9
Ythanbank Abers 159 M11
Ythanwells Abers 158 F10
Ythsie Abers 159 L11

Z

Zeal Monachorum Devon 8 H4
Zeals Wilts 20 E8
Zelah Cnwll 3 L3
Zennor Cnwll 2 D6
Zoar Cnwll 3 K10
Zouch Notts 72 E6
ZSL London Zoo Gt Lon 36 G4
ZSL Whipsnade Zoo C Beds 50 B7

Distances and journey times

The mileage chart shows distances in miles between two towns along AA-recommended routes. Using motorways and other main roads this is normally the fastest route, though not necessarily the shortest.

The journey times are shown in hours and minutes. These times should be used as a guide only and do not allow for unforeseen traffic delays, rest breaks or fuel stops.

For example, the 376 miles (605 km) journey between Glasgow and Norwich should take approximately 6 hours 45 minutes.

Journey times

Distances in miles (one mile equals 1.6093 km)